Mollis'

Skin and Beauty

The Science and Applications of Cosmetics

Published by OAU Press, Obafemi Awolowo University, Ile-Ife, Nigeria

First published 2022

ISBN 978 978 136 097 8

Typesetting by Artpark Studio and Gallery (lanrehighd@yahoo.com)

Indexing and formatting by Books and Copy Publishing (www.booksandcopy.com)

Book cover design – Tosin Afolabi

Foreword

I am really delighted to accept the editor's invitation to write the foreward to this book.
Cosmetology is an essential part of public health. On one hand, it involves the administration and use of active substances but, on the other hand, it is not under the strict regulation of national medicines regulation agencies. Therein lies the potential for public harm given man's age-old pursuit of physical beauty.

Professor 'Lara Orafidiya has undertaken an essential public health service by embarking on this book project. She has assembled an eminent array of authorities to provide the reader with educative information on the history, uses, benefits and downsides of cosmetics use. All shades of interest are catered for as the book deals not only with the beauty aspects of cosmetology and the contents of cosmetics, but also with the health aspects, the law regulating cosmetics production, sale and use, the risks of cancer with cosmetic use and the increasing role of cosmetic surgery in Africa. The environmental aspects of cosmetology have also been discussed such as the use of sunscreens, and the existential threat posed by climate change to our planet has not forgotten in this book.
By presenting the reader with the chemistry of cosmetics ingredients, the health impact of cosmetics in environmental waste, particularly hormones and diphenols in sewage, readily comes to mind.

Cosmetology is an extensive and complex subject, but in addressing the multi-faceted social, physical, environmental, legal and health aspects of the subject, the editor and the contributing authors have provided a reference text that will certainly last for several years to come.

I wish to thank the Editor and all the contributing authors for their brilliant work and I strongly recommend this to you as an essential reading before your next trip to the supermarket.

Professor Stanley OKOLO
Honorary Professor of Global Health,
University College London, United Kingdom
[Director-General of West Africa Health Organisation, 2018-2022]
London, 30 November 2022

Foreword

The untoward effects, arising from the use of cosmetics with abandoned recklessness, especially by persons of Sub-Saharan descent, are of a growing concern among medical practitioners who come across the consumers of cosmetic products almost on a daily basis in their various practice settings. The health (disease) burden arising from the misuse of cosmetics calls for urgent attention for its mitigation. For example, a survey, carried out some years ago, revealed a relationship between the use of certain cosmetics and the incidence of high blood pressure amongst undergraduate female medical students (1). Misinformation or outright lack of information on the appropriate directions for use of cosmetics is one of the major causes of these unpleasant occurrences. The book: Skin and Beauty – the Science and Applications of Cosmetics, has been put together by the editor to address this shortcoming by providing adequate and easy to comprehend literature on cosmetics.

The need for the teaching of the rudimentary of cosmetics as a course or part of a course to medical and related sciences' students in tertiary institutions is gradually being recognised, and institutions that are yet to include the course in their curriculum are making efforts to do so. This has become necessary as these categories of health personnel will be well informed and able to disseminate the much-needed information to the practitioners of cosmetic and beauty applications as well as the consumers of cosmetic products on the proper use of the products. This book will serve as a good textbook for the teachers as well as the students taking the course, as currently available textbooks contain some technical details that may not be required at the undergraduate level. The West African Health Organisation (WAHO) has introduced cosmetics as a course in its curriculum for tertiary institutions of member countries offering Pharmacy at the undergraduate level. It is hoped that the course will be introduced to medical and other allied programmes soon. Postgraduate degree programmes with focus on cosmetics would be a welcome idea to advance knowledge in this field as this will provide experts that will teach the course.

The book provides basic information on the formulation, preparation and stability of cosmetic products which is helpful to those wishing to manufacture cosmetics, especially on a small scale. The necessary regulatory requirements for the sale, importation and manufacture of cosmetic products are clearly spelt out to assist those involved in the cosmetic business. The simple language of the book, which is devoid of the highly technical terminologies, should encourage the lay person to read and comprehend the aspects that may be of interest and concern to them. The untoward effects of cosmetics are well-explained, and consumers are made to recognise their rights to legal procedures when adverse events are encountered in the course of using the products.

I congratulate the Editor as well as the contributing authors for providing this highly educative book that will definitely provide the much-needed information on the proper use of cosmetics, especially in sub-Saharan Africa.

Professor Ibrahim A. Oreagba
Secretary General
West African Postgraduate College of Pharmacists (WAPCP), Lagos, Nigeria.

(1). Olayemi, SO, Oreagba, IA and Mabadeje, AFB. Assessment of rational use and effects of topical steroid creams among female members of an urban higher institution in Nigeria. The Nigerian Journal of Pharmacy 2004; 35(1): 31-34.

Preface

The adorning of the skin and the wearing of cosmetics, no matter how crudely produced and used the cosmetics may be, are ways human beings have made themselves attractive from time immemorial. However, globalisation and the rapid development of cosmetic products and techniques in recent times, have led to the increased desire for better looks with the use of cosmetics than ever before. Unfortunately, the paucity of sources of comprehensive and simple-to-understand information as well as public enlightenment programmes on the appropriateness, suitability and proper use and applications of these beauty enhancement products, have led to the unfortunate and avoidable deleterious and, in some instances, life-threatening and irreversible damages on the consumers' health. There are some products that are expected to be applied on clients only by trained personnel but which are recklessly used and abused by consumers who cannot comprehend the need to engage the services of qualified experts.

This book provides basic but comprehensive information on a wide range of related topics, which are relatively simplified for easy comprehension by the target readers, including teachers and practitioners of cosmetology, formulators and manufacturers of cosmetic products, as well as the consumers and prospective users of cosmetics.

The book, comprising 26 peer-reviewed chapters, has been put together by a team of 31 contributing authors who are pharmaceutical scientists, researchers in drug development and pharmacy administration, dermatologists, as well as those involved in the practice of consumer protection law, cosmetic surgery, cosmetology and the development of cosmetic products. Their expertise has been brought to bear on the various topics addressed in the book.

You are warmly invited to read through and make good use of this simplified but comprehensive book on cosmetics!!!

'Lara Orafidiya,
Editor, December 2022.

Acknowledgements

I am highly indebted to Dr. Taiwo Adebola Ogunleye, a legal practitioner, an educator, and a royal prince of Ile-Ife, Nigeria, who insisted that I must write a book to mark my retirement from the Obafemi Awolowo University (OAU) in August, 2022.

In addition, I wish to acknowledge with thanks, the contributions of the following to the successful outcome of this book project:

All the contributing authors, whose commitment and hard work resulted in the submission of the well-written chapters that make up the book, despite their other important work schedules;

The numerous peer-reviewers (at least two per chapter), who read through the various chapters and contributed to the quality of the book by their comments and corrections;

Professor Tiwalade Olugbade of OAU, Ile-Ife, who worked assiduously, reading through all the chapters of the book and proffering useful comments and corrections;

Miss. Deborah Mayowa Akanji, who assisted immensely with effecting the corrections in the manuscripts;

Dr. Folake Adunola Orafidiya, for not just being a contributing author but for also assisting to enrich some other chapters of the book; and

Mr. Tosin Afolabi, who designed the book cover, gratis.

'Lara Orafidiya,
Editor, December 2022

Authors' Profiles

Awodayo Oluwatoyin Adepiti
B.Pharm. (Ife), MSc. (Phytomedicines, Ife), PhD. (Pharmacognosy, Ife), DAAD Alumna Technical University, Dortmund
Senior Lecturer, Department of Pharmacognosy, Faculty of Pharmacy, Obafemi Awolowo University, Ile-Ife, Nigeria.

Gbadegesin Elubode Adetogun
B.Pharm. (Ife), MSc., MPhil., PhD. (Pharmaceutics, Ife)
Senior Lecturer, Department of Pharmaceutics, Faculty of Pharmacy, Obafemi Awolowo University, Ile-Ife, Nigeria.

Atinuke Arinola Ajani
MBChB (Ife), FWACP (Dermatol)
Consultant Dermatologist and Genito-urinary Physician, Department of Dermatology and Venereology, Obafemi Awolowo University, Ile-Ife, Nigeria.

Ayesha Omolara Akinkugbe
MBBS (Lagos), FWACP (Dermatol)
Senior Lecturer, Faculty of Clinical Sciences, College of Medicine, University of Lagos, Consultant Dermatologist and Genito-Urinary Physician, Lagos University Teaching Hospital, Lagos, Nigeria

Aderonke Doyinsola Dawotola
B.Sc. (Zoology, Lagos), MSc. (Pharmaceutical Sciences, UC)
Founder/CEO Dayspring Cosmeceuticals LLC, Texas, USA.

Rabi Ilemona Ekore
MBBS (Ib), FWACP (Fam. Med), M.P.E. (Ib), MSc. (CAMH, Ib), Dip. (Cosmetics Science, IPCS)
Family Medicine Physician, Health Assurance Hospitals Company, Kuwait

Ademola Olusegun Enitan
MBBS (Ib), FWACP (Dermatol)
Physician, Researcher, Consultant Dermatologist and Venereologist, Obafemi Awolowo University Teaching Hospitals Complex, Ile-Ife, Nigeria.

Funmilola Adesodun Fisusi
B.Pharm. (Ife), MSc (Ife), PhD. (Drug Delivery, UCL)
Research Fellow, Drug Research and Production Unit, Faculty of Pharmacy, Obafemi Awolowo University, Ile-Ife, Nigeria

Sharon Iyobor Igbinoba
B. Pharm. (Ife), PharmD. (Benin), MSc., PhD. (Pharmacology, Ife), FPCPharm
Associate Professor of Clinical Pharmacy,
Department of Clinical Pharmacy and Pharmacy Administration, Obafemi Awolowo University, Ile-Ife, Nigeria.

Maduabuchi Romanus Ihekoronye
B.Pharm. (UNN), MBA, MSc., PhD. (Ife), FPCPharm.
Lecturer, Department of Clinical Pharmacy and Pharmacy Administration, Obafemi Awolowo University, Ile-Ife, Nigeria.

Ayodapo Oluwadare Jegede
B.Pharm. (Ife), PharmD. (Benin), MSc., PhD. (Pharmacy Administration, Ife), FPCPharm. Lecturer, Department of Clinical Pharmacy and Pharmacy Administration, Obafemi Awolowo University, Ile-Ife, Nigeria.

Iain Joseph McEwan
BSc. Hon., (Biochemistry, Strathclyde), PhD. (Molecular endocrinology, Glasgow)
Professor, Research Lead, Institute of Medical Sciences University of Aberdeen, Aberdeen, UK.

Efere Martins Obuotor
BSc. (Biochemistry), MSC., PhD. (Biochemistry, Ife).
Professor, Department of Biochemistry and Molecular Biology, Obafemi Awolowo University, Ile-Ife, Nigeria.

Michael Ayodele Odeniyi
BPharm (Ib), MSC., PhD. (Pharmaceutics, Ib).
Professor, Department of Pharmaceutics and Industrial Pharmacy, University of Ibadan, Ibadan, Nigeria.

Adebola Olufunmilayo Ogunbiyi
MBBS (Ib), FWACP (Dermatol)
Professor of Medicine, University of Ibadan, Consultant Dermatologist, University College Hospital, Ibadan.

Sinmisola Adedunmola Oladeji-Akinsanmi
M.Pharm. (QUB), PhD. (Pharmacy, QUB)
Regulatory Affairs Officer, Norbrook Laboratories Ltd, Belfast, UK.

Ayodeji Olarenwaju Oladele
MBChB (Ife), FWACS (Surgery)
Associate Professor and Head, Plastic Surgery Unit, Department of Surgery, College of Health sciences, Obafemi Awolowo University, Ile-Ife, Consultant Plastic surgeon, Obafemi Awolowo University Teaching Hospitals' Complex, Ile-Ife, Nigeria.

Omoniyi Joseph Ola-Olorun
B. Pharm. (Hons., Ife), MSc., MBA (Lagos), PhD. (Tech. Mgt., Ife), FPCPharm.
Senior Lecturer, Department of Clinical Pharmacy and Pharmacy Administration, Faculty of Pharmacy, Obafemi Awolowo University, Ile-Ife, Nigeria.

Francis Abiodun Oladimeji KSM
B. Pharm. (Hons., Ife), MSc., PhD. (Pharmaceutics, Ife).
Professor, Department of Pharmaceutics and Pharmaceutical Technology, Faculty of Pharmacy, Obafemi Awolowo University, Ile-Ife, Nigeria.

Grace Osarugue Onawunmi
B.Pharm. (Hons., Ife), MSc. (Pharmaceutics, Manc), PhD. (Pharmaceutics, Ife), FNAPharm.
Professor of Pharmaceutics (Pharmaceutical Microbiology), Department of Pharmaceutics, Faculty of Pharmacy, Obafemi Awolowo University, Ile-Ife, Nigeria.

Olumayowa Abimbola Oninla
MBChB (Ife), FMCP (Dermatology & Venereology), FACP
Senior Lecturer, Department of Dermatology and Venereology,
Faculty of Clinical Sciences, College of Health Sciences, Obafemi Awolowo University, Ile-Ife, Nigeria, Consultant Dermatologist and Venereologist, Obafemi Awolowo University Teaching Hospitals' Complex, Ile-Ife, Nigeria.

Folake Adunola Orafidiya
B.Pharm. (Ife), MSc. (Drug Development, Aberdeen), PhD. (Biomedical Sciences (Pharmacology), Aberdeen). Research Associate, Molecular Sciences Research Hub, Imperial College London, London; Research Scientist, Myricx Pharma, UK.

'Lara (Omolara) Olajumoke Orafidiya
B.Pharm. (Hons, Ife), PhD. (Pharmaceutics, Ife)
Professor of Pharmaceutics; retired (2022) from the Department of Pharmaceutics, Obafemi Awolowo University, Ile-Ife, Nigeria.

Kanayo Patrick Osemene.
B.Pharm. (Ife), MBA, MSc., PhD. (Tech. Mgt., Ife), FPCPharm.
Reader, Department of Clinical Pharmacy and Pharmacy Administration,
Obafemi Awolowo University, Ile-Ife, Nigeria.

Bukola Aminat Oseni
B. Pharm. (Ife), MSc. (Pharmaceutical Biotechnology, DMU, Leicester), PhD. (Pharmaceutics & Pharmaceutical Technology, Lagos)
Lecturer I, Department of Pharmaceutics & Pharmaceutical Technology, University of Lagos, Lagos, Nigeria.

Michael Oluwole Osungunna
B.Pharm. (Ife), MSc. (Ib), MPhil. (Pharmaceutics, Ife), PhD. (Pharmaceutical Sciences, USP)
Senior Lecturer, Department of Pharmaceutics, Faculty of Pharmacy, Obafemi Awolowo University, Ile-Ife, Nigeria.

James Yinka Oyeniyi
B.Pharm. (Ife), MBA, MSc., PhD. (Pharmaceutics, ABU)
Associate Professor, & Head, Formulation and Drug Production Unit (FDPU), Department of Pharmaceutics and Pharmaceutical Microbiology, Faculty of Pharmaceutical Sciences, Usmanu Danfodiyo University, Sokoto, Nigeria.

Bamgboye Josiah Taiwo.
B.Pharm. (Ife), MSc., PhD. (Pharmaceutical Chemistry, Ife)
Senior Lecturer, Department of Pharmaceutical Chemistry, and Coordinator, Drug Discovery Laboratory, Faculty of Pharmacy, Obafemi Awolowo University, Ile-Ife, Nigeria.

Modupe Tasala Talabi
BSc Computing and Business Management (Bham), Post Graduate Certificate in Education (UCL), Diploma in Cosmetology (UCB)
Founder/CEO Tasala HQ Hair and Beauty, Lagos, Nigeria.

Abdulwasiu Ojo Yusuff
BL., LL.M. (Ife), LL.M. (Toronto), PhD. (Ife)
Professor, Department of Public Law, Faculty of Law, Obafemi Awolowo University, Ile-Ife, NIGERIA.

Boladale Olanrewaju SILVA
B.Pharm. (Hons.,Ife), MSc., PhD. Pharmaceutics, Miss.), FPCPharm,
Professor of Pharmaceutics, Faculty of Pharmacy, University of Lagos, Lagos, Nigeria.

CONTENTS

CHAPTER ONE

Introduction: Cosmetics – the age-long beauty enhancers

'Lara o.Orafidiya

What are cosmetics?

The word cosmetics is derived from the Greek terminologies: "kosmetikos", "kosmetike" and "kosmos" which in essence connote a feeling of harmony, order and tranquillity, and include the techniques of dressing and use of ornaments. Countries and regions of the world have various definitions for cosmetics; however, these definitions are somewhat similar in that they all emphasise beauty enhancement with the products employed for the purpose, and are expected to have no therapeutic effects on the human body.

According to Nigerian laws and as defined by the National Agency for Food and Drug Administration and Control (NAFDAC), 'a "cosmetic" includes any substance or mixture of substances intended to be rubbed, poured, sprinkled or sprayed, introduced into or otherwise applied to the human body or any part thereof for cleansing, beautifying, promoting attractiveness or altering the complexion, skin, hair or teeth and includes deodorants and detergent powder' (1).

The Food, Drug and Cosmetics Act (FD&C Act) of the United States of America defines cosmetics as "articles intended to be rubbed, poured, sprinkled, or sprayed on, introduced into, or otherwise applied to the human body for cleansing, beautifying, promoting attractiveness, or altering the appearance". The products should not affect body's structure or function. Among the products included in this definition are skin moisturisers, perfumes, lipsticks, fingernail polishes, eye and facial makeup, cleansing shampoos, temporary hair colours and deodorants, as well as any substance intended for use as a component of a cosmetic product. It does not include soap (2).

In Canada, the Food and Drugs Act and Cosmetic Regulations define cosmetics as "any substance or mixture of substances, manufactured, sold or represented for use in cleansing, improving or altering the complexion, skin, hair or teeth and includes deodorants and perfumes" (3). This definition also includes cosmetics used by professional aesthetic services (such as silicone elastomers employed in dermal filling), as well as bulk institutional products (e.g., hand soap in school restrooms).

The European Union Cosmetics Directive defines a cosmetic as "any substance or preparation intended to be placed in contact with the various external parts of the human body (epidermis, hair system, nails, lips and external genital organs) or with the teeth and the mucous membranes of the oral cavity with a view exclusively or mainly to cleaning them, perfuming them, changing their appearance and/or correcting body odours and/or protecting them or keeping them in good condition" (4).

The Council of Ministers of the West African Economic and Monetary Union (Union économique et monétaire ouest-africaine (UEMOA) in October, 2010 adopted the European guidelines as the framework for the harmonised cosmetic regulations for the region which comprises Benin, Burkina Faso, Ivory Coast, Guinea Bissau, Mali, Niger, Senegal and Togo (5).

In Japan, cosmetics as defined by the Pharmaceutical and Medical Devises Act (PMD Act) is stated as "articles with mild action on the human body, which are intended to be applied to the human body through rubbing, sprinkling or other methods, aiming to clean, beautify and increase the attractiveness, alter the appearance or to keep the skin or hair in good condition". Cosmetics include perfume, eau de cologne, skin and hair care products and special-purpose cosmetics such as sunscreen products, shaving cream and soap (6)

In Ghana, "Cosmetic" includes a substance or mixture of substances manufactured, sold, or represented for use in cleansing, improving or altering the complexion, skin, hair, eyes or teeth and includes deodorants and perfumes (7).

In general, cosmetics are substances that enhance the appearance and/or odour of the human body, with "makeup" being a subset that encompasses coloured products intended to alter the user's appearance. Thus, there are care cosmetics and decorative cosmetics. Cosmetics, therefore, are products applied to the skin, teeth and the mucus linings of the mouth with the intent of enhancing the beauty and appearance of the user; they are expected to elicit only topical effects and no systemic manifestation in the body.

As will be seen in the course of this book, some cosmetic agents have systemic connotations which can be deleterious to the health of the consumer. This book will bring to the fore the various types of cosmetic products currently in the market, their effects on the skin of the user, the chemistry of the agents used in their manufacture, the implications of these agents for the endocrine system and eventual cancer development, the laws and guidelines for the registration and sale of cosmetics in different countries, consumer rights and other topics.

The emergence of cosmetics

The earliest use of cosmetics is traced to the ancient Egyptian culture, around 10,000 BC, where cosmetics were used in religious rituals for beauty; this eventually became a status symbol in the society. Cosmetics were also used for the health of the body especially for protection against the adverse effects of the climate which was characterised by harsh sun and drying wind. The Chinese, by 3000 BC, were also known to have applied some substances on the body to enhance beauty as well as to serve as a distinguishing mark in the society. The early cosmetics were prepared mainly with extracts from plants and animals as well as minerals that abound in the soils of these ancient kingdoms.

The early Egyptian women, and even their men, used cosmetics copiously not only to enhance their appearance but also in the belief that this offered the protection of their gods, Horus and Ra. The eyeballs were lined with kohl (ground stibnite powder, Sb_2S_3) to look more beautiful as well as to protect the eyes from the adverse effects of the scourging sun. Children, including neonates, had kohl applied around the eyes with the belief that this would protect from the attack of evil spirits and that the eyes would develop without defects caused by infection. Kohl was prepared as a paint and was applied around the eyes with thin sticks made of ivory, wood or metal. The paint was also applied on the eyebrow and eye lashes for enhanced beauty effects. The use of kohl as an eye liner extended throughout North Africa, the Horn of Africa, West Africa, Middle East, South Asia and some other African and Asian regions. Apart from the black colour from kohl, the green malachite powder, which is a bright green copper carbonate hydroxide mineral ($CuCo_3(OH)_2$), was also applied as an eye liner and on the eyebrow making the eyes look bigger and more attractive. Malachite was later found to have antibacterial properties (8) which protected the eyes from infection. To colour the lips, finely powdered red ochre, which is a light yellow to red-coloured clay mineral containing ferric oxide as well as carmine from cochineal, which is an insect (*Dactylopius coccus*), were applied on the lips and as rouge on the cheeks. Wooden sticks were used as applicators for the lipsticks. The toes and fingertips were stained with leaf extract of henna (*Lawsonia inermis*). The extract was also used to make beautiful patterns on the body, an art that was popularised by Queen Cleopatra VII (69 BC – 30 BC). Generally, the powdered minerals and extracts were incorporated into fat bases, mainly tallow and beeswax, to facilitate application and make the products stay on the skin. Sea salts as well as a mixture of olive oil and honey were applied on the face by the women to exfoliate, heal and rejuvenate the skin as well as to prevent wrinkles and, thus, maintain a smooth skin. Soaps made of clay and olive oil (*Olea europaea*) were used for body cleansing, while oils of olive, sesame (*Sesamum indicum*), and moringa (*Moringa oleifera*) served as body moisturisers. Regular baths of milk (mainly of goat) and honey were part of the women's beauty therapy. The hair was nourished and groomed with castor oil (*Ricinus communis*). Wearing of perfumes obtained by boiling or soaking flowers, leaves and oleoresins of plants such as lavender (*Lavandula* spp.), chamomile (*Chamaemelum nobile*), thyme (*Thymus vulgaris*), lily (*Lilium* spp.), rose (*Rosa* spp.), peppermint (*Mentha piperita*), marjoram (*Origanum majorana*) and myrrh (*Commiphora myrrha*), in almond (*Prunus dulcis*), olive and sesame oils, were perceived not only as being of importance to good appearance but were also pleasing to the gods (9). Protection from the skin-darkening (sun tanning) effect of the scorching sun was achieved using jasmine (*Jasminum officinale*, *Jasminum* spp.), rice bran (*Oryza sativa*) and lupine (*Lupinus albus*), as being lighter-skinned was culturally more desirable during this period. More recently, however, jasmine has been shown to contribute to DNA repair, rice bran absorbs ultraviolet (UV) radiation while lupine lightens the skin (10,11).

The Arab women also adorned their bodies just like the Egyptians. They lined their eyes with kohl and used body care preparations to keep their skin glowing. However, the introduction of the hijab law whereby women covered their hair and most of their face for religious reasons, reduced their use of cosmetics mainly to eye liners.

The ancient Greeks made good use of the abundance of the olive tree in their environment and hence, the olive oil extracted from the fruits of the plant. The skin was cleansed and moisturised regularly with olive oil, the hair was conditioned with the oil and facial masks were prepared with fresh olive berries and goat milk. Perfumed oils were prepared by heating olive oil with fragrant flowers, spices and herbs. Greek women regularly bathed with honey and goat milk as part of their nightly beauty routine and with yogurt as an anti-aging remedy. Having a pale complexion was in vogue at that time, and the women applied a powder, called focus, on the face, counteracting the harsh effect of the powder with the application of olive oil, tallow or lanolin. The powder consisted of white lead (a naturally occurring mineral), lead carbonate complex salt ($Pb_3(OH)_2(CO_3)_2$) (also known as hydrocerussite), mixed with powdered chalk (calcite, a rock mineral calcium carbonate, $CaCO_3$). Lead-poisoning was unknown at that time, but adverse effects which included skin damage, alopecia and even death happened when the powder was used over an extended period (12). The eyebrow was enhanced with the application of a paint made with charcoal, sooth, ashes and kohl dispersed in olive oil; this was also used as an eye liner. Fake eyebrows, made of oxen hair, were fashionable during this era. For the lips and cheeks, a paste made from beetroot powder, (*Beta vulgaris*), red wine or ochre clay mixed with beeswax or olive oil was employed. Henna extract was also used to paint the face. The women, for love of pale instead of the darkly coloured hair, applied vinegar to hair locks and stayed in the sun for bleaching to take place. On the other hand, pale-coloured skin was culturally more desirable; olive oil was used to protect the skin from the harsh effects of the sun and was also used for care after exposure to the sun

(13). Olive oil has, in modern times, been shown to have a sun protection factor (SPF) value of about 8. SPF is a rating for sunscreens and a value of ≥4 to <15 indicates medium/moderate protection (14).

The Indians were known to have the culture of body beautification dating back to between 2500 and 1550 BC (14). Like other cultures of that period, the Indians also applied kohl on the eye lashes and eyebrows and as an eye liner around the eyes for beauty, health and religious purposes. However, the Indian version of kohl, locally referred to as kajal, was prepared by applying sandalwood paste on a muslin cloth, drying it in the sun and then burning the cloth in a castor oil lamp. The carbon thus obtained was incorporated into ghee, a type of clarified butter. Lips were painted by chewing betel leaves (*Piper betle*) while the spiritual red circle of virtue, Bindi, worn by married women on the foreheads was prepared with turmeric and lime. The women in the higher social strata made the skin pale-looking with mixtures of plant parts such as lebbeck leaves (*Albizia lebbeck*), costus root (*Cheilocostus speciosus*), cedarwood (Cedrus spp.), sesame seeds (*Sesamum indicum*), barberry wood (*Berberis vulgaris*) and Pongamia pea plant leaves (*Millettia pinnata*). The young brides had their hands beautifully decorated with exotic designs using henna paste. Aromatic substances, such as sandal wood (*Santalum album*), camphor (*Cinnamomum camphora*), agaru (*Aquilaria agallocha*), saffron (*Crocus sativus*), kasturi (musk, *Moschus* spp.) were also part of the Indian beauty culture, religious beliefs and health protection substances (15,16)

In ancient times, around 300 - 710, the Japanese painted their face with red pigments which were replaced much later with makeups such as face powders and rouge imported from China and Korea. Indigenous cosmetics were, however, prepared by the Japanese when supplies from China were no longer obtainable. Lead-based white powder was applied on the face; eyebrows were plucked off; the upper part of the brow was thickly painted and the teeth blackened. Pigments applied on the cheeks, lips and fingernails were prepared from safflowers (15).

The Chinese similarly used cosmetics just like the Japanese. Rice powder was applied *on the face for a pale look.* Nails were painted with gum arabic, gelatine, beeswax and egg white as well as with different colours to indicate social class (16). *Plum blossom, that is, the flower of the tree, Prunus mume, was used to make designs on the forehead by the ladies while rouge was applied on the lips* (17).

The use of cosmetics is recorded in the old testament of the Bible where Jezebel, around 840 BC, painted her eyelids with kohl (18); and Esther underwent beauty treatments with the oil of myrrh, perfumes and some other cosmetics for six months before she could be brought before King Xerxes (19). Oil of myrrh was also the favourite of the wives of King Solomon as well as of Queen Cleopatra of Egypt. Myrrh oil, an essential oil obtained from oleo-gum resins of the plant *Commiphora myrrha* and other species, apart from its aroma which was used for meditation, has tremendous healing effects on the skin including the relief of dry skin by making the skin supple, prevention of wrinkles and skin rejuvenation (19). Prophets Jeremiah (20) and Ezekiel (21) vehemently preached, in particular, against face-painting by women depicting such practices as vain. Similarly, while Muslim women could use kohl and henna on their faces and bodies, in public, extra adornment such as lipsticks, dazzling eye colours and similar make-ups that could attract amorous attention are forbidden except when worn at home for the admiration of their husbands and other members of the family and household who collectively are referred to as the mahram (22).

Although ancient Roman women made the skin paler with chalk powder, white lead and a cream prepared from starch, tin and animal fat, the use of cosmetics was not universally accepted for a long time in Rome and, indeed, in Europe. Those who initially wore cosmetics were regarded as people of low esteem, prostitutes, heathens and in some countries as evil especially by the church. However, as time went by, the use of cosmetics became gradually acceptable to more people. Queen Elizabeth 1 (1559-1603) of England popularised the use of cosmetics in the 1500s as she was well known for her red hair and a pale skin which was obtained with the application of the popular white foundation known as ceruse that consisted of vinegar and white lead. A concoction that included mercury, sulphur and turpentine was used at that time to remove freckles and blemishes. These ingredients' toxic effects shrivelled the skin and made it greyish. The deleterious effects of these ingredients were, however, counteracted by the application of raw egg whites on the skin which smoothened the skin. She was soon imitated especially by the female English and French aristocrats who added to their cosmetic regime the use of wigs, rouge and the application of beauty spots on their faces. The location of a beauty spot signified the personality of the individual (23).

African women, especially those in the sub-Saharan region, adorned their bodies with products available in their environments such as oils and butters obtained from plants and animals. Different art designs were painted on their bodies with henna extract, white chalk powder and kaolin mixed with oils to get a radiant skin. Their finger and toenails were stained with a pigment obtained from the camwood plant (*Baphia nitida)*. This mode of skin and nail adornment is still in use today in some parts of Africa. For some of these African women, the body cleansing agent was soap prepared with plant oils and aqueous extracts of ash obtained from burnt plantain (*Musa x paradisiaca*) fruit skin and other similar materials that contain potassium and sodium salts. The use of clays to untangle the kinky hair and to prevent shrinkage especially after washing was common in some African cultures. Bentonite clay is presently being used for the same purpose by black Africans especially those who wear their natural hair (24).

The growth of the cosmetic industry

The advancement in science, innovations in cosmetics development, formulation and presentation; coupled with the technology and art of cosmetics as well as the increased access to the internet and the electronic media have all promoted world-wide awareness and use of cosmetics through aggressive advertisements, products launching, innovative and attractive packaging, availability of information on products' constituents and the acclaimed positive effects on the skin and safety of the cosmetic products. However, the cosmetic industry did not take off visibly till the beginning of the 20th century when people in the performing arts and entertainment industries promoted the use of cosmetics by wearing makeups for stage performances. Moreover, the great strides in the modernisation of commercial photography and film industries, the introduction of smart or virtual mirrors and a change in perception of the use of colour in beauty enhancement as well as self-consciousness of personal appearance and self-esteem by the female folk and more recently by men, boosted the growth and diversification of the cosmetic industry world-wide. Positive response by manufacturers to market surveys for consumers' preferences such as the use of natural ingredients in products and women's liking for handy and easy-to-use cosmetics especially while travelling or at social gatherings, have further enhanced cosmetics production and revenue to the industry.

Helena Rubinstein was one of the earliest known commercial cosmetic producers. Prompted by compliments she received from the public about her beautiful complexion, she started off in 1902 with the commercial production of a beauty cream whose main ingredient was lanolin. She later added lavender, pine bark and water lilies to mask the pungent odour of the lanolin. Subsequently, she launched Crème Valaze which was said to include some herbs. She opened the Salon de Beauté Valaze in London making this one of the world's first cosmetic companies. She was also a well-known makeup artist.

Max Factor, full name Maksymilian Faktorowicz (1877 – 1938), a naturalised American citizen who was born in Poland, was the first known famous makeup artist who, in the early 1900s, was popular with the Hollywood's leading film stars, producing the cosmetics he used for his trade by himself. Indeed, he is regarded as the father of makeup, a term he coined. He later founded his own cosmetic company which he named Max Factor & Company. This company's Max Factor brands are available in the market till today.

Earlier before these two cosmetic industry innovators, there was David McConnell who in 1886 founded the California Perfume Company (CPC) which later metamorphosed into the popularly known The Avon Company. Also, Eugene Schueller, a French chemist, in 1907, produced a synthetic dye which he named "Oréal" in 1909. He later, in 1953, established a company - Societé Francaise de Teintures Inoffensives pour Cheveux (Safe

Hair Dye Company of France) - which has since been transformed to the present-day L'Oréal, a topmost cosmetics organisation (25).

A male African American tailor, Garrett Augustus Morgan, in 1909, serendipitously discovered the first chemical permanent hair straightener for the management of the densely, curly Black African hair while trying to find a lubricant for his sewing machine. He quickly commercialised this goldmine and established the G.A. Morgan Hair Refining Company. The lye hair straightener was improved upon to contain petroleum jelly, water, mineral oil and emulsifiers along with the_lye - sodium hydroxide and was, by 1971, officially, commercially manufactured and marketed as a registered product, Dark and Lovely, by Proline, a cosmetic manufacturing company based in the USA (26). Morgan was also known to have developed and marketed hair dye pomades and other hair care products.

History relates the ancient Egyptian women as the earliest users of cosmetics, mascaras inclusive. However, in 1913, the French chemist and perfumer, Eugène Rimmel, produced the first non-toxic mascara, "Rimmel", prepared with petrolatum and coal which was modified and better marketed by Maybelline company owned by T.L. Williams. It was Helena Rubinstein in 1957 (1870 – 1965), whose products, prepared as a lotion and applied with a brush, were more acceptable both in mode of application and presentation and who, through aggressive marketing, made the mascara popular using movie actresses of her time as medium for advertisement. The use of mascaras has since become part of the makeup of the present-day fashionable woman (27).

The cosmetic, beauty and personal care product industry has since grown astronomically and only L'Oréal, of the pioneering companies, has remained among the top players in the industry till date. Among the top 10 cosmetics companies as at 2020 are L'Oréal, Unilever, Estee Lauder as well as Procter and Gamble (28).

The global market for the cosmetic industry was estimated at US$ 380.2 billion for the year 2019 with a projection of US$ 463.5 billion by 2027, at a Compound Annual Growth Rate (CAGR) of 5.3% from 2021 to 2027 (29). These estimates were made before the outbreak of COVID-19 pandemic of 2020 which caused the sector to experience a reduction in sales. However, the impact of the different cosmetic categories on the European market as well as the yearly market value of the top cosmetic consumers, with Germany leading, has been analysed with the effects of Brexit in the United Kingdom and the world-wide Covid-19 pandemic considered (30).

Practitioners of cosmetic applications and therapy

In recent times, and with the explosion in the availability of varied cosmetic and personal care products and therapy, the practitioners of cosmetic applications and therapy have had roles stratified and defined. Most of these practitioners are now certified after undergoing training in recognised institutions designated for this purpose in order that delivery of cosmetic applications can be thorough and safe.

The dermatologist: A dermatologist is a physician, trained in a medical school for general medicine and who later specialises in the field of dermatology for the diagnosis and treatment of skin, hair and nail diseases including cancer of these parts of the body. A dermatologist can further have some additional training in skin care and can work closely with other cosmetics professionals such as the aestheticians who, for example, can do regular facials and other therapies for a patient diagnosed with chronic acne by the dermatologist but who also needs ongoing treatment. Minimally invasive cosmetic procedures such as chemical peels and the administration of injectables like fillers are also under the purview of the dermatologist.

The cosmetologist: Cosmetology is the professional skill or practice of beautifying the face, hair, and skin (31). A person trained in cosmetology and licensed to provide beauty treatments for the skin, hair and nails is referred to as a cosmetologist. In the course of the formal training in certified institutions, the cosmetologist learns about the nature, diseases and means of correcting undesirable disorders of the hair, skin and nails. In respect of hair handling, skills such as special haircuts, hair colouring, chemical perm applications, hair braiding, techniques of hair extensions, sew-in and weave-ons, permanent hair removal processes such as electrology, laser therapy and intense pulsed light, non-permanent hair removal procedures like waxing and sugaring as well as a means of creating thicker and healthier hair are acquired and applied by the cosmetologist. The cosmetologist, as a makeup artist, learns the proper way of applying beauty products like foundation, concealer, bronzer, lipstick, mascara and eyeliner thereby improving clients' facial looks. Manicure and pedicure and nail painting services are rendered by the cosmetologist with the application of acquired knowledge on nail structures, growth and diseases thereby providing the desired nail care and art. The provision and application of appropriate skin care products and use of cosmetics are also performed by the cosmetologist.

The aesthetician/ paramedical aesthetician: An aesthetician is formally trained and licensed basically in the knowhow of making the skin cosmetically beautiful and healthy. Skin conditions such as dryness, wrinkles, unwanted hair, tone fading, dark spots and age spots are handled by the aesthetician. Microdermabrasion, facials, hair removal by various procedures including electrology, laser therapy, chemical resurfacing as well as makeup application and advice are services provided by the aesthetician.

Paramedical aesthetiology is a specialisation that enables the practitioner, the paramedical aesthetician, to work alongside dermatologists and some other physicians for the holistic treatment of patients with medical skin conditions.

The makeup artist: A makeup artist is an expert trained in the chemistry, aesthetic principles and safety of makeup products as well as the art of applying the products and the use of designated tools to transform, make-over and improve a client's personal look and beauty. The makeup artist is highly skilled in the art of face beautification and possesses excellent perception and use of colours for the purpose of tinting, concealing facial defects, highlighting facial features such as the cheek bones and, in the case of the theatre, film, television, commercials and fashion industries, may use prosthetics to achieve desired effects.

The Beautician: The beautician is trained in the art of hair care such as hair colouring, cutting and styling and performs skin care services such as waxing and facials.

Cosmeceuticals

Cosmeceutical is a term coined by Dr. Albert Kligman of the University of Pennsylvania, USA, in 1984 with the intent to find a category under which his newly developed anti-aging compound, tretinoin, could be classified since this affects the physiology of the skin cells and could, therefore, not be acceptably termed a cosmetic agent. Dr. Kligman's concept of a cosmeceutical is "a topical preparation that is sold as a cosmetic but has performance characteristics that suggest pharmaceutical action" (32). The term has since been adopted by the cosmetics industry for products that fall under this category. Cosmeceuticals can be defined as commercial products that, in addition to being used as cosmetics, have therapeutic effects or are able to alter the function or structure of the skin area on which they are applied. These are classified based on product type such as skin care, lip care, hair care and oral hygiene products. The discovery of the alpha-hydroxy acids and certain antioxidants, including vitamin C, as being effective for skin exfoliation and rejuvenation and the subsequent inclusion of these substances in topical products have exponentially expanded the scope and applications of cosmeceuticals. Among the indications for which cosmeceuticals are prescribed by dermatologists and beauty practitioners are moisturisation, anti-wrinkle/ageing effects, skin lightening, scar reduction, oral hygiene, hair health and growth stimulation as well as sunscreens (32–34).

In most cases, cosmeceuticals resolve the cause of skin imperfections unlike makeups that just conceal them; hence, the former are much preferred. Many cosmeceuticals now contain bio-active ingredients and this has increased patronage as consumers are now better informed about the possible deleterious effects of synthetic ingredients on their body. It is, however, a misconception that all bio-active substances used in these cosmeceuticals are without side effects.

It is interesting to note that for over 40 years since this category of skincare products, the cosmeceuticals, has been so designated and put to use, controversies have generated as to the designation of this class of products either as drugs or as cosmetics especially as regards safety test requirements and labelling of the products (33). Neither the United States Food and Drug Administration (US-FDA) nor the European Union has officially recognised nor legislated on these products. As a consequence, some active ingredients are classified differently from country to country. For example, antiperspirants, antidandruff shampoos and sunscreens are classified as drugs in the USA while these fall under ingredients for cosmetics in Europe. The Japanese regulatory body, however, by the Pharmaceutical and Medical Devises Act (PMD Act), classifies products that are neither pure drugs nor pure cosmetics as quasi-drugs (6). Such quasi-drug products are permitted to contain ingredients that are pharmacologically active but which are expected to have demonstrated mild medicinal effects and safety. These include medicated cosmetic products such as depilatories, skin-whitening or bleaching products, anti-acne and oily skin treatment products, hair growth stimulants, anti-ageing products, permanent hair straighteners and dyes (6). In the case of Nigeria, products such as antidandruff shampoos, antiperspirants, sunscreens, toothpastes that contain fluoride, hair growth stimulants and massage oils for relieving body pains or which treat or prevent diseases as well as preparations that reduce cellulite and those that affect melanin production are excluded by NAFDAC's definition of cosmetics (1).

The US-FDA does not require the submission of safety profiles except if the product contains a dye; nor does it control the sale and distribution of cosmetics. However, the Personal Care Products Council (PCPC), a trade organisation representing cosmetics manufacturers in the USA, has put in place the Cosmetic Ingredient Review (CIR) panel to put checks and balances on the safety of cosmetic ingredients used for products. However, this panel is not under the purview of the FDA and has been criticised and accused of permitting certain cosmetic ingredients that are not completely free of side effects on consumers as safe for use in cosmetic products (35). On the other hand, the European Union requires that finished cosmetic products offered for sale must be proven to be safe (36). Hence, the document compiled by the Scientific Committee on Consumer Safety (SCCS) contains information for the testing and safety evaluation of cosmetic substances marketed in member states (37). In Nigeria, NAFDAC requires the submission of the Comprehensive Certificate of Analysis from the quality control laboratory where the cosmetic sample was tested and evaluated as a condition for the registration of cosmetics in Nigeria (38).

With the increase in awareness of personal appearance, cosmeceuticals have grown in areas of research, application, development and formulation of appropriate products using novel and innovative technologies, such as nanotechnology (39), and excipients such as stabilisers and penetration enhancers that enable the production of more effective and safer products. Formulations that can be tested for efficacy and safety using 3D bio-printed live human tissue instead of the laborious animal and human trials are being developed (40).

Beauty enhancement is no longer just the application of makeups but involves the overall wellbeing of individuals especially as regards the health of the skin, hair and nails encompassing healing, rejuvenating and the protective effects of cosmeceuticals. Thus, the use of nutritional supplements such as natural oils, milk peptides, phytonutrients, vitamins and minerals as well as essential oils with bioactivity on the skin has become an integral part of looking good (41).

Other terminologies such as performance cosmetics, functional cosmetics, active cosmetics, dermoceuticals, dermocosmetics and physiologically active cosmetics are more recently being used to refer to marketed products that are not strictly cosmetics (42).

Cosmeceuticals entered the global market in the 1990s on the heels of nutriceuticals which were introduced into the market around 1989 and had gained recognition and patronage but which, like cosmeceuticals, are not recognised by the FD&CA. Cosmeceuticals have since grown exponentially in popularity and use over the years especially the anti-aging, sun care and hair care products as well as injectables due to the increasing awareness of consumers about their physical appearance and self-esteem, especially the 35+ age group who desire to maintain, as much as possible, their youthful looks as they grow older.

The global cosmeceutical market has been growing astronomically and a value of US$ 29.84 billion estimated for 2020 dropped by -26.4% due to the Covid-19 pandemic of that year. However, a growth from US$31.51 in 2021 to US$58.34 in 2028 has been projected at a CAGR of 9.2% during the period. It is expected that demands and use of these products will return to the pre-pandemic era as soon the pandemic subsides (43).

Dermocosmetics

Dermatologists, realising that cosmetics are scientifically developed using appropriate skin models (reconstructed skin) and procedures that are used in the evaluation of dermal pharmaceutical ingredients and products, are well-regulated by relevant regulatory bodies, and could maintain the aesthetic appearance and health of the skin, have introduced dermocosmetics as a branch of dermatology. Dermocosmetics are cosmetic products that are used in the scientific management and treatment of different skin disorders either alone or as adjuncts to regular pharmacotherapeutic agents for improved photoprotection, and enhancement of the management of dry and aged skin conditions as well as inflammatory skin diseases like seborrheic dermatitis, acne, psoriasis, atopic dermatitis and rosacea. Dermocosmetics are also used in the treatment of disorders of the nails and hair as well as for masking of facial scars. These topically applied products may mitigate the side effects of a variety of dermal therapeutic agents, and also enhance patients' quality of life and self-esteem (44). They may also enhance the efficacy of therapeutic agents and other treatments synergistically, increase patients' satisfaction with treatment and thereby encourage patients' adherence to therapy regimen (45). Soothing, moisturising cosmetic creams and lotions are perfect adjuncts that minimise itchiness and redness that accompany skin diseases such as eczema.

Dermocosmetics used as adjuncts in the treatment of acne are about the mostly employed. They contain active ingredients that function as antimicrobial, anti-inflammatory, sebum-controlling, moisturising, keratolytic and/or antioxidant agent(s) which may modulate pathogenic pathways in acne. They have been demonstrated to modify sebum production and to reduce transepidermal water loss (TEWL) thereby improving the clinical signs of acne (45). Moisturisers and anti-ageing cosmetics are of a particular importance in this regard. (See Chapter 3 of this book)

Unruly, thin, easily breaking, dry or excessively oily hair as well as facial hairs on ladies can be psychologically disturbing to a person that is self-conscious. Hair-grooming dermocosmetics are designed to mitigate these hair conditions which invariably are caused by underlying diseases that require the attention of the dermatologist and, in some cases, manifest as side effects of certain medications especially those used in chemotherapy. Anti-dandruff preparations, commonly provided in the form of shampoos, serve as dermocosmetic agents used in the treatment of dandruff and related scalp conditions. Laser therapy and electrology are available for the removal of unwanted facial hairs and there are cosmetic creams and physical devices and procedures that are also used to remove unwanted hair.

Skin-lightening or bleaching preparations are a type of dermocosmetics, designed primarily to remove blotchiness and dark spots on the skin, especially on the face, that are caused by wound scars, black heads, melasma, sun damage and ageing process to give a radiant and clear skin. Also, people born with vitiligo can be advised by dermatologists to use skin-lightening agents to lighten the dark areas of the skin so as to match the lighter parts.

Fibre facial masks or membranes containing facial treatment agents, especially those prepared as nanoparticles, enable more efficient delivery of active ingredients and may be preferred by dermatologists as adjuncts in the treatment of relevant skin disorders (46).

Sunscreens are products prepared to protect the skin from the adverse effects of the ultraviolet (UV) rays of the sun such as photo-toxic reactions, photo-ageing, hyperpigmentation and skin cancer. They are rated according to their sun protection factor (SPF) with the most effective having SPF values greater than 60. These dermocosmetics serve as photo-protective agents when used as adjuncts with therapeutic agents in the management of skin disorders. (See Chapters 7 and 9 for more descriptions of sunscreens).

Patients with overtly visible, skin disfiguring scars and lesions such as acne, vitiligo, psoriasis and rosacea on the face, neck and hands are often emotionally disturbed. They exhibit decreased self-esteem, increased manifestation of depression and anxiety, all of which affect the effectiveness of their daily activities and social interaction. Camouflage dermocosmetics are used as adjuncts in the management of these psychologically disturbing skin disorders, especially if they occur on the face (47). For instance, the health-related quality of life of women with systemic lupus erythematosus and permanent facial skin damage have been shown to improve when camouflage cosmetics were employed in the treatment regimen as adjuncts (48). Camouflage dermocosmetics are makeups which cover up flaws on the face thereby providing emotional benefits to the patients (47). Nail polishes and artificial nails are used to cover up undesirable colour, texture or shape of fingernails and toenails which are caused by some underlying disease conditions, for example, onychomycosis, that are treated by the dermatologists. There are nail polishes that have additional nail strengthening properties that prevent nail breaking, cracking and flaking. (See chapter 3 for a description of makeups).

In general, dermocosmetics are a group of cosmeceuticals and camouflage makeup cosmetics that are used as adjuncts in the treatment of certain dermatological disorders that inflict psychological trauma or disfigure, in one way or the other, the face, hair or nails of the patient.

Personal care products

Personal care products can literally be defined as products that are used for personal skin care and beauty as well as those that are used for personal hygiene. Thus, cosmetics such as skin moisturisers, deodorants, lipsticks, hair colours, perfumes, shaving creams, cleansing shampoos, nail polishes, toothpastes and eye and facial makeups are often also referred to as personal care products. Products that are similarly referred to as personal care include cosmeceuticals such as medicated mouthwashes, antiperspirants, diaper rash products, sun screens with Sun Protection Factor (SPF) numbers, dandruff and acne treatment agents; medical devices such as those used for hair removal and microdermabration procedures; other devices like manicure sets, hair clippers and razors; as well as some consumer hygiene products that include toilet paper, sanitary napkins, cotton swabs, wet wipes, hand soap, hand sanitisers, and baby powder. Dietary supplements are also sometimes referred to as personal care products (49).

Halal cosmetics and personal care products

Halal cosmetics and personal care products have constituted a new, recent and emerging concept in the cosmetic world. Halal, an Arabic word meaning 'permissible' by Islamic laws, refers, among other things, to some food items that are forbidden for a Muslim to eat and sometimes even to touch. In the context of cosmetic products, halal refers to those beauty and personal care products that do not contain ingredients obtained from porcine (lard, gelatine), non-Halal slaughtered animals (tallow, gelatine from sheep and cattle), blood, insects and reptiles. Genetically modified organisms (GMOs) are not to be used for halal cosmetic products as these are considered unclean. Carmine, a red colourant obtained from the cochineal beetle and used in some lipsticks, is not permitted in halal products. However, beeswax and gelatine obtained from marine sources are permissible. Also, application tools such as bristles of brushes manufactured from animal hairs must be certified halal products. Processes such as manufacturing, storage and transportation of halal products are expected to be carried out under hygienic conditions, while brand-labelling including images and logos on labels are expected to conform to Islamic virtues with no obscenity. Nail polish is expected to be water-permeable to allow water to reach the nail during ablution; for this reason there are halal nail polishes that are manufactured with polymers that are breathable (50).

The demand for halal products has further boosted the development and manufacture of organic, vegan and eco-friendly cosmetics which are becoming more preferred by consumers especially the environment enthusiasts and the ethically and ecologically conscious patrons who are particular about the health, safety and the sustainability of the sources of ingredients of their cosmetic products (51). Halal cosmetic industry is estimated to be worth US$ 53.81 billion by 2025, prompting top cosmetic brands like L'Oréal, Unilever and Beiersdorf to manufacture and distribute halal-certified cosmetic products (51).

Men's use of cosmetic products

In the past, men stereotyped cosmetics and their use to women; and in some cultures, for example in Saudi Arabia, men who applied cosmetics, even for skin grooming, were lowly esteemed and regarded as having a low level of masculinity. This notwithstanding, the Egyptian men lined their eyes and brows with kohl not only for religious and health purposes, but also to enhance their looks (9). More recently, encouraged by males in the costumes and performing arts industry who wear cosmetics and makeup for stage outings, the use of skin-grooming products and colour cosmetics is increasingly becoming popular among men. Men are now more aware of their looks than before and would moisturise the body, use skin-whitening products, anti-aging and sunscreen agents as well as enhance their eye brows and apply lightly coloured lipsticks. Some men do go for manicure and pedicure treatments as well as apply hair-grooming products to make their hair look good and manageable. In general, moisturisers, sunscreen, shave care, body cleansers and face wash are the most common among male cosmetics.

The cosmetic industry is giving attention to male cosmetics and is further encouraging male patronage by presenting and packaging male cosmetics in acceptable colours, usually dull grey, and in customised containers with the deliberate intention of differentiating them from female products thereby erasing the stereotype of cosmetics being for females only. Advertisements of male products are specially crafted to make them attractive and convincing to the male audience. With increased aggressive marketing campaigns and electronic advertisement strategies as well as purpose-driven distribution channels, male cosmetics are gradually becoming acceptable world-wide.

In the USA, cosmetics for men are estimated at US$3.4 Billion in the year 2021 projected to reach a value of US$16.3 Billion by 2026, growing at a CAGR of 5.1% over the analysis period, while a projected market size of US$3.3 Billion, at CAGR 7.8%, is forecast for China by 2026. The male cosmetics markets of Germany, Canada and Japan are forecast to grow at approximately CAGR 3.1%, 4.6% and 2.8%, respectively, over the period of analysis (52).

References

1. Food, Drugs And Related Products (Registrations, etc.) japa ACT Cap F.33 LFN 200425 [Internet]. [cited 2021 Oct 25]. Available from: https://www.nafdac.gov.ng/wp-content/uploads/Files/Resources/Regulations/NAFDAC_Acts/FOOD-DRUGS-AND-RELATED-PRODUCTS-REGISTRATION-ACT-Cap.F.33.pdf
2. Federal Food, Drug, And Cosmetic Act [Internet]. [cited 2021 Oct 25]. Available from: https://www.govinfo.gov/content/pkg/COMPS-973/pdf/COMPS-973.pdf
3. Cosmetic Regulations [Internet]. Canada.ca. [cited 2021 Oct 25]. Available from: https://laws-lois.justice.gc.ca/eng/regulations/C.R.C.,_c._869/
4. Cosmetics [Internet]. European Commission. [cited 2021 Oct 25]. Available from: https://ec.europa.eu/growth/sectors/cosmetics_en
5. Vincent Gallon. West Africa: WAEMU to regulate cosmetics approval. [Internet]. 2010. Available from: https://www.premiumbeautynews.com/west-africa-waemu-to-regulate,2426
6. Roger Ying. Japan Cosmetics and Quasi-Drugs Regulation. Japan Cosmetics authetics Regulation [Internet]. [cited 2021 Oct 25]. Available from:

https://www.cosmeticsbridge.com/cosmetics-and-quasi-drugs-regulations-in-japan-exporting-guidance/)

7. Food and drugs authority; Guidelines for the registration of cosmetics and household chemical substance. [Internet]. Vol. 02. 2019 [cited 2021 Oct 25]. Available from: http://fdaghana.gov.gh/images/stories/pdfs/downloads/GUIDELINE%20FOR%20REGISTRATION%20OF%20COS.%20AND%20HOUSEHOLD.pdf
8. Mustafa T.and Fatih G. Antimicrobial effect of CI Basic Green 4 (Malachite Green) against some pathogenic bacteria. January 2012 Tekst Ve Konfeksiyon. 2012 Jan;22(1):48–51.
9. Shannon Boyce. History of Makeup in Egypt. [Internet]. Love to Know. [cited 2021 Oct 25]. Available from: https://makeup.lovetoknow.com/History_of_Makeup_in_Egypt
10. Drissi M, Carr E, Housewright C. Sunscreen: a brief walk through history. Bayl Univ Med Cent Proc. 2022 Jan 2;35(1):121–3.
11. Aldahan AS, Shah VV, Mlacker S, Nouri K. The History of Sunscreen. JAMA Dermatol. 2015 Dec 1;151(12):1316.
12. Kassia St. Clair. The secret lives of colour. John Murray; 2016. 45–46 p.
13. Saraf S, Kaur C. *In vitro* sun protection factor determination of herbal oils used in cosmetics. Pharmacogn Res. 2010;2(1):22.
14. Patkar KB. Herbal cosmetics in ancient India. Indian J Plast Surg Off Publ Assoc Plast Surg India. 2008 Oct;41(Suppl):S134-137.
15. Cultural History of cosmetics [Internet]. JCIA; Cosmetics in Japan. [cited 2021 Oct 25]. Available from: https://www.jcia.org/en/info/history
16. Beccy Koch. Ancient chinese nail polish. [Internet]. 2016 [cited 2021 Oct 25]. Available from: https://prezi.com/pccpylxsf2f_/ancient-chinese-nail-polish/?frame=2d6baeaf92c2ae7d917d5df663074bedd71ddd6c
17. Mei, Hua. Chinese clothing. Cambridge University Press,; 2011. 32 p.
18. Holy bible 2kings 9:30. Cambridge University Press, Cambridge,; 1993. 434 p.
19. Holy Bible Esther 2: 12. Cambridge University Press. Cambridge University Press, Cambridge,; 1993. 575 p.
20. Holy Bible Jeremiah 4:30. Cambridge University Press, Cambridge,; 1993. 878 p.
21. Holy Bible Ezekiel 23: 40. Cambridge University Press, Cambridge; 1993. 985 p.
22. Rosa Safitriin. Is Makeup Haram? – All You Need to Know [Internet]. 2022. Available from: https://halalguidance.com/is-makeup-haram/
23. Elizabeth. Fashion and beauty [Internet]. Royal museums greenwich. [cited 2021 Oct 25]. Available from: https://www.rmg.co.uk/stories/topics/elizabeth-i-fashion-beauty
24. Clay Masks For Hair: Benefits, Best Clay Types & How to Use [Internet]. Lovingkinkycurls. 2020 [cited 2021 Oct 29]. Available from: https://lovingkinkycurls.com/clay-masks-for-hair/
25. A History of Cosmetics from Ancient Times [Internet]. Cosmetics Info. [cited 2021 Oct 25]. Available from: https://cosmeticsinfo.org/Ancient-history-cosmetics)
26. Erika Winston. The History of Hair Relaxers [Internet]. Classroom. [cited 2021 Oct 25]. Available from: https://classroom.synonym.com/the-history-of-hair-relaxers-12078983.html

27. History of Mascara - Invention of the Mascara. http://www.historyofcosmetics.net/history-of-makeup/history-of-mascara/. 2022.
28. Top 10 Largest Cosmetics Companies in the World for 2019 [Internet]. [cited 2021 Oct 25]. Available from: https://blog.technavio.com/blog/top-10-cosmetics-companies
29. Nitesh Chouhan, Himanshu Vig , Roshan Deshmukh. Cosmetics Market [Internet]. 2021 [cited 2021 Oct 28]. Available from: https://www.alliedmarketresearch.com/cosmetics-market
30. The cosmetics market in Europe: today's challenges, tomorrow's opportunities [Internet]. 2021 [cited 2021 Oct 25]. Available from: https://www.cosmoprof.com/en/media-room/news/the-cosmetics-market-in-europe-todays-challenges-tomorrows-opportunities/
31. Cosmetology [Internet]. [cited 2021 Oct 29]. Available from: https://www.lexico.com/definition/cosmetology
32. Pandey A, Jatana GK, Sonthalia S. Cosmeceuticals. In: StatPearls [Internet]. Treasure Island (FL): StatPearls Publishing; 2022 [cited 2022 Jun 23]. Available from: http://www.ncbi.nlm.nih.gov/books/NBK544223/
33. Newburger AE. Cosmeceuticals: myths and misconceptions. Clin Dermatol. 2009 Sep;27(5):446–52.
34. Saint-Leger D. 'Cosmeceuticals'. Of men, science and laws.... october;Int J Cosmet Sci . 2012 Oct;34(5):396-401(5):396–401.
35. Alexandra S, Jamie McConnell. Report Exposes Industry-Funded Cosmetic Ingredient Review (CIR) Panel's Failure to Protect the Public and Manufacturers [Internet]. 2018 [cited 2021 Nov 2]. Available from: https://www.womensvoices.org/2018/04/24/report-exposes-industry-funded-cosmetics-ingredient-review-cir-panels-failure-protect-public-manufacturers/
36. REGULATION (EC) No 1223/2009 OF THE EUROPEAN PARLIAMENT AND OF THE COUNCIL. Off J Eur Union [Internet]. 2009 Nov 30; Available from: https://ec.europa.eu/health/system/files/2016-11/cosmetic_1223_2009_regulation_en_0.pdf
37. Werner Lilienblum, Vera Rogiers. SCCS Notes of Guidance for the Testing of Cosmetic Ingredients and their Safety Evaluation, 9th revision, SCCS/1564/15, [Internet]. 2016 [cited 2021 Nov 2]. Available from: https://www.researchgate.net/publication/302523991_SCCS_Notes_of_Guidance_for_the_Testing_of_Cosmetic_Ingredients_and_their_Safety_Evaluation_9th_revision_SCCS156415_revision_of_25_April_2016
38. National Agency for Food & Drug Administration & Control (NAFDAC) Registration & Regulatory Affairs (R & R) Directorate Guidlines for registration of cosmetics made in Nigeria [Internet]. [cited 2021 Nov 3]. Available from: https://www.nafdac.gov.ng/wp-content/uploads/Files/Resources/Guidelines/R_and_R_Guidelines/LOCAL/Guidelines-for-the-Registration-of-Cosmetics-made-in-Nigeria.pdf
39. Lohani A, Verma A, Joshi H, Yadav N, Karki N. Nanotechnology-Based Cosmeceuticals. ISRN Dermatol. 2014 May 22;2014:1–14.

40. Cubo N, Garcia M, Del Cañizo JF, Velasco D, Jorcano JL. 3D bioprinting of functional human skin: production and in vivo analysis. Biofabrication. 2016 Dec 05;9(1):015006.
41. Das L, Bhaumik E, Raychaudhuri U, Chakraborty R. Role of nutraceuticals in human health. J Food Sci Technol. 2012 Apr;49(2):173–83.
42. Mohammed M, Lakshmi P. Cosmeceuticals: a revolution in the making [Internet]. [cited 2021 Oct 25]. Available from: https://drmajeed.com/pdf/articles/2006CosmeceuticalARevolution.pdf
43. Cosmeceuticals market size, shares & COVID-19 impact analysis by product type [Internet]. Fortune Business Insights. 2022 [cited 2021 Oct 28]. Available from: https://www.fortunebusinessinsights.com/cosmeceuticals-market-102521
44. Dreno B, Araviiskaia E, Berardesca E, Bieber T, Hawk J, Sanchez-Viera M, et al. The science of dermocosmetics and its role in dermatology. J Eur Acad Dermatol Venereol. 2014 Nov;28(11):1409–17.
45. Araviiskaia E, Lopez Estebaranz JL, Pincelli C. Dermocosmetics: beneficial adjuncts in the treatment of acne vulgaris. J Dermatol Treat. 2021 Jan 2;32(1):3–10.
46. Manatunga DC, Godakanda VU, Herath HMLPB, de Silva RM, Yeh CY, Chen JY, et al. Nanofibrous cosmetic face mask for transdermal delivery of nano gold: synthesis, characterization, release and zebra fish employed toxicity studies. R Soc Open Sci. 2020 Sep;7(9):201266.
47. Emer J, Levy LL. Emotional benefit of cosmetic camouflage in the treatment of facial skin conditions: personal experience and review. Clin Cosmet Investig Dermatol. 2012 Nov;173.
48. Oliveira FAP de, Santos F de MM dos, Dias AFM de P, Neiva CLS, Telles RW, Lanna CCD. Cosmetic camouflage improves health-related quality of life in women with systemic lupus erythematosus and permanent skin damage: A controlled intervention study. Lupus. 2020 Oct;29(11):1438–48.
49. Cosmetics Safety Q&A: Personal Care Products [Internet]. [cited 2021 Nov 2]. Available from: https://www.fda.gov/cosmetics/resources-consumers-cosmetics/cosmetics-safety-qa-personal-care-products
50. Aaqilah Alexander. Everything You Need to Know About the Halal Cosmetic Industry [Internet]. 2021 [cited 2021 Oct 25]. Available from: https://www.halalwatchworld.org/everything-you-need-to-know-about-the-halal-cosmetic-industry
51. Technavio. Halal Cosmetics is Booming with Rising Demand for Natural Products [Internet]. 2018 [cited 2021 Oct 25]. Available from: https://blog.technavio.com/blog/halal-cosmetics-rising-demand-natural-products
52. Global Men's Skincare Products Market to Reach $16.3 Billion by 2026 [Internet]. [cited 2021 Nov 2]. Available from: https://www.prnewswire.com/news-releases/global-mens-skincare-products-market-to-reach-16-3-billion-by-2026--301383000.html

CHAPTER TWO

Skin anatomy and physiology

Olumayowa A Oninla, Atinuke A Ajani and Ademola O Enitan

The skin is in continuum with the external environment through exchange of substances and reception of stimuli whilst protecting against ultraviolet irradiation, mechanical/chemical stress, and infections. There is continuous remodelling by the skin itself based on interaction with external stimuli (1). The skin has three different layers which vary in their anatomical structures and function that enables it to adapt to changes (2). Aging, medications, cosmetics, illness, and skin diseases such as psoriasis influences the cellular turnover rate, and the response to environmental stresses and trauma (1).

Skin structure

The skin, the outermost covering of the body, is the largest organ in the body and it covers an average surface area of 1.7 m^2 (1) with a weight over 5 kg in a 70 kg person (2). It has three primary layers - epidermis, dermis, and hypodermis/subcutaneous tissue.

Epidermis

This is the outermost layer of the skin (Figure 1) which developed from the ectoderm (3). The ectoderm is the outermost layer of the three primary germ layers formed in the early embryonic development. This layer differentiates into epithelial and neural tissues (spinal cord, peripheral nerves and brain). The epithelial tissues further develop into the skin, sweat glands, hair and nails, linings of the tooth enamel, mouth, nostrils, and anus. The epidermal layer of the skin is thinnest on the eyelid where it measures 0.1 mm while on the palms and soles of the feet it is thickest with a measurement of 1.5 mm. There are 5 distinct layers in the epidermis. The cells in the epidermis are continually shedding and renewing and are almost completely replaced every three to four weeks (3). The epidermis is avascular but obtains nutrients from the dermal vascular network.

Epidermal layers - The epidermis is divided into five sub-layers (Figure 1):

Stratum corneum: This is the uppermost skin layer with a thickness of about 10–20 µm and the layer that varies most in thickness, particularly in callused skin. It is multi-layered, consisting of 10-20 cell layers and horny scales made up of dead or enucleate squamous cells. The cells contain primarily insoluble bundled keratins fibrils and have cross-linked proteins embedded in covalently- bound lipid bilayers giving rise to the 'bricks and mortar' form of the epidermis (4). These cells also contain defensins which are part of the first immune defence system.

The stratum corneum has two main functions which are:

- External barrier that prevents trans-epidermal water loss (TEWL).
- Formation of an acid mantle. The normal skin pH is 4 - 6 while skin damage to the stratum corneum in an open wound increases skin pH to 6.5 - 8.5. The skin mantle makes the skin less permeable to water and protects the skin from microbial invasion. The acid mantle can be damaged when there is a damage to the skin, by conditions associated with increased skin pH such as eczema and other dermatitis, dry skin, chronic renal failure, diabetes, cardiovascular disease, as well as contact with urine (range from pH 4.6 to 8.0), stool (range from pH 7.0 to 7.5) and perspiration or sweats (from moderately acidic to neutral pH range of 4.5 to 7.0).

Stratum lucidum: It is a clear thin layer of 2-3 cells between the granular and corneal layers in the palms and soles. It consists of eleidin which is a derivative of keratohyalin (3).

Stratum granulosum* or granular cell layer:* It has 3-5 cell layers with diamond shaped cells which contain keratohyalin granules and lamellar granules. Keratohyalin granules are keratin precursors that aggregate and crosslink to form bundles. The lamellar granules contain the glycolipids that are secreted to the surface of the cells and function as 'cement' sticking the cells together (3).

Stratum spinosum* or prickle cell layer:* This layer consists of 8-10 cell layers and contains irregular, polyhedral cells with rounded nucleus in the suprabasal part whereas the cells in the upper layers are generally larger in size and become flatter as they moved towards the surface of the skin and they undergo cytoplasmic processes, referred to as "spines", extending outward and connected to neighbouring cells by desmosomes (3). The spinous cells contain lamellar granules. These are membrane-bound organelles that contain glycoproteins, glycolipids, phospholipids, free sterols, and a number of acid hydrolases (lipases, proteases, glycosidases and acid phosphatases), necessary for the formation of stratum corneum lipids that are later extruded into the intercellular space. Dendritic cells are also found in the prickle cell layer.

***Stratum germinativum or stratum basale* or basal cell layer**: This is a single layer of columnar cells that are mitotically active cells which divide to form new skin cells that migrate upwards to the stratum corneum. Basal cells begin synthesis of tonofilaments which are made of keratin and grouped into bundles called tonofibrils. The keratin makes the cells tough and strong. They are joined together and to overlying cells through the desmosomal junction (5). They have dark-staining oval or elongated nuclei, and the melanin pigments. Basal cells migrate to the corneum in about 28-30 days. Melanocytes are located within the basal layer. They produce melanin which are distributed to other epidermal cells and provide protection from ultraviolet (UV) radiation.

Cells in the epidermis – There are four distinct types of cells (Figure 2.1):

***Keratinocytes*:** These are derived from the ectoderm and make up 80% of the epidermal cells. The basal cells differentiate into other epidermal cells to give rise to horny cells or corneocytesby a process called keratinization (3). This process involves the synthetic phase and the degradation phase (5). Keratin is produced during the synthetic phase and during degradation, cellular organelles such as the nucleus and mitochondria are lost and cell contents are consolidated into a mixture of filaments and amorphous cell envelopes called corneodesmosomes in the cells of the last layer of the skin called the stratum corneum (5).

Melanocytes: these are responsible for melanin pigments which give the skin tone and colour and are present in the same number in all skin types. However, the size and activity of the cells are greater in darker skin. Cells in dark skin are more compact, therefore, the skin is more resistant to injuries such as photodamage from ultraviolet radiation (3).

Merkel cells: they are oval-shaped, modified epidermal cells that are located in the stratum basale above the basement membrane and are attached by desmosomes to surrounding keratinocytes (3). They contain intermediate keratin filaments, function as mechanoreceptors for light touch and their membranes interact with free nerve endings (3). They are found mostly in the fingertips, palms, soles as well as the oral and genital mucosae (3).

***Langerhans cells/dendritic cells*:** These are cells of mesenchymal origin derived from bone marrow stem cells. They are primarily located in the stratum spinosum and serve an immunological function. They are part of the mononuclear phagocytic system. They are the first line of defence and are involved in uptake of antigens in the skin, transportation to the lymph nodes, and antigen presentation for immune responses.

Dermis

The dermis lies immediately below the epidermis (Figure2.2). The cellular components are fibroblasts, macrophages, and mast cells (3). The fibroblast is the most common type of cell found in connective tissues. Fibroblasts secrete collagen proteins that are used to maintain a structural framework for many tissues.

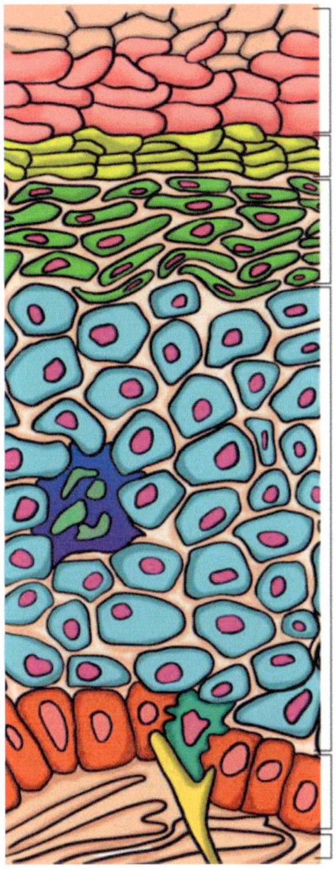

Figure 2.1: Epidermal layers. Contributed by Chelsea Rowe (3).

They also play an important role in wound-healing. The dermis is larger than the epidermis with a thickness of 1–2 mm (6). It contains tough connective tissues, blood vessels, nerves, lymphatics and dermal appendages (hair follicles, sweat glands, sebaceous glands, fingernails and toe nails). The dermis has two layers:

- Papillary (superficial): this is the thinner layer and consists of:
  - Extracellular matrix (ECM)
  - Blood and lymph vessels
  - Epithelial cells
  - Loose connective tissue
  - Nerve tissue

- Reticular (deep): this is the thicker layer and consists of:
  - Sweat glands
  - Hair follicles
  - Blood vessels
  - Nerves
  - Collagen fibers
  - Connective tissue
  - Muscle and fat

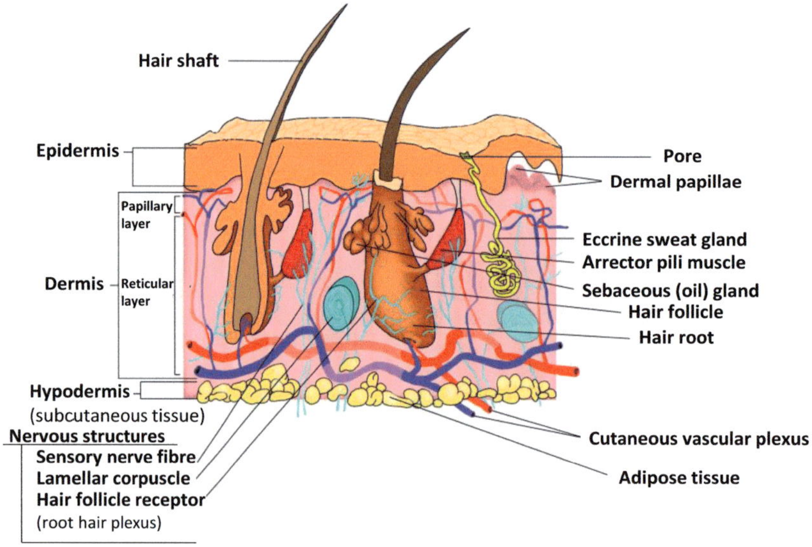

]

Dermal appendages: These include:

Hair follicles: These occur all over the body except in the soles, palms, and glans penis. They are more on the face and scalp and the chest in men. The hair is a derivative of the germinative cells from which melanocytes and keratinocytes arise. The hair shaft consists of an internal medulla surrounded by a cortex made of keratinocytes, an outer cuticle, and then the inner and outer root sheaths. The hair bulb contains the matrix cells from which the hair is formed. The arrector pili muscle supports the hair shaft (Figure 2.2). The muscle responds to environmental and emotional stimulation such as cold and fear-producing "goosebumps" appearance.

Nails: Nails are keratinous structures that protect the tips of the fingers and toes. They are made up of compact plates of hardened keratin of 0.3 to 5 mm thickness. Nails have three parts: the nail matrix, nail bed, and nail plate as shown in Figure 2.3 (8). The nail matrix contains the formative layer of cells made up of dividing keratinocytes and lies at the base of the toenail or fingernail. The cells mature and keratinize to form the nail plate. The lunula is the visible part of the matrix and it is seen as a whitish area at the base of the nail plate.

Sebaceous glands: The glands develop from the epidermal cells and can be found with the follicles of the hair. They are the exocrine glands that secrete sebum, an oily or waxy substance that lubricates skin and hair and impedes skin penetration by microorganisms. Antioxidants are transported through these glands to the rest of the skin, thus protecting the skin surface from damage by UV radiations.

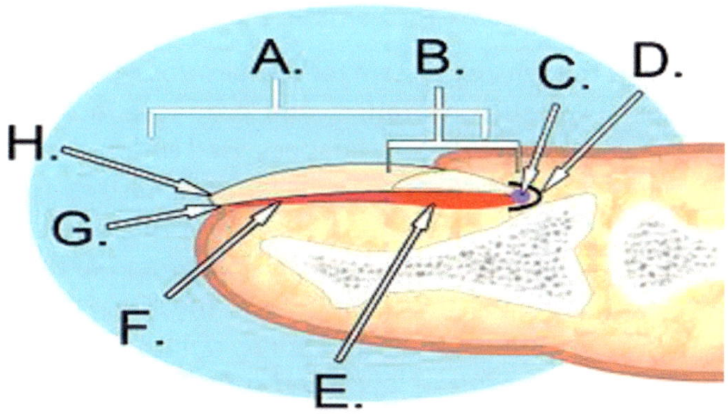

Figure 2.3: Anatomy of the basic parts of a human nail (8). A. Nail plate; B. lunula; C. root; D. sinus; E. matrix; F. nail bed; G. hyponychium; H. free margin. Creative Commons Attribution-Share Alike 3.0 Unported license.

Sweat glands: About 2.5 million sweat glands are present in the dermis and there are two main types: apocrine glands (occurring in axillae, eyelids, ear canals, nostril, areolas and nipples, perianal region, and some parts of the external genitalia) and eccrine glands (all over the body but mostly in palms and soles, and fewer on the extremities and trunk). The activities of the two glands are controlled by the sympathetic nerve fibres. The apocrine glands secrete an odourless fluid which can become an offensive odour when acted upon by bacteria. Sweat is a clear liquid that contains fatty acid, lactic acid, glycoproteins and mucopolysaccharides.

Functions of the sweat glands:

- Provides tensile strength, mechanical support for the appendages and protection to the underlying muscles, bones, and other organs.
- Regulates temperature through the blood vessels (9): increased body temperature causes vasodilation of the blood vessels. Vasodilatation also results from inhibition of the sympathetic centres in the posterior hypothalamus. Reduced body temperature leads to vasoconstriction of skin blood vessels to conserve heat. This process is referred to as thermoregulation. It serves as a very effective mechanism by which body temperature is controlled through the skin. Vasodilatation increases blood flow to the skin thereby transferring heat from within the body to the environment. The heat, providing the heat of vaporisation, causes increased evaporation of sweat from the glands thereby lowering the temperature and cooling the body.

Cutaneous nerves: The skin senses the environment through the nerves (10, 11). There are two types of nerves in the skin - the somatic and autonomic nerves.

Somatic nerves – this is the sensory system for temperature, pain (nociceptors), pressure, light touch, discriminative touch, vibration, and proprioception (joint position sense). These sensations are conducted primarily by specialised cutaneous receptors/end organs; the Merkel disks (senses light touch), Meissner's corpuscles (senses low-frequency stimulation at the dermal papillae level), and Pacinian corpuscles (senses deep pressure), and Ruffini corpuscles (senses pressure). Merkel disks extend to the stratum basale layer whereas the others are found in the deeper parts of the skin. Free nerve endings extend from dermal nerves into the epidermis and sense pain, heat, and cold, and are most numerous in the stratum granulosum layer, and surround most of the hair follicles. Itch receptors are formed from a plexus of free nerve endings closely related to the dermo-epidermal junction. They are stimulated by chemical mediators such as histamine usually released in inflamed itchy skin. Some mediators that are incapable of producing itching alone, potentiate the action of other itch stimulating agents.

Autonomic nerves - control of the vascular tone, pilomotor stimulation ofthe hair root, and sweating process is by the autonomic nerves.

Subcutaneous/adipose/hypodermis layer/panniculus (3): This is the layer of skin below the dermis. It has a variable thickness in different parts of the body. It contains mainly fat cells, blood vessels, and connective tissues. The blood supply varies with the thickness of the adipose tissue. This layer anchors the skin to deep tissues while the fat component insulates the body against cold; hence, it is essential for temperature control. It contains sensory neurons and blood vessels and acts as a fat store which is metabolised to provide energy for cellular activities.

Skin functions

The main function of the skin is protection, both by preventing external damage from the hostile external environment or invasion by noxious chemicals and microorganisms and by maintaining the internal milieu of the body. Though the skin acts as a barrier, it is permeable to many substances such as perfumes, ointments, and dyes. Changes in skin physiology reflect the appearance, texture, or integrity of the skin. Metabolic, immunological, and histological changes occur in the skin in response to various microorganisms, chemicals, and topical formulations used for skin-grooming and transdermal drug delivery.

Mechanism of molecular transportation in the skin

Skin penetration refers to the passage of an active ingredient into the skin to a certain extent. Skin permeation is the term used to describe the passage of an active ingredient or compound through the epidermis to the dermis and then to the circulatory system. The term, skin absorption, can be used for either permeation, penetration, or both occurring simultaneously. Most cosmetics are presented as nanoproducts. Hydrophilic and lipophilic nanoproducts and other particles cannot easily permeate or penetrate the skin due to the constituents of the stratum corneum which consists of 60 - 80% proteins, 5 -20% water, 10% lipids, and 5 - 8% other compounds (12).

Skin transportation occurs through four pathways (7); two transepidermal routes (transcellular route) – intercellular and transcellular, and two transappendageal routes (the shunting route) – the sweat glands and hair follicles.

The transappendageal route is the shortest pathway to dermal microcirculation and the bloodstream and lymph. Transfer of minoxidil through this route plays a major role in hair growth (13). Permeation occurs through the sweat glands and the hair follicles (and sebaceous glands) as their ducts open outside the skin. A combination of all the routes is employed by various compounds and their physicochemical properties determine the route taken (14).

In the transcellular route, the absorbed molecules must first pass through the cellular phospholipid membranes and then into the keratinous matrix of each cell resulting in several partitions causing minor permeability issues. Any molecule such as urea that changes the keratinous structure increases permeability (15, 16).

In the intercellular route, molecules pass through the lipid matrix and the small spaces in-between the cells traversing a diffusional path of 400 mm through the stratum corneum. The increase in distance traversed is due to the impermeability of the cells in the epidermis. Hence, the molecules pass in-between the cells. Most large molecules are usually confined within the lipid matrix. The diffusion rate of small molecules depends on their physicochemical features such as molecular weight, solubility, lipophilicity, and hydrogen bonding ability (10, 17).

Regional differences in skin permeability

The density and size of hair follicles and their appendages, such as sebaceous, eccrine, and apocrine glands, vary in different skin areas. This in turn determines the microbiota composition in topographically different areas of the skin. The microbiota further determines the secretion of various innate immune mediators by keratinocytes and sebocytes such as antimicrobial peptides (AMPs), interleukin-1α, chemokines, and complement factors, as well as stimulation of dermal T-cells and dendritic cells in the skin (18). The level of these mediators and cellular infiltration regulates the antimicrobial property and permeability of skin barriers in different parts of the body. The AMPs are 4- to 9-fold increased in sebaceous gland-rich (SGR) and apocrine gland-rich (AGR) skin areas than the dry gland-poor (GP) skin areas. SGR and AGR regions have higher TEWL levels than GP areas (18).

The permeability barrier of the human skin is not uniform. Gland-poor (GP) skin regions have lesser permeability than gland-rich areas. Factors found in gland-rich areas (sebaceous gland-rich (SGR), and apocrine gland-rich (AGR)) responsible for these differences are (18):

- Significantly lower extracellular protein levels of corneodesmosomes (DSG1, desmoglein; and CDSN, corneodesmosin) and tight junctions (TJs) proteins (OCLN, occludin; and CLDN1, claudin) than in GP areas.
- Kallikrein proteases (KLKs) are significantly higher. KLKs activate multiple enzymes responsible for TJ degradation (e.g., PAR2, matrix metalloproteases) and may be at least partially involved in TJ weakness seen in SGR and AGR regions.
- Prominently disorganised junction structures (corneodesmosomes and TJs).
- Higher transepidermal water loss (TEWL) levels compared to GP skin. Differences between the AGR and GP areas (6.89-fold increase) are more prominent than in SGR versus GP areas (1.57-fold increase).

Major functions of the skin

The skin keeps the biochemical and physiological circumstances of the body in optimum condition. The major functions of the skin are:

- Responsible for physical appearance, a major target of makeup cosmetics. Physical appearance is a factor of psychological well-being and cutaneous defects such as pigmentary disorders and port-wine stains often result in low self-esteem among other psychological disabilities (19). Common alterations most frequently considered unaesthetic with little concern to serious somato-psychic repercussions are: dry or greasy skin, changes in skin colour, wrinkling and hair changes such as unwanted facial or body hair, thin, dull or easily breakable hair (20).

- Physical and biological barrier: Acts as a protective barrier between the external environment and internal organs as well as a two-way barrier preventing loss of body fluids and the penetration of toxic substances and infective organisms into the body. The epidermis mainly acts as the skin barrier while the dermis is permeable.
- Regulates body temperature: by heat regulation - the blood vessels increase perfusion and heat loss, while constricted vessels greatly reduce cutaneous blood flow and conserve heat. Erector pili muscles are significant in man's control of the heat.
- Expels toxic substances with sweat.
- Protects from harmful effects of the sun and radiation.
- Serves as sensory organ: contains various nerve endings for touch, cold, heat, pressure, vibration, sociosexual, emotional sensations, and tissue injury.
- Performs immunological functions. Langerhans cells in the skin are part of the adaptive immune system.
- Synthesis of vitamin D using sunlight: vitamin D is important in production of steroids in the body.
- Storage: acts as a storage centre for lipids and water.
- Absorption: oxygen, nitrogen and carbon dioxide can diffuse into the epidermis in small amounts.
- Control of evaporation: the skin provides a relatively dry and semi-impermeable barrier to fluid loss.
- Water resistance: the skin acts as a water-resistant barrier so that essential nutrients are not washed out of the body.

Skin as a physical and biological barrier

Although the skin acts as a protective barrier between the external and internal environments, it is not an impermeable barrier (21). The most important function of the human skin is creating a watertight enclosure to prevent water loss by the body. The normal physiological function requires strict body-water homeostasis (21). Fluid loss results in fluid and electrolyte imbalance, particularly sodium resulting in harmful effects on the physiological processes in cells and tissues (21, 22).

Corneocytes localised in the stratum corneum (SC) constitute the main physical barrier (Figure 4) along with their cytoskeletal elements, cornified envelope corneodesmosomes as well as lipid-enriched intercellular layers (23, 24). The cytoskeletal elements in the nucleated cells of the epidermis with their tight junctions, adherens junctions, hemidesmosomes, and desmosomes also contribute to the barrier function. The corneocytes envelope lipids, secretions of sebaceous lipids (primarily non-polar lipids - triglycerides, wax esters, and squalene), and the intercellular lipids (made of a mixture of ceramides (41%), cholesterol (27%), and cholesteryl esters (10%) together with fatty acids (9%) and cholesteryl sulphate (1.9%)), and thereby provide a water-resistant barrier to water absorption or loss (25). Transport that is normal to the bilayer structures which are made of a mixture of free fatty acids, ceramides, and cholesterol is necessary for substances to penetrate (25).

The corneocytes' surface is hydrophobic due to covalently bound long-chain ceramides in the corneocytes' envelopes (26). Under normal circumstances, the corneocytes are essentially only permeable to water hence both hydrophilic substances can permeate. The presence of the hydrophobic envelope implies that hydrophobic substances are transported through the extracellular space of the stratum corneum (21). Lipids in this space are arranged in bilayers which provides a space in-between them in which thin water sheets move together with hydrophilic substances while hydrophobic substances can readily diffuse within the plane of the lipid bilayers (21).

Substances penetrate the skin mainly through three routes: through or between epidermal cells; through sweat ducts; or hair shafts (27). Any substance causing dermatitis has penetrated at least the superficial layers for it to trigger an inflammatory response in the skin. Cosmetic substances that are sheathed in a lipid-soluble casing, that is, prepared in an oily milieu, are capable of penetrating the deeper layers of the skin (27). Many cosmetics products have not been subjected to the same stringent testing requirements as drugs. If these penetrate the skin and possibly enter the blood stream, they may exert physiological effects on other structures other than their intended target (28).

Calcium, cytokines, and 3',5'-cyclic adenosine monophosphate control the formation and maintenance of barrier function (29). Factors or substances influencing their control cause changes in epidermal differentiation and skin lipid composition with resultant alterations in the skin barrier. This allows permeability to allergens, environmental pollutants as well as immunological and inflammatory agents.

Protective functions of the skin from harmful effects of the sun and radiation

The harmful effects of ultraviolet radiation (UV) from the sun or other sources range from sunburn to dermatoheliosis (photo-ageing) and skin cancers. UV radiation has a broad spectrum that ranges from 40 to 400nm and consists of Vacuum UV (40–190nm), Far UV (190–220nm), UVC (220–290nm), UVB (290–320), and UVA (320–400nm) (30). Only the last two are of medical importance; ultraviolet C (UVC) in sunlight is filtered out and does not reach the earth's surface. There are two distinct subtypes of UVA radiation: short-wave UVA (320–340nm) and long-wave UVA (340–400nm); the latter constitutes most of UVA radiation. The amount of exposure to UVA usually remains constant, whereas UVB exposure occurs more in the summer.

Ultraviolet A (UVA) with wavelength of 320–400 nm constitutes 95 to 98% of the UV radiation detected on the earth's surface. It is divided into short-wave UVA or UVAI (340–400 nm) and long-wave UVA or UVAII (320–340 nm). UVA causes photo-ageing, hyperpigmentation, photo-toxic reactions, photo-allergic reactions and it may contribute to the development of skin cancer.

The effects of UVA usually manifest after prolonged exposure to the radiation and can occur at low doses of UVA. These are:

- Marked reduction in skin elasticity and/or increased wrinkling which occurs from the degradation of elastic and collagen fibres in the extracellular matrix by matrix metalloproteinase (MMPs), an enzyme postulated to be induced by UVA (30). By penetrating the skin layers, UVA produces reactive oxygen species resulting in acute and chronic skin changes and it is being increasingly recognised as an important cause of photo-aging and skin cancer (30, 31).
- Photo-allergic reactions include polymorphous light eruptions (PMLE), exacerbation of cutaneous lupus erythematosus, and solar urticaria. UVA radiation induces seasonal photodermatosis (a rash that usually appears on areas of the body that are usually covered during winter but are exposed in summer: the upper chest, front of the neck, and the arms) known as polymorphous light eruptions (PMLE) in photosensitive skin (32), though in some it has been shown to reduce PMLE (30) Although sunscreen strategies have been useful for protection against UVB and short-wave UVA, however, complete protection against long-wave UVA has not been achieved (31).

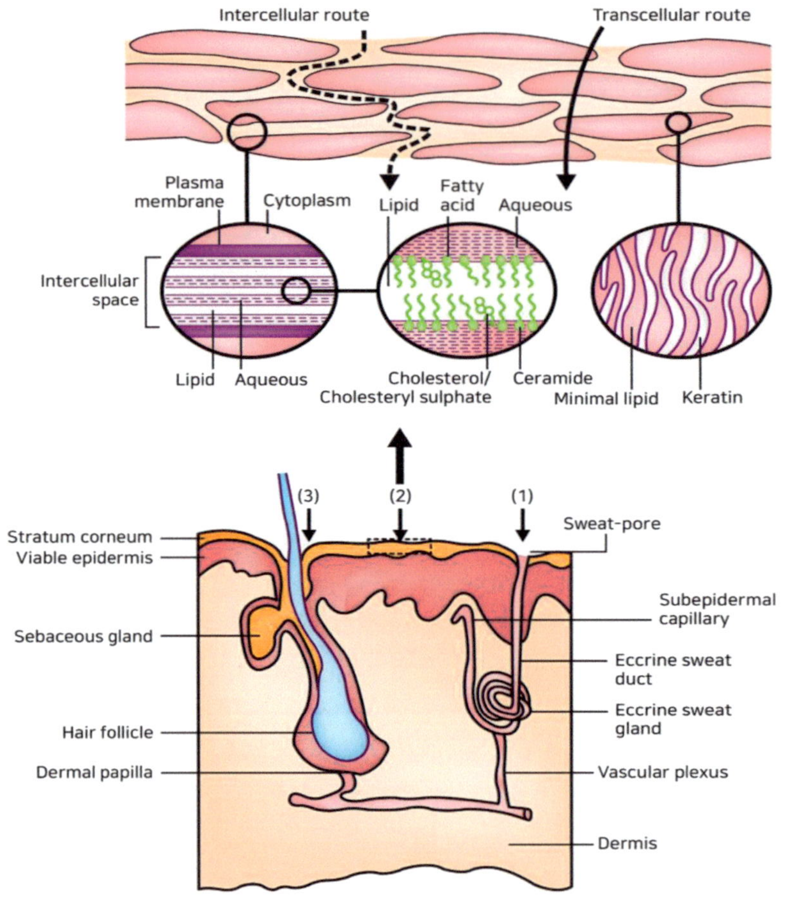

Figure 2.4: Diagram of the brick-and-mortar model of stratum corneum with a simplified lamellar organisation of intercellular domains showing the major stratum corneum lipids. Further shown are the possible actives permeation pathways through intact stratum corneum [Image from Kim et al. (24)].

- Exposure of human skin to UVAI impairs the antigen-presenting cell (APC) activity of epidermal cells by causing Langerhans cell depletion and this results in immune suppression and further contributes to the development of skin cancers. Some sunscreens have been shown to provide significant protection against epidermal APC activity induced by high UVA doses (33).

- UVA radiation cause damages to nuclear and mitochondrial DNA resulting in mutations in the melanocytes; this is one of the proposed reasons.

In summary, UVA radiation can cause nuclear and mitochondrial DNA damage, gene mutations and skin cancer, dysregulation of enzymatic chain reactions, immune suppression, lipid peroxidation (membrane damage), and photoallergic and phototoxic effects.

UVB makes up 2 to 5% of UV radiation reaching the earth's surface. UVB with a wavelength of 280–320 nm can also cause sunburn, hyperpigmentation, solar urticaria, and skin cancer.

Melanocytes are derived from neural crest cells and primarily produce melanin, which is responsible for the pigment of the skin. They are found between cells of the stratum basale. UVB light stimulates melanin synthesis and these pigments serve as built-in sunscreen which protects against damage from UV radiation. Melanin is produced during the conversion of tyrosine to DOPA in a reaction catalysed by the enzyme tyrosinase. Melanin moves to the neighbouring epidermal cells through an elongated cytoplasmic process.

Endocrine functions of the skin

The skin synthesises vitamin D, a prohormone, in the presence of sunlight. Vitamin D is converted into calcitriol in the liver and kidneys (25). Calcitriol is the hormone required for calcium absorption from the small intestine. Photoradiation is the major requirement for vitamin D synthesis. Reduction in UV radiation reaching and penetrating the skin due to large amounts of melanin in dark skins, environmental pollution, high latitudes (particularly during winter), skin aging, and use of sunscreens are factors mitigating against Vitamin D production (25). The main dietary source of the vitamin is fish liver oils. Cod liver oil is a popular vitamin D supplement and contains about 448 IU per teaspoon (4.9 ml) providing 56% of the daily requirements or daily values (DV). It is also a high source of vitamin A with 150% of the DV in one teaspoon (4.9 ml), and very rich in omega-3 fatty acids (34).

Skin as an immunological barrier

Apart from the physical/mechanical barrier, the skin is an immunological barrier. The immune response is vital in wound repairs and infection. The skin also modulates the normal commensals of the skin. Corneocytes continuously check the regular microbiota on the skin surface through pattern recognition receptors (PRRs) which on detection of pathogens initiate the body's innate immune response (35). This stimulates antimicrobial peptides (AMPs), cytokines and chemokines production. AMPs also stimulate the adaptive immune response and directly kill bacteria, fungi, and enveloped viruses.

Constant desquamation of the corneocytes, the acid mantle (pH ~ 5.5), and skin microbiomes makes invasion by pathogenic organisms difficult and also hinders them from establishing permanent residence (36). The surface of the skin is an acidic environment uninhabitable to many microorganisms. The skin microflora further contributes to barrier defences by competing for nutrients and niches required by pathogenic organisms and also expresses antimicrobial molecules that either kill or inhibit the multiplication of these pathogenic organisms.

Different bacterial flora colonises different regions of skin (35): (i) wet regions such as the axilla; (ii) oily regions (for example the face); (iii) dry regions (upper arms). A high degree of specificity of the bacterium is necessary for its adherence to epithelial surfaces in different skin parts. Skin areas with partial occlusion (e.g. axilla) have more microorganisms than do more exposed areas (arms and legs). The quantitative difference is the result of an increased amount of moisture, higher body temperature, and lipid concentrations on the skin surface. Alteration of the microbial flora at these sites will conversely affect these skin parameters: skin hydration, temperature, and lipid content.

Skin as a physical and biological barrier against infections

Skin culture methods have estimated the normal microbial counts of skin commensal organisms ranging from 10^3 to 10^4 per square centimeter with values up to 106 per square centimeter in most humid parts such as the axilla and groin (37). The skin microbiota occupies a range of habitats associated with the three major regions of the body: (i) the moist axilla, perineum, and toe webs, (ii) oily or sebaceous head, neck, and trunk, (iii) the dry forearms and legs (38). Traditional skin culture methods have shown areas of predilection by the bacteria in the skin, such as Corynebacterium spp. and Staphylococcus spp. in moist areas; Propionibacterium acnes and Staphylococcus spp. in oily parts and many members of the phyla beta-Proteobacteria and Flavobacteriales in the dry regions (37).

The skin protects against infection which can stimulate inflammation and thereby affect the epidermal barrier required for the protection of the whole body. For instance, commensal and pathogenic Staphylococci have different abilities to induce the expression of the antimicrobial peptides/proteins (AMPs) and thereby activate different signalling pathways in human keratinocytes (37). The secreted factors of Staphylococci skin commensals induce AMPs human β-defensin 3 (HBD-3) and Ribonuclease 7 (RNase7) expression in primary human keratinocytes via epidermal growth factor receptor (EGFR), Toll-like receptor (TLR)-2, and nuclear factor kappa B (NF-κB) activation while AMPs of pathogenic Staphylococci activate the mitogen-activated protein kinase and phosphatidylinositol 3-kinase/AKT signalling pathways and suppress NF-κB activation. Thus, commensal bacteria tend to amplify the body's innate immune response of keratinocytes to pathogens by increasing induction of AMP expression and preventing NF-κB suppression (37).

The resident cutaneous flora

The average number on the skin surface of an average adult is approximately 1 million per square centimetre (39). They live as small microcolonies stably on the skin (the surface, in the sub-layers, glands, and within the hair follicles). They comprise bacteria, yeasts, some viruses (living both freely or inside bacterial cells), and mites (such as *Demodex folliculorum* and Demodex brevis which live in hair follicles or their environs). The three most predominant bacteria genera are Propionibacterium, Staphylococcus, and Cornynebacterium (40).

Staphylococcus: *Staphylococcus epidermidis* and *Staphylococcus aureus* are the most common types. Staphylococcus epidermidis, a commensal bacterium, commensal bacterium, has recently been demonstrated to modulate the host's innate immune response. S. epidermidis secrete phenol-soluble modulins which selectively inhibit skin pathogens such as S. aureus and Group A Streptococcus and enhance microbial killing by the host antimicrobial peptides (AMPs).

Diphtheroids (Coryneforms)–Diphtheroids (Coryneforms): These are anaerobic Gram-positive pleomorphic bacilli most common in sebum-producing areas. There are generally four groups: anaerobic diphtheroids; lipophilic (normally resides in the axilla) or nonlipophilic (found more generally on glabrous skin) strains; those producing porphyrins (coral red fluorescence when viewed under UV light); and diphtheroids that have keratinolytic enzymes and are associated with the axillary hair infection called Trichomycosisaxillaris (39)

Cutibacteria (formerly Propionibacteria): These are Gram-positive, anaerobic, non-spore-forming, non-motile lipophilic bacteria resident in sebum-producing areas. The most common species, P. acnes, are most numerous on the scalp, forehead, and back and are found in almost 100% of adults (39). It is usually harmless but has been associated with a skin disease known as acne vulgaris.

Micrococci: These are Gram-positive, spherical cells typically appearing in tetrads ranging from about 0.5 to 3 μm in diameter and are regularly present on normal skin, though not as common as the other staphylococci and diphtheroids. Micrococcus luteus is the most predominant type, constituting 20 to 80% of the skin micrococci population, and is the most common specie found in children.

Nail flora: The flora of a normal nail is generally similar to resident skin surface flora.

Dust and other extraneous particles trapped under the nail may carry fungi and bacteria. The major fungus types that infect nails are Aspergillus, Penicillium, Cladosporium, and Mucor, and are usually found under the nails. They infect nails when there is a trauma of excessive exposure of nails to moisture. The normal nail flora also includes mites of the Dermodex genus and certain viruses.

Transient cutaneous flora

Transient organisms are usually present for short periods and so are unstable in durability and protection derived from them by the skin. They are easily transmissible to other individuals and the types present at any time depending on environmental changes. They consist of micro-organisms that are usually derived from the external environment, contaminated environments, or flora from other body sites such as digestive or urogenital systems (41). These organisms easily become pathogenic under favourable environmental changes in skin pH, increased sebum, sweat and protein, hair growth, and break in the epidermal barrier. Common organisms in this group are Enterococcus, Pseudomonas sp., some Staphylococcus sp., Streptococcus sp. and Bacillus sp., and yeasts of the Malassezia genus and Candida genus.

Streptococci: These are rarely seen on normal skin partly due to the presence of lipids that limit their growth, especially β-haemolytic streptococci.

Gram-negative bacilli: These organisms are rare on dry skin and reside mostly in moist intertriginous areas such as the axilla and toe webs. The most common species are Klebsiella, Enterobacter, Acinetobacter and Proteus species, and Escherichia coli.

Candida: Candida species are common on the human skin, particularly in moist areas. They are also normally resident on oral mucous membranes and under immunocompromised states such as HIV infection and diabetes as well as in impaired skin barriers like psoriasis or atopic dermatitis. C. albicans is the most predominant specie (39).

The skin flora is influenced and dependent on both host-specific factors and the external environment.

Factors influencing flora in each individual are (41):

- Genetic
- predispositions

- Age (birth, childhood, puberty, menopausal age, old age). Puberty causes changes in sebum production which corresponds to the level of lipophilic bacteria on the skin
- Gender (men have higher microbial density due to presence of more hair follicles, sebaceous and sweat glands)
- Sebum and sweat production
- Skin thickness
- Immune responses
- Hormonal secretion

External factors influencing skin flora are:

- The environment (climatic changes, geographical location)
- Lifestyle (personal and environmental hygiene)
- Place of residence
- Types of medications
- The use of cosmetics

Biofilm changes in skin microbiota due to cosmetics

The relative abundance of typical symbiotic bacterial groups such as Staphylococcus, Propionibacterium, and Corynebacterium decreases on using basic cosmetics; either because of the growth of other skin bacteria that utilise the components of the basic cosmetics or inhibition of growth of the typical skin bacteria by the cosmetics or environmental changes (37).

The skin microbial count is reduced by washing the body with soap and water. This removes transient microorganisms and other potentially pathogenic from the skin surface. A recent study of skin barrier disruption in the human epidermis showed that women have a significantly greater microbial diversity on their hands than men, and this has been linked to the less acidic skin surface in women and the use of make-up (37). Greater variability of the most important microflora in the armpits (Corynebacterium, Propionibacterium, Staphylococcus, Lactobacillus, Betaproteobacteria, Clostridiales, and Streptococcus species) has been observed following the use of antiperspirants. Aluminium is considered to be toxic to soil bacteria and also interacts with the DNA of bacterial organisms. The Firmicutes are more susceptible to aluminium compared to the Actinobacteria. Increased body odour may occur in cases where the Actinobacteria dominate in the axilla (37).

Cosmetic formulations that are to reduce microbial quantity such as deodorants or germicidal soaps have different impacts on the number and diversity of the skin symbiotes depending on their site of application, whereas, moisturisers' effects of retaining the skin water content may support the skin flora and also reduce skin exfoliation.

Skin types

"The secret to maintaining the skin and keeping it beautiful is to keep it natural." No matter the race, ethnicity, region, age, or gender, skincare is dependent on skin type (43). As skin needs vary according to the type, skincare aims to determine the type of skin and give the most appropriate skincare accordingly. The concept of skin type is ascribed to variable interpretations in different circles. In clinical (dermatology) practice, it is often used interchangeably with "skin phototype," a term used to describe the overall behaviour of the skin in response to sunlight which is predominantly determined by skin colour. In aesthetic practice, however, skin type categorisation is largely based on specific biophysical characteristics of the skin such as the tendency to excess sebum secretion (oiliness), skin hydration, skin texture as well as sensitivity. As a consequence, there are various classification systems for describing skin type. These include, but are not limited to, the Rubinstein classification, Fitzpatrick skin phototype, and Bauman's skin types. Most of the classification systems are based on one or more of the following parameters: skin colour, skin texture, response to sunlight, hydration, sebum secretion, and skin sensitivity.

Classification of skin types

Rubinstein skin types

Helena Rubinstein is credited for describing the traditional classification of skin types in 1915 into 4 main categories: dry, oily, combination, and sensitive skin (42). (1) This classification, which forms the foundation from which newer classification systems have evolved, remains the most commonly used system to describe skin types in aesthetic settings. The category into which an individual fall is determined by the amounts of sebum on the skin (greasiness), the degree of stratum corneum hydration, and the tendency to react to exogenous substances. Under this classification system, skin types are labelled as being oily, dry, sensitive, or combination. This categorisation is very useful in aesthetic practice in guiding recommendations for appropriate skincare products to optimise the efficacy of treatments and treatment outcomes.

Dry skin: This is characterised by a lack of radiance, appearing typically dull or rough with an increased tendency to form wrinkles, scales, and cracks. Individuals with dry skin have lower sebaceous gland activity than normal skin. This skin type has reduced quantities of sebum and other essential skin lipids such as cholesterol, fatty acids, and ceramides. In addition, there is a deficiency of natural moisturising factors required to help the skin to retain water adequately. Dry skin can be associated with impaired skin barrier function depending on the severity of the dryness. This in turn increases the susceptibility of the skin to injury or irritation by environmental factors such as microorganisms, chemical substances including cosmeceuticals, physical elements such as heat, UVR, and dry weather. Individuals with dry skin should avoid harsh soaps or cleansers but rather use non-foaming, lipid-spearing cleansers. The skin also should be treated with barrier-repair moisturisers.

Oily skin: This is characterised by a shiny or greasy appearance, wide pores, and a tendency to develop acne due to excessive sebum production. The manifestation of oily skin typically begins after puberty when the sebaceous glands become active under the influence of androgenic hormones. Older individuals may also develop oily skin for the first time following certain neurological disorders such as Parkinson's disease. Skin oiliness is influenced by a host of factors such as genetics, age, hormones as well as other factors including diet, drugs, and climatic conditions and can similarly be controlled by diet, appropriate cosmeceuticals, and medications.

Sensitive skin: Sensitive skin describes the skin in individuals with an increased propensity for skin redness, irritation, burning, and dryness. This skin type may be either primarily oily or dry. It may also be situational or persistent. Situationally sensitive skin is characterised by triggered or induced sensitivity that resolves once the trigger factor is eliminated, while persistently sensitive skin has a continuation of the skin reactions which continue without any further trigger factor once it has been exposed to an allergen or irritant.

Combination skin: This describes individuals whose skin has both characteristics of dry and oily skin. Typically, the skin over the forehead, nose, and chin (T-zone) tends to be oily appearing greasy with enlarged pores while the cheeks appear comparatively dry.

Fitzpatrick's skin types

The categorisation of skin phototypes based on skin pigmentation was developed by Thomas Fitzpatrick in 1975(Table 1). He classified skin types using a numerical scale based largely on the genetically determined skin colour and the tendency of the skin to either burn or tan on exposure to sunlight. This scale is used clinically for predicting sensitivity to UV radiation (UVR) and risks for adverse effects of sun exposure such as sunburn, premature photo-ageing, and skin cancer. It is also used to estimate the starting dose of UV rays to administer in patients receiving phototherapy (45) and for assessing the need for photo-protection including the use of sunscreens in various populations. In addition, skin phototype is useful in predicting the tendency to hyperpigmentation and may help in choosing appropriate cosmetic and medical skin procedures based on the anticipated risk of hyper- or hypo-pigmentation. There are six categories of skin types based on the Fitzpatrick numerical scale. These range from type I which comprises of individuals that are very fair-skinned, burn easily, and never tan at one end of the spectrum to type VI which comprises dark-skinned individuals with an extremely high threshold for UVR who rarely ever burn but always tan on exposure to sunlight.

An individual's type using the Fitzpatrick system is considered to be static (44) meaning that it does not change throughout the lifetime of the individual as it is genetically determined. However, this concept may not be entirely true because there are acquired diseases (e.g. vitiligo) and cosmeceuticals that alter skin pigmentation and, hence, UVR sensitivity.

Table 2.1: Fitzpatrick skin phototype

Skin phototype	Phenotype	Reaction to sun exposure
Type I	Pale white	Always burns, never tans
Type II	White	Always burns, then tans
Type III	White	Sometimes burns, but can tan without burning
Type IV	Light brown	Occasionally burns but tans easily
Type V	Brown	Rarely burns, tans easily
Type VI	Dark brown to Black	Burns only with very high UVR doses,always tans

Bauman's skin types

The Baumann skin type classification system is a more recent classification system that identifies 16 different skin phenotypes (Table 2) based on four main characteristics: the degree of oiliness, tendency to hyperpigmentation, tendency to wrinkle, and predisposition to skin irritation (46). These characteristics were combined into 4 parameters, and an individual is allocated one characteristic in each group of parameters. The 4 parameters are (42):

a) Dry or oily - D/O;

b) Sensitive or resistant - S/R;

c) Pigmented or nonpigmented;

d) Wrinkled or unwrinkled skin.

Skin type using this classification is determined by computing the results of answers provided by the respondent to a validated questionnaire: the Baumann Skin Type Index (BSTI). Each skin characteristic is represented with the first letter of the response that best describes the respondent's features as follows:

- Individuals with dry skin are ascribed "D" representing Dry while those with normal to oily skin are ascribed "O" representing Oily.
- Individuals with inflammation-prone skin, characterised by an increased tendency for acne, redness, allergic reactions, burning, and/or stinging are ascribed "S" for sensitive skin while those with more tolerant skin are ascribed "R" for Resistant skin.
- People with hyperpigmentation tendencies in response to cutaneous injury or inflammatory processes are designated as having pigmented skin "P" while those without increased risk of hyperpigmentation are designated as having non-pigmented skin type "N."
- Subjects who have wrinkle-prone skin are ascribed "W" for the wrinkle prone, while those who have tighter, firmer, and younger looking skin are ascribed "T" for the Tight skin type.

Skin types are designated using a combination of letters of the parameters above based on the answers provided by the respondent to standardised questions designed to help identify each characteristic.

For instance, a person with oily skin, that is resistant (not prone to inflammation), prone to hyperpigmentation, and with no signs of wrinkling is designated as having ORPT skin type while someone with dry, sensitive, hyperpigmentation, and wrinkling prone is ascribed DSPW skin type. The type of sensitivity the individual has is noted following the skin type designation. For instance, if the individual is acne-prone, has oily and sensitive skin, is hyperpigmentation prone, and is tight, the designation will be: OSPT Acne Type (46).

The Baumann skin type classification is very useful both in clinical and aesthetic practice in guiding not only skincare recommendations for everyday life but also in determining the appropriate choice of treatments and procedures in patients with clinical conditions to improve tolerance to treatments as well as clinical outcomes (46).

Table 2.2: Baumann skin types. Adapted from “BingoCard” © 2014 MetaBeauty Inc. Used with permission. All rights reserved” (47).

Baumann skin type	**Baumann skin type Indicator**	**Interpretation**
1	DSPT	Dry|Sensitive|Pigmented|Tight
2	DSNT	Dry|Sensitive|Non-pigmented|Tight
3	DSPW	Dry|Sensitive|Pigmented|Wrinkle prone
4	DSNW	Dry|Sensitive|Non-pigmented|Wrinkle prone
5	OSPT	Oily|Sensitive|Pigmented|Tight
6	OSNT	Oily|Sensitive|Non-pigmented|Tight
7	OSPW	Oily|Sensitive|Pigmented|Wrinkle prone
8	OSNW	Oily|Sensitive|Non-pigmented|Wrinkle prone
9	ORPT	Oily|Resistant|Pigmented|Tight
10	ORNT	Oily|Resistant|Non-pigmented|Tight
11	ORPW	Oily|Resistant|Pigmented| Wrinkle prone
12	ORNW	Oily|Resistant|Non-pigmented|Wrinkle prone
13	DRPT	Dry|Resistant|Pigmented|Tight
14	DRNT	Dry|Resistant|Non-pigmented|Tight
15	DRPW	Dry|Resistant|Pigmented|Wrinkle prone
16	DRNW	Dry|Resistant|Non-pigmented|Wrinkle prone

Skin care recommendations based on skin type

Prescription or recommendation of skincare products should be guided by both clinical concerns and skin type. Table 3 summarises preferred cosmeceuticals choices for routine skincare for each type.

Table 2.3: Skin care recommendations based on skin type

Skin type	**Cleansing**	**Moisturisers**	**Sun protection**
Dry skin	Non-foaming (soap free cleansers with pH balanced (neutral or	Barrier repair moisturisers rich in ceramides,	Moisturising sunscreen should be recommended and used

	acidic pH) and moisturising properties, moisturising cleansers	cholesterol and fatty acids	routinely as UV radiation can further worsen skin dehydration
Oily skin	Foam cleansers Resistant skin types can tolerate soap cleansers	Light lotions or serum type moisturisers are suitable for oily skin. Humectants such as glycerol and peptide moisturisers can be recommended Avoid heavy or oily moisturisers	Moisturising sunscreens can be used instead of moisturisers but should be preferably oil-free
Sensitive skin	Skincare products should depend on the type of sensitive skin. Mild hypoallergenic soap-cleansers, pH-balanced, and containing minimal or no perfumes or additives are good. Individuals with acne-prone skin may benefit from foaming cleansers if their skin is oily.	Recommendations for moisturisers will depend on the type of sensitivity. Probiotic creams containing *Bidobacteriumlongum* have reduced skin sensitivity in some individuals (48)	Individuals prone to breakouts and irritation should avoid formulations that contain fragrance, essential oils, and preservatives. In general, sensitive skin appears to me more tolerant to products with physical blocks such as zinc oxide. Light weight sunscreens with niacinamide and protective antioxidants could be recommended for those with irritation prone skin

The ideal skin type in terms of cosmetics is characterised by appropriate biophysical characteristics which include normal sebum secretion, and healthy skin barrier function with adequate natural moisturising factors.

The use of appropriate skincare products, together with appropriate lifestyle choices, can promote the development of ideal skin types in individuals with problematic skin types. An individual's skin type is not static and can be influenced by several factors including weather, climate, drugs, hormones as well as cosmeceuticals. Therefore, there is a need to review and re-assess skincare recommendations based on the prevailing skin types.

The human skin is subjected to varying exposures, both external and internal, that can influence its structure and function and ultimately alter the phenotypic expression of skin type. Such factors include UV radiation exposure, environmental pollutants, topical applications, medications, diet, and hormones. In addition, the skin also changes in structure and function with age. Naturally, there is a decline in sebum production above the age of 40 years (48) with a corresponding predisposition to dryness. As such, the classification of an individual's skin using either the Baumann or Rubinstein system is not static.

Subjects with dry skin can, with the treatment of the underlying conditions or use of appropriate cosmeceuticals, become oily. Thus, there is a need to review and re-evaluate skin types as well as recommended treatments over time. In contrast, however, evaluating an individual's type using the Fitzpatrick system is considered to be constant (49). This means that it does not change throughout the lifetime of the individual as it is genetically determined. However, this concept may not be entirely true because there are acquired diseases (e.g., vitiligo) and cosmeceuticals that alter skin pigmentation and, hence, UVR sensitivity.

Rights and permissions

References

1. Kaim, K. Anatomy of Skin and Physiology of Healing. Goondiwindi Hospital. Webpage. (n.d.). Available from: https://www.woundcareresource.com/downloads/Basic.pdf[Cited 20 January 2022].
2. Innoleaguem. Structure and functions of the human skin. Webpage. (n.d.). Available from: *www.innoleague.com/Human Skin.pdf* [Cited 20 January 2022].
3. Yousef, H., Alhajj, M., Sharma, S. (2021). Anatomy, Skin (Integument), Epidermis. [Updated Nov 19 2021]. In: StatPearls [Internet]. Treasure Island (FL): Stat Pearls Publishing; 2022 Jan. Available from: https://www.ncbi.nlm.nih.gov/books/NBK470464/
4. Segre, J. A. (2006). Epidermal barrier formation and recovery in skin disorders. *J Clin Invest.*, 116(5), 1150-1158. doi:10.1172/JCI28521
5. Kolarsick, P. A. J., Kolarsick, M. A. and Goodwin, C. (2011). Anatomy and Physiology of the Skin. *Journal of the Dermatology Nurses' Association*: 3(4), 203-213. doi: 10.1097/JDN.0b013e3182274a98
6. WHO Guidelines on Hand Hygiene in Health Care: First Global Patient Safety Challenge Clean Care Is Safer Care. Geneva: World Health Organization; 2009. 7, Transmission of pathogens by hands. Available from: https://www.ncbi.nlm.nih.gov/books/NBK144014/

7. Nafisi, S. and Maibach, H. I. (2017). Nanotechnology in Cosmetics. In: Kazutami, S., Robert, Y. L.,Howard, I. M., Yuji, Y. (eds.) Cosmetic science and technology: theoretical principles and applications. Oxford, United Kingdom: Elsevier; p.333-337.
8. KDS444. Human nail anatomy. Wikimedia Commons. Publish 3 March 2013. Available from: https://commons.wikimedia.org/wiki/File:Human_nail_anatomy.jpg#filelinks (Creative Commons Attribution-Share Alike 3.0 Unported license.). [Retrieved 04 February 2022].
9. Schlader, Z. J. and Vargas, N. T. (2019). Regulation of Body Temperature by Autonomic and Behavioral Thermoeffectors. *Exercise and Sport Sciences Reviews*, *47*(2), 116–126. https://doi.org/10.1249/JES.0000000000000180
10. Stecco, C., Pirri, C., Fede, C., Fan, C., Giordani, F., Stecco, L., Foti, C. and De Caro, R. (2019). Dermatome and fasciatome. *Clinical Anatomy (New York, N.Y.)*, *32*(7), 896–902. https://doi.org/10.1002/ca.23408
11. Iheanacho, F. andVellipuram, A. R. (2021). StatPearls [Internet]. StatPearls Publishing; Treasure Island (FL): Sep 12, 2021. *Physiology, Mechanoreceptors*.
12. Dreno, B., Araviiskaia, E., Berardesca, E., Bieber, T., Hawk, J., Sanchez-Viera, M, and Wolkenstein, P. (2014). The science of dermocosmetics and its role in dermatology. *Journal of the European Academy of Dermatology and Venereology : JEADV*, *28*(11), 1409–1417. https://doi.org/10.1111/jdv.12497
13. Grice, J. E., Ciotti, S., Weiner, N., Lockwood, P., Cross, S. E. and Roberts, M. S. (2010). Relative uptake of minoxidil into appendages and stratum corneum and permeation through human skin in vitro. *Journal of Pharmaceutical Sciences*, *99*(2), 712–718. https://doi.org/10.1002/jps.21856
14. Bronaugh, R. L. and Maibach, H. I. (1989). Percutaneous absorption: mechanisms, methodology. Drug Delivery. New York: Marcel Dekker.
15. Mccarley, K. D. and Bunge, A. L. (2001). Pharmacokinetic models of dermal absorption. *J. Pharm. Sci.*, 90, 1699-719.
16. Flynn, G. (1996). Cutaneous and transdermal delivery: processes and systems of delivery. Drugs Pharm. Sci., 72, 239-98.
17. Hadgraft J. (2001). Modulation of the barrier function of the skin. *Skin Pharmacology and Applied Skin Physiology*, *14 Suppl 1*, 72–81. https://doi.org/10.1159/000056393
18. Kapitány, A., Medgyesi, B., Jenei, A., Somogyi, O., Szabó, L., Gáspár, K., Méhes, G., Hendrik, Z., Dócs, K., Szücs, P., Dajnoki, Z. andSzegedi, A. (2021). Regional Differences in the Permeability Barrier of the Skin-Implications in Acantholytic Skin Diseases. *International Journal of Molecular Sciences*, *22*(19), 10428. https://doi.org/10.3390/ijms221910428
19. Bassiouny, D., Hegazy, R., Esmat, S., Gawdat, H. I., Ahmed Ezzat, M., Tawfik, H. A., Hegazy, A. A. and Ibrahim, S. (2021). Cosmetic camouflage as an adjuvant to vitiligo therapies: Effect on quality of life. *Journal of Cosmetic Dermatology*, *20*(1), 159–165. https://doi.org/10.1111/jocd.13459
20. Panconesi, E., Cossidente, A., Giorgini, S., Martini, M., Melli, C. andSarti, M. (1983). A psychosomatic approach to dermatologic cosmetology. *International Journal of Dermatology*, *22*(8), 449–454. https://doi.org/10.1111/j.1365-4362.1983.tb02171.x

21. Forslind, B. (2000). The Structure of the Human Skin Barrier. In: Kanerva, L., Wahlberg, J.E., Elsner, P., Maibach, H.I. (eds) Handbook of Occupational Dermatology. Springer, Berlin, Heidelberg. 2000, https://doi.org/10.1007/978-3-662-07677-4_6
22. Weitzman, R. E. andKleeman, C. R. (1980). The clinical physiology of water metabolism. Part III: The water depletion (hyperosmolar) and water excess (hyposmolar) syndromes. *The Western Journal of Medicine*, *132*(1), 16–38.
23. Proksch, E., Brandner, J. M. and Jensen, J. M. (2008). The skin: an indispensable barrier. *Experimental Dermatology*, *17*(12), 1063–1072. https://doi.org/10.1111/j.1600-0625.2008.00786.x
24. Kim, B., Cho, H., Moon, S., Ahn, H., Bae, S., Cho, H., et al. (2020). Transdermal delivery systems in cosmetics. Biomedical Dermatology, 4(10), 1-12. Available from: https://doi.org/10.1186/s41702-020-0058-7
25. Pappas A. (2009). Epidermal surface lipids. *Dermato-endocrinology*, *1*(2), 72–76. https://doi.org/10.4161/derm.1.2.7811
26. Wertz, P. W. (1992). Epidermal lipids. *In Seminars in Dermatology,* 11(2), 106-113.
27. Casey G. (2002). Physiology of the skin. *Nursing standard (Royal College of Nursing (Great Britain): 1987)*, *16*(34), 47–55. https://doi.org/10.7748/ns2002.05.16.34.47.c3193
28. Draelos Z. D. (1997). New developments in cosmetics and skin care products. *Advances in Dermatology*, *12*, 3–18.
29. Proksch, E., Brandner, J. M. and Jensen, J. M. (2008). The skin: an indispensable barrier. *Experimental Dermatology*, *17*(12), 1063–1072. https://doi.org/10.1111/j.1600-0625.2008.00786.x
30. Latha, M. S., Martis, J., Shobha, V., Sham Shinde, R., Bangera, S., Krishnankutty, B., Bellary, S., Varughese, S., Rao, P. and Naveen Kumar, B. R. (2013). Sunscreening agents: a review. *The Journal of Clinical and Aesthetic Dermatology*, *6*(1), 16–26.
31. DeBuys, H. V., Levy, S. B., Murray, J. C., Madey, D. L. and Pinnell, S. R. (2000). Modern approaches to photoprotection. *Dermatologic Clinics*, *18*(4), 577–590. https://doi.org/10.1016/s0733-8635(05)70208-4
32. Ortel, B., Tanew, A., Wolff, K. andHönigsmann, H. (1986). Polymorphous light eruption: action spectrum and photoprotection. *Journal of the American Academy of Dermatology*, *14*(5 Pt 1), 748–753. https://doi.org/10.1016/s0190-9622(86)70088-1
33. Stoebner, P. E., Poosti, R., Djoukelfit, K., Martinez, J. and Meunier, L. (2007). Decreased human epidermal antigen-presenting cell activity after ultraviolet A exposure: dose-response effects and protection by sunscreens. *The British Journal of Dermatology*, *156*(6), 1315–1320. https://doi.org/10.1111/j.1365-2133.2007.07895.x
34. Taylor, J. (2019). 7 Healthy Foods That Are High in Vitamin D. Nutrition. December 18, 2019. *Healthline.* Available from: https://www.healthline.com/nutrition/9-foods-high-in-vitamin-d [Cited 27 Jan 2022]
35. Grice, E. A. and Segre, J. A. (2011). The skin microbiome. *Nature reviews. Microbiology*, *9*(4), 244–253. https://doi.org/10.1038/nrmicro2537
36. Borkowski, A. W. and Gallo, R. L. (2011). The coordinated response of the physical and antimicrobial peptide barriers of the skin. *The Journal of Investigative Dermatology*, *131*(2), 285–287. https://doi.org/10.1038/jid.2010.360

37. Pawlica, P. J. (2019). The influence of cosmetics on the bacterial flora of the skin. *Eur. J. Med. Res*, 3(24), 44-52.
38. Cundell A. M. (2018). Microbial Ecology of the Human Skin. *Microbial Ecology*, *76*(1), 113–120. https://doi.org/10.1007/s00248-016-0789-6
39. Dangi, I. (2021). A review on Normal human skin flora: Exploring the microbial flora of the skin. Experimental and Clinical Microbiology, 1-3. Available from: https://www.pulsus.com/scholarly-articles/a-review-on-normal-human-skin-flora-exploring-the-microbial-flora-of-the-skin.pdf [Cited 2 February 2022].
40. Costello, E. K., Lauber, C. L., Hamady, M., Fierer, N., Gordon, J. I. and Knight, R. (2009). Bacterial community variation in human body habitats across space and time. *Science (New York, N.Y.)*, *326*(5960), 1694–1697. https://doi.org/10.1126/science.1177486
41. OYA Science. What is the skin flora? Know everything about its role and structure. Webpage. Available from: https://inoya-laboratoire.com/en/info/what-is-the-skin-flora-role-and-structure.html [Cited 2 February 2022].
42. Baumann L. (2008). Understanding and treating various skin types: the Baumann Skin Type Indicator. *Dermatologic Clinics*, *26*(3), 359–vi. https://doi.org/10.1016/j.det.2008.03.007
43. Oninla, O. A., Oninla, S. O., Otike-Odibi, B. I., Oripelaye, M. M., Olanrewaju, F. O. and Mohammed, T. (2019). African skin: different types, needs, and diseases. *Int J Trop Dis Health,* 36(3), 1-13.
44. Eilers, S., Bach, D. Q., Gaber, R., Blatt, H., Guevara, Y., Nitsche, K., Kundu, R. V. and Robinson, J. K. (2013). Accuracy of self-report in assessing Fitzpatrick skin phototypes I through VI. *JAMA Dermatology*, 149(11), 1289–1294. https://doi.org/10.1001/jamadermatol.2013.6101
45. Fitzpatrick, T. B. (1988). The Validity and Practicality of Sun - Reactive Skin tyypes I through VI. *Arch Dermatol.*, 124(6), 869–71.
46. Baumann, L. (2016). Validation of a Questionnaire to Diagnose the Baumann Skin Type in All Ethnicities and in Various Geographic Locations. *J Cosmet Dermatol Sci*, 6, 34–40. DOI: 10.4236/jcdsa.2016.61005
47. Baumann skin types. Wikimedia Commons, the free media repository. Available: https://commons.wikimedia.org/wiki/File:BingoCard.png [Cited 10 July 2016].
48. Farage, M. A. (2019). The Prevalence of Sensitive Skin [Internet]. Frontiers in Medicine Frontiers Media SA; May 17, 2019 p. 98. Available from: https://www.ncbi.nlm.nih.gov/pmc/articles/PMC6533878/
49. Ravnbak, M. H. (2010). Objective determination of Fitzpatrick skin type. *Danish Medical Bulletin*, *57*(8), B4153

CHAPTER THREE

Types and modes of application of cosmetics

'Lara O Orafidiya and Rabi I Ekore

A cosmetic is defined by the United States Food and Drug Administration (FDA) as a product that is intended to be applied to the human body for cleansing, beautifying, promoting attractiveness, or altering the appearance (1). The definition of cosmetics by Nigerian laws as published by the National Agency for Food and Drug Administration and Control (NAFDAC), though similar to that of the FDA, contains expanded descriptions for use of the cosmetics (2).

There are several types of cosmetics with widely varying uses and applications but with outcomes that improve skin conditions and outlooks of the consumer. The FDA's and NAFDAC's definition of cosmetics covers skin care products, makeup or colour cosmetics, perfumes and deodorants, and other products that do not clearly fit into these three categories. In this chapter, cosmetics will basically be classified as skin care cosmetics and makeup or colour cosmetics. While cosmetics will be generally discussed in this chapter, few have been selected to be treated as separate chapters in this book.

Skin care cosmetics

Skin care cosmetics are applied on the skin to improve the health of the skin, to repair and/or prevent some skin flaws. Hence, there are different types of skin care products among which are cleansers, toners, exfoliants/chemical peels, masks, moisturisers and hydrators, face oils, eye creams, serums and sun screens which are also categorised as cosmetics.

Cleansers

Cleansers are formulated with ingredients that remove or reduce, from the skin surface, sebum, pollutants, exfoliated cells of the stratum corneum as well as applied products (cosmetics/medications); and control skin odours and microbiome. The art of body cleansing is an age-long practice ever since the discovery of soap, an anionic surfactant, obtained by saponification, a process that involves mixing a vegetable or animal oil/fat with a monovalent alkali such as sodium or potassium salts or hydroxides (lye), traditionally obtained from percolated ashes or an amine such as diethanolamine. Over the centuries, soaps have undergone several modifications in composition and technologies of manufacture culminating in the development of modern-day skin cleansers which basically consist of synthetic surfactants (3).

Surfactants are surface-active substances which structurally consist of two parts, a hydrophilic (water-loving) head which may or may not carry an electric charge, and a hydrophobic (water-hating/fat-loving) tail. Anionic surfactants have negative charges, cationics have positive charges while amphoteric surfactants have both charges on their molecules. Nonionic surfactants carry no charges on their molecules. Surfactants lower the interfacial tension between a hydrophobic substance such as dirt and sebum and a hydrophilic substance, such as water, alcohol or an aqueous medium, causing such hydrophobic substance to be dislodged and dispersed or solubilised in the hydrophilic surfactant-loaded phase and be subsequently wiped off or rinsed off with water. Hence, cleansers are able to remove lipophilic dirt from the skin surface using an aqueous or hydrophilic medium which, ordinarily, water alone could not remove. However, these surfactants also solubilise lipids, enzymes and the natural moisturising factors (NMF) as well as denature proteins of the skin thereby weakening the barrier function of the stratum corneum and eliciting harsh and adverse effects on the skin such as after-bath tightness, irritation, dryness and itching. Molecules of the surfactants remain and penetrate the stratum corneum after rinsing leading to chronic adverse effects, in some instances. Anionic surfactants, such as sodium dodecyl sulphate, which have excellent cleansing ability, are unfortunately also highly irritating to the skin and are responsible for most of the adverse effects. To mitigate this problem, skin cleansing products are formulated with a combination of the different types of surfactants, in such a way that the high cleansing and foaming benefits of anionic surfactants are harnessed while their undesirable irritant properties are reduced by incorporating some mildness from amphoteric (e.g., cocamidopropyl betaine) and nonionic surfactants (e.g., cetearyl alcohol). Other ingredients that are also added to dampen the harsh effects of surfactants as well as leave the skin soft, moist and glowing after cleansing include humectants such as propylene glycol and glycerine, and emollient oils. These mitigate the irritant effects of anionic surfactants on the skin caused by the denaturation of keratin protein and subsequent damage to the cell membrane of keratinocytes (4). Polymers, such as polyethylene oxide, which modify the solution behaviour of surfactants were used earlier to douse the aggressiveness of surfactants on the skin while polyethylene glycol 80 co-processed with sorbitan laurate (PEG-80 sorbitan laurate) was the first to be used to produce mild baby shampoos (5). Addition of hydrophobically modified polymers (HMPs) to surfactant cleansers is able reduce the harsh effects of the surfactants. Micelles of the surfactants bind to the HMP creating large molecules that cannot easily be inserted into the lipid stratum corneum, thereby maintaining the integrity of the skin topmost layer

(6,7). Cleansers that contain these harshness-reducing substances are sometimes classified as 'less-irritating' or mild cleansers. Cleansers with neutral or slightly acidic pH of about the stratum corneum pH of 5.5 are often less irritating than those of about pH 10, that is common with traditional soaps (8). However, studies have shown that a cleanser's pH does not affect the pH-maintaining mechanism of skin even on long term use (9), but may affect the stability of the cleansing product itself, especially if formulated with pH-sensitive ingredients, including polymers and preservatives. The level of irritation caused by surfactants is also dependent on their skin cleanser residue or rinsability factor which reduces when the cleanser is not left on the skin for longer than needed (10). Notwithstanding, the massage action done during cleansing also helps to bring fresh blood flow to the surface of the skin, making it look smoother and healthy after cleansing.

Types of cleansers include:

Solid cleansers – these are cleansers with solid consistency, thickened either due to the nature of the chemical constituents, for example sodium-based soap bars, or hardened with soap hardeners such as stearic acid, sodium stearate, sodium lactate, beeswax, soy wax, shea butter and cocoa butter (Figure 3.1), (11).

Soap-based cleansers: these are traditional soaps, of pH 9 to 10, prepared by the process of saponification and are usually packaged as soap bars. Glycerine is a by-product of the saponification process, although it can also be added to the finished soap batter for enhanced moisturising effects. Soaps enriched with glycerine are referred to as **glycerine or transparent bars**, and these reduce the drying effects of soap. **Superfatted soaps** leave a protective emollient film on the skin after rinsing because of the high content of lipids such plant-based fats, stearic acid, lanolin, mineral oils and paraffin wax. Soaps are superfatted either by adding a small quantity of extra oil, butter or wax (more than the calculated amount) after saponification, or by reducing the amount of calculated lye in order to leave a little quantity of unsaponified lipids in the soap.

Syndet (bar) cleansers: Cleansers prepared mainly with non-soap synthetic surfactants (synthetic detergents) such as fatty acid isothionates and sulfosuccinic acid esters are referred to as syndet cleansers. The high quantity of free fatty acids in these cleansers preserve the lipid and protein regions of the skin by providing good moisturising activity that hydrates the skin, thereby exhibiting much less drying and irritant effects than soaps. Syndet cleansers have near neutral or slightly acidic pH and do not form scums (8). Scums are formed by soaps when used with hard water or in the presence of di- and tri-valent metal ions, for example calcium and magnesium salts in hard water, which displace the monovalent ions of soaps forming di- and tri-valent soaps which are water-insoluble, hence, the scums.

Combination bars (Combars): Surfactants combined with traditional soaps produce combars. These give better cleansing than synthetic surfactants alone and are milder on the skin than soaps.

Liquid cleansers: There are various types of liquid cleansing products based on the constituents and the forms in which they are presented for use. They can be soap based or detergent based. Liquid cleansers formulated with anionic surfactants can irritate the skin, depending on the concentration of the anionic surfactant used. Hence, they are combined with less irritating non-ionic and amphoteric surfactants as well as humectants, to improve mildness. They are less likely to be contaminated since only the quantities required are pressed out of the dispensing bottles or tubes in which they are packaged for use, unlike soap bars that are rubbed upon; they also contain moisturising agents that leave the skin hydrated. With their relatively larger quantity of solvent components, they enhance the active cleansing ingredient in lifting dirt and oil from the skin. They are often used with a washcloth or a foam sponge (Figure 3.2).

Figure 3.1: Solid/bar cleansers

Figure 3.2: Liquid cleansers

Gel cleansers: These are water-based viscid preparations that contain surfactants, gelling agents, moisturisers and some other ingredients that distinguish one product from another in terms of cleansing efficacy and after-use effects on the skin. They are transparent to translucent high viscous liquids and may be lightly coloured and perfumed. They are applied to the face on fingertips and then washed off with water. If not properly washed off the face, residues of the gelling agent may leave the skin sticky or flaky.

Foaming cleansers: Apart from cleansing the dirt on the face, foaming cleansers contain good foam-forming surfactants that further give deep-cleansing effects and also facilitate removal of dirt into water. They are lighter on the skin, penetrate the pores more than gels and may elicit milder adverse effects on the skin. A good lather is first formed before application to the skin. Facial cleansing products, nonetheless, should preferably be less foaming compared to those to be used on other parts of the body.

Oil-based cleansers: Sebum, exfoliated skin cells and most dirt, pollutants and make-ups are lipophilic in nature and would easily mix with the oils in this type of cleansers when applied for cleansing on the face and are subsequently wiped off with a warm and damp washcloth. Oil-based cleansers, unlike surfactant-containing cleansers, while removing excess sebum secretions, do not disrupt but preserve the lipid dynamics of the stratum corneum, clean out clogged pores, cause little or no irritation or dryness to the skin, but serve as emollients that keep the skin hydrated and some oils may have in addition skin-healing and nutritive values. For example, olive oil gives good hydration and is rich in antioxidants and vitamins; avocado oil is highly moisturising, jojoba oil has anti-acne, skin-healing and oil production balancing effects (12), while castor oil has astringent and antibacterial activities. Ceramides are also used as oil cleaners.

Cleansing balms: Cleansing balms are oleaginous products similar to oil-based cleansers but differ in consistency, cleansing balms being semisolid unlike the mobile liquid oil cleansers. The presence of fats such as shea butter and cocoa butter confer the semisolid consistency. The balms remove dirt more effectively than oils.

Cleansing creams: Cleansing creams contain about the same oils and fats as cleansing balms, but have water and emulsifiers added that result in oily creams. They contain less amount of lipids and more of waxy emulsifiers which enhance cleansing and rinsing off of the dirt/oils.

Oil-to-milk cleansers: Oil-to-milk cleansers constitute a currently trending line of oil-based cleansers to which liquid emulsifiers have been added. After being applied and rubbed around the face, the cleanser is washed off as usual with warm or cold water. The difference here is that the presence of an emulsifier converts the cleansing oil(s) to a milky emulsion when water is applied along with the cleanser on the face, which is then easily rinsed off with water, leaving behind a clean, velvety feel on the skin.

Lipid-free cleansers: Unlike oil-based cleansers that contain fatty acids, lipid-free cleansers contain fatty alcohols which are non-irritating compared with soaps and are, therefore, suitable for persons with dry or sensitive skin as well as for oily/acne-prone skin. These types of cleansers leave no pore-clogging residue and are non-comedogenic. The fatty alcohols facilitate evaporation of the lotions in which they are incorporated and confer high rinsability to the products. They can be wiped off or rinsed off with water. Humectants are added to the cleansers for additional hydrating effects.

Micellar water cleansers: As the name implies, these types of cleansers comprise mild surfactants dispersed in purified water at concentrations at which they form micelles. They are gentle on the skin as they elicit little or no irritant effect and are less likely to strip the stratum corneum of its lipid layer. They are more suitable for removing water-based cosmetics. The humectants compounded in the products confer moisturising properties on them.

Facial masks

Facial masks are a type of cosmetic treatment, specially prepared for the purpose, and is carefully applied on the face, avoiding the eyes and mouth, and left for a predetermined period before being removed by rinsing with tepid water or peeling with the hand. Facial masks are formulated to absorb or adsorb, depending on the base used, dirt, pollutants, and excess sebum and to deeply cleanse the pores leaving the skin feeling clean, rejuvenated, revitalised and refreshed. Some of the main base ingredients also have therapeutic properties.

Clay facial masks*:* Face masks were originally prepared with natural clays such as kaolin, bentonite and fuller's earth as bases to which ingredients such as moisturisers, exfoliants and herbal extracts, among others, were incorporated. They unclog pores, reduce blackheads and absorb (particles or molecules penetrate or diffuse into the clay) and adsorb (particles or molecules are attracted, bound and accumulated to the surface of the clay) oils, dirt and impurities from the skin thereby cleansing and refreshing the skin surface and aiding the healing of topical blemishes (13). Clays such as the white, green and pink have been studied as facial masks and found to have similar effects on the different types of skin (14). Clays are highly efficient absorbents on the face absorbing even bacteria and viruses (15). Some types of clay minerals have been found to have antibacterial activity against some bacteria, for example, *Staphylococcus aureus*, an organism implicated in acne and could cure diseases such as Buruli ulcer caused by *Mycobacterium ulcerans* infection (13). Studies have revealed the potential of clay applied on the skin to increase the number of collagen fibres thereby making the skin smoother, softer and firmer (16). Clay is applied as a moist paste on the face. As evaporation takes place, the clay contracts and hardens giving a tightening effect on the face resulting from mechanical stress on the skin which enhances its absorbing effect and firms sagging skin. Clay masks are rinsed off the face or wiped off with a warm washcloth after a stipulated time; the face is patted dry and moisturisers can then be applied.

Mud facial masks: Mud, according to Williams and Haydel "is a slurry of water and sediment dominated by clay and silt sized particles" (13). Hence, clay is usually available as a dry, solid substance while mud occurs as a wet paste. While most muds used in cosmetics are obtained from the beds of the Dead Sea and the Mediterranean Sea, clays are obtained in or on earth's crust. Dead Sea mineral mud has been shown to have protective effects against UV-B induced stress (17) and to demonstrate antimicrobial properties (18). This mud, however, contains chrome and nickel which may affect persons that are already sensitised to the two metals, implying caution for such patrons of Dead Sea facial mask, although there is no toxicological systemic effect. Clay mask and mud mask elicit almost the same effects when applied on the face, the difference being mainly that clay is more drying and suitable for oily skin while mud is less mechanically stressful on the skin and is more suitable for dry skin. Moreover, the ingredients incorporated into the masks determine to a greater extent their effects. Such ingredients include humectants, exfoliators, antioxidants like vitamin C, natural products like honey, plant extracts and sea minerals.

Charcoal facial masks: Charcoal is a black, odourless and tasteless solid substance that is obtained by incomplete combustion of plant and animal products such as wood, coconut shells and bones, respectively (Figure 3.3). Activated charcoal is produced by either physical or chemical activation of charcoal. Physical activation involves heating charcoal at very high temperatures (900–1000°C) and washing with water, while chemical activation involves treating the charcoal with phosphoric acid (H_2PO_4) and then rinsing with water. This may be followed by heating at 450 -900°C to create an extensive pore structure that facilitates adsorption (19) (20). Activated charcoal prepared as a facial mask is more effective in adsorbing oils and dirt from the face than ordinary charcoal, and being an adsorbent is capable of adsorbing and removing pollutants, such as lead, on the skin. Ingredients such as humectants, exfoliators and herbal extracts are included in the preparation of activated charcoal/charcoal facial masks and these are sometimes combined with clay for optimum cleansing and skin rejuvenating outcomes. The mode of application and removal of these masks are similar to that used for mud/clay masks, that is, by rinsing off with tepid water or wet wash cloths.

Figure 3.3: Charcoal mask

Hydrogel/sheet face masks: These are prepared with synthetic polymers such as polyethylene oxide, polyvinyl alcohol and polyvinyl pyrrolidone as well as naturally derived polymers/polymer precursors such as chitosan, hyaluronic acid, plant hydrocolloids and cellulose derivatives like cellulose acetate. They are presented in the form of dry fibre sheets that are wetted before application on the face or in the form of gels that are applied directly on the face. Beauty enhancing agents such as moisturisers, exfoliants, treatment oils, herbal extracts are incorporated in the products during manufacture. These ingredients re-plump, nourish and soothe the skin, especially dehydrated skin.

Recently, a paper-like thin hydrogel facial mask containing gold nanoparticles (Au NPs), ascorbic acid, collagen as well as extracts of green tea and orange-peel has been developed using electrospinning technology which could provide anti-ageing, anti-wrinkling and skin whitening benefits for the user. Au NPs have been shown to brighten and cleanse the skin, reduce wrinkling of the skin probably by slowing down elastin breakdown as well as collagen depletion and provide anti-bacterial, anti-inflammatory and skin-healing effects (21). Sheet masks are mostly peeled off after the stipulated treatment period, and the residual serum is then gently patted into the skin. Rinsing is not advised unless so recommended by the manufacturers of the products.

Other types of sheet masks include knit cotton mask, foil sheet mask, ampoule sheet mask and bubbling sheet mask (22). Ampoule sheet mask are so called because the sheets are pre-dosed from treatment preparations, usually serums, packaged in ampoules. They are, however, fast-acting, being recommended to be left on the face for just five minutes.

Natural products such as extracts of pineapple, aloe vera and kale are used along with other ingredients such as vitamin C, and niacinamide in the preparation of some of these facial masks.

Rinse-off and peel-out masks: Rinse-off masks are those facial masks that are removed, when dried, with a cool or warm wash cloth. Peel-off masks give a deep clean, exfoliating dead skin cells, unclogging pores thereby improving the texture of the skin. They are gel-based and are not as messy as clay masks. They are peeled off the face after they have been left to harden (22).

Night/overnight facial masks: These are also known as sleeping packs, sleeping masks, or leave-on masks. As the name implies, overnight masks are left on the face to elicit their effects of enhancing greater penetration, into the skin, of active ingredients present in the preparations while acting as sealants and barriers all through the night, a leave-on period that can be as long as eight hours. Thus, hydration, skin-brightening effects, calming effects and cell repairs and regeneration processes are increased as the active ingredients remain sealed on the skin while preventing dirt getting into the pores. Ingredients such as ceramides, hyaluronic acid and peptides, which support collagen production and smoothen fine lines and wrinkles, are included in some overnight facial masks where they have a longer period of time to work on the skin cells resulting in optimal treatment outcomes. The masks come as creams that are applied as a thin layer on the face and are removed by washing or with a damp face cloth in the morning. Though they are formulated to be gentler on the skin, it is advisable for those with sensitive skin to seek attention of a dermatologist before using overnight facial masks since these are left on the face for a much longer period of time than the other types of facial masks.

Natural products in facial masks: The composition of many facial masks incorporates natural ingredients and herbal extracts, presumably with positive effects, in the maintenance of facial skin health (23), clinically determined the efficacy of facial masks containing yoghurt and *Opuntia humifusa* Raf. and found these to increase moisture, elasticity and radiance of the treated skin while demonstrating radical scavenging activity also. Recipes and methods of preparation of activated charcoal-based facial masks containing gelatine, honey, lemon juice and eggs have been described (24).

Facial toners

Alcohol-based toners were originally designed to remove scums left on the skin when lye-based soaps are used with hard water for cleansing thereby reducing irritation and harshness of the soap. Toners, being astringents, are now used for purposes such as removing the last traces of water-prove makeup residue, sebum, dirt, grime, impurities and dead cells left on the face which are stuck in the pores after cleansing so as to give a clean and tight feel on the face. Generally, toners are formulated for the types of skin: normal, dry, combination and oily skin types. Most toners available presently are alcohol-free as alcohol is drying and can be irritant, however, toners for oily skin may contain alcohol. Specially formulated toners for dry skin contain propylene glycol and glycerine which are humectants as well as water. Two-phase toners contain a water-miscible solvent and an oily component which when shaken together prior to use form a temporary emulsion that is more easily applied on the face. The water-soluble solvent cleanses the dirt on the face while the oily constituent leaves an emollient film on the skin that makes the skin supple and radiant. Cosmeceutical astringent/acidic toners designed for acne treatment contain salicylic acid (an anti-inflammatory, antibacterial, exfoliating beta-hydroxy acid) as well as menthol (has soothing, cooling effects) and camphor (antibacterial, soothing), both of which give a tingling sensation, while those for anti-aging management contain alpha hydroxy acids, such as glycolic acid, that induce exfoliation (25). Some toners contain herbal extracts, such as witch hazel, eucalyptus, mint, aloe vera, rose water and orange flower water which refresh the skin and may tighten the pores. Toners are also formulated to restore the skin's pH, especially after the use of alkaline bar soaps as cleansers, and tone and also to prepare the skin to absorb moisturisers and other facial treatment products which are applied after toning. Toners are applied either soaked in cotton pads and swept over the face, sprayed on the skin from a spray bottle or poured on the palms and patted directly on the face preferably immediately after cleansing and exfoliating, working with an outward movement on the face.

Moisturisers

Moisturisers are a group of cosmetic products that are basically used to make the skin supple and smooth-looking, thereby enhancing the general outlook of individuals. They have been used since antiquity as grooming agents for the skin, majorly in the form of plant- and animal-derived fats and oils. To the dermatologists, however, a moisturiser is regarded as a bland oleaginous preparation that is used as an adjunct in the treatment of dry skin (xerosis) related dermatosis. Moisturisers comprise emollients, humectants, occlusives, protein rejuvenators and more recently, hydrators. These provide skin moisturisation by different modes of action, mainly to keep the skin moist and to reduce to the barest minimum, loss of moisture or trans-epidermal water loss (TEWL) from the topmost layer of the skin which otherwise would appear dry, rough, scaly and susceptible to some skin diseases and attacks by environmental noxious substances. Normally, the stratum corneum is kept moist by water molecules that move to the surface from the deep epidermal layers of the skin and is sealed by the intercellular lipids of the stratum corneum. However, damage to this layer of the skin results in increased rate and extent of TEWL and the ensuing skin dryness. There are also the natural moisturising factors (NMFs) found within corneocyte skin cells that contribute to the hydration dynamics of the stratum corneum (26). NMFs are hydrophilic substances such as amino acids, salts and urea whose production is stimulated by environmental humidity. At low water content (less than 10%), desquamation of the corneocytes occurs which appear on the skin surface as flakes as seen in dry skin. Table 3.1 shows the types of moisturisers and their mechanism of action. It has been observed that the structural and functioning parameters of the skin vary based on ethnicity, with the Blacks, for example, exhibiting more TEWL than the Caucasians (27). Hence, the effects of weather and environmental conditions, notwithstanding, it can be deduced that the need for and the response to moisturiser therapy will differ from one racial skin type to another with the Blacks requiring more highly moisturising products than the Caucasians. Moisturisers are available as hydrophilic (oil-in-water emulsions) or hydrophobic (water-in-oil emulsions) lotions, creams, ointments (emollients) and gels. In general, an ideal moisturiser should:

- reduce TEWL thereby hydrating the skin,
- provide immediate hydration by being rapidly absorbed,
- make the skin smooth, supple and radiant,

- be non-comedogenic, non-sensitising and hypoallergenic especially for sensitive skin,
- be long-lasting, aesthetically acceptable
- and if possible, be fragrance free as fragrances elicit allergic reactions in some individuals.

Emollients: emollients consist of oils, fats and waxes of animals (lanolin from wool fat, carnauba wax, beeswax, milk fats and oils) and plants (avocado oil, coconut oil, castor oil, olive oil, joboba oil, palm oil, argan oil, canola oil, cocoa butter, mango butter, shea butter); the constituents of which are mainly long chain saturated and unsaturated fatty acids and esters as well as fatty alcohols such as of stearic (stearic acid, octyl stearate, stearyl alcohol), linoleic, linolenic, oleic (oleyl oleate), and lauric (lauric acid, lauric alcohol) and which are also present as diglycerides and triglycerides in fats and waxes (except lanolin), respectively.

Table 3.1: Characteristic properties of moisturisers

Type	Mechanism of action	Examples	Side effects
Occlusives	Form a relatively impermeable layer on the skin surface to physically block the evaporation of water from the skin. They reduce or prevent trans-epidermal water loss	Petrolatum, lanolin, mineral oil	Occlusive folliculitis
Humectants	Attract water to the stratum corneum	Glycerine, urea, propanediol, sorbitol, propylene glycol	Miliaria rubra, prickly heat, heat rash due to sweat retention
Emollients	Fill spaces between skin flakes with oil droplets	Cholesterol, squalene, lanolin, shea butter, olive oil, coconut oil	Contact irritation
Protein rejuvenators	Aid skin renewal by replenishing essential proteins in the skin	Collagen, keratin, elastin	Contact dermatitis

Examples of other fatty esters include PEG-7 glyceryl cocoate, coco caprylate/caprate, myristyl myristate, cetearyl isononanoate and isopropyl myristate. Octyl dodecanol, hexyl decanol and oleyl alcohol are examples of fatty alcohols that are not only with no drying action on the skin but give very good skin-smoothing and moisturising effects. Mineral oils (liquid paraffin, petrolatum, paraffin wax) and non-oily synthetic silicones (dimethicone, cyclopentasiloxane, cetearyl methicone, cyclohexasiloxane) also serve as emollients in cosmetic products.

Ceramides, which are the chief structural intracellular lipid components of the stratum corneum, are available in the market as natural, synthetic as well as synthetic pseudo-ceramides and are effective in preventing and improving dry skin conditions just as cholesterol. Squalene produced by plants and animals (shark liver oil, amaranth seed, wheat germ, olives), is another natural lipid component of sebum that contributes to skin lubrication and protection. It is an isoprenoid compound which is a biochemical intermediate in the synthesis of sterols (including cholesterol) and steroid hormones. However, levels of squalene in the body, and indeed in the skin, begin to decline at about 30 years of age when the skin starts to appear dry and rough. Natural squalene, obtained especially from the liver of shark, is highly unstable being susceptible to oxidation, becoming readily rancid. However, when subjected to hydrogenation it yields the stable squalane, a commercially available emollient for cosmetics (28).

Emollients, when applied, form occlusive layers on the skin that seal in moisture, reducing TEWL, and also fill in fine lines or crevices between the desquamating corneocytes thereby enhancing skin slip or lubricity, giving the skin a soft/supple and smooth texture as well as a radiant look. Most of the oils are comedogenic (that is, can cause acne breakouts), however, plant oils such as grapeseed oil, sunflower seed oil, hempseed oil and sweet almond oil as well as the silicones and squalane have low comedogenicity levels.

Emollients are classified based on their greasiness and spreading characteristics into poor spreading/greasy emollients, medium spreading/creamy emollients and easy spreading/nongreasy emollients (29). Emolliency refers to the ability of a product to fill in the crevices between the desquamating corneocytes; moisturising refers to the net decrease in transepidermal water loss (TEWL) after product application, while lubrication refers to the ability of the product to increase skin smoothness. All three qualities can be achieved through the substance known as an emollient. Therefore, substances with emollient properties can moisturise the skin and improve lubricity (30).

Humectants*:* Humectants are hygroscopic substances that are able to absorb moisture from the atmosphere, especially in humid conditions, and draw water from the dermis unto the stratum corneum and also reduce evaporation of water molecules from the skin surface. Humectants compliment the skin hydration functions of the natural moisturising factor (NMF) found in the skin. NMF is made of low molecular weight hygroscopic substances such as lactic acid, amino acids and pyrollidine-carboxylic acid (29). Humectants used in cosmetics include urea, glycerine, honey, gelatine, sorbitol, hyaluronic acid, panthenol, propylene and butylene glycol, sodium pyrroline-carboxylic acid (Na-PCA) and alpha hydroxy acids such as glycolic acid and lactic acid. However, high concentrations of urea and propylene glycol should be avoided as these can irritate the skin while undiluted glycerine can give a stinging effect. The alpha hydroxy acids are keratolytic whereby they reduce roughness and scaling by increasing cohesion of the stratum corneum cells (30). Urea functions as a humectant at about 10% but is mildly keratolytic at 20 -30%. Aloe vera (*Aloe barbadensis*) gel is humectant (31) and its extract has been shown to be effective at concentrations as low as 0.1 to 0.5% (32).

Hydrators: These constitute a relatively new sub-classification of humectants used by professional cosmetics practitioners and manufacturers, respectively, as a means to introduce a new concept in skin moisturising and promote products containing the hydrators as different in efficacy to similar products. The main agent in this subgroup is hyaluronic acid, a naturally occurring hydrophilic substance found in the body with about 50% present in the basal layer of the epidermis where it functions as the principal component of the skin's extracellular matrix, enhancing the skin's water-binding capacity thereby keeping the skin moist among other functions (33). Hyaluronic acid is basically a dipolysaccharide polymer of the glycosaminoglycan family of polysaccharides that is present in the body mainly as the sodium salt, sodium hyaluronate, in the form of a cationic polyelectrolyte. It is hygroscopic and able to retain large amounts of water which makes it an effective hydrator. It degrades and is reproduced on a daily basis, however, the turnover rate declines with age making the skin to gradually become dehydrated, atrophic with loss of elasticity resulting in the development of fine lines and wrinkles on the skin (34). Notwithstanding, hyaluronic acid is regarded as the gold standard for hydrators that are included in cosmetic moisturiser and anti-wrinkling products as it has been proved to exceedingly improve hydration, turgor and elasticity of the skin thereby reducing fine lines and wrinkles. The duration/retention of its effectiveness when products are applied on the skin is variable depending on formulation and the fact that it has poor skin penetration and deposition and degrades rapidly. To mitigate the short comings of this highly hydrating substance, cross-linked synthetic hyaluronic derivatives with interpenetrating polymer network (IPN) structures that are better able to hold and retain water molecules due to improved visco-elastic properties have been developed. Oka *et al*. developed sodium acetylhyaluronate (AcHA) which has the ability to enhance the intrinsic water-holding abilities of the stratum corneum, eliciting strong skin-softening effect as well as the capability to anchor to the skin surface is generally known as supper hyaluronic acid (39, 40). To further improve on efficacy, Majewski *et al*. have developed a modified hydrophobic IPN using three polymers to obtain a 3-dimentional network structure that entraps hyaluronic acid and water, resulting in a super hydrator that attracts and binds water to the skin surface more efficiently than other derivatives (35).

Occlusives: These are highly hydrophobic substances, which form an impermeable layer on the skin, constituting a physical barrier that prevent trans-epidermal water loss (TEWL). Petrolatum, a mineral hydrocarbon, is highly effective as an occlusive and at a low concentration of about 5% in a moisturiser product is able to reduce TEWL by 98% or more (30). Other types of occlusives include lanolin, mineral oil, dimethicone and zinc oxide (Table 4.1). Occlusives are more effective when applied on moist skin by prior showering, sponge-bathing, spraying of water on the skin or simply by rubbing the product on the palms with a little quantity of water. Occlusives may not be cosmetically acceptable to some persons as they give an obvious shinny look on the skin and can be messy to apply, lanolin may cause sensitisation and irritation (allergic dermatitis) in some individuals and mineral oils may cause folliculitis.

Protein skin rejuvenators*:* Keratin, elastin and collagen are proteins that have been claimed to rejuvenate the skin by replenishing essential proteins when applied topically (Table 4.1). However, these proteins have large molecules that prevent their penetration to the dermis and may therefore be unable to achieve this function. Notwithstanding, by filling irregularities in the stratum corneum, the proteins may provide temporary relief of dry skin and leave a protein film that appear to smoothen the skin since they shrink slightly on drying (30). It is however possible that the moisturisers present in preparations containing these proteins provide most of the acclaimed moisturising activity (36).

Serums

Serums are a relatively new addition to skin care cosmetics. At inception, they were presented as products with very high concentrations of active ingredients, sometimes ten times stronger than the conventional counterpart, and formulated as aqueous or oily liquid preparations, packaged in small or unit dose containers and applied to the affected area as few drops with the tips of one or two fingers, so as to avoid wastage. The very high concentrations of active ingredients in serums make them act promptly, giving noticeable results almost instantly, as they are more quickly assimilated than when present in other forms. Serums are prepared for specific skin care needs and are applied on the affected areas on the face, neck, eyelids and decollate. Thus, they are formulated only to either moisturise, nourish, rejuvenate, sooth, relief stress, tighten up the skin, brighten dark blemishes, as anti-inflammatory or anti-acne. In formulating serums, the pH of the final product is taken into consideration. Products applied to eyelids should have a neutral pH of 7, like that of tears, so as to prevent eye irritation, while products for other parts of the skin should have pH of between 5 and 6.5. Serums are specifically labelled for the purpose for which they have been formulated and the names of the active ingredients that promote the products such as peptides, vitamin C, hyaluronic acid, panthenol, collagen, elastin horse-chest nut extracts (for blood circulation activation), witch hazel (anti-inflammatory) and retinol are also written on the labels. Serums are now available as water-based light emulsion lotions and gels, oil-only and 'pressed' balm which are basically soft, hydrophobic, occlusive, semi-solid preparations containing lipophilic active ingredients (Table 3.2). Serums are usually applied to the face after cleansing and toning or as directed by the manufacturer, over which other skin care products, such as moisturisers, are applied thereby sealing the serum and enhancing its effects on the skin.

Table 3.2: Differences between serum, essence and ampoule

	Toner	Essence	Serum	Ampoule
Purpose	Removes impurities, oil, and dirt left behind after cleansing. May also deliver high-performance actives	Adds a layer of hydration before serum application	Delivery of high-performance actives	Delivery of super concentrated high-performance actives
Application	After cleansing	After cleansing and toning, before serum application	After cleansing, toning and if desired after application of essence	After cleansing and toning
Consistency	Light	Light	Light	Light
Product presentation	Water-based liquid	Water-based liquid	Water-based emulsion and gel, oily liquid and balm	Water-based emulsion and oily liquid
Concentration of active Ingredients	Low	Low	Moderate to high	Very high
Frequency of use	Daily	Daily	Daily	When required (during treatment sessions)
Packaging	Bottles with disc caps or pumps	Bottles with disc caps or pumps	Bottles with airless or regular pump or dropper closures	Single use ampoule (glass or plastic)

The differences between a toner, serum, essence and ampoule, which are cosmetic products that similarly offer benefits to the skin are listed in Table 3.2.

Body odour control agents

Sweating is an important physiological function of the skin that keeps the skin moist and, in the course of evaporation of the exuded sweat, cools and regulates body temperature and also serves as a means of excretion of waste products from the body. Sweats are released from the sweat glands which are distributed in varying densities/concentrations and according to types, mainly eccrine and apocrine glands, all over the body. The eccrine glands are found all over the body while the apocrine glands abound in high densities at those areas of the human body with hair follicles, in particular, the axilla (armpit) where sweating is usually profuse. The eccrine gland secretions consist of water, sodium chloride, fatty acids, lactic acid, citric acid, ascorbic acid, urea, as well as uric acid, and the secretions increase profusely with anxiety, fear, stress and pain. Sweat, when freshly exuded from the eccrine glands in the armpit is odourless and colourless. Evaporation of the salt solutions creates a white sediment which is often found as white stains on clothes of people who sweat profusely. In addition to the constituents of eccrine gland secretions, apocrine gland secretions contain proteins, carbohydrates, lipids, and steroids which, along with the odourless oily sebum secreted by the sebaceous glands of the skin, constitute nutrients on which the skin microflora, especially *Staphylococcus hominis, Staphylococcus epidermidis* and *Corynebacterium* species, thrive. The enzymatic break down of the nutrients by the bacteria produce unpleasant odorous metabolites, especially the volatile fatty acid, trans -3 – methyl - 2- hexenoic acid, which gives a hircine odour that constitutes the greater part of the bad armpit odour; as well as oxidation of oils and lipids that results to rancid smell. The apocrine gland secretion is slightly cloudy because of its higher content of insoluble constituents, it is odourless but when evaporated leaves a white, and sometimes yellowish, residue stain on clothing, especially in the arm pit area, mainly due to its salt and the other insoluble constituents. Apocrine glands do not start secreting sweat until stimulated by hormones at puberty, hence, children normally do not have body odour until they become adolescents except for those with some medical conditions (37).

Men have more apocrine glands than women in the armpits. Europeans and Africans have the largest and most active apocrine glands and are, therefore, more prone to body odour than East Asians (38). Body odour can be masked by application of deodorants while excessive sweating, and consequently body odour, is controlled with the use of antiperspirants.

Hyperhidrosis or highly excessive sweating is a medical condition that often leads to severe and unpleasant body odour that can adversely affect the quality of life (QoL) of an individual. If mild, it could be controlled with frequent use of over-the-counter (OTC) antiperspirants. Severe hyperhidrosis, however, requires the use of prescription antiperspirants that contain high concentrations of aluminium chloride or aluminium zirconium tetrachlorohydrex glycine, the administration of oral anticholinergic (muscle relaxant) medications, Botox (botulinum toxin type A) injection (for underarm sweating only) or surgical intervention.

Chromhidrosis is a rare medical condition whereby secreted sweats are coloured due either to an abnormal physiological process that leads to availability of higher amounts of lipofuscin granules in the apocrine glands (apocrine chromhidrosis) or as a result of excretion of pigmented compounds from ingested drugs such as the quinines, rifampicin, and levodopa; water-soluble dyes such as tartrazine found in colourants and flavourants and heavy metals like copper; through the eccrine sweat glands (eccrine chromhidrosis). Pseudochromhidrosis occurs when the colourless secretion of the eccrine glands turns coloured due to the influence of some exogenous substances such as coloured chemicals (aluminium salts mixed with sweat) and dyes (clothe dye) on the skin, that affect the microflora of chromogenic organisms on the skin surface, e.g., *Corynebacterium* Spp. (brown sweat), *Serratia marcescens* (pink sweat). The stain can occur in any area of the body, especially on the face, neck and palms, and is usually wiped off with moist cloth, but may require medical attention in some cases (39).

Deodorants: The first deodorant, marketed with the trade name, MUM, was invented in 1888 as a waxy cream that contained a low quantity of antibacterial zinc oxide and was applied on the armpit with the fingers, which was rather clumpy. By 1952, it was presented as a roll-on, the formulation has since undergone various modifications and is presently available as roll-on deodorant without aluminium salts, alcohol or perfume but as an all vegan product packaged in sustainable glass bottle (40). Deodorants mask or modify the odour generated in the armpit by killing or inactivating the microorganisms that produce odorous breakdown products of the apocrine sweat gland secretions or by the stronger odour elicited by fragrances and perfumes. Active constituents of deodorants include phenolic and chlorinated antibacterial agents such as chlorhexidine and triclosan; quaternary ammonium compounds, e.g., alkyl dimethyl benzyl ammonium saccharinate; glyceryl fatty acids, e.g., glyceryl caprylate/caprate; sucrose fatty acids, e.g., sucrose hydroxy stearate, sucrose laurate; and fragrances which in most cases, are essential oils some of which have antimicrobial properties, e.g., bergamot oil, lavender oil and sage oil. Although, the FDA, in 2016, banned the use of triclosan in over-the-counter antiseptic products such as bar soaps and body washes, it is still included in deodorants (40). Some other active ingredients of deodorants that do not directly affect the bacterial colony of the armpit but are able to control odour by other means include potassium and sodium bicarbonate, zinc carbonate, zinc glycinate, zinc oxide, silicones and silicates. Derivatives of citric acid reduce the pH of the armpit (approximately 6.0) to acidic pH that inhibit bacterial growth.

Anti-perspirants: Antiperspirants control, reduce or prevent sweating by plugging the pores of sweat ducts on the surface of the skin. This activity affects the normal physiology of sweat glands; hence, anti-perspirants are regarded as drugs by the regulatory agencies of many countries but not by others. In an instance, the FDA classifies them as drugs while the EU legislation considers them as cosmetics. They are, however, classified as cosmeceuticals by manufacturers of cosmetic products. The pore-plugging effect is provided mainly by aluminium and zinc salts such as aluminium chloride and sulphate, aluminium zirconium tetrachlorohydrex gly (glycine), but more especially aluminium chlorhydrate. The salts plug eccrine sweat pores and also form aggregates with sweat proteins of the apocrine glands which bind to the wall of the sweat duct and form a tenuous membrane. This prevents sweat from reaching the surface of the skin (41), the colloidal plug is gradually broken down and normal sweating resumes necessitating re-application of the antiperspirants. Some aluminium salts have demonstrated antibacterial activity which could add to their deodorant activity when used as antiperspirants (42).

Systemic absorption of aluminium in aluminium chlorhydrate, following dermal application, has been shown to be minimal with about 0.01% and up to 0.06% in pre-damaged skin. An equivalent of 4µg mcg of aluminium at 0.012% of systemic absorption following a single application of product was obtained in a study. This value is 2.5% of the amount of aluminium absorbed through the gut from food, determined over the same period (43). Though the results of this study imply that aluminium-containing anti-perspirants may not have deleterious effect on the health of the user, notwithstanding, more studies are still being carried out to fully determine the implication of antiperspirants in breast cancer (44) and neurodegenerative diseases such as Alzheimer's disease. Crystal deodorants/antiperspirants, which contain potassium alum or aluminium alum as active agents are considered safer and lesser allergenic alternatives to conventional products (45). Cyclomethicone (International Nomenclature of Cosmetic Ingredient (INCI): Cyclopentasiloxane), a colourless, odourless, non-irritant, hygroscopic, quick-drying (volatile) silicone also serves as antiperspirant/deodorant by creating a dry environment in the armpit which reduces sweating and prevents the growth of resident microbes. Unlike aluminium salts, cyclomethicone is not absorbed because of the large size of its molecules, and it is, therefore, a safer alternative. It is also used as solvents for these products

Figure 3.4: Spray, stick and roll-on deodorants

It is common to find deodorants being combined with antiperspirants as single products. Deodorants and antiperspirants are available as roll-ons, aerosol sprays, powders and block sticks (Figure 3.4).

Untoward effects of deodorants and antiperspirants include skin irritation (especially when the skin is broken), stained clothing – white residue caused by dried salt constituents, allergy and long-term effects of inhalation of the constituents when aerosols are used. Zirconium-containing active ingredients are not permitted in antiperspirant aerosol products because of the carcinogenic potential of aerosolized zirconium complexes when inhaled.

Makeup, decorative or colour cosmetics

Makeup, decorative or colour cosmetics enhance appearance either by modifying a facial feature, such as the eye lashes, or by adding colours to different parts of the face, nails and the hair in order to promote beauty, and in some instances, conceal conspicuous skin flaws.

Eye makeup

Mascaras

A mascara is a colour cosmetic or a makeup that is used to enhance the appearance of eye lashes through darkening, curling, colouring, thickening and/or lengthening. It is formulated as a liquid preparation packaged in a tube whose cap has the spiral bristle mascara brush applicator attached (Figure 3.5). Mascara is available in different colours and it is mainly obtained from titanium dioxide, a white colourant; carbon black and various iron oxides that give a range of colours that include yellow, orange, red, brown and black. Ultramarine blue and some other colourants and pigments are also used to give the desired colour while some contain glitter in addition. Eyelash curlers may be used with mascara to enhance the natural curl of the eyelashes. The main constituents of today's mascara are pigments, waxes, oils, emulsifiers, viscosity- imparting agents and preservatives, prepared as liquid emulsions better known as lotions. Hydrophobic agents are included where water-resistant mascaras are to be manufactured. Actives such as vitamins, amino acids may be added for growth and structural enhancement.

Mode of application

Mascara is brushed onto eyelashes; the wax contained in the preparation clings and dries out on each of the eyelashes giving a thicker effect to the lashes while the pigments impart a darker shade. Mascaras are removed using cotton pads soaked with either makeup remover or oils cupped on the whole eyelashes and gently wiping off the mascara.

There are some specialised mascaras that give other effects apart from just highlighting the eyelashes. These include lengthening mascara, mascaras with primers, natural lengthening mascaras and 'tubing' mascara (46).

Figure 3.5: Mascara with applicator

Lengthening mascaras: In addition to the basic components of a mascara, lengthening mascaras contain nylon or rayon microfibers which, when the mascara is applied, get attached from the base of hair lashes upwards to the tips giving the effect of lengthening to the lashes. If the mascara also has curling properties, then the eyelashes are curled upwards which gives further lengthening effects to the lashes. A stronger lengthening effect is obtained by application of a second coat of mascara on the lashes. However, to prevent clumping of the mascara on the lashes due to the tiny pieces of the microfibres, not more than two coats are advised.

Mascaras with primers: This type of mascara gives a similar look of eyelash-lengthening. An eyelash primer is first brushed onto the lashes before the coloured mascara is applied resulting in longer-looking lashes.

Natural lengthening mascaras: Natural lengthening fibres as opposed to synthetic ones have been developed for consumers' preference for natural products. In these mascaras, ingredients such as berry pigments, cocoa fibres and black tea are used to replace synthetic pigments as well as nylon and rayon fibres.

Tubing Mascara: The polymer blend contained in this category of mascaras encloses each lash in a narrow black tube that extends beyond the edge of the lash, resulting in longer-looking lashes. While tubing mascara can also thicken the lashes, an initial coat of thickening mascara may give a better thickening effect. Care needs to be taken in removing tubing mascara unlike the conventional lengthening mascaras and this involves the use of warm water and gentle cleaning with a washcloth.

Eyelash extensions

Cosmetic applications that are attached somewhat to the natural eyelashes so as to enhance their length, thickness and fullness are referred to as eyelash extensions. Materials used for their manufacture could be human or horsehair, silk, mink or synthetic. The strands of the extensions are individually attached to each of the natural eyelashes by a trained makeup artist who, after taping down the lower eyelashes, would use a tweezer to isolate the natural eyelash and use another tweezer to apply an eyelash extension 1 – 2 mm from the base of the natural eyelash without touching the eyelid (Figure 3.6). A glue, specific for this purpose, usually a cyanoacrylate adhesive, is applied to keep the eyelash extension in place and care should be taken not to damage the natural lashes which can arise if the extension is too long or too heavy for the eyelash of the individual. The process can take between one to three hours as individuals have from one hundred to two hundred lashes in each eye. When properly attached, eyelash extensions are semi-permanent as they remain in place for two to three weeks after which they can be refilled or replaced with a partial set every four weeks. This is because natural eye lashes, like other hairs on the body, are lost every day and will drop off with the attached extension resulting in loss of fullness of the eyelashes. Wearers of eyelash extensions are advised not to sleep face down and to take proper care when using makeup removers to prevent the extensions from falling off prematurely.

Temporary false eyelashes: Temporary false eyelashes, like eyelash extensions, are used to lengthen, enhance and add to the fullness and volume to natural eyelashes. However, they are expected to be removed after use as they are not designed to be worn to sleep or when swimming or showering and can be applied by individuals without the need for an expert. They are available as a strip lash that is adhered on top of the natural eyelashes with the appropriate adhesive and takes about five minutes to apply. The adhesive is smeared on the strip lash and after about thirty seconds, the strip is pressed against the top root of the natural eyelashes until the adhesive dries off. There are magnetic false lashes which are sandwiched in the natural eyelashes by being placed between the natural lashes. A magnetic eyeliner is first applied to the eyelid on which the magnetic false eyelash is then pressed and put in place.

Eye liners

The eyeliner is a cosmetic product that is applied around the contours of the eyes, highlighting the features of the eyes and producing a variety of looks that depends on the way and the place around the eye that the liner is applied and the colour of the liner employed. It can be applied above the upper eyelid or on the lower eyelid or on both of them as well as on the waterline creating different aesthetic effects to the eyes (Figure 3.7). More exotic looks can be obtained by using a winged eye liner or tight lining eyeliner at the waterline which makes the eye lashes look longer by giving an effect that makes them appear to be farther back on the eyelid, thereby making the use of mascara unnecessary, although it can still be used if desired.

Figure 3.6: Installing eyelash extension

A gel eyeliner and a small, angled brush enables these effects to be easily achieved while waterproof eyeliners are advised because of the close proximity to the eye and eye fluids (47). Eye liners are available in different colours and shades with the commonest being black, grey and brown. Other attractive and more adventurous colours such as bright red, yellow, blue, purple, green, pastel colours, glittered-flecked colours, white as well as shades of frosty silver and gold can be obtained. Eye liners can also be used to depict moods of the individual on the face such as depression especially for castes in movies and in photography. Eyeliners are available as liquid eye liner, powder-based eye pencil, wax-based eye pencils, kohl eye liner, gel eye liner, pen eyeliner, shimmer liner and eyeshadow or cake liner.

Figure 3.7: Applying eyeliner over the upper eyelid

Eye shadow

The eyeshadow is a type of colour cosmetic that is primarily applied on the eyelids, but also to the brow bone and below the eyes, which by adding depth and dimension to the eyes makes them stand out and look more attractive. It comes in different shades of colours, and is applied using either the fingers, brushes or sponges (Figure 3.8). it is available in form of a powder most commonly as a palette of different colour hues, liquid, pencil, cream or mousse. Application of a primer before the eyeshadow is advisable as this prevents creases from appearing the eyeshadow after a while. Colours used should be carefully chosen and blended to give the desired attractive effects.

Figure 3.8: An eyeshadow palette (with foam applicators)

Different types of brushes are used in applying eyeshadow to the eye area in order to achieve the desired effects. Flat brushes are used to place the eyeshadow on the eyelids which is then blended using brushes with fluffy and tapered tips such as foam applicators (Figure 3.8). To apply colour with precision, smaller brushes with dense or angled bristles are employed.

Eye brow makeup

The eyebrows, apart from protecting the eyes by preventing liquids flowing from the forehead into the eyes, contribute to the shape of the face, accentuate the eyes and are a means of communication. When properly groomed, the eyebrows flatter the eyes, enhance appearance giving a more youthful look and thereby serves as a subtle anti-aging agent for the older persons. A roughly and carelessly shaped eyebrow can depict anger, tiredness and even agedness (48). The eyebrow is often trimmed to achieve a desired shape, it can be thinned out to obtain a narrower line of hairs and sometimes outrightly shaved off or plucked and then painted with a liner or tattooed using a stencil or a drawn design of desired eyebrow shape. Eyebrows can also be microbladed. The tweezers, manual or electronic, are the most common tools for removal, trimming and shaping of hairs of the eyebrows. A pair of small scissors can also be used to trim the eyebrow.

Waxing and threading are other hair-removal techniques. Soft waxing involves layering of a thick sticky substance particularly wax on the eyebrow and pressing a strip of cloth or paper on the wax which is then quickly ripped off in the opposite direction of hair growth, thereby removing the wax and uprooting the hair strands from the hair follicles. The wax can be applied cold or molten and then allowed to congeal which enables a good and easily spread layer of wax on the brow. There are pre-made strips which are coated with wax and applied directly on the brow, In the case of stripless or hard wax, molten wax is applied and allowed to congeal as a thick layer on the eyebrow, thereby encapsulating the hair strands as it congeals making the coated strands, especially fine hairs, to be more easily removed manually by trained experts without strips of cloth or paper. This method is less painful than soft-waxing as the wax adheres less firmly on the skin unlike soft-waxing and is preferred by persons with sensitive skin. However, there are certain conditions under which waxing may be undesirable as 'skin-lifting', a condition where the skin top layer is peeled off with the wax, may occur in persons who are using certain medications such as blood-thinners, those that manifest certain allergic reactions and those who have undergone some surgeries and skin treatment like skin peeling.

Eyebrows are also removed by threading, a process involving doubling and then twisting of a thin thread made of cotton or polyester which is rolled over the brow plucking the hair strands from the follicles. This method allows for better control of hair trimming and shaping than waxing and is gentler on the skin than waxing. It is, however, painful especially when improperly performed (49).

Hair transplant, when desired by the client, is performed with hair follicles obtained majorly from the back of the head and injected into the skin of the eyebrows to give fuller looking effects. Also, the eyebrow lift, a cosmetic surgery procedure, is carried out to raise the eyebrow creating a more feminine and youthful outlook.

Makeup cosmetics for the eyebrow

Primers/Waxes*:* Primers are first applied on the eyebrow to give a long-lasting effect to eyebrow pencils and powders which stick to the priming layer of the wax when applied on the brows. A small, angled brush is used to apply the wax along the outline of the eyebrow and then lightly blended in the outlined space with a 'spoolie' brush that is like the mascara brush. The eyebrow pencil or powder is then applied on the wax (54).

Powders: Compact powders of different shades of colours are applied on the eyebrows, preferably on brow wax, using angled eyebrow brushes.

Eyebrow pencils: These are designed to have a powdery consistency to allow for ease of application on the eyebrows and give a perfect effect on thinned or over-plucked eyebrows. They come in various colours and the appropriate colour choice is one with a shade lower than that of the hairs of the brow.

Clear and tinted gels: The clear gel keeps the hair in place giving a more textured, fuller and thicker effects while the tinted gel, gives in addition, desired colours such as grey, blond or overly dark eyebrows.

Pomades*:* These give tinted colours to eyebrows.

Brow makers: The main difference between a brow makers and eyebrow pencil is that the former is felt-tipped and embedded with pigments.

Tattoo pens and mascaras: These give temporary tints to eyebrows when compared to microblading, microshading and brow tinting. There are, however, eyebrow tattoos that are semi-permanent/permanent.

Lip cosmetics

Cosmetics applied to the lips serve to accentuate the lip's appearance by the colour and/or sheen provided and also by improving the lips' texture and conferring some form of protection, mainly emolliency, on the lips. The earliest agents used in lip colouring include crushed gemstones, ochre, carmine and seaweed extracts employed mainly to decorate the lips and, in some cultures, served as a social status (50). This practice has continued till date evolving in gross improvement and development of present-day cosmetics for the lips as regard constituents, formulation and presentation. Lip cosmetics are now available in different forms as lipsticks, lip liquids, lip balms, lip glosses, liners, pencils, stains, crayons and palettes.

Lipsticks

The term lipstick initially connoted the tub into which ingredients used in the preparation of coloured lip products were compacted into a stick-like product. Hence, lipsticks can be defined as compact, stick-like products, packaged in and dispensed from customised metallic tubes from which they are applied to colour, give texture and moisturise the lips. These properties of lipsticks are due to the main ingredients used in their formulation and manufacture that consist of pigments, lake dyes, emollient oils and waxes that confer the semi-solid consistency on the preparations. Lipsticks are made to appeal to current fashion trends. They come in various colours and shades, textures, sizes of tubes used for the packaging, some impart glossy/shimmering effect while some are matted, some are perfumed and some may be sweetened. The tube consists of a cover which can be of transparent plastic to show off the lipstick, and a base in which the lipstick is moulded and which is designed to twist or slide to push the lipstick up for application (Figure 3.9).

Liquid lipsticks: Liquid lipsticks, as they are referred to, contain similar ingredients as traditional lipsticks except the waxes but contain more pigments. They are packaged in special tubes and are applied on the lips using an applicator wand.

Figure 3.9: Lipsticks

Lip balm: Lip balm, also referred to as lip salve, is a waxy product, similar in consistency to lipstick, that provides an occlusive effect on the lips, sealing in moisture and preventing adverse effects of dry air, cold temperature and dry winds which draw moisture away from the skin the effect of which is more prominent on the thin lip skin. Thus, lip balm relieves chapped or dry lips, cold sores, angular cheilitis and stomatitis. Ingredients of lip balm may include menthol which provides analgesic effect, camphor that heals cold sores and salicylic acid which exfoliates dead skin. However, these agents may irritate the thin lip skin. Fragrances present in some lip balms may also irritate the lips and cause allergic reactions. Persons who stay long under the sun may prefer to use lip balms with UV filter agents or sunscreens. Lip balms are presented in lipstick-styled tubes, majorly of plastic material, or in small jars from which the balm is applied using the finger.

Lip gloss: Lip gloss was invented by Max Factor in 1930, to create a lip product that would make the lips of film stars shiny and glossy (56). The primary function of a lip gloss is to give a gentle sheen or soft glow to the lips and, for some product, may subtly add colour to the lips as well as give a frosted, metallic, glittery and/or glossy finish. Thus, it may be applied on top of lipstick to increase the gloss of a colour or to add depth to glittery and glossy lipsticks. Persons who do not want the intense colour of lipsticks but desire some colour and gloss on the lips often go for the milder lip gloss. The ingredients used for the manufacture are similar to those for lipsticks except that less quantities of wax as well as diluted and pale pigments are used and lanolin, a humectant, is added giving a good feel on the lips. Liquid lip glosses are packaged in small cylinders with either a built-in applicator wand or a separately provided applicator (known as a doe foot applicator because of its rounded and sloped tip). Soft solid forms are presented in small, soft, squeezable tubes from which the product can be applied directly on the lips or with the fingertips or with a lip brush (Figure 3.10). Semisolid lip glosses are packaged in tubes like lipsticks or in small boxes.

Figure 3.10: Lip gloss

Lip-plumping glosses contain substances that irritate the lip skin causing inflammatory reactions that make blood to rush to the skin surface resulting in transient swelling that gives a fuller or plumped up appearance of the lips. Such irritants include capsicum oleoresin, cinnamon oil and menthol which can leave a burning sensation on the lips when first applied. While the plumping effect is temporary, continuous application of these type of lip glosses can result in conditioned reflex, a situation where the lip no longer responds to the irritant effects of the substances. Moreover, excessive use of the irritants can cause dry, chapped and irritated lips. Attenuated bee venom also gives the same swelling effect on the lips. However, reaction to the venom by some individuals, especially those with previous history of reaction to bee sting, may occur. Hyaluronic acid, a natural humectant, is a safer lip-plumping agent that is used in some products, including injectable lip filler products, instead of the irritant substances.

Lip liner/lip pencil: This is used to create an outline on the lips within which the lipstick or lip gloss is applied and contained, thereby giving an even edge of lipstick on the lips and creating a defined contrast that makes the lips stand out more. Lip liner can also be applied on the entire lips as a base for lipstick or used in place of a lipstick. It is available in same range and shades of colours as lipsticks, although there are invisible types, and packaged in form of a retractable tube or as a pencil (Figure 3.11) that can be sharpened. The main ingredients are waxes, oils and pigments, with more pigments than in lipsticks and also of a firmer consistency to allow for harder pressing against the lips (51).

Figure 3.11: Lip pencils/lip liners

Face makeups

Primer: A primer, an important cosmetic component in standard beauty routine, is a thin, moisturising serum, that allows the makeup that is applied over it to be smooth, even and crease-free, thereby offering a subtle skin-perfecting glow. Some primers are transparent when applied, while some are tinted either to match the skin tone of the wearer or to even-out the tone, texture, blemishes and discolouration on the face. There are specially prepared primers for some facial skin conditions such as wrinkles, oily/dry skin, acne and sensitive skin. Hence, some primers contain agents such as moisturisers like hyaluronic acid, exfoliating agents like salicylic acid and antibacterial, anti-inflammatory agents like sulphur. Some primers are formulated to plug pores resulting in breakouts. ***Eyelid or eye shadow primers***, have in addition to some of these properties that basically describes ***foundation primers***, the ability to hide veins and smoothen out the creases on the eyelid, while a ***mascara primer***, which may be colourless, thickens and lengthens the eye lashes prior to the application of the mascara and prevents smudging of the mascara when applied. A ***Lip primer***, on the other hand, smoothens the lips, aids the even application of lipstick or lip gloss on the lips and enhances the staying power of the lip colour.

Concealer: A concealer is usually applied over the primer and further covers up dark circles, age spots, fine lines, discolouration, marks and blemishes on the wearer's face. It comes as a cream or liquid product with a colour that matches the user's tone. It is thick in consistency and rich in pigments thereby blending the imperfections into the skin.

Foundation: Foundation, which evolved from Max Factor's "Pan-Cake" is sometimes referred to as 'corrective' makeup, is available as a mousse, cream, liquid or powder in the wearer's skin tone and is applied to cover the entire face, masking flaws, providing a smooth texture and an even base as well as enhancing the natural skin tone (Figure 3.12).

It may be used to cover the skin's natural tone in some instances. The process is also referred to as 'body-painting'. The face is cleaned and moisturised before the foundation is applied. Foundation products, based on the content of pigments which can be between 35% to 50%, are designed to offer varied opacity or coverage which range from sheer, thin, medium to full coverage that is very opaque and covers scars, hyperpigmentation, birthmarks and vitiligo. Foundation is usually applied with a foundation brush, blended with a warm makeup blending sponge; blemishes, pigmentations and redness are then concealed using a concealer applied with the fingers the warmth from which aids blending of the concealer; after which a translucent or pressed powder is applied with a brush to set the foundation and also to get rid of excess oil on the face.

(a) (b) (c)

Figure 3.12(a - c): Semi-solid, compact powder, loose powder foundation

Rouge, blush or blusher: The word rouge is French, meaning red. Rouge was initially a red powder or cream makeup that was applied on the cheek to highlight the cheekbone and sometimes applied to colour the lips red. It metaphorised to present day **blush** or **blusher** which comes in shades of pink, warm tan, brown or gold making the cheekbones to appear more defined when applied.

Highlighter: A highlighter is a makeup that reflects light, highlighting the points on which it has been applied on the face, usually the cheekbones, brow bones, temples, along the nose bridge and the cupid's bow (Figure 3.13). It complements the blush by bringing out its colour more prominently. It contains substances, like mica – a shimmering mineral - which provides shimmer or glitter and is available as a powder, cream or liquid. Powder type is advisable for persons with oily skin while the other two types are suitable for dry and combination skin types. Liquid and cream products are applied using slightly dampened sponges while soft fluffy brushes are good with powder products (52).

Bronzer: This comes as liquids, creams or powders with satin, matte, semi-matte or shimmer finishes (Figure 3.14). Unlike contouring that gives depth and brings out the shape of the face or redefines facial features such as the cheekbones, jaw lines or making the nose look slimmer or the lips bigger, bronzing gives colour and glow to the skin and the products usually come in bronze or tan that mimics sun-tanning effect or simply make the dark-skinned face to glow, or in some other shades of colour to match skin tones. Bronzers are applied to spots hit by light rays especially the cheek bones, eyebrows, forehead, temples and nose bridge.

Figure 3.13: Highlighter and contour palette Figure 3.14: Facial bronzer Face powders

Face powders, when properly matched with the skin tone of the user, serve to complement the colour of the skin and, also, to mask the shine caused by secretions of the sebaceous and sweat glands, as well as to conceal blemishes and skin imperfections such as black heads, sunburn and freckles. Thus, they impart a velvet-like finish and enhance the appearance of the skin. Face powders are available in a variety of forms, with each type having a characteristic feature that differentiates it from the other type.

Loose powder: A loose powder has a light and soft texture, and contains ingredients such as talc and starch, that enable the product to absorb oil from the skin, thereby, eliminating shine from the face. A loose powder also prevents runoff of makeup and locks in foundations and concealers that are applied as layers underneath it, smoothening out the complexion and limiting cracks and lines on the skin. It is available as a translucent or coloured powder and is usually packaged in a shallow jar and is applied with a puff or a soft brush on the face.

Compact powder: Compact or pressed powder is that powder which has been compressed and packaged in such a container that allows it to be more easily carried about and applied than loose powders. It gives a heavier texture on the face than loose powders, having been formulated with oils and moisturisers which also make the face appear oily within hours of its application on the face. It brightens the face and conceals discolouration and blemishes. It can also be used as a light-coverage foundation. It is available in different colour shades, allowing for adequate skin tone-matching before being used.

Setting powder: This powder holds the foundation cosmetic product in place and prevents makeup bases from running off. It maintains an even, matte finish and gives a remarkable glow factor while keeping makeups more durable. A setting powder can be slightly tinted to match the skin tone or just translucent.

Translucent powder: This type of powder reduces oiliness and shine on the face, giving a matte effect. It allows a long-lasting wear of makeups and can be used to brighten up certain areas of the face.

Finishing powder: This product, apparently is the final product that is applied to complete a makeup process. It locks the other products within the makeup and brightens up an uneven makeup, blurring fine lines, concealing pores and thereby, leaving a flawless facial appearance. It is available as loose or compact powder; the loose powder being more commonly employed. The difference between finishing and setting powders is, however, not quite distinct.

Mineral powder: This is a kind of a supplement-enriched powder that contains vitamins and minerals such as iron; as well as zinc and titanium dioxide which are sunscreen agents, thereby providing some health benefits to the skin. in addition, it prevents clogging of pores and it is usually preservative and fragrance free.

High definition (HD) powder: A HD powder reduces shine on the face and provides a softening and a mattifying effect on the skin.

Figure 3.15: A fully madeup face

It prevents camera flashback and that is why it is mainly used for persons featuring in high-definition film and video When professionally applied, these facial makeup products can give an entirely different facial identity to the client (Figure 3.15).

Cosmetic tattoos

The art of tattooing has been for thousands of years dating back to ancient Egypt, as evidenced by tattoos on mummies as far back as in the days of Cleopatra when sharpened sticks and stones were used to drive natural pigments into the skin to give permanently sculptured designs which included those of animals, names and important dates on different parts of the body. The iceman, Otzi, whose body was exhumed 5000 years after he had been buried in ice of the Alps, had fifty-seven tattoos on his body (53), an indication of how far back the art of tattooing had been.

In almost all other parts of Africa, the art of tattooing has been a socio cultural as well as a religious or spiritual phenomenon for ages. Tattooing or scarification served as a means of tribal, ethnic/clan, patrilineal kindred and cult membership identification and beautification. It was also used for record-keeping and identification of persons as important occasions were marked with designated images while marks, such as tribal marks, were made on persons, respectively, and later when western education was introduced, dates such as birthdays and even names of individuals were scarified on different parts of the body.

Tattoo marks were made using sharp and/or hot instruments to make incisions on the skin, into which were rubbed ash, soot or finely ground charcoal and, in some traditions, dyes of plant origin. Henna, the leaf extract of *Lawsonia inermis* was and is still used to draw decorative patterns on the body for special occasions such as bridal adornment for traditional wedding. The patterns made with henna are, however, temporary and wear off with time (usually within three weeks) by exfoliation, unlike scarification marks which are permanent. Since most of the scarification were made on babies and infants who could not give consent for these to be done on their bodies and who grow up embarrassed with the marks, especially on their faces, the practice of scarification has been banned, backed by laws in most countries where the art is practised. An example is the Nigeria's Child Rights Act that forbids making marks or tattoos on a child (54).

Modern day tattoo is an indelible mark of a pattern or picture on the skin. Tattooing is the process of creating a tattoo on the skin (Figure 3.16 a & b). It involves puncturing the skin and introducing pigments into the dermal layer of the skin such that the pigment appears within or under the skin, according to a desired/pre-planned pattern (55). The process of tattooing involves a number of stages which includes planning, execution, and post-care. Planning for a tattoo requires addressing issues pertaining to desired tattoo design, cost of tattooing, pre-existing skin conditions such as keloids and bleeding disorders, among others.

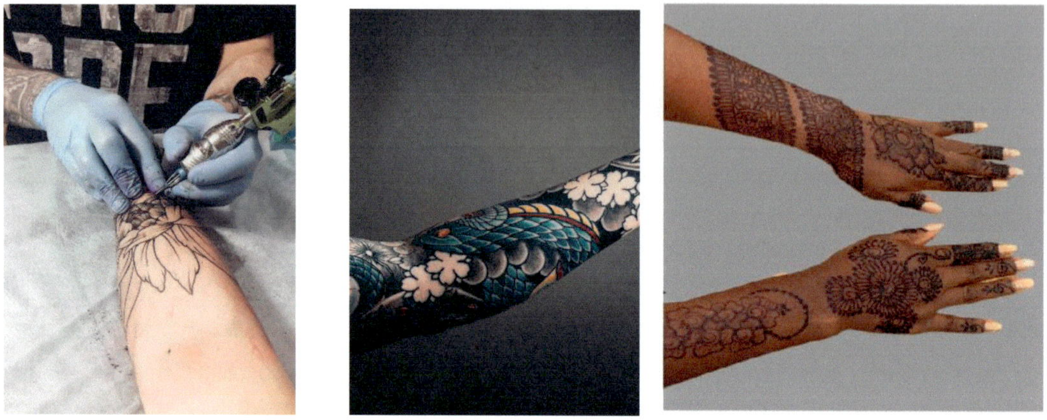

(a) (b) (c)

Figure 3.16 (a, b, & c): Ongoing tattooing, a tattooed arm/forearm, and henna tattooed hands

Tattoos can be temporary (henna) (Figure 3.16c), semi-permanent, or permanent (tattoo pigments) (Figure 3.16 a & b). The insertion of pigments directly into the dermal layer of the skin, with one or more needles on a hand-held equipment which delivers drops of pigments, makes the tattoo marks or designs indelible or permanent. However, the advent of lasers, used for tattoo removal, has made permanent tattoos a thing of the past. Henna, a natural plant pigment, creates temporary tattoos as it is usually placed on the upper (epidermal) layer of the skin and not inserted into it or beneath it. Tattoos can be done intentionally and may occur accidentally. The unintentional or accidental embedding of pigmented materials such as rocks, dirt, and graphite pencils beneath the skin gives rise to traumatic tattoos (55).

Tattoos are made on the skin primarily for cosmetic/aesthetic and therapeutic purposes and have become quite popular as a means of self-expression. They are usually placed on parts of the body that are exposed even while dressed, or parts that can readily be exposed if desired. Other purposes for which tattoos are made include identification with a group, a culture, a cult, or a religion. Cosmetic tattoos can be done by amateurs who usually have low or poor artistic tools or by professionals who use high quality inks, standard equipment, and very good artistic designs.

Tattoos come in very handy in the field of psycho-dermatology where it can be done to provide psychological support or relief for people with permanent skin lesions such as port-wine stains, reddish-violet birthmarks, and vitiligo. Tattoos are also used to create permanent makeup for victims of burns, other physical deformity, and severe forms of alopecia or hair loss (56). They can also be used to mask bodily lesions that are reminders of some form of past trauma, such as a surgical scar or a scar from an injury, "branding" of victims of slavery or kidnapping, and so on. Tattoos also play important roles in the fields of criminology and/or forensic pathology where tattoos can be used as a means of identification and diagnosis.

A wide range of pigments, from natural to synthetic, are used to create tattoos on the skin. These pigments can be in powder or liquid form, usually dispersed in a liquid base. Modern-day techniques employ the use of special equipment on which needles are mounted, to create the tattoo.

Tattoo pigments: The pigments used in creating tattoos can be natural or synthetic, provided as powder or liquid form and are usually dispersed in a liquid base or carrier, such as polyvinylpyrrolidone, propylene glycol, ethanol and glycerol, that keeps the dyes or pigments homogenously dispersed during use. Natural pigments include inorganic mineral pigments like iron oxides, mica, titanium dioxide, and barium sulphate. The iron oxide pigments and mica are mined from the earth and undergo a rigorous process of refinement to reduce their usually high lead content to acceptable levels. Titanium dioxide and barium sulphate (barite) are used to make colours white or to brighten dark colours. Red, brown, and black colours are available in iron oxides, carbon (sooth, ash) and mica. The colours can be used alone or combined to create various blends of colours, including skin/flesh-tone colours. Curcuma yellow (obtained from *Curcuma longa*), logwood violet, purple (obtained from *Haematoxylum campechianum* extract) and henna (obtained from *Lawsonia inermis*) are examples of plant-derived dyes used for tattooing. Synthetic dyes include triphendioxazine (orange), quinoline (yellow), cadmium sulphide (yellow), and 2-naphthol aniline dye (red).

***Procedure*:** After carefully selecting and agreeing on a desired design or pattern, clients are required to sign an informed consent form before the procedure, stating they are over 18 years of age, they understand the procedure is permanent, and understand that it will result in an open wound or abrasion. After the consent form is signed, the tattoo artist checks the skin to ensure it is free of wounds and scrapes. An antiseptic is then applied to the skin to kill any micro-organism on it, and/or lower the risk of getting an infection. The area over which the tattoo is to be created is then shaved.

The pigments/dyes (in the form of ink) to be used for the tattooing process are prepared on a pallet, which has several wells into which the various colours to be used are poured. The tattoo machine (tattoo gun) is then prepared by mounting needles on it.

The artist subsequently draws the desired design onto the skin, using freehand or a pre-made stencil or film which the tattoo artist follows, that is, the artist can use the outline of the stencil as a guide, or tattoo directly over the pattern or design that has been transferred onto the skin from a film.

The tattooing process involves dipping the needles into the colour palette and puncturing the skin within the outlined pattern or design. The needles deposit the pigment in the skin's second layer, the dermis, where they remain indelible unless deliberately removed by laser treatment or other means. It could take an hour, several hours, or even days to complete a tattoo process, depending on its complexity and size. There may also be a need to make several layers of a design, especially if the design contains different colours.

Post-procedure care: It is very important to take proper care of a new tattoo in the early period after the procedure. An antibiotic ointment and a gauze bandage are applied to the tattooed area immediately after the procedure. The application of moisturiser over the tattooed area and the avoidance of swimming, hot tub baths, and hot baths in the early post-procedure period will go a long way to ensure optimal healing of the area (57).

Tattoo removal: It is not unusual for people to have a change of mind about tattoos on their skin, and wanting the tattoos modified or removed. As mentioned earlier, permanent tattoos are indelible and, in the past, were not removable. At that time, it was difficult, expensive, and almost impossible to remove tattoos as most of the techniques used were virtually ineffective. Tattoo removal processes included mechanical abrasion of the skin by "sanding" with any roughly sharp object such as a wire brush, to expose the inner layers with the pigments as much as possible, then the pigments were leached off with salt solutions, or the skin was burned with acid. Other methods used in the past included subjecting the tattooed part of the skin to extremes of temperature (heat from electrocautery or other heat sources, and cold from liquid nitrogen) in a bid to destroy the pigments, the use of chemicals to peel off the skin over the tattooed area, or even outrightly excising the tattooed skin if the area is very small. These techniques are obviously harmful and may result in complications like burns, scarring, infection or outright bodily disfigurement. However, with modern technological advancements in laser and light therapies as well as trichloroacetic acid (TCA) peel, permanent tattoos can now be effectively and completely removed from the skin (57) in as few as one or a couple of laser treatment sessions, with different wavelengths being suited to remove specific pigment colours on the light spectrum (58). This is particularly very effective in people with Fitz-Gerald skin phototypes I, II, and III. The commonly available laser wavelengths are to be avoided or used cautiously for the darker skin types (Fitz-Gerald IV, V, and VI) because of the tendency to burn and develop hypopigmentation (58), hyperpigmentation, hypertrophic scars, and keloids. (59)

Complications of tattooing: The process of tattooing can result in adverse reactions (60) which can be physical/structural, medical, and psychological complications. Complications can result from the piercing/puncturing of the skin by needles or other sharp objects, from the pigments, from constitutional problems with the person receiving the tattoo (such as an existing bleeding disorder, needle anxiety/phobia, or blood anxiety/phobia) or from issues bordering on the procedure itself, like hygiene-related issues. Complications can also result from the use of substandard pigments or inks not originally intended for tattooing purposes (61).

Possible complications that can result from tattooing include allergic reactions to the pigments, skin infection and bruises, development of granulomas, hypertrophic scars, keloids, and even cancerous growths over the tattoo sites, and possible joint contractures if a scar develops across a joint (57,60,62). Other complications include systemic bloodborne diseases from infection with methicillin-resistant *Staphylococcus aureus* (MRSA), hepatitis B, and hepatitis C (56).

It is noteworthy to mention that the presence of tattoos on the skin may pose problems if there is a need to undergo a magnetic resonance imaging (MRI) scan. The energy from the MRI machine may cause swelling or burns in the tattooed areas of the skin, while the pigments in tattoos can result in the degradation of the MRI images.

Complications from tattooing can generally be reduced by engaging the services of a qualified, expert tattoo artist, ensuring the use of good quality, specifically manufactured products for tattoos that are certified safe, adopting and ensuring aseptic procedures (61), ruling out important medical and/or psychological health risk factors or conditions that are contraindicated for tattooing, and strict adherence to recommended post-procedure care.

Cosmetic contact lenses

Cosmetic contact lenses, also known as costume lenses, are coloured lenses worn over the cornea of the eye so as to enhance or alter the colour of the eye for the sake of fashion or for theatrical performances (Figure 3.17). Typically, there is a tear film between the cornea and the contact lens, and the quantity and quality of the tear film in this region determines a wearer's level of tolerance of the contact lenses (63). The lenses, which are mostly non-vision correcting but can also be vision correcting (medicated), are normally expected to be prescribed by a qualified eye doctor who takes measurements of the eye to ensure proper fitting of the lenses. However, cosmetic lenses ordered online or bought off the shelf may not fit snugly on the eye, causing discomfort and eye damage and may reduce vision clarity. On the other hand, there are prosthetic contact lenses which are used to mask discolouration and irregularities as well as improve the function of the eye for conditions caused by eye diseases, trauma or birth defects. Contact lenses are also witnessing technological advancements as they are now being fitted with sensors for continuous disease monitoring and analysis (64). For instance, in combination with optic glucose sensors, contact lenses are developed for novel applications in continuous glucose monitoring for diabetic patients (65).

A cosmetic contact lens, just like the medicated contact lens, is a thin, curved lens that historically have been made with materials that evolved from blown glass, to plastic (polymethyl methacrylate), and now to soft hydrogels (63,66). Cosmetic contact lenses are, however, tinted in various colours that are available for the customer's choices. There are two types currently available namely hard contact lens and soft contact lens.

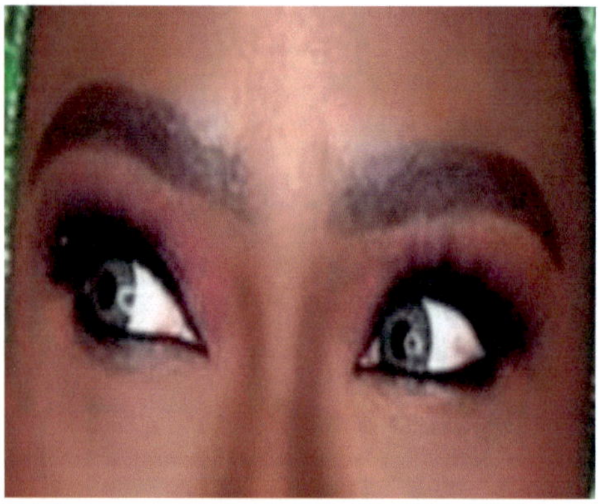

Figure 3.17: A pair of eyes wearing contact lens

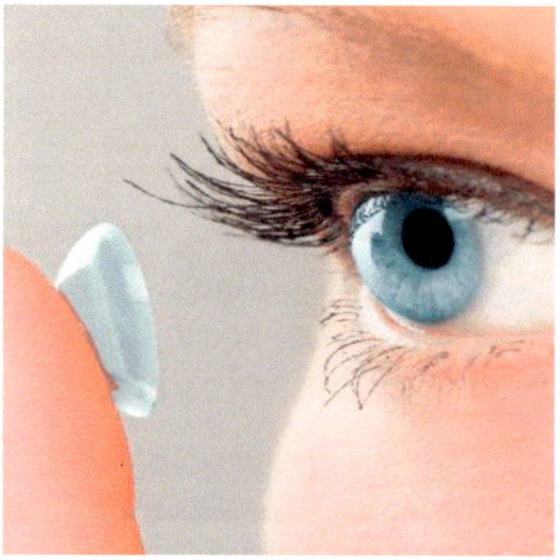

Figure 3.18: A contact lens about to be worn

Wearing contact lenses

Contact lenses should be cleaned with contact lens solutions only before use and strict hygiene must be observed before and while placing them on the eyes. Common sources of contamination of contact lenses are the hands, the environment, and cleaning solutions (67). Available commercial solutions for the cleaning of contact lenses include hydrogen peroxide solutions, rigid gas permeable care systems, daily cleaners and enzymatic protein removers (68). It is strongly unrecommended to use ordinary tap water to clean contact lenses. The lenses should be clean and in good condition and applied with the correct (convex) side facing outwards, giving the impression of a bowl sitting on the fingertip (Figure 3.18). Contact lenses should not be used if visibly damaged

To wear contact lenses, the hands are first properly washed and dried. After properly washing and drying the hands, the first of the already cleaned contact lenses is then taken from its case and placed on the fingertip of the middle or index finger of the non-dominant hand. In front of a mirror, the upper and lower eyelids of the eye are then parted using the non-lens-holding hand. The contact lens is then placed over the cornea of the eye and gently moved until well-positioned. The same process should be repeated to insert the second contact lenses onto the second eye. If any discomfort is experienced in the eye, the lens is removed and rinsed and carefully reapplied.

In a similar vein, removing contact lenses also requires strict observance to basic hygiene, especially thorough hand washing and drying. To remove contact lenses from the eyes, the lower eyelid of the eye is pulled down slightly with the dominant hand's middle finger, and the index finger of the same hand is used to aid in removing the lens. Once removed from the eye, the surface of the contact lens is moistened with contact lens cleaning solution.

Possible Issues with wearing contact Lenses

It is not uncommon to experience discomfort for the first few days when wearing contact lenses for the first time. This is especially true for hard contact lenses and if the eyes become dry. If this happens, the eyes should be repeatedly wetted with hydrating drops made specifically for contact lenses.

Adverse reactions or complications might ensue while using contact lenses and they include pain, stinging, burning, itching, blurred vision, rainbows and halos around objects, sensitivity to light, or an abnormal sensation in the eye. It is recommended that the lens be taken off if any of such symptoms is experienced and if the symptoms persist, expert medical help should be sought immediately.

References

1. Federal Food, Drug, And Cosmetic Act [Internet]. 2021 [cited 2022 May 3]. Available from: https://www.govinfo.gov/content/pkg/COMPS-973/pdf/COMPS-973.pdf
2. Food, Drugs And Related Products (Registration, etc.) ACT Cap F.33 LFN 200425 [Internet]. 2021. Available from: https://www.nafdac.gov.ng/wp-content/uploads/Files/Resources/Regulations/NAFDAC_Acts/FOOD-DRUGS-AND-RELATED-PRODUCTS-REGISTRATION-ACT-Cap.F.33.pdf
3. Ertel K. Modern Skin Cleansers. Dermatol Clin. 2000 Oct;18(4):561–75.
4. Ghosh S, Blankschtein D. The role of sodium dodecyls sulfate (SDS) micelles in inducing skin barrier perturbation in the presence of glycerol. Journal of Cosmetic Science. 2007;58(2):109–133.
5. Walters RM, Fevola M, LiBrizzi J, Martin K. Designing cleansers for the unique needs of baby skin. Cosmet Toilet. 2008;123(12):53–60.
6. Fevola MJ, Walters RM, LiBrizzi JJ. A new approach to formulating mild cleansers: hydrophobically-modified polymers for irritation mitigation. Polymeric Delivery of Therapeutics. 2010;1053:221–242.

7. Walters RM, Mao G, Gunn ET, Hornby S. Cleansing Formulations That Respect Skin Barrier Integrity. Dermatol Res Pract. 2012;2012:1–9.
8. Ananthapadmanabhan KP, Moore DJ, Subramanyan K, Misra M, Meyer F. Cleansing without compromise: the impact of cleansers on the skin barrier and the technology of mild cleansing. Dermatol Ther. 2004 Jan;17(s1):16–25.
9. Takagi Y, Kaneda K, Miyaki M, Matsuo K, Kawada H, Hosokawa H. The long-term use of soap does not affect the pH-maintenance mechanism of human skin. Skin Res Technol. 2015 May;21(2):144–8.
10. Bikowski J. The use of cleansers as therapeutic concomitants in various dermatologic disorders. Cutis. 2001 Dec;68(5 Suppl):12–9.
11. The Secret to the Absolutely Best Soap Recipe [Internet]. The Secret to the Absolutely Best Soap Recipe. [cited 2021 Dec 24]. Available from: https://www.modernsoapmaking.com/blog/secret-to-the-best-soap-recipe
12. Meier L, Stange R, Michalsen A, Uehleke B. Clay jojoba oil facial mask for lesioned skin and mild acne--results sof a prospective, observational pilot study. Forsch Komplementarmedizin 2006. 2012;19(2):75–9.
13. Williams LB, Haydel SE. Evaluation of the medicinal use of clay minerals as antibacterial agents. Int Geol Rev. 2010 May 6;52(7–8):745–70.
14. Velasco et al. Characterization and Short-Term clinical study of clay facial mask. 2016; Available from: https://rcfba.fcfar.unesp.br/index.php/ojs/article/view/7
15. Carretero MI. Clay minerals and their beneficial effects upon human health. A review. Apply Clay Sci. 2002;(21(3-4):155–63).
16. Valenti DMZ, Silva J, Teodoro WR, Velosa AP, Mello SBV. Effect of topical clay application on the synthesis of collagen in skin: an experimental study: Effect of topical clay application on the synthesis of collagen in skin. Clin Exp Dermatol. 2012 Mar;37(2):164–8.
17. Portugal-Cohen M, Soroka Y, Ma'or Z, Oron M, Zioni T, Brégégère FM, et al. Protective effects of a cream containing Dead Sea minerals against UVB-induced stress in human skin. Exp Dermatol. 2009 Sep;18(9):781–8.
18. Ma'or Z, Henis Y, Alon Y, Orlov E, Sorensen KB, Oren A. Antimicrobial properties of Dead Sea black mineral mud. Int J Dermatol. 2006 May;45(5):504–11.
19. Smith L. Historical Perspectives on Water Purification. In: Chemistry and Water [Internet]. Elsevier; 2017 [cited 2022 May 24]. p. 421–68. Available from: https://linkinghub.elsevier.com/retrieve/pii/B978012809330600012X
20. Ilomuanya M, Nashiru B, Ifudu N, Igwilo C. Effect of pore size and morphology of activated charcoal prepared from midribs of Elaeis guineensis on adsorption of poisons using metronidazole and Escherichia coli O157:H7 as a case study. J Microsc Ultrastruct. 2017;5(1):32.
21. Manatunga DC, Godakanda VU, Herath HMLPB, de Silva RM, Yeh CY, Chen JY, et al. Nanofibrous cosmetic face mask for transdermal delivery of nano gold: synthesis, characterization, release and zebra fish employed toxicity studies. R Soc Open Sci. 2020 Sep;7(9):201266.
22. Nilforoushzadeh MA, Amirkhani MA, Zarrintaj P, Salehi Moghaddam A, Mehrabi T, Alavi S, et al. Skin care and rejuvenation by cosmeceutical facial mask. J Cosmet Dermatol.

2018;17(5):693–702.

23. Yeom G, Yun DM, Kang YW, Kwon JS, Kang IO, Kim SY. Clinical efficacy of facial masks containing yoghurt and Opuntia humifusa Raf. (F-YOP). J Cosmet Sci. 2011 Oct;62(5):505–14.
24. Abigail Posne. Activated carbon face mask a step by step recipe. [Internet]. [cited 2022 Jan 12]. Available from: https://www.legit.ng/1327755-activated-carbon-face-mask-a-step-by-step-recipe.html
25. Zoe Diana Draelos, MD. Are facial toners necessary? [Internet]. Dermatology Times. 2018. Available from: https://www.dermatologytimes.com/view/are-facial-toners-necessary-0
26. Loden M, Maibach HI, editors. Effects of Natural Moisturising Factor and Lactic Acid Isomers on Skin Function. In: Dry Skin and Moisturisers [Internet]. 0 ed. CRC Press; 2005 [cited 2022 May 25]. p. 203–26. Available from: https://www.taylorfrancis.com/books/9781420039214/chapters/10.1201/b14251-22
27. Wesley NO, Maibach HI. Racial (Ethnic) Differences in Skin Properties: The Objective Data. Am J Clin Dermatol. 2003;4(12):843–60.
28. Sethi A, Kaur T, Malhotra SK, Gambhir ML. Moisturizers: The Slippery Road. Indian J Dermatol. 2016 Jun;61(3):279–87.
29. Lodén M. Effect of moisturisers on epidermal barrier function. Clin Dermatol. 2012 Jun;30(3):286–96.
30. Lynde CW. Moisturizers: what they are and how they work. Skin Ther Lett. 2001 Dec;6(13):3–5.
31. Javed S, Atta-ur-Rahman. Aloe Vera Gel in Food, Health Products, and Cosmetics Industry. In: Studies in Natural Products Chemistry [Internet]. Elsevier; 2014 [cited 2022 May 25]. p. 261–85. Available from: https://linkinghub.elsevier.com/retrieve/pii/B9780444632944000097
32. Dal'Belo SE, Rigo Gaspar L, Berardo Gonçalves Maia Campos PM. Moisturising effect of cosmetic formulations containing Aloe vera extract in different concentrations assessed by skin bioengineering techniques. Skin Res Technol. 2006 Nov;12(4):241–6.
33. Narurkar VA, Fabi SG, Bucay VW, Tedaldi R, Downie JB, Zeichner JA, et al. Rejuvenating Hydrator: Restoring Epidermal Hyaluronic Acid Homeostasis with Instant Benefits. J Drugs Dermatol JDD. 2016 Jan;15(1 Suppl 2):s24-37.
34. Papakonstantinou E, Roth M, Karakiulakis G. Hyaluronic acid: A key molecule in skin aging. Dermatoendocrinol. 2012 Jul;4(3):253–8.
35. Majewski GP, Rodan K, Fields K, Falla TJ. Characterization of bound water in skin hydrators prepared with and without a 3D3P interpenetrating polymer network. Skin Res Technol. 2019 Mar;25(2):150–7.
36. Nolan K, Marmur E. Moisturizers: reality and the skin benefits. Dermatol Ther. 2012 Jun;25(3):229–33.
37. Lam TH, Verzotto D, Brahma P, Ng AHQ, Hu P, Schnell D, et al. Understanding the microbial basis of body odor in pre-pubescent children and teenagers. Microbiome. 2018 Dec;6(1):213.
38. Prokop-Prigge KA, Greene K, Varallo L, Wysocki CJ, Preti G. The Effect of Ethnicity on Human Axillary Odorant Production. J Chem Ecol. 2016 Jan;42(1):33–9.
39. Suessman A, Srinivasan S. Chromhidrosis: An Unusual Cause of Skin Discoloration. Pediatr Emerg Care. 2021 Dec;37(12): e875–6.

40. U.S Food and Drug Administration. Antibacterial Soap? You Can Skip It, Use Plain Soap and Water [Internet]. 2019 [cited 2022 Jan 27]. Available from: https://www.fda.gov/consumers/consumer-updates/antibacterial-soap-you-can-skip-it-use-plain-soap-and-water
41. Bretagne A, Cotot F, Arnaud-Roux M, Sztucki M, Cabane B, Galey JB. The mechanism of eccrine sweat pore plugging by aluminium salts using microfluidics combined with small angle X-ray scattering. Soft Matter. 2017 May 24;13(20):3812-3821.
42. Aguilar TN, Blaug SM, Zopf LC. A study of the antibacterial activity of some complex aluminum salts. J Am Pharm Assoc Am Pharm Assoc. 1956 Jul;45(7):498–500.
43. Flarend R, Bin T, Elmore D, Hem S. A preliminary study of the dermal absorption of aluminium from antiperspirants using aluminium-26. Food Chem Toxicol. 2001 Feb;39(2):163-8.
44. Klotz K, Weistenhofer W, Neff F, Hartwig A, van Thriel C, Drexler H. The Health Effects of Aluminum Exposure. Dtsch Arztebl Int. 2017 Sep 29;114(39):653-659.
45. Manayi A, Saeidnia S. Cosmetics and Personal Care Products. In: Encyclopaedia of Toxicology [Internet]. Elsevier; 2014 [cited 2022 May 25]. p. 1043–9. Available from: https://linkinghub.elsevier.com/retrieve/pii/B9780123864543009799
46. Coleen Figne. How Does Lengthening Mascara Work [Internet]. [cited 2022 May 25]. Available from: https://www.reviewthis.com/how-does-lengthening-mascara-work/
47. Tightlining Eyeliner How-To: The Makeup Trick That Makes Lashes Longer, Fuller & Thicker [Internet]. Huffpost. 2013 [cited 2021 Nov 18]. Available from: https://www.huffpost.com/entry/tightlining-eyeliner-makeup-tips_n_2853595
48. The Importance of the Brow – Achieve Picture Perfect Eyebrows [Internet]. The Importance of the Brow – Achieve Picture Perfect Eyebrows. [cited 2021 Nov 29]. Available from: https://www.nyib.edu/importance-eyebrows/
49. Litak J, Krunic AL, Antonijevic S, Pouryazdanparast P, Gerami P. Eyebrow epilation by threading: an increasingly popular procedure with some less-popular outcomes--a comprehensive review. Dermatol Surg Off Publ Am Soc Dermatol Surg Al. 2011 Jul;37(7):1051–4.
50. Sarah Schaffer. Reading Our Lips: The History of Lipstick Regulation in Western Seats of Power. (2006), [Internet]. 2006; Available from: http://nrs.harvard.edu/urn-3:HUL.InstRepos:10018966
51. Williams DF, Schmitt WH. 'Color cosmetics' in Chemistry and Technology of the Cosmetics and Toiletries Industry. 1992nd ed.
52. Mishal Cazmi. Everything You Need To Know About Using Highlighter. [Internet]. 2021 [cited 2021 Dec 5]. Available from: https://www.chatelaine.com/style/beauty/how-to-use-highlighter/
53. Marwah M, Kerure A, Marwah G. Microblading and the science behind it. Indian Dermatol Online J. 2021;12(1):6.
54. Child's Right Act [Internet]. Child's Right Act. Available from: http://lawsofnigeria.placng.org/laws/C50.pdf
55. Miranda MD. Forensic Analysis of Tattoos and Tattoo Inks [Internet]. 0 ed. CRC Press; 2015 [cited 2022 May 25]. Available from: https://www.taylorfrancis.com/books/9781498736435
56. Temiz SA, Özlü E. Medical Complications of Tattoos. J Turk Acad Dermatol. 2021 Mar

5;15(1):1–7.
57. Yolanda Smith. The Benefits and Risks of Laser Tattoo Removal. The Benefits and Risks of Laser Tattoo Removal. 2019 [cited 2022 May 25]; Available from: https://www.news-medical.net/health/The-Benefits-and-Risks-of-Laser-Tattoo-Removal.aspx.
58. Henley JK, Zurfley F, Ramsey ML. Laser Tattoo Removal. In: StatPearls [Internet]. Treasure Island (FL): StatPearls Publishing; 2022 [cited 2022 May 25]. Available from: http://www.ncbi.nlm.nih.gov/books/NBK442007/
59. Chandrashekar B, Shenoy C, Madura C. Complications of laser and light-based devices therapy in patients with skin of color. Indian J Dermatol Venereol Leprol. 2019;85(1):24.
60. Bjerre RD, Ulrich NH, Linneberg A, Duus Johansen J. Adverse reactions to tattoos in the general population of Denmark. J Am Acad Dermatol. 2018 Oct;79(4):770–2.
61. Centres for Disease Control and Prevention (CDC). The hidden dangers of getting inked. 2012 [cited 2022 Apr 24]; Available from: https://blogs.cdc.gov/publichealthmatters/2012/08/the-hidden-dangers-of-getting-inked/.
62. Ayanlowo OO, Gold-Olufadi SA, Akinkugbe AO, Otrofanowei E, Nga CN, Olumide YM. Growing trend of tattooing and its complications in Nigeria. Int J Dermatol. 2017 Jul;56(7):709–14.
63. Ruben M. Contact lenses. BMJ. 1984 Feb 25;288(6417):586–8.
64. Farandos NM, Yetisen AK, Monteiro MJ, Lowe CR, Yun SH. Contact Lens Sensors in Ocular Diagnostics. Adv Healthc Mater. 2015 Apr;4(6):792–810.
65. Elsherif M, Moreddu R, Alam F, Salih AE, Ahmed I, Butt H. Wearable Smart Contact Lenses for Continual Glucose Monitoring: A Review. Front Med. 2022 Apr 4;9:858784.
66. Dreyer J. History of Contact Lenses: When, Who, Where and Why Explained. Available at. 2016 [cited 2022 Apr 20]; Available from: https://www.contactlenses.co.uk/education/history-of-contact-lenses.
67. Bloise L. Surveillance, hygiène et entretien des lentilles de contact. J Fr Ophtalmol. 2017 Apr;40(4):329–37.
68. Nichols JJ, Chalmers RL, Dumbleton K, Jones L, Lievens CW, Merchea MM, et al. The Case for Using Hydrogen Peroxide Contact Lens Care Solutions: A Review. Eye Contact Lens Sci Clin Pract. 2019 Mar;45(2):69–82.

IMAGE CREDITS: ©, via Canva.com

Fig 3.1: red2000
Fig 3.2: NatalyaAksenova
Fig 3.3: 1989_s
Fig 3.4: pixelshot
Fig 3.5: Rabi Ilemona Ekore
Fig 3.6: AdamRadoSavljevic
Fig 3.7: Pixelshot
Fig 3.8: doram
Fig 3.9: cclickclick
Fig 3.10: Mladick
Fig 3.11: stanzi11
Fig 3.12a: Aris Leoven
Fig 3.12b: Gam1983
Fig 3.12c: Pogrebkov
Fig 3.13: pavlyukv
Fig 3.14: Kzara Visual
Fig 3.15: Prof Lara Orafidiya
Fig 3.16a: Pexels
Fig 3.16b: Kevin Bidwell
Fig 3.16c: Prof Lara Orafidiya
Fig 3.17: Prof Lara Orafidiya
Fig 3.18: arturmarciniecphotos

CHAPTER FOUR

Skin bleaching and its cutaneous effects

Ayesha O Akinkugbe

Skin bleaching (also referred to as skin lightening, skin whitening, skin brightening, skin peeling), for cosmetic reasons, is the intentional practice of applying chemical substances on the body for the sole purpose of lightening the tone of the skin. Products used for this purpose are manufactured, homemade or a combination and are also available as various 'organic' and 'herbal' skin products, while some products in the market are of unknown composition. They are labelled variously as skin lighteners, skin brighteners, skin toners, skin whiteners and skin fading or skin fairness products (1–3). They are not regarded as cosmetics but as drugs by law (4,5) because they interfere with the structure and function of the skin. However, because these products supposedly enhance beauty, they may be treated as cosmeceuticals (6).

The purported reasons for using skin lightening products by the users vary and range from dermatological to non-dermatological. They include treatment for black heads (acne), freckles, actinic or solar keratoses, ageing, melasma and post inflammatory hyperpigmentation from certain skin disorders such as drug reactions and inflammatory dermatoses as well as wound scars. Individuals with vitiligo sometimes lighten the dark areas of the skin to match the lighter parts. These dermatological conditions of pigmentation are treated by specialists who are trained in the management of skin pigmentation. Non dermatological reasons, however, are mostly to 'lighten' or 'whiten' the colour of the skin for cosmetic purpose. The reasons for skin bleaching are not fully understood; however, culture, economic and psychosocial factors are key to understanding this growing global phenomenon (2,7). Bleaching is seen as a kind of fashion that enhances beauty, popularity, acceptability and self-image.

Skin bleaching or lightening is reported globally, but in particular from countries across Africa and Asia (8–10). The lifetime prevalence obtained from the meta-analysis carried out by Sagoe *et al* (3) was 27.7%, indicating a high global prevalence of skin bleaching practice. Despite regulations, skin lightening products continue to dominate the cosmetic industry (8) and skin bleaching or skin lightening is now of public health concern (7,8). In the year 2020, the global market for skin lighteners was estimated at US$8 billion and is projected, over the period of analysis, to reach a size of US$11.8 billion by 2026 at a compound annual growth rate (CAGR) of 6.6% (11).

Skin lightening agents and their mode of action

Many of the bleaching chemicals affect the melanin in the skin. Melanin is the pigment that gives the skin, the eyes and the hair their colour and is produced by cells called melanocytes. Dark-skinned people have more melanin than light-skinned people. Melanin protects the skin against the harmful effect of the sun and the melanocytes increase the production of melanin in response to sun exposure. Many skin bleaching agents elicit their effects by reducing the production of melanin while some outrightly and irreversibly destroy it. The various substances act on different pathways of melanin biosynthesis (12,13). There are, however, some skin lighteners that exfoliate the dead skin of the topmost layer of the epidermis (1). Hydroquinone as well as glutathione, which is an antioxidant found normally in the liver, but has effects on the skin, inhibit the production of melanin by blocking the activity of tyrosinase. Tyrosinase is a catalytic enzyme involved in the production of melanin. (See Chapter 9 for more information).

Chemical peels

The use of chemical peels in achieving skin lightening involves applying the appropriate chemical agents on the skin, leading to the induction of keratocoagulation or keratolysis, a process that results in the exfoliation, through controlled destruction of the epidermis or dermis of the treated area. Regeneration and remodelling of these layers of the skin follow the initial wounding causing improved texture and appearance of the affected skin area (14). The process of skin lightening with chemical peels is also known as chemabrasion, dermapeeling, chemical face-lifting, facial rejuvenation, chemical exfoliation, surface surgery or chemosurgery (15).

Classification of chemical peels

Chemical peels are classified into three categories namely: superficial, medium depth and deep; based on the depth of penetration attained when applied on the skin, which is dependent on prevailing conditions of the treated area such as anatomical location, skin thickness and density, adnexal structure and epidermal integrity. The type of peeling agent employed, its pH and concentration, skin priming, technique of application, occlusion and contact time also influence the depth of penetration of chemical peels (15).

*AHA, alpha hydroxy acid; BHA, beta hydroxy acid; CO_2, carbon dioxide; TCA, trichloroacetic acid; Baker–Gordon formula contains 88% phenol (USP; 3 mL), croton oil (3 guttae), hexachlorophene (Septisol) soap (Vestal Laboratories, St Louis, MO, USA; 8

Table 4.1: Classification of chemical peels (15)

	Peel depth	Peeling agent	Indications
Superficial	Stratum corneum to papillary dermis (60 µm)	AHA: Glycolic acid 20 – 50%, lactic acid, malic acid, pyruvic acid BHA: Salicylic acid 20 – 35%, carbon dioxide snow, resorcinol Acetic acid analog: TCA 10 – 35% Mixed: Jessner's solution (14% salicylic acid, 14% lactic acid, 14%resorcinol in ethanol base)	Face and body acne, rosacea, actinic keratoses, dyschromia, mild photoageing, post-inflammatory hyperpigmentation Face and body acne, melasma Melasma, post-inflammatory hyperpigmentation, acne, fine rhytides
Medium depth	Papillary dermis to upper reticular dermis (450 µm)	Acetic acid analog: TCA 40 – 50% Mixed: TCA 55% + solid CO^2, TCA 55% + glycolic acid 70% TCA combo peel (TCA 25/35/40% after either Jessner's solution or 70% glycolic acid)	Mild to moderate photoageing, actinic keratoses, medium depth rhytides, solar lentigines, melasma, dyschromias, superficial atrophic scars, blending with laser resurfacing Actinic damage, scarring, dyschromias, blending with laser resurfacing
Deep	Mid-reticular dermis to 600 µm	Phenol Baker-Gordon TCA >50% TCA 70-100% CROSS (chemical reconstruction of skin scars)	Advanced photo-aging, severe acne scarring, peri-oral rhytides, extensive actinic keratoses, Pre malignant skin tumours Ice-pick acne scarring

guttae), and distilled water (2 mL). Croton oil is a vesicant derived from the seed of the *Croton tiglium* plant that promotes deeper penetration and absorption of phenol. Table 4.1 depicts the types of peeling agents, the agents used and the conditions under which they are employed (15).

Naturally derived skin lighteners

The alpha- and beta-hydroxy acids, as superficial chemical peels, exfoliate the hyperpigmented dead cells of the skin's top layer and increase the turnover of new cells resulting in skin lightening (16,17). At high concentrations, however, they may affect melanin production. Lactic acid obtained from milk and citric acid found in citrus fruits such as lime and lemon as well as glycolic acid found in sugar cane and apple are examples of alpha hydroxy acids used as exfoliants while salicylic acid is a beta hydroxy acid with exfoliating activity, obtained naturally from sweet birch, wintergreen leaves and willow tree bark (15,16). Ascorbic acid, naturally found in most fruits especially citrus fruits, also lightens the skin by reducing melanin synthesis (18).

Arbutin is a natural source of hydroquinone obtained from certain fruit berries. Along with its derivatives, α-arbutin acts as a skin lightener by inhibiting tyrosinase activity and melanosome maturation thereby reducing melanin synthesis (19). Kojic acid, a by-product in the fermentation of rice to wine in Japan inhibits melanin production in the skin (20). Azelaic acid which is found in grains such as wheat, rye and barley also inhibits melanin production (21,22). Other natural skin bleaching ingredients used in home-made products include milk, turmeric, liquorice extract, pomegranate and pawpaw.

Other synthetic skin bleachers include mercury and its derivatives (ammoniated mercury, mercuric chloride), fluorinated corticosteroids such as fluocinonide, betamethasone valerate, clobetasol propionate; hydrocortisone; and tretinoin. The use of these substances in skin lightening products have been prohibited in many countries but some of such products are still being smuggled and sold majorly in developing countries. Monobenzone, at low concentrations, and mequinol are recommended for use by people having vitiligo. Others include cysteamine, camphor, and tranexamic acid; caustics, hydrogen peroxide, detergents and hypochloride sodium (7,8,23–26).

In order to circumvent regulations governing the use of skin lighteners, new chemicals of unknown safety are used by some manufacturers of skin lightening products. These include oxybenzone (hydroquinone derivative), triethanolamine, niacinamide and resorcinol.

Glutathione

Recently, especially in ethnic populations with darker skin tones, there has arisen a hype on the 'magical' effect and, subsequently, the use of glutathione as a skin lightening agent of tremendous results especially when administered parenterally (intravenous injection) due to its antimelanogenic properties (27,28). This drug was originally designed and approved for parenteral administration for the treatment of severe liver disorders and the prevention of chemotherapy-associated neurotoxicity. Presently, there is a paucity of controlled studies on the safety of this drug when administered intravenously for general skin lightening and legislation for its use or ban is yet to be announced by many regulating agencies globally (27,28).

Skin lightening surgery or non-cosmetics skin lightening procedures

Skin lightening surgery are means by which the skin is lightened without the use of chemical agents. Some of the procedures are not surgical in the real sense of surgical procedures.

Microdermabrasion

The procedure involves using a stream of fine crystals such as aluminium oxide, sodium chloride, or sodium bicarbonate, or a diamond tip to exfoliate and remove the superficial layer of dry, dead skin cells, allowing for newer brighter skin to emerge. This technique is beneficial to those with uneven pigmentation and melasma. It is, however, not recommended for all skin types and is used cautiously in persons with rosacea, sensitive or thin skin and those with Fitzpatrick skin types IV–VI so as to prevent risks of irritation and hyperpigmentation (29,30). It is actually a non-surgical procedure and it is relatively painless. The procedure is carried out in spas or clinics by trained individuals, aestheticians, or a dermatologist.

Hydradermabrasion

This newly emerging method of skin resurfacing and rejuvenating procedures differs from microdermabrasion in that it uses oxygen combined with aqueous solutions at high supersonic speeds to remove dead cells and debris which are subsequently suctioned off (29).

Laser skin whitening (Ablative laser resurfacing)

In order to achieve skin lightening using laser, short pulsed concentrated beams of light are targeted to the affected part of the skin thereby removing irregular or damaged skin and stimulating the growth of new skin cells. This works by either removing the outer layer of skin or damaging the cells that produce melanin. Activated Platelet-rich Plasma (PRP) is applied on the treated surface to speed up healing of laser treated area of the skin (29). The procedure is usually carried out by a plastic surgeon or dermatologist.

Cryosurgery

This is a non-invasive and non-surgical means of skin lightening. It makes use of liquid nitrogen or argon which freezes affected area causing darkened skin to peel away and destroying melanin cells thereby allowing the skin to regenerate a new epidermis with a lighter shade (31).

Mode of use of skin lighteners

Many skin lightening products are available as creams, lotions, body washes, gels and soaps which are applied topically on the skin through which they penetrate to get to the dermis and affect melanin production. Exfoliants work mainly on the skin surface but because of their small molecules, they penetrate the skin and aid other chemicals to go into the skin.

Glutathione can be applied to the skin, taken orally as tablets or injected intravenously by which route the best and fastest effects (usually within 2 weeks) are manifested. Vitamin C (ascorbic acid) aids the penetration of topically administered glutathione (18). Tranexamic acid is also applied topically, taken orally or injected into a lesion alone or as an adjunct to laser therapy.

Phenol is applied as a liquid with a brush on the affected area for superficial and medium peels. Deep peel affects deeper layers of skin. The procedure often involves the use of a local anaesthetic and a sedative. The blood pressure as well as the heart are monitored during the procedure as phenol can affect the heart and the kidneys. The treatment gives lasting effects that do not require a repeat.

Cutaneous adverse effects of skin bleaching

Long term use of skin bleaching agents causes various adverse effects to the skin and these have been reported in several studies. These cutaneous side effects are influenced by the type of agent used, use of combination of products, the site involved and the duration of use. These adverse effects can be divided into local and systemic. This section will focus on the cutaneous effects.

Hydroquinone (1,4-dihydroxybenzene) is an inhibitor of melanogenesis; and is primarily melanocyte specific. Cutaneous side effects of hydroquinone include nail plate pigmentation; Irritant and allergic contact dermatitis and consequent post inflammatory dyspigmentation. Exogenous ochronosis on sun-exposed parts of the body is also a side effect of hydroquinone.

Topical corticosteroids are a type of steroid medicine (anti-inflammatory agent) applied directly to the skin to reduce inflammation and irritation. They play a major role in the treatment of dermatological conditions such as psoriasis, limited areas of vitiligo, eczema, atopic dermatitis, phimosis, acute radiation dermatitis, lichen planus, lichen simplex chronicus, discoid lupus erythematosus and lichen sclerosus. Their mechanism of action consists of anti-inflammatory, anti-mitotic and immunosuppressive effects. There are various classifications of topical corticosteroids based on their strengths (32). The potency of topical corticosteroid is the amount of the drug required to produce a desired therapeutic effect.

The United States classification of topical corticosteroids consists of seven classes:

Class I super-potent corticosteroids

Class II high-potency corticosteroids

Class II medium- to high- potency corticosteroids

Class IV and V medium-potency corticosteroids

Class VI low-potency corticosteroids

Class VII least- potent corticosteroids

The extensive and prolonged use of the potent topical steroids is what is responsible for most of the side effects noted. The most common cutaneous effect is skin atrophy due to the anti-mitotic effect of topical corticosteroids. They cause the skin to undergo 3 phases: preatrophy, atrophy (due to persistent use in the same region) and tachyphylaxis. There is epidermal thinning and increased resorption within the dermis, leading to thinning and atrophy of the skin.(32 Loss of connective tissue results in erythema, telangiectasia and purpura. Mechanical stress and injury to the dermis result in striae. Degradation of the follicular epithelium and increase in the concentration of free fatty acids on the surface of the skin results in acne formation and comedogenesis.

Other local effects include easy bruising, delayed wound healing, peri-oral dermatitis, folliculitis, rosacea-like eruption, pigment alteration and hypertrichosis (excess hair on the face). Also found are various cutaneous fungal and bacterial skin infections – dermatophytosis, cellulitis, erysipelas, pyoderma and warts. There is usually a masking of the typical presentation of these infections. Topical corticosteroids are recommended for skin conditions and their use should be monitored to avoid cutaneous and systemic adverse effects. They are not recommended to be used unsupervised and in the absence of a skin condition.

Chapter 21 has more information on adverse effects of bleaching agents.

The adverse effects of skin bleaching in pictures

Figures 4.1 to 4.11 show some of the cutaneous adverse effects of improper and long-term use of skin lightening (SL) products and the misuse and abuse of topical corticosteroids (TCS) (7,24,26,33).

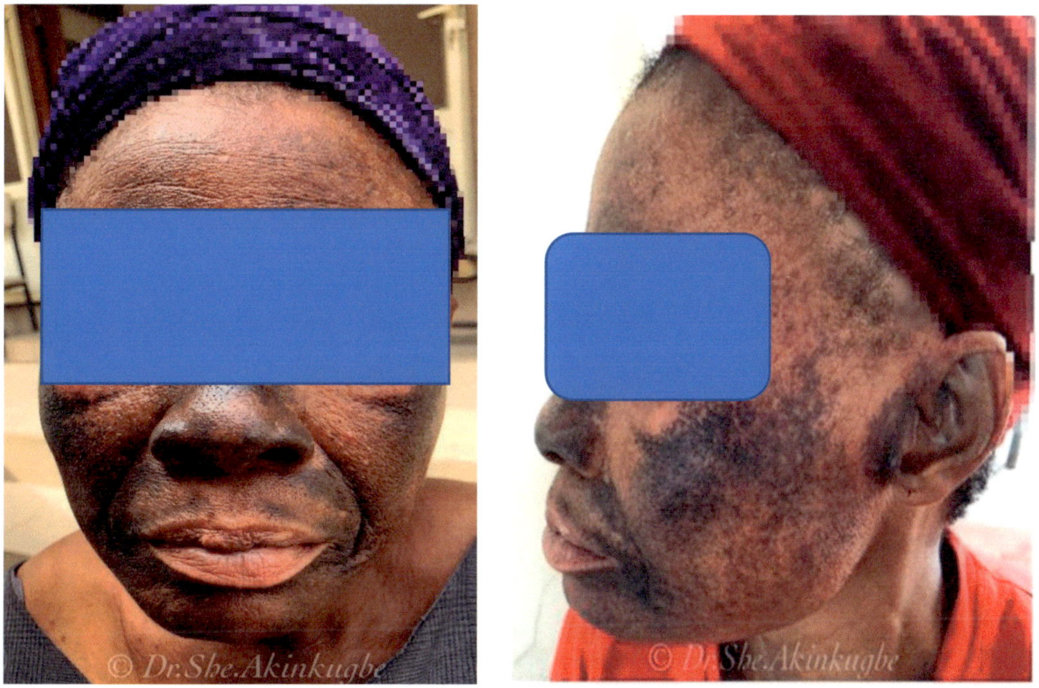

Figure 4.1: Exogenous ochronosis involving different parts of the face

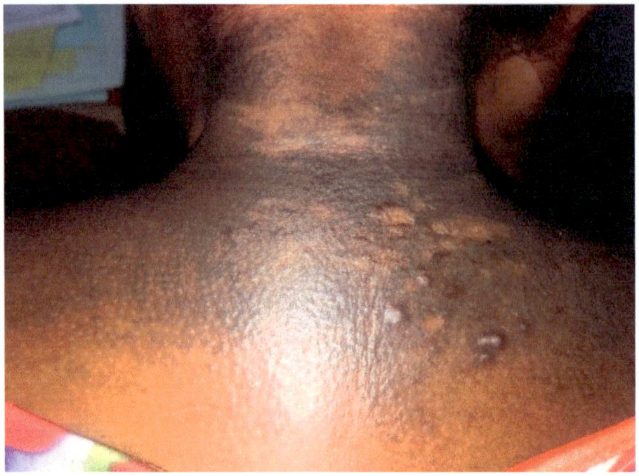

Figure 4.2: Exogenous ochronosis on the neck and upper back

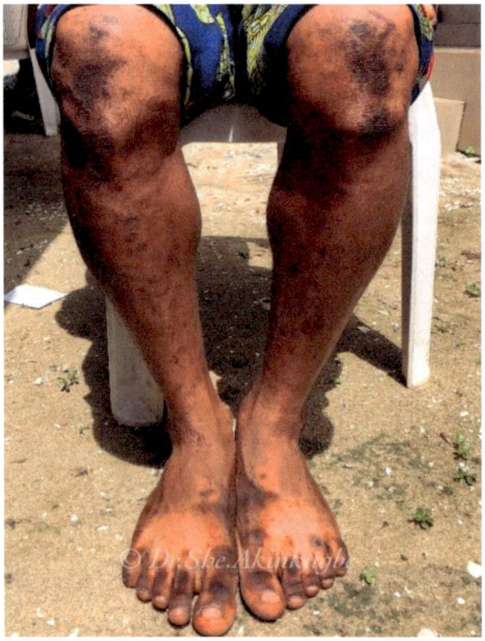

Figure 4.3: Dark knuckles and knees following the use of potent topical corticosteroids

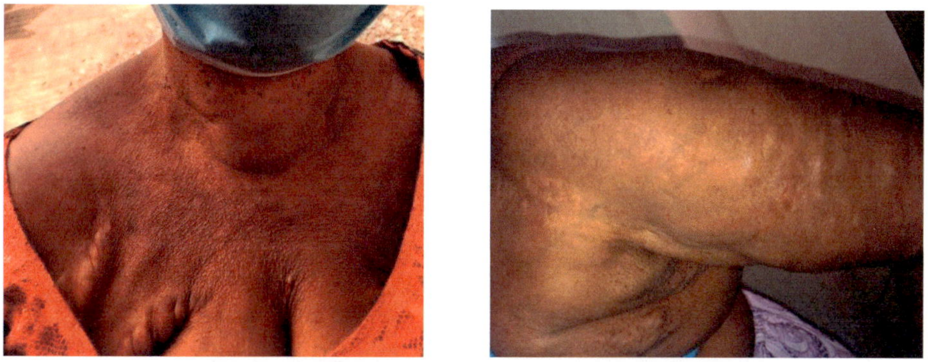

Figure 4.4: Gaping striae on the chest and arm

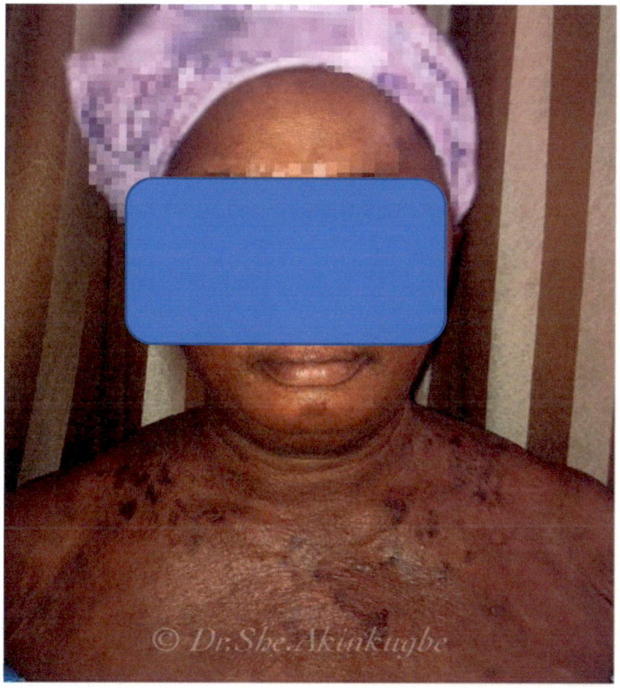

Figure 4.5: Dyspigmentation, erythema and striae from skin lightening agents

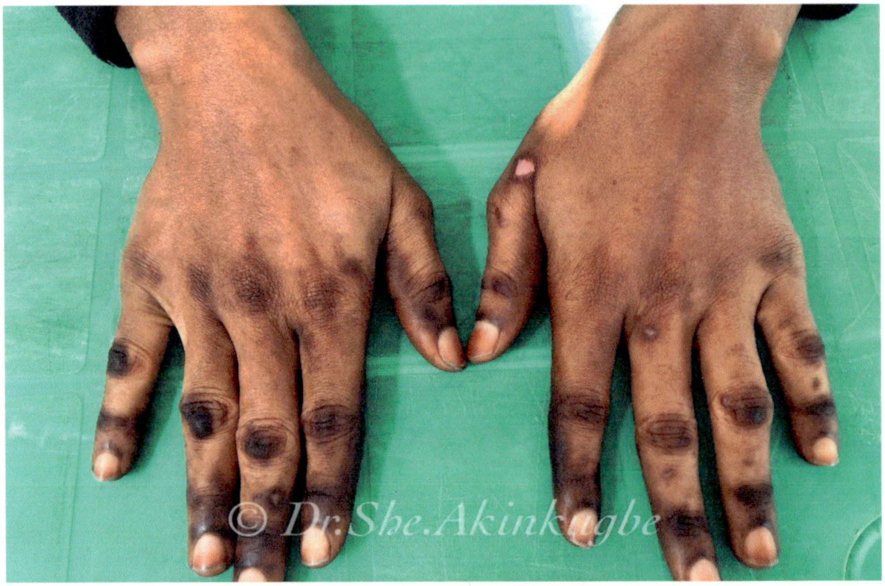

Figure 4.6: Hyperpigmentation of the knuckles

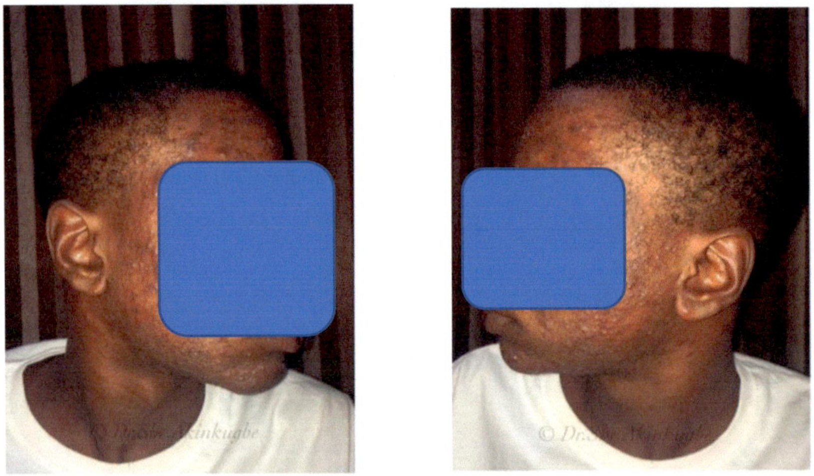

Figure 4.7: Severe acne worsened by use of various 'Triple action' topical agents containing potent corticosteroids

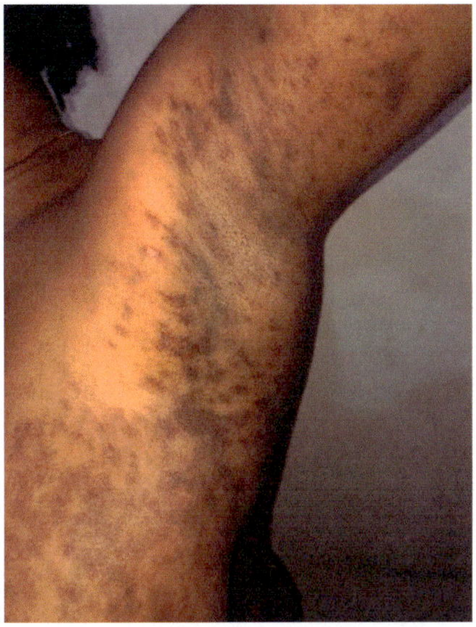

Figure 4.8: Widespread *Candida intertrigo* as a result of prolonged use of potent topical corticosteroids

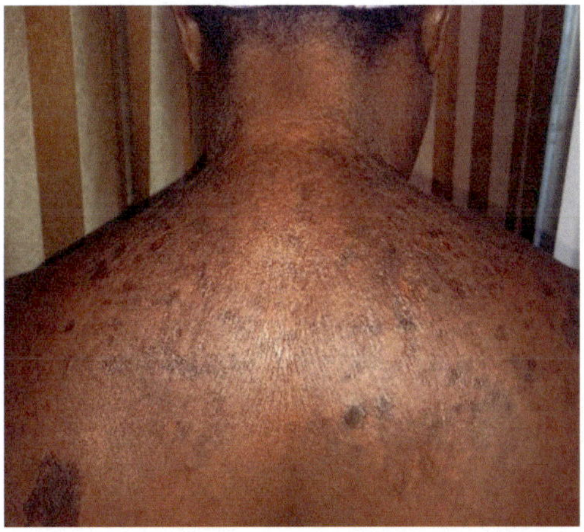

Figure 4.9: Upper back showing photodamage (wrinkling, rough and uneven skin texture, varied pigmentation changes, decreased skin elasticity) and damage from prolonged use of various skin lightening agents and topical corticosteroids (dyspigmentation and tinea corporis)

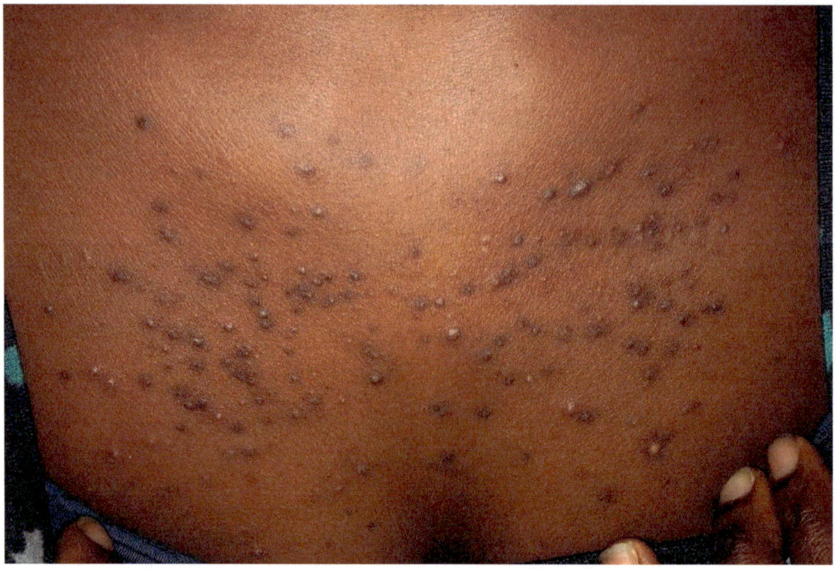

Figure 4.10: Steroid induced acne on the chest

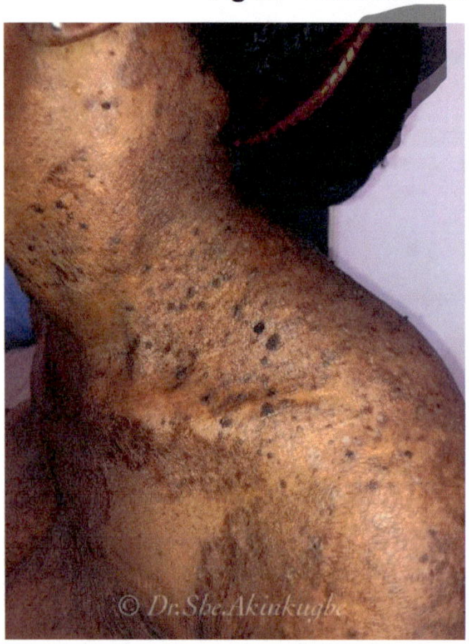

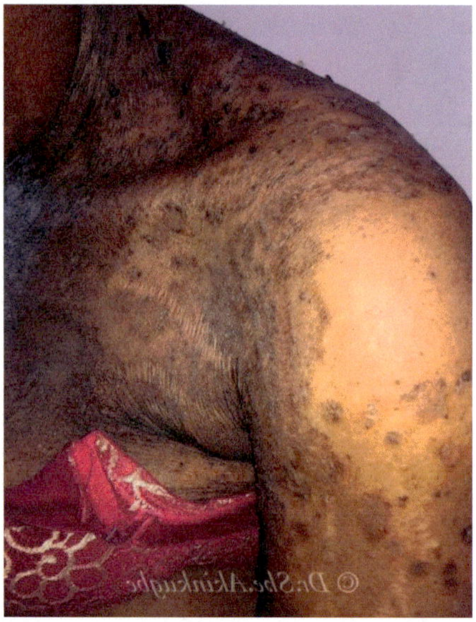

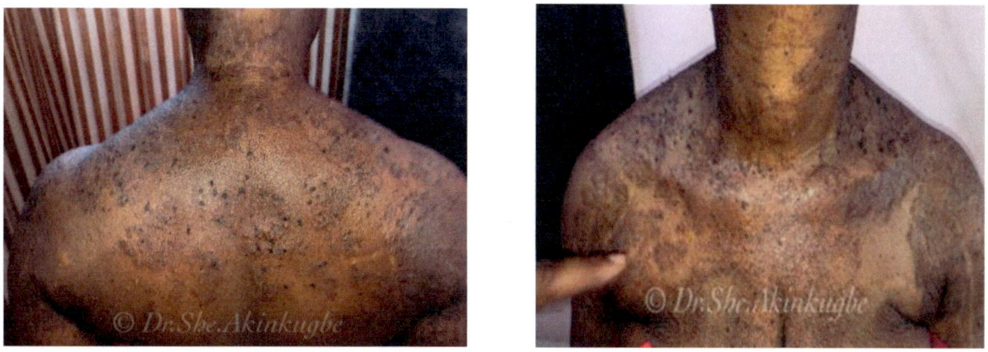

Figure 4.11: Damage to the skin with widespread *Tinea incognito* as a result of prolonged use of skin lightening agents combined with potent topical corticosteroid

Rehabilitation and repair of damaged skin

Many adverse cutaneous changes from prolonged use of skin lightening products are irreversible. Skin infections can be treated appropriately. Damage to the skin requires counselling, behavioural and lifestyle changes, topical and procedural treatments which aid in the repair of the skin.

The following are suggested steps for rehabilitation and repair:

- The first step is to understand and accept that the skin lightening product being used by the subject is harming the skin and its use must be stopped.
- Lifestyle changes which include -
  - Hydration – drinking water is good for the skin. It hydrates the body
  - Regular use of a moisturiser
  - Regular and consistent daily and appropriate use of sunscreen is recommended
  - Diet – a well-balanced diet is important for healthy skin and body
- Regular oral intake of vitamin C which is an antioxidant that protects the skin by neutralising free radical damage caused by exposure to UV radiation from the sun. It also inhibits melanin production, which helps with lightening of areas of hyperpigmentation; it accelerates production of collagen and elastin which keep the skin plump and firm; and it helps in preventing premature ageing.
- Consultation with a dermatologist who evaluates the skin in relation to the damage done and advise accordingly as to the type of skin care required, which

may involve repair and rehabilitation of the skin using chemical peels (light, medium, deep), microdermabrasion and/or laser therapy.

- Skin care products: the contents of skin care products, as listed on the label, should always be checked to ensure absence of mercury and other prohibited skin lighteners. Over-the-counter skin lightener products containing hydroquinone available in countries where hydroquinone is not prohibited should not contain more than 2% of the agent. Kojic acid has antioxidant properties and is safe to use at 2%. Arbutin, a derivative of hydroquinone can also be used safely at very low concentrations.

It is important to reiterate that daily and consistent use of sunscreen is recommended for ALL skin types.

References

1. Aramide OK, Olatunji OS, Ayandele O. Health Information Literacy on the Risks of Using Skin Bleaching Products [Internet]. Rochester, NY: Social Science Research Network; 2019 Sep [cited 2022 May 1]. Report No.: 3458858. Available from: https://papers.ssrn.com/abstract=3458858
2. Benn EK, Alexis A, Mohamed N, Wang YH, Khan IA, Liu B. Skin bleaching and dermatologic health of African and Afro-Caribbean populations in the US: new directions for methodologically rigorous, multidisciplinary, and culturally sensitive research. Dermatol Ther. 2016;6:453–9.
3. Sagoe D, Pallesen S, Dlova NC, Lartey M, Ezedine K, Dadzie O. The global prevalence and correlates of skin bleaching: a meta-analysis and meta-regression analysis. Int J Dermatol. 2019;58:24–44.
4. FOOD-DRUGS-AND-RELATED-PRODUCTS-REGISTRATION-ACT-Cap.F.33.pdf [Internet]. [cited 2022 May 2]. Available from: https://www.nafdac.gov.ng/wp-content/uploads/Files/Resources/Regulations/NAFDAC_Acts/FOOD-DRUGS-AND-RELATED-PRODUCTS-REGISTRATION-ACT-Cap.F.33.pdf
5. COMPS-973.pdf [Internet]. [cited 2022 May 2]. Available from: https://www.govinfo.gov/content/pkg/COMPS-973/pdf/COMPS-973.pdf
6. Baumann L. Cosmeceuticals in skin of color. Semin Cutan Med Surg. 2016;35:233–7.
7. Dadzie O, Petit A. Skin bleaching: highlighting the misuse of cutaneous depigmenting agents. J Eur Acad Dermatol Venereol. 2009;23:741–50.
8. Pollock S, Taylor S, Oyerinde O, Nurmohamed S, Dlova N, Sarkar R, et al. The dark side of skin lightening: An international collaboration and review of a public health issue affecting dermatology. Int J Womens Dermatol. 2021;7:158–64.
9. de Souza MM. The concept of skin bleaching in Africa and its devastating health implications. Clin Dermatol. 2008;26:27–9.
10. Li EPH, Min HJ, Belk RW, Kimura J, Bahl S. Skin Lightening and Beauty in Four Asian Cultures. :7.

11. Global Skin Lighteners Market Growth Opportunities to 2026: Physician-Dispensed Skin Brightening and Lightening Products - ResearchAndMarkets.com [Internet]. 2022 [cited 2022 May 2]. Available from: https://www.businesswire.com/news/home/20220113005476/en/Global-Skin-Lighteners-Market-Growth-Opportunities-to-2026-Physician-Dispensed-Skin-Brightening-and-Lightening-Products---ResearchAndMarkets.com
12. Couteau C, Coiffard L. Overview of Skin Whitening Agents: Drugs and Cosmetic Products. Cosmetics. 2016;3:27.
13. Sarkar R, Arora P, Garg KV. Cosmeceuticals for Hyperpigmentation: What is Available? J Cutan Aesthetic Surg. 2013;6:4–11.
14. Jackson A. Chemical peels. Facial Plast Surg FPS. 2014;30:26–34.
15. O'Connor AA, Lowe PM, Shumack S, Lim AC. Chemical peels: A review of current practice. Australas J Dermatol. 2018;59:171–81.
16. Kornhauser A, Coelho SG, Hearing VJ. Applications of hydroxy acids: classification, mechanisms, and photoactivity. Clin Cosmet Investig Dermatol CCID. 2010;3:135–42.
17. Ravikumar B, R I, Pillai D. Efficacy of Alpha and Beta Hydroxy Acid Chemical Peels in Postacne Pigmentation: A Double Blinded, Randomized, Controlled Trial. J Clin Aesthetic Dermatol. 2022;15:48–52.
18. Al-Niaimi F, Chiang NYZ. Topical Vitamin C and the Skin: Mechanisms of Action and Clinical Applications. J Clin Aesthetic Dermatol. 2017;10:14–7.
19. Alpha Arbutin as a Skin Lightening Agent: A Review. Int J Pharm Res [Internet]. 2021 [cited 2022 May 2];13. Available from: http://www.ijpronline.com/ViewArticleDetail.aspx?ID=21187
20. Lajis AFB, Hamid M, Ariff AB. Depigmenting Effect of Kojic Acid Esters in Hyperpigmented B16F1 Melanoma Cells. J Biomed Biotechnol. 2012;2012:952452.
21. Sardesai VR, Kolte JN, Srinivas BN. A Clinical Study of Melasma and a Comparison of the Therapeutic Effect of Certain Currently Available Topical Modalities for its Treatment. Indian J Dermatol. 2013;58:239.
22. Faghihi G, Taheri A, Shahmoradi Z, Nilforoushzadeh MA. Solution of Azelaic Acid (20%), Resorcinol (10%) and Phytic Acid (6%) Versus Glycolic Acid (50%) Peeling Agent in the Treatment of Female Patients with Facial Melasma. Adv Biomed Res. 2017;6:9.
23. Altraide D, Aladeh DA, Otike-Odibi B. Skin Bleaching Practices: Products, Mechanisms and Effects. Asian J Res Dermatol Sci. 2021;34–42.
24. The widespread use of skin lightening creams in Senegal: a persistent public health problem in West Africa - Del Giudice - 2002 - International Journal of Dermatology - Wiley Online Library [Internet]. [cited 2022 May 2]. Available from: https://onlinelibrary.wiley.com/doi/abs/10.1046/j.1365-4362.2002.01335.x
25. Faye O, Keita S, Diakité FS, Konaré HD, Ndiaye HT. Side effects of de-pigmenting products in Bamako, Mali. Int J Dermatol. 2005;44 Suppl 1:35–6.
26. Nnoruka E, Okoye O. Topical steroid abuse: its use as a depigmenting agent. J Natl Med Assoc. 2006;98:934–9.

27. Sonthalia S, Daulatabad D, Sarkar R. Glutathione as a skin whitening agent: Facts, myths, evidence and controversies. Indian J Dermatol Venereol Leprol. 2016;82.
28. Sonthalia S, Jha AK, Lallas A, Jain G, Jakhar D. Glutathione for skin lightening: a regnant myth or evidence-based verity? Dermatol Pract Concept. 2018;8:15–21.
29. Loesch MM, Somani AK, Kingsley MM, Travers JB, Spandau DF. Skin resurfacing procedures: new and emerging options. Clin Cosmet Investig Dermatol. 2014;7:231–41.
30. Shpall R, Beddingfield FC, Watson D, Lask GP. Microdermabrasion: a review. Facial Plast Surg FPS. 2004;20:47–50.
31. Filho JM, Papaiordanou F. Cryotherapy for Cosmetic Procedures. In: Issa MCA, Tamura B, editors. Chemical and Physical Procedures [Internet]. Cham: Springer International Publishing; 2018 [cited 2022 May 2]. p. 185–96. (Clinical Approaches and Procedures in Cosmetic Dermatology). Available from: https://doi.org/10.1007/978-3-319-16805-0_21
32. Gabros S, Nessel TA, Zito PM. Topical Corticosteroids. In: StatPearls [Internet]. Treasure Island (FL): StatPearls Publishing; 2022 [cited 2022 May 3]. Available from: http://www.ncbi.nlm.nih.gov/books/NBK532940/
33. Olumide YM, Akinkugbe AO, Altraide D, Mohammed T, Ahamefule N, Ayanlowo S, et al. Complications of chronic use of skin lightening cosmetics. Int J Dermatol. 2008;47:344–53.
34. Martínez A, Asensio J, Aran B. Effect of the combination of different depigmenting agents in vitro. J Cosmet Sci. 2014;65:365–75.

CHAPTER FIVE

Hair and hair products

Folake A Orafidiya, Modupe T Talabi and 'Lara O Orafidiya

The hair, an appendage of the epidermis of the skin, is found all over the human body except in the palms, soles of the feet, lips, labia minora and the glans penis. Nonetheless, it is very prominent on the scalp where it contributes to the appearance and beauty of the female gender, in particular. In some cultures, and religious norms, women are required to cover their hair, especially when appearing in the public, due mainly to the fact that the hair, being a thing of beauty, can cause attraction of the opposite sex. Notwithstanding, the hair, when properly groomed and styled, enhances the self-esteem and boosts the self-confidence of the woman. It is, therefore, important that the hair be always maintained in a healthy condition to prevent frizz, split ends, extremely dry condition and the ultimate breakage of the hair shafts. Poor maintenance affects the look of the hair and can lead to hair loss which invariably, affects a person's appearance and self-confidence. The male folks also groom their hair to enhance their appearance and to keep the hair healthy. The condition of the scalp is integral in how the hair grows. Diet, exercise, and a good hair care routine are the best ways to ensure a healthy scalp. For people who suffer scalp conditions such as psoriasis or seborrheic dermatitis, a visit to a dermatologist or trichologist is advised for adequate treatment. The use of cosmetic hair-grooming products, undoubtedly, is how the hair can be properly maintained in a healthy state and presented to enhance beauty.

Structure of the hair

The hair is composed of the hair follicle, and the shaft which is above the epidermis and constitutes the hair that is visible on the scalp (Figure 5.1). The hair root, which is an extension of the shaft, is surrounded by the hair follicle, which is a sheath of connective tissue and the skin. Attached to the hair follicle is the sebaceous gland which produce an oily substance that coats the hair shaft, lubricating it and protecting it from becoming brittle. The hair root widens at its base to form the hair bulb, where new hair cells are formed. The bulb also houses the dermal papilla which are enriched with blood vessels that provide the hair root with blood and nourishment. The arrector pili, which plays a role in thermoregulation, is a tiny muscle attached to the base of each hair follicle at one end and the dermal tissue at the other end. When in cold conditions, the arrector pili muscles contract simultaneously, lifting the hair shafts up into a straight position, creating an insulating layer on the skin that traps heat thereby conserving heat. The process, called piloerection, is also known as goosebumps. As an involuntary reaction that occurs via the sympathetic nervous system, piloerection may also be a fight or flight response as it occurs in tense emotional states. The hair follicle is also well innervated. These nerves are very sensitive and can sense even the slightest movement of the hair.

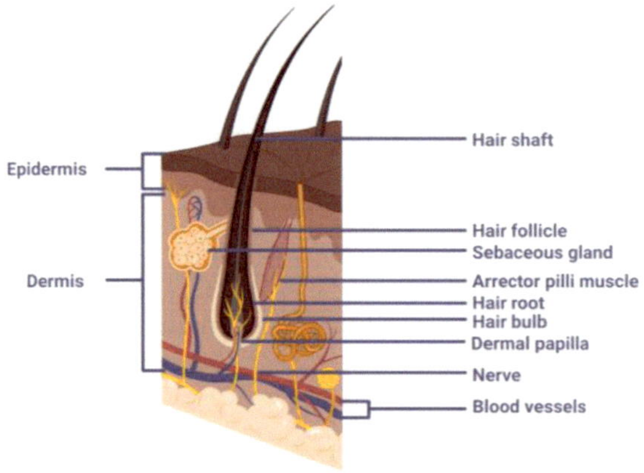

Figure 5.1: The structure of the hair

Each hair fibre is organised into three layers: the cuticle, the cortex and the medulla (Figure 5.2).

Cuticle: The cuticle is the outermost layer which has a scale-like appearance and covers the hair from its root to the tip. It is made of flat overlapping cells and consist of the cell membrane complex and sub-lamellar structures. The cuticle is integral in protecting the hair cortex from physical and chemical insults as well as determining the hair lustre and maintaining the hair in a disentangled state. The state of the cuticle also determines the porosity of the hair, that is, the ability of hair to absorb moisture.

Cortex: The cortex is the second layer and it is the main body of the hair fibre. The cortex plays a role in determining the mechanical and physical properties such as the curl pattern, the hair colour, and the strength of the hair. The cortex contains melanocytes, which produce melanin that gives the hair its colour; keratinocytes which produce keratin that determines curl pattern, strength and elasticity of the hair. The cell membrane complex, which glues hair cells together, is also present in the cortex.

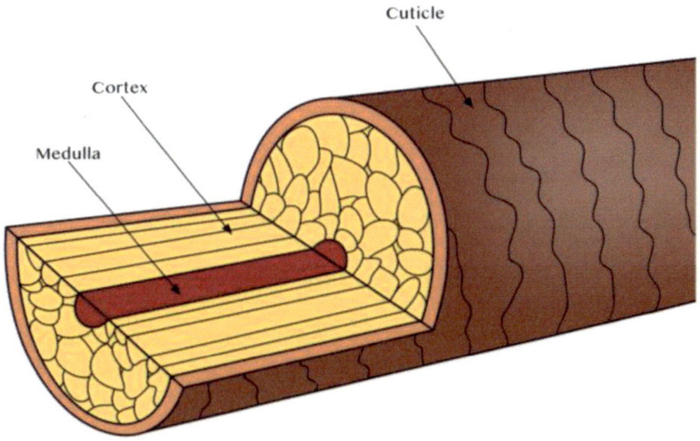

Figure 5.2: Cross section of the hair fibre

Medulla: The innermost layer of the hair is the medulla which is a hollow space. There is no known function of the medulla. In fact, not all hair strands have the medulla as it is mostly found in thick hair strands.

The hair growth cycle

Hair growth is a dynamic process which is influenced by hormones, cytokines, age, nutrition, and environmental factors. The hair grows in the follicle. The maximum number of hair follicles of an individual is present at birth, hence, as the head enlarges, the concentration of hair follicles decreases (1). New hair cells, which are continuously formed in the hair bulb, adhere together, harden, align and become a new full strand of hair. As the new hardened cells keep attaching to the hair base, it gradually pushes the hair above the skin where growth is seen steadily. Each hair strand grows an average of 0.5 inch a month or about 6 inches a year continuously for few years after which growth stops and the old hair is shed off (2). Racial differences have been reported in hair growth rate. A growth rate of 280 µm/day, 411 µm/day and 367 µm/day are attributed to the African, Asian and Caucasian hair respectively (3). Faster growth rate has also been associated with thickness of the hair fibres. Although the study was carried out on Asian and Caucasian hair types, individuals with thick hair fibres had a propensity for faster growth compared with thin fibres (4). The cyclic pattern (Figure 5.3) of hair growth is classified into:

Anagen: This is the active growth stage within the follicle and can last from 2-7 years (1). Approximately 90% of hair are in the anagen phase at any given time (1). The duration of anagen decreases with aging. During anagen, the progenitor cells of the hair proliferate, surround the growing dermal papilla, grow down into the skin and differentiate into the hair shaft. The melanocytes produce the melanin pigments in this phase of the cycle. The duration of anagen is associated with hair length. Individuals with a short anagen phase tend to have short hair and vice versa.

Catagen: This is the transitional stage during which growth stops. About 1% of hairs are usually in this stage and it lasts for few weeks (1). At this point, the hair follicles become thinner, the dermal papilla, which supplies blood, is detached and melanocytes stop producing melanin. The hair bulb gradually loses its root sheath and acquires a club-shaped end known as club hair.

Telogen: Following catagen, the hair enters the resting phase which can last up to 100 days (1). About 10% of hair are typically in the telogen phase (2). The club hair detaches from the root sheath and the epidermal column shortens to form a secondary germ. When anagen recommences, the secondary germ grows down to the dermal papilla forming a new hair bulb. The new hair is formed beside the old one which ultimately falls off (1).

Exogen: Hair shedding is the normal physiological outcome of the hair cycle, and this phase of the hair cycle is referred to as exogen. Typically, in healthy humans, up to 100 strands of hair are shed per day (5).

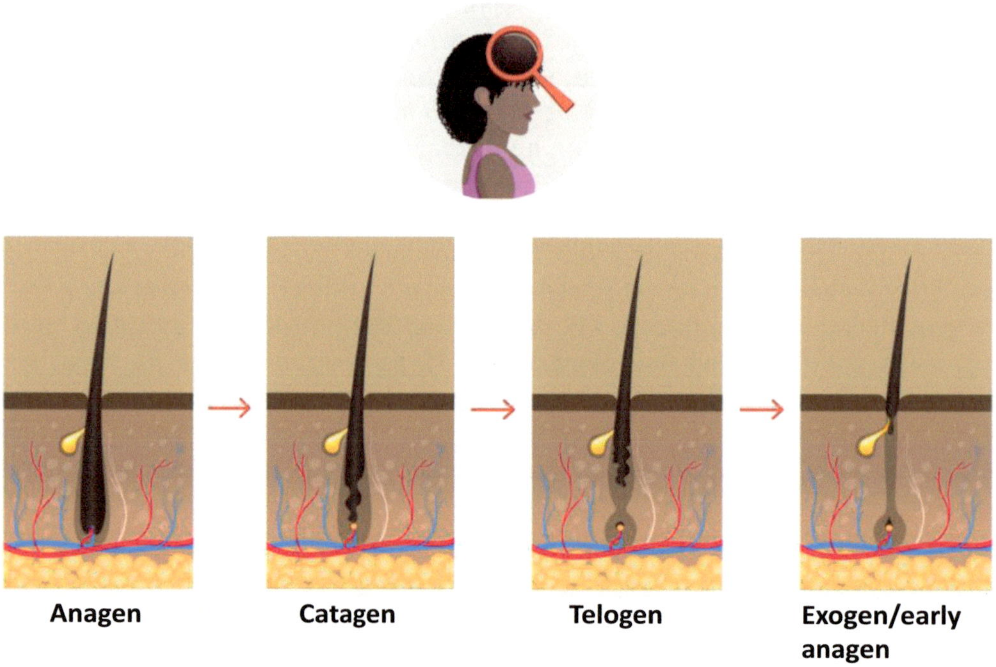

Figure 5.3: The hair growth cycle

Roles of hormones in hair growth

In addition to being enriched in blood vessels, the dermal papilla expresses the androgen receptors which are activated by androgens such as testosterones and the more potent dihydrotestosterone (DHT). Although androgens are regarded as male sex hormones, they are also produced by females. Androgens are the principal regulators of hair growth although their role is paradoxical. Androgens, their prohormones and derivatives are majorly responsible for the growth of terminal hair (6). Excessive androgens result in androgenetic alopecia in susceptible individuals, a disorder characterized by loss of terminal hair on the scalp which affects up to 80% and 50% of men and women, respectively (7,8). In females, excess androgens can cause increased facial hairs or unwanted hair growth known as hirsutism. The role of the female sex hormones in hair growth is debatable. Oestrogens are assumed to extend anagen phase (9). During pregnancy, the effects of oestrogen are more pronounced as the high levels of oestrogen are relatively stable without interruption by menstrual periods. At post-partum, there is a sudden drop in oestrogen levels thus hair that have been in the anagen phase for a long period rapidly transit to the telogen phase as a result of the loss of the stabilizing effect of oestrogen hence, the telogen effluvium or amplified hair shedding associated with post-partum. The increase in female pattern hair loss after menopause is also suggestive of a role of oestrogen in the promotion of hair growth (9). Oestrogen and progesterone are also postulated to make the female hair soft and fine-looking. Progesterone influences hair growth by decreasing androgen synthesis and the conversion of testosterone to DHT (6). Prolactin has been demonstrated to have an inhibitory effect on the elongation of the hair shaft and premature induction of the catagen phase of the hair cycle (6). Excessive production of cortisol, the stress hormone, is also associated with disruption in hair growth (10). Other hormones that affect hair growth and health include, but are not limited to, oestradiol, thyroid gland hormones, melatonin, corticotropin-releasing hormone, and thyrotropin-releasing hormone.

Chemistry of the hair

The hair strand is constituted mainly of dead cells full of keratin, a fibrous protein, along with water, lipids and trace amounts of elements such as chromium, calcium, copper, cadmium, silicon, copper, iron and zinc. Of the amino acids that constitute keratin, l-cysteine, a sulphur-containing amino acid, is the most important as it contributes greatly to the shape of the hair through the characteristic bonds it forms within the hair structure.

Types of chemical bonds in the hair

The chemical bonds in the hair structure are responsible for the shape, strength, elasticity and shine, which characterise the hair strand. There are three main types of bonds in the hair: the disulphide bonds, hydrogen bonds and salt bonds.

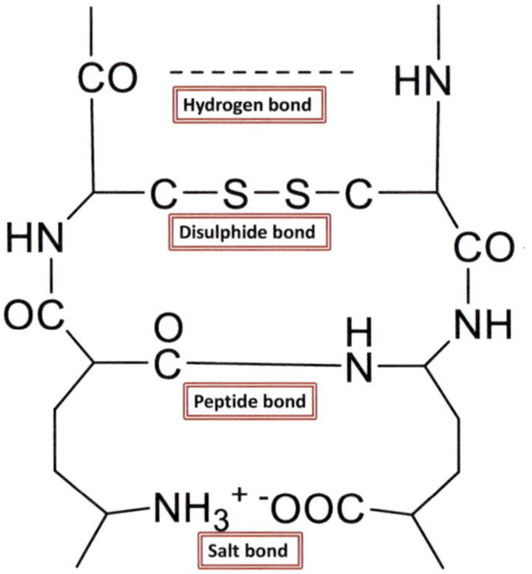

Figure 5.4: The chemical bonds in the hair

Disulphide bonds: These are the strongest bonds which give the hair strand its main shape and curl pattern. The thiol (-SH) group of the cysteine molecule forms disulphide (-S-S-) bond with the thiol group of the cysteine of another keratin (Figure 5.4). The amino acids of the keratin form a helical structure and the formation of disulphide bonds within the structure causes the hair shaft to bend. One helix pairs-up with another and they coil together anti-clockwisely. The pair is attracted to another pair of helices, sticking together to form four helices which further join with another four coiled helices, forming a hair filament. Extensive disulphide bonding occurs among the coiled helices of the hair filaments and the more the cross-bonding among the filaments, the more curved the hair shaft becomes. Hence, curly hairs have more disulphide bonding than straight hairs, and the greater the extent of bonding among the filaments, the curlier the hair. The disulphide bonds permanently keep the hair strand in shape. The bonds, which are found in the hair cortex, also give strength and elasticity to the hair and can only be broken by chemicals such as found in hair relaxers (hair-straighteners) or by extreme damage. Once the disulphide bonds are broken, they cannot be reversed and the hair tends to lose elasticity and is more prone to breakage.

Hydrogen and salt bonds: Hydrogen bonds and salt linkages are the two other important bonds present in the hair shaft (Figure 5.4). These bonds, unlike disulphide bonds, are easily broken by heat and water, respectively. Thus, heat-straightened hair or water-wetted hair reverts to its normal texture due to the permanent disulphide bonds. They, however, allow for the hair to be temporarily styled in different shapes from its original curl pattern.

Hair types

There is an extensive variation in the human hair ranging from length, colour and thickness to curliness or straightness. Various attempts have been made in classifying the hair. A racial category in which hair is classified as African, Asian and Caucasian has been employed. However, this system failed to consider mixed origins which impacts on the nature of the hair. The curl pattern has also been employed in classification. The curl pattern of the hair is determined by the shape of follicle. Straight, wavy and curly hair emanates from a round, oval or flat follicle, respectively (Figure 5.5).

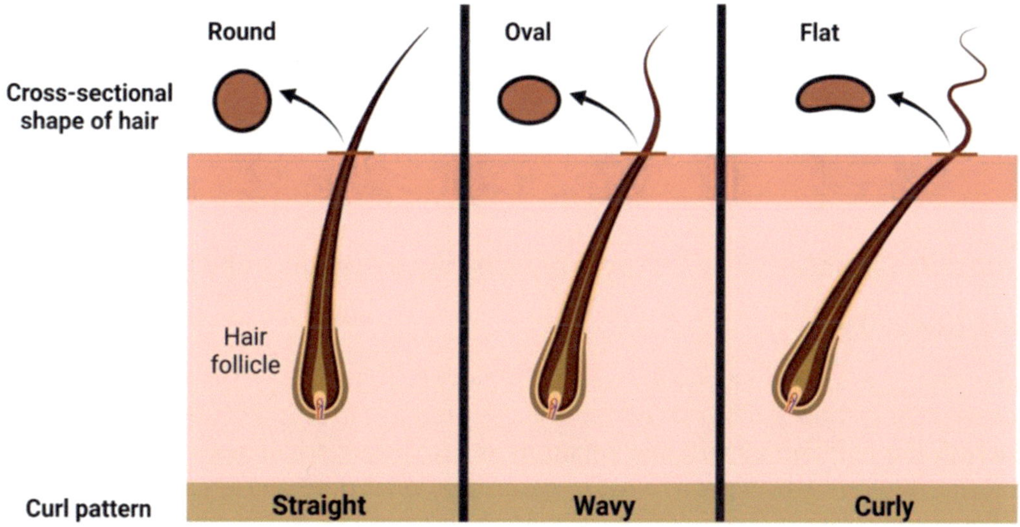

Figure 5.5: The cross-sectional shape of the hair follicle within the dermis and curl pattern of the hair shaft

In the last few years, a numbering and lettering system has been used to make it easier to identify the shape and curl pattern of hair. Andre Walker is famously known to have created this hair typing system. Over the years, modifications have been made to his initial classification system. Based on this, hair is classified into four categories which are further divided into sub-types:

- 1 - straight hair
- 2 - wavy hair (2, 2b, 2c)
- 3 - curly hair (3a, 3b, 3c)
- 4 - Kinky hair (4a, 4b, 4c)

Each category is then ascribed a letter based on the degree of the curl the hair holds (Figure 5.6). Although this classification system is more robust, it is, however, still limited as individuals tend to have more than one curl pattern.

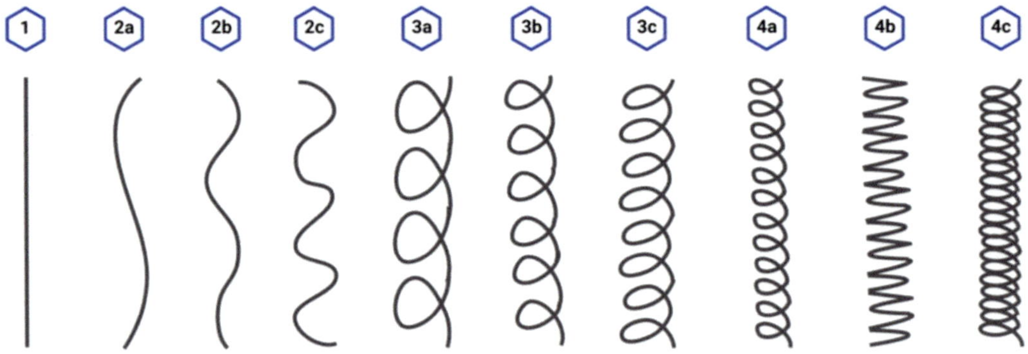

Figure 5.6: Classification of hair shapes using the numbering and lettering system

Hair porosity

The hair strand is a dead tissue and once it grows above the scalp, the health of the hair is dependent on how the hair is treated and the products used in managing it. The extent to which the hair can absorb and retain moisture is called hair porosity. It is used in assessing different hair types in a bid to determine what products are suitable on them. Hair porosity is associated with the extent of tightness of the cuticle. The degree of porosity of the hair (Figure 5.7) is classified into:

Low porosity: The cuticle of the hair is tightly bound together, hence, it is difficult for moisture or water or other hair treatment molecules to penetrate the hair shaft. The hair type that falls into this category is challenging to style. To aid penetration, the pH of the hair must be raised or heat applied.

Medium porosity: This is also referred to as normal porosity. The cuticles in the normally porous hair are less tightly bound and offer appropriate protection to the cortex. They adequately take in moisture and retain moisture. Medium porosity hair typically looks healthy. Such hair is easy to style and can take on products like dyes very well.

High porosity: Hair types that are highly porous are characterised by widely spaced cuticles across the hair shaft. The hair absorbs moisture easily; however, it is unable to retain it. The hair tends to be brittle and frizzy; hence, it is more prone to damage and breakage. The hair strands that have been subjected to harsh treatment with chemicals have a proclivity to have high porosity.

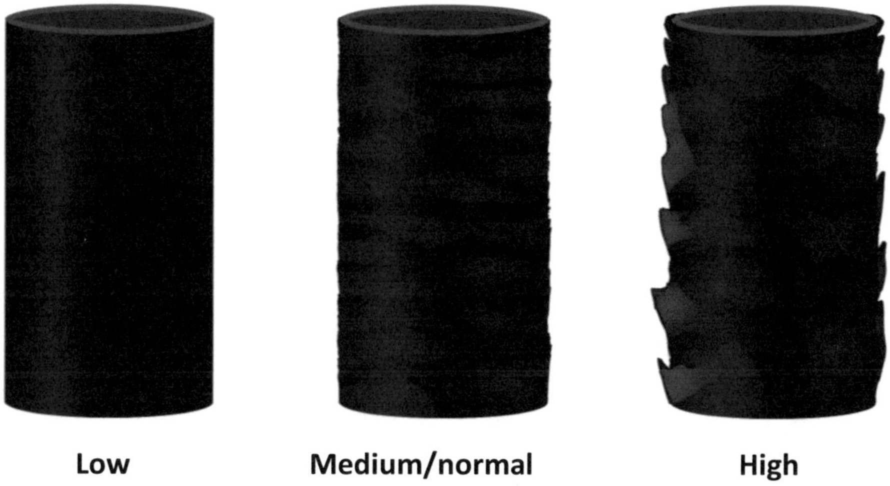

Figure 5.7: Types of hair porosity

The porosity of the hair can be determined by observing the floating properties of clean hair when dropped in water. High porosity hair will sink immediately while low porosity hair will float. The medium porosity hair floats in the middle of the water.

Hair care products

The shape of the hair strands will affect the general condition of the hair and how the hair reacts to products. Straight hair tends to get greasy very quickly as the natural sebum from the scalp travels up the strand easily. People with straight hair tend to wash their hair more often than others; whereas, thickly-curled, afro-typed hair tends to have a drier feel and requires more moisture regularly. Hair care products can be categorized into 3 types: shampoos, conditioners and styling products.

Shampoos

Shampoos are products that cleanse the hair by removing dirt and excess oil from the hair. Shampoos were originally invented to perform as a detergent for washing the hair and offered no other functionality. Over time, using detergents alone was found to be quite harsh on the hair and, more recently, shampoos are formulated to contain other ingredients that better suit the need of the hair.

The main ingredient in a shampoo is a detergent which is a surfactant, examples of which are sodium lauryl or laureth sulphate, ammonium laureth sulphate, cocamidopropyl betaine, cocamidopropyl hydroxsultaine and disodium laureth sulphosuccinate. A surfactant molecule consists of two groups - the hydrophilic or water-loving head, and the hydrophobic or water-hating tail. The latter attaches to dirt and oils in the hair and scalp and is then rinsed away along with the hydrophilic head which is in the water. Other ingredients include moisturisers such as glycerine and oils, as well as fragrances. Some shampoos are made with soaps and are said to be sulphate-free. Soaps, obtained by reacting alkalis with fatty acids of vegetable oils, are milder on the hair, although they produce less suds than the sulphates and are susceptible to forming scums in the presence of hard water. With the advancement in the development of the cosmetics industry, brands now create an array of customised shampoos for specific hair needs. There are different types of shampoos in the market and they include:

Chelating shampoos: These contain chelating agents, such as ethylene diamine tetra acetic acid (EDTA), phytic acid and sodium gluconate, which bind minerals, i.e., metal ions, such as calcium and magnesium ions, that are found in hard water and chlorinated swimming pools; and deposits of certain medications, that might have built-up heavily within the hair shaft. The chelated deposits are removed while the hair is being washed with the shampoos. These shampoos have a low pH and are used occasionally, especially when the hair is to be chemically treated. The shampoos also allow for easy styling and improve the texture and appearance of the hair. Chelating shampoos are sometimes referred to as detox shampoos. Chelating agents, however, are sometimes present at low concentrations, in the regular, daily-use shampoos.

Clarifying shampoos: Unlike chelating shampoos, clarifying shampoos work to remove excess oils, grease, dirt arising from hair products build-up, as well as minerals on (and not within) the hair strands. The shampoos have a high pH, contain a higher quantity of surfactants than the regular shampoos, and remove the dirt and residue without the hair losing its natural moisture. A clarifying shampoo can be used to wash the hair before the use of a chelating shampoo for a more effective outcome.

Conditioning shampoos: These are special shampoos that contain ingredients of both a shampoo and a hair conditioner; thus, allowing for the hair to be conditioned as it is being washed instead of the conditioner being applied after the hair has been shampooed, rinsed and in some cases, towelled till damp.

Shampoos for coloured hair: These are colour-protecting shampoos that enable the colours or dyes applied on the hair to last longer, as the coloured hair has the tendency to become more porous, losing moisture and dye molecules with washing. Sulphate-containing shampoos can cleanse deeply, thus stripping the hair of oils, moisture and dye molecules, thereby making the hair brittle, and the dye appearing faded. Sulphate-free shampoos are, therefore, preferred for coloured hair.

Dry shampoo: Dry shampoos are dry powder preparations that are packaged as pump sprays or aerosols for the purpose of cleansing the hair of dirt, oil and grease, without the use of water. They are usually employed as occasional hair cleansers and are no substitutes for the regular hair-washing shampoos. Dry shampoos are sprayed on the hair, where they absorb the oily dirt substances in the hair and are subsequently removed by blotting the scalp or by brushing the hair. These shampoos basically comprise starch as an absorbent and alcohol as a solvent to dislodge the oily substances from the hair. The starches employed include tapioca, corn and potato starches, which in addition to their absorption abilities, also give a smooth feel to the hair. Preservatives such as benzoic acid and potassium sorbate, as well as fragrances are included in the formulation. Pigments are added to dry shampoos for the black hair, to mask the otherwise visible, lightly coloured particulate residues of the shampoo components on the hair. Some dry shampoos are formulated to contain hair dyes which colour the new hair growth of a previously dyed hair. Rice (*Oryza sativa*) hull powder has been shown to have an exceptionally high capacity to absorb oil and to give a silky, smooth feel to the hair when used in dry a shampoo formulation. Some dry shampoos contain hectorite clay, a type of the smectite clays, which has been found to improve powder flow and to prevent clumping (11). Dry shampoos may give a heavy feel to the hair; while clumps, in poorly prepared powders, which reduce the efficacy of the products, appear as particles on the hair.

Hair conditioners

Hair conditioners are products that affect the way the hair feels and looks after being washed or when used on the unwashed hair. These products address specific hair conditions such as hair breakage, fullness, strengthening, frizziness, and colour. They generally enhance the good qualities of the hair and leave the hair nourished, with a soft and healthier appearance. The effect of conditioners on the hair is temporary and so it is imperative to have a regime whereby the hair is conditioned on a regular basis.

The hair strands carry a negative net static charge, due mainly to the ionization of the proteins in their structure, which causes them to repel each other, a condition that makes the hair to appear frizzy. However, the lipid layer, from the sebaceous glands, enveloping the strands is able to shield them from the effect of these charges, although this may not be totally effective especially where the hair structure has been damaged. Conditioners work mainly on the cuticles of the hair by depositing positively-charged molecules on the cuticles, thereby preventing charge repulsion by neutralizing the negative charges on the hair strands, closing the cuticles and filling the gaps in any broken areas of the cuticles, and in some cases, provide more oil coverage. The primary function of conditioners is, therefore, to reduce the friction between the hair strands and improve manageability of the hair. Some conditioners are used as hair treatments and their effects are enhanced by using steam therapy to allow better penetration of the product into the cuticles.

Hair conditioners are typically applied after the hair has been shampooed. The types of conditioners available include:

Charge-neutralising conditioners: These are acidifiers, such as organic acids, e.g., citric acid. They have a pH of about 3.5 that enables them to tighten up the scaly surface of the hair follicles by strengthening the hydrogen bonds between the keratin molecules and, thereby, give a more compact structure to the hair as they leave a residual positive charge on the hair. Such conditioners also neutralize the effects of the residual basic relaxers on the chemically-treated hair. There are the cationic surfactants that act as charge-neutralising conditioners by binding their hydrophilic heads to the negatively-charged amino acids on the surface of the keratin, with their hydrophobic tails now becoming the new neutral hair surface.

Moisturisers contain high quantities of humectants such as dimethicone and emollients such as coconut, argan, castor and almond oils which are natural oils. Their role is to hold moisture in the hair, thereby making the porous and dry hair softer and more pliable.

Repair/protein conditioners: This class of conditioners enrich the hair with proteins and other nutrients, strengthening the hair and reconstructing badly damaged hair through polymer crosslinking by the hydrolysed proteins which they contain, that also penetrate the hair appreciably.

Detanglers: As acidifiers, detanglers reduce the repulsive charge effects of the hair shafts by modifying the surface pH to neutralise the negative charges; while polymer detanglers coat the shafts thereby by eliminating friction between the hair shafts and improving combability of the hair.

Glossers are light-reflecting polymers that make the hair glossy by binding to its surface. Examples include cyclomethicone and dimethicone which are silicones.

Leave-in conditioners are applied to the hair after shampooing but are not rinsed-off after application.

Rinse-off conditioners are rinsed-off after a specified period on application.

Colour conditioners are applied to either coat the hair temporarily with dyes/pigments or to touch-up the colour already on the hair.

Hair grooming products

The nature of the hair shaft indicates the need that it is properly cared for in order for it to be in a healthy condition and be easily managed. The sebaceous glands supply the scalp and the hair shaft with oil. The straight and curly hair of the Asians and Caucasians allow for smooth flow of the oil from the scalp to the tip of the hair shaft, making the hair to be easily managed as the oil films conserve the moisture within the hair shafts and also shields the negative residual charges on the hair, thereby preventing friction among the hair shafts. The tightly-curled structure of the typical black African hair reduces the extent of the oil coverage on the hair shafts, leaving the hair dry, unable to conserve moisture, and difficult to comb and manage, due to the friction among the shafts that arises from the improperly shielded negative charges on the hair shafts.

Hair-grooming products are available as serums, oil hair sprays, lotions and creams. Products of semisolid, ointment consistency, such as those containing mostly petrolatum and softened butters are often referred to as pomades.

Moisturisers: Moisturisers such as emollients and occlusives, when applied to the hair, complement the effects of the oil films from the sebaceous glands; and humectants, in addition, attract moisture from the environment and seal it into the hair follicles, thus, increase the hair's natural moisture content that results in volumizing of the hair. Moisturisers impact gloss to the hair, reduce frizz, make the hair soft and manageable; thus, enhancing its appearance. Emollients and occlusives, which seal-in the natural moisture and add shine to the hair, include vegetable oils such as coconut oil, olive oil, jojoba oil, argan oil, castor oil, avocado oil, and palm kernel oil; butters like shea butter, cocoa butter and mango butter; as well as liquid paraffin and petrolatum or petroleum jelly which are refined petroleum products. The glycols, e.g., polyethylene glycol (PEG) and polypropylene glycol (PPG or PG) are synthetic humectants that find use as humectants in cosmetic products. Butters, because of their semisolid consistency, do not evenly spread on the hair shafts, and are better mixed with some of the oils to become mobile and to spread more easily. Whipping of butters to give a softer consistency introduces air into them, which increases their susceptibility to oxidation, making them to go rancid quickly. Waxes such as beeswax and wool fat, in the form of lanolin, are also used as occlusives in hair-grooming products. They coat the hair shaft, thereby preventing moisture loss and also add shine to the hair. Examples include glycerine, lactic acid, hyaluronic acid, honey, panthenol, sorbitol, propylene glycol as well as silicones such as dimethicone, lauryl methicone copolyol, and cyclomethicone. Vitamins A, B7 (biotin) and E are sometimes added to hair-grooming products to improve hair health.

Essential oils are added to certain products, sometimes referred to as hair treatments, mainly because of their sensory effects on the scalp as well as their medicinal properties that include antimicrobial activity, anti-inflammatory and hair growth stimulatory effects. Invariably, essential oils that contain menthol as part of their constituents, are likely to stimulate hair growth. The essential oil of *Ocimum gratissimum* has been observed to enhance growth on shaved sites on rabbits, and on humans who used a formulation of the oil to treat acne vulgaris (12,13). Rosemary oil has demonstrated hair growth-stimulating activity and its antifungal effects may be useful in the management of seborrheic dermatitis (14,15). The essential oil extracted from *Zizyphus jujuba* has also demonstrated hair growth-stimulating ability (16). Essential oils are, however, to be diluted with carrier oils such as the vegetable oils, before use so as to prevent their irritant effects on the scalp.

Styling products

Styling products are used to either give the hair a shape and a definition or to impart shine and hold on the hair. These products help to create the final look as desired and can also help with the smooth feel of the hair. They are used in the last steps of the hair care process. Styling products are essential for naturally tightly-coiled hair, as such a texture has a dull appearance and is also prone to frizz and dryness. Using the right combination of products will assist in keeping whatever style is chosen for a period of time, be it a stretched-out style or one with coils or waves. The following are the typical styling products that are used on the hair.

Mousse: The term mousse is a French word that means foam. The styling mousse is presented as a stable foam aerosol spray. It gives the hair definition and shine, reduces frizz, makes curls bouncier and keeps sculpted hairstyles in place for as long as a week to two weeks. It is of a lighter consistency than styling gels and creams and it adds volume and texture to the hair. The main ingredient of mousse is dimethicone, which gives the hair shine and prevents the hair from tangling, giving it a smooth appearance. Other ingredients include panthenol – a moisturiser; behentrimonium chloride which reduces the build-up of static charges and softens the hair; lanolin – an occlusive; lecithin, which apart from being a surfactant that enables a stable product to be attained, also serves to strengthen and soften the hair; as well as fragrances and preservatives. The mousse is applied on wet hair before styling.

Styling gel: Styling gels give strong and stiff hold to the hair, providing glossy and transparent films that coat the hair shaft. Polyvinyl pyrrolidone (PVP), a water-soluble, clear film-forming polymer is a known ingredient of styling gels. It, however, absorbs moisture in highly humid environment, making the hair on which it is applied sticky or tacky. Polyvinyl acetate (PVA) on the other hand, does not absorb moisture, thus giving a better hold in humid weather conditions and a more flexible effect in dry weather. A combination of the two gives an excellent product. Polyurethane, a non-ionic polymer, is another gel that has a good thermal stability. Cationic polymers, such as polyquaternium-4, have an additional advantage over the previously mentioned non-ionic gels, as they, being positively charged, neutralise the negative charges on the hair shafts, thereby decreasing static charge effects. There are styling gels called 'edge control' or 'edge smoothing' gels, which are used to flatten and smoothen the short, curly hair that quickly grows at the headline of chemically treated hair, giving a semblance of similar texture as the bulk of the treated hair.

Serum: A hair styling serum basically consists of silicones that coat the hair, protecting it from fizz, dryness by sealing-in moisture, and environmental pollution, while imparting shine and smoothness. Serums also reduce heat transfer from thermal styling appliances to the hair, thereby acting as thermal protectants. There are water-soluble silicones such as dimethicone and methicone and those that are water-insoluble such as cyclomethicone and amodimethicone. The latter provides better protection against moisture loss from the hair shafts, but require the use of surfactants for removal, unlike the former which can be washed-off with water. There are, however, other serums, often referred to as natural serums that are composed of natural oils, among other ingredients.

Shine and hold sprays: The two types of sprays are applied on the hair after it has been styled. The shine spray, composed mostly of emollient oils, gives gloss and shine to the hair while the hold spray holds the style in place for a long time, gives shine to the hair and also controls frizz and flyaway hair. The hold spray contains polymers as found in serums and styling gels in addition to polydimethylsiloxane, vinyl acetate and acrylates, gums and alcohol solutions. The two products are dispensed as oily liquids sprayed from aerosol containers.

Hair wax: Hair wax products contain waxes such as beeswax and hard paraffin wax, and are used for hairstyling, whereby they give shine, good hold and definition to hairstyles.

They have a hard consistency and may require slight warming or rubbing on the palms before being applied to the hair.

The use of clay for hair care

The use of clay for the cleansing and grooming of the human hair has been since antiquity, especially in some African cultures, where clays were used to untangle kinky hair and to prevent shrinkage after washing. The use of clays has recently been resuscitated and popularised, as people are now more concerned about the health and looks of their hair and would go for the best and latest means of keeping their hair healthy and beautiful, while avoiding, as much as possible, the use of excessive chemicals that are present in other commercial hair care products.

Clay is a type of soil that is rich in mineral elements such as magnesium, potassium and silica. It has the capacity to absorb moisture into the hair, and to cause the hair to absorb the nutrients it contains; while removing dirt, excess oils, environmental pollutants and toxins such as heavy metals, product build-ups, and microbes by adsorption which are then washed off when the scalp and the hair is rinsed with water. The presence of positive charges on clays, enables them to disentangle hair strands caused by the repulsion of the negative charges on the strands. Clays, especially those rich in silica, e.g., rhassoul clay, add shine to the hair and also exfoliate the scalp. In addition, they soften the hair and, in some cases, make the hair voluminous. Clay is also used in hair-grooming and styling, especially among the male folks. Clay-based grooming products give volume, smooth texture, gloss and a matte effect to the hair while also moisturising the hair. Clay-based styling products, on the other hand, provide good hold to styles making them last the whole day, in some instances.

Rhassoul, bentonite, kaolin, fuller's earth, French green, and Australian pink clays are used in hair care products. Excessive use of clays should, however, be avoided as they can strip the hair of the natural oil films.

Natural hair alterations

As an appendage in the body with unique appearance, texture and colour, the natural hair contributes to the identity, ethnic origin as well as the self-esteem of a person. In a bid to express beauty and attractiveness, increase quality of life or general well-being, be accepted in some social classes, or even the ease of day-to-day management of the hair, various modifications are made to the natural hair.

The hair is predominantly made of proteins of which 90% is keratin, which is rich in the amino acid, cysteine. The outer layer, the cuticle, is hydrophobic and made of the lipid 18-methyleicosanoic acid (18-MEA). The unperturbed cuticle has a smooth appearance which reduces friction between the hair shafts as well as reflect light. The texture and lustre of the hair is dependent on the cuticle. The hair cortex is made up of polypeptide chains which are cross-linked by hydrogen, salt and disulphide bonds. These crosslinks and bonds are vital for the elasticity and strength of the hair. The shape and texture of the hair shaft can be changed by altering these chemical bonds in the cortex. The weak salt and hydrogen bonds can be broken by heat and water, resulting in a less-curled hair, and the natural state is restored when the heat-straightened hair comes in contact with moisture or water, and when the hair is dried in the case of water-straightened hair. The disulphide bonds, which are resistant to water, are stronger and require chemical alterations, such as the use of relaxers, to modify the shape of the hair. Some hair types are, however, difficult to modify, i.e., to relax, to colour or to curl, due to a very intact and strong cuticle which prevents heat, chemicals, pigments and dyes from getting to the cortex of the hair. Modifications to the hair can be reversible, as in the case of heat and water treatment, or irreversible when the hair is chemically treated.

Thermal and water alterations

Thermal alteration involves the application of heat to the hair shaft. It is a temporary hair-straightening technique known to give a softer texture and an increased combability to the curly and kinky hair, making the hair more manageable and increasing the styling options. The use of heat to transform the appearance of the curly hair dates to the mid-1900s when Sarah Breedlove, also known as Madame C.J. Walker, used ointments and a heated metal comb that was passed through the hair, to straighten and add shine to it. Hydrogen bonds are broken when the hair is wet. As the hair dries, the hydrogen bonds are reformed and take on the shape of the hair, i.e.; if when wet, the hair is twisted, once dried it remains twisted as the hydrogen bonds are reformed in the twisted pattern. This temporary change in shape also applies when the hair is straightened or curled with heat. The hair reforms to the shape or pattern given by the heating device once cooled. This is a reversible reaction as exposure to moisture or water restores the hair to its native form.

Application of heat to straighten the hair is typically carried out through the use of:

Blow dryer: Blow dryers are used to evaporate water from wet hair as well as straighten it through the blowing of high-speed hot air over the hair. Room temperature air is heated up by the nickel-chromium heating element in the dryer; the hot air is then blown out by a fan onto the hair. Blow dryers can be hooded dryers or hand-held tools.

Hot comb: Combs, made of stainless steel or brass, are heated to about 150-300 ^{o}C by placing them on stoves. The heated comb is then applied to the dry hair from the scalp end or "root" and pulled to the tip of the hair shaft for a straight hair. There are electric combs that are also used to straighten the curled hair.

Flat iron: Flat irons are more modern tools used for hair straightening. They are made of two, smooth metal plates which are electrically heated. Unlike the hot combs whose temperature cannot be inherently determined or adjusted, the flat irons have temperature control knobs which can range from 80-250 °C. The dry hair is parted, placed in between the plates; the plates are pressed together close to the scalp end of the hair shaft and moved along to its tip. To reduce hair damage, flat irons are coated with titanium or ceramic.

Curling iron: This is similar to the flat iron but cylindrical in shape and is used to create straightened, bouncy and curled hair. The dry hair is wrapped around the cylindrical hot iron, left on for about 5-10 seconds, and the iron is gently removed. The hair is allowed to cool and then gently brushed and a finishing spray applied to keep the curls in place.

Alteration with chemical straighteners

This is an irreversible modification to the hair. The pH of the hair shaft is typically 3.67. As the hair is sensitive to pH changes, acidic and alkaline conditions are typically used to alter the curliness of the hair. In acidic condition, the hair cuticle shrinks and hardens whilst it swells and opens up in alkaline conditions (17).

Brazilian keratin/acidic straighteners: The Brazilian keratin straightening is a relatively new method of hair straightening that originated in Brazil in 2003 and has now gained much popularity around the world as a straightening technique that eliminates frizz, with longer staying duration and is used on all hair types (18). The procedure is renowned for making naturally curly hair more manageable, straightening and smoothening naturally wavy hair, as well as improving lustre of the hair. It is also referred to as Brazilian blow out, keratin cure, keratin smoothening, hair botox and Brazilian keratin treatment. This semi-permanent hair straightening method is thought to cause less damage to the hair compared to alkaline-based relaxers or even direct thermal modifications and can be applied on the hair that has been dyed, bleached or relaxed.

Following the washing of the hair which opens up the hair cuticles, a serum which contains formaldehyde (or methylene glycol) and hydrolysed keratin is applied to all sections of the hair with a comb and sealed-in by the application of heat, either through the use of a flat iron or a blow dryer. A period of 48-72 hours is given to allow the chemicals set before the hair is washed with a shampoo formulated for keratin-treated hair. This process does not disrupt the disulphide bonds; however, the initial wash with water changes the hydrogen bonds in the hair's keratin thereby reshaping the hair. In the hair cortex, the amino acids in the hydrolysed keratin are then cross-linked to this newly reshaped keratin of the natural hair by formaldehyde, resulting in a hardened, water-resistant layer on the hair shaft with an increased shine (Figure 5.8) (19).

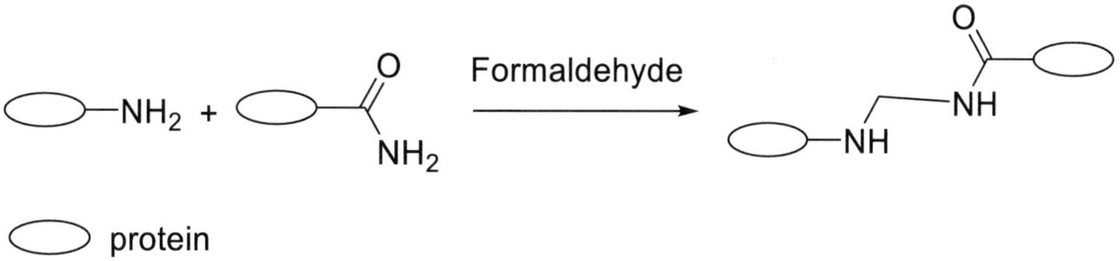

Figure 5.8: Crosslinking by formaldehyde in Brazilian keratin straightening. Formaldehyde molecules diffuse into the hair and cross-links hydrolysed keratin with natural keratin in the hair

Application of heat speeds up this reaction and seals-in the added keratin. Depending on the product used, the straightened hair typically lasts from about 6 weeks to 6 months. As additional keratin is added to the hair, this procedure is thought to strengthen the hair and to make it less prone to damage; however, the release of formaldehyde gas, a carcinogen, whilst in use (see chapter 23) generates concern for the use of this technique. As the concentration of formaldehyde in these products exceeds the accepted limit of 0.2% in cosmetics, some countries such as Canada have banned its use. However, it is in use in many other countries such as the United States of America where consumers are made aware of its potential risks and salon owners are required to ensure adequate ventilation and monitor the concentration of formaldehyde in the air whilst using the products (20,21).

In recent years, there has an been an introduction into the market of non-formaldehyde containing products which in addition to hydrolysed keratin contain glyoxylic acid derivatives such as glyoxyloyl keratin amino-acids, glyoxyloyl carbocysteine and silicone derivatives. These so-called acidic straighteners are recommended to have a minimum pH of 2 (22). It should, however, be noted that glycoxylic acid derivatives also release formaldehyde when heated, thereby constituting a health hazard to salon owners or professional hairdressers following prolonged exposure. Imine and hemiacetal are two products formed in the hair shaft following the reaction of the hair's amino acids with the aldehydes present in glyoxylic acid and formaldehyde (23).

Relaxers/alkaline straighteners

Chemical relaxers are reducing agents with high alkalinity. Chemical relaxation of the hair, using relaxers, is also referred to as lanthionization. It is an irreversible reaction which alters the keratin molecules that comprise the disulphide bonds, weak Van der Waals forces, hydrogen bonds and ionic bonds. When the relaxer is applied to the hair, as a result of its high pH, the hair swells, opening up the cuticle scales to allow penetration of the alkaline agent into the endocuticle and cortex. In the cortex, the hydroxide ions extract acidic alpha protons from cysteine leading to the elimination of the disulphide bonds of keratin's cysteine, (-CH_2-S-S-CH_2-), which is then substituted with lanthionine that has only one sulphur bond (-CH_2-S-CH_2-) (Figure 5.9).

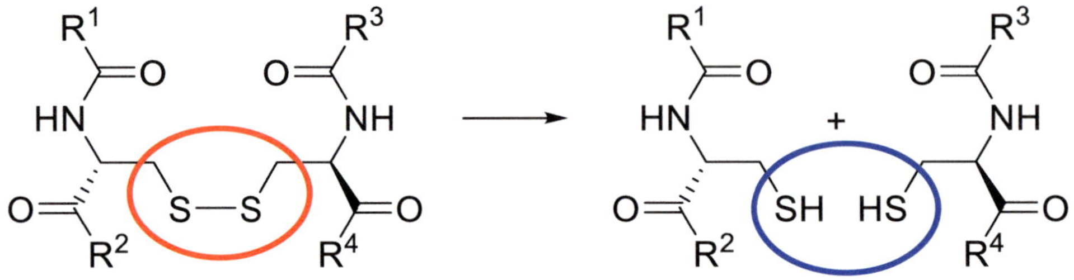

Figure 5.9: Chemical equation showing the process of lanthionization or chemical relaxing.

The disulphide bonds (in red circle) of keratin's cysteine are substituted with lanthionine which has only one sulphur bond (blue circle) following application of relaxer.

The continuous breaking of the disulphide bonds 'relaxes' the curly hair, giving a permanent straight structure. Relaxers are essentially hydroxides of sodium, lithium, guanidine and potassium. Ammonium thioglycolate is also used, although, it has milder effect than the hydroxides. Relaxers are generally classified as lye relaxers and non-lye relaxers depending on the active ingredient. There are also thio-relaxers which are mildly alkaline.

Lye relaxers: Lye relaxers are primarily made of sodium hydroxide. They typically have a pH 13-14 and are fast-acting. Their high alkalinity accounts for their irritating and corrosive nature, hence, they can cause burns on the scalp if application to the hair is poorly done. As they do not leave mineral deposits that prevent absorption of moisture, they are renowned for being moisture-friendly to the hair. When labelled 'base', petrolatum is expected to be applied to the scalp before the relaxer is applied to the hair, whereas no prior use of petrolatum is required for a 'no base' product which contains a lower lye concentration. Notwithstanding, persons with sensitive scalp may still need the prior application of petrolatum when using a 'no base' product. A lye relaxer is stable and does not require mixing with some other agents. The relaxer cream is applied directly to the hair as it is. During application, personal protective equipment such as gloves and other protective clothing should be worn. Sodium hydroxide is also an ingredient of chemical depilatories, thus, 'over relaxing' of the hair can 'dissolve' the hair as seen with the chemical depilatories.

Non-lye relaxers: These relaxers, which are thought to be safer than the lye relaxers, are hydroxides of guanidine, potassium or lithium. They have a pH of 11-13. They have a less burning effect on the scalp; hence, they are more suitable for people with a sensitive scalp. Many a people tend to leave them on the hair for a longer time than recommended by the manufacturer, which leads to breakage of more disulphide bonds, increasing the fragility of the hair and proclivity to breakage. Non-lye relaxers take a longer time to straighten the hair and leave the hair a bit dryer and more brittle as a result of mineral deposits such as calcium, hence, the need for the application of shampoos that contain chelating agents to remove these deposits and, conditioners, to improve the hydration of the hair shaft.

Non-lye relaxer formulations, whose main ingredient is guanidine hydroxide, are typically packaged in two parts. One part, made of a viscous cream base (oil-in-water emulsion), that contains calcium hydroxide; and the second component, the activator, that contains an aqueous solution of guanidine carbonate. The ratio of component one to component two is typically 7:3. Just before use, both components are mixed, providing in a chemical reaction that results in the formation of guanidine hydroxide (Figure 5.10). As the consistencies of the cream and activator are different, mixing both components can be somewhat difficult and can take up to 5 minutes to make a homogeneous mixture. A colouring agent is sometimes added to the activator to serve as a visual guide that indicates homogeneity of the mixing process. If inappropriate amount of either of the two components is used or if they are improperly mixed, the strength of guanidine hydroxide produced will vary; and can either lead to overly or poorly relaxed hair. Guanidine hydroxide is not stable in aqueous solutions for a long period; hence, the relaxer is prepared fresh prior to use and should be used up within a day.

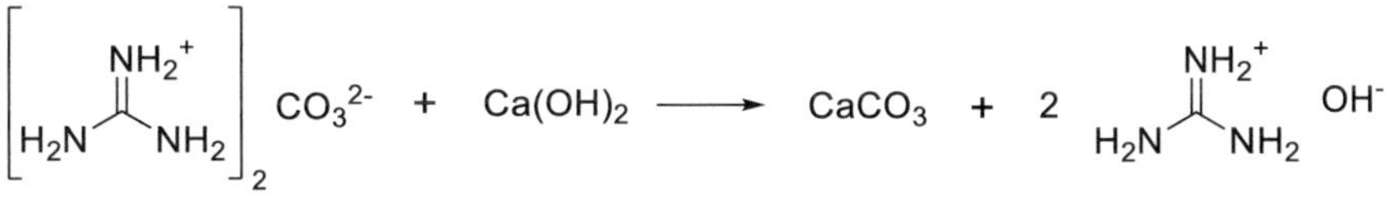

Guanidine carbonate **Calcium hydroxide** **Guanidine hydroxide**

Figure 5.10: Chemistry of non-lye relaxers. Mixing of the two components of the relaxers which are guanidine carbonate and calcium hydroxide produces guanidine hydroxide.

Before the application of relaxers, an assessment of the strength and texture of the hair is made, to determine the appropriate type of relaxer to use. The process of relaxing should be carried out within the stipulated time to avoid 'melting' the hair or damage to the scalp. Upon application, the straightening of the hair becomes visible and, once the desired straightness is achieved, the relaxer must be thoroughly washed off immediately using a neutralizing shampoo, which is typically used on the hair for up to three times to remove all traces of the relaxer. Some shampoos have pH-sensitive colour indicator which changes colour in the presence of the relaxer. The neutralisation process is aimed at rebuilding the hair bonds in a straightened form, closing the cuticle and restoring the pH of the hair. Following shampooing, a rinse-off conditioner is applied to the wet hair, rinsed out and styled to the client's preference. New hair growth is touched-up every 8-12 weeks, on the average. Relaxers should only be applied to the new hair growth, as application to the already 'relaxed hair' predisposes the shaft to damage. As this process is irreversible, straightened hair has to be cut off should a person no longer desire it.

Texturiser

Texturisers are alkaline creams and are similar to relaxers as they are made of guanidine hydroxide and ammonium thioglycolate. However, they are milder than the respective relaxers as they contain lower concentrations of the chemicals. Although texturisers still permanently modify the hair, they maintain some of the natural curls of the hair whilst smoothening and de-frizzing the curls, unlike the relaxers that straighten the entire hair shaft. They cause minimal damage as they are not left to stay for too long on the hair unlike the relaxers. Texturisers loosen the natural curls and the strength of the hair is close to the natural as less disulphide bonds are broken. The hair often feels dry after treatment, hence, the need for a hydrating conditioner.

Although texturisers are used by the female folks, men also use them to create bouncy curls or to give wave-like, sleek and neat effects. Texturisers are marketed to improve the manageability of very thick and coarse hair, however, if left on the hair for too long, the hair becomes straightened as obtained with the relaxers. As it is thought to be milder than relaxers, it is marketed as a safer or more natural alternative. The cream is left on the hair for about 5-10 minutes. Application on pre-texturised hair results in straightening; therefore, texturisers are preferably used on short curly hair for consistency.

Permanent waving/jerry curls

The black African-type hair has natural curly pattern, but its texture makes it challenging to manage. The need for an easy-to-handle hairstyle promoted styles like the jerry curls. Also known as a perm, permanent waving is the process of imparting a stable bending configuration to the hair by two stages of reduction and oxidation. This bond exchange reaction is called sulphydryl/disulphide interchange (SH/SS) (24).

Thioglycolic acid, usually in its salt form as ammonium thioglycolate or monoethanolamine thioglycolate, is used to initiate the process. Under high pH or alkaline conditions (pH 9.2-9.5) the hair cuticle opens up to allow penetration of the thioglycolate which reacts with the cysteine molecules of keratin in the hair cortex, breaking the disulphide bonds to form two cysteine molecules. This reduction reaction gives rise to a new configuration of the hair. A preferred curling device, e.g., curl rods, is then appended on the new hair structure whilst molecular reorganisation takes place in the cuticle and cortex. The thioglycolate is rinsed off and an oxidizing agent, such as hydrogen peroxide, is applied to realign the disulphide bond in its new curly conformation. The shape and size of the resulting curls is determined by the curling device employed before the oxidation process (Figure 5.11).

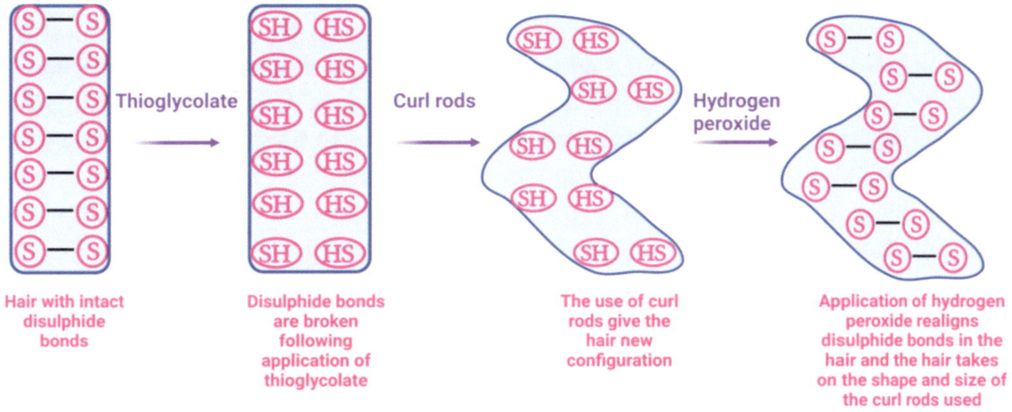

Figure 5.11: Process of permanent waving

Although heating may not be required, the reaction can be hastened by the application of heat (25). Glyceryl monothioglycolate and bisulphites are also used in permanent wave formulations.

Trained personnel are required to carry out the perm procedure as it is a lengthy process and requires expertise to minimize hair damage or possible hair loss. Perms are required to be carried out on virgin or fully natural hair as relaxed or coloured hair increases chances of damage to the hair. The thioglycolate cream is applied to all the hair, from the "roots" to the tips; the shape of the hair begins to change, as the disulphide bonds break, to acquire a straightened form. Once the desired straightening is achieved, the cream is thoroughly rinsed out with water and the hair is sectioned and rolled on curl rods. A fixing lotion, which is a weaker ammonium thioglycolate solution, is applied to the hair on the curl rods to enhance the hair taking the shape of the curl rods and to make it softer. The ammonium thioglycolate is rinsed out and a neutraliser, made of hydrogen peroxide, is applied to reform the disulphide bonds and fix the hair in its new shape.

Hair dyes

The natural colour of the hair is attributed to the amount of melanin in its cortex and medulla. Melanin is formed by the melanocytes, the pigment-producing cells. Melanocytes produce pheomelanin and eumelanin. The type, quantity and size of these pigments determine the hair colour. Pheomelanin granules, which are small, partly oval and partly rod-shaped, produce colours that vary from blond to red, whilst eumelanin granules, which are spherical or ovoid, with sharply defined edges and uniform shape, produce pigments that range from reddish brown to black (Figure 5.12). Natural hair colour comprises a varying mixture and different concentrations of pheomelanin and eumelanin, with different sizes of the granules. Dark hair is predominantly eumelanin whilst red hair has high levels of pheomelanin. In addition to its role in determining hair colour, melanin also plays a role in protecting the hair against UV rays and photobleaching. Eumelanin has a higher photostability compared to pheomelanin, making dark hair more resistant to the effect of UV rays and decay (26).

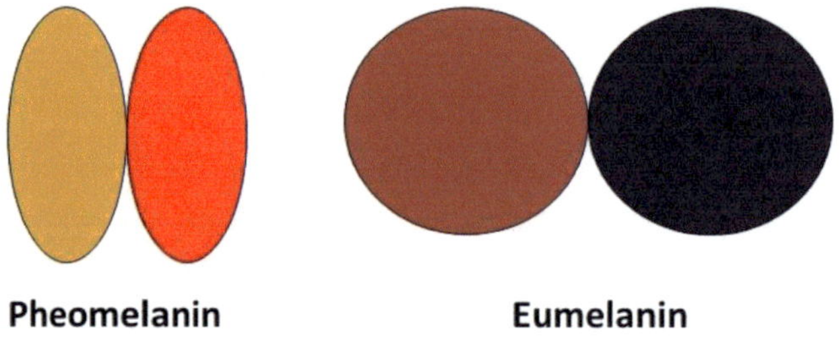

Figure 5.12: The shapes and colours of pheomelanin and eumelanin

The colour of the hair tends to change as one grows in age. Greying of the hair is an irreversible and gradual process which mostly results from declining function of the melanocytes. The hair has less melanin; hence, it becomes white or silver-like as it grows. Aside from ageing, other factors such as stress, ill-health, genetics, reactions to medications, sun-bleaching, chemical products and nutrient deficiencies also result in the greying and other changes to the colour of the hair (27).

Changing the colour of the hair is a common practice with both men and women, either to cover grey hair or to make the appearance of the hair more fashionable or acceptable. For a dye to be used on the human hair, the following criteria have to be satisfied:

- Ratio of the volume of wet hair dyeing formulation to the weight of hair should be 1-2:1
- Dyeing must not distort the natural texture or gloss of the hair

- The hair must not be dyed above a temperature of 40 °C
- Dyeing time must not exceed 40 minutes
- Dyeing must not stain the scalp
- The dye must be stable to perspiration, chlorinated water, light, air, friction and other hair treatments
- The process of dyeing must be safe (28)

Hair colouring products can be classified based on the origin or the degree of permanence of the dyes.

Origin of dyes

Natural/vegetable hair dyes: These dyes are obtained from plants such as henna, cinchona, logwood, chamomile, brazilwood and nutgall. The colour range of natural dyes is limited and the intensity at each application varies. They are generally non-toxic.

Synthetic dyes: Unlike natural dyes, synthetic dyes are synthesised using different chemicals and reactions to produce a wide variety of colours. Upon application of synthetic dyes to the hair, the resulting colour is more predictable than for natural dyes.

Mineral or metallic dyes: Mineral dyes are derived from the salts of lead, silver and bismuth. They can only darken hair with a limited range of colours between brown and black. The colour produced after the application of mineral dyes to the hair can be unpredictable and poor. These inexpensive dyes are deemed to be safe, thus, they can be applied at home. They gradually change the colour of the hair as the metal particles interact with the cysteine residues to form metal sulphides which slowly accumulate on the hair shaft (29). These dyes are potentially toxic and can not be used with hydrogen peroxide.

Degree of permanence of dyes

Temporary dyes: These are also referred to as colour rinses and they have large pigment molecules which are unable to penetrate the hair cuticle but are adsorbed to the hair shaft. However, if applied on chemically treated hair, temporary dyes can penetrate the hair shaft as the cuticle is more porous; hence, they tend to have longer lasting effects on such chemically treated hair. They are synthetic, textile acidic dyes such as anthraquinone, benzoquinoneimine, azo dyes and triphenylmethane, which are water soluble and are used to add colour highlights or to temporarily remove unwanted tones or cover up grey hair. They are easily removed via shampooing. Temporary dyes are formulated as a mousse, shampoo, conditioner, spray or gel. They are harmless to the scalp and hair, although they can easily stain the scalp or clothing when the hair is wet.

Semi-permanent dyes: Natural or synthetic dyes such as henna or non-ionic nitro dyes, respectively, with low molecular weight that can penetrate the hair cortex are classified as semi-permanent dyes. The ability to diffuse in but not to firmly bind hair proteins, as well as to diffuse out when the cuticle opens via washing, gives them a more prolonged effect than temporary dyes. Therefore, they tend to last for weeks and are colour-fast for up to 8 shampooing (30). They are used to add highlight and mask grey hair but cannot be used to lighten hair colour. They are typically formulated as shampoos, mousses, and lotions.

Demi-permanent dyes: These dyes are a hybrid of the semi-permanent and permanent dyes. Demi-permanent dyes are formulated with an oxidizing agent such as hydrogen peroxide (2%) and resorcinol, both of which allow dye penetration into the hair shaft but do not reach the cortex (19). They are used to enhance natural hair colour and shine, blending in grey hairs and subtly darkening the hair. They are colour-fast for up to 15 washes. As they do not contain ammonia, they are milder on the hair compared to permanent dyes. They are marketed as shampoos.

Permanent dyes: These dyes are the mostly used dyes with a high degree of versatility. They are employed to lighten or darken the hair. They cannot be washed out and will remain till the hair grows out. Permanent hair colouration is an oxidation reaction that requires three main components. Firstly, primary intermediates (phenyleneamines, ortho- and para- aminophenol); secondly, couplers (such as p-phenylenediamine, resorcinol) which modify the colour produced by the primary intermediates and oxidants; and lastly, an oxidant (hydrogen peroxide) combined with an alkalizing agent (ammonia or ethanolamine) which oxidise the primary intermediate (28). In the first step of acquiring a permanent hair colour, the primary intermediate is oxidized with alkaline hydrogen peroxide. The high alkalinity (pH 9-10) opens the hair cuticle scales and allows the penetration into the hair cortex of other components. In the cortex, the oxidised primary intermediates react with the couplers (Figure 5.13) to produce indo-dyes, which are large molecules that cannot diffuse out even when shampooed (28). The resulting hair colour depends on molecular conformation of the indo-dyes formed, pH, diffusion rates, concentrations and the competing reaction between the various dye precursors inside the hair fibre (28).

Permanent hair dyes are marketed as a two-component kit. One component contains the primary intermediate, ammonia coupler, and is referred to as the dye precursor, and the second contains a stabilized solution of hydrogen peroxide. Both components are mixed prior to use, and applied to the hair "roots", through the hair shafts to the tips. Application time is typically 20-40 minutes, followed by a rinse with water. The hair can be re-dyed every 4-6 weeks to cover new growth. Sulphate-free or milder shampoos are used to wash the permanently dyed hair to minimize colour loss.

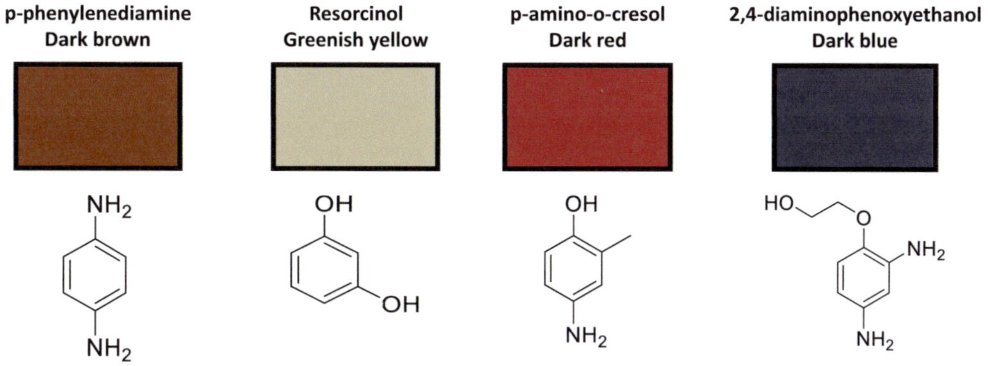

Figure 5.13: Names, colours and chemical structures of some couplers used in permanent hair dyes

The chemical reaction between different components of permanent hair dying procedure is highlighted in Figure 5.14.

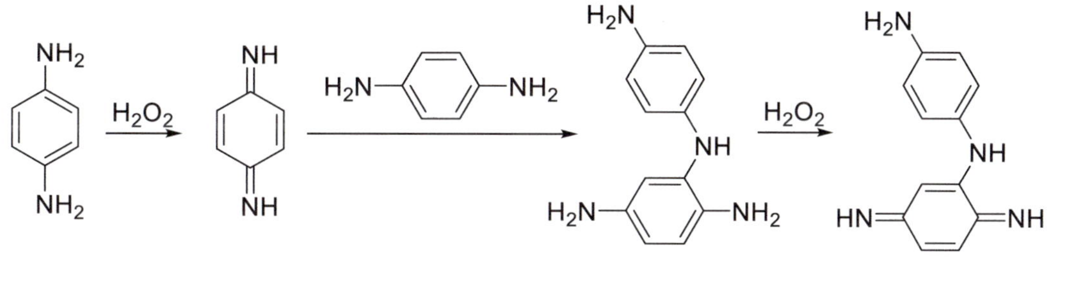

i ii iii iv

Figure 5.14: Chemistry of permanent hair dying process. 1,4-phenylenediamine(i) is oxidised by hydrogen peroxide (H_2O_2) to form cyclohexa-2,5-diene-1,4-diimine (ii). Both (i) and (ii) then react to form N^2-(4-aminophenyl)benzene-1,2,4-triamine (iii) and N^1-(3,6-diiminocyclohexa-1,4-dien-1-yl)benzene-1,4-diamine (iv)

The differences between temporary, semi-permanent, demi-permanent and permanent hair dyes are highlighted in Table 5.1.

Table 5.1: Differences between temporary, semi-permanent, demi-permanent and permanent hair dyes

	Temporary	Semi-permanent	Demi-permanent	Permanent
Dyes	Textile acidic dyes	Ionic/non-ionic dyes	Oxidation dyes	Oxidation dyes
Formulation	mousses, shampoos, conditioners, sprays and gels	shampoos, mousses, and lotions	Shampoos	Two-component kit
Method of application	Applied on clean hair. Mousses, sprays, gels are left on hair whilst shampoo-like products are rinsed off after application	Applied like shampoo and left for 20-30 minutes before rinsing out with water	Applied like shampoo, left on for 20-30 minutes and washed off with water	The two components of the kit are mixed prior to use, applied on hair (preferably dirty) for up to 40 minutes before rinsing out with water
Chemistry/reaction	No chemical reaction	No chemical reaction	Requires hydrogen peroxide (2%) under non-alkaline conditions; oxidation reaction	Carried out under alkaline conditions; requires hydrogen peroxide (6%); oxidation reaction
Hair penetration	Adsorbed on the cuticle	Partially penetrates the hair shaft	Partially penetrates the hair shaft	Penetrates into cortex where chemical reaction takes place
Hair damage	Harmless to hair	May cause damage	May cause damage to the hair as hair cuticle integrity is compromised	May cause damage to the hair as hair cuticle integrity is compromised
Colour fastness/duration	Colour is durable for few days. Fades off after one shampooing	Colour is durable for weeks. Up to 8 shampooing.	Colour is durable for weeks. Up to 15 shampooing	Indefinite duration
Safety	Safe and seldom cause irritation. Can stain fabrics	May cause contact dermatitis	May cause contact dermatitis	May cause contact dermatitis
Reapplication time	As often as required	Every week	6-8 weeks	6-8 weeks

Hair bleaching

Unlike the process of dyeing, where dyes are deposited on/in the hair shaft, bleaching is the partial or complete de-colouring of the natural hair. Bleaching involves the oxidation of melanin pigments in the hair cortex by hydrogen peroxide (up to 12%) in the presence of alkaline agents such as ammonia or monoethanolamine. The following steps are the basics of the bleaching process:

1. Opening of the scales of the hair cuticle;
2. Diffusion of hydrogen peroxide into the hair cortex to reach melanosomes which are organelles that contain melanin;
3. Rupture of the cell membrane of the melanosomes and solubilisation of melanin;
4. Oxidation of melanin (31)

Aside from raising the pH of the hair which allows the hair fibre to swell for the diffusion of the oxidant, the alkalinity of ammonia is also important for the rupturing of the membranes of the melanosomes. In addition, ammonia also plays a role in the deprotonation of hydrogen peroxide and generation of perhydroxyl anion which also plays a role in the oxidation of melanin (31). Bleaching also erodes the hair of the 18-MEA hydrophobic barrier lowering the isoelectric point of the hair (32).

Before bleaching the hair, it is important to consult a colourist who will perform detailed hair and scalp analysis to determine if it is safe to bleach the hair. Bleaching products are supplied in kits that contain hydrogen peroxide solution and an alkali-containing cream, both of which has to be mixed prior to use. The resulting mixture is applied to dry and dirty hair as the sebum from dirty hair tends to protect the scalp from potential irritation that may arise from the product. The hair is sectioned, the mixture is applied firstly to the tip and then mid-length of the shaft before application to the "roots" as the "roots" are processed more rapidly due to their close proximity to the scalp which emits natural body heat. Once the mixture has covered the entire hair, the hair is covered with a plastic cap for a processing period which can be up to 45 minutes. During the bleaching process, there is the dissolution of melanin which is sometimes seen as a change in colour from black to brown, characterised by the breaking of the bonds which maintain the pigment particles. This is then followed by the breaking of the polymeric structure of melanin (30). The degree of bleaching is dependent on the processing time; however, leaving the bleach on the hair for more than an hour may damage the hair. The bleach is completely rinsed out with water, the hair is washed with a sulphate-free, low-pH shampoo which restores the pH of the hair. After bleaching, the colour of the hair can be flat; hence, the use of toners to enhance and brighten the hair. Bleaching may also be employed along with the use of permanent dyes, if lighter shades are desired.

Dark hair, which has more eumelanin, takes a longer time to bleach, whilst red hair that has more pheomelanin is more difficult to bleach than brown (33). In bleaching the dark hair, various stages of colour changes take place; black – brown – red – orange – yellow – pale yellow – white (19).

Hair styles for the black African tightly-curled (kinky) hair

Tightly-curled hair (Figure 5.15), which is peculiar to the black or dark-skinned race of African descent, is not completely amenable to the routine styling of the other types of hair found among the Caucasians and the Asians, in particular. Being tightly curled and knotted along its length, make the hair difficult to comb leading to damages such as breakage, hair loss and split ends.

Figure 5.15: The African curly/kinky hair type

Figure 5.16: Natural kinky hair dyed to golden blond with new hair growth. The hair was straightened by blow-drying and made into cornrows

The tight curls also reduce thorough lubrication by secretions of the sebaceous glands, causing dryness. While chemical treatment can reduce these shortcomings to a great extent, the person that has chosen to wear the hair in its natural state has to pay special attention to the care and grooming of the hair as well as its styling.

Some of the traditional ways by which the natural hair is styled include wearing the hair short which requires frequent combing within a day, plaiting with specialized threads which tend to temporarily stretch the hair, as well as braiding and weaving into "corn" rows. Some individuals also choose to dye their natural hair before styling it (Figure 5.16). While these forms of hairdressing and styling are still embraced by some individuals, some of the other methods by which the hair is worn include dreadlocks and the use of wigs, hair extensions and weaves.

Dreadlocks

Dreadlocks are also referred to as dreads, locs or locks. Any type of hair, when left uncombed, unbrushed or unmanaged in any form, for a long period of time, will become matted into locks of various sizes, shapes and lengths. This is the case with persons, mostly males, who for religious purposes, have pledged not to cut nor comb their hair; or are forbidden, due to vows made on their behalf by their parents, not to cut or comb their hair until a specified age. The Rastafarian movement, for instance, wear dreads for religious reasons and as a form of identity. The appearance of these locks, which could reach the ankles in length, created a semblance of fear of the Rastafarians in people initially, hence, the name dreadlocks. Some individuals are also born with naturally matted hair or dreadlocks. This condition, referred to as plica polonica, is characterized by the irreversible twisting and matting of the hair leading to the formation of a compact mass. These individuals are often referred to as 'Dada' and 'Ezenwa' in the Yoruba and Igbo tribes of Nigeria respectively. Plica polonica is also endemic in Poland (34). The aetiology of plica polonica is not clear however it is believed to be hereditary. Dreadlocks are now fashionable, having become a deliberate hairstyle that has its techniques for formation and maintenance (Figure 5.17). In order to keep locks in place, special gels and waxes are applied on them along with the use of scalp grooming products.

Sister/brother locks

A special looped pin, developed and patented by Dr. JoAnne Cornwell of the University San Diego, in 1993, was created especially for locking the hair of the African women, such that the locks are thinner than the normal dreadlocks and are loosely twisted to enable the hair to be styled (Figure 5.18). Such locks are termed brother locks when worn by men.

Figure 5.17: Fashionable dreadlocks

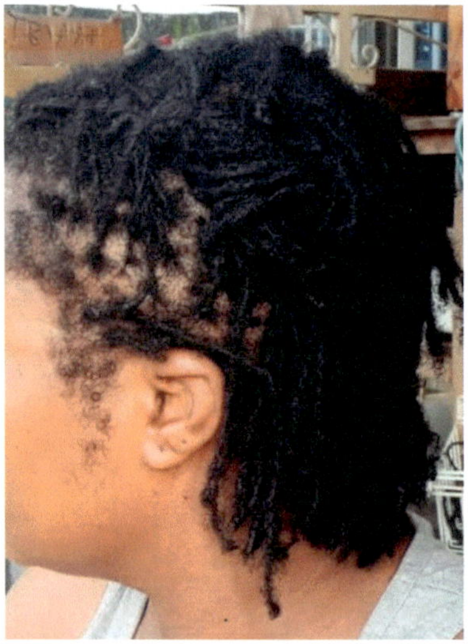

Figure 5.18: Sister locks

Methods of locks formation: There are different types of methods by which locks are formed.

Freeform method: These are formed by simply leaving the hair uncombed or unbrushed; however, the locks take a long time, months or years, to form and lack uniformity in size, shape and length.

Twisting/palm rolling method: The hair is parted into small sections (tresses) and twisted with the fingers or rolled on the palms.

Back-combing method: A comb, with metal bristles, is used to comb the hair backwards from the tip down to the scalp several times and the sections twisted with the fingers or palm-rolled.

Twist and rip method: A parted section of the hair, preferably held with a rubber band at the base, is slightly twisted at the base, then parted into two which are then twisted together, through the entire length of the hair, pulling the two portions apart tightly, intermittently during the process.

Crochet method: This involves the use of a crochet or a latch pin to create locks. Locticians are well trained in this technique.

Interlocking, latch-hooking/root-flicking method: A locking tool is used to twist, especially new hair growth, at the base of an existing lock, moving the tip of the lock through the undergrowth in specific directions.

Two-strand twist method: Two parted sections of the natural hair are twisted from the base to the tips and allowed to grow. As the hair grows, the crotchet method is then applied to the pre-existing twisted strand to create locks.

Maintenance of locks: Locks are to be washed regularly and conditioned, preferably every two to three weeks. The hair should be properly dried after washing, to prevent damp locks that can encourage mould growth. New hair growth is also to be re-locked regularly to keep the hair looking neat and well-kept. Long and heavy locks pull on the hair roots and are likely to cause loss of frontal line hair leading to traction alopecia.

Wigs, hair attachments, weaves and extensions

The use of hair extensions or wigs is common among Africans as with other races. However, the use of attachments/extensions for hair braiding is peculiar to the black African women (Figure 5.19).

The extension or wigs are made from human hair, that is mainly provided by Brazilian and Asian women who purposely grow their hairs, have them harvested, treated and prepared as wigs, attachments and extensions; or from synthetic fibres, such as acrylics, polyesters or nylon which, with the advancement in technology, look and feel like the natural hair. An example is kanekalon hair which is of a high quality, has a human-like texture, and moves more like natural hair than the other synthetics that are cheaper and are more plastic to touch. They are available in different designs, styles, lengths and colours (Figure 5.20).

Figure 5.19: Braiding with hair extensions

Figure 5.20: Diverse styling of wigs

The main advantages of the human hair wigs, attachments and extensions are that these can be easily washed over and over again, heat-dried and styled regularly as desired, while the synthetics come with fixed styles that cannot be changed and cannot be subjected to any form of heat treatment. Heat-friendly synthetic hair, however, can withstand heat treatment to some extent such as the use of boiling water and heated flat iron for hair curling, as well as hot-air blowing. The synthetic hair is more popularly used because it is more affordable than the human hair, although it is not as durable.

Wigs are worn to cover the entire head while hair weaves and extensions are sewn, glued or clipped on the user's hair. Hair attachments are used when the user's hair is being braided, to give fuller braids and to enhance the appearance of the desired styles. Hair damage, especially loss of hair along the hair line, referred to as traction alopecia, is common with hair-braiding when the hair is tightly pulled during the process or when the braids are very long causing a pull on the frontal hair. Tightly fitted extensions and weaves may also cause traction alopecia. Infections can occur when the scalp is scarred during the process of braiding or attaching the hair accessories, more so, since the hair is not washed frequently.

Hair damage

The hair shaft is made of dead cells and, it is, therefore, incapable of the self-repair that is seen in living cells of the body; hence, once damaged, it cannot self-renew. The strength of the hair shaft is associated with the distribution and quantity of cysteine-rich proteins and disulphide bonds, as well as the amount of water in each fibre. The disulphide bonds are key in the stabilization of the keratin structure. The hair is also made of a lipid layer of 18-methyl eicosanoic acid (18-MEA) which plays a key role in its integrity and manageability as well as protection. Procedures that reduce the hydrophobicity and break the disulphide bonds increase the proclivity of the hair to damage.

Wet unperturbed natural hair can stretch up to 30% of its original length. When stretched between 30-70%, there are irreversible changes and stretching up to 80% causes fracture (19). Stretching of the hair can result in splits or cracks in the cuticle as well as damage to the cortex.

Hair damage is visible as split ends and frizz. The hair that is frequently treated with oxidation dyes, peroxide-persulfate, sunbathing or hot irons has been shown to exhibit a higher occurrence of, and most severe splits (35). The African kinky hair, due to its morphology, is the most prone to damage compared to the Asian or Caucasian hair. The causes of hair damage can be broadly divided into physical/mechanical, thermal, UV and chemical causes.

Hair damage by mechanical trauma

Mechanical trauma to the hair is a result of excessive pull and friction on the hair. Daily grooming such as combing or brushing of the hair harshly exposes the cuticle to stress which gradually wears out. For instance, harsh combing to remove tangles results in the falling of the hair which is seen as an increase in the amount of hair on the comb. Combing wet hair has more tendencies to stretch brittle hair to its breaking point, as wet hair has a higher combing friction (36). Tight hairdos ("corn"rows, braids, ponytails, attachment of extensions and weaves) can exert a continual force of up to 100 g on the hair follicles which can result in alopecia, especially around the frontal part of the hair and the hairline above the ears (37). The use of hair accessories that are too tightly fitted, or the rubbing of the hair on headrests/pillows, also cause mechanical trauma. This physical trauma to the hair can lead to split ends, frizz and breakage as the cuticle becomes roughened. Traction alopecia, which affects about a third of women of African descent, is a common form of hair loss associated with mechanical trauma (38). Avoiding tight hairdos, use of silk pillowcases, and gentle hair combing are some few ways to prevent mechanical trauma to the hair.

Hair damage by ultraviolet radiation

Ultraviolet radiation (UV) damages the hair fibre and exposure to the sun causes dryness, lustre and colour changes, brittleness, as well as stiffness of the hair (39). At low wavelengths, the melanin in the hair is photoprotective as it absorbs and filters radiation which it dissipates in form of heat (39). The extensive organisation of conjugate carbonyl groups and double bonds in melanin captures the radiation, immobilises the free radicals formed and prevents the transport of the free radicals into the keratin matrix. In their bid to protect hair proteins from the deleterious effects of UV, the melanin pigments are bleached or degraded. Colour changes to the hair are attributed to the effect of UVA whilst exposure to UVB leads to loss of hair protein (39). At wavelengths of 254-400 nm, the hair protein is degraded (39). The hair that has been chemically altered is more susceptible to UV-damage and this is best prevented by shielding the hair, using scarfs, hats or umbrellas, staying away from the sun at its peak, and using sunscreens.

Hair damage by heat

Exposure of the hair to excessive heat from blow dryers, flat and curling irons are the predominant causes of heat-induced hair damage. The detrimental effects of hair damage by heat include scarring alopecia, bubble hair, dry and brittle hair, poor lustre, loss of natural curls, as well as hair breakage and loss. Aside from temperature intensity, heating duration, frequency of heating, and the moisture content of the hair, the time of heating also plays a role in hair damage by heat. Layers of the hair cuticle and the cell membrane complex are principally susceptible to heat. Leaving the hair to dry by itself at ambient temperature after washing is more protective to the hair surface. The propensity to hair damage by heat is directly proportional to the temperature intensity employed (40). Hair dryers used for daily grooming are usually at temperatures of 80-90 ^{0}C. Repeated cycles of washing and blow-drying can lead to several cracks on the cuticles (40). The hair burns between the temperatures of 228-240 ^{0}C (41). Therefore, exposing the hair to temperatures that exceed 200 ^{0}C using flat or curl irons is detrimental. The moisture content of the hair also plays a role in its proclivity to damage. At normal humidity, there is about 10-15% of water in the hair. Subjecting the hair to temperatures higher than the boiling point of water (100 ^{0}C) can lead to the formation of steam bubbles (bubble hair) which hydrolyses keratin and fractures the hair fibre (42). Direct application of heat to wet hair, such as using the flat or curl iron on wet hair, is more traumatic as the cuticle is opened when wet, exposing the cortex of the hair.

The cuticle of the curly African hair is about one to eight layers thick whilst the straight hair of Caucasians is about six to ten layers thick; thus, the curly African hair is more thermally fragile (17). The ellipsoidal shape and low water content of the afro-hair further add to its high fragility (17). Therefore, caution should be taken when applying heat to the Afro-curly hair. Using a hair dryer at a distance of 15 cm to the hair with continuous motion of the hot air around the hair, has been shown to cause less damage to the hair (40). Also, using flat/curl irons at the lowest temperature possible (<200 °C) to straighten the hair reduces the risk of shaft damage. If the initial temperature used is not effective, then the temperature can be gradually increased. As heat strips the hair of its natural oil, making it dry, it is advised to use heat protectants which act as a barrier between the hot tools and the hair. The use of hot tools everyday should be avoided.

Hair damage by chemical straightening

Chemical treatment of the hair can lead to the loss of lipids on the hair surface which may result in the loss of cohesion between the cuticle cells. Also, the reduction in the levels of cysteine in the hair shaft is associated with greater predisposition to hair fragility (43). Reduced water uptake and retention, susceptibility to breakage, loss of hair mass, reduction in tensile strength of the hair, cuticle irregularities, and colour changes are some of the attributes of the hair that has undergone straightening in acidic/formaldehyde conditions (44,45). The hair shaft that is exposed to acidic straighteners has a higher number of hydrogen ions from the acidic products which has been demonstrated to affect the elasticity of the hair fibre, predisposing it to damage (22). Hair damage is often a result of free radical oxidative treatment that leads to fractures along the cell membrane complex and the medulla, which then results in fibrillated ends and split hairs (35).

Acidic straighteners typically contain formaldehyde and its derivatives. When heat is applied to the hair treated with these products, formaldehyde gas is released. Formaldehyde is associated with allergic contact dermatitis, difficulty in breathing, eye irritation, throat-burning and even cancer. Reports of psoriasiform eczema have been documented with the use of the Brazilian keratin blowout which contains formaldehyde derivatives (45).

The breaking of disulphide bonds during lanthionization increases the fragility of the hair. The treatment of the hair with relaxers reduces the number of cysteine molecules in the hair with a greater loss seen in the hair treated with no-lye relaxers (45). Increase in frizz, hair thinning, split ends (trichoptilosis), scalp desquamation, hair dyschromia and alopecia are some of the features of hair treated with relaxers (45). Scalp burns occur when the relaxer is applied without protecting the scalp with petrolatum or the relaxer is left on the hair for a long period. Recurring scalp burns can predispose scarring and loss of hair.

Hydrogen peroxide, the oxidizing agent used in perm, increases the fragility of the hair, depletes lipids in the cell membrane of the hair fibre making the otherwise hydrophobic hair strands to be more hydrophilic (46).

Hair damage by relaxers can be minimized by reducing the frequency of re-application, and the use of relaxers on only strands that have not been previously treated. In addition, relaxers should not be used together with other hair straighteners and dyes, especially permanent dyes. To avoid scalp burns, about 1 cm should be left between the scalp and the hair when a relaxer is applied.

Hair damage by colouring/decolouring agents

The act of bleaching, and the use of demi-permanent or permanent dyes, alters the natural chemistry of the hair, predisposing it to damage. The high pH of formulations used in enhancing the diffusion of these products into the cortex strips the cuticle of the lipid 18-MEA thereby reducing the hydrophobicity of the hair and making the hair more porous. The reduced hydrophobicity, increased porosity, coupled with the oxidation and weakening of the disulphide bonds, make the hair more brittle (30). The use of products that protect the cuticle can minimize the effects of hair damage caused by dye and bleaching agents. Using relaxers on permanent-dyed or bleached hair should be avoided as the mixture of both further damages the hair, leading to alopecia. Temporary dyes, which adsorb to the hair shaft, are the safest option for relaxed hair. However, demi-permanent dyes, which are formulated with reduced alkalinity, can be used on relaxed hair if a degree of permanence is desired (47).

Hair disorders associated with hair styling and chemical use

As a universal practice mostly in women, hairstyling has long been known to play a role in hair damage. Chronic hair damage is a prerequisite for hair disorders and loss. Normally, up to 100 strands of hair will fall out daily (5). However, effluvium, which is the increased amount of daily hair fall or an obvious alopecia, may be a result of hair damage. Hair disorders associated with styling or the use of cosmetics can be reversed once the underlying cause is disengaged. The use of hair products within the limits specified by the manufacturer as well as astute and appropriate styling techniques which consider the hair type, are practices that minimize hair breakage, disorders and eventual loss. Disorders associated with the use of hair products and styling are highlighted and summarised in Table 5.2.

Table 5.2: Hair disorder associated with hair styling and use of chemicals, their causes, features and prevention

Disorder	Cause	Features	Prevention
Bubble hair deformity	Prolonged exposure of damp hair to temperatures greater than 125 °C for period over one minute	Brittleness, breakage, thinning. Microscopically, bubbles and honeycomb structures are seen in the cortex	Wet hair should not be subjected to prolonged temperatures greater than 125 °C
Trichorrhexis nodosa	Excessive friction, traction, overuse of chemicals	Lack of lustre, dryness, fragility, nodes along the hair shaft	Protecting the hair shaft with oils and conditioners; minimizing and avoiding the use of chemical treatments
Traction alopecia	Repeated and prolonged tension on root of hair follicle through practices such as harsh combing, tight hair dos (cornrows, braids, dreadlocks), use of tight accessories; use of hair glues, weaves and extensions.	Gradual or sudden onset of hair loss along the frontal, temporal and occipital hairline.	Avoid tight hair dos especially in children; braids should be worn not more than 2-3 months; larger diameter of braids; give hair break to recover from stress
Scarring alopecia	Lack of conclusive evidence for cause but it has been associated with traction alopecia. It may also develop secondary to chemical burns from relaxers	Hair breakage, irreversible loss of hair with evidence of follicular damage	Avoid hairstyling practices that are traumatic to the hair

Bubble hair deformity

The formation of air cavity in the hair cortex is described as bubble hair deformity (BHD). It is an acquired hair shaft disorder associated with the protracted exposure (over one minute) of damp hair to temperatures greater than 125 °C, typically from blow dryers or other hot hair styling devices (48). Bubble hair does not occur in dry hair. When the hair is soaked in water, its weight increases by 12-18% (36). The hair retains water when it is wet. High temperatures from heating devices heat up the water in the wet hair shaft, leading to hydrolysis of keratin, air expansion and bubble formation (43). The formation of carbon dioxide following partial decomposition of keratin could also produce the gas seen in the cavity (49). Hair breakage occurs in straight lines and honeycomb structures are seen in the cortex (48). Bubble formations are reported to be a transitional stage to hair combustion as it is accompanied by focal lightening or blackening, curling, fragility and burning smell (50). BHD, which is more common in Caucasian women, is often presented as hair brittleness, breakage and/or thinning (49). Cessation of hair blow-drying at high temperatures and the use of hot styling devices directly on wet hair reverses bubble hair deformity (Table 5.2).

Trichorrhexis nodosa

Trichorrhexis nodosa (TN), also known as paint brush fracture, is characterised by the fragility and presence of nodes along the hair shaft. The hair lacks lustre, appears dry and, in some instances, there is the presence of white spots along the hair shaft. The loss of cuticular cells is thought to be the underlying reason for TN as microscopic examination reveals cuticular cell disruption, breaking of fibres and an appearance likened to that of two paint brushes crushed against each other (51). Although developmental defects and hereditary factors are associated with TN, TN can also be acquired through repeated trauma to the hair shaft. The cumulative effects of excessive shampooing, overuse of chemical (dyes, relaxers, perm) or thermal treatments and excessive pull or traction (brushing, combing) on the hair are some of the causes of TN (51,52). All hair types are prone to TN; however, the Afro curly hair is more susceptible. The curly and kinky nature of the Afro curly hair impairs the distribution of sebum - the hair's natural lubricant-making the hair drier. TN is managed by protecting the hair shaft using hair oils or conditioners which lubricate the hair, minimizing traction, and avoiding or minimizing the use of causative agents (Table 5.2) (51).

Traction alopecia

Traction alopecia (TA) is caused by repeated and prolonged tension on the roots of the hair follicles which damages the follicles and results in hair loss. Practices such as harsh combing, tight hairdos (cornrows, braids, dreadlocks, ponytails), as well as the use of tight/heavy hair accessories predispose to TA. The practice of adding hair accessories such as barrettes and plastic beads on braids of children with African curly hair often adds additional tension to hair and increases the risk of TA in children. Chemically treated hair, which is already weakened, is more prone to TA as it is less resistant to prolonged tension compared to untreated hair (53). The chronic use of weaves with hair weft is also known to result in TA.

This form of alopecia, observed especially at the temporal and frontal hair line, is predominant in women of African descent with about one third of the population affected (54). The asymmetrical shape of the African curly hair follicle creates geometric points of weakness along the hair shaft making the hair more susceptible to traction forces (55). Hair loss is seen in the area where there is tension. TA can be reversed and prevented by discontinuing hairstyles that subject the hair follicles to tension (Table 5.2). However, if the distressing hairstyling continues, TA may progress to irreversible scarring alopecia (56). Applying chemical treatments such as relaxers and dyes, as well as thermal treatment of the hair should be avoided. To manage TA, Haskin and Aguh recommended loosening the braids applied around the hairline, opting for larger diameter of braids and dreadlocks, use of hair extensions for a short period, avoiding hair glues, wearing of braids for not more than three months and giving the hair a styling break to allow it recover from stress (57).

Scarring alopecia

Scarring alopecia (SA) is a hair disorder in which the hair follicles are destroyed and replaced by fibrous scar tissues, consequentially leading to irreversible hair loss. SA is characterised by thinning of the hair in its early stages and a round area featuring smooth and shiny scalp with visible loss of hair in advanced stages (55). Centrifugal cicatricial alopecia (CCA) is a form of scarring alopecia. In CCA, hair loss characteristically begins around the crown or vertex and expands peripherally (centrifugally). There are reports of the development of SA following the use of relaxers; however, no association has been made (45,58). SA may develop secondary to chemical burns from relaxers. Use of hot combs and prolonged history of tight weaves have also been associated with SA. Although there is a lack of conclusive evidence associating SA with hair styling practice, it is frequently advised to avoid chemical and thermal treatments as well as traction styling to prevent further hair loss (55). As hair loss in SA is irreversible, hair transplantation is sometimes explored in persons presenting with this condition (Table 5.2).

Cranial hair prosthesis

Patients or persons who have lost part or the entire hair on their head due to some medical treatments such as chemotherapy; or some medical conditions or diseases such as trichotillomania, alopecia areata, alopecia totalis, hypothyroidism and malnutrition, are often embarrassed by their looks and would prefer to cover these up in a way that makes them have a natural look. Cranial hair prosthesis which comes as custom-made wigs, especially designed and measured to size, for the need of individuals are often used. They differ from the normal fashion wigs as they may not cover the entire head but just the area that is bare of hair and they have similar texture and colour of the remaining hair on the person, except in the case of alopecia totalis when the entire head is bald.

Hair transplant

This is a surgical procedure by which hair is transplanted on the area of the scalp where there are hair loss using hair follicles collected from another area of the patient's head. Chapter 8 of this book has more information on hair transplant.

References

(1) Whiting DA. Male pattern hair loss: current understanding. Int J Dermatol 1998;37(8):561-566.
(2) Buffoli B, Rinaldi F, Labanca M, Sorbellini E, Trink A, Guanziroli E, et al. The human hair: from anatomy to physiology. Int J Dermatol 2014;53(3):331-341.

(3) Loussouarn G, El Rawadi C, Genain G. Diversity of hair growth profiles. Int J Dermatol 2005;44:6-9.

(4) Saint Olive Baque C, Zhou J, Gu W, Collaudin C, Kravtchenko S, Kempf JY, et al. Relationships between hair growth rate and morphological parameters of human straight hair: a same law above ethnical origins? Int J Cosmetic Sci 2012;34(2):111-116.

(5) Murphrey MB, Agarwal S, Zito PM. Anatomy, Hair. StatPearls Treasure Island (FL): StatPearls Publishing LLC; 2022.

(6) Grymowicz M, Rudnicka E, Podfigurna A, Napierala P, Smolarczyk R, Smolarczyk K, et al. Hormonal Effects on Hair Follicles. Int J Mol Sci 2020 Jul 28;21(15):5342. doi: 10.3390/ijms21155342.

(7) York K, Meah N, Bhoyrul B, Sinclair R. A review of the treatment of male pattern hair loss. Expert Opin Pharmacother 2020;21(5):603-612.

(8) Fabbrocini G, Cantelli M, Masarà A, Annunziata MC, Marasca C, Cacciapuoti S. Female pattern hair loss: A clinical, pathophysiologic, and therapeutic review. Int J Womens Dermatol 2018 Jun 19;4(4):203-211.

(9) Desai K, Almeida B, Miteva M. Understanding Hormonal Therapies: Overview for the Dermatologist Focused on Hair. Dermatology 2021;237(5):786-791.

(10) Thom E. Stress and the Hair Growth Cycle: Cortisol-Induced Hair Growth Disruption. J Drugs Dermatol 2016 Aug 1;15(8):1001-1004.

(11) Perfitt, Raoul John Carimbocas, Cicely, Andrea Ruth, inventor. AnonymousDry shampoo composition. . 2016 Nov 3,.

(12) Orafidiya LO, Agbani EO, Abereoje OA, Awe T, Abudu A, Fakoya FA. An investigation into the wound-healing properties of essential oil of Ocimum gratissimum linn. J Wound Care 2003 Oct;12(9):331-334.

(13) Orafidiya LO, Agbani EO, Oyedele AO, Babalola OO, Onayemi O. Original Research Article Preliminary Clinical Tests on Topical Preparations of Ocimum gratissimum Linn Leaf Essential Oil for the Treatment of Acne Vulgaris. Clinical Drug Investigation 2002;22(5):313-319.

(14) Ali B, Al-Wabel NA, Shams S, Ahamad A, Khan SA, Anwar F. Essential oils used in aromatherapy: A systemic review. Asian Pacific Journal of Tropical Biomedicine 2015;5(8):601-611.

(15) al-Sereiti MR, Abu-Amer KM, Sen P. Pharmacology of rosemary (Rosmarinus officinalis Linn.) and its therapeutic potentials. Indian J Exp Biol 1999 Feb;37(2):124-130.

(16) Yoon JI, Al-Reza SM, Kang SC. Hair growth promoting effect of Zizyphus jujuba essential oil. Food and Chemical Toxicology 2010;48(5):1350-1354.

(17) De Sá Dias TC, Baby AR, Kaneko TM, Robles Velasco MV. Relaxing/straightening of Afro-ethnic hair: historical overview. Journal of Cosmetic Dermatology 2007;6(1):2-5.

(18) Weathersby C, McMichael A. Brazilian keratin hair treatment: a review. J Cosmet Dermatol 2013;12(2):144-148.

(19) Gavazzoni Dias MF. Hair cosmetics: an overview. Int J Trichology 2015;7(1):2-15.

(20) U.S Food and Drug Administration. Hair Smoothing Products That Release Formaldehyde When Heated. 2022; Available at: https://www.fda.gov/cosmetics/cosmetic-products/hair-smoothing-products-release-formaldehyde-when-heated. Accessed 29/10/, 2022.

(21) Occupational Safety & Health Administration. Formaldehyde. Available at: https://www.osha.gov/laws-regs/regulations/standardnumber/1910/1910.1048. Accessed 29/10/, 2022.
(22) Goshiyama AM, Dario MF, Lima CRRdC, de Araújo G,Lima Barros, Baby AR, Velasco MVR. Impact of acid straightener's pH value in the hair fiber properties. J Cosmet Dermatol 2020;19(2):508-513.
(23) Boga C, Taddei P, Micheletti G, Ascari F, Ballarin B, Morigi M, et al. Formaldehyde replacement with glyoxylic acid in semipermanent hair straightening: a new and multidisciplinary investigation. Int J Cosmet Sci 2014;36(5):459-470.
(24) Wortmann FJ, Jones C, Davies TJ, Wortmann G. Perm-waved human hair: a thermorheologically complex shape memory composite. Biophys J 2021;120(17):3831-3840.
(25) Barreto TdM, Weffort F, Frattini SC, Martins Pinto G, dos Santos Damasco P, Melo DF. Permanent hair wavings: What dermatologists should know? J Cosmet Dermatol 2021;20(4):1204-1207.
(26) Solano F. Photoprotection and Skin Pigmentation: Melanin-Related Molecules and Some Other New Agents Obtained from Natural Sources. Molecules 2020 Mar 27;25(7):1537. doi: 10.3390/molecules25071537.
(27) Kaur K, Kaur R, Bala I. Therapeutics of premature hair graying: A long journey ahead. J Cosmet Dermatol 2019;18(5):1206-1214.
(28) Morel OJX, Christie RM. Current Trends in the Chemistry of Permanent Hair Dyeing. Chem Rev 2011;111(4):2537-2561.
(29) Johnson DH. Hair and Hair Care. 1st ed.: Routledge; 1997.
(30) Bolduc C, Shapiro J. Hair care products: waving, straightening, conditioning, and coloring. Clin Dermatol 2001;19(4):431-436.
(31) Smith RAW, Garrett B, Naqvi KR, Fülöp A, Godfrey SP, Marsh JM, et al. Mechanistic insights into the bleaching of melanin by alkaline hydrogen peroxide. Free Radical Biology and Medicine 2017;108:110-117.
(32) Dias MFRG, Loures AF, Ekelem C. Hair Cosmetics for the Hair Loss Patient. Indian J Plast Surg 2021 Dec 27;54(4):507-513.
(33) Harrison S, Sinclair R. Hair colouring, permanent styling and hair structure. Journal of Cosmetic Dermatology 2003;2(3-4):180-185.
(34) H19: Plica polonica: a Polish pandemic. Br J Dermatol 2022;187:192-193.
(35) Robbins CR. Morphological, Macromolecular Structure and Hair Growth. In: Robbins CR, editor. Chemical and Physical Behavior of Human Hair Berlin, Heidelberg: Springer Berlin Heidelberg; 2012. p. 1-104.
(36) Sinclair RD. Healthy Hair: What Is it? Journal of Investigative Dermatology Symposium Proceedings 2007;12(2):2-5.
(37) Gummer CL. Cosmetics and hair loss. Clin Exp Dermatol 2002;27(5):418-421.
(38) Khumalo NP, Jessop S, Gumedze F, Ehrlich R. Determinants of marginal traction alopecia in African girls and women. J Am Acad Dermatol 2008;59(3):432-438.
(39) Santos Nogueira AC, Joekes I. Hair color changes and protein damage caused by ultraviolet radiation. Journal of Photochemistry and Photobiology B: Biology 2004;74(2):109-117.

(40) Lee Y, Kim YD, Hyun HJ, Pi LQ, Jin X, Lee WS. Hair shaft damage from heat and drying time of hair dryer. Ann Dermatol 2011 Nov;23(4):455-462.
(41) Kunchi C, Venkateshan KC, Reddy ND, Adusumalli RB. Correlation between Mechanical and Thermal Properties of Human Hair. Int J Trichology 2018;10(5):204-210.
(42) Petrovicova E, Kamath YK. Heat transfer in human hair. Int J Cosmet Sci 2019;41(4):387-390.
(43) Alessandrini A, Starace M, Bruni F, Piraccini BM. Bubble Hair and the Usefulness of Trichoscopy. Dermatol Pract Concept 2020 Oct 26;10(4):e2020081.
(44) Leite MGA, Maia Campos PMBG. Mechanical characterization of curly hair: Influence of the use of nonconventional hair straightening treatments. Skin Res Technol 2017;23(4):539-544.
(45) Hatsbach de Paula JN, Basílio FMA, Mulinari-Brenner FA. Effects of chemical straighteners on the hair shaft and scalp. An Bras Dermatol 2022;97(2):193-203.
(46) Zhang Y, Alsop RJ, Soomro A, Yang FC, Rheinstädter MC. Effect of shampoo, conditioner and permanent waving on the molecular structure of human hair. PeerJ 2015 Oct 1;3:e1296.
(47) Haskin A, Okoye GA, Aguh C. Chemical Modifications of Ethnic Hair. In: Aguh C, Okoye GA, editors. Fundamentals of Ethnic Hair: The Dermatologist's Perspective Cham: Springer International Publishing; 2017. p. 17-29.
(48) GUMMER CL. Bubble hair: a cosmetic abnormality caused by brief, focal heating of damp hair fibres. Br J Dermatol 1994;131(6):901-903.
(49) Li YM, Diaz-Perez J, Obayomi A, Galimberti F, Romanelli P, Tosti A. A review of bubble hair deformity. Int J Dermatol 2022;n/a.
(50) Detwiler SP, Carson JL, Woosley JT, Gambling TM, Briggaman RA. Bubble hair: Case caused by an overheating hair dryer and reproducibility in normal hair with heat. J Am Acad Dermatol 1994;30(1):54-60.
(51) Lawson CN, Hollinger J, Sethi S, Rodney I, Sarkar R, Dlova N, et al. Updates in the understanding and treatments of skin & hair disorders in women of color. International Journal of Women's Dermatology 2017;3(1, Supplement):S21-S37.
(52) Ogunbiyi A, Ogun O, Enechukwu N. Recurrent hair loss resulting from generalized proximal trichorrhexis nodosa in a nigerian female. Int J Trichology 2014 Apr;6(2):83-84.
(53) Khumalo NP, Jessop S, Gumedze F, Ehrlich R. Determinants of marginal traction alopecia in African girls and women. J Am Acad Dermatol 2008;59(3):432-438.
(54) Loussouarn G, El Rawadi C, Genain G. Diversity of hair growth profiles. Int J Dermatol 2005;44:6-9.
(55) Herskovitz I, Miteva M. Central centrifugal cicatricial alopecia: challenges and solutions. Clin Cosmet Investig Dermatol 2016 Aug 17;9:175-181.
(56) Billero V, Miteva M. Traction alopecia: the root of the problem. Clin Cosmet Investig Dermatol 2018 Apr 6;11:149-159.
(57) Haskin A, Aguh C. All hairstyles are not created equal: What the dermatologist needs to know about black hairstyling practices and the risk of traction alopecia (TA). J Am Acad Dermatol 2016;75(3):606-611.
(58) Khumalo NP, Pillay K, Ngwanya RM. Acute 'relaxer'-associated scarring alopecia: a report of five cases. Br J Dermatol 2007;156(6):1394-1396

CHAPTER SIX

Nail cosmetics

Adebola O Ogunbiyi

The desire for nail cosmetics has increased globally. In 2018 the nail cosmetic industry became an \$8.36 billion industry in the United States of America (USA). Globally, the retail market for nail polish increased from \$3 billion in 2007 to \$45 billion in 2012.

Nail cosmetics are products that enhance the appearance of the nails and are generally believed to contribute to a person's overall beauty. The use of nail cosmetics is more common in females, although painting the toenails has recently become fashionable amongst young men. Over the years, the variety of nail cosmetics have increased. They include polishes, hardeners, removers, extensions, artificial nails, and accessories (1, 2).

In this chapter the types the type of nail cosmetics, their uses, and adverse effects will be reviewed.

Historical perspective

Beautification of the nails started with nail colouring, which dates back to ancient Egypt and China. In 5000 BC, the Egyptians used the leaves of the orange henna (*Lawsonia inermis*) to produce semi-permanent stains on the nails. The dried leaves were made into a paste and applied directly on the nail. At the onset, nail colours were associated with social status, with bright colours such as red reserved for the higher socio-economic class. The first true nail polish was developed by the Chinese in 3000 BC; it contained gum Arabic, egg white, gelatine, vegetable dyes, and beeswax. The various dynasties had a characteristic nail polish colour. The Chou Dynasty (600 BC) royalty wore silver and gold nails, while the Ming Dynasty (1300 AD) wore red and black nails (3). In the United States, true nail polish was introduced in 1930 by Charles Revson, who had the idea that the car paint technology could be applied to nails. He first marketed a clear nail polish and then added a variety of pigments when he started the company Revlon, in 1932 (4).

Structure of the nail

The nail plate, which is often referred to as the nail, is a hardened structure made of tough keratin (alpha-keratin), which protects the anterior part of the distal fingers and toes from injury (Figure 6.1). The distal free edge of the nail is useful for picking up items and for scratching the skin and surfaces. The nail plate develops from the nail matrix which is under the proximal nail fold. The top layer of the ventral surface of the proximal nail fold is known as the eponychium which becomes the cuticle as it sheds. The shedding cuticle looks untidy and is usually pushed back or removed during manicure. The cuticle is water-resistant and seals off the area containing the matrix and developing nails, thus, protecting them from invasion by micro-organisms. The nail is sensitive, this is due to the intricate network of nerves situated under the plate. During nail care, in preparation for the application and removal of nail cosmetics, some of the structures in the nail unit get traumatised.

Nail Polish

Nail polish, also known as nail varnish, nail paint and enamel, is applied as a film on the nail plate for beautification, strengthening brittle nails and covering up of nail imperfections. The current formulations of nail polish consist of a film-forming polymer, which is usually nitrocellulose, dissolved in a volatile organic solvent,

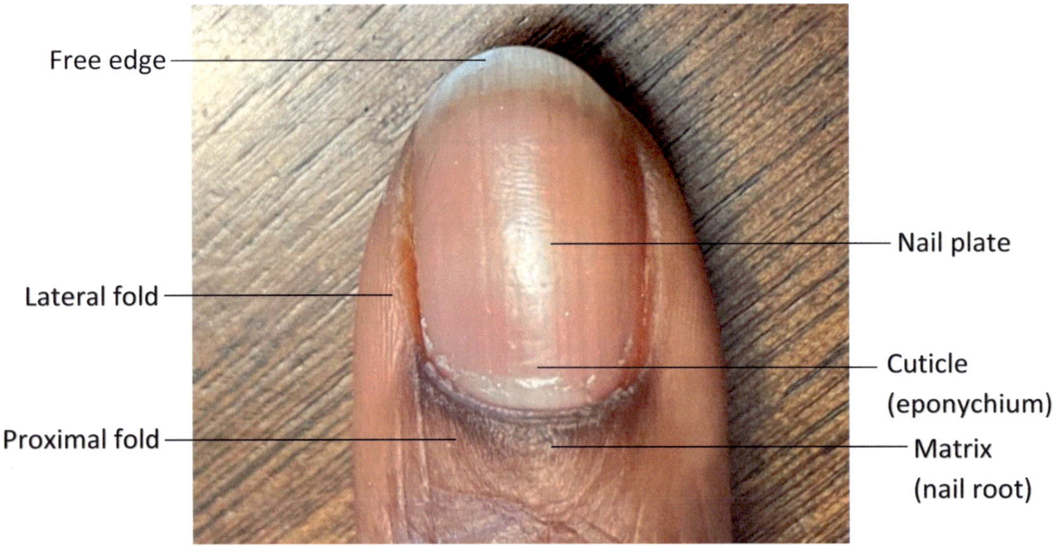

Figure 6.1: Structure of the nail

butyl acetate or ethyl acetate. When the solvent dries, the polymer forms a film on the nail. This basic formulation of the nail polish has multiple components which ensure that the mixture coats the nails smoothly, is flexible, pliable and fluid enough for application.

Most nail polish contain these basic ingredients (4, 5):

Primary film-forming agents: nitrocellulose, methacrylate polymers, and vinyl polymers.

Secondary film forming agents: formaldehyde, p-toluene sulphonamide, polyamide, acrylate, alkyd and vinyl resins. These increase adherence and add resistance to nail polish chipping.

Plasticisers (e.g., dibutyl phthalate) for flexibility, while dibutyl phthalate, dioctyl phthalate, tricresyl phosphate, and camphor keep the nail polish soft and pliable.

Solvents: acetates, ketones, toluene, xylene, and alcohols. Nail polish ingredients are dissolved in a solvent that keeps the polish in a fluid state and dries rapidly when applied to the nails, leaving the coloured film on the nail surface.

Colorants: organic dyes and inorganic pigments – examples of FDA certified colours for nail polish are: (Food, Drug and Cosmetics) FD&C Red No. 4, D&C Yellow No. 7 and External D&C Violet No. 2. Colours used must conform to low heavy metal content standards.

Natural agents: such as guanine, bismuth oxychloride, mica and titanium dioxide are added for enhanced colour, appearance and shine of the nail polish.

Nail polish variants

Technology has led to the development of different types of nail polishes driven by aesthetic requirements.

Photochromic nail polish: The polish contains compounds, such as spiropyrans and spirooxazines, that change structurally when exposed to ultraviolet (UV) rays of the sun and become coloured, thus altering the colour of the nail polish. The technology is similar to that of photochromic lenses. Thus, the colour of polished nails change by the wearer just stepping out into the sun. However, prolonged sun exposure can lead to fading of the nail colour. Some nail polish contain benzophenone which prevents sun induced damage to cosmetics (6).

Thermochromic nail polish: Thermochromic nail polish undergoes a chemical change when there is a change in temperature. The polish contains microcapsules of leuco dyes, a low melting point solvent and an acid. When the temperature is low enough, the dye and the acid molecules are in close proximity, allowing transfer of hydrogen atoms between the molecules and leaving the dye in its coloured form. As the temperature increases, the solvent melts, and the molecules move away from each other; with hydrogen transfer no longer occurring, the dye changes to a colourless form (4). Some nail polishes have a lighter colour when the fingers are cold and get darker when temperature increases, which has been likened to mood changes (6).

Magnetic nail Polish: Magnetic nail polish contain tiny metallic particles which give the nails a textured effect after application. The particles used include nickel, cobalt, iron, gadolinium, terbium and erbium, which vary in shape and are usually darker than the nail polish for contrast. The metals can be employed in any state with magnetic susceptibility. The most preferred metal used is magnetite, iron (II, III) oxide (Fe_3O_4). With the wet paint on the nail plate, a magnetic field is applied on top of the nail, causing the metallic particles to move up to the surface of the polish on the nail plate, producing different types of patterns which can be varied by patterning the magnetic surface (4, 7).

Crackle nail polish: The crackle effect is achieved by applying a regular nail polish first, followed by the crackle polish and then a clear coat to keep the crackle texture from peeling. Varying amounts of ethyl alcohol is poured into different bottles of regular nail polish. The ethyl alcohol leads to uneven drying of the polish giving a crackle effect. More ethyl alcohol leads to thinner cracks, while less ethyl alcohol produces thicker cracks (4).

Caviar Nail Polish: Plastic micro beads resembling caviar (fish eggs) are sprinkled and pushed onto previously applied wet polish on the nail plate. This gives the nail a beaded appearance. Beads may fall off and need to be replaced (4).

Breathable Nail Polish: The polish is commonly used by female Muslims. It is water permeable and allows water to get on to the surface of the nails through the polish while performing wudu (ablution, an essential part of pre-prayer cleansing in Islam) , thus fulfilling the wudu washing mandates which requires that body surfaces must be washed.The nail film is both water and oxygen permeable. It is a resin technology adapted from the extended wear contact lens industry (4).

Hypoallergenic nail polish: This nail polish is free of the common allergens such as tosylamide formaldehyde resin (TSFR) present in regular nail polish which may cause allergic dermatitis. These types of polish contain cellulose, acetate, butyrate, and polyester resins with plasticisers such as dibutyl phthalate for softness and pliability, dissolved in solvents (N-butyl acetate or ethyl acetate). Others contain natural pigments in a water base or argan oi (4, 8, 9).

Nail polish finish and adornment

The final appearance of the nail polish is varied by different additives some of which are brand specific. Finishes include micro-glitter, micro-shimmer (Figure 6.2), frost, matte, translucent and luster. Stickers and colour strips can also be added to the nails (4, 9).

Application of nail polish

To get a smooth application of nail polish on the nail plate, the nails are tidied up with a manicure and pedicure for the finger and toenails respectively. During this process the nails are filed, smoothened and the cuticles are tucked away or trimmed gently. Previously applied polish is removed after which the hands or feet are soaked in warm water with a detergent. This helps to soften the nail plate and cuticle. A cuticle softener is applied on the cuticle allowing it to be pushed back by a wooden stick or trimmed with a cuticle cutter. The surface of the nail is then smoothened using emery boards after which the hands are feet are cleaned and moisturised.

Figure 6.2: shimmering nail finish

Usually, three layers of nail polish are applied. The first is the base coat which is clear and prevents the nails from getting stained by the coloured nail polish. It also creates a smooth surface when ridges are still present on the nails after buffing. It contains the secondary film former resin and improves the adherence of the polish to the nail plate thus reducing nail chipping. The second coat is the coloured polish which can produce various patterns as mentioned earlier. The final coat is the top coat, which is also colourless and contains the primary film former and plasticiser, making the polish dry faster and chip-resistant (4).

Nail polish removers

Nail polish removers commonly contain solvents which dissolve dry nail varnish making removal easy. Removers may contain acetone, ethyl acetate or butyl acetate. The latter being the commonest. The liquid removers can be applied to cotton balls and used to wipe the polish off the nail plate. Nail varnish removers also come as wipes. Under some circumstances, the nail with polish may be soaked in a cup of nail polish remover, or the nail polish remover can be applied on a cotton ball, left on the nail and covered with aluminium foil. Removers containing acetone may lead to dehydration and damage of the nail plate and the surrounding tissues when used frequently. There are nail enamel removers containing fatty materials such as cetyl alcohol, cetyl palmitate, lanolin and castor oil, known as cconditioning nail removers. These oily substances are believed to reduce the solvents' dehydrating effects (4).

Artificial nails

These have become popular over the years especially as long fingernails have become fashionable. They can be pre-formed (nail tips) or custom made (acrylic and gel). Artificial nails are useful for lengthening nails or reinforcing soft, brittle or damaged nails. However, they could also mask diseases on the nails leading to delayed presentation for appropriate treatment (4).

Sculptured nails

These artificial nails are sculpted or cast over the existing nail plate majorly for aesthetic purposes although they have been used by musicians playing string instruments. The nails can be elongated and the shape changed. The nails developed are aesthetically appealing and are more durable than when the traditional nail polish (4, 8).

Acrylic nails

Acrylic nails are made from a mixture of liquid ethyl methacrylate and powdered poly-methacrylate. The polymerised mixture is applied as a thin layer to achieve its desired effect. This is done quickly as the mixture sets rapidly. The powder contains benzyl peroxide, which acts as a catalyst, while hydroquinone acts as an inhibitor of polymerisation. Additional ingredients such as titanium dioxide (sunscreen) and colours are added to individual brands. Acrylic nails can be removed with acetone-containing removers.

Nail tips

These are plastic plates shaped like nails of different lengths. They are glued to the free edge of the nails with adhesives containing methacrylate or ethyl 2-cyanoacrylate. To ensure that the nails are well stuck, the nail surface is filed roughly before gluing. Different lengths of the tips can be stuck on. These artificial nails can be painted and decorated. The tips can be removed with acetone (fingers can be immersed in acetone) (Figure 6.3).

Gel nails

Gel nails basically contain a mixture of ethyl cyanoacrylate and polymethyl-methacrylate monomers. After the mixture is applied to the nail plate, it is exposed to UV light which hardens the polish, similar to the technology used for dental resin (a tooth-coloured restorative material). There are concerns about using UV light to harden the nails in the fair skin with respect to precancerous changes. Gel nails are more flexible than acrylic nails. They are, however, removed by being buffed off the nail plate.

Touch up procedures are required for acrylic and gel nails as the nails grow out thus causing a gap from the nail bed and the artificial nail base (4).

Figure 6.3: Nail tips

Figure 6.4: Acrylic nails

Adverse effects of nail cosmetics

Adverse reactions may develop from manicuring, the nail polish, sculpturing and removing nail polish and artificial nails.

Inflammation and infection of tissue around the nail plate

Traumatic complications may arise during manicure when preparing the nail surface and edge for application of nail polish. The cuticle may be damaged or irritated during manicure or when the sculpture nails are being removed. The irritation of the proximal and lateral nail folds may lead to inflammation and, subsequently, a paronychia (whitlow) which may become chronic. When the cuticle is removed during manicure, the absence of the seal allows bacteria and fungi (candida) into the space below the proximal fold leading to inflammation and paronychia (4, 9).

Irritant dermatitis (non-immunological skin inflammation) around the nail bed may also develop from the frequent use of cuticle softener, nail hardeners, primers and polish removers. Over the years, attempts have been made to remove irritants from nail cosmetics, especially formaldehyde, and when present, it is meant for the nail's free edge. Existing skin disorders affecting the nails can be worsened by use of nail cosmetics (10).

Allergic dermatitis (immunological skin inflammation) as a result of contact to nail polish is seen in about 3% of the general population. Toluene sulphonamide formaldehyde resin is responsible for many of the allergic reactions. Acrylates used in gluing artificial nails can result in allergic contact dermatitis and paronychia when they come in contact with perionychial skin before the rapid polymerisation process. The allergic reaction may develop after months of use (11).

Unsterilised instruments can also spread bacterial, fungal and viral infections in salons. Some individuals with infected nails visit nail studios to camouflage their discoloured nails and may spread infection if the instruments used are not sterilised before being used for other clients. Nail technicians and manicurists with fungal nail infections can also spread the infection to their clients. Pedicure tubs and bowls have been found to harbour infectious organisms. It is best to use personalised equipments in the saloons when not sure of the sterilisation procedures of the saloon and ensure water used for manicure is clean and the sub-sterilised. (4, 9).

Nail plate abnormalities

Onycholysis is the separation of the nail plate from the nail bed which allows air to get under the nail plate giving it a whitish or yellowish appearance (Figure 6.5). This may result from trauma (hitting the free end of the long nail) or from the effect of strong irritants on the sub or periungual area. Onychoschizia, (lamellar dystrophy) which is transverse splitting of the nail plate can also be seen from frequent use of nail cosmetics especially acetone in nail removers and excessive buffing of the nails. Keratin granules which appear as white patches on the nail plate are common with prolonged use of nail polish and removers (Figure 6.6). They are usually misdiagnosed as fungal nail infections. Nail thinning can also occur with use of gel nails leading to brittle nails (4, 12).

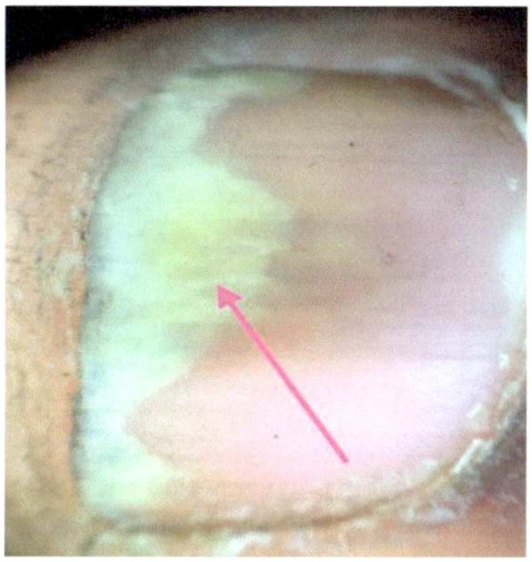

Figure 6.5: Onycholysis; separation of nail plate from the bed

Health hazards of chemicals used in nail cosmetics

Studies have shown that manicurists and nail technicians are exposed to chemicals with adverse effects. In the early 2000s in the USA, animal studies had identified dibutyl phthalate (DBP), a plasticiser, as a reproductive and developmental toxicant. There were also reports of adverse effects of DBP on reproductive health, foetal development, thyroid function, and obesity. Subsequently DBP, toluene and formaldehyde were removed from nail polish in the US and UK.

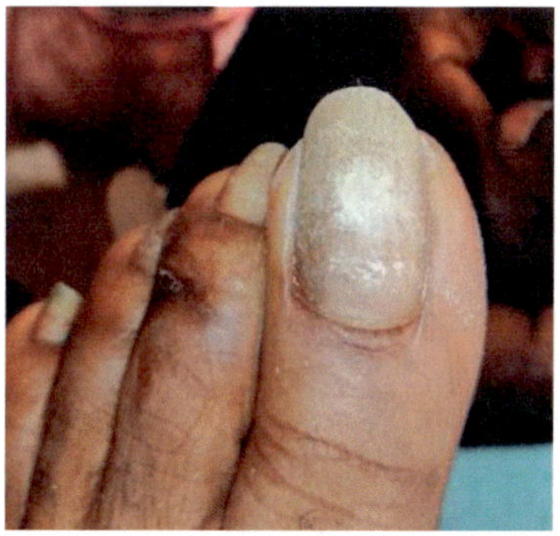

Figure 6.6: Keratin granules on the nail plate

Volatile organic compounds (VOC) are commonly used in nail salons while some of the salons have poor ventilation. Some reports have suggested the need to further scrutinise the contents of the nail polish including the VOC. Nail salons offering acrylic and gel nails should be encouraged to have adequate ventilation. Nail cosmetics should be kept out of the reach of children (13, 14, 15, 16).

References

1. Goldstein Research. Global nail care industry: market trends, size, opportunity and forecast 2016–2024 [Internet]. 2018 [cited 2019 July 1]. Available from: https://www.goldsteinresearch.com/report/nail-care-market-global-industry-analysis.
2. Mazareanu, E. Nail salons in the U.S. – Statistics and facts [Internet]. 2019 [cited 2019 July 22]. Available from: https://www.statista.com/topics/4624/nail-salons-in-the-us/.
3. Shah, Shikha (17 January 2014). "History of nail polish". *The Times of India*. ProQuest 1477854392 (https://search.proquest.com/docview/1477854392).
4. Zoe Diana Draelos. Nail cosmetics and adornment. Dermatol Clin 39 (2021) 351–359.
5. Madnani NA, Khan KJ. Nail cosmetics. Indian J Dermatol Venereol Leprol 2012; 78:309-17.
6. Nail polish. Available from: http://en.wikipedia.org/wiki/Nail_ polish. [access feb 2022.
7. Romanowski, Shannon. "The Science Behind Magnetic Nail Polish" (http://www.self.com/st ory/the-science-behind-magnetic-na). *Self.com*. Retrieved 22 June 2017.
8. Wing HJ. Nail preparations. In: deNavarre MG, editor. The chemistry and manufacture of cosemtics. Wheaton (IL): Allured Publishing Corporation; 1988. p. 983–1005.
9. Daniel CR. Simple chronic paronychia. In: Scher RK, Daniel CR, editors. Nails: diagnosis, therapy, surgery. 3rd edition. Philadelphia7 Elsevier Saunders; 2005. p. 99 – 103.
10. Dahdah MJ, Scher RK Nail diseases related to nail cosmetics Dermatol Clin 24 (2006) 233 – 239
11. Tosti A, Buerra L, Vincenzi C, et al. Contact sensitization caused by toluene sulfonamide-formaldehyde resin in women who use nail cos- metics. Am J Contact Dermatitis 1993; 4:150.
12. Wallis MS, Bowen WR, Guin JD. Pathogenesis of onychoschizia (lamellar dystrophy). J Am Acad Derm 1991; 24:44–8.
13. Young AS, Allen JG, Kim UJ, et al. Phthalate and Organophosphate Plasticizers in Nail Polish: Evaluation of Labels and Ingredients. *Environ Sci Technol*. 2018;52(21) :12841-12850.doi:10.1021/acs.est.8b04495
14. Foster P. M. D.; Thomas L. V.; Cook M. W.; Gangolli S. D. Study of the Testicular Effects and Changes in Zinc Excretion Produced by Some N-Alkyl Phthalates in the Rat. Toxicol. Appl. Pharmacol. 1980, 54 (3), 392–398. 10.1016/0041-008X (80)90165-9. [PubMed] [CrossRef] [Google Scholar]

15. Quach T.; Von Behren J.; Goldberg D.; Layefsky M.; Reynolds P. Adverse Birth Outcomes and Maternal Complications in Licensed Cosmetologists and Manicurists in California. Int. Arch. Occup. Environ. Health 2015, 88 (7), 823–833. 10.1007/s00420-014-1011-0. [PubMed] [CrossRef] [Google Scholar]

16. Tran T. M.; Kannan K. Occurrence of Phthalate Diesters in Particulate and Vapor Phases in Indoor Air and Implications for Human Exposure in Albany, New York, USA. Arch. Environ. Contam. Toxicol. 2015, 68 (3), 489–499. 10.1007/s00244-015-0140-0. [PubMed] [CrossRef] [Google Scholar]

CHAPTER SEVEN

Sunscreens and skin health

Ayodapo O Jegede and Bamgboye J Taiwo

Skin cancer and other forms of skin damage are becoming widespread over the years. Most of these adverse effects have been traced to repeated exposure of the skin to ultraviolet (UV) radiation, which affects the survival of several cell types. It is believed that melanin has some form of photoprotective action; it disperses more than 99% of absorbed UV radiation as heat and has some radical scavenging properties (1). Although melanin is responsible for skin pigmentation, its role in the skin is still debatable as it could also have toxic properties, especially after being exposed to UV radiation (2). In vitro studies have shown that melanin reacts with DNA to produce single strand DNA breaks in skin cells (3). Other effects of melanin include production of hydrogen peroxide after photodegradation and this can cause mutations in melanocytes or other cells (4, 5).

Historical records show that jasmine, from *Jasmine officinale,* lupine from *Lupinus perennis* and other remedies were used as protection by the Egyptians in ancient times against the sun rays because they realised that these substances, some of which are still being used in producing sunscreens till date, could absorb the rays of the sun (6). Sunscreens are basically chemical substances present in creams and lotions that protect the skin from UV rays by deflecting the UV photons thereby preventing their absorption by the skin (7). They are also known as sun blocks or sun protectants. The purpose of sun protection is to reduce the unwanted effects of the sun (UV) rays without affecting the beneficial ones.

Sunscreens have been demonstrated to increase the tolerance of the skin to UV exposure. The discovery of UV rays has led to the continuous evolution of sunscreens, making them well-known in recent times because of their effects on the skin. Since their introduction, compounds with activity as sunscreens have been incorporated into various moisturisers and lip products. Sales of these products have also increased rapidly by roughly 7% on an average per year (8). Other measures of photoprotection include the use of sunhats, umbrellas and sun-protective clothing.

Types of UV radiation

The earth's stratosphere has a shield known as the ozone layer, which absorbs most of the sun's UV radiation. Certain human activities such as the release of chlorofluorocarbons (CFCs) and some other greenhouse gases have caused this layer to be depleted making the UV rays from the sun to reach the earth directly (9). Energy from the sun reaches the earth as solar radiation, of which UV light is a part of the spectrum. The Sunlight is made up of the electromagnetic spectrum (EMS) (Figure 7.1) which consists of different arrays of radiations of different wavelengths. UV light cannot be seen but can be felt (10). For cosmetic purposes, wavelength of the ultra-violet (UV) radiation is critical. Unfettered exposure to UV radiations can lead to dermatological problems. Unfortunately, because of ozone layer depletion, some of these highly energetic radiations find their path to the earth surface to be absorbed by the skin surface (Fig.7.2) with attendant consequences such as: damage to critical biomolecules like deoxyribonucleic acid (DNA), lipids, and proteins; production of inflammation and burns, premature aging and carcinogenesis (11-12).

UVA radiation: These are more abundant than UVB rays. Of the three types, these have the longest wavelength (320 to 400 nm), but lowest energy level. They tend to penetrate the skin deeper, hence easily affect cells. They cause immediate tanning and some skin cancers. Of the UV rays that reach the surface of the earth, 95% are UVA rays (13).

UVB radiation: Also known as burning rays, they have wavelengths that range between 280 and 320 nm. They are the major causes of sunburn which damages the epidermis of the skin. They are mostly absorbed by the cloud hence about 5% reaches the ground (7, 8).

UVC radiation: with the shortest wavelength (about 200 to 280 nm), have the highest energy levels which makes them the most dangerous to any fauna and flora (7).

The ozone layer absorbs a minute amount of UVA, about 95% of UVB and 100% of UVC. As human activity continues to deplete the ozone layer, there is the need to find ways of protecting the skin from the deleterious effects of these rays. Although, photoprotection of the human skin can be achieved by melanin (which acts as an artificial sunscreen), proteins and other internal mechanisms or endogenous substances which aid the conversion of UV photon into harmless amount of heat, photoprotection is accomplished by sunscreens of either the primary or secondary types (15). The primary types can be classified into two: the sunscreens that act as physical barriers, responsible for reflecting and scattering light; and those which act as chemical barriers, responsible for absorption of light. The secondary types are DNA repair enzymes and antioxidants which function by interrupting the photochemical activity of UV sunlight to reduce the damage on the skin caused by the UV light (9).

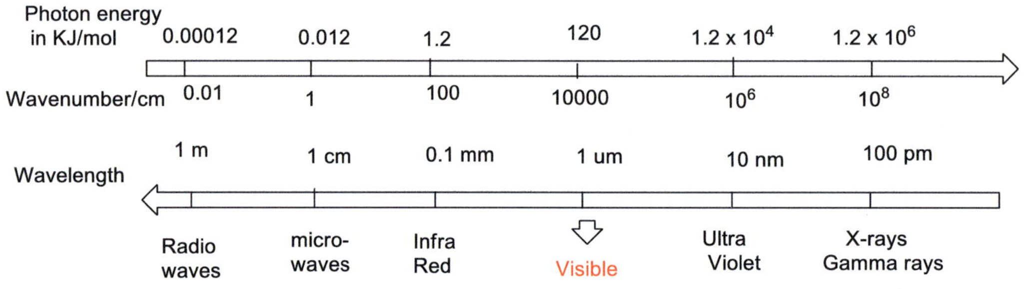

Figure 7.1: Photochemistry: Theoretical Concepts (culled from photobiology.info)

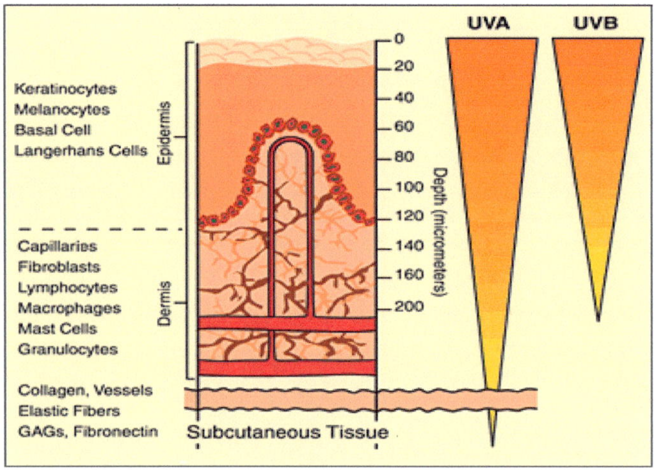

Fig. 7.2: Cross-section of the skin showing its interaction with UV radiation (16)

The chemistry of sunscreens

Sunscreens are agents developed to prevent sunburn and other deleterious effects resulting from excessive exposure to sunlight. They can be physical barriers, e.g., sun radioprotective clothing, glasses, hats, umbrella and shades (16) that have been used to protect against undue exposure to sunlight radiation or through the application of sunscreens. The application of sunscreens, which are cosmetic products, and in some instances, cosmeceuticals, is more popular (17). Sunscreen can be classified into; topical sunscreen which protect skin from harmful effects of radiations either by absorbing or reflecting radiations (18), or oral sunscreen products which are administered orally (cosmeceuticals) and are expected to enter into systemic circulation to elicit their sun screening effects (18-19).

Chemically, the topical sunscreen can be organic, inorganic or natural chemicals.

Sunscreens (sun filters)

Sunscreens are chemical compounds that absorb radiations in the UV region of the electromagnetic spectrum (EMS). This absorption provides the energy for the excitation of the ground state electrons in the material to a higher energy electronic state referred to as the excited state (Fig. 7.3). The electron goes from the excited state (less stable) to the stable ground state by releasing the absorbed energy either in a radiative form, as light (fluorescence, phosphorescence,) or in non-radiative processes, as heat (20).

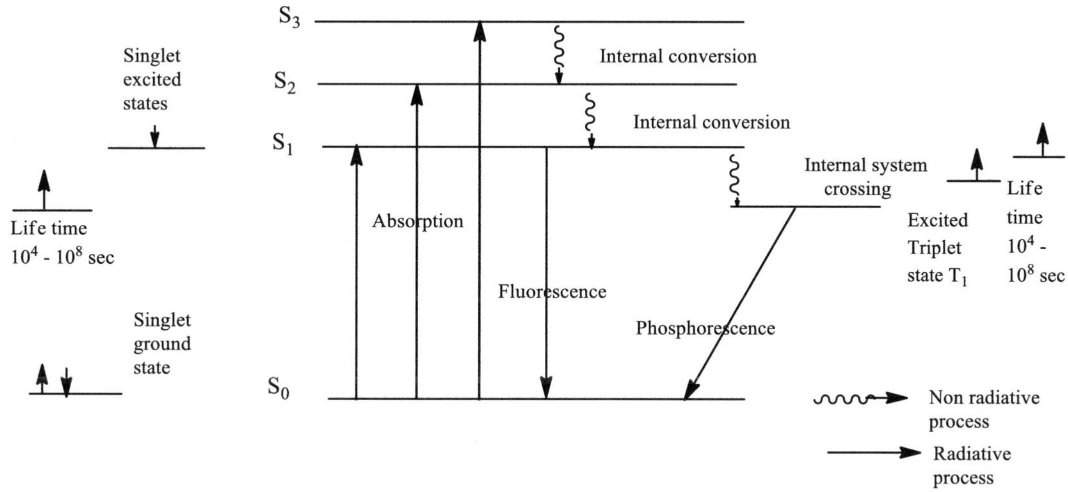

Figure 7.3: The fate of an excited electron.

Classification of sunscreens

Sunscreens are largely grouped into two namely: organic sunscreens and inorganic sunscreens. However, there are other classifications of sunscreens. These classifications include:

Organic sunscreens

Organic sunscreens are also known as chemical sunscreens, they absorb the UV radiation that the sun emits and convert it to heat energy. They are mostly aromatic compounds linked together by a carbonyl group. The active ingredients of organic sunscreens include synthetic compounds like benzophenone, *para*-aminobenzoic acid (PABA) and octocrylene, a common ingredient used in the production of sunscreens with a Sun Protection Factor (SPF) between 30 to 50 (15). They protect the inner layers of the skin from the harmful effects of the UVA rays and prevent UVB rays, which can cause sunburns, from penetrating the skin. An example of a broad-spectrum organic sunscreen that filters UVA and UVB is silatriazole. However, it should be noted that organic sunscreens can cause irritation and allergic reactions although they are easier to rub into the skin (21). **UVB filters** include para-amino benzoic acid derivatives - padimate O (Fig 7.4a); cinnamates – octinoxate or octyl methoxy cinnamate (Fig 7.4c), cinoxate (Fig 7.4f); salicylates – octisalate (Fig 7.4d), homosalate (Fig 7.4i), trolamine salicylate (Fig 7.4e); octocrylene (Fig 7.4j) and ensulizole (Fig 7.4h). **UVA filters** include benzophenones (Fig 7.4g) (UVA1 and UVA2 absorbers) – oxybenzone (Fig 7.4l), sulisobenzone, dioxybenzone, avobenzone (Fig 7.4k) and parsol 1789 (UVA1 absorbers) and meradimate (UVA2 absorber).

Inorganic sunscreens

Inorganic sunscreens are also known as physical sunscreens. They contain fine particles of minerals like titanium oxide (TiO_2) and zinc oxide (ZnO) and they reflect sun rays to the environment thereby creating a physical barrier on the skin surface. ZnO offers true broad-spectrum UV protection, although TiO_2 has better UVB protection. However, both oxides have been used as micro-sized particles (200–500 nanometres) requiring thick applications on the skin which is a disadvantage. The use of nanoparticles (20–100 nanometres) essentially offered cosmetic acceptability (22). Other agents include kaolin, talc, calcium carbonate and magnesium oxide.

They are referred to as broad-spectrum because their protective effects cover the whole UV spectrum. Since they stay on the surface of the skin, they are unlikely to cause skin irritation; therefore, they can be used by people with sensitive skin. However, they have the disadvantage of leaving their heavy residue on the skin (10). Other disadvantages include: not being easily rinsed off, requiring frequent applications, formation of white cast on the skin (scattering extends into the visible region) which is unappealing to the consumers especially those with darker skins and they may require more efforts to rub them in.

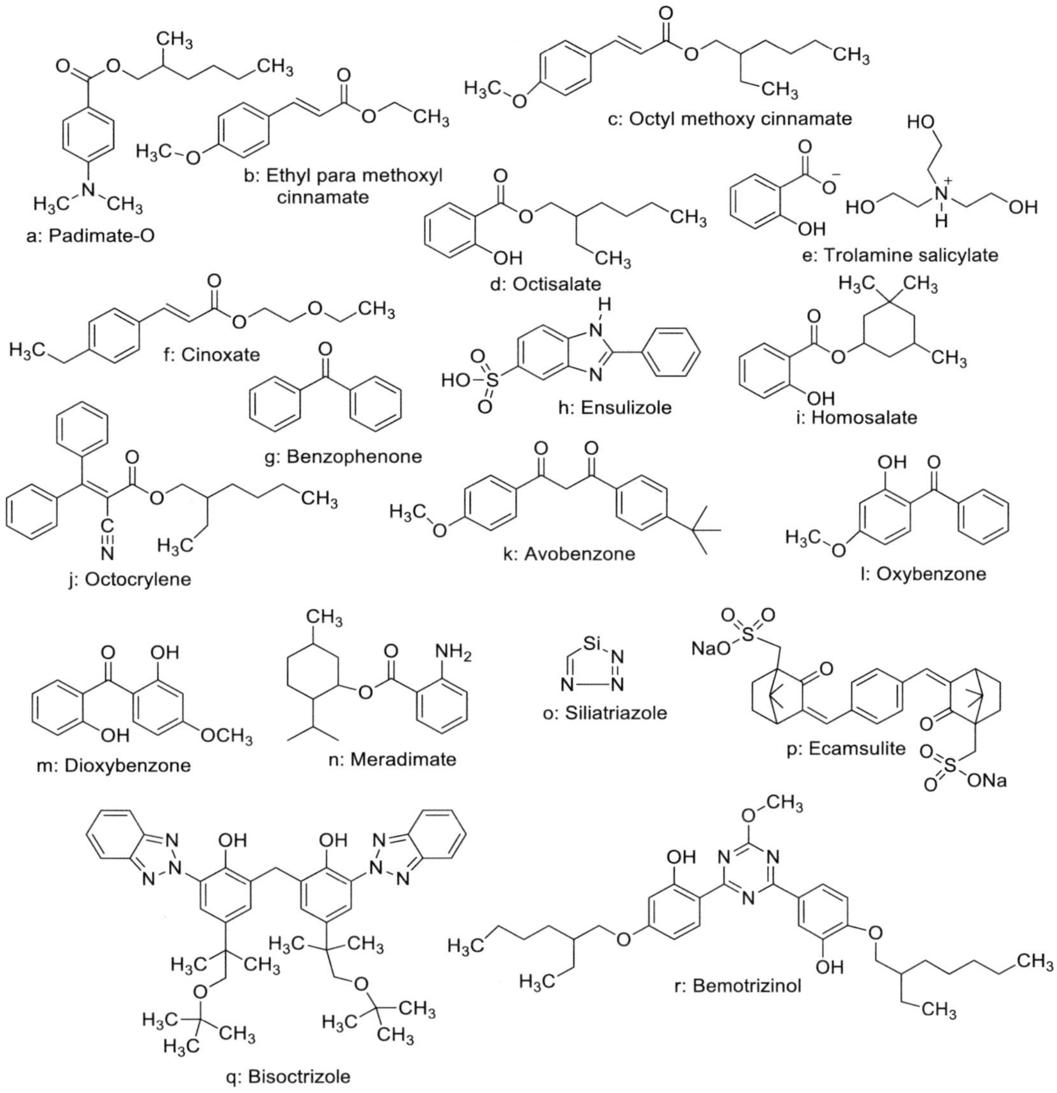

Figure 7.4: Examples of organic UV filters

Table 7.2 shows some examples of products that contain organic and inorganic sunscreen agents.

Table 7.2: Examples of some common organic and inorganic sunscreen products

Product	SPF	Active ingredients	Formulation	Usage
Aveeno positively radiant daily moisturiser	SPF 15	Octinoxate 7.5% Avobenzone 3% Octisalate 2%	Soy extract Non-greasy Cream	Dry skin Brown spots
Neutrogena Sheer Zinc Face Sunscreen	SPF 50	Zinc Oxide (21.6%) Glycerine	Lotion	darker skin tone
Cetaphil DermaControl Daily Moisturiser	SPF 30	Octocrylene (7%), Ethylhexyl Salicylate (5%), Butyl Methoxydibenzoylmethane (Avobenzone) (3%)	ceramide-infused lotion	acne-prone
Biore UV Aqua Rich Watery Essence	SPF 50	Ethylhexyl Methoxycinnamate, Ethylhexyl Triazone, Diethylamino Hydroxybenzoyl Hexyl Benzoate, Bis-Ethylhexyloxyphenol Methoxyphenyl Triazine	Hyaluronic Acid & Royal Jelly Extract	Oily
Cotz Sensitive Sunscreen	SPF 40	Zinc Oxide (20%), C12-15 Alkyl Benzoate, Caprylhydroxamic Acid, Caprylyl Glycol, Etc.	Lotion	Sensitive skin- body and face
Neutogena Invisible Daily Defense Face Mist	SPF 50	Avobenzone 3% Homosalate 10% Octisalate 5% Octocrylene 10%	Spray	Makeup wearer

Natural sunscreen chemicals

These include polyphenols (tannins, flavonoids), lycopenes (23) from tomatoes (*Solanum lycopersicum*), carrots (*Daucus carota*) and present in many red- or orange-coloured fruits and vegetables as well as fixed oils and volatile oils which scavenge for free radicals, thereby protecting the skin from UV-induced free radical-generated damages. Resveratrol (Trans-3′,4′,5′-trihydroxystilbine) from grape (*Vitis vinifera*), nuts and fruits have been found to inhibit ornithine decarboxylase and cyclooxygenase II (COX-2) activity and as well, they decrease the level of lipid peroxidation (23).

Naturally occurring oral/systemic sunscreen agents include polyphenols, flavonoids, tannins, carotenoids, vitamins like chemicals. On oral administration, these compounds exhibit antioxidant effect complimenting the endogenous antioxidant mechanisms and enhancing their photo-protective action (24). For instance, apigenin from fruits and vegetables (lemons, tomatoes, onions, apples, grapes, lettuce, broccoli, kale, cottonseed), beverages (tea, red wine), herbs (*Gingko biloba, Apocynum venetum, Poacynum hendersonii, Opuntia ficusindica*), olive oil and propolis from beehives all inhibit UV-mediated induction of ornithine decarboxylase activity and down-regulates COX-2 expression in macrophages. Quercetin has been found to augment the skin's endogenous antioxidant systems. It also prevents the UVC radiation-induced liposome peroxidation and the SPF of quercetin matches closely that of homosalate, a synthetic sunscreen agent (25). Anthocyanidins from coloured (range from yellow to purple, except green) fruits, flowers, berries, vegetables and cereal grains (e.g., pomegranate (*Punica granatum*) prevents the deleterious effects of exposure to UVB which includes the translocation of transcription factors such as nuclear factor kappa B and activator protein 1, excessive production of the pro-inflammatory cytokine IL-8, cleavage of procaspase-3 (a key step in apoptotic pathway), and DNA fragmentation (24-25).

Mechanism of actions of sunscreens

Sunscreens generally work through two mechanisms:

Absorption of the UV energy

This is specific for organic sunscreens. It is characterised by the chemical structure of the sunscreen which is composed of an aromatic compound in conjugation with a carbonyl group. Excitation of the molecules occurs when the UV rays are absorbed. As they return to their ground state, the lower energy of longer wavelengths is released. The UV energy absorbed is turned to heat energy thereby reducing the distance which it penetrates (26).

Reflection of the UV energy

This forms the basis by which inorganic sunscreens function. The inorganic particles scatter the UV rays that settle on the upper layer of the skin. This leads to an increase in the optical pathway of photons; thus, more photons are absorbed and the sun protection factor is enhanced. The inorganic chemicals, which include minerals like titanium dioxide and zinc dioxide, are responsible for reflecting UV rays, thus, acting as a physical barrier. They provide a coating that blocks sun rays from penetrating through the skin (10).

Measurement of protection of sunscreens

The viability of a sunscreen can be determined by the Sun Protection Factor (SPF) and Immune protection factor (IPF), among other factors. The SPF shows how effective a product is at protecting the skin from the burning rays emitted by the sun. A product with a high SPF tends to be more protective while those with low SPF are less protective but last for a longer period of time (9).

Sun Protection Factor (SPF) is a measure of how the skin protects against UVB rays (10). SPF is also referred to as a simple and international method used to compare sunscreen protection against erythema caused by UVB rays (27). This is because UVB rays are responsible for sunburn and non-melanoma skin cancer (28). On the other hand, UVA rays are responsible for premature ageing, wrinkling and age spots; they penetrate the skin and indirectly destroy the DNA by producing free radicals of oxygen species. Also, they increase the number of inflammatory cells present in the dermis and reduce the antigen-presenting cells (29).

If a sunscreen product is labelled broad-spectrum, this means that it protects the skin against both UVA and UVB rays (9). No SPF has been shown to block a hundred per cent of the sun's UV rays. A sunscreen with an SPF of 15, blocks about 93% of UVB rays while one with an SPF of 30 blocks about 97% of the rays. The SPF is also used to indicate how long it will take for the skin to redden. This is because some UV radiation still eventually gets through the sunscreen and the skin. Therefore, sunscreens with SPF 15 protect the skin from getting red 15 times the regular time it will take without a sunscreen (30).

Also, there are documented evidence that some chemicals in the formulation of sunscreens are carcinogenic, which is harmful to humans. For instance, oxybenzone is absorbed into the skin and is detected in urine even long hours after it is applied (31). It has been suggested that sunscreens that contain oxybenzone should not be used on children. Also, titanium dioxide, which is a mineral present mostly in inorganic sunscreens, has been observed to cause genetic damage in mice (10).

Sun protection ratings

The sun protection factor (SPF) of a sunscreen is determined by a highly controlled clinical test. It makes use of lamps that produce radiations in the UV region on human volunteers to produce erythema. SPF is a measure of the time it takes for a minimal erythema to appear when a sunscreen product is applied, compared to the minimal erythemal dose (MED) without the sunscreen product. For instance, an SPF of 15 indicates that if it takes

10 minutes for skin to start to burn without sunscreen, it will take 150 minutes to do same with sunscreen.

$$\text{SPF} = \frac{Minimum\ erythema\ with\ sunscreen}{Minimum\ erythema\ without\ sunscreen}$$

In vitro SPF determination (absorbance measurement) by UV-Spectrophotometer*:* The absorptions of serially diluted solutions of test sample within the UV range of 290 to 450 nm with every 5 nm increment are taken using a UV spectrophotometer in a 1 cm quartz cell. The readings are taken in triplicates, using ethanol as a blank. The SPF is calculated using Mansur equation as follows (32):

$$SPF = \mathrm{CF} * \sum_{290}^{320} \mathrm{EE}(\lambda) * I * Abs\,(\lambda)$$

EE $*$ I values are constant EE ($\boldsymbol{\lambda}$)–erythemal effect spectrum; I ($\boldsymbol{\lambda}$)–solar intensity spectrum; Abs ($\boldsymbol{\lambda}$)–absorbance of sunscreen product; CF-correction factor (=10).

In vitro determination of SPF by UV 2000S ultraviolet transmittance analyser (Labsphere)*:* The principle of this method is based on the test sample transmittance measurement, where transmittance is defined as the ratio of the illumination that passed through a sample to the illumination incident on the sample. The prepared sample is exposed to Xenon flash lamp and the SPF is determined using the formula below (33–35):

$$\text{SPF} = \frac{\int_{290}^{400} E\lambda * S\lambda * d\lambda}{\int_{290}^{400} E\lambda * S\lambda * e^{-final\ A(\lambda)} * d\lambda}$$

Where, E (λ) is the erythema action spectrum, S(λ) is the solar spectral irradiance, $d(\lambda)$ is the spectral transmittance of the sample with the integral calculated across the 290-400 nm wavelength limit.

In vivo methods of determining SPF: Different approaches have been proposed and they are somehow similar in procedure, except in the outcome and in the way the results are rendered. Mostly, the ratio of the sunscreen-protected minimal immediate pigment darkening dose to the unprotected minimal immediate pigment darkening dose for a set time, after each exposure, is determined.

Procedure: The human skin is exposed to UVA light source (320-400 nm) and the changes in the skin, observed as an instantaneous or chronic pigment darkening, erythema or tanning, after a given period of time following exposure to the radiation are noted; for instance within 60 sec after each exposure (Immediate Pigment Darkening (IPD) test), approximately 2 h after exposure (Persistent Pigment Darkening (PPD) test) or 16-24 h after exposure (Protection factor in UVA (PFA) test or Phototoxic Protection Factor (PPF) test). The irradiated sites are evaluated under bright warm white illumination for pigmentation response and erythema, using the following scales (Table 7.1):

Table 7.1: Scale used for evaluating SPF (36-38)

SN	Scale	Pigmentation	Erythema
1	0.0	No Response	No response
2	0.5	Equivocal response	Equivocal response
3	1.0	Unambiguous dark grey or brown pigmentation	Unambiguous erythema
4	1.5	Well defined dark grey or brown pigmentation with sharp borders	Well defined erythema with sharp borders
5	2.0	Deep pigmentation	Bright erythema

The results are further interpreted as follows:

IPD as designed by Kaidbey and Barnes - the end point for this test is pigmentation producing a grade ≥1 within 60 seconds after each UV exposure (34).

PPD from Chardon et al. - the ratio for approximately 2 h after UVA exposure is determined (35). The end point for this test is pigmentation producing a grade ≥ 1, 2 h following UVA exposure. The benefit of this method, over IPD, is that it enables accurate readings of time because the residual pigmentation developed after radiation exposure is properly established.

PFA by Cole et al.- the ratio is determined approximately 24 h after UVA exposure (32).

PPF by Lowe et al. - here the ratio of sunscreen protected minimal phototoxic dose is measured 72 h after UVA exposure (39). This approach makes use of 8-methoxypsoralen to increase the sensitivity of UV-light. Erythema or tanning producing a grade ≥ 1 within 16-24 hr after UVA exposure is the end point of this method.

Photostability evaluation of sunscreens

After being irradiated by sunlight for a while, many sunscreen agents degrade and lose their photoprotective ability as well as their efficacy. Hence it is essential to evaluate the photostability of sunscreens. This is carried out by measuring the area under the curve index (AUCI) of sunscreens after either natural UV exposure (UVnat) or artificial UV exposure (UVart). The AUCI, is defined as AUCI=AUCafter/AUCbefore. If AUCI is greater or equal to 0.80 then the sunscreen is considered photostable (40).

Administration of sunscreens

There is need for regular application of sunscreens as exposure to UV radiation cannot be avoided. Over the last few decades, sunscreens have evolved notably. As more people get to know about the protection sunscreens provide against sunburns, melanomas and even skin aging (also called photoaging), the demand will constantly increase. Therefore, manufacturing industries will have to balance this demand by manufacturing effective and safe formulations (41). Sunscreens have to be administered rightly to ensure efficacy. Health authorities have advocated that, to adequately cover the average adult body surface, application of $2mg/cm^2$ of sunscreen is required (42). Sunscreens are recommended to be applied 15 to 30 minutes before going outdoors to allow the agent to bind to the skin, and be reapplied every 2 hours of exposure and immediately after swimming or excessive sweating (43). During application, it should not get in contact with the eyes and smoking should be avoided if the sunscreen is flammable. Children younger than 6 months should not be administered sunscreen products, rather, they should be kept away from the sun or be worn photoprotective clothing when exposed to the sun (41-44). Individuals with inflamed skin should avoid using alcohol-based sunscreens and those containing fragrances and chemicals like oxybenzone and octisalate, as these could cause some form of irritation (28).

Benefits of sunscreens

Apart from enhancing beauty by preventing skin damage due to radiations from the sun, sunscreens have various benefits which include:

Prevention of sunburn

Sunburns are usually the most common effects of harmful sun rays on the skin. A short-term effect of the prolonged exposure of the skin to UV rays is erythema or sunburn. Erythema is characterised by the reddening of the skin (45). This also increases the activation of melanocytes which further increases melanin production. As a result, the appearance of the skin darkens which is sometimes known as tanning (1). Therefore, sunscreens are used to prevent sunburn from occurring and keep one's complexion even. Inadequate application of sunscreen may also increase the occurrence of sunburns.

Reducing the risk of skin cancer

Long-term and repeated exposure to the harmful rays of the sun can cause loss of skin elasticity. This loss is usually irreversible and may lead to skin cancers. Although UV radiation is a major cause of skin cancer, other factors that determine the extent of skin damage by UV radiation include geographical location (effect of climate), skin colour, age, immune status and the intensity of the sun. It has been shown that the occurrence of certain types of carcinoma (squamous cell carcinoma (SCC) and basal cell carcinoma (BCC)) are related to the individual's location on the earth, as those that live further away from the equator are at a higher risk of coming down with skin cancer (46). Skin colour also plays a role in the cause of skin melanomas as the SEER (Surveillance, Epidemiology, and End Results programme) cancer statistics review shows that people with white skin are 20 times more likely to have skin cancers than any other skin colour, which is due to the lower amount of melanin in individuals with white skin (46, 47). Older individuals, with weaker immune systems such as those that have had organ transplant are also at risk and may not survive the effects of the cancer (48). Therefore, the use of sunscreens is important in preventing skin cancers especially melanoma and squamous cell carcinoma (49).

Preventing premature ageing

Sunscreens are effective in slowing down the ageing process of the skin. However, since the sun emits harmful rays every day (50), it is especially important to apply sunscreens daily, rather than occasionally, when going out of doors on sunny days (51).

Adverse effects of sunscreens

Allergic reaction

Some of the chemicals used in the formulation of sunscreens, for example, preservatives, have been shown to cause allergic reactions in the form of irritation of the skin such as rashes and intense itching (52). Sunscreens that contain zinc oxide are safer to use as they do not cause skin irritation. However, a patch test should often be done to test if any allergic reaction may occur with the use of sunscreen products. Doing a patch test entails rubbing a small amount of the sunscreen on a plain area of the skin, preferably the inner part of the elbow and exposing it to sunlight. If there are no irritations after a few days, the product is considered safe (53).

Acne

Acne is a skin condition that occurs when the pores of the skin are blocked either by sebum or by hair. Sunscreens cause acne and make it worse for those that have acne-prone skin due to some ingredients, like coconut oil, present in the formulations which are comedogenic and/or cause irritation (54). Body sunscreens should not be applied to the face. Non-oily and gel-based sunscreens are more compatible in oily skin (55).

Eye irritation

On applying sunscreen products on the face, some quantity might get into the eye if care is not taken, such as through sweating, making the eye to sting intensely, causing pain and irritation. This happens because some of the ingredients irritate the eye, e.g., avobenzone, benzophenone and sulisobenzene (55, 56). Care should, therefore, be taken to avoid contact with the eyes. Whether sunscreens cause blindness or not is still debatable, but if in any case they get into the eyes, the eyes should be rinsed thoroughly with water for 15 to 20 minutes (57).

Vitamin D Deficiency

Vitamin D, a vital substance that aids in supporting liver and cardiovascular health is produced by exposing the skin to sunlight for some minutes a day. Studies show that excessive use of sunscreens may reduce the production of vitamin D by 99% (58).

Pain in hairy areas

Sunscreens often come in diverse forms like sticks, gels, lotions, sprays, creams and ointments. However, some sunscreens can cause drying and tightening of the skin, which can lead to pain in hairy areas. This is why it is often advisable to use gel sunscreens for hairy areas like the chest and scalp as they produce a cooling effect (59).

Threat to the environment

Sunscreens serve as a threat to the environment. Studies show that these products support the growth of bacteria and viruses and act as pollutants, and are harmful to several life forms (60).

Blood estrogens levels

Sunscreens have ingredients that can affect cells in breast cancer patients. They can have effects on blood estrogens levels especially those that contain oxybenzone, avobenone and terephthalylidene dicamphor sulfonic acid, as some seep into the bloodstream upon daily usage (61). The use of chemical sunscreens on children should be reduced as their skin tends to absorb the chemicals instantly (62).

Clogged hair follicles

Pus in the hair follicles often occurs as a result of the itchy spots from sunscreens. These itchy spots eventually redden and cause red rashes that may trigger the occurrence of pus around hair follicles (63).

Precautions for sunscreen use

There are certain precautions to take when using sunscreens and these include:

Wear a sunscreen every day and reapply every two hours

Even on cloudy days, sunscreens should be worn and reapplied. This is because the skin is always susceptible to the sun rays and can cause harmful effects over time. Reapplication is crucial especially for those using a spray sunscreen (64). Sunscreens with a high SPF do not last long on the skin. therefore, it is advised to reapply every two hours (65).

Wear it early and in a generous amount

Sunscreens are to be applied 15 to 30 minutes before going out of doors and be adequately applied, making sure that the ears, feet, neck and other exposed areas are well covered.

Use a sunscreen that protects the skin from UVA and UVB rays

Products of this nature protect the skin from sunburns caused by UVB rays and from skin cancers caused by UVA rays such as those containing zinc oxide or titanium dioxide which are known to block both UVA and UVB rays (66).

Use a sunscreen with a Sun Protection Factor of 15 or higher

Cancer can be prevented by the use of sunscreens with an SPF of 15 or above. The higher the SPF, the higher the level of protection (39).

Don't depend only on sunscreens

In addition to sunscreens, the use of sun-protective gadgets such as wearing sunglasses with UV protection, clothing such as a dark long-sleeved shirt, wide-brimmed hat and use of lip balm with SPF 30 or higher guard against skin cancer and sunburns (67).

Minimise exposure to the sun

Of all the precautions associated with sun exposure, staying out of the sun is the best way to avoid sun damage and lesions. 10 am to 2 pm or 11 am to 3 pm are the periods of the day when the sun is at its strongest, hence, exposure should be avoided at these times of the day as much as possible or otherwise, minimised (68).

Reference

1. Brenner M, Hearing VJ. The Protective Role of Melanin Against UV Damage in Human Skin. Photochem Photobiol. 2008;84(3):539–49. Available from: https://onlinelibrary.wiley.com/doi/10.1111/j.1751-1097.2007.00226.x
2. Kvam E, Dahle J. Melanin synthesis may sensitize melanocytes to oxidative DNA damage by ultraviolet A radiation and protect melanocytes from direct DNA damage by ultraviolet B radiation. Pigment Cell Res. 2004;17(5):549–50.

3. Marrot L, Belaidi JP, Meunier JR, Perez P, Agapakis-Causse C. The human melanocyte as a particular target for UVA radiation and an endpoint for photoprotection assessment. Photochem Photobiol. 1999;69(6):686-93.
4. Chedekel MR. Photochemistry and photobiology of epidermal melanins. Photochem Photobiol. 1982;35(6):881-5. doi: 10.1111/j.1751-1097.1982.tb02663
5. Prota G. The chemistry of melanins and melanogenesis. Fortschr Chem Org Naturst. 1995; 64: 93-148. doi:10.1007/978-3-7091-9337-2_2.
6. Moreno-Camacho CA, Montoya-Torres JR, Jaegler A, Gondran N. Sustainability metrics for real case applications of the supply chain network design problem: A systematic literature review. J Clean Prod. 2019;231:600–18. Available from: https://linkinghub.elsevier.com/retrieve/pii/S0959652619318141
7. Parrado C, Gilaberte Y, Philips N, Juarranz A, Gonzalez S. Chapter 34 - Fern extract, oxidative stress, and skin cancer. In: Preedy VR, Patel VB, editors. Cancer (Second Edition). San Diego: Academic Press; 2021. p. 387–98. Available from: https://www.sciencedirect.com/science/article/pii/B9780128195475000341
8. Kullavanijaya P, Lim HW. Photoprotection. J Am Acad Dermatol. 2005;52(6):937–58.
9. Ozone layer depletion: Cause, effects, and solutions | Business Standard News. [cited 2022 Mar 1]. Available from: https://www.business-standard.com/article/current-affairs/ozone-layer-depletion-cause-effects-and-solutions-120091601697_1.html
10. Joshi A, Kumar A. What can we learn from the electromagnetic spectrum? Resonance. 2003;8:8–25.
11. Krutmann J, Morita A, Chung JH. Sun exposure: what molecular photodermatology tells us about its good and bad sides. J Invest Dermatol. 2012;132(3 Pt 2):976-984. Mancebo SE, Hu JY, Wang SQ. Sunscreens: a review of health benefits, regulations, and controversies. Dermatol Clin. 2014; 32(3):427–438.
12. Mancebo SE, Hu JY, Wang SQ. Sunscreens: a review of health benefits, regulations, and controversies. Dermatol Clin. 2014; 32(3):427–438.c
13. UVA vs. UVB Rays: What's the Difference? [cited 2022 Mar 1]. Available from: https://www.healthline.com/health/skin/uva-vs-uvb
14. Gabros S, Nessel TA, Zito PM. Sunscreens And Photoprotection. In: StatPearls. Treasure Island (FL): StatPearls Publishing; 2022 [cited 2022 Mar 1]. Available from: http://www.ncbi.nlm.nih.gov/books/NBK537164/
15. Bhattacharjee D, Patil A, Jain V, preethi.s P. A comparison of Natural and Synthetic Sunscreen Agents: A Review. Int J Pharm Res. 2021;13.
16. Seemal R. Desai MDa, Corey L. Hartman MDb, Pearl E. Grimes MDc, Sana Shah, J Drugs Dermatol. 2021;20(12): 1276-1279. doi:10.36849/JDD.6367 February 3rd 2022.
17. Gies PH, Roy CR, Toomey S, McLennan A. Protection against solar ultraviolet radiation. Mutation Research. 1998;422(1):15-22.
18. Fageon L, Moyal D, Coutet J, Candau D. Importance of sunscreen products spreading protocol and substrate roughness for in vitro sun protection factor assessment. Int J Cosmet Sci. 2009;31(6):405-418.
19. Gilchrest BA. The A-B-C-Ds of sensible sun protection. Skin Therapy Lett. 2008; 13(5):1-5.

20. Kripke ML. The ABCs of sunscreen protection factors. J Invest Dermatol. 2003;121(1):7-8.
21. Hanrahan JR. Sunscreens. Aust Prescr. 2012;35(5):149–51.
22. Schauder S. Bewertung von Lichtschutzmitteln [Evaluation of sunscreening agents]. *Z Hautkr*. 1988; 63 (1):44-48.
23. Donglikar, MM and Deore SL (2016) Sunscreens: A review. Pharmacogn. J. 8(3):171-179
24. Sies H, Stahl W. Non-nutritive bioactive constituents of plants: lycopene, lutein and zeaxanthin. Int J Vitam Nutr Res. 2003;73(2):95-100
25. Ashawat MS, Madhuri BSS, Swarnlata S. Herbal cosmetics: trends in skin care formulation. Pharmacognosy Reviews. 2009;3(5):72-79.
26. Geoffrey K, Mwangi AN, Maru SM. Sunscreen products: Rationale for use, formulation development and regulatory considerations. Saudi Pharm J. 2019;27(7):1009–18.
27. Mori S, Wang SQ. Sunscreens. In: Wolverton SE, editor. Comprehensive Dermatologic Drug Therapy (Fourth Edition). Elsevier; 2021. p. 565-575.e2.
28. D'Orazio J, Jarrett S, Amaro-Ortiz A, Scott T. UV Radiation and the Skin. Int J Mol Sci . 2013;14(6):12222–48.
29. Albini A. Interaction with the environment: Skin. In: Light, Molecules, Reaction and Health. Elsevier; 2020.p. 29–147.
30. How does sunscreen work? | Live Science. [cited 2022 Mar 3]. Available from: https://www.livescience.com/32666-how-does-sunscreen-work.html
31. Wang J, Ganley CJ. Safety Threshold Considerations for Sunscreen Systemic Exposure: A Simulation Study. Clin Pharmacol Ther. 2019;105(1):161–7. Available from: https://onlinelibrary.wiley.com/doi/10.1002/cpt.1178
32. Cole C. Multicenter evaluation of sunscreen UVA protectiveness with the protection factor test method. J Am Acad Dermatol. 1994;30(5):729–36.
33. Pelizzo M, Zattra E, Nicolosi P, Peserico A, Garoli D, Alaibac M. In Vitro Evaluation of Sunscreens: An Update for the Clinicians. ISRN Dermatol. 2012;e352135.
34. Kaidbey KH, Barnes A. Determination of UVA protection factors by means of immediate pigment darkening in normal skin. J Am Acad Dermatol. 1991;25(2):262–266.
35. Moyal D, Chardon A, Kollias N. UVA protection efficacy of sunscreens can be determined by thepersistent pigment darkening (PPD) method. Photodermatol Photoimmunol Photomed. 2000;16(6):250–5.
36. Saewan N, Jimtaisong A. Natural products as photoprotection. J Cosmet Dermatol. 2015;14(1):47-63.
37. Hoppe VU, Kopplow HJ, Wiskemann A. Statistical evaluation of light protection factors. Arzneimittelforschung. 1975; 25(5):817-825
38. Curtis Cole. Multicenter evaluation of sunscreen UVA protectiveness with the protection factor test method. 1994;30(5):729-736.
39. Lowe NJ, Breeding J. Evaluation of sunscreen protection by measurement of epidermal DNA synthesis. J Invest Dermatol. 1980;74(3):181–182.
40. Schauder S. [Evaluation of sunscreening agents]. Z Hautkr. 1988;63(9):764-770.
41. Addor FAS, Barcaui CB, Gomes EE, Lupi O, Marçon CR, Miot HA. Sunscreen lotions in the dermatological prescription: review of concepts and controversies. An Bras Dermatol. 2022;97(2):204-222. Available from: https://doi.org/10.1016/j.abd.2021.05.012

42. Moloney FJ, Collins S, Murphy GM. Sunscreens: Safety, Efficacy and Appropriate Use. Am J Clin Dermatol. 2002;3(3):185–191. Available from: https://doi.org/10.2165/00128071-200203030-00005
43. Diffey BL, Grice J. The influence of sunscreen type on photoprotection. Br J Dermatol. 1997;137(1):103–105.
44. Whiteman DC, Neale RE, Aitken J, Gordon L, Green AC, Janda M, et al. When to apply sunscreen: a consensus statement for Australia and New Zealand. Aust N Z J Public Health. 2019;43(2):171–175. Available from: https://doi.org/10.1111/1753-6405.12873.
45. Government of Ontario M of L. 2. Health Effects of UV Exposure | Ultraviolet Radiation in the Workplace | Ontario Ministry of Labour. Government of Ontario, Ministry of Labour. [cited 2022 Mar 1]. Available from: https://www.labour.gov.on.ca/english/hs/pubs/uvradiation/gl_uvrad_2.php
46. Landow K. Do sunscreens prevent skin cancer? Postgrad Med. 2004;116(1):6–6.
47. Shanbhag S, Nayak A, Narayan R, Nayak UY. Anti-aging and Sunscreens: Paradigm Shift in Cosmetics. Adv Pharm Bull. 2019;9(3):348–59.
48. Qureshi AA, Laden F, Colditz GA, Hunter DJ. Geographic Variation and Risk of Skin Cancer in US Women: Differences Between Melanoma, Squamous Cell Carcinoma, and Basal Cell Carcinoma. Arch Intern Med. 2008;168(5):501–7. Available from: https://doi.org/10.1001/archinte.168.5.501
49. Melanoma Skin Cancer Statistics. [cited 2022 Mar 17]. Available from: https://www.cancer.org/cancer/melanoma-skin-cancer/about/key-statistics.html
50. Melanoma Survival Rates | Melanoma Survival Statistics. [cited 2022 Mar 17]. Available from: https://www.cancer.org/cancer/melanoma-skin-cancer/detection-diagnosis-staging/survival-rates-for-melanoma-skin-cancer-by-stage.html
51. 5 Reasons To Use Sunscreen Every Day. Parrish Healthcare. [cited 2022 Mar 1]. Available from: https://www.parrishhealthcare.com/news/2020/july/5-reasons-to-use-sunscreen-every-day/
52. Sunscreen for Eczema: Why It's Important and the Best Brands. EverydayHealth.com. [cited 2022 Mar 1]. Available from: https://www.everydayhealth.com/products/reviews/best-sunscreens-eczema/
53. Sunscreen Allergy: Symptoms, Treatment, Prevention. [cited 2022 Mar 1]. Available from: https://www.healthline.com/health/sunscreen-allergy#tips
54. James E, Fulton Jr.. Comedogenicity of current therapeutic products, cosmetics, and ingredients in the rabbit ear. Journal of the American Academy of Dermatology. 1984;10(1), 96–105. Available from: https://doi.org/10.1016/S0190-9622(84)80050-X
55. Latha MS, Martis J, Shobha V, Shinde RS, Bangera S, Krishnankutty B, et al. Sunscreening Agents. J Clin Aesthet Dermatol. 2013;6(1):16-26
56. Barbosa TC, Nascimento LED, Bani C, Almeida T, Nery M, Santos RS, et al. Development, Cytotoxicity and Eye Irritation Profile of a New Sunscreen Formulation Based on Benzophenone-3-poly(ε-caprolactone) Nanocapsules. Toxics. 2019;7(4):51. Available from: https://doi.org/10.3390/toxics7040051

57. Protecting your eyes from sunscreen. Charlotte Eye Ear Nose & Throat Associates. [cited 2022 Mar 2]. Available from: https://www.ceenta.com/news-blog/the-danger-of-getting-sunscreen-in-your-eyes
58. Sunscreen may cause vitamin D deficiency, says study. [cited 2022 Mar 2]. Available from: https://www.medicalnewstoday.com/articles/317278#Sunscreen-may-reduce-vitamin-D-3-production-by-99-percent
59. Sunscreen Agent (Topical Application Route) Side Effects - Mayo Clinic. [cited 2022 Apr 22]. Available from: https://www.mayoclinic.org/drugs-supplements/sunscreen-agent-topical-application-route/side-effects/drg-20070255
60. Danovaro R, Corinaldesi C. Sunscreen Products Increase Virus Production Through Prophage Induction in Marine Bacterioplankton. Microb Ecol . 2003;45(2):109–118. Available from: https://doi.org/10.1007/s00248-002-1033-0
61. Lamotte S. Seven sunscreen chemicals enter bloodstream after one use, FDA says, but don't abandon sun protection. WINK NEWS. 2020. [cited 2022 Mar 17]. Available from: https://www.winknews.com/2020/01/22/seven-sunscreen-chemicals-enter-bloodstream-after-one-use-fda-says-but-dont-abandon-sun-protection/
62. All You Need to Know About Sunscreens for Babies. Harper's Bazaar Singapore. [cited 2022 Mar 17]. Available from: https:/ /www.harpersbazaar.com.sg/gallery/all-you-need-to-know-about-sunscreens-for-babies/
63. Heurung AR, Raju SI, Warshaw EM. Adverse reactions to sunscreen agents: Epidemiology, responsible irritants and allergens, clinical characteristics, and management. Dermatitis. 2014;25(6):289-326. Available from: https://doi.org/10.1097/DER.0000000000000079
64. Manikrao Donglikar M, Laxman Deore S. Sunscreens: A review. Pharmacogn J. 2016;8(3):171–179.
65. Novitasari T, Prajitno S, and Indramaya DM. Behavior of Sunscreen Usage Among Medical Students. *Berkala Ilmu Kesehatan Kulit Dan Kelamin*, 2020;*32*(3):174–181. Available from: https://doi.org/10.20473/bikk.V32.3.2020.174-181
66. Collins P, Ferguson J. Photoallergic contact dermatitis to oxybenzone. Br J Dermatol . 1994;131(1):124–129. Available from: https://doi.org/10.1111/j.1365-2133.1994.tb08469.x
67. Sun protection factor (SPF): What is the best sunscreen? 2018 [cited 2022 Mar 3]. Available from: https://www.medicalnewstoday.com/articles/306838
68. Sun Damage: Protecting Yourself. Cleveland Clinic. [cited 2022 Mar 2] Available from: https://my.clevelandclinic.org/health/articles/5240-sun-damage-protecting-yourself

CHAPTER EIGHT

Cosmetic surgery

Ayodeji O Oladele

Cosmetic surgery, also known as aesthetic surgery, is the deployment of surgical procedures to achieve enhancement in appearance of different parts of the body. It has evolved as an aspect of plastic surgery. The term, plastic surgery, is derived from the Greek word, 'plastikos', which means to mould or to form (1). This moulding or forming involves the reconstruction of a deformed, malformed or defective part of the body that does not represent normal anatomy (2), such as the reconstruction of an amputated nose (3). It does not only achieve an improvement in appearance but also impact significantly on function. It is the surgery of form and function.

Cosmetic surgery has evolved to include procedures that aim at improving appearance alone with the absence of a deformity or abnormal anatomy. This has led to its being referred to as 'vanity surgery' (4). The desire and performance of cosmetic surgery have spread across the world, not only limited to the developed economies but also to some low and middle income countries (5), having been influenced by the increasing use of social media (6). The current level of request for cosmetic surgery is, however, relatively sparse in low- and middle-income countries possibly due to ignorance, low socio-economic status, paucity of personnel and lack of facilities for the procedures.

Cosmetic surgery does not commonly deal with disease states, in certain instances, the dividing line is blurred, as some patients may not have a physical ailment but a psychological one. Therefore, cosmetic surgery is considered a medical practice as it has a bearing on psychological health, and its performance has been associated with improvement in the sense of wellbeing.

Cosmetic surgery continues to be a vast and rapidly evolving specialty in the beauty industry. With new and emerging procedures and techniques, many of which are not time-tested, it is important for every prospective cosmetic surgery client to conduct due diligence and be adequately enlightened before embarking on the surgery procedures to avoid unintended outcomes.

Aspects of cosmetics

Achieving an improvement in appearance involves:

- skin care and use of topical pharmacological agents
- non-invasive procedures, e.g., lasers, radiofrequency procedures
- minimally invasive procedures and injections
- open surgical procedures

The latter three groups of procedures are commonly employed in cosmetic surgery.

Ethical considerations and regulation for cosmetic surgery

The field of cosmetic surgery is largely driven by clients' desire for an improvement in appearance (10). The procedures involved are aimed primarily at enhancing appearance and not necessarily as a result of a disease process, as it obtains in traditional fields of surgery. Ethical considerations are, therefore, very important (11) in order to avoid practices that do not conform to ethical standards in medical practice.

The regulation of cosmetic surgery practice is challenging because clients may go out of their way to seek what they consider desirable, regardless of health implications (12). There is also the aspect of media interest in changing appearance, especially among the famous celebrities many of whom are particular about their public appearance due to their career in the show business.

Cosmetic surgery practice

Plastic surgical procedures can be generally grouped into: standard or established procedures; new; and upcoming procedures. The procedures in the former are those which have been scientifically proven or time-tested while the latter are those not yet time-tested. There is a need to distinguish clearly between the two while considering patient information and during counselling before a patient is subjected to cosmetic surgery (21).

The key considerations in cosmetic surgery practice involve the practitioners, the tools, materials and methods employed in its practice.

Practitioners

Cosmetic surgery is practiced by a wide range of surgeons, physicians and sometimes non-physicians such as beauticians, depending on the type of the cosmetic surgery and the part of the body involved (13). In the light of this, "non-plastic surgeons", compared to plastic surgeons who are traditionally known to perform cosmetic surgery, include physicians in other aspects of medicine such as dermatologists, as well as surgeons in other fields of surgery such as orthorhinolaryngologists, ophthalmologists and general surgeons. These personnels, however, have to undergo training and receive certification depending on the aspects of plastic surgery they practice (14). Nonetheless, there is the need to involve trainees, in order to develop manpower for cosmetic surgery (15).

Tools

Cosmetic surgery entails the use of a wide range of tools, some of which are discussed as follows:

The surgeon's knife: As a surgical practice, the cosmetic surgeon employs the use of his knife to cut and, thereafter, sutures are employed to stitch the different tissues together so as to achieve an improvement in aesthetic appearance. This has led to the colloquial term "going under the knife" to describe patients who undergo cosmetic surgery.

Machines: There are different types of machines employed in the performance of cosmetic surgery, such as liposuction machines, ultrasound machines and dermabraiders.

Lasers: Lasers possess qualities that has made it an addition to the arsenal of the cosmetic surgeon. Laser is the acronym for 'light amplification by stimulated emission of radiation'. It acts as a high precision 'knife' and cautery; and its other properties make it very useful in cosmetic surgery. Its major advantage is in the conduct of different procedures with a higher level of accuracy and precision which are essential to outcomes in cosmetic surgery. There are different types of lasers, with a wide range of properties and applications in cosmetic surgery. Some are used to occlude unwanted vessels and to achieve superficial peeling of the skin, among other uses.

Radiofrequency devices: These are newer devices which are non-invasive and are used to achieve effects similar to lasers.

Other materials such as drugs, injections, synthetic implant materials are employed by the cosmetic surgeon.

As advances in biotechnology continue, many new devices, procedures and materials are to be expected to increase the arsenal available to the cosmetic surgeon.

Patient selection

There is a need to choose patients carefully so as to avoid those who have a pathological desire to change appearance and this has led to the description of a psychiatric problem referred to as body dysmorphic disorder. Patients undergoing psychiatric care should receive clean bill of health before embarking on cosmetic surgery. Patients should also be free of diseases and other conditions of ill-health that can adversely affect the outcome of cosmetic surgery (16,17).

Preparing for surgery

Preparatory to surgery, blood thinning drugs such as aspirin and anticoagulants should be discontinued for up to 2 weeks, as these will increase the risk of excessive bleeding and formation of blood clots, respectively, which are common complications in cosmetic surgery. Smoking should also be stopped for at least one month. Investigations, such as a complete blood count, blood electrolytes and clotting profile should be performed. The patients should be screened for diabetes, and an electrocardiogram should be performed to assess the health of the heart, as many of the patients are in their middle age and older and are at increased risk of cardiovascular diseases.

Anaesthesia

The patient is evaluated prior to surgery by the anaesthesiologist. Anaesthesia for cosmetic surgery could be local anaesthesia, regional anaesthesia, conscious sedation or general anaesthesia with intubation of the trachea. The choice will depend on the location of the surgery and the extent and duration of the procedure. The choice of anaesthesia is, therefore, essential and due consideration should be given to avoid anaesthetic complications (19).

Non-surgical procedures

Non-surgical procedures are commonly used to enhance facial appearance.

Face

The face, being the focus of individual identity and beauty, is rarely covered with clothing and, therefore, is a central focus of cosmetic surgery. Acne, scars and wrinkles commonly influence the perception of beauty on the face. Wrinkles are a common occurrence that appear with ageing and result from breaks in the dermal layer of the skin with age. As life span has increased significantly over the years due to advances in medicine, so has the demand for the correction of wrinkles. To correct or reverse wrinkles, certain procedures are employed to fill up the breaks in the dermis using various agents which are injected into the dermis to fill it up.

Injectable fillers: Various types of injectables have been developed and some of them are described as follows:

Collagen: This is the primary component of most of the early injectables and comes in different forms based on the source of the collagen, whether human (from cadavers or from the patient), bovine (from cows) or porcine (from pigs), and in combination with other agents. These agents are absorbed over time and repeated injections may be required depending on how long it takes for them to be absorbed or degraded within the tissues. Once injected, they fill up tissue defects in the dermis which results in a smooth, youthful appearance of the skin.

Hyaluronic acid: With the advancement in biotechnology and genetic engineering, hyaluronic acid, which is normally present in the body, was commercially produced and used as injectable fillers for wrinkles. This has the benefit of being non-allergenic and lasts longer in tissues than collagen, for up to 12 months.

Calcium hydroxyapatite: This injectable product is synthetic and is nontoxic. It also lasts long in tissues.

Silicone: This is no longer used as a tissue filler because of its tissue toxicity.

Botox: This is a form of injectable but works in a different way from filling up the tissues. Botox contains the botulinum toxin obtained from the bacterium, *Clostridium botulinum*, that causes paralysis of muscles by blocking signals from the nerves to the muscles of the face, whose contraction normally causes wrinkles. The injected muscles can no longer contract, thus, making wrinkles to relax and soften. The procedure takes a few minutes, with the provider using a small needle to inject the agent into identified muscles. It does not need anaesthesia, but gives only minor discomfort. The patient is advised not to rub the site for at least 24 hours and to stay upright for 4 hours after the injection. Exercising is also not advised till a day after the procedure. The patient stops taking aspirin and anti-inflammatory medications two weeks and alcohol one week before the treatment; this prevents bruising. The procedure is often used on frown lines, in between the eyebrows, crow's feet (lines around the corner of the eye) and forehead lines. It does not, however, work for wrinkles caused by sun damage or gravity. The effect is fully apparent 7 to 14 days after treatment and lasts up to 2 - 6 months; repeated injections may be required as the lines and wrinkles begin to reappear. In time, the muscles undergo permanent paralysis and effects are irreversible, for which reason it is also called a "chemical knife". Some patients, however, become resistant to the effects of botox over time due to the production of antibodies which neutralise its effects.

Side effects of botox treatment include: bruising, headaches which disappears within 48 hours, eyelid drooping, eye dryness or severe tearing, crooked smiling or drooling, mild pain or swelling around injection site, general unwell feeling, numbness, weakness in nearby muscles and upset stomach. Botox injection is contraindicated for women that are pregnant or breast-feeding, for persons with neurological diseases and those allergic to cow milk proteins.

Botox, being the first to be available, is actually a brand name that is commonly used for botulinum toxin-containing products. Other brands include Dysport and Xeomin.

Many other products are being developed as injectables and the patient should ensure that only products that are approved by the appropriate food and drugs regulatory agencies are injected into them as tissue fillers.

Surgical procedures

This list of cosmetic surgical procedures is by no means exhaustive but the commonly performed procedures are here highlighted.

Facelift (rhytidectomy)

This is a surgical procedure that is used to tighten up the ageing and sagging skin of the cheeks, the jaws, the neck and around the ears. It is a common cosmetic surgical procedure that has undergone evolution over the years (22). Skin markings are done while the patient is awake, with the patient in a sitting position, so as to determine the natural position of the sagging skin. Thereafter, the patient is placed under general anaesthesia, with intubation of the trachea; or local anaesthesia with intravenous sedation and skin incisions made around the ear. The skin of the face in the respective areas is then lifted up, along with varying degrees of underlying tissues, tightened by a pull towards the back, the excess skin is trimmed off and the wounds are closed over a tube to drain blood or fluid which may collect beneath the skin. The complications which may occur include a hematoma (blood clot) within the dissected skin, which may also lead to skin loss, and breathing problems. There is also a risk of injury to abnormally positioned nerves in the face and the patient may develop hair loss from the areas of the lifted skin. Scarring may also be a problem when the wound heals.

Nose Reshaping (rhinoplasty)

The nose, being a central figure on the face, shapes the perception and body image of a person. Nose reshaping is a cosmetic surgical procedure aimed at reshaping the nose based on patient's desired appearance. It is also often performed for cosmetic reasons as well as to improve on breathing. It is common among Caucasians and involves the removal of the hump on the dorsum of the nose. Each surgery has to be individualised due to the high variations in the anatomy of the nose and this makes it one of the most difficult cosmetic surgical procedures. The complications that may result from this surgery include bleeding, bruising and swelling, infection, temporary obstruction of breathing, and patient dissatisfaction which may necessitate another rhinoplasty.

Eye aesthetic surgery

The surgery aims at elevating the eyebrows or removing the bagginess around the eyes because of loose skin that occurs with ageing when the skin loses its elasticity and sags. The bagginess under the eyes gives an impression of an old and tired person. The excess skin is removed at surgery with local anaesthesia or sedation. This procedure can also be performed via endoscopic techniques.

Facial alloplastic implants

The use of synthetic materials, inserted into the bony prominences on the face and in specific regions, has also been used to enhance cosmesis. Such inserts alter the contour of the face and make certain areas prominent depending on where they are placed. The most important of the prominences are the malar (over the cheek bone), the nose, the mandibular (over the jawbone and chin), and the supraorbital (the bony prominence above the eyes). The materials are inserted at surgery, under anaesthesia and may sometimes develop complications such as asymmetry, malpositioning, nerve dysfunction, and patient dissatisfaction.

Peeling

This involves the deliberate removal of the outer layer of the skin (epidermis) to stimulate healing. The new skin that is formed is free of wrinkles and appears more youthful and beautiful. Peeling can be achieved by different means, such as the use of chemicals which include glycolic acid, trichloroacetic acid, salicylic acid, lactic acid and carbolic acid (phenol); mechanical techniques (dermabrasion) and laser carbon peel. They may be used alone or as an adjunct to other cosmetic surgery procedures to improve the appearance of the skin.

Dermabrasion: This is an outpatient procedure. The skin is numbed with a local anaesthesia before removal of its outermost layer with a rotating instrument.

Skin peeling is also used in treating acne scars, uneven skin tone, scars from injury or surgery, rhinophyma or redness and thick skin on the nose, sun-damaged photoaging, melasma, precancerous skin patches, as well as removal of tattoos. It is contraindicated in inflammatory acne; radiation burns and recurrent herpes flare-ups.

Body contouring

This involves surgical procedures that aim at cutting off excess skin and fat that keep the body out of shape. When a person gains weight, there is a disproportionate accumulation of fat in certain areas of the body - the lower abdominal region and around the waist, the buttocks and the thighs. In the upper limbs, the upper arms, especially on the inner aspect, develop a fold of skin and fat. Brachioplasty or upper arm lift is the term used for the removal of fat from the arm while thigh lift refers to the removal of fat and skin from the thighs. All these areas are amenable to surgical correction by excision of the excess skin and fat, in order to achieve a more cosmetically acceptable body contour. An example is abdominoplasty (tummy tuck) shown in Figures 8.1 to 8.6.

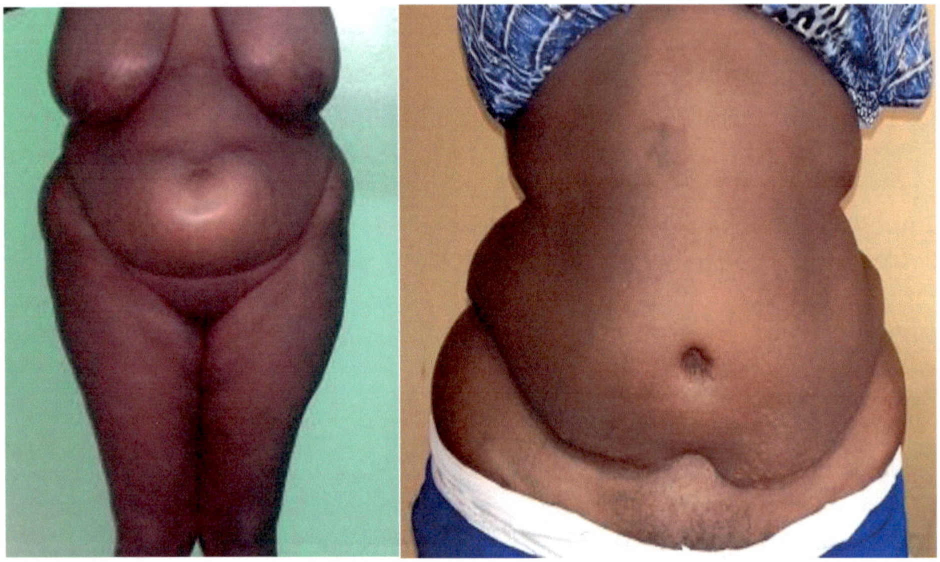

Figures 8.1 and 8.2: Front view of abdominoplasty before and after surgery, respectively

Liposuction

This is the removal of fat beneath the skin by sucking out the fat using small-diameter tubes with multiple holes (cannulas) which are attached to a high vacuum. As the tube is moved back and forth, the fat is dislodged and sucked up along with body fluids and fluids that had been previously injected to make the removal of the fat easier and to minimise bleeding. It is increasingly common (23,24) and best suited to localised deposits of fat which are unresponsive to diet or exercise or as an adjunct to the body-contouring surgeries described earlier. It can be assisted by ultrasound and involves the injection of fluids into the tissues to ease the sucking up of the fat.

Untoward effects of liposuction include: contour irregularities, fat embolism, kidney and heart problems, internal puncture, fluid accumulation, numbness, infection and toxicity of local anaesthetic agents used such as lidocaine.

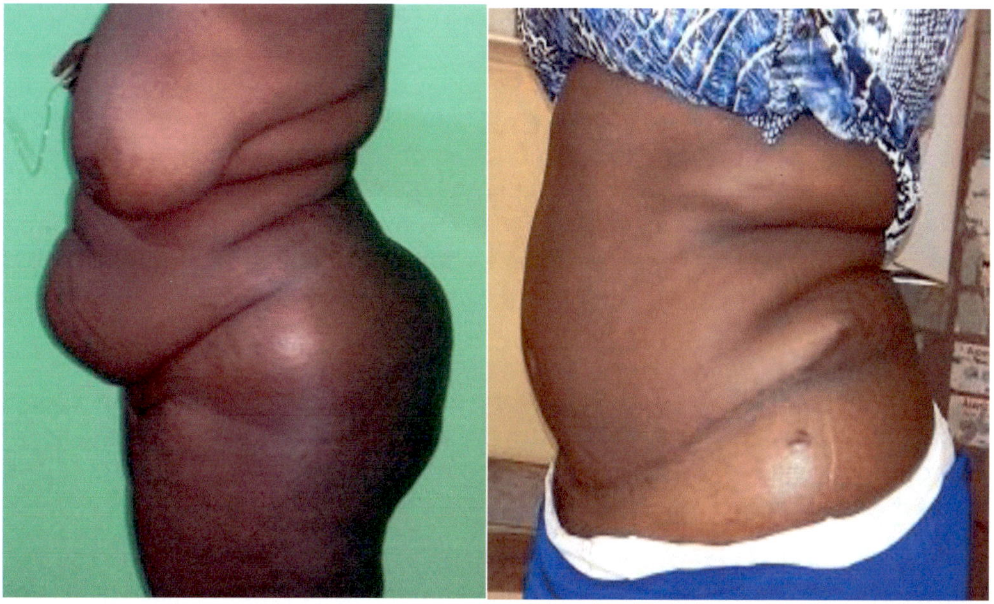

Figures 8.3 and 8.4: Left side view of abdominoplasty before and after surgery, respectively

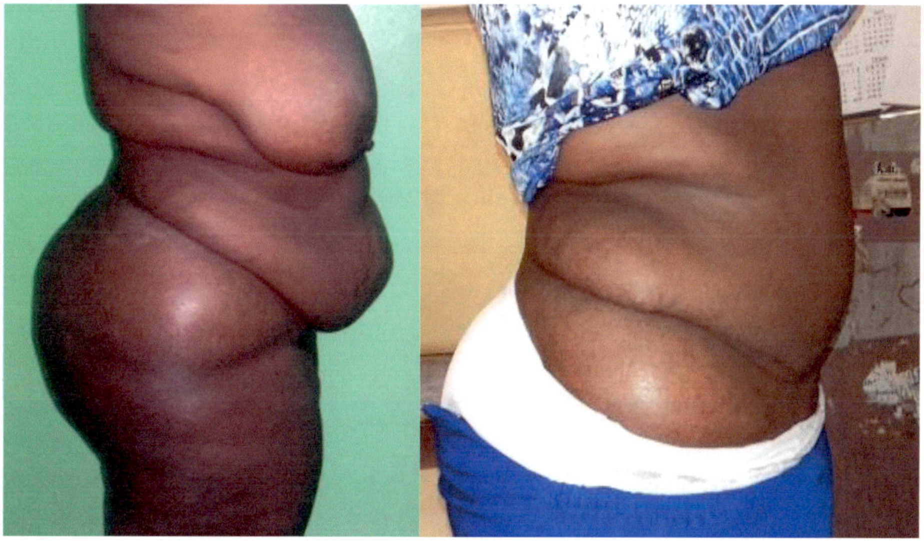

Figures 8.5 and 8.6: Right side view of abdominoplasty before and after surgery, respectively

Fat-grafting

Skin folds that develop with ageing on the face may not be corrected with facelifts due to the more anterior location of the folds close to the nose. Fat grafts are very useful in filling up the folds. The fat is harvested as in liposuction, the accompanying blood and the injected local anaesthetic are removed by placing the fat on an absorbent gauze pad. The fat is then injected into the skin folds to fill up the folds where it gets incorporated into the tissues as living tissue. The results of fat grafting are variable. The results may be lost if the fat-graft atrophies but, generally, at least half of grafted fat is expected to survive.

Cosmetic breast surgery (mammoplasty)

This is one of the most frequently performed cosmetic surgeries among Caucasian females. It may be augmentation of the breast, reduction of the breast, firming up of the breast to reduce sagging, reduction of the size of the nipple-areolar area or a combination of any of these.

Breast augmentation (augmentation mammoplasty)**:** This is usually achieved by the use of breast implants which are made of non-allergenic materials such as silicone, filled with saline. It is placed through a surgical procedure beneath the breast and is filled to the required size to achieve an increase in the projection of the breast. These implants usually fair well but may suffer complication such as infections, blood clots, dislocation or migration of the implant, ruptures, or contractures making them firm and non-supple thereby losing the feel of a natural breast.

Breast reduction (reduction mammoplasty): This involves the surgical removal of some portions of the breast based on carefully designed techniques so as to achieve a uniform overall and cosmetically pleasing appearance of the breast (Figures 8.7 and 8.8).

It is employed in cases of excessively large breasts which, although considered a cosmetic procedure, is commonly associated with other pathology that is responsible for the excessive enlargement of the breast. This enlargement is often accompanied by physical and psychological diseases which are relieved with the surgical reduction of the breast. The reduction is also often accompanied by a breast- lift as the excessively large breasts are almost invariably sagging.

Breast lift (mastopexy): The goal of this procedure is to achieve a more anterior projection of the nipple, giving it a more youthful appearance, as the nipple increasingly assumes a dependent, sagging and downward projection with ageing. It also invariably involves the removal of excessive sagging tissues.

Male breast reduction: This is often required to address excessive growth of the breast in males, a condition that is termed gynaecomastia. Men perceive large breasts as being non-masculine and tend to wear clothing always to cover up, so as to avoid teasing and embarrassment.

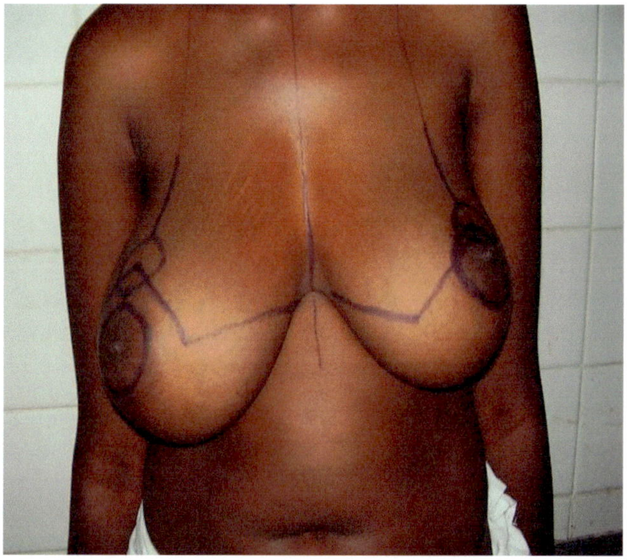

Figure 8.7: Excessively large breasts marked for reduction mammoplasty before surgery

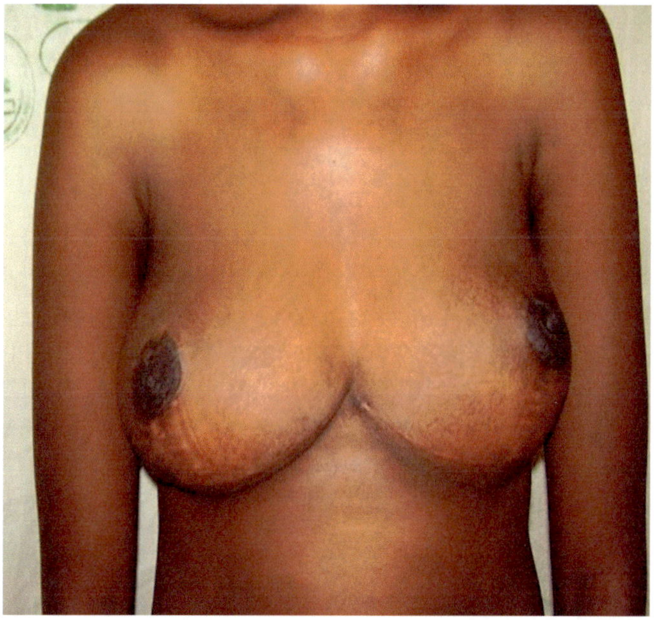

Figure 8.8: The appearance of the breast in Figure 8.7 after reduction mammoplasty

Gynaecomastia may resolve with age after puberty but in later adult life, may reappear due to reducing levels of the testosterone hormone, or due to the side effect of certain drugs like cardiac drugs, AIDS drugs, steroids and marijuana. Thyroid and liver diseases may also be associated with breast growth. The reduction in male breast size may be accomplished by liposuction or by open surgery.

Hand rejuvenation

The process of fat-grafting described earlier is used in hand rejuvenation (25). As ageing proceeds, the hand loses fat and the skin thins and wrinkles. Fat-grafting is used to deposit fat between the skin and the underlying tendons to produce a more youthful, rejuvenated appearance. This procedure is, however, embarked upon very cautiously as complications of infections, if they occur, may lead to loss of hand function to a significant degree which would be a heavy cost for a cosmetic surgery procedure.

Hair removal

Unwanted hairs, especially among females, could constitute a cosmetic embarrassment. Several methods have been employed in hair removal including waxing, bleaching, shaving, plucking, electrolysis and lasers. Modern lasers are by far the most effective in the removal of hairs by being very precise, and their effects most long-lasting. Lasers are most effective in destroying actively dividing hair; therefore, other methods of hair removal should be stopped for months prior to laser hair removal. Multiple sessions are required as 20 – 40% of hairs are killed in each session as not all hair fibres are actively always dividing. Therefore, up to 4 sessions may be required to achieve up to 90% hair removal in whites. In blacks, and the more pigmented races, more sessions are required to achieve the same effect (26).

Hair transplantation/implants

This involves the removal of hair-bearing skin from one part of the scalp to hairless areas, in the treatment of baldness or alopecia. Different sizes of hair-bearing skin are taken, ranging from small sizes of the scalp to transplanting of individual hair follicles. These are implanted in the bald area after careful planning, so as to increase the density of hair in the area. This procedure has, however, been decreasing in popularity over time due to results which are typically poor as some of the hairs are lost after several years. Late scarring may also be a complication.

Tattoo removal

The removal of tattoos, which the wearer considers a cosmetic blemish, is also an aspect of cosmetic surgery. In the use of traditional laser techniques, each colour of ink can only be removed by a single type of laser. For this reason, multiple sessions with different types of lasers are required for laser removal of tattoos. Besides, the tattoo pigments may not completely disappear as they are taken up by adjacent cells and blurry pigmentation may remain. Repeated laser application may also result in scarring of the overlying skin. More recent types of laser have been employed in the removal of tattoos and preliminary studies have showed more promise with shorter treatment times and more effectiveness in removal of tattoos (27).

Genital cosmetic surgery

Genital cosmetic surgery has been assuming importance in recent times. Some females request reduction of the bulky labia which protrudes through dressing or the inner labia which protrudes beyond the outer labia. Laser hair removal has achieved permanent hair removal from the pubic area. Other procedures like labia augmentation, vaginal rejuvenation, hymen repair to restore virginity, vaginal reduction and pubic liposuctions are assuming increasing prominence (28).

In males, procedures like liposuction around the pubic region, penile augmentation to increase the size of the penis by injecting fat and hyaluronic acid, are being performed; but many of the procedures are yet to be time-tested.

Gender reassignment surgery (gender affirmation surgery)

This is a relatively recent aspect of genital cosmetic surgery that involves changing the genitalia from the male to the female form, or vice versa, in patients who suffer gender dysphoria and which could lead to psychosocial sequelae (29). The surgeries form part of the holistic care of these patients which also involves psychotherapy as well as hormonal therapy, among others. Surgeries may also be performed on the face, neck, chest and other parts of the body to enhance the appearance that is consistent with the reassigned gender.

Face transplantation

Since the performance of the first face transplant in France in 2005, face transplantation has become a rapidly emerging field in plastic surgery for patients who have suffered significant facial disfigurement from trauma. As with other transplants, rejection will remain a major challenge (30), but with increasing modulation of the immune system, it is hoped that face transplantation will hold much promise for the future.

Cosmesis in Dentistry

Cosmesis is also very important in the field of dentistry. Procedures to whiten the teeth, ensuring proper order and alignment of the teeth (orthodontics) (31), the use of prosthetic materials to improve or replace defective or missing teeth are also a very important aspect of cosmetic surgery performed by the dental surgeon.

Complications of cosmetic surgery

Allergic reactions (to injectable products), infection, bleeding, blood clots, necrosis of skin, scarring, and poor outcomes are some of the common, general complications that may occur. Some other complications that are specific to some other cosmetic surgery procedures have been mentioned under them.

References

1. Macionis V. History of plastic surgery: Art, philosophy, and rhinoplasty. J Plast Reconstr Aesthet Surg. 2018 Jul;71(7):1086–92.
2. Al-Benna S, Bruce-Chwatt A, Gohritz A. The origins of modern plastic surgery. J Plast Reconstr Aesthet Surg. 2020 Nov;73(11):2086–102.
3. Rana RE, Arora BS. History of plastic surgery in India. J Postgrad Med. 2002 Mar;48(1):76–8.
4. Cosmetic Surgery National Data Bank Statistics. Aesthet Surg J. 2016 Apr;36 Suppl 1:1–29.
5. Hughes CD, Alkire B, Martin C, Semer N, Meara JG. American plastic surgery and global health: a brief history. Ann Plast Surg. 2012 Feb;68(2):222–5.
6. Chen J, Ishii M, Bater KL, Darrach H, Liao D, Huynh PP, et al. Association Between the Use of Social Media and Photograph Editing Applications, Self-esteem, and Cosmetic Surgery Acceptance. JAMA Facial Plast Surg. 2019 Sep 1;21(5):361–7.
7. Yoon S, Kim YA. Cosmetic Surgery and Self-esteem in South Korea: A Systematic Review and Meta-analysis. Aesthetic Plast Surg. 2020 Feb;44(1):229–38.
8. Ambro BT, Wright RJ. Depression in the cosmetic surgery patient. Facial Plast Surg. 2010 Aug;26(4):333–8.
9. Rankin M, Borah GL, Perry AW, Wey PD. Quality-of-life outcomes after cosmetic surgery. Plast Reconstr Surg. 1998 Nov;102(6):2139–45; discussion 2146-2147.
10. Gordon CR, Pryor L, Afifi AM, Benedetto PX, Langevin CJ, Papay F, et al. Cosmetic surgery volume and its correlation with the major US stock market indices. Aesthet Surg J. 2010 Jun;30(3):470–5.
11. Atiyeh BS, Rubeiz MT, Hayek SN. Aesthetic/Cosmetic Surgery and Ethical Challenges. Aesthetic Plast Surg. 2020 Aug;44(4):1364–74.
12. Griffiths D, Mullock A. Cosmetic Surgery: Regulatory Challenges in a Global Beauty Market. Health Care Anal. 2018 Sep;26(3):220–34.
13. Pantelides NM, Highton L, Lamb A, Foden P, Winterton RIS. An analysis of the cosmetic surgery experience acquired through UK plastic surgery training. J Plast Reconstr Aesthet Surg. 2018 Nov;71(11):1532–8.
14. Stuzin JM, Rohrich RJ. Plastic and Reconstructive Surgery and the Evolution of Cosmetic Surgery Education. Plast Reconstr Surg. 2021 Mar 1;147(3):783–8.

15. Ourian AJ, Doval AF, Zavlin D, Chegireddy V, Echo A. Evaluating Patient Outcomes in Breast and Abdominal Cosmetic Plastic Surgery Procedures Involving Residents. Aesthet Surg J. 2019 Apr 8;39(5):572–8.
16. Jafferany M, Salimi S, Mkhoyan R, Kalashnikova N, Sadoughifar R, Jorgaqi E. Psychological aspects of aesthetic and cosmetic surgery: Clinical and therapeutic implications. Dermatol Ther. 2020 Jul;33(4):e13727.
17. Biraben-Gotzamanis L, Aouizerate B, Martin-Guehl C, Grabot D, Tignol J. [Body dysmorphic disorder and cosmetic surgery: assessment of 24 subjects with a minimal defect in appearance 5 years after their request for cosmetic surgery]. Presse Med. 2009 Aug;38(7–8):1062–7.
18. Veale D, Gledhill LJ, Christodoulou P, Hodsoll J. Body dysmorphic disorder in different settings: A systematic review and estimated weighted prevalence. Body Image. 2016 Sep;18:168–86.
19. Bogan V. Anesthesia and safety considerations for office-based cosmetic surgery practice. AANA J. 2012 Aug;80(4):299–305.
20. Nekhendzy V, Ramaiah VK. Prevention of perioperative and anesthesia-related complications in facial cosmetic surgery. Facial Plast Surg Clin North Am. 2013 Nov;21(4):559–77.
21. Retana A. Controversies in Facial Cosmetic Surgery. Oral Maxillofac Surg Clin North Am. 2017 Nov;29(4):441–6.
22. Charafeddine AH, Drake R, McBride J, Zins JE. Facelift: History and Anatomy. Clin Plast Surg. 2019 Oct;46(4):505–13.
23. S W, Dm C, R G. Liposuction: Concepts, safety, and techniques in body-contouring surgery. Cleveland Clinic journal of medicine [Internet]. 2020 Jun [cited 2022 Feb 28];87(6). Available from: https://pubmed.ncbi.nlm.nih.gov/32487557/
24. Oe B, Ja G. Update on Liposuction: What All Plastic Surgeons Should Know. Plastic and reconstructive surgery [Internet]. 2021 Apr 1 [cited 2022 Feb 28];147(4). Available from: https://pubmed.ncbi.nlm.nih.gov/33776041/
25. Cj C, A AG, Mj D, K A, Sj W, Ml E, et al. Fat Grafting for Hand Rejuvenation. Seminars in plastic surgery [Internet]. 2020 Feb [cited 2022 Feb 28];34(1). Available from: https://pubmed.ncbi.nlm.nih.gov/32071579/
26. Lou WW, Quintana AT, Geronemus RG, Grossman MC. Prospective study of hair reduction by diode laser (800 nm) with long-term follow-up. Dermatol Surg. 2000 May;26(5):428–32.
27. V P, E A, E A, M TC. Picosecond laser versus historical responses to Q-switched lasers for tattoo treatment. Journal of cosmetic and laser therapy : official publication of the European Society for Laser Dermatology [Internet]. 2020 Jul 3 [cited 2022 Feb 28];22(4–5). Available from: https://pubmed.ncbi.nlm.nih.gov/33594939/
28. Wilkie G, Bartz D. Vaginal Rejuvenation: A Review of Female Genital Cosmetic Surgery. Obstet Gynecol Surv. 2018 May;73(5):287–92.
29. Selvaggi G, Bellringer J. Gender reassignment surgery: an overview. Nat Rev Urol. 2011 May;8(5):274–82.

30. Siemionow M. The decade of face transplant outcomes. J Mater Sci Mater Med. 2017 May;28(5):64.
31. Mohamed WV, Perenack JD. Aesthetic adjuncts with orthognathic surgery. Oral Maxillofac Surg Clin North Am. 2014 Nov;26(4):573–85.
32. Meier AC, Papadopulos N. [Quality of life after gender reassignment surgery: an overview]. Handchir Mikrochir Plast Chir. 2021 Dec;53(6):556–63.
33. Pan S, Honig SC. Gender-Affirming Surgery: Current Concepts. Curr Urol Rep. 2018 Jun 7;19(8):62.

CHAPTER NINE

The chemical nature of cosmetic agents

Bamigboye J Taiwo

Cosmetic agents consist of chemical compounds that are combined in different proportions to give a perfect blend, resulting in the desired product(s) for the intended purpose(s). Cosmetics are diverse, but preparations for the care of the skin form a major line of cosmetics. The discourse in this chapter is limited only to the chemistry of cosmetic agents.

Chemistry of skin whitening agents

Skin lightening agents are used to give the skin a brighter look and may also be administered for therapeutic purposes in pigmentary disorders, e.g., post-inflammatory hyperpigmentation or melisma (1). Products for skin whitening operate at different stages in melanin synthesis in the skin.

Skin lightening agents act by reducing the amount of melanin, the main source of pigment for skin colour. The colour of the human skin, eyes and hair is derived primarily from melanin which is synthesised from epidermal melanocytes. Melanin is synthesised by the melanocytes upon exposure to irradiations from the ultraviolet B (UVB). The melanin produced in melanosomes is moved to the neighbouring keratinocytes in the epidermis (2). In normal physiological situations, it is the pigmentation of the skin that protects against the deleterious UV injury. However, overproduction of melanin can also lead to dermatological problems like freckles, solar lentigo, melasma, cancer and post inflammatory melanoderma (3-9). Skin pigmentation also has key evolutionary importance in self-defence, animal mimicry and camouflage (10).

Biosynthesis of melanin

Melanogenesis, the process by which melanin is synthesised by the melanocytes present in the melanosomes, involves both enzymatic as well as chemical-catalysed reactions. Two categories of melanin are synthesised: the brown-black eumelanin which is produced from conjugation of indole-5,6-quinone, 5,6-dihydroxyl indole-2-carboxylic acid or indole-2-carboxylic acid-5,6-quinone and the red-yellow pheomelanin which is produced from cysteine or glutathione conjugation (11-13). L-tyrosine's oxidation to dopaquinone (DQ), required for eumelanin synthesis (Figure 9.1) and pheomelanin (14, 15) by tyrosinase (TYR), initiates the melanogenesis process. After DQ formation, which is the slowest step, intramolecular cyclisation of the DQ follows to give leukodopachrome (cyclodopa). This leukodopachrome yields dopachrome, which in a cascade of biosynthetic events gives rise to dihydroxyindole (DHI) and dihydroxyindole-2-carboxylic acid (DHICA) catalysed by tyrosinase related protein-2 (TRP-2). Thereafter, tyrosinase related protein- 1 (TRP-1) catalyses the conversion of both DHI and DHICA to eumelanin (Figure 9.1a). Of TYR, TRP-1 and TRP-2 which are involved in the process of melanogenesis, only TYR is keenly essential.

Tyrosinase enzyme (EC 1.14.18.1, synonym; polyphenol oxidase) is an example of type-3 copper-containing multifunctional membrane-bound glycoprotein, resident in the melanosome membrane (16) and synthesised by only the melanocyte cells. Two moles of copper ions are chelated with three histidine moieties and these majorly carry out the catalytic role of the enzyme (17, 18). For pigmentation to be formed, the active site exists in three forms namely: oxy, met and deoxy forms, though, the two copper ions available at the reactive site, interact with the molecular oxygen to form highly reactive oxygen species (ROS) that are involved in the direct conversion of monophenols to diphenols as well as the ortho diphenols' oxidation to ortho quinones (19, 20).

Agents used for skin whitening

Most skin lightening agents competitively inhibit the activity of tyrosinase enzyme, which is the major enzyme involved in the process of melanogenesis, while the production of this enzyme is inhibited by some other agents, others affect the process of melanosomes (pigment granules) transport from the melanocytes to the surrounding keratinocytes (1). Inhibitors of tyrosinase enzyme are the agents mostly used in commercially available skin lightening agents, as these agents inhibit melanogenesis without known deleterious effects on the integrity of the skin.

Glutathione

Glutathione (Figure 9.2a) is γ-glutamyl-cysteinyl glycine, a water-soluble thiol-tripeptide that is formed from cysteine, glycine and glutamate (21). The sulfhydryl group from the cysteine molecule acts as the reactive site in the molecule. Glutathione exists in two forms in the body: as the reduced form represented as GSH and as the oxidised form represented as GSSG. It is an endogenous antioxidant molecule responsible for the inactivation of reactive oxygen (ROS) and reactive nitrogen species. Its mechanisms of hypopigmentation involve the inhibition of the tyrosinase enzymes.

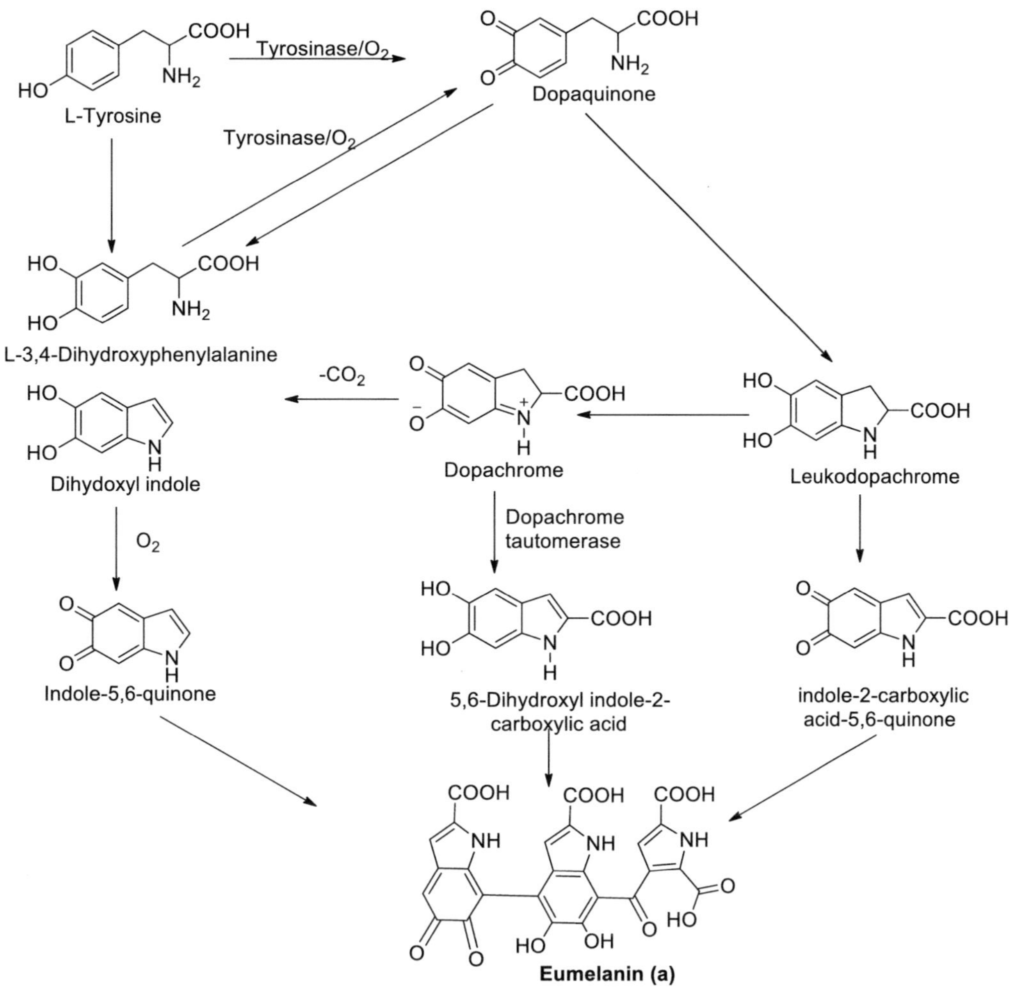

Figure 9.1: Biosynthesis of eumelanin

This involves either of the following:

- Chelating the copper site on the enzyme, using the thiol group
- Intercepting the cellular transfer of tyrosinase enzyme to pre-melanosomes, which is required for melanin synthesis.

- Harnessing its antioxidant effects of scavenging for UV-generated ROS. This inhibits melanin synthesis by forming sulfhydryl-dopa conjugates from the reaction between the thiol group and dopaquinone (22, 23).

GSH can naturally be found in fruits, nuts, vegetables, e.g., tomatoes, avocados, oranges, walnuts, asparagus and whey protein.

Pharmacokinetics and metabolism: When administered orally, the major absorption site has been found to be the upper jejunum. Glutathione is cleared by the kidneys. There is inadequate in human compared to rats, due to faster rate of hydrolysis from hepatic gamma-glutamyl transferase activity (24).

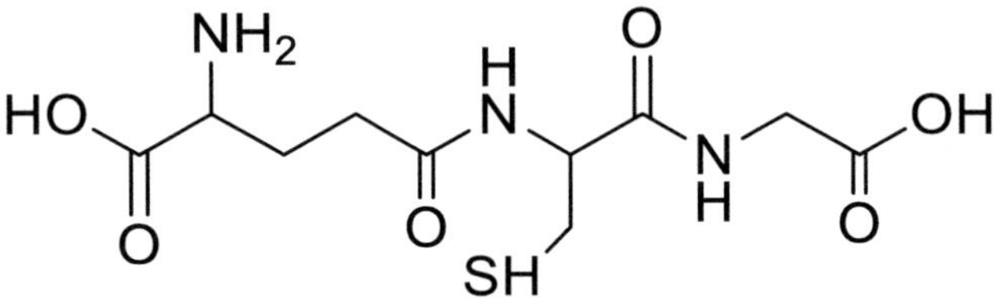

$C_{10}H_{17}N_3O_6S$, Mol. Wt. = 307.3 g/mol

Melting point: 195°C, Solubility: 292.5 mg/ml

Log P = - 6.4

Figure 9.2: Chemical structure of glutathione

Trichloro acetic acid

Trichloro acetic acid (Figure 9.3) is a colourless hygroscopic crystal. The solution of TCA has a shelf life of 2 years. The commonly used solution has a strength of 35 % w/v. It causes light superficial peel with penetration encompassing the full thickness of the epidermis. Other agents are applied alongside TCA, e.g., Jessner's solution, solid ice (CO_2) and exfoliants like glycolic acid. TCA application to the skin causes protein denaturation (keratocoagulation) resulting in the readily observed white frost.

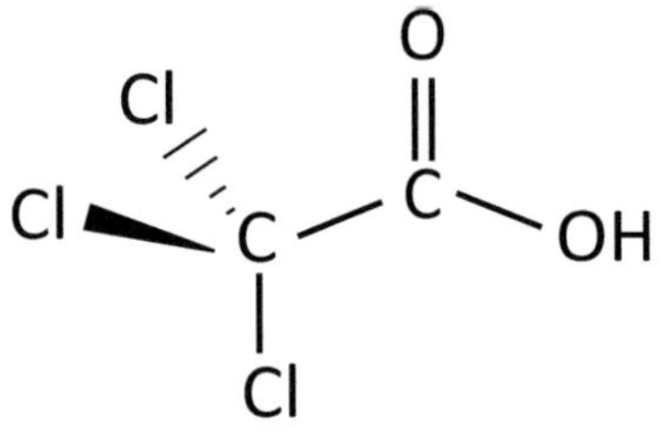

CCl3COOH, Mol. Wt. = 163.38 g/ mol
Density=1.63 g/cm3,
melting point =57-58°C,
b.p.=196-197°C,
water solubility=1000 g/100 mL
pKa=0.66

Figure 9.3: Chemical structure of trichloro acetic acid

The degree of tissue-penetration and keratocoagulation depend on the concentration of the TCA used as well as the skin preparation and the anatomical site involved.

Corticosteroids

The use of corticosteroid in cosmetics has been outlawed. However, since depigmentation is a side effect of topical steroids, they may be applied in some medical preparations for topical uses as whitening agents (26). However, some corticosteroids are being used illegally in cosmetic products for skin whitening. Corticosteroids bleach the skin by: i) initial blanching due to vasoconstriction, ii) slowing down of the skin cell turnover, iii) reducing the number and activity of melanocytes and iv) reducing production of melanocyte-stimulating hormone (27-28). Triamcinolone acetate (Figure 9.4a), clobetasol propionate (Figure 9.4c), betamethasone dipropionate (Figure 9.4d), fluocinonide (Figure 9.4e) and fluocinolone acetonide (Figure 9.4b) are classical examples of corticosteroids found in cosmetic products.

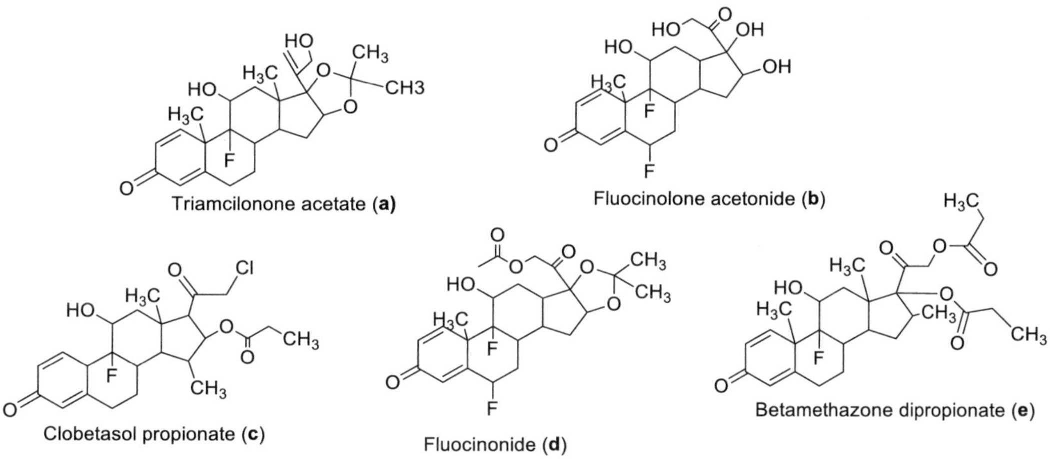

Triamcilonone acetate (**a**)

Fluocinolone acetonide (**b**)

Clobetasol propionate (**c**)

Fluocinonide (**d**)

Betamethazone dipropionate (**e**)

Figure 9.4: Chemical structures of some classical examples of corticosteroids employed as skin-whitening agents in cosmetic products

Kojic acid

Kojic acid (Figure 9.6b) is a heterocyclic antioxidant compound that was identified in 1907 from the mycelia of *Aspergillus oryzae*, cultured on boiled and cooled rice. Kojic acid appeared to be weakly acidic due to the presence of the enolic hydroxyl substituent at carbon C-5. This confers kojic acid with the ability to form salts with some metals (29). Kojic acid was found to be safe in both acute and chronic reproductive and genotoxicity studies. It has anti-inflammatory and pain relief properties. Its use in the cosmetic industry is due to its ability to cause skin whitening as a result of inhibition of tyrosinase enzyme (30, 31).

Phenolic skin whitening agents

Hydroquinone: Hydroquinone (Figure 9.6d) is an odourless white crystalline solid with extremely low vapour pressure, used in the treatment of melasma and is available, in some countries, as a 2% over-the-counter (OTC) formulation, although the purchase of a 4% hydroquinone cream requires a prescription. Hydroquinone exerts its toxicity through the copious generation of hydroxyl free radicals (32) and has been found to be an inhibitor of tyrosinase activity (32-35).

Monobenzyl ether of hydroquinone (MBEH) (Figure 9.6g): MBEH is an FDA approved depigmentation agent in the treatment of vitiligo. While depigmentation by hydroquinone is temporary, depigmentation by MBEH is permanent. This is indicative of its selective elimination of melanocytes from the epidermis. MBEH is structurally related to tyrosine. In the presence of tyrosinase enzyme, it is converted to a highly reactive quinone which react with the enzymatic constituents in the melanosomal organelle (36, 37).

Quinone-binding to the melanosomal compounds occurs in a process referred to as haptenization, whereby the melanosomal enzyme undergoes slight structural changes. This modification is significant because for immunogenic molecules, minor changes in the amino acid composition or even haptenization have been shown to alter their recognition by T cells reactive with the native peptide (39).

4-tertiary butylphenol (Figure 9.6n)**:** Unlike the two previous substances, 4-tertiary butyl phenol interact with the tyrosinase-related protein-1 (38).

Naturally occurring skin whitening agents

Inhibitors of tyrosinase enzyme in commercial skin-whitening products are mostly natural products, e. g., arbutin (Figure 9.6f), (40), ellagic acid (Figure 9.6l), (41) and resveratrol (Figure 9.6i). The tyrosinase from the mushroom, *Agaricus bisporus,* is most widely used for in vitro enzymatic model in the discovery and development of skin whitening substances that can target human tyrosinase (1). There has been a number of reports on compounds from plants (Figure 9.6) with great potentials for application as skin whitening agents. For instance, glabridin (Figure 9.6c), from *Glycyrrhiza glabra* (42-43, 45) is an inhibitor of tyrosinase (44-46), floralginsenoside A (Figure 9.5a) from *Gingko biloba* was shown to have anti-melanogenesis effects through control of microphthalmia-associated transcription factor (MITF) expression and extracellular signal-regulated kinases (ERK) activation (47,48). Betulinic acid (Figure 9.5d) isolated from *Dillenia indica* was a non-competitive inhibitor of tyrosinase enzyme (48) while bixin (Figure 9.5e) and norbixin (Figure 9.5f) isolated from *Bixa orellana* were observed to be an inhibitor of tyrosinase activity and consequently, melanin synthesis (49). Recently, sitogluside (Figure 9.5b) was described as a novel skin-whitening active ingredient through inhibition of TYR expression and activity (50). The ethanolic extracts of the edible mushroom, *Laetiporus sulphureus* and *Agaricus silvaticus*, have also been found to potently inhibit melanogenesis. The inhibition was observed to be in a dose-dependent manner in experimental set-up with zebrafish (*Danio rerio*) used as an animal model in a pre-clinical setting (51).

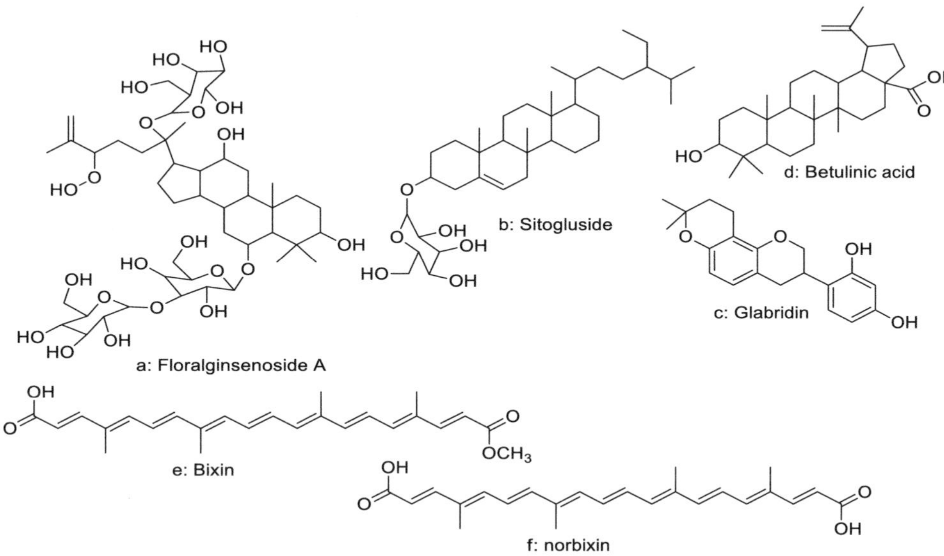

Figure 9.5: Examples of phytochemicals with potent anti-tyrosinase activity

Miscellaneous classes of skin whitening agents

Other classes of compounds that have been evaluated as tyrosinase inhibitors include chalcones and flavones, resveratrol analogues, coumarin derivatives, beta phenyl- alpha beta unsaturated carbonyls, thioureas, e.g., propylthiouracil (Figure 9.6j), methiamizole (Figure 9.6h), thiosemicarbazones, e.g., ethionamide (Figure 9.6k) and peptides (1). Other agents include azelaic acid (Figure 9.6a), (52, 53), ascorbic acid (Figure 9.6e), (54, 55), while others include tranexamic acid (Figure 9.6m), (56-58). A synthetic agent, 2-[2-(2,4-difluorophenyl)-2-propen-1-yl]-1,3-propanediol, which does not exhibit melanocyte toxicity but functions as a tyrosinase inhibitor was found to be capable of inducing skin lightening (59).

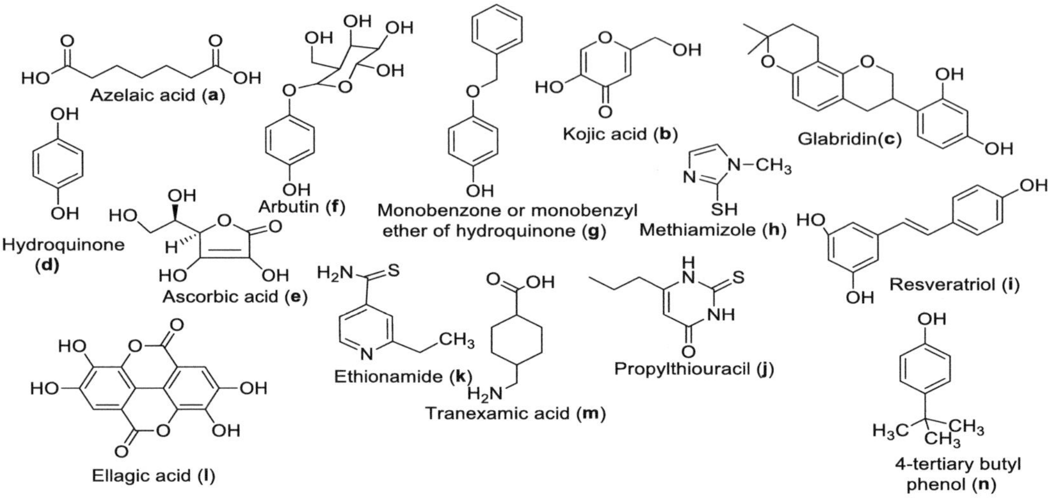

Figure 9.6: Examples of compounds with anti-tyrosinase enzyme activity

Pigments and dyes used in cosmetic products

Colour constitutes an important aesthetic appeal that is given utmost consideration in the development and formulation of cosmetic products. Pigments and dyes are, therefore, used subject to regulatory controls in different countries and regions of the world, mainly because of safety concerns in humans. In the USA, permitted colours used in food, drugs and cosmetics are approved and/or certified by the FDA. The European Regulation of Cosmetic Products (EC 1223/2009, Annex IV) (60) prescribes the rules for the use of dyes in cosmetic products for the European Union, while this duty is carried out by the Ministry of Health, Labour and Welfare (MHLW) in Japan (61).

The FDA classifies colour permitted in cosmetics as: Colour Additives Approved for Use in Cosmetics Part 73, Subpart C: Colour, Additives Exempt from Batch Certification; and as Colour Additives Approved for Use in Cosmetics Part 74, Subpart C: Colour additives subject to batch certification. The latter is further classified as: FD&C (food, drugs and cosmetics), D&C (drugs and cosmetics), external D&C (externally applied drugs and cosmetics). Examples of colour additives exempt from batch certifications are caramel, annatto, carmine, ß-carotene, iron oxides, mica, titanium dioxide. Among those subject to batch certification are: FD&C Red No. 4, FD&C Yellow No. 5, D&C Red No. 31 and Ext. D&C Violet No. 2. Colour additives approved for food and exempt from batch certification have the E code, some of which are also used in cosmetics such as carmine E120 (61).

Among the FDA certified colour additives for lipsticks are D&C Black No. 2, D&C Orange No. 5, D&C Red No. 33 and D&C Red No. 36 while FDA approved colour additives include caramel, annatto, carmine, carotene, iron oxides – yellow, red and black (62).

Colours approved under the International Nomenclature of Cosmetic Ingredients (INCI) are given codes based on the rules dictated by the Personal Care Products Council (PCPC). The codes start with CI (colour index) followed by 5 digits, the first two of which indicate the structural category of the dye. Examples include: iron oxides - yellow (CI 77492), red (CI 77491) and black (CI 77499), Brilliant Blue (CI 42090). Only a restricted number of colours are permitted for global (US/Europe/Japan) use: FD&C Blue # 2 (Indigo Carmine), FD&C Blue # 1 (Brilliant Blue), FD&C Yellow # 6 (Sunset Yellow), Titanium Dioxide, Iron Oxide Red, Iron Oxide Yellow and Iron Oxide Black.

Inorganic pigments

Iron oxides: Iron oxides are compounds made up of oxygen and iron with sixteen of such compounds and oxyhydroxides known. The commonest is the rust which is a compound of iron (III) oxide (63). Of the inorganic pigments, iron oxides are the commonly used in cosmetics products. These consist of three basic shades: yellow (CI 77492), red (CI 77491) and black (CI 77499) which, when properly blended with each other and/or with titanium dioxide and zinc oxide, give various shades of colours.

The natural pigments from iron oxides that meet the required standards for pigments are few, hence, synthetic iron oxides from iron compounds with enhanced uniformity, purity of colour, consistency and strength are made use of. There are different types of iron oxides namely: **hematite, magnetite, maghemite, goethite and ferrihydrite**. **Hematite** (α-Fe_2O_3) has a strongly intense pigmenting power, with the red pigmentation of a lot of natural and synthetic dyes deriving from the colour of the finely dispersed hematite. It is, therefore, the major constituent in a large number of colouring materials.

Magnetite is cubic, with a unit-cell dimension of 8.396 A. It has the molecular formula Fe_3O_4 expressible in the general form as $Fe^{3+}[Fe^{2+}Fe^{3+}]O_4$. It is the only iron oxide that contains both divalent and trivalent iron. Natural magnetites possess relatively good crystallinity and hence, are magnetically ordered at room temperature. They form alloy series referred to as "titanomagnetites" with ulvospinel, Fe_2TiO_4. **Maghemite** is γ-Fe_2O_3 while **goethite** (FeOOH), is the most common iron oxyhydroxide in materials formed in the weathering environment. **Ferrihydrite** ($Fe_5HO_8.4H_2O$), is a hydrous iron oxyhydroxide that is poorly-ordered and is generally formed by the rapid oxidation of iron-containing alloys (64)

Other inorganic pigments: These include ultramarines (natural, synthetic), oxides of chromium (dull yellow/green, bright bluish/green), manganese violet, white pigments such as zinc oxide and titanium dioxide and pearlescent effects obtained mainly by coating pigments with pearlescent agents such as mica and bismuth oxychloride (BiOCl). These pigments are approved colour additives by FDA.

Zinc oxide (ZnO) is white in appearance and it is used to dilute the intensity of coloured pigments.

Titanium oxide (TiO_2) or titanium dioxide, a white water-insoluble powder, is recognised as titanium white, pigment white 6 (PW6) or CI 77891, when it is presented as a pigment. Titanium oxide occurs primarily in three crystalline forms; as **rutile**, which gives a red to reddish brown, hard, brilliant metallic, slender crystals, that is most times surrounded by other minerals, and is the commonest of the three natural forms of titanium dioxide. The other forms are **anatase**, which occur as hard, brilliant crystals of tetragonal symmetry and diverse pigmentations in the veins of igneous and metamorphic rocks and thirdly, **brookite**, which occurs as brown, metallic crystals in the veins of gneiss and schist, and crystals that belong to the orthorhombic system (62). Different proportions of these forms of titanium oxide are used to arrive at desirable colours.

Mica is a phyllosilicate which is made up of any collection of hydrous potassium or aluminium silicate minerals with a dimensional sheet or layer structure. It has a chemical formula $X_2Y_{4-6}Z_8O_{20}(OH, F)_4$, where: X is K, Na, or Ca or less commonly Ba, Rb, or Cs; Y is Al, Mg, or Fe or less commonly Mn, Cr, Ti, Li, etc.; Z is mostly Si or Al, but may also include Fe^{3+} or Ti. Structurally, micas can be classified as dioctahedral (Y = 4), e.g., **muscovite** ($KAl_2(Si_3AlO_{10})(OH)_2$), and trioctahedral (Y= 6), e.g., **biotite** ($K(Mg,Fe)_3AlSi_3O_{io}(OH)_2$, **lepidolite** ($K(Li,Al)_3(Al,Si,Rb)_4O_{10}(F,OH)_2$), **Phlogopite**, **Zinnwaldite**. When X is K or Na, the mica is a common mica, while if the X is Ca, the mica is identified as a brittle mica. The sheet structures of micas are such that the primary gadgets include two polymerised sheets of silica (SiO_4) tetrahedrons. Micas display array of colours for instance purple, rosy, silver, grey (lepidolite), dark-green, brown, black (biotite), yellowish-brown, green-white (phlogopite) and colourless or transparent (muscovite) (65). Just like titanium oxide, the desired colour determines the different proportions of these forms of micas that are used.

Properties of pigments

The visual effects provided by pigments are highly dependent on the size of the particles employed. While particles of 1-15 µm provide velvety, soft and matte shimmer visual effects, those of 20-150 µm give a strong and pronounced sparkle effect, and particles of larger sizes give stronger sparkle effects. Inorganic pigments are relatively stable to light and heat but become unstable at extremes of pH. Pigments are generally either completely or nearly insoluble in water. When combined with mica, they guarantee against corrosion.

Organic dyes

Organic pigments can be grouped into five main groups based on their chemical structure as azoic, triarylmethane, xanthenes, indigoid and quinoline dyes. These are compounds which possess colour because of their ability to absorb radiations in the visible spectrum range (400–800 nm). This ability is due to the presence of at least one chromophore in the compound. Mostly, the intensity of absorption is enhanced with a conjugated system, (i.e., a structure of double bonds alternating with single bonds) and occurrence of resonance stabilising force for the electrons (66). Sometimes, in addition to chromophores, groups like sulfonic acid, amino acid, carboxylic acid, and hydroxyl groups are present as auxochromes which do shift the wavelength of radiation absorption, hence, the ultimate colour of a dye. Table 9.1 indicates the corresponding influence of wavelength and the eventual emitted colour of visible light. Organic dyes are classified as synthetic dyes, lakes and natural dyes. Dyes are either water- or oil-soluble, whereas pigments are not and remain in particulate form.

Table 9.1: Wavelength of absorption versus colour in organic dyes (International Agency For Research on Cancer 2010)

SN	Wavelength absorbed in nm	Colour absorbed	Colour observed
1	400-435	Violet	Yellow-Green
2	435-480	Blue	Yellow
3	480-490	Green-Blue	Orange
4	490-500	Blue-Green	Red
5	500-560	Green	Purple
6	560-580	Yellow-Green	Violet
7	580-595	Yellow	Blue
8	595-605	Orange	Green-Blue
9	605-700	Red	Blue-Green

Synthetic dyes

Synthetic dyes are compounds made out of chemical reactions between chemicals to produce brilliant colour materials. They are cheaper, greater in colour brightness and are stable at extreme environmental conditions and, thus, are preferred.

Azoic dyes - the basic chemical structure of these dyes consists of the functional group, $R\text{-}N{=}N\text{-}R^1$, where R, R^1 are alkyl or aryl radicals which may be symmetrical or asymmetrical. Azo pigments are further divided into mono-azo (greenish to medium yellow, reddish yellow to orange), di-azo (greenish, reddish to orange red), β-naphthol (orange to medium red), naphthol AS (medium red to violet) (67). Azo dyes that are permitted for use in cosmetics are CI 12150, CI 26100 and CI 20170. The use of azo dyes in tattoos and permanent makeups (PMU) are yet to be subjected to legislation nor are there any regulatory stipulations as regards their purity and health safety (68, 69). Azo dyes are the mostly used dyes in consumer products because of their low price, however, the chromophoric azo group in the molecule, is susceptible to chemical breakdown into aromatic amines by the bacterial azoreductase enzyme, that is present in the intestinal and skin microflora. The aromatic amines may cause mutagenic, genotoxic and carcinogenic effects.

Xanthene dyes: Xanthene dyes are compounds with the xanthylium or dibenzo γ-pyran nucleus (xanthene) as the chromophore with amino or hydroxy groups meta to the oxygen as the usual auxochromes. Xanthenes can be divided into two namely, the diphenylmethane (e.g., pyronines) and triphenylmethane (e.g., phthaleins). A very good example of the later, is fluorescein and its mono- and poly-halogenated derivatives. They are popular due to their brilliant hues. Different shades of colour are obtainable; from greenish yellows to dark violets and blues, though the most important colours are the red and pink. As a consequence of their highly rigid chromophores, xanthenes are often fluorescent, thereby enhancing their strength and brightness, though, as is often the case with fluorescent dyes, they have lower lightfastness compared to other chromophores.

Natural dyes

Botanical dyes are extracted from plants and include flavones, which are a class of flavonoids obtained from yellow or orange fruits and vegetables as well as spices such as chili peppers (*Capsicum annum*) from which the flavonoids, capsanthin (Figure 9.8a) and capsorubin (Figure 9.8b) which are orange-red pigments are obtained. Among the botanically sourced colour additives approved by the FDA are: ß-Carotene (Figure 9.8c) - a yellow/orange colour obtained from carrots, *Daucus carota*; annatto (Figure 9.8f) - an orange-red colour obtained from the pericarp of the seeds of *Bixa orellana* containing the red-coloured pigment, bixin (Figure 9.5e); henna - obtained from the leaves of *Lawsonia inermis* and used mainly for hair-colouring and tattoo; and caramel – a brown dye obtained from sugar which is extracted from sugarcane, *Saccharum officinarum*). An FDA approved natural organic dye obtained from animal source is carmine E120 (Figure 9.9b) (70).

Carmine: Carmine (Figure 9.9b) is obtained from carminic acid which is isolated from scale insects, e.g., cochineal (*Dactylopius coccus*), and some *Porphyrophora* species. Carminic acid (Figure 9.9b) has been produced from *Aspergillus nidulans* (71) as a cheaper and more readily available source of the colourant, eliminating the cumbersome processes of extraction and purification from cochineal insects, the supply of which is subjected to weather fluctuations and attacks by other insects and plant pathogens.

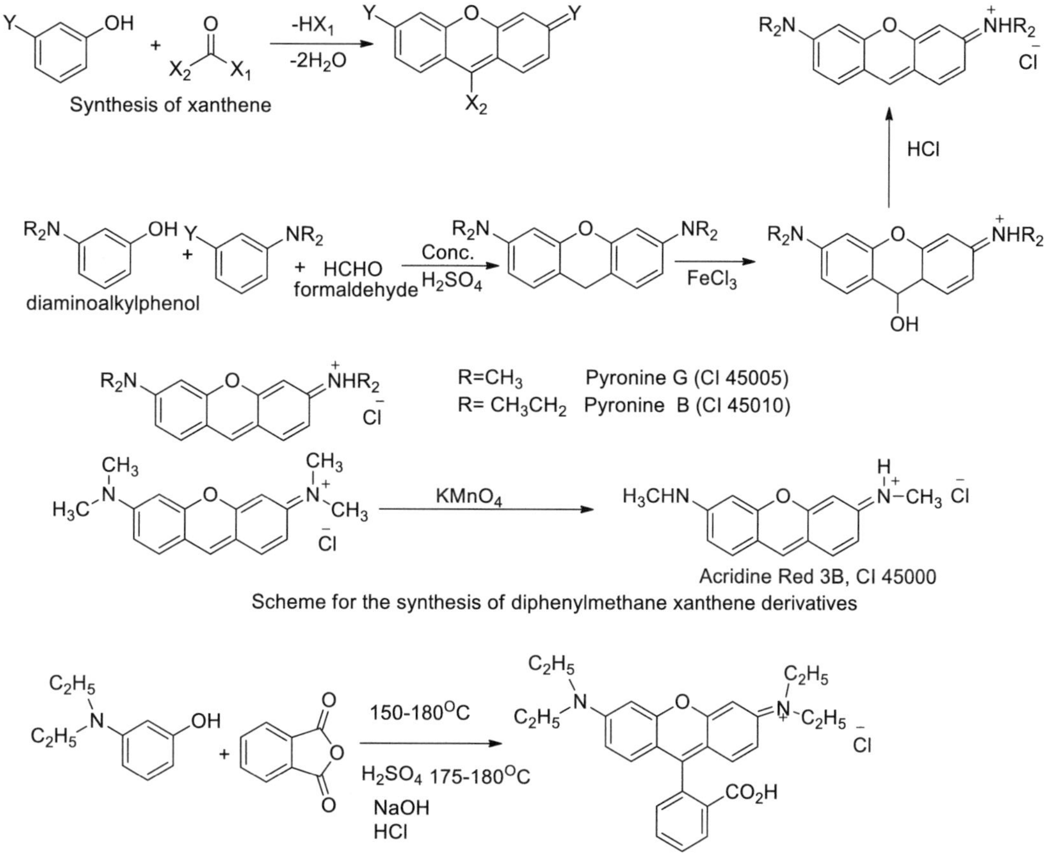

Figure 9.7: A scheme for the synthesis of diphenylmethane and triphenylmethane xanthene derivatives

Lawsone: Henna is one of the most popular vegetable dyes, giving reddish orange colour shades (72). Henna is extracted from the leaf of the *Lawsonia inermis* plant, which is found in most parts of North Africa and Sub-Sharan Africa, including Nigeria. Its colouring properties are strongly linked to the presence of lawsone (Figure 9.8d), a hot water-soluble naphthoquinone with a high affinity for the hair keratin at pH 5.5 (73).

Apigenin: Another dye-producing vegetable usually used to produce yellow shades (74) and which leads to greater light reflection is chamomile, of which only *Anthemis nobilis* (Roman Chamomile) and *Matricaria chamomillae* (German chamomile) are used as hair dye. The active phytoconstituent of the flowers is 1,3,4-trihydroxyflavone (apigenin) (Figure 9.8e) (75).

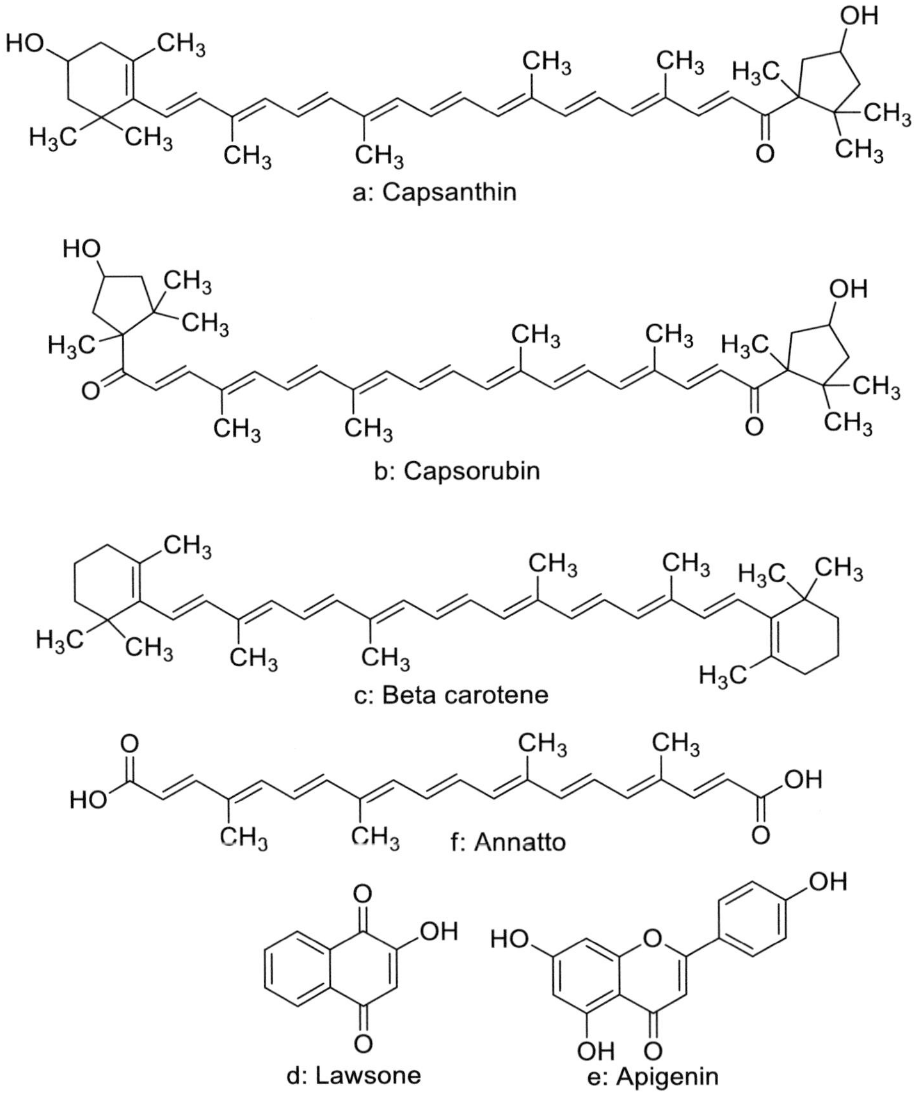

Figure 9.8: Chemical structures of some natural dyes

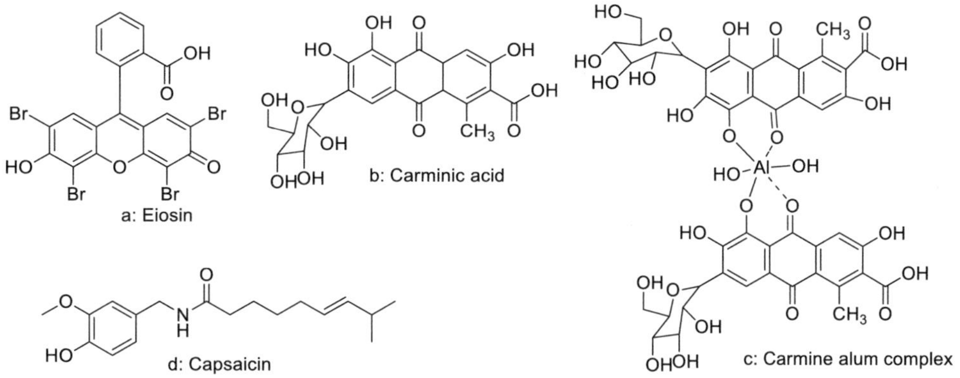

Figure 9.9: Chemical structures of some common naturally occurring dyes/pigments

Hair dyes

The cuticle, cortex, cell membrane complex (CMC), and the medulla (76) make up the hair shaft. However, the ultimate destination of a dye molecule is the matrix which consists of a high concentration of disulphide bonds. The matrix has keratin macrofibrils which are arranged along the hair strand direction, as well as melanin granules which impart colour to the hair and grants its photoprotection. Hair dying methods can be categorised into oxidative and non-oxidative or, based on duration of the colour after application, as temporary, semi-permanent, demi-permanent and permanent (77). The solvents commonly employed in hair dyes include, but not limited to, cetearyl liquor, distearoylethyl hydroxyethylmonium methosulfate, ceteareth-20 and citrus extract (77).

Temporary non-oxidative hair dyes

These dyes are acidic, with high molar weight, and possess anionic characteristics. They are chosen when maximum water solubility and minimum penetration in the hair are desirable (78). The temporary non-oxidative hair dye only interacts with the cuticle and is, thus, washed-off the hair after the first shampoo-washing as a result of its high molecular mass. (79). The temporary dye can be applied to add colourful reflections, remove the yellowish effects of the grey hair or be deposited on the hair strands to impact colour to them. Representative constituents of some dyes, coded according to the International Nomenclature of Cosmetic Ingredients (INCI), are shown in Figure 9.10. However, to get a shade of a particular colour, one may need to mix a number of the dyes. A dye concentration, from 0.1% to 2.0% (w/w), is always adequate. The dyes are presented as shampoos, gels, emulsions (lotions or creams) and solutions for either continuous application or single application.

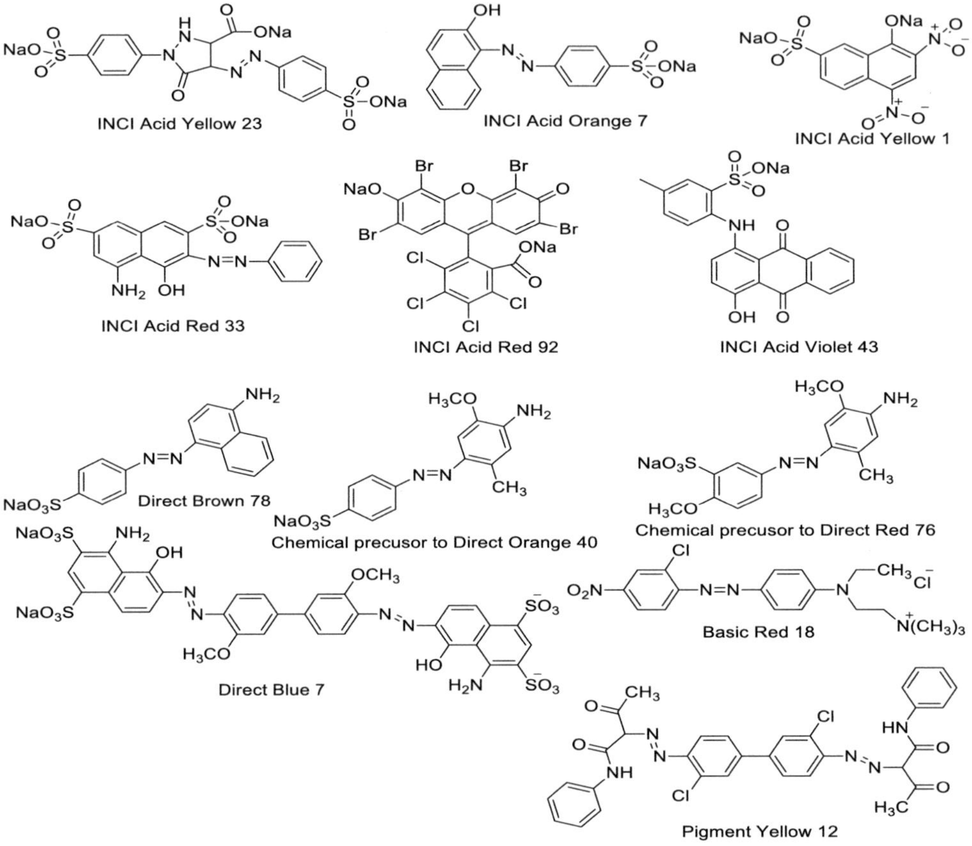

Figure 9.10: Chemical structures of coloured dyes used in tattoo

Semi-permanent non-oxidative hair dyes

These are low molecular weight, basic or cationic dyes, with high affinity for hair keratin as well as with the ability to resist removal, up to between three to six washes. Application does not involve oxidation reaction and takes from 10 to 40 minutes, followed by rinsing (80). Low molar mass enhances slight penetration into the cortex, due to the formulation's high pH value which promotes cuticle-opening (81).

Demi-permanent hair dyes

These produce major hair colour durability. They are made up of oxidising dye precursors that are applied mostly with hydrogen peroxide. On the other hand, the formulation may involve mixing different nitro aniline dyes in addition to acidic or basic dyes. This gives a better colour result with a higher ability to resist removal due to washes because of the high binding strength of the two classes of dyes for the hair keratin. The nitro anilines are made up of a neutral aromatic amine or anthraquinone derivatives which are capable of diffusing through the hair fibre and are held in place by the weak Van de Waals bonds (82). The water solubility index of the demi-permanent dyes influences their activity. Generally, the nitro anilines (Fig. 11) are insoluble in water but require solubility enhancement by the addition of glycol derivatives, e.g., glycerine, or mixtures of high molecular weight quaternary salts, e.g., quaternium-80 and benzyl alcohol, to ensure their dissolution in the formulation as well as during product use and storage (83).

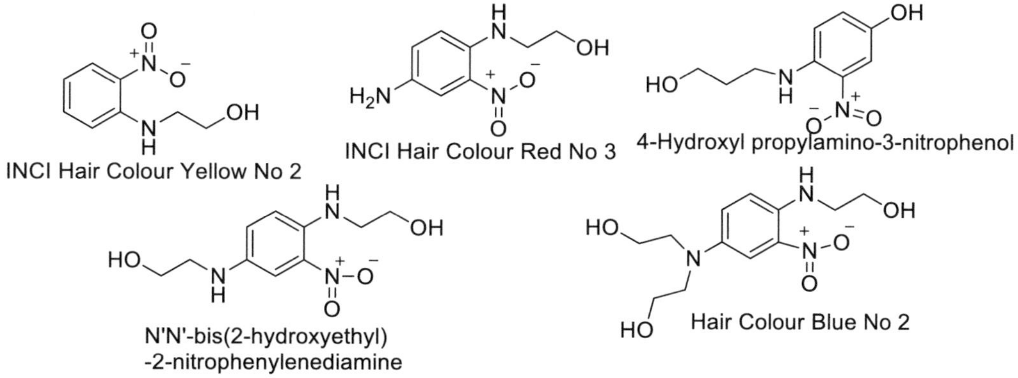

Figure 9.11: Examples of nitro aniline dyes

Cationic dyes

Cationic dyes (Figure 9.12) show very high affinity for the hair keratin, as a result of the chemical interaction between the electrophilic sites of the dye molecule and the nucleophilic sites on the hair fibre, forming an electrovalent bond (84). This allows for better durability due to greater ability to withstand removal due to washing, in comparison to nitro anilines. Though the cationic dyes are soluble in water, there is a need to add co-solvents, to guarantee the uniformity of the colour produced and stop recrystallisation during storage (because in recrystallised form, the dye lacks the cationic sites required to form bond with and bind to hair strands) (85). The control of the pH is also critical to generate stable colour. The development of colours is pH-dependent and extremes of pH must be avoided to maintain appropriate shades of colours; as such, a weak base like monoethanolamine is added to obtain a pH of 9.0, followed by the addition of buffers such as 10% citric solution, a weak acid to adjust the pH value to 6.0 (85).

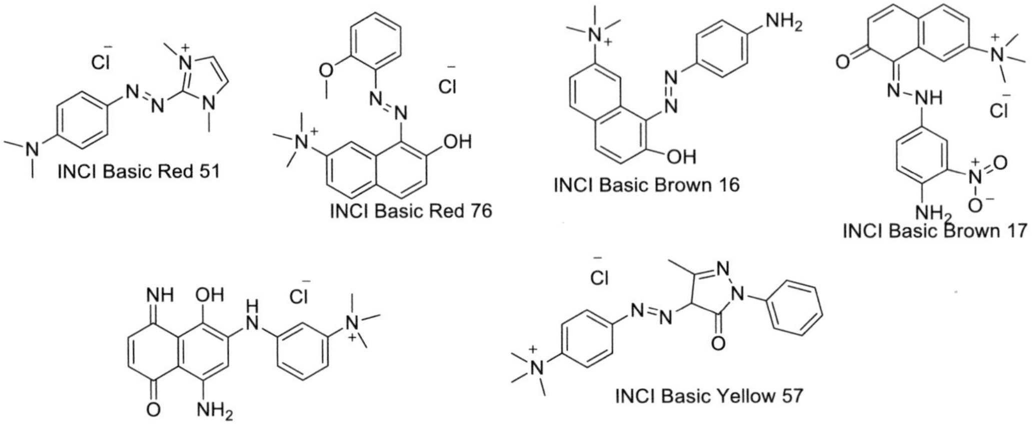

Figure 9.12: Examples of catioinic dyes

Metallic hair dyes

These are made from the salts of silver, lead and bismuth and have long tradition of use by the male gender. The desirable colouring of the hair strands occurs slowly, giving a sense of and feel of natural appearance, which is more acceptable to the client. The drawback of metallic dyes is that application may not be efficient in cases where there are highly extensive grey hair strands (79). Hair dye products made up of diluted lead acetate are administered to the hair on daily basis and do not need washing, so the metallic salt is exposed to atmospheric oxygen in addition to its reaction with sulphur from keratin. This leads to the formation of a mixture of metallic oxides and insoluble sulphides (85), which is responsible for the gradual darkening of grey hair.

Permanent oxidative hair dyeing

When greater permanence of hair dyeing is desired, a permanent hair dye is used. The demi-permanent hair dye is different from the permanent dye. In demi-permanent hair dye, an alkalising agent with low colour lightening ability, such as ethanolamine, is used. Colour formation for permanent hair dye is produced from complex reactions between a number of precursors, catalysed by an oxidising agent (86). The precursors are normally oxidation bases (primary intermediaries) such as *p*-phenylenediamine (Scheme 1) and *p*-aminophenol (Scheme 2) as well as the couplers (reaction modifiers) as shown in Figure 9.13 (85). The occurrence of the reaction in a basic medium enables the opening of the cuticles which enhances the dyes' entrance into the cortex. The chemical reaction that follows is initiated in the cortex by the oxidising agent, e. g., hydrogen peroxide, in aqueous medium, while sodium persulphate is used when the formulation is a powder, which may be stabilised with sodium stannate and penta sodium pentetate because of peroxides which are very unstable and this results in the formation of a colourful complex with high molar mass, which prevents the exit of the complex formed out of the hair (85). The commonly used alkalising agents are hydroxides and ethanolamines. A mixture of surface-active agents and solvents is used to dissolve the dye and to guarantee the achievement of hair wetting. A small quantity of reducing agent such as sodium metabisulphite is added to stop auto-oxidation of the dyes, post formulation and during product storage (87).

Table 9.2: p-phenylenediamine and p-aminophenol, two commonly used coupling bases

Scheme 1	Scheme 2
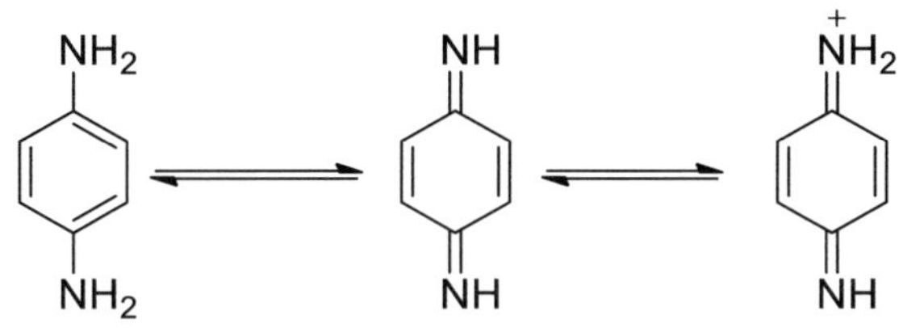 INCI Phenylendiamine	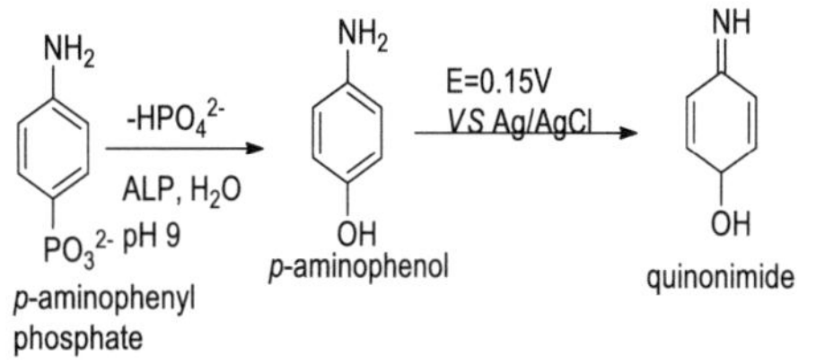 INCl; p-aminophenol

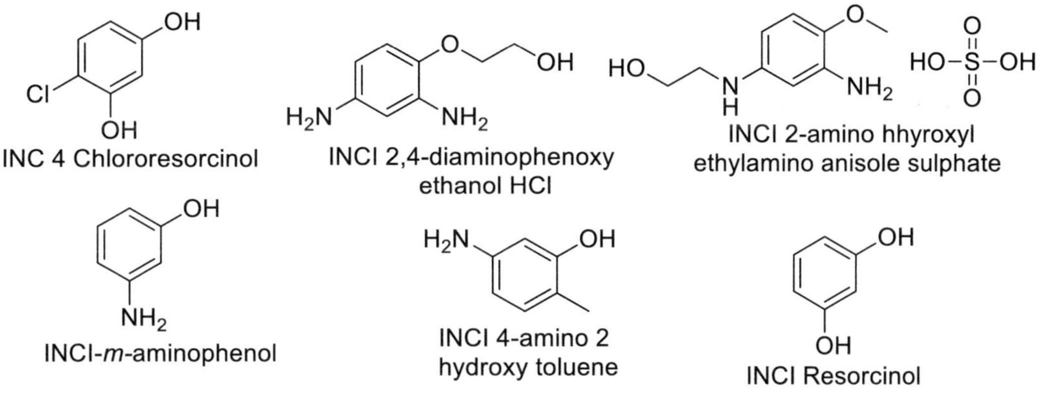

Figure 9.13: Examples of dye reaction modifiers

Antioxidants, especially water-soluble ones, are used to avoid the initial reaction of the chemicals before the addition of the oxidant itself, which may lead to interference with the final colour of the product. Erythorbic acid (Figure 9.14a) is a commonly used antioxidant for this purpose. It is also a lipophilic antioxidant and is recommended when the vehicle used is an emulsion system. Another antioxidant that is mostly used is tert-butyl quinone (Fig. 9.14c) (85).

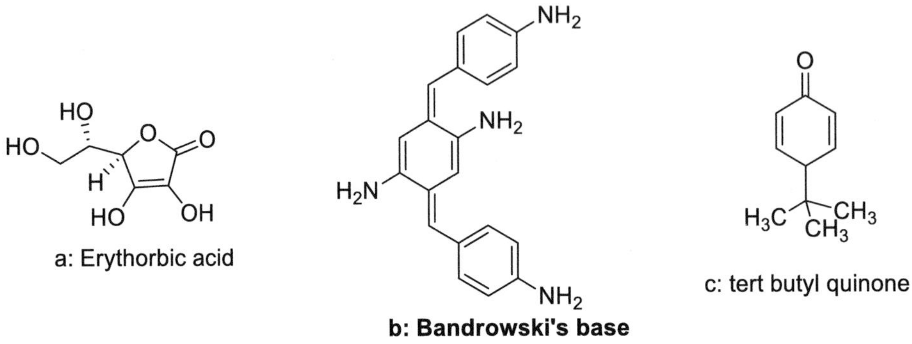

Figure 9.14: Chemical structures of some compounds used in permanent dye formulations

Hair colour formation

The colour formation process entails the generation of the Bandrowski's base (Figure 9.14b). This is produced by the coupling reaction of *p*-phenylenediamine (PPD) base in a basic medium in the presence of hydrogen peroxide (86)· The Bandrowski's base reacts preferentially with a modifier for the formation of coloured compounds which is a gradual process. The desired intensity of the final colour determines the quantities of coupling bases and modifiers that are used (86). About 3% - 5% of PPD is utilised in most oxidation reactions. The intermediate compounds have similar molar sizes, which is about 6.0 Å, enabling an easy and uniform entrance into the hair (87). The required particle size for the occurrence of this penetration is 6.0 Å (80, 88).

Ingredients of deodorant formulations

A deodorant is a product applied to prevent or cover body odour produced from bacterial decomposition of sweat in the armpits, groin, foot, and occasionally, vaginal secretions (89). Deodorant products are often formulated in alcohol that aids quick evaporation of the product when applied on the affected area. Though alcohol initially induces sweating, it has antibacterial effect. Example of other active materials usually present in deodorants are sodium chloride (as a natural deodorant in form of crystal rock), antimicrobials such as triclosan (Figure 9.15v), chlorhexidine (Figure 9.15u), paraben (Figure 9.15b) as well as metal chelating agents such as EDTA (Figure 9.15i). Sodium stearate serves as a thickener for liquid deodorant formulations while stearyl alcohol (Figure 9.15e) functions as an emollient, an emulsifier and a thickener. Also, deodorant products may have perfume fragrances or natural essential oils, desirable to cover the odour of sweat (90). Over-the-counter (OTC) formulations, often labelled as "natural deodorant crystal", contain the chemical rock crystals of potassium alum or ammonium alum, which disallow the effect of bacteria on perspiration (91).

Ingredients of antiperspirant formulations

Antiperspirants disallow the generation of perspiration, primarily by blocking sweat glands (89). Antiperspirants aim to prevent or drastically reduce sweating and thus abolish or limit the humid environment which encourages bacterial grow. Aluminium chlorohydrate and aluminium-zirconium tetrachlorohydrate gly (a complex that consists of aluminum zirconium octachlorohydrate and glycine) are the commonest active ingredients in commercial antiperspirants (92). Complexes of aluminium-based chemicals interact with the ions in the sweat to create a gel plug in the sweat gland duct, thereby disallowing the gland from excreting liquid. These plugs are subsequently removed by the natural sloughing of the skin. Physical plug could also be formed when aluminium salts interact with the keratin fibrils in the sweat ducts. This can prevent sweat from reaching the skin's surface. The slight astringent effect of aluminium salts on sweat ducts causes contraction leading to blockade of the duct, thus preventing sweat from reaching the surface of the skin (93). Methenamine (Figure 9.15t), in the form of cream or spray is effective in the management of profuse sweating and attendant odour.

Other constituents in a deodorant/antiperspirant formulation

Cyclomethicone (Figure 9.15j) is 10-pentaoxapentasilecane ($C_{10}H_{30}O_5Si_5$), a quick-drying chemical that is an odourless, colourless silicone compound which is non-irritant to the skin, has mostly replaced alcohol in deodorant formulations. Cyclomethicone, is a molecule too big, unlike aluminium compounds, to permeate through the initial layer of skin. It is used as a vehicle for deodorant constituents. The other chemicals used in deodorants are brand specific. Humectants such as propylene glycol (Figure 9.15c) and glycerine (Figure 9.15k), prevent the product from drying out while triethanolamine (Figure 9.15h) and diethanolamine (Figure 9.15g) may be used to control the pH. The acronym FCF (For Colouring Food) is a term used to distinguish between a food-grade and an industrial grade batch of dye. However, in the USA, this term has been replaced with the Federal Food, Drug, and Cosmetic (FD&C), Drug and Cosmetics (D&C), External D&C nomenclature). Brilliant Blue FCF (Figure 9.15a) imparts colour, while scent-specific chemicals, e.g., citronellol (Figure 9.15o) (smell of geranium and rose), limonene (Figure 9.15p) (smell of oranges and lemon), hexyl cinnamal (Figure 9.15r), smell of camomile), linalool (Figure 9.15q) (floral smell with a hint of spice), may also be employed to mask malodour. Fixatives, like benzyl benzoate (Figure 9.15l), benzyl salicylate (Figure 9.15m), help the fragrance compounds to blend with other ingredients. Cetyl alcohol (Figure 9.15d), stearic acid (Figure 9.15f) and propylene glycol (Figure 9.15c) are some of the agents used as surfactants, emulsifiers or as gelling agents to improve the product's consistency (94).

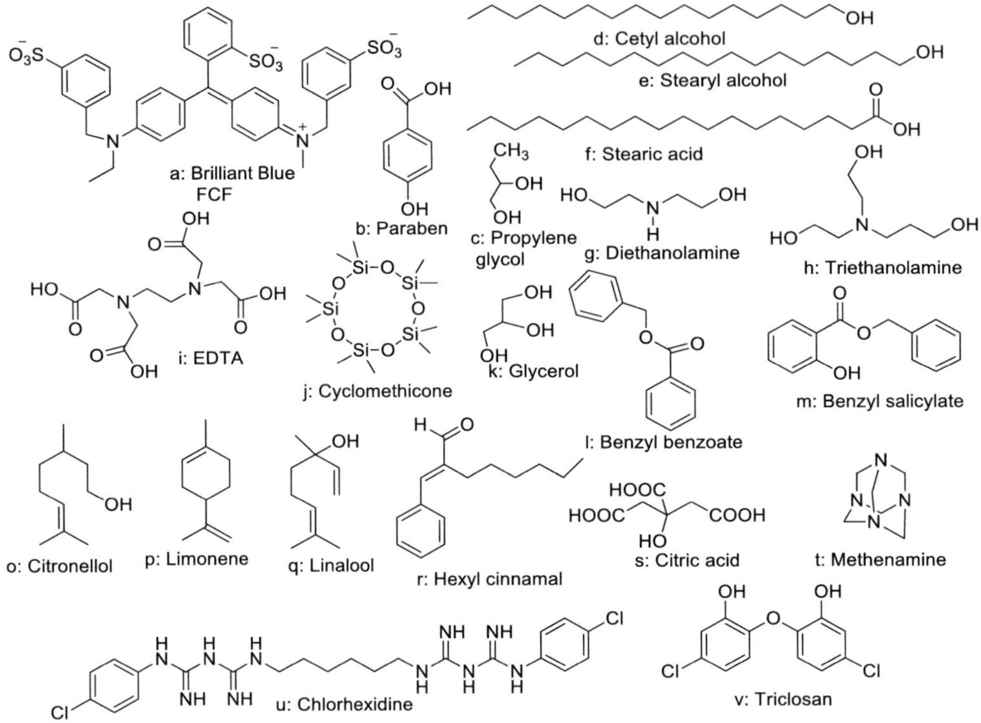

Figure 9.15: Typical chemical constituents in a deodorant formulation

Tattoo colourants

Tattoo colourants are mixtures of complex chemical compounds in which the physicochemical properties influence the degree and the route of transportation inside the skin and/or other organs. Tattoo colourants can either be dyes or pigments. The pigments are of different sizes: monomers, dimers or polymers. Unlike dyes, pigments are not soluble in the solvents in which they are dispersed and are, therefore, mostly formulated as nanoparticles. Tattoo colourants are either inorganic or organic (95).

Currently, the major inorganic pigments are titanium dioxide (TiO_2) (white) and various carbon black (soot) products that give black colour. Because of toxicity, the use of a number of metallic inorganic pigments have been discontinued, apart from TiO_2, which is used to neutralise the intensity of other colours; and soot, for black tattooing, which is still being used (95). The carbon black inorganic pigment always includes polyaromatic hydrocarbon (PAH) contaminants. The increasing desire to produce more colourful tattoos has made the use of organic pigments more popular, with the commonest pigments being azo dyes (Figures 9.12 and 9.13) as they offer a huge range of colours from red, blue, yellow, orange, green to violet, amongst others. The suspensions used for tattooing and permanent makeup (PMU) are not pharmaceutical grade substances and may contain a large number of chemical compounds present in different proportions (96). The formulation of a tattoo pigment is challenging as the particles are not soluble in most solvents applicable on human skin. Thus, to avoid sedimentation of particles, a dispersion is formed using emulsifiers, binders and thixotropic agents which are added to the aqueous solvent. Examples of such agents include polyvinylpyrrolidone and polyethylene glycol. Antifoaming agents, e.g., polydimethylsiloxane, may be added. Any of phenols such as phenoxyethanol, benzoic acid; isothiazolinones and formaldehyde are added as preservatives (97).

Tattoo pigments can be removed from the skin by using trichloroacetic acid (TCA) peels. TCA is a mild acid that works by exfoliating the epidermal layers of the skin and, thereby, remove the tattoo ink. Lasers are, however, the most commonly used methods in recent times.

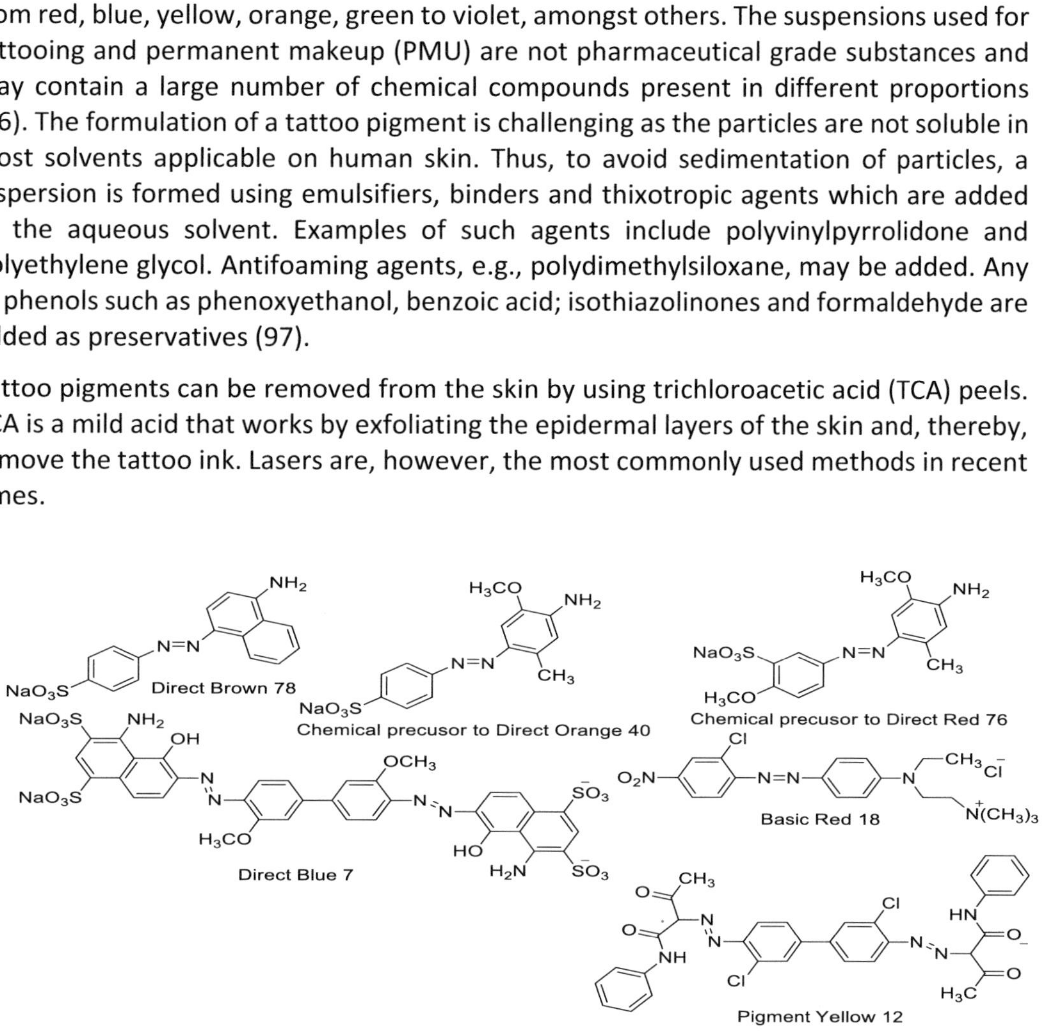

Figure 9.16: Examples of dyes used for tattoo

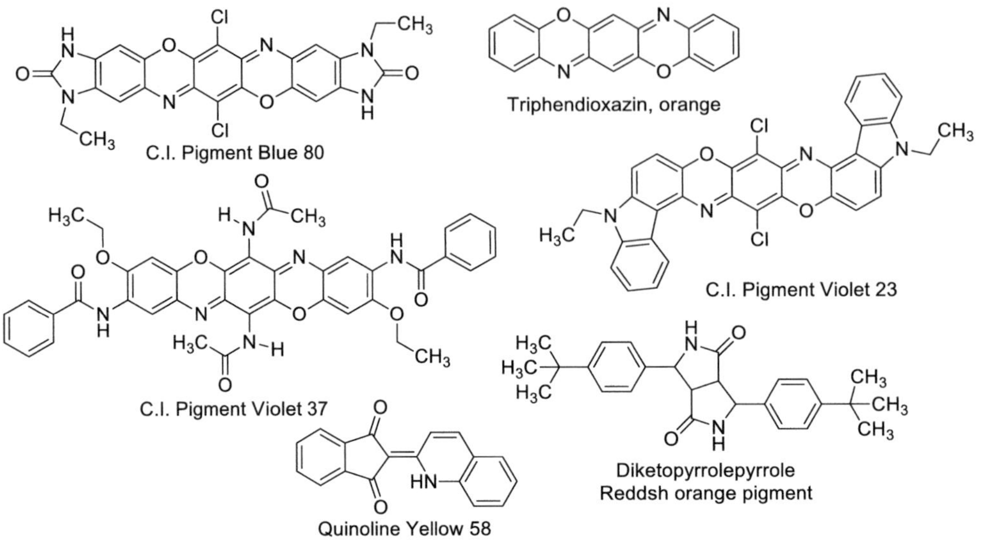

Figure 9.17: Examples of quinophthalone, triphendioxazine and diketopyrrolepyrrole dyes

Metabolism of tattoo colourants

Tattooing introduces polyaromatic hydrocarbons (PAH) into the human body, especially using black inks which majorly consist of carbon black or (PAH). Once administered, a huge amount of the tattooed PAH is absorbed from the skin and can be found in other organs like the lymph nodes, where they may act as carcinogenic agents. Some of the chemical ingredients in tattoos have been found to induce the cytochrome P450 enzyme systems. For example, exposure to 2,3,7,8-tetracholoro dibenzo-para dioxin was observed to induce CYP 1B1 which is involved in metabolic activation of PAH (96-97). Apart from CYP 1B1, CYP 2A13 and 2A6 are important members of the CYP 450 enzyme systems implicated in the activation of PAHs. Metabolic activation of PAHs to genotoxic products leads to the copious production of many procarcinogens (98).

Humectant chemistry

Humectants are mostly skin-conditioning materials added to cosmetic formulation for aesthetics and the moisturising feel they have on the skin and hair. They closely resemble emollients in functions but achieve this in a different manner. Humectants are hygroscopic (that is, can absorb water molecules) because of their ability to form hydrogen-bonding. This ability is referred to as hygroscopicity, which is a physical property of any humectant measured as equilibrium hygroscopicity. Generally, the higher the equilibrium hygroscopicity of a humectant, the better a humectant it is.

Commonly used humectants in cosmetics

Glycerine (Glycerol) (Figure 9.15k): This is the commonest humectant used in cosmetics. It is a clear and odourless liquid. It is obtained primarily as a by-product of chemical and industrial reactions of fats and oils or can be product of synthesis from petroleum sources. It is very close to being ideal as humectant, though with a disadvantage that it gives a feel of stickiness at high concentrations.

Propylene Glycol (Figure 9.15c): It is not toxic; it is low in viscosity and the odour is not strong. It is compatible with many other formulation materials. Its equilibrium hygroscopicity is lower than for glycerine but it is still rated excellent as humectant. It does not have the stickiness effect of glycerine and it is cheaper. The challenge with propylene glycol is that it is prone to being counterfeited with ethylene glycol and di-ethylene glycol.

Sorbitol (Figure 9.19d): This can be derived from glucose and is more hygroscopic than glycerine, without having the feel of stickiness. However, it is more expensive.

Butylene glycol (Figure 9.19f): This is a transparent, low viscosity liquid that works well as a humectant. It has similar humectant property as propylene glycol and it is a good substitute. It effectively solubilises than both glycerine and propylene glycol.

Polyethylene Glycols (PEGs) (Figure 9.19g): PEGs are produced from the polymerisation of ethylene glycol. PEGs, having an average molecular weight of 200 – 2000, exhibit useful humectancy. Their solubility in water is inversely related to their molecular weight.

Sodium pyrrolidone carboxylic acid (Figure 9.19a): This is the sodium salt of pyrrolidone **c**arboxylic **a**cid. It is a humectant found naturally in human skin. It is an excellent humectant with capacity to bind water 1.5 times better than glycerine, which is why it is often included as part of the Natural Moisturising Factor, a mixture of different components that keep the skin's surface supple and intact. It is one of the best performing humectants, though it is relatively higher in cost.

Aloe vera: *Aloe vera* gel is a type of naturally available plant products that enhances the hydration of the skin by means of the humectant mechanism of its chemical constituents. Its humectant effects are connected with its water-holding capacity in the skin. *Aloe vera* gel also stimulates the fibroblasts which yield collagen and elastin fibres making the skin less wrinkled and more elastic (99).

Hyaluronic acid (Figure 9.19e): Hyaluronic acid is a polymer of disaccharides. It is an anionic, non-sulphated glycosaminoglycan comprising of repeating units of D-glucuronic acid and N-acetyl-D-glucosamine, linked via alternating β-(1→4) and β-(1→3) glycosidic bonds. The polymers of hyaluronic acid can range in size from 5,000 to 20,000,000 Da in vivo (100-101).

Panthenol (Figure 9.19b): This is the alcoholic derivative of vitamin B5 (pantothenic acid) which is rapidly transformed into pantothenic acid. It is a viscous and colourless liquid at room temperature. It is applied in cosmetic industry as a moisturiser and in pharmaceuticals to improve wound-healing. In ointments, it is used for the treatment of sunburns, mild burns, minor skin injuries, and disorders (in concentrations of up to 2–5%) (102). It improves hydration, reduces itching and inflammation of the skin. It improves skin elasticity, as well as accelerates epidermal wounds' rate of healing (103).

Allantoin (Figure 9.19c): Allantoin is an imidazolidine-2,4-dione which is a tautomer of a 1-(5-hydroxy-2-oxo-2,3-dihydroimidazol-4-yl) urea (104). In nature, allantoin has been identified from the comfrey plant (*Symphytum officinale* L.) (105) while it is also synthesised for cosmetic use (106). Allantoin has a long history of use to enhance wound-healing and treat skin ulcers (107). Recently, allantoin has been found to possess keratolytic properties, leading to the desquamation of the stratum corneum without being irritating to the skin (107). In cosmetic formulations, allantoin is typically applied at concentrations of 0.0001% – 2.0% w/w, with the FDA approval as skin protectant for use in OTC medications, at a concentration of 0.5% – 2.0% w/w (108).

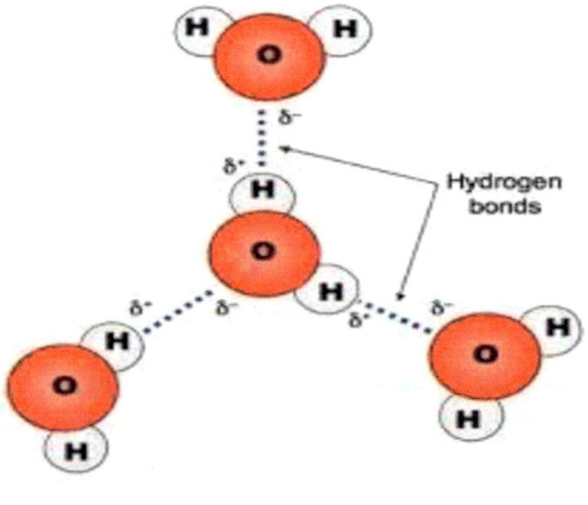

Figure 9.18: The occurrence of hydrogen bonds from humectants (Cosmetic Formulating Basics - Chemists Corner)

Others: Other materials used as humectants or moisturisers, especially in shampoos include amides from low molecular weight acids like acetic acid and lactic acid. Acetamide monoethanolamine (MEA) and lactimide MEA are substantive humectants from surfactant systems. These are compatible with anionic surfactants and possess the ability to react with the cationic groups that are present in the hair.

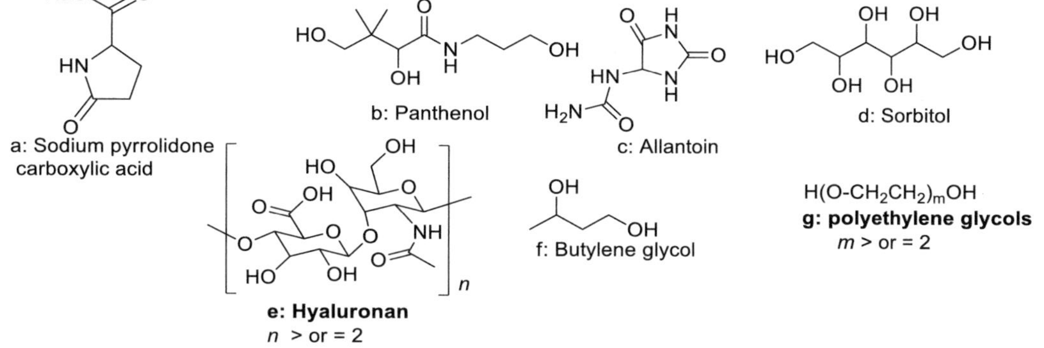

Figure 9.19: Chemical structures of some commonly used humectants in cosmetics

Emollients

Emollients are generally cosmetic agents that are applied directly on the skin to soothe, hydrate and produce moisturising treatments. Like a protective film, they cover the skin to trap in moisture. They are applied to manage dermatological issues such as dry, itchy or scaly skin conditions which include eczema, psoriasis and ichthyosis. Cosmetic emollients (examples of some are listed in Figure 9.20) are oils, which apart from enhancing the skin barrier function, also enhance product spreadability and give a cool feel or effect when applied on the skin. they are mainly made up of long-chain hydrocarbon molecules with small hydrophilic functional groups (109). The lubricity and spreading properties of an emollient product is affected by its rheological properties while the efficiency of the formulation is strongly linked to the polarity of the emollient (110). When cosmetic emollients are applied, they do create a lipophilic, semi occlusive film on the epidermis, thereby reducing the total trans-epidermal water loss (TEWL) and help spread other formulation ingredients [109, 110-112). The occlusive film that is formed has the capacity to fill in the cracks between superficial corneocytes, reduce surface roughness and consequently increase surface 'softness' and 'smoothness' (113-115). Skin transport considerations are critical in determining which organic molecules could be used as cosmetic emollients. The stratum corneum surface of the skin can be penetrated by some emollients and possibly lead to interaction with native intercellular lipids which may be advantageous by further reducing TEWL and/or strengthening the natural barrier to water loss, replenishing damaged physiological lipids, and improving skin hydration (116, 117). On the other hand, a penetrating emollient may have the ability to interact with intercellular lipids, which form the main barrier to water transport through the skin (109, 118-119).

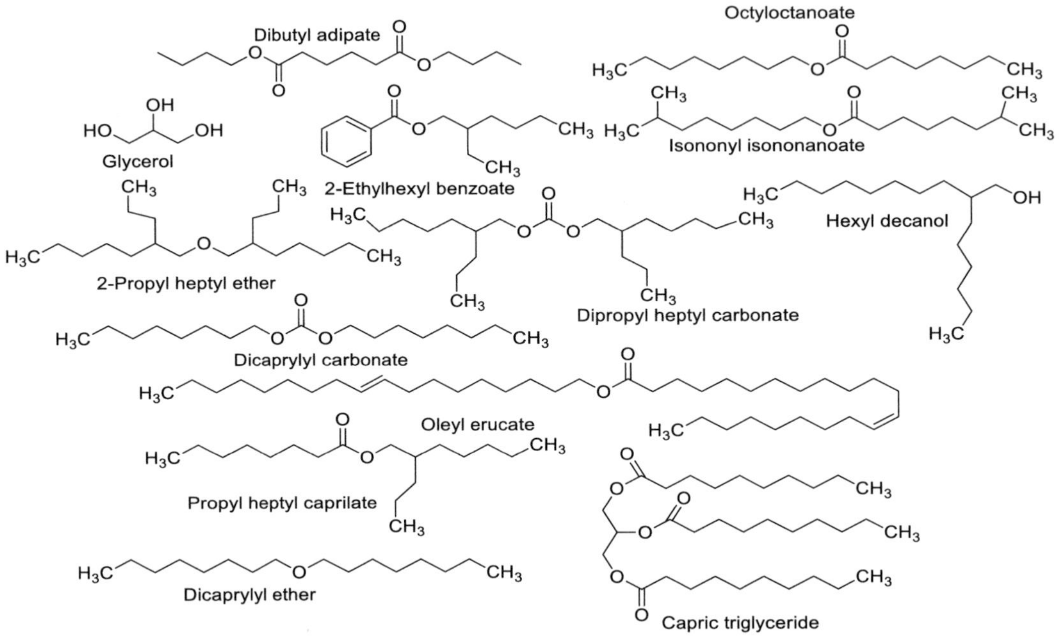

Figure 9.20: Chemical structures of some emollients

Oils and fats

Lipids (oils, fats and waxes) are important components of most cosmetic formulations where they serve as emollients, lipid vehicles for oily solution preparations, oily phase of emulsions, lubricants, e.g., in lipsticks, binders in mascaras and as thickening agents, waxes in particular, especially in stick formulations. Most oils, fats and waxes are of vegetable and animal origin, but there are also oils and waxes that are mineral based or synthesised.

Mineral oils and waxes: these consist of highly refined hydrocarbon oils and white soft solids derived from petroleum, coal or oil shale, e.g., petrolatum (a semi-solid jelly), paraffin oils such as liquid paraffin and paraffin wax. They serve mainly as emollients and are preferred because they hardly cause allergic reactions and they are none comedogenic. Petrolatum gel and paraffin wax are viscosity- imparting while the wax give structure to stick preparations.

Silicone oils: Silicone oils are polymerised organosiloxanes, consisting of alternating atoms of silicone and oxygen (..Si-O-Si-O-Si..). Silicone oils are non-toxic, non-greasy, odourless and tasteless. The most commonly used silicones in cosmetics are cyclopentasiloxane and dimethicone. Silicone oils are used to improve the texture of cosmetic products and provide a feeling of smoothness and silkiness when products are applied on the skin and hair. They are occlusive, preventing the loss of moisture from the skin surface and are non-comedogenic. The oils fill fine lines and wrinkles, making the skin to appear smoother and are, therefore, excellent ingredients for primers. The oils have conditioning effects on damaged, unhealthy hair shafts by reducing friction between the hair shaft and adding shine to the hair. The oils are used as solvents and viscosity- controlling agents. Silicone gel preparation have also been observed to improve the appearance of keloid, hypertrophic and superficial scars (120). Cyclopentasiloxane evaporates quickly when applied on the skin making it a good ingredient in deodorant/antiperspirant products and hair sprays.

Essential oils: these are the volatile, odouriferous compounds produced by aromatic plants and which give the plants their essence. They are mainly terpenoids and phenylpropanoids and are used in cosmetics mainly as fragrances and constituents of perfumes. Certain animals also produce essential oils. Chapter 11 of this book contains more information on essential oils.

Vegetable/animal oils and fats are glycerol esters of higher fatty acids. The esterification process involves a molecule of glycerol reacting with three molecules of fatty acids to produce glycerides (triacylglycerols) (Figure 9.22), where saturated fatty acids give fats and unsaturated fatty acids yield oils. Monoacylglycerols and diacylglycerols, containing one molecule and two molecules of fatty acids, respectively, are also present in oils and fats. In addition, the oils and fats contain small amounts of free fatty acids such as stearic and oleic acids, among other constituents. The hydrocarbon chains in the saturated fatty acids can pack relatively closely together because they are straight, making these fats solid at room temperature. However, when the hydrocarbon chains are loosely packed, it gives rise to liquid oils at room temperature. **Fatty acids** are straight, long-chain hydrocarbon carboxylic acids with even number of carbon atoms. They are subdivided into "saturated" and "unsaturated" fatty acids. Examples are listed below in figure 9.21.

Examples of vegetable oils and fats

Cocoa butter is an oil that contains a high amount of saturated fats and monounsaturated oleic acid, which is found in each triglyceride. It contains arachidic acid (C20:0) and linoleic acid (C18:2) 3.2%, oleic acid (C18:1) 34.5%, palmitic acid (C16:0) 26.0%, Palmitoleic acid (C16:1) 0.3%, Stearic acid (C18:0)34.5%, other fatty acids 0.5% (where the number following 'C' denotes the length of the acid, and the numeral after the colon sign denotes the number of double bond present).

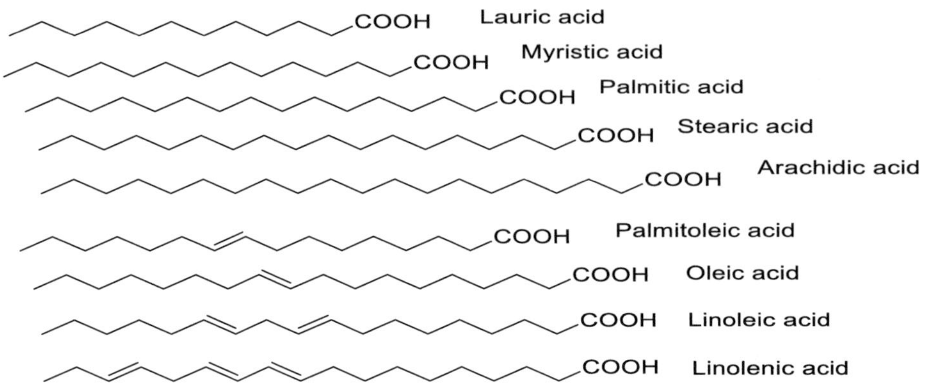

Figure 9.21: Chemical structures of some fatty acids present in oils and fats

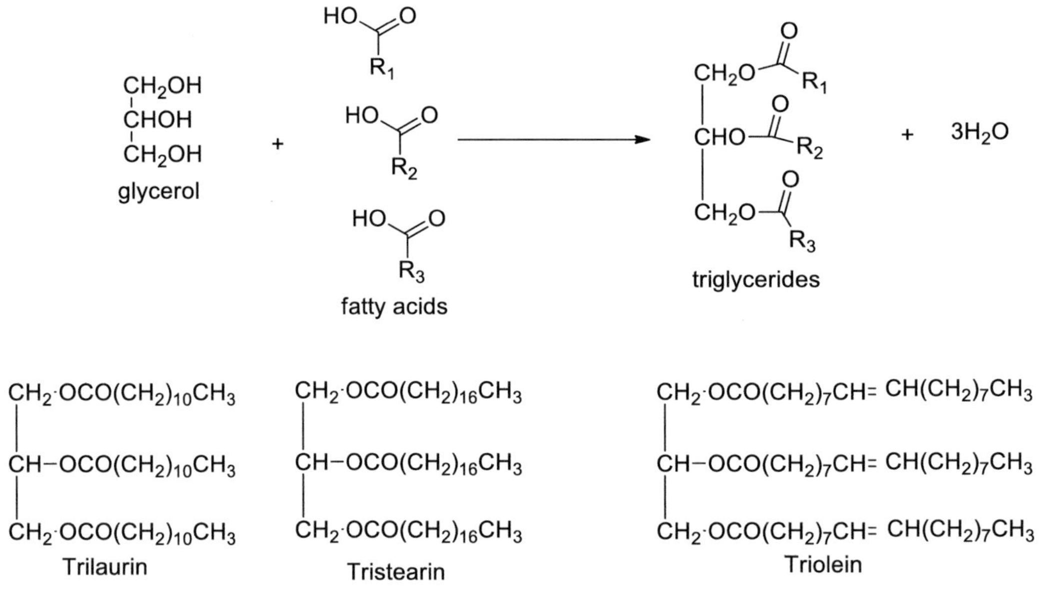

Figure 9.22: Synthesis and examples of triglycerides

Shea butter is made up of the five principal fatty acids: palmitic, stearic, oleic, linoleic, and arachidic with about 85 - 90% being stearic and oleic acids. The relative proportion of these two fatty acids affects shea butter consistency; a higher proportion of stearic acid gives a harder consistency.

Castor oil is a vegetable oil obtained from the seeds of the castor bean, *Ricinus communis*. Castor oil ($C_{57}H_{104}O_9$) has many applications in the cosmetic industry. The main constituent of the oil is ricinoleic acid (85-95 %).

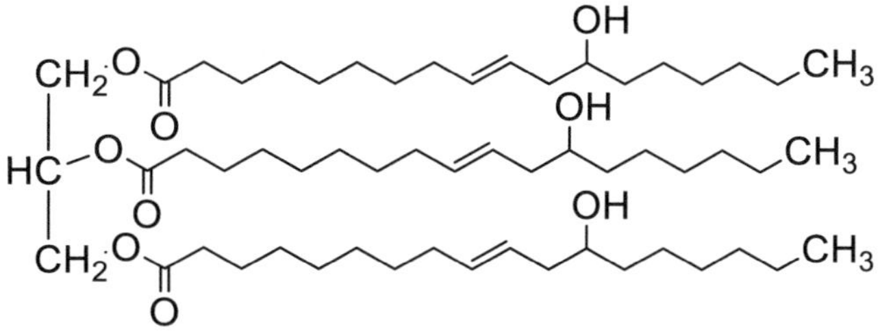

Figure 9.23: Molecular structure of the main constituent of castor oil

Linseed oil is made up of triglycerides, but is distinctive in that it contains an unusually large proportion of α-linolenic acid, which displays a special oxidative reaction with oxygen in air. The composition of the fatty acids in a sample of linseed oil are α-linolenic acid (51.9–55.2%),palmitic acid (about 7%) and stearic acid (3.4–4.6%),oleic acid (18.5–22.6%), linoleic acid (14.2–17%).

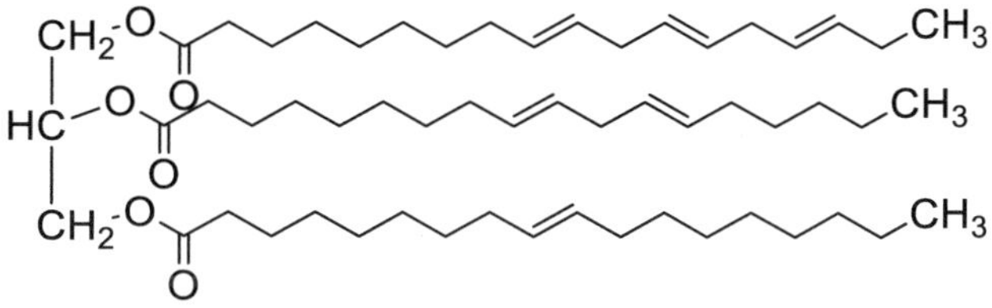

Figure 9.24: Molecular structure of the main constituent of Linseed oil

Sesame oil is made up of linoleic acid (41%), oleic acid (39%), palmitic acid (8%), stearic acid (5%) and others in small amounts (121).

Eucalyptol oil: The major compounds present in the leaf essential oil of *E. maculata* are eucalyptol (54 %), *p*-cymene (10 %), *α*-pinene (7.78%), β-myrcene (7.78%), γ-terpinene (1 %) and citronellal (1 %); while eucalyptol (51 %), α-pinene (23 %), p-cymene (10%), β-myrcene (8 %), Terpinen-4-ol (2 %) and γ-terpinene (2 %) are the major compounds present in *E. globulus* (122**)**.

Natural waxes

Waxes are made up of admixtures of esters from the reaction of higher fatty acids with higher monohydric alcohols such as cetyl ($C_{16}H_{33}OH$) and myricyl ($C_{30}H_{61}OH$) alcohols. A good example is the myricyl palmitate ($C_{15}H_{31}COOC_{30}H_{61}$). Other examples of waxes used in cosmetic products include beeswax, carnauba wax and candelilla wax and cholesterol. They serve as emollients, thickeners, and texturisers in cosmetic products. Some of these waxes are made use of in lipsticks products. Paraffin wax, carnauba wax, and beeswax are commonly found in mascara products.

Carnauba wax, obtained from the carnauba palm, consists of fatty acid esters (80-85%), fatty alcohols (10-16%), fatty acids (3-6%) and hydrocarbons (1-3%). Other constituents include 20% esterified fatty diols, 10% methoxylated or hydroxylated cinnamic acid, and 6% hydroxylated fatty acids. Ceryl palmitate, myricyl ceretate, myricyl alcohol ($C_{30}H_{61}OH$) as well as some other high molecular weight esters and alcohols can be found in carnauba wax_(123).

Candelilla wax, is extracted from leaves of Euphorbia cerifera and E. antisyphilitica and consists mainly of about 50% hydrocarbons, high molecular weight esters, resins and free acids. It is used in the preparation of lipsticks, lip balms and mascaras where it contributes to their shine or gloss, it is a hardening agent and a skin protectant, among other functions.

Beeswax, produced by honey bees, is made up of hydrocarbons (12%–16%), mainly heptacosane, nonacosane, hentriacontane, pentacosane and tricosane; free fatty acids (12%–14%, C24–C32); free fatty alcohols (ca. 1%, C28–C35); linear wax monoesters and hydroxymonoesters (35%–45%, C40–C48), complex wax esters (15%–27%, 15-hydroxypalmitic acid or diols, which are linked to another fatty-acid molecule through their hydroxyl group (124-126).

Lanolin (wool wax), is a typical high-purity grade lanolin is made predominantly of long chain waxy esters (approximately 97% by weight) while the remaining constituents are lanolin alcohols, lanolin acids and lanolin hydrocarbons. Lanolin is extracted from the wool of sheep.

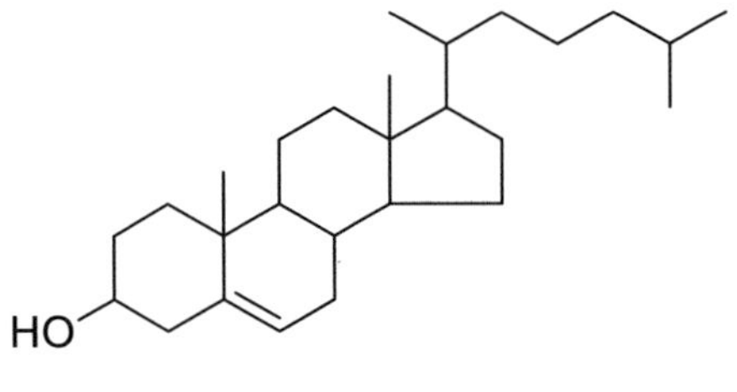

Figure 9.25: Molecular structure of cholesterol

Cholesterol is a waxy, steroidal substance obtained mainly from animal tissues. It has a molecular formula of $C_{27}H_{46}O$, with a structure that consists of a hydrophobic tail, a central non-polar sterol nucleus and a hydrophilic head that enables it act as a water-in-oil promoting emulsifier. In cosmetics, cholesterol is used as an emollient in body lotions and creams, face makeup and hair products.

Other waxes include shellac wax secreted by the scale insect *Kerria lacca*, spermaceti extracted from the head cavities and blubber of the sperm whale.

Chemistry of soaps

Soaps are formed through a chemical process known as saponification, which entails the alkaline hydrolysis of long-chain fatty acid-containing oils, fats or lipids, by an alkaline solution such as that of potassium hydroxide or sodium hydroxide (caustic soda). Traditionally, vegetable and animal fats and oils are used in soap-making. Palm kernel oil, palm oil, olive oil, coconut oil and shea butter are examples of vegetable oils and fat, respectively, used in soap-making while animal fats used are usually lard and tallow. Potassium soaps are soft in texture while soaps produced using sodium hydroxide are hard. A molecule of soap is made up of a lipophilic or hydrocarbon end, and a hydrophilic or polar end. When in contact with a dispersion of aqueous liquid and oily substances including dirt, the molecule orientates itself such that the lipophilic end is in the oily phase while the hydrophilic end is in the aqueous phase, thus, reducing the interfacial tension between the two immiscible phases making them to form a heterogenous mixture called an emulsion. This orientation of soap molecules in the presence of oily dirt in an aqueous environment enables a soap to carry out its cleansing or washing action. Thus, soaps are surface-acting and act as emulsifiers in cosmetic products that contain oily and aqueous ingredients such as creams and lotions or in cleansers that are soap-based. However, soaps used as emulsifiers are usually formed by reacting fatty acids such as palmitic, stearic and oleic acids with the alkaline solutions of sodium, potassium, calcium and di- or tri-ethanolamine, which in most cases, are formed in-situ during the preparation of the emulsion products.

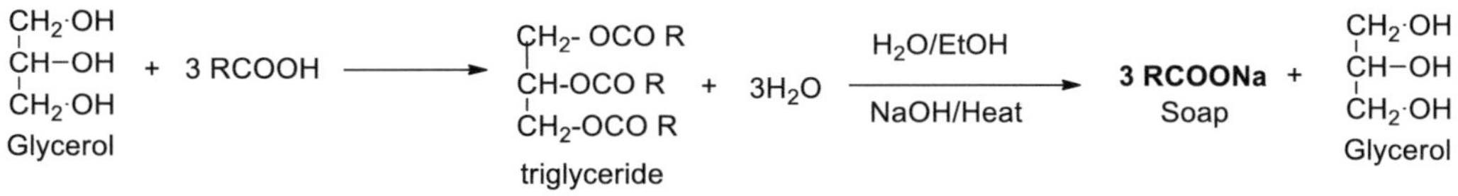

Figure 9.26: The saponification process for the production of soap

Glycerol (glycerine) is a by-product of the process of soap-making. Figure 9.24 shows the chemical reaction that occurs when soap is formed using a triglyceride, the initial reaction that gives the triglyceride is also included in the figure. Triglycerides are typically hydrocarbons consisting of 3 long-aliphatic carboxylic acid chains (long chain fatty acids) attached to a single glycerol molecule. The common soap-making procedure involves heating animal fats or vegetable oils made up of triglycerides in an aqueous or ethanolic solution of sodium hydroxide (or potassium hydroxide (for soft soap) to form carboxylate salts known as soap.

Mineral makeup

The term - mineral makeup, is used to describe those makeup (cosmetic) products that are compounded mainly with ingredients obtained from the earth crust. Such cosmetics or makeups are usually free of fragrances and preservatives as the ingredients may not support microbial growth. They are, therefore, regarded as non-allergenic as fragrances and preservatives could be sources of allergic reactions. The mineral ingredients exhibit many physical properties in one product. For instance, a mineral makeup that glides freely on the skin, sticks properly to it, and masks the defects on the surface of the skin is considered a coverage cosmetic agent. The commonest ingredients of most mineral makeups are ***talc*** and ***mica*** powders. These have the properties of sliding easily on the skin surface and reflecting light, while in addition, mica is capable of displaying an array of different colours (127-128). Titanium dioxide (TiO_2) and zinc oxide (ZnO) powders are also some of the common ingredients in mineral makeup. They are highly useful in getting makeups stick to the skin as well as masking imperfections on the skin. They shield the skin from harmful effect of the ultraviolet (UV) radiation of the sun, due to their ability to reflect the radiation. However, the most important materials in mineral makeup are the oxides of iron which can present as four colours: yellow, black, red and green. The red pigment displays a light salmon colour to a deeper blue-red. There is a need to mix the pigments properly to achieve different colour shades for differing skin tones. Red iron oxide pigments resemble the mineral hematite (Fe_2O_3) in composition and structure, black pigments resemble magnetite (Fe_3O_4) while yellow pigments resemble goethite (FeOOH) (64). Other mineral agents used in cosmetics include mineral oils such as liquid paraffin and petrolatum as well as clays like halite, kaolinite, kieserite and sylvite that are used for mud masks and other mud treatments.

There are many mineral makeup products that contain other materials such as bismuth oxychloride (BiOCl), a synthetic chemical that enhances the feel of mineral makeup powder with added glimmer effect. In addition to the shimmery effect, the reflection and scattering of light gives good coverage property to the makeup. Boron nitride, an inorganic makeup ingredient, functions as a slip modifier, an oil absorbent and increases adherence of product to the skin due to its layered structure where the layers are held together by the weak van der Waals forces, and in addition, in each layer, boron and nitrogen atoms form strong covalent bonds which helps to reinforce the bond within the layers (129).

Among the earliest used mineral makeups were kohl (ground stibnite powder, Sb_2S_3) a black mineral used as eye makeup, and the green malachite powder, which is a bright green copper carbonate hydroxide mineral ($Cu_2Co_3(OH)_2$), that was also applied as an eye liner and on the eyebrow to make the eyes look bigger and more attractive.

Preservatives

There are different classes of compounds used as preservatives in the formulation of cosmetics. Figure 9.22 gives the structures of examples of compounds that are used as preservative agents in cosmetics. A detailed discuss on them will be found in Chapter 19 of this book which is on preservatives. These compounds may be divided into cationic preservatives, the biguanides, alpha hydroxyl alcohols, beta hydroxyl alcohols, parabens and chelating agents.

Quaternium-15 is 1-(3-Chloroallyl)-3,5,7-triaza-1-azoniaadamantane chloride, a quaternary ammonium salt synthesised from hexamethylenetetramine. It is a cationic preservative that is used in many cosmetics.

Chlorhexidine is a member of biguanides and monochlorobenzenes. It derives from a biguanide with a structure consisting of two (p-chlorophenyl) guanide units linked by a hexamethylene bridge. It is an anti-infective and an antibacterial agent that is used as a preservative in cosmetic products and as an anti-effective agent in some personal care products such as antiseptic skin wipes.

Sorbic acid, (2,4-hexadienoic acid), is a colourless naturally occurring carboxylic acid, used as a mild preservative for cosmetic products and also commonly applied as a food preservative. Its chemical formula is $CH_3(CH)_4CO_2H$. It is slightly water-soluble and sublimes easily. It was first obtained from the unripe berries of the *Sorbus aucuparia* (Rowan tree).

Phenoxyethanol (**$C_6H_5OC_2H_4OH$**) is a colourless, oily liquid that can be classified as a glycol ether and a phenol ether. It is an effective and relatively safe preservative used in cosmetic products and is a common preservative in vaccine formulations.

Parabens*:* Para-hydroxy benzoic acid esters (majorly methyl, ethyl, propyl, and butyl esters) (Figure 9.25 a-d), are effective against a broad spectrum of bacteria and fungi. The higher on the homologous series they are, the more their antifungal activity and the less their solubility in water. They are often used in combination with methyl paraben (Fig. 9.25 a). Their activity on underarm bacteria is responsible for odour reduction in deodorant products. They work to eliminate the bacteria that break down sweat to produce foul odour where sweat is found. However, a lot of deodorants are formulated with alcohol-based substances that destroy bacteria, while others make use of synthetic chemicals such as triclosan (Fig. 9.25 g).

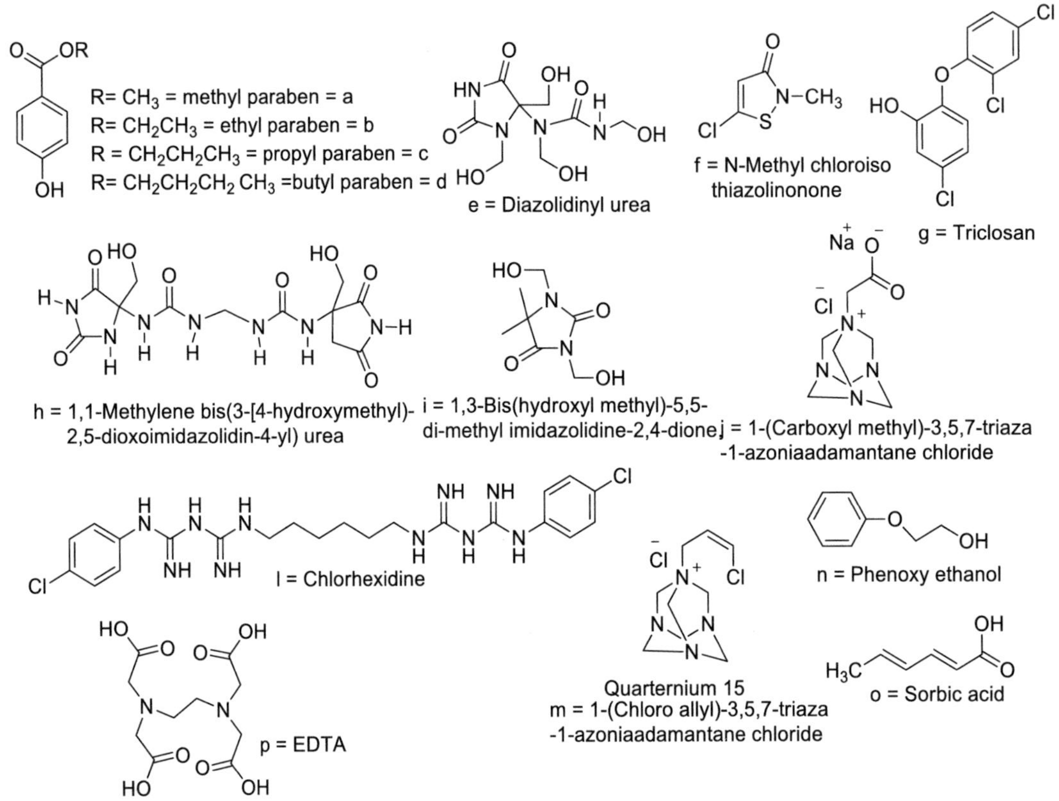

Figure 9.27: Classical examples of compounds used as preservatives in cosmetics

Chelating agents, such as ethylene diamine tetra-acetic acid (EDTA, Fig. 9.25 p), act as antibacterial agents. Specifically, tetrasodium EDTA has the ability to destroy bacterial cell walls and destabilise biofilms by forming complexes with calcium, magnesium, zinc, and iron. This destroys the integrity of the bacterial cell wall, leading to the death of the bacteria (130). This excellent intrinsic antimicrobial and antibiofilm activity will not only preserve the deodorant formulation but have a beneficial effect against biofilm-making colony of bacteria.

Alpha hydroxy acids: These are organic acids that have a hydroxyl group attached to the carbon atom that is one carbon away from the carboxylic acid group. These compounds are formulated in skincare products for their exfoliating properties. They include citric acid (Fig. 9.26b), glycolic acid (Fig. 9.26c), hydroxyl caproic acid (Fig. 9.26d), hydroxyl caprilic acid, lactic acid (Fig. 9.26e), malic acid (Fig. 9.26bv) and tartaric acid (Fig. 9.26a). The structures are simple and are displayed in Fig. 9.26.

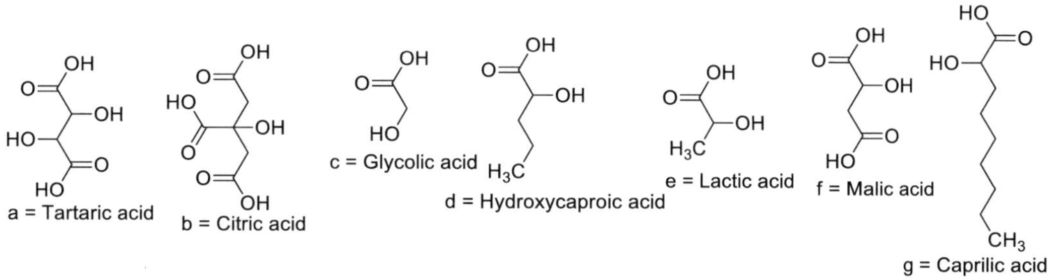

Figure 9.28: Examples of alpha hydroxy acid employed as preservatives

Beta hydroxy acid (β-hydroxy acid) compounds where the hydroxyl group is two carbon atoms away from the carboxylic acid group. The commonest example of this class is salicylic acid (Fig. 9.27d) and, in fact, in cosmetics, it is usual to substitute the term *beta* hydroxy acid specifically for salicylic acid. This compound is employed in some "anti-aging" creams and for acne treatments, possibly as a constituent to combat inflammation. Salicylic acid (SA) is expressed naturally in plants *e.g.* willow bark. It has anti-inflammatory, antibacterial properties, and also works as an exfoliant to remove dead skin cells. Many face washes or skin care products for acne contain SA in varying strengths

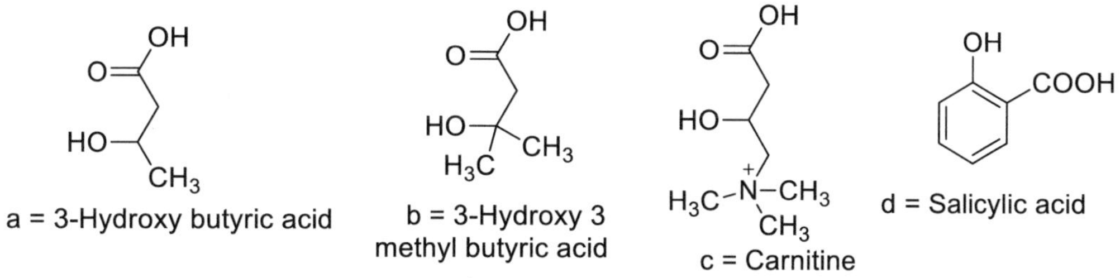

Figure 9.29: Examples of beta hydroxy acid employed as preservatives

Pharmacokinetics of cosmetic ingredients

Pharmacokinetics is an aspect of science that deals with the disposition of xenobiotics (foreign particles) in the body. The xenobiotics could be drugs meant to achieve a particular therapeutic goal, or to diagnose or prevent the advent of diseases. The term also covers any chemical compound that gains entry into an intact body, whether intended for therapeutic purpose of not. On the other hand, a cosmetic product is generally applied to the skin or external body parts, such as the hair, for the purpose of aesthetics, camouflaging, shielding the skin against harmful radiation, for pleasant feel and smell without influencing the normal physiology of the body. To ensure cosmetic products do not change the body's physiology, most cosmetic products are formulated without capacity for substantial penetration into the body. Pharmacokinetics majorly studies the absorption, distribution, metabolism and excretion (ADME) of chemical compounds be it drugs or cosmetics. For a compound that could be absorbed into the body, regulatory bodies limit the amount of such a substance that could be present in a product. The major concerns for any extensive absorption for cosmetic ingredients and their subsequent distribution is the biotransformation of the ingredient (metabolism), a process of converting the agent into a more polar form which enhances its excretion from the body majorly through the renal or biliary route. It is well established that cytochrome P450 enzyme systems are overtly involved in the metabolism of drugs. Examples of these enzyme systems include CYP 3A4 which metabolise majority of drugs, CYP 2D6, CYP 1A2, CYP 2C19, CYP 2C9, CYP 2E1, CYP 1A1 and CYP 1A2 (151). The involvement of any of these enzyme systems in the metabolism of a xenobiotic has consequence on the incidences of drug-drug, drug-cosmetic, cosmetic-cosmetic, drug-food, and cosmetic-food interactions. This is due to the resultant capacity of either the cosmetic ingredient or the food/drug to induce or inhibit particular metabolising enzymes, leading to the accumulation or depletion of required xenobiotics in the body. The consequence of this is the advent of therapeutic failure or toxicity. Metabolism of some cosmetic ingredients, especially those containing polyaromatic hydrocarbons (in tattoos), can lead to the copious production of pro-carcinogens in the body.

With the first stage of pharmacokinetics of a cosmetic being absorption, which is highly limited, it is not expected that an approved cosmetic ingredient will have extensive absorption through the skin. If the absorption is minimal, then the other pharmacokinetic parameters will be negligible.

References

1. Pillaiyar T, Manickam M, Namasivayam V. Skin whitening agents: Medicinal chemistry perspective of tyrosinase inhibitors. Journal of enzyme inhibition and medicinal chemistry. 2017 Jan 1;32(1):403-425.
2. Solano F, Briganti S, Picardo M, Ghanem G. Hypopigmenting agents: an updated review on biological, chemical and clinical aspects. Pigment cell research. 2006 Dec;19(6):550-571.
3. Ahn SJ, Koketsu M, Ishihara H, Lee SM, Ha SK, Lee KH, Kang TH, Kima SY. Regulation of melanin synthesis by selenium-containing carbohydrates. Chemical and pharmaceutical bulletin. 2006;54(3):281-286.

4. Iozumi K, Hoganson GE, Pennella R, Everett MA, Fuller BB. Role of tyrosinase as the determinant of pigmentation in cultured human melanocytes. Journal of Investigative Dermatology. 1993 Jun 1;100(6):806-811.
5. Li G, Ju HK, Chang HW, et al. Melanin biosynthesis inhibitors from the bark of Machilus thunbergii. Biol Pharm Bull 2003; 26:1039–1041
6. Ünver N, Freyschmidt-Paul P, Hörster S, Wenck H, Stäb F, Blatt T, Elsässer HP. Alterations in the epidermal–dermal melanin axis and factor XIIIa melanophages in senile lentigo and ageing skin. British Journal of Dermatology. 2006 Jul;155(1):119-128.
7. Brenner M, Hearing VJ. The protective role of melanin against UV damage in human skin. Photochemistry and photobiology. 2008 May;84(3):539-549.
8. Urabe K, Nakayama J, Hori Y, Norlund JJ, Biossy RE, Hearing VJ, King RA, Ortonne JP. The pigmentary system: physiology and pathophysiology. by Norlund JJ, Boissy RE, Hearing VJ, King RA, Ortonne JP, Oxford University Press, New York. 1998:909-911.
9. YANG JY, KOO JH, SONG YG, KWON KB, LEE JH, SOHN HS, PARK BH, JHEE EC, PARK JW. Stimulation of melanogenesis by scoparone in B16 melanoma cells 1. Acta Pharmacologica Sinica. 2006 Nov;27(11):1467-1473.
10. Pillaiyar T, Manickam M, Jung SH. Inhibitors of melanogenesis: a patent review (2009–2014). Expert opinion on therapeutic patents. 2015 Jul 3;25(7):775-788.
11. Schiaffino MV. Signaling pathways in melanosome biogenesis and pathology. The international journal of biochemistry & cell biology. 2010 Jul 1;42(7):1094-1004.
12. Slominski A, Tobin DJ, Shibahara S, Wortsman J. Melanin pigmentation in mammalian skin and its hormonal regulation. Physiological reviews. 2004 Oct;84(4):1155-1228.
13. Hearing VJ, Jiménez M. Mammalian tyrosinase—the critical regulatory control point in melanocyte pigmentation. International Journal of Biochemistry. 1987 Jan 1;19(12):1141-1147.
14. Halaban R, Patton RS, Cheng E, Svedine S, Trombetta ES, Wahl ML, Ariyan S, Hebert DN. Abnormal acidification of melanoma cells induces tyrosinase retention in the early secretory pathway. Journal of Biological Chemistry. 2002 Apr 26;277(17):14821-14828.
15. Sánchez-Ferrer Á, Rodríguez-López JN, García-Cánovas F, García-Carmona F. Tyrosinase: a comprehensive review of its mechanism. Biochimica et Biophysica Acta (BBA)-Protein Structure and Molecular Enzymology. 1995 Feb 22;1247(1):1-1.
16. Matoba Y, Kumagai T, Yamamoto A, Yoshitsu H, Sugiyama M. Crystallographic evidence that the dinuclear copper center of tyrosinase is flexible during catalysis. Journal of Biological Chemistry. 2006 Mar 31;281(13):8981-8990.
17. Bijelic A, Pretzler M, Molitor C, Zekiri F, Rompel A. The structure of a plant tyrosinase from walnut leaves reveals the importance of "Substrate-Guiding Residues" for enzymatic specificity. Angewandte Chemie International Edition. 2015 Dec 1;54(49):14677-14780.
18. Decker H, Tuczek F. Tyrosinase/catecholoxidase activity of hemocyanins: structural basis and molecular mechanism. Trends in biochemical sciences. 2000 Aug 1;25(8):392-397.

19. Jiménez-Atiénzar M, Escribano J, Cabanes J, Gandía-Herrero F, García-Carmona F. Oxidation of the flavonoid eriodictyol by tyrosinase. Plant Physiology and Biochemistry. 2005 Sep 1;43(9):866-873.

20. Burnett CL, Bergfeld WF, Belsito DV, Hill RA, Klaassen CD, Liebler DC, Marks JG, Shank RC, Slaga TJ, Snyder PW, Andersen FA. Final report of the safety assessment of kojic acid as used in cosmetics. International journal of toxicology. 2010 Nov;29(6_suppl):244S-73S.

21. Dickinson DA, Forman HJ. Glutathione in defense and signaling: Lessons from a small thiol. Ann N Y Acad Sci 2002;973:488-504

22 Yamamura T, Onishi J, Nishiyama T. Antimelanogenic activity of hydrocoumarins in cultured normal human melanocytes by stimulating intracellular glutathione synthesis. Arch Dermatol Res 2002;294:349-54

23. Sonthalia, S., Jha, A. K., Lallas, A., Jain, G., & Jakhar, D. (2018). Glutathione for skin lightening: a regnant myth or evidence-based verity?. *Dermatology practical & conceptual*, *8*(1), 15–21. https://doi.org/10.5826/dpc.0801a04

24. Westerhof, W., Njoo, M.D. (2000). Bleaching Agents. In: Katsambas, A.D., Lotti, T.M. (eds) European Handbook of Dermatological Treatments. Springer, Berlin, Heidelberg. https://doi.org/10.1007/978-3-662-03835-2_130

25. Hagen TM, Wierzbicka GT, Bowman BB, Aw TY, Jones DP. Fate of dietary glutathione: Disposition in the gastrointestinal tract. Am J Physiol 1990;259(4 Pt 1):G530-5.

26. Oakley, A.; Bleaching creams. New Zealand Dermatological Society Incorporated. http://novocosmetica.com/bleaching.pdf (accessed May 8, 2022).

27 Gagliardia, L., De Orsia, D., Rosaria Del Guidice, M.; Development of tandem thin layer chromatography–high-performance liquid chromatography method for the identification and determination of corticosteroids in cosmetic products; Analytica Chimica Acta, (2002); 457: 187–198.

28 Gaudiano, M.C., Lucente, D., Antoniella, E.; "For export only" medicines come back to Europe: A RP-LC method for the screening of six glucocorticoids in illegal and counterfeit anti-inflammatory and lightening creams; Journal of Pharmaceuticals and Biomedical Analysis, (2009); 53: 158–164

30. Gonçalez ML, Correa MA, Chorilli M. Skin delivery of kojic acid-loaded nanotechnology-based drug delivery systems for the treatment of skin aging. BioMed Research International. 2013 Jan 1;2013.

31 Ki DH, Jung HC, Noh YW, Thanigaimalai P, Kim BH, Shin SC, Jung SH, Cho CW. Preformulation and formulation of newly synthesised QNT3-18 for development of a skin whitening agent. Drug development and industrial pharmacy. 2013 Apr 1;39(4):526-533.

32. Arndt KA, Fitzpatrick TB. Topical use of hydroquinone as a depigmenting agent. Jama. 1965 Nov 29;194(9):965-967.

33. Fitzpatrick T, Arndt KA, El Mofty AM, Pathak MA. Hydroquinone and psoralens in the therapy of hypermelanosis and vitiligo. Archives of dermatology. 1966 May 1;93(5):589-600.

34 Kligman AM, Willis I. A new formula for depigmenting human skin. Archives of dermatology. 1975 Jan 1;111(1):40-48.

35 Heilgemeir GP, Balda BR. Irreversible toxic depigmentation. Observations following use of hydroquinonemonobenzylether-containing skin bleaching preparations. MMW, Munchener medizinische Wochenschrift. 1981 Jan 1;123(2):47-48.

36. Hariharan V, Klarquist J, Reust MJ, Koshoffer A, McKee MD, Boissy RE, Le Poole IC. Monobenzyl ether of hydroquinone and 4-tertiary butyl phenol activate markedly different physiological responses in melanocytes: relevance to skin depigmentation. J Invest Dermatol 2010; 130: 211–220.

37 Westerhof W, d'Ischia M. Vitiligo puzzle: the pieces fall in place. Pigm Cell Res 2007; 20:345–359.

38 Manga P, Sheyn D, Yang F, Sarangarajan R, Boissy RE. A role for tyrosinase-related protein 1 in 4-tert-butyl phenol-induced toxicity in melanocytes-implications for vitiligo. Am J Pathol 2006; 169: 1652–1662.

39 Douat-Casassus C, Marchand-Geneste N, Diez E, Aznar C, Picard P, Geoffre S, et al. Covalent modification of a melanoma-derived antigenic peptide with a natural quinone methide. Preliminary chemical, molecular modelling and immunological evaluation studies. Mol Biosyst 2006; 2:240–249.

40. Gallo FR, Pagliuca G, Multari G, Panzini G, D'amore E, Altieri I. New high-performance liquid chromatography-DAD method for analytical determination of arbutin and hydroquinone in rat plasma. Indian journal of pharmaceutical sciences. 2015 Sep;77(5):530.

41 Kumar KS, Vani MG, Wang SY, Liao JW, Hsu LS, Yang HL, Hseu YC. In vitro and in vivo studies disclosed the depigmenting effects of gallic acid: A novel skin lightening agent for hyperpigmentary skin diseases. Biofactors. 2013 May;39(3):259-270.

42. Yao CL, Lin YM, Mohamed MS, Chen JH. Inhibitory effect of ectoine on melanogenesis in B16-F0 and A2058 melanoma cell lines. Biochemical engineering journal. 2013 Sep 15; 78:163-169.

43. Son KH, Heo MY. The evaluation of depigmenting efficacy in the skin for the development of new whitening agents in Korea. International journal of cosmetic science. 2013 Feb;35(1):9-18.

44 Ebanks JP, Wickett RR, Boissy RE. Mechanisms regulating skin pigmentation: the rise and fall of complexion coloration. International Journal of Molecular Sciences. 2009 Sep;10(9):4066-4087.

45 Fisk WA, Agbai O, Lev-Tov HA, Sivamani RK. The use of botanically derived agents for hyperpigmentation: a systematic review. Journal of the American Academy of Dermatology. 2014 Feb 1;70(2):352-365.

46 Chen YS, Lee SM, Lin CC, Liu CY, Wu MC, Shi WL. Kinetic study on the tyrosinase and melanin formation inhibitory activities of carthamus yellow isolated from *Carthamus tinctorius* L. Journal of bioscience and bioengineering. 2013 Mar 1;115(3):242-245.

47 Lee DY, Jeong SC, Jeong YT, Lee MK, Seo KH, Lee JW, Kim GS, Lee SE, Baek NI, Kim JH. Antimelanogenic effects of picrionoside a isolated from the leaves of Korean ginseng. Biological and Pharmaceutical Bulletin. 2015 Oct 1;38(10):1663-1667.

48 Biswas R, Chanda J, Kar A, Mukherjee PK. Tyrosinase inhibitory mechanism of betulinic acid from Dillenia indica. Food Chem. 2017 Oct 1; 232:689-696.
49 Anantharaman A, Hemachandran H, Priya RR, Sankari M, Gopalakrishnan M, Palanisami N, Siva R. Inhibitory effect of apocarotenoids on the activity of tyrosinase: multi-spectroscopic and docking studies. Journal of bioscience and bioengineering. 2016 Jan 1;121(1):13-20.
50 Huang J, Lu J, Hu Y, Zhou Y, Luo L, Zhang Y, Zhang L, Chen J, Zeng Q. Identification of Sitogluside as a Potential Skin-Pigmentation-Reducing Agent through Network Pharmacology. *Oxid Med Cell Longev*. 2021: 23; 1:4883398
51. Pavic A, Ilic-Tomic T, Glamočlija J. Unravelling Anti-Melanogenic Potency of Edible Mushrooms *Laetiporus sulphureus* and *Agaricus silvaticus* In Vivo Using the Zebrafish Model. J Fungi (Basel). 2021 ;7(10):834.
52. Breathnach AC, Nazzaro-Porro M, Passi S, Zina G. Azelaic acid therapy in disorders of pigmentation. Clinics in dermatology. 1989 Apr 1;7(2):106-119.
53. Garcia-Lopez M. Double-blind comparison of azelaic acid and hydroquinone in the treatment of melasma. Acta Derm Venereol (Stockh). 1989; 143:58-61.
54. Shivhare SC, Malviya KG, Malviya KS, Rai NK, Jain V, Kumar A. A Review: Natural Skin Lighting and Nourishing Agents. Research Journal of Topical and Cosmetic Sciences. 2012 Jun 28;3(1):11-15.
55. Huang CH, Sung HC, Hsiao CY, Hu S, Ko YS. Transdermal delivery of three vitamin C derivatives by Er: YAG and carbon dioxide laser pretreatment. Lasers in medical science. 2013 May;28(3):807-814.
56. Eimpunth S, Wanitphadeedecha R, Manuskiatti W. A focused review on acne-induced and aesthetic procedure-related postinflammatory hyperpigmentation in Asians. Journal of the European Academy of Dermatology and Venereology. 2013 Jan; 27:7-18.
57 Hsieh PW, Chen WY, Aljuffali A, Chen CC, Fang JY. Co-drug strategy for promoting skin targeting and minimizing the transdermal diffusion of hydroquinone and tranexamic acid. Current medicinal chemistry. 2013 Oct 1;20(32):4080-4092.
58 Tse TW, Hui E. Tranexamic acid: an important adjuvant in the treatment of melasma. Journal of cosmetic dermatology. 2013 Mar;12(1):57-66.
59 Draelos ZD, Deliencourt-Godefroy G, Lopes L. An effective hydroquinone alternative for topical skin lightening. *J Cosmet Dermatol*. 2020 19(12):3258-3261.
60 The European Parliament and the Council of the European Union. Regulation (EC) No 1223/2009 of the European Parliament and of the Council of 30 November 2009 on Cosmetic products Official Journal of the European Union. L 342/59
61 https://www.fda.gov/industry/color-additive-inventories/summary-color-additives-use-united-states-foods-drugs-cosmetics-and-medical-devices

62 Jones T, Edwards J, Kallioinen J. Titanium compounds, inorganic. Kirk-Othmer Encyclopedia of Chemical Technology. 2000 Dec 4:1-76.

63 Cornell., RM.; Schwertmann, U (2003). *The iron oxides: structure, properties, reactions, occurrences and*. Wiley VCH. ISBN 978-3-527-30274-1

64 Iron oxide (Fe2O3) - Structure, Molecular Mass, Properties & Uses (byjus.com) accessed on 11/04/2022

65 https://geologyscience.com/minerals/mica-group-minerals/ accessed on 09/04/2022

66. Abrahart EN. *Dyes and their Intermediates*. New York: Chemical Publishing, 1977: 1–12).

67 Giuldbudagian M, Schreiver I, Singh A.V., Laux P and Luch A. Safety of tattoos and permanent make-up: a regulatory view. Archives of Toxicology (2020) 94:357–369.

68 Andreou E, Hatziantoniou S, Rallis E, Kefala V. Safety of Tattoos and Permanent Make up (PMU) Colorants. *Cosmetics*. 2021; 8(2):47.

69 Andreou E, Hatziantoniou S, Rallis E, Kefala V. Safety of Tattoos and Permanent Make up (PMU) Colorants. *Cosmetics*. 2021; 8(2):47. https://doi.org/10.3390/cosmetics8020047

70 https://cosmetics.specialchem.com/selection-guide/color-selection-basics

71. Rasmus J. N. Frandsen, Paiman Khorsand-Jamal, Kenneth T. Kongstad, Majse Nafisi, Rubini M. Kannangara, Dan Staerk, Finn T. Okkels, Kim Binderup, Bjørn Madsen, Birger Lindberg Møller, Ulf Thrane & Uffe H. Heterologous production of the widely used natural food colorant carminic acid in Aspergillus nidulans Mortensen Scientific Reports 2018; 8:12853.

72. Sharma, R. K., Goel, A., & Bhatia, A. K. (2016). Lawsonia Inermis Linn: A Plant with Cosmetic and Medical Benefits. *International Journal of Applied Sciences and Biotechnology*, 2016; *4*(1): 15–20. https://doi.org/10.3126/ijasbt.v4i1.14728.

73. López, L., Flores, S.D., Belmares, S.Y., & Galindo, A.S. Naphthoquinones: Biological properties and synthesis of lawsone and derivatives-a structured review *Vitae-revista De La Facultad De Quimica Farmaceutica. 2014; 21:* 248-258.

74. Johnson, W., Heldreth, B., Bergfeld, W. F., Belsito, D. V., Hill, R. A., Klaassen, C. D., Liebler, D. C., Marks, J. G., Shank, R. C., Slaga, T. J., Snyder, P. W., & Andersen, F. A. (2017). Safety Assessment of Anthemis nobilis–Derived Ingredients as Used in Cosmetics. *International Journal of Toxicology*, *36*(1_suppl), 57S-66S. https://doi.org/10.1177/1091581817705620

75. Viola H, Wasowski C, Levi de Stein M, Wolfman C, Silveira R, Dajas F, Medina JH, Paladini AC. Apigenin, a component of Matricaria recutita flowers, is a central benzodiazepine receptors-ligand with anxiolytic effects. Planta Med. 1995 Jun;61(3):213-6. doi: 10.1055/s-2006-958058.

76 Morel, O.; Christie, R.M.; Greaves, A.; Morgan, K.M. Enhanced model for the diffusivity of a dye molecule into human hair fibre based on molecular modelling techniques. Colour. Technol. 2008, 124, 301–309

77 Ballarin, B.; Galli, S.; Morigi, M. Study of dyeing properties of semipermanent dyestuffs for hair. Int. J. Cosmet. Sci. 2007, 29, 49–57

78 de Cássia Comis Wagner R, Kiyohara PK, Silveira M, Joekes I. Electron microscopic observations of human hair medulla. Journal of Microscopy. 2007 Apr;226(1):54-63.

79. Boga C, Delpivo C, Ballarin B, Morigi M, Galli S, Micheletti G, Tozzi S. Investigation on the dyeing power of some organic natural compounds for a green approach to hair dyeing. Dyes and Pigments. 2013 Apr 1;97(1):9-

80 Robbins, C.R. Chemical and Physical Behaviour of Human Hair, 5th ed.; Springer: New York, NY, USA, 2012; p. 724.

81 Harrison S, Sinclair R. Hair colouring, permanent styling and hair structure. Journal of Cosmetic Dermatology. 2003 Jul;2(3-4):180-185.

82. Brown, K.C. Hair colouring. In Hair and Hair Care; Johnson, D.H., Ed.; Marcel Dekker: New York, NY, USA, 1997

83. Robbins CR, Robbins CR. Chemical and physical behaviour of human hair. Berlin: Springer; 2012 Feb 23.

84. Ballarin, B.; Galli, S.; Morigi, M. Study of dyeing properties of semipermanent dyestuffs for hair. Int. J. Cosmet. Sci. 2007, 29, 49–57

85. Aparecida da França, S., Dario, M.F., Esteves, V. B., Baby A.R. and Velasco, M.V.R. (2015). Types of Hair Dye and Their Mechanisms of Action. Cosmetics 2015, 2, 110-126

86. Wolfram, L.J. Hair cosmetics. In Handbook of Cosmetic Science and Technology; Barel, A.O., Paye, M., Maibach, H.I., Eds.; Marcel Dekker: New York, NY, USA, 2001.

87. Hudari FF, de Almeida LC, da Silva BF, Zanoni MV. Voltammetric sensor for simultaneous determination of p-phenylenediamine and resorcinol in permanent hair dyeing and tap water by composite carbon nanotubes/chitosan modified electrode. Microchemical Journal. 2014 Sep 1; 116:261-268.

88. Tucker HH. Hair coloring with oxidation dye intermediates. J. Soc. Cosmet. Chem. 1967; 18:609-628.

89. Vincent U, Bordin G, Rodriguez AR. Validation of an analytical procedure for the determination of oxidative hair dyes in cosmetic formulations. Journal of cosmetic science. 2002 Jan 1; 53(1):43-58.

90. Lukacs VA, Korting HC. Antiperspirants and deodorants--ingredients and evaluation. Dermatosen in Beruf und Umwelt. Occupation and environment. 1989 Mar 1;37(2):53-57.

91. Draelos ZD. Antiperspirants and the hyperhidrosis patient. Dermatologic Therapy. 2001 Sep;14(3):220-224.

92. Baumler W. Chemical Hazard of tattoo colorants. In Quarterly Medical Review-Tattoos. Press. Med.2020;49 (104046):1-6

93. Piccinini P, Pakalin S, Contor L, et al. Safety of tattoos and permanent make-up final report; 2016 [Available from: https://eceuropaeu/jrc/en/publication/eur

94. Moraitis AG, Hewison M, Collins M et al. Hypercalcemia associated with mineral oil-induced sclerosing paraffinomas. Endoc. Pract. 2013; 19:e50-56

95. Akintobi AM, Villano CM, White LA. 2,3,7,8-tetrachlorodibenzo-p-dioxin (TCDD) exposure of normal human derma fibroblasts results in AhR-dependent and independent changes in gene expression. Toxicol Appl Pharmacol. 2007;220:9-17

96. Shimada T, Fuji-Kuriyama Y. Metabolic activation of polycyclic aromatic hydrocarbons to carcinogen by cytochrome P4501A1 and 1B1. Cancer Sci 2004; 95:1-6.

97. Shimada T, Murayama N, Yamazaki H, et al. Metabolic activation of polycyclic aromatic hydrocarbons and aryl and heterocyclic amines by human cytochromes P450 2A13 and 2A6. *Chem Res Toxicol*. 2013;26(4):529-537

98. Lehner K, Santarelli F, Vasold R, et al. Black tattoos entail substantial uptake of genotoxicpolycyclic aromatic hydrocarbons (PAH) in human skin and regional lymph nodes. *PLoS One*. 2014;9(3):e92787

99. Dal'Belo SE, Gaspar LR, Maia Campos PM. Moisturizing effect of cosmetic formulations containing *Aloe vera* extract in different concentrations assessed by skin bioengineering techniques. Skin Res Technol. 2006 Nov;12(4):241-6.) (https://www.sciencedirect.com/science/article/pii/B9780444632944000097
100. Schwarz, K. A bound form of silicon in glycosaminoglycans and polyuronides. Proceedings of the National Academy of Sciences of the United States of America. 1973; 70 (5): 1608–1612.
101. Fraser JR, Laurent TC, Laurent UB. Hyaluronan: its nature, distribution, functions and turnover. *J. Intern. Med.* 1997;**242** (1): 27–33
102. Haberfeld H, ed. (2015). Austria-Codex (in German). Vienna: Österreichischer Apothekerverlag. Bepanthen Crème
103. Ebner F, Heller A, Rippke F, Tausch I (2002). "Topical use of dexpanthenol in skin disorders". American Journal of Clinical Dermatology. 2002; 3(6): 427–33.
104. National Center for Biotechnology Information. "PubChem Compound Summary for CID 204, Allantoin" *PubChem*, https://pubchem.ncbi.nlm.nih.gov/compound/Allantoin. Accessed 19 February, 2022
105. Di Salvo, R.M. "Allantoin" in *The Chemistry and Manufacture of Cosmetics: Vol. III – Ingredients*, Book One, 3rd ed., Ed. M.L. Schlossman, 2002
106. Allantoin, A Safe and Effective Skin Protectant, Akema Fine Chemicals, product literature, accessed June 2017, www.akema.it.
107. Allantoin, An Impressive History, DSM Nutritional Products, product literature, accessed June 2017, www.dsmnutritionalproducts.com
108. Becker, L.C. , W.F. Bergfeld, D.V. Belsito, C.D. Klaassen, J.G. Marks, R.C. Shank, T.J. Slaga, P.W. Snyder, and F. Alan Andersen, Final report of the safety assessment of allantoin and its related complexes, *Int. J. Toxicol.*, 2010; **29**(3):84S-97S.
109. Draelos, Z.D. Therapeutic moisturizers. Dermatol. Clin. 2000; 18:597–607.
110. Alander J.T. Chemical and Physical Properties of Emollients. In: Lodén M., Maibach H. (eds) Treatment of Dry Skin Syndrome. Springer, Berlin, Heidelberg. https://doi.org/10.1007/978-3-642-27606-4_26
111. Cork, M. The importance of skin barrier function. J. Dermatolog. Treat. 2009; 8: S7–13
112. Savary, G., Grisel, M. and Picard, C. Impact of emollients on the spreading properties of cosmetic products: A combined sensory and instrumental characterization. Colloids Surf. B Biointerfaces. 2013; 102, 371–378.
113. Loden, M. Role of topical emollients and moisturizers in the treatment of dry skin barrier disorders. Am. J. Clin. Dermatol. 2003; 4:771–788
114. Nicholls, S., King, C.S. and Marks, R. Short term effects of emollients and a bath oil on the stratum corneum. J. Soc. Cosmet. Chem. 1978; 29: 617–624.
115. Garber, C.A. and Nightingale, C.T. Characterizing cosmetic effects and skin morphology by scanning electron microscopy. J. Soc. Cosmet. Chem. 1976; 27:509–531.
116. Moncrieff, G., Cork, M., Lawton, S., Kokiet, S., Daly, C. and Clark, C. Use of emollients in dry-skin conditions: Consensus statement. Clin. Exp. Dermatol. 2013; 38:231–238.

117. Conti, A., Rogers, J., Verdejo, P., Harding, C.R. and Rawlings, A.V. Seasonal influences on stratum corneum ceramide 1 fatty acids and the influence of topical essential fatty acids. Int. J. Cosmet. Sci. 1996; 18:1–12.
118. Wertz, P.W. and Downing, D.T. Metabolism of topically applied fatty acid methyl esters in BALB/C mouse epidermis. J. Dermatol. Sci. 1990; 1:33–37.
119. Held, E., Sveinsdottir, S. and Agner, T. Effect of long-term use of moisturizer on skin hydration, barrier function and susceptibility to irritants. Acta Derm. Venereol. 1999; 79:49–51.
120. Puri N, Talwar A. The efficacy of silicone gel for the treatment of hypertrophic scars and keloids. J Cutan Aesthetic Surg. 2009 Jul;2(2):104–6
121. Takahashi, K., Sakano, H., Numata, N.,Kuroda, S. and Mizuno, N. Effect of fatty acid diesters on permeation of anti-inflammatory drugs through rat skin. Drug Dev. Ind. Pharm. 2002; 28:1285–1294.
122. "Nutrition Facts for sesame oil per 100 g, analysis of fats and fatty acids". *Conde Nast for the USDA National Nutrient Database, version SR-21. 2014*. Retrieved *11 July* 2015
123. Ismail Almas, Ester Innocent, Francis Machumi, William Kisinza (2021). Chemical composition of essential oils from *Eucalyptus globulus* and *Eucalyptus maculata* grown in Tanzania, Scientific African, 12: e00758
124. Garnier N, Cren-Olivé C, Rolando C, Regert M. Characterization of Archaeological Beeswax by Electron Ionization and Electrospray Ionization Mass Spectrometry. Analytical Chemistry. 2002;74:4868–4877
125. Tulloch AP, Hoffman LL. Canadian beeswax: analytical values and composition of hydrocarbons, free acids and long chain esters. Journal of the American Oil Chemists' Society. 1972;49:696–699
126. Filippo Fratini, Giovanni Cilia, Barbara Turchi, Antonio Felicioli, (2016) Beeswax: A minireview of its antimicrobial activity and its application in medicine, Asian Pacific Journal of Tropical Medicine,2016; 9(9): 839-843.
127. Begoun, P. Mineral Makeup: Powder Perfect or Poor Performer? http://www.cosmeticscop.com/skin-care-facts-mineral-makeup.aspx [Aug 2009]
128. Valhouli, C. Mineral Makeup: Excavated From a Mine. The New York Times, Aug 24, 2006, p G. 3.
129. Gabriel, J. Green Beauty Guide: Your Essential Resource to Organic and Natural Skin Care, Hair Care, Makeup, and Fragrances. Deerfield Beach, FL: Health Communications, Inc., 2008.
130. Finnegan S, Percival SL. EDTA: An Antimicrobial and Antibiofilm Agent for Use in Wound Care. *Adv Wound Care (New Rochelle)*. 2015;4(7):415-421
131. Human Cytochrome P450s – Cytochrome P450 Homepage (uthsc.edu) accessed on 18 April, 2022

CHAPTER TEN

Nanotechnology in cosmetics

Funmilola A Fisusi

Nanotechnology is a dynamic, highly innovative, and versatile field with almost limitless possibilities for application in various areas of scientific endeavours. The cosmetics industry thrives on the quest for novelty and the drive for custom-made products, to deliver optimum customer satisfaction. The introduction of nanotechnology into the cosmetics industry is an innovative move that potentially holds the promise of a nanocosmetics future filled with "super" beauty and personal care products. However, as promising as this may seem, it may turn out to be a double-edged sword, owing to potential risks that are associated with the use of nanosized materials in products for human use. Therefore, to secure the desired nanocosmetics future, there is a need to put adequate measures in place to ensure that only nanomaterials that are safe for both human and environmental health are used in cosmetic products. This chapter covers the different types of nanomaterials used in the cosmetics industry and their applications, safety, toxicity, and regulation in cosmetic products.

Nanomaterials and nanoparticles

Nanomaterials can generally be defined as materials comprising particles with dimensions in the nanometer size range (1). Some definitions of nanomaterials are more specific about the size and resultant properties of constituent particles of such materials. For instance, the United States National Nanotechnology Initiative (US-NNI)'s proposed definition for nanomaterials is as follows: "materials with dimensions of roughly 1–100 nm, where unique phenomena enable novel applications" (2), and the European Commission (EC)'s definition for nanomaterials reads in part, that nanomaterials are ".....materials in which for 50% or more of the particles in the number size distribution, one or more external dimensions is in the size range 1 nm–100 nm...." (3). Although the extremely small particle size is an important property of nanoparticles, the unique properties that such size confer on the particles is equally important. For functional application of nanomaterials, both size and resultant change in inherent properties of the material is important. Therefore, a practical and concise definition of nanomaterials would take the size and properties of the material into consideration. Thus, nanomaterials have been defined as "materials having at least one characteristic length scale in the range 1–100 nm, and with at least one property being considerably different from that of the bulk counterpart as a result of the nanoscale dimensions" (1). Nanoparticles are characterised by a high surface area-to-volume ratio (4,5), which provides more effective surface for interaction with their surrounding (4,6). Thus, some physicochemical properties like dissolution, aggregation, coalescence, and adsorption may not remain constant over time (7). Due to their small size and resulting unique properties, nanomaterials have found wide applications in medicine (diagnostics, drug delivery, tissue engineering), various engineering fields, and cosmetics (7–10).

Application of nanotechnology in cosmetics

Cosmetic products have been used extensively by people of all ages, races, statuses, and clime for the attainment of cleanness (soaps and shampoos) or perpetual youthfulness (creams and serums) (11). As the cosmetics industry continued to grow in leaps and bounds, the quest for novel and custom-made products, based on sound scientific insights, remained a constant feature of the industry (12). Nanotechnology being a highly dynamic, innovative, promising, and versatile field, with wide applicability in various fields of science, is relevant in this regard (5,7,10,13). This may explain why the cosmetics industry was quick to adopt the concept of nanotechnology in the development of products, thus emerging as one of the first industries to embrace the use of nanomaterials (5,9,14).

Nanotechnology was hailed as a major game-changer in the production of superior cosmetic products (9). The penetration of nanotechnology into the cosmetic industry benefitted greatly from the less stringent regulation of cosmetic products, compared to new drug products, and also from the fact that they are typically applied to specific sites on the skin (11). Perhaps another boost for nanotechnology in the cosmetics industry is the great emphasis placed on perceived innovativeness and quality of finished products (14). The first nanoparticle-based anti-ageing products were introduced into the market in 1986 by Lancôme (Niosôme; developed by L'Oreal researchers) and Christian Dior (a liposomal product named Capture™) (7–9). Since that time, the cosmetics industry has welcomed scores of nanoparticle-based products into the market (14), with companies like L'Oreal, Procter & Gamble, Henkel, and Unilever ranking ahead of others in holding patents for nanotechnology-related products (15).

The cosmetics industry uses nanomaterials mostly to improve products' performance, such as prolonging effects and achieving greater stability of products (8,10). Some of the specific advantages derivable from using nanoparticles in cosmetic products include: enhanced stability of degradation-prone ingredients; controlled release of active ingredients; increased contact time at the site of action; improved permeability of ingredients; improved efficacy, efficiency, and tolerability; increased aesthetic appeal of products; and better end-user compliance (5,7,14,16).

Nanomaterials used in cosmetics

Nanomaterials may be used in cosmetic products as the active ingredient, vehicle, carrier, or as an excipient (9,14,17). Nanoparticles have been employed in various categories of cosmetics such as skincare, haircare, and beautification products (14).

Nanoparticles in skincare products

The term "skincare products" is applied to cosmetic products that are used on the epidermis (9). Skincare is considered to be the most relevant area of cosmetics for the application of nanotechnology (18). The ability of the product to produce the desired effect would depend on the active ingredient(s), the base, the formulation technique, access to, and duration of stay of the active ingredient at the desired site of action (9,18). Nanoparticles can be used either as active ingredients or as a delivery vehicle in skincare products (14). Skincare products would usually have agents such as vitamins, proteins, or antioxidants, which have anti-ageing effects incorporated into them. These agents can either be formulated as nanoparticles or delivered via nanocarriers to enhance their bioavailability, stability, and efficacy (14).

Nanoparticles in sunscreens

Cosmetic sunscreens are used to protect the skin from the harmful effects of ultraviolet [UV; UVA (320–400 nm) and UVB (290–320 nm)] rays from sunlight, such as induction of cancers, ageing, inflammation, pigmentation, and so on, which may result from excessive exposure to these rays. Although UVC is also harmful to the skin, it is naturally blocked by the ozone layer. (8,17). Cosmetic sunscreens can exert their protective effect by absorbing the UV light, scattering and/or reflecting it, or by preventing, reducing, or reversing sunlight-induced damage. While inorganic nanoparticles of metal oxides act as UV filters mainly by scattering and reflecting UV rays (though they may also absorb part of the incident UV light), organic compounds such as salicylates and cinnamates amongst others act as sunscreens by absorbing UV light (17). Sunscreens account for a sizeable proportion of the products incorporating nanoparticles worldwide, requiring about 1,000 tons in the 2003/2004 period (13).

Nanoparticles in tattoo inks

Tattoos can be described as body adornments or modifications produced on the skin by injecting ink into the dermis layer (19). The practice of tattooing has been done for ages, cutting across various societies, races, and countries of the world (19–21). A natural mummy (dating back to more than 5,000 years) discovered in the Ötztal Alps in Italy, is thought to be the most ancient evidence of the application of tattoos in humans. Although tattooing has become more of a fad in recent times, it served several purposes in the past, including therapeutic, identification, stigmatisation, and beautification (20,21). The ink suspensions used in the production of tattoos comprise nanosized pigments which are injected into the dermis (20). Like many cosmetic products, regulation of the use of these pigments in tattoo ink was initially loose in many countries. More recently, there have been more regulations in many countries to address toxicity and safety concerns associated with the pigments (19). However, the continued use of tattoos is still associated with different levels of health and safety concerns (19,20).

Nanoparticles in haircare products

Nanoparticles are used for haircare products including shampoos and conditioners (routine haircare); for hair colouring and for improving the general health and aesthetic appeal of the hair (16,22,23).

Routine haircare products: Many important ingredients for the formulation of haircare products such as shampoos and conditioners are insoluble or poorly soluble in water. The incorporation of such ingredients in nanoparticle formulations would improve their solubility and effectiveness. Thus, when nanoparticles are used in such products, they facilitate the moisturising effect of the active ingredients, by increasing contact time with the scalp and follicles, thereby giving them ample time to form protective films which seal moisture within the follicles (16). Silicone oil is a very important ingredient in conventional haircare products, for maintaining hair health and lustre. Silicone does not have good penetrability due to its hydrophobic nature, so, it tends to be deposited on the scalp instead of penetrating the hair (23–25). However, when formulated as nanoemulsion, silicone oil can penetrate the hair fibres to moisturise and restore hair lustre (23). Cationic nanoformulations of ingredients such as sericin for hair conditioning have also been found to help heal damaged hair and restore hair health. Also, nanofibril complexes of zinc and chitin were found to reduce flaky scalp and sebum (16,26).

Hair colouring: Hair colouring is an age-long practice that has carried on into contemporary times (22). The use of conventional synthetic permanent hair dyes to achieve desired hair colour is plagued with unwanted effects including the possibility of increased risk for certain cancers with continuous use (23,27). Although more studies would be required to provide conclusive evidence (27), a safer but more or at least equally efficient platform for the development of hair dyes is required. Nanotechnology and its "off-shoot", nanoarchitectonics which combines nanotechnology with other techniques such as supramolecular chemistry (like self-assembly/self-organisation), organic and material synthesis, atomic/molecular level manipulation, and control amongst others, to produce functional structures (28,29), have been used to produce nanoparticle preparations incorporating hair colouring components. Examples include p-phenylenediamine nanoparticles prepared by ion complexation with poly(γ-glutamic acid), which led to a reduction in the adverse effects of the dye (30); black colouration of hair by lead (II) sulfide nanoparticles which precipitates in hair after treatment with a mixture of lead oxide, calcium hydroxide and a little water (22) and gold nanoparticles generated in situ by treatment of human hair with alkaline gold (III) chloride solution, which produced hair colouration that was resistant to multiple washes (31).

Types of nanoparticles used in cosmetics

The nanoparticles used in the various products may be degradable (organic) nanoparticles such as polymeric nanoparticles, liposomes, and niosomes or non-degradable (inorganic) nanoparticles such as metals or metal oxides (9,17).

Polymer-based nanoparticles

Polymers are large molecules comprising smaller molecules known as monomers, which are chemically linked together, usually forming long chains of repeating units of the monomers. They can be natural, synthetic, or semi-synthetic (24,32). Polymers rate second amongst materials used in cosmetic products (33). Commonly used polymers include those of natural origins such as cellulose, hyaluronic acid, chitosan, starch, collagen, alginate, and pectin; synthetic polymers such as poly (lactic acid) (PLA), poly-lactic-co-glycolic acid (PLGA) and poly-caprolactone; and semi-synthetic polymers like hydroxypropyl methylcellulose (HPMC), polyacrylic acid, nitrocellulose, modified starches and polyamides (9,24,32). In skincare products, polymers can act as rheology modifiers to obtain desired consistency of products, which would impact the ease of application of the product by affecting the ease of removal of the product from the container, spreadability, texture, and retention at the site of the application. Skin hydration is also another important effect produced by cationic polymers such as chitosan. These polymers form a film on the skin, thereby reducing evaporation and in effect "locking in" the moisture (24,33). In products required to be retained in place for long durations while also being water-resistant (make-up) such as lipstick, foundations, mascara, eyeliner, and so on, hydrophobic polymers help to make them waterproof and stay in place for longer durations (24). Polymer-based nanoparticles can be fabricated from these polymers for use as carriers for active compounds and to perform various functions in the formulation of cosmetic products used for skin or haircare (9,24,33). A few examples of these polymers are discussed below.

Cellulose: Cellulose is the most widely available, renewable polymer derivable from natural sources on earth (34). Nanoparticle forms of cellulose (nanocellulose) including microcrystalline cellulose, cellulose microfibrils, cellulose nanocrystals, cellulose nanofibrils, and bacterial nanocellulose have found application in the field of cosmetics (14,34). Nanocellulose can be used as a viscosity enhancer in cosmetic formulations (14,34). The different nanoparticle forms may also perform different functions in cosmetics. Cellulose nanowhiskers suspensions obtained using sulfuric or phosphoric acid produce a chiral nematic liquid crystal phase that reflects visible light, which gives rise to alluring optical effects (14,35). Thus, the nanocrystals may be used in cosmetic products like lipstick and nail polish (14). Cellulose nanocrystals have also been found to be useful as stabilisers for Pickering emulsions (34) and in the preparation of biocompatible, water-resistant, non-penetrating, easy wiping foundation liquid (36).

Chitosan: Chitosan is a natural polymer found in some fungi, but it can be obtained commercially from chitin, the second most abundant biopolymer (after cellulose), by deacetylation. Chitin is abundantly present in the shells of crustaceans like crabs and shrimps, and molluscs (37,38). Chitosan and its derivatives, as well as their nanoparticle formulations, have been shown to possess mucoadhesive and inherent antimicrobial activities which become even more pronounced in solution, and this is a bonus to the usefulness of these polymers in the preparation of cosmetics as well as other consumer products (37,39). Other properties of the polymers have also made them very valuable ingredients in cosmetic products. Thus, nanoparticle preparations of chitosan and its various derivatives have been used as carriers for the delivery and controlled release of different classes of bioactive agents and other formulation agents in various cosmetic and personal care products (30,38–40). The water absorption and retention properties of chitosan and derivatives have an important role in maintaining hydration. Thus, nanoparticles prepared from these polymers are used in skincare products, as they increase the moisture content of the stratum corneum and facilitate skin permeation of loaded active agents (14,39). They have also been used in the preparation of haircare products including shampoos, hair lotions, sprays, creams (14), and sunscreens (41).

Poly (lactic acid) and poly-lactic-co-glycolic acid

Poly (lactic acid): Poly (lactic acid) is a hydrophobic aliphatic polyester that can be obtained synthetically, using lactic acid as starting material. Although lactic acid is enantiomeric and can occur as either L-(+)-lactic acid or D-(-)-lactic acid, L-(+)-lactic acid is the enantiomer useful for application in the biomedical field, as it can be processed by the body's metabolic mechanisms and ultimately eliminated as carbon dioxide and water through the lungs, that is, it is biocompatible and biodegradable. Poly (lactic acid) is also Food and Drug Administration (FDA) approved and has been used extensively in food, pharmaceutical, and cosmetic products (24,42). Poly (lactic acid) has found application in the development of a variety of cosmetic products. Some examples include encapsulation of fragrance molecules in poly (lactic acid) nanocapsules which provided slow and sustained release of the fragrances as perfumes (43) and the use of poly (lactic acid) nanoparticles for encapsulation of olive leaf extracts for use in cosmetic formulation. Olive leaf extract is rich in oleuropein, which possesses antioxidant, anti-inflammatory, and antimicrobial activities among others. The antioxidant activities of the extract can be beneficial in maintaining skin health. However, the extract is poorly aqueous soluble, prone to oxidation, and photo and thermo-labile. Encapsulation of the olive leaf extract in poly (lactic acid) nanoparticles resulted in increased stability of the extract in the cosmetic formulation (44). Furthermore, nanocomposites comprising poly (lactic acid) and organically modified clays (organoclays) have been developed as bio-packaging materials for cosmetic products. It has been demonstrated that the nanocomposites would present minimal toxic effects on the skin. Thus, such poly (lactic acid) based composites represent a potential for biodegradable and more eco-friendly alternative packaging for cosmetic products compared to traditional plastic materials (45). Also, hollow nanoparticles of poly (lactic acid-co-glycidyl methacrylate) copolymer, which demonstrated high ultraviolet (UV) shielding properties and low toxicity have been developed as biodegradable, eco-friendly UV-shielding ingredients in cosmetic products (46).

Poly-lactic-co-glycolic acid: Poly lactic-co-glycolic acid (PLGA) is a copolymer comprising poly (lactic acid) and glycolic acid Similar to poly (lactic acid), PLGA is biocompatible, biodegradable and FDA approved (42,47). The use of the polymer for application in the preparation of cosmetic and personal care products has also been explored for the delivery of active molecules. Poly lactic-co-glycolic acid was used for the preparation of nanospheres loaded with three vitamin derivatives (vitamins A, C, and E), which would be converted to the corresponding vitamins by esterases after application. These vitamins are reputed to produce anti-wrinkling effects and prevent blemishes on the skin, making them popular candidates for anti-ageing and skin whitening products. However, their effectiveness is limited by the barrier action of the outer layer of the skin (stratum corneum) and their poor stability. Hence, the need for an effective means of skin transport and improved stability of the vitamins, which was provided by loading in PLGA nanospheres. The PLGA nanospheres loaded with the vitamin derivatives were prepared and marketed as functional skincare products which could be mixed with beauty essence just before use. The nanospheres were shown to produce the desired skin whitening and anti-ageing effect (48). In another study, ubiquinone (also known as coenzyme Q10 or Q10) was loaded into PLGA nanospheres for application in the development of beneficial cosmetic products, as topical application of ubiquinone has been shown to promote skin health by relieving the effects of stress and exposure to UV irradiation and produce anti-ageing effects on the skin (49). Thymol-loaded PLGA nanoparticles were also developed and evaluated for the treatment of acne. The study showed that the thymol-loaded nanoparticles showed good antimicrobial activity against infecting bacteria while maintaining the balance of the skin microbiota, which is important because treatment of acne with conventional antibiotics leads to disruption of the skin microbiota and development of resistance. Overall, cellular uptake of the nanoparticles enhanced the antioxidant effects in the keratinocytes which could also help in the healing of the acne lesions. Also, adherence of the nanoparticles to the skin surface would potentially cover acne lesions and protect them from further microbial attacks (50).

Nanoliposomes

Liposomes are spherically-shaped vesicles comprising phospholipid bilayers surrounding an internal aqueous core (51,52). Nanoliposomes are liposomes with sizes falling in the nanometer size range (53). Liposomes can serve as carrier systems for a wide variety of ingredients due to their composition (incorporating both lipid and aqueous layers), biocompatibility, biodegradability, and low toxicity (51,52). As mentioned previously, the introduction of a liposomal anti-ageing product (Capture) by Christian Dior (and the introduction of Niosôme by Lancôme) in 1986 signalled the entry of nanoparticle-based products into the cosmetics market (7–9). Liposomes have remained the most widely used nanoparticles in the development of cosmetic products (51,53). Nanoliposomes have been applied to various types of cosmetic products. Nanoliposomes containing safranal (a natural sunscreen agent) were prepared and evaluated against a reference formulation of homosalate. The result of studies conducted suggested that the nanoliposome formulation showed a potentially higher UV shielding effect than the homosalate reference formulation (54). Nanoliposome encapsulation of donkey milk, which has been used since ancient times as a cosmetic agent has also been described. Studies showed that nanoliposome encapsulated donkey milk demonstrated improved skin moisturisation and may also be advantageous in providing some anti-ageing effects (55). Furthermore, another study reported the production of nanoliposomes encapsulating vitamins D3, K2, E, and curcumin using a high-throughput method. These compounds possess demonstrable antioxidant properties but are limited by their low stability and poor absorption profiles. The use of the nanoliposome platform addressed the problems usually associated with the use of the compounds and provide the potential for high-scale production of better-performing cosmetic products from these compounds (56).

Lipid nanoparticles – solid lipid nanoparticles and nanostructured lipid carriers

Solid lipid nanoparticles (SLN) are the first generation of lipid nanoparticles. They are made of solid lipids dispersed in an aqueous medium, stabilised by emulsifiers contained in the aqueous phase, solid lipids are used in place of the oil phase of emulsion systems. Nanostructured lipid carriers (NLC) on the other hand are second-generation lipid nanoparticles comprising both solid and liquid lipids (51,57). Lipid nanoparticles can be used to avoid the pitfalls of other systems like liposomes and emulsions, such as burst release of active ingredients, solubility issues, the possibility for oxidation or hydrolysis of the phospholipids, and huge cost of production (57,58). Moreover, lipid nanoparticles can provide better stability and controlled release of active ingredients and they produce a whitening effect on coloured active ingredients thereby improving the aesthetic appeal of cosmetic products (57). For instance, encapsulation of ingredients for skincare such as vitamins A, E, or coenzyme Q10 in SLN leads to increased stability, better bioavailability, and control of the release of the ingredients (14). Also, SLN and NLC have been developed as potential carrier systems for the delivery of minoxidil for the treatment of hair loss. Both systems effectively delivered the drug without the associated side effects of commercial alcoholic solutions which usually produce redness, irritation, dryness, allergic contact dermatitis, and so on (59,60). Finally, a hydrogel formulation comprising novel NLC based on vegetable oils (rosehip oil or black cumin oils) for the delivery of carrot extract, marigold extract, and azelaic acid was developed. The formulation exhibited excellent antioxidant, anti-inflammatory, and anti-acne activities (61).

Nanoemulsions

Nanoemulsions are colloidal dispersions comprising an aqueous and oily phase, usually stabilised by an emulsifying agent with a droplet size below 1μm, but usually not greater than 200 nm. Either phase can be dispersed in the other, therefore, nanoemulsions (similar to conventional coarse emulsions) can be of the oil-in-water ($^{o}/_{w}$) or water-in-oil ($^{w}/_{o}$) type (9,62,63), with the oil-in-water type being more commonly used (63). The small droplet size in nanoemulsions produces a large interfacial area which results in rapid release of active ingredients from the oil droplets, rapid transfer to the skin surface, and ultimately rapid absorption by the skin and it also leads to a slower creaming rate of the emulsions (9,63,64). Other advantages of using nanoemulsions in cosmetic products include skin hydration due to the production of a strong occlusive effect, improved penetration of narrow gaps including hair follicle structural units and scales spacings, high fluidity, slow creaming rate due to high kinetic stability, improved aesthetics due to the transparent to pearlescent appearance and lustrous effect on the skin. Nanoemulsions are used in wet cosmetic wipes and sprays, creams, gels, and foams (63,64). The ingredients used in nanoemulsions fall under the category of "Generally recognised as safe" (GRAS) ingredients, thus they do not pose additional toxicity risks (65). Nanoemulsions have been employed in various types of cosmetic products (14). An oil-in-water nanoemulsion-based skin moisturising agent containing *Opuntia ficus-indica* (L.) Mill hydroglycolic extract was produced and evaluated for stability and moisturising capacity. The formulation was found to be stable for up to 60 days and increased the water content of the stratum corneum, hence demonstrating moisturising capacity and potential for application as a skin moisturiser (62). Another oil-in-water nanoemulsion product from Chanel namely "Brume Fraîche pour le Corps" Coco Mademoiselle, The Fresh Body Moisturising mist which is a spray product was claimed (by La Maison Chanel) to have improved properties because of the use of nanoemulsions. The product did not undergo creaming and affords a rapid and pronounced moisturising effect by producing an occlusive effect on the skin. Chanel Précision also introduced another product, "Solution Déstressante," Calming Emulsion. The product contains *Centella asiatica* extract which serves as the soothing agent and produces a de-stressing effect felt immediately upon application. The rapid action is attributed to the nanoemulsions facilitating quick skin penetration by the active ingredient (63,64). Nanoemulsions have been used in several haircare products including conditioning shampoos by producing stable nanoemulsions of silicone oil (65). Aqua-Oléum® (Kérastase), an oil-in-water nanoemulsion of avocado and jojoba seed oils is a haircare serum reputed by L'Oréal to be especially beneficial for the restoration of dry hair due to the use of the nanoemulsion platform (63).

Inorganic nanoparticles

Inorganic nanoparticles are essentially insoluble nanomaterials that do not change or disintegrate after skin application, hence more stable than their organic counterparts. This class of nanoparticles includes metals and metal oxides, nanoclays, and mesoporous nanostructures (8,9,17). Although like the organic nanoparticles they can also perform different roles in cosmetic products as active ingredients, carriers for active ingredients, and formulation additives such as rheology and appearance modifiers (17), they are mostly used for their antimicrobial properties and as UV filters in sunscreens (9,17).

Inorganic nanoparticles used as antimicrobial agents

Metals such as silver, gold, copper, titanium, zinc, and their oxides have been recognised to possess antimicrobial activities (8,14). Thus, nanoparticles of these metals are applied as antimicrobial agents in cosmetic products either as active ingredients or as preservatives (9,17,66).

Inorganic nanoparticles in sunscreens

Metal oxides commonly used in cosmetic sunscreens include titanium oxide and zinc oxide nanoparticles (8,14,17). Nanoparticles of these metal oxides have replaced the larger micron-sized particles in cosmetic products as they do not leave visible white marks upon application like the larger particles, and the nanoparticles also possess superior UV-shielding properties than the larger particles (14,17). However, the use of these metal oxides has generated safety concerns due to the possibility of the generation of free radicals when they are exposed to UV radiation. This problem is addressed by using surface coatings of the nanoparticles with materials such as alumina, silica, dimethicone, and stearic acid (17).

Inorganic nanoparticles used in cosmetic products

Silver nanoparticles: Silver nanoparticles are probably the most widely used metal nanoparticles in cosmetics and other products and are frequently used for their antimicrobial properties (9,17). They have a broad spectrum of activity against a wide variety of organisms including bacteria such as methicillin-resistant Staphylococcus aureus (MRSA), multidrug-resistant Pseudomonas aeruginosa, ampicillin-resistant Escherichia coli, and erythromycin-resistant Streptococcus pyogenes, fungi species like Candida albicans, Phoma glomerata, and Trichoderma spp (14,17). They possess antimicrobial activity both to prevent cell growth (bacteriostatic activity) and cause cell death (bactericidal Activity) (8,17). Silver nanoparticles also possess wound healing properties (66), are applied in the treatment of acne (17), can inhibit biofilm formation (66), and have been employed as a preservative for cosmetic products (8). Silver nanoparticles have found application in other cosmetic products including hair colourants, anti-ageing products, shaving products, footcare products, makeup removers, and deodorants (8,17).

Gold nanoparticles: Gold has been used for beautification purposes since antiquity and Queen Cleopatra reportedly used the noble metal in her beauty regimen (9). Gold nanoparticles have both antibacterial and antifungal activities and like silver nanoparticles have been employed in the formulation of various cosmetic products (8). They have been used in products like anti-ageing products, facial gold masks, deodorants, sunscreens, shampoos and conditioners, and makeup removers (8,9,14,17). A recent study demonstrated the potential of a snail-slime and gold nanoparticles hybrid nanomaterial as an ingredient in sunscreens and other cosmetic products (67).

Zinc oxide nanoparticles: Zinc oxide nanoparticles are widely used in sunscreens and day creams. The nanoparticles are very photo-stable, and transparent and are capable of near-total absorption of UVA radiation implicated in photo ageing of the skin and other toxic effects on the skin, including the induction of cancers. They also exhibit antimicrobial and anti-inflammatory activities. They are also used in concealers, eye contour products, face masks, lip, hand, and foot care products, and skin lightening products (9,17,66).

Titanium dioxide nanoparticles: Titanium dioxide nanoparticles are also commonly used ingredients in cosmetic products. They are used as sunscreen, anticaking agents, colourants, eye contour products, face masks, hand and lip care products, shaving products, and skin lightening products (9,17,66).

Carbon nanoparticles

Many types of carbon-based nanoparticles have been applied in the development of cosmetic products. These include carbon black, carbon nanotubes, fullerenes, and nanodiamond (9).

Carbon black is a well-recognised ingredient in cosmetic products. The nanoparticle form is approved for use in the European Union and most parts of the world. It is used as a colourant in some skin products, nail polish, mascara, and other eye cosmetics such as kajal, eyeliner, eye pencil, and eye shadow. It produces intense colour and is light and heat-stable (8,10,18).

Carbon nanotubes and fullerenes are prominent allotropes of carbon and have been used in cosmetic products. Carbon nanotubes may be in the form of single-walled cylindrical tubes made up of one rolled sheet of graphene or multi-walled carbon nanotubes comprising more than one cylindrical sheet of graphene. Carbon nanotubes are mostly used as hair colourants because of their high affinity for hair fibres and the persistent colouring they produce. Fullerenes on the other hand are spherical particles (also called buckyballs) approximately one atom thick. They are reported to demonstrate free radical scavenging activities and are thus used as antioxidants and smoothers in skincare products including anti-ageing creams (9,10,68). Carbon nanobuds are a rather peculiar carbon-based nanomaterial, a hybrid of carbon nanotubes and fullerenes obtained from specific covalent bonding of carbon nanotubes to fullerene-like "sprouts/buds". They exhibit exceptional field emitting properties and so may be very useful in the production of lipsticks and mascaras (8).

Safety and regulatory aspects

Safety and toxicity of nanoparticles used in cosmetics

The question of the safety or otherwise of all ingredients used in cosmetics, whether they are nanosized or not is undoubtedly a very important one. Little wonder that there has been growing concern over the safety of nanocosmetics and the public has been skeptical about the possible threats to human and environmental health (8,13). The safety concerns have been expressed at different levels. For example, a "Friends of the Earth" report in 2006 stressed the issue of increasing the use of nanomaterials in cosmetic products without adequately addressing associated potential risks (13). The safety concerns are not unfounded, as nanotechnology is a relatively new field, and information about the disposition of nanoparticles in humans and the environment is still evolving, with research into the toxicological aspects still lagging far behind the various means being devised to harness the potential benefits of the application of nanomaterials (4). Also, the properties of materials in the nanoform may be completely different from those of the same materials in the bulk form. For instance, nanosized particles may be able to penetrate sites in the human body and the environment which are ordinarily inaccessible to larger particles of the same material; they may also undergo different reactions and interactions than larger-sized materials, leading to unexpected exposures, which may produce toxic effects not usually seen with the bulk material (5,7,10). Research findings also corroborate the fact that harmful effects, including neonatal toxicity, may arise from the use of nanoparticles, and such effects would be a function of the route, quantity, and duration of exposure and the physicochemical properties of the particles. Although cosmetic products are usually applied to the skin surface, nanoparticles in the products may permeate beyond the intended upper surface. Also, broken, or damaged skin may create a breach through which nanoparticles can gain access to unintended areas. Furthermore, there can be accidental inhalation or ingestion of nanoparticles during manufacture (workers) and application (end users), which may lead to nanoparticles being circulated to different organs in the body including the brain, resulting in serious harmful effects (10). Moreover, many nanoparticle types such as carbon-based nanoparticles, titanium dioxide nanoparticles, silver nanoparticles, and other metal-based nanoparticles have been found to exhibit toxic effects on humans and the environment through repeated exposure, causing harmful effects on other members of the ecosystem (10,66). Thus, the perceived advantages of using nanoparticles may easily be upturned by unforeseen adverse effects (4,7,10).

Regulation of nanoparticles in cosmetics

The initial somewhat loose regulation of the use of nanomaterials in cosmetic products allowed for some in the cosmetics industry to use such materials without declaring them. There was also no universally agreed requirement for conducting safety tests on the nanomaterials used before incorporating them into products, further fueling distrust and skepticism about nanocosmetics (5). In a bid to address the safety concerns, stricter regulations were put in place for the regulation of the use of nanomaterials in cosmetic products (9,18). In the European Union, for instance, the laws for cosmetic products were completely overhauled, and by the end of 2009, it was required by law that the use of nanomaterials in cosmetic products be indicated on product labels (18). Also, all materials including nanomaterials used in cosmetic products are required to be subjected to safety tests before use. In the United States of America, the FDA released a "Final Guidance for Industry – Safety of Nanomaterials in Cosmetic Products" in 2014, where they provided an analysis of safety issues and guidance for cosmetic industries. Furthermore, the International Cooperation on Cosmetics Regulation (ICCR), a cohort of cosmetics regulatory authorities from Brazil, Canada, the EU, Japan, and the USA, provides an international regulatory structure for protecting consumers' rights (8).

References

1. de Mello Donegá C. The Nanoscience Paradigm: "Size Matters!" In: de Mello Donegá C, editor. Nanoparticles: Workhorses of Nanoscience [Internet]. Berlin, Heidelberg: Springer Berlin Heidelberg; 2014. p. 1–12. Available from: https://doi.org/10.1007/978-3-662-44823-6_1
2. The National Nanotechnology Initiative. Strategic Plan (2004).
3. European Commission: Recommendation on the definition of nanomaterial. Off J Eur Union L27538-40 2011. 2011;
4. Oberdörster G, Oberdörster E, Oberdörster J. Nanotoxicology: an emerging discipline evolving from studies of ultrafine particles. Environ Health Perspect. 2005 Jul;113(7):823–39.
5. Singh P, Nanda A. Nanotechnology in cosmetics: a boon or bane? Toxicol Environ Chem. 2012 Sep 1;94(8):1467–79.
6. Cristina Buzea, Ivan I Pacheco, Kevin Robbie. Nanomaterials and Nanoparticles: Sources and Toxicity. Biointerphases. 2007;2(4):MR17-71.
7. Mu L, Sprando RL. Application of Nanotechnology in Cosmetics. Pharm Res. 2010 Aug 1;27(8):1746–9.
8. Fytianos G, Rahdar A, Kyzas GZ. Nanomaterials in Cosmetics: Recent Updates. Nanomater Basel Switz. 2020 May 20;10(5):979.
9. Salvioni L, Morelli L, Ochoa E, Labra M, Fiandra L, Palugan L, et al. The emerging role of nanotechnology in skincare. Adv Colloid Interface Sci. 2021 Jul 1;293:102437.
10. Gupta V, Mohapatra S, Mishra H, Farooq U, Kumar K, Ansari MJ, et al. Nanotechnology in Cosmetics and Cosmeceuticals-A Review of Latest Advancements. Gels Basel Switz. 2022 Mar 10;8(3):173.
11. Li BS, Cary JH, Maibach HI. Science Behind Cosmetics and Skin Care. In: Cornier J, Keck CM, Van de Voorde M, editors. Nanocosmetics: From Ideas to Products [Internet]. Cham: Springer International Publishing; 2019. p. 3–15. Available from: https://doi.org/10.1007/978-3-030-16573-4_1
12. Nozaki F. General Aspects of Cosmetics in Relation to Science and Society: Social, Cultural, Science, and Marketing Aspect Translated from Japanese by Izumi Sakamoto. In 2017.
13. Nohynek GJ, Lademann J, Ribaud C, Roberts MS. Grey Goo on the Skin? Nanotechnology, Cosmetic and Sunscreen Safety. Crit Rev Toxicol. 2007 Jan 1;37(3):251–77.

14. Mihranyan A, Ferraz N, Strømme M. Current status and future prospects of nanotechnology in cosmetics. Prog Mater Sci. 2012 Jun 1;57(5):875–910.
15. Tan SH, Loh XJ. CHAPTER 7 Nanoparticle Safety in Cosmetics. In: Polymers for Personal Care Products and Cosmetics [Internet]. The Royal Society of Chemistry; 2016. p. 117–34. Available from: http://dx.doi.org/10.1039/9781782623984-00117
16. Rosen J, Landriscina A, Friedman AJ. Nanotechnology-Based Cosmetics for Hair Care. Cosmetics. 2015;2(3).
17. Vinod TP, Jelinek R. Inorganic Nanoparticles in Cosmetics. In: Cornier J, Keck CM, Van de Voorde M, editors. Nanocosmetics: From Ideas to Products [Internet]. Cham: Springer International Publishing; 2019. p. 29–46. Available from: https://doi.org/10.1007/978-3-030-16573-4_3
18. Huber B, Burfeindt J. Nanotechnology in Cosmetics. In: Cornier J, Keck CM, Van de Voorde M, editors. Nanocosmetics: From Ideas to Products [Internet]. Cham: Springer International Publishing; 2019. p. 17–25. Available from: https://doi.org/10.1007/978-3-030-16573-4_2
19. Rahimi IA, Eberhard I, Kasten E. TATTOOS: What Do People Really Know About the Medical Risks of Body Ink? J Clin Aesthetic Dermatol. 2018/03/01 ed. 2018 Mar;11(3):30–5.
20. Grant CA, Twigg PC, Baker R, Tobin DJ. Tattoo ink nanoparticles in skin tissue and fibroblasts. Beilstein J Nanotechnol. 2015 May 20;6:1183–91.
21. Kent KM, Graber EM. Laser Tattoo Removal: A Review. Dermatol Surg. 2012 Jan 1;38(1):1–13.
22. Walter P, Welcomme E, Hallégot P, Zaluzec NJ, Deeb C, Castaing J, et al. Early Use of PbS Nanotechnology for an Ancient Hair Dyeing Formula. Nano Lett. 2006 Oct 1;6(10):2215–9.
23. Guryanov I, Naumenko E, Fakhrullin R. Hair surface engineering: Combining nanoarchitectonics with hair topical and beauty formulations. Appl Surf Sci Adv. 2022 Feb 1;7:100188.
24. Alves TFR, Morsink M, Batain F, Chaud MV, Almeida T, Fernandes DA, et al. Applications of Natural, Semi-Synthetic, and Synthetic Polymers in Cosmetic Formulations. Cosmetics. 2020;7(4).
25. Kuah HX, Loh XJ. CHAPTER 8 Silicones: The Future for Beauty and Everyday Care. In: Polymers for Personal Care Products and Cosmetics [Internet]. The Royal Society of Chemistry; 2016. p. 135–53. Available from: http://dx.doi.org/10.1039/9781782623984-00135
26. Velazquez Pereda, Maria Del Carme, Polezel, Marcio Antoni, Dieamant, Gustavo De Campo, Nogueira, Cecilia, Marcelino, Amanda Gomes, Rossan, Marcos Roberto, et al. Sericin cationic nanoparticles for application in products for hair and dyed hair. WO2010146415A1. 2010;
27. Zhang Y, Birmann BM, Han J, Giovannucci EL, Speizer FE, Stampfer MJ, et al. Personal use of permanent hair dyes and cancer risk and mortality in US women: prospective cohort study. BMJ [Internet]. 2020;370. Available from: https://www.bmj.com/content/370/bmj.m2942
28. Ariga K, Li J, Fei J, Ji Q, Hill JP. Nanoarchitectonics for Dynamic Functional Materials from Atomic-/Molecular-Level Manipulation to Macroscopic Action. Adv Mater. 2016 Feb 1;28(6):1251–86.
29. Shrestha LK, Mori T, Ariga K. Dynamic nanoarchitectonics: Supramolecular polymorphism and differentiation, shape-shifter and hand-operating nanotechnology. Self-Assem. 2018 May 1;35:68–80.

30. Lee HY, Jeong YI, Choi KC. Hair dye-incorporated poly-γ-glutamic acid/glycol chitosan nanoparticles based on ion-complex formation. Int J Nanomedicine. 2011/11/17 ed. 2011;6:2879–88.
31. Haveli SD, Walter P, Patriarche G, Ayache J, Castaing J, Van Elslande E, et al. Hair Fiber as a Nanoreactor in Controlled Synthesis of Fluorescent Gold Nanoparticles. Nano Lett. 2012 Dec 12;12(12):6212–7.
32. Gad SE. Polymers. In: Wexler P, editor. Encyclopedia of Toxicology (Third Edition) [Internet]. Oxford: Academic Press; 2014. p. 1045–50. Available from: https://www.sciencedirect.com/science/article/pii/B978012386454300912X
33. Lochhead RY. The Role of Polymers in Cosmetics: Recent Trends. In 2007.
34. Trache D, Tarchoun AF, Derradji M, Hamidon TS, Masruchin N, Brosse N, et al. Nanocellulose: From Fundamentals to Advanced Applications. Front Chem. 2020 May 6;8:392–392.
35. Revol JF, Godbout L, Dong XM, Gray DG, Chanzy H, Maret G. Chiral nematic suspensions of cellulose crystallites; phase separation and magnetic field orientation. Liq Cryst. 1994 Jan 1;16(1):127–34.
36. Tang J, He H, Wan R, Yang Q, Luo H, Li L, et al. Cellulose Nanocrystals for Skin Barrier Protection by Preparing a Versatile Foundation Liquid. ACS Omega. 2021 Jan 15;6(4):2906–15.
37. Aranaz I, Acosta N, Civera C, Elorza B, Mingo J, Castro C, et al. Cosmetics and Cosmeceutical Applications of Chitin, Chitosan and Their Derivatives. Polymers. 2018 Feb 22;10(2):213.
38. Ta Q, Ting J, Harwood S, Browning N, Simm A, Ross K, et al. Chitosan nanoparticles for enhancing drugs and cosmetic components penetration through the skin. Eur J Pharm Sci. 2021 May 1;160:105765.
39. Jimtaisong A, Saewan N. Utilization of carboxymethyl chitosan in cosmetics. Int J Cosmet Sci. 2014 Feb 1;36(1):12–21.
40. Mondéjar-López M, López-Jiménez AJ, Martínez JCG, Ahrazem O, Gómez-Gómez L, Niza E. Thymoquinone-Loaded Chitosan Nanoparticles as Natural Preservative Agent in Cosmetic Products. Int J Mol Sci. 2022 Jan 14;23(2):898.
41. Guterres SS, Paese K, Pohlmann AR. Polymeric Nanoparticles. In: Cornier J, Keck CM, Van de Voorde M, editors. Nanocosmetics: From Ideas to Products [Internet]. Cham: Springer International Publishing; 2019. p. 73–94. Available from: https://doi.org/10.1007/978-3-030-16573-4_5
42. Casalini T, Rossi F, Castrovinci A, Perale G. A Perspective on Polylactic Acid-Based Polymers Use for Nanoparticles Synthesis and Applications. Front Bioeng Biotechnol. 2019 Oct 11;7:259–259.
43. Hosseinkhani B, Callewaert C, Vanbeveren N, Boon N. Novel biocompatible nanocapsules for slow release of fragrances on the human skin. New Biotechnol. 2015 Jan 25;32(1):40–6.
44. Kesente M, Kavetsou E, Roussaki M, Blidi S, Loupassaki S, Chanioti S, et al. Encapsulation of Olive Leaves Extracts in Biodegradable PLA Nanoparticles for Use in Cosmetic Formulation. Bioengineering. 2017;4(3).
45. Connolly M, Zhang Y, Brown DM, Ortuño N, Jordá-Beneyto M, Stone V, et al. Novel polylactic acid (PLA)-organoclay nanocomposite bio-packaging for the cosmetic industry; migration studies and in vitro assessment of the dermal toxicity of migration extracts. Polym Degrad Stab. 2019 Oct 1;168:108938.

46. Thananukul K, Kaewsaneha C, Sreearunothai P, Petchsuk A, Buchatip S, Supmak W, et al. Biocompatible Degradable Hollow Nanoparticles from Curable Copolymers of Polylactic Acid for UV-Shielding Cosmetics. ACS Appl Nano Mater. 2022 Mar 25;5(3):4473–83.
47. Makadia HK, Siegel SJ. Poly Lactic-co-Glycolic Acid (PLGA) as Biodegradable Controlled Drug Delivery Carrier. Polymers. 2011/08/26 ed. 2011 Sep 1;3(3):1377–97.
48. Hosokawa M, Nogi K, Naito M, Yokoyama T, editors. DEVELOPMENT OF FUNCTIONAL SKINCARE COSMETICS USING BIODEGRADABLE PLGA NANOSPHERES. In: Nanoparticle Technology Handbook [Internet]. Amsterdam: Elsevier; 2008. p. 501–6. Available from: https://www.sciencedirect.com/science/article/pii/B9780444531223500313
49. Knott A, Achterberg V, Smuda C, Mielke H, Sperling G, Dunckelmann K, et al. Topical treatment with coenzyme Q10-containing formulas improves skin's Q10 level and provides antioxidative effects. BioFactors Oxf Engl. 2015/12/09 ed. 2015;41(6):383–90.
50. Folle C, Marqués AM, Díaz-Garrido N, Espina M, Sánchez-López E, Badia J, et al. Thymol-loaded PLGA nanoparticles: an efficient approach for acne treatment. J Nanobiotechnology. 2021 Nov 8;19(1):359.
51. Khezri K, Saeedi M, Maleki Dizaj S. Application of nanoparticles in percutaneous delivery of active ingredients in cosmetic preparations. Biomed Pharmacother. 2018 Oct 1;106:1499–505.
52. Rahimpour Y, Hamishehkar H. Liposomes in cosmeceutics. Expert Opin Drug Deliv. 2012 Apr 1;9(4):443–55.
53. Fakhravar Z, Ebrahimnejad P, Daraee H, Akbarzadeh A. Nanoliposomes: Synthesis methods and applications in cosmetics. J Cosmet Laser Ther. 2016 Apr 2;18(3):174–81.
54. Golmohammadzadeh S, Imani F, Hosseinzadeh H, Jaafari MR. Preparation, characterization and evaluation of sun protective and moisturizing effects of nanoliposomes containing safranal. Iran J Basic Med Sci. 2011 Nov;14(6):521–33.
55. Kocic H, Stankovic M, Tirant M, Lotti T, Arsic I. Favorable effect of creams with skimmed donkey milk encapsulated in nanoliposomes on skin physiology. Dermatol Ther. 2020 Jul 1;33(4):e13511.
56. Bochicchio S, Dalmoro A, De Simone V, Bertoncin P, Lamberti G, Barba AA. Simil-Microfluidic Nanotechnology in Manufacturing of Liposomes as Hydrophobic Antioxidants Skin Release Systems. Cosmetics. 2020;7(2).
57. Guimarães KL, Ré MI. Lipid Nanoparticles as Carriers for Cosmetic Ingredients: The First (SLN) and the Second Generation (NLC). In: Beck R, Guterres S, Pohlmann A, editors. Nanocosmetics and Nanomedicines: New Approaches for Skin Care [Internet]. Berlin, Heidelberg: Springer Berlin Heidelberg; 2011. p. 101–22. Available from: https://doi.org/10.1007/978-3-642-19792-5_5
58. Ahmad A, Ahsan H. Lipid-based formulations in cosmeceuticals and biopharmaceuticals. Biomed Dermatol. 2020 May 6;4(1):12.
59. Silva A, Santos D, Ferreira D, Souto EB. Minoxidil-loaded nanostructured lipid carriers (NLC): characterization and rheological behaviour of topical formulations. PMID: 19348340. Pharmazie. 2009;64(3):177–82.

60. Padois K, Cantiéni C, Bertholle V, Bardel C, Pirot F, Falson F. Solid lipid nanoparticles suspension versus commercial solutions for dermal delivery of minoxidil. Int J Pharm. 2011 Sep 15;416(1):300–4.
61. Lacatusu I, Istrati D, Bordei N, Popescu M, Seciu AM, Panteli LM, et al. Synergism of plant extract and vegetable oils-based lipid nanocarriers: Emerging trends in development of advanced cosmetic prototype products. Mater Sci Eng C. 2020 Mar 1;108:110412.
62. Ribeiro RC, Barreto SM, Ostrosky EA, Rocha-Filho PA, Veríssimo LM, Ferrari M. Production and Characterization of Cosmetic Nanoemulsions Containing Opuntia ficus-indica (L.) Mill Extract as Moisturizing Agent. Molecules. 2015;20(2).
63. Chevalier Y, Bolzinger MA. Micelles and Nanoemulsions. In: Cornier J, Keck CM, Van de Voorde M, editors. Nanocosmetics: From Ideas to Products [Internet]. Cham: Springer International Publishing; 2019. p. 47–72. Available from: https://doi.org/10.1007/978-3-030-16573-4_4
64. Faria-Silva AC, Costa AM, Ascenso A, Ribeiro HM, Marto J, Gonçalves LM, et al. Nanoemulsions for cosmetic products. In: Nanda A, Nanda S, Nguyen TA, Rajendran S, Slimani Y, editors. Nanocosmetics [Internet]. Elsevier; 2020. p. 59–77. Available from: https://www.sciencedirect.com/science/article/pii/B9780128222867000048
65. Nanda S, Nanda A, Lohan S, Kaur R, Singh B. Nanocosmetics: performance enhancement and safety assurance. In: Grumezescu AM, editor. Nanobiomaterials in Galenic Formulations and Cosmetics [Internet]. William Andrew Publishing; 2016. p. 47–67. Available from: https://www.sciencedirect.com/science/article/pii/B9780323428682000036
66. Niska K, Zielinska E, Radomski MW, Inkielewicz-Stepniak I. Metal nanoparticles in dermatology and cosmetology: Interactions with human skin cells. Nanotechnol Biol Toxicol. 2018 Nov 1;295:38–51.
67. Rizzi V, Gubitosa J, Fini P, Nuzzo S, Agostiano A, Cosma P. Snail slime-based gold nanoparticles: An interesting potential ingredient in cosmetics as an antioxidant, sunscreen, and tyrosinase inhibitor. J Photochem Photobiol B. 2021 Nov 1;224:112309.
68. Jeswani G, Das Paul S, Chablani L, Ajazuddin. Safety and Toxicity Counts of Nanocosmetics. In: Cornier J, Keck CM, Van de Voorde M, editors. Nanocosmetics: From Ideas to Products [Internet]. Cham: Springer International Publishing; 2019. p. 299–335. Available from: https://doi.org/10.1007/978-3-030-16573-4_14

CHAPTER ELEVEN

Essential oils, fragrances, and perfumes in cosmetics

Sinmisola O. Oladeji-Akinsanmi and 'Lara O. Orafidiya

Essential oils, fragrances and perfumes are odoriferous organic substances, usually with pleasant and attractive scents, that are a vital part of cosmetics and personal hygiene products. They impact the selection and increase the attractiveness of the products in which they are incorporated and they beautify an individual by producing an inner feeling of beauty and self-confidence, enriching their spirit and giving them a calming effect. The pleasant scents and effects significantly influence cosmetic assessment. A major role of fragrant substances in cosmetic products is their odour-masking effect because not all cosmetic ingredients have pleasant smells (1).

Scent-producing substances are also formulated singly or in combination to produce fragrant body products that are applied directly on the skin or on clothes. For this purpose, they are available as perfume oils, absolutes, *eau de perfum, eau de toilette* and colognes which are the perfumes designed for men. Fragrances are the raw materials for the preparation of these products and are also used as additives to impact odour to other cosmetic products. While essential oils are natural oils extracted from plants and animals; fragrances and perfumes are either a mixture of essential oils or their isolated compounds dissolved in an appropriate base; or a mixture of a number of synthetic/semi-synthetic odoriferous compounds that produce a distinct and characteristic smell. Some essential oils are now synthesised while some form the bases for semi-synthetic fragrances (1).

Fragrance cosmetics are mainly perfumed products whose manufacture requires high-quality characteristics and assurance, including efficacy, safety, stability, and useability (smell). Examples of some of these quality characteristics include lack of skin sensitivity and oral toxicity (safety), absence of unsolicited smell or quality change (stability), good composition (usability), odour-masking and UV protective effect (efficacy) (1).

Essential oils have been widely used as fragrances in the perfumery and cosmetic industry. They are highly prized and valued ingredients in the manufacture of cosmetic products because they provide a variety of pleasant and unique aromas as well as antimicrobial, antiseptic, sun protection and other benefits. Essential oils are very beneficial in the pharmaceutical, food, beverage, household, cosmetic, and perfume industry because they are natural and are considered less harmful to human health than their synthetic derivatives. Their established health benefits backed by scientific findings have made them attractive to customers, thus, increasing the demands for them by various industries. Although they are generally considered safe, their complex mixture with various diluents, of which some are skin sensitising allergens, has resulted in the need to state this on cosmetic labels so as to alert potential users. This is important for consumers with known allergic sensitive skin or established skin conditions, giving them the choice to perform a patch test before using these products.

Essential oils

Sources

Essential oils (EO), also known as ethereal oils or volatile oils, are a crucial part of the cosmetic industry, commonly composed of completely natural substances extracted from various plant and animal parts (2). Plant oils can be extracted from different morphological parts: flowers e.g., lavender (*Lavandula angustifolia*), rose (*Rosa* species), ylang-ylang (*Cananga odorata*); grasses e.g., lemongrass (*Cymbopogon citratus*) (3), citronella (*Cymbopogon nardus*), palmarosa (*Cymbopogon martini*); roots/rhizomes e.g., ginger (*Zingiber officinale*); resins e.g., frankincense *(Boswella* species), benzoin (*Styrax* species), myrrh (*Commiphora* species); seeds e.g., nutmeg (*Myristica fragrans*), coriander (*Coriandrum sativum*); leaves e.g., peppermint (*Mentha piperita*), basil (*Ocimum basilicum*), clove or African basil (*Ocimum gratissimum*) (4), lippia (*Lippia multiflora*), plectranthus (*Plectranthus aegyptiacus*) (5), geranium (*Pelargonium graveolens*), rosemary (*Salvia Rosmarinus*) polyalthia (*Polyalthia longiflora*) (6); stems e.g., eucalyptus (*Eucalyptus* species); barks e.g., cinnamon *(Cinnamomum* species); fruit peels e.g., lemon (*Citrus limon*), bergamot (*Monarda didyma*), orange (*Citrus sinensis*); and woods e.g., pine (*Pinus* species), cedarwood (*Cedrus* species), sandalwood (*Santalum album*) (7,8). Animal extracts are obtained from animal secretions which include castoreum (beavers), civet (*Viverridae* species), musk (musk deer), and ambergris (sperm whale) (1). Table 11.1(a,b,c) show a list of major essential oils, their main constituents, and their extraction methods.

Table 11.1a: Characteristics of major plant essential oils.

Name	Plant name (plant part)	Major Production country/Region	Extraction Method (Yield %)	Main Components (%)
Ocimum Oil	*Ocimum gratissimum* Lamiaceae (leaves)	Africa, Madagascar	Steam distillation (0.8-1.2)	Eugenol, thymol (48)
Lavender Oil	*Lavandula officinalis* Labiatae (flowers)	Southern France	Steam distillation (0.7-0.85) Solvent extraction (0.7-1.3)	linalyl acetate (30 – 40), limonene, nerol, cineole, linalool esters, geraniol esters, d-borneol, lavandulol
Jasmin Oil	*Jasminium officinale* var. Oleacea (flowers)	Southern France. India, Egypt, Morocco	Solvent extraction (0.14-0.16)	benzyl acetate (65), d-linalool (16), jasmone, indole, phytol, cis-jasmon, benzyl alcohol, jasmin lactone, benzyl benzoate
Neroli Oil	*Citrus aurantium* sub-sp. *A. arnara* Rutaceae (flowers)	Southern France, Italy, Spain, Portugal	Steam distillation (0.08-0.15)	l-linalool (30), linalool acetate (7), d-nerolidol (6), geraniol, terpinol, pinene, nerol, camphene
Rose Oil	*Rosa damascena* and *Rosa centifolia* Rosaceae (flowers)	Bulgaria, Turkey, Southern France, Morocco	Steam distillation (0.01-0.04) Solvent extraction (0.07-0.1)	l-citronellol (30-59), geraniol, l-linalool, damascone, damascenone, β -phenyl ethyl alcohol, farnesol, nonyl aldehyde, rose oxide

Name	Plant name (plant part)	Major Production country/Region	Extraction Method (Yield %)	Main Components (%)
Clove Oil	*Eugenia carophyllata* Myrtaceae (flowers. buds and leaves)	Madagascar, Ceylon, Zanzibar, Indonesia	Steam distillation (15-17) Solvent extraction (4-6)	Eugenol (70-90), acetyleugenol, methyl salicylate, *β*-caryophyllene, methyl-n-amylketone, methyl heptyl-ketone
Tuberose Oil	*Polyanthes tuberosa* Amaryllidaceae (flowers)	Southern France, Morocco, Egypt	Solvent extraction (0.01-0.03)	geraniol, farnesol, benzyl alcohol, methyl benzoate, benzyl benzoate, methyl salicylate, methyl anthranilate, nerol
Pepper Oil	*Piper nigrum* Piperaceae (fruit)	S.W. India, Sumatra, Brazil	Steam distillation (1.0-2.7)	*α*-pinene, sabinene, *β* -caryophyllene, limonene, carene, *β*-pinene
Ylang Ylang Oil	*Cananga odorata forma genuina* Annonacea (flowers)	Reunion Island, Madagascar	Steam distillation (0.5-2.2) Solvent extraction (0.7-2.5)	linalool, geraniol, benzyl alcohol, farnesol, sesquiterpenes
Clary Sage Oil	*Salvia sclaria Labiatae (flowers* *and leaves)*	Southern France, Italy. Spain	Steam distillation (0.5-1.5) Solvent extraction (0.01-0.1)	linalyl acetate, linalool, nerolidol, sclareol

Table 11.1b: Characteristics of major plant essential oils.

Name	Plant name (plant part)	Major Production country/Region	Extraction Method (Yield %)	Main Components (%)
Peppermint Oil	*Mentha piperita* var. Labiatae (flowers and leaves)	Europe. North America	Steam distillation (0.3-1.0)	l-menthol (40-50), menthone (16-25), isomenthone, 1,8-cineole, β-caryophyllene, methyl acetate, menthofuran
Sandalwood Oil	*Santalum album* Santalaceae (wood)	Indonesia	Steam distillation (4.5-6.3)	α-β-santalol (90). santene. santenon, santenol, teresantalol, santalone, α-β-santalene
Bergamot Oil	*Citrus aurantium bergamia* Rutaceae (fruit peel)	Calabrian peninsula, Cote D' Azur	Expression (0.3-0.5)	linalyl acetate (35-40), l-linalool, limonene, citral, p-cymene, decanal
Nutmeg Oil	*Myristica fragrans* Myristicaceae (seeds)	S.W. India, Sumatra, Brazil	Steam distillation (6-16)	Sabinene (20-25), β-pinene, camphene, limonene, linalool, borneol, terpineol
Orange Oil	*Citrus sinensis* Rutaceae (fruit peel)	Florida, California, Italy and Mediterranean region	Expression (0.2-0.4)	d-limonene (90), n-decyl aldehyde, citral, d-linalool, n-nonyl alcohol, d-terpinol, nootkatone
Coriander Oil	*Coriandrum sativum* Umbelliferae (seeds)	Mexico, Morocco, Hungary, India	Steam distillation (0.3-1.0)	d-linalool (60-70), α, β-pinene, limonene, terpinene, phellandrene, geraniol, l-borneol, n-decyl aldehyde

Table 11.1c: Characteristics of major plant essential oils.

Name	Plant name (plant part)	Major Production country/Region	Extraction Method (Yield %)	Main Components (%)
Patchouli Oil	*Pogostemon cablin* Labiatae (dried leaves)	Malaysia, Sumatra	Steam distillation (3-6)	patchouli alcohol (35-40), patchoulene, patchoulenon, *β* - caryophyllene, *α* - guajene, *β*-bulnessene
Lemongrass Oil	*Cymbopogon citratus* Poaceae (leaves)	India, Indonesia, West Africa	Steam distillation (0.8-1.3)	citral, limonene, myrcene, geraniol, citronellol, neral, geranyl acetate, nerol
Lippia Oil	*Lippia multiflora* Verbenaceae (leaves)	Sierra Leone, Nigeria, Uganda, Angola	Steam distillation (0.6-0.9)	Cymene, linalool, geraniol, thymol, limonene (13)
Oakmoss Oil	*Evernia prunastri Usneaceae (oakmoss)*	Yugoslavia, France	Solvent extraction (0.01-0.05)	evernic acid (2-3), α, β-thujone, atranorin, chloroatranorin, camphor, borneol, naphthalene
Cinnamon Oil	*Cinnaniomum zeylanicum Lauraceae (bark)*	Ceylon, Java, Madagascar	Steam distillation (0.2-1.8)	cinnamic aldehyde (65-76), eugenol (2-5), l-phellandrene, pinene, linalool. 1, 8-cineole, caryophyllene
Lemon Oil	*Citrus limon Rutaceae (fruit peel)*	Florida, California. Italy and Mediterranean region	Expression (0.2-0.3)	d-limonene (70), γ-terpinene (7), citral, α, β -pinene, camphene, methyl heptenone, β-phellandrene, α - bergamotene, β - bisabolene

Categories of essential oil fragrances (1):

- Floral base - forms an important group of flower scents made from rose, jasmine, ylang-ylang, tuberose, and lilac.
- The citrus base is commonly used in light perfumes and it is made from lemon, grapefruit, orange, bergamot, and lime.
- Woody bases are sweet sandalwood, elegant and dry vetiver, cedarwood, and exotic patchouli.
- Green bases create a scent of leaves, vegetables or cut grass such as tomato or cucumber.
- Oriental bases have a strong powdery sweet fragrance with a balance of vanilla and balsamic notes mixed with animal and woody notes.
- Chypre bases have a scented mixture of oakmoss, musk, rose, amber, bergamot, jasmine, and orange.
- Spicy bases create a stimulative impression composed of pepper, cinnamon, nutmeg, clove, thyme, and cardamom.
- Fruity bases are non-citrus bases characterised by banana, peach, apple, strawberry, raspberry, melon, and pineapple.
- Animal bases are made up of musk, amber, castoreum and civet.

The increasing interest in essential oils by the cosmetic industry originates from the strong demand for pure organic ingredients that are plant-based. This heightened demand resulted in the production of large quantities of essential oils globally to meet the needs of the cosmetics, aromatherapy, and fragrance industries (9). These industries account for 29% of the market demand for essential oils, which is the second largest after the beverage and food industry which accounts for 35% of the market demand, and the pharmaceutical and household/domestic industry each accounts for 16 % of the market share (10).

Essential oil production methods

Essential oils are extracted from their sources by different methods. The commonest mode of extraction is through steam distillation, water distillation, cold compression or expression, volatile solvent extraction, non-volatile solvent extraction which consists of enfleurage and maceration, as well as supercritical carbon dioxide extraction methods

(1,9). The method applied largely depends on the type of essential oil to be extracted, and the plant part used (10).

The extracted oils are not processed, manipulated, or diluted with additives or solvents, making them neat oils and 100% pure. Reproducibility can be tough due to variability in the chemical components of specific essential oils based on the plant's growing condition, time and season of collection, genetic factors, physiological factors (plant organ and age) (11), geographical variation and distribution, production parameters, and climate. In addition, post-harvest processing, handling, packaging, and storage may vary resulting in various grades and quality (12,13). Essential oils are usually expensive because the production process is expensive and the yield can be very small (2).

Steam distillation is widely used to extract essential oils into steam vapour by blowing steam on dried or fresh plant materials. The steam frees the essential oil from the oil glands present in the plant's tissues. The oil-water vapour mixture is then condensed, with the oil separated from the distillate using a separator. It is advantageous for extracting heat-resistant oils, compared to other extraction processes (7).

Water distillation is similar to steam distillation only that the plant materials are immersed in water which is heated to boiling point (7).

Cold-compression or expression is an extraction method used for unstable volatile oils since no heat is required. It is mainly used for citrus essential oils such as lemon or orange oil. The process involves pressing the fruit peel to remove oils from the glands with the oil washed from the mashed peel using fine water spray. Centrifugation is then employed to separate the resultant oil-water emulsion (7). This process can be performed either by hand through a sponge-pressing technique or via a machine using the Ecuelle technique. The sponge-pressing process involves soaking the fruit peel in water before being squeezed with a sponge to directly absorb the oil, after which the sponge is pressed in a container. The resultant mixture is left to stand to separate the oil from the aqueous phase. On the other hand, the Ecuelle process can be divided into sfumatrice or pelatrice techniques. The pelatrice technique involves slowly rotating the citrus fruits against the machine's abrasive shell using an Archimedean screw which bursts the oil glands and releases their contents. A fine spray of water is used to remove the oil-water emulsion from the fruit which is then passed through a centrifugal separator to obtain the pure oil. Sfumatrice technique involves bending and pressing fruit peels against machine walls using ribbed rollers. This process enables the peels to release their oil which is washed by a fine spray of water, filtered, centrifuged and decanted to obtain the pure oil from the mixture (14).

Enfleurage is an extraction method used for delicate plant parts such as fresh flower petals, which have very minute oil contents that limit other extraction processes. This method involves repeatedly placing fresh flower petals for some hours or days on odourless fat or fixed oil that has been spread thinly on glass plates mounted on rectangular wooden frames called chassis. Odourless fat is used because of its high absorption strength. Defleurage is the delicate process of removing the withered or exhausted flower petals with tweezers before being replaced with fresh flowers (14). Once the scented molecules have infused and saturated the oil or fat, that is, 'complete' absorption of all possible fragrances by fat or oil, alcohol can then be used to extract the essential oil (15).

Hot maceration involves a similar process as enfleurage with the immersion of the flower petals in odourless fat that has been heated for 1 to 2 hours at 45 - 60 ºC. Although this process is less common, it reduces the extraction time, it is, however, unsuitable for delicate flowers. After multiple immersions of batches of the flowers, the fat is separated from the flower wastes by sieving. Scalding water is then used to wash off adhering fat on the separated flower wastes thereby ensuring substantial, if not complete, removal of the fat from the exhausted flowers. The fat is then separated from the water. The scented fat produced is called a pomade which can be used as such or further processed using ethanol to produce alcoholic extract which when concentrated in vacuo, gives an absolute (1).

Solvent extraction is another method commonly used in the perfume industry to produce essential oils by soaking plant materials in slightly warmed volatile solvents, such as hexane and petroleum ether. A major benefit of this process is the use of a uniform temperature throughout the extraction process, thereby giving a purer odour to the extracted oils. It is commonly used for essential oils with low yield due to thermolability during steam distillation (7). The product obtained is called a concrete which can be used as such, but commonly undergoes further reprocessing using cold ethanol to give an absolute oil (1). Absolutes are products typically generated by reprocessing concretes, supercritical fluid extracts and pomades through solvent extraction using ethanol (16).

Super critical carbon dioxide extraction method involves getting carbon dioxide to reach a supercritical state at 1071 psi and 31.1°C, when it exhibits both gaseous and liquid properties. In this state, it diffuses into the oil glands like a gas and dissolves the constituents as a liquid. The liquid goes into a collection jar from where the extracted oil and carbon dioxide are separated, and the carbon dioxide recycled for subsequent extraction. Although this method takes the longest period for extraction (about 6 hours in some cases), it produces oils of the highest purity and yields than the other methods. The low temperature used prevents degradation of the constituents of the oil, there is no residual solvent in the oil and all microorganisms that may be present in the plant parts are killed due to the presence of carbon dioxide (17).

Essential oil chemistry

The major components of essential oils, that contribute to their aroma which may be odious or pleasant (18), include aromatic compounds (phenol, aldehyde, methoxy derivative, alcohol), and terpenes (sesquiterpenes and monoterpenes). Generally, essential oil compounds are divided into oxygenated compounds and terpene hydrocarbons. Hydrocarbons may exist as aromatic, alicyclic (monocyclic, bicyclic, tricyclic), or acyclic. Terpene hydrocarbons are the most frequently occurring constituents of natural fragrances in essential oils; they consist mainly of monoterpenes (90%) and sesquiterpenes, while diterpenes, triterpenes, tetraterpenes are present at low concentrations (8). Monoterpenes and sesquiterpenes are naturally occurring chiral compounds typically found in enantiomers that have evolved through enzymatic biosynthesis. Moreover, variations in the chirality of these compounds result in difference in taste and odour. Citronellal, geraniol/nerol, citral, citronellol, and linalool are the mostly used terpenes in the perfume industry (9).

Oxygenated compounds including ketones, phenols, alcohols and lactones are derived from terpenes. Some specific examples of these groups of compounds are (8):

- Ketones – menthone, carvone, camphor
- Oxides – 1,8-cineole (eucalyptol), rose oxide
- Lactones – nepetalactone, citroptene
- Esters – geranyl acetate, linalyl acetate, citronellyl acetate
- Phenylpropanoids – myristicin, anethole
- Phenols – thymol, carvacrol, eugenol
- Alcohol – monoterpene alcohol (lavanduol, isopulegol), sesquiterpenes alcohol (santalol, nerolidol

An essential oil may contain a mixture of 20 to 60 constituents (or even more than 100 individual constituents) at different concentrations (19), two to three of which are usually significant at relatively high concentrations of 20 to 70% while others occur in trace amounts (20). The contribution of an individual compound to the odour or flavour of a mixture, largely depends on its odour threshold, which is governed by its volatility and structure rather than by its concentration. Subsequently, even though a degradation or oxidation product is present in small concentrations, if it has a high aroma value, it could strongly impact the odour or flavour of the mixture (9). The oxidation of essential oils also affects their antimicrobial properties leading to decrease or increase in activity depending on the new compounds that are formed (12,13,21). Furthermore, these volatile essential oils are mostly colourless, although some have some tints of the colour of the plant parts from which they are extracted, e.g., Nerioli oil, obtained from the flower blossoms of the bitter orange tree, is pale yellow to orange in colour. They are liquid at room temperature with solubility in fixed oils, alcohol, and ethers, but are water-insoluble (9,22).

Chemical stability of essential oils

The constituents of essential oils are highly susceptible to chemical degradation giving rancid odours. Proper storage of essential oils is crucial because of the need to be protected from light, air (oxygen), trace elements and presence of water or moisture which are potential triggers of degradation; thus, they should be stored in air-tight amber bottles that are fully filled and properly closed and the oil devoid of water (16,21). Inappropriate storage conditions could result in oxidation, ketone hydrolysis, peroxidation, photo-isomerisation, alcohol decomposition and photocyclization, which cause chemical degradation of the oils and alter their effects and safety (12,13,23). The International Organisation for Standardisation (ISO) has published standards (ISO/TS 210:2014) which constitute general rules for conditioning, storage and packaging of essential oils to prevent degradation (24).

Regulations for the inclusion in cosmetic products

Essential oils, though natural, do not go well for everyone. This factor is an important aspect that is pertinent to their use. Individuals react differently to the components of the oils and may develop adverse allergic reactions. A major risk factor for allergic contact dermatitis is the concentration and presence of potent allergens, contaminants, and adulterants in the oils (2,16). Constituents of essential oils can oxidise due to reactive peroxides and oxides, thereby increasing the risk of skin reactions (9). Therefore, it is crucial that essential oils are properly stored in tightly sealed amber bottles placed in a cool, dark place or refrigerator (21,25). Sensitisation to specific essential oils, essential oil adulterants, or a combination of essential oils with similar components could result in toxic effects in some persons while remaining non-toxic in others. In the presence of ultraviolet A (UVA) radiation or sunlight, applying essential oils containing phototoxins to the skin may cause photosensitisation. The inflammatory reactions during photosensitisation include blistering, pigmentation or severe burns (9). The severity of the effects of essential oils classed as dermal irritants depends on the concentration used. They should be properly diluted before use and should not be applied to allergic or inflammatory skin conditions. After applying essential oils that are photosensitising, it is important to avoid exposure to UV rays or sunlight for at least 24 hours (26).

The use of undiluted essential oils and synthetic aroma chemicals has resulted in many dermatological sensitivity issues. The co-reactivity and complexity of fragrance chemical compositions make identifying the allergens responsible for contact allergy due to a specific essential oil difficult. Skin reactions can be detected and avoided by performing a patch test using 2 to 5 % essential oil concentrations dissolved in carrier oil. Typically, 1 mL of a fragrance product contains 20 drops of essential oil. Patch tests are highly recommended for the detection of potential risks to patients as this helps to quickly test for irritation (9).

The potential allergenic substances that must be stated on cosmetic packaging are listed in the EU Cosmetic Regulation Annex II and III. The ISO/TS 211:2014 standard states the general regulated labelling rules. There is a list of 26 regulated individual fragrance allergens, of which 18 are constituents of essential oils. Therefore, it is a legal requirement to state these allergens on the product packaging or label if the maximum acceptable concentration that should be present in cosmetic products for use in various applications are exceeded (16). The maximum acceptable concentration of allergens in baths (rinse-off products) and shower gels is 0.01%, while body oils, creams (leave-on products), and massage oils are 0.001%. Moreover, the cosmetic directive requires products containing other fragrances to state the fragrance, perfume, or aroma on their labels (27). Manufacturers of cosmetic products are responsible for supplying products with high quality, and to achieve this, the list of ingredients are commonly required by the Food and Drug Administration (FDA) (9). The following are 26 potential fragrance allergens (16):

- Amylcinnamal
- Amylcinnamyl alcohol
- Anisyl alcohol
- Benzyl alcohol
- Benzyl benzoate
- Benzyl cinnamate
- Benzyl salicylate
- Cinnamyl alcohol
- Cinnamal
- Citral
- Citronellol
- Coumarin
- Eugenol
- Geraniol
- Farnesol
- Hexyl cinnamaldehyde
- Hydroxy-citronellal
- Hydroxy-methylpentylcyclohexenecarboxaldehyde

- Isoeugenol
- D-Limonene
- Linalool
- Methyl heptin carbonate
- 3-Methyl-4-(2,6,6-tri-methyl-2-cyclohexen-1-yl)-3-buten-2-one
- Oakmoss and treemoss extract
- Treemoss extract
- 2-(4-tert-Butylbenzyl) propionaldehyde

Aromatherapy

Essential oils have found use in other areas of health management applications apart from cosmetics. The antimicrobial activities of many essential oils have been reported in literature, an example of which is the broad-spectrum antimicrobial activity of the essential oil (ocimum oil) extracted from the leaves of *Ocimum gratissimum*. The oil and its preparations have demonstrated marked activity on bacteria isolated from wounds, boils and pimples (acne) (28,29). Honey increased and surfactant type affected the wound healing activity of the oil while the ability to increase vascular permeability improved healing (4,30). Studies by Orafidiya *et al.*, have demonstrated the suitability of ocimum oil as a prospective drug for the management of acne vulgaris. Preparations containing ocimum oil, especially at 2% and 5% concentrations in alcohol and cetomacrogol blend bases, have been proven to be more effective and act more quickly in reducing lesion counts than the reference drug product, benzoyl peroxide 10% lotion, which is a commonly used topical medication for acne (29); the anti-acne activity of ocimum oil was increased by aloe vera gel (31). In addition, ocimum oil at 3%v/v, have been shown to demonstrate remarkable activity against clinical isolates of *Neisseria sicca* of similar resistance profile. Thus, the oil may be suitable for further development for the treatment of *N. sicca* infections (32). Similarly, ocimum oil was shown to enhance hair growth at shaved sites on experimental rabbit models (29), and to prevent hair loss and damage to skin structure caused by the administration of cyclophosphamide in a rat model (33). Taken together, these studies demonstrate the remarkable potential of ocimum oil for remedies and aromatherapy. In addition, the essential oil of *Polyalthia longiflora* has demonstrated pesticidal activity against termites, cobweb spider and ants (6), lippia oil (*Lippia multiflora* leaves) has pediculocidal and scabicidal activity higher than that of benzyl benzoate (34,35), while lemongrass oil (*Cymbopogon citratus* leaves) is mosquito-repellent (3).

The efficacy of essential oils in relieving pain and inflammation (36), migraine and stress and their use in hair grooming, skin softening and as anti-ageing agent make them valuable. Furthermore, essential oils can be taken internally, applied directly to the skin, or used in baths (2). In the cosmeceutical industry, orange peel essential oil has provided multiple health benefits such as skin firmness, skin elasticity, acne treatment, stretch marks, and scars. Orange peel and lemon essential oils have exhibited antimicrobial and antiseptic properties, making them suitable ingredients for hair and skincare products. Furthermore, alongside scented oils, essential oils play a crucial part in producing scented candles (37). In addition, some essential oils have been shown to possess sunscreen properties, although these may be low. Examples of such oils and their approximate Sun Protection Factor (SPF) values include rose oil, 1; tea tree oil, 2; eucalyptus, 3; orange oil, 4; lavender oil, 6; peppermint oil and tulsi oil, 7 (38).

Aromatherapy has been exploited by studying the psychological and physiological impact of smell on the mind and body. It has been discovered that rose fragrance produces a tranquilising and calming effect, citrus fragrance enhances concentration, the lavender fragrance gives a calming effect, and jasmine fragrance gives stimulating effect. These discoveries, among others, have been exploited by formulators in the development of cosmetic products and are used in massage therapy (39–41).

Fragrance oils

Fragrance oils (FO) are oils produced in the laboratory by mixing various odorous compounds. The oils have more long-lasting scents than essential oils. Fragrance oils comprise natural and synthetic fragrant compounds. Natural fragrance oils (NFO) are fabricated from natural complex scents by isolating aromatic chemical components, while synthetic fragrance oils (SFO) are created artificially by chemical reactions. Although NFOs are obtained from natural sources, they are produced by human science through crystallisation, extraction, and purification (2). Many cheap scented commercial products contain SFOs because they maintain their aroma for longer; however, these should be avoided if an individual has skin sensitivities to any of the constituents. Processes such as steam distillation and cold compression employed in extracting essential oils are unable to effectively extract the oils from some plant parts. Hence, constituents of natural fragrance oils are used to semi-synthetically produce these scents, e.g., blueberry seed oil, and to chemically produce scents that do not occur naturally as essential oils. Although fragrance oils are beneficial in mimicking or recreating scents in perfumed cosmetic products, they do not provide the health benefits attained from essential oils. Fragrance oils are cheaper to produce than essential oils making them cheaper to purchase (2). Fragrance oil components are grouped into lactones, acetals, hydrocarbons, oxides, ketones, phenols, aldehydes, esters and alcohols, based on their functional groups and structures (Table 11.2a,b,c). Advances in synthetic chemistry have resulted in the current research of converting aroma chemicals, previously used as racemic compounds, into optically active chemicals. Methods used for this process include microorganisms or

Table 11.2a: Properties of the major groups of chemical compounds of essential oils

Chemical Classification		Aroma Chemicals	Chemical Structure	Molecular Formula and Weight	Odour
Alcohols	Sesquiterpene alcohols	Farnesol	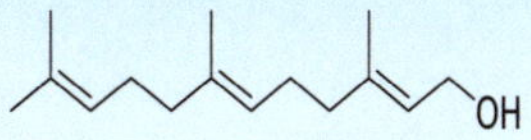	$C_{15}H_{26}O$ 222.37	Fresh Green and floral
	Fatty Alcohols	cis-3-hexenol	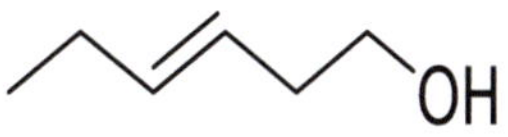	$C_6H_{12}O$ 100.16	Fresh Green leaves
	Aromatic alcohols	β-phenylethyl alcohol	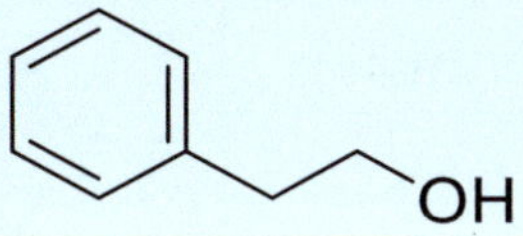	$C_8H_{10}O$ 122.17	Rosy
	Monoterpene alcohols	Linalool	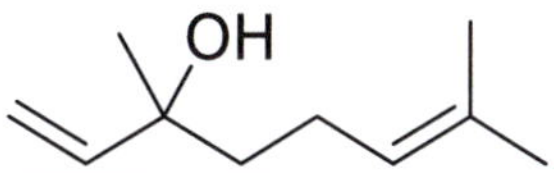	$C_{10}H_{18}O$ 154.25	Lily of the Valley
Ketones	Terpene ketones	l-carvone	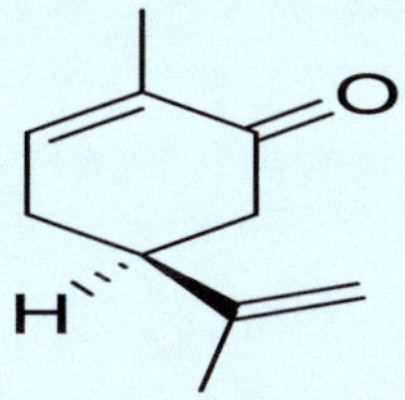	$C_{10}H_{14}O$ 150.22	Spearmint
	Alicyclic ketones	β-ionone	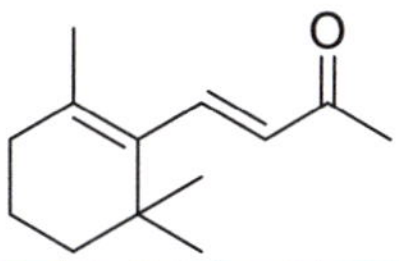	$C_{13}H_{20}O$ 192.30	Violet when diluted
	Macrocyclic ketones	Cyclopentadeca none	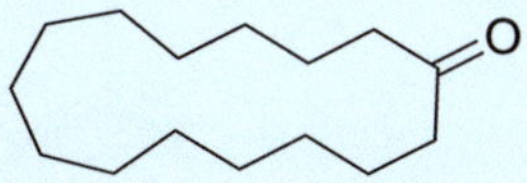	$C_{15}H_{28}O$ 224.39	Musky

enzyme bio-exchange, optical cleavage based on crystallisation and chromatography, or optically active enzymes or catalysts (1).

Table 11.2b: Properties of the major groups of chemical compounds of essential oils

Chemical Classification		Aroma Chemicals	Chemical Structure	Molecular Formula and Weight	Odour
Hydrocarbons	Sesquiterpenes	β-carophyllene	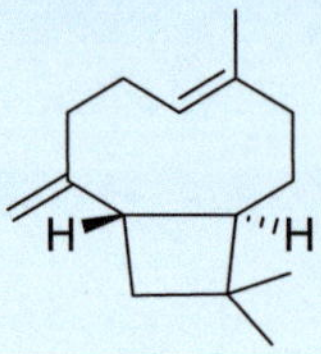	$C_{15}H_{24}$ 204.36	Woody
	Monoterpenes	Limonene	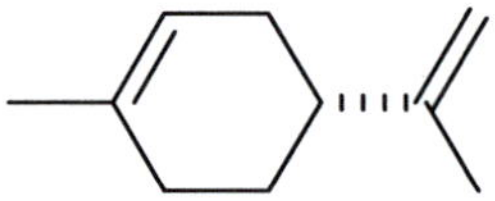	$C_{10}H_{16}$ 136.24	Orange
Aldehydes	Terpene aldehydes	Citral	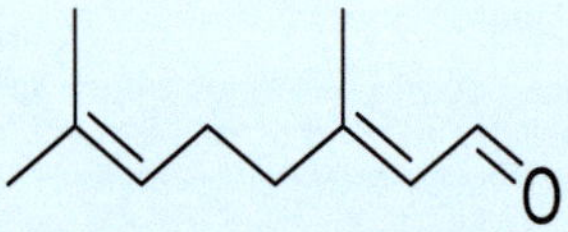	$C_{10}H_{16}O$ 152.24	Lemon
	Fatty aldehydes	2,6 nonadienal		$C_9H_{14}O$ 138.21	Violet, cucumber
	Aromatic aldehydes	α-hexylcinnamic aldehyde	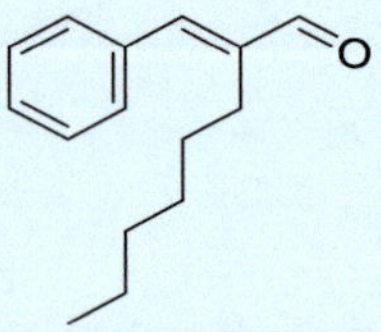	$C_{15}H_{20}O$ 216.33	Jasmin
Esters	Terpene esters	linalyl acetate	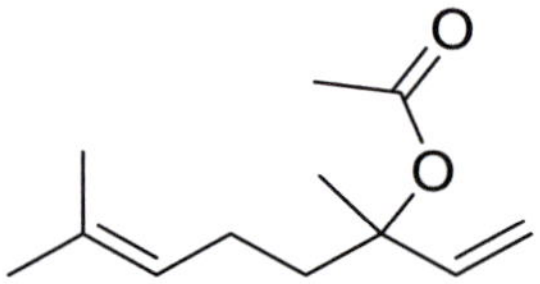	$C_{12}H_{20}O_2$ 196.29	Bergamot and lavender
	Aromatic esters	benzyl benzoate	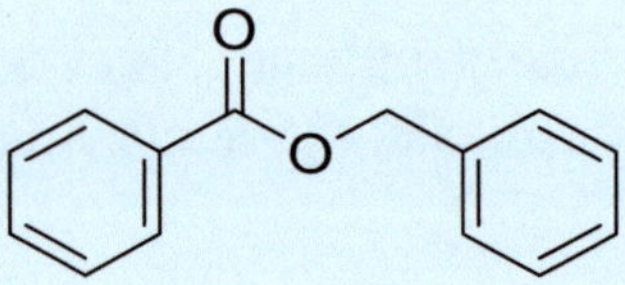	$C_{14}H_{12}O_2$ 212.25	Faint balsamic

Table 11.2c: Properties of the major groups of chemical compounds of essential oils

Chemical Classification	Aroma Chemicals	Chemical Structure	Molecular Formula and Weight	Odour
Acetals	phenyl acetaldehyde dimethyl acetal	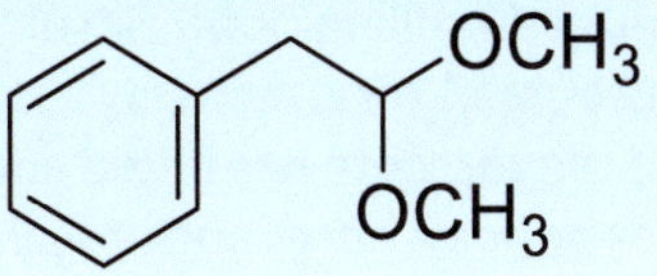	$C_{10}H_{14}O_2$ 166.22	Faint hyacinth
Oxides	rose oxide	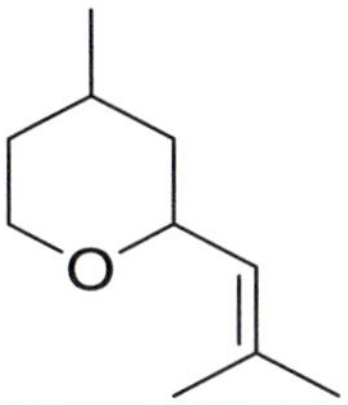	$C_{10}H_{18}O$ 154.25	Green and floral
Phenols	Eugenol	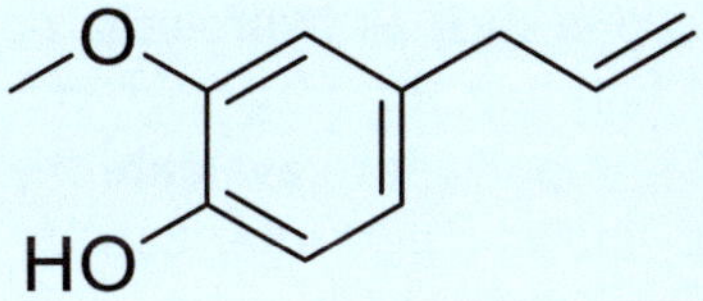	$C_{10}H_{12}O_2$ 164.21	Clove
Lactones	y-undecalactone	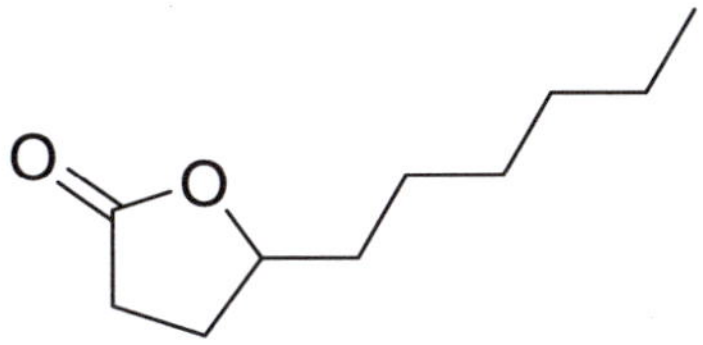	$C_{11}H_{20}O_2$ 184.28	Peach
Nitrogen compounds	Indole	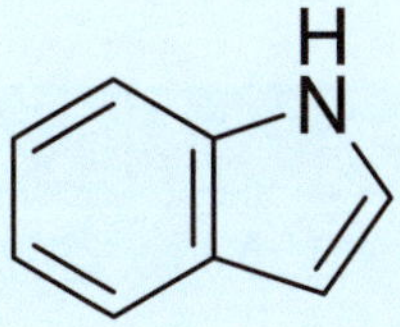	C_8H_7N 117.15	Fecal when strong, jasmin when dilute

Perfumes

Perfumes are created for cosmetic purposes by perfumers. There are about 1000 synthetic aroma chemicals and 500 natural aromatic materials or fragrances that are blended to produce a perfume with a distinct scent. Complex or more sophisticated perfumes are usually composed of 50 – 100 fragrance compounds, while simple perfumes are composed of 10 – 30 compounds. The formulation of the perfume determines how beautiful the fragrance would be (1).

Fragrances are divided into perfumery notes such as top, middle, and base notes based on their odorous strength, scent duration, volatility, and air diffusion rate (42). Top notes majorly impact the first impression as they have high volatility but do not last for longer than 2 hours and are a perfume's selling note. Citrus or fruity fragrances are commonly used as top notes due to the need for originality and freshness (1). Middle notes help establish the fragrance once the top note has faded and give body to the blends. Common examples include spicy notes or floral notes such as jasmine, ylang-ylang, geranium, clove and rose (42). They have medium volatility and last for 2 to 6 hours. On the other hand, base notes are long-lasting and last for over 6 hours. Base notes have low volatility, with common examples such as balsamic notes, woody notes, myrrh, frankincense, oakmoss, and animal notes, and are used in higher proportions when designing oriental fragrances (1). There should be a balance between these notes when formulating perfumes, and consideration should also be given to the cosmetic bases used. Oxygen, temperature, humidity, and light can affect the physical and chemical properties of fragrance compounds, causing reactions such as hydrolysis, polymerisation, and oxidation; thus, changing the colour and harming the fragrance by the rancid smell of the degraded compounds. Therefore, it is important to evaluate the choice of container and packaging used. Fragrance products include perfume, Eau de toilette, Eau de parfum, Eau de cologne, and perfumed oils and soaps (1).

Perfumes are formulated using an alcohol, mainly ethyl alcohol, as a basis, into which fragrance compounds are dissolved in fixed proportions (1). Various types of perfumes are formulated using different essential oils or fragrance compositions at varying ratios as displayed in Table 11.3.

Table 11.3: Examples of fragrance/perfumed products and their fragrance or essential oil compositions (1)

Name of fragrance or perfumed product	Fragrance or essential oil ratio (%)
Perfume/Parfum	15 – 30
Eau de Parfum	7 – 15
Eau de Toilette	5 – 10
Eau de Cologne	2 – 5
Perfumed Oil/Soap	1.5-4

Toxicity and untoward effects of essential oils, fragrances and perfumes

Essential oils, though of natural origin, do have toxic and untoward effects (43), especially when used for the wrong indications and at concentrations that are not recommended. While perfumes and fragrances are available in diluted forms, ready to be applied on the skin, essential oils are known to cause skin irritations when applied undiluted to the skin and oxidised oils are even more irritant (23). For instance, oxidised tea tree oil, containing peroxides, endoperoxides and epoxides was three times stronger in eliciting skin hypersensitivity than the unoxidised oil (44).

Certain essential oils and components of fragrances and perfumes are known to cause photosensitisation, photo-contact dermatitis or phototoxicity in susceptible individuals; a condition that arises from a chemical reaction that occurs when a chemical compound, absorbs UV radiation, usually from the sun, while in contact with the skin. The furocoumarins, e.g., bergapten and oxypeucedanin, present in essential oils especially those obtained from citrus fruits such as lime, orange and bergamot oils, are examples of compounds that may cause photosensitisation in products in which they are present. Other oils implicated in photosensitisation include oakmoss, lavender, cedar, tea tree and sandalwood oils (45). Geraniol, benzaldehyde, cinnamic aldehyde, linalool, neroli oil and terpenes from lemon and orange oils were found to be the main cause of allergic contact dermatitis observed in workers of a perfumery factory (46). These essential oils and their constituents, employed as fragrances and perfumes are present in cosmetic products such as body creams, moisturisers, bath oils, perfume sprays and oils, and hair shampoos. Damage to the skin caused by photosensitisation commonly manifests as redness, itching, blisters, burns and permanent skin discoloration while repeated exposure can lead to more serious conditions such as squamous cell and basal skin cancer or even the malignant melanoma. Also, the photosensitivity of the skin, and hence the harmful effects of implicated essential oils, is increased by certain drugs such as tetracycline.

Although fragrant cosmetic products are applied on the skin, it has been observed that transdermal absorption of essential oils and, by extension, perfumes and fragrances, into the circulatory system is feasible. Studying the effects of ocimum oil on hair growth enhancement and the ability to prevent damage to hair and other skin structures elicited by cyclophosphamide that was applied on shaved skin cites on rats, it was found that the oil elicited similar effects at skin sites to which the test drug was not applied on the same animals, indicating systemic absorption of the oil from test cites (29,33). Thus, extensive applications of essential oils on the body may lead to systemic side effects. Ocimum oil, in an acute and subchronic toxicity study in rats, has been shown to cause a significant increase in the weights of rats' liver and brain and to have sedative and central nervous system depressant activities that manifested as susceptibility to fatigue, a dose dependent weakness and sedative and sleep-inducing effects (47). The cytotoxicity and genotoxicity studies carried out on the essential oils of *Myrtus communis, Thymus vulgaris, Achillea millefolium, Salvia somalensis, Pistacia lentiscus, Rosmarinus officinalis* and *Helichrysum italicum* indicated that most essential oils exhibit cytotoxic and genotoxic effects on human peripheral lymphocites as well as having marked antiestrogenic activity (48). Gynaecomastia was observed in three prepubertal boys who used topical products that contained tea tree and lavender oils, an indication of antiandrogenic and oestrogenic activities of the oils. The effects, however, subsided when the use of the oils was discontinued (49).

Credit for chemical structures - Dr. Zhangping Xiao, Postdoctoral Research Fellow, Imperial College, London, UK.

References

1. Mitsui T. New cosmetic science [Internet]. Amsterdam; New York: Elsevier Science; 1997 [cited 2022 Jul 2]. Available from: http://www.sciencedirect.com/science/book/9780444826541
2. Jessie and Clare. How do essential oil and fragrance oil differ and why does it matter? – bare-soaps [Internet]. Bare Soap. 2016 [cited 2022 Jan 12]. Available from: https://www.bare-soaps.com/blogs/good-reads/77988165-difference-between-essential-oil-and-fragrance-oil
3. Oyedele AO, Gbolade AA, Sosan MB, Adewoyin FB, Soyelu OL, Orafidiya OO. Formulation of an effective mosquito-repellent topical product from lemongrass oil. Phytomedicine. 2002;9(3):259–62.
4. Orafidiya LO, Adesina SK, Igbeneghu OA, Akinkunmi EO, Adetogun GE, Salau AO. The effect of honey and surfactant type on the antibacterial properties of the leaf essential oil of Ocimum gratissimum Linn. against common wound-infecting organisms. Int J Aromather. 2006;16(2):57–62.
5. Elusiyan CA, Olawuni I, Olugbade TA, Orafidiya O, McDonald A. Acetylcholinesterase Inhibitory Effect and Characterization of the Essential Oil of Plectranthus aegyptiacus (Forssk.) C. Chr. Growing in Nigeria. Med Aromat Plants. 2018;07(02). DOI: 10.4172/ 2167-0412.1000316
6. Orafidiya LO, Kaloustian J, Agbani EO, Portugal H, Adewoyin FB, Wojuola A, et al. Pesticidal and antimicrobial profile of the sesquiterpenerich leaf essential oil of Polyalthia longifolia (Sonn.) Thwaites. Int J Essent Oil Ther. 2010;4(1–2):11–6.
7. Talati A. Extraction Methods of Natural Essential Oils [Internet]. 2017. p. 1–13. Available from: https://www.researchgate.net/publication/313638030_EXTRACTION_METHODS_OF_NATURAL_ESSENTIAL_OILS

8. Tongnuanchan P, Benjakul S. Essential Oils: Extraction, Bioactivities, and Their Uses for Food Preservation. J Food Sci. 2014;79(7). doi: 10.1111/1750-3841.12492.
9. Sharmeen JB, Mahomoodally FM, Zengin G, Maggi F. Essential oils as natural sources of fragrance compounds for cosmetics and cosmeceuticals. Molecules. 2021;26(3):666. doi: 10.3390/molecules26030666.
10. Barbieri C, Borsotto P. Essential Oils: Market and Legislation. In: Potential of Essential Oils El-Shemy, H., Ed.; Potential of Essential Oils, IntechOpen: London, UK, 2018; pp. 107–127. doi: 10.5772/intechopen.77725
11. Oyedele AO, Lamikanra A, Orafidiya LO. Physical and antibacterial characteristics of the volatile oil of Hemizygia welwitschii (Rolfe). Phyther Res. 1992;6(4):224–6.
12. Orafidiya LO. The effect of autoxidation of lemon-grass oil on its antibacterial activity. Phyther Res. 1993;7(3):269–71.
13. Oladimeji FA, Orafidiya OO, Okeke IN, Dagne E. Effect of autoxidation on the composition and antimicrobial activity of essential oil of Lippia multiflora. Pharm Pharmacol Lett. 2001;11(2):64–7.
14. B Burger P, Plainfossé H, Brochet X, Chemat F, Fernandez X. Extraction of Natural Fragrance Ingredients: History Overview and Future Trends. Chem. Biodivers. 2019.16. doi: 10.1002/cbdv.201900424.
15. Joie Power. What are Enfleurage Essential Oils? | Artisan Aromatics [Internet]. [cited 2022 Jan20]. Available from: https://artisanaromatics.com/what-are-enfleurage-essential-oils/.
16. Sarkic A, Stappen I. Essential oils and their single compounds in cosmetics - A critical review. Cosmetics. 2018, 5, 11. doi: 10.3390/cosmetics5010011
17. Yousefi M, Rahimi-Nasrabadi M, Pourmortazavi SM, Wysokowski M, Jesionowski T, Ehrlich H, et al. Supercritical fluid extraction of essential oils. Trends in Analytical Chemistry. Elsevier; 2019:118: 182–93. doi: 10.1016/j.trac.2019.05.038
18. Sadgrove N, Jones G. A Contemporary Introduction to Essential Oils: Chemistry, Bioactivity and Prospects for Australian Agriculture. Agriculture. 2015;5(1):48–102. doi: 10.3390/agriculture5010048
19. Turek C, Stintzing FC. Stability of essential oils: A review. Comprehensive Reviews in Food Science and Food Safety. 2013, 12, 40–53. doi: 10.1111/1541-4337.12006
20. Chouhan S, Sharma K, Guleria S. Antimicrobial Activity of Some Essential Oils—Present Status and Future Perspectives. Medicines [Basel]. 2017;4(3):58. doi: 10.3390/medicines4030058
21. Oladimeji FA, Orafidiya LO. A study on the autoxidation profile of leaf essential oil of Lippia multiflora Modenke under different storage conditions. Int J Essent Oil Ther. 2007;1:39–44.
22. Oladimeji FA, Orafidiya LO, Okeke IN. Physical properties and antimicrobial activities of leaf essential oil of Lippia multiflora Moldenke. Int J Aromather. 2004;14(4):162–8.
23. Matura M, Sköld M, Börje A, Andersen KE, Bruze M, Frosch P, et al. Not only oxidized R-(+)- but also S-(-)-limonene is a common cause of contact allergy in dermatitis patients in Europe. Contact Dermatitis. 2006;55(5):274–9.

24. Guidance on Essential Oils in Cosmetic Products | EDQM - European Directorate for the Quality of Medicines [Internet]. [cited 2022 Jan 31]. Available from: https://www.edqm.eu/en/guidance-essential-oils-cosmetic-products
25. Vostinaru O, Codruta Heghes S, Filip L. Safety Profile of Essential Oils. In: Essential Oils - Bioactive Compounds, New Perspectives and Applications. IntechOpen: London, UK, 2020. doi: 10.5772/intechopen.91363
26. Balick R. A peek into safe use of essential oils. Pharm Today [Internet]. 2019 Aug 1 [cited 2022 Mar 1];25(8):22–3. Available from: http://www.pharmacytoday.org/article/S1042099119308904/fulltext
27. European Commission. Fragrance Allergens Labelling [Internet]. 2019 [cited 2022 Jan 31]. Available from: https://ec.europa.eu/growth/sectors/cosmetics/cosmetic-products-specific-topics/fragrance-allergens-labelling_en
28. Orafidiya LO, Agbani EO, Oyedele AO, Babalola OO, Onayemi O. Preliminary clinical tests on topical preparations of Ocimum gratissimum linn leaf essential oil for the treatment of acne vulgaris. Clin Drug Investig. 2002;22(5):313–9. doi: 10.2165/00044011-200222050-00005
29. Orafidiya LO, Agbani EO, Abereoje OA, Awe T, Abudu A, Fakoya FA. An investigation into the wound-healing properties of essential oil of Ocimum gratissimum linn. J Wound Care. 2003;12(9):331–4. doi: 10.12968/jowc.2003.12.9.26537
30. Orafidiya LO, Fakoya FA, Agbani EO, Iwalewa EO. Vascular permeability-increasing effect of the leaf essential oil of Ocimum gratissimum Linn as a mechanism for its wound healing property. African J Tradit Complement Altern Med. 2005;2(3):253-58 doi: 10.4314/ajtcam.v2i3.31123
31. Orafidiya LO, Agbani EO, Oyedele AO, Babalola OO, Onayemi O, Aiyedun FF. The effect of aloe vera gel on the anti-acne properties of the essential oil of Ocimum gratissimum Linn leaf - A preliminary clinical investigation. Int J Aromather. 2004;14(1):15–21. doi: 10.1016/j.ijat.2003.12.005
32. Orafidiya LO, Kaloustian J, Agbani EO, Portugal H, Abudu A, Igbeneghu OA, et al. A study on the composition, autoxidation and antimicrobial activity of the leaf essential oil of Ocimum gratissimum Linn. against Helicobacter pylori and Neisseria sicca. Int J Essent Oil Ther. 2007;1(3):103–9.
33. Orafidiya LO, Agbani EO, Adelusola KA, Iwalewa EO, Adebanji OA, Adediran EAF, et al. A study on the effect of the leaf essential oil of Ocimum gratissimum Linn. on cyclophosphamide-induced hair loss. Int J Aromather. 2004;14(3):119–28.
34. Oladimeji FA, Orafidiya OO, Ogunniyi TAB, Adewunmi TA. Pediculocidal and scabicidal properties of Lippia multiflora essential oil. J Ethnopharmacol. 2000;72(1–2):305–11.
35. Oladimeji FA, Orafidiya LO, Ogunniyi TAB, Adewunmi TA, Onayemi O. A comparative study of the scabicidal activities of formulations of essential oil of Lippia multiflora Moldenke and benzyl benzoate emulsion BP. Int J Aromather. 2005;15(2):87–93.
36. Iwalewa EO, Oladimeji FA, Adewunmi CO, Osoniyi OR, Orafidiya LO, Adeloye O, et al. Involvement of nitric oxide and other antioxidant markers in the anti-inflammatory and

analgesic effects of Lippia multiflora (Moldenke) leaf essential oil emulsion. Int J Essent Oil Ther. 2007;1(3):126–34.

37. Ahuja K, Singh S. Essential Oils Market Size By Application (Orange oil, Lemon oil, Eucalyptus oil, Clove oil, Peppermint oil, Jasmine oil, Rosemary oil, Cornmint oil, Citronella oil, Geranium, Spearmint oil, Lavender oil, Tea tree oil and others). Industry Analysis Report, Regional Outlook, Growth Potential, Competitive Market Share & Forecast, 2019–2026. [Internet]. Global Market Insights, Inc. 2019 [cited 2022 Feb 28]. Available from: https://www.gminsights.com/industry-analysis/essential-oil-market
38. Kaur CD, Saraf S. In vitro sun protection factor determination of herbal oils used in cosmetics. Pharmacognosy Res. 2010;2(1):22–5. doi: 10.4103/0974-8490.60586
39. KIKUCHI A, YAMAGUCHI H, TANIDA M, ABE T, UENOYAMA S. Effects of Odors on Cardiac Response Patterns and Subjective States in A Reaction Time Task. Tohoku Psychol folia. 1993;51:74–82.
40. Torii S, Fukuda H, Kanemoto HM. R., Hamauzu, Y. & Kawasaki, M. Contingent negative variation (CNV) and the psychological effects of odour. Perfum Psychol Biol Fragrance New York Champaign Hall. 1989;107–20.
41. Shibata H, Fujiwara R, Iwamoto M, Matsuoka H, Yokoyama MM. Recovery of PFC in mice exposed to high pressure stress by olfactory stimulation with fragrance. Int J Neurosci. 1990;51(3–4):245–7. doi: 10.3109/00207459008999710
42. Irshad M, Ali Subhani M, Ali S, Hussain A, Subhani MA, Ali S, et al. Biological Importance of Essential Oils. In: Essential Oils - Oils of Nature [Internet]. IntechOpen; 2020 [cited 2022 Mar 1]. Available from: https://www.intechopen.com/chapters/68027
43. Orafidiya LO. Essential oils in the treatment of diseases: aspects of efficacy and toxicology. In: Evaluation of herbal medicinal products. Edited by Houghton P and Mukherjee PK. the Pharmaceutical press, Uk; 2009. p. 359 – 366.
44. Fritz TM, Burg G, Krasovec M. [Allergic contact dermatitis to cosmetics containing Melaleuca alternifolia (tea tree oil)]. Ann Dermatol Venereol. 2001;128(2):123–6
45. Placzek M, Frömel W, Eberlein B, Gilbertz KP, Przybilla B. Evaluation of phototoxic properties of fragrances. Acta Derm Venereol. 2007;87(4):312–6.
46. Schubert HJ. Skin diseases in workers at a perfume factory. Contact Dermatitis. 2006;55(2):81–3.
47. Orafidiya LO, Agbani EO, Iwalewa EO, Adelusola KA, Oyedapo OO. Studies on the acute and sub-chronic toxicity of the essential oil of Ocimum gratissimum L. leaf. Phytomedicine. 2004;11(1):71–6.
48. Contini A, Di Bello D, Azzarà A, Giovanelli S, D'Urso G, Piaggi S, et al. Assessing the cytotoxic/genotoxic activity and estrogenic/antiestrogenic potential of essential oils from seven aromatic plants. Food Chem Toxicol. 2020;138.
49. H Henley D V., Lipson N, Korach KS, Bloch CA. Prepubertal Gynecomastia Linked to Lavender and Tea Tree Oils. N Engl J Med. 2007 Feb;356(5):479–85.

CHAPTER TWELVE

Antioxidants as agents of cosmetics products

'Efere M Obuotor

Many cosmetics and pharmaceutical products that are currently being marketed for the care and improvement of skin or hair appearance often contain, antioxidants, as one of the ingredients. Antioxidants are compounds or macromolecular systems that can donate electron to free radicals thereby inhibiting the oxidation reaction elicited by the free radicals and preventing radical chain reactions in biological systems (1). The cosmetic products which are available as creams, lotions, shampoos or powders are often used for cleansing, protecting, and moisturising the skin or hair for the purposes of enhancing beauty by boosting the skin's radiance, minimise age spots, sun spots, and fine lines (2). Generally, antioxidants in cosmetic preparations interrupt oxidation reactions and prevent the effects of reactive oxygen species (ROS) and ultraviolet radiation (UVR), from dam ageing the integrity and function of various biological molecules present in the skin and hair (3,4). Although, the human body has its own natural mechanism of protection from free radical induced damage, this protective capacity diminishes with age and time of exposure especially when the magnitude of free radicals formed overwhelms the body's natural ability to neutralise them. Consequently, there is need to fortify cosmetic products with antioxidant agents to strengthen and render it more effective in combating free radical induced damages in the skin. Antioxidants are useful in two ways: On the one hand, they prevent degradation of active pharmaceutical ingredients in the cosmetic product while on the other hand they protect the skin cells from being damaged and slow down the ageing process. Antioxidants in skin and hair care products are capable of penetrating into the deepest layer of the skin and scalp and consequently enabling living cells to repair and renew itself [4].

Free radicals and skin ageing

Free radicals include any chemical species that have one or more unpaired electrons in its last electron layer. They are highly reactive, short lived and unstable molecules (5) which in a bid to gain stability, often reacts with other molecules, triggering a chain of events that damage macromolecules and cellular substructures leading to cell death

(6). Free radicals derived from either molecular oxygen are known as reactive oxygen species (ROS) while those from nitrogen are reactive nitrogen species (RNS). Examples of ROS include superoxide anion [$O2^{\bullet -}$], hydroperoxyl [$HOO^{\bullet}$] and hydroxyl [$^{\bullet}OH$] radicals while RNS include peroxynitrite [$ONOO^{\bullet}$] and nitric oxide [$NO^{\bullet}$] radicals. Our bodies naturally produce free radicals, but they can also come from exposure to environmental factors like UV rays, pollution, cigarette smoke and some chemicals the body is exposed to in the course of our daily activities (6).

The human skin, being the largest and outermost organ in the body, is constantly being assaulted by free radicals (7). These free radicals are formed in the skin as well as in other cells of the body through normal cellular processes of mitochondrial oxidative metabolism in the skin and through solar ultraviolet radiation (UVR). Furthermore, exposure of the skin to environmental pollutants such as smoke, smog, pesticides and other chemicals the body is exposed to in course of daily activities, are also capable of generating free radicals such as reactive oxygen species and reactive nitrogen species (ROS/RNS) (8). These radical species cause oxidative damage to lipids, proteins, carbohydrates, and DNA. They also stimulate matrix metalloproteinases formation (MMP-1, MMP-3, MMP-8, and MMP-9), as well as activate enzymes such as collagenase, elastase, tyrosinase, and xanthine oxidase, resulting in degradation of collagen and elastin, damage to the dermal connective tissue, and consequent premature skin ageing (9).

The cascade of (ROS/RNS) formation in the skin, which amounts to about 80% of ROS, are initiated by UVR-absorption, predominantly in the UVA region, by both endogenous and exogenous chromophores in the skin. The UVA radiation includes those with longer waves that span between 320 and 400 nm while UVB radiations are of medium wavelengths ranging between 280 and 320 nm. Specifically, UVB radiation acts predominantly on the epidermal basal layer of the skin to produce free radicals amongst other biochemical derailments including the formation of pyrimidine photoproducts, stimulation of DNA synthesis and cell cycle growth arrest (10). Furthermore, UVB radiation increases reactive oxygen species (ROS) formation, which activates complex signaling pathways and induces proinflammatory cytokines release from epidermal keratinocytes and dermal fibroblasts. Neutrophils are also activated and these stimulate the activity of myeloperoxidase (MPO), an enzyme that generates ROS. UVB rays constitute approximately 2-5% of total solar UV light and are primarily responsible for sunburn. They represent an important agent in the development of melanoma and non-melanoma skin cancers (10).

In contrast, UVA radiation, which constitute more than 90% of solar radiation, readily penetrates deeper into the cutaneous layers of the skin and contributes to photo ageing. This process occurs through multiple mechanisms, such as reactive oxygen species (ROS) formation, DNA damage, and induction of inflammation. ROS-induced oxidative stress in the skin has been linked to cancer, ageing, inflammation, and photodamage (11).

Skin antioxidant defense systems

Fortunately, the healthy and young skin has an intrinsic defense system to mitigate the deleterious effects of oxidative reactions initiated by free radicals. However, with age, the defense system gets impaired, so much so, that an exogenous supply of oral and topical antioxidants is required to maintain the balance of the skin's defense system. (12) Several studies have indicated that the inclusion of antioxidants in skin care preparations can help the skin fight free radical damage and recover from oxidative stress. (13, 14)

Antioxidants are substances that neutralise free radicals or their actions. They act through a number of mechanisms such as reduction of free radicals by scavenging them and by inhibiting the oxidation reaction elicited by the free radicals. They also function as singlet and triplet oxygen quenchers, peroxide decomposers and enzyme inhibitors as well as metal chelating agents (15). In cosmetic preparations, antioxidants can be conveniently categorised into natural and synthetic types. The natural antioxidants which are obtained from natural sources comprise mineral antioxidants such as the trace minerals (selenium, manganese), the vitamins (Vit A, C, and E) and the phyto-antioxidants which are mainly the polyphenols and the terpenoids (16). On the other hand, synthetic antioxidants are compounds synthesised through chemical processes; they include butylated hydroxyl anisole (BHA), butylated hydroxytoluene (BHT), (PG) propyl gallate, tertiary butylhydroquinone (TBHQ) and idebenone (Co Q10 analogue) (16).

Antioxidants act at different levels of prevention, interception and repair of damaged macromolecules [proteins, DNA, lipids carbohydrates] by the free radicals. This defense system comprises enzymatic and nonenzymatic components, both of which work synergistically to eliminate free radicals from the skin (17). The endogenous non-enzymatic antioxidants are low–molecular weight compounds such as glutathione (GSH), ubiquinol (Co Q10), melanin, uric acid and thio-containing proteins which are found in the stratum corneum and *stratum basale* of the epidermis. The enzymatic defense systems are achieved through the skin's "interceptive" antioxidant network of enzymes which directly neutralizes ROS and RNS. The skin also possesses mechanisms of "antioxidant repair" enzyme network which can reverse oxidatively damaged proteins as well as regenerate small molecule antioxidants (18). Enzymes in the interceptive network system include catalase [CAT], glutathione peroxidase [GSH-Px] and superoxide dismutase [SOD] while the antioxidant repair network comprises glutathione reductase, glutathione –S-transferase (GST), thioredoxin reductase and the glutathione–methionine sulfoxide reductase (MSR) system [Figure 1]. For instance, though the accumulation of oxidised amino acids in proteins is mostly irreversible, oxidised methionine and cysteine can be

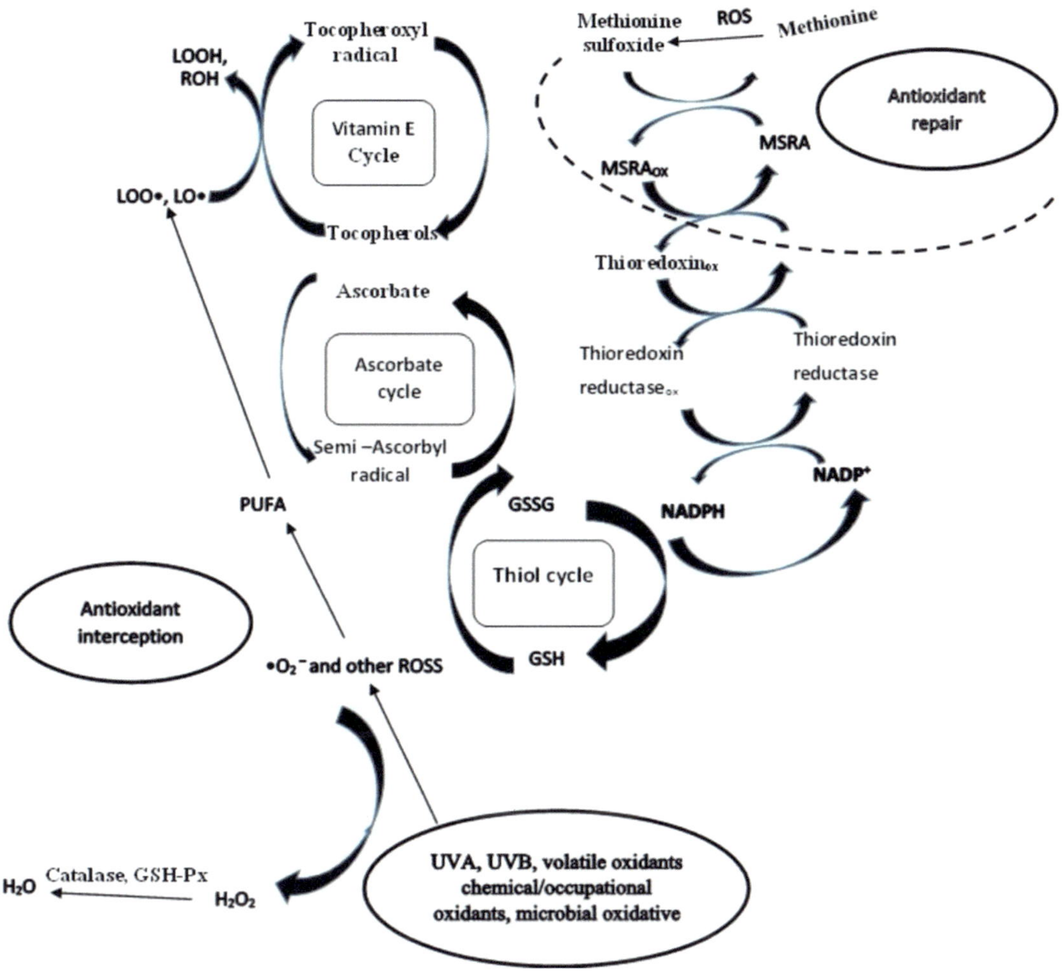

Figure 12.1: Activation of the skin interactive network of antioxidants and antioxidant enzymes by oxidative stress (20).

reversed to their reduced forms by the (MSR) system. Methionine sulfoxide accumulation in protein oxidative damage occurs, as two different forms, methionine-R-sulfoxide and methionine-S-sulfoxide. These two forms of protein oxidation can be reversed by methionine-S-sulfoxide reductase A (MSRA) and methionine-R- sulfoxide reductase B (MSRB), respectively. Accumulated studies have shown that MSRA levels appear directly proportionate to oxidative resistance and that during the cellular ageing process, MSRA/B activity is decreased, with an increase in the accumulation of oxidatively damaged proteins

(20). MSRA activity has been detected in keratinocytes in all epidermal layers of human skin, as well as in sebaceous glands, eccrine glands, hair follicles, and the blood vessels of human skin, while certain isoforms of MSRB have been localised to melanocytes and blood vessels only. It has been suggested that the presence of MSR is indicative of significant oxidative protein stress in these cutaneous components requiring particularly efficient antioxidant repair mechanisms. It has also been speculated that the lack of/or a reduced MSR system may be associated with UV-induced oxidative protein modifications in human skin leading to photocarcinogenesis and photo ageing (20). Moreover, it has been demonstrated that the levels of these different antioxidant enzymes vary within the different skin cells. For instance, fibroblasts have the highest level of antioxidant enzymes as compared to the other skin cells such as the melanocytes, a property that confers a higher resistance to oxidative stress on these cells (21).

Plant antioxidants and skincare

It is well known that plants produce phytoconstituents, products of secondary metabolism, which are natural compounds that could inhibit environmental stressors such as oxidative stress caused by UVR and oxygen. A good number of these natural compounds have antioxidant properties and they fall into two major classes of secondary metabolites, namely terpenes and polyphenols (22). Many plant extracts containing natural antioxidants have been used for centuries, in ancient and modern cultures, for the purpose of caring for the skin and the application of antioxidants in cosmetics is ever increasing. Many patents and commercial cosmetic products contain various combinations of plant extracts. For example, green tea, rosemary, grape seed, basil grape, blueberry, tomato, acerola seed, pine bark, and milk thistle have been used in various cosmetic formulations, while some others contain pure natural compounds such as quercetin, curcumin, kojic acid, and resveratrol (22). The choice of the right active plant extracts or compounds, the confirmation of their activity, their stability and synergistic effects in cosmetic products are important factors often considered in the formulation of an effective product. Some natural antioxidant compounds and extracts that have been used in cosmetic preparations are now discussed.

Vitamin C

Vitamin C (ascorbate) can be obtained from fruits such as citrus fruits, and it is a very potent water-soluble antioxidant. Chemically, it predominantly exists in its reduced form, ascorbic acid, while its oxidised form, dehydro-L-ascorbate, which exists in trace quantities can be regenerated by reduction back to ascorbate by other stronger reducing biological compounds. However, an irreversible opening of the lactone ring leads to the formation of diketogulonic acid which completely lacks activity. This often happens when vitamin C preparations are oxidised, rendering them biologically ineffective (23).

Topical vitamin C as a photo-protectant, has been investigated in *in vitro* and *in vivo* experimental models and its effects in preventing UVB and UVA- induced skin damage by reducing the level of sunburn cells and decreasing erythema has been demonstrated.

Furthermore, the addition of topical vitamin C to "after–sun" products has been shown to scavenge UV-induced reactive oxygen species (24). Clinical studies have reported that there was improvement in the appearance of skin wrinkles upon topical application of vitamin C based cosmetic product and that vitamin C preparations are useful in preventing or lessening the detrimental effects of UV radiation (24).

Vitamin E

Vitamin E (tocopherol) is a lipid-soluble antioxidant that is present in the skin and found in various foods, such as vegetables, seeds, and meat. It consists of 8 active forms that are grouped into tocopherols and tocotrienols. Amongst the four tocopherols (α (alpha), β (beta), γ-(gamma) and δ (delta)), alpha-tocopherol has the highest activity. In animals, a topical application of α-tocopherol has been shown to exert photoprotective effects by causing reduction in the number of sunburn cells, reduction in ultraviolet B (UVB)-induced damage, and inhibition of photo-carcinogenesis (25). In a clinical study, the application of 5%-8% tocopherol-based cream on the skin caused improved signs of photo ageing when compared with placebo. Furthermore, the application of vitamin E (5%) to human skin under light-tight occlusion for twenty-four hours before UV treatment was shown to inhibit human macrophage metalloelastase, an enzyme involved in the degradation of elastin (26).

Recent studies have shown that combined application of various antioxidants does enhance their potency synergistically in terms photo protection outcomes as compared with single antioxidant application. Consequently, it has been suggested that the combination of vitamins E and C in cosmetic preparations holds a good photoprotection benefits in skin care (26).

Curcumin

Curcumin, the most biologically active curcuminoid, comprising 2-8%, in turmeric (*Curcuma longa*) has been demonstrated to have a very potent antioxidant activity in addition to its reported antimicrobial, anti-inflammatory and antineoplastic activities (27). Particularly, it can scavenge reactive oxygen species, such as hydroxyl radicals, superoxide anion radicals, and nitrogen dioxide radicals. Additionally, it serves as an anti-inflammatory agent by down- regulating the production of pro-inflammatory cytokines (e.g., IL-1 and TNF-α) and inhibiting the activation of specific transcription factors (e.g., NF-κB and AP-1). Curcumin has also been demonstrated to have antiproliferative properties (27). Specifically, curcumin inhibits UV radiation-induced skin cancer in SKH-1 hairless mice and reduces UVB-induced matrix metalloproteinase-1/3 expression in human dermal fibroblasts via MAPK-p38/JNK pathway suppression (27).

Coenzyme Q10

Coenzyme Q10 (Co Q10), or ubiquinone, is a fat-soluble antioxidant that is found in all human cells as a component of the respiratory chain, as well as in some foods, e.g., fish and shellfish. Up to 95% of the body's energy requirements seem to be provided by Co Q10. (61) It is a common topical antioxidant ingredient that is included in several over-the-counter (OTC) cosmetic products with no adverse effects reported, to date

In vitro studies have showed that Co Q10 suppresses the expression of collagenase following ultraviolet A (UVA) irradiation in human skin models (28).

Green tea

The extract of *Camellia sinensis* (tea plant) leaves contains catechins, a class of polyphenols with remarkable antioxidant properties. In fact, one of these catechins, epigallocatechin gallate (EGCG), is considered as one of the most studied green tea polyphenols (GTP) in relation to its several health promoting benefits (28). Green tea extracts and EGCG have been shown to reduce the amount of ROS in the skin and as well as reversing the impact of photo ageing elicited by UV irradiation to the skin. Furthermore, the topical use of cosmetic products containing green tea extract have been reported to reduce the production of collagen-degrading enzymes in the skin. Apart from their potent antioxidant activity, GTP, which can be administered either orally or topically, also act as anti-inflammatory and anticarcinogenic agents. For example, an *in vivo* topical application of GTP in mice has been shown to suppress chemo- and photo-carcinogenesis and to prevent UV-induced oxidative damage and induction of matrix metalloproteinases. In the human skin, GTP reduced UV- induced erythema, the number of sunburn cells, immunosuppression, and DNA-damage. Consequently, a number of OTC cosmetic products containing green tea have been recommended for use every morning for photo protection (28).

Lycopene

Lycopene, a powerful antioxidant, is a carotenoid found in red fruits and vegetables. It is, in fact, responsible for their red colour. Although the effect of topical lycopene is not well characterised, its chemoprotective properties against photo-induced tumours have been demonstrated in mouse models. An in vivo study using SKH-1 hairless mice found that topical lycopene reduced the activity of ornithine decarboxylase (ODC) and myeloperoxidase (MPO), enzymes that have been implicated in the carcinogenic and acute inflammatory effects of UVB irradiation (29)

Caffeine

Caffeine is a naturally occurring alkaloid found in leaves, seeds, and fruits of the coffee plant, *Coffea arabica,* and the leaves of *Camellia sinensis* (tea plant). Caffeine has become increasingly popular as an additive in topical skin care products for the purpose of improving the appearance of skin owing to its antioxidant and anticarcinogenic properties (30).

In addition to its antioxidant effects on the skin, its ability to protect cells against ultraviolet (UV)-induced non-melanoma skin cancers, and anti-inflammatory properties has been well- documented. In an *in vitro* study to evaluate effective topical antioxidants capable of inhibiting ROS-induced oxidative damage, pre-treatment with caffeine was observed to significantly reduce fibroblast necrosis as well as improve cell morphology induced by 30 min of exposure to H2O2. Accumulated studies on the effect of caffeine on the skin support the use of caffeine as an effective anti- ageing cosmeceutical (30).

Resveratrol

Resveratrol is a polyphenolic phytoalexin compound that is found in the skin and seeds of grapes, peanuts, fruits, and red wine, among others. (31). Its antioxidant activity has been reported based on *in vitro* and *in vivo* studies that, when topically applied to mice, it protected against UVB-mediated generation of hydrogen peroxide and infiltration of leucocytes cutaneous damage. It also inhibited UVB-mediated oxidative stress in the skin by reducing the expression of Activator protein 1 (AP-1) and nuclear factor kappa B (NF-KB) factors. Although the effect of resveratrol on human skin and photo ageing is still under investigation there are a few products with claims of anti ageing benefits and its antiproliferative properties has been related to the inhibition of cellular events associated with tumour initiation, promotion, and progression, and the triggering of apoptosis in tumour cells. (31).

Grape seed extract

Grape seed extract is obtained from the seeds of the common grape vine, *Vitis vinifera,* and is rich in proanthocyanidins, which belong to the flavonoid family. Grape seed proanthocyanidins (GSP) are polyphenolic compounds with potent free radical scavenging properties (32). Grape seed extract has been reported to have stronger free radical scavenging activities than vitamins C and E. A possible antioxidant mechanism of photoprotection by GSP has been suggested. GSP has been shown to inhibit the depletion of antioxidant defense components induced by UVB, and topical application of grape seed extract seems to enhance the sun protection factor in humans. It is often incorporated in a number of topical cosmetic formulations for anti ageing purposes (32).

Pomegranate

Pomegranate extracts can be obtained from various parts of the fruits of *Punica granatum*, such as the juice, seed, and peel. In particular, the phenolic components have shown potent antioxidant activity. Topical application of the peel extract was shown to restore catalase, peroxidase, and superoxide dismutase enzyme activities *in vivo*. The fruit extract has been shown to ameliorate UVA-mediated damages and protect against the adverse effects of UVB radiation *in vitro.* Pomegranate extract has also been incorporated in many skin care products (33, 34).

Genistein

Genistein, an isoflavone extracted from soybeans, has the capacity to inhibit UV-induced oxidative DNA damage. Genistein, either topically applied or orally supplemented, has been shown to effectively protect human skin against UVB-induced skin photo damage. It is often included in various products such as facial moisturisers, sunscreens, and other skin care formulations that claim to provide anti- ageing effects (35).

Pycnogenol

Pycnogenol is a standardised extract obtained from the French maritime pine, *Pinus pinaster*. It contains primarily monomeric and oligomeric procyanidins, flavonoids and phenolic compounds, which possess multiple biological effects. It elicits potent free-radical scavenging, immunosuppression and anti-inflammatory properties (36). For instance, a reduction of inflammatory sunburn reaction has been observed in mice after topical application of a formulation containing 0.05%–0.2% pycnogenol. It modulates the expression of proinflammatory cytokines in macrophages to induce an anti-inflammatory effect and has been shown to selectively induce apoptosis within specific human cancer cell lines (36).

Niacinamide

Niacinamide, or nicotinamide, is the biologically active amide of vitamin B3. Besides its antioxidant activity, it has also been shown to exhibit anti-inflammatory, depigmenting, and immunomodulant properties. The use of niacinamide has been shown to improve the texture and tone of the skin, and reduce fine lines, wrinkles, and hyperpigmentation]. Topical niacinamide has been reported to be well tolerated and is often incorporated in some skin care products (37).

Rosemary

The leaves of *Rosmarinus officinalis* are the source of various antioxidant substances. Most of the antioxidant activity comes from carnosol and carnosic acid, but ursolic, rosmarinic, and caffeic acids also contribute to the antioxidant activity by working as free radical scavengers. Rosemary essential oil contains monoterpenes such as 1,8-cineol and alpha-pinene that act as antioxidants too (38).

Silymarin

Silymarin, derived from the milk thistle plant, *Silybum marianum*, is a natural polyphenolic flavonoid. Its main component silybin (silibinin), is considered to be the most biologically active with strong antioxidant properties. *In vivo* studies have shown photoprotective effects with topically applied silybin prior to, or immediately after, UV irradiation. Thus, there is reasonable evidence to include the compound into sunscreen preparations (39, 40).

Cosmetic antioxidant capacity determination

For the antioxidant ingredient in a cosmetic product to achieve its desired activities in the product, it is desirable that it must remain stable in the cosmetic product being admixture with the other ingredients. Currently, a number of *in vitro* analytical methods are available for the determination of antioxidant capacities in cosmetic formulations. However, there is no single universally accepted method by which the antioxidant capacity in cosmetic formulations can be assessed accurately and quantitatively. In order to determine the total antioxidant activity, testing methods which consider the presence of both hydrophilic and hydrophobic compounds are often considered (41). The methods can be categorised into three main groups based on the reaction platforms being used. These are *in vitro*, *in vivo* and *ex vivo*. The *in vitro* assays rely on the ability of the antioxidant to neutralise free radicals in a cell-free medium or in cell cultures, while the *in vivo* and *ex vivo* assays require the use of an intact animal or human subjects. The *in vitro* cell free assays can be further categorised based on the mechanism of the reaction as either through electron transfer (ET) or hydrogen atom transfer (HAT) (42).

Electron transfer based methods

The ET-based assay involves a redox reaction with a single electron transfer mechanism. One of the most used techniques based on the ET mechanism involves the use of the stable synthetic radical, 2,2- diphenyl-1-picrylhydrazyl [DPPH•]. A solution of this compound, in methanol or ethanol, s exhibits a maximum absorbance in the visible range at a wavelength of 515–520 nm. The radical solution has a purple colour which changes because of electron transfer reactions after the addition of an antioxidant. This reaction is accompanied by a change in the absorbance which is a function of the antioxidant concentration in the sample. Another common ET-based method that has found practical application in the cosmetic industry involves the use of 2,2'-azino-di-(3-etylobenzotizoline-

6-sulfonate), [ABTS]. This compound is converted to ABTS•+ cation radical by an enzymatic reaction with metmyoglobin, haemoglobin, horseradish peroxidase and hydrogen peroxide, or by chemical reaction with potassium persulfate ($K_2S_2O_6$) or manganese dioxide (MnO_2) or with 2,2'-azo-bis (2-aminopropane) (ABAP) radicals) (42). The ABTS•+ cation radical is blue-green and has a maximum absorbance at several wavelengths: 417, 645, 734, 815 nm. In the presence of antioxidants in the solution, it is reduced and accompanied by the disappearance of the colour of the solution. Reduction in colour intensity is proportional to the antioxidant content in the sample. In this method, the antioxidant activity is expressed in Trolox equivalents as TEAC (Trolox Equivalent Antioxidant Capacity). Trolox (6-hydroxy-2,5,7, 8- tetramethylochroman-2-carboxylic acid) is a synthetic, water-soluble analogue of vitamin E which is used as a reference substance, due to its high antioxidant activity. The advantage of using ABTS• + cation is that it permits the determination of both hydrophilic and lipophilic antioxidants, which are widely used in the cosmetics industry (43).

Hydrogen atom transfer based method

The hydrogen atom transfer (HAT-based) method measures the ability of antioxidants to neutralise free radicals by the reaction of hydrogen atom transfer. The method is often recommended to measure lipophilic antioxidants due to peroxide radicals that are involved in the process of lipid oxidation in cosmetics, food and other biological systems. The method is based on the requirement that the antioxidant and substrate compete for thermally generated peroxyl radicals via decomposition of an azo compound, 2,2-azobis-(2-amidino- propane)-dihydrochloride (AAPH). The relative antioxidant activity is determined by monitoring the kinetics of quenching the free radicals through the bond dissociation energy of the antioxidant which is the hydrogen donor group in the reaction mix (44).

Another method that is based on the HAT mechanism is the oxygen radical absorbance capacity, (ORAC). This method measures the loss of fluorescence intensity or fluorescent decay of a molecular probe through the reaction of thermally generated free hydroperoxyl radicals in the presence (test sample) and absence (blank sample) of antioxidants. The kinetics of this reaction is then compared with that of a reference substance, such as Trolox. In the measurement of the antioxidant activity of cosmetics, fluorescent substances that are often employed include β-phycoerythrin (B-PE), and dichlorofluoroscein diacetate (DCFH-DA)-(DCF). Furthermore, the DCFH-DA assay also allows *in vitro* assessment of antioxidant capacity of cosmetics to be carried out in the living cell cultures (45).

The total peroxyl radical trapping antioxidant parameter (TRAP) assay is also a HAT based assay often applied in cosmetic antioxidant assessment. This method is based on luminol (3- amino phthal hydrazide)-enhanced chemiluminescence (CL) for determining the antioxidant capacity of a substance. Alkyl peroxyl radicals from the decomposition of 2,2' – azobis (2- amidinopropane (AAPH) in the presence of luminol produces luminescence which is quenched by the addition of antioxidants. The TRAP value is determined by the duration of the time period in which the sample quenches the CL signal in the presence of antioxidants. Trolox is also often used as the reference inhibitor. This method is suitable for measuring the antioxidant capacity in both hydrophilic and lipophilic compartments of plasma and tissue homogenates (45). Activity of the antioxidant in the testing sample is determined by comparing the kinetics reaction of the control sample without antioxidants to the sample containing antioxidants. A variant of this method uses Pholasin, a bioluminescence protein, for measuring the relative activity of both water and fats soluble antioxidants. This method has also been found useful in assessing the quality of finished cosmetic products and monitoring different stages of the manufacturing process of cosmetics. The advantages of the fluorescent and chemiluminescent methods include their low threshold of detection of antioxidants whether hydrophilic or hydrophobic, and their ability to determine the content of reactive oxygen species in different biological systems and cosmetic preparations (46).

Electrochemical methods

Voltammetry is a simple, cost-effective electrochemical technique that measures the intensity of current flowing through a test sample inside a cell, depending on the voltage applied to the electrode. This technique measures the redox capacity of antioxidants and does not require reagents nor absorbance characteristics of the antioxidant compounds.

This technique has two variants, the linear sweep voltammetry (LSV) and the cyclic voltammetry (CV), with the latter giving more quantitative information on the redox properties of the substance being tested. The CV method have been adapted for the quantification of the overall reducing capacity of antioxidants in different biological fluids and recently a validation process for measuring global antioxidants in the stratum corneum by cyclic voltammetry have been described. Voltammetry has become one of the fastest, easy to use, and effective methods for measuring the antioxidant activity of cosmetics products (47).

Resonance spectroscopic (ESR)/(EPR) methods

Currently, the increasingly employment of resonance-based techniques for the indirect determination of antioxidant activity of cosmetics enables the assessment of new parameters known as Radical Protection Factor (RPF) and Radical Skin/Status Factor (RSF) (48). These techniques allow for a simple classification of cosmetic products, which are designed for neutralising free radicals. It is also useful to monitor changes in the antioxidant properties over a long period of time, thus making the methods suitable for quality control of cosmetic formulations. The measurement of the RPF defines the scavenging activity of an antioxidant against a tested substance. In this method, nitroxides such as: Proxo (2,2,5,5-tetramethyle-1-dihydropyrrolinoxy-nitroxide), Tempol (2,2,6,6-tetramethyl-1-piperidinoxy-4-ol-nitroxide), DTBN (di-tert-butyl-nitroxide) or preferably DPPH (1,1- diphenyl-2-picryl-hydrazyl) are used as reactive radicals and the RPF measurement is carried out using the electron spin resonance spectroscopy (ESR) or electron paramagnetic resonance (EPR). These magnetic resonance-based techniques allow detection of species with unpaired electrons and thus indirectly assess the antioxidant capacity of the test cosmetics sample. With the RPF technique, the effect of external skin treatments by cosmetic antioxidants and UV filters influence the free radical status of the skin (49). This influence can be quantitatively characterised in terms of the RSF. The RSF describes the relation between the radical status (RS) of the untreated vs treated skin and the measurement is based on ESR spectroscopy. By this method it is possible to characterise the whole radical status as a function of various exogenous and endogenous influences and also to distinguish between a substance acting as a radical protector or promoter. Furthermore, RSF values, measured as a function of time, give information about the penetration behaviour of reactive ingredients (50).

Cell culture–based methods

Cultured cells have become an invaluable model for evaluation of the antioxidant activity of cosmetics ingredients and for control of lipid peroxidation. A large amount of literature concerning the *in vitro* effects of cosmetics antioxidant activity were determined in cell-free systems. However, this approach, it is argued, does not take into cognisance the skin's microenvironment and the cellular mechanisms, and therefore is considered incomplete (56). Thus, to assess the antioxidative capacity of cosmetic compounds in a more physiological microenvironment, evaluations have been performed using *in vitro* cell-based cultures. For instance, human keratinocyte cell lines, HaCaT, and *in vitro* homogeneous fibroblasts and keratinocytes have been suggested to reflect the skin's microenvironment. Studies on the effects of antioxidant on cell viability, proliferation, free radical generation, lipid peroxidation, and intercellular enzymes level measurements have been carried out. For example, the effects of skin moisturisers on total antioxidant capacity of human skin using glutathione peroxidase activity as a marker of antioxidant capacity was undertaken with EpiDerm™ (MatTek Corporation, Ashland, MA, USA) skin model (51). Other studies have also used the HaCaT cell line to assess the antioxidant activity of vitamins C and E in cosmetics using 2′, 7′-dichlorodihydrofluorescein diacetate (H2DCF-dA) as the detector. The presence of free radicals in a cell, especially the superoxide anion, causes the transformation of the detector compound into dichlorofluorescein (DCF), which emits a characteristic fluorescence spectrum with a wavelength maximum at 520 nm. Thus, this method allows the monitoring of specific cellular mechanisms in response to oxidative stress-inducing factors (52).

In vivo and ex vivo methods

Currently, a number of instrumental techniques for the non-invasive and indirect assessment of the antioxidant activity of cosmetics using in vivo models of skin assessment has been employed (53). For instance, in vivo measurement of lipid peroxidation using proton- transfer reaction mass spectrometry (PTR-MS) has been found to be quite a useful model.

This model was also used for in vivo and ex vivo assays to indirectly determine anti- ageing properties of cosmetics formulation with different antioxidant capacities. With this technique, markers of lipid peroxidation such as aldehydes and hydrocarbons in multicomponent mixtures of various volatile organic compounds (VOCs) can be measured (54).

Experimental models exploring ex vivo techniques have been found to be specifically helpful in the evaluation of the inhibition of lipid peroxidation by natural skin antioxidants and cosmetics ingredients. The model which involves the stripping of stratum corneum of the epidermis has also been used in the evaluation of the kinetic and penetration depth of topically applied pharmaceutical preparation and cosmetics products. It has also been applied in the determination of the degree of inhibition of the subcutaneous lipid peroxidation and thus indirectly allows for the assessment of the antioxidant capacity of the topical cosmetics (55).

Electron spin resonance (EPR) technique

Another invaluable and complementary technique for the direct and non-invasive measurement of free radicals is the Electron Spin Resonance (EPR) technique and its modifications, such as the nitroxide-based EPR spectroscopy and imaging (EPRI) of spin labels. These techniques allow for the measurement of the kinetics and mapping of the spatial distribution of free radicals in biological systems (56). The EPRI technique uses resonators like nitroxides as redox indicators and spin labels, which when topically applied, penetrate the skin surface into the dermis and react with skin antioxidants, such as ascorbate, ubiquinone, glutathione, alpha-tocopherol to form stable adducts. The EPR-based techniques allow indirect evaluation of cosmetics antioxidant capacity as well as the monitoring of the complex enzymatic and nonenzymatic redox processes in human tissues and the distribution and metabolism of nitroxides in the body (57).

Considerations for the inclusion of antioxidants in cosmetic formulations

At present, market development of cosmetics products is growing very rapidly worldwide and this might be due to the increasing demands of consumers for safe and effective cosmetics. However, for a relatively good, stable, acceptable cosmetics formulations, the selection of antioxidants and other active ingredients, including excipients, must be optimised. In this regard, a good quality control measure of the cosmetics ingredients must be performed. Accumulated evidence from both animal and clinical studies have demonstrated that topical antioxidants help limit UV-induced skin damage. In humans, the protective effects of ascorbic acid, tocopherol, ferulic acid, and a few other natural antioxidant mixtures including extracts from green tea, which is rich in EGCG, curcumin, pycnogenol, etc., have been well documented. These studies indicated that the efficacy of antioxidants is significantly increased when applied in combination. The combination of ascorbic acid, tocopherol, and ferulic acid, or the combination of ascorbic acid, tocopherol, and green tea extract or EGCG, have been shown to be particularly potent, synergistic, antioxidant combinations. In this regard, regular use of skin care products with such natural antioxidants can efficiently protect skin against exogenous and endogenous oxidative stressors occurring during daily life is strongly advocated.

However, formulating cosmetic products with high antioxidant capacity as well as having an efficiency can be quite challenging as certain considerations must be brought to bear because, generally, antioxidants tend to be inherently unstable. Firstly, the antioxidants should have high antioxidative capacity and be present in appropriate concentrations. Secondly, the antioxidants must be stable in the final formulation. In the case of vitamins E and C, stable ester forms (tocopheryl acetate, sodium ascorbyl phosphate, etc.) are often used as substitutes. Also, these substitutes have lower biological activities, since they need to be hydrolysed with the help of esterases in the skin before eliciting their antioxidant properties. Thirdly, antioxidants need to penetrate through the stratum corneum and maintain adequate concentrations in the epidermis and dermis in order to provide relevant antioxidant efficacy.

References

1. Dreher, F, Thiele, J, and Levin J. Antioxidants. In: Sivamni RK, Jagdeo J, Elsner P, Maibach HI, editors. Cosmeceuticals and Active Cosmetics, (3rd Edition) CRC Press 2015[cited 2022 Apr 2]. Chapter 12. Available from: https://bookshelf.vitalsource.com/reader/books/9781482214178/pageid/10
2. Oresajo, C., Pillai, S., Manco, M., Yatskayer, M. McDaniel, D. Antioxidants and the skin:

Understanding formulation and efficacy. 2012 Aug, [cited 2022 feb 14] 25:252-59.

3. Perez-Sanchez, A., Barrajon-Catalan, E., Herranz-Lopez, M and Micol, V. Nutraceuticals for skin care: Comprehensive review of human clinical studies. Nutrients, 2018; 10: 403
4. Kusumawati, I and Indrayanto, G. (2013). Natural Antioxidants in Cosmetics. Studies in Natural Product Chemistry. 2013 Dec [cited 2022 Jan 18]; 40485-505.
5. Devasagayam,TPA, Tilak JC, Boloor, kk, Sane KS, Ghaskadbi SS, Lele RD. Free radicals and antioxidants in human health: Current status and future prospects. *J. Assoc Physicians India*. 2004; 52:794-804.
6. Chen L, Hu JY, Wang SQ. The role of antioxidants in photoprotection: a critical review. *J Am Acad Dermatol*. 2012; 67:1013-1024.
7. Oroian M, Escriche I. Antioxidants: characterization, natural sources, extraction and analysis. *Food Res Int*. 2015; 74:10-36.
8. Cuelho CHF, Alves GdAD, Lovatto MO, Bonilha, IF, Barbisan, F, da Cruz, IBM et al. Topical formulation containing *Ilex Paraguariensis* extract increases metalloproteinases and myeloperoxidase activities in mice exposed to UVB radiation. *J Photochem Photobiol B*. 2018; 189:95-103.
9. Lee JH. In vitro phototoxicity test using artificial skin with melanocytes. *Photodermatol Photoimmunol Photomed* 2007: **23** (2–3): 73–78.
10. Masaki H. Role of antioxidants in the skin: anti- ageing effects. J Dermatol Sci. 2008; 58: 85–90.
11. Chen, LL and Wang, SQ. From the bottle to the skin: challenges in evaluating antioxidants. *Photodermatol Photoimmunol Photomedicine,* 2012, 28 (5): 228-34.
12. Arct J, Pytkowska K. Flavonoids as components of biologically active cosmeceuticals. *Clin Dermatol*. 2008; 26:347-357.
13. Menaa F, Menaa A. Skin photoprotection by polyphenols in animal models and humans. In: Watson RR, Preedy VR, Zibadi S eds. Polyphenols in Human Health and Disease. Cambridge: Academic Press, Elsevier; 2014:831-838.
14. Saito M, Tanaka M, Misawa, E, Yao R, Nabeshima K, Yamauchi K, Abe F, Yamamoto Y, Furukawa F. Oral administration of *Aloe vera* gel powder prevents UVB-induced decrease in skin elasticity via suppression of overexpression of MMPs in hairless mice, *Biosci. Biotechnol. Biochem.* 2016; 80: 1416–1424, https://doi.org/10.1080/09168451.2016.1156480.
15. Greul, A.K., Grundmann, J.U., Heinrich, J., Pfitzner, I., Bernhardt, J., Ambach, A., Biesalski, H.K., Gollnick, H. (2002). Photoprotection of UV-irridiated human skin: an antioxidative combination of vitamins E and C, carotenoids, selenium and proanthocyanidins. Skin Pharmacology and Physiology, 15 (5): 307-315
16. Moreira LC, de Ávila RI, Veloso D, Pedrosa,TN, Lima, ES, Olivera do Conto, R et al. *In vitro* safety and efficacy evaluations of a complex botanical mixture of *Eugenia dysenterica* DC. (Myrtaceae): prospects for developing a new dermocosmetic product. *Toxicol in vitro*. 2017; 45:397-408.
17. Briganti S, Picardo M. Antioxidant activity, lipid peroxidation and skin diseases. What's new?

J Eur Acad Dermatol Venereol. 2003: **17**: 663–669.

18. Thiele, JJ, Schroeter, C., Hsieh, SN, Podda, M. and Packer, L. The antioxidant network of the stratum corneum. In: J. Thiele, P. Elsner, Editors. Oxidants and antioxidants in cutaneous biology. Current Problems in Dermatology, 2001 ; 29, Basel: Karger, pp 26-42.
19. Heng, MCY. Curcumin in cosmetics: Biochemical basis for skin repair with use of topical curcumin. In: Sivamni RK, Jagdeo J, Elsner P, Maibach HI, editors. Cosmeceuticals and Active Cosmetics, (3rd Edition) CRC Press; 2015 [cited 2022 Apr 2]. Chapter 12. Available from: https://bookshelf.vitalsource.com/reader/books/9781482214178/pageid/9
20. Khaiat, A. and Saliou C. Botanical extracts. In: Sivamni RK, Jagdeo J, Elsner P, Maibach HI, editors. Cosmeceuticals and Active Cosmetics, (3rd Edition) CRC Press 2015 [cited 2022 Apr 2]. Chapter 12. Available from: https://bookshelf.vitalsource.com/reader/books/9781482214178/pageid/9
21. Sta BF, Wolber R, Blatt T, Keyhani R, Sauermann G. Topically applied antioxidants in skin protection. Methods Enzymol 2000; 319: 465–478.
22. Leopoldini M, Russo N, Toscano M. The molecular basis of working mechanism of natural polyphenolic antioxidants. *Food Chem*. 2011 Jan [cited 2022 feb 17]125 (2):288-306.
23. Al-Niaimi, F. and Yi Zhen Chiang, N. Topical vitamin C and the skin: Mechanism of action and clinical applications. The Journal of Clinical and Aesthetic Dermatology, 2017 July: 10(7):14-17
24. Telang, P.S. Vitamin C in dermatology. Indian Dermatology Online Journal. 2013, 4(2): 143-146.
25. Abid Keen, M and Hassan I. Vitamin E in dermatology. Indian Dermatology Online Journal. 2016 7(4): 311-315
26. Casas, C. Vitamins In: Amparo Salvador and Alberto Chisvert, editors. Analysis of Cosmetics Products Cosmetics, Elsevier, 2007, pp 364-379. [Cited 2022 May 14].
27. Gopinath, H and Karthikeyan K. Tumeric: A condiment, cosmetic and cure. Indian Journal Of Dermatology, Venereology and Leprology. 2018 Mar [cited 2022 mar16]; 84:16-21.
28. Ganeti, M. D, Mercurio, D. G. Maia Campus, P.M.B.G. The use of green tea extract in cosmetic formulations: not only an antioxidant active ingredient. Dermatol. Ther. 2013 26(3): 267-71.
29. Marchena, A.M., Franco, L., Romero, A.M., Barriga, C.Rodriguez, A.B. Lycopene and melatonin: Antioxidants compounds in cosmetic formulations. Skin Pharmacology and Physiology, 2020: 33: 237-243.
30. Herman, A. and Herman, A.P. Caffeine's mechanism of action and its cosmetic use. Skin Pharmacology and Physiology. 2013; 26(1): 8-18.
31. Ratz-Lyko, Aand Arct, J. Resveratrol as an active ingredient for cosmetic dermatological applications: A review. Journal of Cosmet Laser Ther. 2019: 21(2): 84-90.
32. Tao, K., Guo, L., Hu, X., Fitzgerald, C., Rouzard, K., Healy, J., Tamura, M., Stock, J., B., Stock, M., Perez, E. and Fernandez, J. R. Encapsulated activated grape seed extract: A novel formulation with anti- ageing, skin-brightening, and hydrarion properties.Cosmetics, 2022, 9,4.
33. Aslam, M. N., Lansky, E., P., and Varani, J.Pomegranate as a cosmeceutical source:

pomegranate fractions promote proliferarion and procollagen synthesis and inhibit matrix metalloproteinase-1 production in human skin cells. Journal of Ethnopharmacology, 2006, 20 103(3): 311-318.

34. Marini, A., Grether-Beck, S.Jaenicke, T., Weber,M, Burki, C., Foremann, P., Brenden, H., Schonlau,F., Krutmann, J. (2012). Pycnogenol(r) effects on skin elasticity and hydration coincide with increased gene expressions of collagen type1 and hyaluronic acid synthase in women. Skin Pharmacology and Physiology, 2012 July [cited 2022 Apr 10]; 25:86-92
35. De Lima Cherubim, DJ, Farina, LO, Silva De Lucca, RA. Polyphenols as natural antioxidants in cosmetics applications. J. Cosmet Dermatol. 2019:00;1-5 doi:10.1111/jocd.13093
36. Saliou, C, Rimbach, G., Moini, H. , McLaughlin, L., Hosseini, S., Lee, J., Watson, R., Parker, L. (2001). Solar ultraviolet-induced erythema in human skin and nuclear factor-kappa-B- (NF-Kβ)-dependent gene expression in keratinocytes are modulated by a French maritime pine bark extract. Free Radical Biologyand Medicine, 30 (2): 154-160.
37. Bose B, Choudhury H, Tandon P, Kumaria S. Studies on secondary metabolite profiling, anti-inflammatory potential, *in vitro* photoprotective and skin- ageing related enzyme inhibitory activities of *Malaxis acuminata*, a threatened orchid of nutraceutical importance. *J Photochem Photobiol B*. 2017; 173:686-695.
38. Syed, D.N., Malik, A., Hadi, N., et al . Photochemopreventive effect of pomegranate fruit extract on UVA-mediated activation of cellular pathways in normal human epidermal keratinocytes. Photochem Photobiology, 2006, 82 (2): 398-405.
39. Irrera, N., Pazzino, G.,D'Anna, R., Vaccaro, M., Arcoraci, V., Squadrillto, F., Altavilla, D and Bitto, A. Dietary management of skin health: Role of genistein. Nutrients, 2017, 9(6):622
40. Haneke, E., and Baran, R. Micronutients for hair and nails. In: Krutmann, J. and Humbert, P. (eds). Nutrition for healthy skin. Springer-Verlag, Berlin Hiedelberg, 2011. pp 149-163.
41. Ratz-Lyko, A Arct, J. and Pytkowska K. Methods for evaluation of cosmetic antioxidant capacity. Skin Research Technology. 2012 Oct [cited 2022 Apr 6]; 18(4):421-30.
42. Compos, P.M., Goncalves, G.M. and Gasper, L.R. *In vitro* antioxidant and *in vivo* efficacy of topical formulations containing vitamin C and its derivatives studied by non-invasive methods. Skin Res. Technol., 2008, 14(3): 376-80.
43. Munteanu, G.I and Apetrei, C. Analytical methods used in determining antioxidant activity: A review. International Journal of Molecular Sciences, 2021, 22: 3380.
44. Molyneux P. The use of the stable free radical diphenylpicrylhydrazyl (DPPH) for estimating antioxidant. J. Sci. Technol 2004; 26: 212–219.
45. Cao G, Alessio HM, Culter RG. Oxygen radical absorbance capacity assay for antioxidant free radicals. Free Radic Biol Med 1993: **14**: 303–311.
46. Niki E. Assessment of antioxidant capacity *in vitro* and *in vivo*. Free Rad Biol Med 2010; 49: 503–515
47. Korotkova, E.I., Karbainov, Y.A and Shevchuk, A.V.. Study of antioxidant properties by voltammetry. Journal of Electroanalytical Chemistry, 2002, 518:56-60.
48. Khabiri F, Hagens R, Smuda C. Non-invasive monitoring of oxidative skin stress by ultraweak

photon emission (UPE)-measurement. I: mechanisms of UPE of biological materials. Skin Res Technol 2008: **14**: 103–111.

49. Ziosi P, Besco E, Vertuani S, Solaroli N, Manfredini S. A non-invasive method for the *in vivo* determination of the skin antioxidant capacity (IAC-S). Skin Res Technol 2006: **12**: 303–308.
50. Guitton C, Gros P, Comtat M. Evaluation of antioxidant properties of dermocosmetic creams by direct electrochemical measurements. J Cosmet Sci 2005; 56: 79–90.
51. Gelo-Pujic M, Desmurs JR, Kassem T, Delaire S, Adao A, Tawil D. Synthesis of new antioxidant conjugates and their *in vitro* hydrolysis with *stratum corneum* enzymes. Int J Cosmet Sci 2008: **30** (3): 195–204.
52. Weber SU, Thiele JJ, Cross CE, Packer L. Vitamin C, uric acid and glutathione gradients in murine *stratum corneum* and their susceptibility to ozone exposure. J Invest Dermatol 1999: 113: 1128–1132.
53. Fonseca-Santos B, Antonio CM, Chorilli M. Sustainability, natural and organic cosmetics: consumer, products, efficacy, toxicological and regulatory considerations. *Braz J Pharm Sci*. 2015; 51:17-26.
54. Zhai H, Choi MJ, Arens-Corell M, Neudecker BA, Maibach HI. A rapid, accurate and facile method to quantify the antioxidative capacity of topical formulations. Skin Res Technol 2003; 9: 254–256.
55. Menaa F, Menaa A. Skin photoprotection by polyphenols in animal models and humans. In: Watson RR, Preedy VR, Zibadi S (eds). Polyphenols in Human Health and Disease. Cambridge: Academic Press, Elsevier; 2014:831-838.
56. Franen M, Rode T, Steinhart H. Determination of green tea catechins in cosmetic formulations and *in vitro* skin extracts by HPLC with electrospray ionization mass spectrometry. Chromat 2002; 55: 43–48.
57. Regoli, F., Winston, G.W. Quantification of total oxidant scavenging capacity of antioxidants for peroxynitrate, peroxyl radicals and hydroxyl radicals. Toxicol. Appl. Pharmacol., 1999, 156: 96-105.

CHAPTER THIRTEEN

Natural products in cosmetics

Awodayo O. Adepiti

Natural products are naturally occurring substances obtained from plant, animal and mineral sources. These substances include whole plant or animals, tissues/organs, resins, secretions and extracts. In recent times, the marine environment has been included as a large reservoir of natural products of cosmetic, economic, and therapeutic benefits. Natural products could also be defined as organic compounds with molecular weight range of 100-2000 (1).

In cosmetics use, as with other aspects of life, there is a growing shift from the use of synthetics to natural substances. Synthetic products such as the parabens, phthalates and silicones are avoided due to dermal toxicity and carcinogenicity, among other untoward effects (2). Some perceived advantages of natural cosmetics include: safety of use - many people believe these products are not toxic or harmful to the body (3); they have relatively less side-effects compared to the synthetic ones; there is the belief that natural cosmetics are compatible with all skin types; it is believed that, although natural cosmetics may still be relatively new in the beauty industry, they already offer a variety of beauty products for all, apart from the fact that they are affordable (2).

Although naturally-sourced cosmetic ingredients can be of plant, animal or marine origin, they are further classified on the basis of products for which they are employed as: cosmetics for enhancing the appearance of skin and for skin protection; cosmetics for hair growth and care; and cosmetics for topical use such as shampoos, soaps, powders and perfumery (4).

In this chapter, further classification and specific examples of each category will be highlighted.

Plant-based cosmetics

Plants constitute a major source of natural cosmetic products. Plant extracts can be obtained from all morphological parts of the plants including the leaf, stem bark, fruit,

Table 13.1: Plant sources of some cosmetic agents with their mode of action

S/No	Name of plant	Common name	Local name	Morphological part used	Mechanism of cosmetic action	Citation
1.	*Aloe vera* L. /A. barbadensis Mill (Liliaceae)	Aloe	Eti erin oyinbo/Ahon erin (Yoruba), Ebube-Agu (Igbo) and Zabuwa (Hausa)	Mucilage of leaf	Anti-inflammatory properties, wound-soothing effect	(22,23)
2.	*Camellia sinesis* L. (Theaceae)	Green tea, Black tea	Tii (Yor)	Leaf	Protects skin from UV irradiation-induced photo-aging	(27, 28)
3.	*Citrus sinensis* L. Rutaceae	Orange	Osan (Yor)	Leaf	Phenolic compounds and Vitamin C have anti-photoaging activity	(7)
4.	*Curcuma longa* L. (Zingiberaceae)	Turmeric	Ata ile pupa, Laali-pupa (Yor)	Rhizome	Reduces skin wrinkling	(32)
5.	*Glycine max* L. (Fabaceae)	Soybean	Soya	Seed	Anthocyanin modulates UV B-Induced photoaging	(7)
6.	*Allium sativum* (Liliaceae)	Garlic	Aayu (Yor)	Bulb	Anti-dandruff	(7)
7.	*Panax ginseng* L. (Araliaceae)	Ginseng		Rhizome	Ginsenosides possess anti-aging activities	(19,33)
8.	*Theobroma cacao* L. (Sterculiaceae)	Cocoa	Koko (Yor)	Seed	Polyphenol and xanthine derivatives –antiaging	(34)
9.	*Zingiber officinale* L. (Zingiberaceae)	Ginger	Ata Ile; Laali funfun (Yor)	Rhizome	Inhibits wrinkle formation	
10.	*Curcubita pepo*		Elegede (Yor)	Root; seed	Anti-acne; anti-aging	
11.	*Azadirachta indica*	Neem	Dongoyaro (Yor), Dongo yaro (Hausa)	Leaf	Anti-acne	
12.	*Ocimum gratissimum*	Scent leaf	Efirin (Yor), Nchianwu (Ibo)	Leaf	Anti-acne	(14,24,35)
13.	*Lawsonia inermis* (Lythraceae)	Henna	Laali (Yor)	Fruit	Hair colourant, hair growth stimulant, anti-dandruff	(15,36)
14.	*Cucumis sativa* L. (Cucurbitaceae)	Cucumber		Fruit	Treatment of hyperpigmentation	(7,37)
15.	*Allium cepa* (Liliaceae)	Onion	Alubosa (Yor)	Bulb	Hair colourant	(7)

flower, seed and the root. Furthermore, juices, exudates, secretions from plants are all potential sources of ingredients for cosmetic products. In addition, plant-based cosmetics may comprise single chemical compounds belonging to any of these classes of natural products: coumarins, terpenoids, alkaloids, flavonoids, tannins, non-protein amino acids and glycosides, which can also be referred to as botanical extracts. Plant extracts, though may be from the same plant, are obtained from various processing methods that produce tinctures, juices, waxes, fixed oils, lipids, plant carbohydrates, essential oils, as well as purified plant components, such as vitamins, antioxidants, and other substances with recognised biological activity (3). Table 13.1 lists plant sources of some cosmetic agents while the pictures of some of the plants are shown in Plate 13.1.

Plate 13.1: Some plants used in cosmetic products

A – *Azadirachta indica* leaf; B – *Aloe vera* leaf; C. *Lawsonia inermis* leaf and flower bud; D. *Ocimum gratissimum* leaf; E. *Curcubita pepo* aerial part (Habitat – Medicinal Garden, Faculty of Pharmacy, OAU [A, B, C]; Private Garden, Ede road, Ile-Ife, Nigeria [D, E)

Cosmetics for enhancing the appearance of skin and for skin protection

The skin is a protective barrier that helps to regulate fluid balance and temperature, keeps off dangerous microorganisms and chemicals as well as protects from sunlight. It comprises the epidermis, dermis and subcutaneous layers. The epidermis, consisting of the outermost layer, the stratum corneum, comes in direct contact with the environment. The human skin manifests conditions ranging from simple dryness, scaling to severe erythema. Emollient natural products usually contain mucilage, made up of polysaccharides, complex sugars and derivatives of starch that relieve dryness and provide a soothing membrane. Plants that confer firmness and tone the skin are rich in tannins and are valuable for their astringent effect. The presence of high levels of flavonoids makes some plants beneficial as anti-inflammatory agents while those for skin healing possess antimicrobial constituents (5).

Natural product cosmetics for different skin conditions

Care of dry skin: A dry skin can arise as a result of water loss from the epidermis due to a compromise of the outer epidermal layer arising from a medical condition, harsh weather or use of harsh soaps. The protection afforded by skin hydration and the softening of the skin and hair can be achieved by the use of herbal moisturisers which usually contain fixed oils. Fixed oils are esters of fatty acids and triglycerides that are capable of reducing trans-epidermal water loss. The chemical structures of some constituents of fixed oils are shown in Figure 13.1. The following are some fixed oils that are components of herbal products for the care of dry skin.

Coconut oil: This is the oil expressed from the fresh or the dried solid portion (copra) of the endosperm of *Cocos nucifera* L. (Palmae). Coconut oil is a liquid at warm temperatures but becomes semisolid at relatively low temperatures. It consists of majorly the triglycerides of lauric and myristic acids with minor quantities of palmitic, caproic, stearic, and oleic acids (6). It is excellent as an emollient, skin moisturiser and softener (7).

Olive oil: The expressed oil from the ripe fruits of the evergreen tree, *Olea europoea* L. (Oleaceae), is a pale-yellow liquid, with a slight odour and a bland taste. The tree is usually found in Italy, Spain, France and Greece. The major constituents of the oil are oleic, linoleic, palmitic and stearic acids. These constituents vary with different varieties of the tree and show climatic differences (6). Other constituents of olive oil include tocopherols, squalene, polyphenols and carotenoids. Usually, olive oil is successively expressed from the fruits and the oil obtained from the first extraction is called virgin oil or extra virgin oil depending on the method of extraction, while those of subsequent extractions are of lower quality and are referred to as pomace oil. In addition to its use as a moisturiser for dry skin, olive oil is employed as an ingredient of lip balm, shampoo, body soap, massage oil, hair conditioner and for dandruff treatment, often in combination with coconut oil. Furthermore, olive oil exhibits anti-inflammatory effect, exerted by the unsaponifiable and polar compounds it contains while its antioxidant effect is due to the presence of polyphenols (5).

Sunflower oil: The oil is extracted from the seed of *Helianthus annuus* L. (Asteraceae). Sunflower oil contains lecithin, tocopherols, carotenoids and waxes. It has smoothening properties as it increases the linoleic acid levels of the skin, lowers trans-epidermal water loss and eliminates scaly lesions (7).

Cocoa butter or theobroma oil: This is the fixed oil obtained by hot expression of the roasted beans (seeds) of *Theobroma cacao* L. (Sterculiaceae). It contains triglycerides of stearic, arachidic, palmitic and oleic acids (8). It is widely used as an emollient and is known as a natural antioxidant source.

Castor oil: Castor oil is obtained from the seed of *Ricinus communis* L. (Euphorbiaceae), a tree that is indigenous to India. Commercial production of the oil takes place in Brazil, Thailand and India. The seed contains about 50% of fixed oil comprising ricinoleic, isoricinoleic and stearic acids (8).

***Jojoba oil*:** It is a mixture of esters extracted from the seed of *Simmondsia chinensis* (Link) Schneider (Simmondsiaceae). Jojoba oil is often used in cosmetics as a moisturiser and as a carrier oil for exotic fragrances. Jojoba oil replenishes the moisture of the skin and hair and restores them to their natural pH balance.

Amino acids: In addition to fixed oils, amino acids are constituents of the natural moisturising factor (NMF), which are responsible for skin hydration control. Amino acids, such as alanine and serine, play important physiological roles for the generation and integration of skin function.

Cosmetic care for eczema or atopic dermatitis: Eczema is a chronic inflammatory skin condition with symptoms such as swelling, redness, itching and scaling. Ethnomedicinally, natural products used in the management of eczema in Asia include curcumin (9), the yellow polyphenolic compound obtained from the powdered rhizome of *Curcuma longa* L. (Zingiberaceae). In Southwest Nigeria, *C. longa* is known as *Laali pupa* or *Ata ile pupa.*

Plant products for skin protection: The exposure of the skin to stress agents generate reactive oxygen species (ROS) (10). Although ROS are constantly generated in skin cells, they are usually neutralised by a network of non-enzymatic (for example, glutathione and ascorbic acid) and enzymatic antioxidants. Some plants with free radical scavenging activities include:

Green tea: Green tea is the tea obtained from the dried leaf of *Camellia sinensis* (L) O. Kuntze (Theaceae). Four different types of tea are produced from *C. sinensis* depending on the method of preparation.

- **White tea**: this is made from the youngest buds of the plant.
- **Green tea**: the leaf is dried immediately after harvesting in order to prevent oxidation of the catechins/polyphenols (fermentation).
- **Oolong tea** is obtained from semi-fermented tea leaves before drying.
- **Black tea** is the completely fermented leaf. The green and black teas have ROS scavenging properties, though the green tea exhibits the higher effect.

In the green tea, four major polyphenolic catechins are present in the leaves and these are gallocatechin, 2-epicatechin, (2)-epicatechin-3-gallate, and epigallo-catechin-3-gallate, which is the most abundant (about 65%).

Calendula oil: The oil is obtained from the flowers (marigold flowers) of *Calendula officinalis* L. (Asteraceae) and is reported to have remarkable antioxidant, anti-inflammatory, wound-healing, and anti-acne activities. The essential oil of Calendula consists mainly of α-thujene, α-pinene, 1,8-Cineole and T-muurolol and is used mainly in the treatment of foot infections and the elimination of pests, such as lice and bed bugs from the body.

Red wine: The polyphenolic proanthocyanidins of the seed of *Vitis vinifera* L. (Vitaceae) are also strong antioxidants comparable to Vitamins C and E. The mechanism usually is by inhibition of lipid peroxidation (11).

Plant products used for acne: Acne is a skin condition that affects the sweat glands and hair follicles, causing inflammation and pustules that result in black and white head spots on the skin. The following plants have been assessed for their potential usefulness in the treatment of acne.

Ocimum oil: the essential oil is extracted from *Ocimum gratissimum* L. (Lamiaceae) leaf and has been shown to be an effective antibacterial agent for the treatment of acne (12). Furthermore, a synergistic effect was observed in the anti-acne activity of the oil when combined with aloe vera gel. This activity was highest with aloe vera gel at 50% and the combination was more effective than clindamycin (1%) in the treatment of acne (13).

Pea: The seed of *Pisum sativum* L. (Leguminosae) has been used to treat acne in the form of face masks.

Pumpkin: The root and seed oils of *Cucurbita pepo,* (Curcubitaceae) commonly known as pumpkin, are used for acne (pimples, blackheads) and some venereal sores (Table 13.1).

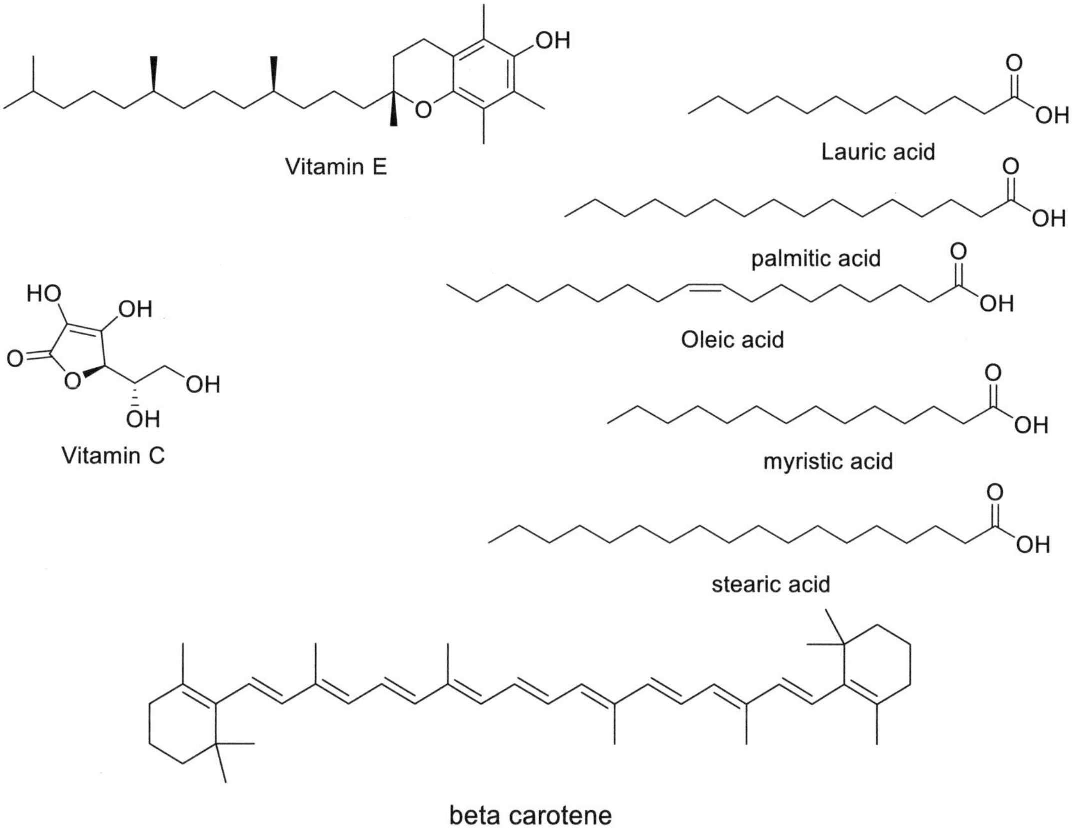

Figure 13.1: Chemical structures of some constituents of fixed oils

Others: *Azadirachta indica* A. Juss, *Rosmarinus officinalis* L., *Eucalyptus globulus* Labill. and *Citrus aurantium* L. are plants reported for activity against acne (14).

Plant Products used in dandruff treatment: Dandruff is a skin condition characterised by flaking and scaling of the scalp. It is also associated with a decrease in free lipid level, large reduction in ceramides, cholesterol and fatty acids. *Salvia officinalis* L (sage) oil has long been in use for dandruff, *Allium sativum* L. (garlic), *Thymus vulgaris* L. (thyme), *Juglans regia* L. (walnut) leaves are employed in the management of dandruff. Also, the leaves of *Azadirachta indica*, (Meliaceae), commonly called neem, is employed as a treatment for dandruff. Neem leaves possesses antifungal, antibacterial, pain-relieving, and anti-dandruff compounds. In addition, *Lawsonia inermis* L. (Lythraceae) leaves, commonly called henna and containing a naphthoquinone derivative, lawsone, is ethnomedicinally useful for the treatment for hair and scalp problems including dandruff (15).

Plant products used as anti-ageing cosmetics: Ageing is characterised by thinning and wrinkling of the epidermis, the appearance of lines, crevices and creases and furrows, which become more prominent on varying facial expressions. There are changes in the underlying dermis, characterised by loss of collagen and elastin fibres. There are two types of ageing: one which is due to the passage of time, called chronological ageing, and the other which is due to environmental factors, called premature or photo-ageing. Chronological ageing is characterised by loss of firmness and fine wrinkles, while photo ageing is characterised by coarse wrinkles, irregular dryness, hyperpigmentation, inelasticity, roughness, pre-malignant lesions, and a leathery appearance (16).

Herbal cosmetics play a major role in slowing down, reversing, alleviating and preventing the process of ageing and help people to live longer and healthier lives. Many anti- ageing natural products are antioxidants that scavenge free radicals and eliminate by-products of metabolism. They are available as flavonoids, carotenoids and polyphenols, especially in the diet. There are antioxidants that are topically applied which are quickly absorbed by the superficial layers of the skin and are usually hypo-allergenic in nature (17). Herbal products that can prevent or reduce the signs of ageing skin include products that offer photoprotection, decreased transepidermal water loss (TEWL), increased skin elasticity, increased collagen formation, decreased facial pigmentation, or offer antioxidant effects on the skin (18) The following plants are documented to have anti- ageing effects.

***Panax ginseng* C.A. Meyer (Araliaceae)**: This is commonly known as Korean or Chinese or Asian ginseng root. It hydrates and softens the skin as well as alleviates the wrinkling of the skin (7). The major effects are due to enhanced skin nutrition, increase in blood circulation and cell proliferation leading to increased metabolism that results in an 'anti-ageing' effect. Also some studies indicate that the anti-ageing activity may be due to the action of radical-scavenging effect and the inhibition of lipo-peroxidation by some of the chemical constituents such as ginsenosides and lignans (19–21).

Aloe vera gel: Another product that is relevant in anti- ageing cosmetics is aloe vera gel. This is one of the most widely used natural product for the treatment of skin conditions of different varieties. The gel is obtained from *Aloe vera* L., also known as *A. barbadensis* (Liliaceae). In Nigeria, *A. vera* is locally known as *Eti erin oyinbo/Ahon erin* (Yoruba), *Ebube-Agu* (Igbo) and *Zabuwa* (Hausa). Aloe gel is a colourless and mucilaginous gel obtained from the parenchymatous cells of the leaf and it comprises proteins, water and polysaccharides such as glucomannans and pectic substances (8). Aloe gel should not be confused with aloe juice, which is an exudate of the pericyclic tubules found beneath the epidermis of the leaves and comprises purgative anthraquinones(8). Aloe gel can be useful as an emollient for burns, sunburn, and has anti-inflammatory properties. It is also employed for its wound-soothing and cooling properties due to its high water and mineral contents. The activity has been ascribed to the presence of polysaccharides which stimulate connective tissue cells to produce more collagen, which, therefore, remodels and fills in the wound area (22,23). An example of a commercial herbal anti- ageing product is an anti-wrinkle serum that is made up of aloe vera leaf gel (85%) and many other ingredients of herbal origin.

***Camellia sinesis* L. (Theaceae)**: Commonly known as black or green tea, it contains many chemical constituents including flavonoids, tannins, caffeine and polysaccharides. Black tea which is produced from fermented tea leaves, has more than 90 % of its vitamin C destroyed during the fermentation process while green tea, produced by immediately steaming and drying the leaf after harvesting, retains most of its vitamin C, having 100 mg in 100 g tea leaf; which is similar to that found in lemon (*Citrus limon*). Although black tea possesses a lower quantity of polyphenols, it is still considered a good antioxidant that prevents premature ageing as earlier discussed.

***Daucus carota* L. (Apiaceae):** This is commonly known as carrot and it is rich in vitamin A along with other essential vitamins. The characteristic, bright orange colour of the carrot is due to β-carotene, a 40-carbon chain terpenoid, and lesser amounts of α-carotene and γ-carotene. The α- and β-carotenes are partly metabolised into vitamin A in humans. Carrot seed oil is used as an anti- ageing, revitalising and rejuvenating agent (24,25).

***Avena sativa* L. (Graminae)**: It is commonly known as oats. Apart from its food property, it is also used in the cosmetic industry. However, oat fractions are more beneficial than the entire oats. These natural products protect and repair the skin and hair from UV irradiation, smoke, and free radicals. They also repair damages from bleaching agents and surfactants. Cosmetic oat fractions include oatmeal, oat flower, oat oil, bran, oat β-glucan and hydrolysed oat protein (7).

Plant products used in hair growth and care

Humans have about 100,000 hair strands on their heads. Each hair shaft has three layers with the cuticle, the outer layer, protecting the two inner layers of the cortex and medulla. In healthy hair, the layers of the cuticle lie flat, overlap tightly and reflect light. The inner layers are then well protected from heat, sun, chlorine and other environmental stressors. When the hair is damaged, the cuticles can be separated and hair may be dry. As the cuticles no longer protect the two inner layers, the hair becomes brittle, can break, and looks dull. Humans have direct control on their hair in terms of its length, colour and style. Problems with the hair include oily hair, dandruff and hair loss (alopecia) while hair care involves caring for hair quality and scalp care.

Hair cosmetics can be categorised into two, as those that work on the exocuticle (shampoos, conditioners, hair sprays, waxes, gels and mousses) and those that work on the cortex such as hair colour, bleaching agents, straightening and perming agents (26,27). Herbal hair growth stimulants are used in the prevention of alopecia by stimulation of the hair follicle. Plants such as *L. inermis* (henna), *A. cepa* (onion), *Eclipta alba* and *Tridax procumbens* (tridax), *Vitis vinifera* L. (grape), *Panax ginseng* L. (ginseng), *Curcubita pepo* (cucumber) and aloe vera gel have been reported to promote hair growth by various mechanisms. In addition, in pre-clinical tests, the essential oil of *Ocimum gratissimum* leaf was reported to possess hair growth-enhancing ability. It was also observed to stimulate hair growth in cancer therapy-induced hair loss (28,29).

An example of herbal shampoos is Everclean herbal shampoo® comprising allantoin, aloe vera whole leaf gel, henna extract, rosemary extract (*Rosmarinus officinalis*), among other ingredients.

Plant products used as colourants

Examples of some plant-derived dyes are shown in Table 13.2. these are used singly, but more often in combination with other colourant for various cosmetic products.

Mineral-based cosmetics

Minerals are used as active ingredients and also as excipients in some cosmetic products such as sunscreens, powders, creams, and emulsions, as well as in deodorants (38).

Aluminium silicate hydroxide: In Nigeria, some minerals are used for skin care. An example is the *Calabash chalk,* known as Calabar stone, which is made up of aluminium silicate hydroxide from kaolin clay group. It is made up of fossilised seashells, mixed with clay mud and other ingredients such as sand, wood ash and sometimes salt. It is usually sold as powder, blocks and pellets. The calabash chalk is ground into a fine powder and applied to the face as facial powder and as an antiperspirant which makes the face to remain dry.

Black antimony: Another mineral cosmetic is black antimony, known locally as "*Tiro, Otanjele* and *Buje*", which reportedly contains up to 81% lead. It is ground into fine crystalline powder and poured into a metallic cone-shaped container from where, with the aid of thin stick, it is used as an eye-liner (39).

Clay minerals: The most commonly used clays are kaolinite, smectites and talc (38). They can be found in cosmetics such as powders and creams where they provide opacity, remove shine, and cover skin imperfections. These minerals produce a film by sticking to the skin and protecting it against external, physical or chemical agents (40). By absorbing the skin's secretions, they also exhibit a refreshing action, together with a gentle antiseptic action.

Sea water minerals: These are also known to have beneficial properties (20). Sea water notably contains minerals such as sodium, calcium, magnesium, potassium, sulphates, and chlorides which are of benefit to the skin. Invariably, sea salts are notably used in cosmetics for skin care (41). The health benefits are claimed to be related to the type of minerals contained in the sea water and to the quality of the deep-sea water sources (42).

Table 13.2: plant-derived dyes

S/N	Name of dye/ colour	Plant source
1.	Annnatto extract; yellow to orange	Seed of *Bixa Orellana* L. (Bixaceae)
2.	Dehydrated beet (beet powder); red	Taproot of *Beta vulgaris* L. (Amaranthaceae)
3.	[beta]-Carotene; yellow to orange	Root of *Daucus carota* (Hoffm) Schubl. (Apiaceae) (carrot)
4.	Grape colour extract; red in acid solution, blue in alkaline solution	Fruit of *Vitis labrusca* L. hybrid (Vitaceae)
5.	Turmeric; bright yellow to deep orange Turmeric oleoresin; deep brownish-orange	Rhizome of *Curcuma longa* L. (Zingiberaceae)
6.	Tomato lycopene extract; tomato lycopene concentrate; bright red to brown or dark brick red	Berry of Solanum lycopersicum (Solanaceae)
8.	Saffron; yellow or orange	Stigma of flower of *Crocus sativus* L. (Iridaceae)
9.	Riboflavin; yellow to orange-yellow	Vitamin B_2
10.	Paprika, bright red Paprika oleoresin; bright red, orange hues	Dried fruit of *Capsicum annum* L. (Solanaceae)
11	Indigo; blue	Leaf of *Indigofera tinctorial* L. (*Fabaceae)*
12	Alizarin; red	Root of *Rubia Tinctorum* L. (Rubiaceae) (madder plant)

Sea mud: It contains nutrients and minerals and is useful in skin care formulations particularly for its activities on psoriasis and other skin-related disorders. Sea mud has anti-acne activity, equilibrates skin pH, and exhibits anti- ageing properties (42).

However, sea water and sea mud may contain naturally-occurring toxic elements or those derived from pollution and must, therefore, be subjected to strict control analysis. Metals such as nickel and chromium naturally occur in the Dead Sea mud at low levels. Therefore, users have to be informed of the presence of these metals by the proper labelling of the products (43).

Mica-based/potassium aluminium silicate-based pearlescent pigments: These are pigments that are prepared by depositing iron salts or/and titanium dioxide on mica or potassium aluminium silicate. These offer soft shimmering, glitter or bright sparkling effects due to the reflection of light on the platelets that make up the pigments, whose particle size determines the intensity of lustre that is obtained. Some of these pigments, being iridescent, portray luminous colours that change depending on the angle from which they are viewed. Makeup products such as lipstick, nail polish, lip gloss, blush, highlight and bronzer are coloured with pearlescent pigments.

Iron oxide pigments: Iron oxide pigments are about the most used colourants, as they are relatively cheap and are stable under ambient conditions especially to the effect of sunlight. Depending on the source, they occur as red, yellow, brown and black pigments. They are used as colourants in cosmetic products such as lip products, eyeliners, blushes, face powders and eyeshadows.

Titanium oxide and carbon black: Titanium dioxide, a white pigment, and carbon black are mixed with other colourants to achieve a desired colour shade.

Animal-based cosmetics

Animal-based cosmetics are derived from terrestrial animals. Although animal-derived products are used with caution and are avoided in some instances, the products from the bee are generally well-accepted. Honey, propolis, bee pollen, bee bread, royal jelly, beeswax and bee venom are naturally produced by the bee, *Apis mellifera*, and they are used for cosmetic purposes. The chemical composition of bee products are subject to geographical location, botanical composition of the plants from which nectar is obtained by the bee, and time/period of collection (44).

Honey

Honey contains about 180 ingredients (45). It is a supersaturated carbohydrate solution containing mainly sugar (glucose and fructose) and water deposited by *A. mellifera* and other species of *Apis* in the cells of the honeycomb. In addition, honey can have little amount of dextrin, sucrose, formic acid, volatile oil, enzymes, vitamins, minerals, wax and pollen grains (8). Honey exhibits moisturising and emollient properties and is used in cosmetic products at concentrations at about 10 %. Higher concentrations (up to 70%) are obtained by dispersing it in oils, gels or polymer entrapment. Moreover, derivatives of honey such as hydrogenated honey and hydroxypropyltrimonium honey are used in shampoos and hair conditioners(46).

Propolis

Propoliis is also called bee glue, is a chemically diverse product derived from activities of bees in the building of the hives, with at least 300 active compounds identified as resin, wax, essential oils, pollen grains and organic acids. The organic acids comprise of phenolic acids (e.g ferulic, chlorogenic, p-coumaric acid, cinnamic acid) and flavonoids (chrysin, luteolin, kaempherol, quercetin etc.) (46). Propolis also contains minerals (calcium, magnesium, manganese, zinc, copper, iron, cobalt and selenium), vitamins (B1, B2, B6, C and E) and enzymes. Propolis, is used as the aqueous or ethanol extract. The ethanol extracts of propolis are most frequently used and are available as propolis and propolis extract (44,45). Propolis is an anti-acne agent and has regenerative and skin repair effects and also protects the skin against environmental factors. In addition, an aqueous extract of propolis is used in antifungal products, while propolis dissolved in fats is used to produce lipsticks.

Bee pollen

This is used in the form of aqueous, lyophilised and lipid extracts. Bee pollen extracts are used in cosmetics at concentrations of 0.5–5% w/v (47). In natural cosmetics, dried grains of micronised bee pollen are also used.

Beeswax

Beeswax is prepared by the purification of honeycombs after the removal of honey. Yellow beeswax (*Cera flava*) or white beeswax (*Cera alba*) is used in the production of cosmetics (44) as emulsifiers, stiffening agents in lipsticks and viscosity-imparting agents in creams. Beeswax is a humectant and does not clog pores. It also serves as an emollient that soothes the skin.

Royal jelly

This comprises water (50-60 %), proteins (18%), peptides (jelleines I, II, III, IV), proteins, carbohydrates (15%), lipids, vitamins and minerals (44,45). The proteins are rich in exogenous amino acids while the carbohydrates are mainly monosaccharides such as fructose and glucose, and oligosaccharides. The main lipid component of this product, used as a marker, is 10-hydroxy-trans-2-decenoic acid. Royal jelly is most frequently found in cosmetics in a lyophilised form and creams with royal jelly (0.5 and 1%) have moisturising properties (44).

Bee venom or apitoxin

This is the yellow, light powder obtained by collecting a large amount of bee venom by electric stunning using a bee venom collector without harming the honey bee. It includes a complex mixture of peptides, enzymes, lipids, and bioactive amines (48). Bee venom possesses anti- ageing, anti-acne, anti-inflammatory and antimicrobial effects (44,48). It is also used in the treatment of psoriasis.

Lanolin (wool fat)

Lanolin is the purified fat-like substance that is obtained from the wool of sheep (*Ovis aries* L.). It is used as an emollient in products such as moisturising body creams and lotions, hair conditioners and pomades, lip gloss and balm. Anhydrous lanolin has more capacity for added water. Lanolin is a skin sensitiser to which some persons are allergic.

Glycerine

Glycerine is obtained by heating tallow (fat from beef or mutton) or pork with water. It is an emollient commonly used in many cosmetic products.

Gelatine

This is obtained by acid or base hydrolysis of the skin, tendons and bones of cows or pigs. It serves as a gelling or viscosity-imparting agent in many cosmetic products and may also be used as a moisturiser.

Collagen

Collagen is a fibrous protein that is mostly found in the ligaments, skin, bones and tissues of animals but is mostly obtained for commercial purposes from beef or fish. It is employed in cosmetic products for its ability to improve skin's elasticity and to reduce fine lines and wrinkles.

Carmine

Carmine, the aluminium salt of carminic acid, is a bright-red pigment that is obtained as the aluminium salt of carminic acid, a red colouring principle, extracted from the scaly insect, *Coccus cacti* (cochineal). Carmine is a commonly used colourants in cosmetic products such as lipstick, nail vanish, blush and eye shadow to which it imparts red, orange or pink colour.

Shellac

The tiny scales of the lac insect, *Kerria lacca*, produces an amber-coloured resin that is shinny and thermoplastic in nature, which effects lend their usefulness in hair lacquers and nail vanishes.

Restrictions on some animal-based cosmetic ingredients

There are some restrictions on some animal-based cosmetics due to religious considerations. By Islamic law, there are permissible as well as prohibited ingredients and these are referred to as halal and haram cosmetic products, respectively. Halal products must not contain substances obtained from blood, human body parts, reptiles, pig, predatory animals, insects and some others. Even the permissible animals must be sacrificed according to the Islamic law. Thus, products bearing the halal logo should be taken as being prepared with all cleanliness and purity in line with the religious law. However, some prohibited animals and products thereof cannot be used by Islamic adherents; these are called haram cosmetic ingredients(49). For more information, check chapter 1 of this book.

Musk, a perfume that was obtained from the pod found under the abdominal skin of the male musk deer, the civet and other animal-derived fragrances, have been prohibited due to the cruel manner the fragrances are obtained and are now replaced by similar synthetic versions.

Marine-derived cosmetics

The oceans, which cover about 70% of the earth's surface, serve as enormous resources that provide abundant bioactive substances in the form of food, cosmeceuticals, and pharmaceutical products. Marine organisms possess the capacity to produce molecules with unique chemical and structural features, and they represent an underexploited source of highly diverse valuable natural products.

Marine cosmetics, also known as phycocosmetics, comprise products with ingredients obtained from the oceans and seas with activities such as antioxidant, sunscreen, hydrating, emollient and functional characteristics such as colour, texture and emulsifying properties (50). The sources of marine cosmetic ingredients include microalgae and macroalgae; fish (a source of gelatine and collagen); corals and crustaceans (can provide diguanosine tetraphosphate, chitin and chitosan); as well as sea muds and sea salts. Macroalgae are also called seaweeds and can be separated into the following groups: brown algae (*Phaeophyta*), red algae (*Rhodophyta*), green algae (*Chlorophyta*), and blue-green algae (*Cyanophyta*) (51).

Moisturisers and anti-ageing agents

Moisturisers have beneficial effects in treating dry skin. Orange roughy (*Hoplostethus atlanticus*) fish oil, a marine-derived wax ester, performed comparably to a petrolatum-based moisturiser in clinical trials in subjects with moderate to severe skin dryness (52). Mycosporines and mycosporine-like amino acids (MAAs), which are accumulated by a wide range of microorganisms, prokaryotic (cyanobacteria), as well as eukaryotic (microalgae) organisms are useful as anti- ageing products. Several pure algal compounds have shown this activity, for example, sargaquinoic acid and sargachromenol from *Sargassum sagamianum* dieckol from *Ecklonia cava* or fucoxanthin from *S. siliquastrum* (50) (Table 13.2). Peptides, such as matricines, have potentials for stimulating collagen synthesis. *Alaria esculenta*, a brown alga, and are therefore, helpful in the management of wrinkles.

Depigmenting or skin lightening agents

Skin lightening, also known as skin bleaching, is a common global practice. It aims to lighten dark areas of the skin by reducing the melanin level in the skin. Although melanin protects the human skin, its accumulation can cause hyperpigmentation, with undesirable effects. Most of the skin-lightening products are formulated based on tyrosine inhibitors. Tyrosinase, a polyphenol oxidase, is the rate-limiting enzyme in the production of melanin. Marine-sourced inhibitors include the fucoxanthin extract of *Laminaria japonica* (53), kojic acid from selected strains of marine fungi (54), phlorotannins, from marine brown algae, eckol, and dieckol from *Ecklonia cava* (Table 13.2). Furthermore, zeaxanthin (from Nannochloropsis oculata) and asthaxanthin, both carotenoids, are also of particular interest. In addition, *Pistacia lentiscus*, a traditional medicinal halophyte plant of the Mediterranean area, is reported for its anti-hyperpigmentation property (43).

UV-protecting agents

Ultraviolet (UV) radiation is one of the major stress factors for most phototrophic organisms found in land and sea ecosystems. Natural products of marine origin that are worthy of mention are the mycosporine-like amino acids (MAAs) such as usujirene and shinorine. Some red algae are also exploited because of their high MAA content. Palythine, shinorine, usujirene, and others are found in numerous marine organisms. Certain red algae (*Porphyra umbilicalisi)* are relevant on commercial scale because of their high MAA content (54). These photoprotective compounds are incorporated into sunscreen cosmetics and they will be further discussed under that section.

Antioxidant agents

The antioxidant activities of marine substances have been extensively studied. They prevent the oxidation induced by the reactive oxygen species. Marine antioxidants include carotenoids, MAAs and mycosporines (55). Algae are one of the most documented sources of marine antioxidants and it has been noted that extracts from brown algae are more effective than extracts from red and green algae with reference to their antioxidant activities. This may be due to the phlorotannin content (Table 13.2).

Marine fish-derived products

Gelatine and collagen are proteins that could be obtained from marine fish and these are more acceptable, in terms of halal, than those from terrestrial animals.

Gelatine: Gelatine is a mixture of reversible gel-forming proteins; it had cosmetic relevance based on its gel-forming and viscoelastic properties, but more recently, it has been used as a moisturiser in cosmetic creams for dry skin (53).

Collagen: This is a main structural protein in connective tissues of the skin and bone. Marine-derived collagen has an ability to scavenge free radicals, and thus, can be utilised for skin care products. Collagen from these marine sponges: *Ircina fusca* and *Chondrosia reniformis*, sea urchins, the marine crab, *Scylla serrata,* is a safer alternative to those of terrestrial origin (56).

Squalene: Shark fish liver oil, squalene, with its high omega-3-fatty acid content, is found in moisturisers, deodorants, shampoos, lip balms, lipsticks, tanning oils, perfumes, anti-ageing products, eye makeups and foundations. It easily goes rancid; however, subjecting squalene to hydrogenation gives squalane which does not undergo autooxidation. There is the advocacy for the replacement of shark squalene with plant-derived squalene in order to preserve shark populations in the oceans.

Guanine: This is a crystalline substance obtained by crushing fish scales, giving a shiny and shimmery effects that makes it a preferred ingredient for lipsticks, mascaras, bronzers, eyeshadows, nail vanishes and highlighters.

Marine fish peptides: These have afforded the development of many categories of cosmetics such as anti- ageing, skin care and anti-wrinkle products. Despite this great potential, there is the limitation as most of them need further investigation (57).

Chitosan and chitin products: Chitosan is a natural polysaccharide, an N-deacetylated derivative of chitin, one of the most abundant polysaccharides in nature. Chitins are synthesised by sea animals, and microorganisms such as green algae (56). They are useful in oral health care, as moisturisers, anti- ageing and antioxidant cosmetic products (58)

Other marine sources of cosmetic ingredients: The following are other marine sources of ingredients used as cosmetics

Seaweed: This is useful in skincare products to balance natural moisture levels. Seaweed has a high content of mineral salts, amino acids and the water-soluble vitamins B and C as well as the lipid-soluble vitamins A, D, E and K.

Coral: Coral powders have been used in numerous cosmetic products, to scrub and to supply trace minerals to the skin.

Jelly fish: The mucus from jellyfish is vital for some anti- ageing beauty cosmetics products.

Hydra: Hydra gel comprises antioxidants and proteins used in the preparation of lipsticks and some other products related to lips.

Phytoplankton: Extracts from the phytoplankton consist of lipids and omega-3 fatty acids and they are mainly used as de-pigmentation, anti-wrinkling and anti- ageing agents.

Sea fennel: Sea fennel comprises the antioxidant and anti- ageing components which are vitamins A, C and E (59).

Carrageenans: These are relevant in oral health care as well as for their moisturising effects.

Seaweeds as sources of cosmetic pigments

Algae are also sources of pigments which are called phycobiliproteins. These are water-soluble fluorescent proteins that are commonly present in *Cyanobacteria* (blue-green algae) and *Rhodophyta* (red algae). The phycobiliproteins include phycoerythrin, phycocyanin and phycoerythroanthocyanin. Phycocyanin, is a blue molecule known for its antioxidant and anti-free radical properties while phycoerythrin is the most valued for its intense pink colour in the cosmetic industry (53,56,60). In addition, carotenoids, which are C_{40} tetraterpenoids compounds, distributed in both plant and marine sources, comprise carotenes and xanthophylls as yellow/orange lipo-soluble pigments. Carotene pigment is the main carotenoid produced by the halotolerant microalga *Dunaliella salina.*

Fucoxanthin, identified as the predominant carotenoid found in the chloroplast of the brown algae, has tyrosinase inhibitory, anti-inflammatory, anti- ageing and moisturising effects (Table 13.2). Some species of brown algae used in cosmetics are *Isochrysis spp., Postelsiapa maeformis, Laminaria digilata*. It is noted that many micro- and macro-algae produce carotenoids which also aid in the absorption of light from the sun (61).

Table 13.2: Seaweeds with cosmetic properties of interest

S/No	Component	Seaweed	Cosmetic action/Property	Citation
1.	Fucoidans	*Ascophyllum nodosum, Chnoospora minima, Ecklonia maxima, Hizikia fusiforme, Saccharina japonica, Sargassum* spp.	Inhibits photo-aging, Promotes skin-whitening, antioxidant, anti-inflammatory	(60)
2.	Ulvan	*Ulva pertusa, Ulva* sp.	Anti-aging	(56,60),
3.	Carrageenan	Red seaweeds, *Porphyra haitanensis, Gracilaria chouae, G. blodgettii*	Antioxidant, antitumor, antiaging, protection against radiation	(62,63)
4.	Mycosporine-like amino acids extract	*Phorphyra umbilicalis*	Anti-aging	(60)
		Curdieara covitzae, Iridaea cordata	Antioxidant, UV-protective effect, anti-aging	(64)
		Rhodymenia pseudopalmata	Antioxidant	(65)
5.	Phycobiliproteins (phycoerythrin allophycocyanin and phycocyanin)	*Gracilaria gracilis*	Antioxidant	(60)
6.	Eckol	*Eisenia bicyclis, Ecklonia stolonifera*	Anti-inflammatory, anti-tyrosinase	(60)
7.	Fucoxanthin	*Sargassum siliquastrum*	Skin protective (antiphotodamage, anti-pigmentary, antiphotoaging, anti-wrinkling,	(66)
		Myagropsis myagroides	Anti-inflammatory	(67)
		Laponaria japonica	Antityrosinase	(60)
		Sargassum fusiforme	Antioxidant	

Cosmetics from mushrooms

Mushrooms are fungal members of the Thallophyta division of the plant kingdom. They lack chlorophyll and are not differentiated into leaf, stem and root. Mushrooms, also called superfoods, are an important part of the human diet as rich sources of proteins, vitamins, minerals, but low sources of sugars and fat. They also possess flavonoids, alkaloids and terpenoidal compounds (68). Several types of mushroom extracts and bioactive compounds are incorporated into topical creams, lotions, ointments, serum, and facial preparations as cosmetic ingredients for their moisturising, free radical scavenging, anti-inflammatory, anti- ageing, and anti-hyperpigmentation effects(69).

Nutricosmetics or nutraceuticals

These are the newest trend in skin care and this involves the consumption of dietary and nutritional supplements to produce a visual benefit and improve the health of the skin. These products usually include the following ingredients: carotenoids, polyphenols, several vitamins, mushroom extracts (e.g., polyphenolic isoflavones), micronutrients, glycopolyglycans, amino acids, other mushroom-based elements, and polyunsaturated fatty acids(69).

Moisturisers: Significant moisturising effects have been observed with a polysaccharide from *Tremella* as well as water extracts of *Auricularia fuscosuccinea* (Montagne) Farlow. The mushroom powder of *Fomes officinalis* (also known as *Laricifomes officinalis*) also showed the potential application of mushrooms as effective moisturising agents in cosmetics.

Skin bleaching agents: Many mushrooms such as *Agaricus bisporus, A. hortensis, Ganoderma* spp., and *Phellinus baumii* have anti-tyrosinase effect, thereby proving useful against hyperpigmentation.

Anti-wrinkle/anti-ageing agents: the extracts of the mycelium of *Tricholoma matsutake* (pine mushroom) and the fruiting body of *Dictyophora indusiata* (veiled lady mushroom) are anti-wrinkle skin agents. In addition, *Lentinula edodes* has several applications in cosmetics, ranging from an exfoliant to an anti-inflammatory, encourages faster skin renewal, and increases skin elasticity as a skin brightener (68,70).

References

1. Heinrich M, Barnes J, Gibbons S, Williamson EM. A text book of Fundamentals of Pharmacognosy and Phytotherapy. Elsevier USA. 2004;18:60–105.
2. Kumar D, Rajora G, Parkash O, Antil M, Kumar V. Herbal cosmetics: An overview. Int J Adv Sci Res. 2016;1(4):36–41.
3. Antignac E, Nohynek GJ, Re T, Clouzeau J, Toutain H. Safety of botanical ingredients in personal care products/cosmetics. Vol. 49, Food and Chemical Toxicology. 2011. p. 324–41.
4. TIWARI M, DUBEY V, LAHIRI A. COMPARATIVE STUDY OF VARIOUS HERBAL COSMETICS: A SURVEY. Asian J Pharm Clin Res. 2020;31–4.
5. Aburjai T, Natsheh FM. Plants Used in Cosmetics. Vol. 17, Phytotherapy Research. 2003. p. 987–1000.
6. Evans WC. Trease and Evans' Pharmacognosy: Sixteenth Edition. Trease and Evans' Pharmacognosy: Sixteenth Edition. 2009. 1–603 p.
7. Aburjai, Talal, Natsheh, Feda M. Plants Used in Cosmetics. Phytother Res. 2003;17(9):987–1000.
8. Evans WC. Trease and Evans' pharmacognosy. Elsevier Health Sciences; 2009.
9. Gupta SC, Kismali G, Aggarwal BB. Curcumin, a component of turmeric: From farm to pharmacy. Vol. 39, BioFactors. 2013. p. 2–13.
10. Woodby B, Penta K, Pecorelli A, Lila MA, Valacchi G. Skin health from the inside out. Annu Rev Food Sci Technol. 2020;11:235–54.
11. Bijauliya RK, Alok S, Kumar M, Chanchal DK, Yadav S. A comprehensive review on herbal cosmetics. Int J Pharm Sci Res. 2017;8(12):4930–49.
12. Orafidiya LO, Agbani EO, Oyedele AO, Babalola OO, Onayemi O. Preliminary clinical tests on topical preparations of Ocimum gratissimum linn leaf essential oil for the treatment of acne vulgaris. Clin Drug Investig. 2002;22(5):313–9.

13. Orafidiya LO, Agbani EO, Oyedele AO, Babalola OO, Onayemi O, Aiyedun FF. The effect of aloe vera gel on the anti-acne properties of the essential oil of Ocimum gratissimum Linn leaf – a preliminary clinical investigation. Int J Aromather. 2004 Jan 1;14(1):15–21.
14. Reddy DM, Jain V. An overview on medicinal plants for the treatment of acne. J Crit Rev. 2019;6(6):7–14.
15. Badoni Semwal R, Semwal DK, Combrinck S, Cartwright-Jones C, Viljoen A. Lawsonia inermis L. (henna): Ethnobotanical, phytochemical and pharmacological aspects. J Ethnopharmacol. 2014 Aug 8;155(1):80–103.
16. Ferreira MS, Magalhães MC, Oliveira R, Sousa-Lobo JM, Almeida IF. Trends in the use of botanicals in anti- ageing cosmetics. Molecules. 2021;26(12).
17. Patidar DK. Unmet Need and Challenges of Skin ageing by Herbal Anti- ageing Cosmeceuticals: An Overview. Asian J Pharm AJP Free Full Text Artic Asian J Pharm [Internet]. 2018 Aug 18 [cited 2022 Apr 9];12(02). Available from: https://asiapharmaceutics.info/index.php/ajp/article/view/2368
18. Mukherjee PK, Maity N, Nema NK, Sarkar BK. Bioactive compounds from natural resources against skin ageing. Phytomedicine. 2011;19(1):64–73.
19. Oliveira Zanuso B, Dos Santos AR de O, Miola VFB, Campos LMG, Spilla CSG, Barbalho SM. Panax ginseng and ageing related disorders: A systematic review. Exp Gerontol. 2022;111731.
20. Ma'Or Z, Yehuda S, Voss W. Skin smoothing effects of Dead Sea minerals: comparative profilometric evaluation of skin surface. Int J Cosmet Sci. 1997;19(3):105–10.
21. Choi W, Kim HS, Park SH, Kim D, Hong YD, Kim JH, et al. Syringaresinol derived from Panax ginseng berry attenuates oxidative stress-induced skin ageing via autophagy. J Ginseng Res. 2021;
22. Sharma P, Kharkwal AC, Kharkwal H, Abdin MZ, Varma A. A review on pharmacological properties of Aloe vera. Int J Pharm Sci Rev Res. 2014;29(2):31–7.
23. Saleem A, Naureen I, Naeem M, Murad HS, Maqsood S, Tasleem G. Aloe Vera Gel Effect on Skin and Pharmacological Properties. Sch Int J Anat Physiol. 2022 Jan 7;5(1):1–8.
24. Gediya SK, Mistry RB, Patel UK, Blessy M, Jain HN. Herbal plants: used as a cosmetics. J Nat Prod Plant Resour. 2011;1(1):24–32.
25. Dwivedi AK, Jhade D. Cosmetic potential of selected medicinal plants: A. J Pharmacogn Phytochem. 2021;10(4):381–6.
26. Okole B, Pillai SK, Ndzotoyi P, Phasha V. Use of herbal extract-based nanoemulsions for hair care application. In: Nanotechnology for the Preparation of Cosmetics Using Plant-Based Extracts. Elsevier; 2022. p. 203–33.
27. Kotnala A, Verma K, Sharma A, Parashar S, Rathi B, Kumar R, et al. Indian Medicinal Plants for skin care and cosmeceuticals: A review. J Integr Sci Technol. 2019;7(2):35–70.
28. Orafidiya LO, Agbani EO, Abereoje OA, Awe T, Abudu A, Fakoya FA. An investigation into the wound-healing properties of essential oil of Ocimum gratissimum linn. J Wound Care. 2003;12(9):331–4.
29. Orafidiya LO, Agbani EO, Adelusola KA, Iwalewa EO, Adebanji OA, Adediran EAF, et al. A study on the effect of the leaf essential oil of Ocimum gratissimum Linn. on cyclophosphamide-induced hair loss. Int J Aromather. 2004;14(3):119–28.

30. Noviani V, Thauresia S, Apriani EF, Simanjuntak P. Hair Growth Promoting Activity of Green Tea Leaves (Camellia sinensis l.) Ethanolic Extract. Maj Obat Tradis. 24(2):104–9.
31. Koch W, Zagórska J, Marzec Z, Kukula-Koch W. Applications of tea (Camellia sinensis) and its active constituents in cosmetics. Molecules. 2019;24(23):4277.
32. Zheng Y, Pan C, Zhang Z, Luo W, Liang X, Shi Y, et al. Anti ageing effect of Curcuma longa L. essential oil on ultraviolet-irradiated skin. Microchem J. 2020 May 1;154:104608.
33. Peng X, Hao M, Zhao Y, Cai Y, Chen X, Chen H, et al. Red ginseng has stronger anti- ageing effects compared to ginseng possibly due to its regulation of oxidative stress and the gut microbiota. Phytomedicine. 2021;93:153772.
34. Journal of Applied Pharmaceutical Science [Internet]. [cited 2022 Apr 11]. Available from: https://japsonline.com/abstract.php?article_id=3005
35. Joshi LS, Pawar HA. Herbal cosmetics and cosmeceuticals: An overview. Nat Prod Chem Res. 2015;3(2):170.
36. Himangshu Kalita, Jyochhana Priya Mohanty, Gopal Pokhrel. Formulation and Evaluation of Natural Herbal Hair Dye Gel Using Lawsonia inermis (Henna Leaves) and Skin Irritation Studies in Albino Rats. J Pharm Pharmacol [Internet]. 2022 Jan 28 [cited 2022 Apr 11];10(1). Available from: http://www.davidpublisher.com/index.php/Home/Article/index?id=46833.html
37. Dwivedi AK, Jhade D. Cosmetic potential of selected medicinal plants: A review. :7.
38. Carretero MI, Pozo M. Clay and non-clay minerals in the pharmaceutical and cosmetic industries Part II. Active ingredients. Appl Clay Sci. 2010;47(3–4):171–81.
39. Popoola OE, Bisi-Johnson MA, Abiodun A, Ibeh OS. Heavy metal content and antimicrobial activities of some naturally occurring facial cosmetics in Nigeria. Ife J Sci. 2013;15(3):637–44.
40. Carretero MI. Clay minerals and their beneficial effects upon human health. A review. Appl Clay Sci. 2002;21(3–4):155–63.
41. Blanco-Dávila F. Beauty and the body: the origins of cosmetics. Plast Reconstr Surg. 2000;105(3):1196–204.
42. Kim SK. Marine cosmeceuticals. J Cosmet Dermatol. 2014;13(1):56–67.
43. Guillerme JB, Couteau C, Coiffard L. Applications for Marine Resources in Cosmetics. Cosmetics. 2017 Sep;4(3):35.
44. Kurek-Górecka A, Górecki M, Rzepecka-Stojko A, Balwierz R, Stojko J. Bee Products in Dermatology and Skin Care. Molecules. 2020 Jan;25(3):556.
45. Viuda-Martos M, Ruiz-Navajas Y, Fernández-López J, Pérez-Álvarez J a. Functional Properties of Honey, Propolis, and Royal Jelly. J Food Sci. 2008;73(9):R117–24.
46. Burlando B, Cornara L. Honey in dermatology and skin care: a review. J Cosmet Dermatol. 2013;12(4):306–13.
47. Basista K, Sodzawiczny K. Bee pollen—A new natural material, possibilities of use in medicine and cosmetology. Gaz Farm. 2011;12:30–2.
48. El-Wahed AAA, Khalifa SAM, Elashal MH, Musharraf SG, Saeed A, Khatib A, et al. Cosmetic Applications of Bee Venom. Toxins. 2021 Nov;13(11):810.
49. Sugibayashi K, Yusuf E, Todo H, Dahlizar S, Sakdiset P, Arce Jr F, et al. Halal cosmetics: A review on ingredients, production, and testing methods. Cosmetics. 2019;6(3):37.

50. Balboa EM, Conde E, Soto ML, Pérez-Armada L, Domínguez H. Cosmetics from marine sources. In: Springer Handbook of Marine Biotechnology. 2015. p. 1015–42.
51. MacArtain P, Gill CI, Brooks M, Campbell R, Rowland IR. Nutritional value of edible seaweeds. Nutr Rev. 2007;65(12):535–43.
52. Domoto N, Koriyama T, Chu BS, Tsuji T. Evaluation of the efficacy of orange roughy (Hoplostetbus atlanticus) oil in subjects with dry skin. Int J Cosmet Sci. 2012;34(4):322–7.
53. Couteau C, Coiffard L. Seaweed application in cosmetics. In: Seaweed in health and disease prevention. Elsevier; 2016. p. 423–41.
54. Li X, Li Y, Jeong JH, Lee KT, Choi HD, Son BW. Screening of tyrosinase inhibiting activity from the marine-derived fungus. Korean J Pharmacogn. 2003;34(2):138–41.
55. Wada N, Sakamoto T, Matsugo S. Mycosporine-like amino acids and their derivatives as natural antioxidants. Antioxidants. 2015;4(3):603–46.
56. Balboa EM, Conde E, Soto ML, Pérez-Armada L, Domínguez H. Cosmetics from marine sources. In: Springer handbook of marine biotechnology. Springer; 2015. p. 1015–42.
57. Venkatesan J, Anil S, Kim SK, Shim MS. Marine fish proteins and peptides for cosmeceuticals: A review. Mar Drugs. 2017;15(5):143.
58. Aranaz I, Acosta N, Civera C, Elorza B, Mingo J, Castro C, et al. Cosmetics and cosmeceutical applications of chitin, chitosan and their derivatives. Polymers. 2018;10(2):213.
59. Uppala L. A Review on Active Ingredients from Marine Sources used in Cosmetics. SOJ Pharm Pharm Sci. 2015;2(3):01–3.
60. López-Hortas L, Flórez-Fernández N, Torres MD, Ferreira-Anta T, Casas MP, Balboa EM, et al. Applying seaweed compounds in cosmetics, cosmeceuticals and nutricosmetics. Mar Drugs. 2021;19(10):552.
61. Miyagawa K, Yamamotoyoichi CI. Production of phycocyanin-containing blue pigment from blue-green alga and cosmetic containing said pigment. JP Pat. 1989;123865:16.
62. Quantification of 3,6-anhydro-galactose in red seaweed polysaccharides and their potential skin-whitening activity | SpringerLink [Internet]. [cited 2022 Apr 20]. Available from: https://link.springer.com/article/10.1007/s13205-020-02175-8
63. Algal polysaccharides: potential bioactive substances for cosmeceutical applications: Critical Reviews in Biotechnology: Vol 39, No 1 [Internet]. [cited 2022 Apr 20]. Available from: https://www.tandfonline.com/doi/full/10.1080/07388551.2018.1503995
64. Rangel KC, Villela LZ, Pereira K de C, Colepicolo P, Debonsi HM, Gaspar LR. Assessment of the photoprotective potential and toxicity of Antarctic red macroalgae extracts from Curdiea racovitzae and Iridaea cordata for cosmetic use. Algal Res. 2020 Sep 1;50:101984.
65. Pliego-Cortés H, Bedoux G, Boulho R, Taupin L, Freile-Pelegrín Y, Bourgougnon N, et al. Stress tolerance and photoadaptation to solar radiation in Rhodymenia pseudopalmata (Rhodophyta) through mycosporine-like amino acids, phenolic compounds, and pigments in an Integrated Multi-Trophic Aquaculture system. Algal Res. 2019 Aug 1;41:101542.
66. Heo SJ, Ko SC, Cha SH, Kang DH, Park HS, Choi YU, et al. Effect of phlorotannins isolated from Ecklonia cava on melanogenesis and their protective effect against photo-oxidative stress induced by UV-B radiation. Toxicol In Vitro. 2009 Sep 1;23(6):1123–30.

67. Heo SJ, Yoon WJ, Kim KN, Ahn GN, Kang SM, Kang DH, et al. Evaluation of anti-inflammatory effect of fucoxanthin isolated from brown algae in lipopolysaccharide-stimulated RAW 264.7 macrophages. Food Chem Toxicol. 2010 Aug 1;48(8):2045–51.
68. Wu Y, Choi MH, Li J, Yang H, Shin HJ. Mushroom cosmetics: the present and future. Cosmetics. 2016;3(3):22.
69. Taofiq O, González-Paramás AM, Martins A, Barreiro MF, Ferreira IC. Mushrooms extracts and compounds in cosmetics, cosmeceuticals and nutricosmetics—A review. Ind Crops Prod. 2016;90:38–48.
70. Rahman T, Choudhury MBK. Shiitake mushroom: a tool of medicine. Bangladesh J Med Biochem. 2012;5(1):24–32.

CHAPTER FOURTEEN

Nutraceuticals for skin care

Olumayowa A Oninla

Nutraceuticals are foods or part of a food that provide both health benefits by reducing or preventing diseases and supplying basic nutritional needs. Examples are natural foods containing antioxidants, vitamins, and minerals, dietary supplements, milk and fortified dairy products, herbals and cereals. They remain to be fully defined and legally recognised as separate entity (1). Prakash (2) defines nutraceuticals as bioactive compounds that are extracted from their original food matrix. Food provides nutrients (fats, proteins, carbohydrates, vitamins, carotenoids, flavonoids, minerals and non-nutrients (fibre, antioxidants, glucosinolates, prebiotics, and probiotics and beneficial enzyme inducers). Among the nutraceuticals, the most widely used ingredients are bioactive peptides, oligosaccharides, plant polyphenols, carotenoids, vitamins, and polyunsaturated fatty acids. Topical preparations and supplements containing these products have been used in many human trials to ameliorate the signs of ageing and protect against photo- ageing from UV radiation (2).

The skin provides protection for the body against microorganisms, chemicals and ultraviolet (UV) radiation which may result in photo-ageing, skin inflammation and immune dysfunction following exposures to them (3). Supplementations with nutraceuticals have been found to prevent or minimise these effects as well as provide treatment for some skin disorders (3). Nutraceuticals are well known to strengthen physiological skin defences by their antioxidant properties providing protection from UV radiation involved in photo- ageing, improvement in skin appearance by collagen stimulation and improvement in skin pigmentation (4,5). An *in vivo* study of red orange extract supplements (100 mg/daily) in humans using reflectance spectrophotometry following ingestion for 15 days by Purglia *et al.* (4), showed a significant reduction in the degree of solar lamp UV-induced erythema. Also, in skin age spots pigmentation, the melanin content decreased from 27% to 7% following UV-radiation after administration of the supplements.

Nutraceuticals used as cosmetics (cosmeceuticals)

The use of cosmetics has moved from the traditional topical application to enhance beauty into the biomedical revolution stage. It presently involves employing biologically active products to enhance the structure and function of healthy skin (6).

Vitamins

These are low-molecular-weight organic compounds required in trace amounts for essential metabolic reactions that are indispensable for life activity and their deficiencies cause specific disease symptoms.

Retinoids: Retinoids (Vitamin A and its derivatives) are common ingredients in topical anti ageing products. They are lipophilic in nature hence diffuse through cellular membranes to specific nuclear receptors to modulate expression of the genes regulating cellular proliferation and differentiation. There are two types: naturally occurring and synthetic retinoids (7). The synthetic retinoids are the prescription types (tretinoin, isotretinoin, alitretinoin, tazarotene and adapalene) and they are not used in cosmetics. The natural types (retinol, retinyl-palmitate, retinyl-acetate and retinaldehyde) are common ingredients in cosmetics. Retinoids are naturally found in the skin (7), retinol and retinyl esters being the most abundant types. Retinyl esters are the storage form of vitamin A and mostly concentrated in the epidermis (8). Retinol is produced in the small intestine by hydrolysis of retinyl esters or by oxidation of carotenoids (9). It is then oxidised first to retinaldehyde then to the active form tretinoin (9).

Carotenoids constitute a class of plant chemicals called phytonutrients that occur in a wide variety of plants, algae and bacteria whose main function is the absorption of light energy for photosynthesis. There are three types of carotenoids, namely: carotene, β-carotene, and β-cryptoxanthin, which are provitamin A and can be converted into retinol while some such as lycopene, lutein, and zeaxanthin are known as non-provitamin A carotenoids (10).

Retinoids also have ultraviolet (UV) absorption, antimicrobial, antioxidant, and pigment reduction properties (7). Retinyl esters concentrate in the epidermis, and with retinol strongly absorb UV radiation between 300 and 350 nm up to a maximum of 325 nm (UVB radiations) (8). A study of topical retinyl palmitate in human subjects, showed that it has the same efficiency as a sunscreen with sun protection factor 20 in preventing sunburn erythema and inhibits thymine dimer formation in human skin (8). Thymine dimer is a primary marker of DNA damage in skin cells and represents a risk factor for skin cancers (8).

In a study carried out by Pechere *et al.* (11) to analyse the potential anti-infective activities of topical retinoic acid (RA), retinol (ROL) and retinaldehyde (RAL), the only retinoid that was found to possess antibacterial activity was retinaldehyde. A 0.05% retinaldehyde topically applied for two weeks to the forehead and forearm had a positive correlation with decrease in bacterial counts (11). The activity was found against Gram-positive bacteria such as *Staphylococcus aureus*, *Micrococcus* species and *Propionibacterium acnes*. There was no activity against Gram-negative bacteria. The pigment reduction properties of topically applied retinoids diminish melanin production in the skin. Retinoids reduce the activity of stimulated melanocytes, block transport of melanosomes to surrounding keratinocytes, control distribution of melanin in the epidermis, increase the synthesis and activity of tyrosinase inhibiting melanogenesis (12).

Common side effects of retinoids when used as a cream are limited to the skin and they are mostly skin redness, peeling, and sun sensitivity. Retinaldehyde and retinol considerably cause fewer irritant reactions such as burning, scaling or dermatitis that are usually associated with tretinoin and tazarotene (13). People with sensitive skin should avoid using any cream or lotion with strong drying effect, astringents, alcohol, spices, lime, sulphur, resorcinol and aspirin with the topical form of retinoids to prevent interactions or exacerbation of side effects (14).

Nicotinamide: Nicotinamide (Vitamin B3) is a precursor of nicotinamide adenine dinucleotide phosphate (NADP), a cofactor that has antioxidant properties and mostly acts in oxidative processes to reduce free radicals (6). Topical application increases skin lipids and epidermal protein (15). This smoothens out the unevenness of skin texture, reduces wrinkling, and skin ageing. Clinical trials revealed smoothening of skin surface and marked improvement in skin wrinkling following 4-5% niacinamide topically applied on wrinkles for 8 weeks (16, 17). Vitamin B3 prevents dyspigmentation through inhibition of melanosome transfer to keratinocytes (18). In ageing facial skin, topical niacinamide has been found to reduce wrinkling, skin yellowing, red blotchiness, improve skin texture (makes skin smooth, soft, and supple) and hyperpigmented spots (19). Niacinamide improves skin elasticity in ageing skin (17).

Vitamins C and E: Vitamin C (L-ascorbic acid) has been reported to have anti-inflammatory and antioxidant properties and to stimulate collagen biosynthesis (6). Topical 3% vitamin C reduced erythema, facial wrinkles, and at 5-17% ascorbic acid improved skin texture and effects of photo ageing (6, 20). Fruits and vegetables are the best food sources particularly guavas, citrus fruits, pawpaw, pineapples, mangoes, peppers, tomatoes, blackcurrants, strawberries, broccoli and potatoes.

A high concentration of the non-esterified, optical isomer of the antioxidants, vitamins C and E, respectively, inhibited the acute UV damage of erythema, sunburn, and tanning as well as chronic UV photo ageing and skin cancer. Both vitamins are highly effective depigmenting agents. Topical vitamin C also increases collagen synthesis in both young and old fibroblasts. As vitamin C regenerates oxidised vitamin E, the combination in a cosmeceutical formulation is synergistic, particularly in UV protection (21).

Vitamin E is synthesised by plants and available from dietary sources. Nuts, whole grains, spinach, broccoli, olive oil, almond, almond oil and sunflower oil are among the richest sources (22). Eight types of the vitamin are known and these are α- tocopherol, β-tocopherol, γ- tocopherol, and σ-tocopherol and their corresponding tocotrienols. While γ-tocopherol is the most abundant in diet, α-tocopherol is the most abundant in human skin and sera (22). It exhibits antioxidant action by inhibiting lipid peroxidation in unsaturated fatty acids mainly by reacting with the peroxyl radical (HOH•) and singlet oxygen ($^1O_2$), thereby preventing damages to cell membranes and intracellular organelles (23). Alpha-tocopherol is the main type responsible for removing peroxyl radicals from the membranes (23). This effect of vitamin E on melanocyte membranes as well as its effects on inhibiting tyrosinase activity and increasing intracellular glutathione content results in depigmentation (22).

The antioxidant protection of the skin by a-tocopherol for effective skin care measures is obtained at a concentration that varies from 0.1% to 1% in topical formulations (24). Combination of vitamin E with other co-antioxidants, particularly vitamin C, enhances its antioxidant effects and stability in topical products (24). Cosmetic chemicals like vitamin E acetate and sodium ascorbyl phosphate in sunscreens are bio-converted to vitamins E and C, respectively, and reported to reduce reactive oxygen species generated in viable epidermal layers thereby improving photoprotection (25).

Polyphenols

Polyphenols are organic chemical compounds which have two or more hydroxyl groups attached to an aromatic ring and consist of 5 groups: flavonoids, tannins, phenolic acids, diferuloylmethane and stilbenes; the most studied group are the flavonoids (26). Polyphenols are widely available in plants giving different colours to flowers and fruits, and the richest sources are spices and herbs (cloves, oregano, peppermint and rosemary), fruits (berries, grapes, and drupe fruits - apples, apricots, peaches and pears), nuts (walnuts, hazelnuts, chestnuts, and almonds), seeds (flaxseeds and soybeans), and vegetables (broccoli, lettuce, spinach, black and green olives, onions and spinach) (27). They have many important functions such as smoothing, softening and hydrating, soothing and astringent effects on skin by inhibition of skin enzymes (collagenase, elastase, and hyaluronidase) which degrade collagen fibres, elastin fibres, and hyaluronic acid, respectively (26). Polyphenols also reduce skin irritation and redness, promote epidermal regeneration, improve blood supply and prevent micro-haemorrhages such as petechiae by strengthening the capillaries, thus, mitigating the negative effects of external factors like UV radiation (26).

Flavonoids, also called Vitamin P, are the major active nutraceutical compounds in plants which are polyphenolic molecules with a flavan structure consisting of three rings with 15 carbon atoms, which are soluble in water and found naturally in many fruits, vegetables, grains, barks, roots, stems, flowers, teas, chocolates and wines (28). They are rich in anti-oxidative activity providing protection against UV radiation, possess anti- ageing, anti-inflammatory, anti-allergic, anti-cellulite, anti-couperose (rosacea), antiviral, antiseptic, antithrombotic, hepatoprotective, and anti-mutagenic, anti-carcinogenic, and skin-lightening properties with the capacity to modulate many cellular enzyme functions (29). Flavonoids such as flavones and catechins provide the most powerful protection against superoxide radicals. Kaempferol, morin, quercetin, myricetin and rutin, act as strong antioxidants against reactive oxygen species (30).

Polyphenols, particularly flavonoids, used as cosmetic ingredients are based on scientifically proven skin benefits such as strengthening capillaries and preventing haemorrhages, stimulation of fibroblast proliferation, reduction of collagen breakdown, prevention of lipid oxidation, as well as moistening, soothing, and softening (31). Plant extracts with flavonoids used in many known cosmetic products for their antioxidant properties include *Arnica montana, Crataegus monogyna, Pulmonaria officinalis, Helichrysum italicum, Sophora japonica, Arctium lappa, Polygonum aviculare, Centella asiatica, Melilotus officinalis* and *Hippophae rhamnoides* (31).

Hydroxy acids

The anti- ageing effects of hydroxy acids (HA) have become a prominent factor in cosmetic dermatology, leading to the proliferation of HA-containing cosmetic products and skin care systems (32, 33) because of their exfoliating properties and rejuvenating effect on photoaged skin (34). The group comprises α-hydroxy acids (AHAs), β-hydroxy acids (BHAs), polyhydroxy acids (PHAs), and bionic acids (6). The alpha-hydroxyl acids consisting of glycolic acid (found in sugar cane), lactic acid (found in sour milk and tomato juice), malic acid (found in apples), tartaric acid (found in grapes), and citric acid (found in citrus fruits) are water soluble while β-hydroxy acids consisting of salicylic acid (SA) or 2-hydroxybenzoic acid and its derivatives such as C8-lipohydroxy acid (C8-LHA) are lipophilic. BHAs occur naturally in milk, yogurt, fresh fruit (such as pawpaw, berries, and pineapples), sweet birch, and some other plants.

The SA derivative, C8-LHA, has wide applications in cosmetics due to its much lower skin penetration (34). The relatively slow penetration of C8-LHA in the skin is due to its more lipophilic nature than other SA derivatives resulting in its efficiency at low concentrations in exfoliation. The anti-ageing benefit of these compounds is due to increased production of glycosaminoglycans, collagen, and elastic fibres causing dermal thickening and thereby reducing skin wrinkles and fine lines (35). AHAs and BHAs are used to reduce hyperkeratinized skin. Hence, they are useful in the treatment of dry skin, ichthyosis and verrucous growths (36). β-hydroxy acids have antimicrobial, antifungal, anti-inflammatory, anti-comedogenic and exfoliating properties making them effective against acne and for combating dandruff (34).

The polyhydroxy acids and bionic acids are similar with improved skin barrier functions resulting in better moisturisation, and antioxidant properties. Gluconolactone, a polyhydroxy acid, protects against UV radiation skin damages by trapping free radicals (37). Glycolic, salicylic and lactic acids accelerate skin exfoliation and are used as chemical peeling agents in cosmetics, and for reducing hyperpigmentation as in acne-prone skin and pigmentary disorders, and for improving skin texture (6).

Peptides

Peptides are short amino acid sequences usually between 2 and 20 amino acids but less than 50 with bioactivity that is different from the larger proteins from which they are derived (38). There are four main categories based on the mechanism of actions: signal peptides, neurotransmitter-affecting peptides, enzyme-inhibitor peptides, and carrier peptides (39, 40).

Acetyl hexapeptide-8: Botulinum neurotoxins (BoNTs) are used in cosmetic science for their antiwrinkle property but are of limited use due to high neurotoxicity. Acetyl hexapeptide-8 (also called Acetyl hexapeptide-3 or Ac-EEMQRR-NH_2 or Argireline) is a non-toxic, antiwrinkle peptide that mimics the action of BoNTs. Acetyl hexapeptide-8 is a hexapeptide with the sequence Ac-Glu-Glu-Met-Gln-Arg-Arg-NH2 (41). It is a fragment from the N-terminal end of the protein SNAP-25 (Synaptosomal-Associated Protein, 25kDa) which is a substrate of botulinum toxin (*Botox*) (42). There is concern that peptides in cosmetic creams marketed as anti- ageing/anti-wrinkle may penetrate into the deep layers of the skin and may potentially stimulate biological activity. However, the amount of Ac-EEMQRR-amide that penetrates the skin remains mostly in the stratum corneum and the peptide levels decreases with each layer of the epidermis and no peptide is detectable in the dermis (43).

Ac-EEMQRR reduces the depth of deep wrinkles that occur around the forehead and eyes (44). It inhibits facial muscle movements or contractions (41) to a significant effect by decreasing the anisotropy property of facial skin resulting in increased firmness or tensor effect. Anisotropy of a substance is caused by asymmetry and specific orientation of the molecules themselves in the

GHK-Cu: The tri-peptide, GHK (glycyl-L-histidyl-L-lysine), is released during tissue injury and occurs naturally in the plasma. It forms a complex with copper 2+ (Cu^{2+}) to produce GHK-Cu which is presently a common component of many hair and skin products. GHK-Cu has been found to have these effects on the skin (46):

- Improves elasticity, tightens skin and smoothens rough skin
- Stimulates skin barrier proteins
- In aged skin, it reverses skin thinning, reduces fine lines, and depth of wrinkles
- Protects from skin damages from UV radiation
- Reduces hyperpigmentation
- Reduces inflammation
- Reduces free radical damage
- Enlarges hair follicle size, and stimulates hair growth and thickness,
- With its regenerative property it promotes wound healing.

According to Pickart (47), GHK-Cu effects on ageing skin and wound repair result from activation of tissue remodelling by:

- Inducing cellular infiltration for tissue repair (mostly macrophages, mast cells, and platelets),
- Stimulating anti-inflammatory reactions such as diminishing the formation of free radicals, thromboxane (TXA2),
- Transforming growth factor beta-1 (TGF β-1), tumor necrosis factor alpha (TNF-α),
- Release of oxidising iron (Fe^{2+}) and protein glycation (48) while preventing ultraviolet damage to keratinocytes,
- Increasing superoxide dismutase levels, increasing vasodilation and improving fibroblast recovery following X-ray treatments;
- Increasing synthesis of collagen, elastin, metalloproteinases, anti-proteases, growth factors (vascular endothelial growth factor (VEGF), fibroblast growth factor 2, and nerve growth factor), neutrotropins 3 and 4, and erythropoietin
- Stimulating the proliferation of fibroblasts and skin keratinocytes, hair follicle size; nerve outgrowth, and angiogenesis.

pal-KTTKS (Matrixyl): Palmitoyl pentapeptide-4 (palmitoyl-KTTKS) is a pro-drug that is degraded by aminopeptidase in the epidermis, deaminases and esterases in the extracellular spaces of the stratum corneum, sebaceous glands and near hair follicles (49). KTTKS is a pentapeptide Lys-Thr-Thr-Lys-Ser released *in situ* and exacts the biological activity of palmitoyl-KTTKS (49, 50). KTTKS acts in the post-transcriptional phase (50, 51) by the up-regulation of transforming growth factor-β(TGF-β) expression (52) which maintains the stability of the messenger RNAs (mRNAs) encoding type I procollagen and fibronectin, thus, stimulating type I and III collagen and fibronectin production (53). A study comparing topical use of palmitoyl-KTTKS twice daily for 12 weeks with the placebo-treated skin showed that it reduced the total length of fine lines and wrinkles (54). Some other skin benefits include skin firmness, age spot reduction, and improvement of dark circle under the eyes (53).

Minerals

Minerals are essential micronutrients as they cannot be synthesised in human body but are available from dietary sources. There are two types of minerals: macroelements (sodium, potassium, calcium, phosphorus and magnesium) and microelements (iron, iodine, zinc, sulphur, chlorine, cobalt, manganese, molybdenum, copper, and selenium). Zinc, copper, selenium and silicon are important in the prevention of skin ageing (26, 55). As cofactors and coenzymes in different enzyme systems, minerals regulate many important biochemical and physiological functions vital to skin, endocrine, circulatory, skeletal, and nervous systems.

Zinc (Zn): Zinc (Zn) is an essential microelement involved in the structure and function of over 300 enzymes, hence, controls many physiological processes. It is present in all body tissues and fluids. The skin is the third most Zn-abundant body tissue. Zinc is more abundant in the epidermis than dermis and in the stratum spinosum than in the other epidermal layers, while in the dermis, the concentration is more in the reticular part. Adequate intake is mainly from a balanced diet containing plant and animal products or dietary supplements. Common food sources include pumpkin seeds, sunflower seeds, nuts, legumes, whole grains, fish, poultry, red meat, dairy products and seafood (shrimps, oysters) (26).

Effects of zinc on the skin:

- Prevents photodamage from UV radiation – zinc is important in the function of antioxidant enzymes such as copper-zinc superoxide dismutase (Cu/Zn-SOD), which is required for neutralising the superoxide radical and commonly used as zinc oxide in sunscreens (56);

- It stimulates skin morphogenesis, repair and maintenance – the formation of skin ridges, creases and furrows is referred to as morphogenesis. The ridges in the skin produce friction which is important in grasping and walking. These ridges contain numerous sweat glands with their pore openings located on the top. The sweat produced hydrates the hands and feet. The creases, together with the furrows between the ridges ensure flexibility of the skin. The ridges and furrows are unique to individuals and are used for identification of individuals in forensic science (57, 58, 59);
- Modulates the activity of 5α-reductase-type 1 isozyme which is present in cytoplasm of human sebocytes, keratinocytes, fibroblasts, dermal microvascular endothelial cells, hair dermal papilla cells, and melanocytes. This enzyme is an autocrine mediator facilitating skin growth and differentiation (60);
- Essential element for collagen synthesis necessary for wound healing;
- Zinc deficiency causes pale and rough skin, stretch marks, poor wound healing and skin disorders such as acne, greasy skin, atopic dermatitis, epidermolysis bullosa and acrodermatitis enteropathica.

Silicon (Si): Silicon can be found in all human tissues - the skin, hair and nails, liver, heart, kidneys, lungs, connective tissues, bones, and muscle (26, 61, 62). It is converted in the stomach to orthosilicic acid (OSA) and absorbed by the thymus. Plant sources are dried fruits (raisins), nuts, grains and grain products (rice, barley, oats, wheat, cereals, bread, pasta), beans, maize, root vegetables (carrots, onions, potatoes) and fruits (bananas).

***Functions in the skin*:**

- OSA stimulates neocollagenesis in fibroblasts leading to synthesis of collagen, elastin and glycosaminoglycans (GAGs) or mucopolysaccharides;
- It improves skin surface and its mechanical properties;
- It improves keratin structure, increases the resistance and thickness of nails and hair fibers;

In a study by Barrel et al., oral intake of 10mg/day for 20 weeks produced improved skin surface and mechanical properties and reduced hair and nail brittleness (62).

Deficiencies of zinc are associated with: faster appearance of skin wrinkles, soft and brittle nails, alopecia, and slow wound healing.

***Copper (Cu)*:** Copper is involved in very many important physiological and metabolic processes required for the proper functioning of the human body as it is a constituent of

30 essential proteins (26). Many enzymes such as cytochrome c oxidase, superoxide dismutase, dopamine β-hydroxylase and tyrosinase contain copper (63). It occurs naturally in dietary sources as cupric copper (Cu^{2+}) which is reduced to cuprous copper (Cu^{+}) and absorbed into the body (64). It is most commonly found in the skin, muscles, bones, liver and brain in the human body (26). Plant and animal sources include seeds, nuts, whole grains, legumes, chocolate, cocoa, liver, seafood, and oysters.

Effects of copper in the skin and other body areas (26):

- It exhibits antimicrobial activity against viral, bacterial and fungal organisms (65),
- Copper stimulates collagen maturation enhancing wound healing,
- It modulates melanin synthesis as a constituent of tyrosinase which is the main enzyme in the synthesis of melanin pigments,
- As a cofactor of superoxide dismutase (SOD), it prevents oxidative damage by UV radiation to cell membranes,
- Copper ions are commonly used in cosmetics as these enhance the penetration of active ingredients into the skin,

Copper deficiency reduces the activity of copper-dependent enzymes which promote the activities of free radical scavengers. This results in lipid peroxidation in the cells of the skin, erythrocytes, plasma, liver and heart and the resultant cellular damages.

Selenium (Se): Selenium is a part of the structure of many enzymatic proteins such as glutathione peroxidases, selenoprotein P and thioredoxin reductases. Synthesis of the various selenoproteins have different responses to changes in selenium availability. Dietary deficiency of selenium causes redistribution of intracellular selenium among the different selenoproteins and GPx proteins (69). Hence, dietary intake must be adequate. Plant and animal sources are: cereals and cereal products, nuts, broccoli, white cabbage, asparagus, garlic, onion, mushrooms and legumes (26). Selenium is commonly used as selenium sulphide in skin care applications such as shampoos for dandruff (66).

Effects of selenium in the body:

- it has strong antioxidant properties through its effect on selenium-dependent enzymes, such as thioredoxin reductase and glutathione peroxidase which scavenge free radicals and oxidative stress induced by UV radiation (67, 68) and, thus, it has anti-ageing role in the skin.
- It plays significant role in preventing ageing and ageing-related diseases.

- It is an essential cofactor for approximately 25 selenoproteins, one of which is glutathione peroxidases (GPx1–8). These are a group of enzymes that removes harmful peroxides from reactive oxygen species (ROS), reducing oxidative stress-mediated inflammation and DNA damage in cells (69).
- It regulates skin flora, skin flaking and discomfort caused by microorganisms such as *Propionobacterium acnes*.

Selenium deficiency is associated with many skin diseases including acne vulgaris, fluffy hair, blue-black nail hyperpigmentation, psoriasis, atopic dermatitis, pruritic papular eruption, xeroderma, and oral candidiasis (70, 71).

Coenzyme Q10 (CoQ10): CoQ10 is an endogenous lipophilic compound that is an essential component of metabolism in the mitochondria which produces adenosine triphosphate (ATP), the main source of energy for all cellular metabolisms. It is naturally made in the human body, and the highest levels are found in the heart, liver, kidneys and pancreas, and also naturally found in food (26). In a study by Žmitek *et al.* (72), a dosage of 50 mg or 150 mg CoQ10 taken for 3 months reduced features of skin ageing such as fine lines, wrinkles, loss of skin elasticity and micro-relief lines as well as improved skin texture.

CoQ10 occurs in two forms, ubiquinone and ubiquinol. The body converts ubiquinone to ubiquinol. Ubiquinol is the most abundant form constituting 99% of the total plasma CoQ10 in healthy people, and it is the form used in most therapies (73). It prevents free radicals produced from oxidative stress in the body, and stimulates production of adenosine triphosphate (ATP) (73). Other effects of the antioxidant property include reducing risk of heart disease and high blood pressure, neurodegenerative diseases, infertility, and migraine (73).

CoQ10 levels in the body progressively decline with ageing and intake through food provides the additional amounts needed for healthy skin (74). Daily amounts of less than 1200 mg is considered safe (73) (See Table 1). Cosmeceutical components from plant and animal sources provide CoQ10 for the body (See Table 2).

Polyunsaturated Fatty Acids (PUFAs): There are two types of unsaturated fatty acids: monounsaturated fatty acids – mainly omega-9 (ω-9; n-9) and polyunsaturated fatty acids (PUFAs) – mainly omega-3 (ω-3; n-3) and omega-6 (ω-6; n-6). The PUFAs, Omega-3 (ω-3; n-3) and omega-6 (ω-6; n-6), are essential fatty acids (EFAs) (See Table 3) relevant to cosmetics production (26). Recent research reports that gamma linolenic acid (GLA), an omega-6 fatty acid, reaches the stratum corneum when topically applied as a cream while it penetrates to the dermis when taken orally, thus, enhancing epidermal cohesiveness and preventing excess fluid loss (75, 76).

Table 14.1: Sources of Coenzyme Q10 (73, 74)

Food types		**Sources**	**CoQ10 (mg/kg)**
Plants	Oils	soybean oil	166.4
		olive oil	82
		peanut oil	77
		corn oil	76
		rapeseed oil	68.5
		sesame oil	32
		cottonseed	17.3
		sunflower oil	9.6
	Seeds	sesame seeds	20.3
		Soybean	12
	Nuts	Peanuts	26.7
		Walnuts	19
		Hazelnuts	16.7
		Almond	9.4
	Vegetables	Broccoli	7.3
		sweet pepper	3.3
		sweet potato	3.3
		Garlic	3.1
		pea	2.5
		Cabbage	2.1
	cereals	corn germ	7
		wheat germ	5.2
		rice bran	4.9
Animal	meat	chicken	14
		Pork	24
		Beef	31

	fish (fatty)	Mackerel	67.5
		Trout	8.5

Functions of omega-3 and omega-6 EFAs - these EFAs act as:

- Components of cell membrane essential for epidermal barrier
- Constituents of intracellular cement together with ceramides (GLA is a component of ceramide 1) and cholesterol limiting trans-epidermal water loss (TEWL) thereby ensuring adequate cellular hydration and protection against external factors.
- Precursors of eicosanoids – leukotriens (LT), prostacyclins (PGI), prostaglandins (PG), and thromboxanes (TX)which are essential in defensive and regulatory functions in many tissue processes
- Anti-inflammatory and anti-allergic chemicals preventing skin inflammation and reducing allergic responses and skin irritation
- Protective effect against ultraviolet radiations
- Facilitator of metabolic processes and cell division

Deficiencies cause skin dryness, skin inflammations, increased exfoliation and susceptibility to skin irritation by external irritants, flabby skin and slow healing from skin injuries (26).

Table 14.2: Classes of Coenzyme Q10 content in plant sources (74)

Class	**CoQ10 content**	**Level**
A	> 50 mg/kg	very rich
B	10-50 mg/kg	Rich
C	5-10 mg/kg	Moderate
D	1-5 mg/kg	Poor
E	< 1 mg/kg	very poor

Table 14.3: Polyunsaturated fatty acids of cosmetic importance - Omega-3 and Omega-6 (26)

PUFA types			
Omega-3	**Stucture**	**Omega-6**	**Structure**
alpha-linolenic acid (ALA)	C18:3N-3	linoleic acid (LA)	C18:2N-6
docosahexaenoic acid (DHA)	C22:6N-3	gamma-linolenic acid (GLA)	C18:3N-6
eicosapentaenoic acid (EPA)	C20:5N-3	arachidonic acid (AA)	C20:4N-6

References

1. Santini, A., Cammarata, S. M., Capone, G., Ianaro, A., Tenore, G. C., Pani, L., and Novellino, E. (2018). Nutraceuticals: opening the debate for a regulatory framework. *British journal of clinical pharmacology*, *84*(4), 659–672. https://doi.org/10.1111/bcp.13496
2. Prakash, V. and van Boekel, M. A. J. S. Chapter 19 - Nutraceuticals: Possible Future Ingredients and Food Safety Aspects, Editor(s): Christine E. Boisrobert, Aleksandra Stjepanovic, Sangsuk Oh, Huub L.M. Lelieveld, Ensuring Global Food Safety, Academic Press, 2010, Pages 333-338. *https://doi.org/10.1016/B978-0-12-374845-4.00019-9*
3. Pérez-Sánchez, A., Barrajón-Catalán, E., Herranz-López, M. and Micol, V. (2018). *Nutraceuticals for Skin Care: A Comprehensive Review of Human Clinical Studies. Nutrients, 10(4), 403.* doi:10.3390/nu10040403
4. Puglia, C., Offerta, A., Saija, A., Trombetta, D., & Venera, C. (2014). *Protective effect of red orange extract supplementation against UV-induced skin damages: photo ageing and solar lentigines. Journal of Cosmetic Dermatology, 13(2), 151–157.* doi:10.1111/jocd.12083
5. Heinrich, M. "Nutraceutical". Encyclopedia Britannica. [Internet] 19th March 2019. [Cited 2021 Sept. 30]. Available from: https://www.britannica.com/science/nutraceutical
6. Martin, K. I. and Glaser, D. A. (2011). Cosmeceuticals: the new medicine of beauty. *Missouri Medicine*, *108*(1), 60–63.
7. Babamiri, K. and Nassab, R. (2010). Cosmeceuticals: the evidence behind the retinoids. *Aesthetic Surgery Journal*, *30*(1), 74–77. https://doi.org/10.1177/1090820X09360704
8. Antille, C., Tran, C., Sorg, O., Carraux, P., Didierjean, L. and Saurat, J. H. (2003). Vitamin A exerts a photoprotective action in skin by absorbing ultraviolet B radiation. *The Journal of Investigative Dermatology*, *121*(5), 1163–1167. https://doi.org/10.1046/j.1523-1747.2003.12519.x
9. Sorg, O., Antille, C., Kaya, G. and Saurat, J.-H. (2006). Retinoids in cosmeceuticals. *Dermatologic Therapy, 19(5), 289–296.* doi:10.1111/j.1529-8019.2006.00086
10. Bhatt, T. and Patel, K. (2020). Carotenoids: Potent to Prevent Diseases Review. *Natural Products and Bioprospecting*, *10*(3), 109–117. https://doi.org/10.1007/s13659-020-00244-2

11. Pechère, M., Germanier, L., Siegenthaler, G., Pechère, J. C. and Saurat, J. H. (2002). The antibacterial activity of topical retinoids: the case of retinaldehyde. *Dermatology (Basel, Switzerland)*, *205*(2), 153–158. https://doi.org/10.1159/000063903
12. Zasada, M. and Budzisz, E. (2019). Retinoids: active molecules influencing skin structure formation in cosmetic and dermatological treatments. *Postepy Dermatologii i Alergologii*, *36*(4), 392–397. https://doi.org/10.5114/ada.2019.87443
13. Mukherjee, S., Date, A., Patravale, V., Korting, H. C., Roeder, A. and Weindl, G. (2006). Retinoids in the treatment of skin ageing: an overview of clinical efficacy and safety. *Clinical Interventions in ageing*, *1*(4), 327–348. https://doi.org/10.2147/ciia.2006.1.4.327
14. "Tretinoin Cream- tretinoin cream". *DailyMed.* [Internet] *1 December 2018.* [Cited 2021 Sept. 30]. *Available from:* https://dailymed.nlm.nih.gov/dailymed/drugInfo.cfm?setid=745cc3ce-60b4-4479-a055-316817567949
15. Gehring W. (2004). Nicotinic acid/niacinamide and the skin. *Journal of Cosmetic Dermatology*, *3*(2), 88–93. https://doi.org/10.1111/j.1473-2130.2004.00115.x
16. Kawada, A., Konishi, N., Oiso, N., Kawara, S. and Date, A. (2008). Evaluation of anti-wrinkle effects of a novel cosmetic containing niacinamide. *The Journal of Dermatology*, *35*(10), 637–642. https://doi.org/10.1111/j.1346-8138.2008.00537.x
17. Bissett, D. L., Oblong, J. E. and Berge, C. A. (2005). Niacinamide: A B vitamin that improves ageing facial skin appearance. *Dermatologic Surgery: official publication for American Society for Dermatologic Surgery [et al.]*, *31*(7 Pt 2), 860–865. https://doi.org/10.1111/j.1524-4725.2005.31732
18. Hakozaki, T., Minwalla, L., Zhuang, J., Chhoa, M., Matsubara, A., Miyamoto, K., Greatens, A., Hillebrand, G. G., Bissett, D. L. and Boissy, R. E. (2002). The effect of niacinamide on reducing cutaneous pigmentation and suppression of melanosome transfer. *The British Journal of Dermatology*, *147*(1), 20–31. https://doi.org/10.1046/j.1365-2133.2002.04834.x
19. Bissett, D. L., Miyamoto, K., Sun, P., Li, J. and Berge, C. A. (2004). Topical niacinamide reduces yellowing, wrinkling, red blotchiness, and hyperpigmented spots in ageing facial skin. *International Journal of Cosmetic Science*, *26*(5), 231–238. https://doi.org/10.1111/j.1467-2494.2004.00228.x
20. Raschke, T., Koop, U., Düsing, H. J., Filbry, A., Sauermann, K., Jaspers, S., Wenck, H. and Wittern, K. P. (2004). Topical activity of ascorbic acid: from in vitro optimization to in vivo efficacy. *Skin Pharmacology and Physiology*, *17*(4), 200–206. https://doi.org/10.1159/000078824
21. Burke K. E. (2007). Interaction of vitamins C and E as better cosmeceuticals. *Dermatologic Therapy*, *20*(5), 314–321. https://doi.org/10.1111/j.1529-8019.2007.00145.x
22. Keen, M. A. and Hassan, I. (2016). Vitamin E in dermatology. *Indian Dermatology Online Journal*, *7*(4), 311–315. https://doi.org/10.4103/2229-5178.185494
23. Pinto, C. A. S., Martins, T. E. A., Martinez, R. M., Freire, T. B., Velasco, M. V. R. and Baby, A. R. (2021). Vitamin E in Human Skin: Functionality and Topical Products. In: PınarErkekoglu and Júlia Scherer Santos (eds). *Vitamin E in Health and Disease - Interactions, Diseases and Health Aspects*. London, UK: IntechOpen; 7th June 2021. DOI: 10.5772/intechopen.98336. Available from: https://www.intechopen.com/chapters/77087

24. Thiele, J. J. and Ekanayake-Mudiyanselage, S. (2007). Vitamin E in human skin: organ-specific physiology and considerations for its use in dermatology. *Molecular Aspects of Medicine*, *28*(5-6), 646–667. https://doi.org/10.1016/j.mam.2007.06.001
25. Hanson, K. M. and Clegg, R. M. (2003). Bioconvertible vitamin antioxidants improve sunscreen photoprotection against UV-induced reactive oxygen species. *Journal of Cosmetic Science*, *54*(6), 589–598.
26. Michalak, M., Pierzak, M., Kręcisz, B. and Suliga, E. (2021). Bioactive Compounds for Skin Health: A Review. *Nutrients*, *13*(1), 203. https://doi.org/10.3390/nu13010203
27. Pérez-Jiménez, J., Neveu, V., Vos, F. and Scalbert, A. (2010). Identification of the 100 richest dietary sources of polyphenols: an application of the Phenol-Explorer database. *European Journal of Clinical Nutrition*, *64 Suppl 3*, S112–S120. https://doi.org/10.1038/ejcn.2010.221
28. Panche, A. N., Diwan, A. D. and Chandra, S. R. (2016). Flavonoids: an overview. *Journal of Nutritional Science*, *5*, e47. https://doi.org/10.1017/jns.2016.41
29. Burak, M. and Imen, Y. (1999). Flavonoids and their antioxidant properties. *TurkiyeKlin Tip BilDerg.*, 19, 296–304.
30. DeGroot, H. (1994). Reactive oxygen species in tissue injury. *Hepatogastroenterology*, 41,328–332.
31. Malinowska, P. (2013). Effect of flavonoids content on antioxidant activity of commercial cosmetic plant extracts. *Herba Pol.*, 59(3), 63-74. DOI: 10.2478/hepo-2013-0017
32. Green B. (2005). After 30 years ... the future of hydroxyacids. *Journal of Cosmetic Dermatology*, *4*(1), 44–45. https://doi.org/10.1111/j.1473-2165.2005.00159.x
33. Kornhauser, A., Coelho, S. G. and Hearing, V. J. (2010). Applications of hydroxy acids: classification, mechanisms, and photoactivity. *Clinical, Cosmetic and Investigational Dermatology*, *3*, 135–142. https://doi.org/10.2147/CCID.S9042
34. Saint-Léger, D., Lévêque, J. L., & Verschoore, M. (2007). The use of hydroxy acids on the skin: characteristics of C8-lipohydroxy acid. *Journal of Cosmetic Dermatology*, *6*(1), 59–65. https://doi.org/10.1111/j.1473-2165.2007.00296.x
35. Yu, R. J. and Van Scott, E. J. (2005). Hydroxyacids, polyhydroxyacids, aldobionic acids and their topical actions. In: Baran R, Maibach HI, editors. Textbook of Cosmetic Dermatology. 3rd ed. New York: Taylor & Francis; 77-93.
36. Green, B. A., Yu, R. J. and Van Scott, E. J. (2009). Clinical and cosmeceutical uses of hydroxyacids. *Clinics in Dermatology*, *27*(5), 495–501. https://doi.org/10.1016/j.clindermatol.2009.06.023
37. Bernstein, E. F., Brown, D. B., Schwartz, M. D., Kaidbey, K. and Ksenzenko, S. M. (2004). The polyhydroxy acid gluconolactone protects against ultraviolet radiation in an in vitro model of cutaneous photo ageing. *Dermatologic Surgery: official publication for American Society for Dermatologic Surgery [et al.]*, *30*(2 Pt 1), 189–196. https://doi.org/10.1111/j.1524-4725.2004.30060.x
38. Karami, Z. and Akbari-Adergani, B. (2019). Bioactive food derived peptides: a review on correlation between structure of bioactive peptides and their functional properties. *Journal of Food Science and Technology*, *56*(2), 535–547. https://doi.org/10.1007/s13197-018-3549-4

39. Lupo, M. P. (2005). Cosmeceutical peptides. *Dermatologic Surgery: official publication for American Society for Dermatologic Surgery [et al.]*, *31*(7 Pt 2), 832–836. https://doi.org/10.1111/j.1524-4725.2005.31728
40. Gorouhi, F. and Maibach, H. I. (2009). Role of topical peptides in preventing or treating aged skin. *International journal of Cosmetic Sscience*, *31*(5), 327–345. https://doi.org/10.1111/j.1468-2494.2009.00490.x
41. Blanes-Mira, C., Clemente, J., Jodas, G., Gil, A., Fernández-Ballester, G., Ponsati, B., Gutierrez, L., Pérez-Payá, E. and Ferrer-Montiel, A. (2002). A synthetic hexapeptide (Argireline) with antiwrinkle activity. *International Journal of Cosmetic Science*, *24*(5), 303–310. https://doi.org/10.1046/j.1467-2494.2002.00153.x
42. Wang, Y., Wang, M., Xiao, X. S., Pan, P., Li, P. and Huo, J. (2013). The antiwrinkle efficacy of synthetic hexapeptide (Argireline) in Chinese Subjects. *Journal of Cosmetic and Laser Therapy: official publication of the European Society for Laser Dermatology*, Advance online publication. https://doi.org/10.3109/14764172.2012.759234
43. Kraeling, M. E., Zhou, W., Wang, P. and Ogunsola, O. A. (2015). In vitro skin penetration of acetyl hexapeptide-8 from a cosmetic formulation. *Cutaneous and Ocular Toxicology*, *34*(1), 46–52. https://doi.org/10.3109/15569527.2014.894521
44. Ruiz, M. A., Clares, B., Morales, M. E., Cazalla, S. and Gallardo, V. (2007). Preparation and stability of cosmetic formulations with an anti- ageing peptide. *Journal of Cosmetic Science*, *58*(2), 157–171.
45. Tadini, K. A., Mercurio, D. G. and Campos, P. M. B. M. (2015). Acetyl hexapeptide-3 in a cosmetic formulation acts on skin mechanical properties - clinical study. *Brazilian Journal of Pharmaceutical Sciences* [online]. 51(4), 901-909. https://doi.org/10.1590/S1984-82502015000400016.
46. Pickart, L. and Margolina, A. (2018). Regenerative and Protective Actions of the GHK-Cu Peptide in the Light of the New Gene Data. *International Journal of Molecular Sciences*, *19*(7), 1987. https://doi.org/10.3390/ijms19071987.
47. Pickart, L. (2008). The human tri-peptide GHK and tissue remodeling. *J Biomater Sci Polym Ed*, 19(8), 969-988. DOI:10.1163/156856208784909435.
48. Luevano-Contreras, C. and Chapman-Novakofski, K. (2010). Dietary advanced glycation end products and ageing. *Nutrients*, 2(12), 1247-1265. DOI: 10.3390/nu2121247.
49. Pouillot, A., Dayan, N., Polla, A. S., Polla, L. L. and Polla, B. S. (2008). The stratum corneum: a double paradox. *J Cosmet Dermatol,* 7(2), 143-148. DOI:10.1111/j.1473-2165.2008.00379.x
50. Katayama, K., Armendariz-Borunda, J., Raghow, R., Kang, A. H. and Seyer, J. M. (1993). A pentapeptide from type I procollagen promotes extracellular matrix production. *J Biol Chem*., 268(14), 9941-9944.
51. Katayama, K., Seyer, J. M., Raghow, R. and Kang, A. H. (1991). Regulation of extracellular matrix production by chemically synthesized subfragments of type I collagen carboxypropeptide. *Biochemistry,* 30(29), 7097-7104. DOI: 10.1021/bi00243a009.
52. Tsai, W. C., Hsu, C. C., Chung, C. Y., Lin, M. S., Li, S. L. and Pang, J. H. (2007). The pentapeptide KTTKS promoting the expressions of type I collagen and transforming growth factor-beta of tendon cells. *J Orthop Res.*, 25(12), 1629-1634. DOI:10.1002/jor.20455

53. Abu Samah, N. H. and Heard, C. M. (2011). Topically applied KTTKS: a review. *Int J Cosmet Sci.*, 33(6), 483-490. DOI:10.1111/j.1468-2494.2011.00657.xv
54. Robinson, L. R., Fitzgerald, N. C., Doughty, D. G., Dawes, N. C., Berge, C. A. and Bissett, D. L. (2005). Topical palmitoylpentapeptide provides improvement in photoaged human facial skin. *Int J Cosmet Sci.*, 27(3), 155-160. DOI:10.1111/j.1467-2494.2005.00261.x
55. Park, K. (2015). Role of micronutrients in skin health and function. *Biomo. Ther.,* 23,207–217.
56. Devi, C. B., Nandakishore, T., Sangeeta, N., Basar, G., Deni, N. O., Sungdirenla, J., et al. (2014). Zinc in human health. *IOSR-JDMS.*, 13, 18–23.
57. Kimura, S. (1991). Embryological development of flexion creases, *Birth Defects: Original Article Series,* 27(2), 113–129.
58. Babler, W. (1991). Embryonic development of epidermal ridges and their configurations, Birth Defects: *Original Article Series,* 27(2), 95–112.
59. Maceo, A. (2009). Friction ridge skin: Morphogenesis and overview. In *Wiley Encyclopedia of Forensic Science,* 1-9. DOI:10.1002/97804700061589.fsa358
60. Chen, W., Zouboulis, C. C., Fritsch, M., Blume-Peytavi, U., Kodelja, V., Goerdt, S., et al. (1998). Evidence of Heterogeneity and Quantitative Differences of the Type 1 5α-Reductase Expression in Cultured Human Skin Cells – Evidence of its Presence in Melanocytes. *J Invest Dermatol.*, 110(1), 84-89. https://doi.org/10.1046/j.1523-1747.1998.00080.x
61. Boguszewska-Czubara, A. and Pasternak, K. (2011). Silicon in medicine and therapy. *J Elem.*, 3, 489–497.
62. Barel, A., Calomme, M., Timchenko, A., de Paepe, K., Demeester, N., Rogiers, V., et al. (2005). Effect of oral intake of choline-stabilized orthosilicic acid on skin, nails and hair in women with photodamaged skin. *Arch. Dermatol. Res.*, 97, 147–153.
63. Karlin, K. D. (1993). Metalloenzymes, structural motifs, and inorganic models. *Science,* 261, 701–708.
64. Linder, M. C., Wooten, L., Cerveza, P., Cotton, S., Shulze, R. and Lomeli, N. (1998). Copper transport. *Am J ClinNutr,* 67, 965–971.
65. Borkow, G. and Gabbay, J. (2005). Copper as a biocidal tool. *Curr Med Chem,* 12, 2163–2175.
66. Mitchell, S. C., Nickson, R. M. and Waring, R. H. (1993). The Biological Activity of Selenium Sulfide. *Sulfur Reports*, 13(2), 279-289. DOI: 10.1080/01961779308048957
67. Park, K. (2015). Role of micronutrients in skin health and function. *Biomol Ther*, 23, 207–217.
68. Zhu, X., Jiang, M., Song, E., Jiang, X. and Song, Y. (2015). Selenium deficiency sensitizes the skin for UVB-induced oxidative damage and inflammation which involved the activation of p38 MAPK signaling. *Food Chem Toxicol.*, 75, 139–145.
69. Bermingham, E. N., Hesketh, J. E., Sinclair, B. R., Koolaard, J. P. and Roy, N. C. (2014). Selenium-enriched foods are more effective at increasing glutathione peroxidase (GPx) activity compared with selenomethionine: a meta-analysis. *Nutrients,* 6(10), 4002-4031. DOI:10.3390/nu6104002
70. Akinboro, A. O., Mejiuni, D. A., Onayemi, O., Ayodele, O. E., Atiba, A. S. and Bamimore, G. M. (2013). Serum selenium and skin diseases among Nigerians with human immunodeficiency virus/acquired immune deficiency syndrome. *HIV AIDS (Auckl),* 5, 215-221. DOI:10.2147/HIV.S46364

71. Seshadri, D. and De, D. (2012). Nails in nutritional deficiencies. *Indian J Dermatol Venereol Leprol*, 78, 237-241.
72. Žmitek, K., Pogačnik, T., Mervic, L., Žmitek, J. and Pravst, I. (2017). The effect of dietary intake of coenzyme Q10 on skin parameters and condition: Results of a randomised, placebo-controlled, double-blind study. *Biofactors*, 43(1), 132-140. DOI:10.1002/biof.1316
73. Brennan, D. (2020). *Foods High in CoQ10*. Nourish by WebMD. 3rd November 2020. [Cited 18th January 2022]. Available from: https://www.webmd.com/diet/foods-high-in-coq10#2
74. Cudmore, D. (2021). *The Best Vegan Sources of CoQ10 [List].*VegFAQs. May 24, 2021. [Cited 18th January 2022]. Available from: https://vegfaqs.com/vegan-sources-of-coq10/
75. Michalak, M. and Kiełtyka-Dadasiewicz, A. (2018). Oils from fruit seeds and their dietetic and cosmetic significance. *Herba Pol.*, 64, 63–70.
76. Burris, J., Rietkerk, W. and Woolf, K. (2013). Acne: The role of medical nutrition therapy. *J. Acad. Nutr. Diet.*, 113, 416–430.

CHAPTER FIFTEEN

Formulation and preparation of cosmetic products

'Lara O Orafidiya, Francis A Oladimeji, Michael A Osungunna, Folake A Orafidiya and Yinka J Oyeniyi

Cosmetic products are presented for use in appropriate forms that are not only attractive to the consumer but are also functional, based on the intended use, convenience of application to the desired part of the body and, above all, remaining safe and stable throughout the stated shelf life. The formulation of cosmetics is both an art, a science and a systematic and technical process that requires basic knowledge of the ingredients employed and, more importantly, the peculiar formulation and stability characteristics of the particular product being designed. While the art aspect of cosmetic formulation, which invariably distinguishes one product from the other, involves the choice of colourants and dyes, fragrances, as well as the consistency of the final product and packaging; the technical process involves using appropriate ingredients in the right quantities, which are systematically mixed or processed together as prescribed, using the specified equipment designed for the type of product desired. In the process of product formulation and development, a series of test formulations are prepared and subjected to stability and functionality tests in order to choose the optimal formulation.

The ingredients of a formulation consist of the **active ingredients**, which elicit the desired effects of the product being formulated, e.g., moisturisers and antiperspirant agents; as well as the **excipients**, also referred to as additives or adjuncts, which are agents employed in formulations to obtain the desired characteristics of a particular form of product, e.g., emulsifiers, suspending agents and gelling agents. Cosmetic products are presented as creams, gels, pastes and ointments, which are semisolids; lotions and oily solutions which are in the form of liquids; as well as powders (loose or compact), capsules, pencils and sticks (deodorant sticks) which are solid preparations.

Rheology, which is defined as the study of the flow and deformation of matter, that is, the viscosity and flow characteristics of solids, gases, liquids and semisolids; is paramount to the formulation of liquid and semisolid cosmetic products, as well as ensuring the reproducibility of the physical characteristics of each batch of the products.

The quality of water used in the preparation of cosmetic products is of utmost importance as the use of poor-quality water ultimately affects the overall quality of the products, especially their microbial stability.

Unlike pharmaceutical products for which all ingredients used and their concentrations must be listed on the label, the **labelling of cosmetic products** requires that the ingredients used in a product are only listed in descending order of the quantities or concentrations employed, the values of which need not be stated. Fragrances and perfumes are trade secrets and their identity are often not disclosed on the label. However, the instruction to shake the container before use for lotions, and to store the products in a cool place should be on the label as the droplets of fluid emulsions and fine particles of suspensions tend to segregate on storage and be unevenly distributed, and extremes of storage temperatures can cause instability that can lead to a complete breakdown of the products. The directions for the use or application of cosmetic products are often written on the labels that appear on the product containers and sometimes in the form of literature inserts. Certain ingredients of a product to which some users may be allergic, e.g., gluten, are stated on the label of such a product.

All cosmetic products must have, stamped on their containers, information on the **batch number,** so that they can be easily traced in case there is a need for a recall of a batch**;** **date of manufacture**, and **expiry or 'best before' (BB) date**. Expiry dates of products are usually determined by subjecting the products to accelerated stability tests that involve storage at temperatures ranging from 25° to as high as 65°C for a specified period and observing for changes in the physical and chemical parameters of the product. Manufacturers determine the test procedures and end points for their products. Samples of the products are expected to be kept on the shelf by the manufacturer and observed throughout the stipulated shelf life. Chapter 18 of this book has more information on procedures for these determinations.

In a nutshell, this chapter aims to discuss the quality of water used for preparations, rheology in general, as well as the various ingredients and methods employed in the formulation and preparation of the basic forms in which cosmetics are presented. Information on the formulation and preparation of individual types of cosmetic products are discussed in the book entitled: *Textbook of Cosmetic Formulations* (1).

Water quality for preparation of cosmetics

One important application of water is its industrial use in the preparation of pharmaceuticals and cosmetics, among others. Water is referred to as the "universal solvent" because it dissolves a large number of substances than any other solvent. Water also serves as a vehicle for the dispersion of insoluble or partially soluble solids in suspensions, gases in aerosols and oils in emulsions. Even though water can be used alone as a solvent, it can also be used in combination with other solvents such as ethanol and glycerine as a co-solvent. **In the formulation of cosmetics, water is the most commonly used ingredient and may account for some 60%, or even more, of the product, depending on the product category. For instance,** while bar soaps, face powders, serums and some makeup products may contain only traces of water or none at all; hair shampoos and rinse-off conditioners, body creams and lotions, may contain up to 60% of water.

Unlike the water that is used for the manufacture of pharmaceutical products, which is highly regulated and requires strict compliance by manufacturing plants, water for the preparation of cosmetics is generally not regulated by appropriate regulatory agencies, leaving manufacturers to choose the type of water for the manufacture of their products.

Potable water, also referred to as tap water, drinking water or municipal water: Although this is treated to meet standards that are determined by the respective state and federal regulatory agencies of various countries for consumption, it is not always suitable for the manufacture of cosmetics. This is because it often contains high levels of ionic compounds such as nitrates, sulphates and phosphates; and minerals such as magnesium, calcium and iron; which can affect the chemistry of the constituent ingredients, as well as reactive compounds that can affect the pH, viscosity, odour and colour of the product for which the water is used. Also, seasonal changes do affect the growth of microorganisms and this can lead to high levels of microbial contamination, especially of stored potable water. Invariably, potable water does not conform with the United States Pharmacopeia's (USP) requirements for Total Organic Carbon (TOC), which indicates the presence of unwanted organic compounds in water and, that of Conductivity, which indicates the level of ions in water. It is because of these drawbacks of potable water that manufacturers of cosmetics opt for purified water, which is used for the manufacture of non-sterile pharmaceutical products.

In this section, emphasis will be placed on different sources of water; water as a vehicle in cosmetic products; different types of water used for pharmaceutical and cosmetic products; types of purified water; and microbial quality of water.

Sources of water

Water, a gift of nature, is a renewable resource that cannot be used up. It can be obtained from different sources as shown in Table 15.1. However, a large proportion of water comes from oceans, while a negligible proportion is from rivers. It has been reported that only about 2.7 - 3.0% of the world water resources is fresh water (2). The corollaries to this submission are that a large proportion of water sources are inaccessible and those that are accessible are not of good quality. The inaccessibility of water has led to global water scarcity, while the poor quality of the accessible ones has resulted in the outbreak of infections. According to the World Health Organisation (WHO), over 2 billion people live in water-stressed countries, and climate change and population expansion are predicted to make the situation worse in some areas (3). Similarly, it has been claimed that drinking water that has been contaminated by microorganisms can spread diseases that include cholera, dysentery, typhoid, and polio, as well as causing 485,000 diarrheal deaths annually (4).

Table 15.1: Sources of water

Water Source	% of total water
Oceans	97.24%
Icecaps, glaciers	2.14%
Ground water	0.61%
Fresh-water lakes	0.009%
Inland seas	0.008%
Soil moisture	0.005%
Atmosphere	0.001%
Rivers	0.0001%

Sources of water contamination

Water can be contaminated through several sources:

Basin contamination: This includes salts that are washed from the soil during irrigation as well as toxic substances that are flushed from fields and highways.

Channel contamination: The release of organic and inorganic water from private, public, and industrial sources causes channel contamination. While toxic waste products from chemical sources are the predominant contaminants from industrial concerns, sewage makes up a considerable portion of waste from domestic and communal sources. Moreover, significantly contributing to channel contamination are ship waste dumps.

Thermal contamination: When hot waste water from industries and thermal power plants is dumped into a body of water, thermal contamination occurs. As a result, fish stocks and oxygen levels decline. Additionally, it encourages the growth of algae, which further reduces the oxygen level.

Hydro-biological contamination: Farms utilise an ever-increasing quantity of herbicides, insecticides, fungicides, fertilisers, and other similar chemicals, which flow into streams and rivers after being applied to plants and soils, leading to hydro-biological contamination.

Due to the threat it poses to the environment and, ultimately, to people, the contamination of water from any of the aforementioned sources is of utmost concern. It poses a threat to the ecosystem since it may alter the biological balance of the area, which might have very catastrophic repercussions, by destroying some of the plant and animal life in any body of water. Humans may be affected directly or indirectly. For instance, poisonous substances ingested by fish from contaminated waters would build up in its body which, when eaten, transmits the toxins to humans. People who use contaminated water for drinking and cooking are also at risk. To prevent any of these scenarios, all water sources must be safeguarded from severe contamination. Undoubtedly, a welcome and constructive development is the growing awareness of the necessity of environmental conservation, at least in developed nations.

The control measures that should be taken to protect water supplies are:

- Purification of waste water from homes and industry
- Dilution of waste water
- Shifting surface water to underground channels
- Reducing the discharge of waste water to a minimum by using closed production cycles
- Using waste water for agricultural purposes.

Water as a vehicle in cosmetics

Several ingredients are incorporated into cosmetic products in different forms as solutions, suspensions, gels, aerosols or emulsions, which require a suitable vehicle to produce. This implies that a vehicle is an indispensable component of cosmetic products.

In order that a vehicle may be considered suitable for the formulation of a cosmetic product, it is expected to have the following characteristics:

- Should be pharmacologically inert

- Non-toxic
- Compatible with several ingredients
- Non-sensitising
- Non-irritating
- Effective in maintaining solubility
- Stable physically and chemically
- Unaffected by changes in pH
- Easily available and inexpensive.

The solvent that comes closest to satisfying these specifications is water which, consequently, is the vehicle of choice for most cosmetics.

Types of water for pharmaceutical and cosmetic preparations

Water for preparations or purified water and water for injections, are the types of water used in the manufacture of pharmaceutical products. The manufacture of medications, that are not intended to be sterile but for which water of good bacteriological quality is necessary, uses water for preparations (purified water) rather than water for injections, which is used in the manufacture of preparations designed for parenteral administration and other sterile products. For some specific uses, other forms of water, such as sterile water and bacteriostatic water for injection, may be provided. Sterile cosmetics, which are a type of cosmetics that contain no preservatives but are not for parenteral administration or other sterile uses, are also prepared using sterile water. Some manufacturing industries have access to potable water of acceptable biological quality, which can be utilised for non-sterile preparations as long as the mineral impurities it contains do not interact with the active ingredients or other ingredients. However, to eliminate adulteration by chemical and microbiological contaminants in cosmetic products, the use of purified water has been advocated.

Purified water

Purified water is a term used to describe water that has been filtered or processed by some other means to remove impurities that may otherwise render the water unsuitable for its intended use. There are many techniques developed for producing high-quality water required for industrial operations. These include ion-exchange, reverse osmosis, ultrafiltration, distillation, and electro-dialysis. The USP defines Purified Water USP, as water obtained by these processes or other suitable processes. Unfortunately, there is no single system for producing high-quality purified water; the selection of the system to use is dependent on such factors as raw water quality, intended use, flow rate, and cost of production.

Types of purified water

Purified water is named according to the purification technique employed for the production:

Deionised water: A well-known, traditional technique for purifying water is deionisation. With the help of hydronium and hydroxide ions (H_3O^+, OH^-), specific ion-exchange resins remove anions and cations that are present in the water leading to the production of deionised water. Salts like sodium chloride and magnesium sulphate, make up the majority of dissolved water pollutants. Anion exchangers hold onto anions (sulphate^{---}, chloride$^-$, etc.) and release hydroxide ion (OH-), while cation exchangers hold onto cations (magnesium^{++}, calcium^{++}, sodium$^+$, etc.) and release hydronium ion (H_3O^+). The ion-exchange resins become saturated and are regenerated for additional usage after being used for a certain number of time cycles (depending on the original quality of the water). Microorganisms, volatile substances, organic contaminants, and suspended materials cannot be removed using this technique.
Microbial contamination is rarely a major issue with ion-exchange resins when maintained properly. However, this may become a problem if the resins are left unused for a protracted period, or if certain types of organic compounds that support microbial growth are present in the input water. *Acinetobacter*, *Alcaligenes*, and *Pseudomonas* species are the organisms most frequently found with deionisers. UV lamps, operating at 254 nm, may be employed along with deionisers to regulate the microbiological load, as long as the deionisers have been appropriately scaled to handle the flow rate, optical clarity, and projected bioburden of the water (6). Deionised water is frequently filtered with 0.45µ or 0.20µ membrane filters to lessen the microbiological load. Ion-resins also tend to shed particles or resin fines into the water processed through them.

Demineralised water: Most frequently, deionisation and demineralisation of water are confused; however, the resultant water obtained by the use of these two processes differ. The basic goal of demineralisation, which can be carried out via the use of ion exchangers or other filtration devices, is to make the water softer by eliminating calcium and magnesium ions. Sodium chloride, which is absent in deionised water, is, however, present in demineralised water, which is most effectively obtained using a reverse osmosis filtration method.

Distilled water: One of the earliest methods of water purification is distillation. It is, however, one of the costliest and most energy-intensive water treatment processes.

During distillation, the water is heated to a boil, and the water vapour that results is condensed back into the water at the other end of the system. All suspended matter (if any), mineral, and microbiological pollutants are removed during this process. With the right aseptic collecting and storage measures, distilled water can be kept sterile for a long time after condensation. In the workplace, distilled water is frequently kept at 80°C and circulated in a ring system. This procedure preserves the quality of water by eliminating any vegetative organism that may accidentally be present as a pollutant and also prevents the production of pyrogen.

Bidest, or doubly distilled water: This is obtained as a result of a second distillation process that is done to produce water for certain scientific laboratory experiments and uses, and the technique is, therefore, only applicable in specific laboratories.

Nano-filtered water: The process of nano-filtration is described as a form of partial reverse osmosis. This process eliminates bivalent ions such as calcium, magnesium and sulphate, as well as heavy metal ions, and is mostly used in the manufacture of drinking water. However, its effectiveness in eliminating sodium chloride from water is only marginal.

Reverse osmosis (RO): This approach to water purification is getting more popular and cost-effective. Due to osmotic pressure forcing water through a semi-permeable membrane that only permits molecules with a molecular weight of less than 250 daltons to flow through, reverse osmosis-processed water can be sterile and pyrogen-free. As shown in Figure 15.1, a semi-permeable membrane through which water, but not electrolytes and organic compounds can pass, is placed between two compartments. When external pressure is applied, water will move from the compartment with the higher ion concentration (the left compartment) to the compartment with the lower ion or no ion concentration, depending on the osmotic pressure, while leaving behind dissolved minerals, big molecules, lipids, and germs.

Infiltration of microorganisms into the storage or distribution vessel downstream of the membrane can result in post-RO contamination. However, there is proof that bacteria, and more specifically, Gram-negative bacteria, can flourish in RO water and on the membrane (7).

Purified water should be prepared from water of potable quality and should contain no added substances. Not even chlorine is allowed to be present in Purified Water USP because it ionises in water to form chloride ion and hypochlorous acid. Chlorine being a strong oxidising agent, also reacts readily with constituents of products it is contained with, including cosmetic products, if the purified water contains any trace of it. Such reactions can result in cosmetic product degradation.

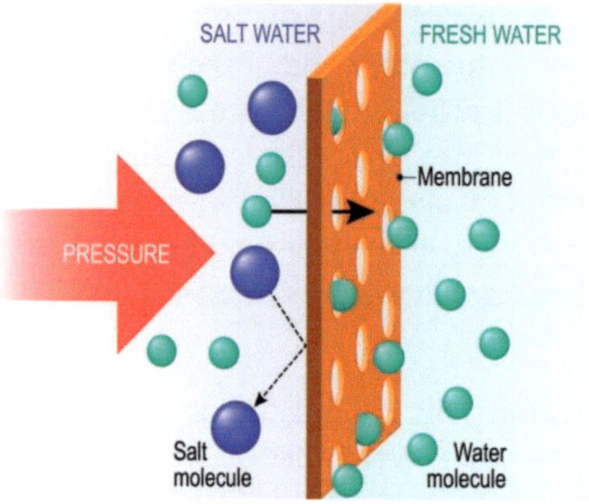

Figure 15.1: The process of reverse osmosis

Though chlorine may be removed from processed water by the use of activated charcoal, it is still necessary to determine its residual amount in purified water quantitatively. Presently, ozone is increasingly being used in place of chlorine in view of the fact that it can be destructively decimated by the action of UV light of 254 nm wavelength.

Concept of compendial water

Purified waters obtained from sources that meet pharmacopoeial standards are known as compendial water. They are classified based on the nature of their preparation and the type of usage they are subjected to as: Purified Water, Water for Injection, Sterile Water for Injection, Bacteriostatic Water for Injection, Water for washing and rinsing, and Water for drug product cooling.

Characteristics and types of compendial water

The general characteristics of compendial waters include:

- They are low conductivity waters and should contain no added disinfectant or preservatives
- Total aerobic count should not be more than 100 cfu/mL or should be based on the intended use
- Their physicochemical limits are given in Table 15.2
- They should be free of indicator microorganisms such as *Staphylococcus aureus*, *Escherichia coli*, *Salmonella* spp, *Pseudomonas* species, *Serratia marcescens*, *Klebsiella* species or any other pathogen.
- Microbiologically, they must satisfy the limit specified in Table 15.3

It is to be noted that the presence of the indicator organisms has implications for the quality of water. For instance, the presence of *E. coli* is an indication of recent faecal pollution of the water source; *Staphylococcus aureus*, an index of unhygienic production of the water; *Salmonella* spp., a causal agent of typhoid fever and food poisoning; and *Pseudomonas* species, a common wound pathogen capable of causing systemic infections. The presence of any of these indicator organisms in water renders it unsuitable for use.

Table 15.2: USP physicochemical standards for compendial waters (8)

Parameter	Purified water	Water for injection
pH	5.0 – 7.0	5.0 – 7.0
Chloride (mg/L)	0.5	0.5
Sulphate (mg/L)	1.0	1.0
Ammonia (mg/L)	0.1	0.1
Calcium (mg/L)	1.0	1.0
Carbon dioxide (mg/L)	5.0	5.0
Heavy metals (mg/L)	0.1 as Cu	0.1 as Cu
Oxidisable substance	Pass USP permanganate test	Pass USP permanganate test
Total solid (mg/L)	10.0	10.0
Limit of Pyrogens (EU/mL by LAL)	-	0.25

LAL: Limulus Amoebocite Lysate.EU: Endotoxin Unit

From Table 15.2, it can be inferred that both purified and water for injection have similar physicochemical standards except for pyrogen whose limit has been set at 0.25 endotoxin units per millilitre as determined by the Limulus Amoebocyte Lysate (LAL) test but with no limit for purified water.

Pyrogens**,** lipopolysaccharides (LPS) from Gram-negative bacterial cell-walls, are released upon bacterial death or lysis and generate a fever (pyrogenic) reaction when present in the blood stream. Contamination with pyrogen is better managed by strictly preventing water from being contaminated by microorganisms. However, infrequent sanitisation increases the risk of pyrogen release from established biofilms (9).

It can be deduced from Table 15.3 that the set microbial levels in compendial waters depend and vary with the reference used. However, while all the references support the total absence of microbes in water for injection, limited numbers are set for purified water.

Table 15.3: Microbial levels for compendial and other waters (8)

Reference	Microbial levels (cfu/mL) in			
	Potable water	Packaged water	Purified water	Water for injection
NAFDAC	-	100	100	Nil
USP XXII	-	-	100	Nil
GMP/LVP	-	-	50	0.1
BP	-	-	100	Nil

NAFDAC: National Agency for Food and Drugs Administration and Control; USP: United States Pharmacopoeia; GMP: Good Manufacturing Practice; LVP: Large Volume Parenteral; BP: British Pharmacopoeia

Rheology of liquid and semi-solid cosmetic products

Rheology is the science of deformation and flow of matter, which includes fluids, gases and solids. Generally, liquids and semisolids flow when poured or when a certain amount of force is applied to them, while solids are merely deformed by such a force. The term, viscosity, is a measure of the extent of internal friction in a fluid and defines the resistance of a fluid to flow. Rheology characterises the flow properties of liquids and semisolids. The viscosity of the final product of a fluid formulation is fundamental to its development, preparation, and evaluation.

Viscosity is expressed in the Centimetre-Gram-Second (CGS) system as dynes/cm^2-sec^{-1} or g/cm-s, which is represented as poise (P); where the unit of shear stress is dynes/cm^2 (force per unit area) and shear rate is expressed as cm/s. A centipoise (cP) is 1/100 of a poise, for example, water has a viscosity of 1.0 cP. In the International System of Units (SI), viscosity is expressed as Newton/m^2-s^{-1} or Pascal.s (Pa.s) which is equivalent to 10 P.

Plotting the shear rate as a function of applied stress (shear stress) for a fluid yields a rheogram that describes the flow characteristics as well as defines the viscosity of the fluid. When the rate of flow (shear rate) is directly proportional to the applied stress, the fluid is said to exhibit Newtonian flow or is Newtonian. Fluids which deviate from this relationship are termed non-Newtonian. A fluid is either Newtonian or non-Newtonian. However, non-Newtonian fluids exhibit other characteristic flows.

Effect of temperature on viscosity

The determination of the viscosity and flow characteristics of fluids are made under controlled temperatures, the value of which is quoted with the viscosity values and rheograms obtained, as viscosity reduces with an increase in temperature due to an increase in the kinetic energy of the particles of the test materials that makes them flow faster; the reverse occurs with a decrease in temperature.

Types of viscous flow

Newtonian flow: Newtonian flow is characterised by a straight-line rheogram which starts from and passes through the origin (Figure 15.3-2); indicating the direct proportionality of shear rate to shear stress that characterises Newtonian fluids, and is represented by the Newtonian equation:

$$\tau = D\eta$$

$$\eta = \tau / D$$

where τ is the applied stress; D is the rate of flow; and η is the constant of proportionality or the coefficient of dynamic viscosity and is simply referred to as viscosity.

The slope of the rheogram or the tangent of the angle it makes with the vertical axis gives the viscosity of the test liquid which is independent of shear stress or shear rate. Newtonian fluids are simple, pure liquids with small molecules as well as solutions of small-molecule solutes and solvents. The molecules neither agglomerate nor form a network structure, and their viscosity is, therefore, unaffected by how fast and for how long they are stirred or the previous stirring profile of the liquid at a constant composition and temperature, that is, they are time-independent. The viscosity of Newtonian liquids increases with a decrease in temperature and decreases with an increase in temperature; and, for solutions of solid solutes, the viscosity increases with an increase in concentration. Examples include glycerine, water, alcohol, sodium chloride solution and vegetable oils such as castor and olive oils. Mascaras and serums are Newtonian liquids.

Non-Newtonian flow: This is further divided into time-independent flow and time-dependent flow.

Time-independent, non-Newtonian flow: Shear-thinning, shear-thickening and plastic flows are types of time-independent, non-Newtonian flows.

Shear-thinning (pseudoplastic) flow: Fluids whose viscosity reduces the faster they are stirred at a constant temperature and composition, are termed shear-thinning (or pseudoplastic) and their viscosity is time-independent. This type of flow is exhibited by polymer solutions and flocculated dispersions of macromolecules. The rheogram begins at the origin, because the fluid flows immediately shear stress is applied, but is concave towards the shear rate axis since an increase in shear rate is higher than the respective shear stress. Hence, the slope of a tangent, taken at a specific point on the rheogram, gives the apparent viscosity (η_{app}) of the fluid for which the shear rate, at the point of determination, is quoted. Shear-thinning arises from the disentanglement and alignment of the entangled chains of polymers and high molecular weight molecules in solution along the direction of flow, creating less resistance to flow (Figure 15.2). However, with continuous stirring and increase in shear stress, the chains become fully aligned; the viscosity of the fluid becomes Newtonian and the rheogram tends towards linearity, an indication of the attainment of minimum viscosity (Figure 15.3-4). The viscosity of the substance can also be determined at this point. However, because equilibrium is established at any particular shear rate and the corresponding shear stress due to the re-entanglement of the particles by Brownian movement, the up-curve of the rheogram coincides with the down-curve. Colloidal dispersions, such as hydrocolloids used as thickening agents, e.g., gum mucilages, methyl cellulose and polyvinylpyrrolidone, exhibit shear-thinning. Body creams and lotions are shear-thinning when rubbed on the palms, thereby enhancing spreadability when applied on the skin. Suspensions are better formulated as shear-thinning preparations to allow for thorough redispersion of settled suspended particles when shaken. This is unattainable with Newtonian products of relatively high viscosity.

***Shear-thickening (dilatant) flow*:** Dilatant flow is opposite to shear-thinning as viscosity increases with an increase in shear rate and the material under test appears to increase in volume, appearing dry, when sheared quickly. The effect reverses when the shear is removed and the suspension appears wet again. The rheogram starts from the origin but is convex towards the shear rate axis (Figure 15.3-1). The up-curve and the down-curve coincide as the shear rate is reduced because the bunched-up particles tend to return to their initial state as the shear rate is reduced. The phenomenon is exhibited by dispersions of high concentrations (approximately 50%) of small, deflocculated particles that do not stick together or aggregate and which contain just enough liquid to lubricate the particles and fill the voids between them. When such suspensions are stirred very fast, the particles get into each other's way and bunch up, while the liquid around them sip into the void created, giving a dry appearance and an apparent increase in volume. Concentrated starch suspension (40 -50%) in glycerine, water or ethylene glycol, as well as concentrated dispersions (12%) of deflocculated inorganic pigments, e.g., red iron oxide, in water or nonpolar liquids, exhibit dilatancy when stirred very fast. This behaviour can cause overload and damage to the motor of mixers when operated at high speeds. Dilatancy is, however, less common than the other types of time-independent flows.

Plastic (Bingham) flow: Plastic flow is exhibited by semisolids that are made up of polymers, particulates or macromolecules with cross-linked 3-dimensional (3D) network, as well as concentrated suspensions with flocculated particles or with structured dispersion medium. The rheogram of a plastic fluid does not start at the origin but at some point (yield point) on the shear stress axis, known as the yield value, that represents the value of stress needed to break down the network structure or floccules of the material, after which the material starts to flow (Figure 15.3-5). The material, thereafter, may exhibit Newtonian or pseudoplastic flow depending on the nature and extent of the breakup of the network structure or deflocculation. At shear stress values below the yield value, the material behaves like an elastic solid. Materials that exhibit plastic flow are known as Bingham bodies. Plastic flow is observed for fluid lotions which appear immobile in their containers such that the containers can be turned upside down with no movement of the contents until shaken. Creams, gels, pastes and ointments, because of their semisolid consistency, exhibit plasticity which prevents them from running off the hands till they are rubbed on the palms and applied on the skin or from sinking into applicators such as brushes.

Time-dependent, non-Newtonian flow: This type of flow comprises thixotropy, negative thixotropy or anti-thixotropy and rheopexy.

Thixotropy: Thixotropy means "to change by touch" and indicates a time-dependent, reversible decrease in the apparent viscosity of a material. It is an isothermal transformation of a fluid material from the gel state, when at rest, to a sol when sheared, and back to the gel state when shearing is gradually reduced back to the state of rest. The apparent viscosity of such a material is dependent on its composition, its previous shear history, and as for all the other types of flow, the temperature at the time of determination.

Thixotropic materials are composed of macromolecules or asymmetric particles that interact by many secondary bonds forming a loose, 3-dimensional network that confers a gel-like state to the material at rest. Also, the dispersion medium of some thixotropic suspensions consists of polymeric colloids whose polymer chains entangle one another. Under shear, the 3-dimensional network structures are broken, the entangled polymer chains disentangle and viscosity reduces. However, because of the high viscosity of the medium and the large size and weight of the particles, Brownian motion is unable to quickly restore the broken links of the particles or the re-entanglement of the polymers as the shear rate is gradually reduced. Hence, the apparent viscosity of the material is lower when shear is gradually being reduced than when being increased or constant, that is, the upward curve of the rheogram of a thixotropic material does not coincide with the downward curve, creating the hysteresis loop (Figure 15.3-3). The area of the loop is an index of the degree of structural breakdown or the disentanglement of the polymers of the dispersion medium under shear.

At times, plasticity is superimposed on thixotropy. For materials that exhibit this phenomenon, the restoration of structures is not substantially completed by the time shear is reduced to zero and the down-curve rests, with a reduced yield value, on the shear stress axis (Figure 15.3-6a). Subjecting such a material immediately to another cycle of shear will yield a rheogram with a lower apparent viscosity and a smaller hysteresis loop. With subsequent cycles of shear, the structures become completely broken, are unable to be restored by Brownian motion, are irreversibly destroyed and no hysteresis can be obtained thereafter if the material is subjected to another shear cycle as the down curve has ended at the origin of the graph (Figure 15.3-6b). In some other instances, the broken-down structure of the materials is not restored, no matter how long the material is left at rest, after being subjected to a single shear cycle. The down-curve at this instance, is either Newtonian or pseudoplastic and ends at the origin of the graph (Figure 15.3-5). This phenomenon is referred to as shear destruction and is observed with high molecular weight gels whose structures, formed by a large number of secondary bonds (especially when the dispersions are prepared by heating) are extensively reorganised while being sheared, reducing the initial 3-dimensional network structures to 2-dimensional structures that are unable to form network structures. As an example, starch gels are formed when water molecules, by the aid of heat, form hydrogen-bonding bridges between starch molecules that are adjacent to one another, as well as intramolecular van der Waals interactions between the hydroxyl groups on the molecules. The bonds are irreversibly broken by shear.

Pastes that consist of a high concentration of deflocculated particles suspended in highly viscous thixotropic materials exhibit dilatancy with thixotropy when sheared fast, for example, toothpaste gels containing particulate ingredients.

Thixotropy lends an advantage to cosmetic suspensions and emulsions in that it allows products to pour easily from the container when shaken, that is, viscosity is reduced, but prevents sedimentation or creaming at rest or on storage, when the initial high viscosity is re-established and the dispersed particles or droplets are immobilised within the restored 3-dimensional structure, thereby enabling a shelf-stable product. The addition of thixotropic agents, such as microcrystalline cellulose, bentonite magma and colloidal silicon dioxide, to liquid products confers high apparent viscosity that may result in a product that exhibits plasticity along with thixotropy.

Negative thixotropy or anti-thixotropy or rheopexy: The full restoration of the network structure by Brownian motion of a gel that has been subjected to shear may take a while to be achieved after shearing is discontinued. However, subjecting the material to low shear rates by gently shaking the container or by applying moderate, rhythmic vibration, accelerates the rate of restoration of the network structure and, consequently, the product to its initial consistency. This phenomenon is referred to as anti-thixotropy or negative thixotropy. Rheopexy is, however, reversible as the material reverses to its original mobile state when the shear is removed.

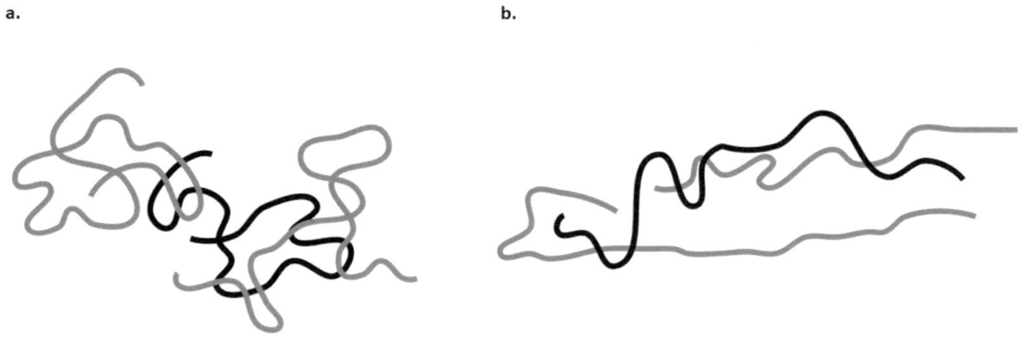

Figure 15.2: Behaviour of entangled polymers in pseudoplastic flow (a) three entangled polymers at rest (b) the three entangled polymers alligning along the direction of flow when sheared

Measurement of the flow properties of materials

The instruments used for the measurement of the viscosity and flow characteristics of fluids are basically of two types – single-point viscometers and rotational viscometers.

Single-point viscometers: These are of two basic types: the capillary viscometers and the falling or rolling sphere viscometers. Single-point viscometers are not suitable for non-Newtonian fluids as the rheological characteristics of such fluids cannot be observed with these viscometers.

Capillary viscometers: These are used to measure the viscosity of Newtonian fluids since the shear rate is directly proportional to shear stress for these fluids and a flow curve; involving the use of a rotational viscometer, may not be necessary. The viscometers operate on the principle of the flow of a liquid through a standard capillary tube, under the influence of gravity or an externally applied pressure. The tubes are clamped vertically and placed in a thermostatic water-bath and the tube, filled appropriately with the test liquid, is allowed to equilibrate with the temperature of the water-bath. The flow of the liquid from one designated point to another on the instrument is taken as the flow time (Figure 15.4-a, b).

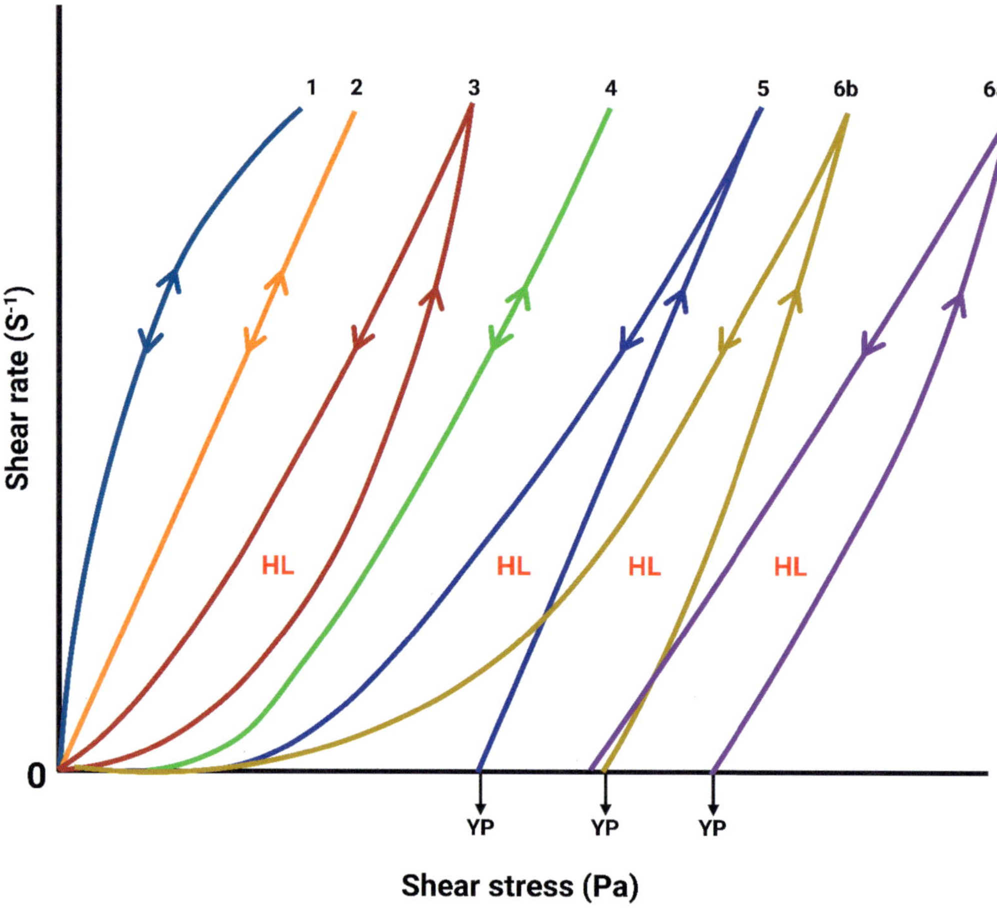

Figure 15.3: Characteristic rheograms of fluid products

1 = dilatant flow, 2 = Newtonian flow, 3 = pseudoplastic flow with thixotropy, 4 = pseudoplastic flow, 5 = plastic flow with complete loss of network structure after a single shear cycle, 6a = plastic flow with incomplete network structure destruction after a single shear cycle, 6b = plastic flow with complete network structure destruction after a second shear cycle of the sample used in 6a. YP = yield point at which yield value is calculated, HL = hysteresis loop

The flow time of the test liquid, of known density, is related to that of a known liquid whose density is known and the viscosities are calculated using these equations:

$\eta_1 / \eta_2 = t1\rho1/t2\rho2$ dynamic viscosity (Poise P or Pascal Pa)

$V_1/V2 = t_1/t_2$ kinematic viscosity (Stoke St)

$$V = Kt(\frac{\rho s}{\rho 1} - 1)$$

t = flow time sec, ρ = density, 1= test fluid, 2= known fluid, K is a constant that may be determined using a liquid of known kinematic viscosity

Examples of capillary viscometers are the Ubbelohde, Ostwald, and Cannon-Fenske viscometers.

Falling or rolling sphere viscometer: The viscometer (Figure 15.5) measures the time it takes for a sphere or a ball to fall or roll through a test fluid from one point (A) on the viscometer to another (B) under the influence of gravity, which is referred to as the fall time. The movement of the sphere is monitored with the aid of a microscope. The fall time is used to calculate the kinematic viscosity of the fluid using the equation:

$$V = Kt(\frac{\rho s}{\rho 1} - 1)$$

t = flow time sec, ρ = density, 1= test fluid, 2= known fluid, K is a constant that may be determined using a liquid of known kinematic viscosity

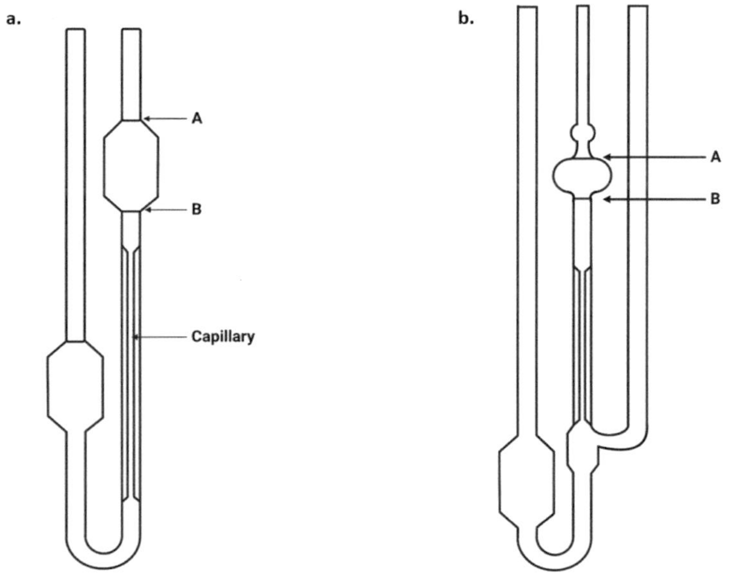

Figure 15.4: Capillary viscometers a. = Ostwald U-tube viscometer, b. = Ubbelohde viscometer, A, B =liquid flow from point A to B

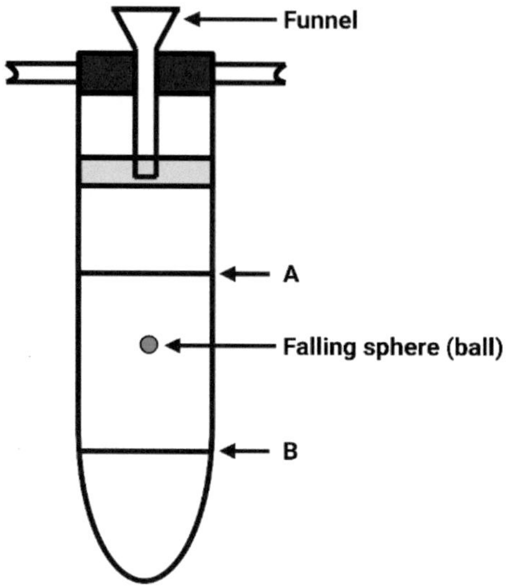

Figure 15.5: Falling sphere viscometer A, B, = falling sphere travel from A to B

Rotational viscometers: Non-Newtonian fluids are assessed using continuous shear instruments that are connected to a recording machine which plots the shear rate and shear stress of a material as a flow curve or rheogram. Rotational viscometers are available in two measuring geometries namely:

Concentric cylinder (Couette) geometry: Viscometers of this type consist of two coaxial cylinders; the outer cylinder is the cup that contains the test material while the inner cylinder or bob is centrally placed about the cup (Fig. 15.6a). The cylinder that is rotated for measurement is dependent on the design of the viscometer. For the MacMichael type of viscometer, the outer cup is rotated and the bob is stationary, while the bob is rotated and the cup is stationary in the Stormer type of viscometer. Water from a thermostatic water-bath is circulated within the walls of the cup to maintain a constant sample temperature during the measurement.

Cone and plate geometry: This type consists of a circular, flat plate above which is a centrally placed cone that has a wide angle and whose tip just touches the plate. The test sample fills into the gap between the cone and the plate (Figure. 15.6b). The set-up is surrounded by an anti-evaporation hood (10), and water at a controlled temperature is circulated under the plate. The viscometer is connected to a recorder that gives a rheogram for the sample under test.

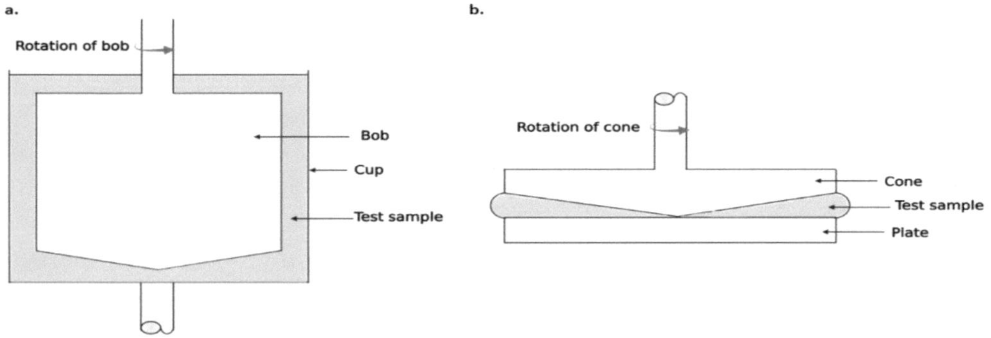

Figure 15.6: Rotational viscometers. a, concentric cylinder geometry b, cone and plate geometry

Applications of rheology in formulation and stability studies

Rheology determination is of great value when a product is being formulated as it ensures the reproducibility of the consistency of the product. Factors that may affect the viscosity of the product are taken into consideration and appropriate ingredients are used. The viscosity of a product determines the type of equipment that is used in its preparation. For instance, a propeller mixer can be used for fluid preparations, a turbine mixer for a more viscous fluid, and a planetary mixer for a semisolid product. The final viscosity of a product determines the type of container in which it is packaged, for example, while lotions can be packaged in rigid bottles with a narrow mouth; semisolid creams, ointments and pastes will be difficult to remove from such containers unless with a wide mouth that allows the fingers to get at the product or a soft squeezable tube with an appropriate orifice is used.

It is expected that the viscosity of a product will remain constant throughout its shelf life. A reduction or increase in viscosity during storage indicates poor formulation and requires a reformulation after the factors causing the instability have been identified. For example, hydrolysis of polymer chains, especially hydrocolloids, into shorter chain lengths during storage will lead to a reduction in viscosity, while swelling of polymers with time will lead to an increase in viscosity. An increase in viscosity can increase the stability of creams and suspensions but can negatively affect the pourability of the product from the container. A decrease in viscosity will encourage the creaming of emulsions and settling of suspended particles of suspensions which are indicators of instability for these types of products.

Preformulation studies

Preformulation studies are carried out on the prospective ingredients, both the active ingredients and the excipients, of an intended product formulation. It involves the determination, understanding and utilisation of the physico-chemical properties of the ingredients. In the pharmaceutical industry, preformulation involves the chemical substance known as the drug or the active pharmaceutical ingredient (API) and the excipients, also known as the adjuvants. Excipients are invariably used for the various dosage forms, such as injections, tablets, capsules, emulsions, lotions, creams, and powders for preparations, by which APIs are presented for use to the patients. The main role of excipients in these dosage forms is to enable the attainment of the desired characteristics, physical form and the stability of the desired dosage forms, and examples include: emulsifiers, buffers, binders for tablets, colourants, antioxidants and preservatives. Hence, preformulation, carried out on these ingredients, which involves determination of their efficacy, stability and compatibility with the API to be used, assist in their proper selection. Similarly, the active ingredients and excipients used for the formulation of cosmetic products are subjected to preformulation.

Most of the APIs employed in the formulation of medicaments are solid drug substances and preformulation requires the determination of their several physico-chemical properties such as the chemical form (e.g., salt forms), solubility, crystal properties (e.g., polymorphism, optical isomers, crystal habit), physico-mechanical properties (e.g., particle size analysis, powder flow, degree of wetting, hygroscopicity), stability (kinetics and order of reaction, hydrolysis, oxidation, photolysis), organoleptic properties (e.g., taste, colour, smell) and compatibility with excipients. On the other hand, most of the active ingredients of cosmetic products are essential oils, fixed oils, fats, waxes and other liquid ingredients such as the glycols and silicones.

The oils, fats and waxes employed for cosmetic product formulation are mostly obtained from natural sources and, as such, have variable constituents and quality with each batch. Preformulation is, therefore, imperative to set quality standards as required by each manufacturer, to ensure the same quality is obtained with each batch of product. Quality tests may involve determining which of the constituents of a particular naturally-sourced ingredient is unacceptable and using physico-chemical processes, such as fractionation and chemical extraction techniques, to remove such compounds. For example, some manufacturers only need the long chain glycerides of shea butter for their cosmetic products, which are extracted and the residue (marc) discarded. In the same manner, only certain chemical compounds of an essential oil may be all that are needed. Oxidation of the fatty acid components of natural oils, fats and waxes is the predominant form of instability of these ingredients and appropriate tests are carried out to determine the level of the oxidative deterioration in a batch sample to ascertain its acceptability. Preformulation of cosmetic ingredients involves testing for some of the following properties.

Organoleptic properties

Colour: The colour of the degradation product of a substance that has undergone oxidation may be easily observed even before chemical tests are carried out. A well-whipped sample of shea butter appears whitish compared to the original butter-yellow to ivory colour, although decoulorised shea butter is white in colour. Whipped shea butter is highly susceptible to oxidation because of the much air it contains.

Smell: Some substances have their characteristic smell; deviation from this may indicate adulteration or a degradative chemical change, e.g., the rancid smell of vegetable fats and oils due to oxidation.

Taste: it is not advisable to taste new chemical entities; notwithstanding, test-tasting of batches of well-known supplies of ingredients may give-off rancid samples.

Particle size of powdered ingredients

The particle size of powdered ingredients such as metallic dyes and sunscreen agents, and those employed in the preparation of face powders, facial scrubs and masks, plays an important role in the efficacy and stability of the products prepared using the powders. The optimum particle size and size distribution are studied in the preformulation of such products.

Solubility

Active ingredients of cosmetic products are often mixed with each other and with excipients in a formulation. Oils, fats and waxes are non-polar and do not mix with water which is a polar substance. Organic solvents such as acetone, alcohol, propylene and ethylene glycols are used, singly as solvents or mixed together in certain proportions as cosolvents for these oily substances. Essential oils, however, contain some compounds which impart their aroma to water while not dissolving completely in the water. Oily substances can be solubilized in water using appropriate surface-active agents.

Stability

The stability profile of the ingredients of a product formulation is determined in preformulation to obtain information that guides their use and the possible means of preventing their deterioration.

Hydrolysis: Hydrolysis occurs in aqueous environment and is affected by changes in pH and temperature. Fats and some oils, undergo hydrolysis, breaking down to fatty acids, mono- and di-glycerides and glycerol.

Oxidation: Fats, oils and waxes, in the presence of oxygen (air), and catalysts like heat, sunlight, and di- and tri- valent metal ions such as those of iron and copper, undergo oxidation reaction that results in rancidity with changes in smell, and in some cases, in colour and consistency. Such fatty substances should be stored protected from air, heat, sunlight and metallic ions. Antioxidants, employed at the effective concentrations, can prevent oxidative degradation of susceptible substances.

Excipients and active ingredients

The physico-chemical properties, compatibility and efficacy of the active ingredients and excipients chosen for the formulation of a product are determined in preformulation.

Formulation and preparation of creams and lotions (emulsions)

General properties of emulsions – creams and lotions

Creams and most lotions, though of semisolid and liquid consistencies, respectively, are emulsions. An emulsion is a heterogeneous dispersion of two immiscible liquids, (usually oily and aqueous substances), where one liquid is dispersed as droplets (dispersed phase) within the other liquid (continuous phase) and stabilised by the inclusion of an emulsifying agent or emulsifier. The emulsifier lowers the interfacial tension between the immiscible liquids and forms films around the dispersed droplets, thereby stabilising the dispersion by preventing droplet coalescence.

The dispersed phase of an emulsion could be the oily liquid and such an emulsion is regarded as an oil-in-water (o/w) emulsion which is easily diluted or mixed with water or other aqueous liquids. Thus, aqueous o/w emulsions do not appear oily on the skin and are easily washed off the skin with water. Water-in-oil (w/o) emulsions, on the other hand, have the aqueous liquid phase dispersed as droplets within the oily continuous phase and can be diluted or mixed with oily liquids. Such emulsions are said to be oily; they give a shiny look on the skin and are not miscible with water nor easily washed off the skin with water.

Emulsions are classified according to their droplet sizes, which also determine the colour of the emulsions. Macroemulsions have droplet sizes of $\geq 0.1\mu$ - 100μ and constitute the normal emulsions which are usually whitish, unless highly concentrated, when they appear yellowish. Microemulsions are translucent to transparent with droplet sizes of 1nm - 1μ while nanoemulsions are transparent with droplet sizes of < 1nm.

There are also multiple emulsions: water-in-oil-in-water (w/o/w) emulsion where an initial w/o emulsion is dispersed as droplets within an aqueous continuous phase; and oil-in-water-in-oil (o/w/o) emulsion, the dispersed phase of which are droplets of o/w emulsions. Multiple emulsions serve as controlled release systems where the active ingredient is enclosed within the dispersed phase of the primary emulsion and diffuses slowly through the dispersion medium of the secondary emulsion before it is released to elicit its effects at the site where the emulsion is applied.

The consistency of an emulsion is determined by the physical nature and the viscosity of the oily materials and the emulsifiers, (for example, hydrocolloids - the excess of which increases the viscosity of the continuous phase), employed as well as the inclusion of viscosity-imparting agents in the dispersion medium. Thus, a fluid emulsion contains liquid oily substances and is termed a lotion. A cream, on the other hand, may contain semi-solid fatty substances (such as fats and waxes) that impart their semi-solid consistency to the product, or may have, included in the formulation, other viscosity-imparting agents such as carbomer gels and hydrocolloids.

Components of emulsions – creams and lotions

Oils: The oils included in creams and lotions serve mainly as emollients, and, in some instances, as lubricants, in most of the cosmetic products in which they are present. Oils used in cosmetics include: avocado oil, coconut oil, castor oil, olive oil, jojoba oil, palm oil, argan oil, and canola oil which are plant-derived. These contain fatty acids and form emollient films on the skin and hair and also acts as lubricants. Liquid paraffin is a petroleum-derived oil that serves the same purpose as natural oils.

Fats and waxes: Fats and waxes are employed in the preparation of creams and lotions either as emollients or as viscosity-imparting agents and may sometimes serve both functions. Shea butter, cocoa butter, mango butter, lanolin from wool fat, carnauba wax and beeswax, consist mainly of triglycerides (esters of glycerol and fatty acids) with some phospholipids and unsaturated hydrocarbons, and are obtained from plants and animals while paraffin wax is a petroleum product.

The oil phase: This is composed of oils, fats, waxes and oil-soluble ingredients of a product.

The aqueous phase: This consists mainly of water and aqueous solutions of water-soluble or water-miscible ingredients of an emulsion preparation.

Emulsifiers (Emulsifying agents): Emulsifying agents are regarded as the third phase of an emulsion. Most emulsifiers are surface active agents (SAAs) which are amphiphilic as their molecules consist of a hydrophilic (polar) head and a hydrophobic (non-polar) tail.

Surfactants orientate themselves at the water-oil interface, with the hydrophilic head within the aqueous phase and the hydrophobic tail in the oily phase, thereby reducing the interfacial tension between the two immiscible phases, making them to have less repulsion for each other and be dispersed one in the other. Emulsifiers, after the two phases have been mixed such that one phase is dispersed as droplets within the other, form films around the dispersed droplets and prevent coalescence, thereby stabilising the dispersion. Emulsifiers with surfactant activity (e.g., sodium oleate) form monomolecular films around the dispersed droplets while hydrocolloids (e.g., gum acacia) form multimolecular films and particulate emulsifiers (e.g., veegum) form films of particulate matter around the droplets.

The chemical nature of an emulsifier determines the type of emulsion that it forms, whether o/w or w/o, while some, like the particulate film formers can produce both types depending on the phase in which they are placed before the two phases are mixed. The phase in which the emulsifier is more soluble becomes the continuous phase. However, if the concentration of the dispersed phase is much more than that required for such an emulsifier to form a particular type of emulsion, phase inversion can occur and the type of emulsion obtained is reversed, for example, calcium oleate normally give w/o because it is more soluble in the oil than in the aqueous phase. However, such an emulsion can invert to o/w type if the concentration of the aqueous phase is increased beyond a tolerable level or the temperature of the emulsion is increased beyond its phase inversion temperature, which as the name implies is the temperature at which an emulsion changes from its initial type (o/w or w/o) to the other type (w/o or o/w), respectively.

Synthetic emulsifiers

Synthetic emulsifiers are classified as ionic surfactants - those that dissociate in water and carry charges on their molecules; and non-ionic surfactants, those that are neutral.

Ionic emulsifiers

Anionic emulsifiers: These consist of soaps of monovalent, di- and tri-valent metal hydroxides as well as amine bases. Examples include sodium oleate, calcium laurate and triethanolamine stearate, which are formed in situ when sodium hydroxide (monovalent alkali base), calcium hydroxide (divalent alkaline base) and triethanolamine (amine base) are added to the aqueous phase and mixed vigorously with the oil phase that contains fatty acids of oleic acid, lauric acid and stearic acid, respectively. These fatty acids are components of vegetable oils and fats, but pure fatty acids, such as oleic and stearic acids, are often added to complement the efficacy of the fatty acids of the oils in forming very stable emulsions.

A special type of anionic soap is formed when the fatty acid fraction of beeswax reacts with the sodium hydroxide released when borax is dissolved in water. The o/w emulsion formed, referred to as beeswax-borax emulsion, can sustain a high proportion of the oil internal phase, but when applied with rubbing on the skin, inverts to w/o type during which process a cooling effect of the water is felt on the skin while the inverted oil continuous phase enhances the cleansing action of the cream, hence the term **cold cream.**

Monovalent and amine soaps give o/w emulsions while di- and tri-valent soaps produce w/o emulsions. The emulsifiers are very effective and relatively cheap, but must be used at a high pH as low acidic pH causes a breakdown of the soaps. They may cause stinging in the eyes, skin irritation as well as increased trans-epidermal water loss (TEWL) by interacting with interstitial skin lipids. They are incompatible with cationic emulsifiers, such as found in conditioning products and other cationic substances such as hard water which contains magnesium and calcium ions. They reduce the antimicrobial properties of positively-charged preservatives such as the parahydroxy benzoic acids and the parabens (11).

Alkyl sulphates and sulphosuccinates are also a type of ionic surfactants and examples include sodium lauryl sulphate, sodium laureth sulphate, alkyl polyoxyethylene sulphate, ammonium lauryl sulphate, perfluorooctanesulphonate, sodium dodecyl sulphate, and dioctyl sodium sulphosuccinate (docusate). These produce o/w emulsions and are less irritant than soap emulsifiers.

Cationic emulsifiers: The emulsifiers in this group are quaternary ammonium compounds and examples include cetyl trimethyl ammonium bromide, benzalkonium chloride and lauryl dimethyl benzyl ammonium chloride. They have marked bactericidal activities and are used in anti-infective products. They produce o/w emulsions and may require auxiliary emulsifiers such as cetyl alcohol to enhance the stability of the emulsions formed. The pH of products prepared with these emulsifiers is between 4 - 6 which is within the pH of the skin, hence, such emulsions are minimally irritant to the skin (12); they are incompatible with anionic emulsifiers.

Amphoteric emulsifiers: The molecules of amphoteric emulsifiers exhibit both anionic and cationic characteristics depending on the pH of the environment in which they are, being anionic at low pH, cationic at high pH and neutral at the isoelectric point when both ions are present on the molecule. They have a protein-like structure and are relatively mild on the skin. They are stable in the presence of cationic, anionic and non-ionic surfactants and act synergistically with these surfactants. They are also stable to acids, alkalis, hard water and electrolytes. Examples include cocamidopropyl betaine, cocoamphoacetate, alkyldimethylamine N-oxide, and alkylamidopropylamine. They do not irritate the eyes; hence, they are employed in shampoos and bath washes for babies and infants.

Nonionic emulsifiers

Nonionic surfactants do not ionise nor do they carry charges on their molecules. However, to act as a surfactant and emulsifier, each molecule must have well-balanced hydrophilic and lipophilic groups. Where the hydrophilic group is higher, then the compound is water-soluble and supports o/w emulsion formation; while a more lipophilic compound is oil-soluble and supports w/o emulsion formation. The lipophilic portion of the molecule comprises fatty acids of 12 -18 carbon atoms while the hydrophilic group is made up of alcohol or ethylene oxide group. These emulsifiers exhibit optimum emulsion stabilisation profile when combined at the appropriate ratio, which is calculated based on the hydrophile-lipophile balance (HLB) numbers that are assigned to the surfactants, and the type of emulsion desired. As emulsifiers, a surfactant with an HLB number of between 3 - 6 will support w/o emulsion while that with HLB number of 8 – 18 will support o/w emulsion formation (12).

Types include:

Glycol and glycerol esters: Examples are propylene glycol monooleate and glyceryl monostearate; which give weak w/o emulsions. However, the addition of small quantities (approximately 3 - 6%) of sodium, potassium or triethanolamine salts to glyceryl esters produces more effective emulsifiers. Such emulsifying agents are referred to as 'self-emulsifying', e.g., self-emulsifying glyceryl monostearate.

Sorbitan esters: These are a combination of fatty acids with sorbitol or mannitol and are commonly marketed in the form of a series as 'Spans^{R} 'or 'Arlacels^{R}; e.g., sorbitan mono-oleate = Span 80^{R} with an HLB of 4.3. They promote w/o emulsion.

Polysorbitan esters: These are polyoxyethylene glycol or macrogol derivatives of sorbitan esters. They have similar series as the Spans called Tweens^{R} or Polysorbates^{R}; e.g., Polyoxyethylene sorbitan mono-oleate = Tween 80^{R} (HLB 15). They promote o/w emulsion formation and are often combined with the sorbitan esters to give good emulsions.

Other nonionics include fatty acid polyglycol esters, e.g., polyoxyethylene stearate Myrj 52^{R} which gives o/w emulsions; poloxalkol or poloxamers – polyoxyethylene/ polyoxypropylene co-polymers which impart structure to vehicles; higher fatty alcohols or long chain alcohols, e.g., cetostearyl alcohol, cetyl alcohol, stearyl alcohol; polyoxyethylene alkyl ethers (macrogols), polyoxyethylene polyoxypropylene block copolymers (poloxamers), polyethylene glycol 400 monostearate, lanolin alcohols, ethoxylated lanolin and polyvinyl alcohols.

Nonionic emulsifiers have low toxicity and irritancy, are more compatible with other materials than ionic emulsifiers, are less sensitive to pH changes and are stable at pH 4-9. However, they are more expensive than most other emulsifiers, they have an unpleasant taste and tend to bind and inactivate preservatives with phenolic or carboxylic acid groups.

Natural and semisynthetic emulsifiers

There are some other types of emulsifiers which have little or no surface activity but can form tenacious films around the dispersed droplets of an emulsion, preventing coalescence of the droplets, hence, making the dispersion stable. Such emulsifiers include natural and semisynthetic colloids such as gum exudates, e.g., acacia gum (*Acacia senegal*); tragacanth (*Astragalus gummifer*); alginates (brown algae); chondrus/carrageenan (Irish moss -*Chondrus crispus*); guar gum (*Cyamopsis tetragonoloba*); xanthan gum produced by fermentation of sugars by the bacterium *Xanthomonas campestris*; pectin - a heteropolysaccharide that is usually obtained from the rinds of citrus fruits; and cellulose derivatives such as methyl cellulose and carboxymethyl cellulose. These hydrophilic polysaccharide colloids, which form multimolecular film layers around the droplets, produce o/w type of emulsions. They further enhance the stability of emulsions by imparting viscosity to the aqueous internal or continuous phase of the emulsion. However, the major drawbacks of these excipients are that, being of natural origin, there is the likelihood of batch-to-batch variation and contamination with microorganisms which may affect their emulsifying activity and the microbial quality of the emulsion product, respectively. Also, the viscosity of the polysaccharides dispersed in the aqueous phase reduces with storage due to the hydrolysis of their polymeric chains to shorter chain lengths and, if the effect is extensive, may cause a reduction of the stability of the emulsions in which they are employed due to a reduction in the viscosity of the continuous phase of the emulsion that may lead to creaming of the product. The hydrocolloids are also used as co-emulsifiers and as viscosity-imparting agents along with some other types of emulsifiers. They are non-toxic and are safe for use but may not be suitable in some preparations, e.g., topical products, especially when used in relatively high concentrations as they may cause clothes to stick to the skin.

Carnauba wax (obtained from the wax leaves of *Copernicia prunifera*) and candelilla wax (obtained from the wax leaves of *Euphorbia cerifera, E. antisyphilitica*) are sometimes used as a form of emulsifiers in cosmetics for oily, w/o products.

Some emulsifiers that are obtained from animal sources. These include gelatine which is obtained by acid or alkaline treatment of bovine and porcine skins and bones; egg yolk; casein - a milk protein, as well as lecithin that is produced mainly from soy (soya beans), eggs and sunflower seeds. These are amphiphilic, possessing both polar and non-polar groups as described earlier, and they give o/w emulsions. Wool fat; lanolin (anhydrous wool fat); cholesterol - sterols obtained from wool fat; and beeswax obtained from honeycombs (*Apis mellifera*) produce w/o emulsions.

Bioemulsifiers

Bioemulsifiers, also known as exopolysaccharides or high molecular weight biopolymers, are complex mixtures of lipopolysaccharides, heterosaccharides, lipoproteins and proteins that are derived from microbial metabolic processes. The presence of polysaccharides, lipoproteins and proteins in these emulsifiers enhances their emulsifying and emulsion-stabilising ability. They are amphiphilic and, the polysaccharide polymer being the hydrophilic moiety that is covalently attached to the hydrophobic protein moiety. Hence, they have a surface activity that enables them to adsorb at the oil-water interface, lowering the interfacial tension and increasing the kinetic stability of the dispersed droplets of an emulsion by binding tightly to the surface of the dispersed oil droplets. While biosurfactants are similarly derived, their molecules are of lower molecular weight and act mainly to reduce surface and interfacial tensions but give less stable emulsion than bioemulsifiers which, incidentally, do not reduce surface tension appreciably (13). Also, much lower concentrations are required for bioemulsifiers than biosurfactants and, indeed, other emulsifiers for the production of stable emulsions, for example, Emulsan^{R}, a lipopolysaccharide produced by *Acinetobacter calcoaceticus* RAG 1, has a use concentration range of 0.01 – 0.001% as an emulsifying agent (13). Other bioemulsifiers include lauryl fructose obtained from *Pseudomonas* spp.; liposan obtained from *Candida lipolytica*; phaffia yeast from *Phaffia rhodozyma;* and alasan obtained from *A. radioresistens* KA53 which is an anionic alanine-containing bioemulsifier (14).

Bioemulsifiers have superior properties and advantages over chemically synthesized emulsifiers, such as being produced from natural substrates under mild environmental conditions, being biodegradable, non-toxic, efficient at low concentrations, biocompatible as well as having a high tolerance to pH and temperature changes (13). Patented cosmetic products, in the form of shampoo, lotion, ointment, cream, soap and dentifrice containing 0.02 to 0.5% by weight of a bioemulsifier obtained from *Acinetobacter calcoaceticus* species, are examples of cosmetic products prepared using bioemulsifiers (15).

Particulate film-forming emulsifiers

Finely powdered, solid materials that are partially wetted by water (partially hydrophilic) and oil (partially hydrophobic) can serve as emulsifiers. This type of emulsifiers form coherent particulate films that are irreversibly adsorbed at the oil-water interface of dispersed droplets of an emulsion and such emulsions are termed Pickering emulsions, after the person that first described the phenomenon (16). The emulsifiers form either the o/w or w/o type of emulsions depending on whether they are added to the aqueous phase or oily phase, respectively, when the emulsion is being prepared. Examples include montmorillonite clays such as bentonite, veegum and attapulgite; metallic hydroxides such as aluminium and magnesium hydroxides; as well as carbon black and colloidal mica.

Auxiliary emulsifiers

Auxiliary emulsifiers are unable to form stable emulsions but are used in conjunction with some emulsifiers to enhance the stability of the emulsions formed by the latter. Some have a minimal surface activity such as cetyl alcohol and glyceryl monostearate, which being waxy solids like stearic acid also increase the viscosity of the emulsions in which they are employed. Stearic acid is also added in the formulation of emulsions prepared using plant oils that contain fatty acids with anionic bases so as to increase the quantity of fatty acids available to form the required anionic soap emulsifier for a stable emulsion. Methylcellulose and sodium carboxymethylcellulose, on their own, do not form stable emulsions but increase the viscosity of emulsions thereby preventing the creaming or coalescence of the dispersed droplets.

Self-emulsifying wax, an anionic emulsifier, consists of cetyl stearyl alcohol and sodium cetyl stearyl sulphate.

Other essential constituents of emulsions

Emulsion-based cosmetic products are customarily formulated according to the intended use and applications; hence the components may include additives such as colourants, fragrances, moisturisers (humectants, emollients, occlusives), viscosity-improvers, and pearlescents. However, there are other excipients, apart from emulsifiers and stabilisers, that must be included in the formulation to achieve a product that remains stable and acceptable throughout a shelf-life period. These are antioxidants that prevent the oxidation of natural oils, fats, waxes, and other susceptible components, and preservatives that prevent microbial growth.

Antioxidants

The main causes of rancidity of fixed oils, comprising mainly fatty acid esters, are hydrolysis of the ester group to fatty acids and oxidation of the double bonds in the free fatty acids or in the fatty acid portion of the esters to produce ketones and aldehydes, which give an off odour, known as the rancid smell. Factors that accelerate the oxidation of these compounds include the presence of water, exposure to air and relatively high temperatures as well as sunlight. Double bonds, which are present in the carbon chain of some fatty acids, such as oleic acid, are also susceptible to oxidation and so are other components of an emulsion that are prone to oxidation such as fragrances. Antioxidants, also referred to as chemical preservatives, are compounds that prevent the oxidative breakdown of susceptible substances by being preferentially oxidised. Examples of antioxidants used in cosmetics are propyl gallate, butylated hydroxytoluene (BHT), butylated hydroxyanisole (BHA), ascorbyl palmitate, pentaerythrityl tetra-di-t-butyl hydroxyhydrocinnamate and tocopherol (vitamin E). More information on antioxidants is available in chapters 12 and 18 of this book.

Preservatives

Microbial preservatives are added to emulsions to prevent the growth and proliferation of microorganisms that may be present in cosmetic products while being prepared or introduced during use by the consumer. The presence of microorganisms in products may pose health hazards to the consumer, may affect aesthetics where such growth is obvious to sight or results in the production of gas and colour change; and may also lead to the breakdown of the emulsion. The presence of oils, water, certain emulsifiers (e.g., natural colloids) and some other ingredients of an emulsion preparation constitute a conducive environment and nutritive medium for microorganisms to thrive, hence preservatives must be added to emulsions to prevent the growth of the microorganisms. Most, if not all, preservatives employed have an affinity for both the oil and aqueous phases and, therefore, partition into the two phases. Thus, an antimicrobial agent that is more soluble in oil than in water is not suitable for emulsion preservation as the effective concentration of the preservative must be in the aqueous phase. Examples of preservatives include phenoxyethanol, benzyl alcohol, dimethylol-dimethyl (DMDM) hydantoin, bronopol, imidazolidinyl urea, benzisothiazolinone, benzoic and sorbic acid derivatives, and esters of parahydroxy benzoic acid such as methyl parahydroxybenzoic acid (m-paraben).

Preservatives are often used in combinations, each with differing mechanisms of antimicrobial action. Preservative potentiators, which have no antimicrobial activity of their own, significantly increase the activity of preservatives and are, therefore, employed along with preservatives for more effective preservation. Chelators such as disodium ethylenediamine tetraacetic acid (EDTA) and sodium citrate; diols such as pentylene glycol; monoglycerides, e.g., glyceryl monolaurate; acids, e.g., citric and lactic acids; ethers, e.g., ethylhexylglycerine; metals, e.g., copper, zinc and silver salts; and peptides, e.g., polylysine; are groups of compounds that act as potentiators for preservatives. Chapter 19 of this book has more information on preservation and preservatives.

Stability of emulsions

A stable emulsion product is characterised by the absence of creaming, which is the occurrence of a layer of a more concentrated dispersed phase droplets; cracking/breaking that occurs when the dispersed droplets begin to coalesce and separate as a layer in the emulsion; as well as demulsification, which is the complete coalescence of the droplets of the dispersed phase resulting in two immiscible layers of the initial oil and aqueous phases. An emulsion must also be free of microbial growth and the ingredients, especially the oils and fats, must remain chemically and physically stable throughout the shelf-life of the product.

The factors that cause emulsion instability and how these can be prevented are discussed in Chapter 18 of this book.

Formulation process

Formulation involves having the basic knowledge of the characteristics of a product which includes the physical and chemical nature of the active ingredients, excipients and additives that are required to produce the desired product. The quantities needed for each ingredient of the formulation; the steps needed for the mixing of the ingredients as well as the appropriate equipment for the manufacture of the products are considered in the preliminaries of the formulation of a product.

Type of emulsion: The type of emulsion required for a formulation determines the type of emulsifier(s) that will be employed as well as the concentrations of the primary ingredients of oil and water and the method of preparation. For instance, o/w type of emulsion will require o/w-promoting emulsifier(s) and vice versa. Waxy solid emulsifiers will increase the viscosity of the emulsion and the presence of viscosity-imparting agents, such as the carbomers, will result in the formation of a highly viscous lotion or a semi-solid cream preparation.

Oil-water ratio for emulsions: The ratio of the oil phase to that of the aqueous phase is critical to the formulation of a stable emulsion and depends, in part, on the type of emulsion desired, that is, o/w or w/o type. Ideally, stable emulsions are formed when the concentration of the internal phase is 40 – 60% (40: 60 to 60:40, oil: water) although this may be as low as 25% and as high as 70% in some cases depending on the type(s) and concentration of emulsifier(s) employed and the nature of the oil phase especially its consistency: liquid oils or semisolid butters and waxes. For example, it is possible to form an o/w emulsion containing 75% of oil using acacia gum as emulsifier, while such a concentration of internal phase for an ionic emulsifier, for example, calcium oleate that forms w/o emulsion, will lead to inversion of the emulsion to o/w type. Notwithstanding, ocimum oil, an essential oil, at internal concentrations of 1% and 2%, have been shown to give stable emulsions using Tween 80^{R}, a sorbitan emulsifier at 1 to 5%. The oil, at 0.5% produced transparent microemulsions with the emulsifier (17).

All ingredients used are better weighed and the quantities expressed as percentage weight in weight (% w/w) because the liquid ingredients are of different specific gravities and some, like the semisolids and solids, cannot be efficiently measured in a measuring device.

Choice of emulsifiers: There is a vast array of emulsifiers at the disposal of the formulator. Invariably, a combination of emulsifiers is used to achieve the desired product, based on whether the emulsion is o/w or w/o and whether the product is a cream (semi-solid consistency) or a fluid lotion. There is no hard and fast rule as to the concentrations of the emulsifiers to be employed as these are determined based on experience and by experimenting with various emulsifiers and at varying concentrations to obtain an optimal consistency and stability. Notwithstanding, the nature of the oils employed contributes in no small measure to the choice and concentration of emulsifiers that are eventually used. Semisolid fats such as cocoa butter and waxy materials like paraffin wax, are not as easily emulsified as liquid oils such as olive oil and mineral oil and may require higher concentrations and entirely different types of emulsifiers. Generally, emulsifiers are used at 3 - 7%, however, there are suggested concentrations of emulsifiers that may serve as a guide to emulsion formulation (18).

Choice and concentrations of preservatives and antioxidants: Preservatives and antioxidants are integral components of an emulsion formulation that ensure the microbial stability of the product and prevent the oils and other susceptible components from undergoing oxidation, respectively. The choice and concentrations of these two additives are determined through preliminary studies, as factors such as oil-water ratio, solubility in water (for microbial preservatives), the nature of other ingredients of the formulation such as the presence of naturally-derived substances like gums, lecithin and vegetable and animal oils; and even the containers (communal jars) in which the product is packaged, affect the efficacy of preservatives and antioxidants. Even though the manufacturers of preservatives and antioxidants indicate use concentration ranges for these substances, the eventual concentrations and types are still determined for each formulation. As examples, methyl paraben, a preservative, is recommended at a use concentration of 0.1 –0.2% while propyl gallate, an antioxidant, is 0.1%. A combination of preservatives and of antioxidants, respectively, is often used for optimal effects. Combinations of preservatives are often employed along with potentiators for effective microbial preservation. Combinations of the parabens, caprylyl glycol, phenoxyethanol, pentylene glycol, ethylhexyl glycerine, 1,2 hexanediol, sodium dehydroacetic acid and disodium/trisodium EDTA are examples of preservatives and potentiators that are commonly used in emulsion product formulation.

Other ingredients that enhance the effectiveness, physical stability and aesthetics of emulsion formulation

Cosmetic creams and lotions are used for various purposes which determine the ingredients that are added to the basic formula. Creams such as vanishing creams, night creams, massage creams and body/hand creams vary mainly in their contents of oils, moisturisers and types of emulsion (o/w or w/o).

Moisturisers (Occlusives, humectants, hydrators): These are important agents that are present in all creams and lotions as they keep the skin soft and supple. The nature, types and examples of moisturisers used for cosmetic products are discussed in chapter 3 of this book.

Increased moisturising effect: The moisturising effects of a lotion or cream can be enhanced by carefully increasing the quantities of the oil phase without causing a breakdown of the emulsion. Occlusives such as cocoa butter, lanolin and dimethicone will reduce TEWL, while glycerine can be added to the aqueous phase.

Stabilisers/thickeners/viscosity-improvers: Liquid emulsions, especially those prepared with ionic emulsifiers are often very fluid. Cetyl alcohol at 2% is commonly added to stablise liquid emulsions to prevent the dispersed droplets from segregating (creaming, flocculating, cracking). Polymers, such as the carbomers, e.g., Cabomer 940, improve the consistency of lotions and creams; preventing separation (creaming) in lotions and giving a creamier and a soft texture to creams. Gums and hydrocolloids such as cellulose derivatives are also used. Xanthan gum at a concentration of 0.3% is an emulsion stabiliser but it is incompatible with cationic emulsifiers such as behentrimonium methosulphate and can be replaced with guar gum, 0.3%, which is cationic. Gums form lumps in water but can be mixed with a little quantity of glycerine or added to the oil phase to avoid this phenomenon.

Spreadability and soaping improvers: There are synthetic, oil-like, quick-spreading substances such as hemisqualene, silicones, coco caprylate, isohexadecane, dicaprylyl carbonate and dicaprylyl ether, which are used as substitutes for emollient oils, the quantities of which may need to be reduced in order to increase the spreadability of products and to reduce the soaping effects of products, especially those emulsified with ionic surfactants. The quantities of waxes and stearic acid are also reduced to increase spreadability while not compromising the stability of the emulsion.

Colourants: Colourants enhance the aesthetic appeal of cosmetic products. However, most body creams, except foundation creams, do not contain colourants. The choice and quantities of colourants to be included in a formulation rests on the formulator entirely.

Pearlescents: These are translucent and shimmery pigments that make a product shine and be luminous on the skin. Titanium dioxide and mica may be added to enhance the glare of products.

Fragrances and perfumes: These agents are added to creams and lotions to enhance their aesthetic appeal to the consumer. The type and quantity employed are the prerogatives of the formulator as these contribute, in no small measures, to distinguishing one product from another and determines the market share of the products. Thus, they are regarded as secrets and are not required to be disclosed.

Preparation of emulsions (creams and lotions)

The oil and water solubilities of ingredients determine in which of the two phases of an emulsion they are placed before mixing. There are two basic methods of emulsion preparation namely: mixing at room temperature; and the fusion method which involves heating the two phases before mixing.

Mixing at room temperature: This method is used when the oils and emulsifiers employed are of liquid consistencies. The water-soluble ingredients of the recipe (formula) are dissolved in water while the oil-soluble ones are added and mixed with oils. Where the emulsifiers are formed in situ, for example, the anionic soaps, the hydroxides of the mono-, di- and tri-valent ions as well as the amine bases are dissolved in the aqueous phase while the fatty acids and/or vegetable oils containing fatty acids are added to the oil phase. The two phases are then mixed vigorously, using appropriate mixers, until the mixture turns whitish when the emulsion is formed. Viscosity improvers such as the carbomers can be added to the aqueous phase or added to the formed emulsion and mixed. The fluid emulsion formed, a lotion, is then passed through a mechanical homogeniser, although the homogeniser can also be used as the initial mixer. Ingredients of the formulation that are salts of divalent and trivalent metals are mixed with the prepared emulsion to prevent interaction with the monovalent ions of anionic emulsifiers during the emulsification process.

Fusion method: The fusion method is employed where semisolid fatty ingredients are components of an emulsion formulation. This enables the entire oil phase to be mobile and, therefore, to mix homogeneously with the aqueous phase.

Oil soluble ingredients, except those that are susceptible to degradation at elevated temperatures and volatile ingredients such as fragrances and perfumes, are heated together to 70° – 75°C, on a water-bath or in a steam-jacketed kettle (by which means the heating temperature is controlled to avoid over heating of the oil phase). The aqueous phase, containing water-soluble ingredients is heated to about 5°C higher than the oil phase to prevent the high-melting fatty substances from congealing and separating as tiny lumps if colder water is added. Water evaporates on heating and the loss of water vapour reduces the calculated quantity of the water needed, hence, the aqueous phase should not be heated to boiling and necessary adjustment for the calculated quantity of water is made before mixing with the oil phase. When carbomers are used, they are better prepared separately and added to the formed cream at about 50°C to prevent the effect of heat on the polymer. The heated aqueous phase is then added to the heated oil phase with continuous stirring till the emulsion has cooled to about 35°C when the volatile constituents are added and mixed. Heat-sensitive ingredients may be added at 45°C. The cream is then passed through a three-roller mill to obtain a very smooth product after which it is packed in appropriate containers that are determined by the ultimate use and application of the product.

Table 15.4 indicates the ingredients for a simple o/w cream preparation. In this recipe, olive oil, coconut oil, liquid paraffin, cetyl alcohol, propyl gallate and stearic acid constitute the oil phase, while glycerine, dimethicone, triethanolamine and phenoxyethanol are mixed with water to make the aqueous phase. The fragrance is added after the phases have been heated to 70°C and 75°C, respectfully, mixed vigorously and continuously together, and cooled to about 35°C.

Equipment used for emulsion preparation: Equipment used include high-shear mixers such as vacuum colloid mills and homogenizers; mechanical mixers, e.g., propellers, turbine-type impellers mounted on shafts that are placed off-centre and used with containers that have baffles on the inner walls, and ultrasonifiers which use ultrasonic energy and give extremely fine droplets of fluid emulsions.

Stability of product: Emulsions are thermodynamically unstable and tend to separate into the two initial phases if not properly formulated, prepared and stored. The stability of emulsions is discussed in chapter 18 of this book.

Performance evaluation of creams: Formulated body creams are evaluated to ensure they meet the criteria for which they are formulated. Some of the methods employed are discussed in the book on cosmetic formulation (19).

Table 15.4: A typical formula for an o/w cream preparation

Ingredients	Quantity (g)
Glycerine	10
Olive oil	10
Coconut oil	5
Light liquid paraffin	10
Cetyl alcohol	6
Triethanolamine	3
Stearic acid	12
Phenoxyethanol	0.1
Dimethicone	2
Propyl gallate	0.03
Fragrance	As needed
Water for preparations sufficient to make up to	100

Formulation and preparation of mascaras

Mascaras are colour cosmetics that are applied to eye lashes to enhance their appearance. They colour, thicken, lengthen, add volume, and are used to curl eye lashes. They are formulated and prepared mainly as either w/o or o/w emulsions although there are non-aqueous preparations which are oil-based. The w/o and oleaginous mascaras are water-proof and stay longer on the eye lashes. However, the oleaginous types are more difficult to remove than the w/o types, though both of them tend to smudge when applied because they dry slowly and the film takes long to stay firm on the lashes.

Emulsion-based eye lashes differ from the basic emulsions earlier described as they contain, in addition to the basic ingredients for emulsion preparation, pigments, waxes, film-forming polymers, volatile solvents that accentuate drying in water-based formulations, as well as lash-lengthening fibres, if the product is designed to lengthen the lashes. Examples of these additives are:

Pigments: Iron oxides, D&C Black No.2 (carbon black), titanium dioxide, ultramarines, chromium oxide green and manganese violet are among the pigments employed for mascara formulation. Dispersing surfactants, such as sodium polymethacrylate and lecithin, are first used to disperse the pigments in the aqueous phase before emulsification.

Waxes: These increase the thickness of the film formed on the lashes and, hence, the volume of the lashes. Examples include beeswax, carnauba wax, hard paraffin, hydrogenated vegetable oils like that of palm oil and synthetic waxes. These are added to the oil phase of the emulsion.

Film formers: Formulations for mascaras contain film formers that form quickly on drying, are wash- and wear- resistant, are flexible and non-tacky films that contract on drying thereby lifting and curling the lashes and prevent the waxes in the preparations from flaking off. There are water-soluble or water-dispersible (hydrophilic) as well as oil-soluble (lipophilic) polymers that serve as film formers. These are sometimes combined to give the desired effects. The hydrophilic film formers include shellac, polyvinyl pyrrolidone (PVP), acrylate copolymers, polyurethane 35, polyvinyl acetate/ alcohol and acacia gum; while examples of lipophilic polymers are acrylates/octylacrylamide copolymer, behenyl methacrylate/T-butyl methacrylate copolymer, (vinyl pyrrolidinone) VP/eicosene copolymer and pentaerythrityl hydrogenated rosinate.

Lash lengthening/volume building fibres*:* Nylon 6 and rayon are the commonly used fibres for this purpose.

Preservatives: The mode of application of mascara on the eye lashes involves dipping the wand or brush applicator into the tube container for each use and returning the same back into the tube after use, thus, exposing the remaining contents to microbial contamination which puts the user at risks of eye infection by the contaminating microorganisms. It is imperative, therefore, that adequate quantities and types of preservatives are added to the formulation to take care of the microorganisms introduced by the user. This involves challenging the products with prospective contaminants and observing the ability of the preserved product to prevent the growth of the organisms. The challenge test is described in Chapter 19 of this book.

Preparation of mascaras

Oil-based mascaras are prepared by heating the oleaginous ingredients together and stirring until cool. Heating becomes necessary to allow for homogenous mixing of the waxy ingredients with the oily liquid ones.

Emulsion-based products are prepared with the oil-soluble ingredients heated to 70 -75° C and mixed vigorously with the water-soluble ingredients, previously heated 5° hotter than the oil phase, until cool, using appropriate equipment as described earlier. Anionic soap-based emulsifiers such as triethanolamine oleate, palmitate and stearate, are commonly employed. Emulsion stabilisers are also used to ensure the stability of the preparation, being a liquid product.

Packaging

Mascaras are packaged in specially designed tubes with screw-on wands or brushes that also serve as the lid. The design of the wand controls the quantity applied, how quickly the mascara dries and the proper layering of the coating on the lashes. Hence, for a new formulation, the appropriate wand should also be designed.

Formulation and preparation of solution-based cosmetic products

A solution is a homogenous mixture of two or more substances that are soluble or freely miscible one in the other. Gases are freely miscible and so are finely powdered solids. In the case of liquids, the substance that dissolves in the other is referred to as the solute, and the liquid in which it is dissolved is known as the solvent. In some cases, the two substances freely mix with, while in some, the extent of solubility is dependent on the concentration of the solute employed. Highly concentrated solutions contain very high quantities of solutes that may eventually lead to the precipitation of the solutes when the solutions become super-saturated. For oily solutions, the solute may be an oil or an oily or oil-soluble substance such as essential oils and waxes dissolved in an oil such as a vegetable oil. Some oils such as vegetable oils and liquid paraffin have limited solubility in organic solvents such as benzene, methanol and ethanol. The solubility of a substance (the solute), for example, plant extracts, in a particular solvent can be increased by using co-solvents in conjunction with the intended solvent. Ethanol and methanol are common co-solvents used with water. Propylene glycol, polyethylene glycol 400 (PEG 400) and glycerine are also co-solvents used with water.

Cosmetic solution products contain the active agent(s) as the solute(s) and the solvent as the vehicle for the preparation. However, in some instances, the vehicle also serves some other purposes such as moisturisers, e.g., glycerine and propylene glycol; and preservatives such as when alcohol is used at its preservative concentrations. Solutions are applied on cotton swabs and dabbed on the skin; examples include serums, which in most cases, are oily solutions and face cleansers, that may contain alcohol.

Excipients employed in solution formulation

Vehicles or solvents: Cosmetic solution products are mainly aqueous, having water, buffers, and hydro-alcoholic and polyhydric alcohols as vehicles. There are also oily solutions where the solute and solvent are oily substances.

- **Water** is a universal solvent and it is mostly used in the preparation of solution products that contain water-soluble ingredients.

- **A buffer** solution contains a mixture of a weak acid and its conjugate base or a weak base and its conjugate acid. Buffers resist pH changes when diluted or when small quantities of acids and alkalis are added to their solutions. They are used as solvents for substances, such as ionic compounds, whose solubility is affected by pH changes in the environment. Buffers are used to adjust or stabilise the pH of solutions making them less irritant when present in solutions that contain acidic or basic ingredients that affect the pH of the resultant solution. For example, the alkalinity of detergents used in the formulation of shampoos can damage the scalp, however, the inclusion of buffers, such as sodium citrate or citric acid, adjusts the pH of the shampoo to slightly acidic. To prevent eye irritancy, baby shampoos are usually adjusted to pH around 6.0 which is slightly acidic.

- **Alcohol:** ethanol (ethyl alcohol) and methanol (methyl alcohol) are the types of alcohol used as solvents in solution products. They are used diluted with water. While ethanol is safe when ingested, methanol is used only for externally applied products because of its systemic toxicity. Both are freely miscible with water, glycerine, as well as propylene and polyethylene glycols. Ethanol and methanol are also used in the extraction of phytochemicals. They are more polar than water They are less polar than water and, therefore, provide higher solubility to organic substances.

- **Glycols:** Propylene glycol and polyethylene glycol 400 (PEG 400) are slightly viscous fluids that dissolve a wider range of substances than water, alcohol and glycerine. Propylene glycol has the added advantage of being a preservative and a better solvent than glycerine for a wider variety of substances such as vitamins A and D, phenolic compounds and alkaloids.

- **Glycerine (glycerol):** This is a viscous and hygroscopic liquid with a sweet taste. It is miscible with water, alcohol, PEG 400, and propylene glycol. It is as good a solvent as ethanol but substances dissolve slowly in it because of its viscosity. However, warming increases the rate of its solubility.

- **Oils:** Oils are used in the formulation of solution cosmetic products as solvents for oil-soluble constituents and as vehicles for mixing other oils. Vegetable oils, such as coconut oil and mineral oils such as liquid paraffin, are used as diluents for oily solutions such as serum. Invariably, these oils also perform other functions such as emolliency in the preparations.

- **Co-solvents**: Co-solvents increase the solubility of non-ionisable substances that are sparingly soluble in water by increasing the polarity of the dissolving medium.

Solvents such as glycerine, ethanol, propylene glycol and PEG 400 are used alone with water or combined in varying proportions as co-solvents.

- **Solubilising agents**: solubilisers are surfactants which, above the concentrations at which they aggregate to form micelles (critical micelle concentrations CMCs), can enclose small particles of substances within their micelles that thereby enables homogeneous dispersion of such substances in water, hydrosols and gels, producing clear products. Small quantities of oils such as essential oils and fragrance oils are often solubilised in water-based products such as facial toners, gels and micellar waters. Examples of solubilising agents include polysorbate 20, poloxamers, polyglyceryl-3 cocoate and PEG 40 hydrogenated castor oil. Combinations of solubilisers along with solvents such as 1,2 hexanediol, 1,2 pentanediol, dimethylene glycol and dimethyl isosorbide give better effects.

Preservatives: solutions, especially aqueous solutions, can be good substrates for microbial proliferation and, therefore, require the use of preservatives. Hydroalcoholic and polyglycolic solutions may not require preservatives if properly formulated to be at their effective preservative concentrations in the final product. The preservatives employed must be water-soluble to prevent clouding of the product. Examples of such preservatives are sodium benzoate, sorbic acid, benzoic acid, phenoxyethanol, potassium sorbate and Germall™ Plus which is a combination of diazolidinyl urea and iodopropynyl butylcarbamate solubilised in propylene glycol.

Antioxidants: Easily oxidisable constituents of aqueous solutions require the inclusion of water-soluble antioxidants in their preparations. Examples are ascorbic acid (vitamin C), sodium metabisulphite and uric acid. Also, vegetable and animal fats and oils as well as essential oils are susceptible to oxidation, especially when exposed to air and sunlight. Oil-miscible antioxidants such as propyl gallate, ascorbyl palmitate, tocopherol and butylated hydroxyl anisole are examples of antioxidants used.

Colourants: Colourants are added to solutions, if needed, at concentrations and at such a solubility that maintain the clarity of the product.

Fragrances/perfumes: these are added in the solubilised form to solution cosmetic products as needed.

Preparation

Solutions are very easy to prepare and require the use of simple mixers. Viscous solutions tend to entrap air as bubbles which may dissipate very slowly. The choice of a mixer, along with a controlled slow speed of mixing are techniques that are employed to prevent such bubbles.

Solid ingredients are first dissolved in sufficient quantity of the vehicle (solvent) and other ingredients are then added to the solution and mixed appropriately, with attention paid to preventing contamination of the preparation by extraneous matter.

Packaging

Solution cosmetic products are used for a variety of purposes that determine the type of packaging to be employed. Examples include sprays, dropper bottles and squeeze bottles. More information on the packaging of liquid preparations can be found in chapter 17 of this book.

Formulation and preparation of suspension products

Suspensions are liquid preparations that consist of finely divided solid particles of the ingredients of a formulation which are insoluble or partly soluble in the liquid vehicle used for the preparation. The dispersed solid particles are referred to as the suspensoids and constitute the dispersed phase, while the liquid vehicle is the dispersion medium of the 2-phase dispersion system. Coarse suspensions have particle size of $\geq 0.5\mu$, while the particle size of colloidal dispersions is between 1nm and 0.1μ. The suspensoids of coarse suspensions tend to sediment when left undisturbed, unless if properly formulated using appropriate suspending agents and techniques to produce non-sedimenting preparations. The rate of sedimentation is dependent on particle size; hence, particle size reduction retards the sedimentation rate. A particle size that is greater than 5μ imparts a gritty texture to the product. The suspensoids of colloidal suspensions, on the other hand, are small enough to be maintained suspended by Brownian motion, hence, they rarely sediment on storage. Micronisation is the technique used to produce particles of colloidal dimensions using the appropriate equipment such as the colloid mills and, more recently, the use of supercritical fluid techniques. Cosmetic products that are formulated as suspensions include facial scrubs, liquid make-ups, mascaras, blushers, nail polishes, and sunscreens which contain finely divided metals such as titanium dioxide (TiO_2) and zinc oxide (ZnO) as colloidal dispersions. In some instances, the suspensions are incorporated into oil-in-water or water-in-oil emulsions that contain other desirable cosmetic agents, such as moisturisers, to give a multi-functional cosmetic product. Such preparations are referred to as **suspoemulsions**.

Types of suspensions

Deflocculated suspensions: The suspensoids of a deflocculated suspension remain as discrete units within the dispersion liquid and settle slowly on standing. The repulsive forces between the particles make them slip past each other as they sediment while the slow rate of settling prevents the entrapment of liquid within the sediment; thus, the sediment becomes compacted into a hard cake at the bottom of the container which is difficult to redisperse by shaking.

Flocculated suspensions: The suspensoids of flocculated suspensions aggregate into loose floccules which sediment faster than deflocculated particles, but because the liquid vehicle permeates the floccules, they form fluffy sediments that do not cake on storage and are readily redispersed when shaken. The sedimentation volume of a flocculated suspension is much larger than that of a deflocculated suspension. Flocculation of particles is obtained by:

- **Addition of electrolyte:** The addition of an electrolyte to an aqueous suspension reduces the zeta potential of the suspensoids and, thus, the repulsive effects between them. The suspensoids are, therefore, able to form loose flocs. The Schultz-hardy rule quantifies the ability of electrolytes to cause particles to flocculate; the higher the valency of the oppositely charged ions of the electrolyte, the more the efficacy of flocculation of the suspensoids. The quantity of electrolyte used should be controlled as an excess may cause charge reversal on the suspensoids leading to deflocculation. Examples of electrolytes used are sodium and potassium acetates, phosphates, citrates, and chlorides.

- **Addition of surfactants:** Ionic surfactants, like electrolytes, can neutralise charges on particles and flocculate suspensoids, e.g., anionic sodium dodecyl sulphate. Non-ionics do not influence the charge density of suspensoids but form loose floccules by being adsorbed to more than one particle due to their linear configuration, e.g., Triton X-100.

- **Polymeric flocculating agents**: The linear and branched chains of hydrophilic polymers enable them to form gel-like structures in aqueous media which are adsorbed onto the surfaces of the suspensoids, shielding the charges on them and enabling them to flocculate. An excessive blending of the agents with the suspensoids should be avoided as this may prevent cross-linking of adjacent polymer molecules and this may lead to deflocculation. Starch, alginates, cellulose derivatives, carbomers and silicates are examples of agents that are used.

Flocculated suspension in a structured vehicle: Hydrophilic polymers form a 3-dimensional network structure in aqueous dispersions that entrap flocculated particles and prevent them from sedimenting; thus, producing suspensions that remain evenly dispersed during storage, that is, non-sedimenting suspensions. The net charge on the floccules should be the same as that of the structure vehicle employed, as having opposite charges can affect the formation of the 3-dimensional structure and results in decreased viscosity and inadequate suspending effect. Examples of polymers used include carboxymethylcellulose, natural gums, acid and alkaline gelatine, and polyvinylpyrrolidone.

Excipients used in the formulation of suspensions

Vehicle or dispersion medium: The vehicle is the liquid medium in which the insoluble solid particles, which invariably are the ingredients, are dispersed in a formulation. While water is the major vehicle for most preparations, other liquids, such as oils, are also employed depending on the ultimate use of the product. The dispersion medium often contains other ingredients of the formulation that are soluble or miscible in it, e.g.**,** moisturisers, as well as excipients such as colourants, wetting agents, suspending agents and fragrances.

Wetting agents: Some finely divided solid particles adsorb air films on their surfaces while some have waxed surfaces which prevent them from being easily wetted by water (or some other liquids), or from spreading on a surface with which they are in contact. They float on the liquid instead of being dispersed within it. There are solid particles that agglomerate forming porous clumps within the liquid in which they are suspended. The foam produced by some particles when shaken in a liquid medium is slow to subside because of the stabilising effect of the small particles at the air/liquid interface. Such particles exhibit hydrophobic characteristics and demonstrate a contact angle that is higher than 90° when in contact with the liquid or surface. Wetting agents, which are a class of surfactants, reduce the interfacial tension between the solid particles and the liquid, the adsorbed air films are displaced, the particles spread more easily and are dispersed within the bulk of the liquid. Wetting agents improve the distribution of solid particles, for instance, pigments, and prevent the agglomeration of the particles within the dispersion medium. Wetting agents generally have hydrophile-lipophile balance (HLB) numbers of between 6 and 9. Examples include lauramide diethanolamine (DEA), cocamide diethanolamine, sodium lauryl sulphate, sodium dioctyl sulphosuccinate, quillaia extract (saponins), as well as water-miscible substances such as ethanol, glycerine and propylene glycol. Hydrocolloids such as acacia, bentonite, alginates, and cellulose derivatives, behave as protective colloids by coating solid hydrophobic particles with multimolecular film layers and imparting hydrophilic character to the particles, thereby acting as wetting agents. They are, however, used more commonly as suspending and viscosity-imparting agents.

Suspending agents: Solid particles used in the preparation of suspensions are of two types: **diffusible solids** that remain sufficiently dispersed in the vehicle for a quantity of the product to be dispensed, and **indiffusible solids** that settle rapidly immediately after the product is shaken, preventing a homogeneous dispersion to be dispensed.

Notwithstanding, suspensions that are manufactured to be available for some time and are to be stored on the shelf, need to be adequately formulated using, at least, suspending agents to keep the suspensoids sufficiently dispersed and to prevent caking when they eventually settle. Suspensoids tend to settle in a dispersion especially when they are of such sizes (> 0.1μ) that cannot be maintained suspended by Brownian motion. With time, the particles form a hard, not easily re-dispersed cake at the bottom of the container, reducing the effective concentration of the active ingredients of the product. Suspending agents, which are mostly hydrophilic colloids, form a 3-dimensional network structure that enmeshes the suspensoids within the dispersion medium and increase the viscosity of the medium, thereby reducing the rate of settling of the suspensoids, and when properly formulated, prevent caking on storage. The quantity and type of suspending agents used to determine the stability of a suspension. Examples of suspending agents include gums such as xanthan gum; cellulose derivatives such as methyl cellulose, hydoxypropylmethylcellulose and sodium carboxymethylcellulose (NaCMC); clays such as bentonite; and glycols such as polyethylene glycol. Acrylates such as carboxypolymethylene (carbopol); and silicones such as colloidal silicon dioxide are also used.

An ideal suspension should have a high apparent viscosity at rest, which enables the suspensoids to settle slowly or not at all; and at high shear rates, when the container is shaken, the apparent viscosity reduces to allow the suspensoids to be homogenously dispersed and the product to pour out or be dispensed from the container easily; and to spread evenly when applied on the skin or hair, a rheological phenomenon known as pseudoplasticity. The initial viscosity should reform within a short time after use to maintain adequate stability, thus exhibiting thixotropy. Plasticity is a rheological phenomenon by which the suspensoids are completely immobilised within the dispersion medium due to its viscosity and structural nature such that the suspension does not flow until shaken with a force that exceeds the yield value. The yield value is an indication of the extent and strength of the network structure of the suspending agent or structured vehicle, which must be broken before flow can be initiated. Suspending agents, e.g., glycols, that only increase the viscosity of suspensions without forming network structures produce suspensions that exhibit Newtonian flow which does not allow for homogeneous mixing of the suspensoids when the products are shaken, as the viscosity does not become reduced with shaking.

Flocculating agents*:* Solid particles carry charges on their surface that make them repel one another due to high zeta potentials, thereby preventing aggregation of the particles in a suspension. Flocculation is a process whereby such particles are made to aggregate to form loose flocs with a resultant high sedimentation volume, which do not form a cake when they eventually settle at the bottom of the container. Controlled flocculation involves the addition of a controlled quantity of a flocculating agent to a dispersion of deflocculated particles. Ionic flocculating agents possess charges that are opposite to those on the dispersed particles, whereby they neutralise such charges and make the particles to form loose flocs. Excessive use of ionic agents causes charge reversal on the suspensoids which now carry a net charge of the flocculating agent and become deflocculated. Ionic flocculating agents include ionic surfactants, e.g., sorbitan monooleate, and electrolytes such as sodium and potassium chlorides (NaCl, KCl), acetates, phosphates, and citrates. On the other hand, hydrophilic colloids such as starch, alginates, cellulose derivatives, carbomers, silicates, are adsorbed on to the surfaces of the dispersed particles shielding the charges on them and keeping them in a flocculated state.

Structured vehicles*:* Hydrophilic polymers form 3-dimensional network structure in an aqueous medium which can entrap suspended particles and floccules, retarding the rate of sedimentation and increasing the viscosity of the medium. When the suspension is shaken, the network structure breaks down, causing a reduction in the viscosity, thereby allowing for easy pourability of the product. However, the floccules must not have a net charge that is opposite to that of the polymer as this may reduce the extent of the formation of the 3-dimensional network, thereby reducing the viscosity of the suspension and increasing the rate of sedimentation of the floccules. Examples of polymers that give structured vehicles are acacia gum, sodium carboxymethylcellulose, gelatine and methylcellulose.

Preservatives: Aqueous suspensions **are** susceptible to microbial contamination and proliferation. Preservatives, therefore, become essential ingredients of the formulation. The choice of type and concentration of preservatives to be employed in a suspension formulation should be carefully determined for each product as some ingredients of the formulation, including the suspensoids, may adsorb preservatives thereby reducing their effective concentrations. Chapter 19 of this book deals with preservation and preservatives.

Fragrances/perfumes and colourants: These are examples of additives that are employed in cosmetic suspension formulations. Colourants can be adsorbed on the suspensoids, reducing the desired colour shade for the product and may result in a blotchy appearance of the product. For instance, the finer the particles (exposing more surface area) of the suspensoids in a formulation, the more the quantity of a dye that can be adsorbed on the particles, and the paler may appear the colour of the product for a given concentration of a dye.

Methods of preparation of suspensions

Wetting agents are triturated with suspensoids that are not easily wetted by water. Powdered suspending agents are then added and mixed before some quantity of the vehicle, usually water, is added to form a slurry. Other ingredients and excipients are added and mixed thoroughly using the remaining vehicle. In most cases, the dispersion medium already contains the suspending agents and it is added to the wetted particles to give a uniform dispersion of deflocculated particles. The other processes from this point depends on the type of suspension that is desired as the final product:

Deflocculated suspension in structured vehicle: A structured vehicle is added to the dispersion of deflocculated suspensoids.

Flocculated suspension: A flocculating agent is added to the dispersion of the deflocculated suspensoids.

Flocculated suspension in structured vehicle: To the flocculated suspension is added a structured vehicle.

Factors that affect the stability of suspensions as well as the assessment of suspension stability are discussed in chapter 18 of this book.

Packaging and labelling

Suspension products are packaged in screw-cap glass or plastic containers with a narrow mouth from which they can be easily poured or used with an applicator such as for mascaras. Suspensions are also packaged in squeeze bottles as well as in pressurised cans as aerosols. Because of the tendency of the suspensoids to settle on standing, the instruction to shake the container before use should be part of the label placed on the product container.

Gels

A gel is a semi-solid and homogeneous substance in which the liquid phase is embedded within a three-dimensional (3D) polymeric matrix which possesses a high degree of chemical or physical cross-linking. This polymeric matrix or 3D colloidal network, formed by the addition of appropriate solvents to gelling agents, restricts the movement of fluid, thereby immobilising solvent molecules. The 3D network confers on the gel its viscoelastic properties which makes it unique as it is both rigid and elastic. Gels are also referred to as aqueous colloidal suspensions made up of a minimum of two components, the dispersed constituent (solid), and the dispersion medium (liquid), both of which are uniformly distributed within the network structure. Although they behave as solids, their liquid components are relatively higher than the solid dispersion.

Gels tend to be transparent or translucent when formulated as a single phase, however, in a two-phase system, they are opaque. Upon contact with the skin, gels, which are characteristically thick, non-greasy, except when formulated as oily gels, liquefy and dry to form a non-occlusive film which hydrates the skin. Due to their ability to retain water, gels can facilitate the transport of active ingredients into the skin.

Non-greasy gels are easily applied and give a cooling sensation when applied to the skin; however, they are washed off during perspiration. Greasy gels, on the other hand, are lipophilic and have the advantage of being water-resistant. Gels are widely accepted and are used on the face and the hair-bearing parts of the body.

Types of gels

Gels are classified based on the nature of the liquid continuous phase or the nature of the bond involved in the 3D network.

Continuous phase classification – hydrogels, organogels and xerogels

Can be classified based on the nature of their liquid phase. Gel based system are categorised based on the physical state of gelling agent – organogels and hydrogels. They can also be classified based on the nature of solvents into xerogels or aqueous gels

Hydrogels: These consist of a dispersed phase that is made up of cross-linked hydrophilic polymeric gelling agents which form the 3D network that enmeshes the aqueous dispersion medium of a gel. They are highly absorbent. Gelling agents can be natural such as chitosan, gelatine, hyaluronic acid and gums; while synthetic agents include acrylate polymers, silicone, polyvinyl alcohol and polyethylene glycol. Aloe vera gel and gum exudates are naturally occurring hydrogels.

Organogels: They are made of a liquid organic phase within a 3D network containing lipophilic liquids as their dispersion medium. Organogels, also referred to as oleogels, have a large number of oleaginous materials that form an occlusive barrier, preventing moisture escape from the skin.

Biphasic gels (bigels): Bigels are a combination of hydrogels and organogels. They have the advantage of delivering both aqueous and lipophilic active agents on the skin, thereby enhancing the hydration of the skin. They also have improved spreadability and washability.

Emugels: These are hydrogels or oleogels with an emulsion. Emugels are designed to have a gelling agent in the hydrophilic phase of an emulsion. They have improved viscosity, adhesion, and spreadability compared to hydrogels or organogels.

Pronisomal/niosomal: These gels are liposomes formulated as either hydrogels or oleogels.

Xerogels/aerogels: Gels in which the liquid phase has been removed leaving a polymer network are referred to xerogels or aerogels. They are typically made of silica gel which have been dried. Drying at normal atmospheric pressure results in a xerogel which is dense and has relatively small-sized pores. Aerogels on the other hand, have larger pore sizes and are less dense after supercritical drying. In aerogels, the liquid component of the gel is replaced by a gas. Xerogels swell when they come in contact with water. Dried gum tears are also examples of xerogels.

Responsive gels or smart gels: These are novel gel formulations which release active agents upon response to stimuli such as light, temperature, pH, enzymes, and others. In addition to their controlled-release delivery, smart gels have higher biocompatibility, reduced propensity for side effects and tend to be more biodegradable.

Uses of gels in cosmetics

Gels are used as facial masks, body lotions, cleansers, exfoliating scrubs, shaving gels, hair products and antiperspirants/deodorants.

Ingredients used in the preparation of gel

The primary ingredients required in making gels are the gelling agents or bases or polymers (Table 15.5). They fall into four categories - natural polymers which are either proteins or polysaccharides; inorganic; synthetic and semi-synthetic which are cellulose derivatives. The effectiveness and aesthetic appeal of a gel is dependent on the base used. An ideal polymer should:

- Allow the diffusion and release of active agents
- Be stable in the presence of active agents/excipients and when applied on the skin
- Not react chemically or physically with the active agent
- Be malleable and easy to work with
- Be non-toxic
- Withstand the stress associated with the formulation process (pH, temperature, homogenisation, etc.)

Smart gels, which release their active components as a response to a stimulus, have bases unique to them. Polymers which are capable of temperature-triggered phase transition such as poly (N-isopropylacrylamide), poly (tetramethylene ether glycol) poly (N,N-diethylacrylamide) are used in preparation of temperature-sensitive hydrogels or thermogels. These polymers have lower critical solution temperature. Addition of surface active Pluronic^{R} (poloxamer) or Tetronic^{R} (poloxamine) can lead to thermally reversible gels.

Enzyme-responsive hydrogels release active agents when in contact with enzymes. Cellulose is often used in this type of hydrogel, which releases active components when exposed to protease or glycosidase-catalysed enzymatic reactions.

Poly acrylic acid ionised at a high pH and poly (N,N'-diethylaminoethylmethacrylate) ionised at a low pH are both used in pH-responsive smart gels.

Table 15.5: Categories of gel-forming polymers

Category/examples			
Natural (proteins or polysaccharides)	Inorganic	Synthetic	Semi-synthetic (cellulose derivatives)
• Agar • Alginic acid • Gelatine • Carrageenan • Cassia tora • Gellan gum • Guar gum • Pectin • Tragacanth gum • Xanthan gum	• Aluminium hydroxide • Bentonite	• Carbomer (Carbopol -934, Carbopol -940, Carbopol -941) • Poloxamer, • Polyacrylamide • Polyethylene polymers • Polyvinyl alcohol	• Carboxymethyl cellulose • Hydroxyethyl cellulose • Hydroxypropyl cellulose • Hydroxypropyl methyl cellulose • Methylcellulose

Aside from gelling agents, active ingredients are essential in gel preparations. They constitute the essence of the gels. Actives used in gels should:

- Not irritate the skin
- Have adequate lipophilicity
- Have optimal pH

Gels can also be formulated with ingredients that promote skin permeability. These permeation enhancers act by disrupting the stratum corneum via altering the lipid-protein partitioning or by exfoliating the stratum corneum cell membranes thereby eliminating the barrier function of the stratum corneum, and increasing the penetration of actives (20). A polar enhancer leads to protein conformational changes and solvent swelling, while a non-polar enhancer increases the fluidity of the lipid portion of the stratum corneum. Examples include water, terpenes, urea, glycol, fatty acids, dimethylsulphoxide, azone, surfactants and pyrrolidine. They are required to be:

- Non-toxic, non-irritating, non-allergenic
- Inert
- Compactible with gelling agents and actives
- Incapable of causing a loss in body electrolytes

Methods of gel preparation

The methods for the preparation of gels are dependent on the physicochemical properties of the gelling agents employed. These include:

- Cold method
- Dispersion method
- Fusion method

Cold method: Water is cooled to between 4-10 ^{O}C, the gelling agent is added slowly with agitation until it is dissolved; the active ingredient in liquid form is then added slowly with gentle mixing.

Dispersion method: The gelling agent is dispersed in water and stirred, the active ingredient in a non-polar solvent is added with continuous stirring.

Fusion method: The gelling agent in a non-polar medium and the active ingredient are melted by fusion and slowly stirred until a uniform gel is formed.

The order of mixing of the ingredients in a gel is critical and dependent on the effect of the ingredients on the gelling process. Active ingredients and other excipients can be added prior to the gel swelling process if they do not influence the extent and rate of the swelling of the gelling agent. If they do, they are preferably added after the gel has been formed. Conditions such as temperature, pH and duration of swelling are rate-limiting parameters in the process of the manufacture and they vary with each gelling agent. For instance, hot water is preferred for making gelatine gel whilst cold water is the preference for methylcellulose gel.

Flow properties, swelling capacity, morphology, surface charge, physical appearance, extrudability, homogeneity, spreading coefficient, viscosity, content of active agents, skin test, and grittiness are some of the parameters used to evaluate the efficacy of gels.

Aerosols

An aerosol, also known as a pressurised package, consists of a colloidal dispersion of a liquid, a semi-solid or a solid in a gaseous (propellant) medium, packaged in a container that is hermetically sealed under an applied pressure and whose contents are discharged or dispensed by the action of a gas, the propellant, that also serves as the dispersion medium. The dispersed phase of an aerosol consists of either a solution, an emulsion, a suspension, an ointment, a powder or a gel. Cosmetic products packaged as aerosols include perfume and fragrances, hair setting and conditioning agents, deodorants and antiperspirants.

Aerosols differ from **pump sprays** even though they both perform the same function of product packaging and dispensing. Aerosols are pressurised packages and release products contained in them through the pressure created by the propellant; while a pump spray, discharges its contents by the pressure applied manually on the nozzle of the container. Moreover, the discharged contents of an aerosol are aerosolised, that is, dispensed in a gaseous medium. Products packaged in aerosol containers are hermetically sealed and cannot, therefore, be contaminated by microorganisms and extraneous substances, and are also protected from the effects of air (oxygen) and moisture. Pump sprays are eco-friendly as they do not contain propellants that may affect the environment and, sometimes, the health of the consumer when the propellant and/or some aerosolised ingredients are inhaled.

Containers for aerosols are made of glass and metal, especially aluminium because of its low reactivity with water and gases. An aerosol container consists of the can or bottle, and a valve system that includes an actuator which when pressed releases the product through the nozzle to which a dip tube, made of plastic, is attached and through which the contents are drawn up to the nozzle from the bottom of the container. The design of the nozzle and the formulation of the product concentrate are responsible for the form the product attains when released into the atmosphere – fine mists, stream of liquid, quick-breaking or stable foam, creams, ointment, fine powder and gels.

The aerosol consists majorly of two constituents namely the propellant and the product concentrate:

Propellants

The propellant is a gaseous chemical substance whose vapour pressure is higher than that of the atmosphere at 40°C. Its pressure within the pressurised container expels the product concentrate and leaves it as either a foam, a semisolid, a powder or a spray. Liquefied propellants also serve as solvent or vehicle for the product concentrate. There are four types of propellants. Chlorofluorocarbons, hydrochlorofluorocarbons and hydrocarbon gases are filled into pressured packs in the liquefied form which serves as a reservoir for the gases when the aerosol is being used, as the liquefied form escapes to fill up the spaces on top of the product concentrate from where the gaseous form has been depleted. The fourth type are the compressed gases.

Chlorofluorocarbons (CFCs): These were the earliest propellants but which are no longer permitted for use, except for certain medications, because of their ozone layer-depleting activity. Examples include P-11 trichloromonofluoromethane CCl_3F, P-12 dichlorodifluoromethane CCL_2F_2 and P-114 dichlorotetrafluoroethane $CClF_2ClF_2$.

Hydrochlorofluorocarbons (HCFCs) and hydrofluorocarbon (HFCs): These have a lower effect on the ozone layer because they break down at a faster rate in the atmosphere than the CFCs. They are more miscible with water than other propellants and serve as solvents for the product concentrates. Examples are P-22 chlorodifluoromethane $CHClF_2$, 142b chlodifluoroethane CH_3CClF_2 and 152a difluoroethane CH_3CHF_2.

Hydrocarbons: Hydrocarbons are eco-friendly and have low toxicity. Being immiscible with water, they remain on top of the product concentrate, providing the pressure that pushes out the concentrate. They are used for water-based products because they do not contain halogens (chlorine, fluorine) that can cause hydrolysis of susceptible ingredients. They are flammable and can explode; the degree of which can be reduced by mixing with other types of propellants or the use of valves with a vapour tap. Examples include A-108 propane C_3H_8, A-31 isobutane C_4H_{10}, and A-17 butane C_4H_{10}.

Compressed gases: Product concentrates that are insoluble in compressed gases are emitted mainly as placed in the container while the sprays produced are wet and foams are unstable, due to the low expansion rates of the gases. The pressure in the container diminishes with use as there is no reservoir of pressure, unlike liquefied gases; hence, higher gas pressures are used. Nitrogen, nitrous oxide and carbon dioxide are examples of compressed gases used in aerosols.

Product concentrate

The product concentrate consists of the active ingredients and excipients such as solvents, co-solvents, surfactants, antioxidants, emulsifying agents and suspending agents. Liquefied propellants sometimes serve as solvents for ingredients that are soluble in them and as the dispersion medium for suspensions and powders.

The aerosol principle

The aerosol is configured by pouring the product concentrate into the can and sealing the upper casing that houses the valve system onto the can. The propellant, under pressure, is pumped into the can through the valve system. After filling is completed, the spring in the valve system pushes up the head piece and the can is sealed. An equilibrium between the liquefied and the vapourised portions of the propellant is quickly established. The vapour exacts pressure against the walls of the container, the valve system and the liquid phase which consists of the product concentrate and the liquefied gas. It is this pressure that pushes the liquid phase up the dip tube and out through the orifice of the nozzle into the atmosphere when the valve is actuated by pressing on the nozzle. On getting out of the container, the propellant evaporates as it gets in contact with air due to a drop in pressure, leaving the product concentrate airborne as a mist or foam, or deposited on the skin in the form the product has been formulated – lotions, creams, powders, gels, ointments, stable or quick-breaking foam. As the liquid phase is being removed from the container, equilibrium between the liquefied propellant left in the container and that in the vapour phase is quickly reestablished such that a continuous stream of the contents at an even rate can be released without a drop in the pressure until there is an appreciable depletion of the propellant. Hence, a small quantity of the product is usually left in the depleted aerosol container. Compressed gas propellants are more quickly exhausted and unable to maintain a constant pressure for the continuous product release than those of liquefied gases because they lack reservoir of the gases.

Manufacture of aerosols

Aerosols are usually contract-manufactured, whereby, the manufacturer is supplied the product concentrate along with the instructions for the type of container, propellant and nozzle design by the company that owns the product.

Formulation and manufacture of lipsticks

Lipsticks are cosmetics that colour, moisturise, cover up defects, and give texture to the lips. They consist of dyes and pigments which are available in a wide range of colour shades and are dispersed in a fragranced oil-wax base. The oils, waxes and pigments are typically combined in proportions of: oils 50 -70%; waxes 20 -30%; and pigments 5 -15% (21).

Ingredients used in the formulation of lipsticks

Waxes: Waxes give the solid structure to lipsticks and allow for the formulation to be shaped as desired. White beeswax, carnauba wax, candelilla wax, microcrystalline waxes, ozokerite wax, ceresin wax and hard paraffin are some of the waxes used in the formulation of lipsticks.

Liquid components: The liquid components consist mainly of oils such as mineral oil and castor oil. Other liquid components are butyl stearate, silicone fluids, isopropyl maleate and glycols. These agents add gloss to lipsticks and serve as solvents or dispersing fluids for the pigments and dyes that are used as colourants. Some colourants are initially dissolved in a little quantity of water before being incorporated into the lipstick formulation. Silicone fluids aid mould-release of the lipsticks when formed. The oils, propylene glycol and butyl stearate also serve as emollients.

Texture improvers: Petrolatum, lanolin and lecithin are used to give the desired texture to lipsticks by softening the waxes employed. They are also emollient.

Colourants: Colourants are essential additives in the formulation of lipsticks. Some of the FDA certified colour additives for lipsticks are D&C (Drug and Cosmetics) Orange No. 5, D&C Red No. 36 and No. 33. Caramel, iron oxides – yellow, red and black, carmine, carotene and annatto are also FDA approved colours permitted for use in lipsticks (22).

Opacifying agents: Titanium dioxide is commonly used to give translucent effect to lipsticks.

Pearlescent pigments: Titanium dioxide flakes, micaceous iron oxide flakes, bismuth oxychloride and guanine crystals are used to impart shimmering effects on lipsticks.

Preservatives and antioxidants: Examples of these are the parabens and propyl gallate, respectively, and they are added to lipstick formulations as appropriate.

Fragrances and perfumes*:* These are added to lipsticks, most times, as signatures that distinguish one brand from another, and which inform the choice of the consumers. Examples include natural fragrant oils such as lavender oil and rose oil.

Flavourants: Flavourants complement the sensory effects of colour, aromas and sweeteners in a product as they are perceived by the taste, smell, sight, touch and even sound sensory organs. Hence, they are carefully selected to rhyme with the fragrance and colourant used for a lipstick product. Examples are wild cherry, mint, anise, passion fruit, chocolate, orange, raspberry and citric acid syrups.

Sweeteners: Artificial sweeteners such as sodium saccharin and ammonium glycyrrhizate; as well as the natural sweetener, stevia, are used to improve the taste of lipsticks.

Manufacture of lipsticks

Melting and mixing process: The oils are heated separately in the process vessel to 80 – 85°C. The waxes are also separately melted in a steam-jacketed kettle that is fitted with an anchor mixer/scrapper. The molten wax mixture is added to the oil phase and mixed continuously till a homogenous mass is obtained. Powdered pigments are dispersed in a quantity of oil to make a paste. The paste is passed through a three-roller mill to obtain a smooth paste that is devoid of 'grainy' feel for the lipstick, except if the pigments have been pre-micronised which only require trituration to break agglomerated particles. The pigment pastes or the ready-to-use liquid pigment dispersions, if these are to be used instead of powdered pigments, are added to the hot oil/wax mixture and mixed appropriately to obtain a homogenous mixture which may sometimes require being passed through a colloid mill. Fragrances, antioxidants, preservatives and the remaining ingredients of the formulation are then added after the mixture has been slightly cooled.

The mixture is stirred continuously for a while, preferably with a vacuum mixer, at a maintained temperature (that keeps the mixture in a fluid state), to ensure homogeneity and to get rid of entrapped air bubbles.

Moulding process: The mixture, maintained at the desired temperature while being continuously stirred to prevent components from separating, is poured into moulds which have previously been lubricated with liquid paraffin or isopropyl myristate. The filled mould is kept refrigerated for the lipstick to solidify after which the lipstick is removed from the mould and passed through a flaming chamber to seal pinholes and to give it a glossy finish. It is then inspected for the presence of blemishes, mould lines and air holes. If the product is unsatisfactory, it is reworked and reprocessed.

Labelling

Lipsticks are labelled with batch number, expiry date and direction to store in cool place.

Quality tests for lipsticks

Lipsticks are the only cosmetics that are ingested and, therefore, are subjected to standards set by relevant agencies of the governments of individual countries such as the FDA in the USA. Only specified and approved pigments and dyes are used. All raw ingredients and processes are subjected to quality control, and good manufacturing practice must be put in place. Colour control of lipstick is critical as the colour shade must be reproducible for each batch. Colorimetric equipment that gives numerical values are best used for colour control.

Quality tests for lipsticks: Two main tests are usually carried out to determine the quality of lipsticks after being manufactured.

- ***Heat test***: The lipstick, in an extended position, is placed in a holder and kept in a thermostatic oven set at 54° C for 24 hours after which the lipstick is expected neither to droop nor become distorted.
- ***Rupture test or Breaking Load Point test:*** To the lipstick, extended horizontally an inch from the base, is added loads of increasing weights at intervals of 30 seconds and the weight at the point at which it begins to rupture or break is called the breaking load point. The test determines the hardness and tensile strength of the lipstick. Each manufacturer sets its own parameter for this test.

Microbiological tests to determine the efficacy of the preservatives employed, chemical tests to assess rancidity propensity of the product as well as storage tests that determine the expiry dates are some of the other tests carried out for lipsticks.

Samples of each batch are kept on the shelf by the manufacturer to observe for any breakdown throughout the shelf-life period and beyond.

Formulation and manufacture of lip balm/gloss

Lip balms, also referred to as lip salves, are applied to the lips to relieve chapped lips and similar conditions of the lips caused by unfavourable environmental conditions and minor health conditions such as angular cheilitis. Lip gloss, on the other hand, gives a gentle gloss or glow to the lips.

The formulation and manufacture of lip balms and lip gloss are similar, in some ways, to those for lipsticks. They contain waxes and oils. However, the quantity of oils that constitute the moisturiser contents are higher than for lipsticks. While lip balm may contain no pigments and dyes, the quantities of these agents in lip gloss are much lower than for lipsticks. Moreover, lip balms may contain menthol for its analgesic activity, salicylic acid that exfoliates chapped skin and camphor that heals cold sores.

Moulds are usually not used for lip balm and lip gloss, rather the molten mass is poured directly into the package tube or other containers to congeal, since the tips are not shaped like lipsticks.

Packaging: Soft, solid lip balm and lip gloss are packaged in glass, plastic or cardboard push- or roll-up tubes and in jars or pots made from tin, glass or plastics. Small, soft, squeezable tubes from which the product can be applied directly on the lips or with the fingertips or with a lip brush are also used. Fluid products are packaged in glass or plastic roll-on containers or in small cylinders with either a built-in applicator wand or a separately provided applicator (known as a doe foot applicator because of its rounded and sloped tip).

Formulation and manufacture of deodorants and anti-perspirants

Deodorants and antiperspirants are two types of products that are used to control body odour and sweating in the armpit, respectively. Deodorants kill or inhibit the growth of the bacteria (microflora) that reside in the armpit, which thrive on sweat secretions, breaking down the constituents of the secretions into unpleasant, odorous compounds that result into body odour. There are, however, some deodorants that merely mask the unpleasant odour generated by the microflora with fragrances. Antiperspirants, on the other hand, plug sweat gland ducts and prevent sweat secretions from getting to the surface of the skin. Antiperspirants are also able to control odour since they reduce or prevent sweat secretions on which the bacteria thrive. Some of the active ingredients of antiperspirants, the aluminium salts in particular, also have inhibitory effects on the microflora of the armpit.

Deodorants are regarded as cosmetics, but antiperspirants, by the regulatory agencies of some countries, for example the FDA, are classified as drugs since they plug sweat glands, preventing sweat from getting to surface of the skin, thereby affecting some physiological functions of the skin. While the two types of products differ in function and hence their active ingredients, they are presented similarly for use as roll-ons, gels, aerosol sprays and sticks, generally as water-in-oil emulsions and, where the oily phase is replaced by silicone, as water-in-silicone emulsions.

Active ingredients employed in deodorant formulations

Fragrances: Most fragrances used in deodorants are essential oils some of which, apart from masking unpleasant odour of the underarm, are also able to inhibit or kill the causative bacteria. These include clove oil, rose oil, orange oil, vanilla, tea tree oil, eucalyptus oil, coconut essential oil, and lavender oil. Other natural fragrances include (pressed) oils of cucumber, and cashmere. Isolated constituents of essential oils are also used such as farnesol, eugenol, geraniol, limonene, linalool, citronellol, hydroxy citronellal and hexyl cinnamal. Synthetic fragrances such as α-isomethyl ionone, benzyl alcohol, benzyl salicylate, synthetic musks, benzyl benzoate and butyl phenyl propional are also employed.

Antibacterial agents: Chlorinated antibacterial agents, e.g., chlorhexidine gluconate; phenolic agents, e.g., triclosan; quaternary ammonium compounds, e.g., alkyl dimethyl benzyl ammonium saccharinate; glyceryl fatty acids, e.g., glyceryl caprylate/caprate; sucrose fatty acids, e.g., sucrose hydroxy stearate and sucrose laurate; as well as benzyl alcohol are examples of synthetic chemical substances used as antibacterial ingredients in the formulation of deodorants. Essential oils with proven antibacterial activity such as sage oil, tea tree oil and lemongrass oil are also used in combination with other agents. Zinc oxide and zinc glycinate (23), especially nanosized, serve as antibacterial agents in deodorants.

Agents that absorb/adsorb/neutralise odour: These ingredients absorb or adsorb odour-producing molecules of the bacterial decomposed sweat secretion, thereby, reducing their volatility. Examples include calcium silicate; zinc ricinolate and hydroxyapatite which also adsorbs bacteria. Sodium bicarbonate and zinc glycinate neutralise body odour through an acid/base chemical reaction with the fatty acids of sweat secretions. However, the zinc hydroxide produced by the chemical reaction involving zinc glycinate is milder on the skin than the sodium hydroxide produced from sodium bicarbonate, hence, the former is preferred and used (23).

Enzyme-inhibiting agents*:* The enzymes that are mostly responsible for the breakdown of the odourless components of apocrine gland secretions into malodour compounds, of which the thiol alcohols are the most pungent, have been identified as the cysteine-thiol lyases (C-T Lyases), the C-S lyases (chondroitin sulphate lyases) being more broad-acting

(24). Inhibition of the activity of the enzymes serves as a means of reducing axillary malodour (25). Amino-oxyacetic acid, a hydroxylamine derivative, inhibits amino acid beta-lyase enzyme produced by the underarm bacteria. It is an example of enzyme-inhibiting agents, and it is used in deodorant formulations.

Substrate substitution: Substitution of substrates of apocrine gland secretion, which on bacterial decomposition produce malodour, with amino acids and amino acid analogues that are preferentially acted upon by the enzymes implicated in axillary bacteria activity, gives by-products that are either odourless or have pleasant odours. Examples of such substitutes include O-benzylserine, which is lysed by the enzymes to produce odourless benzyl alcohol. Menthol is the breakdown product of 0-menthylserine, and O-phenethylserine is metabolised to give phenethyl alcohol, a compound with the smell of rose (26). The use of these compounds as active ingredients in deodorant products is a means of controlling underarm malodour.

pH-lowering agents: The growth of bacteria is retarded at low pH of the environment. Citric acid and its derivatives are sometimes used to reduce the pH of the underarm skin, thereby, inhibiting the growth of the odour-producing bacteria.

Active ingredients employed in antiperspirant formulations

Aluminium salts: These constitute the major types of active ingredients used in antiperspirants as they plug the apocrine and eccrine sweat glands, reducing underarm secretions and wetness and, thereby, also control odour formation by bacteria that reside in the underarm. Aluminium salts are used singly but are often combined with zirconium salts and glycols (PG, PEG) forming chemical complexes. Examples include aluminium chloride, aluminium chlorohydrate (ACH), aluminium sesquichlorohydrate, Aluminum zirconium chloride, aluminum zirconium tetrachlorohydrex-gly, aluminum zirconium pentachlorohydrex-gly, aluminum sesquichlorohydrex PG or PEG and aluminum zirconium tetrachlorohydrex PG or PEG. These substances are used at concentrations that range between 5% to 30%. Aluminium zirconium compounds, however, have been banned by the FDA since 1977 in aerosol formulations as they form zirconium particulates in the lungs leading to granulomatous changes (27). Aluminum chlorohydrate is used in aerosol formulation.

Occlusive film-forming antiperspirant polymers: Hydrophobic polymers, such as octylacryl amide alone or combined with a PVP/Eicosene copolymer (28), have been explored as antiperspirants instead of the metallic aluminium salts, or in combination with a reduced quantity of aluminium salts. The polymers form a tenacious film over the armpit preventing sweat secretions from being extruded from the sweat glands. Ethyl cellulose is also a hydrophobic film former that is used, combined with other film formers as occlusive film-forming antiperspirants.

Excipients for deodorant and antiperspirant formulations

These include:

Organic solvents dissolve solid ingredients or otherwise non-aqueous soluble substances and, in some cases, increase the volatility of the product thereby enhancing the drying of the product when applied, e.g., ethanol, toluene, isododecane, glycerol, di- and tripropylene glycols, isopropyl myristate, oleyl alcohol, isostearyl alcohol, ricinoleic alcohol, ethers, ethylene, hexylene and propylene glycols.

Emulsifiers stabilise the mixture of oily ingredients or silicones and aqueous ingredients to give a stable emulsion These include polysorbates, e.g., Tween^{R} 80; sorbates, e.g., Span^{R} 60; ionic emulsifiers e.g., triethanolamine oleate; glycols, e.g., polyethylene glycol (PEG) distearate; steareth-2, glyceryl stearate; and sucrose hydroxystearate.

Solubilisers are surfactants that enable oils to form clear solutions with water, e.g., propylene glycol, polysorbates (e.g., Tween^{R} 80) and propanediol.

Suspending agents/thickening or viscosity-imparting agents ensure even distribution of insoluble particulate substances in a liquid vehicle and increase the consistency of a dispersion, respectively, e.g., xanthan gum, guar gum, sodium carboxymethyl cellulose, macrogols and behenyl alcohol.

Gelling agents give forms to semi-solid products such as sticks, e.g., hydrogenated castor oil, glyceryl stearate, cetyl alcohol, stearyl alcohol, castor wax, paraffin wax, carbowax, talc, fumed silicas, polyvinyl alcohol, hydroxyethyl cellulose and starches.

Emollients moisturise the skin, e.g., plant oils, mineral oil, plant butters and glycerine.

Colourants make products more attractive to the consumers, e.g., approved cosmetics colours - Drug and Cosmetics (D&C) certified colours.

Perfumes/fragrances improve the aesthetics and customers' preference for a product, e.g., essential oils and their isolated compounds, synthetic fragrances and perfume blends.

Microbial preservatives inhibit microbial growth and examples include parahydroxy benzoic acid esters (parabens), e.g., methyl paraben; phenoxyethanol, benzyl alcohol, sodium benzoate, and imadozolidinyl urea.

Antioxidants prevent the rancidity of ingredients that are susceptible to oxidation, e.g., vitamin E (α-tocopherol), propyl gallate, calcium disodium EDTA, and pentaerythrityl tetra-di-t-butyl hydroxyhydrocinnamate.

Plasticizers reduce the brittleness and increase the flexibility of films formed when products are applied to the underarm by increasing the elasticity of the films, making them softer, e.g., triethyl citrate, cetyl alcohol, polypropylene oxide, stearyl alcohol, and cottonseed oil.

Coupling agents improve clarity of products, e.g., propylene carbonate, hexyl alcohol, phenyl dimethicone, and ethanol.

pH or acidity regulators maintain the acidity of the formulation, e.g., potassium lactate, citric acid and its derivatives with di- and tri-ethanolamine as bases to moderate the acidity.

Methods of preparation

The formulation of deodorants and antiperspirants is an art on its own that involves the careful selection of desired ingredients and processes in order to achieve a product with characteristics that is peculiar to the product designer. Notwithstanding, most products contain the same basic ingredients and the different forms in which the products appear are differentiated by the excipients required to give the characteristic forms.

Stick forms: Sticks are semi-solid in nature and they maintain their shapes when outside their packaging and during use. The basic ingredients, dispersed in form of a suspension, are further dispersed homogenously by fusion in waxy substances, combined with gelling or thickening agents to obtain the desired stick form. Sticks are packaged in a two-part container with the lower part housing the stick which can be pushed or rolled up to expose the stick for use, while the upper part is the cover for the package.

Gel/paste forms: These are like sticks in composition but contain less quantities of waxy materials, but contain more gelling and thickening agents and are, therefore, of fluid consistency. They are packaged in containers that have apertures on their top through which the contents are applied onto the underarm directly or on to the fingers with which they are then applied on the underarm.

Roll-on forms: The basic ingredients are dispersed as fluid emulsions or fine, translucent suspensions, packaged in specially designed containers with rolling balls at the top.

Aerosol forms: Aerosol spray products are formulated to contain the desired ingredients as emulsions, suspensions, solutions and dry powders which are dispensed from hermetically sealed aerosol containers. They are filled with the appropriate propellant gases at predetermined pressures. The propellants propel the product concentrates out of the container in a form previously determined by the formulator such as a mist, liquid stream or dry powder spray. Aerosols are usually contract-manufactured, the product formulations are, however, provided by the products' owner company.

A typical deodorant/antiperspirant formula

Table 15.6 shows a prototype formula for the manufacture of deodorants and antiperspirants when combined in a product, otherwise, without the antiperspirant agent, for a deodorant-only product. By working around this formula, adding other excipients for the product desired, such as gelling and thickening agents, other product types, such as sticks, can be obtained.

General method of preparation

Water-soluble ingredients and those soluble in solvents are dissolved in the aqueous phase while oil-soluble ingredients are mixed to constitute the oily phase. The two phases, along with the required emulsifiers, are then thoroughly mixed using an appropriate equipment to obtain a stable emulsion preparation. However, where there are semisolid fatty or oily substances, e.g., cetyl alcohol, the oily phase is heated to melt the fatty solids and the aqueous phase is similarly heated to a slightly higher temperature before the two are mechanically mixed. Stick deodorants/antiperspirants usually do not contain water, the ingredients are dispersed in the oily phase. Volatile ingredients such as volatile active ingredients and fragrances; colourants, as well as thickening and gelling agents are added after the emulsion formed has been cooled appropriately. The product is then poured into the container selected for it.

Tests for efficacy of deodorants

A protocol for the assessment of the odour-masking efficacy of deodorants has been developed (29). This is an in vivo test, also referred to as indirect sniffing, that involves sniffing of the underarms of volunteers by a panel of trained sniffers, 24 hours and 48 hours of the use of deodorants by the volunteers and the assessment of the odour perceived by rating the intensity of the odour on a 6-point scale of 0 - 5. Antibacterial activity of deodorants is determined using the appropriate anti-microbial activity determination methods as well as the quantification of volatile materials found in the sweat collected from the armpit (30).

Tests for efficacy of antiperspirants

The ability of antiperspirants to reduce or prevent underarm perspiration is evaluated using these methods:

Table 15.6: A prototype formula for a deodorant/antiperspirant formulation

Ingredient	Function of ingredient	Percentage composition
1. Aluminium chlorohydrate	Antiperspirant (not for deodorant only products)	13%w/w
2. Polysorbate oleate, sorbitan oleate	Emulsifiers	3%w/w
3. Mineral oil, beeswax, stearic acid	Emollients	8%w/w
4. Sucrose dilaurate	Emollient/emulsifier	0.5%w/w
5. Perfume/fragrance	Odour-masking, aesthetic effect	qs.ad. (as needed) (approx. 0.5%w/w)
6. Propylene glycol	Solvent, viscosity-imparting	0.4%w/w
7. Di-ethanolamine and Triethanolamine	pH regulator	qs.ad (as needed)
8. Water	Vehicle	qs.ad. (as needed)
9. Preservatives a) Microbial preservatives b) antioxidants	a) Prevent microbial growth b) Prevent rancidity of oils and fats	As previously determined

Gravimetric method*:* Weighed absorbent pads placed in the armpit of subjects are used to collect sweat for a specific period, usually four hours, while the subjects go about their normal daily routine. Accelerated tests are carried out with the subjects kept in a controlled and heated environment or made to undergo some form of physical exercise. The pads are collected and reweighed to determine the amount of sweat secreted within the test period. The test is carried out without and with the application of the antiperspirant under test. Details of the protocol for this test can be obtained (29).

Silicone test: A film of silicone is applied onto the skin and the subject is exposed to a controlled temperature environment or made to undergo some form of physical exertion for a period. The film is peeled off and the number of holes created by sweat drops on the film is counted and compared to a standard.

Visualisation method: The skin is painted with a solution of alcohol, castor oil and iodine and allowed to dry. A layer of starch powder is applied to whiten the area on which dark spots are observed as sweat is exuded.

Infrared gas sensor method: Infrared sensors that detect moisture loss are employed in this method. The method analyses the moisture content of the gas stream previously passed over the subject's armpit.

Other tests employed in the determination of the efficacy of antiperspirants and deodorants have been further described (30).

Formulation and manufacture of soft gelatine capsules

Certain cosmetic products are packaged in soft gelatine gels and are often referred to as soft gels. These include serums, fragrant oils, some types of colour cosmetics and makeup preparations. The soft gels come in various colours, sizes and shapes such as round, oval, oblong, tubs and twist-offs; the twist-off soft gels being the most convenient to use. Soft gelatine capsules, unlike the hard gelatine capsules that consists of two parts, are one-piece hermetically sealed capsules, that have the advantages of being able to effectively keep liquids, semisolids (creams, pastes) and powders packaged in them and serve as a form of tamper-evident packages.

Basically, the capsule is made up of gelatine, a substance obtained by acid (Type A) or base (Type B) hydrolysis of the skin, bones and connective tissues, mostly of bovine or porcine animals. The gelatine is plasticized to make it more flexible by being treated with glycerine, sorbitol, maltitol, and polypropylene glycol singly or combined with glycerol. Preservatives are important components of a gelatine capsule because of its vulnerability to serve as a medium for microbial growth. Colourants and /or opacifiers and added to the capsule to create aesthetic effects and to distinguish products marketted by different manufacturers.

Manufacture of gelatine capsules

The methods employed in the manufacture of soft gelatine capsules Include: plate process, reciprocating die process, rotary die process, seamless process and accogel process. The plate method is the oldest of them and involves placing a sheet of gelatine on a mould, filling the prepared product into the gelatine sheet, applying another sheet on top and pressing this onto the lower sheet to form, seal and cut the capsules into individual units.

Formulation and manufacture of body and face powders

The word, powder, defines the state of subdivision of a solid material. Powders in the plural sense, are dry, free-flowing preparations consisting of one or a mixture of finely divided substances that are intended for pharmaceutical or cosmetic applications. Powders as a pharmaceutical dosage form could be used orally (divided or individual dose-wrapped powders, antacid powders, antibiotic powders for reconstitution), as a topical application or as an injectable formulation which is reconstituted with water for injections prior to use. Cosmetic powder products, on the other hand, include foundations, eye shadows, primers, blushers, bronzers, as well as body and face powders.

There are different types of cosmetic powders and these include: loose powder, compact powder, setting powder, finishing powder, mineral powder, translucent powder, and high definition (HD) powder. Nonetheless, the formulation of the different powders usually entails similar basic ingredients to which are added the components that distinguish one type of powder from the other. In this section, the basic ingredients and manufacturing processes of facial loose and compact powders, as well as body powders will be discussed.

Required features of face powders

Face powders are made from a blend of ingredients that are expected to impact the following good characteristics into the product: covering power, absorbency, adhesiveness, slip and bloom (31,32).

Covering power: Covering power is the quality that enables a powder to conceal blemishes, skin imperfections and shine. Ingredients such as titanium dioxide, zinc oxide, kaolin and magnesium oxide are used for their covering power. Titanium dioxide is the most potent covering agent.

Slip: This is the ease of spreadability of the powder over the skin, without dragging, and giving the characteristic smooth feeling. There should be sufficient slip to enable the powder to be applied to the skin with a suitable applicator, such as a puff or a soft brush, without dragging or producing a blotchy effect. Good powder flowability and spreadability are two important parameters that are always considered at the time of formulation and evaluation of topical powders. Slip is hard to define in any quantifiable manner, but like powder grittiness, it can be felt with the fingers on the face. While a few ingredients can contribute to giving a powder slip, such as the kaolin, the stearates and starch, by far the most important substance is talc (magnesium silicate). Thus, it usually makes up to 50% or more of some face powders. Other substances used for softness and slip are zinc stearate, magnesium stearate, zinc undecanate, magnesium undecanate. Tapioca starch has also been found to give a very smooth feel to face powders.

Adhesiveness: This is the ability of a face powder to cling to the skin surface and produce a lasting effect, thereby preventing frequent application within a period of use. It must adhere to the skin and be reasonably resistant to the mixed secretions of the skin. Adhesiveness improves the consistency of face powders, ensuring a smooth application. Lack of adhesion was a common problem with early face powders and many women resorted to applying a vanishing or cold cream before powdering to help their face powder stay in place.

Absorbency: Absorbency refers to the capability of a powder component(s) to absorb the skin secretions, i.e., sebaceous secretions and perspiration; to take up such other oily substances that are not easily dislodged by water and to cover up the shiny areas of the face without getting damp. Materials for this purpose should have a high absorptive capacity, and, at the same time, should not change the appearance of the powder on the skin. There are several components of face powders which have this absorptive property, such as kaolin, starch, microcrystalline cellulose, magnesium and calcium carbonate. Zinc oxide and titanium dioxide are better at masking skin greasiness but calcium carbonate (chalk powder), kaolin and starch have better moisture absorption capacity.

Bloom: This is the ability of a powder to impart a velvety, peach-like finish to the skin. The preparation should make the face pleasant to look at and to touch. Shine on or around the nose should be eliminated. The materials chiefly used to impart bloom are chalk, rice starch and silk powder.

Raw materials

It is essential that all raw materials employed in the production of face and body powders are of the cosmetic grade with minimal impurities. The natural mineral ingredients, e.g., talc and kaolin, are susceptible to heavy contamination with bacteria that includes *Clostridium tetani* and *Bacillus anthracis*. Such ingredients should be sterilised thoroughly by heat before being incorporated into a formulation. Alternatively, the final product is subjected to sterilisation before being packaged, provided it contains no volatile ingredients (31–33).

Blends of specific raw materials are often employed to obtain the desired characteristics of good face and body powders. While the different types of powder formulations may contain the same basic ingredients, their functions, mode of production and application may necessitate variation in the composition of the formula. Hence the basic formula for loose face powder will differ from that of compact face powder and for body powders.

Ingredients for the formulation of loose face and body powders

Talc: Talc is the sole component of face powders that may comprise up to 75% of the formulation in some products. It is a mineral composed of hydrated magnesium silicate with the chemical formula $3MgO_2.4SiO_2.H_2O$ (34). Talc is not soluble in water, but it is slightly soluble in dilute mineral acids. It absorbs oils, makes makeup more translucent and prevents caking of pressed powders. Its colour ranges from white to grey or green and it has a distinctly greasy feel. Grades of talc should be judged on slip, smoothness, fineness, grit, density, colour and odour (35). In addition, a check should be made for impurities such as carbonates and water-soluble iron, and the talc must be free from asbestos impurities (36). The highest grade of talc are mined in France, Italy and the United States of America (USA) (32). Particle size of talc is an essential criterion for determining its standard of quality. It is expected that for a high-quality grade talc, at least 98% should pass through a mesh 200 screen (not larger than 74μ). The particle size of the talc can significantly affect the appearance and feel of the finished formulation; the smaller the particle size, the smoother the feel on the skin. However, the use of excessively micronised talc may lead to loss of some of its basic characteristics, causing light scattering and appearing to be of higher opacity, which are not required for a quality face powder product (35). Care must be taken to ensure that the talc has been adequately treated to overcome any possible microbial contamination, the major concern being tetanus spores. Talc is used mainly because of outstanding spreadability (slip) and low covering power (translucency). Talc is a major component of baby powder, an astringent powder used for preventing rashes, especially on the area covered by a diaper. In recent times, however, the use of talc in cosmetic products, especially in powders, has become controversial as talc has been suspected to be a carcinogen, although the FDA classifies it as a 'generally recognised as safe (GRAS)' substance for use in cosmetics and other products. Talc that does not contain asbestos, a known carcinogen, is generally safe for use in cosmetic products.

Titanium dioxide: Titanium dioxide is a naturally occurring metallic element that is opaque, bright and UV-resistant. It is used widely in sunscreens and pigmented products that are likely to be exposed to light, such as in a wide variety of personal care products, including colour cosmetics like eye shadow and blushers, loose and pressed powders, and in sunscreens (32,37). Titanium dioxide is a better absorber of UV light, and is three to four times better as a covering agent than zinc oxide, but it has less adhesive property and does not blend quite as well as zinc oxide. For any powder formulation in which an appreciable covering effect is desirable, the judicious use of titanium dioxide or zinc oxide or a blend of the two is necessary at concentrations of 10 to 15% (38).

Zinc oxide: Zinc oxide, a white powder with a chemical formula of ZnO, is a topical skin product ingredient that is used as a protective coating for mild skin irritations and abrasions. It can promote the healing of chapped skin and diaper rash. Zinc oxide works as a mild astringent and has some antiseptic properties (32). It is also used in a wide range of cosmetics and personal care products including makeup, nail products, baby lotions, bath soaps and foot powders. It is a substance that effectively works in drying excess oil on skin. Unlike chemical sunscreens that can cause hormonal disturbance, using products containing zinc oxide as one of the main ingredients is a perfect choice even for those with sensitive skin. However, its excessive use may result in a drying effect and may produce a mask-like effect, which are not desirable. Hence, its recommended usage in a powder formulation is not more than 25%. Zinc oxide has moderate adhesive properties, and when employed in the formulation of face powders, it should be of high quality with very whitish colour, odourless, and fine characteristics without grittiness (32,39).

Kaolin: Kaolin, a hydrated aluminium silicate natural clay mineral, also known as China clay, has been used in healing skin infections since ancient times. The high adsorption and absorption capacities, cation exchange capacity, as well as the extremely fine particle size of the clay, are the important reasons kaolin and its other varieties are used to remove oils, secretions, toxins, and contaminants from the skin. By adsorbing and absorbing moisture and impurities from the skin, the clays also serve to cleanse and refresh the skin surface and aid the healing of topical blemishes (31,40). Kaolin possesses good covering power and adhesion as well as grease-resistant and perspiration-absorbent characteristics. It does not have a good slip and may feel harsh on the skin if used in very high concentrations. Kaolin helps to remove the shine of talc and has certain soothing effects on the skin. Its high density is an advantage in the in the formulation of a less bulky powder with moderate fluffiness. Kaolin is hygroscopic, which may require storage from damp environment. Its hygroscopicity may limit its use in face powder to less than 25% (31).

Starch: Starch has beneficial advantages such as low-cost, low-toxicity, biodegradability, and renewability. Corn starch is used as a thickener in liquid and semisolid cosmetic products, as a diluent in powder preparations and, more recently, as a replacement for talc in natural baby powders (31). Rice starch was very common as a basic ingredient in formulations and was considered to give a 'peach-like' bloom to the face. Starch gives a very smooth feel when applied to the skin because the particles are spherical. It has excellent absorptive properties and, in addition, has good covering power. Starch can be modified by acid hydrolysis, oxidation, etherification, esterification and cross-linking. Such modified starches can be very beneficial in new powder products with new desirable properties (41). However, starches and their modified forms are ideal media for microbiological growth; which requires that the grades for production are adequately sterilised prior to use (31).

Calcium carbonate: Calcium carbonate, otherwise known as precipitated chalk or white chalk, is one of the most abundant minerals in the earth's crust. Fossils and marble, formed from metamorphosised sedimentary rocks, are the sources of natural calcium carbonate which occurs in the form of limestone and chalk. It consists mostly (>98%) of pure calcium carbonate ($CaCO_3$), with trace amounts of magnesium carbonate, iron oxide, and aluminium silicates (31). In make-up products, it is used as a pigment extender or prolonger, a whitener and an oil absorber. Calcium carbonate absorbs moisture, and as such, it is frequently used as an ingredient in face powders to upsurge the capacity of the makeup to absorb moisture. Its high absorbency nature makes it an essential component of other cosmetic products such as primers, foundations, and finishing powders. It is known in the cosmetic industry for its absorbent power, translucency, opacity, skin protecting properties, adhesion power that makes make-up to stay long on the body, and light scattering properties (42). The brightness and opacity of calcium carbonate make it suitable for use in white and coloured cosmetics. It readily reduces the shine of talc and has a good covering power, but it lacks slip. It is a useful ingredient for the absorption of perfume during production processes. When used in excess, the powder gives a dry feel, but moderate usage is most helpful to face powder formulations where the chalk powder preserves certain balances between slip and adhesion, coverage power and transparency, and develops the "bloom effect" when applied on the face (43).

Magnesium carbonate: Magnesium carbonate ($MgCO_3$) is used as an absorbent, opacifying agent, or to adjust the pH of cosmetic products. It is a white, tasteless, odourless, amorphous, fine powder. It is used in cosmetic industries especially in products such as talcum powder, face powder and body powder. It is incorporated in special soaps due to its marked absorptive power. The white powder is used in pharmaceutical preparations, hair bleach, powdered shampoo, cosmetic powder formulations as well as foot care and skin care products (31,32). In dry skin conditions, oil-absorbing products containing powders such as magnesium carbonate should be avoided (43). It is used topically for the treatment of acne and acne rosacea. Magnesium carbonate cosmetic grade is packed with utmost care in order to prevent moisture absorption due to its hygroscopic property. It has tremendous capacity to absorb oil from skin and prevent formulations from lump formation; and acts as a fragrance enhancer. As a result of its very high absorbency, it is often used to absorb the fragrance as a separate step before being added to the face powder during formulation (31). It has a lower density than calcium carbonate, which may result in a fluffy type of powder. It should be used in moderation as excessive use may result in a drying effect on the skin.

Silk Powder: Silk powder is produced from high quality silk, using a sophisticated technology to retain its chemical properties. It is made up of 100% fibroin, which contains 18 types of amino acids and trace elements that are essential to the human body. It serves as an ideal protein enricher for high quality cosmetics. It is in the form of a yellow powder of 200 mesh (74μ) diameter, that can be applied to a wide range of cosmetics. It helps to maintain moisture levels in the skin and prevents dryness. Superfine silk powder is useful as a filler in mineral makeup formulations in that it provides moisture balance and absorbs excess oil, thereby providing a silky slip (44). Superfine silk powder can also be used in any type of powdered formulations where oil absorption and a silky slip are desired. It is an exceptional alternative to talc in body and face powders.

Metallic stearates: The materials primarily used for imparting adhesive characters are soaps of anionic metals, primarily zinc stearate and magnesium stearate, as well as talc, magnesium and calcium salts of myristic acid. Magnesium stearate has a better adhesive property than zinc stearate and is more preferred in face powders, but zinc stearate is more predominantly used in talcum powders. Magnesium stearate is used at 3-10% in face powders and any other pharmaceutical topical powders (32).

Colourants: The sources of colourants used in face powders are the inorganic pigments like iron oxides as well as organic lakes and toners. Inorganic pigments were originally sourced from nature, but synthetic forms were later preferred. Synthetic pigments are less likely to have contaminants, are free from grit, more uniform in colour from batch to batch and, being purer, have a greater strength of colour than their natural counterparts (31,32). Any lake colour selected for use, need to be tested for stability and checked to ensure that it does not readily dissolve in water or oil, otherwise the colour in a product, would bleed when applied to areas of the body, where perspiration or sebum is present. Many face powders suffer colour change after they have been on the skin for a while, a problem exacerbated by the fact that colour changes are greater where more sebum is produced, making an evenly applied face powder look blotchy with time. Various synthetic and natural inorganic pigments used include iron oxides for yellow, red, and brown colour shades, and ultramarine for green and blue colours (31). Lead and arsenic compounds, which are toxic substances, are not used as colourants. Other colouring agents that could be added to face powder include metallic powders (mica, aluminium, bronze) to give gold, silver and other metal effects; synthetic bismuth oxychloride and synthetic pearl pigments to give the powder a pearlescent sheen; and various forms of resins and plastics (45). Under the Federal Food, Drug and Cosmetic Act, the organic colour additives must be government-certified; however, inorganic pigments do not require such certification. It is essential that the pigment used must be of uniform particle size in other to bring out the maximum colour effect and uniformity in each batch of a face powder.

Perfumes/fragrances: The odour of a powder product plays an important role in its acceptability and sales potential, hence, the need for the selection of a proper perfume or fragrance that is dispersed in the face powder. The odour must be pleasant in order for the powder to enjoy good patronage. It is an essential requirement that the perfume used is nonirritating, stable to mildly alkaline conditions and does not undergo oxidation or volatilisation very readily under various storage conditions (31,32). In addition, the perfume must be very compatible with all the ingredients of the powder. The rancidity of the perfume could result in change in the colour (discolouration) of the powder on storage. The reasonable concentration of perfume in face powder is between 0.2 and 1.0%, as too low a concentration may not be perceptible and properly mask the odour of the raw materials. A higher concentration may cause lumping of the powder because of over-wetting. Such a higher concentration of the perfume may also cause skin irritation.

The dispersion of the perfume in the powder requires skill because of its relatively small quantity in a formulation, since it is essential that the perfume is homogeneously dispersed in the powder. The incorporation of the perfume into the powder mass, may involve mixing it initially with one of the ingredients that has good absorbent property, e.g., magnesium carbonate, or it may be sprayed into the entire preparation. It is required that on addition of the perfume to a powder product, the powder must be stored for up to a month, an ageing process, before it is finally packaged for marketing (31,32). The ageing procedure depends on the method of incorporating the perfume into the powder.

Ingredients for formulation of compact face powders

A compact (pressed) powder is a dry powder which has been compressed into a cake and is usually applied with a powder puff or a soft brush. The basic ingredients for the formulation are the raw materials, binding agents and preservatives. Essentially, the raw materials constituting the pressed powder are identical to those employed for loose face powder. However, there are three characteristics of utmost importance for pressed powder which do not present a problem in loose powder. These are binding ability, payoff and preservation (31,32). It is essential that the base for a compact cake compresses easily, holds the powder ingredients together and does not crumble or chip under normal conditions of usage and transportation. To achieve this, binding agents are employed. A compact powder must also have sufficient payoff when applied with a powder puff, that is, it should come off easily onto the applicator. Too low a compaction pressure will result in a cake that will easily disintegrate, while too high a pressure will result in a hard, glazed cake which will not payoff sufficiently (46).

Binding agents: In the formulation of a compressed or compact face powder, the binder may be introduced as a solution or in a dry powder form. The binder impacts cohesiveness into the powder mixture so that when compressed, the product remains solid, stable and can withstand transportation and handling stresses. Manufacturers use a wide range of materials as binders, and at times, mixtures of the binders are used to achieve a specific purpose. Generally, gum mucilages, e.g., tragacanth, karaya, Arabic, quince seed and carrageenan; sugars, aromatic tinctures, starches and some celluloses may be used as binders in compressed face powder formulation (47).

The binders employed in face powders are classified into five groups:

- Dry binders
- Oil binders
- Water-soluble binders
- Water-repellent binders
- Emulsion binders

Dry binders: Dry binders, such as the metallic stearates (zinc or magnesium stearate), have been discussed in the section on loose face powders. The use of dry binders requires increased pressure for firm compacting.

Oil binders: Oils such as mineral oil, isopropyl myristate, and lanolin derivatives can be used alone as binding agents in a variety of compact face powders.

Water-soluble binders: Natural gums such as tragacanth, karaya, and Arabic and synthetic varieties such as polyvinylpyrollidone (PVP), methyl cellulose, and carboxylmethyl-cellulose have been used as water-soluble binders in the manufacture of compact face powders. As a result of bacterial proliferation in gum solution, preservatives are required in the formula. The parabens (p-hydroxybenzoates) are considered to be very effective preservatives (32)

Water-repellent binders: Mineral oil, fatty esters of all types, and lanolin derivatives are water-repellent binders that may be used alone or mixed with appropriate quantity of water to aid in the formation of smooth, compact face powders. There may be a need to include a wetting agent that will aid in uniform distribution of the moisture in the powder.

Emulsion binders: Emulsions are a heterogeneous mixture of oil and water. The use of emulsion-type binders in compact face powder formulation is to overcome the difficulties in incorporating water-repellent binders homogeneously in the powder and to prevent the formation of lumps that may occur when oils alone are used as binders in face powders (32). The emulsion allows for a uniform distribution of both the oil and water phase, which is essential for the satisfactory pressing of the powder. Emulsion binder has the advantage of retaining the moisture unlike water-repellent binder, thus allowing for a smoother running of the manufacturing procedure. Emulsion binding agents may be prepared with ionic emulsifiers such as soaps, e.g., such as triethanolamine stearate; and non-ionic emulsifiers such as glyceryl monostearate, in mineral oil-water combinations. The required quantities of the binders needed in compaction process vary based on the base formula. For oil-type binders, a 3% concentration has been suggested as starting point, while for emulsion-type binders, the baseline concentration may be 10% (32).

Table 15.7: Formulas for light loose face powers

Ingredient	Formula 1 (%)	Formula 2 (%)	Formula 3 (%)	Formula 4 (%)
Talc	70	63	75	60
Kaolin	10	20		10
Starch (rice)			10	
Calcium carbonate	10	5		15
Zinc oxide	5	5	10	5
Zinc stearate		5	5	5
Magnesium carbonate	5	1		5
Colourant	q.s.	0.5	q.s.	
Perfume	q.s.	0.5	q.s.	q.s.

q.s. =sufficient quantity

Formulation and manufacturing processes

Loose face powders

The early face powders were generally simple mixtures of not more than three substances that were readily combined. In imparting all the desired characteristics (spreadability, slip, adhesiveness, absorbency, bloom) into a face powder product, mixtures of a variety of substances are used in the formulation. The market consideration is also essential for the manufacturer, e. g., is it a standardised product formulated for a more conservative clientele? Is the product designed for teenagers or for more mature women? (31,47). For the consumer, the desired benefits will depend on the type of the skin of the user. It may be tasking creating a formula for a loose face powder that functions well and meets all the required conditions. For example, the opacity of the zinc oxide and titanium dioxide, and the transparency of talc will greatly influence the concentration of the colourant to be employed in the formulation. Thus, the formulae for loose face powders will be classified under light powder, medium powder and heavy powder types (32,48).

Light powder: The products are illustrated in Table 15.7 by Formulas 1 to 4. They are meant for application on dry skin, with virtually no oil secretion. The formulas have low covering power but large amount of talc to provide slip. Formula 4 is a white-base face powder (no colourant) with zinc oxide in which the magnesium carbonate can be substituted with calcium carbonate.

Medium powder: The powder products indicated in Table 15.8 (Formulas 5 to 7) are applied on normal skin or moderately oily skin. The products contain less quantity of talc, with the kaolin providing good covering power compared to the light powder. Formula 7 is a white-base face powder (no colorant) with zinc oxide in which the magnesium carbonate is substituted with calcium carbonate as absorbent.

Table 15.8: Formulas for medium loose face powers

Ingredient	Formula 5 (%)	Formula 6 (%)	Formula 7 (%)
Talc	40	50	54
Kaolin	37	15	12
Calcium carbonate	5		8
Zinc oxide	7	5	25
Zinc stearate	7	5	5
Magnesium carbonate	3		
Colourant	0.3	q.s.	
Perfume	0.7	q.s.	1

Heavy powder: This type of powders is applied on extremely oily skin, which have more shine due to excessive secretions of the sebaceous glands. The formulas in Table 15.9 contain ingredients with high covering power to cover the shine of the skin. The inclusion of talc and calcium carbonate is to provide the slip and absorbent properties. Formulas 8 and 10 are white-base face powders (no colourant) with zinc oxide. Titanium dioxide in Formula 10 increases the covering power and provides a brilliant, white and inert powder.

Manufacturing procedures for loose face powders

The procedure for mixing the ingredients employed in loose face powder production is the same for both small- and large-scale production, which is the dry mixing method. Also, the same method is used in the manufacturing of all the different grades of loose face powders. The traditional method for making face powder on a small scale involves pulverising all the ingredients and sifting to a uniform size. The perfume and colourants are mixed separately with portions of the powder until they are evenly distributed, after which the two mixtures are combined and mixed thoroughly with the rest of the powder base; the resulting powder is then sifted. The pulverising and mixing procedures are carried out using the pestle and mortar.

Table 15.9: Formulas for heavy loose face powers. q.s = sufficient quantity

Ingredient	Formula 8 (%)	Formula 9 (%)	Formula 10 (%)
Talc	20	35	38
Kaolin	20		25
Calcium carbonate	39	35	5
Titanium dioxide			5
Zinc oxide	15	25	21
Zinc stearate		5	5
Magnesium carbonate	5		
Colourant		q.s.	0
Perfume	1	q.s.	1

In the manufacture of loose face powders on a large scale, pulverisation is carried out using size-reducing equipment such as the ball mill (Figure 15.7). Powder sifter and mixing machines that are provided with a spray arrangement for the addition of the perfume are then used. The procedures may be divided into the following stages:

Stage 1: The perfume is added to some part of the absorbent in the formula, e.g., calcium carbonate, and mixed thoroughly. This preparation is kept aside for some time (ageing process).

Stage 2: The colourant is pulverised, added to one of the basic ingredients, e.g., talc and mixed thoroughly for a few hours. The remaining ingredients in the formula are added to the mixture and mixed properly.

Stage 3: The mixture in stage 1, containing the perfume is added to the mixture in stage 2 that contains the colourant and mixed thoroughly using an efficient V-shape or double cone mixer (figures 15.8, .9) The powder is sieved using either a silk mesh or nylon cloth. The fineness of the powder is determined by the pore size of the sieve. Ideally, sieve with mesh size not greater than 125µ is suitable.

Some of the equipment used in the manufacturing processes are indicated below.

Figure 15.7: Industrial ball mill

Figure 15.8: The V-shape mixer

Figure 15.9: Double cone mixer

Packaging of loose face powder

The container for filling loose face powders must be selected carefully to ensure that there is no interaction between the powder ingredients and the box used. It must be ascertained that there will be no odour development or any incompatibility between the plastic material of the package being employed and the powder. The machine employed in the filling process may fill by volume or weight. This makes the density of the powder relevant to the filling process. If a powder is too bulky (very light), the container may not be filled to the required weight, if it is too dense, the container may appear to be under-filled. Loose powders are packed in relatively smaller plastic jars fitted with reclosable perforated lids or in jars equipped with applicators (puff and brushes). Some of the containers for packaging loose face powders are shown in Figure 15.10.

Figure 15.10: Containers for packaging loose face powders

Formulation and manufacture of compressed face powders

Compressed face powders are manufactured using either the wet-casting on mould or compression techniques. The two techniques are classified into three procedures namely: the wet moulding process, the damp compression method, and the dry compression method. The wet moulding process is now virtually obsolete and most cosmetic industries make use of the damp or dry method for the manufacture of compressed face powder. The amount of pressure required for compacting a cake will vary considerably, depending on the basic formulation, type and quantity of binder employed, the powder moisture content, and other variables (32,49).

The basic formulas for compressed face powders to which any of the three compression methods can be applied are illustrated in formulas 11 to 14 (Table 15.10).

Table 15.10: Formulas for compact face powers. q.s. = sufficient quantity

Ingredient	Formula 11 (%)	Formula 12 (%)	Formula 13 (%)	Formula 14 (%)
Talc	60	40	65	69
Kaolin	12	12		18
Calcium carbonate	12			
Titanium dioxide	12		5	8
Rice starch		10		
Zinc stearate	4	8		5
Zinc oxide		20	20	
Magnesium carbonate		10	5	
Magnesium stearate			5	
Colour, perfume, binder	q.s.	q.s.	q.s.	q.s.

The compression method that is used by the manufacturer will depend on the powder formula and the binder type. If an aqueous binder is used, the method is referred to as damp or wet compression, otherwise, the process is known as dry compression when a dry binder is used (46). As indicated in Table 15.10, the colour, perfume and binder requirements for the production of the compressed powders vary and are best determined by the manufacturer during a pilot study.

Wet moulding or casting: Wet moulding or casting involves the use of a wet binder to dampen the powder mass that converts it into a paste, which is, thereafter, cast into a lubricated shallow mould of the required shape that is made of glass, porcelain, nickel or any other suitable metal. The cake is then dried and transferred into the final packaging material. The whole process is a two-stage technique that is automated in most factories, thereby, ensuring mass production.

- **Dry compression:** Dry compression involves the introduction of a dry binder into the powder mass and, thereafter, the powder mixture is charged with a little quantity of a liquid vehicle of the manufacturer's choice. The mixture is then thoroughly blended and the powder is pressed. The method requires increase in pressure when materials such as magnesium stearate and zinc stearate are used as the effective binders. The use of a liquid binder, in some instances where none of the ingredients are sensitive to water, are becoming popular (48).

- **Damp compression method:** This method is most widely used for commercial purposes since very little binding agents are required. The base powder, colourant and perfume are properly mixed to form a uniform mixture. The liquid binder, i.e., aqueous mucilage or emulsion (oil-in-water type) are added to the mixture. The mixture is properly blended until the desired plasticity is obtained. The powder is then screened and passed to the compression machines where it is compacted; the finished compacts are dried at a predetermined elevated temperature (48).

Compression equipment

Compressed face powders could be homemade with the use of the hand press equipment shown in Figure 15.11, while on a laboratory level, the hand-held face powder compressing machine is very applicable (Figure 15.12). The compression of the powder into a compact cake at the pilot or large- scale level involves the use of either pneumatics, hydraulics or ram-type pressing machines. The pneumatic presses are excellent for producing very fine quality compacts. The hydraulic press is an extremely high-speed machine and is very well adapted to extensive runs with a high level of quality performance. The ram press is considerably cheaper and is better suited for shorter runs (32). Some of the equipment used in the compression of compact face powders at pilot or industrial scale are illustrated in Figures 15.13 and 15.14.

Figure 15.11: Hand compression equipment for homemade compact face powders

Figure 15.12: Laboratory hand-held face powder compressing machine

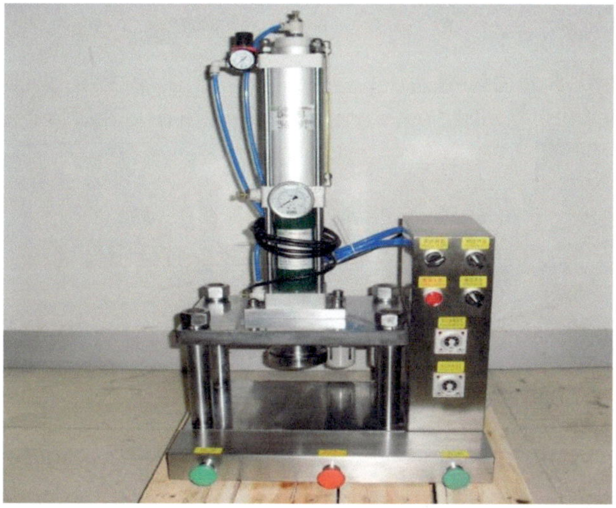

Figure 15.13: Pilot scale production hydraulic press machine for compact face powder

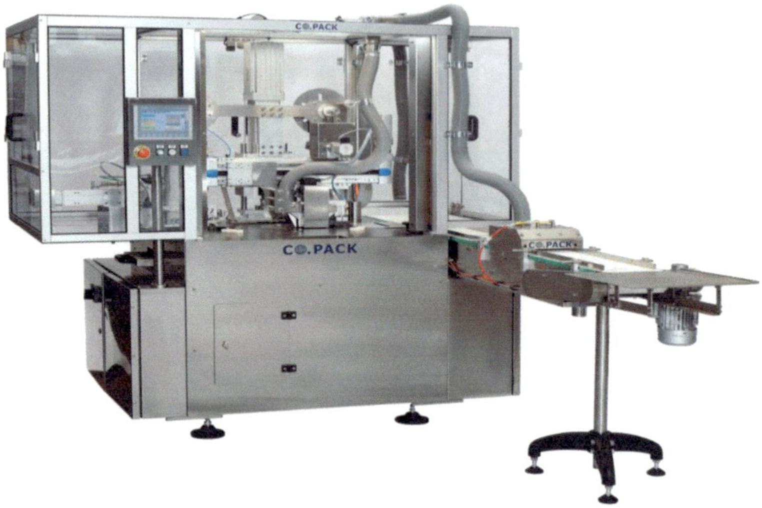

Figure 15.14: Industrial hydraulic press machine for compact face powder (Source: www.copackonline.com)

Samples of packaged compressed face powders for different skin shades are illustrated in Figure 15.15. They can be applied with a brush, sponge or powder puff (Figure 15.15A).

A: Normal skin, medium light

B: Perfect light pressed powder, translucent

Figure 15.15: Compact face powders of different shades

Formulation and manufacturing of body powders

Body powders, otherwise called talcum or dusting powders, are most-widely used preparations for multiple purposes: providing cooling and lubrication character with the ability to prevent irritation of the skin. Like the loose face powders, they contain slip, covering, adhesive, absorbency materials, perfumes and in some cases, antiseptic agents, and, rarely, a colouring agent. The main function of body powder is the absorption of perspiration (sweat) and as a counter-irritant.

The Pharmaceutical Codex, eleventh edition (PC_x) (50), contains four official formulations of dusting powders which are: Talc Dusting-Powder; Zinc, Starch and Talc Dusting-Powder; Zinc Undecenoate Dusting-Powder; and Chlorhexidine Dusting-Powder. Talc and starch as the major components, provide slip and absorbent properties, respectively, for the formulations. Both talc and starch, acting as glidant materials, also improve the flowability of the powder, ease of application and provide good body coverage. Other formulations of body powders with or without antiseptic/dermatological properties are depicted by Formulas 15 to17 in Table 15.11 (48).

Table 15.11: Formulas for body powers

Ingredient	Formula 15 (%)	Formula 16 (%)	Formula 17 (%)
Talc	75	70	20
Kaolin	10		25
Calcium carbonate		25	
Colloidal silica	5		
Maize Starch			35
Magnesium carbonate	5		
Zinc oxide			19.5
Zinc stearate		4	
Aluminium stearate	4		
Chlorhexidine hydrochloride			0.5
Boric acid	0.3	0.3	
Perfume	0.7	0.7	

The procedures and equipment for the manufacturing of body powders are essentially the same as indicated for loose face powders. Where perfumes are not incorporated into the formula, e.g., Formula 17, heat sterilisation of the final product can be carried out just before the final packaging. Body powders generally are packed in plastic jars fitted with reclosable perforated lids. These containers are relatively bigger than those used in the packaging of loose face powders.

Quality control and evaluation of body and face powders

In the manufacturing industry, the development of a formulation is the responsibility of the Research and Development (R &D) department, while the evaluation of the finished product is carried out by the Quality Control (QC) department, using in-process quality control (IPQC) and final product testing procedures. Thus, the final quality of the product is a joint responsibility of the two departments. Each developed formula should be subjected to intensive testing in the laboratory to assure that unexpected problems will be at a minimum when the product is presented to the manufacturing department and, ultimately, to the consumer. Panel-testing is most useful in this respect. Extensive and controlled stability tests should be run to determine if the formulated product will remain as manufactured when stored for an extended period of time (31,32,49). The following are the essential quality control tests for body and face powders.

Shade control and test

It may be difficult to determine the exact point at which a new batch is considered to be different from a commercial match or the standard batch. Ladies expect their powder shades to remain the same, batch after batch and would change brands if they found too much variation from one purchase to another. Therefore, there is a need to rigidly enforce production control so that shades do not differ to any appreciable degree from batch to batch and with the standard batches.

Among the procedures for checking the shade of a powder are:

- Spreading the powder sample on a white paper and observing the appearance in comparison with the standard batch.
- Applying the powder sample and the standard one with a puff on the skin and then making a comparison of the shade of the two samples. The puff or device used to perform this test should be the one to be used for the final product.

It is essential that colour evaluation of products must be carried out under the same quality of light, preferably using artificial light.

Colour dispersion test

Non-homogeneous dispersion of pigments in face powders may be due to poor pulverisation, mixing or colour bleeding. Colour uniformity of a powder can be checked by spreading it on a white paper and examining it with a magnifying glass. A non-colour uniformity powder can be further processed to achieve the maximum colour development and homogeneity. The introduction of a colour measurement procedure with a colorimeter has greatly improved the accuracy of the colour dispersion test.

Payoff test

This test is essentially for compact powders and is dependent on the pressure applied in its compaction. The payoff of a compressed powder cake is checked on the skin using the puff. If the pressure applied on the cake is too high, there will be insufficient adhesion of the material to the puff, and if the pressure is too low, the cake will tend to crumble and break.

Pressure test

Uniformity in hardness of a powder cake is determined using a penetrometer (drop testing system). The readings on the compacts are taken at various points to ensure that the product is of the proper hardness and that the pressure has been applied homogeneously. Non-uniformity in pressure applied may be due to the presence of air pockets, which may result in a cake that is easily broken.

Breakage test

This test is used to ascertain the stability of the compact powder during handling and transportation. The tendency of a pressed powder cake to break or chip is determined by dropping the assembled compact on a wooden surface several times from a height of 20 to 25 centimetres (8 to 10 inches). If the compact powder remains unbroken, it is an indication that the compact can withstand the handling and transportation stresses.

Flow property test

This test is carried out mainly for body and loose face powders to determine their cohesiveness and flow properties which are essential for the pourability of the powder from the container and its ease of application on the skin. Poor powder flow would limit dispensability and could cause textural inconsistencies, which can block the apertures of dispensers and limit dosing efficiency. Flowability of a powder can be determined by the indirect method (angle of repose, bulk and tapped densities, Carr's compressibility index and Hausner ratio) and the direct method using a powder flow tube or machine.

Particle size determination

The fineness of a body or loose face powder is defined by its particle size. The expected particle sizes of body and loose face powders should not be greater than 125μ and 106μ, respectively. The particle size of a powder can be determined by microscopy, sieve analysis or any other suitable methods.

Moisture content test

The moisture content of a powder affects its flowability, spreadability, cohesiveness, and the stability of the ingredients. The moisture content of a powder can be determined on a "Wet weight" basis (% Moisture Content) or on a "Dry weight" basis (% Loss on Drying) using the Ohms moisture balance apparatus. The moisture content of body and face powders, inclusive that of compact powders, should be kept as low as 0.5% to prevent damping and microbial growth.

Further information on the formulation of different types of cosmetics can be found in the book entitled: Textbook of Cosmetic Formulations (1).

References

1. Sharma, Gaurav & Gadhiya, Jayesh & Dhanawat, Meenakshi. Textbook of Cosmetic Formulations. 2018.
2. Raut KS, Shinde SE, Pathan TS, and Sonawane DI. Monthly variation of physicochemical parameters RavivarPeth Lake at Ambajpgai Dist. Beed Marathwada Region, India. Vol. 5 (2): 70 – 4. Global Journal of Environmental Research,; 2011.
3. WHO (2022). Drinking water. https://www.who.int/news-room/fact-sheets/detail/drinking-water.
4. Sylvester CI and Ebinyo RI (2015). A review of the microbial quality of potable water sources in Nigeria. Journal of Advances in Biological and Basic Research.
5. Water Facts - Worldwide Water Supply. [Internet]. Bureau of Reclamation California-Great Basin. Available from: https://www.usbr.gov/mp/arwec/water-facts-ww-water-sup.html
6. Mendie U (2005). The Theory and Practice of clean water production for domestic and Industrial use: Purified and Packaged Waters. Lacto-Medals Publishers, Lagos, Nigeria.
7. Chaitanya RK (2020). Systematic Study and Review of Water Standards Requirement for Synthesis of Pharmaceutical Products. IOSR Journal Of Pharmacy And Biological Sciences, 15(4):52-58.
8. WHO good manufacturing practices: Water for pharmaceutical use. https://www.who.int/docs/default-source/medicines/norms-and-standards/guidelines/production/trs970-annex2-gmp-wate-pharmaceutical-use.pdf?sfvrsn=39eb16b8_0.

9. El-Radhi AS (2019). Pathogenesis of Fever. Clinical Manual of Fever in Children. doi: 10.1007/978-3-319-92336-9_3.
10. Orafidiya,'Lara O. Continuous shear rheometry of o/w emulsions: control of evaporation in cone/plate geometry. J Pharm Pharmacol. 1989;41:341–2.
11. Orafidiya, L. O., Adesina, S. K. (Jr.), Igbeneghu, O. A., Akinkunmi, E. O., Adetogun, G. E. and Salau, A. O. (2006): The effect of honey and surfactant type on the antibacterial properties of the leaf essential oil of Ocimum gratissimum Linn. against common wound-infecting organisms.
12. R Pichot, Fotios Spyropoulos Ian T. Norton. O/W emulsions stabilised by both low molecular weight surfactants and colloidal particles: The effect of surfactant type and concentration December 2010. J Colloid Interface Sci. 352(1):128-35.
13. Chibuzo Uzoigwe1, J. Grant Burgess2, Christopher J. Ennis1 and Pattanathu K. S. M. Rahman1*. Bioemulsifiers are not biosurfactants and require different screening approaches. Front Microbiol 07 April 2015.
14. Mahmood. Bioemulsifiers derived from microorganisms: Applications in the drug and food industry.
15. Cosmetic and pharmaceutical compositions containing bioemulsifiers [Internet]. 2022. Available from: EPO178443B1
16. Pickering spencer umfreville. emulsions. J Chem Soc Trans. 91:2001–21.
17. Orafidiya, Oyedele, Shittu, Elujoba. The formulation of an effective topical antibacterial product containing Ocimum gratissimum leaf essential oil. Int J Pharm. 224:177–83.
18. Rowe, R. C., Sheskey, P. J., Owen, S. C., & American Pharmacists Association. List of Emulsifying agents (Emulsifiers or Emulgents) Handbook of pharmaceutical excipients. London: Pharmaceutical Press; 2006). Handb Pharm Excip Lond Pharm Press 2006.
19. Gaurav Kumar Sharma, Jayesh Gadhiya, Meenakshi Dhanawat. Textbook of Cosmetic Formulations. https://www.researchgate.net/profile/Meenakshi-Dhanawat; 2018.
20. Kim B, Cho HE, Moon SH, Ahn HJ, Bae S, Cho HD, et al. Transdermal delivery systems in cosmetics. Biomed Dermatol. 2020 Dec;4(1):10.
21. Lipstick manufacture. https://www.silverson.com/us/resource-library/application-reports/lipstick-manufacture.
22. Summary of Color Additives for Use in the United States in Foods, Drugs, Cosmetics, and Medical Devices [Internet]. U.S Food and Drug Administration. Available from: https://www.fda.gov/industry/color-additive-inventories/summary-color-additives-use-united-states-foods-drugs-cosmetics-and-medical-devices#table3A.
23. Frank W. Marschner. Deodorant composition [Internet]. Available from: https://patents.google.com/patent/US4565693A/en.
24. Rudden M, Herman R, Rose M, Bawdon D, Cox DS, Dodson E, et al. The molecular basis of thioalcohol production in human body odour. Sci Rep. 2020 Dec;10(1):12500.

25. Egert M, Höhne HM, Weber T, Simmering R, Banowski B, Breves R. Identification of compounds inhibiting the C-S lyase activity of a cell extract from a *Staphylococcus* sp. isolated from human skin. Lett Appl Microbiol. 2013 Dec;57(6):534–9.
26. Sue Brockett LyonClifford O'nealHermes Van D. Alternative enzyme substrates as deodorants [Internet]. Available from: https://patents.google.com/patent/EP0521871A1/en
27. CFR - Code of Federal Regulations Title 21 [Internet]. U.S Food and Drug Administration. Available from: https://www.accessdata.fda.gov/scripts/cdrh/cfdocs/cfcfr/CFRSearch.cfm?fr=700.16
28. TOPICAL ANTIPERSPIRANT COMPOSITION CONSISTING ESSENTIALLY OF NON-TOXIC WATER-INSOLUBLE OCCLUSIVE FILM-FORMING ANTIPERSPIRANT POLYMER. https://patentscope.wipo.int/search/en/detail.jsf?docId=WO1993024105.
29. Deodorant and antiperspirant testing [Internet]. [cited 2022 Jul 19]. Available from: https://www.sensenet.net/deodorant-and-antiperspirant-testing/
30. Piérard GE, Elsner P, Marks R, Masson P, Paye M. EEMCO Guidance for the Efficacy Assessment of Antiperspirants and Deodorants. Skin Pharmacol Physiol. 2003;16(5):324–42.
31. Mohiuddin AK. An Extensive Review of Face Powder Formulation Considerations. Auctores Publishing LLC, editor. Dermatol Dermat. 2019 Nov 13;4(3):01–18.
32. Balsam MS, Sagarin E, Sagarin E. Cosmetics, science and technology. 2d ed. New York: Wiley-Interscience; 1972. 3 p.
33. Di Maiuta N, Schwarzentruber P. (2011) Molecular detection of bacteria in calcium carbonate powder used in cosmetic formulations. Int J Cosmet Sci. 2011;33(5):426-431.
34. Talc [Internet]. 2022 [cited 2022 Aug 23]. Available From: https://www.fda.gov/cosmetics/cosmetic-ingredients/talc.
35. Singh SK. Handbook on cosmetics (Processes, formulae with testing methods). Asia Pacific Business Press Inc; 2010. P. 336. ISBN 8178331292, 9788178331294.
36. Gordon RE, Fitzgerald S, Millette J. Asbestos in commercial cosmetic talcum powder as a cause of mesothelioma in women. Int J Occup Environ Health. 2014 Oct;20(4):318–32.
37. Barel AO, Paye M, Maibach HI, editors. Handbook of cosmetic science and technology. Fourth edition. Boca Raton: Taylor & Francis; 2014. 711 p.
38. Powders and compacts. In: Mithal BM, Saha RN, eds. A handbook of cosmetics. Vallabh Prakashan; 2006. p. 23. ISBN 9788185731223, 8185731225.
39. The Ultimate Guide to Zinc oxide [Internet]. 2022 [cited 2022 Aug 23]. Available From: https://www.alyaka.com/magazine/ultimate-guide-zinc-oxide/.
40. Williams LB, Haydel SE. Evaluation of the medicinal use of clay minerals as antibacterial agents. Int Geol Rev. 2010 May 6;52(7–8):745–70.

41. Kaur M, Oberoi DPS, Sogi DS, Gill BS. Physicochemical, morphological and pasting properties of acid treated starches from different botanical sources. J Food Sci Technol. 2011 Aug;48(4):460–5.
42. Schaefer K. Natural Calcium carbonates for oral care and color cosmetics. Cosmetics & Toiletries® Magazine, June 11, 2010.
43. Draelos ZD. Cosmetics and dermatological problems and solutions: a problem based approach. 3rd ed. London: Informa Healthcare; 2011. 280 p.
44. Silk powder (200 Mesh) raw material [Internet]. 2022 [cited 2022 Aug 23]. Available from: https://www.newdirectionsaromatics.com/products/raw-materials/silk-powder-200-mesh.html.
45. Marzec A, Szadkowski B, Rogowski J, Maniukiewicz W, Szynkowska M, Zaborski M. Characteristics of Hybrid Pigments Made from Alizarin Dye on a Mixed Oxide Host. Materials. 2019 Jan 24;12(3):360.
46. Cosmetics and skin: Compressed face powders [internet]. 2022 [cited 2022 August 23]. Available from: https://www.cosmeticsandskin.com/ded/compressed-face-powders.php.
47. Barel A, Paye M, Maibach H. 2001 Handbook of cosmetics science and technology. New York: Marcel Dekker Inc; 2001.
48. Classification of powders [internet]. 2022 [cited 2022 August 23]. Available from: https://www.pharmacy180.com/article/classification-of-powders-825/.
49. iTsolis P. Approaches and issues in powder formulations [Internet]. 2014 [cited 2022 Sep 19]. Available from: https://www.cosmeticsandtoiletries.com/formulas-products/color-cosmetics/article/21836310/approaches-and-issues-in-powder-formulations.
50. Royal Pharmaceutical Society of Great Britain, Editor. The pharmaceutical codex: incorporating the British Pharmaceutical Codex. 11. ed. London: Pharmaceutical Press; 1979. 1101 p.

CHAPTER SIXTEEN

Good manufacturing practice for cosmetic products

Grace O. Onawunmi

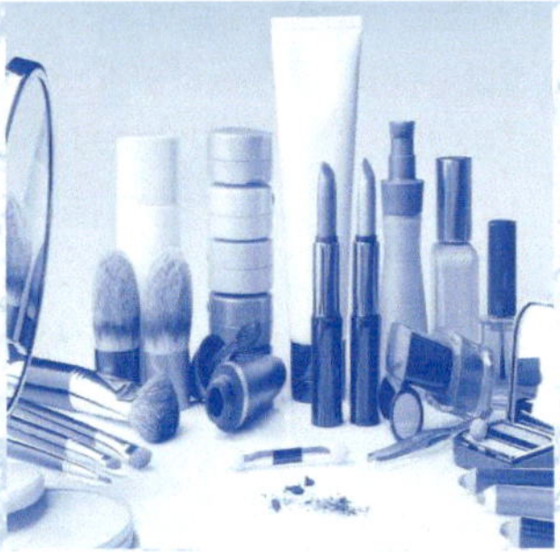

Good Manufacturing Practice (GMP) is a set of regulations, codes and guidelines controlling the manufacture of products such as drugs, foods, dietary supplements and cosmetics. It is designed to ensure that a product is consistently manufactured to a quality that not only meets the specifications of the regulatory bodies but also promotes brand name, opens doors of opportunities for exportation and saves costs that may arise from wastage, criminal contravention of regulations or laws and civil liabilities. Chapters 24 and 25 provide details of the legal responsibilities that a manufacturer of cosmetics bears to the state and to the consumer. The term current Good Manufacturing Practice (cGMP) commonly used in the United States of America (US) is to emphasise the dynamic nature of the expectations.

GMP is a key component of the overall Quality Assurance of a product (QA) and as a general concept, QA can be defined as the sum of all the organised arrangements made to ensure that products will be of the pre-set quality standards required for the intended use and for presentation in the market.

Regulatory authorities in several countries/regions have versions of GMPs for use in the manufacture of products. The World Health Organisation (WHO) version is used mainly in developing countries while the European Union (EU) GMP is used in the European Union and the Food and Drug Administration (FDA) version is used in the US. Other versions of GMP are available for use in Australia, Japan, Canada, Singapore etc. The National Agency for Food and Drugs Administration and Control (NAFDAC) GMP version is used in Nigeria. Harmonisation to obtain a universal version of GMPs has many advantages and would facilitate trade of products across borders. This is ongoing under the auspices of the International Cooperation on Cosmetics Regulation which is a voluntary cooperation between regulatory authorities from Brazil, Canada, Chinese Taipei, the European Union, Japan, the Republic of Korea, and the United States (1).

NAFDAC was established by the NAFDAC Act Cap N 1 LFN 2004 (2) "with the functions among others to regulate and control the importation, exportation, manufacture, advertisement, distribution, sale, and use of food, drugs, cosmetics, medical devices, bottled water and chemicals". The Agency is further empowered by the provisions of the Food and Drug Act Cap F.32 LFN 2004 (3) and the various regulations published by the Agency on food, drug, cosmetic and medical device are derived from these two principal laws. The current NAFDAC GMP Guidelines document (2021) (4) stipulates the minimum standards to be adhered to by manufacturers. The good practices are considered as general guides which may change as comparable methods, new technology and important but relevant new knowledge are available with the current NAFDAC guidelines statutorily due for review in April, 2026, while relevant updates on any aspects are gazetted as regulations from time to time.

All the national or international versions of GMPs address key elements such as equipment, buildings including facilities, personnel, processes, documentation, internal quality control system and records. Although all the GMP versions for different countries are similar, a Nigerian company wishing to export a product to another country must note that the product must conform to the GMP regulations of that country.

GMP for cosmetics

The Food and Drugs Act provides a more general definition for cosmetics in terms of their intended use. However, the term has been more elaborately defined in section 21 of the advertisement regulation (2021) (5) as "any substance or mixture of substances intended to be rubbed, poured, sprinkled or sprayed on, introduced into or otherwise applied to the human body or any part thereof for cleansing, beautifying, promoting attractiveness or altering the complexion, skin, hair or teeth and includes deodorants and detergent powder". Such products include skin moisturisers, perfumes, lipsticks, fingernail polishes, eye and facial makeup preparations, cleansing shampoos, permanent waves, hair colours and deodorants, as well as any substance intended for use as a component of a cosmetic product (6).

However, if the labelling has any therapeutic claims, the product ceases to be treated as a cosmetic but as a drug and the more stringent regulatory controls for drugs will now apply. According to the NAFDAC Cosmetics Products Labelling Regulations 2021 (7) "Labelling shall not be false, misleading, deceptive or likely to create an erroneous impression regarding its character, quality, quantity and origin. Any claims on the cosmetic product shall be substantiated and any information on the label which misleads or deceives a consumer shall constitute an offence ". The Sri Lanka National Medicines Regulatory Authority Guidelines (2018) on cosmetic claims provides a classification guide to help identify products and claims as cosmetics. It also lists unacceptable claims for cosmetic products in label or advertisement (8).

GMP for cosmetics are detailed guidelines concerning the production process that ensure safety, consistency and satisfactory quality of the final product. It includes rules for operation and organisational guidelines which avoid costly production errors such as mix up in labels or cosmetic ingredients, contamination of equipment and products from raw materials, environment and personnel as well as deviations in quality due to lack of documentation of manufacturing procedures.

Cosmetic GMP guidelines

The International Organisation for Standardisation (ISO) 22716 guidelines (9), which are the internationally accepted standards for cosmetics, have been incorporated in the Cosmetic GMP guidelines of various countries such as the US. EU, Canada, Japan and Nigeria. The objective of the NAFDAC Good Manufacturing Practice Guidelines for Cosmetic Products (2021) is to ensure that cosmetics manufactured in Nigeria meet acceptable standards consistently (4). NAFDAC Guidelines are also available for individuals intending to engage in manufacturing of cosmetics in Nigeria (10).

Adherence to GMP for cosmetics are not legally binding for certain countries such as the US (11) and Canada (12) where compliance to the guidelines is only recommended, although the US FD&C Act prohibits adulterated or misbranded cosmetics. The risk of adulterating or misbranding can, however, be reduced by adherence to GMP recommendations while manufacturers must adhere to GMP guidelines in the production of cosmetics to be sold in the European Union (13).

Implementation of Cosmetic GMP guidelines helps to identify and control all possible areas that can affect product quality and it ensures manufacture of safe, consistent and high-quality products that meet required specifications. The low microbial counts obtained in the final product also allows added preservatives to function effectively at low concentrations thereby protecting the product during storage, shelf life and use by the consumer. While cosmetic products are hardly required to be sterile, it is mandatory that they meet some specific level of hygiene with respect to total microbial count and absence of specific bacterial species as discussed in Chapter 19. Beyond hygiene, microbes (bacteria or fungi) can facilitate product deterioration.

In this section the main GMP guidelines for cosmetics will be discussed under the following headings:

- Documentation, standard operating procedures (SOPs) and records
- Buildings, facilities and environment

- Equipment
- Personnel
- Raw materials
- Production process
- Quality Control
- Internal Audit
- Complaints and Recalls

Documentation, standard operating procedures (SOPs) and records

Documentation, development and use of (SOPs) as well as keeping of records are interwoven but salient GMP requirements. Documentation is a comprehensive process and starts at the stage of process design, includes developing a dossier or series of documents to meet premise registration on one hand, and the specific product registration on the other hand. It continues beyond production as quality check procedures and results must be documented for each batch of product. Documentation of sales and distribution records are very important for tracking, in case of any controversy or recall of product.

Specifically, documentation at the stage of production is the process of writing down how a production process and work flow is undertaken or conducted. The record of the master formula for each batch is mandatory for GMP. This important component of GMP can be done by writing on paper or electronically. As a guide, for each batch, all production operations, processes and practices must be documented using detailed (SOPs). Indeed, every operation must have a record of written SOP which must be in simple language. The procedure for handling and storage of new stock of raw materials, equipment operation and maintenance, production processes, packaging and sampling of final products or intermediates, where required, must be guided by written operating procedures. The written operating procedure must be available at the respective point of operation and must be reviewed or updated routinely but only by the approved authority.

A central feature of GMP is management of records such as production records. The WHO (14) defines a batch or lot as "a defined quantity of starting material, packaging material, or product processed in a single or series of processes so that it is expected to be homogeneous. It may sometime be necessary to divide batch into a number of batches which are later brought together to form a final batch". It, therefore, follows that each batch of a product must have a Master Formula that provides the history of each batch, with each batch of final product assigned a unique code (number or alphanumeric) with full documentation of the batch size, the source or reference code and batch number and quantities of each ingredient, a code for the analysis report on the batch, final packing details and date of release. In practice, a template or format is available for entering the appropriate details for each batch.

The records of the facility need to be stored safely until required for legal or other purposes. Access to the documents must be limited to prevent loss or alteration. The availability of records helps to identify the source of the problem and provides evidence that GMP guidelines were complied with during the manufacturing process. The master formula for each batch of the product must be kept secure. Beyond regulatory requirements, records of manufacturing data are very important for internal research and development towards improvements and innovations with respect to products or processes.

Buildings, facilities and environment

This has to do with the plant's external and internal environment. It includes how the buildings are designed, constructed, the environment around the buildings, pest control, sewage, air conditioning, water systems, and the like. Facilities, buildings and utilities not only need to be operating correctly, but maintenance, cleaning, sanitising and pest control schedules and records must be kept for GMP purposes. The facilities should be organised in such a way that there is separation of production, storage and packaging activities. Only authorised personnel should enter the production facility. The facility is, therefore, designed, constructed and maintained to facilitate good workflow and prevent contamination of the cosmetic product.

Equipment

Appropriate equipment used in the manufacture of cosmetics should be installed in the facility in such a way as to ensure easy operation, cleaning, sanitising and maintenance. Detailed SOPs for routine calibration, cleaning/sanitising and maintenance of equipment should be established and recorded when undertaken. Each equipment is expected to have a logbook as a record of its use and performance.

Personnel

The organisation must have a clearly defined organogram with adequate number of staff manning each level. Personnel involved in cosmetic manufacturing and control must have prerequisite training and experience in their duties. There is also a need for periodic retraining of personnel on assigned tasks. The personnel have responsibilities to wear clean clothing and the necessary protective gear such as gloves and hair covers to prevent contamination. They should be adequately supervised during the manufacturing process and access to production, storage and control areas should be restricted to staff members. Personal hygiene and good health condition are mandatory for all production personnel.

Raw materials

The raw materials used for manufacturing cosmetics should be of appropriate standard and specification, given that several quality grades of the same raw material are sometimes available in the market, but for different purposes. Raw materials should be stored properly to avoid mix-ups or selection errors and to prevent microbial contamination and environmental degradation. They should be identified, sampled and tested for compliance with the company's established specifications prior to usage. The widely used principle of first-in, first-out (FIFO) applicable to warehouse storage for both the raw material and the finished product sections would help to prevent deterioration while in storage.

Water used for cosmetic production must be of acceptable quality for the purpose and should be monitored regularly to ensure compliance with chemical, physical and microbiological specifications. The water system must be designed to avoid areas of stagnation and must be routinely cleaned and sanitised.

Only approved colour additives should be used in production while prohibited and restricted ingredients are listed in the US GMP guidelines (11). Similarly, NAFDAC Cosmetics Products (Prohibition of Bleaching agents) Regulations (2019) prohibits the importation, manufacture, distribution and sale of any cosmetic containing corticosteroids, mercury and mercury compounds or more than 2% hydroquinone alone or 1% hydroquinone in combination with other lightening ingredients and any of the three forms of arbutin (15).

Production process

Detailed manufacturing and control SOPs should be established for all aspects of production. Microbiological, physical and chemical contaminations should be prevented during production and packaging. In-process samples and final products should be checked to ensure adequate mixing during production and consistency of final products. Finished products should be properly labelled with specified requirements for labelling on internal and external containers or packages and records for each batch produced should be maintained. Current labelling regulation (2021) (7) emphasises, among others, accuracy, prominence and legibility of information. It stipulates that labelling "must not be false, misleading, deceptive or likely to create an erroneous impression regarding its character, quality, quantity and origin". The regulation further requires that any claims on the product must have been substantiated, apparently at the point of registration. The labelling must include a complete list of all ingredients with even fragrance, flavour and colour specified by internationally accepted names or codes. The labelling regulation requires that the prescribed storage condition, expiry date, National Agency for Drug and Food Administration and Control (NAFDAC) product registration number, and any relevant caution concerning use, storage or disposal of container must be included. The current cosmetic product advertisement regulation (2021) (5) is consistent with the above labelling requirements in several respects and specifically regulates advertisement of cosmetics in a comprehensive manner covering media (including social media), digital or printed material or even oral advertisements.

Quality control (QC)

Production and quality teams are headed by different people and are not responsible to each other. Adequate laboratory facilities for the testing and monitoring procedures should be available in the QC unit where possible. Otherwise, analysis can be contracted out to qualified analysts to complement available internal resources. The first challenge is to develop or adopt appropriate monograph of specifications and methods of analysis for each ingredient, product and intermediate, where necessary. Such would normally be expected at the initial point of documentation for product registration. The quality unit must apply appropriate sampling techniques and analytical methods to test the raw materials including water, packages, labels, intermediate/in-process materials and, finally, each finished product before release and ensure that released products meet all applicable specifications including ensuring the effectiveness of preservative systems used. It is also customary for the QC unit to keep voucher samples of each batch of finished product for a specified period as reference material and for the purpose of validating the initial accelerated shelf-life prediction submitted at the point of product registration.

Internal audit

To evaluate the overall performance of GMP in a company, an internal audit is conducted. This assesses the strengths and weaknesses of the system and recommends remedial action to overcome any failings in GMP. The recommendations made and the action implemented because of the audit must be documented. The QA unit has the autonomy and authority to act independently and can, therefore, undertake internal audits to determine if the company is adhering to GMP requirements. In addition, it can conduct periodic GMP training for personnel at all levels of the organisation.

Complaints and recalls

A person must be designated to receive and review complaints. Any complaint or adverse event reported should be documented. The review process should be in response to both written and verbal complaints using SOPs established for such reviews. Complaints about a product, for example, may suggest problems such as spoilage or contamination. It may even assist the company to detect any fake of its product in circulation.

Adverse events such as undesired body reactions to the product should be investigated. If a serious safety or quality issue is suspected, a company may conduct a total product recall after NAFDAC has been informed of the situation. The effectiveness of the recall process should be evaluated.

Enforcement

All cosmetics available for use in many countries, including Nigeria, must be produced according to the GMPs of the relevant regulatory authorities. Like best practices in other countries such as the US (16) and EU (13), inspectors from NAFDAC have the power to enter and carry out periodic inspections of cosmetic premises at reasonable times without prior notice, to check for compliance with regulations/guidelines (2). The inspector may also collect or seize samples of cosmetics, anything used for manufacturing and any labels or advertising materials. The inspector can examine any document that may contain relevant information. Test samples can also be obtained from typical retail stores to help the investigation. From the information collected and results from the samples examined by the analyst, the seized articles may be returned to the owner if found to be satisfactory. If the findings are not satisfactory, the owner of the articles will be informed of the results and face subsequent proceedings. Other factors that may initiate inspection of a cosmetic establishment include consumer complaints received and the company's compliance history/record.

Consequences of non-compliance to cosmetic GMP guidelines/regulations

Voluntary actions are actions undertaken by the firm while regulatory actions are those taken by regulatory authorities against the firm and those responsible for non-compliance. As part of voluntary action, it is advisable for firms to respond to the forms used by inspectors to record their observations on corrective measures to be taken by the firm on issues raised in the forms. Removal of product from the market or recall may have to be done by the firm.

Regulatory actions include the following:

- Regular review of regulatory inspection findings and defective products reports.
- A warning letter alerting the firm of non-compliance and the need to address the problem before regulatory action is taken against the firm and responsible individuals.

- Instructions to Custom Services to block product entry into the country.
- Seizure, when there is imminent public health threat that the firm is not addressing on its own
- Criminal proceedings against individuals and /or body corporate with penalties for contravention as stipulated under the various laws and regulations.

References

1. International Cooperation on Cosmetics Regulation. What is ICCR? [Internet] 2022 [cited 2022 Jul 16]. Available from https://www https://www.iccr-cosmetics.org/about
2. National Agency for Food and Drug Administration and Control Act Cap N1 LFN 2004 (Ng).
3. Food and Drug Act Cap F32 LFN 2004 (Ng)
4. NAFDAC Good Manufacturing Practice Guidelines for Cosmetic Products 2021 [Internet] 2021 [cited 2022 Jul 16]]. Available from https://www.nafdac.gov.ng/wp-content/uploads/Files/Resources/Guidelines/Updated_Drug_Guidelines/NAFDAC-GMP-GUIDELINES-FOR-COSMETICS-PRODUCTS-2021-DER-GDL-004-01.pdf
5. NAFDAC Gazette No 127 Vol 108 B3031-3038 on Cosmetics Products Advertisement Regulation [Internet] 2021 Aug 3 [cited 2022 Jul 16] Available from https://www.nafdac.gov.ng/wp-content/uploads/Files/Resources/Regulations/REGULATIONS_2021/COSMETICS-PRODUCTS-ADVERTISEMENT-REGULATIONS-2021.pdf
6. Federal Food, Drug, and Cosmetic Act (USA) Chapter II sec.201(i) [21 U. S. C. 321] Amended through P. L. 117-103, Enacted Mar 15 2022 [Internet} 2022 [cited 2022 Jul 16] available from https://www.govinfo.gov/content/pkg/COMPS-973/pdf/COMPS-973.pdf
7. NAFDAC Gazette No 151 VOL 108 B3243-3255 on Cosmetics Products Labelling Regulation [Internet] 2021 Sep 10 [cited 2022 Jul 16]. Available from https://www.nafdac.gov.ng/wp-content/uploads/Files/Resources/Regulations/REGULATIONS_2021/COSMETIC-PRODUCTS-LABELLING-REGULATION.pdf
8. NMRA. Guideline on Cosmetic Claims [Internet] 2018 [cited 2022 July 16]. Available from https://nmra.gov.lk/images/2021/Publicconsultation/Guideline-on-Cosmetic-Claims-.pdf
9. The International Organization for Standardization. ISO 22716. Guidelines on Good Manufacturing Practices. Edition 1. Geneva, Switzerland. International Organization for Standardization. 2007.
10. NAFDAC. Guidelines for production inspection of Large and Medium Scale Cosmetics manufacturing facilities. [Internet] 2021 [cited 2022 July 16]. Available from https://www.nafdac.gov.ng/wp-content/uploads/Files/Resources/Guidelines/Updated_Drug_Guidelines/GUIDELINES-FOR-PRODUCTION-INSPECTION-OF-LARGE-MEDIUM-SCLAE-COSMETICS-MANUFACTURING-FACILITIES-DER-GDL-001-01.pdf

11. The United States Food and Drug Administration. Guidance for Industry: Cosmetic Good Manufacturing Practices [Internet] 2013 [cited 2022 Jul 16] Available from https://www.fda.gov/media/86366/download
12. Food and Drugs Act (R.S.C., 1985, c. F-27) (Can) Sections 16 and 18 [Internet} [cited 2022 Jul 16] Available from https://laws-lois.justice.gc.ca/eng/acts/f-27/page-2.html#h-234163
13. European Union (Cosmetic products) Regulation 2013. I. R. S.I No. 440, 2013 [Internet] 2013 [cited 2022 Jul 16]. Available from https://www.irishstatutebook.ie/eli/2013/si/440/made/en/print
14. World Health Organization WHO Technical Report Series, No. 908, 2003 Annex 4 Good Manufacturing Practices for pharmaceutical products: main principles [Internet] 2003 [cited 2022 Jul 16]. Available from https://cdn.who.int/media/docs/default-source/2021-dha-docs/trs996_annex4.pdf?sfvrsn=c44d141a_1&download=true
15. National Agency for Food and Drug Administration (NAFDAC) Cosmetics products (Prohibition of Bleaching agents) Regulation, 2019 [Internet] 2019 [cited 2022 Jul 16]. Available from https://www.nafdac.gov.ng/wp-content/uploads/Files/Resources/Regulations/All_Regulations/Cosmetics-Products-Prohibition-of-Bleaching-Agents-Regulations-2019.pdf
16. Federal Food, Drug, and Cosmetic Act (USA) sec.704 [21 U. S. C. 374] Amended through P. L. 117-103, Enacted Mar 15 2022 [Internet} 2022 [cited 2022 Jul 16] available from https://www.govinfo.gov/content/pkg/COMPS-973/pdf/COMPS-973.pdf

CHAPTER SEVENTEEN

Packaging in cosmetics

Bukola A Oseni

Packaging in cosmetics refers to the art and processes that are involved in ensuring that cosmetic products are kept intact from the point of manufacture till they get to the consumer. This process employs the use of a package to enclose the cosmetic product as a guard against hazards such as contamination, spoilage, spillage, counterfeiting, as well as pilferage during transportation, storage and handling (1). Furthermore, packaging provides convenience in handling, dissemination of detailed information about the product (such as identity, quality, and direction for use), and portrays very important aesthetic values such that the product is sufficiently appealing to the consumer to trigger impulse for its purchase. In other words, the quality and functionality of packaging play a major role in the protection of a product and its perceived quality such that high-quality packaging usually translates to a perceived high-quality product and high selling price (1,2).

Development and design of packages for cosmetic products

Packages include all that is used to contain a product, from the containers to closures, labels, literature inserts and even advertisement. Packaging development and design are important for the manufacture of new cosmetic products, or when improvement in existing packaging and or reduction of cost is desired. Considering the availability of different cosmetic products, the choice of an ideal package for the various types of cosmetic products will depend on the physico-chemical properties of the product, as well as the form (liquid, semisolid, solid) in which it is presented for use, and in some case, the mode of application of the product. In addition to the major function of containment, protection, and marketing, packaging materials should not react with the cosmetic product and vice versa to prevent the deterioration of the products, packages, or both (1). The choice of packaging should, therefore, be considered as early as possible during the development of new cosmetic products to enable considerable time for the determination of product-package compatibility. In the manufacture of packages, in-process quality control is adopted to achieve the desired performance of the end products. This entails incorporating quality tests that will ensure product-package compatibility, the ability of the package to withstand the abrasion and rigours encountered during packaging operation in the factory, stacking and storage in the warehouse, and transportation to various wholesalers and retailers (1). In other words, the package should be subjected to a simulated abuse test in the laboratory, a performance test in the factory and warehouse, as well as for transportation and storage systems. Tests that demonstrate the ease of opening, filling, and closing of packages; ease, and effect of product spillage on the package, product-package compatibility test, and shelf-life determination are also mandatory.

Factors considered in the design and development of cosmetic packages and labels

Customer identity: the identity of clients for the cosmetic products such as gender, age, etc., is defined (3). This will enable the choice of appropriate design and package concepts that will appeal to the category of clients. For example, packages for hair treatments for girls may have warm bright colours that suggest the product is for children on being sighted.

Brand personality: It is important to determine the message that the brand stands for. Incorporating the brand identity on packages will enable the customer to easily identify the different cosmetic products, for example, soaps, creams, and hair shampoos from the same manufacturer (4). The brand personality dictates the style to be employed, such as incorporating nature photography for natural cosmetic products (3,4).

Trends in cosmetic packaging: This can serve as a source of inspiration for packaging design. A modern and trending design combined with a timeless and universal design can render the package an all-time design. Some trending designs include intricate line drawing, unique fonts, bold patterns and floral colours (3).

Colours: Distinct eye-catching colours should be chosen to stand out from competitor brands (if any) and portray the brand personality.

Fonts: Unique, legible fonts that complement the brand style should be employed. For example, a sophisticated style will go with a 'sans serif' font and a classic look will employ a 'serif' font (3).

Design focal point: This refers to the unique selling point of the cosmetic product. Examples are '100% natural', 'chemical-free with no additives', 'vegan', 'cruelty-free' and 'hypoallergenic'. The presence of a unique ingredient can also be indicated.

Package/label material and printing options: The type, properties, and function of the cosmetic product will largely determine the type of packaging material and label printing to be employed. For example, bath gels are used and stored in the shower room, therefore, plastic containers, compatible with the ingredients of the formulation and label prints that are steam- and water-resistant will be appropriate (3). Printing options, such as foil prints, create a special effect and a luxurious feel.

Regulatory guidelines: In the design of packages, the guidelines and required information stipulated by regulatory bodies in countries and states where the cosmetic product is to be marketed should be reflected on the package (4). This ensures that the customer obtains as much information as possible to assist in making a well-informed decision when buying a product.

Elements and characteristics required of an ideal package

- The package should be sturdy to preserve the quality of the product it contains.
- The package should be easy to brand and use.
- The package should contain the name of the product, brand, instructions for use, ingredients, warnings, precautions, brand logo, and specific product information if any.
- The package should allow the product to be pressed out but not sucked back to avoid contamination of the remaining product in the container, e.g., tubes and squeezed bottles used for lotions and creams.
- The package should have a tamper-proof seal and counterfeiting tools such as holograms to assure the consumer that the container has neither been previously opened nor tampered with and that the product is of good quality (1,5).

Regulatory requirements for packaging and labelling of cosmetics

The regulations and guidelines for packaging and labelling of cosmetic products in each country are unique even though they are intended to serve a similar purpose of providing required information to ensure safe use by the consumer. It is, therefore, important for the manufacturer or distributor to understand the local regulations in the intended country of use for a successful product entry.

In most countries, the constituted guideline requires the package to withstand physical, mechanical, chemical, radiation, thermal, biological and electrical stresses, as well as compression forces (6–8). In addition, it must provide adequate **labelling information** such as:

- The names of all ingredients, in internationally accepted names or codes, contained in a cosmetic product, including flavourants and fragrances, must be written on its label. The common name of the product, e.g., 'Moisturising cream', its use, and net quantity of constituents in descending order, with appropriate units of measure or numerical counts. Some countries require only the listing of the ingredients in the order of prominence and not necessarily their quantities. Active ingredients in cosmeceuticals should be displayed before other ingredients.
- The net quantity of the product in the container, either in terms of volume or net weight, must be written on the product.
- The name and address of the manufacturer and the main distributor.
- Possible harmful substances, side effects, label warning on potential hazards, and instructions for safe use must be included on the package or in the leaflet placed in the outer package (9,10).
- Cosmetic products intended for internal use such as toothpastes and douches must have tamper-proof features on the immediate or outer container (11–13).
- Prescribed storage conditions, 'best before' or expiry date, and in Nigeria, NAFDAC product registration number, must be on the product container.

All information on the package must be legible, conspicuous, and presented in English language and or a national language or a local language where the product is marketed (11–13).

Packages used for cosmetic products

In the selection of appropriate containers for various cosmetic products, the important factors to consider are the type of packaging material, functionality of container, compatibility with and protection of products, sustainability, eco-friendliness, ease of shipping, and logistics (5).

Packages can be classified based on their function or type of material used for their manufacture (1). Based on function, packages are classified as primary, secondary, and tertiary packaging.

Primary packaging also known as product packaging is that which is in direct contact with the product. For example, a lipstick tube, a jar used for cream formulations.

Secondary packaging or inner packaging encloses the primary packaging. For example, the small rectangular box that houses the lipstick tube, and the paper box that houses the cream jar.

Tertiary packaging or outer packaging is used for storage and transportation of many units of the product, e.g., the box or carton used to ship orders from warehouses to retail stores or the bag used to package the product at retail stores (1).

Materials used for the manufacture of cosmetic packages

Packages for cosmetic products are either made of glass, plastic, metal, or paper.

Glass – This is one of the oldest materials used in cosmetic packaging. It is versatile because of its properties. It is basically made from sand (silica or silicon dioxide), soda ash (sodium bicarbonate) and limestone (calcium carbonate) which along with sand are natural substances. Oxides of potassium, calcium, magnesium, boron, and iron are also components of glass structure. Addition of boric acid during the manufacturing process makes glass to be heat- resistant. Glass is used to make jars, bottles, and ampoules for packaging of skin care products.

Advantages: Glass is resistant to degradation, impermeable to solvents, gases, and moisture, and can be recycled (5). It can also be moulded into different shapes, sizes, and designs of different forms. It provides clear view of contents (it is transparent), shades (it can be coloured for aesthetics), and sparkle for a good product presentation as well as offer protection to ingredients with special requirements such as those that are hygroscopic, effervescent, or oxidisable since it is impermeable to extraneous moisture and oxygen (air), respectively. Incorporation of metallic oxides for green and brown glasses; nickel, sulphur, and carbon for amber glass; copper or cobalt oxide for blue glass; or ultraviolet (UV) absorbing substances, e.g., cerium oxide, into the composition of glass enables glass containers to protect ingredients that are light-sensitive.

Disadvantages: The use of glass is limited because it is heavy, fragile, and can be expensive to ship and handle due to the risks of breakages (1). Apart from boric acid that enters the structure of glass, the oxide components are loosely bound and are relatively free to migrate. Thus, they may be leached into solutions contained in glass containers where they hydrolyse, raising the pH of such solutions that may cause instability for the solutions such as affecting the solubility of dissolved salts. Glass flakes can also be dislodged into the solutions.

Plastic – Plastics are synthetic materials made up of polymers of large molecular-weight organic substances. In addition to polymers, plastics contain certain substances that modify their properties, stability, and ease of production such as plasticizers, e.g., phthalates, resins, antioxidants, antifungal agents, colourants, opacifiers, lubricants and mould-release agents, respectively. Plastic material for packaging offers a readily available and widely used alternative material to glass in the packaging of cosmetic products.

Plastic containers for cosmetic products are mostly made from high density polyethylene (HDPE), polyethylene terephthalate (PET) and polypropylene (PP) polymers for rigid containers and low density polyethylene (LDPE) for flexible containers; other types of plastics used are high-end acrylics that have the same clarity as glass but are unbreakable (5). Acrylics and polycarbonates (PC) are also synthetic polymers that are transparent and can be coloured to give containers aesthetic effects. Plastics are made into jars, bottles, tubes, ampoules, caps, and closures for a variety of cosmetic products.

Advantages: It is cheap, resistant to breakage, durable, odourless and has lightweight. It can be moulded into numerous shapes, sizes with various colours, tints and designs such as squeeze bottles and droppers (5,14).

Disadvantages: In contrast to glass, plastics are prone to:

- **Alteration of shape and appearance**: cracking, crazing, deformations, hardening, and softening are changes that can occur with plastic containers on storage due to physical stress exerted on them during handling and transportation, changes in temperature and reaction of some constituents of the products with the containers.

- **Permeation**: this occurs when certain constituents of the product within a plastic container, such as volatile substances (e.g., essential oils) and water, migrate through the walls of the container to the outside and are lost, thereby affecting the integrity of the product. The reverse is the migration of volatile substances (strong odours), gases such as the air and moisture from the surroundings through the walls of the container into the contents of the container. Hence, products stored in plastic containers are not to be stored in surroundings of strong-smelling substances. Inks used for printing of labels on plastic containers can permeate into the contents while permeated oxygen can cause oxidation of susceptible ingredients. Co-extruded two-layer polyethylene bottles prevent ingress of moisture which can cause hydrolysis of susceptible ingredients and, when the inner layer is black polyethylene, protects from the effects of sunlight.

- **Leaching**: leaching occurs when certain substances of the plastic formulation, e.g., plasticizers, migrate into the contents of plastic containers affecting the quality of the product. Leaching is enhanced by excessive shaking of the container, increase in environmental temperature and the presence of a solubilising substance for one or more additives of the plastic container in the liquid content.

- **Sorption**: certain solutes of liquid contents can be adsorbed on to the inner surface of plastic container and with time may diffuse into the plastic and be bound to it. Sorption reduces the concentration of such solutes, e.g., vitamin A, in the product. The sorption of excipients such as dyes, preservatives and stabilisers affect the quality of the product.
- **Label printing**: certain types of plastics are resistant to inks used for printing.
- **Disposal after use**: Plastics are not easily biodegradable and, therefore, have become a major waste nuisance worldwide (14). However, plastics made from polyethylene terephthalate (PET), poly vinyl chloride (PVC), high density polyethylene (HDPE), and low-density polyethylene (LDPE) are recyclable while those made with polypropylene (PP) and polystyrene (PS) are usually not recycled because their recycled outcomes are not amenable to desired re-use. Nevertheless, Post Consumer Recycled (PCR) packaging, made from recycled plastics is used in cosmetics packaging, and its use enables brands to fulfil one of their sustainability goals.
- **Health concerns***:* plastics contain some substances such as phthalates (plasticizers) and bisphenol A (BPA) (common with polycarbonates) that are leached into liquid contents, which are implicated in some disease conditions.

Metals - Metallic materials used for packaging cosmetic products contain varying proportions of aluminium, tin and, rarely, lead (5). Metallic materials are made into collapsible tubes for pastes, gels, and creams as well as cans for aerosols.

They are also combined with plastics to offer more elegant packaging options, for example, metals and plastics are used in the production of lipstick cases and sachet packages (14).

Advantages: metallic packaging materials offer protection against permeation of gases and moisture, are resistant to low and high temperatures, unbreakable, have lightweight, are environmentally friendly due to their recyclable properties, and are available in different shapes, sizes, and designs (1,14).

Disadvantages: Metals are non-transparent, prone to corrosion, and can react with the product, this is usually prevented by coating the surfaces of the container with lacquer.
Paper – This is used in the manufacture of secondary and tertiary packages that consist of rigid and semi-rigid paperboards of different sizes such as cartons and boxes(1).

Advantages: the use of paper packaging is cost-effective, and packages can contain large quantities of products. Paper is obtained from sustainable sources (plants), and it is highly degradable and, therefore, eco-friendly.

Disadvantages: the packages can be easily damaged during handling and transportation and as such need to be handled carefully. Paper can be laminated with polyethylene for more durability. Paper packages are not quite appealing to high-end users. Paper is not recyclable.

Silicone: silicone, a flexible, rubber-like synthetic substance, is an inorganic polysiloxane whose monomers are made up of naturally occurring silicon dioxide (silica). It is used in packaging liquid cosmetic products such as brush head squeeze facial cleanser and mascara wand tube. It is also used to line container caps as a flexible, water-repellent seal that prevents product from spilling as well as the ingress of air.

***Advantages*:** silicone is highly durable, lasts longer and withstands high and low temperatures better than plastic as a packaging material. It is recyclable and does not give off toxic fumes when incinerated unlike plastics but returns into its composite ingredients of silica, water vapour and carbon dioxide. It is ocean-friendly as it does not turn into microparticles unlike plastics. In addition, it does not contain lead, phthalates nor bisphenol A (BPA) and does not leach into products.

***Disadvantages**:* It is non-biodegradable.

Composite materials: The inability of a single material, in many instances, to meet all the requirements of packages for cosmetics has brought about the use of composite materials in laminar form as packaging materials, for example, the production of sachets and collapsible tube laminates as alternatives to pure metal tubes for pastes, gels and creams; combines the appearance of plastics with the impermeability and collapsibility properties of aluminium (1). Paper is also laminated with polyethylene and other plastic materials to allow for packaging of cosmetic products and for labels.

Closures

A closure is an important component of a package that protects the product against external contaminants, prevents spillage of content, allows for easy dispensing of products in some designs, and prevents fragrances and other volatile constituents from escaping from the container (15). The choice of closure depends on its compatibility and functionality with the product and other components of the package and the intended method of application of the cosmetic product (16).

Types of closure used in the packaging of cosmetics include screw caps that are mainly produced from plastic with spiral threads that fit the threading on the neck of containers;

they are suitable for glass or plastic jars or bottles and metal tubes. The flat metal lug caps fit a glass container and open by a slight turn in an anticlockwise direction; brush caps have brushes attached to the caps for the application of products as seen in mascara tubes. Other closure types made from plastic materials are pumps and sprayers for rigid bottles; flip top spout caps, push and pull caps, snap top caps, and disc top caps for squeezable plastic bottles and tubes to effectively dispense their liquid or semi-solid content (17).

Desiccants

Desiccants, which can adsorb and hold moisture that is present in their vicinity, are placed either in the primary package or fixed onto the inner part of the closure of the container of a solid product, e.g., a tablet, gel or powder, that is affected by the presence of moisture. Silica gel, made of silicon dioxide, prepared in the form of tiny beads and packaged in small packets, is the most commonly used desiccant in packaging. The silica gel can be presented in the form of a moisture-indicating packet that changes colour when it has adsorbedssss a significant amount of moisture. Other less commonly used desiccants for packaged products include molecular sieve, calcium chloride, activated alumina and activated charcoal.

Types of cosmetic packages

Jars – Jars are made from glass or plastic material and are fitted with airtight screw caps, They are used for products that do not pour freely but are to be dispensed in small quantities (18). Jars have a flat plastic shield that fits into them to prevent contamination. The various types of jars readily available include straight-sided glass jars with plastic lids that come in clear, amber, and blue colours. These are mostly used for bath, body, and beauty products such as face powders, creams, bronzers, and glitters (5). Round jars with double-walled closures are commonly used for face powders and lip balms (5). Thick-walled glass jars with caps are used for lip balms, eye shadows, creams, powders, creams, and foundations (5,14). Pots made from glass or plastic with screw caps provide trendy and sophisticated packaging for lip balms, hand creams, aromatherapy oils, and hair products (19).

Bottles – These are made from glass, plastic, or acrylic materials fitted with capped tops or pump dispensers and are available in different colours, shapes, and sizes. They are used for products that are free-flowing such as liquid soaps, shampoos, conditioners, lotions, perfumes, loose powders, facial cleansers, and toner nail polish remover (15,18). The ingredients and type of the cosmetic product generally determine the type, shape, and size of containers used. For example, skin lotions, shower gel, liquid soaps, shampoos, and conditioners come in tall plastic bottles with a narrow opening at the top or cylindrical plastic bottles with pump dispensers. Perfumes are packaged in glass, airless bottles of different sizes, nail polishes are stored in small bottles made of glass, while nail polish remover comes in larger plastic bottles (15).

Sticks and pens – Cosmetic sticks and pens fitted with caps are oval, round, rectangular, or cylindrical containers made from plastic or metal, designed to be pushed up or twisted to reveal their content or sometimes accompanied by an applicator.

Sticks and pens are attractive and offer ease of application of products (5). They are mostly suitable for lipsticks, lip glosses, highlighters, eyeliners, and concealers (5,19).

Vials – These are containers with brushes for application attached to the cap and inserted into the tubes. Vials are made from glass, plastic, or acrylic material into cylindrical, convex, round, or square shapes. They are used for lip glosses, mascaras, and nail polishes (5).

Tubes – Tubes are produced from metallic, plastic, or acrylic materials of different compositions and are designed into rigid or squeezable tubes fitted with canula, snap-on lids, or screw caps with or without an applicator. The squeeze tube offers a soft body design that is squeezed to get the product out while the rigid tube has a hard body whose content is drawn using an applicator or by twisting the base (20).

They offer the opportunity to dispense a controlled amount of a product and prevent contamination due to the inability of the product to be sucked back into the container once dispensed (5).

The squeezed tubes are used for liquid concealers, lip gloss, hand and foot lotions, highlighters, creams, toothpastes, hair serums, and gels while the rigid tubes are used for eyeliner, mascara, and lipsticks (19,20).

Compact containers – These are made from plastic and acrylic materials into round, square, and rectangular attractive finishes to accommodate beauty and makeup products such as compact powders and eye shadow colour palettes (19).

Pressurised containers – Metallic materials and glass are used as pressurised packs, whereby the contents are filled under pressure and the containers, with a valve system, a dip-tube attached to a nozzle are sealed hermetically. Pressurised containers depend on the propellants, which are gases, to dispense their contents. The design of the nozzle determines whether the product will be dispensed as fine mists or a stream of liquids, quick-breaking or stable foam, suspensions (lotions), emulsions (lotions or creams) or a spray of fine powder. Having been sealed hermetically, products packaged in pressurised containers are free from microbial contamination and from effects of moisture and oxygen in the air.

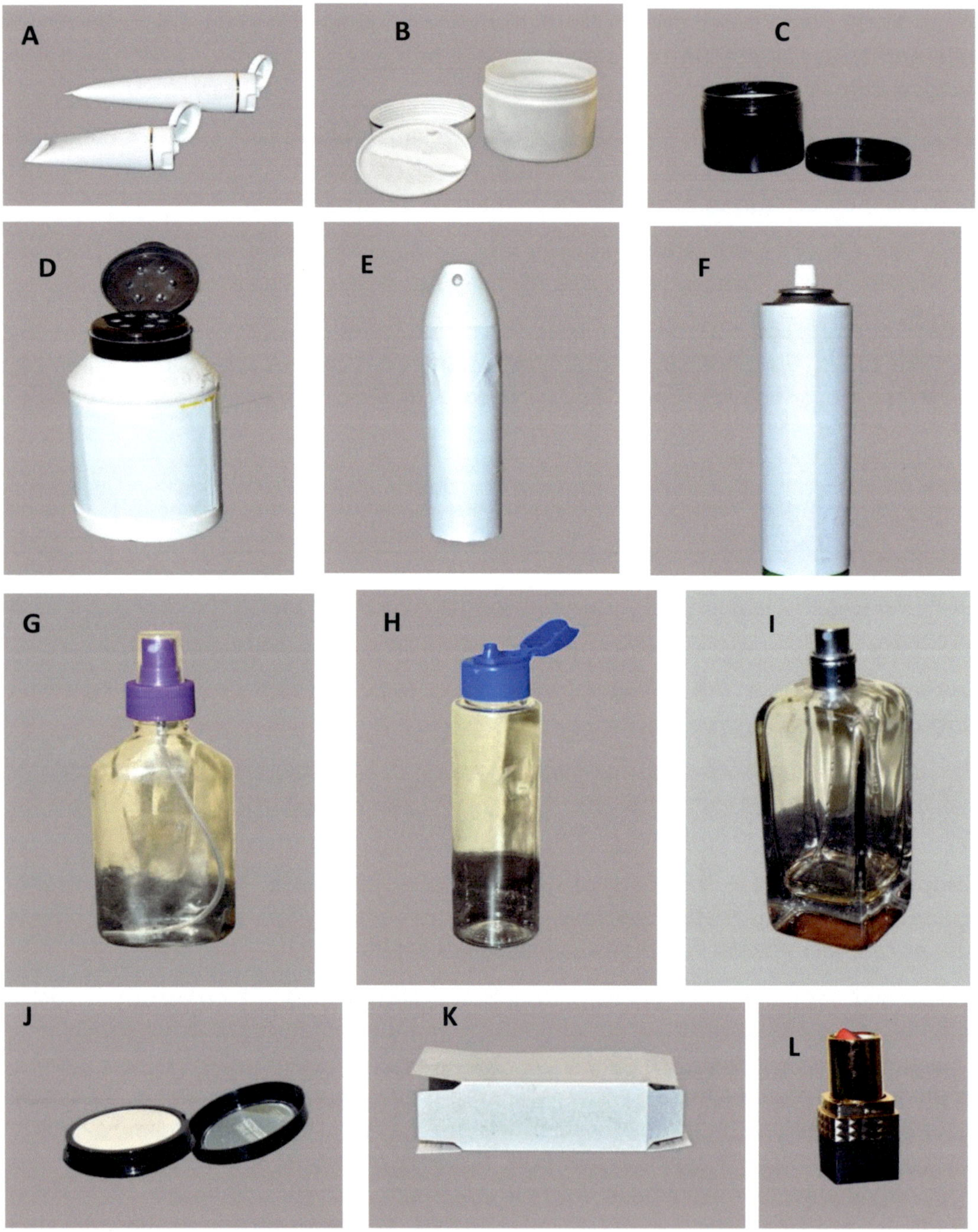
A
B
C
D
E
F
G
H
I
J
K
L

Figure 17.1: Types of packages used in cosmetics – namely: plastic squeezable tubes with snap on lids (A); white plastic jar with a screw cap and a flat shield fitted with a spoon (B); black plastic jar and a screw cap (C); plastic bottle with perforated lid (D); metal pressurised cans with spray pump (E & F); plastic bottle with sprayer (G) or snap top caps (H); glass bottle with sprayer (I); plastic compact container with lid (J); paper package (K); plastic cosmetic stick container (L)

Table 17.1: Comparison of materials used in packaging of cosmetic products

Material	**Advantages**	**Disadvantages**	**Application**
Glass	Impermeable to moisture, gas, and solvent; recyclable; clear container for elegant showcasing of product	Prone to breakage; heavyweight; expensive	Bottles for perfumes and creams; vials for nail polish
Metal	Unbreakable, thermal resistant, recyclable	Causes corrosion and undesirable reaction with product; non-transparent and conceals product	Tubes for creams, gels, pastes; cans for aerosol antideodorants, lip balms
Paper	Cheap, contains large quantities of cosmetic products	Prone to damage during handling and transportation	Boxes for soaps; cartons for cosmetic products
Plastic			
Low density polyethylene (LDPE)	Highly flexible, chemically inert, fair moisture barrier, translucent, resistant to acid, bases, and oils	High gas permeability, prone to stress cracking, less firm than HDPE, difficult to recycle	Tubes for skin and beauty products such as hand and body lotion, concealers, highlighters
High density polyethylene (HDPE)	Fair moisture and oxygen barrier, strong and durable, recyclable (21,22)	Prone to environmental stress	Bottles for hair and skincare products

		cracking, not as clear as PET	such as lotions; caps
Polyethylene terephthalate (PET or PETE)	resistant to breakage; good moisture, chemical and gaseous barrier, cheap, clear packaging, recyclable	Resources for manufacturing are limited	Bottles for hair and skin care products such as shampoos, facial washes, body lotions
Polypropylene (PP)	Resistant to chemicals and high temperature, moisture barrier, sturdier than PET, recyclable	Poor oxygen barrier, brittle at low temperature	Jars and tubes for skincare products; caps and shield
Polyvinyl chloride (PVC)	Cheap, lightweight, thermal resistance	Poor moisture and oxygen barrier, environmentally harmful due to high chlorine content; difficult to recycle	Bottles for skincare and beauty products
Poly(methyl methacrylate) (PMMA)	Lightweight, clear, unbreakable alternative to glass	Limited heat and chemical resistance	Lipstick cases, mascaras, compact containers, eyeliners (23)

Environment-friendly packaging materials

In recent times, there has been increased awareness on preservation of the environment in the cosmetic industry through the development of environment-friendly ingredients and manufacturing processes. This involves the use of recyclable materials for packages and their production in an eco-friendly manner (24). Some of the emerging environment-friendly packaging are highlighted below.

Bamboo packaging – Bamboo offers a biodegradable replacement for plastics. It is lightweight and comes in different varieties; bamboos have been made into containers for organic products such as creams, concealers, facial cleansers, and sunscreen lotion (5,24).

Beeswax packaging – beeswax is moulded into covers and packages of different colours and patterns for cosmetic products; it possesses antibacterial properties which provide additional protection to its content (24).

Seaweed packaging – Seaweed packaging can serve as an alternative to plastic for liquid based cosmetic products and face masks. In an early stage of development, however, seaweed is being made into transparent film packaging (24).

Other packaging options such as corn starch packaging and post-consumer recycled (PCR) packaging are being explored.

Although environment-friendly packaging options are beneficial, they might be difficult to implement in their totality especially considering the cost implication to consumers. Therefore, making the packaging as eco-friendly as possible, the use of minimum packaging where possible, and maximising the product-to-package ratio can be useful in the reduction of resources for packaging (22).

References

1. PACKAGING OF COSMETICS [Internet]. PharmaTutor. [cited 2022 Mar 29]. Available from: https://www.pharmatutor.org/articles/packaging-of-cosmetics
2. The Importance of Product Packaging in the Cosmetic Industry [Internet]. Printex Transparent Packaging. 2020 [cited 2022 Apr 4]. Available from: https://www.ptpackaging.com/blog/the-importance-of-product-packaging-in-the-cosmetic-industry/
3. How to Design Cosmetics Packaging: The Ultimate Guide [Internet]. 99designs. 2022 [cited 2022 Apr 4]. Available from: https://99designs.com/blog/packaging-label/cosmetics-packaging-design/
4. A Beginner's Guide to Cosmetic Labeling and Packaging | Luminer [Internet]. [cited 2022 Mar 29]. Available from: https://www.luminer.com/articles/a-beginners-guide-to-cosmetic-labeling-and-packaging/
5. Shivsharan U, S R, M S. PACKAGING OF COSMETICS: A REVIEW. J Pharm Sci Innov. 2014 Sep 9;3:286–93.
6. Nutrition C for FS and A. Summary of Cosmetics Labeling Requirements. FDA [Internet]. 2022 Mar 17 [cited 2022 May 25]; Available from: https://www.fda.gov/cosmetics/cosmetics-labeling-regulations/summary-cosmetics-labeling-requirements
7. Commissioner of the Legislation - Fair Packaging and Labeling Act [Internet]. Office of the Commissioner; [cited 2022 May 25]. Available from: http://wayback.archive-it.org/7993/20161022071126/http:/www.fda.gov/RegulatoryInformation/Legislation/ucm148722.htm
8. Koons ESK. Government Regulations of Cosmetic Packaging in the USA and the EU [Internet]. [cited 2022 Apr 4]. Available from: https://www.desjardin.fr/en/blog/government-regulations-of-cosmetic-packaging-in-the-usa-and-the-eu
9. Cosper A. What you should know when packaging cosmetics compliant to EU regulations [Internet]. [cited 2022 May 26]. Available from: https://www.desjardin.fr/en/blog/what-you-should-know-when-packaging-cosmetics-compliant-to-eu-regulations

10. Regulation (EC) No 1223/2009 of the European Parliament and of the Council of 30 November 2009 on cosmetic products (Text with EEA relevance) [Internet]. OJ L Nov 30, 2009. Available from: http://data.europa.eu/eli/reg/2009/1223/oj/eng
11. Branch LS. Consolidated federal laws of canada, Consumer Packaging and Labelling Act [Internet]. 2019 [cited 2022 May 25]. Available from: https://laws.justice.gc.ca/eng/acts/C-38/page-1.html#h-95984
12. Cosmetics Regulations in ASEAN countries [Internet]. Cosmetri software for cosmetics businesses. 2021 [cited 2022 May 25]. Available from: https://www.cosmetri.com/cosmetics-regulations-asean/
13. International Laws [Internet]. Safe Cosmetics. [cited 2022 May 26]. Available from: https://www.safecosmetics.org/get-the-facts/regulations/international-laws/
14. Cosper A. Cosmetic Packaging - Suitable Materials for Cosmetic Containers [Internet]. [cited 2022 Mar 29]. Available from: https://www.desjardin.fr/en/blog/cosmetic-packaging-suitable-materials-for-cosmetic-containers
15. What Are the Different Types of Cosmetics Containers? [Internet]. Beauty Answered. [cited 2022 May 26]. Available from: http://www.beautyanswered.com/what-are-the-different-types-of-cosmetics-containers.htm
16. Cosmetics Products Packaging & Container Closure | Arbro Pharma [Internet]. [cited 2022 Jun 2]. Available from: https://arbropharma.com/packaging-and-container-closure-for-your-cosmetics-products/
17. Resources - Closures and Liners.pdf [Internet]. [cited 2022 Jun 2]. Available from: https://www.pipelinepackaging.com/images/uploaded/Closure%20&%20Liner/Resources%20-%20Closures%20and%20Liners.pdf
18. Best Cosmetics Packaging and Types [Internet]. [cited 2022 May 26]. Available from: https://packagingoptionsdirect.com/best-cosmetics-packaging-and-types
19. Walker S. Essential Cosmetic Containers for Skincare & Beauty Packaging [Internet]. 2021 [cited 2022 May 31]. Available from: https://www.raepak.com/essential-cosmetic-containers-for-skincare-beauty-packaging/
20. What Are the Different Types of Cosmetics Bottles? [Internet]. Beauty Answered. [cited 2022 May 26]. Available from: http://www.beautyanswered.com/what-are-the-different-types-of-cosmetics-bottles.htm
21. Plastics Packaging for Pharmaceutical Products [Internet]. [cited 2022 Jun 20]. Available from: https://www.researchgate.net/publication/351379300_Plastics_Packaging_for_Pharmaceutical_Products
22. Successful Cosmetic Packaging For Beauty and Personal Care Brands [Internet]. [cited 2022 May 31]. Available from: https://www.newdirectionsaromatics.com/blog/products/successful-cosmetic-packaging-for-beauty-and-personal-care-brands.html
23. Packaging 360. Packaging of Cosmetic Products [Internet]. Packaging 360. 2018 [cited 2022 Jun 20]. Available from: https://packaging360.in/insights/packaging-of-cosmetic-products/
24. 7 Eco-Friendly Cosmetics Packaging Ideas [Internet]. PakFactory Blog. 2021 [cited 2022 May 26]. Available from: https://pakfactory.com/blog/7-eco-friendly-cosmetics-packaging-ideas/

CHAPTER EIGHTEEN

Physical and chemical stability of cosmetic products

Boladale O Silva, Michael A Odeniyi and Gbadegesin E Adetogun

The stability of a cosmetic product is its ability to maintain its aesthetics and functionality from the time of production to that of its use under conditions specified (1). Developing a stable cosmetic product requires an understanding of the formulation process and the ingredients employed. To ensure that a quality product is obtained, a number of stability tests must be conducted (2).

The measurements of the resistance of the product to common stressors such as extreme environmental condition, microbial growth, changes to physical properties and chemistry of the ingredients, especially the active ones, are standard approaches to predict the stability of cosmetics. Instability of a cosmetic product leads to a less attractive product, decreased usability and, in extreme cases, complete spoilage of the product. Therefore, quality control processes should be put in place starting from the choice of compatible ingredients and packaging as well as adopting appropriate manufacturing processes.

Furthermore, stability tests are carried out on the cosmetic preparation alone as well as the product in the proposed package to ascertain the compatibility between it and the packaging material. There is no standard stability testing for cosmetics because these products are of diverse forms with unique characteristics, therefore, the manufacturers of cosmetics can develop their stability testing procedures to effectively address and demonstrate the integrity of a particular product. However, there are guidelines that can serve as the starting point, for example, most elevated temperature testing are carried out at 45°C (113°F) and 37°C (98°F). If a cosmetic product is stable for 12 weeks at 45°C, it is deduced that it should be stable at room temperature (RT) or on the shelf for up to two years (2). Lower temperatures serve as controls and reveal the possibility of any occurrence of crystallization. Another stability setting is the freeze/thaw testing which involves alternating temperature testing between 37°C (98°F) and –10°C (14°F) in three cycles (2).

Stability concerns in cosmetic products

Powders

Stability issues in pressed and loose powder cosmetic products, such as foundations, blushes, shimmer powders, eyeshadows, and bronzers, are usually associated with compatibility of the ingredients contained in the products as well as the interaction between the ingredients and the packaging materials (3). The common forms of instabilities encountered in powder products include:

Caking: This is apparent in loose powders which become compacted when caked. Caking might occur over time because of settling and agglomeration of the solid particulate ingredients of the product. The finer the particles, the faster the settling and the quicker the onset of caking. The occurrence of caking from the time of production to the time of use can, therefore, be prevented by adjusting the particle size of the solid ingredients such that it is fine to avoid grittiness during application but not too fine so as to prevent rapid settling and clumping of solid particles (3). In addition, anti-caking agents, such as silica and calcium silicate, can be added during the manufacturing process. Agglomeration of particles can occur due to an increase in temperature generated by equipment used in production (4); thus, temperature control is crucial during manufacture. Excessive moisture in the loose powder may result into caking of the solid particles.

Glazing: Glazing refers to the shiny appearance that is observed following the use of applicators in pressed powder products. It is due to a high binder concentration that leads to the migration of the binder components of the formulation unto the surface (3). Therefore, the use of the appropriate quantity of the binder is important to prevent glazing while effecting the desired compressibility of ingredients in the preparation of the product. The use of dry binders such as zinc stearate, and an anti-caking agent such as silica, has been found to be effective in attaining the balance required in this type of cosmetic product (3). Glazing can also occur when there is a change in the size of the packaging material, specifically, when the powder is filled and compressed unto a smaller pan than normally used (5). In other words, a stable product is affected by the size of the container; hence, a change in the container for a formulation might necessitate an adjustment to the formula and further pre-formulation studies may be carried out to obtain a non-glazing product.

Colour variation: Inconsistency in the colour of a final powder product can occur due to uneven dispersion of pigments during the manufacturing process (3). This challenge can be averted by employing the geometric mixing method. This entails the initial mixing of ingredients with small quantities followed by gradual addition of larger quantity ingredients to effect even mixing (3). Similarly, the use of pre-pulverized pigment extenders (made up of a high concentration of pigments in the filler component of the product) during production can help achieve a consistent shade of colour in powder cosmetic products. An example of a pigment extender is Red 7 Lake in talc extender.

Lipsticks

Lipsticks are subjected, after manufacture, to quality tests that determine their ability to withstand breaking during use. These include the heat test and the rupture or breaking load point test which are described in Chapter 15 of this book. Other stability concerns for lipsticks include:

Sticky product: A sticky lipstick product is due to rancidity of the oil components of the formulation. Antioxidants such as gallic acid are added to lipstick formulations to prevent rancidity (6).

Crystal and wrinkle formation: The presence of crystals or wrinkles on the surface of a lipstick is a defect that occurs due to improper temperature control during the manufacturing process, especially during the cooling phase (2) when natural butters such as shea butter and mango butter are present in the formulation. Shea butter exists in three main polymorphic forms which solidify at different temperatures when the butter is heated to more than 36°C while being melted. Melting at 30 - 36°C, forms the stable beta (β) crystals which solidify quickly on cooling, but when overheated, it forms the unstable gamma (γ) crystals with a melting point of 15°C or the alpha (α) crystals with a melting point of 20°C, both of which solidify slowly over an appreciably long period of time and eventually appear as crystals on the surface of the lipsticks in which the shea butter is used. Adequate temperature control is, therefore, required during the manufacturing process. Hydrogenated shea butter that does not exhibit polymorphism is a preferred substitute for the natural shea butter. Crystallization of waxes and some other ingredients can also occur. These Ingredients, such as preservatives, can be dissolved in a solubilizer before being incorporated into the preparation, while the molten mixture is cooled gradually with stirring to avoid crystallization of the waxes.

Blooming, surface 'sweating' or syneresis: These forms of instability occur as a result of fluctuation in storage temperature that causes the emollients present in the lipsticks to move out from the inner part to the surface of the lipstick in the form of small liquid beads (7). This is caused by the disruption in the wax-oil complex that is responsible for the formation of a stable product (8). The loss of binding forces between the wax and oil ingredients is due to several factors. These factors are:

- addition of natural butters such as shea and cocoa butters

- use of elevated temperatures or fluctuations in temperature during melting, mixing, and moulding
- excessive flaming and spraying of lipsticks using silicone for improved surface appearance (9)
- the type of pigments, pearls, lanolin, and colour concentrates utilized in the formulation
- incorporation of a high quantity of glycerine in the formulation (7)

Figure 1: Blooming in lipstick

Blooming in lipsticks can be prevented or rectified by adopting one or more of the following methods:

- Introduction of branched-chain type of waxes such as C18-C32 triglycerides to the formulation; this prevents the disruption of the wax-oil matrix
- The use of hydrogenated butter such as hydrogenated shea butter helps to stabilize the wax-oil complex
- control of temperature as well as flaming and silicone spraying during production
- utilization of titanium-coated mica pearls, pigments that are highly soluble in the oil component, and lanolin derivatives such as lanolin wax prevents the deposition of oil droplets on the surface of lipsticks (10)
- inclusion of emulsifiers as gelling agents (8,11)

Nail polish/vanish

Change in viscosity: An increase or reduction in viscosity can be attributed to the type and blend of solvents used in the formulation of a nail polish or vanish. Solvents with low boiling points are usually less viscous and vice versa. The selection of appropriate blends of solvents will maintain the viscosity of a nail polish. In addition, the incorporation of a co-solvent such as ethyl alcohol helps to maintain the viscosity of nail polish (12). A change in viscosity may lead to alteration of the rheological profile of the product especially when being applied on the nails. Thus, it may give a rough outcome on the nails, if highly viscous due to low temperatures, or run off the nails, when it becomes very fluid due to higher temperatures. The solvents in nail polishes evaporate when the containers are not properly closed or left uncovered, resulting in highly viscous products that, with time, may turn into a semisolid. Hence, nail polishes are to be properly stored as recommended by the manufacturer.

Sedimentation: The settling of ingredients such as pearlescent pigments that make up nail lacquer can occur over time. The rate of sedimentation is dependent on the densities difference between the dispersion vehicle or medium and the dispersed particles, the particle size of the dispersed ingredients, as well as the viscosity of the dispersion medium as described by Stokes' law (13). Sedimentation can be prevented by increasing the vehicle's viscosity, reducing the dispersed particles size and the incorporation of suspending agents. Examples of suspending agents used in the preparation of nail polishes are Bentone-27 and Bentone-34 (14).

Creams and lotions

Change in colour: Colour change in creams and lotions might occur because of the instability of some of the ingredients in the formulation to light. This form of instability might not necessarily mean deterioration of the product, e.g., fading of colourants. However, a type of colour change that is an indicator of instability is the decay of some ingredients such as vitamin C which gives a yellowish colour, or the inactivation of preservatives which can result in the growth of colour-producing microorganisms in the products (15). The colour change can be prevented using adequate and appropriate antioxidants and preservatives, and by protecting the product from light through the appropriate choice of packaging materials, e.g., the use of coloured or opaque containers and non-communal jars that prevents unintended introduction of microorganisms during use. Also, specific storage instructions should be included on the package for consumers to protect the products from light.

Changes in pH: pH changes in creams and lotions are caused by the instability of some ingredients in the formulation such as the hydrolytic breakdown of some esters. Some plant colourants, such as the anthocyanins, used in cosmetic formulations are sensitive to pH resulting in a change in colour (15).

Presence of bubbles and water droplets: The appearance of bubbles in creams and lotions is usually due to the breakdown of some ingredients, especially by microorganisms, resulting in the evolution of gas which is mostly oxygen or carbon dioxide. Microbial contamination of products is one of the major causes of product deterioration and the use of appropriate type and quantity of preservatives can prevent this type of instability (15). In addition, the use of a suitable package that prevents the ingress of contaminants, such as dirt and especially microorganisms, during use of cosmetic products can prevent microbial contamination. Creams packaged in communal jars are highly susceptible to microbial contamination.

Shrinkage: Creams tend to shrink with a harder texture and a darker colour especially on the surface, when exposed to the atmosphere for a long period due to the evaporation of the water molecules in the aqueous phase. This phenomenon occurs mainly with creams stored in communal jars that are not properly closed and on the exposed tips of creams stored in tubes whose caps are not properly replaced after use.

Creaming: This is the upward movement of the dispersed droplets of an oil-in-water emulsion or the downward movement in the case of a water-in-oil emulsion formulation of creams and lotions. This phenomenon can be reversed by agitation. However, the proximity of the droplets to one another can lead to the breaking of the emulsifier films around the droplets, if not sufficiently tenacious, causing the droplets to coalesce and resulting, ultimately, in complete separation of the product into the two distinct oil and aqueous phases.

The factors that determine the product's creaming rate is explained by Stokes' law (16) which is represented by the following equation:

$$v = \frac{2r^2(d_1 - d_2)g}{9\,\eta}$$

Where v = creaming rate; r = droplets' radius; d_1 = dispersed phase density; d_2 = dispersion medium density; g = acceleration due to gravity; η = dispersion medium's viscosity.

In other words, a decrease in the dispersed droplet size, a decrease in the densities difference between the dispersion vehicle and the dispersed phase, and a dispersion medium with a relatively high viscosity, will cause a decrease in the rate of creaming, resulting in a prolonged stability of the product. Creaming is a reversible phenomenon, and shaking redisperses the droplets.

Cracking, coalescence and demulsification: Coalescence is a major problem in emulsion formulation. It is an irreversible process where larger droplets are formed by the merging together of the dispersed droplets (emulsion cracking) and ultimately leads to the separation of the water and oil phases, a condition that is known as demulsification or the breaking of the formulation. Coalescence and eventual demulsification of an emulsion formulation is caused by creaming, microorganisms, changes in temperature, presence of a common solvent for the oil, emulsifying agent and water which gives a clear solution, incompatibility of surfactants used as emulsifying agents, insufficient emulsifier concentration, insufficient amount of viscosity improvers, and the decomposition of the emulsifying agents employed (2,17).

The use of an appropriate blend of emulsifying agents to maintain the interfacial film between the oil and water phases, viscosity improvers that prevent droplets from coming close to each other and from creaming, storage at the recommended temperatures, and the inclusion of preservatives that prevents microbial growth, will prevent the breaking of the emulsions prepared as creams and lotions. Cracking, coalescence and demulsification are irreversible processes and require a reformulation of the emulsion.

Figure 2: Creaming of an emulsion formulation – the upper cream layer of concentrated dispersed phase droplets with the lower aqueous layer devoid of dispersed phase droplets, shaking redisperses the droplets.

Ostwald ripening: This is a molecular diffusion phenomenon that takes place due to the solubility difference of the small and large droplets contained in the emulsion formulation (18). It involves the dissolution of the small droplets in an emulsion into the continuous phase, due to an increase in solubility of the dispersed phase molecules in the phase, and their subsequent redeposition on and diffusion into the larger droplets of the dispersed phase. This, eventually, as the droplets grow bigger, can lead to the emulsion separating into the water and oil phases. Ostwald ripening can be inhibited by the addition of a third component that has a lower solubility and vapour pressure than the dispersed phase, such as long-chain alkanes; the use of polymeric emulsifiers that increase the viscosity of the dispersion medium, and the use of appropriate surfactants to produce an almost mono-sized dispersion. Ostwald ripening is irreversible.

Phase inversion: This refers to a change from one type of an emulsion to another type, for example, a change from an emulsion formulation of the water-in-oil type to that of oil-in-water type and vice versa. Phase inversion can be caused by the addition of an electrolyte to an emulsion prepared with anionic or cationic surfactants which may suppress their ionisation due to a common ion effect, thereby resulting in the formation of a water-in-oil emulsion instead of an oil-in-water emulsion expected of the surfactants. The addition of divalent and trivalent salts to emulsions prepared with monovalent soaps, e.g., sodium oleate, will result in the inversion of the oil-in-water emulsion to a di- or tri-valent metal soap-based water-in-oil emulsion. Extreme changes in temperature and the phase volume ratio, especially when the internal phase concentration is higher than 70% in some instances, can lead to phase inversion of an emulsion (16). Phase inversion, if carefully carried out, can be used to prepare emulsions of finer droplet sizes. It is, however, an irreversible phenomenon.

Flocculation: The coming together of droplets of the dispersed phase of an emulsion to form larger aggregates within the bulk of the emulsion, without the rupture of the emulsifier films is referred to as flocculation. The flocks are held together by weak Van der Waal's forces and, as such, they are easily redispersed by shaking. Nonetheless, flocculation may lead to creaming and eventually to coalescence.

Assessment of emulsion stability

The stability of emulsions is studied on emulsion samples stored for a period of time on the shelf or samples that have been subjected to accelerated storage conditions. The process enables the monitoring of the possible increase in the droplet sizes, changes in viscosity, as well as the extent of creaming and cracking of the emulsion which indicate instability. The tests are conducted at least 24 hours after the emulsions are prepared to allow the droplets to stabilise, and subsequently after predetermined time intervals. The values obtained for each of the tests can be plotted against time to give a good representation of the results.

Creaming/phase separation: A properly formulated emulsion should not show any traces of creaming which is reversed by shaking; nor phase separation (cracking or demulsification) which is irreversible. Samples of the emulsion under test are stored in graduated and transparent cylinders and observed for any separated layer, the height of which is recorded over a period of storage. The percentage creaming or the degree of creaming is calculated and plotted against storage time.

$$\% \text{ Creaming} = V_a/V_b \times 100$$

Where: V_a = volume/height of separated aqueous layer, V_b = volume/height of the total emulsion sample

Droplet size analysis: The following methods are used for droplet size analysis:

Microscopy method: An eye piece graticule is calibrated with a stage micrometer. The emulsion sample is diluted using fluids such as 50% v/v aqueous propylene glycol to prevent agglomeration of the droplets. A drop of the diluted emulsion, placed on a microscope slide and covered with a cover slip, is observed and the droplets from different fields of view are observed, measured and counted and fitted into an already determined size ranges that give a size distribution of the sample. A minimum of a total of 1500 droplets from more than three fields of view are counted (19,20,21). A camera lucida, attached to the microscope, enables the images of the droplets to be seen on a calibrated sheet of paper on which the droplets can be drawn and later analysed for particle size. The results obtained are used to calculate the geometric mean diameter (M) and the geometric standard deviation (δg) of the sample using the following equations derived by Smith and Jordan (22):

$$\log M = \frac{\Sigma_i n_i \log x_i}{\Sigma_i n_i}$$

$$log\ \delta g = \sqrt{\frac{\Sigma_i n_i (log\ x_i - log\ M)^2}{\Sigma_i n_i}}$$

n_i
$= number\ of\ droplets\ whose\ diameter\ lies\ in\ an\ interval\ of\ which\ the\ midpoint\ is\ x_i$

Coulter counter method: The Coulter principle allows the dispersed droplets move through an aperture, under the influence of an electric field of known characteristics. The passage of the droplet causes a momentary change in impedance and gives rise to voltage pulses, the heights of which are proportional to volume (consequently, to volume diameter) of the droplet traversing the passage between two electrodes. These pulses are expressed as a size distribution and are sized, amplified and counted, (23).

Laser diffraction method: In this method, there is a transmission of a beam of monochromatic laser light through a dilute emulsion. A series of light-sensitive detectors is used to measure the diffraction pattern resulting from the transmission. The droplets in the emulsion that are being analysed scatter the laser beam which results in the formation of the diffraction pattern. The resultant diffraction pattern indicates precisely the characteristics of the droplets (i.e. complex refractive index, size and concentration). The determination of the concentration and size distribution of the droplets is done by finding the values that give the best agreement between the measured diffraction pattern and that predicted by light-scattering theory. In this theory, there is the assumption that each photon of light is scattered only by a single droplet. This means that there must be adequate dilution of the emulsion in order to avoid multiple scattering (24).

Rheological assessment: Changes in the rheological characteristics of an emulsion over a period are indications of droplet size changes and/or changes in the viscosity of the continuous phase. The rheograms of undisturbed samples of the emulsion are determined using a rotational viscometer (see Chapter 15 of this book) and their viscosities calculated and monitored over a predetermined period. The samples are, however, mixed prior to measurement by gently rolling the container between the palms as well as turning the containers up and down to get a homogenous dispersion, as the emulsions might have settled on storage. The Brookfield viscometer with the Helipath attachment is, however, particularly useful in investigating changes in viscosity as the spindle is lowered in the undisturbed emulsion while the spindle rotates (usually at low speed). Various resistances are met at different levels by the descending rotating spindle due to the separation of the emulsion and viscosity fluctuations are also registered. This makes the early detection of sedimentation or creaming possible before it becomes visible. Generally, a decrease in viscosity with time reflects a droplet size increase due to coalescence and it is an indication that the system is not stable. Also, a decrease in the viscosity of the emulsion may indicate a reduction in the viscosity of the viscosity-imparting agents employed, which may be due to a breakdown (hydrolysis) of the chain lengths of the polymeric agents into shorter chains that gives a lesser resistance to flow. A stable emulsion should retain its initial rheological profile, as much as possible, from the time of production to use (25,26).

Accelerated stability studies for emulsions

In the design and development of a new emulsion-based product, series of emulsion formulations are often prepared from which the most stable is selected for the product. Accelerated stability tests that employ exaggerated stress conditions, are carried out on the preparations to enable a quicker means of selecting the best in a series of test preparations and to indicate the shelf stability of a product formulation.

Temperature: Elevated temperatures can be used as an exaggerated stress to accelerate creaming or cracking of an emulsion. Notwithstanding, the effect of temperature changes on emulsions needs a careful approach as an emulsion is likely to break down completely when subjected to high temperatures. Creaming, droplet size, coalescence, and viscosity are parameters that are assessed after subjecting the test samples to the stress conditions (27).

Centrifugation: Centrifugation introduces a mechanical stress into an emulsion system. Samples of each formulation are subjected to cycles of a predetermined speed, in revolution per minute (rpm), for a duration that may depend on the stability of the test emulsion. Parameters to evaluate after this procedure are creaming, droplet coalescence and turbidimetric measurements, by which the centrifuged samples are observed in a colorimeter or a nephelometer to determine the extent of phase separation in samples where this may not be visible to the eye or the separation is not clearly demarcated (28).

Phase inversion temperature: The temperature at which an emulsion interconvert between water-in-oil and oil-in-water emulsions, is known as the phase inversion temperature (PIT). It has been used as a tool to assess the stability of emulsion formulations and the emulsion with the highest PIT in a series, shows the highest stability (25,29).

Challenge test for preservatives: Preservative efficacy tests are used to determine if an emulsion is adequately protected against microbial spoilage. The procedure for this test is described in Chapter 19 of this book.

Suspensions

Suspensions are regarded as physically stable if the suspensoids or suspended particles do not settle, aggregate, nor undergo Ostwald ripening, but remain uniformly distributed throughout the dispersion for a relatively long period. Ostwald ripening is a condition where small crystals of the suspensoids dissolve in the vehicle and are deposited on larger crystals forming suspensoids of larger particle sizes. The ideal stability condition is rarely met except for suspensions that have been carefully formulated to be non-sedimenting (see Chapter 15 of this book). With flocculated suspensions, the floccules of the suspensoids settle rapidly but are easily re-suspended by shaking. However, suspensoids of unflocculated suspensions sediment and over time form a hard cake that is not re-dispersed with shaking. This is a type of instability as the quantity of the available dispersed phase particles is reduced with time and the product becomes substandard.

The stability of suspensions can be theoretically estimated before the formulation process based on the size of the particles in the solid phase as well as the viscosity and density of the liquid phase; using the Stoke's equation (13,16), thereby saving time and resources. The sedimentation rate of a suspension is controlled by:

- Increasing the vehicle viscosity;

- Decreasing the size of the particles of the suspensoids which can be achieved by either dry or wet milling, as appropriate;
- Developing a structured vehicle with the use of appropriate polymers, this prevents settling;
- The formulation of a suspension by flocculation of the suspensoids and the inclusion of a structured vehicle that exhibits plasticity to such a formulation. This provides a non-sedimenting product that is very stable.

Chapter 15 of this book provides information on the formulation of suspensions.

Assessment of suspension stability

Rate of sedimentation: To determine the rate of sedimentation, the suspension is left undisturbed in a graduated and transparent cylinder, and at predetermined time intervals; the ratio of the sediment height (ultimate height, H_U) in the container to the total initial suspension height (H_O), H_U/H_O, as the suspension settles in a cylinder under standard conditions, is noted. The larger this fraction or the closer the value is to 1, the better is the suspendability, and this becomes evident as the plot is more horizontal or remains flattened throughout. Values closer to zero is an indication of a suspension in which the suspensoids will settle rapidly.

A plot of H_U/H_O as ordinates against time on the abscissa gives a curve starting at 1 on the ordinate. It can either be gradually sloping downward to the right with time or horizontal. The steeper the plot, the larger the negative slope value obtained from the plot that indicates a poor suspension in which the suspensoids settle rapidly. Comparison can be made between different formulations and the best chosen by observing the lines, the better formulations obviously producing lines that are more horizontal and/or less steep.

Ease of re-dispersion: This is employed to qualitatively assessed suspension stability by shaking of the product in a container. The use of a mechanical shaker eliminates variation in the shaking ability (30,31,32). The ease of re-dispersion is often linked to the sedimentation volume measurement.

Particle Size Changes: Samples withdrawn at predetermined time intervals from undisturbed suspension are diluted by a convenient factor for ease of counting with the aid of an ocular grid, and are also subjected to particle-sizing using microscopic or photographic techniques, in which photomicrographs may be taken for permanent records. It is, however, important to note that dilution may affect the aggregation behaviour of the samples. This method involves evaluation of a large number of samples which makes it quite tedious. A plot of the particle size distribution and mean particle size changes against time would reveal particle/crystal growth (Ostwald ripening), leading to large-sized particles. This phenomenon would affect suspension stability (31,33,34).

Flocculation value (Degree of flocculation, β): In this test, comparison is made between the sedimentation volume of a flocculated suspension, F_1, and the sedimentation volume of the suspension when it is deflocculated, F_∞.

Shown as: $\beta = F_1 / F_\infty$

The degree of flocculation is an expression of the increased sediment volume resulting from flocculation. The value of β is an indication that the volume of the sediment in the flocculated system is larger than that in the deflocculated system by that number of folds. This shows that the flocs are quite porous and the desirable scaffold-like structure is present (36).

Measurement of zeta potential: A direct current electric field is applied across a suspension; particles of the suspension move towards the electrode of opposite charge to that on their surface. An electrophoresis apparatus is employed in the measurement of the migration velocity of the particles in the suspension. The migration of the particles towards an electrode of opposite charge is in respect to the surface electric charge or the zeta potential measured in volts. Certain zeta potentials produced more stable suspensions in suspension systems where aggregation was controlled and optimized (30,36,37,38).

Rheological techniques: A Brookfield viscometer is commonly employed for the rheological evaluation of suspension stability. The viscometer consists of a T-bar spindle which rotates around its axis. The T-bar spindle is lowered into an undisturbed suspension sample and, at low shear rates, the dial reading on the viscometer, which is a measure of the resistance to the rotation of the spindle, is recorded for that point in the suspension. The spindle is further made to descend slowly into the suspension, and the dial readings on the viscometer are noted at the predetermined levels in the suspension. The values indicate the levels of the suspension at which the structures are greater, owing to particle agglomeration, because as the T-bar descends, it rotates, and the bar is continually entering new and essentially undisturbed material. Data obtained on samples that have been variously aged and stored, indicate whether undesired changes are taking place. The overall result of the determination shows how the particles are settling with time, and changes in aggregation as well as settling behaviour can be followed. From a plot of the rate of spindle turns against depth, a good suspension would show a lesser rate of increase of dial reading with spindle turns, where, the curve is horizontal for a longer period (30,31).

Accelerated tests for suspension stability

Accelerated methods employed to evaluate the physical stability of suspensions are aimed at simulating conditions that naturally would lead to the degradation phenomenon observable in a suspension.

Centrifugation: This test involves subjecting a suspension to a force that is several folds the force of gravity (g), which causes an increase in the sedimentation rate. The ratio of the final sediment volume (or height) to the original volume (or height) of the suspension, also affects the ease of redispersion of the suspension as well as alter the rheological properties and size distribution of the dispersed particles. Centrifugation at a force several hundred times that of gravity (g), however, has the disadvantage of breaking down the structure of flocculated suspensions and producing a closely packed sediment regardless of the stability of the product; an effect that would not occur under normal gravity even on prolonged storage. Low speed centrifugation producing an effect equivalent to about four times that of gravity may be of value in some cases and can be a useful stress when comparing the stability of some suspensions (39,40).

Temperature cycling: This method is employed to mimic the changes in the environmental temperature in which the suspension is likely to be kept. Hence, the suspension product is subjected to extreme temperature fluctuations and at an increased frequency which may accelerate crystal growth. The product is stored at about 40 – 50 °C for about 48 hours and then at a lower temperature, e.g., 4 °C, for another 24 hours which represent a cycle. This cycle could be repeated for up to 8 times. Alternatively, suspensions are stored at elevated temperatures (40 – 60 °C) for 4 – 8 months, and the samples are examined at regular intervals for sedimentation, flocculation value, ease of redispersion and particle size, among other indices that may be employed to assess stability (39,41,42).

Ointments

The use of excessive shear on a congealed ointment base or product can lead to loss of the physical structure of the ointment composition as well as a reduction in the viscosity of the product. The loss of structure manifests as oil "bleed" or syneresis by which tiny droplets of oil are seen on the surface of the product which may eventually result in a layer of oil, due to the separation of the lighter oil fractions of the base from the bulk formulation on storage. The nature and physicochemical properties of the active ingredients and excipients of an ointment preparation also influence the stability of the product. Microbial growth may not be excluded in ointments packaged in communal jars as the presence of moisture can encourage the growth of microorganisms, especially moulds, introduced during use. Ointments are to be stored in a cool place as exposure to heat causes the product to melt, leading to the segregation and subsequent precipitation of incorporated solid ingredients which, unless the product is stirred until cool, are not redispersed when the ointment re-solidifies at a lower storage temperature. Thus, the upper layer of the ointment will contain little or no active ingredients, while the lower part will be highly concentrated.

Gels

The degradation of a gel may manifest as changes in its physical or chemical properties which may be due to environmental factors such as heat and light; as well as chemicals or applied forces. The degradation manifests as changes in viscosity, tensile strength, colour and molecular weight of the gel. Changes in the physical stability of a gel are manifested mainly by changes in the viscosity and colour of the gel product. The breakdown of the polymeric structures of gelling agents into shorter chain lengths leads to the reduction in their viscosity. The degradation may be due to acid hydrolysis, e.g., chitosan, gums; enzymatic breakdown of glycosidic bonds of polysaccharides by glycoside hydrolase, lysozyme-mediated degradation of chitosan and chitin into oligomers and later into monomers, microbial degradation of polysaccharides, and degradation of the alginates by lyases. Metal ions that may be present in the water employed in the preparation of gels can affect the swellability, the quality of the gel formed as well as the staying properties of the gel. A study determined the effects of municipal potable water from different sources and solutions of chloride salts of sodium, potassium, calcium and magnesium ($NaCl$, KCl, $CaCl_2$, $MgCl_2$ ($NaCl$, KCl, $CaCl_2$, $MgCl_2$), on the physicochemical characteristics of sodium and potassium polyacrylate hydrogels. A progressive degradation of the gels was observed that affected their swelling capacity and their shelf life. Sodium polyacrylate was less susceptible to the effects of sodium, potassium and magnesium salts on swelling capacity than potassium polyacrylate while calcium chloride caused a significant reduction in the swellability of the two gels. The effects of the water obtained from different sources were ascribed to the presence of the metallic ions they contained. Breaks in the cross-linking of the gel polymers as well as ion exchange between the polymeric and aqueous phases were responsible for the reduction in the chain lengths and, consequently, the viscosity of the hydrogels. Distilled water and water obtained by osmosis did not affect the swelling capacity and staying power of the gels (43). This study, therefore, emphasises the use of treated water for the preparation of gels and cosmetics, generally.

Colour change may indicate chemical degradation of the included ingredients in a gel, such as the oxidation of pigments and dyes which results in fading or the colour change arising from oxidation of some ingredients such as ascorbic acid.

Solutions

Storage at elevated temperatures and temperature cycling provide accelerated stability testing processes for the determination of the stability of solutions. The products are examined for the precipitation of solutes, crystal formation, colour change, cloudiness and changes in pH. Microbial stability of the product is also determined as solutions can provide media for microbial growth.

Chemical stability of ingredients of cosmetic products

Ingredients of cosmetic products are chemical compounds that are susceptible to chemical reactions which can lead to their degradation when exposed to unfavourable conditions. Such reactions include oxidation, hydrolysis and complexation.

Oxidation

Oxidation reaction involves the reaction of a compound with oxygen or the removal of electrons from a molecule or a compound. Fading of dyes and pigments incorporated in a product is an example of an oxidation reaction. Ingredients such as ascorbic acid (vitamin C) and retinol (vitamin A) undergo oxidation producing orange-brown and yellow compounds, respectively, which invariably are less effective or may have lost their activity completely.

Oxidation of fats and oils: The term, rancidification, defines the oxidation and hydrolysis of oils, fats and essential oils, in the presence of air, water, light, and microorganisms, leading to the release of unpleasant odours and flavours. The breakdown of lipids or triglycerides into volatile free fatty acids and glycerol in the presence of water is called hydrolytic rancidity. Oxidative rancidity involves the degradation of fats and oils caused by the cleavage of the double bonds present in the triglycerides by oxygen (of the air), through a free radical reaction that produces volatile ketones, aldehydes and alcohols which give the malodour to such lipids. Sunlight and the presence of transition metals such as copper, zinc and iron catalyse oxidative rancidity. Microbial rancidity is the degradation of lipids in the presence of water by microbial enzymes such as the lipases. Fats and oils are, therefore, best protected from degradation by being stored in fully filled containers that are protected from light, adequately preserved, with minimal contact with water and stored in a cool place. Antioxidants employed at their effective concentrations will prevent the oxidation of well-formulated and packaged products containing oils and fats. The acid number and the peroxide value can be used to determine the state of oxidation of a lipid.

The active oxygen number (A.O.N.) is also used to determine the oxidation state of lipids and essential oils and to determine the type and concentration of antioxidant to be employed for a product. The method is an accelerated test that involves aeration of the test sample at elevated temperatures for a period, with samples taken at predetermined intervals and subjected to iodometric titration. The volume of sodium thiosulphate used up in the titration is equivalent to the amount of peroxide present in the oil samples and this signifies the level of oxidation of the oil. The titre values obtained are used to calculate the A.O.N. of the samples using the equation (44):

$$\text{A.O.N.} = \frac{(\text{Actual titration} - \text{blank}) \times \text{factor of thiosulphate} \times 2}{\text{Weight of the oil (g)}}$$

Thus, the A.O.N. is defined as the number of milligram equivalent of the primary oxidation product (peroxide) that liberates one mole of iodine from an acidic solution of potassium iodide.

The determination is based on the ability of peroxides, which are the first products of an autoxidation reaction, to liberate, in an acidic medium, iodine from potassium iodide. The liberated iodine is then titrated against sodium thiosulphate as illustrated in the equations (45):

$$ROOH + 2I^- + 2H^+ = I_2 + ROH + H_2O$$

$$I_2 + 2Na_2SO_2O_3 = Na_2S_4O_6 + 2NaI$$

Hydrolysis

Hydrolysis involves reaction of a compound with water resulting in cleavage of chemical bonds in its molecular structure. Molecules containing esters and amide functional groups are prone to hydrolysis, especially the ester derivatives, which may lead to the formation of carboxylic acid and the corresponding alcohol. The effectiveness of the compounds in cosmetics, therefore, depends on their hydrolytic stability.

Complex formation

Complex formation can occur between molecules of two excipients, for example, between phenolic preservatives, like the parabens, and macrogols in a cosmetic formulation which leads to a reduction in the efficacy of the preservatives. Complex formation could be beneficial if reversible. Macromolecules like cyclodextrins are non-toxic cyclic polysaccharides used in complex formation. They form inclusion complexes with a lot of organic molecules. The chemical and physical properties of the guest molecules are therefore changed as a result of complex formation. For instance, the stability of the complexed molecule against oxygen and light increases and the vapour pressure reduces. There is an increase in the solubility of slightly soluble molecules in a cyclodextrin complex. All these and further advantages of cyclodextrins and their complexes can be used to produce cosmetic products (1)

Crystallisation or precipitation: This occurs in solution formulations due to changes in temperature, pH, evaporation of solvents or microbial growth and results in supersaturation and increased concentration of the soluble solid ingredients in the vehicle and subsequent deposition of particles in form of crystals or precipitates for crystalline and amorphous substances, respectively. The adoption of suitable packages that prevent loss of solvents, the use of compatible non-volatile solvents and preservatives, control of storage temperature and the formulation of cosmetic solutions below their saturation concentrations can prevent crystallisation or precipitation instability (46).

Accelerated stability tests/ determination of shelf-life or Best Before dates for cosmetic products

The need for testing for stability of cosmetics is necessary for the following reasons: the development of a new product; reformulation of an existing product; modification of the method of production; acquisition of a new facility/vendor for production; and/or change of packaging. There is, however, a paucity of currently published studies to support specific testing methods for the prediction of the shelf life cosmetic products. This has been attributed to the complexity and wide variety of cosmetic formulation and packaging, the proprietary nature of most cosmetic products, the associated methods of testing for stability which include the scope of potential physical, chemical and microbial changes that are to be examined as well as the functional or aesthetic properties of the products (5).

The main aim of testing the stability of cosmetic products is to ensure the maintenance of the intended chemical, physical and microbiological quality standards of a modified or newly formulated product as well as the aesthetics and functionality when kept under specified conditions. The development cycle of cosmetic products is relatively short; hence, manufacturers design their own stability testing programme in such a way that is economically reasonable and which addresses the testing required efficiently. Factors that may be measured in determining the extent of product degradation include:

- The rate of natural degradation of key ingredients
- The ability of the product to resist microbial contamination
- The reactivity of the product to the materials of the package
- Impurities exacerbated by the manufacturing process

- The response of the product to humidity, light and heat,

Tests for stability can be carried out under accelerated conditions or in real time with the purpose of assessing the stability of a product under appropriate conditions of use, storage and transport. This is mainly for the determination of the shelf life of formulated products or the Period After Opening (PAO) which is the period when the product is stable and poses no risk to the health of the user. The determination of PAO also takes into consideration the type of product and its purported use or indication. For instance, a short PAO would be essential for cosmetics products manufactured for use on specific populations like children under 3 years, on specific populations (children under 3 years, people with compromised immune responses and the elderly people and those used on sensitive parts of the body (around the eyes, on damaged skin or on mucous membranes). The PAO is printed on the packaging with a symbol representing an opened cream jar and a number that is followed by the letter M, where the number indicates the months the product can be safely used after the container is opened. According to the EU Cosmetics Regulation EC 1223/2009, if the determined shelf life is lower than 30 months, an expiration date must be printed on the product packaging. However, if the shelf life is more than 30 months, expiration date may not be necessary on the packaging, but a PAO is mandatory (6).

Need for accelerated stability testing

Real-time stability testing is a challenge in the formulation of cosmetic products because time is a critical factor. Accelerated testing for stability, where samples of the cosmetic product are stored at different elevated humidity and temperature conditions, as determined by market demands and product type, is therefore a better alternative.

Accelerated testing for stability is carried out within a short time scale but at extremes of conditions of storage that hasten the manifestation of degradation products of instability that can be used to forecast the potential shelf life of a product.

Accelerated stability tests can include:

Elevated temperature stress testing: This involves exposing the finished product briefly to temperatures far higher than those encountered during storage. The aim is to generate data that will be used to predict the product's shelf life or to compare the relative stability of several formulations to choose the most suitable. Data obtained are fitted into the Arrhenius equation for shelf-life determination or 'best before' dates. The shelf life at the intended temperature for storage is obtained by extrapolation on the graph. The Arrhenius equation is:

$$\log\frac{k2}{k1} = \frac{Ea}{2.303R}\left(\frac{1}{T2} - \frac{1}{T1}\right)$$

Where k is the rate constant of degradation, Ea stands for the activation energy of degradation, T is the temperature and R is the universal gas constan in absolute value.

Freeze-thaw testing (cyclic temperature testing): This involves the storage of the product at alternating high and low temperatures to accelerate physical deterioration of the product (usually from less than 0° C to 40° C). The duration of each cycle is usually 24 hours to simulate the earth's diurnal temperature. Temperature fluctuations may show the precipitation of solutes in solutions, cracking of emulsions and creams and particle growth in suspensions (2).

Photostability testing: This involves the assessment of the effects of light on the cosmetic product. It gives information on the handling, packaging and labelling criteria for the product. The product in its proposed final package is exposed to fluorescent lamps within a cabinet. After a specified period of storage, the product is analysed for degradation products due to the exposure to light.

Centrifugation testing – This involves subjecting the cosmetic product to centrifugation. Here the product is heated to 50° C and centrifuge for 30 minutes (or more) at 3000 rpm. The dispersed phase (of an oil-in-water emulsion) tends to separate and rise to the top of the emulsion forming a layer of coalesced oil droplets. This phenomenon is called creaming. Creaming is one of the first signs of impending emulsion instability. This test is very critical for those products that contain powders of any kind, such as a liquid or cream makeup (3).

Extremes of humidity testing: This test is used for powdered products such as compact and loose powders. Based on the history of their exposure to moisture, different materials used in cosmetic formulations such as maize, potato and corn starches, vary in their capacity to retain water at the same relative humidity (RH). For instance, if a completely dried starch powder is exposed to an environment that is humid, it will absorb and adsorb moisture at the same temperature to the maximum equilibrium moisture content at 100% RH. However, when the powder, saturated with moisture, is exposed to an environment that is low in humidity, desorption occurs slowly because of the amylase chemical bonding that takes place during sorption, which prevents the rapid desorption of molecules of water.

Microbial stability testing: This is discussed in Chapter 19 of this book.

References

1. ISO/TR 18811:2018(en), Cosmetics — Guidelines on the stability testing of cosmetic products [Internet]. [cited 2022 Apr 7]. Available from: https://www.iso.org/obp/ui/#iso:std:iso:tr:18811:ed-1:v1:en
2. Uncovering Stability Issues: The Obvious and Not So Obvious [Internet]. Cosmetics & Toiletries. 2014 [cited 2022 Apr 4]. Available from: https://www.cosmeticsandtoiletries.com/formulas-products/skin-care/blog/21837745/uncovering-stability-issues-the-obvious-and-not-so-obvious
3. Approaches and Issues in Powder Formulations [Internet]. Cosmetics & Toiletries. 2014 [cited 2022 Apr 5]. Available from: https://www.cosmeticsandtoiletries.com/formulas-products/color-cosmetics/article/21836310/approaches-and-issues-in-powder-formulations
4. Buell D, Barclay K, Block P, Junker J, Victor B, Melenkevitz D, et al. The Manufacture of Cosmetics, ch 35. In: Harry's Cosmetology. 8th Edition. Revere, MA USA: Chemical Publishing Co.; 2000. p. 787–874.
5. Hollenberg J. Color Cosmetics, ch 26. In: Harry's Cosmeticology. 8th ed. Revere, MA USA: Chemical Publishing Co.; 2000. p. 560–88.
6. Evaluation of Lipsticks - Cosmetic Formulation [Internet]. pharmacy180.com. [cited 2022 Apr 7]. Available from: http://www.pharmacy180.com/article/evaluation-of-lipsticks-817/
7. Inc F. The causes of blooming in lipsticks and the solutions to avoid it [Internet]. Farachem. [cited 2022 Apr 5]. Available from: https://farachem.com/the-causes-of-blooming-in-lipsticks-and-the-solutions-to-avoid-it/
8. Seo SY, Lee IS, Shin HY, Choi KY, Kang SH, Ahn HJ. Observation of the sweating in lipstick by scanning electron microscopy. Int J Cosmet Sci. 1999 Jun;21(3):207–16.
9. Geoffrey Finkenaur, The chemistry and manufacture of cosmetics chapter 22, Lipsticks p. 629-657 - Google Search [Internet]. [cited 2022 May 10]. Available from: https://www.google.com/search?q=Geoffrey+Finkenaur%2C+The+chemistry+and+manufacture+of+cosmetics+chapter+22%2C+Lipsticks+p.+629-657&rlz=1C1NHXL_enNG761NG763&oq=Geoffrey+Finkenaur%2C+The+chemistry+and+manufacture+of+cosmetics+chapter+22%2C+Lipsticks+p.+629-657&aqs=chrome..69i57.872j0j7&sourceid=chrome&ie=UTF-8
10. Dixit S. Lanolin for silky, soft, smooth, skin. [cited 2022 May 10]; Available from: https://www.academia.edu/31299510/Lanolin_for_silky_soft_smooth_skin
11. David et al. Non-sweating lipsticks, The P&G company. 1995. USP 94/11510 - Google Search [Internet]. [cited 2022 Apr 26]. Available from: https://www.google.com/search?q=David+et+al.+Non-sweating+lipsticks%2C+The+P%26G+company.+1995.+USP+94%2F11510&rlz=1C1NHXL_enNG761NG763&oq=David+et+al.+Non-sweating+lipsticks%2C+The+P%26G+company.+1995.+USP+94%2F11510&aqs=chrome..69i57j69i59.1230j0j7&sourceid=chrome&ie=UTF-8
12. Sharma G, Gadhiya J, Dhanawat M. Textbook of Cosmetic Formulations. 2018.

13. Pharmapproach. Physical Stability Issues Frequently Encountered In Suspensions [Internet]. Pharmapproach.com. 2020 [cited 2022 Aug 15]. Available from: https://www.pharmapproach.com/physical-stability-issues-frequently-encountered-in-suspensions/
14. Formulation of Nail Lacquers - Cosmetic Formulation [Internet]. pharmacy180.com. [cited 2022 May 11]. Available from: http://www.pharmacy180.com/article/formulation-of-nail-lacquers-828/
15. Early Signs of Instability of Your Cosmetic Products - Swettis Beauty Blog [Internet]. [cited 2022 Apr 7]. Available from: https://skinchakra.eu/blog/archives/393-5-Early-Signs-of-Instability-of-Your-Cosmetic-Products.html
16. Shikha Thakur. Stability of emulsion [Internet]. 15:52:40 UTC [cited 2022 Aug 15]. Available from: https://www.slideshare.net/ShikhaThakur25/stability-of-emulsion
17. Rajkumar Kumawat. Pharmacy Emulsion Physical Pharmaceutics II [Internet]. [cited 2022 Aug 15]. Available from: https://www.slideshare.net/RajkumarKumawat6/pharmacyemulsionphysical-pharmaceutics-ii
18. De Gruyter, 2016. Ostwald ripening in emulsions and its prevention. In: 10 Ostwald ripening in emulsions and its prevention [Internet]. [cited 2022 Aug 15]. p. 129–40. Available from: https://www.degruyter.com/document/doi/10.1515/9783110452242-011/pdf
19. Staniforth, J.N., and Aulton, M.E. (2009). Particle size Analysis. In: Aulton's Pharmaceutics. The Design and Manufacture of Medicines. 3rd Edn. Ed. Aulton M.E. Elsevier. pp 121 – 136.
20. Parrot, E.L. (2009). Milling. In: Theory and Practice of Industrial Pharmacy. Special Indian Edition. Eds. Leon Lachlan and Herbert A. Lieberman. CBS Publishers & Distributors Pvt. Ltd. India. pp21 – 46.
21. Manisha Garg. Camera Lucida Available from: https://www.biologydiscussion.com/microbiology-2/instruments/camera-lucida-with-diagram/54974
22. Smith, J. and Jordan, M.L. (1964). Mathematical and graphical interpretation of the log-normal law for particle size distribution. J. colloid Sc. 19; 549-559
23. Oleg, D.N., and Nikolay, A.Y., (2019). Powder Characterization and Testing. In: Handbook of Non-Ferrous Metal Powders. Technologies and Applications. 2nd Edn. Ed. Oleg D. Neikov. Elsevier. pp 3 – 62.
24. Carlos, A.M.S., Samuel V.S., Darlan, B., Ricardo T.H., Rosiane L.C., Luiz, O.V.P., Flavio, V.S., and Ana M.F.F., (2022). Measurements of bimodal droplet size distribution of emulsions using ultrasonic spectroscopy in the long and intermediate wavelength regimes. Chemical Engineering Science. 10.1016/j.ces.2021.117274, 252, (117274),
25. Billany, M.R. (2009). Suspensions and Emulsions. In: Aulton's Pharmaceutics. The Design and Manufacture of Medicines. 3rd Edn. Ed. Aulton M.E. Elsevier. pp 383 – 405.

26. Martin, M.R. (2009). Emulsions. In: Theory and Practice of Industrial Pharmacy. Special Indian Edition. Eds. Leon Lachlan and Herbert A. Lieberman. CBS Publishers & Distributors Pvt. Ltd. India. pp 502 – 533.
27. Witta, K.R., Yulianti, S., Yenny, M., and Agus H. (2015). Effect of Accelerated Stability Test on Characteristics of Emulsion Systems with Chitosan as a Stabilizer. International Symposium on Applied Chemistry. Procedia Chemistry. **16:** 171 – 176.
28. Estanqueiro, M., Conceição, J., Amaral, M.H., Santos, D., Silva, J.B. Lobo, J.M.S. (2014). Characterization and stability studies of emulsion systems containing pumice. Brazilian Journal of Pharmaceutical Sciences **50**(2): 361 – 369.
29. Attwood, D. (2009). Disperse systems. In: Aulton's Pharmaceutics. The Design and Manufacture of Medicines. 3rd Edn. Ed. Aulton M.E. Elsevier. pp 70 – 98.
30. Suspensions. (1994). In: The Pharmaceutical Codex, Principles and Practice of Pharmaceutics. 12th Edition. Ed. Walter Lund. The Pharmaceutical Press. London. pp 72 – 81.
31. Patel, N.K., Lennon, L., and Levinson, R.S. (2009). Pharmaceutical Suspensions. In: Theory and Practice of Industrial Pharmacy. Special Indian Edition. Eds. Leon Lachlan and Herbert A. Lieberman. CBS Publishers & Distributors Pvt. Ltd. India. pp 479 – 501.
32. Nutan, M.T. and Reddy, I.K., (2010). General principles of suspensions. In: Pharmaceutical Suspensions. Springer, New York, NY. pp. 39-65.
33. Jones, D. (2008). Fasttrack Pharmaceutics: Dosage Form and Design of Drugs. London, UK: Pharmaceutical Press.
34. Kulshreshtha, A., Singh, O., and Wall, M. (2010). Pharmaceutical Suspensions: From Formulation Development to Manufacturing. London, New York, Dordrecht Heidelberg: Springer.
35. Higuchi, W.I., Swarbrick, J., Ho, N.F.H., Simonelli, A.P., and Martin, A.N. (1985). Particle Phenomena and Coarse Dispersions. In: Remington's Pharmaceutical Sciences. Ed. Gennaro R. Alfonso. MACK Publishing Company. USA. pp 301 – 329.
36. Haines, B.A., and Martin, A.N. (1961). Interfacial Properties of Powdered Material; Caking in Liquid Dispersions II: Electrokinetic Phenomena. Journal of Pharmaceutical Sciences. **50**(9): 753 – 756.
37. Schott, H. (1985). Colloidal Dispersion. In: Remington's Pharmaceutical Sciences. Ed. Gennaro R. Alfonso. MACK Publishing Company. USA. pp 271 – 300.
38. Nutan, M.T. and Reddy, I.K., 2010. General Principles of Suspensions. In Pharmaceutical Suspensions. Springer, New York, NY. pp. 39 – 65.
39. Stability of Medicinal products. (1994). In: The Pharmaceutical Codex. Principles and Practice of Pharmaceutics. 12th Edn. Ed. Walter Lund. The Pharmaceutical Press, London. pp 277 – 310.
40. Kathpalia, H., Mittal, S., Bhatia, V. and Pillai, P., (2011). Development and evaluation of a ready to use Cefpodoxime proxetil suspension. International Journal of Pharmaceutical Sciences and Research, **2**(8), 2173.

41. Stability of Medicinal Products. (1994). In: The Pharmaceutical Codex. Principles and Practice of Pharmaceutics. 12th Edn. Ed. Walter Lund. The Pharmaceutical Press, London. pp 277 – 310.
42. Carless, J.E., and Foster, A.A. (1966). Accelerated crystal growth of sulphathiazole by temperature cycling. Journal of Pharmacy and Pharmacology. **18**(11): 697 – 708.
43. Degradation of Hydrogels Based on Potassium and Sodium Polyacrylate by Ionic Interaction and Its Influence on Water Diego David Pinzon-Moreno , Isabel Rosali Maurate-Fernandez, Yury Flores-Valdeon, Antony Alexander Neciosup-Puican and María Verónica Carranza-Oropeza
44. Boehm E. and Williams R. (1943). A study of the inhibiting actions of propyl gallate (normal propyl trihydroxy benzoate) and certain other trihydric phenols on the autoxidation of animal and vegetable oils. Quarterly Journal of Pharmacy and Pharmacology 16:232-243.
45. Olaniyi a. a. and Ogungbamila F.O. (1991). Experimental pharmaceutical chemistry. Shaneson C. I. Limited, Ibadan, Nigeria, pp 26-31
46. Stability - Pharmaceutical solutions [Internet]. pharmacy180.com. [cited 2022 Aug 15]. Available from: http://www.pharmacy180.com/article/stability-2821/

CHAPTER NINETEEN

Microbiological quality and preservation of cosmetic products

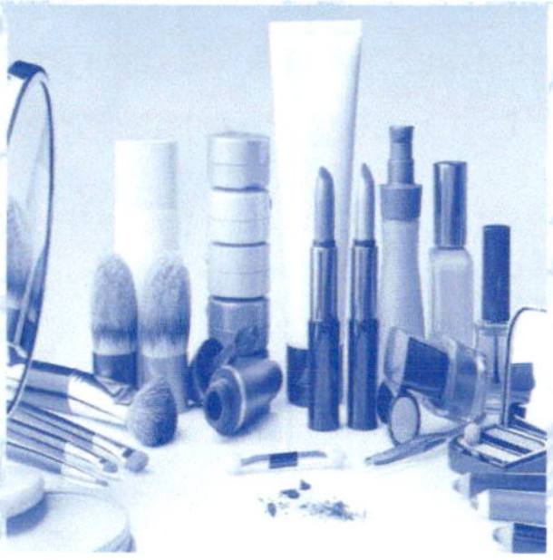

Michael O Osungunna

Cosmetic products represent the most complex and diverse examples of non-sterile products. While this category of consumer products is not strictly required to be free from all forms of microbial contaminants, there are limits as to the permissible levels and types of micro-organisms that can be present in the products, including those that are likely to be introduced by the consumer during the period of use.

However, microbial contamination of cosmetic products, whether during their preparation, transportation and/or use often leads to the spoilage of the products and exposure of consumers of such spoilt products to infection(s). It follows, therefore, that efforts should be directed at curtailing contamination of cosmetic products with micro-organisms. One major method of achieving this is through adhering to current Good Manufacturing Process (cGMP) during manufacture and the inclusion of preservatives.

Microbiological quality of cosmetic products

In evaluating a cosmetic product for its microbial quality, interest is focused on two points: the extent of the contamination and the nature of the contaminants. While the extent of contamination focuses on the limits of permissible levels of microbial contamination, the nature of the contaminants focuses on the presence or otherwise of objectionable organisms in cosmetic products. To date, there is no single universal limit of permissible levels of microbial contamination in cosmetic products. The extent of contamination in cosmetic products is regulated according to the acceptance conditions and standards for microbial quality specified in Pharmacopeia monographs. A standard published in 2015 by the International Organisation for Standardisation (ISO 17516:2014 Cosmetics-Microbiology-Microbiological limits) requires that each manufacturer be responsible for the microbiological safety and quality of their products and must ensure that they have been produced under hygienic conditions (1). As such, the extent of contamination allowed in cosmetic products varies from country to country and from region to region. Notwithstanding the variation, the same parameters, as used for non-sterile pharmaceutical products, are used in setting the conditions for the acceptance of cosmetics.

The acceptance standards for cosmetic and other related non-sterile products as specified in the United States Pharmacopeia (USP) are shown in Table 19.1.

Table 19.1: United States Pharmacopeia (USP) standards for microbial quality of cosmetic and other related non-sterile products (as colony-forming unit (CFU) in 1 g or mL) (2)

Route of Administration	Total Aerobic Colony Count	Total Combined Yeasts/Moulds Count	Objectionable microorganism(s)
Oral (non-aqueous)	10^3	10^2	*Escherichia coli*
Oral (aqueous)	10^2	10^1	*Escherichia coli*
Rectal usage	10^3	10^2	None designated
Oro-mucosal usage	10^2	10^1	*Staphylococcus aureus, Pseudomonas aeruginosa*
Gingival usage	10^2	10^1	*Staphylococcus aureus, Pseudomonas aeruginosa*
Nasal usage	10^2	10^1	*Staphylococcus aureus, Pseudomonas aeruginosa*
Cutaneous usage	10^2	10^1	*Staphylococcus aureus, Pseudomonas aeruginosa*
Auricular usage	10^2	10^1	*Staphylococcus aureus, Pseudomonas aeruginosa*
Vaginal usage	10^2	10^1	*Pseudomonas aeruginosa, Staphylococcus aureus and Candida albicans*

Transdermal patch (drug matrix, adhesive layer and backing)	10^2	10^1	*Pseudomonas aeruginosa, Staphylococcus aureus*
Inhalation	10^2	10^1	*Staphylococcus aureus, Pseudomonas aeruginosa* and bile-tolerant Gram-negative bacteria
Substances for pharmaceutical usage	10^3	10^2	None designated

Table 19.1 can be interpreted thus: maximum acceptable count is 20, 200, 2000 when the USP standard for microbial quality is 10^1, 10^2 and 10^3 CFU per g or mL, respectively. From the table, it can be deduced that *Pseudomonas aeruginosa* and *Staphylococcus aureus* are objectionable in products for cutaneous use while the maximum total aerobic colony count allowed is 200 and the total combined yeasts/moulds count allowed is 20.

According to the Japanese Pharmacopoeia, standards for microbial quality are that total aerobic colony count in articles for cutaneous, gingival, oromucosal and nasal usage should not exceed 10^2 CFU per g or mL while total combined yeasts/moulds count should not exceed 10^1 CFU per g or mL. However, *Pseudomonas aeruginosa and Staphylococcus aureus* are considered objectionable in one gram or one millilitre of the product (3).

Two different classes of cosmetic products with respect to microbial quality control limits were identified by the European Union's Scientific Committee on Consumer Safety Guideline: Category 1—products to be applied in the eye area as well as on mucous membranes of children under three years; and Category 2—other products. For Category 1, the total aerobic colony count should not exceed 10^2 CFU per g or mL of the product while for Category 2, the count should not exceed 10^3 CFU per g or mL of the article. *Pseudomonas aeruginosa*, *Candida albicans* and *Staphylococcus aureus* are considered objectionable and must not be detected in 1.0 g or mL of Category 1 products and in 0.1 g or 0.1 mL of Category 2 cosmetic products (4). It is worthy of note that for cosmetic products to have been adjudged suitable for use implies that the products have passed the tests for the extent of contamination and the nature of contaminants.

Need for preservatives in cosmetics

Contamination of cosmetic products may result in spoilage which manifests in the form of a change in organoleptic properties of the product. For instance, colour development in contaminated cosmetic products may be characteristic of pigmentation produced by contaminants such as the purple violacein of *Chromobacterium violaceum,* the red prodigiosin of *Serratia marcescens*, and the greenish pyocyannin and pyoverdin pigments of *Pseudomonas aeruginosa,* apart from the degradative capabilities of such typical cosmetic contaminants. The clouding of clear fluids represents visible degradation, but also at risk are opaque products such as emulsions which are subject to microbe-mediated phase separation, a phenomenon that can result from the mere presence of dead bacteria (5-7).

A special quality variable of importance in cosmetics is product perfume/fragrance which often functions as a potent symbol for a product. While product fragrance involves great formulation input and effort, it is easily undermined by compounds as indole, skatole, hydrogen sulphide, and various fungal volatiles which are synthesised volatile organic compounds of microbial origin with intensity of detection at parts-per-million if not parts-per-trillion levels (8-10).

Another important consequence of cosmetic products' contamination is consumer health risk following the use of contaminated product. Morbidity and mortality associated with the use of contaminated cosmetic products have been linked to microbes present in such a contaminated product. Several outbreaks of infections associated with contaminated cosmetic products as well as recalls have been reported. Application of a shampoo heavily contaminated with *Pseudomonas aeruginosa* by neutropenic patients about to undergo chemotherapy resulted in infections and death (11).

Outbreak of 74 nosocomial infections in an intensive care unit following exposure to contaminated mouthwash has been reported (12). The report of indirect exposure to contaminated cosmetic products leading to secondary infections has been made following an outbreak of nosocomial infections traced to the use of a contaminated hand cream by a nurse (13). An outbreak of invasive mycoses as well as its cutaneous manifestation caused by *Paecilomyces lilanus* from a contaminated skin lotion was reported in Switzerland (14,15). In USA, a link between an outbreak of *Pseudomonas aeruginosa* in a neonatal intensive care unit and contaminated skin lotion has been established and reported (16).

Infections related to contaminated cosmetic products can occur during use by consumers. Ocular infections have resulted in significant eye diseases and even blindness following the application of contaminated mascara products; the infection is facilitated by mascara brushes through abrasion of the eye surfaces (17, 18). The list of microorganisms that have been implicated in cosmetics contamination and health hazards is inexhaustible and some are shown in Table 19.2 (19)

Table 19.2: Cosmetics-associated bacteria and fungi contaminants (19)

Consumer-Derived	Manufacturing-Derived
Bacteria	
Acinetobacter spp.	*Acinetobacter spp.*
Bacillus spp.	*Aeromonas sobria*
Citrobacter freundii	*Bacillus spp,*
Clostridium perfringens, C. tetani	*Burkholderia cepacian*
Enterobacter spp.	*B. picketii*
Klebsiella oxytoca	*Citrobacter freundii*
Klebsiella pneumonia	*Enterobacter spp.*
Moraxella spp.	*Klebsiella oxytoca*
Propionibacterium spp.	*Klebsiella pneumoniae*
Pseudomonas aeruginosa	*Moraxella spp.*
Pseudomonas spp.	*Ochrobactrum anthropic*
Sarcina spp.	*Proteus spp.*
Serratia spp.	*Pseudomonas aeruginosa*
Staphylococcus aureus	*Pseudomonas spp.*
S. epidermidis	*Salmonella spp.*
Stenotrophomonas maltophilia	*Serratia marcescens*
Streptococcus mutans	*Serratia spp.*
Fungi	
Aureobasidium pullulans	*Aureobasidium pullulans*
Candida albicans	*Candida lipolytica*
Penicillium spp.	*Paecilomyces variotii*
Rhodotorula sp.	*Penicillium spp.*
Scopulariopsis sp.	*Saccharomyces cerevisiae*

Contamination of cosmetics products has led to several product recalls which serve as an important intervention in controlling the use of cosmetic products contaminated with pathogens. Between October 1, 1993 and September 30, 1999 for instance, the FDA engaged in the recall of a total of 3,793 cosmetic products as shown in Table 19.3 (20). Of these, 1,370 (36%) products, of which 56 (4%) were cosmetic products, were recalled as a result of microbial contamination, being the major cause of recalls during the period reviewed. Also, for this period, some microbial contaminants were isolated of which *Pseudomonas aeruginosa* was the predominant bacterium associated with recalls of cosmetic products (Table 19.4).

Similarly, between 2004 and 2011, approximately 75% of non-sterile product recalls were as a result of contaminated over-the-counter (OTC) or personal care products. The majority of these recalls were attributed to the following: (i) presence of 'objectionable' organisms, 72%; (ii) contamination levels exceeding microbial limits, 15%; (iii) sterility or microbial diagnostic kit error, 7%; (iv) failed microbiological tests, 5%; and (v) GMP manufacturing deficiencies, 1% (21).

Table 19.3: Recall of cosmetic products resulting from microbial contamination (20)

	Recalls	
Product type	Number	Percentage
Beverage	94	7
Condiment	36	3
Cosmetic	56	4
Dairy	304	22
Dip/sauce	108	8
Fruit	21	2
Grain	80	6
Pastry	147	11
Salad	126	9
Sandwich	124	9
Seafood	157	11
Vegetable	81	6
Others	36	3
Total	1,370	100

Evidently, efforts should be directed at curtailing or eliminating all forms of contaminant in cosmetic products. One of the ways this can be achieved is by the addition of "preservatives" which have been defined as chemicals added to products in small amounts to inhibit the growth of and to destroy microbes arising from contamination.

Cosmetics preservation serves the dual roles of preventing product deterioration and preventing infections, which may not always be traced or attributed to the offending product. The term 'preservative' refers to the circumstances of use rather than the chemical nature of the substance.

Table 19.4: Bacteria and fungi isolated from recalled cosmetic products (20)

Microbe	Number of products recalled	Percentage
Burkholderia cepacian	19	33
Pseudomonas spp.		
Pseudomonas aeruginosa	25	45
Other spp.	6	11
Klebsiella oxytoca	1	2
Enterobacter gergoviae	1	2
Mould/yeast	4	7
Total	56	100

Concept of Good Manufacturing Practice (GMP) in cosmetic products manufacture

The fact that a cosmetic product is to contain preservative(s) is not enough grounds to compromise its microbial quality during production. One of the ways to certify that a cosmetic product possesses the desired therapeutic properties and is safe for administration by the intended route, is to ensure that the principle of Good Manufacturing Practice (GMP) is strictly obeyed during its production. GMP aims at ensuring that a product is constantly produced to meet the requirements of regulatory bodies as well as the quality appropriate for its intended use (22). GMP requires that: [1] the manufacturing procedure is fully clarified before it commences; and [2] the mandatory facilities are provided. In practice, this means that: (i) buildings and facilities for production are of acceptable and appropriate quality in terms of size, design, and construction, and maintained in a clean and orderly manner (ii) equipment and utensils for production are of suitable design, size, material and workmanship for the intended purpose (iii) personnel involved in the manufacture of cosmetic products are adequately trained to perform their assigned functions (iv) raw materials conform to appropriate standards and specifications (v) good quality water that has been treated is used as a cosmetic ingredient (vi) approved colour supplements are used in defined cosmetic products. Suffice it to say that qualification of personnel, equipment disinfection, microbial control of raw materials, and water treatment can reduce the chance of contamination (23,24).

However, following the September 2007 meeting in Belgium of the International Cooperation on Cosmetic Regulation (ICCR), the provision of the current International Organisation for Standardisation (ISO) standard for cosmetic GMPs (ISO 22716:2007) was adopted by the regulators from the United States, Canada, the European Union, and Japan as an institutionalised scheme for GMPs that could apply to their regions (25).

More information on GMP can be obtained in chapter 16 of this book.

Preservatives

There are many chemicals with antimicrobial activity. However, not all can be employed as preservatives. It, therefore, follows that those that are to be employed as preservatives must possess some attributes such as they:

- should be effective at low concentrations against a wide range of organisms
- should be non-toxic and non-sensitising externally or internally at the concentrations required for activity
- should be soluble in the formulation at use-concentration
- should be compatible with a wide range of active ingredients, solubilising and dispersing agents
- should be free of objectionable odour, taste and/or colour
- should be active with long-term stability over a wide range of pH and temperature; and
- should be inexpensive relative to the cost of the product (26).

Preservative agents with all these attributes are said to be "ideal". However, no single preservative has been found to possess all these attributes and, hence, there is no ideal preservative. An ideal state can be created through combination of two or more suitable preservatives.

In this section, emphasis will be on five major classes of preservatives often used in the preservation of cosmetic products.

Classes of chemical preservatives used in cosmetic products

Esters of parahydroxybenzoic acid (parabens): Included in this class are methyl paraben, ethyl paraben, propyl paraben, and butyl paraben. These are highly economical preservatives that are closest to the ideal and are the first choices in many situations. They have a broad spectrum of activity against bacteria and fungi at low concentrations, and remain active over a wide pH range although they are optimally active at low pH. They are compatible with many other chemical substances and can be used in the preservation of a large variety of cosmetics including both the rinse-off and the leave-on products. Although, there have been some concerns about their estrogenic activity, they have been adjudged innocuous for application in cosmetic products at concentrations up to 25 percent. Generally, parabens are used at concentrations ranging from 0.01 to 0.3% (27).

Formaldehyde releasers: Examples include Quaternium 15 (triaza-azoniaadamantine chloride), dimethyl dimethylol hydantoin (DMDM hydantoin), imidazolidinyl urea, diazolidinyl urea. The use of formaldehyde-releasing preservatives ensures that the actual level of free formaldehyde in the products is always very low, yet sufficient to maintain microbial quality. They have broad spectrum activity against bacteria but weak antifungal efficacy (28).

Isothiazolinones: These include: chloromethyl isothiazolinone and methyl isothiazolinone. They have broad spectrum activity against both the Gram-positive and the Gram-negative bacteria. They are effective over the entire pH range normally encountered in cosmetics and are best for rinse–off products. Toxicological data have shown them to be non-carcinogenic but may produce skin irritation in some end users (29).

Organic alcohols: Commonly used members of this class include: ethyl alcohol, benzyl alcohol and phenoxyethanol. They are considered a "milder alternative" to traditional preservatives. They are usually combined with EDTA (ethylenediaminetetraacetic acid), sorbic acid and its potassium salt (potassium sorbate), or caprylyl glycol to create broad spectrum activity. They have good antibacterial effect with best activity against Gram-negative bacteria. They are highly stable and their activity is not pH dependent. They are used in most preparations at up to 1% w/v. Although, they are found not to be irritating or sensitising up to 2.2% w/v, however, there have been concerns about their possible carcinogenic effect.

Organic acids and their metallic salts: These include: benzoic acid, sodium benzoate, sorbic acid, potassium sorbate, and dehydroacetic acid. They are "natural alternatives" despite the fact that they are usually produced synthetically. They are often combined with other organic acids or diazolidinyl urea for broad spectrum effectiveness. They are effective against most fungi with weak efficacy against bacteria. Their effectiveness requires an aqueous base and a pH range 2-6, although they precipitate when water

Table 19.5: Preservative combinations in major cosmetic products (31)

Product Class	Possible preservatives that can be combined
Shampoo	Dimethyl dimethylol hydantoin, EDTA, methyl paraben
	Dimethyl dimethylol hydantoin, Methylisothiazolinone/chloromethylisothiazolinone/EDTA
	Diazolidinyl urea, benzyl alcohol, iodopropenylbutylcarbamate, EDTA
	Methylisothiazolinone/chloromethylisothiazolinone, sodium benzoate, EDTA
Conditioner	Methylisothiazolinone/chloromethylisothiazolinone, benzyl alcohol
	Methyl paraben, chlorhexidine
	Dimethyl dimethylol hydantoin, Methylisothiazolinone/chloromethylisothiazolinone, EDTA
	Methylisothiazolinone/chloromethylisothiazolinone, benzyl alcohol, EDTA
Body wash	Dimethyl dimethylol hydantoin, EDTA
	Dimethyl dimethylol hydantoin, Sodium benzoate, EDTA
	Methylisothiazolinone/chloromethylisothiazolinone, EDTA
	Quaternium 15, EDTA
Lotion	Dimethyl dimethylol hydantoin, iodopropenylbutylcarbamate, EDTA
	Benzyl alcohol, phenoxyethanol
	Dimethyl dimethylol hydantoin, methyl paraben, EDTA
	Benzyl alcohol
Mascara	Methyl paraben, propyl paraben
	Diazolidinyl urea, methyl paraben, propyl paraben
	Parabens (methyl, ethyl, propyl, isopropyl, butyl, isobutyl), phenoxyethanol, EDTA, sodium
	Dehydroacetic acid
	Diazolidinyl urea, methyl paraben
Mousse	Dimethyl dimethylol hydantoin
	Diazolidinyl urea
	Phenoxyethanol, methyl paraben

	Sodium benzoate
Make-up powder	Sorbic acid, parabens (methyl, propyl, butyl), EDTA
	Methyl paraben, propyl paraben
	Phenoxyethanol, parabens (methyl, propyl, butyl)
	Sorbic acid, methyl parabens, propyl parabens

content is high and become inactive. They are required in high concentrations leading to higher costs (30).

Preservative combinations in cosmetic products

To achieve synergism and broad-spectrum activity, two or more suitable preservatives are often combined in cosmetic products. The choice of suitable preservatives for possible combination is often determined by the product type while combinations may be between preservatives of broad efficacy and compounds of more selective efficacy. Table 19.5 provides possible combinations based on product category.

Cosmetic preservatives and associated toxicity

One of the criteria for the choice of suitable preservatives for use in cosmetic products is their freedom from irritation and toxicity. As a result, tests for skin irritation and toxicity are consumer safety considerations of cosmetic preservation through which the use of some cosmetic preservatives have been restricted or prohibited. The US FDA has estimated 12,500 chemicals used in cosmetics, 20% of them are safe according to the review by the Cosmetic Ingredient Review (CIR), only 11 of them are banned in the US but more than 1300 are banned or restricted in the EU (32). This implies that the list of prohibited and restricted ingredients, such as preservatives in cosmetics, varies from country to country. For instance, while the use of some mercury compounds, tetrabromosalicylanilides, dichlorosalicylanilides, tetrachlorosalicylanilides, dibromoslicylanilides, captan, sodium pyrithione, bithionol, hexachlorophene and tribromosalicylanilides have been prohibited in cosmetics in the European Union according to Annex II of the EU Cosmetic Directive, preservatives like dichlorophen, bithionol, mercury and its compounds, halogenated salicylanilides, hexachlorophene and formalin are prohibited in Japan. Moreover, some preservatives have been found to act as carcinogens, neurotoxins, endocrine disruptors, mutagens, and reproductive toxins, and to cause harm to the ocular surface (33). Reports have demonstrated that several adverse reactions such as allergic reactions, ocular irritation, contact dermatitis, corneal epithelial cell toxicity, tear film instability, blepharitis and dry eye disease may be associated with eye cosmetics (34). The corollary to this submission is that the effects and toxicity associated with different preservatives vary. For example, while some parabens such as methyl, ethyl, propyl, butyl, isopropyl and isobutyl paraben have been listed as endocrine disruptors, causing congenital malformations, growth and metabolic disorders (overweight, type-2 diabetes), fecundity, neurological disorders, cardiovascular disease and cancers in hormonally-sensitive tissues such as the breast, prostate, testis (35); phenoxyethanol, methylparaben, propylparaben, imidazolidinyl urea, and DMDM hydantoin have been associated with skin irritation and contact allergies which may manifest in the form of erythema, oedema or unusual itching (36).

Other components of cosmetic products with preservative activity

Apart from preservatives, several other compounds known as "preservative adjuncts", whose role is to facilitate preservative activity are included in cosmetic products. Preservative adjuncts may be effective alone at high concentrations and complement the activities of better-known preservatives at low concentrations. Ethanol at concentrations higher than 15% has direct preservative activity while it complements other preservatives at lower concentrations. Propylene, butylene and longer chain glycols may regulate water activity levels sufficiently to prevent microbial growth at high concentrations but facilitates preservation at low levels. EDTA may compromise the integrity of the cell wall and capsule of microorganisms such that it permits greater and improved penetration of antimicrobial agents into microbial cells by its ability to chelate divalent cations such as calcium and magnesium.

Cosmetic products may also contain perfumes and natural materials that have been reported to have some level of preservative efficacy as components. The preservative efficacy of a perfume is limited as such a preservative loses its activity following dilution in formulation and such activity may be dependent on pH. The difficulty often encountered in assuring the consistency of natural materials because their active principles are rarely known, limits their preservative efficacy in cosmetic products. For instance, commercial grapefruit seed oil was reported to have antimicrobial activity which was later ascribed to the quaternary ammonium compound found in the oil (37).

Antioxidants may also be present in cosmetic products. These are substances that inhibit oxidation or reactions promoted by oxygen, peroxides or free radicals. They can be synthetic such as butylated hydroxytoluene (BHT) and butylated hydroxyanisole (BHA) or natural such as tocopherol (Vitamin E), ascorbic acid (Vitamin C), polyphenols and flavonoids. However, only phenolic antioxidants have been found to possess pronounced antimicrobial properties among the reducing agents used (38). Although the reported antimicrobial activities may not be enough to afford adequate preservation of complex cosmetic systems, the proven potentiating effects of these compounds on Bronopol,

Bronidox L, Glydant, Germall 115 and Kathon CG can be utilised to reduce the concentrations of the preservatives to lower levels (39).

The concept of non-preservative preservatives

When an agent, despite having a preservative potential, is not listed on Annex VI of the EU Cosmetics Directive, it cannot be considered a preservative. It, therefore, means such an agent must have a different role in the formulation. The concept of non-preservative preservative excludes the use of high concentrations of salts, polyols or glycols to decrease the extent of water activity. Non-preservative preservatives must exhibit killing activities and act as essential oils, emulsifiers, or humectants.

Essential oils: The antimicrobial activities of some essential oils found in fragrances have been known and reported (40). However, the concentrations of essential oils needed as preservatives exceed those needed as fragrances in formulations. Often, the antimicrobial activity is lost upon emulsification. For instance, undiluted (100%) tea tree leaf oil shows good antimicrobial activity which is lost upon emulsification. It is, therefore, important to note that fragrances may have activity against microbes and when the need arises, chemical preservatives can be used at lower concentrations than otherwise would be required.

Emulsifiers: Some emulsifiers have been reported to have antimicrobial activities and one of the earliest emulsifiers whose antimicrobial activity has been promoted is 90% (purity) monoester of glyceryl monolaurate. However, the use of this emulsifier has been limited due to its weak antimicrobial and emulsifying activities.

Humectants: The promotion of the preservative property of some hydroxyl-containing compounds, such as farnesol, pentylene glycol, caprylyl glycol and 1,2 hexanediol, used as humectants has been limited due to the fact that the concentration needed for preservation has been found to be toxic to humans. For example, propylene glycol at high concentrations can function as preservative but the safety of the products which contain it cannot be guaranteed. Similarly, the concentration of glycol needed to reduce water activity in products to ensure inhibition of microbial proliferation impacts negatively on the aesthetics (high viscosity) of such products thereby making the products unacceptable to the consumers.

Packaging as a means of cosmetic products preservation

Packaging is an effective physical element that offers protection against contamination during consumer use and against accumulation of contaminants in the distribution system. The potential of packaging to prevent product contamination depends on the components and properties of primary packaging materials. The properties include, but are not limited to, the type of the packaging (jars, boxes, flasks, bottles, tubes, aerosol propellants, sachets, etc.). The composition as well as the nature of the materials used for packaging also plays some roles (polymers, glass, etc.) (41). Aside this, the delivery orifices and the packaging sizes do have an effect on products' contamination. For instance, packaging in aerosol containers presents a total barrier to contamination during use by consumer, and the aerosol propellant alone offers some preservative functions (42). Furthermore, limited- or single- use packaging such as sample size bottles and sachets reduce the chances for contamination.

As regards volume control, product quality has been shown to be maintained through the design of pump and closure that curb ingress of contaminants (43). Notwithstanding their functions in product preservation, several packaging types entail supplementary preservative considerations. Cellulosic packaging and labels may require preservation against fungal growth provided that conditions of high humidity are anticipated (44). Such conditions may come from the environment in which the product is distributed or from the product itself.

Device for Exclusive Formula Integrity (D.E.F.I.)

Not all cosmetic products need preservatives. Usually, products that contain water such as moisturisers, shampoos or make-up need preservatives. However, the following cosmetic products do not usually require preservatives: (i) water-free (anhydrous) products such as body oils and oil-based hair serums; (ii) products which are acidic, such as antiperspirants, or alkaline, such as depilatory (hair-removal) creams; (iii) products with a high alcohol content, generally 20% or above, such as perfumes and after shaves; and (iv) aerosol products with airtight packaging which prevents contact with air, for example, aerosol hair sprays. These products that do not need preservatives are known as preservative-free cosmetic products and are usually kept protected and sterile in a large tube often referred to as **"Device for Exclusive Formula Integrity".** D.E.F.I. guarantees that the product remains sterile throughout use. It is usually made up of a cap which is the actual D.E.F.I., a sealing system (lower part) and a sleeve, the flexible part which has been specially designed to fit the D.E.F.I. cap. Both parts, sleeve and cap, interlock perfectly and guarantee complete airtightness that allows the formula to remain sterile throughout use. The D.E.F.I cap is made of 4 parts, namely: the external cover, internal element, lip and a flexible membrane that rises when pressure is exerted on the tube and goes back into place when the pressure is released. A D.E.F.I. system differs from an airless dispenser which prevents any entry of air and oxidation of the product, in that the D.E.F.I system does not have a "dead volume" at the top. This "dead volume" contains some of the product and poses a contamination risk for the product which suggests the need for the use of preservatives. In the D.E.F.I system, there is no dead volume and no contamination is possible. The formula is sterile and remains so for the entire duration of the product's use.

Preservative failure in cosmetic products

It is a common occurrence to experience preservative failure in cosmetic products despite using the appropriate preservative at the right concentration. Failure may arise especially when some parameters of a product's formulation and packaging are not considered thereby affecting preservative efficacy and stability. Some of these parameters, based on the assumption that cosmetic products are multiphase systems, are considered below.

Partition coefficient: This is a measure of the tendency of a preservative to distribute itself between oil and water phases of an emulsion. It is designated as:

$$K^{o}_{w} = \frac{\text{Equilibrium concentration in oil phase}}{\text{Equilibrium concentration in water phase}}$$

Partition coefficient is constant only for a particular oil-water system. The oil/water partition coefficient of a bactericide often varies widely for different oils, causing great variation in the preservative concentration in the aqueous phase. However, the greater the value of K°_{w}, the smaller the amount of preservative that will remain in the aqueous phase and available to the contaminating micro-organisms.

Temperature: As temperature is increased, the partition coefficient usually changes in favour of the oil phase. Hence, attention must be given to the storage temperature of cosmetic products as the proximity to the growth temperature, such as 37°C for mesophilic bacteria and 25°C for fungi, can encourage proliferation of contaminating organisms at a rate beyond the scope of the preservative. Also, increase in temperature almost always increases the antimicrobial activity of the preservative, although the effect is more marked with some agents than with others. In general, as temperature is increased in arithmetical progression, the rate of kill increases geometrically. The effect of temperature increase on the aqueous concentration of preservative at a fixed inoculum size is expressed quantitatively as a temperature coefficient, usually in terms of a specified 10°C rise in temperature (designated ($\emptyset^{10}$ or Q10). Thus:

$$\emptyset^{10} = \frac{\text{Time required to kill at X°C}}{\text{Time required to kill at (X+ 10)°C}}$$

under stated condition or for the general case,

$$\emptyset^{T2-T1} = t_1/t_2$$

where T_2 and T_1 are two temperatures differing by 10°C and

t_1 and t_2 are the corresponding lethal times.

The $Ø^{10}$ value is characteristic of a particular preservative and the values for different agents vary widely. The effectiveness of agents with a high coefficient, such as aliphatic alcohols, is increased by raising the temperature more than that of agents with a low coefficient, such as formaldehyde. For example, the $Ø^{10}$ value for aliphatic alcohols is 30-50 and for formaldehyde, it is 1.5. This, therefore, implies that a drop from 30°C to 20°C can result in a 30-50 fold reduction in the antimicrobial activity of aliphatic alcohols.

pH: This is a measure of acidity and alkalinity of a medium. The value of pH does not only affect the activity and stability of preservatives but also the rate of growth of bacterial cells and the physico-chemical states of their surfaces. Optimum growth of many bacteria occurs at pH 6-8 while growth falls on either side of these ranges. A number of preservatives are active in their unionised states, e.g., benzoic acid, esters of parahydroxybenzoic acid; while some are active as either anions (e.g., EDTA), or cations (e.g., quaternary ammonium compounds). The degree of ionisation of acidic or basic preservatives depends on pH; hence, the activity of preservatives increases at a pH which favours the formation of their active species. For example, the effects of organic acids are greatly impaired and undermined in neutral and alkaline formulations; in the same manner the stability of isothiazolinone preservatives is compromised when amines are present (45-47).

For some products, the effect of pH goes beyond the properties of the bulk product to the microenvironments provided by some product designs and constructs. For instance, paraben hydrolysis can be mediated in emulsions when the pH changes from neutral to alkaline.

Interaction with other formulation components: Many hydrocolloids, such as methylcellulose, alginates, polyvinylpyrolidone and tragacanth, when used in cosmetic products can interact to some extent with preservatives and diminish their activity. In some cases, it is a direct incompatibility, such as between alginates, which are anionic, and cation-active preservatives; whereas in many other cases, interactions with components of cosmetic products like sugar alcohols, sugars, polymers, and sunscreen actives, have led to both interference and synergy with preservative efficacy (48-52).

Water activity (A_w): This is another moderator of preservative efficacy in cosmetic products. It has been defined as a measure of the amount of water available to microbial contaminants for growth. It also represents water that is not complexed with solutes, especially glycols or salts, and does not correspond directly to product's percentage of water. When A_w level is less than 0.9, pseudomonads and some other Gram-negative bacteria are inhibited whereas Gram-positive bacteria such as staphylococci are inhibited at A_w less than 0.8. A_w levels lower than those inhibitory to bacteria are required to inhibit *Cryptococcus neoformans* and *Candida albicans* (yeast-like fungi). However, systems with A_w less than 0.6 do not need additional preservatives as they are considered to be water-free. However, formulating A_w values restrictive for all microbial growth in a single cosmetic product may not be practicable because a small change in the water activity may significantly affect microbial proliferation. Examples of A_w modulators include glycerol, carboxymethyl cellulose, sodium chloride, glucose, sucrose, ethanol and urea.

Effects of containers: This is of considerable significance especially with plastic containers as there is very little or no interaction between the majority of preservatives and neutral glass and so there is little danger of preservative loss from cosmetic products stored in glass bottles. Preservative activity is affected by plastic containers through permeation, sorption and leaching.

Plastic containers, because they are usually formed at molecular level by chains of polymers, may present voids that may not be large enough to allow leakage of the cosmetic products but large enough to allow air and water vapour to enter the product thereby subjecting the preservative to degradation through oxidation or hydrolysis. Volatile substances such as alcohols used as preservatives may move out through the walls of plastic containers in which they are present, causing a reduction in effective concentration. This phenomenon is known as permeation. Sorption, on the other hand, may be adsorption which is a surface phenomenon in which some molecules of preservatives in the product are held to the interior surface of the container; or absorption in which some molecules of the preservatives are taken into the voids of the plastic container. However, sorption leads to a reduction in the effective concentration of preservative in the product. It is also possible that some components of plastic containers are released into the product and interact with the preservative contained therein. This phenomenon is referred to as leaching. Such an interaction reduces the effective concentration of preservative in the cosmetic product.

Preservative resistance

One major consequence of exposing contaminating microorganisms to sub-inhibitory concentrations of preservatives is "preservative resistance" in which an organism which is initially sensitive to a preservative becomes insensitive to the same preservative. Resistance to many preservatives has been reported as shown in Table 19.6 (53). The mechanisms involved include modification of cellular permeability, inactivation, and biofilm growth. However, organisms may utilise one or combinations of the mechanisms.

Cellular permeability to preservatives can be modified to exclude preservatives from the cytoplasm in Gram-negative bacteria through the loss of porins (water-filled pores and channels associated with the modulation of cellular permeability in the membranes of bacteria), by elimination of specific transport proteins in both Gram-negative and Gram-positive bacteria, or by altering membrane structure. A link between reduced susceptibility to isothiazolone of a diverse range of Gram-negative bacteria isolates from isothiazolone-preserved consumer products and loss of porin has been reported (54). Similarly, reduced susceptibility to a series of parabens has been attributed to porin deficiency in *E. coli*. The corollary to these observations is that reduced permeability to preservatives through the loss of porin can be a successful mechanism for bacteria developing resistance to preservatives

Inactivation, a process by which an active antimicrobial agent becomes converted to an inactive form, is another mechanism of developing resistance to preservatives. Some resistant strains of organisms are capable of synthesising substances which degrade or change preservatives in such a way that they become ineffective. For instance, resistance to formaldehyde and formaldehyde-releasing preservatives has been linked to the formation and overexpression of formaldehyde dehydrogenase, an enzyme that utilises formaldehyde as a substrate and converts formaldehyde to a non-toxic metabolite (55).

Table I9.6: List of selected preservatives to which resistance has been reported (53)

Benzalkonium chloride	Imidazolinyl urea
Benzisothiazolone	Iodine
Benzoic acid	Methylchloro/methyl isothiazolone
Chloramine	Methylenevischlorophenol
Chlorhexidine	Methyl paraben
Chloroallyltriazine-azoniadamantane	Phenoxyethanol
Chlorophenol	Phenylethyl alcohol
Dibromodicyanobutane	Phenylmercuric acetate
Dimehtyloxazolidine	Povidone iodine
Dimethoxydimethyl hydantoin	Propyl paraben
Dimethyldithiocarbamate	Quaternary ammonium compounds
Formaldehyde	Sorbic acid
Glutaraldehyde	Tetrahydrothiadiazinthione
Hexahydrotriethyl triazine	Trifluoromethyl dichlorcarbanilide

It is to be noted that resistance to preservative through modification of cellular permeability and preservative inactivation can be displayed when bacteria exist in planktonic (free swimming) form. The mechanisms of resistance to preservatives differ when the organisms exist in sessile or biofilm form. Biofilm, a consortium of microbial communities enclosed in self-produced extracellular polymeric substances, and attached to a surface, can be formed following the processes of attachment (reversible and irreversible), microcolonies formation, maturation and dispersion. Resistance to preservatives by microbes in a biofilm may be due to reduced penetration of antimicrobials, variation in the chemical microenvironment within a biofilm, in which bacterial cells have differing access to nutrients and oxygen due to the heterogeneous nature of a biofilm and formation of recalcitrant phenotypic stages often referred to as "persisters" (56).

Preservative efficacy tests of cosmetic products

These are specific tests that must be carried out on all preserved cosmetic products and which serve to evaluate the efficacy of preservative in cosmetic products. It is necessary since it is not normally possible to predict how the activity of a chemical preservative will be influenced by the various components of cosmetic products and the container coupled with the reported lack of correlation between preservative efficacy *in vitro* and *in vivo*. The specific tests may take the form of a single or series of challenge tests whereby the preserved cosmetic product is inoculated with relevant organisms whose fate is determined at various time intervals, depending on the nature and the use of the product. The relevant organisms in this context require that such organisms are associated with contamination of the product, have a high level of resistance to antimicrobial agents, have appreciable opportunistic contamination capacity, low nutrients demand, and adaptivity. According to the United States Pharmacopeia (USP), such organisms include: *Candida albicans, Aspergillus niger, Escherichia coli, Staphylococcus aureus and Pseudomonas aeruginosa. O*ther regulatory bodies, such as the Personal Care Products Council, include the use of *Penicillium luteum* and *Bacillus subtilis.*

Inoculum levels of 10^6-10^7 viable organisms per gram or mL have been recommended with a test period of 28 days. However, a 3-month test period should not be considered excessive. Sampling periods of 0 h, 6 h, 48 h, 7, 14 and 28 days have also been recommended. Although the procedures for the test remain similar interpretation of results varies from country to country as shown in Table 19.7.

For a preservative to be deemed suitable for use in cosmetic products, according to USP, requires that it is able to bring about a 2log reduction in bacterial count with no increase in the initial number of yeast/mould on day 14 and maintained through to day 28 of the test. However, EP provides that there should be a 2log reduction in bacterial count within 48h (day 2) of the test and a 3log reduction on day 7 and a 2log reduction in the yeast count on day 14 of the test and maintained through to day 28 of the test. Japanese

Pharmacopoeia requires that there should be a 2log reduction in bacterial count by day 14 with no increase in the number of the yeast and maintained through to day 28 of the test (57).

Table 19.7: Log reduction values for preservative efficacy test according to the United States Pharmacopoeia (USP), European Pharmacopoeia (EP) and Japanese Pharmacopoeia (JP) (57)

	Day 2		Day 7		Day 14		Day 28	
	Bacteria	Yeast	Bacteria	Yeast	Bacteria	Yeast	Bacteria	Yeast
USP	-	-	-	-	2	NI	NI	NI
EP	2	-	3	-	-	2	NI	NI
JP	-	-	-	-	2	NI	NI	NI

NI = No increase

References

1. International Organization for Standardization (ISO). Cosmétiques—Microbiologie—Limites Microbiologiques European Committee for Standardization; ISO 17516:2014; ISO: Geneva, Switzerland, 2014.
2. United States Pharmacopeia Convention Inc. *United States Pharmacopeia 36- National Formulary, 31*. Chapters 61, 62, 610, 1111, 1112, 1163, 1191. Rock-Ville, MD: US Pharmacopeia Convention Inc.: 2021.
3. Pharmacopeia, T.J., The Japanese Pharmacopeia, 64th ed.; Japan Ministry of Health, Labour and Welfare: Tokyo, Japan, pp. 2486–2489, 2016.
4. Scientific Committee on Consumer Safety. The SCCS Notes of Guidance for the Testing of Cosmetic Ingredients and Their Safety Evaluation, 9th ed.; SCCS, Ed.; European Union: Brussels, Belgium, Volume SCCS/1564/15, 2016.
5. Nagata, Y., Measurement of odor threshold by triangle odor bag method. *Odor Measure Rev.*, 2003, 118, 2003.
6. O'May, G.A., Allison, D.G., and Gilbert, P., A rapid method for the evaluation of extrinsic and intrinsic contamination and resulting spoilage of water-in-oil emulsions. *J. Appl. Microbiol*, 96,1124, 2004.
7. VaJderama M.J., Marquina, D., Peinado, J.M., Isolation, characterization and effect of *Candida albicans* isolated from a deteriorated cosmetic. *Int. J. Biodeter. Biodegrad.* 40,151,1997.
8. Bento, F.M. and Gaylarde, C.C., The production of interfacial emulsions by bacterial isolates from diesel fuels. *Int. J. Biodeter. Biodegrad.,* 38, 31, 1999.

9. *Bergey's Manual of Systematic Bacteriology*, Krieg, N. R. and Holt, J.G., Eds., Williams & Wilkins, Baltimore, 1984.
10. Wheatley, R.E., The consequences of volatile organic compound-mediated bacterial and fungal interactions. *Antonie Van Leeuwenhoek J. Microbiol.*, 81, 257, 2002.
11. Fainstein, V., Andres, N., Umphrey, J., and Hopfer, R. Hair clipping: another hazard for granulocytopenic patients. *J. Infect. Dis.*, 158, 655, 1988.
12. Anon., Nosocomial *Burkholderia cepacia* infections and colonization associated with intrinsically contaminated mouthwash: Arizona. *MMWR* 47, 926, 1998.
13. Passaro, D.J. Waing, J., Armstrong, L., Bolding, F., Bouvier, B., Rosenburg, J., Reingold A.W., McQuitty, M. PhilPott, S.M., Jarvis, W.R., Werner, S.B., Tompkins, L.S., and Vugia D.J., Postoperative *Serratia marcescens* wound infections traced to an out-of-hospital source. *J. Infect. Dis.*, 175, 992, 1997.
14. Orth, B., Frei, R., Itin, P.H., Rinaldi, M.G., Speck, B., Gratwohl, A. and Widmer, A.F., Outbreak of invasive mycoses caused by *Paecilomyces lilacinus* from a contaminated skin lotion. *Annals of internal medicine*, *125*(10), 799–806, 1996.
15. Itin, P.H., Frei, R., Lautenschlager, S., Buechner, S.A., Surber, C., Gratwohl, A. and Widmer, A.F., Cutaneous manifestations of *Paecilomyces lilacinus* infection induced by a contaminated skin lotion in patients who are severely immunosuppressed. *Journal of the American Academy of Dermatology*, *39*(3), 401–409, 1998.
16. Becks, V. and Lorenzoni, N., *Pseudomonas aeruginosa* outbreak in a neonatal intensive care unit: a possible link to contaminated hand lotion. *Am J Infect Control* 23, 396–398, 1995.
17. Taub, S.J., Contaminated cosmetics as a cause of eye infections. *Eye Ear Nose Throat Mon.*, 54, 81, 1975.
18. Brannan, D.K., Dille, J.C.and Kaufman. D.J., Correlation of *in vitro* challenge testing with consumer use testing of cosmetic products. *Appl. Env. Microbiol.*, 53, 1827, 1987.
19. Sutton, S. and Jimenez, L., A review of reported recalls involving microbiological control 2004–2011 with emphasis on FDA considerations of 'objectionable organisms'. *Am Pharmaceut Rev.*, 15, 42–57, 2012.
20. Wong, S., Street, D., Delgado, S. I. and Klontz, K.C., Recalls of foods and cosmetics due to microbial contamination reported to the U.S. Food and Drug Administration, *Journal of food protection*, 63(8), 1113–1116, 2000.
21. Vu, N., Lou, J.R. and Kupiec, T.C., Quality control analytical methods: microbial limit tests for nonsterile pharmaceuticals, Part 1. *International journal of pharmaceutical compounding*, *18*(3), 213–221, 2014.
22. Sharp, J. R., Good Manufacturing Practice, Philosophy and Applications, Buffalo Grove, IL: Interpharm Press, p47,1991.
23. Mitsui, T. (Ed.) Preservation of cosmetics. In New Cosmetic Science; Elsevier: Amsterdam, The Netherlands, 1997; pp. 199–208.
24. Geis, P.A. Cosmetic microbiology: A practical approach. In Cosmetic Microbiology: A Practical Approach; Geis, P.A., Ed.; Taylor & Francis: New York, NY, USA, 2006; pp. 163–180.

25. De Boer, E., Understanding and Implementing the Requirements of the ISO 22176 Good Manufacturing Practices (GMP) Certification Standard for Cosmetics Products. URL: SGS Offices & Labs. Available online: https://www.sgs.com/en/white-paper-library/cosmetics-gmp
26. De Villiers M.M., Antimicrobial preservatives In: A practical Guide to Contemporary Pharmacy Practice 3rd Edition, Lippincott Williams & Wilkins, pp.203-215, 2009.
27. Cosmetic Ingredient Review, Amended Safety Assessment of Parabens as Used in Cosmetics, Draft Tentative Amended Report for Panel Review, 211,2018.
28. Latorre, N., Silvestre, J.F. and Monteagudo, A.F., Allergic Contact Dermatitis Caused by Formaldehyde and Formaldehyde Releasers. *Actas Dermosifiliogr*. 102(2), 86–97, 2011
29. Silva, V., Silva, C., Soares, P., Garrido, E.M., Borges, F., and Garrido, J., Isothiazolinone Biocides: Chemistry, Biological, and Toxicity Profiles. *Molecules,* 25(4), 991, 2020.
30. Gurtler, J. B. and Mai, T. L., Traditional Preservatives – Organic Acids. *Encyclopedia of Food Microbiology, 119–130, 2014.* doi:10.1016/b978-0-12-384730-0.0
31. Rosen, V.E. and Berke, P A., Germall 115: a safe and effective preservative, in *Cosmetic and Drug Preservation*, Kabara, J.J., Ed., Marcel Dekker, New York,1984, p. 191
32. Mohiuddin, A.K., Cosmetics' Safety: Gray Areas with Darker Inside. *Journal of Dermatological Research,* **4(1),** 163-166, 2019.
33. Sheikh, A.G., Harmful effects of beauty care products on human health. *Int J Med Sci Public Health*, 7(1), 1-8, 2018.
34. Wang, M.T. and Craig, J.P., Investigating the effect of eye cosmetics on the tear film: current insights. *Clinical optometry,* 10, 33–40, 2018. https://doi.org/10.2147/OPTO.S150926
35. Diamanti-Kandarakis, E., Bourguignon, J.P., Giudice, L.C., Hauser, R., Prins, G.S., Soto, A.M., Zoeller, R.T. and Gore, A.C., Endocrine-disrupting chemicals: an Endocrine Society scientific statement. *Endocrine reviews,* 30(4), 293–342, 2009. https://doi.org/10.1210/er.2009-0002
36. Ma, X., Wang, H., Song, Y. and Pan, Y., Skin irritation potential of cosmetic preservatives: An exposure-relevant study. *Journal of Cosmetic Dermatology,* 20(1), 195–203, 2020.
37. Takeoka, G., Dao, L., Wong, R.Y., Lundin, R., and Mahoney, N., Identification of Benzethonium Chloride in Commercial Grapefruit Seed Extracts. *Journal of Agricultural and Food Chemistry,* 49(7), 3316–3320, 2001.
38. Post, L.S. and Davidson, P.M., Lethal effect of butylated hydroxyanisole as related to bacterial fatty acid composition. *Applied and Environmental Microbiology*, 7, 214-216, 1986.
39. Scholtyssek, R., Protection of cosmetics and toiletries. *Directory of Microbicides for the Protection of Materials,* 263–266, 2004.
40. Chouhan, S., Sharma, K. and Guleria, S., Antimicrobial Activity of Some Essential Oils - Present Status and Future Perspectives. *Medicines (Basel, Switzerland)*, 4(3), 58, 2017. https://doi.org/10.3390/medicines4030058
41. Varvaresou, A., Papageorgiou, S., Tsirivas, E., Protopapa, E., Kintziou, H., Kefala, V., and Demetzos, C., Self-preserving cosmetics, *Int. J. Cosmet. Sci.*, 31, 163–175, 2009.

42. Ibrahim, Y.K. and Sonntag, H.G., Effect of formulation pH and storage temperatures on the preservative efficacy of some gases used as propellants in cosmetic aerosols. *J. Appl. Bacterial*, 74,20,1993.
43. Brannan, D.K. and Dille, J.C., Type of closure prevents microbial contamination of cosmetics during consumer use. *Appl. Env. Microbiol.*, 56, 1476,1990.
44. Narcisco, J.A. and Parish, M.E., Endogenous mycoflora of gable-top carton paperboard used for packaging fruit juice. *J. Food. Sci.*, 62, 1917, 1997.
45. Wallhauser, K.H., Antimicrobial preservatives used by the cosmetic industry, in *Cosmetic and Drug Preservation*, Kabara, J.J., Ed., Marcel Dekker, New York, 1984, p. 605.
46. Sedlewicz, L.B., Preservatives demystified: a guide to choosing the correct preservative for your product. New York SCC Technical Note, 2005. http://www.nyscc.org/news/archive/tech0903/html
47. Collier, P.J., Ramsey, A., Waigh R.D., Douglas, K.T., Austin, P. and Gilbert, P., Chemical reactivity of some isothiazolinone biocides. *J. Appl. Microbiol.*, 69, 578, 1990.
48. Ma, M., Lee, T. and Kwong, E., Interaction of methyl paraben preservative with selected sugars and sugar alcohol. *J. Pharm. Sci.* 91,1715, 2002.
49. Kurup, T.R., Wan, L.S. and Chan, L.W., Interaction of preservatives with macromolecules I: natural hydrocolloids. *Pharm. Acta Helv.*, 67, 301,1992.
50. Scalzo, M., Orlandi, C., Simonetti, N. and Cerreto, F., Study of interactive effects of polyacrylic acid polymers (Carbopol 940) on antimicrobial activity of methyl parahydroxybenzoate against some Cram-negative, Gram-positive bacteria and yeast. *J. Pharm. Pharmacol.*, 48, 1201, 1996.
51. Orth, D.S., Lutes-Anderson, C.M., Smith D.K. and Milstein, S.R., Synergism of preservative system components: use of survival curve slope method to demonstrate anti-Pseudomonas synergy of methyl paraben and acrylic acid homopolymer/copolymer *in vitro. J. Soc. Cosmet. Chem.*, 40, 347, 1989.
52. Rassat, F., Gonzenbach, H. and Pittet, G.H., Use of sunscreen and vitamins in daily-use cosmetics. *Drug Cosmet. Ind.*, December, 16, 1997.
53. Chapman, J. S., Diehl, M. A. and Fearnside, K. B., Preservative tolerance and resistance. *International journal of cosmetic science*, *20*(1), 31–39, 1998.
54. Chapman, J.S., Characterizing bacterial resistance to preservatives and disinfectants. *Int. Biodegrad.*, 41, 241, 1998.
55. Chapman, J.S., Diehl, M.A., and Fearnside, K.B., Characterization of preservative-resistant bacteria, in *Abstracts of the 95th Meeting of the American Society for Microbiology*, Washington, D.C., 1996.
56. Stewart, P.S. and Costerton, J.W., Antibiotic resistance of bacteria in biofilms. *Lancet*, 358: 135 – 138, 2001.
57. Halla, N., Fernandes, I. P., Heleno, S. A., Costa, P., Boucherit-Otmani, Z., Boucherit, K., Rodrigues, A. E., Ferreira, I. and Barreiro, M. F., Cosmetics Preservation: A Review on Present Strategies. *Molecules (Basel, Switzerland)*, 23(7), 1571, 2018.

CHAPTER TWENTY

Cosmetics clinical trials and evaluation

Sharon I Igbinoba

Entrenched in the stages of drug product development is a process where medicines to be used in/on humans are subjected to scrutiny to ensure their safety and efficacy. Like pharmaceuticals, it is also equally expected and expedient that cosmetics are safe when used as instructed by the manufacturer (1). Processes of drug development are divided into the pre-clinical and clinical stages with the latter involving studies done in human subjects. Clinical trials, a stage in drug development process, are instrumental for evidence-based medicine and practice. The main purpose of clinical trial stage of drug development is to establish **safety** and **efficacy** of the developed pharmaceutical products (2). Unlike clinical trials for pharmaceuticals or medicines which have been well established and regulated by regulatory bodies, the need to subject cosmetics products to rigorous clinical trials have only started to gain momentum over the recent years (3).

The essence of clinical studies is to obtain reliable proof for the claims of products or procedures that influence their approval for use by the public. The technological revolution of the century has continued to improve the testing methods employed in clinical studies. A good clinical study relies on a robust research design and appropriate statistical analysis. The rapid influx of cosmetic products into the markets only strengthens the need for reliable evidence-based clinical studies of cosmetics. The role of clinical testing of cosmetics will continue to validate the product claims that are used in packaging and advertising and, at the same time, ensure that safe and effective cosmetic products are available to consumers. This has become vital in an era where consumers have access to a huge amount of information leading to more demands and expectations from consumers on the use of their cosmetics coupled with advertising companies which are now being more stringent and diligent with their responsibilities. Conducting clinical trials are not without challenges but going all out to ensure that robust clinical data are generated is important for overcoming challenges in conducting successful clinical trials.

What clinical trials entail

In brief, clinical trials are researches or studies conducted to test new treatments or products and assess their impact on human health. These trials are carefully designed and approved by ethical committees before commencement. Volunteers for the study would normally participate in the test involving a new product either under normal conditions of use that is referred to as "in use" tests, or under appropriate experimental conditions (2).

The four stages of clinical trials for medicines which can also be applied to cosmetics clinical trials, depending on the type of cosmetics, are:

Phase I studies: This phase involves the first-time test of new products/drugs on a few numbers of people (who have no underlying health conditions) to determine the safe dose and side effects.

Phase II studies: Here, the test agent, at a dose that has been found to be safe for use in phase I, is monitored in large numbers of humans, usually several hundred participants, for adverse effect if any.

Phase III studies: These are carried out on a larger number of people across regions and countries and for longer durations, before a new drug product or treatment is approved.

Phase IV studies: This phase is the post-marketing surveillance (PMS) study and begins with the approval to market the drug. The safety of the drug is closely monitored in larger populations over a very long period and can reveal adverse effects that were not captured in Phase III.

Purpose of cosmetics clinical trials

According to the efficacy evaluation guideline of the European Cosmetic Association, cosmetic claim substantiation should be integrated into product development and should serve the purpose of supporting the communication of product performance and benefits. The clinical evaluation or trial of cosmetics is intended to provide evidence confirming a manufacturer's claims of safety; ascertain product compliance with the requirements of high level of safety and health as it relates to the properties, functionality and the suitability of the ingredients under normal conditions of use; assess the undesired potential adverse situations that may result from the use of the product and the collection of the information on user's experience on the product of interest (4).

A manufacturer or company involved in clinical evaluation of its cosmetics product is expected to gather specific safety and efficacy data. It is necessary to monitor if the original activity of the cosmetic product is achieved in the end-users. It is also important to ensure the appropriate application of the cosmetic product, both in terms of appropriately identifying the product by recipients as well as proper use of the product itself (1).

Regulation of cosmetic products for safety and efficacy purpose

The main purpose of regulatory agencies and framework is to ensure consumers are protected from erroneous or false claims regarding efficacy of cosmetic products. Cosmetic products are expected to demonstrate efficacy when used by consumers following the labelled instruction, normal use or unexpected conditions of use. Regulations of cosmetic products vary from country to country and from one regulatory body to another and there are no distinctively clear and harmonised guidelines for efficacy testing of cosmetic products (5). For example, the regulation in India does not mandate clinical trials for all cosmetic products that are imported into the Indian market provided they are already approved in markets outside India. In the United States of America (USA), the Food and Drug Administration (FDA), an agency of the government, does not have to approve cosmetics before marketing but requires that labelling of cosmetics meets certain FDA requirements, such as inclusion of common name of the product, net weight, names of ingredients in order of prominence, name and address of manufacturer, warning statement, and statement on drug claim. Violation of cosmetics labelling requirement may attract detention of shipment at the port of entry. In the United Kingdom (UK), the manufacture and supply of all cosmetic products is governed by both the UK cosmetics regulation and the European Union (EU) cosmetics regulation. The main objective of the UK regulation is to ensure that a cosmetic product does not cause harm, does not contain any prohibited product and is correctly labelled. Most regulatory agencies have similar goals of ensuring that cosmetics supplied to consumers satisfy their requirements for safety and efficacy.

The problem with the lack of common ground or guideline for efficacy-testing leaves a gap which could lead to misleading claims of cosmetic products' efficacy, thus, compromising consumer protection. The regulatory prerequisites may not be effective in substantiating cosmetics claims and efficacy if well spelt out methods of testing are not made available to cosmetic manufacturers (5,6).

Safety of cosmetics - Is it a point of concern?

The different definitions and descriptions of what qualifies as cosmetics have been explicitly presented in the introductory chapter of this book. The definitions suggest that cosmetics are traditionally not meant or intended to have significant or appreciable systemic effects. Even though cosmetics are expected to produce low risks to the end-users or consumers, since they are typically not meant to be absorbed into the body for systemic action, certain risks may be inherent in their use. Irrespective of the region from which a definition of cosmetic products emanates, there is an agreement that these products need to be subjected to a review process by regulatory bodies before being accepted for use. This consensus arose out of the understanding that cosmetics have chemical components that could, potentially, cause harm to the individual using them. Examples of such chemicals include mercury which can damage the kidneys and nervous system; formaldehyde and coal tar (a known carcinogen); ethanolamines (that are linked to liver tumors and other organ damages); parabens (that are used as preservatives in cosmetics, and which can be absorbed through the skin to affect the blood and digestive system and can disrupt the endocrine system). A manufacturer of cosmetic products is, therefore, expected to conduct product-testing to ensure the safety of their products. Adverse effect from cosmetics use is not common, and certain individuals, when exposed to cosmetic ingredients, may experience a range of adverse effects in the form of mild tingling sensations or soreness/redness to more serious allergic reactions (6,7).

Toxicological test is an aspect of safety-testing which ascertains if any risk is associated with the cosmetic product's ingredient or its mixture. Examples of such tests include skin irritation, corrosion and sensitisation (patch testing) test, as well as eye corrosion and irritation test (8). The safety health issues that could arise from using a cosmetic product is known as **Endpoints of Concern**. For instance, when a compound can be ingested, penetrate the skin or be absorbed dermally, the metabolism, distribution throughout the body, and excretion of the compound should be investigated. For such a compound to be acceptable for use and for regulatory labelling purposes, an important toxic endpoint for such a product will be to understand whether the compound is a mutagen or genotoxin (7). This detailed process of not only identifying but quantifying the risk in cosmetics is known as **Cosmetic Risk Assessment.** The current opinion on risk assessment of cosmetics is that it consists of four steps: hazard identification, dose-response assessment, exposure assessment and risk characterisation.

Hazard identification or analysis: This is the process of evaluating the type of harm or danger that could be caused by a cosmetic product. The analysis is often done by specially trained scientists known as toxicologists, who evaluate the risk associated with each of the components in the eventual product, in order to determine what the overall risk of using the product is. Examples of hazards in cosmetics could be skin irritation (7).

Dose-response assessment: As relating to cosmetics, this assesses the association between the dose or amount of the cosmetic agent and the incidence of a defined biological effect in an exposed population, for example, association between bleaching creams and incidence of skin cancer in patients.

Exposure assessment: This is the process of estimating or measuring the magnitude, frequency, and duration of exposure to an agent, along with the number and characteristics of the population exposed, for instance, exposure assessment of a population exposed to the heavy metals in cosmetics.

Risk characterisation: This is the last of the four steps of risk assessment. It is defined as an estimation of the probability of occurrence and severity of known or potential adverse health effects in a population based on the preceding steps of hazard identification, hazard characterisation, and exposure assessment (9,10). Although most risks evaluated are based on the intended method of use of the product, some risks that are peculiar with cosmetics may also arise from unintended use or misuse. An example will be a face moisturiser that gets ingested. This type of risk must also be investigated by the toxicologist. Evaluation for ocular irritation or ingestion harm are quite common with cosmetic products even if they are not intended to be used around the eyes or lips. This evaluation would also be taken into consideration when designing the labels for such products (7).

Numerous organisations are available to provide guidance for assessing the risks of use of cosmetic products. Examples include: Cosmetic Ingredient Review (CIR) expert panel in the USA and the European Chemicals Agency (ECHA) in Europe (11). The National Agency for Food and Drug Administration and Control (NAFDAC) has been empowered by an act to regulate clinical trials in Nigeria. Here, the law stipulates that only a holder of a valid clinical trial certificate can conduct clinical tests on cosmetics (12). The knowledge that risks and hazards can be associated with the use of cosmetics requires the establishment of regulations to assure safety and efficacy of cosmetic products when used following the labelling instruction. Clinical trial research of a cosmetic product before it is accepted for use is necessary for ensuring safety and efficacy (12,13). Cosmetics safety-testing can be conducted on varieties of cosmetic products ranging from oral care, skin, foot, hair care products, and colour cosmetics (foundations, lip sticks, eye shadow) (14).

Clinical efficacy studies and evaluation of cosmetic products

Extensive and comprehensive safety assessment of individual ingredients in cosmetic products should be carried out prior to efficacy testing to rule out local or systemic adverse reactions. Clinical evaluation of cosmetics for efficacy should be objective and quantitative, as much as possible, and the study protocol that allows the same effect of the cosmetics to be assessed at different endpoints is highly recommended. This is particularly of advantage as a linear relationship between the results of each endpoint further gives credence to the effect under study. At the same time, the influence of confounders should be put in perspective and made adjustment for, in the effect observed (3). Efficacy testing should only be conducted in humans when there is established evidence of safety of the product, and even at that, there should be a lookout for adverse effect alongside the efficacy testing (5). The schematic diagram in Figure 20.1 depicts the steps in the clinical evaluation of cosmetics.

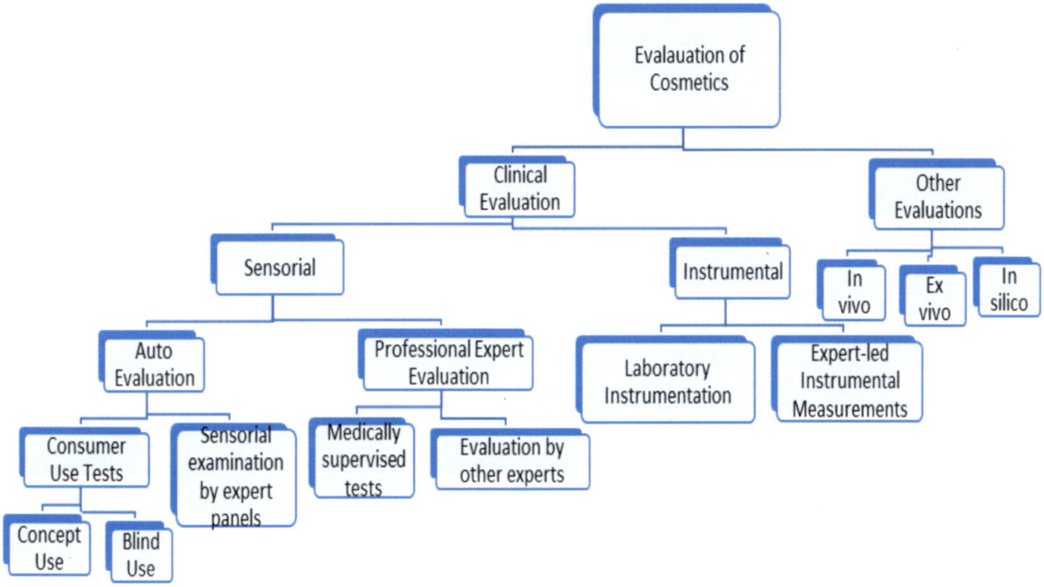

Figure 20.1: Various tests involved in cosmetics evaluation

Approaches to conducting cosmetic products' clinical trials and evaluation

Ethical considerations are an essential aspect of the biomedical research involving the use of human participants. Cosmetics testing on humans, employing skin measurement techniques, is a form of biomedical research that is both basic and applied (5). The World Medical Association (WMA) General Assembly, in the declaration of Helsinki in Finland, in June 1964, provided ethical consideration principles on any biomedical research involving human subjects and the principles declared should be adhered to in cosmetics clinical trials (15).

The intended use of a cosmetic product determines the type of test or experiment required. In other words, "the claim dictates the test". The claim could be for ingredients, performance or sensory based. Usually, a combination of methods may be employed to arrive at the final decision on the quality, safety and efficacy of cosmetic products. Clinical trials give scientific validity to the cosmetics available in the market, further establishing its safety. The tests are described as follows:

Sensorial tests

The sensory attributes of cosmetics are pertinent in cosmetics science and determines whether the product is liked and used by consumers. The method of assessment of the product will depend on the sensory properties of interest and the required claims. These tests evaluate the product based on the professional/expert view or the consumer'/user's experience of the product (5). The tests could be:

Auto-tests: In this test, consumer and the expert panels are involved. The *consumer-use tests* could be *"concept use"* or *"blind use"* based. In the concept use, the communication of the product to the user is evaluated to ensure that the message communicated by the manufacturer matches that understood by the end-user. The evaluation of the communication is important since cosmetic products usually have certain peculiar instructions for their use. The blind use tests exclude brand information or it supplies the cosmetic product in an anonymous pack which would not influence the consumer's evaluation of the product.

Professional evaluation test: This is usually done by medical professionals, e.g., dermatologists and other professionals with relevant expertise such as aestheticians, make-up artists or basic scientists, and such evaluation usually involves comparison with a placebo or a reference (4). In this, expert-grading, based on a reference scale for scoring a product is used, and it is preferred that the scoring scales should factor in a consumer perception of the product. The expertise (whether conducted by a dermatologist, ophthalmologist or non-clinical scientist) and training required for a study must be sustained throughout the duration of the study (5,16). Sensory assessment can be affected by several factors which may be environmental or human related. A drawback of the sensory test may be subjectivity of assessment of the cosmetics if the physical and mental states of health, the sensitivity in respect of senses of smell and taste, of the evaluator is not normal. For effective sensory evaluation, the purpose of the study should be recognised by the analyst who should also ensure that the choice of appropriate experimental design, selection of panelists who fit the purpose, and the proper method for preparing and presenting the samples, and analysis of the data, are correctly done (17).

Instrumental tests

Instrumental testing of cosmetics has been made feasible due to the advances in technology, particularly in the aspects of bioengineering. Instrumentation tests often involve determination of certain parameters such as the roughness or the protection afforded by the cosmetic products against ultraviolet (UV) radiation. Many of these tests are done with standard apparatuses and compared against certain pre-determined standards. The complexity of the tests would determine the type of expertise required. For instance, trichogram analysis for hair products would need to be performed by highly skilled persons (4). Current science makes available a variety of methods for safety- and efficacy-testing of cosmetic products, as is the case of 3D image analysis devices and software that are applicable for the quantification of features such as facial wrinkles, eye bags, cellulite, and scalp hair. A draw-back to instrumentation test is when the effect quantified by the instrument is so small that it is not noticeable by the consumer and, thus, does not find relevance to the consumer. To overcome this, grading by expert or consumer assessment test should always be done alongside instrumentation test so as to improve the relationship between the instrumental measurement and the claim.

Interestingly, a number of devices are available for the efficacy-testing of cosmetics. Examples are the C+K devices which are used for efficacy and claim support of cosmetics and other products. Examples of some efficacy tests that can be done by these devices include: skin hydration measurement, assessment of trans-epidermal water loss, skin elasticity measurement, measurement of gloss of skin, hair product and decorative cosmetics, as well as analysis of macro- wrinkles (18).

Alternative testing to clinical evaluation of cosmetics in humans

Animal testing: The use of animals as an alternate option to using human clinical trials for the testing of cosmetics is sometimes preferred by manufacturers and consumers. The FDA recommends the development of alternatives rather than whole-animal testing for the testing of the safety of cosmetic products (6). The FDA policy on developing alternative methods provides information on the legal criteria for cosmetic safety. For instance, the Federal Food, Drug and Cosmetics Acts (FD&C Act) does not specify the use of animals for the testing of the safety of cosmetics prior to market approval. The agency however advises manufacturers of cosmetics to employ any appropriate test that effectively substantiates the safety of their products before marketing (6). FDA supports and adheres to the provisions of applicable laws, regulations, and policies governing animal-testing, and where animals must be used, a most humane approach should be employed while also not compromising the scientific validity of the test (10). To date, over 41 countries have passed laws to limit or ban cosmetics animal-testing, some of which include every country in the European Union, Australia, Colombia, Guatemala, Iceland, India, Israel, Mexico, New Zealand, Norway, South Korea, Switzerland, Taiwan, Turkey, the United Kingdom, and several states in Brazil.

Ex vivo and in vitro testing*:* There are some evaluations done in/with animal tissues or cell parts (ex vivo and in vitro studies, respectively) and these tests provide supplementary decisions to those used in clinical tests. Ex vivo tests involve using animal tissues in an artificial environment with conditions to mimic the natural conditions. In vitro tests usually involve using a part of an organism that has been isolated from its original environment (20). Ex vivo methods are gaining much popularity because they provide a more reliable observation of how the subject is affected. Common examples of ex vivo test in cosmetic evaluations include: skin explants used in testing the properties of a skin preparation. A common ex vivo method available for evaluation of skin irritants and subsequently for classification of irritant/non-irritant cosmetic products is the use of OECD TG439 Reconstructed Human Epidermis (RHE) (21,22). In a cosmetics evaluation using ex vivo irritation test performed on human skin explants, it was found that irrespective of the part of the body where the human skin originated, a reproducible and graded irritancy, which was comparable to human patch test with high accuracy and specificity, was observed (22).

The proliferation of 3-D reconstructed tissue models in product-testing is relatively new. Use of such 3-D reconstructed tissue models is getting regulatory approval as this approach will spare animals pains and even death. These models are also reliable, cost-effective, and a predictive alternative to animal experimentation. A recognised cosmetics company, EpiDerm, uses human skin cells that have been retrieved from surgical waste materials after cosmetic surgeries and circumcisions, or through procurement from tissue banks or commercial outlets, to assess the efficacy and tolerability of cosmetics ingredients premarketing (23). Table 20.1 shows a list of in vitro and in vivo efficacy testing done by a cosmetics company, Eurofins Scientific, on a range of cosmetic products (24).

***In silico* testing:** A new type of test, known as *in silico* testing, is yet to be employed fully in cosmetics testing but it has great potentials. This test is performed via computer simulation by collecting data from human parts, such as the hair and the skin, and feeding them into a model to predict how a material will function in the real world (25). The utilisation of the test is expected to increase in the future with rising clamour for the restriction of animal testing.

The guiding principles in designing a test remains that they should rely on sound scientific principles and the methods employed must be robust, reproducible and validated. The fact that many of such tests would be performed on living organisms (including humans) requires that all ethical principles, with respect to the conduct of scientific research, be respected and complied with.

Table 20.1: Efficacy testing done by a cosmetics company, Eurofins Scientific (24)

• **Oral hygiene products**	
In vitro tests	***In vivo tests***
Action against biofilms	Mouthwash cleansing activity Breath freshener activity
Cleaning efficacy	
• **Hair products**	
In vitro tests	***In vivo tests***
Inhibition of 5-a-reductase	Seboregulator activity
Inhibition of lipase	Anti-fall and anti-dandruff
	Resistance to humidity (curl-retention)
	Assessment of hair-damages
	Curl fixation
	Sensory characterization
• **Skin care products**	
In vitro tests	***In vivo tests***
Anti-ageing activity	Anti-cellulite and anti-stretch
Anti-oxidant activity	Moisturising and firming activity
Collagen and elastin synthesis	Barrier effect and absorption of fats
Hyaluronic acid synthesis	Activity emollient (soothing test)
Anti-inflammatory analyses	Sensory characterization
Percutaneous absorption	Evaluation of the cutaneous microcirculation
Depigmenting activity	Anti-perspirant and deodorant activity
Barrier or protective effect	Reduction / elimination of comedones
Exfoliating activity	Anti-wrinkle
Action healing	Activity depigmenting

	Exfoliating activity
	Tonic activity
	Relaxing activity

Setting up a cosmetics evaluation committee

In order to ensure that the principles of safety and efficacy of cosmetic products are adhered to, a committee of experts is required to constituted, which will address the varying parts of the process. One of the major tasks of this committee is to oversee the design of the study protocol which ensures that acceptable methods have been employed in the evaluation of the efficacy of the product(s) in question (4). The committee is also to ensure that during the process of evaluation, the tests are carried out exactly the way they were described in the study protocol and that all ethical principles are upheld. The committee also ensures that the data obtained is analysed with acceptable statistical methods and that the results obtained from the analysis are not exaggerated or misrepresented. To ensure that such a committee can carry out all these functions, it must be constituted of individuals who:

- are suitably qualified,
- have the requisite knowledge/skills to evaluate the tests, and
- are respected for their professional integrity.

It is also necessary that the committee oversees the qualifications of those working on the test procedures so as to be sure that there are no gaps in knowledge, and to address these early enough before the evaluations begin. This may be particularly relevant if different types of cosmetic products need to be evaluated simultaneously, or if the technician do not have experience with a particular testing protocol to be employed.

Components of a study protocol for cosmetic testing

The study protocol usually contains two major types of information:

General information: The general information usually refers to the information pertaining to the reason for the study, the type of product, details about the study procedure to be employed, data acquisition and management and the equipment to be used in the study.

Specific information: The specific information covers information about the study subjects, an in-depth look at the tests employed such as use tests and the sensorial evaluation tests.

Table 20.2: Components of a clinical research protocol

• Idea/Hypothesis/question - This portion states the claim that is to be investigated by the study.
• Literature summary and rationale for the study in question, or background to the study - This describes the background of the study and the scientific basis for the study.
• Study Objectives - The study protocol should give as much as possible a comprehensive description of the study objective and purposes.
• Methodology - Method to be employed should be appropriate to the study
• Study design (Interventional or observational) - The description of the study design should include the following information or details: (i) a detailed description on the endpoints (primary and secondary) to be measured during the study, (ii) a description of the study type/design (e.g., is it a placebo-controlled, uncontrolled, double blind, etc.), (iii) a detailed diagram of the study flow, (iv) a chart reporting the schedule of the assessments, (v) the expected duration of the study, (vi) a description of the "stopping rule" or "discontinuation criteria" for individual subjects, and (vii) the maintenance of study treatment randomisation codes and/or the measures taken in order to safeguard the study blindness (when applicable). a) Randomised controlled clinical trials (RCT) are the best approach for determining intervention efficacy in specific situations. In RCT treatments, active ingredient and placebo are assigned to subjects in a randomised and unpredictable pattern. b) Observer-blind or single-blind design is another study that may suffice where the assessor or subject is unaware of the test product assigned. Design that minimises interindividual variability is preferred in cosmetics testing, for instance applying a product to half of the body or face where test products or placebo/control group are allocated in this design. Researchers can make use of other study designs that are applicable to cosmetics.
• Selection and withdrawal of subjects – Inclusion and Exclusion criteria should be explicitly stated. The criteria must be specified before the recruitment of volunteers to ensure credibility and reduce confounders.

• Treatment - The treatment on human subjects should be well described to include information about; the name (including the reference and the batch numbers of the product and a statement to indicate that the products were formulated in compliance to the required regulation, and also including that the product safety has been considered and addressed and safe on humans following the usage instruction.
• Efficacy and safety measures or assessment: The specific efficacy or safety test, the methods to assess, record the test, and analyse the efficacy and safety parameters should be clearly described in the study protocol.
• Statistical Analysis - The data obtained from the research experiments need to be interpreted in a way that is meaningful. Descriptive and inferential statistical methods, to be employed, the level of significance to be used, the way to account for missing data etc., the selection of subjects to be included in the analyses (e.g., all randomised subjects, all dosed subjects, all eligible subjects, evaluable subjects) should be clearly described in the study protocol before the study starts to avoid statistical mistakes that could affect the credibility of the results obtained. Also, a statistician needs to be consulted before the study begins, to review the robustness of the proposed statistical methods.

In designing the general aims of the study, the consideration should be on the identification and interpretation of novel findings. The evaluation should aim to investigate the new product, vis-à-vis, the claims that have been put forward by the manufacturers. The results of the study should reject, confirm or modify the knowledge presented by the manufacturers of the product. The overall goal is to produce reliable and reproducible results that could assist regulatory agencies, healthcare practitioners, other researchers and the end-users in making an informed decision about the product (2). Regardless of the type of clinical area that is being investigated, a typical protocol based on sound ethical and scientific bases (5,26,27) should include the following as shown in Table 20.2.

References

1. Healthy Cosmetics: Safety, Ingredients, and More [Internet]. Healthline. 2014 [cited 2022 Mar 25]. Available from: https://www.healthline.com/health/beauty-skin-care-cosmetics

2. Clinical trials [Internet]. [cited 2022 Mar 19]. Available from: https://www.who.int/westernpacific/health-topics/clinical-trials
3. innovationsite.pl. Clinical evaluation of cosmetic products | Flow Clinical Evaluation Institute EN [Internet]. [cited 2022 Mar 19]. Available from: https://www.instituteflow.com/clinical-evaluation-of-cosmetic-products
4. Cosmetic Europe. COLIPA Guidelines Efficacy Evaluation of Cosmetic Products [Internet]. Cosmetics Europe the Personal Care Association; 2008. Available from: https://www.cosmeticseurope.eu/files/4214/6407/6830/Guidelines_for_the_Evaluation_of_the_Efficacy_of_Cosmetic_Products_-_2008.pdf
5. Nobile V. Guidelines on Cosmetic Efficacy Testing on Humans. Ethical, Technical, and Regulatory Requirements in the Main Cosmetics Markets. J Cosmetol Trichology [Internet]. 2016 [cited 2022 May 11];02(01). Available from: https://www.omicsonline.org/open-access/guidelines-on-cosmetic-efficacy-testing-on-humans-ethical-technical-and-regulatory-requirements-in-the-main-cosmetics-markets-jctt1000107.php?aid=68398
6. FDA/Company Cosmetic Registration Program [Internet]. Cosmetics Info. [cited 2022 Mar 19]. Available from: https://www.cosmeticsinfo.org/regulation-and-oversight/fda-company-cosmetic-registration-program/
7. Toxicological Evaluation of Cosmetics: A Primer [Internet]. Cosmetics & Toiletries. 2021 [cited 2022 Mar 19]. Available from: https://www.cosmeticsandtoiletries.com/testing/safety-stability/article/21836410/toxicological-evaluation-of-cosmetics-a-primer
8. Cosmetic Product Safety & testing: Which Tests are Required? [Internet]. CPG, F&B and Cosmetic: a blog on NPD issues and software. 2018 [cited 2022 May 11]. Available from: https://www.inno-foodproducts-brainbox.com/2018/05/31/which-tests-to-ensure-cosmetic-product-safety/
9. European Commission. Directorate General for Health and Consumers. Addressing the new challenges for risk assessment. [Internet]. LU: Publications Office; 2013 [cited 2022 Jun 7]. Available from: https://data.europa.eu/doi/10.2772/37863
10. Kim KB, Kwack SJ, Lee JY, Kacew S, Lee BM. Current opinion on risk assessment of cosmetics. J Toxicol Environ Health Part B. 2021 May 19;24(4):137–61.
11. Expert Panel for Cosmetic Ingredient Safety [Internet]. Personal Care Products Council. [cited 2022 May 14]. Available from: https://www.personalcarecouncil.org/science-safety/cosmetic-ingredient-review/
12. NAFDAC. NAFDAC-Good-Clinical-Practices-Guidelines-2020.pdf [Internet]. 2015 [cited 2022 Mar 19]. Available from: https://www.nafdac.gov.ng/wp-content/uploads/Files/Resources/Guidelines/CTD_Guidelines/NAFDAC-Good-Clinical-Practices-Guidelines-2020.pdf
13. Clinical Testing of Cosmetics and Personal Care Products [Internet]. [cited 2022 Mar 19]. Available from: https://www.intertek.com/consumer-healthcare-trials/
14. VibeThemes. Product categories in the cosmetic industry [Internet]. Chemists Corner. 2015 [cited 2022 Mar 25]. Available from: https://chemistscorner.com/product-categories-in-the-cosmetic-industry/

15. WMA - The World Medical Association-WMA Declaration of Helsinki – Ethical Principles for Medical Research Involving Human Subjects [Internet]. [cited 2022 May 14]. Available from: https://www.wma.net/policies-post/wma-declaration-of-helsinki-ethical-principles-for-medical-research-involving-human-subjects/
16. Lemperle G, Holmes RE, Cohen SR, Lemperle SM. A classification of facial wrinkles. Plast Reconstr Surg. 2001 Nov;108(6):1735–50; discussion 1751-1752.
17. Busch P, Gassenmeier T. Evaluation of Cosmetics by Sensory Assessment. In: Schwindt DA, Maibach HI, editors. Cutaneous Biometrics [Internet]. Boston, MA: Springer US; 2000 [cited 2022 Jun 5]. p. 65–80. Available from: http://link.springer.com/10.1007/978-1-4615-1199-1_6
18. Courage + Khazaka Electronic, Köln - Efficacy Tests [Internet]. [cited 2022 May 11]. Available from: https://www.courage-khazaka.de/en/scientific-products/efficacy-tests
19. Nutrition C for FS and A. Animal Testing & Cosmetics. FDA [Internet]. 2022 Mar 4 [cited 2022 Mar 19]; Available from: https://www.fda.gov/cosmetics/product-testing-cosmetics/animal-testing-cosmetics
20. Costa A, Lindmark L, Arruda LHF, Assumpção EC, Ota FS, Pereira M de O, et al. Clinical, biometric and ultrasound assessment of the effects of daily use of a nutraceutical composed of lycopene, acerola extract, grape seed extract and Biomarine Complex in photoaged human skin. An Bras Dermatol. 2012 Feb;87(1):52–61.
21. OECD. Test No. 439: In Vitro Skin Irritation: Reconstructed Human Epidermis Test Method [Internet]. Paris: Organization for Economic Co-operation and Development; 2021 [cited 2022 Mar 19]. Available from: https://www.oecd-ilibrary.org/environment/test-no-439-in-vitro-skin-irritation-reconstructed-human-epidermis-test-method_9789264242845-en
22. Matarrese P, Beauchef G, Peno-Mazzarino L, Lati E, Fitoussi R, Vié K. Assessment of an ex vivo irritation test performed on human skin explants and comparison of its results with those of a 24-/48-h human patch test for the evaluation of cosmetics. Toxicol In Vitro. 2021 Feb;70:105030.
23. CNBC.com BW special to. Companies are making human skin in labs to curb animal testing of products [Internet]. CNBC. 2017 [cited 2022 Mar 25]. Available from: https://www.cnbc.com/2017/05/25/loreal-is-making-lab-produced-human-skin-to-curb-animal-testing.html
24. Cosmetics Efficacy studies [Internet]. Efficacy studies. [cited 2022 May 11]. Available from: https://www.eurofins.com/human-safety-toxicology-testing/our-testing-services/for-cosmetics/efficacy-studies/
25. How in silico screening can guide product development in cosmetics [Internet]. QIMA Life Sciences. 2020 [cited 2022 Mar 19]. Available from: https://qima-lifesciences.com/en/in-silico-screening-cosmetics/
26. Bagatin E, Miot HA. How to design and write a clinical research protocol in Cosmetic Dermatology. An Bras Dermatol. 2013;88(1):69–75.
27. International Nomenclature of Cosmetic Ingredients (INCI) [Internet]. [cited 2022 May 14]. Available from: https://www.cirsreach.com/Cosmetic_Inventory/International_Nomenclature_of_Cosmetic_Ingredients_INCI.html

CHAPTER TWENTY-ONE

Adverse reactions to cosmetics

Aderonke D Dawotola

Adverse reactions can arise from exposure to a variety of ingredients and compounds found in household items. These unintended and untoward reactions even occur from the use of cosmetics, which are supposed to make the user feel more beautiful. An average number of adults use cosmetics daily; however, their use has been associated with many adverse reactions, generally traced to either the active ingredients or the excipients/vehicles in a particular formulation. The rapid proliferation and diversification of cosmetics products come with increased cases of irritant and contact dermatitis that are associated with the use of cosmetics. Data from studies conducted in Africa, Asia and the Middle East show a high incidence of adverse reactions to cosmetics (1). The increased usage of cosmetics in the general population is also fueled by the fact that there is a wide range of ingredients available to the cosmetic formulators to make a variety of products that are pleasing and attractive to consumers. In a research conducted by the Environmental Working Group, an average adult uses nine cosmetic products while more than 25% of women use 15 or more. On the average, a woman uses 12 personal care products daily, which comprise 168 ingredients, while a man uses 6 personal care products daily with 85 ingredients (2).

A high prevalence of cosmetic use-related adverse reactions occurs but are generally underreported or overlooked compared to adverse drug reactions. This may be because cosmetic products have less stringent regulatory requirements in many countries. For instance, in the United States of America (USA), there is no clear regulation by the Food and Drug Administration (FDA) requiring cosmetic manufacturers to conduct safety and efficacy testing before products are marketed or to report adverse reactions of products to the FDA (3). The FDA does not have a premarket approval system for cosmetic products or ingredients, with the important exception of colour additives, unlike pharmaceutical products and over-the-counter (OTC) drugs. The level of regulation in developing countries is generally poor compared to that of the United States, European Union (EU), United Kingdom, Canada, and Japan.

Types of adverse reactions to cosmetics

Cosmetics manufacturers conduct safety tests to protect users against possible adverse reactions. However, because cosmetics are not well regulated nor require premarket approval in most countries before being launched into the market, adverse reactions to cosmetics do occur, even though they are generally safe and well-tolerated by most users (4). The use of cosmetics is known to cause a wide array of adverse reactions, including pigment disorders, irritant contact dermatitis, allergic contact dermatitis, contact urticaria, photosensitisation, damage of hair and nails, and acneiform eruption; with contact dermatitis reported most frequently. Adverse reactions to cosmetics represent a small, but significant, proportion (10%) of contact dermatitis cases, and this can be irritant or allergic or a combination of both. It is generally difficult to differentiate irritant dermatitis from allergic dermatitis without doing a skin patch test of the suspected skincare products and their ingredients (5).

Figure 21.1: Contact dermatitis reported in most patients (6)

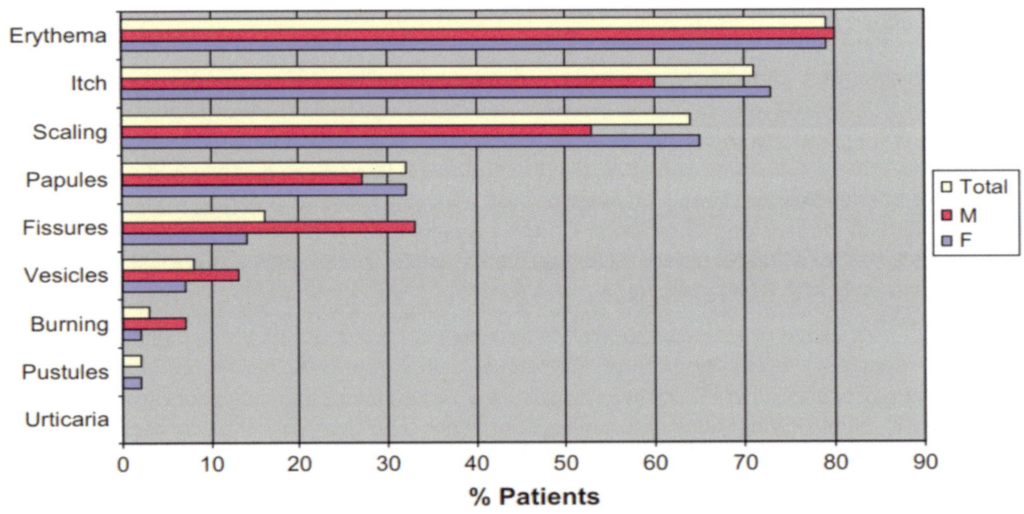

In a study involving 151 patients reported to have used 533 products in total, mostly moisturisers and eye make-up, the most common signs and symptoms of adverse reactions observed were those related to contact dermatitis (Figure 21.1).

The face was the most affected site of the body among females, while the hand was the most affected among men (6). The final observation recorded after patch testing, demonstrated irritant dermatitis (41 cases, 27%) to be as common as allergic contact dermatitis (42 cases, 28%), among the 530 products that were tested (Table 21. 1) (6).

Figure 21.2: Affected body sites of females and males by cosmetics (6)

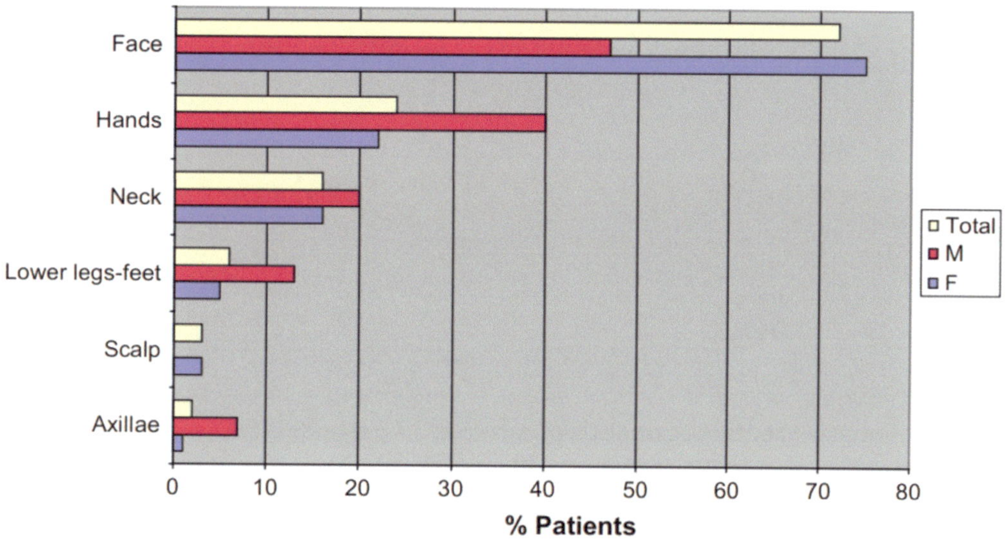

Table 21.1: Study of adverse reactions of 151 patients who used cosmetic products (6)

Diagnosis	Females	Males	Total
Allergic contact dermatitis	41	1	42
Irritant contact dermatitis	37	4	41
Unspecified eczema	33	5	38
Atopic eczema	29	4	33
Seborrhoeic eczema	7	1	8
Others (psoriasis and rosacea)	10	3	13

The frequency of adverse reactions to cosmetics usage was also demonstrated in another study where 176 patients who presented at a medical dermatology practice with dermatosis caused by cosmetics were observed and evaluated over a period of 10 years. The most common dermatoses related to cosmetics were (Table 21.2): contact dermatitis, seborrhoeic dermatitis, and alopecia. Some participants were noted to have developed irritant contact dermatitis due to lack of sun protection, use of products not for their skin type, and excessive use of products. Allergic contact dermatitis was also noted to occur in participants from use of facial moisturisers, body creams, and lipsticks. The main sites of the body affected by cosmetic dermatitis were the face, followed by the body, axillae, scalp, and legs. The clinical manifestations of these adverse reactions were erythema, scaling, hyperpigmentation, pruritis and burning (4).

Table 21.2: Dermatoses related to cosmetics in 80 patients from 1996–2006 (4)

Dermatoses	N	%
Contact Dermatitis*	49	28
Inadequate use of cosmetic	25	14
Seborrhoeic dermatitis worsens by the use of cosmetics	5	2.5
Alopecia	1	0.5
Total	80	45

*Irritant dermatitis contact dermatitis occurred in 17 patients (10%), Allergic in 4 patients (2%), and inconclusive in 28 patients (16%).

Irritant contact dermatitis from cosmetics

Irritant contact dermatitis (ICD) or primary skin irritation to cosmetics is a non-immunological, non-infectious, local inflammatory cutaneous reaction of the skin to some of the ingredients in a cosmetic product. Cosmetics can damage the stratum corneum layer of the skin by chemicals or physical/abrasive agents, especially in damaged, compromised, or susceptible skin. An ICD reaction involves skin barrier disruption, cellular damage to keratinocytes; and the release of inflammatory mediators, creating rashes that are mostly pruritic and erythematous, and develop a burning sensation when the affected body part is exposed to water. Individuals with diminished skin barrier function, such as those with atopic dermatitis, are predisposed to cosmetics-induced ICD (7). Prolonged and chronic exposure to irritants may lead to hyperkeratosis (thickening of stratum corneum), diffuse epidermal thickening (acanthosis), and fissured skin. When exposed to an irritant, the type of skin irritation that occurs depends on the area of the body. The most frequent areas of the skin that are affected are the face, upper back, the retroauricular area, and the hand.

ICD from use of cosmetics can be triggered by exposure to numerous irritants, such as water, alkalis, acids, oils, fragrances, preservatives, dyes, and organic solvents used to formulate the products (8). Also, the use of antiperspirants, associated with the friction of clothing and shaving products, can induce irritation of the armpit. Hairdressers and beauticians can experience irritation of the hands, often caused by thioglycolates, water, degreasers, detergents, soaps, and hair dyes.

Unintended misuse of cosmetic products can also result in strong irritant reactions. A patient developed severe ICD after using a shower cream as a moisturising cream due to lack of instruction on how the shower cream should be used. Dermatological examination showed an erythematous and well demarcated scaly rash on the arms (9).

Rinse-off products: Rinse-off products such as shampoos, body washes and shower gels, hair conditioners, and shaving lotions are formulated to remain on the body or hair for a very short period. They rarely cause significant adverse reactions unless used incorrectly, either by being left in contact with the skin for too long, applied in quantities higher than advised, used under occlusion, in which case irritant reactions can occur, or used for a different purpose other than what they are formulated for (9). Shampoos mostly contain sodium lauryl sulfate, a surfactant that is commonly known to irritate the skin. Medicated shampoos may also contain benzalkonium chloride, a quaternary ammonium cationic surfactant and a strong irritant that is widely used in cosmetic formulations and as a skin antiseptic agent. Benzalkonium chloride is generally considered to be an irritant, and cases of allergic contact dermatitis due to it have been reported (10).

Leave-on products: Leave-on cosmetics, such as eye makeups and foundations, are tolerated by most people but may cause irritant reactions with frequent use. Eye makeups such as mascara, eyeliner, eye shadow, and eyebrow pencil, are the most widely used cosmetics products that are applied to the eyelid, which is the thinnest part of the skin. People with preexisting skin diseases or those who wear contact lenses must be careful in selecting eye makeup.

In a randomised, blinded study, mascaras were applied to normal skin in aluminum chambers, and the skin reaction was evaluated by visual assessments of erythema and noninvasive measurements. Mascaras with volatile petroleum distillate induced pronounced skin inflammation under occlusion, while those with conventional emulsion ingredients, such as stearates as the main emulsifiers, did not produce significant inflammatory responses. These findings suggest that solvent-based mascaras are more likely to induce cosmetic ICD (11).

Irritant reactions of the eyelids and face were also observed in a patient who used eye make-up base and foundation cream, both of which contained C11-13 isoparaffin and isododecane. These ingredients were added to the formulation of these cosmetics as solvents and emollient/perfume, respectively, (12), and are usually found in a variety of other cosmetic products. The Cosmetic Ingredient Review Expert Panel concluded that these ingredients are safe, but may cause eye irritation. Leave-on cosmetics, especially those close to the eye, have a higher likelihood of causing ICD.

Allergic contact dermatitis from cosmetics

An allergic contact dermatitis (ACD) reaction to cosmetics is a T-cell–mediated delayed-type hypersensitivity reaction that occurs after skin exposure to a specific hapten in previously sensitised individuals. A hapten is a small molecule that can induce an immune response when attached to a larger carrier molecule, mostly skin self-proteins. Following an initial sensitisation, a subsequent exposure above the individual elicitation threshold will result in clinically visible ACD (13), leading to a hypersensitivity reaction that develops over the course of 2 to 3 days. Cosmetics can act as haptens that causes ACD in some users.

The circulating or resident sensitised T cells are activated by the offending allergen to release pro-inflammatory cytokines. Sensitisation depends on several factors which include product composition, concentration of potential allergenic components, amount of product applied, application site, skin barrier integrity, and frequency and duration of application (14). ACD to cosmetics could be observed in different parts of the body, including the face, neck, hands, back, legs, axilla, and scalp. Cosmetic allergens can reach the skin through direct application, occasional contact with an allergen-contaminated surface, airborne contact (e.g., vapors or droplets), transfer from the hands to more sensitive areas of the skin (e.g., eyelids, around the nose), transfer from another person, or photoinduction by exposure to sunlight, particularly ultraviolet A (UV-A) light. The most frequent contact allergens in cosmetics are fragrance components and preservative agents, even though any cosmetic ingredient can cause ACD. There are many studies exploring new allergens in cosmetics, including a recent monograph on contact allergy that profiles fragrance components, essential oils, and other known cosmetic allergens (15), such as hair dyes, acrylates, and methacrylates in nail products.

Facial dermatitis is a common presentation of cosmetic ACD because the face is exposed to the greatest number of cosmetics daily. As a result, the eyelids are frequently vulnerable to common sources like facial cleansers, makeup removers, mascaras, makeup sponges, eyelash curlers, shampoos, conditioners, and allergens transferred from the hands (16). Other common facial distributions of ACD include lateral facial dermatitis, central facial dermatitis, and generalised facial dermatitis, each with its own unique set of likely causes. Lateral facial and/or neck dermatitis is often caused by rinse-off face wash, shampoo, and/or conditioner while rinsing down over these areas. Central facial dermatitis is caused by makeup foundation or ingredients in moisturisers, anti-wrinkle creams, and topical medications. Generalised facial dermatitis is caused by airborne contaminants, facial cleansers, makeup foundation, moisturisers and medications.

Types of cosmetic products causing allergic dermatitis

Rinse-off products: Shampoos, shower gels, shaving creams, and makeup removers are common rinse-off cosmetic products that rarely cause significant allergic reactions because they mostly stay on the skin for a short period of time. However, with repeated application and cumulative exposure from multiple products that contain potential allergens, an allergic reaction is possible. Potential sensitisers in rinse-off products include fragrances, preservatives, excipients, surfactants, and antimicrobials, such as triclosan and chlorhexidine, among others (17).

Reactions to allergens in rinse-off products often present with dermatitis of the eyelids, face, neck, or hands. The eyelids are one of the most sensitive areas of the skin because of their thin stratum corneum and epidermis, and because much of the upper eyelid skin is occluded while the eye is open. Any substance used on the scalp, hair, face, or hands may produce ACD of the eyelids; for example, people who normally wash their hair with their eyes closed and then open their eyes, allowing occlusion of residual allergens in the eyelid fold (18). This could lead to allergic reactions unless the eyelids and the entire face are washed with non-allergenic facial wash after the use of hair shampoo. One of the main allergens in hair care products are paraphenylenediamine or glyceryl monothioglycolate, which can cross-react with ammonium thioglycolate to cause an allergic reaction of the scalp.

Leave- on products: Leave-on products such as sunscreens, serums, moisturisers, anti-ageing lotions, skin-lightening creams, and leave-in hair conditioners are formulated to remain on the skin for a longer period than rinse-off products, making them a common source of ACD from use of cosmetics.

Common allergens in leave-on products include active ingredients, fragrances, preservatives, antioxidants, vehicles, excipients, emulsifiers, surfactants, UV filters, as well as pigments and resins used in nail cosmetics. Arising from the increased awareness of the harmful effects of sun exposure in terms of skin cancer risk and photoageing, many cosmetic products, especially daytime moisturisers, lip balms, and liquid makeup, now contain UV filters. These may be responsible for allergic and photoallergic reactions. Adverse reactions to sunscreen agents include photoallergic, phototoxic, and irritant reactions. The benzophenones have also been reported to cause contact urticaria (19).

Face/eye makeup: Makeup products such as eye shadows, foundations, and lipsticks are considered leave-on products, but they are usually formulated with the inclusion of colour additives. They generally contain the same potential allergens as other leave-on cosmetics because they are formulated with similar excipients, fragrances, and antioxidants; however, there is one allergen specific to eye makeup and lip care products.

Most cases of adverse reactions to eye makeup are ICD, despite the wide array of known allergens in eye makeup. Mascara, eyeliner, eye shadow, and eyebrow pencils are the mostly used eye makeups.

The emulsifiers and organic solvents in water-based and waterproof mascara, respectively, can be irritating and lead to ACD. In terms of allergy, shellac is the one allergen that seems to be specific to mascara (16). Shellac, or *gomme-laque*, CAS number [9000-59-3], is the purified resinous secretion of *Coccus lacca*, an insect that is found on certain trees in southern Asia. Processed shellac has emollient and film-forming properties that make it suitable for use in the formulation of cosmetics such as hair sprays, nail polishes, lipsticks, eyeliners, and mascaras (20). Pigments in mascara are another possible cause of ACD, although, there are fewer instances than from shellac. Presently, due to consumer awareness and the shift towards natural and vegan products, some mascaras do not contain shellac.

Since eye makeups are usually formulated without fragrance, allergies arise from preservatives and antioxidants. Allergies to eye shadow are quite rare. Common allergens in lipstick include dyes, emollients (e.g., lanolin), UV filters, preservatives, antioxidants, excipients (e.g., propylene glycol), and fragrance.

Deodorants and antiperspirants: Deodorants are the leading cause of fragrance allergies, especially ACD in eczema patients. They are formulated with an 'unhealthy' composition of the fragrance chemicals present in Fragrance Mix II (21), due to the deodorising function they are meant to perform. Deodorant-antiperspirant products also contain antimicrobials and active antiperspirant agents, such as aluminum chloride hexahydrate, which can cause irritation in some users. Propellants in spray-on formulations (isobutene, butane, and propane) can also be allergenic and irritant.

Common ingredients that cause allergic reaction to cosmetics

Fragrance

Fragrance components are the leading cause of allergic reactions to cosmetics products (19). Sensitisation is most often induced by highly perfumed products such as deodorants, anti-perspirants, and after-shave lotions. However, any fragrance-containing skin care products may also cause allergic reactions. A review and analysis of data obtained from 19 studies involving 19,440 individuals tested from 2007 – 2017, indicate the prevalence of Fragrance Mix I (FM I) contact allergy among the general population with 3.5% prevalence (3.4% for women, 2.9% for men) (22). In a retrospective study of 24,168 eczema patients patch-tested from 1986 to 2015 to examine trends in contact allergy to FM I, 7 – 8% were sensitised to FM I, with clinical relevance established in 78.2% of them and an increasing rate of prevalence in recent years (23).

Since 2005, because of the increasing cases of fragrance allergy, and to ensure that sensitised consumers are adequately informed, current European regulations (Annex 3 of the Cosmetic Directive 2003/15/EC), require 26 fragrances (Table 21.3), known to be contact allergens, to be disclosed on the labels of cosmetic and household products, if their concentrations exceed 10 parts per million (ppm) in leave-on products and 100 ppm in rinse-off products. The prevalence of sensitisation to these products is 7.6%, with leave-on products more often responsible for fragrance allergies than rinse-off products (24). Linalool, limonene, and citronellol are the ones most widely found in hygiene products and daily-use moisturisers (25).

Table 21.3: List of 26 fragrances that must be Included on the labels of cosmetic products, according to the Seventh Amendment of the European Cosmetics Directive (26)

Cinnamal	**Farnesol**
Geraniol	**Benzyl alcohol**
Evernia prunasti	**Benzyl salicylate**
Cinnamyl alcohol	**Linalool**
Eugenol	**Limonene**
Hydroxycitronellal	**Butylphenyl methylpropional**
Isoeugenol	**Anisyl alcohol**
α-Amylcinnamal	**Benzyl cinnamate**
Citral	**Benzyl benzoate**
Coumarin	**Methyl 2-octionate**
Hydroxyisohexyl 3-cyclohexane carboaldehyde	**Evernia furfuracea**
α-Isomethyl ionone	**Amylcinnamaldehyde**
Citronellol	**α-Hexylcinnamal**

Fragrance Mix I: There are eight substances that comprise 1% of the mix: amylcinnamaldehyde, cinnamyl alcohol, cinnamic aldehyde, hydroxycitronellal, geraniol, eugenol, isoeugenol, and oak moss extract (*Evernia prunaastri*), all diluted in petrolatum and emulsified with sorbitan sesquioleate. Of these substances, oak moss extract is the most common allergen, while amylcinnamaldehyde is the least common. The estimated prevalence of sensitisation to FM I in the general population ranges from 7.2% to 11.5%, and approximately 70% to 80% of fragrance allergies are due to FM I (27).

Fragrance Mix II: This contains six ingredients which are lyral, 3,7 dimethyl- [2,6]-octadienal or citral, farnesol, hexyl cinnamic aldehyde, coumarin, and citronellol. The prevalence of sensitisation in the general population is estimated to be 5%, and it is considered the second most important marker for detecting allergies to fragrances. Overall, 42% of patients who react positively to Fragrance Mix II also have a positive reaction to FM I (28). It has been shown that an allergic reaction is greater when the two fragrance mixes are used together in a formulation rather than individually, and that irritated skin is at higher risk of being sensitised by singly used fragrances (21).

Lyral (hydroxyisohexyl 3-cyclohexene carboxaldehyde): This is a fragrance component with a lily-like scent. It is a prominent allergen in deodorants that is responsible for allergic contact reactions. It is also used in shampoos, soaps, and fine fragrances (29). In Europe, the contact allergy rate to lyral is between 1.5% and 3%, compared to the US where it is 0.4%, which is due to higher concentrations of lyral in European deodorants (30).

Limonene: This is a commonly used fragrance in cosmetics. It is a component of essential oils, including rosemary, peppermint, lemongrass, lavender, eucalyptus, caraway, and tea tree oils (31). It was first used industrially during the late 1980s, then it became widely used because it was regarded as more environmentally friendly than its organic solvent equivalents. However, on exposure to air, limonene easily oxidises into compounds with considerable sensitising capacity, such as limonene oxide, l-carvone, and the limonene hydroperoxides. A study in Sweden patch-tested 2800 patients with different concentrations of fresh and aged d-limonene. Contact allergies were recorded in 5.1% of patients tested with 5% of d-limonene that had been exposed to air for 10 weeks (32).

Linalool (dimethyl octadienol): Linalool is another fragrance that is present in many essential oils. The pure form of linalool has a lower sensitisation rate compared to its oxidation products that are highly allergenic.

Balsam of Peru: This is a natural resin extracted from the *Myroxylon pereirae* tree. It is composed of approximately 250 different chemical substances, many of which are unidentified. Some fragrances in Balsam of Peru include eugenol, isoeugenol, cinnamyl alcohol and cinnamic aldehyde. It has been shown to induce allergenic reactions in approximately 50% of patients with suspected fragrance allergy (19).

Preservatives

Preservatives are generally added to cosmetic formulations to prolong the shelf-life and to prevent microbial contamination of the products (33). Cosmetics are packaged for repeated use in a variety of containers that continually come in contact with the environment and the bacteria on the skin (e.g., fingers during application). In addition, the constituents of the products provide an extremely good medium for microorganisms to thrive. The inclusion of preservatives, thus, becomes imperative to protect the consumer from possible microbial infections and to prevent the deterioration of the product. There are different kinds of preservative systems devised to keep cosmetics safe for long-term use depending on the type of product. Dry anhydrous products like eyeshadows tend to have a longer shelf life than water-based moisturisers. Most preservatives contain low molecular-weight compounds, making them potential sensitisers. Preservatives are the second most common cosmetic contact allergens, with the parabens being one of the most widely used, followed by formaldehyde-releasing agents and isothiazolinones (34).

Types of preservatives causing allergic reactions in cosmetics

Parabens: These are a family of alkyl esters (methyl-, ethyl-, propyl-, butyl-, and benzyl esters) of p-hydroxybenzoic acid, and are found in cosmetics in any of these forms, but mostly in combination. They are one of the most widely used preservatives in cosmetics, drugs, and food because of their optimal properties (35). The FDA ranks them second in the most widely used ingredients in cosmetic formulations, after water. A study in Europe estimated 99% of leave-on and 77% of rinse-off cosmetics used parabens as a preservative (34). Their broad antimicrobial activities can be enhanced by combining them with other biocides, such as formaldehyde releasers, methylchloroisothiazolinone /methylisothiazolinone, or phenoxyethanol (36).

Parabens rarely cause irritant reactions when applied to healthy skin and are present at a concentration of around 1%. They have one of the lowest rates of sensitisation of all preservatives (37). However, sensitization, due to a combined effect with therapeutic preparations that are applied to damaged skin, are much more common.

Most cosmetics manufacturers have stopped the use of parabens in their products. This is largely due to consumer bias that parabens have carcinogenic and estrogenic effects, even though those effects have not been demonstrated in humans and seem unlikely from their use in cosmetics (38).

Formaldehydes and formaldehyde-releasing agents: These are preservatives that are added to a wide range of cosmetic, domestic, and industrial products to inhibit the growth of bacteria, particularly *Staphylococcus aureus* and *Pseudomonas* spp., which can flourish in an aqueous environment. Although the use of formaldehyde has decreased remarkably in cosmetics, the use of formaldehyde-releasers has increased (39) and have been shown to be present in approximately 20% of cosmetics and personal care products in the USA (40).

Formaldehyde-releasing preservatives (FRPs) function by releasing formaldehyde in the presence of water through hydrolysis in varying quantities depending on the type of the preservative used, its concentration, and the amount of water present in the product (41). TFRPs include quaternium-15, diazolidinyl urea, imidazolidinyl urea, 2-bromo-2-nitropropane-1,3-diol (bronopol), and dimethylol-dimethyl hydantoin (DMDM hydantoin). The most widely used FRP in cosmetic products is bronopol, because it releases less formaldehyde compared to other FRPs. This explains the estimated 15% of positive allergic reactions to bronopol compared to 40% - 60% of positive reactions to other formaldehyde-releasing agents (40). Imidazolidinyl urea and diazolidinyl urea were observed in a study to give the same reaction in patch test, and both caused allergic reaction in the same population, which may be explained by a common metabolite (4-hydroxymethyl-2,5-dioxo-imidazolidin-4-yl urea) of the two substances (42).

FRPs cause allergic reactions similar to formaldehyde, with 34% of patients with allergies to formaldehyde also experiencing sensitisation to a formaldehyde-releasing agent, especially quaternium-15 and, to a lesser extent, bronopol. Cosmetics are the most prevalent sources of exposure to FRPs. However, not all allergies to formaldehyde-releasing agents are due to release of formaldehyde, but may likely be due to components of FRPs that can induce sensitisation that leads to an allergic reaction (43).

Isothiazolinones, such as methylchloroisothiazolinone (MCI) and methylisothiazolinone (MI), are known preservatives that are among the most important allergens found in cosmetics and other personal care and household products. Sources of exposure include shampoos, dishwashing liquids, cosmetics, and moist cleansing wipes.

MCI/MI, also known as Kathon CG or Euxyl K 100, is recommended initially up to 30ppm and later to 15 ppm to be used only in rinse-off products; however, it is still found in several leave-on products such as moisturisers (19). The use of such products or any other leave-on product containing MCI/MI in nonkeratinised areas or under occlusion has caused allergic reactions (43).

MI is a less potent allergen than MCI, but the increased use of MI in many "gentle" or "green" cosmetics and wet wipes for children and adults, has caused significant sensitisation and alarming allergic reactions (44). In 2005, MI was approved as a stand-alone preservative in cosmetic products at a maximum concentration of 100 ppm, which is a considerably higher concentration than when used in combination with MCI. This also resulted in an epidemic of contact allergies (45).

As an example of the prevalence of MI allergies, in a study of 23 patients tested between March and July 2014, 14 subjects (61%) showed a negative reaction to MCI/MI and MI, 8 subjects (35%) showed a positive reaction to MCI/MI and MI, and only one subject (4%) showed a positive reaction to MI and a negative reaction to MCI/MI. Among those patients who showed a positive reaction to MI, 90% had disseminated lesions on the legs, trunk, abdomen, hands, scalp, and face (46).

Antioxidants

Antioxidants are added to cosmetics to counteract the effects of free radicals and to prevent the deterioration or to delay oxidation of unsaturated fatty acids and other compounds that are susceptible to oxidation. Some antioxidant compounds, such as gallates, caffeic acid, coumaric acid, ferulic acid, citric acid, and tartaric acid, have demonstrated antimicrobial activity. They rarely cause cosmetic allergies, but cases do occur. Gallates (dodecyl, octyl, propyl) are the main sensitisers among the antioxidants. They are mostly found in lipsticks, moisturisers, and eye cosmetics. Allergic reaction to gallates in lipsticks usually presents as cheilitis (29). Butylated hydroxyanisole (BHA), butylated hydroxytoluene (BHT), and t-butylhydroquinone (TBHQ) are used in cosmetic products, particularly in lipsticks and hair dyes, where they have been reported to cause contact allergy (47).

Other antioxidants include tocopheryl acetate (vitamin E), retinyl palmitate, ascorbyl palmitate, and ascorbic acid (vitamin C). They are mainly employed in sunscreens and anti-ageing creams and are rarely responsible for allergy to cosmetic products (48).

Emollients/humectants

Emollients and humectants are generally added to cosmetic formulations for skin conditioning and moisturising purposes.

Lanolin: It is produced from the sebaceous glands of sheep and is utilised in cosmetic products mainly for its emollient properties. Lanolin contains sterols, fatty alcohols, and fatty acids (49). ACD caused by lanolin typically develops after repeated or prolonged topical exposure, especially on damaged skin (50). Individuals with atopic dermatitis, leg ulcers, and lower-extremity venous stasis dermatitis are at higher risk of developing allergic reactions from lanolin (49). Hydrogenated lanolin is preferably used in cosmetic formulations because of its colourless, odourless, less tacky, and more hydrophilic nature than lanolin. In a study of 594 patients, 170 patients had a positive patch test reaction to at least one lanolin derivative and were defined as allergic to lanolin (51).

Caprylyl maleate - Dicaprylyl maleate (DCM): This is also known as dioctyl maleate; it is an emollient and solvent and is a common ingredient in tanning lotions, moisturisers, foundations, and sunscreens (52). Initial chemical testing of DCM indicated that it does not cause ACD, but 10 years after its introduction into cosmetic products, it has been found to cause contact allergy in some patients. In a recent study, 22 patients suspected to have allergic reactions to DCM were tested with freshly manufactured DCM and deliberately aged DCM. Twelve patients tested positive to the freshly manufactured DCM and 6 developed a positive reaction to the aged DCM (53).

Sunscreens/UV filters

The use of sunscreens or UV filters as part of skincare regimens have increased greatly in recent years. This is mostly due to consumers' awareness and media attention on accelerated skin-ageing and the carcinogenic effects of excessive sunlight exposure. UV absorbers are increasingly used, not only in sunscreen-specific products, but also in other cosmetic products including moisturisers and face makeup (19). The use of sunscreens prevents sunburn and skin pigmentation. They are also used to prevent photodegradation of other cosmetic products and may have a sensitising potential in products where they are present (54).

UV filters are classified as either organic or physical agents depending on their mechanism of action. Organic or chemical UV filters absorb UV rays, while physical UV filters (titanium dioxide and zinc oxide) act as protective barriers and reflect UV rays. Physical UV filters are chemically and biologically inert and unlikely to cause irritation or skin sensitisation (55). But the opaque appearance of physical agents on the skin, especially the purplish look on darker skin, makes them less desirable to consumers.

Chemical UV filters include the benzophenones, dibenzoylmethanes, para-aminobenzoic acid (PABA) and its esters, cinnamates, salicylates, and anthranilates. They can potentially cause ACD or photoallergic contact dermatitis, which occurs in more than 15% of users. Benzophenones (oxybenzone) and dibenzoylmethanes (avobenzone/ Parsol 1789) are the main sensitising agents in sunscreens (56).

Hydroxybenzophenone UV filter: Oxybenzone, also known as benzophenone 3, is an aromatic hydrocarbon that acts as an UV light filter. It is a broad-spectrum UVA/UVB absorber that is used up to 6% concentration in sunscreen preparations and up to 0.5% in personal care products as a photo-stabiliser, minimising colour and odour changes. It is used in over 2000 personal care formulations, ranging from skin and hair care to colour cosmetics and fragrances (57). Oxybenzone is present in 68% of sunscreens. In 2013, the North American Contact Dermatitis Group documented it as the most common cause of sunscreen allergy, representing 70.2% of sunscreen reactions (58). A case of an anaphylactoid reaction to benzophenone-3 was reported 24 hours after the application of a sunscreen. The allergic reaction presented as oedematous, painful, pruritic eruption on arms and neck, with increased amount of phlegm, voice changes, and tachycardia, and required hospitalisation. Patch test result showed urticarial reactions to benzophenone-3 and other hydroxybenzophenone derivatives (benzophenone 8 and benzophenone 10) and delayed reaction to propyl gallate (59).

Avobenzone (butyl methoxydibenzoylmethane, AVO): This is the second most widely used organic UV-filter, mostly because of its ability to protect against UVA rays. However, it is not photostable, given that it photodegrades 60% in one hour and 90% in four hours after UV exposure (60). The photo degradants in avobenzone are responsible for photo allergy. Photoallergic reactions to AVO have been reported in the literature more than allergic reactions, which may be in part due to its photo-instability (60).

Octocrylene (Parsol® 340): This is an organic UV filter that mainly absorbs UVB radiation and short UVA wavelengths. It is mostly used in stabilising other UV filters such as avobenzone for optimal protection. Octocrylene used as a UV filter in cosmetic products at concentrations up to 10% can be considered safe. It rarely causes allergic reactions (61). A study conducted in Germany reported two weak positive reactions to 10% octocrylene in a patch test among 2,577 participants (62). However, in another study that included both adult and pediatric patients with a history of adverse skin reactions from sunscreen products, contact and photo contact allergy to octocrylene was observed more frequently and severely in children than in adults, likely due to the immaturity of the skin epidermal barrier and the prevalence of atopic dermatitis in young children (63). As with a benzophenone UV filter, photoallergic reactions to octocrylene occur particularly in patients previously photosensitised by ketoprofen, a nonsteroidal anti-inflammatory drug, which is attributed to cross-reactivity (64).

Surfactants

Surfactants are ubiquitous compounds found in almost all cosmetics, household, and personal care products. Because of their versatility, they are used for different purposes, such as detergents, wetting agents, emulsifiers, foaming agents, or dispersants in formulations. Their primary attribute is their amphiphilic ability to lower the surface tension between two or more inmiscible liquids, between a liquid and a gaseous substance, or between a liquid and a solid. This makes them important ingredients in formulations of cosmetic products. They can interact with proteins and lipids of the stratum corneum layer of the skin when applied topically and can cause damage to the skin barrier (65). Surfactants can cause both ICD and ACD. Sodium lauryl sulphate is one of the most irritation-causing detergents.

Sodium lauryl sulphate (SLS): This is the most widely used of the lauryl sulfate surfactants in cosmetics and personal care products. It is the fourth most prevalent individual surfactant and is found in 298 (6.6%) of 4,519 products in Contact Allergen Management Program (66). It is mostly used in shampoos and cleansers and is a well-recognised irritant.

Cocamide diethanolamine (DEA): Cocamide DEA is a non-ionic surfactant frequently used in industrial, household, and cosmetic products for its foaming and stabilising properties.

Contact allergy to cocamide DEA has been reported in the past to be rare, but recently several cases were published, suggesting an increase in the frequency of allergic dermatitis caused by this agent. In a study of 1,767 patients patch-tested for allergic reaction to cocamide DEA, 18 (1%) presented with hand dermatitis. The results of this study show that allergic reaction to cocamide DEA is rare, despite frequent use in cosmetics and household products formulation (67).

Alkyl glucosides: These are often used as mild surfactants and are common in products marketed as "green" because of their eco-friendly properties. They are used for their cleansing, foaming, and emulsifying properties in both rinse-off products (e.g., shower gels, shampoos, soaps, cleansers, hair dyes) and leave-on cosmetics (e.g., sunscreens, fragrances, tanning products, moisturisers, deodorants). They can also be found in certain baby products, such as wipes and cleansers (68).

Although alkyl glucosides are considered to have lower irritancy and allergenicity than harsher surfactants like SLS and sodium laureth sulfate, positive reaction rates to decyl glucoside have increased from 1.6% in 2013–2014 to 2.1% in 2015–2016 (69). Because of their increasing prevalence, alkyl glucosides were ranked by the American Contact Dermatitis Society as Contact Allergen of the Year for 2017 (70).

A 19-year study (1993–2012) patch-tested 11,842 patients with suspected contact dermatitis. A total of 30 patients (24 women and 6 men) presented with a positive reaction to one or more alkyl glucosides. The products causing the reactions were shampoos, skin-cleansing products, intimate hygiene wipes, sunscreens, and deodorants. Sixteen patients showed multiple sensitivities (defined as three or more contact allergies) not only to other glucosides, but also to non-related chemicals (68).

Skin-lightening agents

The cosmetic use of bleaching products is common among women in sub-Saharan Africa, with a prevalence of 67% in certain urban areas. Most of these products contain corticosteroids, such as clobetasol propionate and hydroquinone. The skin diseases associated with this practice are various and often severe. The most commonly reported are cellulitis, acne, eczema, and dyschromia including exogenous ochronosis. Other skin diseases are striae, macular hyperchromia involving the face, and lichen-like or lupus-like dermatitis (71).

Hydroquinone

Hydroquinone (HQ) is a hydroxy phenolic compound known for its depigmenting properties. It acts as a depigmenting agent by competitive inhibition of tyrosinase. It is generally prescribed at 4% for treatment of post-inflammatory hyperpigmentation, melasma, and other skin dyschromia. It is also available in 2% or less in over-the-counter products. HQ in high concentrations is commonly abused as skin whitening agents in dark-skinned populations, and overexposure of the skin to HQ and other bleaching cosmetics makes hyperpigmentation worse and achieving clear skin almost impossible. Commonly reported adverse effects include erythema, pruritus, mild oedema, burning, scaling, and exogenous ochronosis. However, in a rare case, permanent leukoderma and cutaneous squamous cell carcinoma have been reported (Figure 21.3). A case study of a woman who applied 4% hydroquinone for 8 months without supervision of a dermatologist presented with white patches over her face (Figure 21.4). A histopathology study of the white patches showed blunt rete ridges, melanophages in the dermis, and perivascular chronic inflammatory infiltrate, which is consistent with chemical leukoderma (72).

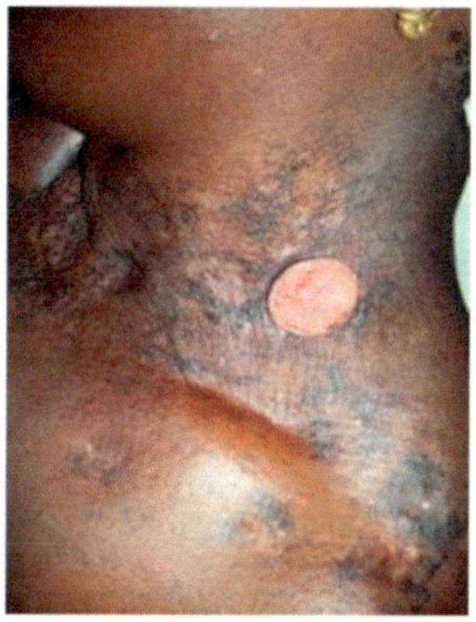

Figure 21.3: The neck showing squamous cell carcinoma (71)

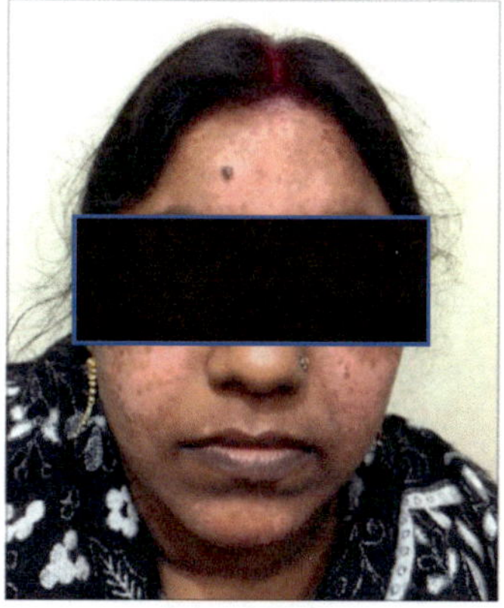

Figure 21.4: Depigmented macules and patches over the face (72)

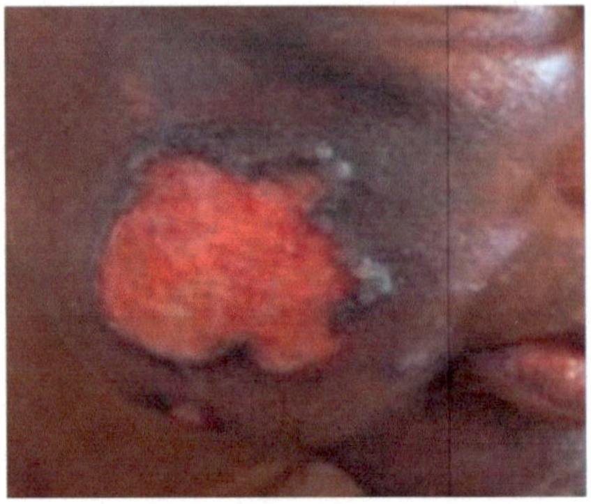

Figure 21.5: The cheek showing exogenous ochronosis and squamous cell carcinoma (71)

Another rare adverse effect of misuse of hydroquinone was reported in a multicenter study in Senegal from August 2005 to January 2016. A total of 8 female patients were reported to have cutaneous squamous cell carcinoma (Figure 21.3) associated with skin-bleaching from the use of topical hydroquinone and highly potent corticosteroids over the whole body, for an average duration of 20.3 years (71).

Exogenous Ochronosis (EO) is a rare skin disorder characterised by an asymptomatic hyperpigmentation of the face, sides and back of the neck as well as the back and extensor surfaces. EO appears on the skin as either blue-black, brown, and/or black pigment mottled macules in areas where topical lightening agents such as hydroquinone, resorcinol, phenol, mercury and/or picric acid have been applied for a prolonged period (Figure 21.5). It can also occur following the use of systemic antimalarials, such as quinine (73).

EO is mostly seen among the indigenous black population in African countries. The prevalence in African populations could be a result of their unsatiated search and use of products that promise clearer and brighter skin, which could result in the use of skin-care products containing resorcinol in combination with hydroquinone or use of hydroquinone in a hydroalcoholic lotion that could result in EO (74).

Glutathione (GSH)

Glutathione (GSH) is a water-soluble, tri-peptide thiol that consists of cysteine, glutamate, and glycine amino acids. It is known for its antioxidant effect of protecting cells from oxidative stress and damage. It is available naturally in fresh leafy vegetables, walnuts, oranges, avocados, meat, poultry, broccoli, chestnuts, asparagus, whey protein, tomatoes, and other fresh fruits. In vitro studies of the reduced form of GSH have been shown to have good skin-whitening/bleaching effect in humans. It is reported to disrupt melanogenesis by binding and chelating copper at the active site of tyrosinase, increasing cysteine levels, and to enhance pheomelanin production, thereby causing lightening of the skin and antioxidative effects of combating free radicals (75).

GSH is considered a magic drug for skin-lightening and bleaching of darker skin tones. It is popular in countries such as Singapore, Thailand, Malaysia, and Indonesia. It is also commonly used in beauty parlours in Nigeria. It is available in topical, oral, and injectable formulations. Topical and oral formulations have shown significant improvement in skin-lightening on continuous use for certain period and are considered safe with mild adverse effects (76). Studies on efficacy and safety of GSH are still limited. There is a need for comprehensive, double-blind, vehicle-controlled study of its efficacy. There are not enough published studies to validate safety and efficacy of intravenous (IV) injections (75). A comparative, placebo control study of an oral formulation of reduced and oxidised GSH at 250 mg taken daily for 12 weeks, reported decreased Melanin Index, UV spots, transepidermal water loss, wrinkles, and increased skin elasticity compared to placebo. Side effects reported include transaminitis, gastrointestinal upset (flatulence), pruritus, erythema, and fatigue (77). Another study in the Philippines that used lozenges to administer 500 mg of GSH daily for 8 weeks reported an adverse effect of sore gums (78).

Intravenous injection of GSH has shown more adverse effects due to the lack of a standardised dose, greater risk of overdose, or unapproved additives that might be present in the GSH injection. Common adverse effects include headaches, mild to severe skin reaction such as fatal Stevens-Johnson syndrome, toxic epidermal necrolysis, kidney, thyroid and liver dysfunction, abdominal pain, and serious adverse effects such as air embolism or sepsis that may lead to death. There is also increased risk of communicable diseases, such as hepatitis B and C, or human immunodeficiency virus (HIV), particularly when administered by a non-professional in an illegal medical spa or beauty parlour. A controlled clinical study of 25 participants administered with 1,200 mg GSH twice a week for 6 weeks did not report any significant result to indicate IV GSH as an effective or safe treatment for skin tone lightening. However, adverse effects like liver, renal, and thyroid dysfunction were reported (75).

In 2017, the FDA ordered Flawless Beauty LLC (Ocean Township NJ, USA) to stop selling and recall all IV skin whitening/bleaching GSH products (Advanced Glutathione and Tatiomax Glutathione Collagen Whitening kits) from the market due to reported issues of infection, systemic reactions, necrosis, and for containing an unapproved ingredient (human placenta) (79).

The Philippines and the United Kingdom (UK) have also issued warnings against the use of IV GSH for skin lightening.

Mercury

Mercury is a toxic heavy metal that is found in some skin lightening/ bleaching products, primarily due to its ability to produce a dramatic whitening effect, especially when used at a very high concentration. It commonly occurs in cosmetic products as inorganic salts, such as mercurous chloride (calomel), mercuric chloride, and mercuric oxide. It is considered a skin lightening agent because of its competitive ability to inhibit tyrosinase. It competes with copper and cysteine in the active site of tyrosinase leading to inactivation of the enzyme and disruption of melanogenesis to block the production of melanin, leading to a lighter skin tone (80).

Inorganic mercury in cosmetic formulations applied to the skin is absorbed into the body through the transepidermal route, sebaceous glands, sweat glands, hair follicles, and even parenterally though inhalation (81). The high rate of systemic absorption leads to adverse effects and fatal complications, which is why it has been banned in most countries. The World Health Organisation (WHO) also set the limit of mercury in skin-lightening products to less than one part per million (ppm) (82). However, consumers still have access to concentrations higher than the acceptable limit from unlicensed sale and mislabeling of products (83).

Prolonged use and exposure to mercury through repeated cosmetic applications may lead to damaging adverse effects. Common cutaneous side effects of mercury include rashes, paradoxical hyperpigmentation, scarring, and discoloured, fragile nails. Serious adverse effects due to systemic exposure from inhalation of fumes or ingestion include pneumonitis, gastric disturbance, glomerulonephritis, nephrotic syndrome, peripheral neuropathy, and psychosocial issues. A case report of a 34-year-old woman who used skin-lightening cream containing 30,000 ppm mercury presented with nephrotic syndrome due to accumulation of mercury in her kidneys (81).

The adverse effects of using mercury for skin-lightening are not limited to the users, but also to people in the same household as users, like family members. A case study of a 17-month-old child indicated acute mercury toxicity from a skin-lightening cosmetic used by her mother and grandmother. Heavy metal screening reported a blood mercury level of 26 mcg/L (normal <10 mcg/L) and a urine creatinine level of 243 mcg/g (normal <35 mcg/g creatinine). Adverse effects observed in the child included fussiness, weight loss, mild resting tremor, shyness with other children, stereotypical hand-flapping behavior when stressed, hypertension, constipation, and arthralgia (84).

Topical corticosteroids

The adverse effects of corticosteroids are discussed in Chapter 4 of this book.

References

1. Pollock S, Taylor S, Oyerinde O, et al. The dark side of skin lightening: An international collaboration and review of a public health issue affecting dermatology. *Int J Womens Dermatol.* 2021;7(2):158-164.
2. Environmental Working Group's Skin-Deep Cosmetic Safety Database 2011. https://www.ewg.org/skindeep/. Accessed 01/10/2018.
3. FDA Authority Over Cosmetics: How Cosmetics Are Not FDA-Approved, but Are FDA-Regulated. US Food and Drug Administration. Cosmetic Laws & Regulations Web site. https://www.fda.gov/cosmetics/cosmetics-laws-regulations/fda-authority-over-cosmetics-how-cosmetics-are-not-fda-approved-are-fda-regulated. Published 2018. Updated 03/02/2022. Accessed 1/10/2018, 2018.
4. Duarte I, Campos Lage AC. Frequency of dermatoses associated with cosmetics. *Contact Dermatitis.* 2007;56(4):211-213.
5. Pereira JX, Pereira TC. Cosmetics and its Health Risks. *Global Journal of Medical Research: B Pharma, Drug Discovery, Toxicology & Medicine.* 2018;18(2):63-70.
6.
7. Reich D, Psomadakis CE, Buka B. Irritant Dermatitis. In: *Top 50 Dermatology Case Studies for Primary Care.* Cham: Springer International Publishing; 2017:303-307.
8. Schnuch A, Carlsen BC. Genetics and Individual Predispositions in Contact Dermatitis. In: Johansen JD, Frosch PJ, Lepoittevin J-P, eds. *Contact Dermatitis.* Berlin, Heidelberg: Springer Berlin Heidelberg; 2011:13-42.
9. Opstrup MS, Yazdanyar S. Irritant contact dermatitis caused by a shower cream used as a leave-on product. *Contact Dermatitis.* 2019;81(5):399-400.
10. Oiso N, Fukai K, Ishii M. Irritant contact dermatitis from benzalkonium chloride in shampoo. *Contact Dermatitis.* 2005;52(1):54.
11. Lodén M, Wessman C. Mascaras may cause irritant contact dermatitis. *Int J Cosmet Sci.* 2002;24(5):281-285.
12. Goossens A, Huygens S, Gilissen L. Irritant reactions to leave-on cosmetics and other products. *Contact Dermatitis.* 2020;82(4):227-228.
13. Johansen JD, Aalto-Korte K, Agner T, et al. European Society of Contact Dermatitis guideline for diagnostic patch testing - recommendations on best practice. *Contact Dermatitis.* 2015;73(4):195-221.
14. Robinson MK, Gerberick GF, Ryan CA, McNamee P, White IR, Basketter DA. The importance of exposure estimation in the assessment of skin sensitization risk. *Contact Dermatitis.* 2000;42(5):251-259.
15. de Groot AC. *Monographs in Contact Allergy: Volume 2: Fragrances and Essential Oils.* CRC Press; 2021.
16. Zirwas MJ. Contact Dermatitis to Cosmetics. *Clin Rev Allergy Immunol.* 2019;56(1):119-128.
17. Deza G, Giménez-Arnau AM. Allergic contact dermatitis in preservatives: current standing and future options. *Curr Opin Allergy Clin Immunol.* 2017;17(4):263-268.

18. Huang CX, Yiannias JA, Killian JM, Shen JF. Seven Common Allergen Groups Causing Eyelid Dermatitis: Education and Avoidance Strategies. *Clin Ophthalmol.* 2021;15:1477-1490.
19. Goossens A. Contact-allergic reactions to cosmetics. *J Allergy (Cairo).* 2011;2011:467071.
20. Le Coz CJ, Leclere JM, Arnoult E, Raison-Peyron N, Pons-Guiraud A, Vigan M. Allergic contact dermatitis from shellac in mascara. *Contact Dermatitis.* 2002;46(3):149-152.
21. Heisterberg MV, Menné T, Andersen KE, et al. Deodorants are the leading cause of allergic contact dermatitis to fragrance ingredients. *Contact Dermatitis.* 2011;64(5):258-264.
22. Alinaghi F, Bennike NH, Egeberg A, Thyssen JP, Johansen JD. Prevalence of contact allergy in the general population: A systematic review and meta-analysis. *Contact Dermatitis.* 2019;80(2):77-85.
23. Bennike NH, Zachariae C, Johansen JD. Trends in contact allergy to fragrance mix I in consecutive Danish patients with eczema from 1986 to 2015: a cross-sectional study. *Br J Dermatol.* 2017;176(4):1035-1041.
24. Nardelli A, Drieghe J, Claes L, Boey L, Goossens A. Fragrance allergens in 'specific' cosmetic products. *Contact Dermatitis.* 2011;64(4):212-219.
25. Arribas MP, Soro P, Silvestre JF. Allergic Contact Dermatitis to Fragrances. Part 1. *Actas Dermosifiliogr.* 2012;103(10):874-879.
26. González-Muñoz P, Conde-Salazar L, Vañó-Galván S. Dermatitis alérgica de contacto a cosméticos. *Actas Dermo-Sifiliográficas.* 2014;105(9):822-832.
27. Heras F, Díaz-Recuero JL, Cabello MJ, Conde-Salazar L. [Sensitization to Lyral]. *Actas Dermosifiliogr.* 2006;97(6):374-378.
28. Krautheim A, Uter W, Frosch P, Schnuch A, Geier J. Patch testing with fragrance mix II: results of the IVDK 2005-2008. *Contact Dermatitis.* 2010;63(5):262-269.
29. Watkins S, Zippin J. Allergic contact dermatitis and cosmetics. *Cutis.* 2012;90(4):201-204.
30. Bruze M, Andersen KE, Goossens A. Recommendation to include fragrance mix 2 and hydroxyisohexyl 3-cyclohexene carboxaldehyde (Lyral) in the European baseline patch test series. *Contact Dermatitis.* 2008;58(3):129-133.
31. Matura M, Sköld M, Börje A, et al. Not only oxidized R-(+)- but also S-(-)-limonene is a common cause of contact allergy in dermatitis patients in Europe. *Contact Dermatitis.* 2006;55(5):274-279.
32. Karlberg AT, Dooms-Goossens A. Contact allergy to oxidized d-limonene among dermatitis patients. *Contact Dermatitis.* 1997;36(4):201-206.
33. Thyssen JP, Engkilde K, Lundov MD, Carlsen BC, Menné T, Johansen JD. Temporal trends of preservative allergy in Denmark (1985-2008). *Contact Dermatitis.* 2010;62(2):102-108.
34. Orton DI, Wilkinson JD. Cosmetic allergy: incidence, diagnosis, and management. *Am J Clin Dermatol.* 2004;5(5):327-337.
35. De Groot AC. Fatal attractiveness: the shady side of cosmetics. *Clin Dermatol.* 1998;16(1):167-179.

36. Cashman AL, Warshaw EM. Parabens: a review of epidemiology, structure, allergenicity, and hormonal properties. *Dermatitis.* 2005;16(2):57-66; quiz 55-56.
37. Svedman C, Andersen KE, Brandão FM, et al. Follow-up of the monitored levels of preservative sensitivity in Europe: overview of the years 2001-2008. *Contact Dermatitis.* 2012;67(5):312-314.
38. Revuz J. [Long live parabens]. *Ann Dermatol Venereol.* 2009;136(5):403-404.
39. Lundov MD, Johansen JD, Carlsen BC, Engkilde K, Menné T, Thyssen JP. Formaldehyde exposure and patterns of concomitant contact allergy to formaldehyde and formaldehyde-releasers. *Contact Dermatitis.* 2010;63(1):31-36.
40. de Groot AC, White IR, Flyvholm MA, Lensen G, Coenraads PJ. Formaldehyde-releasers in cosmetics: relationship to formaldehyde contact allergy. Part 1. Characterization, frequency and relevance of sensitization, and frequency of use in cosmetics. *Contact Dermatitis.* 2010;62(1):2-17.
41. Emeis D, de Groot AC, Brinkmann J. Determination of formaldehyde in formaldehyde-releaser patch test preparations. *Contact Dermatitis.* 2010;63(2):57-62.
42. Lehmann SV, Hoeck U, Breinholdt J, Olsen CE, Kreilgaard B. Characterization and chemistry of imidazolidinyl urea and diazolidinyl urea. *Contact Dermatitis.* 2006;54(1):50-58.
43. Latorre N, Borrego L, Fernández-Redondo V, et al. Patch testing with formaldehyde and formaldehyde-releasers: multicentre study in Spain (2005-2009). *Contact Dermatitis.* 2011;65(5):286-292.
44. García-Gavín J, Vansina S, Kerre S, Naert A, Goossens A. Methylisothiazolinone, an emerging allergen in cosmetics? *Contact Dermatitis.* 2010;63(2):96-101.
45. Latheef F, Wilkinson SM. Methylisothiazolinone outbreak in the European Union. *Curr Opin Allergy Clin Immunol.* 2015;15(5):461-466.
46. Scherrer MA, Rocha VB, Andrade AR. Contact dermatitis to methylisothiazolinone. *An Bras Dermatol.* 2015;90(6):912-914.
47. Field S, Hazelwood E, Bourke B, Bourke JF. Allergic contact dermatitis from tertiary-butylhydroquinone and Laureth 12 in a hair dye. *Contact Dermatitis.* 2007;56(2):116.
48. Watkins SA, Maibach HI. The hardening phenomenon in irritant contact dermatitis: an interpretative update. *Contact Dermatitis.* 2009;60(3):123-130.
49. Lee B, Warshaw E. Lanolin allergy: history, epidemiology, responsible allergens, and management. *Dermatitis.* 2008;19(2):63-72.
50. Thyssen JP, McFadden JP, Kimber I. The multiple factors affecting the association between atopic dermatitis and contact sensitization. *Allergy.* 2014;69(1):28-36.
51. Knijp J, Bruynzeel DP, Rustemeyer T. Diagnosing lanolin contact allergy with lanolin alcohol and Amerchol L101. *Contact Dermatitis.* 2019;80(5):298-303.
52. Chan I, Wakelin SH. Allergic contact dermatitis from dioctyl maleate in a moisturizer. *Contact Dermatitis.* 2006;55(4):250.
53. Lotery H, Kirk S, Beck M, et al. Dicaprylyl maleate--an emerging cosmetic allergen. *Contact Dermatitis.* 2007;57(3):169-172.
54. Hughes TM, Stone NM. Benzophenone 4: an emerging allergen in cosmetics and toiletries? *Contact Dermatitis.* 2007;56(3):153-156.

55. Scheuer E, Warshaw E. Sunscreen allergy: A review of epidemiology, clinical characteristics, and responsible allergens. *Dermatitis.* 2006;17(1):3-11.
56. Wong T, Orton D. Sunscreen allergy and its investigation. *Clin Dermatol.* 2011;29(3):306-310.
57. DiNardo JC, Downs CA. Dermatological and environmental toxicological impact of the sunscreen ingredient oxybenzone/benzophenone-3. *J Cosmet Dermatol.* 2018;17(1):15-19.
58. Warshaw EM, Wang MZ, Maibach HI, et al. Patch test reactions associated with sunscreen products and the importance of testing to an expanded series: retrospective analysis of North American Contact Dermatitis Group data, 2001 to 2010. *Dermatitis.* 2013;24(4):176-182.
59. Tawfik ME, Atwater AR. Anaphylactoid reaction to benzophenones, with recurrence during patch testing. *Contact Dermatitis.* 2019;81(4):303-304.
60. Beasley DG, Meyer TA. Characterization of the UVA protection provided by avobenzone, zinc oxide, and titanium dioxide in broad-spectrum sunscreen products. *Am J Clin Dermatol.* 2010;11(6):413-421.
61. Berardesca E, Zuberbier T, Sanchez Viera M, Marinovich M. Review of the safety of octocrylene used as an ultraviolet filter in cosmetics. *J Eur Acad Dermatol Venereol.* 2019;33 Suppl 7:25-33.
62. Uter W, Lessmann H, Geier J. Is octocrylene a frequent contact allergen? *Contact Dermatitis.* 2017;77(2):127-128.
63. Avenel-Audran M, Dutartre H, Goossens A, et al. Octocrylene, an emerging photoallergen. *Arch Dermatol.* 2010;146(7):753-757.
64. Karlsson I, Vanden Broecke K, Mårtensson J, Goossens A, Börje A. Clinical and experimental studies of octocrylene's allergenic potency. *Contact Dermatitis.* 2011;64(6):343-352.
65. Hanson JL, Warshaw EM. Contact Allergy to Surfactants in a Hypoallergenic Liquid Cleanser. *Dermatitis.* 2015;26(6):284-286.
66. Weinhammer AP, Scheman A, Reeder MJ. Prevalence of Surfactant in the Contact Allergen Management Program. *Dermatitis.* 2019;30(6):358-362.
67. Mertens S, Gilissen L, Goossens A. Allergic contact dermatitis caused by cocamide diethanolamine. *Contact Dermatitis.* 2016;75(1):20-24.
68. Gijbels D, Timmermans A, Serrano P, Verreycken E, Goossens A. Allergic contact dermatitis caused by alkyl glucosides. *Contact Dermatitis.* 2014;70(3):175-182.
69. DeKoven JG, Warshaw EM, Belsito DV, et al. North American Contact Dermatitis Group Patch Test Results 2013-2014. *Dermatitis.* 2017;28(1):33-46.
70. Sasseville D. Alkyl Glucosides: 2017 "Allergen of the Year". *Dermatitis.* 2017;28(4):296.
71. Ly F, Diousse P, Ndiaye C, et al. Cutaneous squamous cell carcinomas (SCC) associated with cosmetic skin whitening: 8 cases reported in Senegal. *Ann Dermatol Venereol.* 2018;145(2):83-88.
72. Das A, Ghosh A, Kumar P. Chemical leukoderma due to hydroquinone: An unusual phenomenon. *Indian J Dermatol Venereol Leprol.* 2019;85(5):567.

73. Bhattar PA, Zawar VP, Godse KV, Patil SP, Nadkarni NJ, Gautam MM. Exogenous Ochronosis. *Indian J Dermatol.* 2015;60(6):537-543.
74. Levitt J. The safety of hydroquinone: a dermatologist's response to the 2006 Federal Register. *J Am Acad Dermatol.* 2007;57(5):854-872.
75. Mohan S, Sangal R, Singh N. Glutathione for skin lightening for dermatologists and cosmetologists. *International Journal of Research in Dermatology.* 2020;6:284.
76. Wahab S, Anwar AI, Zainuddin AN, Hutabarat EN, Anwar AA, Kurniadi I. Combination of topical and oral glutathione as a skin-whitening agent: a double-blind randomized controlled clinical trial. *Int J Dermatol.* 2021;60(8):1013-1018.
77. Weschawalit S, Thongthip S, Phutrakool P, Asawanonda P. Glutathione and its antiaging and antimelanogenic effects. *Clin Cosmet Investig Dermatol.* 2017;10:147-153.
78. Handog EB, Datuin MS, Singzon IA. An open-label, single-arm trial of the safety and efficacy of a novel preparation of glutathione as a skin-lightening agent in Filipino women. *Int J Dermatol.* 2016;55(2):153-157.
79. Juhasz MLW, Levin MK. The role of systemic treatments for skin lightening. *J Cosmet Dermatol.* 2018;17(6):1144-1157.
80. Naidoo L, Khoza N, Dlova NC. A Fairer Face, a Fairer Tomorrow? A Review of Skin Lighteners. *Cosmetics.* 2016;3(3):33.
81. Abbas HH, Sakakibara M, Sera K, Nurgahayu, Andayanie E. Mercury Exposure and Health Problems of the Students Using Skin-Lightening Cosmetic Products in Makassar, South Sulawesi, Indonesia. *Cosmetics.* 2020;7(3):58.
82. Mercury in skin lightening products. 2019. https://www.who.int/publications/i/item/WHO-CED-PHE-EPE-19.13. Published 11-3-19.
83. Dlova NC, Ajose F. Communication on the dangers and abuse of skin lighteners in Africa. *Int J Dermatol.* 2014;53(6):e335-337.
84. Ori MR, Larsen JB, Shirazi FM. Mercury Poisoning in a Toddler from Home Contamination due to Skin-Lightening Cream. *J Pediatr.* 2018;196:314-317.e311.

CHAPTER TWENTY- TWO

Endocrine disrupting chemicals in cosmetics: More than skin deep?

Iain J. McEwan and Folake A. Orafidiya

The presence of and exposure to endocrine disrupting chemicals (EDCs) has been widely reported in different parts of the world and in multiple biological models since the term was first used over thirty years ago (1). EDCs are defined as exogenous chemicals that can disrupt the synthesis, metabolism and/or action of natural hormones in the body, in particular the sex hormones (2). EDCs can typically have oestrogenic activity, mimicking the natural hormone oestradiol or act as anti-androgens, impairing the function of the hormone testosterone. Generally, reports on EDCs focus on environmental exposure due to the use of certain families of chemicals in pesticides, food wrappings and industrial processes. However, there is a source much closer to home, one we unwittingly expose ourselves to on a daily basis, namely, cosmetics and also personal care products (PCPs) (3, 4). In this chapter, we consider chemicals found in cosmetics and PCPs, that may act as endocrine disrupters and discuss their potential mechanisms of action and impact on human health. For a broader discussion on the topic of EDCs the reader is directed to some excellent reviews (1,2, 5, 6).

Cosmetics

Cosmetics and personal care products

Today cosmetics and PCPs represent multibillion-dollar global industries manufacturing products for hair, skin, nails, personal hygiene, teeth and mouth (4). Although the inclusion of steroids in cosmetics and PCPs has been banned, the presence of parabens, benzophenones, bisphenols and phthalates (Figure 22. 1, Table 22.1), which are considered to be EDCs raises questions concerning the use of cosmetics and PCPs and human health; especially the health of women and, in particular, those of childbearing age, as EDCs may also have generational impact on off-springs.

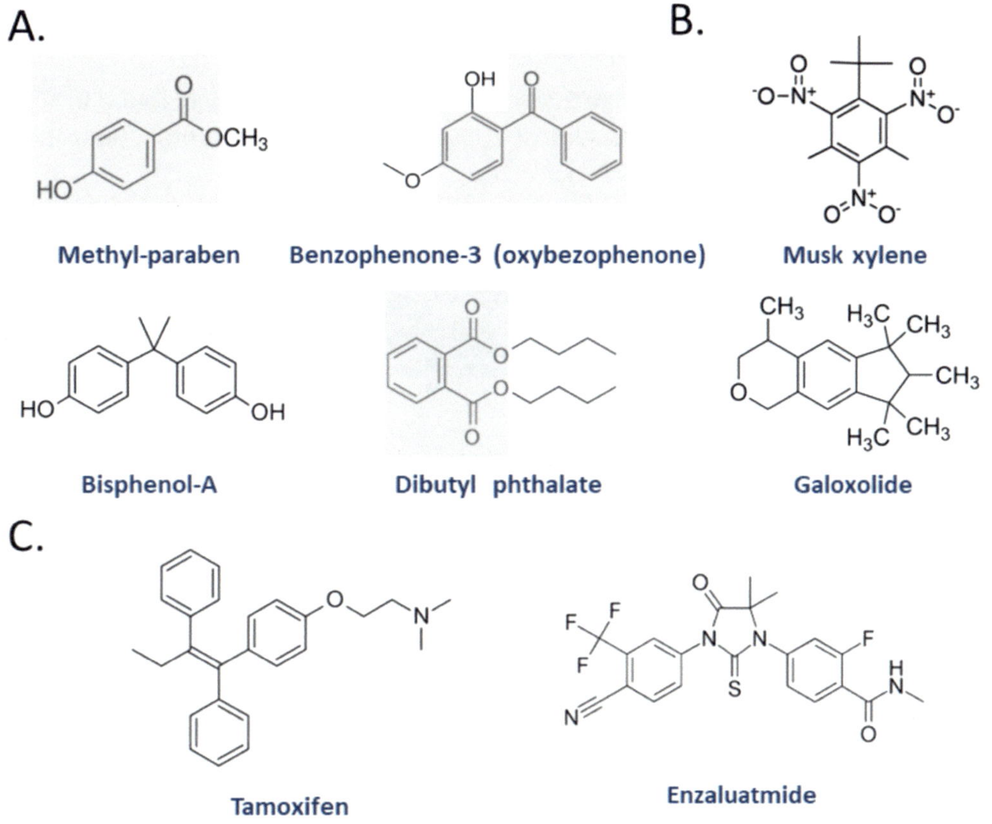

Figure 22.1. Structures of chemical families found in cosmetics, PCPs and fragrances with endocrine disrupting properties. *A. Illustration of the diverse chemical structures of some common examples of EDCs found in cosmetics. The core structure of parabens, benzophenones and phthalates are shown in grey boxes. B. Examples of nitro (musk xylene) and polycyclic musk (galoxlide) found in fragrances. C. For comparison the structures of the selective oestrogen receptor modulator, tamoxifen and the antiandrogen enzalutamide are shown.*

Parabens: Parabens (Table 22.1) are used for their antimicrobial properties and are found in a range of products (over 40 % of cosmetics and PCPs tested), with methyl-paraben (Figure 22.1), frequently found in cosmetics and PCPs.

Phthalates: Phthalates (Table 22.1) are used as plasticizers and are found in bactericidal creams, deodorants, skin lotions, nail- and hair-products. They have also been recorded in more than 90 % of feminine hygiene products.

Benzophenones: This family (Table 22.1) of chemicals are commonly found in sunscreen products as they act as UV filters. Almost 20 % of these products contain benzophenone-1 and benzophenone-3 (Figure 22.1).

Table 22. 1. Chemicals found in cosmetics and PCPs with endocrine disrupting properties.

Compound	Use in cosmetics	Effects on hormone signalling	Refs
Benzophenones	Ultraviolet filters	Oestrogenic activity	2, 4, 5, 17, 31
Bisphenol A	Packaging (banned as an ingredient in 2006)	Oestrogenic activity	2, 4, 5, 17, 33
Octamethylcyclo-tetrasiloxane	Moisturizers	Oestrogenic activity	2, 4, 5, 17
Parabens	Preservative-antimicrobial properties	Oestrogenic activity	2, 4, 5, 17
Phthalates	Plasticizer	Anti-androgenic activity	2, 4, 5, 17
Poly-fluorinated chemicals	Antiaging products	Altering sex hormone levels?	2, 17

Other chemicals found in cosmetics and PCPs with possible endocrine-disrupting properties include bisphenols, camphenes, dimethicones and oxycinnamates which are present in epoxy resins, polycarbonate plastics and are added to products for mechanical and thermal stability. As illustrated in Figure 22.1 these compounds have diverse chemical structures, but are generally aromatic and planar in structure, properties shared with selective oestrogen receptor modulators (SERMs) and anti-androgens and to a lesser degree steroid hormone.

Although not named on PCPs or cosmetics labels, some EDCs such as dioxin are by-products of manufacturing. Dioxins are absorbed and stored in adipose tissue and have been implicated in the pathogenesis of deep infiltrating endometriosis in humans (7).

Steroid hormones and the endocrine system

Biosynthesis and metabolism

There are five groups of steroid hormones which play critical roles in reproductive health (androgens, progestins, oestrogens), development (androgens, oestrogens), metabolic regulation (androgens, glucocorticoids, oestrogens) and salt balance (mineralocorticoids) (Figure 22.2, Table 22.2). The major classes of sex steroids were initially isolated and chemically synthesised in the first half of the 20th century, which led to major advances in the understanding of the mechanisms of action and their use as therapeutic agents.

The key organs in steroid biosynthesis are the ovaries and placenta in women and the testes in men and the adrenal glands of both sexes. However, it has also been recognised that steroid synthesis and metabolic enzymes are widely expressed in peripheral tissues of the body, including adipose, regions of the brain and prostate gland. For example, in the prostate the hormone testosterone is metabolised to the more potent androgen dihydrotesterone (DHT) by the enzyme 5α-reductase (8, 9). Steroid hormones are synthesised from cholesterol through a series of enzyme-catalysed reactions involving cytochrome P450 and hydroxysteroid dehydrogenase enzymes (Figure 22.2). The rate-limiting step in steroid biosynthesis is catalysed by the steroid 20,22-lyase, Cyp11A1, which cleaves the side-chain of cholesterol to produce pregnenolone, which represents a common precursor for all classes of steroid hormone (Figure 22.2).

Two classes of P450 enzymes are required for steroid biosynthesis: type I found in the mitochondria and type II located in the endoplasmic reticulum (8, 9). In addition to de novo biosynthesis, the levels of active steroid hormone can be regulated by metabolising enzymes which add or remove sulphate or glucuronic acid groups at the 3, 17 or 21 position of the steroid structure (9).

Receptors and mechanisms of action

Steroid hormones bind to and activate intracellular receptor proteins that function as ligand-activated transcription factors regulating networks of target genes in a cell-or tissue-selective manner (Figure 22.3). Steroid receptors have a well-defined structural and domain organisation, consisting of a C-terminal ligand binding domain, linked via a hinge region to the highly conserved DNA-binding domain and, lastly, a structurally flexible and variable amino-terminal domain (Figure 22.3) (10).

Natural hormones, such as the androgen, testosterone (T) and the oestrogen, oestradiol (E2) bind to the ligand binding pocket in the LBD (Figure 22.3). This is also the site of binding of clinically important drugs, for example, the anti-androgen enzalutamide and selective oestrogen receptor modulator (SERM) tamoxifen (Figures 22.1C and 22.3), which modulate signalling by the androgen and oestrogen receptors respectively. Enzalutamide acts as a competitive inhibitor of T or DHT binding to the androgen receptor and is thought to block nuclear translocation and/or productive interactions with co-regulatory proteins, thereby repressing androgen signalling (11) (Figure 22.3). In contrast, the SERMs tamoxifen and raloxifene exhibit both tissue selective agonist and antagonist activity when bound to the oestrogen receptor: competing for oestradiol binding and inhibiting signalling in breast tissue, while promoting oestrogenic activity in the uterus and bone respectively (12) (Figure 22.3).

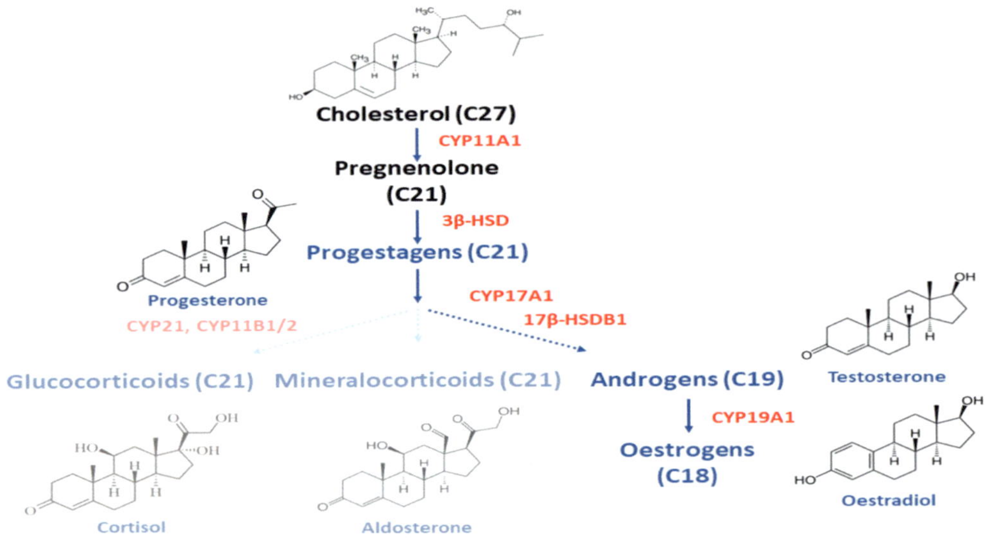

Figure 22.2: Summary of steroid hormone biosynthesis. *Simplified pathway of steroid hormone synthesis from cholesterol through a series of hydroxylation and reduction reactions, which take place in the mitochondria and endoplasmic reticulum. Figure emphasises the sex hormones - progesterone, testosterone and oestradiol and some of the key biosynthetic enzymes (in red) involved.*

Steroid hormone receptor represents a sub-family of the nuclear receptor superfamily which also includes receptors for thyroid hormones, fatty acids, xenobiotics, retinoic acid derivatives and vitamin D_3 (10). In addition to the above classical pathway of steroid hormone action, sex steroids can act through several non-classical mechanisms (13-15). These include association of steroid receptors with the plasma membrane and binding of hormone to transmembrane, G-protein coupled receptors (i.e. GPER1 for oestradiol and ZIP9 for testosterone) (13, 15). Non-classical signalling can involve cross-talk with growth factor signalling and the involvement of multiple kinase cascades, resulting in phosphorylation of both cytoplasmic and nuclear substrates: one common pathway involves mitogen active kinases (MAPs) (13-15). As with the classical pathway, EDCs can impact on the non-classical signalling pathways to altered physiological responses (16).

Table 22.2. Physiological actions of steroid hormones.

Steroid	Functions	
	Development	Adult
Androgens	Male differentiation and development	Male secondary sexual characteristics (puberty); anabolic actions
Oestrogens	Maintenance of pregnancy	Female secondary sexual characteristics (puberty); bone strength
Progesterone	Maintenance of pregnancy	Female fertility (implantation and maintenance of pregnancy); metabolic regulation
Glucocorticoids	Embryo development and maintenance of pregnancy; foetal programming	Stress response; metabolic regulation; immune system; anti-inflammatory actions
Mineralocorticoids	Salt balance	Salt balance; metabolic syndrome and cardiovascular disease

See Endotext (https://www.endotext.org/) for more details

Endocrine disrupting chemicals

Any exogenous compound that may interfere with the synthesis, secretion, transport, metabolism, receptor binding or elimination of endogenous hormones, thereby altering the endocrine and homeostatic systems, is defined as an endocrine disrupting chemical (EDC) according to the US Environmental Protection Agency (5). EDCs can interact with nuclear hormone receptors such as thyroid hormone receptors, androgen receptor, oestrogen receptors as well as non-nuclear receptors, for example, dopamine receptor, a cell surface G-protein coupled receptor that binds the neurotransmitter dopamine. Interaction of EDCs with hormone-signalling pathways alters the synthesis of steroid hormones from cholesterol, compete for binding sites on receptors (as agonist or antagonist), modulates transport and gene expression as well as epigenetic profiles and metabolic/clearance. Collectively, this leads to imbalances in the hormone homeostasis and signalling (17, 18). Also known as endocrine modulators or environmental hormones, these chemicals have been shown in both animal models and human cohorts to play a role in reduced fertility, endometriosis, obesity, diabetes, cognitive deficits and even cancer (19-27). EDCs are ubiquitous and commonly found in everyday products such as metal food cans, plastics, detergents, toys, pesticides, flame retardants as well as cosmetics and PCPs.

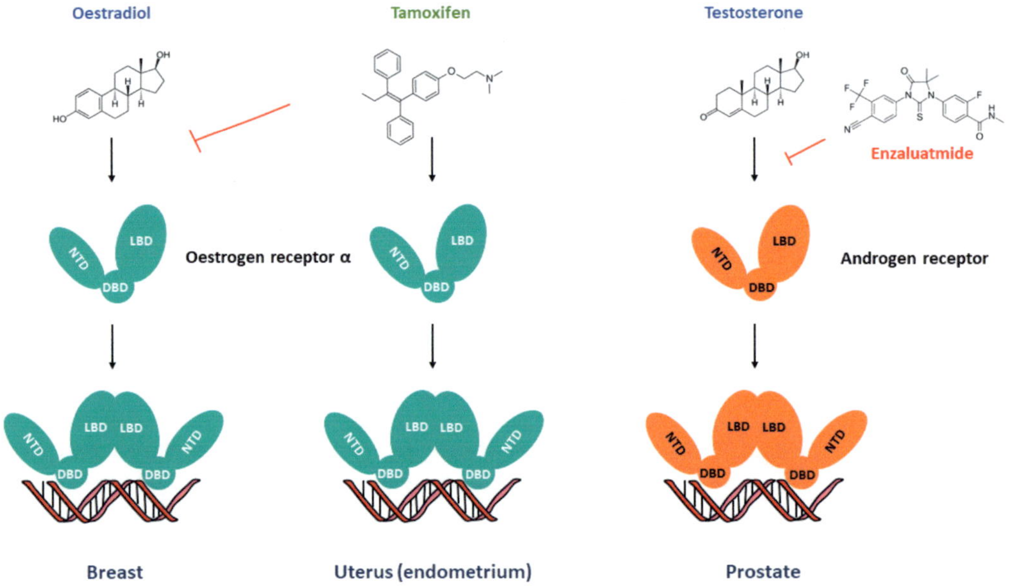

Figure 22.3. Domain organisation and mechanism of action of steroid hormones. *Steroid hormone receptors are part of a large family of nuclear receptors and have a characteristic domain organisation: LBD, ligand binding domain; DBD, DNA binding domain; and NTD, amino-terminal domain. In the absence of steroid, these receptors (e.g. oestrogen and androgen receptors) are localised in the cytoplasm, upon binding hormone (agonist), the receptor moves from the cytoplasm to the nucleus, where it binds target sites in the genome (DNA response elements) as homodimers to upregulate or down regulate networks of target gene expression. The SERM tamoxifen exhibits antagonist action in breast, but pro-oestrogenic activity in uterus. The anti-androgen, enzalutamide is an androgen receptor antagonist and inhibits androgen activity in target tissues such as the prostate. EDCs can act by competing for the binding of the natural hormone to the LBD, or binding could result in alternative receptor structures and alterations in co-regulatory protein binding leading to changes in gene expression.*

Classification of EDCs

Based on their origin, EDCs can be naturally occurring or synthetic. Naturally occurring EDCs include phytoestrogens found in soy-based foods as well as natural hormones produced by a species which has an impact on another species. Synthetic EDCs are man-made chemicals or by-products which include, but are not limited to bisphenol A (BPA), phthalates, polychlorintated biphenyls, dichlorodiphenyltrichoroethane (DDT), parabens and diethylstilbestrol (DES) (Table 22.1, Figure 22.1) (1, 2, 4, 5). They typically originate from chemical, agricultural and pharmaceutical industries where they are used as industrial solvents, plastics, pesticides and as contents of some cosmetic products like creams and shampoos. Drugs such as oral contraceptives, cimetidine and diethylstilbestrol can similarly be classified as EDCs (5). As many EDCs have lipophilic properties, they tend to bioaccumulate in the adipose tissue otherwise referred to as body fat and can be released to systemic circulation following weight loss (28).

EDCs can also be classified as persistent and non-persistent depending on their degree of liposolubility or resistance to degradation. Persistent EDCs have low biodegradability, high lipophilicity and tend to accumulate in adipose tissues and biomagnify in the food chain, for example, organochlorine pesticides (27). Phthalates, BPA and parabens fall into the category of non-persistent EDCs as they are less lipid-soluble, more easily metabolized or rapidly excreted (29, 30). As the primary point of exposure to these non-persistent EDCs is via the skin, they are able to avoid hepatic first-pass effect and tend to have high bioavailability in the body.

Mechanism of action(s) impacting human health

The skin, as the largest organ in the body, is the main route of exposure to EDCs found in cosmetics and PCPs, through the topical application of creams and lotions which can be directly absorbed. EDCs can also be inhaled via fragrances and hair sprays. They can also get into the systemic circulation via ingestion using lipsticks and related products. In addition, EDCs can be transferred to an unborn child via embryonic exposure and to new-born infants through breast milk (see below).

Bisphenol A, parabens, phthalates, and benzophenones found in cosmetics and PCPs are described as 'non-persistent' EDCs and may impact negatively on human health by disrupting the synthesis, metabolism, or action of steroid hormones, in particular the sex hormones. As described above and in Table 22.1, phthalates are known to have antiandrogen properties, while bisphenol A, parabens and benzophenones can act as oestrogenic compounds, promoting oestrogenic signalling. It is therefore noteworthy, that the UV filter 4-methyl-benzlidene camphor (4-MBC) disrupted male development (delayed puberty and reduced weight of the prostate in adult animals) and at the molecular level altered the expression of the androgen and oestrogen receptors, at both the mRNA and protein level. In this study five- to six-week-old male and female mice were treated with 0.7 up to 47 mg/kg/day 4-MBC for ten-weeks prior to mating. Treatment of female animals was continued during pregnancy and lactation and in off-spring until adulthood (31). Furthermore, oestradiol repression of AR and IGF-1 mRNA expression was antagonised by 4-MBC possibly because of altering the expression of the nuclear receptor co-repressor protein, NCoR (31). Collectively, these results suggest a complex modulation of steroid signalling by 4-MBC exposure.

EDCs found in cosmetics and PCPs have been associated with the aetiology of cryptorchidism (see Box 1), infertility, and possibly prostate and testicular cancers in men (Figure 22.4) (for recent reviews see 5, 25 and references therein). In females, different

Box 1 Reproductive health terminology

Term	Definition
Cryptorchidism	Failure of one or both testicles to descend into scrotum during development.
Endometriosis	Endometriosis is a painful condition where tissues similar to lining of the uterus (womb) grows in other places e.g. ovaries, fallopian tubes tissues lining the pelvis.
Gynaecomastia	Enlargement of the breast tissue in boys or men caused by hormonal imbalance.
Hypospadias	Abnormal formation urethra in boys, where the opening is not at the tip of the penis.
Menarche	First menstrual cycle in in girls reaching puberty.
Menopause	The point in a woman's life when the body stops producing the hormones oestrogen and progesterone that cause the menstrual period, which eventually stop. Other symptoms include hot flushes, reduced sex drive and mood changes.
Polycystic ovarian syndrome (PCOS)	PCOS is a condition where woman produce excess male hormones (androgens), which causes problems menstrual periods, infertility and face and body hair growth.
Premenstrual syndrome	A collection of symptoms that include and not limited to changes in mood, headaches, fatigue, breast tenderness which can occur in women roughly two weeks before their period.
Spermatogenesis	The production and development of sperm cells in the testes of male.
Testicular atrophy	The shrinkage of the testicles in male which may lead to a loss of function.
Thelarche	Onset of adult breast development normally associated with puberty.

groups of EDCs have been associated with endometriosis, hormone-dependent cancers (breast, ovarian) and risks of exposure in-utero (Figure 22.4) (for reviews see 5, 25, 26).

Of particular concern is the evidence linking bisphenol A compounds and phthalates with reproductive defects in both women and men (Figure 22.4) (2, 5, 25, 26, 32-38). In rodent, both mouse and rat, models maternal exposure to BPA caused altered prostate gland and breast development in male and female animals respectively (5). Elevated levels of BPA have been associated in boys with cryptorchism (34). Exposure to phthalates or phthalate mixtures caused cryptorchism in male rats (5) and disrupted normal female reproduction in mice, having a negative impact on follicle growth and health (35, 36). In the study by Zhou et al (35), two-month-old female mice were mated and at gestational day 10, dosed orally with a phthalate mixture (20 µg/ kg/ day up to 500 mg/kg/day) until birth. In the subsequent study (36) ovaries and follicles were collected from 32- to 42-day old mice and treated in culture with a phthalate mixture (0.065 to 325 µg/ ml) based on proportions measured in the urine from pregnant woman. It has been proposed these effects are because of altered steroid hormone biosynthesis and/or increased expression of oestrogen receptor alpha or androgen receptor (5, 34). There are increasing evidence to suggest the association between a decline in the quality of semen and presence of BPA in the urine of men exposure to this EDC (37, 38).

In woman, phthalate metabolite levels were associated with occurrence of menopausal hot flushes (39). In addition, a number of studies have reported disruption of puberty. In a study of 31 Puerto Rican girls, precocious thelarche (Box 1) in girls has been associated with high levels of phthalate esters (40). In a USA study that recruited 1051 culturally diverse girls between age 6-8 years old, followed up for 8-11 years and whose urinary levels of phthalates and phenols were measured, a 7-month earlier onset of menarche was associated with higher 2,5-dichlorophenol. In contrast, the phthalate metabolite, mono-3-carboxypropylphthalate was associated with 4-5 months delay in thelarche and menarche (41). The UV-protectant benzophenone-3 and triclosan, which is a component of PCPs mainly used in soaps for its antimicrobial activity, were associated with earlier thelarche (41).

Phthalates have anti-androgenic activity (Table 22.1). In twenty five-day old male Sprague-Dawley rats, exposure to phthalates (for up to 14-days) resulted in testicular atrophy and impaired spermatogenesis (42). However, a study of US men, examining phthalate exposure, measured in urine during adulthood and semen quality revealed negligible effects of phthalates on semen quality (motility and morphology of spermatozoa) (43). In contrast, an earlier study did reveal an association between low sperm motility, concentration, and abnormal sperm morphology and some phthalate monoesters, again measured in urine (44). Collectively, such studies reveal the importance of the window of exposure and the challenges in translating laboratory studies to human populations.

Features of metabolic syndrome (obesity, insulin resistance, hypertension, and dyslipidaemia) in both men and women, as well as oxidative stress and inflammation, have also been linked with cosmetic use and EDCs. The question is how strong is the evidence that the use of cosmetics and PCPs is the source of a particular EDC or directly the cause of impaired endocrine signalling?

Figure 22.4. Impact on human reproductive health of different classes of EDC found in

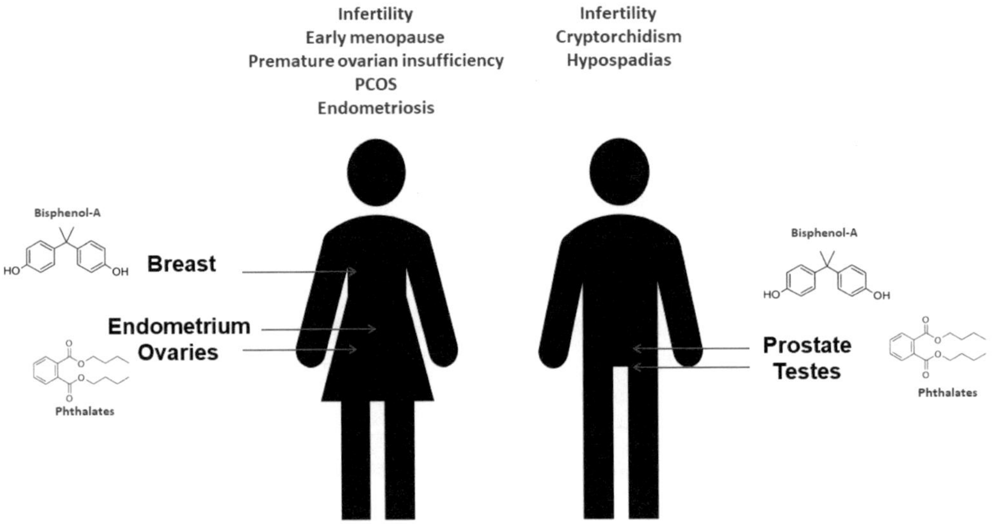

cosmetics and PCP.*Illustrated are some of the suspected impacts of EDCs present in cosmetics and PCPs on reproductive health in woman and men. EDC have been associated with infertility in both sexes and conditions such as endometriosis and polycystic ovarian syndrome (PCOS) in woman and failure of the testes to descend or defects in penis development in boys.*

A major challenge with EDC research is being able to directly link exposure to different chemicals and disruption of normal hormone signalling and determining the active levels in endocrine target tissues. It is significant, therefore, that in addition to correlating the use of particular cosmetics or PCPs and pathophysiological changes (as described above), endogenous levels of EDCs have been measured in serum, menstrual discharge and urine (4). Also, absorption through the skin avoids first-pass metabolism, potentially enhancing bioavailability and biological impact (4).

The timing and duration of exposure to EDCs are critical determinants of their effects on the endocrine system. Exposure during development – pregnancy, lactation and puberty – have been linked to severe health outcomes such as developmental abnormalities and the risk of chronic diseases later in life. The window of susceptibility to endocrine-associated cancers is usually opened at early life. In prostate cancer for instance, exposure to BPA and other EDCs have been shown to be capable of reprograming the developing foetal prostate gland, predisposing it to carcinogenic tendency in the mature gland (45). EDCs may also affect hormonal balance during puberty which may lead to molecular changes in later years. A time dependent exposure to xenoestrogens, EDCs that mimic oestrogen, during development of the mammary glands may disrupt signalling which may lead to early menarche or prolonged puberty (31, 46, 47).

Lavender oil and tea tree oil, which are essential oils, are also reported to have endocrine disrupting properties. Topical administration of products containing lavender, or tea tree oils have been associated with precocious puberty in males who developed gynaecomastia and premature thelarche in females in clinical studies (48, 49). The presence of anti-androgenic and pro-oestrogenic activity was determined in laboratory studies using human cell-lines, expressing the androgen and/or oestrogen receptor α. Discontinuation of products containing these oils reversed the breast growth in both sexes (48, 49).

Musk ketone and xylene are components of fragrances. Analysis of the association between musk ketone and xylene blood levels and gynaecological/endocrine dysfunction in premenopausal women found that women with premenstrual syndrome had higher blood levels of musk ketone compared with women without premenstrual syndrome (50). A significant inverse association between musk xylene levels and levels of luteal phase hormones, oestrogen and progesterone was observed (50). Infertile women also had higher serum levels of musk xylene compared to those who had been pregnant once (50). This study brings to light a potential endocrine disruptive property of nitromusk which is a component of some fragrances.

A comprehensive 2010 study, with pairs of mothers and infants from Switzerland, highlighted another challenge associated with determining the health impacts of EDC present in cosmetics, namely inter-individual variability (51). Mothers were sampled at either 4 to 21 days postnatally (n=49) or after day 34 (n=5). No differences were seen between the two groups. However, in the case of UV filters and synthetic musk fragrances greater than 80% of breast milk samples tested positive, while parabens were measured in 15 to 34% cases (sample size 54 mother infant pairs) (51). Significantly, using information from a questionnaire the authors correlated cosmetic use with the presence of UV filers in breast milk. Levels of monophthalate esters were also detected, but due to small sample size (n=20) no statistical correlations could be drawn (51). In a recent systematic review of the literature, covering the last two decades (2000-2020), the authors found evidence for the presence of bisphenols, parabens and benzophenones in

63.6%, 27.9-63.4% and 39.5% of studies respectively (52). A number of studies related exposure to the use of facial cleansers, sun-blockers, make-up or skin care products: overall, a small fraction (16%) of these studies identified socio-demographic and lifestyle factors as likely source for the EDC (46 and references therein). Interestingly, the authors found both geographical and temporal variation in the concentrations of bisphenols, parabens and benzophenones in breast milk: BPA was higher in Asia, when compared with USA and Europe, while benzophenone-3 was considerably higher in European studies and dramatically increased in the last ten years (2011-2020). During the same period BPA increased by 2-fold and methylparaben showed a 6-fold decrease (52). The authors related these changes to the production, availability and/or use of these families of EDCs. Collectively, these studies demonstrate infant exposure to a range of chemicals found in cosmetics and PCPs with potential endocrine disrupting properties. However, as stressed by Artacho-Cordón and colleagues (52) determining the health impacts of this exposure is more challenging and clearly more research in this area is required, with consideration given to study design, sample collection and data reporting to avoid biases and facilitate comparative analysis across studies.

Summary

Steroid hormones act as crucial signals at all stages of life, from conception, to maintaining a healthy pregnancy, through to adult life. The biosynthesis, metabolism of the hormones as well as the tissues selective expressing of specific intracellular receptor proteins work in balance to ensure appropriate temporal and spatial regulation of our reproductive and metabolic physiology. The wide-spread use of cosmetics and PCPs represent a major source of exposure to a range of chemicals, some of which have demonstrated endocrine-disrupting properties in laboratory studies. The major families of EDC in cosmetics and PCPs are bisphenols, parabens, phthalates and benzophenones which have oestrogenic or antiandrogenic activities. Therefore, the use of cosmetics and PCPs is indeed more than skin deep, as these compounds, separately or in combination, have the potential to upset the normal endocrine balance and adversely affect the health not only of the individual, but also their off-springs.

References

1. Giwercman, A and Jégou B. Editorial overview: Current Opinion in Endocrinology and Metabolic Research: Endocrine disruptors. Current Opinion in Endocrine and Metabolic Research. 2019; 7: iv-vii.

2. Laws MJ, Neff AM, Brehm E, Warner GR, Flaws JA. Endocrine disrupting chemicals and reproductive disorders in women, men, and animal models. Adv Pharmacol. 2021; 92: 151-190. doi: 10.1016/bs.apha.2021.03.008.
3. STRAUSS JS. Hormones in Cosmetics. JAMA. 1963; 186: 759-762. doi: 10.1001/jama.1963.03710080031006.
4. Francisco M. Peinado, Luz M. Iribarne-Durán, Olga Ocón-Hernández, Nicolás Olea and Francisco Artacho-Cordón (June 29th 2020). Endocrine Disrupting Chemicals in Cosmetics and Personal Care Products and Risk of Endometriosis, Endometriosis, Courtney Marsh, IntechOpen, DOI: 10.5772/intechopen.93091. Available from: https://www.intechopen.com/chapters/72654
5. Diamanti-Kandarakis E, Bourguignon J, Giudice LC, Hauser R, Prins GS, Soto AM, et al. Endocrine-Disrupting Chemicals: An Endocrine Society Scientific Statement. *Endocrine reviews.* 2009; 30 (4): 293-342. Available from: doi: 10.1210/er.2009-0002 Available from: https://doi.org/10.1210/er.2009-0002 [Accessed 11/24/2021].
6. Gore AC, Chappell VA, Fenton SE, Flaws JA, Nadal A, Prins GS, Toppari J, Zoeller RT. Executive Summary to EDC-2: The Endocrine Society's Second Scientific Statement on Endocrine-Disrupting Chemicals. Endocr Rev. 2015; 36(6): 593-602.
7. Martínez-Zamora MA, Mattioli L, Parera J, Abad E, Coloma JL, van Babel B, et al. Increased levels of dioxin-like substances in adipose tissue in patients with deep infiltrating endometriosis. Hum Reprod 2015;30(5):1059-1068.
8. Miller WL, Auchus RJ. The molecular biology, biochemistry, and physiology of human steroidogenesis and its disorders. Endocr Rev. 2011; 32(1):81-151. doi: 10.1210/er.2010-0013.
9. Schiffer L, Barnard L, Baranowski ES, Gilligan LC, Taylor AE, Arlt W, Shackleton CHL, Storbeck KH. Human steroid biosynthesis, metabolism and excretion are differentially reflected by serum and urine steroid metabolomes: A comprehensive review. J Steroid Biochem Mol Biol. 2019; 194:105439. doi: 10.1016/j.jsbmb.2019.105439.
10. McEwan IJ. The Nuclear Receptor Superfamily at Thirty. Methods Mol Biol. 2016; 1443: 3-9. doi: 10.1007/978-1-4939-3724-0_1.
11. Tran C, Ouk S, Clegg NJ, Chen Y, Watson PA, Arora V, Wongvipat J, Smith-Jones PM, Yoo D, Kwon A, Wasielewska T, Welsbie D, Chen CD, Higano CS, Beer TM, Hung DT, Scher HI, Jung ME, Sawyers CL. Development of a second-generation antiandrogen for treatment of advanced prostate cancer. Science. 2009; 324(5928):787-90.
12. Sporn MB and Lippman SM. Agents for chemoprevention and their mechanism of action. In Holland-Frei Cancer Medicine 6th Edition. 2003. Editors: Donald W Kufe, Raphael E Pollock, Ralph R Weichselbaum, Robert C Bast, Jr, Ted S Gansler, James F Holland, and Emil Frei, III.
13. Rahman F, Christian HC. Non-classical actions of testosterone: an update. Trends Endocrinol Metab. 2007; 18(10): 371-8.
14. Garg D, Ng SSM, Baig KM, Driggers P, Segars J. Progesterone-Mediated Non-Classical Signaling. Trends Endocrinol Metab. 2017; 28(9): 656-668.
15. Pillerová M, Borbélyová V, Hodosy J, Riljak V, Renczés E, Frick KM, Tóthová Ľ. On the

role of sex steroids in biological functions by classical and non-classical pathways. An update. Front Neuroendocrinol. 2021; 62: 100926. doi: 10.1016/j.yfrne.2021.100926.

16. Sonavane M. Classical and Non-classical estogen receptor effects of bisphenol A. In Toxicology 2022; No. 43 Bisphenol A: A Multi-modal Endocrine Disruptor. Edited by NR Gassman.
17. Balaguer P, Delfosse V, Grimaldi M, Bourguet W. Structural and functional evidences for the interactions between nuclear hormone receptors and endocrine disruptors at low doses. C R Biol. 2017; 340(9-10): 414-420.
18. La Merrill MA, Vandenberg LN, Smith MT, Goodson W, Browne P, Patisaul HB, et al. Consensus on the key characteristics of endocrine-disrupting chemicals as a basis for hazard identification. *Nature Reviews Endocrinology.* 2020; 16 (1): 45-57. Available from: doi: 10.1038/s41574-019-0273-8 Available from: https://doi.org/10.1038/s41574-019-0273-8 .
19. Axelstad M, Hass U, Scholze M, Christiansen S, Kortenkamp A, Boberg J. EDC IMPACT: Reduced sperm counts in rats exposed to human relevant mixtures of endocrine disrupters. *Endocrine connections.* 2018; 7 (1): 139-148. Available from: doi: 10.1530/EC-17-0307 [doi] .
20. Johansson HKL, Svingen T, Fowler PA, Vinggaard AM, Boberg J. Environmental influences on ovarian dysgenesis - developmental windows sensitive to chemical exposures. *Nature reviews.Endocrinology.* 2017; 13 (7): 400-414. Available from: doi: 10.1038/nrendo.2017.36 [doi] .
21. Ghassabian A, Trasande L. Disruption in Thyroid Signaling Pathway: A Mechanism for the Effect of Endocrine-Disrupting Chemicals on Child Neurodevelopment. *Frontiers in Endocrinology.* 2018; 9 204. Available from: https://www.frontiersin.org/article/10.3389/fendo.2018.00204 .
22. Cano-Sancho G, Salmon AG, La Merrill MA. Association between Exposure to p,p'-DDT and Its Metabolite p,p'-DDE with Obesity: Integrated Systematic Review and Meta-Analysis. *Environmental health perspectives.* 2017; 125 (9): 096002. Available from: doi: 10.1289/EHP527 [doi] .
23. Alonso-Magdalena P, Vieira E, Soriano S, Menes L, Burks D, Quesada I, et al. Bisphenol A exposure during pregnancy disrupts glucose homeostasis in mothers and adult male offspring. *Environmental health perspectives.* 2010; 118 (9): 1243-1250. Available from: doi: 10.1289/ehp.1001993 [doi] .
24. Scsukova S, Rollerova E, Bujnakova Mlynarcikova A. Impact of endocrine disrupting chemicals on onset and development of female reproductive disorders and hormone-related cancer. *Reproductive Biology.* 2016; 16 (4): 243-254. Available from: doi: https://doi.org/10.1016/j.repbio.2016.09.001
25. Sifakis S, Androutsopoulos VP, Tsatsakis AM, Spandidos DA. Human exposure to endocrine disrupting chemicals: effects on the male and female reproductive systems. *Environmental toxicology and pharmacology.* 2017; 51 56-70. Available from: doi: https://doi.org/10.1016/j.etap.2017.02.024

26. Gibson DA, Saunders PT Endocrine disruption of oestrogen action and female reproductive tract cancers. Endocr Relat Cancer. 2014; 21(2):T13-31. doi: 10.1530/ERC-13-0342.
27. Arrebola JP, Fernández MF, Martín-Olmedo P, Molina-Molina JM, Sánchez-Pérez MJ, Sánchez-Cantalejo E, et al. Adipose tissue concentrations of persistent organic pollutants and total cancer risk in an adult cohort from Southern Spain: Preliminary data from year 9 of the follow-up. *Science of The Total Environment.* 2014; 500-501 243-249. Available from: doi: https://doi.org/10.1016/j.scitotenv.2014.08.043 Available from: https://www.sciencedirect.com/science/article/pii/S0048969714012224 .
28. Darbre PD. Endocrine Disruptors and Obesity. Current Obesity Reports 2017;6(1):18-27.
29. Peinado FM, Ocón-Hernández O, Iribarne-Durán LM, Vela-Soria F, Ubiña A, Padilla C, Mora JC, Cardona J, León J, Fernández MF, Olea N, Artacho-Cordón F. Cosmetic and personal care product use, urinary levels of parabens and benzophenones, and risk of endometriosis: results from the EndEA study. Environ Res. 2021; 196: 110342. doi: 10.1016/j.envres.2020.110342.
30. Søeborg T, Frederiksen H, Andersson AM. Considerations for estimating daily intake values of nonpersistent environmental endocrine disruptors based on urinary biomonitoring data. *Reproduction (Cambridge, England).* 2014; 147 (4): 455-463. Available from: doi: 10.1530/REP-13-0458.
31. Durrer S, Ehnes C, Fuetsch M, Maerkel K, Schlumpf M, Lichtensteiger W. Estrogen sensitivity of target genes and expression of nuclear receptor co-regulators in rat prostate after pre- and postnatal exposure to the ultraviolet filter 4-methylbenzylidene camphor. Environ Health Perspect. 2007; 115 Suppl 1(Suppl 1):42-50. doi: 10.1289/ehp.9134.
32. Rodprasert W, Toppari J, Virtanen HE. Endocrine Disrupting Chemicals and Reproductive Health in Boys and Men. Front Endocrinol (Lausanne). 2021; 12: 706532.
33. Li Y, Burns KA, Arao Y, Luh CJ, Korach KS. Differential estrogenic actions of endocrine-disrupting chemicals bisphenol A, bisphenol AF, and zearalenone through estrogen receptor α and β in vitro. Environ Health Perspect. 2012; 120(7): 1029-35.
34. Komarowska MD, Grubczak K, Czerniecki J, Hermanowicz A, Hermanowicz JM, Debek W, Matuszczak E. Identification of the Bisphenol A (BPA) and the Two Analogues BPS and BPF in Cryptorchidism. Front Endocrinol (Lausanne). 2021; 12: 694669. doi: 10.3389/fendo.2021.694669.
35. Zhou C, Gao L, Flaws JA. Prenatal exposure to an environmentally relevant phthalate mixture disrupts reproduction in F1 female mice. Toxicol Appl Pharmacol. 2017; 318: 49-57.
36. Meling DD, Warner GR, Szumski JR, Gao L, Gonsioroski AV, Rattan S, Flaws JA. The effects of a phthalate metabolite mixture on antral follicle growth and sex steroid synthesis in mice. Toxicol Appl Pharmacol. 2020;388: 114875.

37. Meeker JD, Ehrlich S, Toth TL, Wright DL, Calafat AM, Trisini AT, et al. Semen quality and sperm DNA damage in relation to urinary bisphenol A among men from an infertility clinic. Reproductive Toxicology 2010;30(4):532-539.
38. Knez J, Kranvogl R, Breznik BP, Vončina E, Vlaisavljević V. Are urinary bisphenol A levels in men related to semen quality and embryo development after medically assisted reproduction? Fertil Steril 2014;101(1):215-221.e5.
39. Ziv-Gal A, Gallicchio L, Chiang C, Ther SN, Miller SR, Zacur HA, Dills RL, Flaws JA. Phthalate metabolite levels and menopausal hot flashes in midlife women. Reprod Toxicol. 2016; 60: 76-81.
40. Colón I, Caro D, Bourdony CJ, Rosario O. Identification of phthalate esters in the serum of young Puerto Rican girls with premature breast development. Environ Health Perspect 2000;108(9):895-900.
41. Wolff MS, Pajak A, Pinney SM, Windham GC, Galvez M, Rybak M, et al. Associations of urinary phthalate and phenol biomarkers with menarche in a multiethnic cohort of young girls. Reproductive Toxicology 2017;67:56-64.
42. Park JD, Habeebu SSM, Klaassen CD. Testicular toxicity of di-(2-ethylhexyl)phthalate in young Sprague–Dawley rats. Toxicology 2002;171(2):105-115.
43. Thurston SW, Mendiola J, Bellamy AR, Levine H, Wang C, Sparks A, et al. Phthalate exposure and semen quality in fertile US men. Andrology 2016;4(4):632-638.
44. Duty SM, Silva MJ, Barr DB, Brock JW, Ryan L, Chen Z, et al. Phthalate Exposure and Human Semen Parameters. Epidemiology 2003;14(3).
45. Prins GS, Calderon-Gierszal E, Hu W. Stem Cells as Hormone Targets That Lead to Increased Cancer Susceptibility. *Endocrinology.* 2015; 156 (10): 3451-3457. Available from: doi: 10.1210/en.2015-1357 Available from: https://pubmed.ncbi.nlm.nih.gov/26241068.
46. Cohn BA, Cirillo PM, Terry MB. DDT and Breast Cancer: Prospective Study of Induction Time and Susceptibility Windows. *JNCI: Journal of the National Cancer Institute.* 2019; 111 (8): 803-810. Available from: doi: 10.1093/jnci/djy198 Available from: https://doi.org/10.1093/jnci/djy198 [Accessed 8/22/2021].
47. Özen S, Darcan Ş. Effects of environmental endocrine disruptors on pubertal development. *Journal of clinical research in pediatric endocrinology.* 2011; 3 (1): 1-6. Available from: doi: 10.4274/jcrpe.v3i1.01 Available from: https://pubmed.ncbi.nlm.nih.gov/21448326.
48. Henley DV, Lipson N, Korach KS, Bloch CA. Prepubertal Gynecomastia Linked to Lavender and Tea Tree Oils. N Engl J Med 2007;356(5):479-485.
49. Ramsey JT, Li Y, Arao Y, Naidu A, Coons LA, Diaz A, et al. Lavender Products Associated With Premature Thelarche and Prepubertal Gynecomastia: Case Reports and Endocrine-Disrupting Chemical Activities. J Clin Endocrinol Metab 2019;104(11):5393-5405.
50. Eisenhardt S, Runnebaum B, Bauer K, Gerhard I. Nitromusk Compounds in Women with Gynecological and Endocrine Dysfunction. Environ Res 2001;87(3):123-130.
51. Schlumpf M, Kypke K, Wittassek M, Angerer J, Mascher H, Mascher D, Vökt C, Birchler M, Lichtensteiger W. Exposure patterns of UV filters, fragrances, parabens, phthalates,

organochlor pesticides, PBDEs, and PCBs in human milk: correlation of UV filters with use of cosmetics. Chemosphere. 2010; 81(10):1171-83. doi: 10.1016/j.chemosphere.2010.09.079.

52. Iribarne-Durán LM, Peinado FM, Freire C, Castillero-Rosales I, Artacho-Cordón F, Olea N. Concentrations of bisphenols, parabens, and benzophenones in human breast milk: A systematic review and meta-analysis. Sci Total Environ. 2022; 806(Pt 1):150437. doi: 10.1016/j.scitotenv.2021.150437.

CHAPTER TWENTY-THREE

Cosmetics and their implication in cancer

Folake A. Orafidiya

A plethora of chemicals found in cosmetics or personal care products (PCPs) are considered safe. However, a growing number of studies in animal models and humans indicates that some of these chemicals may be associated with the onset and progression of cancer. As PCPs and cosmetics are mostly used daily, it is important to take into consideration the potential long-term effects of exposure to these chemicals. Following the use of some of these PCPs, some of their metabolites are found in breast milk which not only has implications for breast cancer but can also be transferred to breastfed infants with potentially deleterious consequences later in life. This chapter contains evidence for the implication of the use of cosmetics and their potential associations with cancer. In addition, it also highlights the anticancer properties of some natural products. As there are conflicting pieces of evidence in published studies, a definitive conclusion on the role of certain cosmetics or ingredients used therein, and their impact in carcinogenesis cannot be drawn. However, this chapter summarises the current state of the literature surrounding the links between cosmetics and PCPs and their implications in cancer.

History and epidemiology of cancer

Cancer, now ranked as one of the leading causes of death in most countries, continues to be a burden to public health and its increased frequency in recent times has posed questions surrounding its causes and natural history (1).

The discovery of the fossil of an early human ancestor with malignant neoplastic disease dating back to about 1.6 million years is evidence that cancer has plagued humans since primeval times (2). Prates and colleagues reported prostate cancer bone metastasis in a Ptolemaic Egyptian mummy (285-30 BC) (3).The Edwin Smith Papyrus, dating back to about 3000 BC, gives the earliest description of human cancer possibly written by Imhotep, a Physician-Architect, who chronicled breast cancer as being incurable if it is cool to touch, bulging and has spread over the breast (4). The George Ebers Papyrus of

1500 BC, on the other hand, documented the use of herbs and magic for cancer treatment (5). These findings and similar ones support the existence of cancer in antiquity. In 2020, an estimated 19.3 million new cancer cases and approximately 10 million deaths were reported, with female breast cancer described as the most diagnosed cancer, closely followed by lung cancer (6). The markedly increased prevalence in recent times may be attributed to an aggregate of factors which include but are not limited to genetics and family history, lifestyle modifications because of socioeconomic development, longer life expectancy, advances in medical diagnosis as well as an increase in carcinogens in consumer products and in the environment.

Classification of cancer

Cancers can be classified histologically based on the type of cells from which they arise.

- Lymphomas - which emanate from the glands of the lymphatic system, subcategorised into Hodgkin lymphoma and non-Hodgkin lymphoma
- Carcinomas – malignancies of epithelial cells, further subcategorised as adenocarcinoma (organ or gland) and squamous cell carcinoma (squamous epithelium)
- Sarcomas which are solid tumours of the connective tissues- muscles, bones, cartilage
- Myelomas are cancers with origin in the plasma cells of the bone marrow
- Leukaemia – bone marrow cancer

Furthermore, they can also be classified by the primary site where they develop, e.g., breast cancer originating from breast tissue, melanoma from the skin etc.

Risk factors for cancer

Genetics and family history

Although most cancers are a result of genetic aberrations that occur over a lifetime, the implication of heritage is now apparent for cancer risk. Inherited genetic mutations account for approximately 5-10% of all cancers (7). Mutations in genes such as tumour protein 53 (TP53), Kristen Rat Sarcoma Viral Proto-oncogene (KRAS), breast cancer 1/2 (BRCA1/2), Ataxia-telangiectasia mutated (ATM), Phosphatase and Tensin Homolog (PTEN) are implicated in various cancers. Hereditary breast and ovarian cancer syndrome, an autosomal dominantly inherited cancer typified by breast cancer or ovarian cancer or both in multiple family members, is an example. It is associated primarily with mutation in the BRCA1/2 genes although mutations in other tumour suppressors such as PTEN and TP53 as well as oncogenes have also been documented to drive this cancer (8). Tumour suppressor genes encode proteins that regulate cell division by inhibiting cell proliferation whereas oncogenes stimulate cell growth and survival.

Breast cancer gene 1/2 (BRCA1/2) are tumour suppressor genes which maintain genomic stability. The likelihood of a woman developing breast cancer by the age of 70 years is 8%, however, this increases to 65% and 45% for BRCA1 and BRCA2 mutation carriers, respectively (9). A similar pattern is seen in ovarian cancer where risk of carcinogenesis is 39% for females with inherited BRCA1 variant and 11% in those with BRCA2 variant (10). Inheriting a dysfunctional BRCA1/2 also increases the chances of developing fallopian tube and peritoneal cancers in women, as well as acute myeloid leukaemia and childhood solid tumours as a result of Fanconi anaemia (11,12). Evidence is conflicting regarding melanoma and non-melanoma skin cancer and BRCA mutation status. However, carriers of this deleterious mutation should be made aware of the potential risk of skin cancer (13).

Founder mutations are alterations in genetic composition that are highly prevalent in a group of individuals who are or were culturally or geographically isolated wherein an ancestor(s) carried an altered copy of the gene. Founder mutations in the BRCA1/2 genes are reported among Blacks, Ashkenazi Jews and Hispanics and may account for an increase in incidence of BRCA mutation-associated cancers in these populations (14-16).

Mutations in BRCA1/2 are also associated with increased risk of prostate, male breast and pancreatic cancers (17). The impact of BRCA mutation in prostate cancer includes adverse clinical features and poor prognosis. An individual with a first degree relative that has prostate cancer has a 2.57-fold lifetime risk of developing this disease (18). The authors of this work went on to reveal an increase of 5.08-fold risk in men who have two or more family members affected by prostate cancer (PC) and further noted a 57% genetic influence compared to a 43% environmental influence in the variability of a twin liability to develop PC (18). The risk of developing the disease was also higher in men with an affected brother (18). It is reported that the risk of one twin developing PC, giving that the other has had PC, is approximately four times higher in monozygotic twins – who share genetic makeup – compared with dizygotic twins and this further emphasizes the component of genetics in cancer development (19). Although mutations in BRCA1/2 is given as an example here, mutations in other genes such as tumour suppressors or oncogenes also predisposes to cancer. Martinez-Jimenez and colleagues provide a comprehensive review on mutated genes that drive cancer (20).

Lifestyle and cancer

Diet, the quality and quantity of food a person habitually eats, is a significant factor in the prevention and/or causation of chronic diseases. The risk of developing certain cancers is associated with some diets. For example, diets rich in processed meat and animal fats are associated with an increased risk of colorectal cancer; and the development of nasopharyngeal cancer is associated with some types of salted fish (21). On the other hand, a diet high in vegetables, nuts, legumes, non-refined cereals, fresh fruits, olive oil, low intake of red meats, moderate consumption of fish, dairy products and alcohol mainly red wine, otherwise known as the 'Mediterranean diet', has been documented to lower the risk of cancer onset as they contain high contents of antioxidants and anti-inflammatory agents (22).

Body mass index (BMI), an anthropometric used to indirectly estimate body fat and mass, has over the years been used as an indicator of whether someone is underweight, of normal weight, overweight or obese. A BMI of between 25-29.9 kg/m^2 and 30 kg/m^2 is regarded as overweight and obese, respectively, conditions which are associated with a number of chronic and non-infectious diseases including cancer (23). Overweight/obese status is associated with increased risk of thirteen cancer types which include colorectal, breast, ovarian and pancreatic cancers according to the International Agency for Research on Cancer working group (24). A worldwide study in 2012 revealed that 3.6% of all new cancer cases in adults were attributed to high BMI (23). In the United Kingdom (UK) specifically, it was revealed that being overweight and obese is associated with 6.3% of cancers, whilst alcohol intake and tobacco smoking accounts for 3.3% and approximately 16% of cases, respectively (21). Smoking of tobacco has long been associated with lung cancer and the duration of smoking is the strongest determinant of developing this malignancy (25).

A sedentary lifestyle, in addition to other unhealthy habits, accelerate tumorigenesis partly via immunological and metabolic dysregulation, whereas being physically active is strongly associated with a 10-20% reduction in relative risk of stomach, colon, breast cancers, and improved survival amongst individuals diagnosed with certain cancers (26,27). Exercise has also been proposed as a strategy to improve the function of tissues by reprograming metabolic and immune-specific pathways (26).

Life expectancy and cancer

Over the past century, there has been an increase in life expectancy worldwide with more people surviving to older ages. According to the World Health Organisation (WHO), between 2015 and 2050, the number of people older than 60 years is expected to nearly double to 22% from 12% (28). The implication of this change is the propensity for the development of chronic diseases in older population, cancer being one of them. In the USA, it is projected that between 2010 and 2030, the incidence of cancer will increase to about 45% owing to an older population (29). There is an increase in the risk of developing cancer up to 70 years, after which there is a reduced risk (30). In fact, there is a threefold decrease in incidence and cancer related death at the age of 90 years and over (31).

Chronic infections and cancer

Exposure to some pathogens and the development of infections can also drive transformation of normal cells to malignant ones. These pathogens can disrupt cell homeostasis, weaken the immune system or cause chronic inflammation leading to cancer. The Epstein-Barr virus, hepatitis (B, C), human immunodeficiency virus (HIV), human papillomaviruses (HPV) and *Helicobacter pylori* are associated with Burkitt's lymphoma, liver cancer, Kaposi sarcoma, cervical cancer and stomach cancer, respectively (32). Cholangiocarcinoma and bladder cancer can also result from infection with the parasites *Opisthorchis Viverrini* and *Schistosoma hematobiumi* (32).

Environmental influence and cancer

In 1775, Percivall Pott described an association between exposure to chimney soot and scrotal cancer in chimney sweepers. However, causative links between environment and cancer was not proven till 1918 when Yamagiwa and Ichikawa demonstrated that repetitive application of coal tar to the inner surface of rabbits' ears leads to chronic irritation, which over a period, causes precancerous epithelial alterations that may lead to carcinoma (33,34). This provided evidence for the role of some chemicals in the pathogenesis of cancers and further led to the identification of polycyclic aromatic hydrocarbons as carcinogens. Since then, exposure to chemicals in pesticides and some industrial chemicals (including those used in making cosmetics) or trace concentrations of radioactive materials in rocks such as granite has been associated with carcinogenesis.

Humans are constantly exposed to electromagnetic waves of varying frequencies. These are broadly divided into ionizing radiations which are emitted at high frequency, and non-ionizing radiations which include Wi-Fi, radio waves, infra-red radiation, emission from power lines, microwaves and visible light. Exposure to ionizing radiation, which includes X-rays, gamma rays and ultraviolet rays can damage DNA, initiating cancer (35).

The development of cancer

Cancer is a disorder at the cellular level, and it can be broadly described as an alteration in the process of cell division.

Cell division and growth is a highly controlled and coordinated process involving a plethora of proteins responsible for progression to the next phase of the cell cycle (cyclins and cyclin dependent kinases – CDKs) as well as checkpoints which can be likened to quality control systems that monitor the integrity of critical events and prevent progression to the next phase of the cell cycle should there be irregularities (Figure 23.1).

In cancer, cells become resistant to regulatory signals that control their growth and death leading to rapid and sustained uncontrolled proliferation and consequently metastases to other sites. This unchecked cell growth is a multistep process involving accumulation of mutations in several genes associated with cell homeostasis.

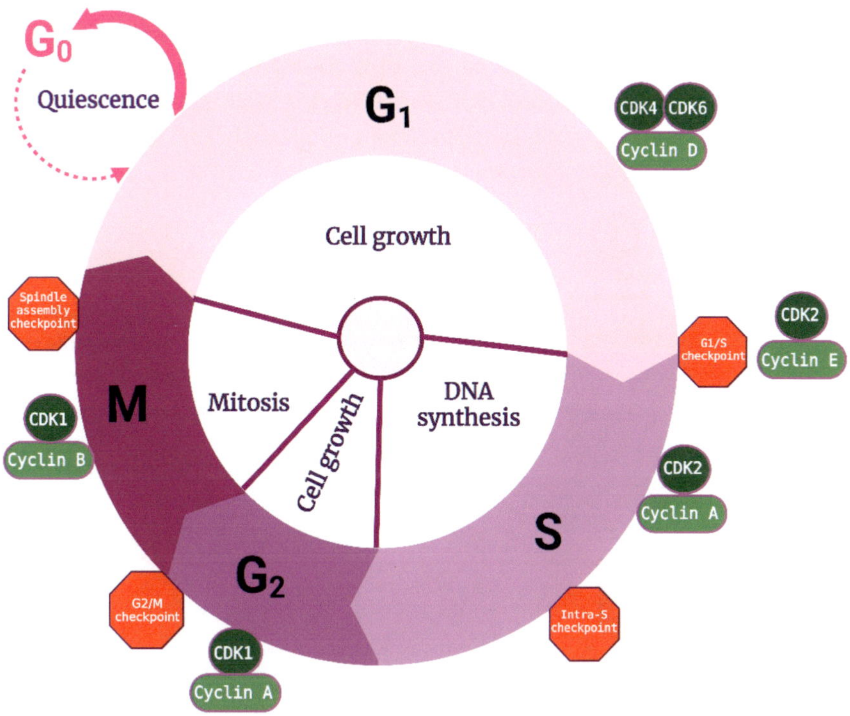

Figure 23.1: **The cell cycle**. *The progression of the cell cycle is controlled by cyclins and cyclin dependent kinases (CDKs) whilst checkpoints prevent the cell from progressing to next phase if there is a defect or an error. G_0-quiescent state; G_1-gap phase 1; G_2-gap phase 2; S-DNA synthesis; M-mitosis. Created with BioRender.com.*

The first step in tumour development is genetic alteration as a result of inherited or acquired somatic mutation which leads to the clonal expansion of a single cell in an unregulated manner. More mutations continue to accumulate in these cells as they divide. These mutations which may confer a growth advantage on the cells may arise from exposure to exogenous and endogenous substances that damage the DNA, or the inability of the cells to repair a faulty DNA (Figure 23.2). In a study carried out in prostate cancer, it was revealed that somatic mutations accumulate at a rate of about 16 mutations per year per cell and this somatic mutation in the epithelium is likely to be constant throughout life (36). Although most cancers are thought to have developed from a single cell, there is now mounting evidence indicating that different cells or clonal populations are required for tumorigenesis (37,38).

Genetic aberration causes changes in the function of proto-oncogenes and tumour suppressor genes. If the genetic aberration or mutation leads to loss of activity of a protein, it is called a loss-of-function mutations. If the mutation generates a new protein isoform which has a new function, then it is referred to as gain-of-function mutation. Proto-oncogenes are genes encoding proteins that drive cell cycle progression. Gain-of-function mutations, chromosomal translocation or amplification of proto-oncogenes can convert them to oncogenes which stimulate cell growth and division. Examples include mutation of Ras and amplification of c-MYC.

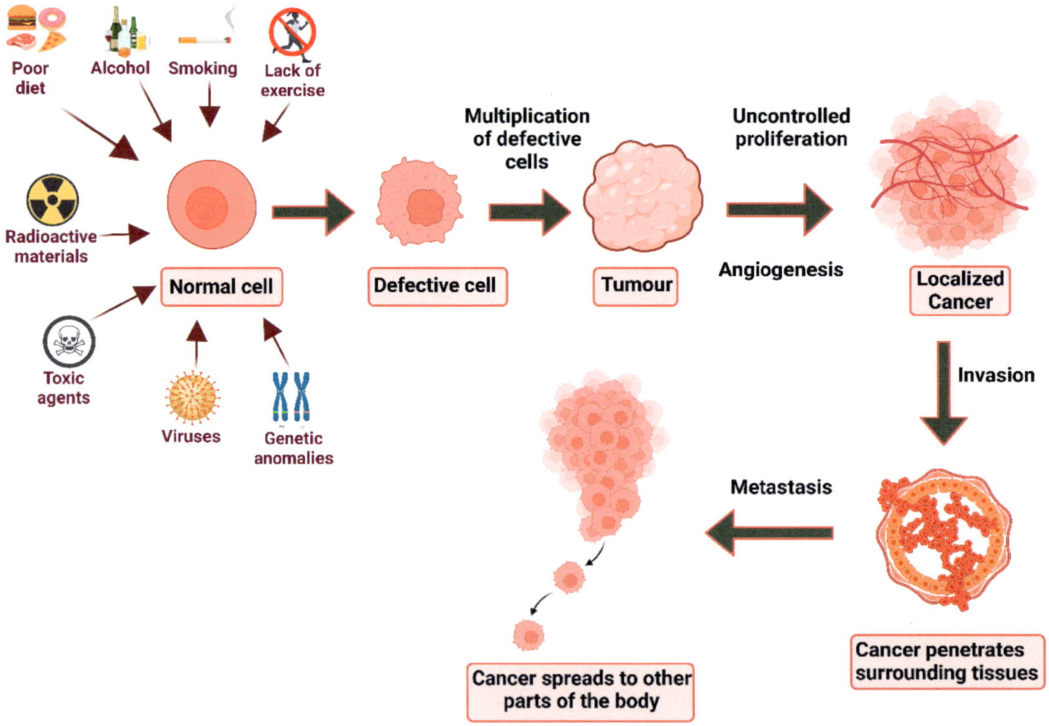

Figure 23.2: **The development of cancer**. *Exposure to exogenous or endogenous factors that damage the DNA changes confers a growth or survival advantage, leading to uncontrolled proliferation and angiogenesis. The tumour is now characterized as a cancer which may be confined to tissue of origin in early stages. Invasion and metastasis lead to migration of the cancer cell to distant sites in the body. Created with BioRender.com*

Tumour suppressors, on the other hand, are genes that encode proteins that negatively regulate the cell cycle by preventing cell division and promoting apoptosis, for example, pRb, which stops the expression of genes required for cells to progress into S-phase. Inactivation of tumour suppressor genes leads to a loss of function, thus, both gene copies must be mutated or altered for development of cancer. A frequently mutated tumour suppressor gene is Tumour Protein 53 (TP53), also known as the 'guardian of the genome', which makes the protein p53. In response to cellular stress or DNA damage, p53 inhibits the cell cycle to allow for DNA repair, cells can then re-enter the cell cycle after repair. In instances where the repair fails, p53 initiates the destruction of the damaged cell (apoptosis) to prevent transfer of damaged genetic materials to new daughter cells, maintaining genomic integrity(39). Over 50% of human cancers carry mutations in p53 which can lead to loss of function, hence, malignant transformation (40). Following genetic aberration and accumulation of mutations, the architecture of the tissue changes, leading to formation of preneoplastic nodules and then cancer which may then spread to distant sites in the body (Figure 23.2).

Features of cancer

Continuous proliferation

One of the main features of cancer cells is the ability to proliferate abnormally, surviving beyond their normal life span. Growth and survival in normal cells are regulated by growth factors, hormones and signalling pathways such as Nuclear Factor Kappa B (NFκB), phosphoinositide-3-kinase/AKT, insulin-like growth factor (IGF), androgen and oestrogen signalling, amongst others. These growth signals control entry and progression through the cell cycle. Following a multistep tumorigenesis process which include epigenetic changes and mutations, there are changes in the characteristics of cells rendering them resistant to homoeostatic signalling thus boosting growth and survival by: (i) constitutively stimulating these pathways which promote proliferation, (ii) dysregulating receptor signalling which become hyperresponsive to growth factors.

Apoptosis escape

Asides from the ability of malignant cells to sustain growth signals through oncogene activity and evasion of tumour suppressors, they are also characterised by resistance to programmed cell death or apoptosis. Apoptosis is the cell's intrinsic mechanism of programmed death which under physiological conditions is triggered following cellular stress, DNA damage or exposure to genotoxic substances. Malignant cells acquire the ability to shut off this signalling pathway by either upregulating anti-apoptotic proteins or downregulating pro-apoptotic proteins giving the cell a growth advantage.

Angiogenesis

Angiogenesis, the development of new blood vessels and lymphatic vessels, is another hallmark of cancer which takes place early in preneoplastic stages of tumour development. The influx of oxygen and nutrients as well as efflux of carbon dioxide and metabolic waste via the blood vessels are required for the sustenance of tumours. During tumour progression, activation of the angiogenic switch triggers the expression of pro-angiogenic factors such as Vascular Endothelial Growth Factor-A (VEGF-A) and repression of angiogenic inhibitors (e.g., thrombospondin-1) resulting in the transition of poorly vascularized tumour to a well vascularized one (41). Furthermore, these newly formed blood vessels are also required for invasion and metastasis to distant sites (41).

Invasion and metastasis

Most cancer-related death can be attributed to the development of secondary tumours in body parts that is distant from the primary cancer site. Invasion and metastasis are typified by the ability of cancer cells to be detached and released from primary site, intravasate into blood or lymphatic vessels, circulate in the blood stream, evade immune cells, adhere to and colonize new sites (42,43). Epithelial cells are tightly bound by extracellular matrix and typically immobile. However, the onset of metastasis in a cancerous epithelial cell is characterised by epithelial-mesenchymal transition (EMT) in which the cell develops the capacity to resist stress, disseminate and invade (42,43).

Reprogramming cellular metabolism

Cancer cells also have the attribute of reprogramming cellular energy metabolism. As cancer cells are continuously growing and rapidly proliferating, there is a need for increased energy supply. With a faster metabolic rate, cancer cells tend to consume more glucose than normal cells. They preferentially generate energy via glycolysis, a phenomenon called Warburg effect. In normal cell, glycolysis takes place only in conditions of limited oxygen supply. Although energy production in glycolysis (two adenosine triphosphate [ATP] molecules generated) is not as efficient as normoxic mitochondrial respiration (36 ATP molecules generated), cancer cells compensate for this by upregulating glucose transporters which increases the uptake of glucose as well as increase the expression of glycolytic enzymes (44,45). Aside from the altered energy generation, there is also reprogramming in amino acid and lipid metabolism, biosynthesis of macromolecules, mitochondrial biogenesis, pentose phosphate pathway and glutaminolysis to compensate for increased energy requirements (45).

Evasion of the immune system

Finally, cancer cells are characterised by the ability to evade detection and destruction by the immune system. The body's immune system protects against infectious microorganisms such as bacteria and viruses. Aside from this, it can distinguish between healthy and unhealthy cells, detect abnormal or damaged cells and target them for destruction via cytotoxic T- lymphocytes (CTL). Cancer cells evade recognition by CTLs through expression of inhibitory molecules such as Programmed Death Ligand 1 (PDL1), antigen modulation or downregulation of major histocompatibility class I (46).

Other features of cancer such as evading growth suppressors, enabling replicative immortality, tumour promoting inflammation, genome instability and mutation are comprehensively discussed by Hanahan and Weinberg (47).

Ingredients used in cosmetics and their impact on cancer development

There are a plethora of cosmetic products in the market and most of them are made up of a combination of several synthetic chemicals as well as natural ingredients. The amount of chemicals in any given product can typically range from about 10 – 60 ingredients. Although manufacturers will not, in good conscience, intentionally add carcinogenic chemicals to their products, these substances do exist in cosmetics as impurities from ingredients such as pigments, waxes and oil. According to the International Agency for Research on Cancer (IARC) monograph series, carcinogenic hazards are classified into four categories based on evidence supported by human, experimental studies on animals and mechanistic evidence (48) (Table 23.1).

Table 23.1: The International Agency for Research Cancer monograph series classification of chemicals- Examples in cosmetics (49)

Group	Description	Examples in cosmetics
1	Carcinogenic to humans	Formaldehyde, lindane, asbestos, benzene, ultraviolet radiation (UV), cadmium
2A	Probably carcinogenic to humans	Acrylamide, occupational exposure of hairdresser or barber
2B	Possibly carcinogenic to humans	Talc, methyl eugenol, safrole, aloe vera whole leaf extract, methyl mercury compounds, di(2-ethylhexyl) phthalate, benzophenone
3	Not classifiable as to its carcinogenicity to humans	Kojic acid, captan, isopropyl alcohol, musk xylene, benzoyl, eugenol peroxide, xylene, hydroquinone, mercury and inorganic mercury compounds, butyl benzyl phthalate

It is worth noting that it is the concentration of the above chemicals in a given product that will determine the risk it poses. Some cosmetic products may contain carcinogenic chemicals or chemicals that release carcinogens, for example, formaldehyde, a class I carcinogen, albeit the concentration in which they are used is typically deemed safe (Table 23.1). Formaldehyde/methylene glycol can be found at concentrations up to 2%, 0.1% and 0.2% in nail hardeners, toothpaste and shampoos, respectively. Formaldehyde is a gas, however, in aqueous form it is referred to as methylene glycol. Dehydration of methylene glycol or exposure of methylene glycol to low PH results in formation of formaldehyde, hence, heating a product that contains methylene glycol, for example, hair straighteners, will potentially emit formaldehyde which is toxic and carcinogenic. In accordance with European regulations, cadmium, a class 1 carcinogenic (Table 23.1) is prohibited in cosmetic products, however, it is found in trace amount in lipsticks, eyeshadows, compact powders and blushes as a result of the minerals used as pigments or fillers in these products. Studies from Nigeria have detected high levels of cadmium in some lotions and creams as well as facial cosmetics (50,51). Exposure to cadmium has been associated with the development of lung, kidney prostate and breast cancers (52,53).

Scientific research into the effects of various cosmetic ingredients and products as well as their association with cancer and its management are discussed. Readers should be aware that some of these studies are limited in scope as they were carried out in laboratory grown cells or animals. Furthermore, some of the studies carried out in humans have used a limited number of participants.

Talc

Talc occurs naturally and is commonly used as a moisture absorbent, opacifier, abrasive, anticaking or texturing agent. It is found in deodorants, creams, powders, feminine hygiene products, lipsticks and some other cosmetic products. Some women preferentially use talc in the perineal area, apply it to sanitary towels, underwear or diaphragms to absorb moisture, prevent rashes and odours as well as reduce friction. Over 60 years ago, the first report documenting the possible association between ovarian cancer and the use of talc-containing powders in the genital areas was published (54). In 2016, a study carried out in over 4,000 women with data collected over a period of 16 years, noted that the regular use of talc in the genital area was associated with a 33% increase in risk of ovarian cancer (55). More recently, a meta-analysis study revealed that women with greater than 3600 lifetime applications of talc powder were slightly at higher risk of ovarian cancer compared with those with less than 3600 lifetime applications (56). The study went on to show a positive association between ovarian cancer and use of talc powder in perineal areas and a 24 - 39% increased risk of this cancer (56). Prior to this study, Terry *et al.* also reported a small to moderate increase in risk of most types of ovarian cancer with genital use of the powder (57). In contrast, O'Brien and colleagues reported no statistically significant association between ovarian cancer and use of powder in the pubic area in the analysis of pooled data from four cohorts of women in the USA (58).

As talc and asbestos are found in proximity in the earth crust, cross contamination of talc with asbestos, a known carcinogen, is not uncommon. Regulation for the use of talc in cosmetics came to effect in 1976 with the stipulation that no detectable fibrous asbestos minerals were to be present in talc (59). Marketed to prevent diaper rash in babies, the talc in the Johnson & Johnson baby powder has been implicated to be contaminated with asbestos which may have predisposed infants to the development of ovarian cancer later in life. In 2018, an allegation suggesting that Johnson & Johnson had knowledge that the talc used in its product were contaminated with asbestos as far back as the 1970s but failed to inform consumers of the risk of using talc-containing products emerged (60). There are ongoing lawsuits against the company worth billions of dollars as plaintiffs ascertain the relationship between ovarian cancer and the use of the company's talcum powder. In the light of these litigations, Johnson & Johnson announced it would end the sales of the talc-based baby powder in North America although international sales continue (61).

Aloe vera

Universally known for its soothing, hydrating and calming effects as well as anti-inflammatory, antimicrobial and laxative properties, *Aloe vera* is employed in many cosmetics and PCPs with an history of about 2000 years in folk medicine. There are over 400 species of the *Aloe spp* plant. However, the most common and widely used species is *Aloe barbadensis* Miller commonly called Aloe vera. Aloe vera leaf extract, gel and latex are components of the plants that are frequently used. The fleshy green leaves covered by a thick cuticle store large amount of water and within the inner leaf pulp is the gel whilst the latex is obtained from the yellow drippings when the leaf is cut.

Laboratory animals that were orally administered *Aloe vera* whole leaf extract for up to two years demonstrated dose-related increase in the incidence of intestinal tumours and colon carcinomas (62,63). Application of creams of Aloe whole leaf or decolorized whole leaf on hairless mice for a year demonstrated a weak enhancing photocarcinogenic effect of simulated solar light evidenced by an increase in the multiplicity of squamous cell neoplasms (64). These studies provide clear evidence of the carcinogenic effect of the whole leaf extract of *Aloe vera* and has promoted the IACR to designate it as a group 2B agent - possible human carcinogen (Table 23.1).

Aloe vera latex is found along the margin of the leaf and it is exuded as a yellow-brownish coloured fluid once the leaf is cut. Also referred to as Aloe juice or sap, it is made up of hydroxyanthraquinones such as aloe-emodin, emodin and danthron. Melanin-containing skin tumours were observed on the skin of mice painted with aloe emodin and exposed to UVB radiation which was not seen in animals treated with aloe emodin alone in the absence of UVB radiation, demonstrating the photocarcinogenic potential of aloe-emodin to induce cutaneous melanomas (65). Aloe emodin was also demonstrated to have weak enhancing effect on the photocarcinogenic activity of simulated solar light in female mice but not in male (64).

In a study investigating the carcinogenic potential of emodin, F344/N and B6C3F1 rats were fed with emodin for two years. The study found no evidence of carcinogenic effect in male F344/N animals whilst an increase in the Zymbal's gland – an auditory sebaceous gland -carcinoma was observed in the females. Incidence of uncommon renal tubule neoplasm was reported in male B6C3F1 rats fed emodin while no carcinogenic event was reported in their female counterpart (66).

The inner most part of the Aloe vera leaf contains the pulp which is a transparent mucilaginous jelly-like aqueous substance which is popularly referred to as aloe vera gel. Although one study demonstrated that aloe vera gel can weakly enhance the photocarcinogenic activity of simulated solar light leading to multiplicity of squamous cell neoplasm (64), there is paucity of information associating it with the development of cancer and it is generally considered safe. Unlike the whole leaf extract or latex, the gel has been shown to induce apoptosis in lung and breast cancer cells (67). Oral administration of processed aloe vera gel in mice prevented colon carcinogenesis by inhibiting chronic inflammation, cell cycle progression, activation of NF-κB as well as increasing the expression of the tumour suppressor, CDX2 (68).

Endocrine disrupting chemicals (EDCs) in cosmetics and hormone driven cancers

From embryo through to critical developmental stages such as puberty to fully developed adults, exposure to EDCs pose a risk through life and its impacts can be seen over generations. The growth of breast, prostate, endometrial, ovarian and testicular cancers is driven by hormones, thus, exposure to EDCs, which increase the amount of circulating hormones, could feasibly drive accelerated progression of these cancers. The window of susceptibility to endocrine associated cancers is usually opened at early life. In prostate cancer for instance, exposure to bisphenol-A (BPA) and other EDCs have been shown to be capable of reprograming the developing foetal prostate gland, predisposing it to carcinogenic tendency in the mature gland (69). Women who are 40 years old and above exposed to diethylstilbesterol (DES) *in utero* via their mothers were shown to have a cumulative risk of 3.9% of developing breast cancer compared with 2.2% in those not exposed (70). This risk may also extend to their daughters and granddaughters implicating a three-generation effect of exposure to this EDC (71). DES, previously prescribed to pregnant women to prevent miscarriage, is not commonly found in cosmetic products. However, its carcinogenic tendency brings to light the potential impact of EDCs in the development of cancer later in life.

According to Cancer Research United Kingdom (CRUK), one in seven women will develop breast cancer (BC) in her lifetime (72). As the development of BC is associated with exposure to exogenous or endogenous oestrogens and knowing how ubiquitous the use of cosmetics is among women, the role of EDCs in the aetiology of BC is worth considering.

In a study to determine the oestrogenic and anti-oestrogenic activity of commonly used hair and skin care products, petroleum jelly, oil hair lotions, intensive and extra-dry skin lotions were found to have measurable oestrogenic activity in oestrogen-sensitive cell lines whilst cocoa butter cream, tea-tree oil and placenta hair conditioner had anti-oestrogenic activity (73). The human placenta promotes the proliferation of hair follicles hence its use in products to promote growth and thickness of the hair (74,75). Oestrogen, progesterone or estrone may be found in placenta extracts and these have been associated with premature sexual development in African American girls which increases their risk of BC prior to menopause later in life (76).

Triclosan is an antimicrobial with potent antibacterial and antifungal properties, hence, its use in antiseptic products and as preservative in many cosmetic products. Although the use of triclosan in soap products was banned by the FDA in 2016, its use in toothpaste, mouthwash and hand sanitizers is still permitted at concentration between 0.1-0.3%. As it is readily absorbed into the human skin and oral mucosa, the detection of triclosan in human serum, urine and breast milk has incited an interest in its role in cancer development (77,78). As a xenoestrogen, triclosan can bind to the oestrogen receptor as an agonist or antagonist. Its agonistic property has implications in the development of breast cancer. Farasani *et al.* show that long term exposures at concentrations reported in human milk increase migration and invasion in breast cancer cell lines (79). Epithelial-mesenchymal transition (EMT), which is a predictor of the aggressiveness of cancer, was shown to be induced by triclosan in lung cancer cell lines (80). Breast tumour volumes in mice exposed to triclosan were shown to be increased compared to control animals (81). This tumour-promoting effect was demonstrated to be mediated in an oestrogen receptor signalling-dependent manner, further validating the role of triclosan as an EDC (81).

Per-and polyfluoroalkyl substances (PFAS) are added to cosmetic products such as mascara, lipstick, eyeshadow and eyeliner amongst others to improve consistency, texture and durability. **Perfluorooctanoic acid** (PFOA), an example of PFAS, is used for its water-resistant properties, hence, a constituent of water-proof products. In breast cancer cells, PFOA was shown to stimulate migration, invasiveness and metastasis as well as activate the NF-κB pathway, indicating its potential role in the growth and progression of breast cancer (82,83). In a Greenland Inuit study, an association was shown between the risk of developing BC and serum levels of these perfluorinated compounds (84).

Aluminium is a metalloestrogen – a metal that exert oestrogenic effects – and, together with its salts, a component of many deodorants. The implication of aluminium salts and cancer are discussed below in the deodorant section.

Used primarily as an antimicrobial, **parabens** possess oestrogenic activity and have been detected in human breast tissue (85). Parabens are associated with increased proliferation of oestrogen-responsive breast cancer cells, migration and invasiveness, evasion of apoptosis as well as inhibition of growth suppressors (86). Parabens are found in foundations, moisturizers, shampoos, shaving products and other related products.

Aside from their use as plasticizers, **phthalates** are also vehicles for fragrances in perfumes and PCPs, hence they are common in cosmetics. An increased risk of BC was associated with exposure to diethyl phthalate but not monobenzyl phthalate in a Mexican study (87). In a nationwide cohort study carried out in Denmark, exposure to high levels of dibutyl phthalate was associated with a two-fold increase in the rate of incidence of oestrogen receptor positive BC (88). Dibutyl phthalate is also implicated in prostate carcinogenesis as it was shown to promote proliferation of prostate cancer cells and activation of the MAPK/AP1 growth signalling pathway (89).

A meta-analysis found no association between **bisphenol-A** (BPA) and BC. However elevated breast density, a marker of BC risk, was observed in post-menopausal women who had high serum levels of BPA (90,91). BPA has been shown to induce proliferation and metastasis in ovarian cancer cells (92). Although since banned in cosmetic products in the European Union, BPA are typically found in nail polish, eye makeups and lipsticks.

To reduce exposure to UV light and protect the skin from its deleterious effects, **UV filters** are added to some cosmetic products such as sunscreen lotions. Products containing UV filters are typically used topically, however, they are absorbed into the systemic circulation. Components of UV filters and their metabolites have been reported in human urine, placenta and breast milk (93-96). Benzophenone (BP-1, -2,-3), homosalate, 4-methylbenzilidenecamphor, octylmethoxycinnamate and related compounds have the ability to absorb and dissipate UV rays and are used extensively as UV filters. Long term exposure to these UV filters increases the migration and invasion of breast cancer cells (97).

Cosmetics/personal care products and their association with cancer

Deodorants/antiperspirants

There has been a long debate on the role of deodorants/antiperspirants in the development of breast cancer. They are typically applied under arm which is near the breast and lymph nodes. Some deodorants/antiperspirants contain aluminium-based compounds such as aluminium chloride which prevent the flow of sweat to the skin surface. Aluminium salts have been described as having endocrine disrupting properties, therefore, when absorbed by the skin may have oestrogen-like effects on breast cells – promoting growth, and potentially increased risk of breast cancer (BC) (98). Significant amounts of aluminium have been measured in human breast milk, tissue and nipple-aspirate fluid of healthy women and those with breast cancer (99,100).

In a study of 104 women split into 54 women with breast cancer and 50 women grouped in the control unit, no association was found between the use of antiperspirants and occurrence of breast cancer (101). In a related population-based case control study in which the relationship between the use of antiperspirant and risk of BC in over a thousand women aged 20-74 was carried out, the risk of BC did not increase with the use of antiperspirant (102). Albeit, exposure of normal mouse breast epithelial cells to the concentration of aluminium salt found in human breast over a period of 14-16 weeks resulted in malignant transformation of these cells with metastatic capability (103). A 32–37-week exposure of human breast cancer cells to aluminium salts increased the migratory and invasiveness features of these cells thus suggesting that aluminium salts can promote metastasis of breast cancer (104). In a more recent 1:1 age-matched case control study made up of 418 participants investigating the self-reported use of underarm PCPs and the risk of BC, Linhart and colleagues report an accumulation of aluminium in breast tissue and found a significant association between use of underarm PCPs and the risk of BC (105). The risk of BC was increased in women who used underarm PCPs several times daily starting under the age of thirty years old (105).

As there are limited studies and contradictory evidence as to the role of aluminium salts in the breast carcinogenesis, some people avoid the use of aluminium-containing deodorants/antiperspirant.

Anti-ageing creams

The ageing of the skin is characterized by loss of elasticity, elastic fibre degeneration, reduction in collagen content, dryness, reduction in thickness and increased wrinkling. Reduction in the levels of oestrogen exacerbates ageing in postmenopausal women. The skin is an oestrogen-responsive tissue; thus, oestrogen plays a key role in maintaining the skin's structural composition and integrity. Collagen, the main constituent of the skin, is modulated by the presence of oestrogen. A study in postmenopausal women suggested that reduction in the levels of collagen is related to declining oestrogen levels rather than chronological age (106). Oestrogen is added to some anti-ageing creams to increase collagen and improve hydration of the skin. A significant improvement in skin firmness and elasticity, moisture content as well as wrinkles was observed in pre-climacteric women with skin ageing symptoms who applied 0.01-0.3% oestriol cream over their face and neck daily over a period of six months (107). This demonstrated the effectiveness of oestrogen-containing products in the prevention and treatment of skin ageing. Although there is paucity of data on the implication of oestrogen-containing anti-ageing creams on carcinogenesis, caution should be taken in the use of these products as exposure to increased levels of oestrogen is associated with the risk of developing breast cancer.

Nail polish

The nail is a plate-like, translucent structure made of keratin and grows from the dermis of the skin. It protects the nail tip and is involved in tactile sensation. Well-manicured and healthy nails are considered part of an attractive, neat and well-groomed appearance in some communities.

Exposure to volatile organic compounds which are components of many nail salon products may increase risk of carcinogenesis. These compounds include formaldehyde, acetone, methyl acrylate, toluene, ethyl acetate and others (108,109). Formaldehyde is classified as a group 1 carcinogen (Table 23.1). Investigation by Lamplugh *et al.*, revealed that the levels of benzene, toluene, ethylbenzene and xylene in indoor air samples collected in nail salons in Colorado, USA, were similar to those in auto garages and oil refineries, thus, posing a significant health risk (109). In addition, they estimated an increased lifetime risk of cancers such as leukaemia, squamous cell carcinoma, nasopharyngeal cancer and Hodgkin's lymphoma in nail technicians who work in this environment for more than 20 years (109). Nail polishes also contain phthalates which are known EDCs capable of altering hormone signalling and may advance the rate of carcinogenesis such as breast cancer.

Shellac and gel manicures and pedicures are increasing in popularity as they have improved lustre and last longer without chipping compared to traditional nail polish. Gel nail polishes are pre-mixed semisolid monomers and oligomers acrylics that harden to polymers via curing. Curing is carried out using light boxes referred to as UV lamps or LED lamps, both of which emit high intensity UV-A which is associated with ageing of the skin and higher risk of cancer, hence, a cause for concern. UV-A rays penetrate the skin and damage collagen and elastin, resulting in photoageing. There are various models of the curing lamps and there is currently no regulation as to how much emission output is required or considered safe. In a bid to evaluate the risk associated with exposure to curing lamps, it was revealed that in less than ten minutes, a person's hand receives an energy dose of between 15-22 J/m^2. The international commission on non-ionizing radiation protection set a limit of 30 J/m^2 for eight hours for recreationalists and outdoor workers. This therefore implies that within the short period of nail curing, a person is exposed to almost a day-long recommended limit of UVA (110). In their study of seventeen curing lamps, Shipp *et al.* revealed that these devices had varied UV-A irradiance and the higher the wattage, the higher the UV-A irradiation. They also observed that exposure of the hands to these devices for a longer period of time increases the possibility for cutaneous damage. Comparing the emission from these lamps to the energy density of 60 J/cm^2 attributed to DNA damage in keratinocytes, they show that for each visit to the nail salon, exposure to UV-A is low and that it will take multiple visits to attain the threshold for potential DNA damage (111). They, however, recommended the use of UV-A protective gloves or sun blocking screens whilst using the light boxes for curing (111).

Hair relaxers/keratin hair treatments

Hair relaxers are commonly used by black women to straighten natural textured curls, making hair easier to style and manage. They are generally classified as lye - made of sodium hydroxide and non-lye - made of potassium hydroxide, guanidine carbonate, lithium hydroxide or ammonium thioglycolate. Use of hair relaxers often result in scalp burns which compromise the skin barrier thus enabling systemic uptake of contents of hair relaxer. In 2007, Rosenberg *et al.* published a prospective study in which they reported that relaxer use was not associated with breast cancer (BC) risk in African-American women (112). In another large case-control study, within the African-American population studied, the regular use of relaxers was not significantly associated with BC compared with non-users, albeit, there was a 74% increased risk of BC associated with the use of relaxers in white women (113). In a study that enrolled women aged 35-74 years, Eberle *et al.* revealed that the use of relaxers twelve months before enrolment into the study was associated with 18% higher risk of BC. Furthermore, they showed that more frequent use of at least every 5-8 weeks increases the risk to 31% (114). In Ghanaian study of 3237 participants, 58% increase in BC was associated with women who had ever used hair straightener (115). The study reported a higher risk in women who used non-lye relaxers compared to lye users and a higher risk for former/long term users as against current users (115). In an investigation into the role of relaxers and ovarian cancer, it was revealed that frequent adult use of relaxers/straighteners, defined as greater than four times per year, is associated with about two times the risk of developing ovarian cancer (116).

Aside from the use of chemical relaxers to straighten hair, it is now increasingly popular to use Brazilian Keratin hair treatments which are renowned for straightening naturally wavy hair, increasing shine, decreasing frizz for a longer period and pose less damage to the hair compared to hair relaxers. The main components of this treatment are hydrolysed keratin, a natural occurring constituent of the hair, skin and nails as well as formaldehyde or its derivative (methylene glycol, formalin) which is used to crosslink the hydrolysed keratin to the hair via the application of heat. Upon applying and heating the keratin hair treatment, there is release of formaldehyde gas which is a known irritant and carcinogen (117) (Table 23.1). There are currently no reports associating the use of Brazilian Keratin hair treatment to cancer (118). However, caution should be exercised in the use of this product especially by salon professionals who are constantly exposed to toxic fumes.

Hair dyes

There are debates on the relationship between the use of hair dyes and carcinogenesis. Hair dyes can be permanent, semi-permanent or temporary. In a national prospective cohort study carried out in the USA to investigate the association between hair dye use and breast cancer (BC) risk by ethnicity, it was revealed that there was no association between temporary dye use and BC risk, however, the authors showed a 45% higher BC risk in black women who use any permanent hair dye in the twelve months before enrolment compared to non-users, and a 7% higher risk in white women. They further showed that an increase in frequency of use of dye was positively associated with risk. A use of at least every 5-8 weeks increases BC risk to 60% in black women (114). This association was more evident and less precise in dark-coloured dye and light-coloured permanent dye respectively in black women however in white women, use of light-coloured permanent dye but not dark-coloured permanent dye was associated with breast cancer risk (114). In a related finding, following a meta-analysis of 210,319 subjects from 14 studies, a significantly higher BC risk was observed in users of permanent hair dye compared with individuals with natural hair. There was no association seen with the use of semi-permanent hair dye and BC. In contrast to the Eberle study (114), the authors showed that neither the timing of use nor race had an impact on the correlation between BC risk and use of hair dyes (119). The use of dark hair dye shades in African-American women was associated with higher risk of BC compared to non-users, even more interesting was the finding that oestrogen receptor positive BC was associated with higher frequency of use (113). The study further revealed that amongst white women, the dual use of both hair dyes and relaxers is associated with BC and that increased oestrogen positive BC was associated with dark-coloured dyes (113).

Prior to the 1980s, aromatic amines such as 4-aminobiphenyl benzidine were components of hair dyes. These aromatic amines can bind DNA, forming adducts and were associated with urothelial cancers, an occupational health hazard (120,121). In a meta-analysis to ascertain this association, hairdressers were reported to be at a higher risk of bladder cancer, especially if they had held the job for more than 10 years (122). These carcinogenic constituents have since been banned in hair dyes in the European Union. Tagged the 'silent killer', ovarian cancer which is rated as the gynaecological cancer with the worst prognosis and highest mortality, has been documented to be associated with hair dyes (123). Frequent use of semi-permanent hair dye, defined as greater than four times in a year, was reported to be possibly associated with higher risk of ovarian cancer compared to never-use of the dye (116). A positive association between non-serous ovarian cancer and ever-use of permanent hair dye was also reported (116).

In a prospective cohort study reported in 2020 in which over 100,000 women were enrolled, the authors report no positive association between the risk of most cancers and the personal use of permanent hair dye (124). However, on stratifying participants by hair colour, they report novel findings which show a higher risk of Hodgkin lymphoma in women with naturally dark hair, who were presumed to use dark-coloured permanent hair dyes, and basal cell carcinoma in women whose hair is naturally light (124).

Skin lighteners

Aside from haemoproteins and carotenoids, the presence, amount and distribution of melanin in the human skin is the chief determinant of skin colour. The dark skin tone has more melanocytes which produce the melanin required to protect the skin from the harmful effects of solar radiation, hence, conferring on the black skin a photoprotective advantage. The levels of melanin in the black skin are approximately four times higher than found in the white skin (125). The measure of how much UV radiation from the sun is required to produce sunburn on a protected skin relative to an unprotected skin is referred to as Sun Protection Factor (SPF). SPFs are rated on a scale of 2 to 50+, consequently, the higher the SPF, the more protection from sunburn. The epidermis of the black skin is estimated to have an intrinsic SPF of 13.4 compared to the light skin with an SPF of 3.3 (126). The concept of colourism, in which people with lighter skin tone are found more attractive and acceptable than individuals with darker skin tone is one of the reasons for the use of skin lighteners. Having a lighter skin tone is also associated with higher social standing in some cultures. The act of lightening the skin is increasingly popular in black communities. Up to 75%, 60% and 30% of women in Nigeria, Senegal and Ghana routinely engage in this practice, respectively, (127-129) citing increase in attractiveness and fashion trend as reasons for skin bleaching. Skin lighteners are also used to improve the appearance of blemishes such as dark patches or birth marks as well as correct cosmetic or medical skin conditions such as melasma.

Skin lightening, brightening, whitening or bleaching are terms used synonymously to refer to the act of using chemical substances to lighten skin tone. These chemical substances act by inhibiting the synthesis of melanin thereby reducing its concentration in the skin. They are formulated as creams, soaps, pills and even injectables and typically contain mercury, arsenic, topical steroids, hydroquinones, phthalates, kojic acid and glutathione.

Cancer of the skin tend to be rare in black skin, however, squamous cell carcinoma (SCC), a type of skin cancer, is the most common skin cancer among black Africans followed by basal cell carcinoma (130). In a single case from Ivory Coast reported by Gbandama *et al.*, SCC was associated with the daily use of formulations containing hydroquinone, lemon and dermocorticoid extracts for many years (131). In a related study from Senegal, 8 cases of SCC were associated with the cosmetic use of skin lightening products (132) whilst in Mali, a 30-year-old woman was diagnosed with SCC following the use of bleaching cream over a period of ten years (133). Skin carcinogenesis, in addition to other risk factors, can be associated with the lack of photoprotection because of the destruction of melanin, the possible 'carcinogenic' effect of hydroquinone and immunosuppression by topical corticosteroids following long term use of products that contain these ingredients.

Exposure of female Wistar rats to hydroquinone revealed disruptions in the epidermal layer of the skin increasing susceptibility to damaging effect of UV rays as well as an increase in expression of p65, a component of the Nuclear Factor kappa B (NF-κB) which has been shown to be essential for skin carcinogenesis (134,135). Application of aloe vera to the skin of the hydroquinone treated rats was, however, demonstrated to preserve the epidermis thereby reversing the lethal effect of hydroquinone (134). Hydroquinone has also been implicated in DNA damage, a precursor to genomic instability leading to cancer in cell lines (136,137).

According to the IARC, the summation of data emanating from carcinogenic studies of hydroquinone, also referred to as 1,4-Benzenediol, indicate that there is inadequate evidence in humans to classify it as a carcinogen, whereas in experimental animals, limited evidence exist, hence, it is classified as a group 3 substance (138) (Table 23.1). Caution and regular assessment are, however, recommended with the use of hydroquinone (139). Due to safety concerns of hydroquinone, it is banned in European countries, South Africa, Kenya, Tanzania, Ivory Coast, Ghana, Rwanda, amongst others.

Kojic acid, a natural metabolite of fungi (*Aspergillus spp., Penicillium spp.*) with the ability to competitively inhibit tyrosinase activity thereby reducing the synthesis of melanin, is used as a substitute of hydroquinone. In addition to its skin lightening properties, it is known to have antioxidant, anti-inflammatory, anti-proliferative and radioprotective effects (reviewed in (140)). Treatment of human malignant melanoma cells with kojic acid suppressed melanogenesis and tumorigenesis (141). Further, its anti-cancer properties have also been demonstrated in C6 glioma cell line (142). As ionizing radiation is a risk factor for carcinogenesis, it is interesting to note that kojic acid did protect Chinese hamster ovary cells and C57BL/6 mice against gamma irradiation demonstrating its radioprotective effect (143).

Arbutin is another skin lightening compound which occurs naturally in dried leaves of pear, blueberry and cranberry trees. It is also a derivative of hydroquinone; however, it is less cytotoxic. Like kojic acid, it inhibits the activity of tyrosinase competitively, however, it is thought to be less effective than kojic acid for hyperpigmentation treatment.

Glutathione, which has anti-melanogenic properties, is often administered intravenously to achieve skin whitening. Documented to have antioxidant properties, it has also been demonstrated to improve skin elasticity and wrinkles (144). There is currently no reported evidence for its role in carcinogenesis nor its safety in chronic use (145).

Essential oil obtained from lime mint oil, which contains carvone, δ-selinene, β-caryophyllene and D-limonene, has been shown to reduce melanogenesis and, hence, is considered a potential skin-brightening agent (146). The rind of citrus fruits such as lemon and orange also contain D-limonene.

Tanning products

In contrast to the choice of lightening of the skin, there is a preference for 'bronzed' or tanned skin tones particularly in white women from colder climates and this is associated with being healthier and a more attractive appearance sometimes in anticipation of sun holidays. In pursuit of darker skin complexion, sunless tanners such as sunlamps, tanning lotions and even injections are employed.

Sunlamps are devices in the form of sunbeds, tanning beds or booths which use UV lamps which emit both UVA and UVB rays to irradiate any part of the body to induce skin tanning. Although the UV emission spectra of sunlamps are similar to those of the sun's UVB (280-320 nm) they can go up to 10-15 times higher in the UVA range (147). As UVA can penetrate more deeply into the skin, it has the propensity to cause DNA damage, a prerequisite for carcinogenesis. UV radiation emitted from sunlamps are of health concerns especially as it increases the risk of skin cancer. In a meta-analysis to estimate the risk of skin cancer in relation to the use of tanning devices, a Canadian study demonstrated that 7.0%, 5.2% and 7.5% of melanomas, basal cell carcinomas and squamous cell carcinomas respectively are associated with the use of tanning devices (148). In a related study, an association was found between an increased risk of early onset (age <50 years) of non-melanoma skin cancer as well as melanoma and the use of indoor tanning devices. In addition, the authors found that first exposure at an age less than 20 years and an annual exposure frequency of greater than ten times to tanning is associated with an increased risk of both melanoma and non-melanoma skin cancer (149).

In response to UV radiation, the keratinocytes in the skin increase the synthesis of the α-melanocyte stimulating hormone which binds melanocortin receptor increasing the production of tyrosine and consequently an increase in the production of eumelanin, inducing skin hyperpigmentation which creates a partial barrier against UV rays. The synthetic analogue of this hormone namely melanotan I and the more potent variant, melanotan II are popularly used to produce a natural tan. Melanotan II, also referred to as the barbie drug, is further used for its ability to increase sexual function as it causes penile erection and aid weight loss by reducing appetite. These unlicensed analogues are marketed as a tanning product in some tanning salons, beauty shops, spas, gyms and on the internet as nasal sprays or subcutaneous injections.

Following histological examination and immunohistochemical staining of the skin lesion of a 42-year old white woman who had self-administered melanotan II for a period of seven days to her abdominal region, and who occasionally visited tanning parlours and participated in other sun-seeking activities, Paurobally et al. reported a case of melanoma in the woman (150). Although the authors did not directly associate the use of the melanotan II with the melanoma, they suggested a possible causative effect as they saw rapid changes in an existing naevus within three months following the administration of melanotan II (150). In a related case, a 20-year old Caucasian woman with history of use of sunbeds was diagnosed with melanoma three months after completing a three to four - week course of melanotan II (151). Other reports have also documented increase in pigmentation of existing and development of new naevi following injection of melanotan (152,153). Although there is no documented evidence to suggest a relationship between the use of these synthetic analogues of α-melanocyte stimulating hormone, these cases bring to awareness a possible causal association which calls for larger studies.

Dermal fillers

Dermal fillers, also referred to as injectable implants or soft tissue fillers, are used for lip augmentation, cheekbone lifting, smoothening of under-eye circles and wrinkles reduction amongst others. To increase attractiveness, they are injected into the dermis layer of the skin where they increase the bulk of the soft tissues. Based on the type of material(s) they are made from, they are classified as biodegradable (hyaluronic acid,

Poly-L-lactic acid, collagen, autologous fat, calcium hydroxylapatite) or non-biodegradable (silicone, polyalkylimide, polymethyl methacrylate, polyacrylamide gels) (154). Depending on the duration of their effect, they are also classified as permanent, semi-permanent and temporary fillers.

Although dermal fillers are considered safe, once injected or implanted, these biomaterials may trigger an immune response as they are perceived as foreign by the body resulting in inflammation which may be an early or late onset reaction. These dermal fillers can also leak and may migrate to distant sites where they can provoke inflammatory reactions (155,156). Granuloma, accumulation of immune cells in response to chronic inflammation, is a delayed adverse event associated with the use of soft tissue fillers (157,158). Continuous chronic inflammation is a risk factor for cancer.

In a retrospective study carried out in ten females who had used orofacial dermal fillers, it was observed that all types of fillers used were associated with host inflammatory response and salivary gland neoplasm was observed in 30% of participants (159). Although the development of lymphomas following the use of dermal fillers is very rare, B-cell lymphoma was reported in a 72-year-old female patient who had used dermal fillers for cheek augmentation about 50 years earlier (160). Diffuse large B-cell non-Hodgkin's lymphoma has also been reported following the use of a dermal filler in the buttocks of a 40-year-old man who also presented with an autoimmune/inflammatory syndrome (161).

Hyaluronic acid is a component of the extracellular matrix of the dermis. Together with its cell surface receptor, Cluster of differentiation-44 (CD44), hyaluronic acid functions to hydrate the extracellular matrix, regulate tissue homeostasis and resist compressive forces by forming a resilient gel-like substance (162). Hyaluronic acid/CD44 have been implicated in cell adhesion, migration, inflammation and cancer progression (163-165). High levels of hyaluronic acid/CD44 are associated with poor prognosis in some cancers such as hepatoblastoma, gastric, breast and prostate cancers (166-170).

Due to its hydrophilicity, biocompatibility, non-immunogenicity and high affinity for CD44, hyaluronic acid is being explored as drug conjugates or carriers to deliver cytotoxic payloads to cancer cells that express high levels of CD44. This approach mitigates challenges to the efficacy of cancer therapeutics such as poor solubility, which prevents drugs from reaching tumour sites, as well as poor selectivity which accounts for various adverse effects associated with therapeutics. A micellar formulation of hyaluronic acid conjugated with folic acid was used to deliver the chemotherapeutic agent, doxorubicin, to cancer cells and tumour bearing mice. Cellular uptake was via CD44 receptor-mediated endocytosis and the micelles demonstrated good *in vivo* tumour targetability. This demonstrated the potential of hyaluronic acid as a delivery system in cancer therapy (171).

The non-biodegradable and permanent filler, polymethyl methacrylate, has also been explored as a conduit for drug delivery in cancer. Formulations made of polymethyl methacrylate have been used to effectively deliver chemotherapeutics such as tamoxifen, paclitaxel as well as plant extracts with anticancer properties such as *Curcuma longa* and *Piper cabralanum* to cancer cells (172-175).

Botox

As the physiological function of the body begins to decline due to ageing, there is a gradual reduction in the renewal of the skin cells, synthesis of structural proteins, dermal thickness and collagen density leading to the loss of dermal integrity and pliability which manifests as wrinkles (176). Aside from these intrinsic factors, wrinkles are also exacerbated by exposure to the sun, pollution, chronic inflammation, sedentary lifestyle, poor nutrition and smoking (176). Wrinkles are more prominent on the face as it is more exposed to the elements.

Botulinum toxin injection, more commonly referred to as Botox, is frequently administered to reduce the appearance of wrinkles as well as frown lines and crow's feet. It is one of the most performed non-invasive cosmetic procedure (177). Medically, the toxin is also used to treat excessive sweating, neck spasms, lazy eyes, chronic migraines and overactive bladder. The Botulinum toxin, a potent neurotoxin which inhibits the release of acetylcholine at neuromuscular junction resulting in chemical denervation and muscle paralysis, is obtained from the bacterium, *Clostridium botulinum*. Injection of small amounts of the toxin results in muscle relaxation thereby reducing wrinkles at the site of administration with its effect visible from about two weeks and can last up to 3-4 months (178).

Pain is one of the most common symptoms of cancer and it may be caused by the tumour itself or the tumour pressing on nerves and organ, as well as from surgery, chemotherapy or radiotherapy. A decrease in the intensity of a persistent upper limb pain for up to six months has been reported in breast cancer survivors who were administered Botulinum toxin A in addition to physical therapy (179). The toxin is deemed to be effective in the management of pain resulting from radiation and surgery (180-182).

There are also reports on the cytotoxic effect of botulinum toxins in cancer cells. Rust *et al.* showed that differentiation of neuroblastoma cells sensitises them to botulinum toxin-C inducing apoptosis, therefore, proposing a potential utility of this toxin in the treatment of neuroblastomas (183). Botulinum toxin-A has been shown to inhibit the growth of prostate cancer cell lines as well as slow the growth of tumours in xenograft model (184). Evaluation of Botox-treated prostate cancer tissues obtained from patients in a phase I clinical trial was observed to have increased apoptosis (185). In the breast cancer cell line

T47D, botulinum toxin-A was shown to induce apoptosis via caspases leading to cell death in this cell line (186).

Based on their ability to inhibit neurogenic contractions, botulinum toxins have been explored as promising adjuvants to anti-cancer therapies. Botulinum toxin A was shown to interfere with neurotransmitter release leading to inhibition of contractions of tumour blood vessels, improving tumour perfusion and oxygenation which led to a substantial improvement in the response of tumours to chemotherapy and radiotherapy (187,188). As we move to the era of more precise and targeted therapy in cancer, drugs are now designed to target specific proteins on cancer cells. An example is trastuzumab which has a high affinity for human epidermal growth factor 2 (HER2) receptors which are abundantly expressed in certain breast cancers. Trastuzumab was conjugated with Botulinum toxin and the effect investigated in breast cancer cell lines. An increase in the efficacy of trastuzumab, characterized by a significant reduction in cell viability, was observed in the treatment group compared to the control arm (189).

Fragrance

Following metabolism, the human body produces odours which are given off via breath, sebum and sweat. To mask such odour, give off a pleasant scent and increase attractiveness, fragrances are employed. Fragrances are also used in thousands of cosmetic products to mask undesirable odours of surfactants, fatty acids and various excipients are used in fragrance formulations which in turn increases their marketability. Fragrances are formulated as mixtures of essential oils, natural fragrance oil and several chemical compounds including alcohols to produce perfumes. Cosmetic products do carry on their labels the name of the fragrance employed, however, the fragrance listed is not just one product but a cocktail of compounds which give off a pleasant scent, thus, it is often difficult to determine which component is responsible for adverse effects. The contents of fragrances are trade secrets, hence, not given away publicly as they are commercially valuable and confer economic benefit to their holders. Nevertheless, the International Fragrance Association have published a list of about 4000 compounds used in consumer goods (190) . Aside from the basic compounds used to mask odour, the list is also made of functional ingredients which are necessary for stability and utility of fragrances (190). Some of these ingredients and their association with cancer are discussed below. It should be noted that most of the studies reported are carried out in cancer cell lines and in instances where patient studies are included, they are carried out in a small number of patients.

Benzophenone (BP) are UV filters capable of absorbing UV-A and UV-B radiation. In perfumes they are used to prevent loss of scents and colours caused by exposure to UV light. They are lipophilic, hence the tendency to bioaccumulate (191,192).

Benzophenone-3 (BP-3), known as oxybenzone is one of the most common and it is also found in nail polish, lip balm and sunscreens. In a bid to assess the estrogenic effects of benzophenone in breast cancer cells, MCF7 cells were treated with ten BP derivatives. Of the ten, 6 were found to significantly stimulate proliferation of this breast cancer cell line which was dependent on the oestrogen receptor alpha (ERα) whilst BP, BP1, BP3 and 234BP had very little or no effect on proliferation (193). Using environmental relevant levels of BP1 (0.2-200 µg/L), Liu *et al.*, revealed binding of BP1 to ERα in an agonistic manner in the ovarian cancer cell line, SKOV3, where it promoted cell proliferation, migration and invasion (194). Although these studies were conducted in cell lines, it warrants further detailed mechanistic studies to access the ability of these chemicals to influence human cancer progression. However, this finding begs for precautionary measures for the use of BP and its derivatives in humans especially persons with breast or ovarian cancer.

Musk is one of the most frequently used bases in perfumes. This highly valued olfactory stimulant was originally obtained from the secretion in the preputial gland of the male musk deer, *Moschus moschiferus*, and is believed to have aphrodisiac properties (195). Other natural sources include the plant, *Angelica archangelica*, and *Abelmoschus moschatus* (195). Due to its high demand and in a bid to protect musk deer from extinction, synthetic versions such as 1,3,4,6,7,8-hexahydro-4,6,6,7,8,8-hexamethylcyclopenta[g]-2-benzopyran (HHCB) and 7-acetyl-1,1,3,4,4,6-hexamethyltetrahydronaphthalene (AHTN) patented as Galaxolide and Tonalide, respectively, were developed and about 4000 tons of these polycyclic musks are produced per year (195).

Examination of HHCB and AHTN for genotoxic effect via micronucleus formation revealed musks had no such effects on the human hepatoma cell line and lymphocytes (196). Api and Ford also reported that there was no toxic effect observed in rats treated with HHCB for 90-days (197). Although reported to have neuro-degenerative effects in animals, both HHCB and AHTN were revealed to reduce cell viability and induce apoptosis (up to 200 µM and 5 µM employed, respectively) in the lung cancer cell line, A549 and SH-SY5Y, which is a neuroblastoma cell line (198). In a contrary study, Doğanlar *et al.* showed that long term exposure of glioblastoma cells to AHTN or HHCB at sub-lethal doses (2.5-5 µM) induced angiogenesis, invasion and migration in these cell lines as well as in its tumour spheroids indicating potential carcinogenic property of these polycyclic musks (199). Dermal absorption and inhalation are the main routes through which synthetic musks get into systemic circulation. Synthetic musks have been detected in human breast milk (200). Caution is, therefore, advised in the use of products containing synthetic musks.

Essential oil

As the campaign to use more natural products is gaining momentum in the cosmetic industry, the demand for cosmetic products dubbed 'natural' is increasing shifting from synthetic products to ones obtained from nature, there has, therefore, been a surge in demand for essential oils as fragrances in cosmetics.

Essential oils are mixtures of aromatic or aliphatic compounds and terpenes which are produced as secondary metabolites in specialized secretory tissues of aromatic plants for attraction of pollinators, defence and other regulatory and signalling processes. They are also produced in animals, for example, musk. They are mainly used in cosmetics for their pleasant odour. Essential oils are also used as preservatives, owning to their antimicrobial properties. Some essential oils used as fragrances include floral oils such lavender, citrus and eucalyptus. They are also used as anti-acne, anti-aging, skin lightening and sun protection agents.

Constituents of some essential oils such as methyl eugenol have been documented to be possibly carcinogenic to humans (Table 23.1). Methyl eugenol is found in some essential oils like tea tree (*Melaleuca* spp.), basil (*Ocimum* spp.), citronella (*Cymbopogon* spp.), bay (*Laurus nobilis*) and rose (*Rosa* spp.) oils. Investigation into the role of methyl eugenol in cancer revealed an association with the development of tumour of the liver, stomach and kidney in animals that were either administered methyl eugenol orally or intraperitoneally (201-203). Although it can be argued that methyl eugenol may not be ingested, however, it should be noted that it can be absorbed into systemic circulation via inhalation and dermal contact. Phenylethyl isothiocyanate found in mustard or papaya essential oils has been demonstrated to induce bladder cancer in rats (204). The phorbol ester, 12-O-tetradecanoylphorbol-13-acetate (TPA), is an active component of croton oil. It stimulates cell division and induces changes in cell morphology and it is well documented as a potent tumour promoter (205). It is often used in combination with the mutagen 7,12-dimethylbenz[a]anthracene to model skin carcinogenesis in animal models (206).

Essential oil contents with anticancer properties

Surgery, radiotherapy, chemotherapy and immunotherapy are used in the management of cancer, however, there tends to be relapse of disease prompting the need for more effective and targeted therapy with fewer side effects. As natural sources are associated with fewer untoward effects, their effectiveness as chemo-preventive and anticancer agents are being explored. As a result, a number of research have demonstrated the effects of essential oils in the prevention and treatment of cancers in pre-clinical models. Although there is paucity of clinical data to ascertain their efficacy in treating and preventing cancer clinically, some components of essential oils have been documented to alter signalling pathways in cancer cells as well as demonstrate antiproliferative and antimutagenic effects in animal models. Some of these are discussed.

Carvone

This terpenoid which gives off a minty, spicy and slightly flora odour is found in the essential oils of dill, spearmint and caraway plants. Carvone decreased the melanin content and inhibited the proliferation of melanoma cells in a dose-dependent manner (207). Apoptosis, a mechanism of natural physiological self-destruction used to remove aged, unwanted or malignant cells, is mediated by proteins called caspases. Apoptosis is often used as a reliable indicator of the efficiency and effectiveness of anticancer agents. (+) Carvone was shown to persistently activate caspase-3 which is the primary executioner of apoptotic death in cancer cells, bringing to light its anticancer properties (208). In a study in which skin cancer was induced using 7,12-dimethylbenz[a]anthracene (DMBA) in Swiss albino mice, D-carvone significantly prevented carcinogenesis, increased expression of pro-apoptotic proteins in treated animals compared to control. Apoptosis was mediated by caspase-3 and -9. The authors suggested a role for D-carvone as a chemo-preventive agent against skin cancer (209). In breast cancer, L-carvone inhibited proliferation and migration, induced apoptosis via caspase-3, initiated cell cycle arrest at the S-phase as well as increased the expression of the tumour suppressor p53 in cell lines (210). Although the data obtained from studies in gastric cancer cells are preliminary, it is evident that D-carvone does inhibit cell proliferation and induce apoptosis (211). Its capability to induce G2/M cell cycle arrest, induce apoptosis and inhibit cell invasion has also been documented in myeloma cells (212).

Bisabolol

Also referred to as levomenol, bisabolol is obtained from the essential oil of German chamomile. In addition to its pleasant smell, it is purported to have anti-inflammatory, healing and soothing features. The anticancer effects of bisabolol have been documented in glioma, leukaemia, breast and non-small cell lung cancers (213-216) Bisabolol's ability to suppress invasiveness and motility of pancreatic cancer cells has been associated with the upregulation of kisspeptin receptor (KISS1R), a receptor for KISS1 which suppresses metastasis (217). One of its synthetic derivatives have also been shown to demonstrate antiproliferative and tumoricidal effects in models of pancreatic cancer via inhibiting the serine/threonine protein kinase (AKT), which plays a significant role in tumorigenesis (218). It has also proved to be a promising clinical treatment adjuvant as it enhanced radiotherapy-induced apoptosis in endometrial cancer cells (219). The essential oil of *Teucrium alopecurus* has been used traditionally for its anti-inflammatory properties. Guesmi *et al.* demonstrated the cytotoxic effect of this oil in a number of cancer cell lines and further showed that the hydrophobic fraction of this oil, which contains bisabolol, suppressed the expression of genes involved in proliferation, invasion, metastasis, angiogenesis and survival of human colon cancer cells (220).

Anethole

Anethole is a component of essential oils obtained from anise, star anise and fennel plants. It is also obtained synthetically. Aside from its aroma, it has a sweet taste (thirteen times sweeter than sugar), hence, it is employed in cosmetic products used for oral care. In a dose-dependent manner, anethole was shown to selectively induce toxicity, reduce cell proliferation and induce apoptosis in oral cancer cells (221). It was further shown to suppress migration and invasion – characteristic of metastasis, inhibit the expression of oncogenes, whilst increasing the expression of the tumour suppressor gene, p53 (221). The potency of anethole in other cancers has also been explored. It was revealed to have suppressed survival and induced apoptosis in breast cancer cell lines irrespective of their oestrogen receptor status (222). Combination of anethole with the chemotherapeutic doxorubicin is observed to have demonstrated a synergistic effect in mediating cell cycle arrest, inducing endoplasmic reticulum stress and promoting apoptosis in triple-negative breast cancer cell lines (223). Similar anticancer properties have been reported in osteosarcoma and prostate cancer cells (224,225).

Citral

Citral, which is a component of lemon grass, citrus fruits, verbena and ginger amongst others, has been demonstrated to have antiproliferative effect in cancer cell lines (226,227). Citral has been delivered to multiple cancer cell lines as nanoparticles and shown to inhibit proliferation and induce apoptosis (228). The antiproliferative effect is attributed to the oil's ability to increase intracellular oxygen radicals leading to oxidative stress, decreased proliferation and apoptosis in p53 dependent cancers (228,229). In the absence of p53, citral can induce endoplasmic reticulum stress which ultimately leads to cell death (228). Chronic exposure of the skin to UVB is a major cause of skin cancer and it is often mitigated using sunscreen. Application of citral to hairless mice five minutes after exposure to UVB resulted in reduced oxidative stress, decreased pro-inflammatory cytokines, increased apoptotic rate thereby ultimately reducing skin carcinogenesis in treated animals compared to control and, thus, demonstrating its chemoprotective effect against UVB-induced cancer (230). In a bid to decipher the mechanism of the antiproliferative and cytotoxic effect of citral on melanoma cells, Sanches *et al.* demonstrated that citral can induce oxidative stress through production of reactive oxygen species, reduction of nitric oxide levels and reduced activity of proliferation-promoting signalling pathways such as AKT, eventually leading to cell death (231). Using an animal model of triple negative breast cancer, citral was effectively delivered using a nanostructured lipid carrier where it was shown to delay tumour progression by suppressing the expression of the oncogene c-myc, induce apoptosis, impede invasiveness and inhibit the metastasis of cancer cells to the bone marrow and lungs via the downregulation of pro-metastases and pro-angiogenic proteins (232,233). Olfactory receptors which detect odour of molecules, including those used in perfumes and cosmetics, are expressed in breast tissues (234). An investigation to understand the role of citral as an odorant in breast cancer revealed it induces cell cycle arrest and exert antiproliferative and anti-apoptotic effects in breast cancer cell lines (235).

Limonene

Limonene is the main constituent of the essential oil of the peels of citrus fruits such as orange, mandarin, grapefruit, lemon and lime. It has been suggested to have wound healing, bactericidal and anti-inflammatory properties (236-238). Nitric acid is a ubiquitous free radical that regulates a number of physiological processes. Its role in cancer is bimodal depending on a number of factors. It has been described as tumoricidal in some instances and in other cases involved in cancer development and progression. The induction of apoptosis and antiproliferative effect of limonene was attributed to its ability to increase in the synthesis of nitric oxide (239). Topical application of limonene prior to tumour induction on the skin of mice delayed tumorigenesis and promoted pro-apoptotic proteins attesting to its chemo-preventive effects (240). In a case control study carried out in Arizona, USA, to evaluate the association between the consumption of citrus products and squamous cell carcinoma (SCC), 74.5% and 64.3% of the participant indicated weekly consumption of citrus fruits and citrus juices, respectively, whilst 34.7% indicated consumption of citrus peels (241). The study found no association between the consumption of citrus fruits or juices and SCC, however, a protective effect following consumption of citrus peel was noted as a significant inverse association was seen between the consumption of citrus peel and SCC risk (241).

Following the extraction of essential oil of blood orange (*Citrus sinensis*), it was shown to be made up of 95.35% D-limonene, this was formulated into an emulsion and its effects explored in colon cancer cells *in vitro*. The researchers report a dose-dependent decrease in colon cancer cell proliferation, induction of apoptosis, inhibition of angiogenesis and metastasis in treated cells compared to the control group, proposing a role for limonene in cancer therapy and as a chemo-preventive (242). Jia and colleagues further showed that D-limonene induced apoptosis in colon cancer cells which was mediated via activation of caspase-3, and that this essential oil component inhibited AKT signalling, a pathway renowned for promoting cell survival and proliferation (243).

In an attempt to investigate the anticancer properties of the peels of citrus fruits, Nair *et al.*, demonstrated D-limonene to constitute up to 87.54% of the major constituents of the peel oils. They showed that mandarin orange (*Citrus reticulata*) peel water extract resulted in cell cycle arrest, nuclear condensation, apoptotic body formation, DNA damage and apoptosis in Dalton's lymphoma ascites (DLA) cell line. In vivo, mice pre-treated with this peel water extract were reported to be significantly protected from tumour development following challenge with DLA compared to the post-treated animals, suggesting a cancer preventive role of the essential oil of mandarin orange (244). Investigation into the therapeutic effect of D-limonene in lung cancer revealed it inhibited the growth of cells, induced apoptosis and repressed the growth of tumours in animal xenograft models of lung cancer (245). In addition to activating caspases, inducing apoptosis and triggering cell cycle arrest, limonene suppressed cell migration and invasion – essential events in metastasis - in bladder cancer cells (246). The antiproliferative and apoptosis-inducing effect of limonene has also been attributed to the suppression of hepatocarcinogenesis in Sprague-Dawley rats signifying its anticancer effects in liver cancer (247).

A phase I clinical trial made of thirty-two patients to assess the pharmacokinetic profile and the toxicity of limonene in patients with advanced cancer, revealed it was well tolerated and one breast cancer patient showed a partial response characterized by a 50% reduction in supraclavicular lymphadenopathy which was sustained for eleven months before disease progression (248). Further, there was stabilization of colorectal cancer in three patients for longer than six months (248). In women with newly-diagnosed operable breast cancer who received two grams of limonene daily for 2-6 weeks prior to excision of tumours surgically and metabolic profile interrogated, the levels of circulating adrenal steroids - which fuels hormone-dependent cancers - were reduced and levels of cyclin D1 – which is overexpressed and dysregulated in breast cancer – were reduced, suggesting an anticancer effect of limonene (249).

Essential oil obtained from lemon and orange formulated as chitosan nanoparticles showed improved potency and efficacy as they reduced cell viability in melanoma and breast cancer cell lines (250). Limonene inhibits cell viability in prostate cancer cells (251). D-limonene (Table 23.1) has been demonstrated to enhance the cytotoxic profile of docetaxel, a potent therapeutic used in the management of castrate-resistant prostate cancer. The combination of both agents resulted in an enhanced antiproliferative effect, increase in expression of the tumour suppressor, p53 and activation of caspase-9 and caspase-3 (252).

Linalool

Essential oils obtained from coriander, lavender, basil, cinnamon, spearmint, cypress, rose and lemon contain linalool in form of two stereoisomers commonly referred to as licareol and coriandrol. It is noted to have a sweet, floral, flesh and clean odour. This terpene is reported to have anti-inflammatory, antimicrobial and antioxidant properties.

Essential oil obtained from the English lavender (*Lavandula angustifolia*) contains linalool. The endocrine disrupting properties of Lavender oil are described in chapter 22. In human prostate cancer cell lines, the essential oil and linalool had antiproliferative effects that were characterized by significant reduction in cell viability as well as cell cycle arrest and induction of apoptosis. Furthermore, from results of in vivo studies using mouse xenograft model of prostate cancer, no obvious toxic effect of the lavender oil or linalool were noted in major organs such as spleen, liver and heart, however, a significant reduction in tumour volume was observed in treated animals compared to controls, there was a reduction in ki67 and PCNA – both markers of cell proliferation – in xenograft tumours. Immunostaining also confirmed a moderate rate of apoptosis in tumour specimen of animals treated with either lavender oil or linalool (253). A similar observation was made by Zhao *et al.* who further demonstrated an increase in expression of the tumour suppressor p53 and induction of caspases-9 and-3 in prostate cancer cells treated with linalool (254). Although linalool was shown to be unable to induce apoptosis via the activation of caspase-3 or -9 in lung cancer cells, it was shown to inhibit cell migration, initiate cell cycle arrest and inhibit proliferation via production of reactive oxygen species (255). Oxidative stress associated with treatment of lung cancer cells and xenograft model using linalool resulted in inhibition of cell proliferation and a significant decrease in tumour volume, respectively (256). Apoptosis and cell cycle arrest in leukaemia and cervical cancer cell following treatment with linalool have also been reported (257). As a result of its pro-apoptotic properties, linalool has been proposed for future development in the management of T-cell acute lymphoblastic leukaemia (258).

Aside from its antiproliferative and anti-migratory effects, Becker *et al.* demonstrated the ability of linalool to inhibit angiogenesis by targeting various mediators of angiogenesis independently (259).

Chronic exposure of mice to UV-B radiation thrice weekly for 30 weeks led to the development of SCC which was mitigated in animals who had topical application on the skin or intraperitoneal administration of linalool, demonstrating the chemo-preventive effect of linalool in skin carcinogenesis (260).

Cachexia, a syndrome characterized by weight loss, skeletal muscle atrophy, anaemia, anorexia and asthenia, negatively affects the quality of life of cancer patients and it is one of the side effects of chemotherapeutics. *In vivo* studies revealed that linalool can improve symptoms of cachexia resulting from the use of cisplatin (261).

Ability to evade the immune system is one of the hallmarks of cancer progression and a number of strategies are now being developed to harness the killing ability of the immune system to fight cancer. Linalool has been shown to induce CD4 T helper type 1 (Th1) immune response which triggered the secretion of cytokines such as interferon gamma (IFNγ), tumour necrosis factor alpha (TNF-α) and other interleukins (262). Following the induction of apoptosis in a xenograft model of breast cancer, linalool was shown to reduce B cell counts but increased natural killer (NK) cells in peripheral blood and, consequently, a significant increase in TNF-α (263).

In addition to improving delivery and reducing toxicity, formulation as linalool-incorporated nanoparticles or linalool loaded glutathione-modified gold nanoparticle conjugates has proven to have superior antiproliferative and pro-apoptotic effects compared to unconjugated counterpart in ovarian cancer (264,265).

To explore the potential of both doxorubicin and linalool, both compounds were formulated as doxorubicin-containing liposomes encapsulating linalool nanoemulsion and their therapeutic efficacy was evaluated in mouse model of epithelial ovarian cancer. A synergistic effect characterized by a significant decrease in tumour growth, decrease in cell proliferation markers and induction of apoptosis compared to monotherapy was observed. Furthermore, the delivery system proved to have minimal side effects as against single agent (266).

Linalool has also been described as a chemosensitizing agent. Although it demonstrated weak antiproliferative effect in the breast cancer cell line MCF7, linalool potentiated the cytotoxic and pro-apoptotic effects of doxorubicin when both compounds were combined. Linalool was also demonstrated to increase the accumulation of doxorubicin by interfering with drug efflux in the multidrug-resistant model of MCF7 cells (267).

The action of linalool on cancer can be attributed to its antiproliferative, pro-apoptotic, anti-migratory, anti-angiogenic as well as the ability to suppress EMT, induce cell cycle arrest and modulate immune response.

Eugenol

Eugenol and its isomer, isoeugenol, are components of the essential oils of clove, basil and nutmeg. Synthetic vanillin is obtained from isoeugenol. Eugenol is renowned as an antioxidant hence its speculative role in anticancer mechanism.

In a study which investigated the chemo-preventive efficacy of eugenol in skin cancer, Kaur *et al.* demonstrated that eugenol inhibited all pro-inflammatory and tumour promotion markers as well as NF-κB signalling in the mice that were pre-treated with eugenol prior to chemical induction of carcinogenesis. Although eugenol did not prevent tumour formation in this model, the onset of tumour formation was significantly delayed, and tumour volume reduced in animals that were pre-treated with eugenol. The induction of apoptosis in pre-treated cells was pinned down to eugenol's ability to increase the expression of the tumour suppressor p53. it was shown to induce apoptosis via increased expression of p53 (268). A significant decrease in tumour size and growth as well as an inhibition to metastasis is reported in melanoma xenograft model following exposure to eugenol (269).

Investigation into its tumour suppressive role indicates that eugenol can reduce cell viability in lung cancer cells as well as inhibit cell migration and invasion via modulation of AKT signalling and expression of matrix metalloproteinase-2 respectively (270). Eugenol has been demonstrated to potentially restrict the generation of toxic reactive species by boosting enzyme detoxification, thus protecting against the harmful effects of carcinogen in a lung cancer model. It was further revealed that the chemo-preventive mechanism of eugenol may be ascribed to its ability to significantly downregulate the expression of β-catenin, whose enhanced expression is correlated with poor prognosis in lung cancer (271).

Downregulation of oncogenic proteins such as NF-κB, E2F1, β-catenin which are highly expressed in breast cancer and induction of p53 apoptosis has been associated with eugenol treatment in breast cancer cells using *in vitro* and *in vivo* models (272). Eugenol has also been suggested to be a potent anticancer in triple negative breast cancer as it significantly inhibited cell proliferation and induced autophagic cell death in cell line models (273).

Eugenol has been reported to sensitise ovarian cancer cells to cisplatin resulting in enhanced cytotoxic effect. Combination of both eugenol and cisplatin significantly repressed tumour growth and consequently increased tumour free survival in ovarian cancer xenograft models compared to animals treated with either eugenol or cisplatin alone. The combination therapy also seems to reverse cisplatin-associated drug resistance in ovarian cancer by preventing drug efflux, hence, a promising therapeutic option in patients with ovarian cancer (274). In a related study in breast cancer, eugenol enhanced the cytotoxic and pro-apoptotic effect of cisplatin by inhibiting NF-κB signalling in addition to inhibiting breast cancer stem cells which contribute to chemoresistance and recurrence in aggressive triple negative breast cancer models (275). A heightened cytotoxic effect of doxorubicin in combination with eugenol is also reported in hormone-receptor positive breast cancer where the synergistic effect may have been mediated by the accumulation of doxorubicin via prevention of drug efflux by eugenol (276).

The synergistic effect of eugenol in combination with ionizing radiation in cervical cancer cells resulted in an increase in the expression of pro-apoptotic proteins such caspase-3 indicative of cell death by apoptosis (277).

Menthol

Menthol, obtained principally from peppermint (*Mentha spp*) oil and other mint oils, is characterized by its minty, sweet, fresh and cooling scent. It is one of the most ubiquitous essential oils used in the cosmetic industry. It is also used for its antipruritic and analgesic effects stemming from its ability to expand the blood vessel and produce a cooling soothing relief.

The essential oil obtained from *Mentha piperita* made up of 30.69% menthol amongst other terpenoids, was subjected to cytotoxic test where it was revealed to mediate antiproliferative effect in liver, gastric, lung and leukaemia cell lines (278). This effect may not be singly attributed to menthol alone as it may be due to the synergistic effect of the terpenoid cocktail present in the extracted essential oil. Menthol was unable to reduce cell viability in hepatic cancer cell model. However, when the cell line was pre-treated with menthol and either vincristine or paclitaxel added, a significant decrease in cell viability was observed (279).

The analgesic and cooling effect of menthol is elicited via the transient receptor potential melastatin 8 (TRPM8) receptor which has been deemed to be necessary for the initiation and progression of tumours and a plethora of its expression is seen in a wide range of tumours (280). Nevertheless, preliminary research from Naziroglu and colleagues reveal that although TRPM8 was highly expressed in both prostate and breast cancer cell lines, treatment of prostate cell line with menthol resulted in apoptosis - evident by expression of caspase-3 and -9 - independently of the presence of TRPM8 channels (281). In another study, it was shown that menthol was able to inhibit cell growth and migration and induce cell cycle arrest, albeit without activating apoptosis, in prostate cancer cells which express TRPM8 (282). Mitochondrial depolarization and loss of electrochemical gradients are some of the events that precede cell death. Menthol was shown to increase calcium ions dose-dependently through TRPM8 in bladder cancer cells which led to cell growth arrest and induction of mitochondrial membrane depolarization and consequently cell death (283).

Menthol is being explored as an agent in cancer theranostics – a treatment modality that uses diagnostic imaging to identify targets followed by precision radiation. Menthol and the infrared dye IR-780 were formulated as a liposome and upon exposure to laser irradiation, resulted in phototoxicity in colon and pancreatic cancer cell line (284). The menthol/IR780 liposome was deemed a potent photoabsorber for effective photothermal therapy of tumours as apoptosis and tumour shrinkage were seen in mice exposed to this theranostic intervention (284).

Geraniol

This terpene is noted for its sweet rose floral odour. It is found in rose, palmarosa and citronella oils. Low concentrations are found in lavender, geranium, lemon and bergamot oils. In addition to its use as a fragrance, it is renowned for its anti-inflammatory and antiseptic properties.

The transcription factor, E2F8, is an important regulator of the cell cycle progression and is implicated in carcinogenesis. In metastatic prostate cancer, E2F8 is overexpressed and associated with poor prognosis via regulation of the G2/M phase of the cell cycle. Geraniol was shown to target E2F8 and reduce its expression thereby suppressing the growth and survival of prostate cancer cells (285). In addition, geraniol inhibited AKT signalling, induced cell cycle arrest and apoptosis in prostate cell lines and tumour-grafted mice models (286,287).

Chronic inflammation, which is mediated by the continuous production of cytokines such as TNF-α, IL-6 through activation of NFκB signalling, is one of the processes that drive carcinogenesis. Geraniol reduced the expression of the pro-inflammatory factors, TNF-α, NFκB, preventing chemical-induced oral carcinogenesis in rats thereby demonstrating its chemo-preventive attribute (288).

As geraniol could inhibit various tumour angiogenic factors in endothelial-like cell line model as well as animal model, in addition to its anti-proliferative activities, it has been proposed to be an anti-angiogenic (289).

In hepatocarcinoma cells, the anti-cancer effects of geraniol were demonstrated by its ability to inhibit cell proliferation and promote apoptosis by increasing expression of pro-apoptotic factors such as caspase-3 (290).

By modulating the molecular targets involved in the initiation and progression of cancer, geraniol inhibited the proliferation of lung and skin cancer cells and further reduced tumour size in treated swiss albino mice, indicating its potential as a potent antiproliferative in cancer (291).

Farnesol

Farnesol is a component of the tuberose, citronella, cyclamen and neroli essential oils. It has a flowery odour. Addition of farnesol to prostate cancer cells revealed that this isoprenoid decreased cell proliferation in a dose and time dependent manner, induced apoptosis and inhibited tumour growth in mouse mode. The expression of p53, caspase-3 and caspase-9 were increased whilst AKT signalling was repressed (292). Combination of farnesol with docetaxel and ibandronate further inhibited the growth of prostate cancer cells (293).

Farnesol inhibited migration and invasion via modulation of the expression levels of epithelial-mesenchymal transition markers, inhibited AKT signalling and suppressed growth in lung cancer cells and xenograft model (294)

Farnesol inhibited the progression of diethyl nitrosamine-induced liver cancer via depletion of inflammatory markers such as TNFα and COX-2 and regulation of cellular oxidation thus indicating its role as a chemo-preventive (295).

Cisplatin was combined with farnesol and formulated as nanoparticles. An additive effect of the combination was observed in hepatocellular carcinoma compared to single agent treatment. This effect was characterized by increase in apoptosis, upregulation of p53 and increase expression of caspase-3 (296).

In multiple myeloma, farnesol significantly suppressed the activation of STAT3, a transcription factor in a dose dependent manner. In addition to inhibiting proliferation, induction of cell cycle arrest, activation of caspase-3 and sustaining pro-apoptotic signals, it was shown to potentiate the anticancer effect of the targeted therapy bortezomib (297). Inclusion of the terpenes discussed in this chapter into personal care products does not constitute a treatment of cancer.

The use of these terpenes as chemotherapeutic agents requires the approval of the national regulatory agency based on established evidence of efficacy and safety and such use will require special formulation for the cancer target and effective delivery with other treatment strategies under the supervision of a proficient medical personnel and expert care.

References

(1) Bray F, Laversanne M, Weiderpass E, Soerjomataram I. The ever-increasing importance of cancer as a leading cause of premature death worldwide. Cancer 2021 Aug 15;127(16):3029-3030.

(2) Odes EJ, Randolph-Quinney PS, Steyn M, Throckmorton Z, Smilg JS, Zipfel B, et al. Earliest hominin cancer: 1.7-million-year-old osteosarcoma from Swartkrans Cave, South Africa. S Afr J Sci 2016;112(7-8):1-5.

(3) Prates C, Sousa S, Oliveira C, Ikram S. Prostate metastatic bone cancer in an Egyptian Ptolemaic mummy, a proposed radiological diagnosis. International Journal of Paleopathology 2011;1(2):98-103.

(4) Dawson WR. BREASTED, JAMES HENRY. The Edwin Smith Surgical Papyrus (Book Review). Journal of the Royal Asiatic Society of Great Britain and Ireland 1931:882.

(5) The Papyrus Ebers : the greatest Egyptian medical document. 1937.

](6) Sung H, Ferlay J, Siegel RL, Laversanne M, Soerjomataram I, Jemal A, et al. Global Cancer Statistics 2020: GLOBOCAN Estimates of Incidence and Mortality Worldwide for 36 Cancers in 185 Countries. CA A Cancer J Clin 2021;71(3):209-249.

(7) National Cancer Institute. Genetic Changes and Cancer. 2017; Available at: https://www.cancer.gov/about-cancer/causes-prevention/genetics. Accessed 01/10/21.

(8) Hoang LN, Gilks BC. Hereditary Breast and Ovarian Cancer Syndrome: Moving Beyond BRCA1 and BRCA2. Adv Anat Pathol 2018;25(2).

(9) Antoniou A, Pharoah PD, Narod S, Risch HA, Eyfjord JE, Hopper JL, et al. Average risks of breast and ovarian cancer associated with BRCA1 or BRCA2 mutations detected in case Series unselected for family history: a combined analysis of 22 studies. Am J Hum Genet 2003 May;72(5):1117-1130.

(10) Chen S, Parmigiani G. Meta-analysis of BRCA1 and BRCA2 penetrance. Journal of clinical oncology: official journal of the American Society of Clinical Oncology 2007;25(11):1329-1333.

(11) Howlett NG, Taniguchi T, Olson S, Cox B, Waisfisz Q, De Die-Smulders C, et al. Biallelic inactivation of BRCA2 in Fanconi anemia. Science 2002 Jul 26;297(5581):606-609.

(12) Alter BP. Fanconi anemia and the development of leukemia. Best Pract Res Clin Haematol 2014;27(3-4):214-221.

(13) Gumaste PV, Penn LA, Cymerman RM, Kirchhoff T, Polsky D, McLellan B. Skin cancer risk in BRCA1/2 mutation carriers. Br J Dermatol 2015 Jun;172(6):1498-1506.

(14) Roa BB, Boyd AA, Volcik K, Richards CS. Ashkenazi Jewish population frequencies for common mutations in BRCA1 and BRCA2. Nat Genet 1996 Oct;14(2):185-187.

(15) Weitzel JN, Lagos VI, Herzog JS, Judkins T, Hendrickson B, Ho JS, et al. Evidence for Common Ancestral Origin of a Recurring *BRCA1* Genomic Rearrangement Identified in High-Risk Hispanic Families. Cancer Epidemiol Biomarkers Prev 2007;16(8):1615-1620.

(16) Mefford HC, Baumbach L, Panguluri RC, Whitfield-Broome C, Szabo C, Smith S, et al. Evidence for a BRCA1 founder mutation in families of West African ancestry. Am J Hum Genet 1999 Aug;65(2):575-578.

(17) Reichl F, Muhr D, Rebhan K, Kramer G, Shariat SF, Singer CF, et al. Cancer Spectrum, Family History of Cancer and Overall Survival in Men with Germline BRCA1 or BRCA2 Mutations. Journal of Personalized Medicine 2021;11(9).

(18) Zeegers MPA, Jellema A, Ostrer H. Empiric risk of prostate carcinoma for relatives of patients with prostate carcinoma. Cancer 2003;97(8):1894-1903.

(19) Page WF, Braun MM, Partin AW, Caporaso N, Walsh P. Heredity and prostate cancer: a study of World War II veteran twins. Prostate 1997 Dec 1;33(4):240-245.

(20) Martínez-Jiménez F, Muiños F, Sentís I, Deu-Pons J, Reyes-Salazar I, Arnedo-Pac C, et al. A compendium of mutational cancer driver genes. Nature Reviews Cancer 2020;20(10):555-572.

(21) Key TJ, Bradbury KE, Perez-Cornago A, Sinha R, Tsilidis KK, Tsugane S. Diet, nutrition, and cancer risk: what do we know and what is the way forward? BMJ 2020;368:m511.

(22) Mentella MC, Scaldaferri F, Ricci C, Gasbarrini A, Miggiano GA. Cancer and Mediterranean Diet: A Review. Nutrients 2019;11(9).

(23) Arnold M, Pandeya N, Byrnes G, Renehan AG, Stevens GA, Ezzati M, et al. Global burden of cancer attributable to high body-mass index in 2012: a population-based study. The Lancet Oncology 2015;16(1):36-46.

(24) Lauby-Secretan B, Scoccianti C, Loomis D, Grosse Y, Bianchini F, Straif K. Body Fatness and Cancer — Viewpoint of the IARC Working Group. N Engl J Med 2016;375(8):794-798.

(25) Doll R, Peto R, Boreham J, Sutherland I. Mortality in relation to smoking: 50 years' observations on male British doctors. BMJ 2004;328(7455):1519.

(26) Koelwyn GJ, Zhuang X, Tammela T, Schietinger A, Jones LW. Exercise and immunometabolic regulation in cancer. Nature Metabolism 2020;2(9):849-857.

(27) McTiernan A, Friedenreich CM, Katzmarzyk PT, Powell KE, Macko R, Buchner D, et al. Physical Activity in Cancer Prevention and Survival: A Systematic Review. Med Sci Sports Exerc 2019;51(6):1252-1261.

(28) World Health Organization. Ageing and Health. 2018; Available at: https://www.who.int/news-room/fact-sheets/detail/ageing-and-health. Accessed 22/08/, 2021.

(29) Smith BD, Smith GL, Hurria A, Hortobagyi GN, Buchholz TA. Future of cancer incidence in the United States: burdens upon an aging, changing nation. J Clin Oncol 2009 Jun 10;27(17):2758-2765.

(30) White MC, Holman DM, Boehm JE, Peipins LA, Grossman M, Henley SJ. Age and cancer risk: a potentially modifiable relationship. Am J Prev Med 2014;46(3):S7-S15.

(31) Pavlidis N, Stanta G, Audisio RA. Cancer prevalence and mortality in centenarians: A systematic review. Crit Rev Oncol 2012;83(1):145-152.

(32) Jacqueline C, Tasiemski A, Sorci G, Ujvari B, Maachi F, Missé D, et al. Infections and cancer: the “fifty shades of immunity” hypothesis. BMC Cancer 2017;17(1):257.

(33) Pott P. Chirurgical observations relative to the cataract, the polypus of the nose, the cancer of the scrotum, the different kinds of ruptures, and the mortification of the toes and feet. London: T.J. Carnegy for L. Hawes, W. Clarke & R. Collins; 1775.

(34) Yamagiwa K, Ichikawa K. Experimental Study of the Pathogenesis of Carcinoma. J Cancer Res 1918;3(1):1.

(35) Gilbert ES. Ionising radiation and cancer risks: what have we learned from epidemiology? Int J Radiat Biol 2009;85(6):467-482.

(36) Grossmann S, Hooks Y, Wilson L, Moore L, O’Neill L, Martincorena I, et al. Development, maturation, and maintenance of human prostate inferred from somatic mutations. Cell Stem Cell 2021.

(37) Parsons BL. Multiclonal tumor origin: Evidence and implications. Mutation Research/Reviews in Mutation Research 2018;777:1-18.

(38) Yuan D, XiuJuan W, Yan Z, JunQin L, Fang X, Shirong Y, et al. Use of X-Chromosome Inactivation Pattern to Analyze the Clonality of 14 Female Cases of Kaposi Sarcoma. Medical science monitor basic research 2015;21:116-122.

(39) Sionov RV, Haupt Y. The cellular response to p53: the decision between life and death. Oncogene 1999 Nov 1;18(45):6145-6157.

(40) Vousden KH, Lu X. Live or let die: the cell's response to p53. Nature Reviews Cancer 2002;2(8):594-604.

(41) Hanahan D, Folkman J. Patterns and Emerging Mechanisms of the Angiogenic Switch during Tumorigenesis. Cell 1996;86(3):353-364.

(42) Fouad YA, Aanei C. Revisiting the hallmarks of cancer. Am J Cancer Res 2017 May 1;7(5):1016-1036.

(43) Fares J, Fares MY, Khachfe HH, Salhab HA, Fares Y. Molecular principles of metastasis: a hallmark of cancer revisited. Signal Transduction and Targeted Therapy 2020;5(1):28.

(44) Vander Heiden M,G., Cantley LC, Thompson CB. Understanding the Warburg effect: the metabolic requirements of cell proliferation. Science (New York, N.Y.) 2009;324(5930):1029-1033.

(45) Phan LM, Yeung SJ, Lee M. Cancer metabolic reprogramming: importance, main features, and potentials for precise targeted anti-cancer therapies. Cancer biology & medicine 2014;11(1):1-19.

(46) Muenst S, Läubli H, Soysal SD, Zippelius A, Tzankov A, Hoeller S. The immune system and cancer evasion strategies: therapeutic concepts. J Intern Med 2016;279(6):541-562.

(47) Hanahan D, Weinberg RA. Hallmarks of Cancer: The Next Generation. Cell 2011;144(5):646-674.

(48) Samet JM, Chiu WA, Cogliano V, Jinot J, Kriebel D, Lunn RM, et al. The IARC Monographs: Updated Procedures for Modern and Transparent Evidence Synthesis in Cancer Hazard Identification. J Natl Cancer Inst 2019;112(1):30-37.

(49) International Agency for Research on Cancer. IARC monographs on the identification of carcinogenic hazards to humans. 2021; Available at: https://monographs.iarc.who.int/list-of-classifications/. Accessed 16/01/, 2022.

(50) Sani A, Gaya MB, Abubakar FA. Determination of some heavy metals in selected cosmetic products sold in kano metropolis, Nigeria. Toxicology Reports 2016;3:866-869.

(51) Orisakwe OE, Otaraku JO. Metal Concentrations in Cosmetics Commonly Used in Nigeria. The Scientific World Journal 2013;2013:959637.

(52) Luevano J, Damodaran C. A review of molecular events of cadmium-induced carcinogenesis. Journal of environmental pathology, toxicology and oncology: official organ of the International Society for Environmental Toxicology and Cancer 2014;33(3):183-194.

(53) Huff J, Lunn RM, Waalkes MP, Tomatis L, Infante PF. Cadmium-induced cancers in animals and in humans. International journal of occupational and environmental health 2007 Apr;13(2):202-212.

(54) Cralley LJ, Key MM, Groth DH, Lainhart WS, Ligo RM. Fibrous and mineral content of cosmetic talcum products. Am Ind Hyg Assoc J 1968;29(4):350-354.

(55) Cramer DW, Vitonis AF, Terry KL, Welch WR, Titus LJ. The Association Between Talc Use and Ovarian Cancer: A Retrospective Case-Control Study in Two US States. Epidemiology 2016 May;27(3):334-346.

(56) Penninkilampi R, Eslick GD. Perineal Talc Use and Ovarian Cancer: A Systematic Review and Meta-Analysis. Epidemiology 2018;29(1).

(57) Terry KL, Karageorgi S, Shvetsov YB, Merritt MA, Lurie G, Thompson PJ, et al. Genital Powder Use and Risk of Ovarian Cancer: A Pooled Analysis of 8,525 Cases and 9,859 Controls. Cancer Prev Res (Phila) 2013;6(8):811.

(58) O'Brien KM, Tworoger SS, Harris HR, Anderson GL, Weinberg CR, Trabert B, et al. Association of Powder Use in the Genital Area With Risk of Ovarian Cancer. JAMA 2020;323(1):49-59.

(59) CTFA compendium of cosmetic ingredient composition. 1990.

(60) Lisa Girion. Johnson & Johnson knew for decades that asbestos lurked in its Baby Powder. 2018; Available at: https://www.reuters.com/investigates/special-report/johnsonandjohnson-cancer/. Accessed May 17, 2022.

(61) Tiffany Hsu and Roni Caryn Rabin. Johnson & Johnson to End Talc-Based Baby Powder Sales in North America. New York Times 2020 May 19.

(62) Boudreau MD, Mellick PW, Olson GR, Felton RP, Thorn BT, Beland FA. Clear evidence of carcinogenic activity by a whole-leaf extract of Aloe barbadensis miller (aloe vera) in F344/N rats. Toxicol Sci 2013 Jan;131(1):26-39.

(63) Boudreau MD, Beland FA, Nichols JA, Pogribna M. Toxicology and carcinogenesis studies of a nondecolorized [corrected] whole leaf extract of Aloe barbadensis Miller (Aloe vera) in F344/N rats and B6C3F1 mice (drinking water study). Natl Toxicol Program Tech Rep Ser 2013 Aug;(577)(577):1-266.

(64) National Toxicology Program. Photocarcinogenesis study of aloe vera [CAS NO. 481-72-1(Aloe-emodin)] in SKH-1 mice (simulated solar light and topical application study). Natl Toxicol Program Tech Rep Ser 2010 Sep;(553)(553):7-103 passim.

(65) Strickland FM, Muller HK, Stephens LC, Bucana CD, Donawho CK, Sun Y, et al. Induction of Primary Cutaneous Melanomas in C3H Mice by Combined Treatment with Ultraviolet Radiation, Ethanol and Aloe Emodin ¶. Photochem Photobiol 2000;72(3):407-414.

(66) National Toxicology Program. NTP Toxicology and Carcinogenesis Studies of EMODIN (CAS NO. 518-82-1) Feed Studies in F344/N Rats and B6C3F1 Mice. Natl Toxicol Program Tech Rep Ser 2001 Jun;493:1-278.

(67) Tong X, Li M, Li D, Lao C, Chen J, Xu W, et al. Aloe vera gel extract: Safety evaluation for acute and chronic oral administration in Sprague-Dawley rats and anticancer activity in breast and lung cancer cells. J Ethnopharmacol 2021;280:114434.

(68) Im S, Kim J, Kim H, Park C, Shin E, Do S, et al. Prevention of azoxymethane/dextran sodium sulfate-induced mouse colon carcinogenesis by processed Aloe vera gel. Int Immunopharmacol 2016;40:428-435.

(69) Prins GS, Calderon-Gierszal E, Hu W. Stem Cells as Hormone Targets That Lead to Increased Cancer Susceptibility. Endocrinology 2015;156(10):3451-3457.

(70) Hoover RN, Hyer M, Pfeiffer RM, Adam E, Bond B, Cheville AL, et al. Adverse Health Outcomes in Women Exposed In Utero to Diethylstilbestrol. N Engl J Med 2011;365(14):1304-1314.

(71) Hilakivi-Clarke L. Maternal exposure to diethylstilbestrol during pregnancy and increased breast cancer risk in daughters. Breast Cancer Research 2014;16(2):208.

(72) Cancer Research UK. Breast Cancer Statistics. Available at: https://www.cancerresearchuk.org/health-professional/cancer-statistics/statistics-by-cancer-type/breast-cancer#heading-Four. Accessed 05/09/, 2021.
(73) Myers SL, Yang CZ, Bittner GD, Witt KL, Tice RR, Baird DD. Estrogenic and anti-estrogenic activity of off-the-shelf hair and skin care products. J Expo Sci Environ Epidemiol 2015 May;25(3):271-277.
(74) Yoon S, Yoon J, Jo SJ, Shin CY, Shin J, Kim J, et al. A role of placental growth factor in hair growth. J Dermatol Sci 2014;74(2):125-134.
(75) Kim MH, Kim K, Lee H, Yang WM. Human placenta induces hair regrowth in chemotherapy-induced alopecia via inhibition of apoptotic factors and proliferation of hair follicles. BMC Complementary Medicine and Therapies 2020;20(1):230.
(76) Donovan M, Tiwary CM, Axelrod D, Sasco AJ, Jones L, Hajek R, et al. Personal care products that contain estrogens or xenoestrogens may increase breast cancer risk. Med Hypotheses 2007;68(4):756-766.
(77) Bever CS, Rand AA, Nording M, Taft D, Kalanetra KM, Mills DA, et al. Effects of triclosan in breast milk on the infant fecal microbiome. Chemosphere 2018;203:467-473.
(78) Weatherly LM, Gosse JA. Triclosan exposure, transformation, and human health effects. Journal of toxicology and environmental health.Part B, Critical reviews 2017;20(8):447-469.
(79) Farasani A, Darbre PD. Long-term exposure to triclosan increases migration and invasion of human breast epithelial cells in vitro. J Appl Toxicol 2021;41(7):1115-1126.
(80) Winitthana T, Lawanprasert S, Chanvorachote P. Triclosan potentiates epithelial-to-mesenchymal transition in anoikis-resistant human lung cancer cells. PloS one 2014;9(10):e110851.
(81) Lee H, Hwang K, Nam K, Kim H, Choi K. Progression of Breast Cancer Cells Was Enhanced by Endocrine-Disrupting Chemicals, Triclosan and Octylphenol, via an Estrogen Receptor-Dependent Signaling Pathway in Cellular and Mouse Xenograft Models. Chem Res Toxicol 2014;27(5):834-842.
(82) Pierozan P, Jerneren F, Karlsson O. Perfluorooctanoic acid (PFOA) exposure promotes proliferation, migration and invasion potential in human breast epithelial cells. Arch Toxicol 2018;92(5):1729-1739.
(83) Zhang W, Wang F, Xu P, Miao C, Zeng X, Cui X, et al. Perfluorooctanoic acid stimulates breast cancer cells invasion and up-regulates matrix metalloproteinase-2/-9 expression mediated by activating NF-κB. Toxicol Lett 2014;229(1):118-125.
(84) Bonefeld-Jorgensen E, Long M, Bossi R, Ayotte P, Asmund G, Krüger T, et al. Perfluorinated compounds are related to breast cancer risk in greenlandic inuit: A case control study. Environ Health 2011;10(1):88.
(85) Barr L, Metaxas G, Harbach CAJ, Savoy LA, Darbre PD. Measurement of paraben concentrations in human breast tissue at serial locations across the breast from axilla to sternum. J Appl Toxicol 2012;32(3):219-232.
(86) Darbre PD, Harvey PW. Parabens can enable hallmarks and characteristics of cancer in human breast epithelial cells: a review of the literature with reference to new exposure data and regulatory status. J Appl Toxicol 2014;34(9):925-938.

(87) López-Carrillo Lizbeth, Hernández-Ramírez Raúl U, Calafat Antonia M, Torres-Sánchez Luisa, Galván-Portillo Marcia, Needham Larry L, et al. Exposure to Phthalates and Breast Cancer Risk in Northern Mexico. Environ Health Perspect 2010;118(4):539-544.

(88) Ahern TP, Broe A, Lash TL, Cronin-Fenton D, Ulrichsen SP, Christiansen PM, et al. Phthalate Exposure and Breast Cancer Incidence: A Danish Nationwide Cohort Study. JCO 2019;37(21):1800-1809.

(89) Zhu M, Huang C, Ma X, Wu R, Zhu W, Li X, et al. Phthalates promote prostate cancer cell proliferation through activation of ERK5 and p38. Environ Toxicol Pharmacol 2018;63:29-33.

(90) Sprague BL, Trentham-Dietz A, Hedman CJ, Wang J, Hemming JD, Hampton JM, et al. Circulating serum xenoestrogens and mammographic breast density. Breast Cancer Res 2013 May 27;15(3):R45.

(91) Liu G, Cai W, Liu H, Jiang H, Bi Y, Wang H. The Association of Bisphenol A and Phthalates with Risk of Breast Cancer: A Meta-Analysis. Int J Environ Res Public Health 2021 Mar 1;18(5):2375. doi: 10.3390/ijerph18052375.

(92) Sang C, Song Y, Jin TW, Zhang S, Fu L, Zhao Y, et al. Bisphenol A induces ovarian cancer cell proliferation and metastasis through estrogen receptor-α pathways. Environ Sci Pollut Res Int 2021 Jul;28(27):36060-36068.

(93) Kunisue T, Chen Z, Buck Louis GM, Sundaram R, Hediger ML, Sun L, et al. Urinary concentrations of benzophenone-type UV filters in U.S. women and their association with endometriosis. Environ Sci Technol 2012 Apr 17;46(8):4624-4632.

(94) Valle-Sistac J, Molins-Delgado D, Díaz M, Ibáñez L, Barceló D, Silvia Díaz-Cruz M. Determination of parabens and benzophenone-type UV filters in human placenta. First description of the existence of benzyl paraben and benzophenone-4. Environ Int 2016;88:243-249.

(95) Schlumpf M, Kypke K, Wittassek M, Angerer J, Mascher H, Mascher D, et al. Exposure patterns of UV filters, fragrances, parabens, phthalates, organochlor pesticides, PBDEs, and PCBs in human milk: Correlation of UV filters with use of cosmetics. Chemosphere 2010;81(10):1171-1183.

(96) Rodríguez-Gómez R, Zafra-Gómez A, Dorival-García N, Ballesteros O, Navalón A. Determination of benzophenone-UV filters in human milk samples using ultrasound-assisted extraction and clean-up with dispersive sorbents followed by UHPLC–MS/MS analysis. Talanta 2015;134:657-664.

(97) Alamer M, Darbre PD. Effects of exposure to six chemical ultraviolet filters commonly used in personal care products on motility of MCF-7 and MDA-MB-231 human breast cancer cells in vitro. J Appl Toxicol 2018;38(2):148-159.

(98) Darbre PD. Metalloestrogens: an emerging class of inorganic xenoestrogens with potential to add to the oestrogenic burden of the human breast. J Appl Toxicol 2006;26(3):191-197.

(99) Mannello F, Tonti GA, Medda V, Simone P, Darbre PD. Analysis of aluminium content and iron homeostasis in nipple aspirate fluids from healthy women and breast cancer-affected patients. J Appl Toxicol 2011;31(3):262-269.

(100) Exley C, Charles LM, Barr L, Martin C, Polwart A, Darbre PD. Aluminium in human breast tissue. J Inorg Biochem 2007;101(9):1344-1346.

(101) Fakri S, Al Azzawi A, Al Tawil N. Antiperspirant use as a risk factor for breast cancer in Iraq. EMHJ - Eastern Mediterranean Health Journal, 12 (3-4), 478-482, 2006 2006.

(102) Mirick DK, Davis S, Thomas DB. Antiperspirant Use and the Risk of Breast Cancer. J Natl Cancer Inst 2002;94(20):1578-1580.

(103) Mandriota SJ, Tenan M, Ferrari P, Sappino A. Aluminium chloride promotes tumorigenesis and metastasis in normal murine mammary gland epithelial cells. Int J Cancer 2016;139(12):2781-2790.

(104) Darbre PD, Bakir A, Iskakova E. Effect of aluminium on migratory and invasive properties of MCF-7 human breast cancer cells in culture. J Inorg Biochem 2013;128:245-249.

(105) Linhart C, Talasz H, Morandi EM, Exley C, Lindner HH, Taucher S, et al. Use of Underarm Cosmetic Products in Relation to Risk of Breast Cancer: A Case-Control Study. EBioMedicine 2017;21:79-85.

(106) Affinito P, Palomba S, Sorrentino C, Di Carlo C, Bifulco G, Arienzo MP, et al. Effects of postmenopausal hypoestrogenism on skin collagen. Maturitas 1999;33(3):239-247.

(107) SCHMIDT JB, BINDER M, DEMSCHIK G, BIEGLMAYER C, REINER A. TREATMENT OF SKIN AGING WITH TOPICAL ESTROGENS. Int J Dermatol 1996;35(9):669-674.

(108) Swenberg JA, Moeller BC, Lu K, Rager JE, Fry RC, Starr TB. Formaldehyde Carcinogenicity Research: 30 Years and Counting for Mode of Action, Epidemiology, and Cancer Risk Assessment. Toxicol Pathol 2013;41(2):181-189.

(109) Lamplugh A, Harries M, Xiang F, Trinh J, Hecobian A, Montoya LD. Occupational exposure to volatile organic compounds and health risks in Colorado nail salons. Environmental Pollution 2019;249:518-526.

(110) Curtis J, Tanner P, Judd C, Childs B, Hull C, Leachman S. Acrylic nail curing UV lamps: High-intensity exposure warrants further research of skin cancer risk. J Am Acad Dermatol 2013;69(6):1069-1070.

(111) Shipp LR, Warner CA, Rueggeberg FA, Davis LS. Further Investigation Into the Risk of Skin Cancer Associated With the Use of UV Nail Lamps. JAMA Dermatol 2014;150(7):775-776.

(112) Rosenberg L, Boggs DA, Adams-Campbell LL, Palmer JR. Hair Relaxers Not Associated with Breast Cancer Risk: Evidence from the Black Women's Health Study. Cancer Epidemiol Biomarkers Prev 2007;16(5):1035-1037.

(113) Llanos AA, Rabkin A, Bandera EV, Zirpoli G, Gonzalez BD, Xing CY, et al. Hair product use and breast cancer risk among African American and White women. Carcinogenesis 2017;38(9):883-892.

(114) Eberle CE, Sandler DP, Taylor KW, White AJ. Hair dye and chemical straightener use and breast cancer risk in a large US population of black and white women. Int J Cancer 2020;147(2):383-391.

(115) Brinton LA, Figueroa JD, Ansong D, Nyarko KM, Wiafe S, Yarney J, et al. Skin lighteners and hair relaxers as risk factors for breast cancer: results from the Ghana breast health study. Carcinogenesis 2018;39(4):571-579.

(116) White AJ, Sandler DP, Gaston SA, Jackson CL, O'Brien KM. Use of hair products in relation to ovarian cancer risk. Carcinogenesis 2021;42(9):1189-1195.
(117) Formaldehyde, Report on Carcinogens, Fourteenth edition. . Accessed 14/11/, 2021.
(118) Weathersby C, McMichael A. Brazilian keratin hair treatment: a review. J Cosmet Dermatol 2013;12(2):144-148.
(119) Xu S, Wang H, Liu Y, Zhang C, Xu Y, Tian F, et al. Hair chemicals may increase breast cancer risk: A meta-analysis of 210319 subjects from 14 studies. PLOS ONE 2021;16(2):e0243792.
(120) Ambrosone CB, Abrams SM, Gorlewska-Roberts K, Kadlubar FF. Hair dye use, meat intake, and tobacco exposure and presence of carcinogen-DNA adducts in exfoliated breast ductal epithelial cells. Arch Biochem Biophys 2007;464(2):169-175.
(121) Bolt HM, Golka K. The debate on carcinogenicity of permanent hair dyes: new insights. Crit Rev Toxicol 2007;37(6):521-536.
(122) Harling M, Schablon A, Schedlbauer G, Dulon M, Nienhaus A. Bladder cancer among hairdressers: a meta-analysis. Occup Environ Med 2010;67(5):351-358.
(123) Coburn SB, Bray F, Sherman ME, Trabert B. International patterns and trends in ovarian cancer incidence, overall and by histologic subtype. Int J Cancer 2017;140(11):2451-2460.
(124) Zhang Y, Birmann BM, Han J, Giovannucci EL, Speizer FE, Stampfer MJ, et al. Personal use of permanent hair dyes and cancer risk and mortality in US women: prospective cohort study. BMJ 2020;370:m2942.
(125) Tadokoro T, Kobayashi N, Zmudzka BZ, Ito S, Wakamatsu K, Yamaguchi Y, et al. UV-induced DNA damage and melanin content in human skin differing in racial/ethnic origin. FASEB J 2003;17(9):1177-1179.
(126) Kaidbey KH, Agin PP, Sayre RM, Kligman AM. Photoprotection by melanin—a comparison of black and Caucasian skin. J Am Acad Dermatol 1979;1(3):249-260.
(127) Blay YA. Skin bleaching and global white supremacy: By way of introduction. The Journal of Pan African Studies 2011;4(4):4-46.
(128) Dlova NC, Hamed SH, Tsoka-Gwegweni J, Grobler A. Skin lightening practices: an epidemiological study of South African women of African and Indian ancestries. Br J Dermatol 2015;173:2-9.
(129) Dadzie OE, Petit A. Skin bleaching: highlighting the misuse of cutaneous depigmenting agents. J Eur Acad Dermatol Venereol 2009 Jul;23(7):741-750.
(130) Hogue L, Harvey VM. Basal Cell Carcinoma, Squamous Cell Carcinoma, and Cutaneous Melanoma in Skin of Color Patients. Dermatol Clin 2019;37(4):519-526.
(131) Gbandama KKP, Diabaté A, Kouassi KA, Kouassi YI, Allou AS, Kaloga M. Squamous Cell Carcinoma Associated with Cosmetic Use of Bleaching Agents: About a Case in Ivory Coast. Case Rep Dermatol 2019 Dec 4;11(3):322-326.
(132) Ly F, Diousse P, Ndiaye C, Déme A, Diatta BA, Ndiaye MT, et al. Cutaneous squamous cell carcinomas (SCC) associated with cosmetic skin whitening: 8 cases reported in Senegal. Annales de Dermatologie et de Vénéréologie 2018;145(2):83-88.

(133) Faye O, Dicko AA, Berthé S, Cissé L, Traoré B, Keita A, et al. Squamous cell carcinoma associated with use of skin-lightening cream. Ann Dermatol Venereol 2018 Feb;145(2):100-103.

(134) Owolabi JO, Fabiyi OS, Adelakin LA, Ekwerike MC. Effects of Skin Lightening Cream Agents - Hydroquinone and Kojic Acid, on the Skin of Adult Female Experimental Rats. Clinical, cosmetic and investigational dermatology 2020;13:283-289.

(135) Kim C, Pasparakis M. Epidermal p65/NF-κB signalling is essential for skin carcinogenesis. EMBO Mol Med 2014 Jul;6(7):970-983.

(136) Yang X, Lu Y, He F, Hou F, Xing C, Xu P, et al. Benzene metabolite hydroquinone promotes DNA homologous recombination repair via the NF-κB pathway. Carcinogenesis 2019;40(8):1021-1030.

(137) Pereira P, Enguita FJ, Ferreira J, Leitão AL. DNA damage induced by hydroquinone can be prevented by fungal detoxification. Toxicology reports 2014;1:1096-1105.

(138) IARC Working Group on the Evaluation of Carcinogenic Risks to Humans. Re-evaluation of Some Organic Chemicals, Hydrazine and Hydrogen Peroxide. Lyon (FR): International Agency for Research on Cancer; 1999. (IARC Monographs on the Evaluation of Carcinogenic Risks to Humans, No. 71.) Hydroquinone.

(139) Tse TW. Hydroquinone for skin lightening: Safety profile, duration of use and when should we stop? J Dermatol Treat 2010;21(5):272-275.

(140) Saeedi M, Eslamifar M, Khezri K. Kojic acid applications in cosmetic and pharmaceutical preparations. Biomedicine & Pharmacotherapy 2019;110:582-593.

(141) Nawarak J, Huang-Liu R, Kao S, Liao H, Sinchaikul S, Chen S, et al. Proteomics Analysis of Kojic Acid Treated A375 Human Malignant Melanoma Cells. J Proteome Res 2008;7(9):3737-3746.

(142) Yoo DS, Lee J, Choi SS, Rho HS, Cho DH, Shin WC, et al. A modulatory effect of novel kojic acid derivatives on cancer cell proliferation and macrophage activation. Pharmazie 2010 Apr;65(4):261-266.

(143) Wang K, Liu C, Di CJ, Ma C, Han CG, Yuan MR, et al. Kojic acid protects C57BL/6 mice from gamma-irradiation induced damage. Asian Pac J Cancer Prev 2014;15(1):291-297.

(144) Dilokthornsakul W, Dhippayom T, Dilokthornsakul P. The clinical effect of glutathione on skin color and other related skin conditions: A systematic review. J Cosmet Dermatol 2019 Jun;18(3):728-737.

(145) Davids LM, Van Wyk JC, Khumalo NP. Intravenous glutathione for skin lightening: Inadequate safety data. S Afr Med J 2016 Jul 6;106(8):782-786.

(146) Yang C-, Huang Y-, Tsai M-, Cheng C-, Liu L-, Yen Y-, et al. Inhibition of melanogenesis by β-caryophyllene from lime mint essential oil in mouse B16 melanoma cells. Int J Cosmet Sci 2015;37(5):550-554.

(147) Gerber B, Mathys P, Moser M, Bressoud D, Braun-Fahrländer C. Ultraviolet Emission Spectra of Sunbeds¶. Photochem Photobiol 2002;76(6):664-668.

(148) O'Sullivan DE, Brenner DR, Demers PA, Villeneuve PJ, Friedenreich CM, King WD. Indoor tanning and skin cancer in Canada: A meta-analysis and attributable burden estimation. Cancer Epidemiology 2019;59:1-7.

(149) An S, Kim K, Moon S, Ko K, Kim I, Lee JE, et al. Indoor Tanning and the Risk of Overall and Early-Onset Melanoma and Non-Melanoma Skin Cancer: Systematic Review and Meta-Analysis. Cancers 2021;13(23).

(150) Paurobally D, Jason F, Dezfoulian B, Nikkels AF. Melanotan-associated melanoma. Br J Dermatol 2011;164(6):1403-1405.

(151) Hjuler KF, Lorentzen HF. Melanoma associated with the use of melanotan-II. Dermatology 2014;228(1):34-36.

(152) Langan EA, Ramlogan D, Jamieson LA, Rhodes LE. Change in moles linked to use of unlicensed "sun tan jab". BMJ 2009;338:b277.

(153) Reid C, Fitzgerald T, Fabre A, Kirby B. Atypical melanocytic naevi following melanotan injection. Ir Med J 2013 May;106(5):148-149.

(154) Chiang YZ, Pierone G, Al-Niaimi F. Dermal fillers: pathophysiology, prevention and treatment of complications. J Eur Acad Dermatol Venereol 2017;31(3):405-413.

(155) Shahrabi-Farahani S, Lerman MA, Noonan V, Kabani S, Woo S. Granulomatous foreign body reaction to dermal cosmetic fillers with intraoral migration. Oral Surgery, Oral Medicine, Oral Pathology and Oral Radiology 2014;117(1):105-110.

(156) Hamed-Azzam S, Burkat C, Mukari A, Briscoe D, Joshi N, Scawn R, et al. Filler Migration to the Orbit. Aesthet Surg J 2020;41(6):NP559-NP566.

(157) Alijotas-Reig J, Fernández-Figueras MT, Puig L. Inflammatory, immune-mediated adverse reactions related to soft tissue dermal fillers. Semin Arthritis Rheum 2013;43(2):241-258.

(158) Chiang YZ, Pierone G, Al-Niaimi F. Dermal fillers: pathophysiology, prevention and treatment of complications. J Eur Acad Dermatol Venereol 2017;31(3):405-413.

(159) Martin LHC, Hankinson PM, Khurram SA. Beauty is only mucosa deep: a retrospective analysis of oral lumps and bumps caused by cosmetic fillers. Br Dent J 2019;227(4):281-284.

(160) Lee SH, Kim HC, Kim YJ. B-Cell Lymphoma in a Patient With a History of Foreign Body Injection. J Craniofac Surg 2017;28(2).

(161) Vera-Lastra O, Rojas-Milán E, Peralta-Amaro A, Sánchez-Uribe M, Cruz-González LI, Hernández-Sánchez M, et al. Autoimmune/inflammatory syndrome induced by methylmethacrylate associated to seronegative antiphospholipid syndrome and diffuse large B-cell non-Hodgkin's lymphoma. Lupus 2020;29(10):1292-1296.

(162) Abatangelo G, Vindigni V, Avruscio G, Pandis L, Brun P. Hyaluronic Acid: Redefining Its Role. Cells 2020;9(7).

(163) Hill A, McFarlane S, Johnston PG, Waugh DJJ. The emerging role of CD44 in regulating skeletal micrometastasis. Cancer Lett 2006;237(1):1-9.

(164) Sironen RK, Tammi M, Tammi R, Auvinen PK, Anttila M, Kosma V. Hyaluronan in human malignancies. Exp Cell Res 2011;317(4):383-391.

(165) Caon I, Bartolini B, Parnigoni A, Caravà E, Moretto P, Viola M, et al. Revisiting the hallmarks of cancer: The role of hyaluronan. Semin Cancer Biol 2020;62:9-19.

(166) Lipponen P, Aaltomaa S, Tammi R, Tammi M, Ågren U, Kosma V-. High stromal hyaluronan level is associated with poor differentiation and metastasis in prostate cancer. Eur J Cancer 2001;37(7):849-856.

(167) Auvinen P, Tammi R, Parkkinen J, Tammi M, Ågren U, Johansson R, et al. Hyaluronan in Peritumoral Stroma and Malignant Cells Associates with Breast Cancer Spreading and Predicts Survival. The American Journal of Pathology 2000;156(2):529-536.

(168) Wu W, Chen L, Wang Y, Jin J, Xie X, Zhang J. Hyaluronic acid predicts poor prognosis in breast cancer patients: A protocol for systematic review and meta analysis. Medicine 2020;99(22).

(169) Bahnassy AA, Fawzy M, El-Wakil M, Zekri AN, Abdel-Sayed A, Sheta M. Aberrant expression of cancer stem cell markers (CD44, CD90, and CD133) contributes to disease progression and reduced survival in hepatoblastoma patients: 4-year survival data. Translational Research 2015;165(3):396-406.

(170) Chen Y, Fu Z, Xu S, Xu Y, Xu P. The prognostic value of CD44 expression in gastric cancer: A meta-Analysis. Biomedicine & Pharmacotherapy 2014;68(6):693-697.

(171) Yang Y, Zhao Y, Lan J, Kang Y, Zhang T, Ding Y, et al. Reduction-sensitive CD44 receptor-targeted hyaluronic acid derivative micelles for doxorubicin delivery. International journal of nanomedicine 2018;13:4361-4378.

(172) Mendes AN, Filgueiras LA, Siqueira MRP, Barbosa GM, Holandino C, de Lima Moreira D, et al. Encapsulation of Piper cabralanum (Piperaceae) nonpolar extract in poly(methyl methacrylate) by miniemulsion and evaluation of increase in the effectiveness of antileukemic activity in K562 cells. Int J Nanomedicine 2017 Nov 21;12:8363-8373.

(173) Sahu A, Solanki P, Mitra S. Curcuminoid-loaded poly(methyl methacrylate) nanoparticles for cancer therapy. International journal of nanomedicine 2018;13(-):101-105.

(174) Gibbens-Bandala BV, Ocampo-García BE, Ferro-Flores G, Morales-Avila E, Ancira-Cortez A, Jaimes-Aguirre L. Multimeric System of RGD-Grafted PMMA-Nanoparticles as a Targeted Drug- Delivery System for Paclitaxel. Curr Pharm Des 2017;23(23):3415-3422.

(175) Alomari M, Balasamy RJ, Almohazey D, Ravinayagam V, Al Hamad M, Ababneh D, et al. Nile Red-Poly(Methyl Methacrylate)/Silica Nanocomposite Particles Increase the Sensitivity of Cervical Cancer Cells to Tamoxifen. Polymers (Basel) 2020 Jul 8;12(7):1516. doi: 10.3390/polym12071516.

(176) Bonté F, Girard D, Archambault J, Desmoulière A. Skin Changes During Ageing. In: Harris JR, Korolchuk VI, editors. Biochemistry and Cell Biology of Ageing: Part II Clinical Science Singapore: Springer Singapore; 2019. p. 249-280.

(177) John Hopkins Medicine. Cosmetic Plastic Surgery Overview. Available at: https://www.hopkinsmedicine.org/health/treatment-tests-and-therapies/cosmetic-plastic-surgery-overview. Accessed 29/12/, 2021.

(178) Small R. Botulinum toxin injection for facial wrinkles. Am Fam Physician 2014 Aug 1;90(3):168-175.

(179) De Groef A, Devoogdt N, Van Kampen M, Nevelsteen I, Smeets A, Neven P, et al. Effectiveness of Botulinum Toxin A for Persistent Upper Limb Pain After Breast Cancer Treatment: A Double-Blinded Randomized Controlled Trial. Arch Phys Med Rehabil 2018;99(7):1342-1351.

(180) Mailly M, Benzakin S, Chauvin A, Brasnu D, Ayache D. [Radiation-induced head and neck pain: Management with botulinum toxin a injections]. Cancer radiotherapie : journal de la Societe francaise de radiotherapie oncologique 2019;23(4):312-315.

(181) Mittal S, Machado DG, Jabbari B. OnabotulinumtoxinA for Treatment of Focal Cancer Pain After Surgery and/or Radiation. Pain Med 2012;13(8):1029-1033.

(182) Rostami R, Mittal SO, Radmand R, Jabbari B. Incobotulinum Toxin-A Improves Post-Surgical and Post-Radiation Pain in Cancer Patients. Toxins 2016;8(1).

(183) Rust A, Leese C, Binz T, Davletov B. Botulinum neurotoxin type C protease induces apoptosis in differentiated human neuroblastoma cells. Oncotarget 2016 May 31;7(22):33220-33228.

(184) Karsenty G, Rocha J, Chevalier S, Scarlata E, Andrieu C, Zouanat FZ, et al. Botulinum Toxin Type A Inhibits the Growth of LNCaP Human Prostate Cancer Cells In Vitro and In Vivo. Prostate 2009;69(11):1143-1150.

(185) Coarfa C, Florentin D, Putluri N, Ding Y, Au J, He D, et al. Influence of the neural microenvironment on prostate cancer. Prostate 2018;78(2):128-139.

(186) Effect of Botulinum Toxin A on Proliferation and Apoptosis inthe T47D Breast Cancer Cell Line. APJCP 2013;14(2):891-894.

(187) Ansiaux R, Baudelet C, Cron GO, Segers J, Dessy C, Martinive P, et al. Botulinum toxin potentiates cancer radiotherapy and chemotherapy. Clin Cancer Res 2006;12(4):1276-1283.

(188) Cron GO, Beghein N, Ansiaux R, Martinive P, Feron O, Gallez B. 19F NMR in vivo spectroscopy reflects the effectiveness of perfusion-enhancing vascular modifiers for improving gemcitabine chemotherapy. Magn Reson Med 2008;59(1):19-27.

(189) Preparation of Immunotoxin Herceptin-Botulinum and Killing Effects on Two Breast Cancer Cell Lines. APJCP 2015;16(14):5977-5981.

(190) International Fragrance Association. IFRA Transparency List. Available at: https://ifrafragrance.org/priorities/ingredients/ifra-transparency-list. Accessed 26/11/, 2021.

(191) Martín J, Hidalgo F, Alonso E, García-Corcoles MT, Vílchez JL, Zafra-Gómez A. Assessing bioaccumulation potential of personal care, household and industrial products in a marine echinoderm (Holothuria tubulosa). Sci Total Environ 2020;720:137668.

(192) González-Rubio S, Vike-Jonas K, Gonzalez SV, Ballesteros-Gómez A, Sonne C, Dietz R, et al. Bioaccumulation potential of bisphenols and benzophenone UV filters: A multiresidue approach in raptor tissues. Sci Total Environ 2020;741:140330.

(193) Kerdivel G, Le Guevel R, Habauzit D, Brion F, Ait-Aissa S, Pakdel F. Estrogenic Potency of Benzophenone UV Filters in Breast Cancer Cells: Proliferative and Transcriptional Activity Substantiated by Docking Analysis. PLOS ONE 2013;8(4):e60567.

(194) Liu X, Zhan T, Gao Y, Cui S, Liu W, Zhang C, et al. Benzophenone-1 induced aberrant proliferation and metastasis of ovarian cancer cells via activated ERα and Wnt/β-catenin signaling pathways. Environmental Pollution 2022;292:118370.

(195) David ORP. A Chemical History of Polycyclic Musks. Chem Eur J 2020;26(34):7537-7555.

(196) Kevekordes S, Mersch-Sundermann V, Diez M, Dunkelberg H. In vitro genotoxicity of polycyclic musk fragrances in the micronucleus test. Mutation Research/Genetic Toxicology and Environmental Mutagenesis 1997;395(2):145-150.

(197) Api AM, Ford RA. Evaluation of the oral subchronic toxicity of HHCB (1,3,4,6,7,8-hexahydro-4,6,6,7,8,8-hexamethylcyclopenta-γ-2-benzopyran) in the rat. Toxicol Lett 1999;111(1):143-149.

(198) Ayuk-Takem L, Amissah F, Aguilar BJ, Lamango NS. Inhibition of polyisoprenylated methylated protein methyl esterase by synthetic musks induces cell degeneration. Environ Toxicol 2014;29(4):466-477.

(199) Doğanlar O, Doğanlar ZB, Chasan T, Kurtdere AK. Prolonged sub-lethal exposure to galaxolide (HHCB) and tonalide (AHTN) promotes the metastatic potential of glioblastoma tumor spheroids. Neurotoxicology 2021;87:219-230.

(200) Yin J, Wang H, Li J, Wu Y, Shao B. Occurrence of synthetic musks in human breast milk samples from 12 provinces in China. Food Addit Contam Part A Chem Anal Control Expo Risk Assess 2016 Jul;33(7):1219-1227.

(201) Williams GM, Iatropoulos MJ, Jeffrey AM, Duan JD. Methyleugenol hepatocellular cancer initiating effects in rat liver. Food Chem Toxicol 2013 Mar;53:187-196.

(202) Johnson JD, Ryan MJ, Toft JD,II, Graves SW, Hejtmancik MR, Cunningham ML, et al. Two-year toxicity and carcinogenicity study of methyleugenol in F344/N rats and B6C3F(1) mice. J Agric Food Chem 2000 Aug;48(8):3620-3632.

(203) National Toxicology Program. NTP Toxicology and Carcinogenesis Studies of Methyleugenol (CAS NO. 93-15-2) in F344/N Rats and B6C3F1 Mice (Gavage Studies). Natl Toxicol Program Tech Rep Ser 2000 Jul;491:1-412.

(204) Sugiura S, Ogawa K, Hirose M, Takeshita F, Asamoto M, Shirai T. Reversibility of proliferative lesions and induction of non-papillary tumors in rat urinary bladder treated with phenylethyl isothiocyanate. Carcinogenesis 2003 Mar;24(3):547-553.

(205) ROHRSCHNEIDER LR, BOUTWELL RK. Phorbol Esters, Fatty Acids and Tumour Promotion. Nature New Biology 1973;243(128):212-213.

(206) AU - Vähätupa M, AU - Pemmari T, AU - Junttila I, AU - Pesu M, AU - Järvinen T,AH. Chemical-Induced Skin Carcinogenesis Model Using Dimethylbenz[a]Anthracene and 12-O-Tetradecanoyl Phorbol-13-Acetate (DMBA-TPA). JoVE 2019(154):e60445.

(207) Kang W, Choi D, Park S, Park T. Carvone Decreases Melanin Content by Inhibiting Melanoma Cell Proliferation via the Cyclic Adenosine Monophosphate (cAMP) Pathway. Molecules 2020;25(21).

(208) Masood N, Dubey V, Luqman S. Activation of Caspase-3 by Terpenoids and Flavonoids in Different Types of Cancer Cells. Curr Top Med Chem 2020;20(21):1876-1887.

(209) Gopalakrishnan T, Ganapathy S, Veeran V, Namasivayam N. Preventive effect of D-carvone during DMBA induced mouse skin tumorigenesis by modulating xenobiotic metabolism and induction of apoptotic events. Biomedicine & Pharmacotherapy 2019;111:178-187.

(210) Patel PB, Thakkar VR. L-Carvone Induces p53, Caspase 3 Mediated Apoptosis and Inhibits the Migration of Breast Cancer Cell Lines. Nutr Cancer 2014;66(3):453-462.

(211) Lv L, Yang N, Cao Y, Dang J, Cheng L, El-Sheikh M, et al. d-Carvone inhibits the JAK/STAT3 signaling pathway and induced the apoptotic cell death in the human gastric cancer AGS cells. J Biochem Mol Toxicol 2021;35(5):e22746.
(212) Ding X, Chen H. Anticancer effects of Carvone in myeloma cells is mediated through the inhibition of p38 MAPK signalling pathway, apoptosis induction and inhibition of cell invasion. J BUON 2018;23(3):747-751.
(213) Costarelli L, Malavolta M, Giacconi R, Cipriano C, Gasparini N, Tesei S, et al. In vivo effect of alpha-bisabolol, a nontoxic sesquiterpene alcohol, on the induction of spontaneous mammary tumors in HER-2/neu transgenic mice. Oncol Res 2010;18(9):409-418.
(214) Cavalieri E, Mariotto S, Fabrizi C, de Prati AC, Gottardo R, Leone S, et al. α-Bisabolol, a nontoxic natural compound, strongly induces apoptosis in glioma cells. Biochem Biophys Res Commun 2004;315(3):589-594.
(215) Cavalieri E, Rigo A, Bonifacio M, de Prati AC, Guardalben E, Bergamini C, et al. Pro-apoptotic activity of α-bisabolol in preclinical models of primary human acute leukemia cells. Journal of Translational Medicine 2011;9(1):45.
(216) Wu S, Peng L, Sang H, Ping Li Q, Cheng S. Anticancer effects of α-Bisabolol in human non-small cell lung carcinoma cells are mediated via apoptosis induction, cell cycle arrest, inhibition of cell migration and invasion and upregulation of P13K/AKT signalling pathway. J BUON 2018;23(5):1407-1412.
(217) UNO M, KOKURYO T, YOKOYAMA Y, SENGA T, NAGINO M. α-Bisabolol Inhibits Invasiveness and Motility in Pancreatic Cancer Through KISS1R Activation. Anticancer Res 2016;36(2):583-589.
(218) MURATA Y, KOKURYO T, YOKOYAMA Y, YAMAGUCHI J, MIWA T, SHIBUYA M, et al. The Anticancer Effects of Novel α-Bisabolol Derivatives Against Pancreatic Cancer. Anticancer Res 2017;37(2):589-598.
(219) Fang D, Wang H, Li M, Wei W. α-bisabolol enhances radiotherapy-induced apoptosis in endometrial cancer cells by reducing the effect of XIAP on inhibiting caspase-3. Biosci Rep 2019;39(6):BSR20190696.
(220) Guesmi, F., Tyagi, A., Prasad, S., Landoulsi,A. Terpenes from essential oils and hydrolate of *Teucrium alopecurus* triggered apoptotic events dependent on caspases activation and PARP cleavage in human colon cancer cells through decreased protein expressions. Oncotarget 2018;9(64).
(221) Contant C, Rouabhia M, Loubaki L, Chandad F, Semlali A. Anethole induces anti-oral cancer activity by triggering apoptosis, autophagy and oxidative stress and by modulation of multiple signaling pathways. Scientific Reports 2021;11(1):13087.
(222) Chen CH, deGraffenried LA. Anethole suppressed cell survival and induced apoptosis in human breast cancer cells independent of estrogen receptor status. Phytomedicine 2012;19(8):763-767.
(223) Arumugam P, Sampathkumar B, Perumalsamy H, Balusamy SR, Ramesh V, Sundaravadevel S. Synergistic effect of anethole and doxorubicin alleviates cell proliferation, cell cycle arrest, and ER stress and promotes ROS-mediated apoptosis in triple-negative breast cancer cells. J Biochem Mol Toxicol 2021;35(12):e22928.

(224) Pandit K, Kaur S, Kumar A, Bhardwaj R, Kaur S. trans-Anethole Abrogates Cell Proliferation and Induces Apoptosis through the Mitochondrial-Mediated Pathway in Human Osteosarcoma Cells. Nutr Cancer 2021;73(9):1727-1745.

(225) Ha B, Ko H, Kim B, Sohn EJ, Jung JH, Kim JS, et al. Regulation of Crosstalk between Epithelial to Mesenchymal Transition Molecules and MMP-9 Mediates the Antimetastatic Activity of Anethole in DU145 Prostate Cancer Cells. J Nat Prod 2014;77(1):63-69.

(226) Farah IO, Trimble Q, Ndebele K, Mawson A. Retinoids and citral modulated cell viability, metabolic stability, cell cycle progression and distribution in the a549 lung carcinoma cell line - biomed 2010. Biomed Sci Instrum 2010;46:410-421.

(227) Chaouki W, Leger DY, Liagre B, Beneytout J, Hmamouchi M. Citral inhibits cell proliferation and induces apoptosis and cell cycle arrest in MCF-7 cells. Fundam Clin Pharmacol 2009;23(5):549-556.

(228) Kapur A, Felder M, Fass L, Kaur J, Czarnecki A, Rathi K, et al. Modulation of oxidative stress and subsequent induction of apoptosis and endoplasmic reticulum stress allows citral to decrease cancer cell proliferation. Scientific Reports 2016;6(1):27530.

(229) Sanches LJ, Marinello PC, Panis C, Fagundes TR, Morgado-Díaz JA, de-Freitas-Junior J,Cesar Madureira, et al. Cytotoxicity of citral against melanoma cells: The involvement of oxidative stress generation and cell growth protein reduction. Tumour Biol 2017;39(3):1010428317695914.

(230) Kremer JL, Melo GP, Marinello PC, Bordini HP, Rossaneis AC, Sábio LR, et al. Citral prevents UVB-induced skin carcinogenesis in hairless mice. Journal of Photochemistry and Photobiology B: Biology 2019;198:111565.

(231) Sanches LJ, Marinello PC, Panis C, Fagundes TR, Morgado-Díaz JA, de-Freitas-Junior J,Cesar Madureira, et al. Cytotoxicity of citral against melanoma cells: The involvement of oxidative stress generation and cell growth protein reduction. Tumour Biol 2017;39(3):1010428317695914.

(232) Nordin N, Yeap SK, Rahman HS, Zamberi NR, Mohamad NE, Abu N, et al. Antitumor and Anti-Metastatic Effects of Citral-Loaded Nanostructured Lipid Carrier in 4T1-Induced Breast Cancer Mouse Model. Molecules (Basel, Switzerland) 2020;25(11):2670.

(233) Nordin N, Yeap SK, Rahman HS, Zamberi NR, Abu N, Mohamad NE, et al. In vitro cytotoxicity and anticancer effects of citral nanostructured lipid carrier on MDA MBA-231 human breast cancer cells. Scientific Reports 2019;9(1):1614.

(234) Flegel C, Manteniotis S, Osthold S, Hatt H, Gisselmann G. Expression profile of ectopic olfactory receptors determined by deep sequencing. PloS one 2013;8(2):e55368.

(235) Klauser A, Hirschfeld M, Ritter A, Rücker G, Jäger M, Gundarova J, et al. Anticarcinogenic Effects of Odorant Substances Citral, Citrathal R and Cyclovertal on Breast Cancer in vitro. Breast cancer (Dove Medical Press) 2021;13:659-673.

(236) d'Alessio PA, Ostan R, Bisson J, Schulzke JD, Ursini MV, Béné MC. Oral administration of d-Limonene controls inflammation in rat colitis and displays anti-inflammatory properties as diet supplementation in humans. Life Sci 2013;92(24):1151-1156.

(237) d'Alessio PA, Mirshahi M, Bisson JF, Bene MC. Skin repair properties of d-Limonene and perillyl alcohol in murine models. Antiinflamm Antiallergy Agents Med Chem 2014 Mar;13(1):29-35.

(238) Espina L, Gelaw TK, de Lamo-Castellví S, Pagán R, García-Gonzalo D. Mechanism of bacterial inactivation by (+)-limonene and its potential use in food preservation combined processes. PLoS One 2013;8(2):e56769.

(239) Manuele MG, Barreiro Arcos ML, Davicino R, Ferraro G, Cremaschi G, Anesini C. Limonene exerts antiproliferative effects and increases nitric oxide levels on a lymphoma cell line by dual mechanism of the ERK pathway: relationship with oxidative stress. Cancer Invest 2010 Feb;28(2):135-145.

(240) Chaudhary SC, Siddiqui MS, Athar M, Alam MS. d-Limonene modulates inflammation, oxidative stress and Ras-ERK pathway to inhibit murine skin tumorigenesis. Hum Exp Toxicol 2012;31(8):798-811.

(241) Hakim IA, Harris RB, Ritenbaugh C. Citrus peel use is associated with reduced risk of squamous cell carcinoma of the skin. Nutr Cancer 2000;37(2):161-168.

(242) Chidambara Murthy KN, Jayaprakasha GK, Patil BS. D-limonene rich volatile oil from blood oranges inhibits angiogenesis, metastasis and cell death in human colon cancer cells. Life Sci 2012;91(11):429-439.

(243) Jia S, Xi G, Zhang M, Chen Y, Lei B, Dong X, et al. Induction of apoptosis by D-limonene is mediated by inactivation of Akt in LS174T human colon cancer cells. Oncol Rep 2013;29(1):349-354.

(244) Nair S A, SR RK, Nair AS, Baby S. Citrus peels prevent cancer. Phytomedicine 2018;50:231-237.

(245) Yu X, Lin H, Wang Y, Lv W, Zhang S, Qian Y, et al. d-limonene exhibits antitumor activity by inducing autophagy and apoptosis in lung cancer. OncoTargets and therapy 2018;11:1833-1847.

(246) Ye Z, Liang Z, Mi Q, Guo Y. Limonene terpenoid obstructs human bladder cancer cell (T24 cell line) growth by inducing cellular apoptosis, caspase activation, G2/M phase cell cycle arrest and stops cancer metastasis. J BUON 2020;25(1):280-285.

(247) Kaji I, Tatsuta M, Iishi H, Baba M, Inoue A, Kasugai H. Inhibition by D-limonene of experimental hepatocarcinogenesis in Sprague-Dawley rats does not involve p21ras plasma membrane association. Int J Cancer 2001;93(3):441-444.

(248) Vigushin DM, Poon GK, Boddy A, English J, Halbert GW, Pagonis C, et al. Phase I and pharmacokinetic study of D-limonene in patients with advanced cancer. Cancer Research Campaign Phase I/II Clinical Trials Committee. Cancer Chemother Pharmacol 1998;42(2):111-117.

(249) Miller JA, Pappan K, Thompson PA, Want EJ, Siskos AP, Keun HC, et al. Plasma Metabolomic Profiles of Breast Cancer Patients after Short-term Limonene Intervention. Cancer Prev Res (Phila) 2015;8(1):86-93.

(250) Alipanah H, Farjam M, Zarenezhad E, Roozitalab G, Osanloo M. Chitosan nanoparticles containing limonene and limonene-rich essential oils: potential phytotherapy agents for the treatment of melanoma and breast cancers. BMC Complementary Medicine and Therapies 2021;21(1):186.

(251) Yang C, Chen H, Chen H, Zhong B, Luo X, Chun J. Antioxidant and Anticancer Activities of Essential Oil from Gannan Navel Orange Peel. Molecules (Basel, Switzerland) 2017;22(8):1391.

(252) Rabi T, Bishayee A. d -Limonene sensitizes docetaxel-induced cytotoxicity in human prostate cancer cells: Generation of reactive oxygen species and induction of apoptosis. J Carcinog 2009;8:9-3163.51368.

(253) Zhao Y, Chen R, Wang Y, Qing C, Wang W, Yang Y. In Vitro and In Vivo Efficacy Studies of Lavender angustifolia Essential Oil and Its Active Constituents on the Proliferation of Human Prostate Cancer. Integr Cancer Ther 2017;16(2):215-226.

(254) Zhao Y, Cheng X, Wang G, Liao Y, Qing C. Linalool inhibits 22Rv1 prostate cancer cell proliferation and induces apoptosis. Oncology letters 2020;20(6):289.

(255) Rodenak-Kladniew B, Castro MA, Crespo R, Galle M, García de Bravo M. Anti-cancer mechanisms of linalool and 1,8-cineole in non-small cell lung cancer A549 cells. Heliyon 2020;6(12):e05639.

(256) Iwasaki K, Zheng Y, Murata S, Ito H, Nakayama K, Kurokawa T, et al. Anticancer effect of linalool via cancer-specific hydroxyl radical generation in human colon cancer. World journal of gastroenterology 2016;22(44):9765-9774.

(257) Chang MY, Shieh DE, Chen CC, Yeh CS, Dong HP. Linalool Induces Cell Cycle Arrest and Apoptosis in Leukemia Cells and Cervical Cancer Cells through CDKIs. Int J Mol Sci 2015 Nov 26;16(12):28169-28179.

(258) Gong X, Wang B, Yan L, Lu X, Zhao X. Linalool inhibits the growth of human T cell acute lymphoblastic leukemia cells with involvement of the MAPK signaling pathway. Oncol Lett 2020 Nov;20(5):181.

(259) Becker V, Hui X, Nalbach L, Ampofo E, Lipp P, Menger MD, et al. Linalool inhibits the angiogenic activity of endothelial cells by downregulating intracellular ATP levels and activating TRPM8. Angiogenesis 2021;24(3):613-630.

(260) Gunaseelan S, Balupillai A, Govindasamy K, Muthusamy G, Ramasamy K, Shanmugam M, et al. The preventive effect of linalool on acute and chronic UVB-mediated skin carcinogenesis in Swiss albino mice. Photochem Photobiol Sci 2016;15(7):851-860.

(261) Zhang H, Chi M, Chen L, Sun X, Wan L, Yang Q, et al. Linalool Prevents Cisplatin Induced Muscle Atrophy by Regulating IGF-1/Akt/FoxO Pathway. Front Pharmacol 2020 Nov 30;11:598166.

(262) Chang M, Shen Y. Linalool exhibits cytotoxic effects by activating antitumor immunity. Molecules (Basel, Switzerland) 2014;19(5):6694-6706.

(263) Zhao Y, Meng X, Zeng Y, Wang C, Chen J, She Z. Linalool Inhibits MCF-7 Tumor Growth in a Xenograft Model by Apoptosis Induction and Immune Modulation. Natural Product Communications 2021;16(5):1934578X211015125.

(264) Jabir M, Sahib UI, Taqi Z, Taha A, Sulaiman G, Albukhaty S, et al. Linalool-Loaded Glutathione-Modified Gold Nanoparticles Conjugated with CALNN Peptide as Apoptosis Inducer and NF-κB Translocation Inhibitor in SKOV-3 Cell Line. Int J Nanomedicine 2020 Nov 17;15:9025-9047.

(265) Han HD, Cho Y, Cho SK, Byeon Y, Jeon HN, Kim H, et al. Linalool-Incorporated Nanoparticles as a Novel Anticancer Agent for Epithelial Ovarian Carcinoma. Mol Cancer Ther 2016;15(4):618-627.

(266) Wi TI, Won JE, Lee CM, Lee J, Kang TH, Shin BC, et al. Efficacy of Combination Therapy with Linalool and Doxorubicin Encapsulated by Liposomes as a Two-in-One Hybrid Carrier System for Epithelial Ovarian Carcinoma. International journal of nanomedicine 2020;15:8427-8436.

(267) Ravizza R, Gariboldi MB, Molteni R, Monti E. Linalool, a plant-derived monoterpene alcohol, reverses doxorubicin resistance in human breast adenocarcinoma cells. Oncol Rep 2008 Sep;20(3):625-630.

(268) Kaur G, Athar M, Alam MS. Eugenol precludes cutaneous chemical carcinogenesis in mouse by preventing oxidative stress and inflammation and by inducing apoptosis. Mol Carcinog 2010;49(3):290-301.

(269) Ghosh R, Nadiminty N, Fitzpatrick JE, Alworth WL, Slaga TJ, Kumar AP. Eugenol Causes Melanoma Growth Suppression through Inhibition of E2F1 Transcriptional Activity*. J Biol Chem 2005;280(7):5812-5819.

(270) Fangjun L, Zhijia Y. Tumor suppressive roles of eugenol in human lung cancer cells. Thorac Cancer 2018;9(1):25-29.

(271) Choudhury P, Barua A, Roy A, Pattanayak R, Bhattacharyya M, Saha P. Eugenol emerges as an elixir by targeting β-catenin, the central cancer stem cell regulator in lung carcinogenesis: an in vivo and in vitro rationale. Food Funct 2021;12(3):1063-1078.

(272) Al-Sharif I, Remmal A, Aboussekhra A. Eugenol triggers apoptosis in breast cancer cells through E2F1/survivin down-regulation. BMC Cancer 2013;13(1):600.

(273) Abdullah ML, Al-Shabanah O, Hassan ZK, Hafez MM. Eugenol-Induced Autophagy and Apoptosis in Breast Cancer Cells via PI3K/AKT/FOXO3a Pathway Inhibition. International journal of molecular sciences 2021;22(17):9243.

(274) Islam SS, Aboussekhra A. Sequential combination of cisplatin with eugenol targets ovarian cancer stem cells through the Notch-Hes1 signalling pathway. Journal of Experimental & Clinical Cancer Research 2019;38(1):382.

(275) Islam SS, Al-Sharif I, Sultan A, Al-Mazrou A, Remmal A, Aboussekhra A. Eugenol potentiates cisplatin anti-cancer activity through inhibition of ALDH-positive breast cancer stem cells and the NF-κB signaling pathway. Mol Carcinog 2018;57(3):333-346.

(276) Fouad MA, Sayed-Ahmed M, Huwait EA, Hafez HF, Osman AM. Epigenetic immunomodulatory effect of eugenol and astaxanthin on doxorubicin cytotoxicity in hormonal positive breast Cancer cells. BMC Pharmacology and Toxicology 2021;22(1):8.

(277) Fathy M, Fawzy MA, Hintzsche H, Nikaido T, Dandekar T, Othman EM. Eugenol Exerts Apoptotic Effect and Modulates the Sensitivity of HeLa Cells to Cisplatin and Radiation. Molecules (Basel, Switzerland) 2019;24(21):3979.

(278) Sun Z, Wang H, Wang J, Zhou L, Yang P. Chemical Composition and Anti-Inflammatory, Cytotoxic and Antioxidant Activities of Essential Oil from Leaves of Mentha piperita Grown in China. PLOS ONE 2014;9(12):e114767.

(279) Nagai K, Fukuno S, Omachi A, Omotani S, Hatsuda Y, Myotoku M, et al. Enhanced anti-cancer activity by menthol in HepG2 cells exposed to paclitaxel and vincristine: possible involvement of CYP3A4 downregulation. Drug Metabolism and Personalized Therapy 2019;34(1).

(280) Liu Z, Wu H, Wei Z, Wang X, Shen P, Wang S, et al. TRPM8: a potential target for cancer treatment. J Cancer Res Clin Oncol 2016;142(9):1871-1881.

(281) Nazıroğlu M, Blum W, Jósvay K, Çiğ B, Henzi T, Oláh Z, et al. Menthol evokes Ca2+ signals and induces oxidative stress independently of the presence of TRPM8 (menthol) receptor in cancer cells. Redox Biology 2018;14:439-449.

(282) Wang Y, Wang X, Yang Z, Zhu G, Chen D, Meng Z. Menthol inhibits the proliferation and motility of prostate cancer DU145 cells. Pathol Oncol Res 2012 Oct;18(4):903-910.

(283) Li Q, Wang X, Yang Z, Wang B, Li S. Menthol Induces Cell Death via the TRPM8 Channel in the Human Bladder Cancer Cell Line T24. Oncology 2009;77(6):335-341.

(284) Zhang C, Liu J, Guo H, Wang W, Xu M, Tan Y, et al. Theranostic Nanomedicine Carrying L-Menthol and Near-Infrared Dye for Multimodal Imaging-Guided Photothermal Therapy of Cancer. Adv Healthcare Mater 2019;8(16):1900409.

(285) Lee S, Park YR, Kim S, Park E, Kang MJ, So I, et al. Geraniol suppresses prostate cancer growth through down-regulation of E2F8. Cancer Med 2016;5(10):2899-2908.

(286) Kim SH, Park EJ, Lee CR, Chun JN, Cho NH, Kim IG, et al. Geraniol induces cooperative interaction of apoptosis and autophagy to elicit cell death in PC-3 prostate cancer cells. Int J Oncol 2012 May;40(5):1683-1690.

(287) Lee S, Park YR, Kim S, Park E, Kang MJ, So I, et al. Geraniol suppresses prostate cancer growth through down-regulation of E2F8. Cancer Med 2016;5(10):2899-2908.

(288) Madankumar A, Tamilarasi S, Premkumar T, Gopikrishnan M, Nagabhishek N, Devaki T. Geraniol attenuates 4NQO-induced tongue carcinogenesis through downregulating the activation of NF-κB in rats. Mol Cell Biochem 2017;434(1):7-15.

(289) Wittig C, Scheuer C, Parakenings J, Menger MD, Laschke MW. Geraniol Suppresses Angiogenesis by Downregulating Vascular Endothelial Growth Factor (VEGF)/VEGFR-2 Signaling. PloS one 2015;10(7):e0131946.

(290) Shen X, Cui X, Cui H, Jin Y, Jin W, Sun H. Geraniol and lupeol inhibit growth and promote apoptosis in human hepatocarcinoma cells through the MAPK signaling pathway. J Cell Biochem 2019;120(4):5033-5041.

(291) Fatima K, Wani ZA, Meena A, Luqman S. Geraniol exerts its antiproliferative action by modulating molecular targets in lung and skin carcinoma cells. Phytotherapy Research 2021;35(7):3861-3874.

(292) Park JS, Kwon JK, Kim HR, Kim HJ, Kim BS, Jung JY. Farnesol induces apoptosis of DU145 prostate cancer cells through the PI3K/Akt and MAPK pathways. Int J Mol Med 2014 May;33(5):1169-1176.

(293) Epplen R, Stöckle M, Engelmann U, Heidenreich A, Ohlmann CH. Differential effects of ibandronate, docetaxel and farnesol treatment alone and in combination on the growth of prostate cancer cell lines. Acta Oncol 2011 Jan;50(1):127-133.

(294) Lee JH, Chinnathambi A, Alharbi SA, Shair OHM, Sethi G, Ahn KS. Farnesol abrogates epithelial to mesenchymal transition process through regulating Akt/mTOR pathway. Pharmacological Research 2019;150:104504.
(295) Balaraman G, Sundaram J, Mari A, Krishnan P, Salam S, Subramaniam N, et al. Farnesol alleviates diethyl nitrosamine induced inflammation and protects experimental rat hepatocellular carcinoma. Environmental Toxicology 2021;36(12):2467-2474.
(296) Mondal J, Khuda-Bukhsh A. Cisplatin and farnesol co-encapsulated PLGA nano-particles demonstrate enhanced anti-cancer potential against hepatocellular carcinoma cells in vitro. Mol Biol Rep 2020;47(5):3615-3628.
(297) Lee JH, Kim C, Kim S, Sethi G, Ahn KS. Farnesol inhibits tumor growth and enhances the anticancer effects of bortezomib in multiple myeloma xenograft mouse model through the modulation of STAT3 signaling pathway. Cancer Lett 2015;360(2):280-293.

CHAPTER TWENTY-FOUR

Regulatory framework for the Cosmetic Industry

Omoniyi J. Ola-Olorun

The global importance of cosmetics coupled with advancement in technology has facilitated not only the development and trade in a myriad of cosmetic products today but, also, the risk of circulation of adulterated and misbranded ones. There is hardly any person in today's world who does not use at least one cosmetic product or the other in any single day. This growing demand for cosmetic products has, in turn, led to the growth of the cosmetics industry not only in Nigeria, but across the whole world (1). The primary purpose of cosmetic regulation is to ensure the safety of the cosmetic products thereby avoiding adverse effects on consumer health (2).

This chapter covers the principles of cosmetic regulation; the processes devised for the regulation of cosmetic products and a comparison of the world's major cosmetic jurisdictions namely the European Union (EU), the United States of America (USA), the People's Republic of China (PRC), Brazil, Japan and the Association of Southeast Asian Nations (ASEAN), and some selected countries in Africa including Nigeria, South Africa and Ghana.

The European Union (EU) is an association of twenty-seven countries comprising Austria, Belgium, Bulgaria, Croatia, Cyprus, Czechia, Denmark, Estonia, Finland, France, Germany, Greece, Hungary, Ireland, Italy, Latvia, Lithuania, Luxembourg, Malta, Netherlands, Poland, Portugal, Romania, Slovakia, Slovenia, Spain and Sweden. UK has been covered to represent a single country from EU. UK is no longer part of EU following BREXIT and has been included in this review to see how a single independent country is doing in that region. The ASEAN, as a conglomerate comprises ten member States namely Brunei Darussalam, Cambodia, Indonesia, Laos, Malaysia, Myanmar, Philippines, Singapore, Thailand and Vietnam and is included to enable comparison with the EU. South Africa is a known major cosmetic market in Africa and Ghana is a fast-growing nation as a cosmetic market in the West Africa subregion to which Nigeria belongs in Africa and so were covered. Data for this review was obtained by surfing through the search engines Google and Bing as well as Google Scholar and visiting the Government and competent regulating authority websites of the various jurisdictions.

Principles and models of cosmetic regulation

There are seven principles identified in literature which provide the features or elements of cosmetic regulation which include the competent authority's definition of a cosmetic; product safety as an incontrovertible goal of regulation; adequate and non-misleading information to be provided to consumers by the person responsible for placing the cosmetic on the market in form of product claims; responsibility for compliance of the person responsible for placing the cosmetic on the market (the issue of responsible person); a model for the regulation of cosmetics by the competent authority; registration of cosmetic manufacturers & importers; in-market control of compliance by the regulating authority through market surveillance; and regulation of specific substances through ingredient lists (3,4). At the global level, two major regulatory models exist for regulating the cosmetic products industry; they are the lengthy 'pre-market approval' model in which the government primarily assumes responsibility for product safety and the 'in-market control' which is without the lengthy review process and usually involves product notification through an online notification portal to the regulating authority (4). Ten key features of the in-market control and five features of the pre-market approval' approaches have been presented in literature (4).

The elements of the 'in-market control' approach are reported to include:

- Avoidance of time-consuming and expensive pre-market licensing/registration of products
- The company responsible for placing the cosmetic on the market is also responsible for regulatory compliance and for the safety and efficacy of the product, and must be able to justify this on authority investigation
- The notification of the appointed competent authority of data concerning the company
- Competent national authorities have effective in-market control by monitoring the market to check compliance with regulations which is by market surveillance through random control on the market (in retail shops), by routine checks on compliance with regulations or by systematic control of given product categories, in the event of a problem arising, such as a consumer complaint
- In case of non-compliance there can be penalties of varying strength, and if the manufacturer fails to prove the cosmetic is safe for use the product is withdrawn from the market

- It encourages companies to ensure product safety and therefore it offers better health protection benefits
- Administrations must be aligned and compatible, not identical. 8. It has one safety standard for consumers
- It increases the competitiveness of the market, ensuring that new products will be available to consumers more quickly
- It guarantees equal treatment of all companies.

The key features of pre-market approval on the other hand are listed to include:

- ➢ Lengthy registration time which delays the launch of cosmetics that change quickly in line with developments in technology and/or fashion
- ➢ Restriction of availability of new products on the market, discouraging innovation and investments
- ➢ Failure to prevent fraud or stop illegal products from reaching the market, and thus, not necessarily increasing product safety
- ➢ In-market surveillance is still needed to monitor the system, implying a duplication of enforcement procedures and,
- ➢ The time-consuming, and somewhat uncertain, procedures and high registration fees imply higher costs for companies and consequently more expensive products. The key features can be grouped into two stages namely, first, registration for market entry; and second, regulatory control for maintenance of the product's legitimacy in the market which are now discussed below.

Key features of cosmetic products registration process

The key features of cosmetic products registration process collated from literature are summarised in Table 24.1.

Pre-market approval model of registration

Four of the ten jurisdictions listed in Table 24.1 namely Ghana (5), Brazil (6) Japan (7) and PRC (4) employ the pre-market approval model of registration. Countries that clearly categorise cosmetic products into ordinary and special categories, such as China and Japan (4,8) have the specialised ones registrable under the pre-market approval model while the ordinary ones are registered in the other, product notification model (4). South Africa, ASEAN, EU, UK and USA do not employ the pre-market approval approach in their cosmetic regulation.

Validity of the registration certificate following pre-market approval

In Nigeria and Brazil the validity period for cosmetic product approval is five years from the day of market authorisation (6,9,10) while it is three years in Ghana and PRC (11,12). In PRC, if the product contains a "new ingredient," the approval is given for three years to monitor its safety because China distinguishes between "existing ingredient" and "new ingredient" (12).

Timeline for registration application processing

The timeline for the processing of registration application varies among jurisdictions depending on whether the product (or single ingredient) is new and for new uses. In Nigeria, the timeline for registration application processing is one hundred or twenty working days for cosmetic products manufactured in Nigeria (10). The timeline may range from 30 days in some cases within the ASEAN jurisdictions to up to ten years for new ingredients and new use in Japan (7). A study found median approval time to be 795 days in Brazil (13)

Product notification model of registration

A cosmetic can be marketed after notification has been sent to the competent authority and acknowledgment received (25). Some jurisdictions such as Brazil, Japan, and PRC employ this approach for ordinary cosmetics while the pre-market approval model is employed for the registration of specialised cosmetic products or substances (14). For instance, in Japan, mandatory notification of product name and function, plus quantitative or semi-quantitative ingredients list must be notified ten days at the latest after placing the product on the market (8,15). Among the ten reviewed jurisdictions, only Nigeria, Ghana and South Africa do not employ this model.

Table 24.1: Registration procedures for cosmetic products in world's major cosmetic markets and some other selected countries

S/N.	Item	Nigeria	Ghana	South Africa	ASEAN	Brazil	EU	Japan	PRC	UK	USA
1	Pre-market approval model of registration	Yes (10,16,17)	Yes (11)	No (18)	No (3)	Yes, for Group 2 cosmetics (14)	No	Yes (4,8)	Yes (4)	No (19)	No
2	Validity of the registration certificate following pre-market approval	Five years for product manufacture (9,10)	Three years (11)	NAp	Nap	10 years, renewable for equal and successive periods (6)	NAp	5 years (4)	3 years for new ingredients (12)	NAp	NAp
3	Timeline for registration application processing	120 working days for manufacture (9,10)	180 days (5)	NAp	Nap	ANVISA takes 90 days to assess the application for approval; 7 days to issue importation license (6)	NAp	6-12 months for ordinary cosmetics to ten years for medicated cosmetics (4,7,20)	3 months (21)	NAp	NAp

ASEAN = Association of Southeast Asian Nations; EU = European Union; PRC = People's Republic of China; UK = United Kingdom; USA = United States of America; ANVISA = Brazilian National Health Surveillance Agency; NAp = Not applicable

Table 24.1 (cont'd): Registration procedures for cosmetic products in world's major cosmetic markets and some other selected countries

S/N.	Item	Nigeria	Ghana	South Africa	ASEAN	Brazil	EU	Japan	PRC	UK	USA
4	Product notification model of registration	No	No	No (18)	Yes (3,4)	Yes (distinct for Group I and Group II) (22,23)	Yes, All cosmetic products must be notified at commission level to the CPNP at the time of first placement on the market (4,24)	Yes, Mandatory notification of product name and function, plus quantitative or semi-quantitative ingredients list to be notified ten days at the latest after placing the product on the market (8,15)	Yes (12,21)	Yes (19)	Yes (voluntary registration) (4,8,18,24)
5	Timeline between notification and product launch	Nap	NAp	NAp	30 working days (25)	At least 30 days before marketing for Class I products. For Class II cosmetics, ANVISA takes 90 days to	Nil	One week for Primary distributor of ordinary cosmetics and 6-12 months for medicated cosmetic (7)	Nap	Up to 7 months (17,19)	Nil

						assess the application for approvals (22)					
6	Validity of certificate following Notification (in years)	Nap	NAp	Nap	5years subject to renewal (25)	5 years, renewable for equal and successive periods (23)	Nap	NAp	Nap	NAp	Permanent

ASEAN = Association of Southeast Asian Nations; EU = European Union; PRC = People's Republic of China; UK = United Kingdom; USA = United States of America; ANVISA = Brazilian National Health Surveillance Agency; NAp = Not applicable

Timeline between notification and product launch

The timeline provides the regulating authority in the jurisdiction the opportunity to do a spot or normal check on the product and to acknowledge the presence of the product in the market. The timeline varies and ranges between receiving acknowledgment within three working days in the ASEAN jurisdiction (26), to twelve months for specialised a cosmetic in Japan (7). A study found median approval time to be 795 days in Brazil (13)

Validity of certificate following Notification

For the countries that have notification in place, the registration validity of certificate following notification is supposed to be permanent subject to annual renewal with payment of fees. However, in the ASEAN, it is for five years (25).

Products regulatory control systems of the world's major cosmetics markets and some other selected countries

Table 24.2 presents, in summary, the key features of the cosmetic products regulatory control systems of some selected markets collated from literature.

Presence of enabling laws

Except for South Africa, all the reviewed jurisdictions have government-enacted enabling laws, which guide and provide the force of law to the competent regulating authorities and the regulating guidelines. South Africa is the only example of cosmetics self-regulation in the world, having a self-regulatory code of practice, formulated by her cosmetic industry (4).

Competent regulating authority

The competent regulating authority in each jurisdiction formulates guidelines to interpret the legislation enacted by the legislative arm of the government and provide specific steps on how to comply with them (4,27). Each of all the ten reviewed jurisdictions have competent regulating authority empowered by their jurisdictions' enabling laws.

Competent authority's definition of cosmetic product

The different jurisdictional approaches to the regulation of cosmetics are not unconnected to the divergent cosmetic definitions, among other things (18). Differences in regulatory frameworks result in differences between markets and imposes barriers in interjurisdictional trade (8). For a clear understanding of regulatory requirements in the various jurisdictions, we need to understand how they define cosmetics within their various legislations (4). The terms 'cosmetics' and 'cosmetic products' are often used interchangeably especially when referring to a particular type of product. Cosmetics are constituted from a mixture of chemical compounds derived from either natural sources, or synthetically created ones. They are usually presented as liquids, semi-solids or solids (28). The specific definitions of a cosmetic in each of the jurisdictions covered are presented in Table 24.3. All the jurisdictions have their differing definitions for a cosmetic or cosmetic product.

The Nigeria definition states that a cosmetic 'includes any substance or mixture of substances intended to be rubbed, poured, sprinkled or sprayed, introduced into or otherwise applied to the human body or any part thereof for cleansing, beautifying, promoting attractiveness or altering the complexion, skin, hair or teeth and includes deodorants and detergent powder' (16,29).

With regards to composition, the Nigerian definition appears to be adequate but with respect to the field of application, it simply specifies "the human body or any part thereof" without mentioning whether it pertains to internal or external part. Furthermore, as to functions, it only addresses four of the six identified functions in the UK definition. There is therefore an imperative need to review the quality of the definition of cosmetic products by the authorised regulating agency in Nigeria.

Cosmetic product categorisation

Cosmetics are generally categorised into general (ordinary) and specialised cosmetics which may be medicated or therapeutically functional (4). The Nigerian categorisation of cosmetic products is not clear. However, three categories are mentioned in NAFDAC guidelines, namely, general cosmetics (16,29), veterinary cosmetics (30), and veterinary medicinal cosmetics (31). Out of the nine remaining jurisdictions reviewed, six namely, South Africa, ASEAN, Brazil, Japan, PRC and USA have their cosmetic products categorised while three, including Ghana, EU and UK do not.

Presence of intermediate/borderline products

The term 'borderline product' is used when a product lies on the edge of one product category and verges on another (32). The overlap between the definitions of cosmetic products and medicinal products is the reason for these borderline issues (4,32–34) Out of the ten reviewed jurisdictions, only Japan and USA have clear identification of intermediate/borderline products (4,20). The remaining eight jurisdictions do not have borderline categories.

Employment of public regulation for the safety of cosmetics

Public regulation, is the regulation of cosmetics through a government organ. As used in UK and many other jurisdictions, it exercises a greater control on cosmetics, and it is thought to offer the most efficient system of safety (3) South African cosmetics regulations represent the only example of cosmetics industry self-regulation in the world through Self-Regulatory Code of Practice by the industry, the South African National Standards (4). All of the remaining nine jurisdictions employ public regulation for the safety of cosmetic products.

Product safety focus

The need for the safety of products placed on a market for cosmetic purpose cannot be over flogged for reasons bothering on public health (69). Cosmetic manufacturers are required to prove the safety of each of the ingredients incorporated into their final products as well as the final cosmetic product (70). All of these ten jurisdictions had some specifications for the safety of any cosmetic product placed on their markets and specified product safety as the manufacturer's responsibility for any cosmetic product placed on their markets (4,70).

Product safety as manufacturer responsibility: A person putting a product on a market for the purpose of public wellbeing, should be ready to defend the intention and good will of the product (4,70). All the ten jurisdictions specified product safety as the manufacturer's responsibility for any cosmetic product placed on their markets.

Obligations of the manufacturer to provide a cosmetic product safety report: Product safety information is normally in form of safety information report which contain data on the quantitative and qualitative composition of the products, toxicological profiles of the ingredients, exposure conditions, and undesirable effects, and a safety assessment report which comprises the report of full chemical safety assessment (CSA) provided by technical experts prior to placing a cosmetic product on the market (3,34,36,71,72). Nigeria and Ghana do not have specifications for obligation of the responsible person to provide a cosmetic product safety report. Seven of the jurisdictions: South Africa, ASEAN, EU, Japan, PRC, UK and USA. Brazil has for Group II products only, which are special purpose cosmetics (6).

Product Information File (PIF) that is readily accessible: The company responsible for placing a cosmetic on the market is supposed to complete a Product Information File (PIF) that is readily available (4). All of the reviewed jurisdictions with the exception of Nigeria, Brazil, and the USA specify requirement for a PIF that is readily accessible in their guidelines. However, for the USA, in the absence of product data submission, compulsory warning "The safety of this product has not been determined" must appear on packaging. (13).

Table 24.2. Key features of cosmetic products regulation in world's major markets and some selected countries (i)

S/N.	Features	Nigeria	Ghana	South Africa	ASEAN	Brazil	EU	Japan	PRC	UK	USA
I	Presence of enabling laws	NAFDAC Act Cap N.1 LFN 2004; Food, Drugs and Related Products Act Cap F33 LFN 2004 (16,29)	Public Health Act, No. 851 of 2012 (5)	Self-Regulatory Code of Practice guided by South African Cosmetics, Toiletry, and Fragrance Association Cosmetics Compendium; Foodstuffs, Cosmetics and Amendment Act; Consumer Protection Act; ISO standards related to cosmetics (4)	The ASEAN Cosmetic Directive and Agreement on the ASEAN harmonised cosmetic regulatory scheme (35)	Law no. 6.360 of September 23, 1976 and Decree no. 8077 of August 14, 2013; Resolution RDC No. 79, for Cosmetics, Personal Hygiene Products and Perfumes (22)	EC Regulation No. 1223/2009 (36)	Pharmaceutical and Medical Device Act (7)	Regulations concerning the Hygiene Supervision over Cosmetics from 1989; Technical Safety Standard for Cosmetics, 2015 (21)	Product Safety and Metrology etc. (Amendment etc.) (EU Exit) Regulations 2019 (19)	Federal Food, Drug, and Cosmetic Act; Fair Packaging and Labeling Act; Microbead-Free Waters Act of 2015 (4)

Table 24.2: (contd., a): Key features of the cosmetics regulation in the world's major markets and some selected countries (ii-iii)

S/N.	Features	Nigeria	Ghana	South Africa	ASEAN	Brazil	EU	Japan	PRC	UK	USA
Ii	Competent regulating authority	NAFDAC (16,17,29)	Food and Drugs Authority, Ghana (5)	Medicines Control Council; Advertising Standards Authority (ASA), South African National Standards; Cosmetics, Toiletry, and Fragrance Association of South Africa (CTFA-SA) (37–39)	Individual countries implementation of legislation as part of its national laws (35,40)	The General Office of Cosmetics within the Brazilian Ministry of Health; ANVISA (22)	European Commission is for legislation ("EC"); Member countries health Authorities are for enforcement (4,33,36)	Pharmaceutical and Food Safety Bureau of the MHLW (20)	SAMR, NMPA and the MPAs (4,21)	Secretary of State (19)	FDA (4)
Iii	Competent authority's definition of cosmetic product	Present (10,29)	Present (5)	Present (37)	Present (25)	Present (6)	Present (36)	Present (15,41)	Present (12)	Present (19)	Present (4)

ASEAN = Association of Southeast Asian Nations; EU = European Union; PRC = People's Republic of China; UK = United Kingdom; USA = United States of America; ANVISA = Brazilian National Health Surveillance Agency; NAp = Not applicable; NFd = Not found.

Table 24.2 (contd., b): Key features of the cosmetics regulation in the world's major markets and some selected countries (iv-vi)

S/N.	Features	Nigeria	Ghana	South Africa	ASEAN	Brazil	EU	Japan	PRC	UK	USA
Iv	Cosmetic product categorisation	No formal categorisation, some are classified as veterinary and veterinary medicinal cosmetic (16,29,30,42)	None found	Yes, Cosmetics for the purpose of treating or preventing disease' are exempted OTCs (38,39)	Yes (25)	Yes, Group 1 and Group 2 (22)	No, cosmetics or not cosmetics (4)	Yes, cosmetics or quasi-drugs (15,43)	Yes, general or non-special use cosmetics (non-SUC) and special use cosmetics (SUC) (44)	No, cosmetics or not cosmetics as carried over from EU (4)	Yes, cosmetics or OTCs or drugs (4)
V	Clear identification of intermediate / borderline products	No	No	No	No	No	No	Yes, (4)	No	No	Yes (4)
Vi	Employment of public regulation for the safety of cosmetics	Yes (16,29)	Yes (5)	No (4)	Yes (35)	Yes, ANVISA (22,23)	Yes (4,36)	Yes, MHLW (20)	Yes (4)	Yes (19)	Yes (4)

ASEAN = Association of Southeast Asian Nations; EU = European Union; PRC = People's Republic of China; UK = United Kingdom; USA = United States of America; ANVISA = Brazilian National Health Surveillance Agency; NAp = Not applicable; NFd = Not found.

Table 24.2 (contd., c): Key features of the cosmetics regulation in the world's major markets and some selected countries (vii-viic)

S/N.	Features	Nigeria	Ghana	South Africa	ASEAN	Brazil	EU	Japan	PRC	UK	USA
vii	Product safety focus with demand for conformity of cosmetic product with regulatory laws and guidelines	Yes	Yes (5)	Yes, those for the purpose of treating or preventing disease are exempted OTCs (18)	Yes (35)	Yes (23)	Yes (4,36)	Yes (20)	Yes (12)	Yes (19)	Yes (4)
viia	Product safety as manufacturer's responsibility	Yes	Yes (5)	Yes (18)	Yes (35,45)	Yes (23)	Yes (18)	Yes (4,20)	Yes (12)	Yes (19)	Yes (4,24)
viib	Obligations of the manufacturer to provide cosmetic product safety report	No	No	Yes (18)	Yes (35,45)	No (46) Yes for Grade 2 products (6)	Yes (18)	Yes (20)	Yes (12)	Yes (19)	No (24)
viic	Product information file (PIF) that is readily accessible	No	No	Yes (18)	Yes (35,45)	NFd	Yes (4,36)	NFd	Yes (4,12)	Yes (19)	No. (4,24)

ASEAN = Association of Southeast Asian Nations; EU = European Union; PRC = People's Republic of China; UK = United Kingdom; USA = United States of America; ANVISA = Brazilian National Health Surveillance Agency; NAp = Not applicable; NFd = Not found.

Table 24.2 (contd., d): Key features of the cosmetics regulation in the world's major markets and some selected countries (viii-x)

S/N.	Features	Nigeria	Ghana	South Africa	ASEAN	Brazil	EU	Japan	PRC	UK	USA
viii	Requirement for Compliance with GMP for imported cosmetics in the originating country	Yes (16,29)	No	Yes (18)	Yes (25)	NFd	Yes (4,36)	Yes (41)	Yes (47)	Yes (19)	Yes (4)
ix	Specification that product information be already approved in another state/country	Yes (16,29)	No	No	Yes (35,48)	NFd	Yes (4,36)	No	Nf	Yes (19)	Yes (4)
x	Demand for use of INCI names for ingredients	No, INN required (49)	Yes, as an optional condition (50)	Allowed (18)	Yes (25,35,51)	Yes (22)	Yes (8)	Yes, (in Japanese) (4,15)	Yes, (in Chinese) (4, 47)	Yes (19)	Yes (4)

ASEAN = Association of Southeast Asian Nations; EU = European Union; PRC = People's Republic of China; UK = United Kingdom; USA = United States of America; ANVISA = Brazilian National Health Surveillance Agency; NAp = Not applicable; NFd = Not found.

Table 24.2 (contd., e): Key features of the cosmetics regulation in the world's major markets and some selected countries (xi-xiii)

S/N.	Features	Nigeria	Ghana	South Africa	ASEAN	Brazil	EU	Japan	PRC	UK	USA
xi	Availability of negative lists of ingredients	Yes (4,16)	Yes (52)	Yes (4,18)	Yes (25,35,51)	Yes (22)	Yes (4,36)	Yes (15,41)	Yes (4)	Yes (19)	Yes (4)
xii	Availability of positive lists of ingredients	No	No	Yes (4,18)	Yes (25,35,51)	Yes (22)	Yes (4,36)	Yes (15,41)	Yes (4)	Yes (19)	Yes, for colours and for UV filters as OTCs but not for preservatives (4)
xiii.	Specification for CMR substances and nanomaterials	No	No	No	No. Some carcinogens are listed on the list of banned and restricted ingredients (51)	No	Yes (4,36)	Yes (4)	No, under development (21)	Yes (19)	Yes (4)

ASEAN = Association of Southeast Asian Nations; EU = European Union; PRC = People's Republic of China; UK = United Kingdom; USA = United States of America; ANVISA = Brazilian National Health Surveillance Agency; NAp = Not applicable; NFd = Not found.

Table 24.2 (contd., f): Key features of the cosmetics regulation in the world's major markets and some selected countries (xiv-xv)

S/N.	Features	Nigeria	Ghana	South Africa	ASEAN	Brazil	EU	Japan	PRC	UK	USA
xiv.	Specifications for labelling	No	No. although in passing, require names of any excipient known to be a safety concern (50)	Yes (4,53)	Yes (3,51)	No	Yes (4,36)	NFd	No	Yes (19)	Yes (4)
xiva.	Demand for warning provision for CMR- and nanomaterial-containing substances on label to consumers	Yes (16, 29)	Yes (11)	Yes (18,38)	Yes (3,35)	Yes (22,23)	Yes (4,36)	Yes (4)	Yes (4,12)	Yes (19)	Yes (4)
xv.	Specification for Product claims	No	No, in passing, requiring preapproval application for advertising (50)	Yes (38)	Yes (3,35)	Yes (22,23)	Yes (4,36)	Yes (4)	Yes (4,12)	Yes (19)	Yes (4)

ASEAN = Association of Southeast Asian Nations; EU = European Union; PRC = People's Republic of China; UK = United Kingdom; USA = United States of America; ANVISA = Brazilian National Health Surveillance Agency; NAp = Not applicable; NFd = Not found

Table 24.2 (contd., g): Key features of the cosmetics regulation in the world's major markets and some selected countries (xvi-xviii)

S/N.	Features	Nigeria	Ghana	South Africa	ASEAN	Brazil	EU	Japan	PRC	UK	USA
xvi.	Cosmetovigilance in place	No	No	No	Yes (3,35)	Yes (54)	Yes (4,36)	Yes (4)	Yes (12)	Yes (19)	No
xvii.	Ban on animal testing for cosmetics	Not banned	Not banned	Yes (55)	No formal stance on animal testing; depends on each member State (40)	Yes, 2014	Yes (4,36)	Yes (4)	Partially. Post-market animal testing stopped in 2019 (47,56)	Yes (19)	No definite position on animal testing. Safety comes first (44,57)
xviii.	Scientific advisory committees	No	No	No	Yes, ASEAN Cosmetic Scientific Body (ACSB) (3,48)	Yes, e.g., Advisory Technical Committee on Cosmetics (CTAC) (13,46)	Yes e.g., Scientific Committee on Cosmetic Products and Non-Food Products (58)	Government officials and experts. Cosmetics Advisory Committee is in charge of positive lists (8)	Yes (4,59)	Yes, e.g., The Aromatherapy Trade Council (19)	No. But there is Cosmetic Ingredients Review (voluntary committee of experts organised by industry) (18)

ASEAN = Association of Southeast Asian Nations; EU = European Union; PRC = People's Republic of China; UK = United Kingdom; USA = United States of America; ANVISA = Brazilian National Health Surveillance Agency; NAp = Not applicable; NFd = Not found.

Table 24.2 (contd., h): Key features of the cosmetics regulation in the world's major markets and some selected countries (xix-xx)

S/N.	Features	Nigeria	Ghana	South Africa	ASEAN	Brazil	EU	Japan	PRC	UK	USA
xix.	Involvement of Cosmetic Industry Association	Yes e. g., Toiletries & Cosmetics Group of Manufacturing Assocition of Nigeria; International Federation of Societies of Cosmetic Chemists (60)	Yes, e.g., Cosmetics Association of Ghana (1)	Yes. E.g., South African Cosmetics, Toiletry, and Fragrance Association (CTFA-SA) (39)	Yes (The ASEAN members all have their individual cosmetic industry associations) (61)	Yes (Brazilian Association of the Cosmetic, Toiletry and Perfumery Industry) (23)	Yes, EU countries all have their individual cosmetic industry associations (4,36)	Yes e.g., Japanese Cosmetic Industry Association (62,15,18,8)	Yes e.g., China's National Medical Products Association (12)	Yes. E.g., Cosmetic, Toiletry & Perfumery Association Ltd (63)	Yes, American Cosmetic Manufacturers Association (64)
xx.	Membership of The International Cooperation on Cosmetics Regulation (ICCR)	No	No	Observer since 2017 (65)	One member, Thailand as Member; Observer since 2015 conference (4,65)	Regulator – Member; Industry – Member (65,66)	Regulator – Member; Industry – Member (65)	Regulator – Member; Industry – Member (66)	PRC as an observer since 2012 (65)	Yes in EU but following Brexit, participated as an observer in 2021 (65)	Regulator – Member; Industry – Member (65,67)

ASEAN = Association of Southeast Asian Nations; EU = European Union; PRC = People's Republic of China; UK = United Kingdom; USA = United States of America; ANVISA = Brazilian National Health Surveillance Agency; NAp = Not applicable; NFd = Not found.

Table 24.3: Definitions of cosmetic or cosmetic product in each of the selected regulatory jurisdictions

Nigeria: "Cosmetic includes any substance or mixture of substance intended to be rubbed, poured, sprinkled or sprayed, introduced into or otherwise applied to the human body or any part thereof for cleansing, beautifying, promoting attractiveness or altering the complexion, skin, hair or teeth and includes deodorants and detergent powder" (16).
Ghana: "Cosmetic refers to a substance or mixture of substances manufactured, sold or represented for use in cleansing, improving or altering the complexion, skin, hair, eye or teeth and deodorants and perfumes" (5).
ASEAN: "A cosmetic product shall mean any substance or preparation intended to be placed in contact with the various external parts of the human body (epidermis, hair system, nails, lips and external genital organs) or with the teeth and the mucous membranes of the oral cavity with a view exclusively or mainly to cleaning them, perfuming them, changing their appearance and/or correcting body odours and/or protecting them or keeping them in good condition" (35).
Brazil: "Cosmetics are part of a category of products involving Personal Care Products, Cosmetics and Perfumes. Therefore, the information presented relates to these 3 types of products: Personal Care Products, Cosmetics and Perfumes are preparations consisting of natural or synthetic substances, for external use on various parts of the human body, skin, capillary system, nails, lips, external genital organs, teeth and mucous membranes of the oral cavity, with the sole or main purpose of cleaning them, perfuming them, altering their appearance, correcting body odours and or protecting or maintaining them in good condition" (34).
European Union (EU): "Cosmetic product means any substance or mixture intended to be placed in contact with the external parts of the human body (epidermis, hair system, nails, lips and external genital organs) or with the teeth and the mucous membranes of the oral cavity with a view exclusively or mainly to cleaning them, perfuming them, changing their appearance, protecting them, keeping them in good condition or correcting body odours" (36).
Japan: "Applied by spreading, sprinkling or other similar ways for the purpose of cleaning, beautifying, promoting attractiveness, altering appearance, or keeping the health of skin hair, with a moderate effect on the applied site. Not including the products also having pharmaceutical purpose or quasi-drugs." (56).
Peoples' Republic of China (PRC): "Daily chemical industry products intended to be applied by spreading, spraying or other similar ways to human body surfaces, such as skin, hair, nails, and lips, for the purpose of cleaning, protecting, beautifying and decorating" (12).
United Kingdom (UK): "The definition of a cosmetic product comprises three parts: a function, field of application, and product composition. All parts of the definition must be satisfied. The Regulation specifies six functions in relation to external parts of the human body for products that may be cosmetic products, namely: to clean; to perfume; to change the appearance; to protect; to keep in good condition; or to correct body odours. The field of application of cosmetics is to the external parts of the human body; that is one or more of the following sites: the epidermis; the hair system; the nails; the lips; the external genital" (19).

United States of America (USA): "The FD&C Act defines cosmetics as articles intended to be rubbed, poured, sprinkled, or sprayed on, introduced into, or otherwise applied to the human body ... for cleansing, beautifying, promoting attractiveness, or altering the appearance. Included in this definition are skin care products, fragrance preparations, manicuring products, lipsticks, eye and facial make-up preparations, bath preparations, hair preparations (non-colouring), hair colouring preparations, oral hygiene products, baby products, personal cleanly ness products, shaving products, tanning products and deodorants. Soaps consisting primarily of an alkali salt of a fatty acid and making no label claim other than cleansing of the human body are not considered cosmetics under the law" (4,68)

Request for compliance with good manufacturing practice (GMP) for imported cosmetics in the originating country

For imported cosmetic products, compliance with GMP in the originating country as a regulatory condition may be seen as a step further to assure the protection of public health (4). Nigeria, with seven other jurisdictions namely South Africa, ASEAN, EU, Japan, PRC, UK and USA have, in place, stipulations that the manufacture of imported cosmetics comply with GMP guidelines in the originating country. Ghana does not have this regulation and the information could not be ascertained for Brazil.

Specification that product information be already approved in other state/country

This specification is a step further to guarantee the safety of the product, particularly new ingredients (or substances). Five jurisdictions: Nigeria, ASEAN, EU, GB, and the USA have specifications that product information be already approved in one or more jurisdictions. Three jurisdictions namely Ghana, South Africa, and Japan did not have this requirement in their legislation. The information could not be ascertained for Brazil and PRC.

Use of International Nomenclature for Cosmetic Ingredients (INCI)

International Nomenclature for Cosmetic Ingredients (INCI) are systematic names internationally recognised to identify cosmetic ingredients (i.e., plant extracts, oils, chemicals) (4,15,73–75). Nigeria does not have specification for the use of INCI names for cosmetic ingredients. Ghana has INCI specified as an option and South Africa specifies it as "allowed" among other names. The remaining seven jurisdictions namely ASEAN, Brazil, EU, Japan, PRC, UK and USA make use of the INCI.

Availability of negative lists of ingredients

The management of ingredients through positive and negative lists is one of the essential elements of cosmetic regulation (4). The two negative lists are the banned (prohibited) and restricted cosmetic ingredients/substances. All the reviewed jurisdictions including Nigeria possessed a list of prohibited or restricted cosmetic ingredients (4, 16). Examples of banned ingredients in the EU jurisdiction are hydroquinone, tretinoin and corticosteroids (76).

Availability of positive lists of ingredients

Positive lists contain ingredients (or substances) that are authorised to be used in cosmetic product formulations for specific intended use and they are of three types namely preservatives, ultra violet (UV) filters, and colourants with concentration limits (4,77). For a substance in a cosmetic product to be permitted for use as either a colourant, preservative, or UV–filter in a jurisdiction, the substance ought to be listed in the appropriate regulatory document. Out of the ten jurisdictions reviewed, only Nigeria and Ghana do not have positive (authorised) list for colourants, preservatives or UV–filters.

Specification for CMR substances and nanomaterials

CMR means "carcinogenic, mutagenic or toxic to reproduction" (4) and CMR substances are chemicals that are carcinogenic, mutagenic or toxic to reproduction (78). They are of specific concern due to the long term and often non-reversible effects that they may exert on human health, often after only low-dose exposures (78). Examples are heavy metals, benzene, acrylamide, formamide, petroleum refinery streams, fuels, pesticides and asbestos (79). Their use is prohibited, unless in exceptional cases (4,79). The manufacturer of a cosmetic product containing nanomaterials should state this on the label. (80). Only EU, Japan, UK and USA have specifications for CMR substances and nanomaterials (4,18). ASEAN have some carcinogens listed on their list of banned and restricted ingredients (51). Nigeria, Ghana, South Africa and Brazil do not have specification for CMR substances and nanomaterials while the one for PRC is documented to be under development (21).

Demand for warning provision on label to consumers for CMR- and nanomaterial-containing substances: Nigeria, Brazil and PRC do not have specification for warning provision on label to consumers for CMR- and nanomaterial- containing substances. Ghana also does not, but in passing, requires names of any excipients known to be of safety concern. The remaining six jurisdictions comprising South Africa, ASEAN, EU, Japan, UK, and USA have requirement for warning provision on label to consumers for CMR- and nanomaterial- containing substances.

Specifications for labelling

Labelling of cosmetic products provides a set of obligations (80) and labels provide a concrete purpose of cosmetics and indicate the type of ingredients used in formulations (81). The language requirements on labelling among cosmetic jurisdictions continue to be a major challenge still facing the cosmetic industry (15). Seven mandatory items of information are expected to be listed on cosmetic products' labels and they include name and address of the Responsible Person; country of origin for imported products; nominal quantity of contents; date of minimum durability ("Best Before" date), or (where the minimum durability is more than 30 months) a 'Period After Opening' (PAO); warning statements and precautionary information; batch number (to ensure the traceability of the product); product function, when not obvious from its packaging/presentation; and the list of the ingredients (19,24,36,80). Nigeria and all the other nine jurisdictions have specifications for labelling in their cosmetic regulation documents.

Specification for product claims

Studies have shown that exposure to advertisements tend to cause changes in the behaviour and purchase decisions of individuals and that advertisers employ advertising appeals to influence purchase decisions (82) (Ucheanya, 2020). In many cases, cosmetic product manufacturers, importers and marketers conceal the real constituent of cosmetics by not listing them in the product label or even making outrightly false claims (83,84) (Odigie & Odion, 2011; Nduka et al., 2019). Jurisdictions normally legislate against inaccurate, false and misleading claims under product claims which essentially addresses advertisement claims of cosmetic producers and product claim is a key feature of cosmetic product regulation in any jurisdiction. Product claims signify adequate and non-misleading information to be provided to the final consumers by the person responsible for placing the cosmetic on the market (4) and six principles for correct communication of product claim are: compliance with regulations, truthfulness, evidential support, honesty, accuracy and well-informed decisions (80). Nigeria does not have specification for product claims. Ghana has it only in passing, requiring pre-approval of labels for advertising. The remaining eight jurisdictions: South Africa, ASEAN, Brazil, EU, GB, Japan, PRC and USA all have specification for product claims.

Cosmetovigilance

Cosmetovigilance refers to the monitoring of cosmetic product safety (85). It is an adverse reactions monitoring and reporting system, that includes communication of confirmed serious and undesirable effects (SUEs) as well as performing product recalls, when necessary (86–88). Another aspect of cosmetovigilance is the communication, to national competent authorities, by responsible persons and distributors, of confirmed serious undesirable effects (SUEs), linked to the use of a cosmetic product (11,32,34). Nigeria, Ghana and South Africa have no cosmetovigilance in place. Six of the remaining seven countries namely ASEAN, Brazil, EU., UK, Japan, and PRC have a clause addressing cosmetovigilance in their cosmetic regulations (11,34,59). In the US, there is no mandatory obligation to report adverse event information, although there are alternative channels like MedWatch and The Center for Food Safety and Applied Nutrition (CFSAN) to make such reports (4).

Ban on animal testing for cosmetics

A lot of discussions have gone into the issue of ban on animal testing for cosmetics with several unanswered questions (90,91), and it is believed that presently, there are no alternative methods that could fully assess all toxicological endpoints (90). Ban on animal testing for cosmetics was not addressed in cosmetic product regulations of Nigeria and Ghana. Ban on animal testing for cosmetics has been implemented in six of the jurisdictions reviewed, namely, South Africa, Brazil, EU, GB, Japan and USA. In the ASEAN jurisdiction, there is no formal stance on animal testing and each member state is mandated with setting its policies regarding this (40). In China, animal testing has been banned for domestic non-special use cosmetics since 2014, but still required for special use cosmetics (SUC) and imported cosmetic products while post-market animal testing was stopped in 2019 (47,56).

Scientific advisory committees

These are committees appointed for the scientific and technical questions concerning consumer health that relates to cosmetic products and non-food products intended for the consumer especially substances used in the preparation of these products, their composition, the intended use as well as the types of packaging. The committees assist government departments (and their arms-length bodies) to access, interpret and understand the full range of relevant scientific information, and to make judgements about its relevance, potential and application, providing opinions on health and safety risks of non-food consumer products such as cosmetic products (63,92,93). Nigeria, Ghana and South Africa, do not have scientific advisory committees. US also does not have one but has Cosmetic Ingredients Review which is a voluntary committee of experts organised by the cosmetic industry (93). However, six of the jurisdictions namely ASEAN, Brazil, EU, Japan, PRC and UK have within their system scientific advisory committees.

Involvement of cosmetic industry association

It is believed that through the cooperation of the many facets of the cosmetic industry via cosmetic industry associations, the differences and challenges facing the cosmetic industry can continue to reduce both in scope and specifics in order to better facilitate the free flow of cosmetic products (4,15) All of the ten jurisdictions reviewed, have documented involvement of cosmetic industry associations.

Membership of The International Cooperation on Cosmetics Regulation (ICCR)

ICCR is a voluntary international group of cosmetics regulatory authorities and industry associations, and has assumed the role of advancing cosmetic products regulation and its harmonisation globally (4,65,67,94). Nigeria and Ghana are not yet members of ICCR. PRC and South Africa have been participating on observer status since 2012 and 2017, respectively. UK, as part of EU, was a member and following BREXIT, attended as an observer in 2021. As for the ASEAN, only one member, Thailand, participated as Observer since 2015 (4,65). Brazil transitioned to a member in 2014 and Chinese Taipei (Taiwan) and Republic of Korea in 2020 (65). The remaining three jurisdictions namely the EU, Japan, and the USA are fully represented as members.

Some decided court cases involving cosmetics

Serious problems and cosmetic related injuries are not unusual in the course of cosmetic use leading to litigations (95–97). Majority of court cases pertaining to cosmetics revolve around the labels and advertisements representing the products, patents, trade secrets within the cosmetic industry and packaging of the products mostly in form of consumer class-action litigations (98).

The definition of cosmetics often presents opportunity for litigation. In a particular case, the major issue was whether the FDA could categorise the skin care product labelled 'Sudden Change ™' as a "drug" and thus subject it to the extensive regulatory requirements for new drugs (with which the manufacturer had not complied). The court held that on the basis of the product's intended use and the relevant standard a normal consumer faced with such representations, 'Sudden Change' was a drug. Three other decided court cases in the US, cited by the same author (99) are briefly presented here:

- Johnson & Johnson Talc Baby Powder Litigation in which Johnson & Johnson Company had become the subject of major litigation because of their baby powder product that contains talc, which many persons have claimed to contain cancer-causing asbestos, and which has led to thousands of lawsuits being filed against the company. The company has successfully defended some lawsuits and are appealing almost all of the lawsuits it has lost, which includes a judgment for approximately $4.69 billion dollars in 2018.
- Another company that has been the subject of much scrutiny in the media is Chaz Dean due to many reports of adverse events from the use of one of its products - WEN Hair products the adverse effects of which include hair loss, balding, and itching. As a result, in 2016, a group of approximately 200 people joined together in a class-action lawsuit against the popular hair care brand, which eventually resulted in a preliminary settlement for approximately 26.25 million dollars.

- The Honest Company: In the case of Michael v. Honest Co. in the US, two class action cases were filed against the Honest Company (as Defendant) in 2015, that the company "deceptively and misleadingly labelled, advertised and marketed" various Honest products, including Honest Sunscreen™, "as both natural and effective, when in fact, the 'Natural Products' contained non-natural ingredients, and that Honest Sunscreen™ was ineffective.
- Another example is an interesting case involving "Heavenly" Trade Mark. An application to register the trade mark Heavenly for use for cosmetics was denied on the ground that cosmetics were such that in relation to them "Heavenly" had a laudatory meaning (99,100).

Registration process for cosmetic products in Nigeria

The existing regulatory framework governing cosmetic products in Nigeria has its root in the laws enacted by the legislative arm of the Federal Government of Nigeria which include the Food, Drugs and Related Products Act Cap F33 LFN 2004 (29) and National Agency for Food and Drugs Administration and Control (NAFDAC) Act Cap N.1 LFN 2004 (16,29). NAFDAC was officially established in October 1992, and by virtue of the Acts, the NAFDAC organisation has the mandate to regulate and control the manufacture, importation, exportation, distribution, advertisement, sale, and use of cosmetics in Nigeria, in addition to food, drugs, medical devices, packaged water, chemicals and detergents (collectively known as regulated products) (17).

Cosmetic manufacturers and importers within or outside Nigeria intending to market their products in Nigeria are to first register their products with NAFDAC accompanied with appropriate documentation (9,10,16,29). Registration is defined as the submission of information on the product which undergoes an evaluation and approval process prior to marketing the product (25). There are also cognate Government Ministries, Departments and Agencies that support NAFDAC in the regulation of cosmetic products in Nigeria such as the Corporate Affairs Commission of Nigeria charged with the registration and incorporation of the companies, Trademark Registry in the Ministry of Industry, Trade and Investment charged with registration of brand name, Federal Ministry of Commercecharged with registration of trademark, the Pharmacists' Council of Nigeria for registration of Pharmacist and renewal of Annual License / registration and retention of premises and the Veterinary Council of Nigeria for the registration of Veterinary Doctor and renewal of annual license / registration and retention of premises. They are referred to in various NAFDAC guidelines (9,10).

Registration process for cosmetics manufactured in Nigeria

The flowchart in Figure 24.1 summarises the process for the registration of cosmetics manufactured in Nigeria as documented in NAFDAC guidelines (10).

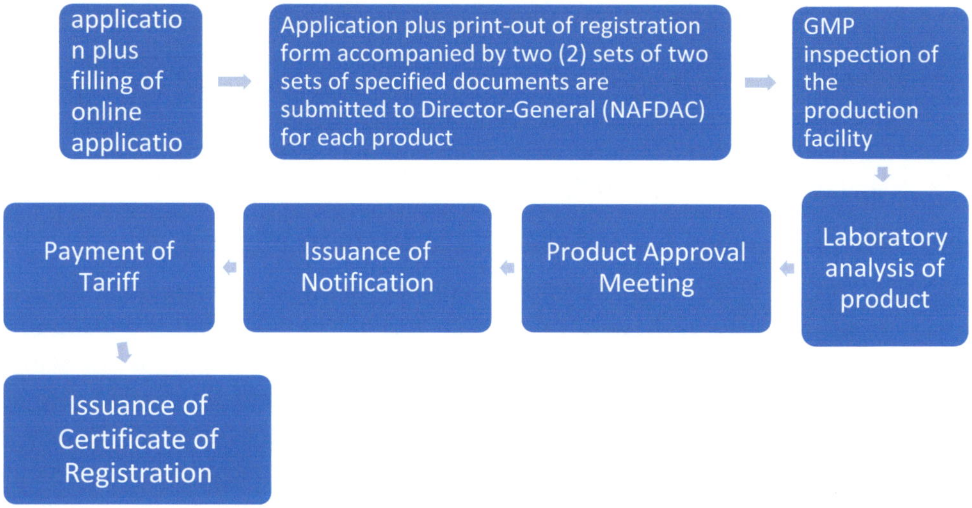

Figure 24.1: Flow chart of the process for registration of cosmetics made in Nigeria

First, a written application by the intending manufacturer is prepared along with a filled online application form for each product. The application letter along with a print-out copy of the registration form as well as two sets of specified documents are then submitted to the Director-General of NAFDAC. Secondly, a good manufacturing practice (GMP) inspection of the production facility is carried out and samples of the product(s) taken. Thirdly, the products are subjected to laboratory analysis by NAFDAC. The fourth step is the holding of the Product Approval Meeting, at the end of which the fifth step, which is the issuance of notification for approved products or Compliance Directive for those not approved are pronounced. The payment of tariff and the issuance of certificate of registration constitute the sixth and seventh steps, respectively..

Registration process for imported cosmetics in Nigeria

The flowchart in Figure 24.2 provides the steps for registration of imported cosmetics in Nigeria (9). The prospective importer of cosmetics writes an application that includes the common name of the product and its brand name and fills an online application form which are submitted to the Director-General of NAFDAC for each product. Hard copies of these document along with two sets of specified documents (all originals) and two sets of photocopies are submitted at the NAFDAC office after which the agency issues an import permit to the prospective importer.. Samples of the products are then submitted for laboratory analysis, which if found acceptable are recommended for approval at the Product Approval Meeting. The meeting directs the issuance of Notification of Approval for the importation of the said products and the importer can then pay the stipulated tariff after which the Certificate of Registration is issued.

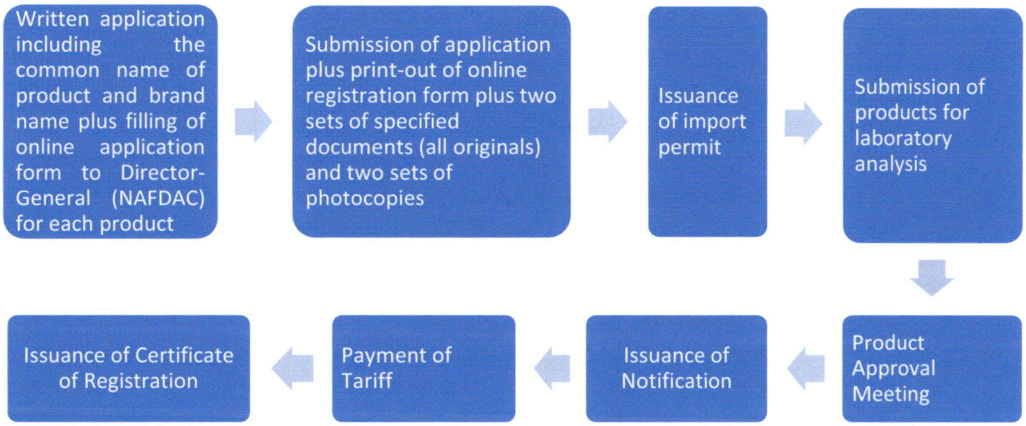

Figure 24.2: Process for registration of cosmetics to be imported into Nigeria

There are other guideline documents uploaded by NAFDAC for the regulation of cosmetic products which could be located online at NAFDAC website (101).

References

1. Kraus TL. Caring about personal care products, regulation in the US, the European union, and China in the age of global consumption. Wis Int'l LJ,. 2014;33(1):167–91.
2. Zakaria Z. COSMETIC SAFETY REGULATIONS: A COMPARATIVE STUDY OF EUROPE, THE USA AND MALAYSIA. 2012.
3. Zakaria Z. Regulation of cosmetics: what has Malaysia learnt from the European system? J Consum Policy. 2015;38(1):39–59.

4. Dorato S. General concepts, Current legislation on cosmetics in various countries. In: Analysis of Cosmetic Products [Internet]. Elsevier; 2018 [cited 2022 May 10]. p. 3–37. Available from: https://linkinghub.elsevier.com/retrieve/pii/B9780444635082000011
5. Ghana Federal Government. Public-Health-Act-851 - FDA, Ghana..pdf [Internet]. FDA, Ghana; 2012 [cited 2022 May 13]. Available from: https://www.moh.gov.gh/wp-content/uploads/2016/02/Public-Health-Act-851.pdf
6. Ferreira A. Overview of the regitration process of cosmetics in brazil. N. d.;22.
7. Hayashida M. Cosmetic Regulation in Japan. Adv Med Health Beauty 1 2-15 2018. 2018;5(1):12–5.
8. Shweta K, Swarnlata S. A note on dire need of harmonisation of cosmetic legislation. Int J Trade Glob Mark. 2008;1(4):419–31.
9. Nigeria NAFDAC (a). Guidelines for Registration of Imported Cosmetics in Nigeria.pdf [Internet]. R&R-GDL-OO4-OO Dec 13, 2021 p. 7. Available from: https://www.nafdac.gov.ng/wp-content/uploads/Files/Resources/Guidelines/DR_And_R_Guidelines/Guidelines-for-Registration-of-Imported-Cosmetics-in-Nigeria.pdf
10. Nigeria NAFDAC (b). Guidelines for Registration of Cosmetics Made in Nigeria.pdf [Internet]. Jan 6, 2018 p. 4. Available from: https://www.nafdac.gov.ng/wp-content/uploads/Files/Resources/Guidelines/DR_And_R_Guidelines/Guidelines-for-Registration-of-Cosmetics-Made-in-Nigeria.pdf
11. Ghana Food and Drugs Authority. Guidelines for the registration of cosmetics and household chemical substances in Ghana [Internet]. Government of Ghana; 2019 [cited 2022 Oct 4]. Available from: https://globi-reg.com/wp-content/uploads/2019/05/GUIDELINE-FOR-REGISTRATION-OF-COS.-AND-HOUSEHOLD.pdf
12. Su Z, Luo F ya, Pei X rong, Zhang F lan, Xing S xia, Wang G li. Final Publication of the "Regulations on the Supervision and Administration of Cosmetics" and New Prospectives of Cosmetic Science in China. Cosmetics. 2020 Dec 17;7(4):98.
13. Patel P, Cerqueira DM, Santos GML, de Lima Soares R, Sousa VD, Liberti L, et al. A Baseline Analysis of Regulatory Review Timelines for ANVISA: 2013–2016. Ther Innov Regul Sci. 2020 Nov;54(6):1428–35.
14. Cancian M de L, Leonardi MS, Mosca MM, Guerra LO, Hengeltraub SF, Leonardi GR. Safety assessment of cosmetic products, with emphasis on the ocular area: regulatory aspects and validation processes. Braz J Pharm Sci. 2014 Dec;50(4):667–76.
15. Blaschke JW. Globalization of cosmetic regulations. Food Drug Law J. 2005;60(3):413–9.
16. Federal Government of Nigeria (a). NAFDAC Act Cap N.1 LFN 2004.pdf [Internet]. p. 81. Available from: https://www.nafdac.gov.ng/wp-content/uploads/Files/Resources/Regulations/NAFDAC_Acts/NAFDAC-ACT-Cap-N.-1-LFN-2004.pdf

17. Nigeria NAFDAC (c). NAFDAC Mandate [Internet]. 2017. Available from: https://www.nafdac.gov.ng/about-nafdac/nafdac-organization/nafdac-functions/?msclkid=c2b6b924d05e11ec88e9f91f143ddb08
18. Gagliardi L, Dorato S. General Concepts and Cosmetic Legislation - Gagliardi and Dorato, 2007. In: Salvador A, Chisvert A, editors. Analysis of Cosmetic Products [Internet]. 1st ed. Amsterdam ; London: Elsevier; 2007 [cited 2022 May 10]. p. 25. Available from: https://www.semanticscholar.org/paper/1.1-%E2%80%93-General-Concepts.-Current-Legislation-on-in-Gagliardi-Dorato/e5cdb9c7aea300d8d3adb50feb0457c7e8a7f8d0
19. UK Government. Regulation 2009/1223 and the Cosmetic Products Enforcement Regulations 2013: Great Britain [Internet]. 2021. Available from: https://www.gov.uk/government/publications/cosmetic-products-enforcement-regulations-2013/regulation-20091223-and-the-cosmetic-products-enforcement-regulations-2013-great-britain
20. Blaschke JW. Regulatory Developments in Canada, Japan, Australia, China, and India. In: Global Regulatory Issues for the Cosmetics Industry [Internet]. Elsevier; 2007 [cited 2022 May 8]. p. 21–33. Available from: https://linkinghub.elsevier.com/retrieve/pii/B978081551567850005X
21. Rogiers V. A comparison study between Chinese and EU technical guidelines for cosmetic safety assessment final. 2021 Mar p. 24.
22. Schneider SB. Global Cosmetic Regulations? A Long Way To Go .... In: Global Regulatory Issues for the Cosmetics Industry [Internet]. Elsevier; 2009 [cited 2022 May 8]. p. 189–233. Available from: https://linkinghub.elsevier.com/retrieve/pii/B9780815515692500166
23. Inmetro IN de M Qualidade e Tecnologia. A Guide to Brazil Toiletry, Perfume and Cosmetic Products Compliance Requirements [Internet]. Inmetro (Instituto Nacional de Metrologia, Qualidade e Tecnologia); 2017 [cited 2022 Jan 7]. Available from: https://www.nist.gov/system/files/documents/2017/05/31/aguidetobraziltoiletryperfumeandcosmeticproductscompliancerequirements-170504154110.pdf
24. Ravi P, Reddy DDS, Ramu B, Rajkamal DB. Comparative Study on Cosmetics Legislation in INDIA US and EU. World J Pharm Pharm Sci. 2016;5(6):10.
25. ASEAN Governments. ASEAN DEFINITION OF COSMETICS AND ILLUSTRATIVE LIST BY CATEGORY OF COSMETIC PRODUCTS [Internet]. [cited 2022 May 11]. Available from: https://www.aseancosmetics.org/docdocs/technical.htm
26. ASEAN Cosmetics Association. Notification webpage on ASEAN ACD [Internet]. [cited 2022 Apr 21]. Available from: https://aseancosmetics.org/asean-cosmetics-directive/notification/
27. WHO. WHO Guide for the review of drug regulatory systems [Internet]. WHOa; 2007 [cited 2022 May 11]. Available from: https://www.globalforumljd.com/sites/default/files/documents/virtualLibrary/WHO%

20Guide%20for%20the%20review%20of%20drug%20regulatory%20systems%20%282007%29.pdf?msclkid=a53222ecd16a11eca210e02457e49868

28. Patil A, Sandewicz RW. Cosmetic science and polymer chemistry: Perfect together. In: ACS Symposium Series. American Chemical Society; 2013. p. 13–37.
29. Federal Government of Nigeria (b). FOOD, DRUGS AND RELATED PRODUCTS (REGISTRATION, ETC.) ACT Cap F.33 LFN 2004 [Internet]. 2004 p. 8. Available from: https://www.nafdac.gov.ng/wp-content/uploads/Files/Resources/Regulations/NAFDAC_Acts/FOOD-DRUGS-AND-RELATED-PRODUCTS-REGISTRATION-ACT-Cap.F.33.pdf
30. Nigeria NAFDAC (d). Guideline for Inspection of Facilities for Manufacture of Veterinary Cosme.pdf [Internet]. Jan 11, 2021 p. 4. Available from: https://www.nafdac.gov.ng/wp-content/uploads/Files/Resources/Guidelines/VETERINARY_GUIDELINES/Guidelines-for-Inspection-of-Facilities-for-Manufacture-of-Veterinary-Cosmetics-1.pdf
31. Nigeria NAFDAC (e). Guidelines for Inspection of Facilities for Manufacture of Veterinary Medicinal.pdf [Internet]. VMAP-GDL-016-12 Jan 11, 2021 p. 6. Available from: https://www.nafdac.gov.ng/wp-content/uploads/Files/Resources/Guidelines/VETERINARY_GUIDELINES/Guidelines-for-Inspection-of-Facility-for-the-Manufacture-of-Veterinary-Medicinal-Cosmetics-in-Nigeria-1.pdf
32. Wunderskirchner M, Cosmetic II, Functions B. Borderline Products in the EU : Obstacles for Manufacturers and Importers. 2021;2009(1223):2020–2.
33. Foley E. Cosmetic Industry, Comparing the Industry Oversight in the European Union and the United States – Foley, 2019.pdf. Creighton Int Comp Law J. 2019;11(1):4–22.
34. Raj RK, Chandrul KK. Regulatory Requirements for Cosmetics in Relation with Regulatory Authorities in India against US, Europe, Australia and Asean Countries. Int J Pharma Res Health Sci. 2016;4(5):1332–41.
35. ASEAN Governments. ASEAN Cosmetic Directive (ACD) agreement.pdf [Internet]. Available from: http://agreement.asean.org/media/download/20140119114643.pdf
36. European Parliament. Regulation (EC) No 1223.2009 of the European Parliament and of the Council on cosmetic products.pdf [Internet]. European Parliament; [cited 2021 Dec 10]. Available from: https://ec.europa.eu/health/sites/health/files/endocrine_disruptors/docs/cosmetic_1223_2009_regulation_en.pdf
37. South Africa Government M. FOODSTUFFS, COSMETICS AND DISINFECTANTS ACT 54 OF 1972 [Internet]. May 19, 1972 p. 15. Available from: https://www.gov.za/sites/default/files/gcis_document/201504/act-54-1972.pdf
38. South African cosmetics industry. Cosmetic advertising code of practice – South Africa.pdf [Internet]. Available from: http://www.arb.org.za/assets/appendix-b-(2020).pdf

39. The Cosmetic, Toiletry & Fragrance Association of South Africa (CTFA). The Cosmetic, Toiletry & Fragrance Association of South Africa (CTFA) [Internet]. [cited 2022 Dec 1]. Available from: https://ctfa.co.za/
40. Gonzales L. Overview of Asean Cosmetic Regulations [Internet]. Overview of Asean Cosmetic Regulations. 2019 [cited 2022 Mar 22]. Available from: https://www.qse-academy.com/overview-of-asean-cosmetic-regulations/
41. Zhan M. Overview of Cosmetic Regulations in Korea and Japan.pdf [Internet]. 2018 [cited 2022 Dec 1]. Available from: https://www.life-vermeer.eu/wp-content/uploads/2019/01/W05122018-8_Zhan-Reach24h-Korea-Japan-cosmetic-legislation.pdf
42. Nigeria NAFDAC (f). Guidelines for inspection of facilities for manufacture of veterinary medicinal cosmetics [Internet]. VMAP-GDL-016-12 Jan 11, 2021 p. 6. Available from: https://www.nafdac.gov.ng/wp-content/uploads/Files/Resources/Guidelines/VETERINARY_GUIDELINES/Guidelines-for-Inspection-of-Facility-for-the-Manufacture-of-Veterinary-Medicinal-Cosmetics-in-Nigeria-1.pdf
43. Rähse W. Cosmetic Creams: Development, Manufacture and Marketing of Effective Skin Care Products [Internet]. 2020 [cited 2022 May 20]. Available from: https://books.google.com.ng/books?hl=en&lr=&id=M2XBDwAAQBAJ&oi=fnd&pg=PR11&ots=yXNbieVA2g&sig=sVbBlGqO_gE2ARt4-ykhcEVLsbo&redir_esc=y#v=onepage&q&f=false
44. Núñez NS. The International Cosmetic Regulatory Framework [Internet]. [Spain]: Universidad de Barcelona; 2015 [cited 2022 Oct 4]. Available from: http://diposit.ub.edu/dspace/bitstream/2445/67016/1/TFG_Shaw_Nunez_2015.pdf
45. ASEAN Governments. ASEAN G uidelines for safety evaluation of cosmetic products [Internet]. ASEAN Governments; [cited 2022 Apr 5]. Available from: https://www.npra.gov.my/images/Guidelines_Central/Guidelines_on_Cosmetic/Annex_I_Part_6_.pdf
46. Garbossa WAC, Campos PMBGM. Evaluation of the Brazilian Cosmetic Legislation and its impact on the industries during the 20th century. Braz J Pharm Sci. 2016 Jun;52(2):319–28.
47. Daxue Consulting. Required cosmetics animal testing in China is loosening: "Ordinary" products no longer required to do animal testing [Internet]. Beijing; 2021 Mar [cited 2022 May 5]. Available from: https://daxueconsulting.com/cosmetics-animal-testing-in-china/#:~:text=In%202019%2C%20the%20regulations%20stopped%20requiring%20post-market%20animal,alternative%20for%20non-animal%20skin%20%2F%20eye%20irritation%20test
48. ASEAN Governments. ASEAN Cosmetic Directive Guidelines for Product Information File (PIF).pdf.

49. Nigeria NAFDAC (g). Guidelines for the Preparation of Product Dossiers`in The Common Technica.pdf [Internet]. DR&R-GDL-018-01 Dec 13, 2021 p. 4. Available from: https://www.nafdac.gov.ng/wp-content/uploads/Publications/Others/QMS_Documents/GUIDELINES-FOR-CLINICAL-TRIAL-APPLICATION.pdf
50. West Africa Competitiveness Programme. Ghana Cometic-regulations matrix-table [Internet]. [cited 2022 Apr 29]. Available from: https://wacompghana.org/wp-content/uploads/Cometic-regulations_matrix-table-final.pdf
51. ASEAN Governments. ANNEXES OF THE ASEAN COSMETIC DIRECTIVE.pdf.
52. Ghana Standards Authority. CATALOGUE-2019_04_03 [Internet]. 2019 [cited 2022 Apr 29]. Available from: https://gsa.gov.gh/wp-content/uploads/2019/06/CATALOGUE-2019_04_03.pdf
53. Klaschka U, Rother HA. Read this and be safe!' Comparison of regulatory processes for communicating risks of personal care products to European and South African consumers. 2013;25(30):18.
54. ANVISA, Brazil. Cosmetic Products Stability Guide, Brazil. National Health Surveillance Agency; 2005.
55. Wilson AP. Animal Law in South Africa: "Until the lions have their own lawyers, the law will continue to protect the hunter". Derecho Anim Forum Anim Law Stud. 2019 Jan 11;10(1):35.
56. Dal Zotto A. The Chinese Cosmetics industry, an attractive Market for Foreign Companies.pdf [Internet]. 2021 [cited 2022 May 13]. Available from: http://dspace.unive.it/bitstream/handle/10579/20471/882972-1260615.pdf?sequence=2
57. Food and Drug Administration, US. Animal Testing & Cosmetics [Internet]. 2014. Available from: https://www.fda.gov/cosmetics/product-testing-cosmetics/animal-testing-cosmetics
58. Pauwels M, Dejaegher B, Vander Heyden Y, Rogiers V. Critical analysis of the SCCNFP/SCCP safety assessment of cosmetic ingredients (2000–2006). Food Chem Toxicol. 2009 Apr;47(4):898–905.
59. Luo F ya. The current status of alternative methods for cosmetics safety assessment in China. ALTEX. 2019;36(1):136–9.
60. Umoh IO. CHALLENGES IN THE COSMETICS & MEDICAL DEVICES INDUSTRIES [Internet]. Lagos: Stellarchem Nigeria Ltd; 2017 Oct [cited 2022 Mar 28]. Available from: https://stellarchem.com.ng/2017/10/10/national-agency-for-foods-drug-administration-and-control/
61. Gill D, Yeabsley J. International regulatory cooperation Case studies and lessons learnt. Wellington, New Zealand; 2018 p. 47.
62. Vernon J, Nwaogu TA. Comparative Study on Cosmetics Legislation in the EU and Other Principal Markets with Special Attention to so-called Borderline Products [Internet]. London, UK: European Commission, DG Enterprise; 2004 [cited 2022 May 15] p. 142.

Available from: https://rpaltd.co.uk/uploads/report_files/j457-final-report-cosmetics.pdf

63. UK Government Office for Science. Guidance Code of Practice for Scientific Advisory Committees and Councils: CoPSAC 2021 [Internet]. 2021 [cited 2022 Mar 20]. Available from: https://www.gov.uk/government/publications/scientific-advisory-committees-code-of-practice/code-of-practice-for-scientific-advisory-committees-and-councils-copsac-2021
64. American Cosmetic Manufacturers Association A. American Cosmetic Manufacturers Association – ACMA [Internet]. American Cosmetic Manufacturers Association – ACMA. 2010 [cited 2022 Sep 1]. Available from: http://www.americancosmetics.org/about/about.html
65. ICCR. ICCR Outcome Document [Internet]. ICCR Meeting Reports. 2021. Available from: https://www.iccr-cosmetics.org/meetings
66. ICCR. ICCR General SOP-2021.pdf [Internet]. ICCR; 2021 [cited 2022 Oct 2]. Available from: https://www.iccr-cosmetics.org/downloads/topics/iccr%20general%20sop-2021.pdf
67. USA Food & Drug Administration. US Food and Drug Administration on International Cooperation on Cosmetics Regulation (ICCR) [Internet]. 2022 [cited 2022 May 15]. Available from: https://www.fda.gov/cosmetics/cosmetics-international-activities/international-cooperation-cosmetics-regulation-iccr
68. USA Food & Drug Administration. Cosmetics & U.S. Law [Internet]. USA Food & Drug Administration; 2022 [cited 2022 May 13]. Available from: https://www.fda.gov/cosmetics/cosmetics-laws-regulations/cosmetics-us-law#U.S._Law
69. Rai S, Gupta A, Punetha V. Regulations of Cosmetics Across the Globe. Applied Clinical Research, Clinical Trials and Regulatory Affairs. Appl Clin Res Clin Trials Regul Aff. 137AD 144;2(3):8.
70. Geoffrey K, Mwangi AN, Maru SM. Sunscreen products: Rationale for use, formulation development and regulatory considerations. Saudi Pharm J. 2019 Nov;27(7):1009–18.
71. Beg MR. Cosmetic-Regulations, Research & Marketing challenges and global compliance, An overview – Beg, 2020.pdf. 2020.
72. Knight. Continuing Animal Tests on Cosmetic Ingredients for REACH in the EU – Knight et al, 2021. 2021 p. 16.
73. Giordano-Labadie F. Cosmetic products: learning to read labels. Eur J Dermatol. 2012 Sep;22(5):591–5.
74. Abrutyn ES. International Nomenclature Chemical Ingredient Dictionary and Handbook: Back-Label Ingredient Statement. In: Draelos ZD, editor. Cosmetic Dermatology [Internet]. 1st ed. Wiley; 2022 [cited 2022 May 13]. p. 106–13. Available from: https://onlinelibrary.wiley.com/doi/10.1002/9781119676881.ch11

75. González Abellán EF, Martínez Pérez D. Quality Control of Cosmetic Products. In: Analysis of Cosmetic Products [Internet]. Elsevier; 2018 [cited 2022 May 13]. p. 39–53. Available from: https://linkinghub.elsevier.com/retrieve/pii/B9780444635082000023
76. Desmedt B, Van Hoeck E, Rogiers V, Courselle P, De Beer JO, De Paepe K, et al. Characterization of suspected illegal skin whitening cosmetics. J Pharm Biomed Anal. 2014 Mar;90:85–91.
77. Wallenhorst T. Registration and Approval in Regulatory Toxicology. In: Reichl FX, Schwenk M, editors. Regulatory Toxicology [Internet]. Berlin, Heidelberg: Springer Berlin Heidelberg; 2020 [cited 2022 May 14]. p. 1–19. Available from: http://link.springer.com/10.1007/978-3-642-36206-4_82-2
78. Backhaus T, Scheringer M, Ubl-Kägi DS, Arrhenius Å. Chemicals of Global Concern. Sweden: Swedish Chemicals Agency; 2020 Jun p. 39.
79. Stanković M, Tadic V, Arsic I. Safety and efficacy of cosmetic_dermocosmetic products – et al, 2014.pdf. In: Roj E, editor. Supercritical CO2 Extraction and its applications. Lublin, Poland; 2014. p. 137–60.
80. Lionetti N, Rigano L. Labeling of Cosmetic Products. Cosmetics. 2018 Mar 13;5(1):22.
81. Romero V, Khury E, Aiello LM, Foglio MA, Leonardi GR. Diferenças entre cosméticos orgânicos e naturais: literatura esclarecedora para prescritores. Surg Cosmet Dermatol [Internet]. 2018 [cited 2022 May 10];10(3). Available from: http://www.surgicalcosmetic.org.br/detalhe-artigo/646/Diferencas-entre-cosmeticos-organicos-e-naturais--literatura-esclarecedora-para-prescritores
82. Ucheanya F. Influence of Emotional Appeals in Television Cosmetics Advertisements on Purchase Decisions of Female Students of Higher Institutions in Niger State, Nigeria [Internet] [M.Sc. Mass Communications]. [Kwara State University, Nigeria.]; Florence [cited 2022 Aug 6]. Available from: https://www.proquest.com/openview/9b5c3a46700f5f2bb2282ca870ecd3d1/1?pq-origsite=gscholar&cbl=18750&diss=y
83. Odigie D, Odion J. THE IMPACT OF CONSUMERS' PROTECTION LAWS AND THE REGULATORY SCHEMES IN NIGERIA. 2011;2(1):13.
84. Nduka JK, Kelle HI, Odiba IO. Review of Health Hazards and Toxicological Effects of Constituents of Cosmetics. In: Poisoning in the Modern World - New Tricks for an Old Dog? [Internet]. IntechOpen; 2019 [cited 2022 Jun 12]. p. 18. Available from: https://www.intechopen.com/books/poisoning-in-the-modern-world-new-tricks-for-an-old-dog-/review-of-health-hazards-and-toxicological-effects-of-constituents-of-cosmetics
85. Toklu H, Antigua A, Lewis V, Reynolds M, Jones J. Cosmetovigilance: A review of the current literature. J Fam Med Prim Care. 2019;8(5):1540.
86. Theophilus Kureh G, Ndesangia A, Opio RD, Umoh IO, Aruwa JO, Okoruwa GA. Use of Cosmetic Products and Related Adverse Reactions among Health Science Students. J Young Pharm. 2020 Sep 22;12(3):271–4.

87. Almeida LS. Proposal of Scope of Clinical Assays of Safety and Effectiveness of Cosmetic Products. J Phys Conf Ser. 2015 Jan 6;575:012043.
88. Getachew M, Tewelde T. Cosmetic Use and Its Adverse Events among Female Employees of Jimma University, Southwest Ethiopia. Ethiop J Health Sci [Internet]. 1970 Jan 1 [cited 2022 May 14];28(6). Available from: https://www.ajol.info/index.php/ejhs/article/view/186860
89. Assuris. China Cosmetic Supervision and Administration Regulation (CSAR) (Global) [Internet]. Available from: https://www.intertek.com/assuris/cosmetics/regulatory/china-cosmetic-regulation-csar/
90. Sreedhar D, Manjula N, Pise A, Ligade D. Ban of Cosmetic Testing on Animals, A Brief overview. J Curr Res Rev. 2020;12(14):113–6.
91. Zencovich VZ. LAW, BEAUTY AND WRINKLES. FIRM POINTS AND OPEN ISSUES AFTER THE EU COSMETICS REGULATION. Comp LAW Rev. 2014;5:14.
92. Europian Commission. Europian Commission Scientific Committee on Consumer Safety (SCCS) [Internet]. Europian Union; [cited 2022 May 15]. Available from: https://ec.europa.eu/health/scientific-committees/scientific-committee-consumer-safety-sccs_en#contact
93. Nohynek GJ, Antignac E, Re T, Toutain H. Safety assessment of personal care products/cosmetics and their ingredients. Toxicol Appl Pharmacol. 2010 Mar;243(2):239–59.
94. ICCR. ICCR Terms of Reference [Internet]. 2022 [cited 2022 May 15]. Available from: https://www.iccr-cosmetics.org/component/attachments/?task=download&id=113
95. Torjesen I, Chinthapalli K. Cosmetic interventions need tighter controls. 2013;346:6.
96. Digiovanni C, Arcoraci V, Gambardella L, Sautebin L. Cosmetovigilance survey: Are cosmetics considered safe by consumers? Pharmacol Res. 2006 Jan;53(1):16–21.
97. Termini RB, Tressler L. American Beauty: An Analytical View of the Past and Current Effectiveness of Cosmetic Safety Regulations and Future Direction. Food Drug Law J. 2008;63(1):257–74.
98. Weiss CA. Legal Issues and Challenges in the Cosmetics Industry. Holl Kn. 2019;21–7.
99. Rodriguez M. Dying to Be Beautiful: An Assessment of How a Self-Regulating Cosmetic Industry and Biotechnology Are Impacting Public Health. Hous J Health Pol. 2020;20:457–91.
100. Board of Trade. 'HEAVENLY' TRADE MARK. Rep Pat Des Trade Mark Cases. 1967 Sep 21;84(12):306–11.
101. Nigeria NAFDAC (h). Cosmetics Guidelines – NAFDAC [Internet]. [cited 2022 May 11]. Available from: https://www.nafdac.gov.ng/herbals-cosmetics/cosmetics-guidelines/

CHAPTER TWENTY-FIVE

Legal framework for product liability and consumer protection in cosmetics

Abdulwasiu O Yusuff

Until the last few decades, people generally accepted their natural facial and bodily features and had very limited options to improve their outlook or make modifications to their features. Today, however, people have at their disposal, an array of products, treatments and procedures that are able to modify how they appear physically. These cosmetic interventions or treatment could include simple application of body care products, such as, powder, lotions, and creams; or more drastic dermatological interventions and procedures as well as surgical and non-surgical enhancement.

In most nations of the world, there exists the normal desire for attractiveness and beautiful appearance preponderantly by women, although men are not excluded from the use of cosmetics and beauty products. The cosmetics and personal care industry (PCI) is heavily and strictly regulated in the western countries (1). The reasons for this are not far-fetched, manufacturers, marketers and distributors of cosmetic products often make ludicrous, untrue, deliberate misrepresentations and even fraudulent claims to attract patronage and acceptance of the products. Sometimes the products could contain ingredients that might be harmful to users or the environment generally. Hence, the weight of regulatory attention focused in this area (2).

Chapter 24, (Regulatory framework for the cosmetic industry), focused on the core principles of cosmetic regulation and the processes devised for the regulation of cosmetic products. It equally provided a comparison of the world's major cosmetic jurisdictions. This chapter focuses on product liability and protection of rights of consumers of cosmetic products and services. Product liability as used here simply means legal responsibility for the manufacturing and sale or distribution of defective or harmful products to users of those products. Nigeria is one of the most populous countries in the world, with extensive availability and access to cosmetic products and services. Drawing from this, the chapter examines the actual legal (statutory) and institutional frameworks for the protection of consumers of cosmetic products and liability for harmful products, using Nigeria as an example.

Legal framework for product liability and consumer protection

A user or consumer can be defined as the individual who voluntarily purchased or acquired a product or services for a specific use or purpose (3). Implicit in this definition is the assumption that a consumer must have exercised a freedom of choice in the purchase or acquisition of the product or service with the hope that it would meet a need or satisfy an expectation. In modern societies, there would normally be a number of manufacturers of products and providers of services competing for the attention of consumers. Consumer choice could therefore be more influenced as the consumer opts for one out of many brand options guided by what is normally expected or claimed about the product or service. The relevant issue then is whether the consumer needs to be protected from his own ignorance and failure to exercise due diligence in freely exercising his right of choice to purchase and, or use a product or service. Beyond ignorance, however, consumers might well be taken advantage of through fraud or deceit by cosmetic product manufacturers and service providers (4).

As Monye posited:

'To ensure that consumers are not short-changed in dealings with suppliers of products and services, governments often put in place various measures... to protect the interests of consumers. Supply of defective products and services constitutes a big problem to the consumer, ...the supply of fake or substandard products denies the victim proper worth for money. Worse still, the product may be injurious to health thus exposing the user to health hazards' (5).

The author further noted:

'Most often, consumers find themselves saddled with shoddy services, or even non-performance of the obligation bargained for. Unfortunately, victims of fake and substandard products rarely seek redress due to some reasons, the most prominent being lack of knowledge about the laws and agencies protecting the rights of consumers as well as the channels of redress' (5).

This chapter examines the legal framework for product liability and consumer protection under three subheads: the statutory, institutional and judicial.

Statutory framework on product liability and consumer protection in Nigeria

There is an extensive statutory outlay for consumer protection in Nigeria. These are legislative foundations upon which consumer rights, inclusive of product liability claims, might rest.

Pharmacy Council of Nigeria (Establishment) Act, 2022

Cosmetic products sometimes come within a broad definition of drugs or pharmaceutical products that could be used externally on the skin or applied to work in the body. The practice of Pharmacy is strictly regulated in Nigeria. The Pharmacy Council of Nigeria (Establishment) Act establishes the Pharmacy Council of Nigeria (PCN) which generally regulates and controls the practice of the profession in all its aspects and ramifications in Nigeria (6, 7). This is to ensure that only people with the necessary training, qualifications and experience handle or discharge pharmaceutical duties which includes, "importation, exportation, compounding, preparing, supply, delivery, storage, distribution, preservation, dispensing, selling, procuring, processing, evaluating and manufacture" (8). Regulating the pharmaceutical profession directly and indirectly protects members of the public from potential hazards of improper dealings in drugs by non-qualified persons, including quackery, substandard drugs, drug adulteration and abuse (8).

Accordingly, anyone who contravenes the Pharmacy Council of Nigeria (Establishment) Act with respect to production and distribution of cosmetics could incur liability under the Act.

Standards Organisation of Nigeria (SON) Act 2015

More closely related to the PCN Act is the SON Act (9). Even where a product is not strictly considered as a drug or pharmaceutical, it is expected to attain a reasonable standard in terms of quality and fitness for purpose as stated in the SON Act. This could be a function of the use of genuine and reliable components in the making or the adoption of proper process of manufacturing for the best industrial result as far as the end users or consumers are concerned. In general terms, however, standard or standardization refers to the establishment of rules, procedures, order and guidelines deemed acceptable for doing things (10, 5).

In Nigeria, the SON Act 2015, established the Standards Council of Nigeria (11). The Act provides for standards to be known as Nigerian Industrial Standards (NIS) as well as Certification marks (11, 12).

In the wild jungle of cosmetics market, as the situation in many countries might be described, having standards would not only be required but is a necessity. Standards in the cosmetics market would ensure 'that products and services are fit for intended purpose' and are 'comparable and compatible' and 'that only good quality and safe products and services are offered to consumers' (5, 13).

This Nigerian Act, therefore, offers a good legal and particularly preventive template for the protection of consumers of cosmetics product and services by seeking to ensure that consumer products meet national and international standards. The Act mandates the Standards Council to 'organize tests and do everything necessary to ensure compliance with standards designated and approved by the Council'(14), 'coordinate all activities relating to its functions throughout Nigeria and cooperate with corresponding national or international organisations in such fields of activity as it considers necessary with a view to securing uniformity in standards'(15), and 'undertake appropriate investigations into the production premises and raw materials; and establish relevant quality assurance systems including certification of production sites for regulated products' (16).

It is not clear if the Standards Organisation of Nigeria or Council, have established industrial standards specifically in the field of cosmetics, nevertheless, it could work hand-in-hand with sister organisations in this regard. The Organisation is also empowered to prosecute offenders (17) and most importantly to recall defective products (18). In exercising the power of recall, the Organisation is required to disclose to the public or any specified class of persons the nature of the defect in the commodity to be recalled and the circumstances in which the use of the commodity may be dangerous, as well as the procedure for the disposal of the commodity (18).

In addition to power to recall products, the Organisation is empowered to detain and order the destruction of products if testing indicates that the goods did not meet the relevant Nigerian Industrial Standards and it is reasonable to destroy the goods because they are in a dangerous state or injurious to the health of human beings, animals or plants (19). Where a product is tested for safety and effectiveness or fitness for purpose before it enters the consumer market, or where it is recalled if found to be potentially hazardous, the consumer is thereby protected from harm.

Federal Competition and Consumer Protection Act 2018

The Federal Competition and Consumer Protection Act 2018 (20) of Nigeria is unarguably the most comprehensive consumer protection specific law in Nigeria today. The Act established the Federal Competition and Consumer Protection Commission as well as the Competition and Consumer Protection Tribunal (20, 21). It seeks, among others, to 'protect and promote the interests and welfare of consumers by providing consumers with a wider variety of quality products at competitive prices'; and applies to 'all commercial activities aimed at making profit and geared towards the satisfaction of demand from the public' (20, 22).

Section 17 of the Act provides an extensive outlay of functions for the Commission geared towards protection of interests of consumers and elimination of injuries to them. Specifically, the Act mandates the Commission to, among other functions, protect and promote consumer interests; regulate and seek ways and means of removing or eliminating from the market, hazardous goods and services, including emission, untested, controversial, emerging or new technologies, products or devices whatsoever, and cause offenders to replace such goods or services with safer and more appropriate alternatives; encourage trade, industry and professional associations to develop and enforce in their various fields quality standards designed to safeguard the interests of consumers; ensure that consumers' interests receive due consideration at appropriate fora and provide redresses to obnoxious practices or the unscrupulous exploitation of consumers by companies, firms, trade associations or individuals; ensure the adoption of appropriate measures to guarantee that goods and services are safe for intended or normally safe use; act generally to reduce the risk and injury which may occur from consumption of certain consumers items and other services rendered to consumers which action may include restriction or prohibition (20, 23).

These functions provide relevant legal template for the protection of consumers of cosmetic products and services in Nigeria. However, beyond these, the Act contains additional provisions on rights of consumers and certain duties of manufacturers, importers, distributors and suppliers of goods and services. Few examples are as follows:

General standards for the marketing of goods and services (Section 123): A producer, importer, distributor, retailer, trader or service provider shall not, in pursuance of trade and for the purpose of promoting or marketing, directly or indirectly, goods or services make any representation to a consumer: (a) in a manner that is likely to imply any false or incorrect representation concerning those goods or services; (b) that is reasonably misleading or likely to be misleading in any material respect concerning those goods and services; (c) in a manner that is erroneous, fraudulent or deceptive in any way, including in respect of:

- the nature, properties, advantages or uses of the goods or services (24)

    - **Consumer's rights to safe, good quality goods** (section 131): Every consumer has a right to receive goods that: (a) are reasonably suitable for the purposes for which they are generally intended; (b) are of good quality, in good working order and free of defects; (c) will be useable and durable for a reasonable period of time, having regard to the use to which they would normally be put and to all the surrounding circumstances of their supply (24, 25).

- **Duty to withdraw hazardous goods from the market** (section 135): Upon becoming aware of any unforeseen hazard arising from the use of goods already placed on the market, the manufacturer or distributor of such goods shall notify the general public immediately of such risk or danger and cause such goods to be withdrawn from the market (24, 26).
- **Liability for defective goods** (section 136): (1) Where a damage is caused wholly or partly by defective goods or the supply of a service, the undertaking that supplied the goods or service is liable for the damage

➢ For the purpose of this Act, damage includes personal injury and damage to the consumer's property.

➢ An undertaking that supplied the defective goods or services is liable whether or not the user or consumer bought the goods or service from or entered into any contractual agreement with the undertaking.

➢ A person affected by the defective goods or services has the right to sue under this section.

➢ The liability of any undertaking under this section shall not be excluded or restricted (24, 27).

The importance of these provisions in the cosmetic market in Nigeria is quite obvious. It is rather common to see cosmetic products being marketed or promoted with fantastic but fraudulent and unrealistic claims which unfortunately many consumers believe. It is also material that manufacturers and retailers are required to pull defective, unfit, harmful and hazardous products from circulation. This imposes responsibility on such people to closely study effects of their products on consumers and generally monitor complaints about the products to enable them take immediate and appropriate action. If such steps are taken whenever called for, they minimize injury and would mitigate any possible legal consequences.

National Agency for Food and Drug Administration and Control (NAFDAC) Act 1993

The NAFDAC Act established the National Agency for Food and Drug Administration and Control with extensive functions covering cosmetics in Nigeria. As far as cosmetics are concerned, the Agency under Section 5 of the Act, is empowered to:

- regulate and control the importation, exportation, manufacture, advertisement, distribution, sale and use of food, drugs, cosmetics, medical devices, bottled water and chemicals;
- conduct appropriate tests and ensure compliance with standard specifications designated and approved by the Council for the effective control of the quality of food, drugs, cosmetics, medical devices, bottled water and chemicals and their raw materials as well as their production processes in factories and other establishments;
- undertake appropriate investigations into the production premises and raw materials for…., cosmetics….and establish relevant quality assurance systems, including certificates of the production sites and of the regulated products;
- undertake inspection of imported…, cosmetics…, and establish relevant quality assurance system, including certification of the production sites and of the regulated products;
- compile standard specifications and guidelines for the production, importation, exportation, sale and distribution of food, drugs, cosmetics, medical devices, bottled water and chemicals;
- undertake the registration of food, drugs, cosmetics, medical devices, bottled water and chemicals;
- pronounce on the quality and safety of food, drugs, cosmetics, medical devices, bottled water and chemicals;
- issue guidelines on, approve and monitor the advertisement of food, drugs, cosmetics, medical devices, bottled water and chemicals; and
- determine the suitability or otherwise of medicines, drugs, food products, cosmetics, medical devices or chemicals for human and animal use.

Specifically, the NAFDAC Act strictly regulates production and availability of cosmetics in Nigeria which is expected to offer advanced protection to consumers of the products and ensure safety of the products that are marketed or offered for use in the country as cosmetics (29). The NAFDAC Act ensures that cosmetics and other regulated products are of good quality, are effective and safe for human and animal use and or consumption, as applicable. It also establishes appropriate frameworks and programmes for the quality, safety and rational use of the concerned products. The Agency is granted extensive powers to effectively carry out its statutory functions including powers to enter premises, carry out inspection of articles, take sample or specimen of any article, examine records and seize and detain any article to which the Act or the Agency's regulatory functions apply (30). It is a punishable offence to contravene the provisions of regulations made under the Act or obstruct officers of the Agency in the performance of their duties (28, 31).

NAFDAC has been very active in Nigeria in controlling the use of food, drugs and cosmetics (32). However, it would appear that the enormity of the functions and the territory over which it is expected to extend its powers stretches the Agency beyond its resources and operative capacity making inter-agency and international collaboration with sister agencies a necessity (33).

Other relevant statutory templates

There is a sizeable number of other legislative and regulatory templates applicable to the protection of consumers of cosmetics products and services in Nigeria. This sub-section will provide brief highlights of a few of these.

- **Food, Drugs and Related Products (Registration, etc.) Act 1993:** This provides that no processed food, drug, drug product, cosmetic, medical device or water shall be manufactured, imported, exported, advertised, sold or distributed in Nigeria unless it has been registered in accordance with the provisions of this Act or regulations made under it (34). The Act equally provides that no person shall import, procure, supply or manufacture cosmetic products in Nigeria for the purpose of conducting clinical trials of same without a valid clinical trial certificate issued by NAFDAC (34, 35).

- **Advertisement of products and services:** Consumers can easily be taken advantage of through advertisement of products and services. Advertisements generally make wide claims and seek to induce people by playing on their emotions and psychology to take steps that they perhaps would not have taken. Nigeria has laws and regulations in place to ensure that advertisements and advertisers have some rules to play by, particularly the Advertisement Practitioners (Registration, etc.) Act 1988 (36). This Act created the Advertising Practitioners Council of Nigeria (APCON) which regulates and controls the practice of advertising subject to the approval of the Minister of Health where the advertisement relates to matters of food, cosmetics, beverages and drugs (37, 5). As part of its statutory functions, APCON issued the Code of Advertising Practice, Sales Promotion and Other Rights/Restrictions on Practice 2012. Article 22 of this Code states that advertisements shall not contain any description, claim or illustration which directly or by implication conveys an erroneous or misleading impression about the product or service advertised or about its suitability for the purpose recommended. The Code notably provides, and this is arguably applicable in the context of cosmetic and beauty treatments, that adverts for drugs or devices relating to treatment of diseases, complaints, conditions or symptoms which rightly require the attention of a registered medical practitioner shall not be exposed in any public medium except in relevant professional media (38). Furthermore, advertisement for drugs, including cosmetological or dermatological drugs, shall not contain any claim to provide rejuvenation or to prevent, retard or reverse the physiological changes and degenerative conditions brought about by, or associated with advancement in age (39). It is noteworthy that many adverts for cosmetics and beauty products in the print and electronic media make precisely the claims prohibited by the Code (40).

- **National Health Act 2014:** This Act is perhaps the most comprehensive legislative provisions in the health/medical field in Nigeria currently. The Act provides a framework for the regulation, development and management of a National Health System and sets standards for rendering health services in the country. The Act is applicable to the rendering of cosmetic services and the personal care industry in the country to the extent that they are part of the health services and involve practices and practitioners/professionals covered by the provisions of the Act. Health services are defined under the Act as health care services that are preventive, protective, promotive, curative and rehabilitative in respect of physical, mental and social well-being (41). To this extent, health care providers in the dermatology, cosmetics, beauty and personal care practice fields, in general, would be expected to possess necessary skills and attain reasonable levels of professional competence for proper and safe care of their patients. Practitioners would be answerable where they display negligence or show reckless attitude to human life in treating their patients, including while rendering cosmetic services. Liability here could range between payment of fines and damages, suspension from or withdrawal of professional licence to practice or criminal prosecution, depending on the extent of the negligence or professional shortcoming. Importantly, the Act requires health care providers to provide relevant information to consumers of health services generally as part of the provision of wholesome services and obtaining valid consent without which any treatment could be regarded as a trespass to the person (42). Specifically, section 23 provides that user of services (43) must be given information as to their health status or condition, the range of diagnostic procedures and treatment options available to the user and the benefits, risks, costs and consequences generally associated with each option. In the provision of cosmetic services, inclusive of use of a range of alternative brands of products, users must be offered proper guidance. Treatments should ideally be preceded by necessary investigations and tests for the purpose of diagnoses. This is to be followed by determination of treatment options, a consideration of the benefits, risks, costs and consequences associated with each option and finally a choice most suitable among the options. It is debatable whether many providers of cosmetic services follow this pattern which would have afforded consumers and users of cosmetic services the benefit of services tailored to their health needs, taking their individual physiological peculiarities into account and considering their overall best interest (43a).

- **Food and Drugs Act 1974**: The Act made provisions for the regulation of the manufacture, sale and advertisement of food, drugs, cosmetics and devices. Section 1(3) of the Act provides that no person shall sell, import, manufacture or store any article of food or any drug or cosmetic which was manufactured, prepared, preserved, packaged or stored under insanitary conditions. This provision appears to be more respected in breach rather than obedience in Nigeria today. Many cosmetic products are apparently prepared and packaged in such conditions, especially fake and substandard cosmetic products. Furthermore, section 1(4) of the Act states that no person shall sell, import, manufacture or store any cosmetic which has in it or upon it any substance which may cause injury to the health of the user when the cosmetic is used according to the direction or label accompanying it or used for such purposes and by such methods of use as are customary or usual. The subsection equally prohibits selling, importing, manufacturing or storing any cosmetic which contains any filthy or decomposed substance or of any foreign matter (44, 45).

  To protect consumers against fraudulent and unscrupulous merchants in the cosmetic and personal care industry, the Food and Drugs Act also forbids advertising or selling any cosmetic product as treatment, preventative or cure for some diseases, disorders or abnormal physical states that were listed in the First Schedule to the Act, including Autoimmune deficiency syndrome (AIDS), blood disorders, cancer, any genital or urinary diseases, glaucoma, goitre, measles, mumps, hernia, sexual impotence, tumours, etc. (46).

  The Act appears to clearly limit the purpose or use of cosmetics to substances manufactured, sold or advertised for use in cleansing the skin, hair or teeth, and improving or altering the complexion, and, therefore, not what would normally be used as a drug (47). This definition seems restrictive. Admittedly, most cosmetic products would be for external use only but some could be applied or introduced into the body for any of the purposes stated above (48). Besides, some cosmetic products which contain active medicinal ingredients could also come under the definition of 'drug or drug product' depending, probably, on the registration and or licence obtained for them (49). The provision is, nevertheless, justifiable for the sake of public safety and protection of public health and in consideration of the level of literacy in the country.

- **Civil and Criminal Law:** Consumers of cosmetic products and services are also availed of the general templates of civil and criminal law systems in Nigeria for their protection. This could be through the application of law of contract and or sales of goods law where consumers could seek redress for breach of express or implied terms or warranties regarding cosmetic products. Consumers are also afforded protection from injury because of product defects or negligence in the provision of cosmetic services under torts law. Consumers of cosmetic products and services can also take advantage of the criminal law system where attending practitioners contravene applicable provisions with respect to or while rendering services or show such disregard for the life and safety of others as to amount to a crime against the State and conduct deserving punishment (50). For example, under the Criminal Code Act of Nigeria (51).

- **Duty of persons doing dangerous acts (Section 303 C.C.):** It is the duty of every person who...undertakes to administer surgical or medical treatment to any other person, or to do any other lawful act which is or maybe dangerous to human life or health, to have reasonable skill and to use reasonable care at doing such act, and he is held to have caused any consequences which result to the life or health of any person by reason of any omission to observe or perform that duty. Section 335 C.C. provides that any person who unlawfully does grievous harm to another is guilty of a felony and is liable to imprisonment for seven years. Furthermore, Section 343 (1) C.C. on Criminal recklessness or negligence leading to harm, injury or death, states- Any person who in a manner so rash or negligent as to endanger human life or to be likely to cause harm to any other person- (i) Gives medical or surgical treatment to any person whom he has undertaken to treat; or (ii) dispenses, supplies, sells, administers, or gives away, any medicine, or poisonous or dangerous matter;...is guilty of a misdemeanour and is liable to imprisonment for one year (52).

It is, therefore, clear that persons who provide cosmetic services or dispense, supply, sell or administer cosmetic products in a manner that endangers the life of consumers or causes them harm could face criminal prosecution.

This chapter has so far shown that there is a robust legal framework for the protection of consumers of cosmetic products and services in Nigeria. This framework is complemented by agencies and institutions which are established to enforce and give effects to the provisions of the law. Persons who are aggrieved or suffer harm because of the use of cosmetic products or services are at liberty to explore any of these remedial channels.

Institutional framework for the protection of consumers of cosmetic products and services: the channels of redress

It is imperative, as Ekanem observed, for the State to protect itself and the populace from the antics of unscrupulous producers and service providers by way of administrative intervention, in view of the vulnerable position of the consumers (4, 53). Protection is also necessary because of the overall negative social and economic impacts of unwholesome or defective products on the public in general. Hence, the government, through legislative and regulatory measures, has created appropriate and complementary administrative and institutional channels for protective and remedial actions by affected individuals.

The existence of relevant legal structure is, however, not quite meaningful where it is not exploited or activated. Consumers should not only know but must also be ready and willing to activate the channels and trigger the processes to protect their rights and obtain remedies when the rights are breached. The current reality in this regard in Nigeria is not so encouraging, prevailing ignorance about product liability and the structure for consumer protection is partly to blame for this. Even where some are aware that there are laws and institutions for the protection of consumer rights, they presume that the processes would be cumbersome because the laws are too formal and, thus, inaccessible. Therefore, the moment some consumers complain to the retailer or seller of whatever product they are dissatisfied with and the retailer or seller angrily retort that she/he is not the cause of whatever problem that has resulted from the use of the product and that, in any case, she/he is not the manufacturer; and that the receipt issued on purchase already declared that 'goods once received in good condition cannot be returned', invariably the consumer gets discouraged and does not pursue the matter any further. Sometimes, the distributor, retailer or seller at the end of the supply chain flaunt the policy of 'no refund, no return and no replacement' in the face of the buyer/consumer (54). In many cases, all these are not acceptable and cannot stand in view of the existing laws of product liability and consumer protection in the country.

As Monye rightly observed:

"...the role of consumers remains paramount. Consumers can serve as active drivers of the system by making demands on the agencies and product/service providers in a manner that spurs activism. They can drive the system by taking steps to seek redress in the event of violation of protected rights. Without the active participation of consumers by way of enforcement, many laws may remain redundant" (54, 55).

The same author went ahead to list the channels of redress which are available to aggrieved or dissatisfied consumers of products and services, namely-

- the manufacturer/supplier of the product or service;
- any regulatory agency;
- relevant professional body;
- any voluntary consumer organisation;
- court action; or
- class and representative actions (55).

These channels are individually broad enough to afford due redress to aggrieved consumers, they are, however, not mutually exclusive and a consumer might take advantage of a combination of them at the same time. This section will briefly look at some of these channels while the involvement of courts in enforcing the law on consumer protection and product liability in Nigeria would be considered in the next section.

Direct complaint to the manufacturer

The first step for a displeased consumer is to complain to the manufacturer, supplier or seller about the product or service in question. This is not guaranteed to solve the problem, but it gives both parties an opportunity to explore an amicable settlement. It might afford the manufacturer, supplier or seller of a product or a provider of services a chance to know that there is a defect or other issues with the product or service and, thus, be able to give a prompt response to investigate the situation, recall the product if necessary, pay closer attention to the manufacturing process or the distribution chain, as the case may be, and generally help the manufacturer to improve on the product or service. The result could be satisfactory to the customers/consumers and possibly enlarge the market share and increase the profit margin of the product. If all these happen, it definitely is a win-win situation for the manufacturer, supplier, seller or provider concerned. The consumer's displeasure can be assuaged and more costly choices, particularly litigation, avoided. Reassuringly, there is no formality to the mode or content of the complaint. A simple oral or written complaint by the customer/consumer would suffice if it is clear and provides necessary information about the product or service transaction concerned. This channel of redress is, therefore, the easiest and cheapest, although it is only deceptively simple (56). Not all complaints would receive positive response from the providers of the products or services and may not even be entertained at all. This is where a consumer might need to take more engaging remedial measures to enforce her or his rights.

Formal complaint to a regulatory agency

The other channel for a dis-satisfied customer/consumer is to lodge a formal complaint with any of the regulatory agencies or report to the relevant professional body. As previously discussed, there are statutory agencies and institutions with specific powers and functions to provide assurance on product quality and also provide appropriate redress for aggrieved consumers. These agencies include Federal Competition and Consumer Protection Commission; the National Agency for Food and Drugs Administration and Control; the Standard Organisation/Council of Nigeria; Advertising Practitioners Council of Nigeria; Ministries/Departments of Health at the Federal and State levels; and, where the situation is drastic and portends danger to the public, law enforcement agencies, particularly the Police Force. These agencies and institutions have clear procedures and processes to receive and treat complaints for the best possible outcomes.

For example, the Federal Competition and Consumer Protection Act, 2018, recognises that a consumer may seek to enforce any right under the Act, transaction or agreement or resolve any dispute with an undertaking that supplied the goods and services by direct complaint to the supplier, by referring the matter to the relevant industry regulator, if any, by approaching a competent court or by filing a complaint directly with the Federal Competition and Consumer Protection Commission (20, 57). Section 148 lays out the process for the consumer to file a complaint in the prescribed manner and form and how the complaint is to be treated with proper investigation and other consequential actions. Necessary orders could be made against the undertaking in question, including order for compliance and compensation in favour of the consumer/complainant (20, 58).

Seeking redress through consumer rights advocacy groups

In addition to the agencies and institutions mentioned earlier, aggrieved consumers could also channel complaints to, or through any of the consumer rights protection advocacy or civil society groups (59). Groups such as these could deploy their structure, organisational strength, financial resources and personnel to tackle recalcitrant manufacturers, suppliers, sellers or service providers against which complaints have been made by an aggrieved consumer. The consumer rights group can also more easily relate with relevant industry regulators and/or government ministry, department or agency.

Report to relevant/applicable professional bodies

In appropriate circumstances, a consumer might report to applicable professional bodies, for example, the Pharmacy Council of Nigeria, the Nigerian Medical Association, the Medical and Dental Council of Nigeria, the Nigerian Dermatology Association, the Manufacturers Association of Nigeria, Chambers of Commerce, other Trade Associations and so on. Where a manufacturer, undertaking or person against whom a consumer has complaints is a member of these professional bodies, there is a possibility that a consumer who properly tender complaints would receive some attention and redress. Some of these professional bodies have disciplinary committees or panels which entertain complaints from aggrieved individuals, investigate, conduct hearings and take appropriate measures. A practitioner purporting to be a registered member of a particular professional body/association may be punished where she/he is adjudged by the disciplinary committee, panel or tribunal to be guilty of infamous conduct in any professional respect, or found involved in an act considered incompatible with the status of a professional in good standing in that profession or even found to be fake or fraudulently practicing as a registered professional. Punishments range from striking the person's name off the relevant register, suspending the person from practice for a specified period and admonishing such a person (60).

Consumers of cosmetic products and services in the personal care industry can take advantage of the legal structure and framework discussed above. They can also, perhaps as a last resort, approach a court of competent jurisdiction to seek appropriate redress in the area of consumer protection and product liability. This is discussed subsequently.

Judicial roles in enforcing the law on consumer protection and product liability: the Nigeria example

The plight of consumers in Nigeria and their susceptibility to unwholesome products from unscrupulous manufacturers and sellers was recognized and decried by the Supreme Court of Nigeria by Aniagolu JSC in: *Nigerian Bottling Co. Ltd. v Ngonadi,* when he stated-

"Nothing appears to be more elementary in this country where it is often the unhappy lot of the consumers to be inflicted with shoddy and unmerchantable goods by some pretentious manufacturers, entrepreneurs, shady middlemen and unprincipled retailers whose avowed interest seems only, and always, to maximise their profits leaving honesty a discounted and shattered commodity" (61).

Consumers aggrieved about a cosmetic product or service would have the burden to establish their case in court and justify why adverse action should be taken against the defendant. Fortunately, there is no dearth of judicial precedents to draw on in issues of product liability and consumer protection in Nigeria as shown below.

Lawsuit for fake, substandard or defective cosmetic

Consumers of cosmetic products and services could be aggrieved and go to court where they believe that they were sold fake, substandard, or defective product or one which contains foreign objects. The complaint might be that the product or service was not fit for the purpose and did not meet the expectation or warranties given by the manufacturer, distributor, seller or service provider (62). The grouse could also be that the 'professional' who attended to them or provided the cosmetic service did not possess or use adequate skill, knowledge or competence expected of him or her and that they suffered injury or harm traceable to such breach of care or negligence on his or her part. Ultimately, the consumer might be demanding damages or compensation from the product or service provider.

It is rather difficult to determine when a product may be said to be defective because defect is a relative term; a skin lotion might fail to tone or lighten skin complexion, as claimed by the maker or seller, but might not in fact be defective (63). Anyone who alleges that a product is defective must strictly prove the defect and be ready to debunk or disprove assertion that the product was not properly used as directed. Product defect could be understood in two distinct senses. Firstly, under the law of contract, that the product was not fit for its purpose from the perspective or expectation of the consumer. The product was not of 'merchantable quality', being inherently tainted or possessive of deleterious materials to cause damage to the user. The Supreme Court of Nigeria decided in: *Nigerian Bottling Co. Ltd. v Ngonadi* (61) that a refrigerator which showed faults few days after delivery and eventually exploded after a month of purchase thereby causing injury to the buyer was defective and unmerchantable. Secondly, reference to a product being defective under torts law means that the product is unsafe and can cause injury to the user. In this case, a cosmetic product might not, strictly speaking be proved to be fake or substandard but nevertheless is capable of causing or caused harm to the user. Thus, anything that could adversely affect the health of the consumer would render a product defective (54, 64).

Apart from the hurdle of proving that the product is defective or caused harm, another challenge which a consumer might face is determining which entity in the usual distribution chain of products it could successfully proceed against. For many products, the chain starts from and go through the manufacturer, distributor, marketer, wholesaler, retailer, to outlets like small shops or kiosks before reaching the final user or consumer. The general legal rule where a claim is founded on contract is that it would fail where there is no privity of contract, in other words, where there is no formal, direct or implied contractual link between one party against which a claim is made and the other who is making the claim. Where a user of a cosmetic product alleges that the product was harmful or defective, for example, she/he might not be able to proceed in a court action against the mighty corporation which manufactured or distributed the product, especially if the consumer was not a direct buyer from them. This principle, therefore, constitutes a great limitation to court actions arising from product liability based on allegation of defect in the product (65).

Lawsuit founded on negligence of cosmetic product manufacturer

While absence of privity of contract might constitute an impediment to an aggrieved consumer who wishes to maintain an action against the manufacturer or others in the distribution chain of a defective or harmful product, there is no such impediment where the action is founded on the tort of negligence (54, 62, 66). The foundation of the tort of negligence, and particularly liability for defective and or harmful product, was laid in the old English case of *Donoghue v Stevenson* (67) where Lord Atkin established the popular neighbour principle. In the case, the English House of Lords decided that the defendant manufacturer of ginger beer which contained the decomposed remains of a snail, which the plaintiff consumed unknowingly and became sick, owed a duty of care to the plaintiff and was liable to her for the injury consequently suffered. It did not matter, the court held, that the drink was not purchased from the manufacturer directly by the plaintiff but was bought for her by a friend. Lord Atkin in the lead judgment in the case stated that:

"A manufacturer of products, which he sells in such a form as to show that he intends them to reach the ultimate consumer in the form in which they left him with no reasonable possibility of intermediate examination, and with the knowledge that the absence of reasonable care in the preparation or putting up of the products will result in an injury to the consumer's life or property, owes a duty to the consumer to take that reasonable care" (67, 68).

The principle established in this case had been applied in many other cases, to hold manufacturers, distributors, retailers, service providers and other intermediate handlers of products liable for the tort of negligence, in Nigeria and elsewhere (69). In the case of *Okwejiminor v Gbekeji and Nigerian Bottling Co Plc* (70), for instance, the plaintiff claimed that he felt an object in his throat while drinking the liquid content of the bottle of Fanta Orange drink he purchased from a retailer and discovered on closer look at the content that there was remains of a dead cockroach in the bottle. This caused him stomach pains which landed him in hospital where tests showed that the drink was contaminated by the germ *Shigella.* He filed an action in negligence against the retailer and the manufacturer of the drink and the trial court held them liable. Although upturned by the court of appeal, the supreme court of Nigeria agreed with the decision of the trial court when it held that the manufacturer owed a duty of care to the ultimate consumer, that the orange drink was manufactured and bottled by the respondent company, sealed in such a manner as to exclude interference with or examination by an intermediate handler and was received in the ordinary form in which it was bottled and sealed by the manufacturer.

The requirements that consumer goods should be made or packaged to reach the final consumer in the condition or form it left the manufacturer and that the consumer would not have had an opportunity for closer examination of the product are factors that might affect liability in negligence with respect to defective or harmful product. Thus, if there was a probability of intermediate examination or interference, a court might give the benefit of the doubt to the manufacturer and decide against a claim of negligence. A string of cases concerning complaints of foreign substances in beer drunk by consumers and which allegedly harmed them were dismissed by courts on the basis that the claimants were not able to prove that those substances were there when the products left the manufacturers (71, 54). This condition obviously places a heavy burden on claimants, but it appears to be geared towards doing substantial justice in cases of this nature. However, a manufacturer would escape liability in negligence for defective and or harmful product only if there is reasonable probability that a test or examination, even if carried out, would be sufficient to reveal any defect in the product, and a proper warning was enclosed in the product package or attached or displayed at a visible part of the product that it should not be used without prior examination or check (72, 62, 54). For many cosmetic products, simple examination by consumers might not reveal an inherent defect and thus might not avail the manufacturer.

To succeed in an action for negligence generally, the plaintiff must not only establish existence of a duty of care and breach of such duty, but must additionally prove that the injury suffered was caused by the breach. In the case of *Okwejiminor v Gbekeji and Nigerian Bottling Co Plc* examined above, the claimant succeeded notably because he was able to establish a clear link between the contaminant in the Fanta drink he drank and the harm he subsequently suffered. The damage must not only be established, but it must also be linked to the defect in the product in question. The damage suffered by the plaintiff must directly emanate from the negligent act, or defect in the product of the defendant. Failure to prove that link would be fatal to the case of any claimant (73). Where a court finds, in favour of the consumer, a monetary award might be made to compensate him or her for the resulting injury.

As noted by Babatunde Sodipo:

"The injured party in a product liability claim is entitled to damages for bodily injury, such as pain or illness, and for psychological injury such as agony, discomfort or negative feeling. Damages may also either be purely economic, such as loss of income, loss of or damage to property, loss of business or expectation of profit; or non-economic, such as loss of life expectancy. In addition, the injured party may also recover the cost of medical expenses and purchase of the defective product" (74).

Liability for harmful cosmetic services

In addition to use of cosmetic and beauty products, consumers could also take advantage of assorted professional cosmetic services. This could also attract liability where the consumer suffered an injury traceable to the act or omission of the service provider. Professionals are liable in law where they provide advice, counsel or guidance to their clients which they reasonable should know would be relied upon as expert opinion by the clients. The professional would incur liability where the client suffers physical or economic injury because of reliance on his or her statement if the statement amounts to negligent misstatement or fraudulent misrepresentation. Untenable statement or exaggeration made to a consumer of cosmetic services might thus give rise to liability, as examples would show in some medical scenarios. In the Californian case of *Crawford v Duncan* (75), the defendant agreed to give the plaintiff radium treatment for swollen glands on the right side of her neck. He also assured the plaintiff that the treatment would not leave any permanent scar; in fact, the treatment left permanent and disfiguring scars on the plaintiff's neck, the defendant was held liable. In *Minich v Balzinger* (76), the defendant agreed to improve the appearance of the plaintiff's nose through plastic surgery. After 3 operations, however, the nostrils of the plaintiff collapsed. The doctor was held liable. Similarly, in the case of *Bailey v Hammond* (77) the defendant, a plastic and cosmetic surgeon, undertook to make the plaintiff, a woman, 'a model of harmonious perfection'. When he finished with her, it was apparent that she ended up worse than she was before the operation. He was held liable for breach of a promise to achieve a particular result.

Globally, many people avail themselves of different cosmetic surgeries. These vary from facial procedures on nose, cheeks, lips; breast reduction, enlargement or augmentation; waist narrowing, butt enlargement, tummy tuck, and general liposuction (78). These procedures become increasingly common as models, celebrities, socialites, actors and actresses, on-air personalities, social medial influencers and some other people pay greater attention to their looks and images and are willing to do or take any risk to get the body of their desire (79). Many of these procedures have the expected outcome with consumers being largely satisfied while some others have morbid or fatal consequences (80).

In the first instance, many of the providers of these services are not properly trained, certificated or licensed to perform the cosmetic operations and interventions they get involved in, although, they generally hold themselves out to clients that they possess the necessary skill, level of knowledge, professional competence and requisite experience to so act. Secondly, even where these practitioners are prima facie qualified or licensed to carry out the cosmetic services or procedures, questions remain whether they do so competently or negligently. In many cases there would be dismal failure of informed consent whereby clients and consumers were not honestly counselled or appropriately examined for suitability for the cosmetic procedure requested. In addition to lack of proper diagnosis or investigation prior to the procedures, it is doubtful if most consumers were afforded the opportunity to know and choose among alternatives, or warned on the probable risks and side effects of the cosmetic procedures (81). Lastly, the primary motivation for some of the service providers in the cosmetic surgery practice is the money derivable from the clients/patients even when they lack the necessary equipment and expertise. Hence, many consumers of cosmetic services turn out to be victims of unwholesome, substandard and negligent treatments.

Nigerian courts would not hesitate to appropriately punish fake or unlicensed practitioners or those who are licensed to practice but are found to have exhibited professional incompetence or negligence leading to injury, loss or harm to those who seek their services (82).

In the final analysis, a streamlining of the jurisdictions of the regulatory agencies in the area of consumer protection is strongly needed in many countries having agencies with overlapping powers and functions. In addition, more extensive public enlightenment, education and guidance on channels of redress for consumers of harmful or defective cosmetic products and services might be of significant benefit.

Appreciation

The author appreciates Oduniyi Oreoluwa, Adegbite N. Kehinde and Ogundepo Okikijesu for the research assistance provided towards this chapter. The author, however, accepts full responsibility for the chapter in its entirety.

References

1. See generally, Karl Lintner, ed, Global Regulatory Issues for the Cosmetics Industry, USA, William Andrew, 2009.
2. For example, claims that cosmetic products are free of "paraben", "fluoride", "preservatives"; "not tested on animals," "100% natural," "better than surgery", enable users to "lose inches within days" and so on are claims that are really problematic. Furthermore, abuses such as inclusion of "Mercury and hydrocortisone in skin whiteners, hormones in body care, Belladonna extracts in baby creams", and "the general public's perception that cosmetics in general (and skin care/body care products with their often far reaching claims in particular) are futile and outrageously overpriced", all contribute to near suffocating regulatory attention in this area. See (1), p. xxii.
3. For more definitions of the term 'consumer', see, Augustus NU. Consumer Rights in a Democratic System and the emerging market in Nigeria. International J on Consumer Law and Practice. 2018;6:31-33; Eseyin M. and Chukwuemeka CW. Articulating Consumer's Rights as Human Rights in Nigeria. J of Law, Policy and Globalisation. 2018;72:125. See also, Akinrinmade G. The Jurisprudence of Product Liability in Nigeria: A need to complement the existing fault theory. Afe Babalola Univ. J of Sustainable Dev't Law and Pol. 2016;7(2):190-194 for wider conceptual definition and analysis.

4. Ekanem EE. Institutional Framework for Consumers Protection in Nigeria. International Journal of Advanced Legal Studies and Governance. April 2011;2(1):34.
5. Monye Felicia, Law of Consumer Protection, Vol. 1, 2nd ed, Ibadan, Kraft Books Limited, 2021 p.2, 3.
6. Pharmacy Council of Nigeria (Establishment) Act, 2022 which replaced the Pharmacist Council of Nigeria Act, Cap. P 17, Vol. 13, Laws of the Federation of Nigeria 2004.
7. *(8)*, S.1.
8. Igweze EO. "Forensic Pharmacy", in Umerah, B.C., Ed, Medical Practice and the Law in Nigeria, Nigeria, Longman Nig. Ltd. 1989 p. 189.
9. Standards Organization of Nigeria Act No 14, 2015, Federal Republic of Nigeria Official Gazette, (FGP/I/8311/2201/S/L200), No. 91, Vol. 10, 23rd June, 2015.
10. As stated by Monye, standardisation is also defined as 'formulation, publication and implementation of guidelines, rules, and specifications for common and repeated use aimed at achieving optimum degree of order or uniformity in a given context, discipline or field'; Monye F, (5), p. 163-164.
11. S. 3 Standards Organisation of Nigeria Act 2015.
12. (11), sections 23-26.
13. Monye, (5), p. 164.
14. S. 5 (1) (a) SON Act 2015.
15. S. 5 (1) (r) SON Act 2015.
16. S. 5 (1) (t) SON Act 2015.
17. S. 34 SON Act 2015.
18. S. 46 SON Act 2015.
19. S. 47 (1) SON Act 2015
20. Federal Competition and Consumer Protection Act No 1, 2018, Federal Republic of Nigeria Official Gazette, (FGP 5/052019/250), No 18, Vol 106, 1st February, 2019.
21. Part II, section 3 and Part VII section 39, respectively.
22. Sections.1 and 2 on Objectives and Scope of Application of the Act.
23. Section 17 (l), (m), (p), (s), (t), & (x).
24. S. 123 (1), Federal Competition and Consumer Protection Act No 1, 2018. Under s. 123 (2), the representation mentioned by this section could be expressed on the goods and services offered or displayed for sale, it could also be attached to, inserted in or accompanying goods offered or displayed for sale, their wrapper or container, or anything on which the goods are mounted for display or sale. The representation as to the qualities or other assurances about the product or service might also be made expressly in the course of selling goods and services to the ultimate consumer or contained in or on anything that is sold, sent, delivered, transmitted or in any other manner made available to a member of the public.
25. Section 131 (1).
26. Section 135 (1).
27. Section 136 (1)- (5).
28. National Agency for Food and Drugs Administration and Control Act, Cap. N 1, Vol. 10, LFN 2004.

29. Consistent with its mandate to issue appropriate guidelines, NAFDAC has made a number of regulations on cosmetics, namely, Cosmetics Products Prohibition of Bleaching Agents Regulation 2019; Cosmetics Product Labelling Regulations 2019; and Cosmetics Advertisement Regulations 2018. For these and related Regulations, see http://www.nafdac.gov.ng/resources/nafdac-regulations/ (accessed 2nd April, 2022).
30. National Agency for Food and Drugs Administration and Control Act, Cap. N 1, Vol. 10, LFN 2004. section 24.
31. Section 25.
32. See also the Cosmetics and Medical Devices (Advertisement) Regulations, a subsidiary legislation to the NAFDAC Act.
33. Iyioha IO, Yusuff AO and Metiboba S. "Regulation of Healthcare Practice" in Comparative Health Law and Policy-Critical Perspectives on Nigerian and Global Health Law, IO Iyioha and RN Nwabueze, eds, UK, Ashgate Publishing Limited, 2015 p. 62.
34. S. 1 (1) Food, Drug and Related Products (Registration, etc) Act 1993.
35. Section 5 (1).
36. Advertisement Practitioners (Registration Etc) Act 1988, Cap A7 Laws of the Federation of Nigeria, 2004. The Act has been amended in 1992, 1993 and lastly 2016.
37. Section 1, Advertising Practitioners (Registration ETC) Act 1988 (as amended). Monye, (5) p. 249.
38. Art. 61, Code of Advertising Practice, Sales Promotion and Other Rights/Restrictions on Practice 2012.
39. Art. 56, Code of Advertising Practice, Sales Promotion and Other Rights/Restrictions on Practice 2012.
40. The Code equally prohibits in art. 66, the use in advertisements of words of exaggeration such as magic, miraculous or claims that products are 'safe', 'without risk', or 'harmless' when such are not backed or supported by medical authorities.
41. S. 64, National Health Act 2014.
42. For a detailed analysis and examination of the doctrine of patient consent in medical practice, see, Yusuff AO. The Significance of the Supreme Court of Nigeria's Decision on Patients' Consent to Medical Treatment in *Dr. Rom Okekearu* v. *Danjuma Tanko*. The Appellate Rev. September 2009:1(1):53-65.
43. The National Health Act 2014 did not use the word 'patient' to describe persons receiving treatment in a health establishment but rather used the term 'user'.
1. 43 a. Factors responsible for this include proliferation of cosmetic services providers in response to increased demands and the pervasive ignorance of many consumers of cosmetic services, particularly cosmetic surgeries, which makes them more vulnerable to exploitation and abuse.
44. Food and Drugs Act 1974, Cap F 32, Laws of the Federation of Nigeria 2004.
45. Section 1 (4) (a) –(b).
46. Section 2 (a) & (b).
47. Section 21 on interpretation of words used in the Act.
48. A position that is supported by the definition of cosmetic in later and more recent statutes, namely, Food, Drugs and Related Products (Registration, Etc) ACT 1993, Cap F

33, Laws of the Federation of Nigeria, 2004 and National Agency for Food and Drug Administration and Control Act 1993, Cap N 1, Laws of the Federation of Nigeria, 2004.

49. S. 12 of the Counterfeit and Fake Drugs and Unwholesome Processed Foods (Miscellaneous Provisions) Act 1999, Cap C 34, Laws of the Federation of Nigeria 2004, defined 'drug or drug product' to include a cosmetic product containing an active medicinal ingredient.
50. See *R v Bateman* (1925) 19 Cr. App. R. 8.
51. Criminal Code Act, Cap C 38, Laws of the Federation of Nigeria 2004.
52. For similar provisions under the Penal Code applicable in the Northern part of Nigeria, see, S. 196 on rash or negligent conduct causing danger to person or property and s. 253 on causing hurt by act endangering life or personal safety of others, Penal Code (Northern States) Federal Provisions Act, Cap. P 3, Vol. 13. LFN 2004.
53. Ekanem (4) p. 34.
54. Monye F., Law of Consumer Protection, Vol. 2, Ibadan, Kraft Books Limited, 2021 p. 228.
55. Monye, p. 231-232.
56. The situation might be different with products and services of big wholesalers, marketers, distributors and national or multi-national corporations; or where questions of warranties and or privity of contracts are involved and where end users or buyers do not even have or know how, to whom or where to lodge a complaint. For a detailed discussion of these and related issues; Monye F. (54) p. 227-262.
57. Section 146 (1) FCCP Act, 2018.
58. Sections 148, 150 and 154 of the FCCP Act 2018.
59. This is legally recognized under s. 151 of the FCCP Act 2018 which gives the Commission power to accredit, collaborate with, facilitate or support certain activities of consumer protection or civil society groups.
60. For example, see, Medical and Dental Practitioners Act, Cap M 8, vol. 8, Laws of the Federation of Nigeria, 2004, Sectios 15, 16 (1) & 16 (2).
61. *Nigerian Bottling Co Ltd v Ngonadi* [1985] 5 SC 313; also reported in [1985] 1 Nigerian Weekly Law Reports (Pt. 4) 739, at p. 753.
62. Malemi EO. Law of Tort, Lagos, Princeton Publishing Co, 2013, p. 346-347.
63. Monye F. (54) p. 1-2.
64. Monye F. (54) p. 8.
65. On this point, see the detailed discussion of Monye (54) p.13-15.
66. Monye F. (54) p. 15; Malemi E. (62) p. 346-347; Babatunde A Sodipo (Ajumogobia & Okeke-NIGERIA), in Product Liability 2019, eds, Gregory L Fowler and Simon Castley, U.K., Law Business Research, 2019, p. 83, Available at <http://www.ajumogobiaokeke.com/wp-content/uploads/2019/08/edition-767-chapter-18-190809130237968-product-liability-2019-nigeria.pdf> accessed 28 February 2022.
67. *Donoghue v Stevenson* (1932) AC 562.
68. At p. 599.
69. Malemi E. (62) p.347.
70. [2008] 5 NWLR (Pt. 1079) 172 SC.

71. See the discussion by Monye F. (54) pp 16-18 of the decisions of Nigerian courts in *Boardman v Guinness (Nig) Ltd [1980] 1 PLR, Okonkwo v Guniness (Nig.) Ltd [1980] 1 PLR 583, Ebelamu v Guinness (Nig.) Ltd*, FCA/LII01/82 (Delivered on 24th January 1993). However, see the case of *Okwejiminor v Gbekeji and Nigerian Bottling Co Ltd* [2008] 5 NWLR (Pt. 1079) 172 SC which reached a different conclusion where the defendant company was held liable for the consequent harm caused to the plaintiff when he consumed their beverage sealed in such a way as to exclude interference with or examination by an intermediate handler.
72. Malemi E. (62) p. 348; Monye F. (54) p.17-18.
73. For example, see, *Nsima v Nigerian Bottling Co Plc* (2014) LPELR 22542 (CA); *Okonkwo v Guinness (Nig.) Ltd* (1980) 1 PLR 58.
74. Babatunde A Sodipo (Ajumogobia & Okeke-NIGERIA), in Product Liability 2019, eds, Gregory L Fowler and Simon Castley, U.K., Law Business Research, 2019, p. 80, Available at <http://www.ajumogobiaokeke.com/wp-content/uploads/2019/08/edition-767-chapter-18-190809130237968-product-liability-2019-nigeria.pdf> accessed 28 February 2022.
75. *Crawford v Duncan* 61 Cal. App 647. (Cal. Ct App, 1923).
76. *Minich v Balzinger* (1942) 28 Cal. App 103.
77. *Bailey v Hammond* (1924) 74 Colo 390.
78. Stephanie Gardner, "Liposuction: What You Should Know", <https://www.webmd.com/beauty/cosmetic-procedure-liposuction> accessed 28 February 2022; Rosemary Bassey, "Nigerian Women And The Rush For Cosmetic Surgery" <https://dailytrust.com/nigerian-women-and-the-rush-for-cosmetic-surgery> accessed 28 February 2022; Njideka Agbo, "The Rise Of Cosmetic Surgery in Nigeria" <https://guardian.ng/life/the-rise-of-cosmetic-surgery-in-nigeria/> accessed 27 February 2022; Njideka Agbo, "Cosmetic Surgery: The Idea of Perfection?" <https://guardian.ng/life/cosmetic-surgery-the-idea-of-perfection/> accessed 27 February 2022.
79. Abuja Plastics, "Tummy Tuck in Nigeria" <https://www.abujaplastics.com/procedures/tummy-tuck/> accessed 26 February 2022; Samson Toromade, "Senate moves to regulate distribution, marketing of bleaching cream" <https://www.pulse.ng/business/senate-moves-to-regulate-bleaching-cream-cosmetics/g0pmvqw> accessed 27 February 2022; Balogun Harold, "Beauty Regulation: Hydroquinone Use in Nigeria" <https://balogunharold.com/beauty-regulation-hydroquinone-use-in-nigeria/> accessed 27 February 2022; Nike Adebowale, "Silent dangers in methods of bleaching Nigerians adopt" <https://www.premiumtimesng.com/health/health-features/333150-silent-dangers-in-methods-of-bleaching-nigerians-adopt.html> accessed 27 February 2022.
80. Chioma Obinna & Yinka Latona, "Cosmetic surgery: Death by Choice?" <https://www.vanguardngr.com/2019/09/cosmetic-surgery-death-by-choice/> accessed 27 February 2022.
81. For a critical and detailed examination of the nature of patient consent to medical treatment and a supreme court of Nigeria decision on the subject, see, Yusuff AO. The

Significance of the Supreme Court of Nigeria's Decision on Patient Consent to Medical Treatment in *Dr. Rom Okekearu v. Danjuma Tanko.* The Appellate Rev. September 2009;1(1):53-65.

82. For a comprehensive, critical and multi-dimensional exposition on negligence of medical practitioners in Nigeria, see, Odunsi S. B., "Glancing back at Eden: A Note on Medical Negligence in Nigeria", a Public Lecture delivered at the Ogun State Bar and Bench Forum 10th Public Lecture, on 17th October, 2019, at Ogun State Judiciary Complex, Abeokuta, Ogun State.

CHAPTER TWENTY-SIX

The cosmetics market and its marketing strategies

Kanayo P. Osemene and
Maduabuchi R. Ihekoronye

Cosmetics form an important part of the global beauty industry. They include a wide range of products such as colour cosmetics (make-up), hair care, skin care, fragrances, and health supplements (1). In year 2020 the global cosmetics market was estimated at US $ 277.67 billion which translates to over 1.2 trillion Nigerian naira (2). As with other markets, the COVID-19 pandemic has had a significant impact on the cosmetics market resulting in a lower growth of minus10.57% in 2020, compared to the year-on-year growth rates in the preceding 2017-2019 (2). A recent report by ***TABS Analytics***, (a US-based technology-enabled analytics firm that services the CPG [Consumer Packaged Goods] industry) found that millennial women, that is, those aged roughly between 18 and 34 years in the early 2020s, were the highest consumers of beauty products (3). Global projections expect the cosmetics market to grow from $287.94 billion in 2021 to $415.29 billion in 2028 at a Composite Annual Growth Rate (CAGR) of five per cent. While women will continue to consume cosmetics more than men in the foreseeable future, online sales are projected to make up 48% of all beauty sales by 2023 (3). According to the ***Fortune Business Insights Forecast 2021-2028***, the distribution of cosmetics happens via a complex set of channels including online sales, hypermarkets/supermarkets, pharmacies, personal sales, beauty salons, specialty stores, direct sales firms etc. (2). Cosmetics producers often employ a blend of several of these distribution channels to reach their consumers. While prices of beauty products are not usually subject to government regulations, product contents and labelling are closely regulated by the food and drug regulatory authorities in various jurisdictions.

It is to be noted that the cosmetics market has features consistent with the paradigm of monopolistic competition (3). This is due to the fact that there are many producers and consumers with no single player really able to exert a sustainable control over market prices. While many producers compete for the attention of consumers, the products they sell are not perfect substitutes for each other but are usually differentiated either by way of functional attributes, marketing/distribution patterns or their targeted buyers. Since cosmetics producers know that consumers are aware of the fact that non-price differences exist between competing cosmetic products, each producer can independently make decisions regarding its own product prices without the fear of provoking a conscious rivalry or some other reciprocal actions by competitors. The cosmetics market is so dynamic that no supplier or consumer can boast of having complete information on the demand and supply situations at any point in time. There are little or no barriers to market entry hence no supplier can make and sustain super-normal profits for a long time. Any highly profitable group of items quickly attracts new suppliers into the market space thereby forcing prices down. As more suppliers compete for the market space, the market soon gets saturated affording only marginal profits which drive fringe players out of the market. There is, therefore, the need for cosmetics producers to pay a close attention to innovative technologies and techniques so as to minimize the cost of production while at the same time ensuring high quality products. This is important because evidence shows that unlike other categories of consumer-packaged goods (CPGs) where loyalty rates are often over 50 percent, average loyalty rates for cosmetics consumers is only about 42 percent (3). This implies a relatively high tendency for customers to switch to other competitors. For this reason, organisational performance requires substantial investments in advertisements and publicity both of which add up to high selling costs. For selling costs not to significantly impact profitability, there is a need for an effective marketing strategy in the cosmetics ecosystem.

Marketing strategies for cosmetics

Strategies describe the set of choices that the cosmetics suppliers make concerning which customers they want to serve, which of the customers' needs (or wants) they want to meet, how they are to meet these needs better than their competitors and how to do so on a long-term basis (4). Strategy formulation here entails a choice between two sets of options namely: option 1 - product differentiation or low-cost strategy; and option 2 - mass-marketing or focused strategy. Differentiation aims to find a unique position in the cosmetics market driven by innovative designs, image, quality, better trained and equipped workforce, superior technologies among others. The goal of the differentiation strategy is to deliver better performance, higher quality and an exceptional appeal for a particular cosmetics brand. The cosmetics supplier who chooses to differentiate will also target a unique (usually high-end) set of customers and will do well to charge a premium for doing this. To win a sufficient number and quality of loyal customers that will sustain a differentiated strategy, emphasis must be placed on advertising and sales promotion both of which will highlight the unique value proposition of the cosmetics product. In other words, customers will buy the product not necessarily because they will pay the lowest price but because they are convinced that they will get the highest value for their money (5). On the other hand, the supplier who chooses a low-cost strategy will focus on improving operational efficiencies all along the value chain. The goal will be to achieve cost leadership by operating at an overall cost below those of competitors (6). This can be accomplished by several initiatives that include sourcing cheaper input materials, cutting down on the number of middlemen and the size of the sales forces, adopting smarter digital technologies to reduce production and sales costs, eliminating wastes, targeting only those customers who are profitable to the organisation etc. Though the profit margin per cosmetics item may be lower than those of the differentiated strategy, the higher volume of customers, including those won from competitors, will ensure that the brand remains profitable while the market shares are higher (7).

In addition to differentiation and cost-based strategies, cosmetics suppliers may adopt an approach that targets either a broad market (sometimes global) or a narrow (focused) and well-defined niche (6). Mass marketing seeks to generate demand for the cosmetics from anyone anywhere who can use the product. Little attention is paid to how these demands can be fulfilled. Marketing experts contend that generating demands without adequate plans for supply fulfilment usually leads to customer dissatisfaction which may eventually trigger a conflict between the marketing and the sales teams (7). Meanwhile, the focus strategy identifies those market segments currently underserved, neglected and under-exploited by competition and develops products and services that speak to the unique attributes of such market segments [8, 9]. Nevertheless, the identity, size, location, purchasing power, motivations and behaviour of the customers will drive all the other elements of the marketing strategy (5).

Given the keen competition in the cosmetics market, detailed marketing research and market analytics must precede any marketing strategy formulation (9). In the cosmetics industry, proper market segmenting can reveal certain relevant niches which may be targeted by marketing efforts. Niches may be associated with any or some of the following:

- geographic characteristics such as specific locations and regions;
- demographic features such as socioeconomic indices of different customer populations;
- firmographic variables describing relevant organisational characteristics such as location, industry, size, and structure, among other features that may be relevant in business-to-business franchise marketing decisions;
- behavioural attributes such as customer backgrounds, habits and emotions which affect their purchasing behaviour including impulses, repeat purchases,

and obsessions (These can be targeted by the messaging and timing of marketing communication); or

- psychographic features such as different customer personality types, lifestyles, social status, interests, and attitudes (10).

Once the business strategy has been decided, the marketing strategy has the responsibility of communicating this in every detail to all the firms' operations. To achieve a high degree of success, marketing efforts must utilize big data to address certain fundamentals that include:

Customer specification: Customers differ according to their wants, needs, motivations and buying behaviours. While almost everybody on earth uses one form of cosmetics or another, suppliers of cosmetics must first identify and characterize who will actually buy their products.

Changing customer preferences: Customers do not only differ one from another, but each individual customer is also constantly in a process of change. In this era of easy access to information, customer preferences are constantly being shaped by the availability of new information from competing products and services (11).

Market segmentation: No cosmetics supplier can achieve superior economic performance in all segments of the cosmetics market at the same time (12). The marketing strategy must be clear on whether the supplier wishes to achieve superior competitive positioning in fragrances, hair care, skin care, colour cosmetics, or whether he wishes to focus on the organic products market.

Unpredictable moves by competitors: Though suppliers of cosmetics operate in an imperfectly competitive market, every move by each supplier will provoke some reaction from competitors which must be anticipated by the marketing strategy (13).

Resource constraints: The marketing strategy must be designed to operate within the confines of limited organisational resources including human, material and financial resources. The value proposition of the strategy must be such that the marketing/sales costs must not only be justified by attendant revenues but also be within the scope of available organisational resources.

Building blocks for the formulation of marketing strategies for cosmetics business

Certain time-tested building blocks are critical to the formulation of an effective marketing strategy for any cosmetics business (14).

Vision and Mission

The foundation of every marketing strategy must be built on the vision and mission of the organisation. These will determine the specific objectives the organisation intends to accomplish in the cosmetics market. A cosmetics supplier must first set out to solve social problems. In the current globalized market, the vision must be global in perspective, addressing such basic needs of humanity as happiness, self-esteem and good health. A new entrant into the market must target those markets with the highest potentials for growth. In other words, the strategy should be to go where the market is going, not where the market is. The strategy should, for example, aim to establish a strong presence in markets such as China, India, and Africa.

People

Marketing experts believe that marketing strategy should be people-centric, with consideration for those within the organisation (employees), those outside (customers), as well as those relatively unconnected with the organisation (humanity) (15). All these people-groups should be perceived as customers. There is a need for the strategy to draw from customer hindsight, insight, and foresight (16). Customer hindsight tells us what worked with customers in the past and what did not work. This guides the organisation to avoid repeating the mistakes of the past or committing scarce resources to "re-inventing the wheel". Customer insight reveals what currently drives customer preferences because what worked well yesterday may not work so well today. Insight helps the organisation to form an amalgam with the culture and become a corporate citizen. For instance, the marketing strategy of any cosmetics supplier in the 21st century must be in sync with the ideals of gender equality, environmental sustainability and digitalisation. On the other hand, customer foresight enables the organisation to predict where the market is going in the foreseeable future. It also helps the supplier to identify the triggers and signals of change and so take up a strategic position in the unfolding market scenario.

The same attributes of hindsight, insight and foresight are applicable to competitor analysis in terms of what competitors did, what they are doing, and what they will likely do next. Some scholars equally emphasize peripheral vision. This is the vision that addresses an analysis of developments in the wider market outside the cosmetics ecosystem which may impact the business. Though global evidence shows that the average life span of most cosmetics manufacturers range between 10 and 20 years, organisations that survive for longer durations have been shown to demonstrate significant hindsight, insight, foresight and peripheral vision. In the cosmetics market, Unilever, L'Oreal of France established some 112years ago, Shiseido of Japan established some 150years ago, as well as Procter and Gamble are good examples here.

Organising for marketing

Building an organisational structure to drive the marketing effort is key to achieving organisational success. Learning from recent trends in the healthcare ecosystem, the Head of Marketing in the cosmetics business requires 'high-tech' and 'high-touch' competences (17, 18). High-tech capabilities describe the technical know-how in relation to nature, scope, drivers, competitors and other elements of cosmetics and the cosmetics market. High-touch competences refer to relationship-marketing capabilities which enable the marketer to connect with different stakeholders beyond shareholders; as well as build trust and commitment from the other units in the organisation (such as finance, logistics, human resources) all the way up to the Chief Executive Officer (CEO). The marketing strategy works better if the CEO is a marketer, and even best if the entire organisation adopts a marketing orientation (19). Building a solid structure for marketing cosmetics requires establishing an alliance for seamless continuity between marketing (demand generation) and sales (supply fulfilment).

Approaches to the formulation of a marketing strategy for a cosmetics business

A number of approaches can be adopted in formulating a marketing strategy for cosmetics marketing. The preferred approach must acknowledge fundamental shifts that have occurred in the market space over time. For example, in the 1950s and 1960s, competitive advantage depended mainly on ability to offer superior products. In the 1970s and 1980s, marketing strategies focused mainly on superior customer satisfaction. Between 1990 and 2010, superior branding was enough to confer competitive edge. By 2015, organisations that delivered superior value to customers became market leaders (15). However, at present (2022), digital technologies have empowered co-creation and crowd-sourcing innovations thus co-opting cosmetics consumers into the backend research & development (R&D) processes. For an instance, it is easy nowadays to ask end users what features they would like to see in their hair care products which are not available in the products they are currently using and to incorporate this intelligence into new product development.

The strategic positioning approach

This approach is built on developing the best fit between the internal capabilities of the cosmetics supplier and the developments in the external environment of the business (19, 20). A popular tool employed to achieve this is the analysis of SWOT, an acronym for strengths, weaknesses, opportunities, and threats. Originally proposed by Albert Humphrey of the Stanford Research Institute International (SRI International) of

California, USA, in the 1960s and 1970s, SWOT analysis has emerged as a popular approach to strategic planning across many industries. It facilitates a realistic, fact-based, data-driven approach to strategic planning in line with real-life contexts of performance, risks, competition, and potentials of a product, service, business, an industry or an entity. Strengths and weaknesses relate to the internal environment of the organisation while the opportunities and threats relate to the attributes of the external environment of the business organisation (20).

Strength factors of an organisation include:

- The characteristics of the cosmetics supplier or its team that confers competitive advantage in the marketplace.
- The internal features of the organisation that are beneficial – these include tangible and intangible assets.

Some examples of the strengths of the organisation which include brand equity, access to raw materials, superior technologies, competent workforce, R & D capabilities etc.

Weaknesses of an organisation include:

- Attributes of the business organisation itself or its team which places it at a disadvantage relative to competition.
- Attributes of the organisation that reduces the focus on and that slows down progress towards set objectives.
- Organisational assets that fall short of expected quality standards.
- Liabilities that may be intangible or tangible but which are internal to the organisation.

Some examples of weaknesses of the organisation include obsolete technologies, high staff attrition, and poor access to capital.

Opportunities for any organisation will comprise attributes such as:

- Factors in the environment that facilitate successful planning and implementation of marketing campaigns and that also enhance the capacity of the organisation to achieve sales targets.
- Developments in the marketplace that promote the organisation's odds of making additional financial gains from existing services and products.

- ❖ Sudden catastrophic events that happen to key competitors which limit their capacity to fulfil customer expectations. This increases the tendency of customers to switch.
- ❖ Novel government policies that the organisation can exploit to its own advantage.
- ❖ Availability of new techniques and technologies that can be adopted to enhance efficiency and productivity.
- ❖ Policy developments in the industry that present new opportunities for organisations to increase their market share. Examples of these developments include a sudden regulatory recall of major competing brands, the development of new technologies or techniques that significantly reduce production costs etc.

Threats to the organisation will come from factors such as:

- ❖ Uncontrollable variables in the external environment which threaten the core goals of the organisation.
- ❖ Negative market trends that complicate current weaknesses of the organisation.
- ❖ Novel market trends that can wipe out the bottom line of the organisation's core business. Examples of these trends include the impact of COVID-19 pandemic on supply chains; new government policies that limit access to key production inputs etc.

It must be noted that there are other frameworks related to SWOT that may be used to formulate a marketing strategy. Examples include PEST (political, economic, social, and technological), PESTEL (political, economic, social, technological, environmental, and legal) analysis (20). Whether the cosmetics supplier adopts SWOT, PEST, or PESTEL framework, the resultant marketing strategy must specify, among other factors, what market segments, which products, which customer groups, which geographical location, what distribution channels etc. should be targeted by the marketing effort. Beyond the traditional approaches to strategic marketing, emerging consensus seems to favour the adoption of an integrated approach. This approach draws internal capabilities from the resource-based view (RBV) and external possibilities from the market-based view (MBV).

The competitive marketing approach

This approach draws heavily from Porter's five forces framework which is premised on the fact that the cosmetics supplier will tend to maximize opportunities and minimize the impact of threats in the external environment of the business. Hence organisational success depends to a large extent on the supplier's understanding of market structures and the extent to which its marketing strategy is aligned to these structures especially as regards changing policy and macroeconomic environments (21). First proposed in 1979 by Michael Porter in a ***Harvard Business Review*** article titled "How Competitive Forces Shape Strategy", this framework is built on the possibility of threats from new entrants, threats of substitutes, the bargaining power of customers, the bargaining power of suppliers and general competitive rivalry (22).

New entrants and substitute products are described as horizontal competitive forces. They represent threats that come from outside the present set of actors within the industry. Their entrance increases the competitive 'entropy' which is defined as a gradual decline into disorder or a lack of order or predictability. This eventually results in alignments and realignments of market forces. For example, the ascendancy of organic skin and hair care products, with claims of superior long-term safety profiles both to the human body and the environment, continues to present significant threats to existing synthetic brands (23). Another example is the evolving market of "nutricosmetics". These combine nutritional supplements with cosmetics thus providing micronutrients needed for healthy skin and hair while delaying the aging process. Moreover, the so-called "green cosmetics "utilize only organic inputs for beauty products and are perceived to resonate with the current global emphasis on ecology and sustainability. In terms of disruptive technological innovations in supply chains, the projection that online sales channels will contribute 48% of all beauty sales by 2023 means that new suppliers with superior online distribution capabilities may exploit the low barriers to market entry in online sales to disrupt current competitive balance in various markets (24).

The bargaining power of suppliers and customers are described as vertical competitive forces. They impact the value chain that flows from suppliers to their customers. At the interface of business transactions, suppliers often want to charge higher prices for fewer goods while customers want to be supplied with more goods at lower prices. The ultimate balance will tilt towards the relative strengths of the two parties. Marketing strategists must, therefore, identify the unique strengths of their value propositions and leverage them to exploit existing opportunities for competitive advantage.

In the cosmetics market, the competing products are not perfect substitutes for one another. The unique attributes (benefits) of a particular item therefore offer strategists the lever for competitive positioning at the bargaining table. However, for customers, there is a low cost of switching in the cosmetics market and this offers them a strong bargaining power. Ongoing marketing research in each organisation therefore remains important because what constitutes strength today may turn out to be weakness tomorrow. For this reason, the strategy must remain flexible enough to adapt to these vagaries if the cosmetic offering is to remain attractive and profitable (25).

Competitive rivalry refers to the jockeying for positions among the current competitors. It must be emphasized that individual suppliers find it difficult to remain as market leaders among co-competitors for a long time in the cosmetics industry. The marketing strategy must anticipate all possible market scenarios and make provisions to maximize, where applicable, the forces of first mover advantage, economies of scale, superior logistics management systems, R & D capabilities, online presence etc.

In adopting Porter's five forces framework for strategy formulation, it may not be out of place to suggest that only market segments (such as cosmetics) and not the entire industry (such as the beauty market) should be analysed. It should also be noted that the beauty industry encompasses beauty appliances, services and cosmetics.

Marketing mix modelling

Marketing mix variables are tools in the hands of marketing experts for the formulation and implementation of the marketing strategy (26). The variables are traditionally presented as a set of letter Ps which has grown from four (product, price, place, and promotion), to about nine and still counting (27). These Ps include:

Product: what cosmetics category - skin and skincare, makeup and colour, hair care, deodorants and fragrances - should be provided and for what market segment? Should it be for men, women, unisex, European, American, African or Asian segment?

Price: what pricing strategy – low-cost, premium, discount regimes - should be adopted? A recent study in the Sultanate of Oman (a country in the Middle East) found that price was the most impactful variable for competitive advantage (28).

Place (of Distribution): should it be a storefront; hypermarkets/supermarkets, specialty stores, pharmacies; or by direct shipping, online?

Promotion: what mix of advert channels should be used – rating companies, celebrity endorsements, search engine optimization, social media marketing, and influencer networks, among others? What good causes should the brand support? How can the supplier ensure that customer communication is credible, consistent, clear and competitive?

Positioning: will the strategy target low-cost or differentiated approach; market leadership, market share, or a unique niche? (28).

Packaging: what brand image is best for the cosmetics line? What of the brand image of the persons behind the product? What colour code, product logo, and website design etc. should be adopted?

Performance: how will the entire value chain of the cosmetics line deliver superior economic profitability on a sustainable basis? How can the supplier identify the best practices in each operation along the value chain, and subsequently attain and perhaps even improve on these best practices so as to achieve specific financial and nonfinancial outcome measures? (29).

Processes: will the organisational goals be better served by direct delivery to consumers, online sales, warehousing or using salesmen? Should the organisation adopt customization or mass-marketing? Note that properly planned processes make it possible for platforms to deliver profitable performance.

People: what quantity, quality, training, empowerment and motivation of the workforce will be needed to deliver on the marketing goals? What customer service and relationship marketing practices will deliver superior value to customers?

Note that in practice, marketing-mix modelling develops a mathematical relationship between the various variables on the one hand and their impact on market share as the primary outcome measure on the other hand. The model deploys specialized algorithms to determine what the outcome of a change in any one marketing mix variable will be on the market share (30).

Product life cycle approach

The concept of product life cycle (PLC) describes the stages every product (including cosmetics) goes through from cradle to graveyard that is from development and entry into the market to the time it leaves the marketplace (31). Originally postulated by Professor Raymond Vernon of Harvard University in 1966, PLC typically comprises four distinct stages namely: introduction, growth, maturity and decline (Figure 26.1). Each stage presents unique opportunities and challenges to marketers in terms of crafting and implementing an appropriate marketing strategy. By its very nature, strategy takes a long-term view, up to five years and beyond. This time frame is usually enough for most cosmetic products to navigate more than one phase in their life cycles.

Effective marketing strategies for cosmetics are therefore designed to sustain demand for the products indefinitely. This requires on-going attention to product performance and changing customer preferences. Although product performance will be judged based on the accurate calibration of the present position of the item on its product life cycle, it is a correct understanding and interpretation of changing customer preferences that will determine what marketing actions the supplier must implement to sustain demand for the product beyond the present. An accurate estimation of the potential market size for a cosmetics product must inform the applicable marketing strategy meant to attain the maximum possible market share. The difference in the performances between one cosmetics product and another usually depends on the extent to which their supplier organisations are able to strike a match between the state of the product on the PLC and the marketing strategies deployed. Hence, an understanding of the critical elements of the product life cycle becomes an important success factor in the cosmetics market (31).

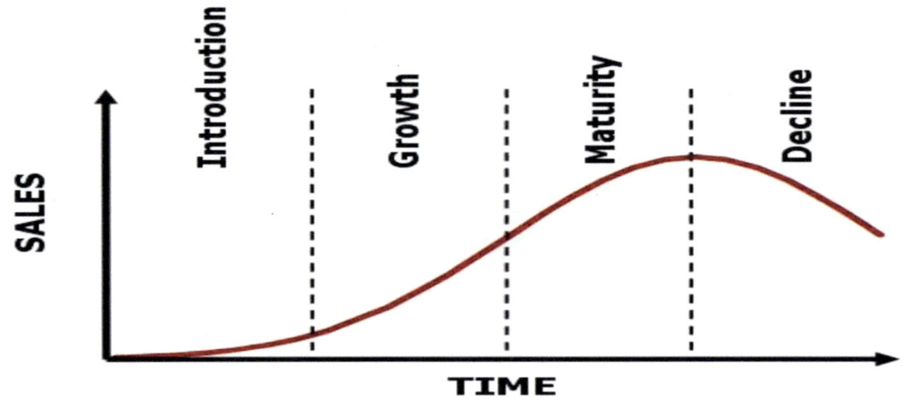

Figure 26.1: Product Life Cycle (PLC)

The Introduction Phase

Let us take for example a new perfume brand that has just come through the R & D department and that has just been introduced to the market. The brand name is new and unfamiliar. Only a few inquisitive early starters will buy mainly out of curiosity. Production and marketing costs are high compared to sales revenue thus yielding a net loss (12). Marketing challenges at this phase are to create awareness, encourage people to try the perfume and educate potential consumers on its unique attributes. For a differentiated marketing strategy, focus will be placed on exotic packaging, celebrity endorsements, high-end advertising, targeted product placement, digital marketing, all of which will be backed up by price-skimming since at this time there are only a few competitors. For a low-cost strategy, marketing focus will be to create massive awareness in the general population using a mix of advertising channels while adopting a market penetration pricing strategy to maximize unit sales, increase market shares and encourage more perfume users to switch from their traditional brands to the new product. The price can be carefully adjusted later to a cost-based approach after a sufficient market share has been attained.

The growth phase

As more consumers begin to use the perfume, the brand awareness and talk value increases along with sales and profits. The rapid revenue growth causes an upward movement in net income, thereby gradually ending start-up losses. New competitors usually begin to emerge at this stage. The marketing challenge at this point is to switch from awareness creation to brand building (4, 12). For the perfume brand that we are presently looking at, competitive pressure means there may be the need to expand market share by the introduction of lower–priced units and smaller pack sizes while retaining the brand name, logo, colour codes and other brand artefacts. For a differentiated marketing strategy, focus will be placed on sustaining the same brand image originally associated with the primary perfume brand while operational efficiency will be required for a low-cost strategy.

The maturity phase

With many competitors, stabilized production and demand levels along with well-established distribution channels, the growth in unit sales flattens out while profit margins decline (4, 5, 11). Competitors are content with incremental market shares rather than breakthrough gains while offering price discounts and promotional bargains to customers.

For a differentiated marketing strategy, the challenge is to re-invent (revitalize) the brand via brand extension. For the perfume, brand extension may include the introduction of perfume oils, body sprays, deodorants, antiperspirant sprays among others. These will require R&D re-investments in product development, product testing and new market entries, thereby reducing the operating profits from the original perfume brand. Co-branding has proven helpful at this stage. Advert messages such as "if you like ABC, you'll also like our new XYZ", or "new improved" are all too familiar slogans at this stage as consumers will likely associate the new with the old. However, most low-cost strategies will intensify sales promotion and optimal demand fulfilment via supply chain operational efficiencies.

The decline phase

Cutting edge technologies and techniques used in producing cosmetics of today will eventually grow obsolete. Customer preferences change rapidly and new products are always on the way to the market. No cosmetic product sits on top of the chain forever. As the demand for the cosmetics declines year after year, marketing challenge will shift to introducing the product in new markets where the brands will have a chance to trigger new product life cycles. Many organisations fail to realize the point in time when their flagship products attain the critical decline phase. They continue to invest marketing assets on the products when in fact they should be negotiating a franchise in a different market while the decline is not yet obvious to untrained eyes (20). Depending on the level of penetration in the original markets, it is often necessary to maintain supplies to a certain baseline customer population who will remain loyal to the brand despite the prevailing market trends. However, investing additional organisational assets within the same markets have proven not to achieve commensurate returns, hence the need to explore other new markets.

The Boston Consulting Group (BCG) Matrix approach

Most cosmetics suppliers do not offer just one item, such as a hair cream, to the market. They would rather provide one or more groups (portfolio) of cosmetics. For an instance, L'Oreal Paris offers a variety of product portfolios to the African market, including skin care (moisturizers, masks, cleansers); make-up (that includes L'Oreal Paris Face, L'Oreal Paris Lips and L'Oreal Paris Eye Treatment); hair care (L'Oreal Paris Elvive Dream Lengths Long Hair Regime Set, L'Oreal Paris Elivive Dream Lengths 8, L'Oreal Paris Extraordinary Oil, among others); and L'Oreal Paris Men (hair colour, anti-perspirants, among others) (32). Across different product portfolios and within any given portfolio, the different cosmetic items exist at different phases in their product life cycles. While the baseline marketing communication of L'Oreal Paris "because *I'm worth it*" speaks to the consumer's sense of self- esteem, adopting a one-size-fits-all marketing strategy for all the cosmetic ranges can be a sure recipe for organisational failure.

The Growth Share Matrix (Figure 26.2) - popularly known as BCG matrix was originally proposed in 1970 by Bruce D. Henderson (1915-1992), founder of the Boston Consulting Group (BCG), as a strategic framework for portfolio management with the aim of ensuring competitiveness and generating optimal returns on investment (14, 20). The 2 x 2 matrix has four quadrants describing products at various levels of profitability. These quadrants are code-named 'question marks', 'stars', 'cash cows' and 'pets' (33). Note that 'pets' is often represented as 'dogs'

"Question marks" represent products with low market share but in high growth markets. The company has to decide either to invest in the product or discard it altogether depending on the chances of it becoming a star.

"Stars" represent products with high market shares and in high growth markets. The company should invest heavily here as the products have high potentials.

"Cash cows" represent products with high market shares in low growth markets. The company should optimize the supply pipelines and milk these cash cows for maximum returns with which to re-invest.

"Dogs" represent products with low market shares in low growth markets. Investing organisational assets here will always result in losses. The company should reposition these products, divest or liquidate them to minimize losses.

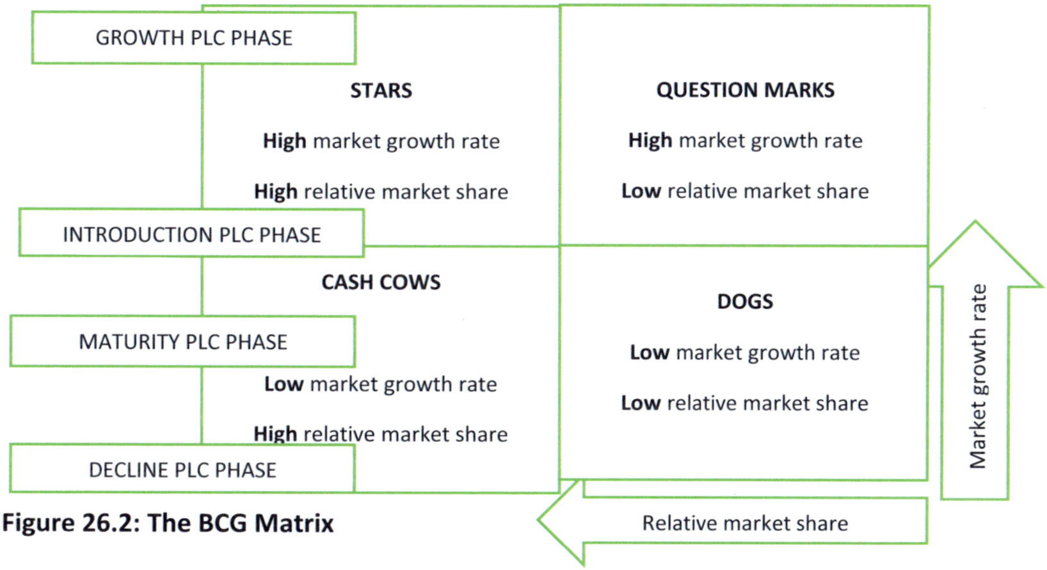

Figure 26.2: The BCG Matrix

As a general rule, market share is synonymous with cash generation (inflow) while market growth requires cash investment (outflow). On-going market research based on product performance and competitive mapping are required to guide suppliers of multiple cosmetics products to determine the current status of each item. By assigning different cosmetics products to one of these quadrants, business leaders determine how best to invest organisational assets to yield the best returns and where best to minimize losses. The BCG matrix is all about company competitiveness (market share) and market attractiveness (market growth). The market leader achieves sustainable superior returns on investments which in turn generates a self-re-enforcing cost advantage relative to competition. The value of any cosmetics product depends on how much market share the company is able to achieve before growth slows down. This is because every product will eventually attain a cash cow or a dog status.

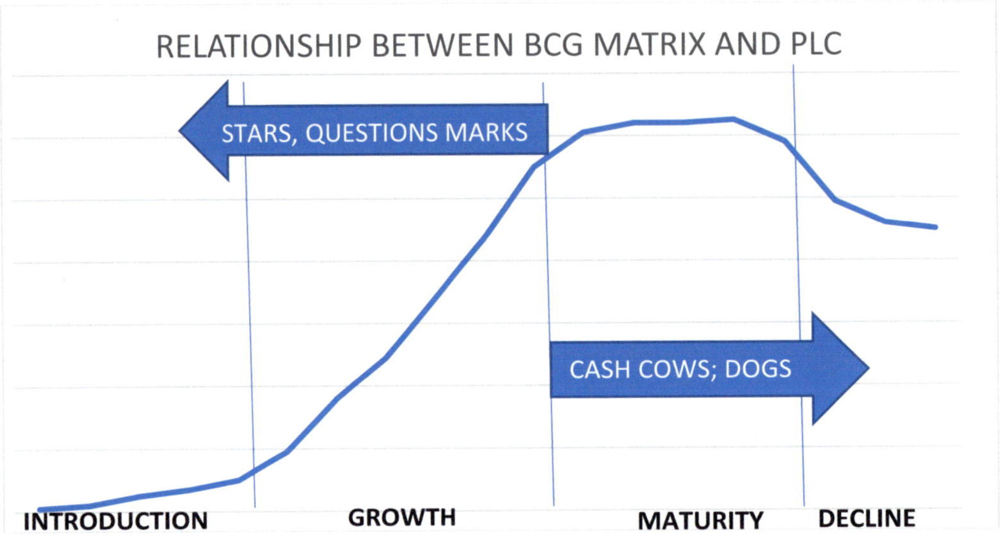

Figure 26.3: Portfolio Management Using the BCG Matrix

In formulating and implementing the marketing strategy of cosmetics, the investment of marketing assets should be tailored to their present and potential future positions on the product life cycle (Figure 26.3). Therefore, the metrics for product performance as well as monitoring and evaluation regimes should take cognizance of the product life cycle.

Marketing strategies for cosmetics in a digital economy

Digital technologies continue to drive rapid changes in virtually every area of human endeavour. Unlike traditional marketing which employs channels such as face-to-face calls, television, radio, newspapers, billboards, handbills, magazines, direct mail, and trade shows to reach potential consumers, the digital economy offers faster, direct, personalized business to consumer (B2C) interfaces that challenge several existing theoretical models of marketing (34). Several disruptive technological innovations currently promote products or services and reach consumers using internet-based channels such as websites, podcasts, emails, YouTube, LinkedIn, Twitter, WhatsApp, pop-ups, Wikipedia among others. Digital marketing extends beyond internet marketing; it includes channels that do not require the use of the internet such as mobile phones (both Short Message Service and Multimedia Messaging Service - SMS and MMS), display advertising, search engine marketing, and many other forms of digital media (35).

Digital marketing is related to, but is distinct from, "e-commerce". While digital marketing focuses on demand generation using the internet and digital channels to advertise products and services, e-commerce uses the internet (websites) for supply fulfilment -

buying and selling of products and services (36). Cosmetics are typical consumer goods, that is, finished (final) goods purchased by individuals for their personal consumption and they are amenable to both digital marketing and e-commerce (37). Depending on the preferred competitive positioning (differentiated or low-cost, wider market or niche), applicable SWOT variables, as well as item profitability and placement along the product life cycle, the digital economy offers a number of platforms for the marketing of cosmetics. These platforms include the following:

Search Engine Optimization (SEO): This is the process of achieving a higher ranking of the products of the cosmetic supplier's websites on the Search Engine Results Page (SERP) such that the search engine directs a larger quantity and quality of traffic to the supplier (38). Several on-page and off-page design strategies are available free of charge to achieve SEO for cosmetics websites.

Search Engine Marketing (SEM): A successful SEO usually prepares the ground for SEM in which the designs and contents of websites can be further developed and deployed for paid advertisement campaigns using models such as pay-per-click, cost-per-click, and cost-per-thousand impressions (34, 39). Platforms such as Google AdWords and Bing Ads are popularly employed for SEM and can significantly improve the competitive performance of cosmetics, particularly those that have attained the rank of 'stars' on the BCG matrix.

Social Media Marketing (SMM): Social media platforms such as Instagram, Facebook, LinkedIn, WhatsApp, Twitter, Pinterest, YouTube, Reddit, Snapchat, Yelp, TikTok, etc. can be used to increase traffic to a cosmetics supplier's website. Different platforms appeal to different categories of consumers and so cosmetics marketers usually exploit a combination of different social medium platforms to increase their brand visibility. Marketing strategists can also improve their brand talk value by setting the agenda and driving interactions between groups, individuals and virtual communities. The latter are the actual and potential consumers who utilize the internet to create, share, exchange ideas, photographs, and videos about the cosmetics products (40).

Email marketing: A cosmetics supplier with a focused and differentiated marketing strategy may choose to send newsletters to a specific list of registered clients via their emails. This low-cost channel delivers detailed information about the product and offers an opportunity for customer feedbacks (41).

Content marketing: High-quality content, images and professionally-created videos of the cosmetics product can be provided in a blog post where consumers can access an accurate knowledge of the product. This gives a professional image to the brand and improves customer loyalty (42).

Mobile marketing: Mobile marketing is a direct business to customer (B2C) marketing which allows the cosmetics supplier to contact and engage with customers in a relevant and interactive way using any mobile device or network (43). It usually requires informed consent and the explicit permission of customers as well as their active participation (44).

Influencer marketing: This novel marketing technique rides on the popularity of social media influencers to drive a positive public perception of the product (45). These influencers are individuals who have become famous, with a large on-line followership due to their exceptional success and expertise in specific areas of endeavour such as sports, music, politics, fashion, entertainment, technology, education etc. The flip side of influencer marketing is that one scandal about the influencer may be sufficient to turn popularity to notoriety which in turn may affect public perception of the product.

Affiliate marketing: A cosmetics supplier may hire a third-party publisher (an affiliate marketer) to promote the cosmetics through their website by providing product data files, text links, or banners. Whenever a visitor to the affiliate marketer's website clicks on the link (click), contacts the cosmetics supplier (leads), or makes a purchase (sale) of the recommended item, the affiliate marketer receives a commission from the organisation (46). Crafting a win-win arrangement between the affiliate and the cosmetics supplier is critical to the success of this marketing technique.

In summary, for long-term performance of cosmetics portfolios, it is strongly recommended that a contextually relevant mix of traditional and digital marketing techniques be employed (47). This mix must be dynamic enough to respond to the changing competitive environments and market vagaries along the entire life cycle of the product.

Marketing strategies for cosmetics in the sharing economy

According to a market research firm, the ***Euromonitor***, the sharing economy holds important possibilities for cosmetics suppliers to reach new streams of customers via curated, flexible retail and distribution channels (48). Powered by innovative digital technologies, on-demand Apps can be deployed to link relatively new market entrants to consumers. Such emerging brands can accelerate their market entry by associating their relatively unknown brand with a professional endorsement or influencer marketing (45, 49). In Nigeria's $1.2b cosmetics market, for example, several beauty service providers within local neighbourhoods in city centres are increasingly deploying on-demand Apps to connect with patrons to offer curated and personalised make-up services. This model has proven to be a win-win proposition for both consumers and suppliers. Many cosmetics consumers find no need to spend huge sums on subscriptions and exotic make-up kits; they would rather call up service providers within minutes. For suppliers, emerging cosmetics brands easily find their ways into the market by connecting with the burgeoning army of beauty service providers. It must be noted that while the shared economy facilitates market entry for emerging brands, experts remain divided on the scalability of this model to facilitate the achievement of sustainable performance and profitable portfolio performance down the product life cycle (49).

The shared economy also provides a new marketplace for peer-to-peer transactions for consumers to exchange unwanted and unused items from their subscription boxes. Such peer-to-peer transactions are becoming commonplace within virtual communities of cosmetics users.

Another variant of the sharing economy is the shareable beauty booths (also called shareable make-up booths) which emerged in China (50) a few years ago but which have now spread to some cities in the world including the USA. Each booth is the size of a walk-in closet which contains an assortment of cosmetics products, make-up tools and styling appliances. Located in convenient spots within shopping malls, airports, railway stations, and similar places, consumers can access these unmanned booths by scanning a QR code and paying specified fees for various time durations. Some cosmetics items in the booth, including new and relatively unknown brands, can be displayed and purchased by consumers by scanning the QR codes. These booths are increasingly becoming attractive to busy executives who want to look fresh on the go. However, in the wake of COVID-19, important health concerns have been raised regarding the potentials for disease transmission through the sharing of personal make-up items (50). These concerns remain unresolved.

Recent developments in the African cosmetics market

The cosmetics market in Africa has enormous potentials for growth driven by burgeoning population and rapid urbanisation. According to ***Technavio***, a global market research and advisory firm, the Middle East and Africa (MEA) region accounted for 9.30% of the global cosmetics market size of USD 334.5 million in the year 2019 (51). The same report projects the African beauty and personal care market to accelerate by a compound annual growth rate (CAGR) of 2% or USD 1.26billion between 2022 and 2025. The structure of the current market is largely fragmented with many players occupying market shares and this trend will likely continue till 2025. However, any important consolidation between the major players will likely impact the projected growth rate. The South African cosmetics market is dominant in the continent, and is estimated to contribute 53% of the projected growth in the time under consideration (52).

The cosmetics market is wide. In fact, it represents one of the most prosperous industrial sectors in Ghana and South Africa. It is also very competitive and profitable. Customers of cosmetic products usually prefer well-packaged and attractive products that are of high quality. Most manufacturers of cosmetics and personal care products engage in wholesale and retail activities. Ghana for instance, is the largest exporter of Shea butter in West Africa. The country is equally involved in large scale production of cosmetics ingredients such as Shea butter, Avocado oil, Castor oil, Baobab oil and Neem oil (53).

In addition to South Africa and Ghana, other leading markets include Kenya and Egypt. In all these markets, product innovation, product line extension as well as rising demands for men's personal care products are expected to drive market growth. However, the availability of counterfeit ingredients and rising awareness of adverse health effects of synthetic chemicals used in cosmetics production will present important drawbacks to market growth (54). In terms of evolutions in distribution channels, marketing experts believe that offline channels will continue to be employed more than online channels in Africa by 2025.

The current most prominent cosmetics suppliers in the African continent include Avon Products Inc., Beiersdorf AG, Coty Inc., Godrej Consumer Products Ltd., Johnson and Johnson, L'Oreal SA, Revlon Inc., The Estee Lauder Companies Inc., The Procter and Gamble Co., and Unilever Group. In the absence of any consolidations, these suppliers are expected to remain predominant by 2025. Moreover, among the various cosmetics product portfolios (skin care, hair care products, colour cosmetics and fragrances) analysts expect that skin care ranges will remain dominant especially because of increasing demand for skin brightening products a wrinkle remover mainly among female consumers in Africa (55).

Key learning points

- ❖ The cosmetics market remains a fast-growing part of the beauty industry.
- ❖ Millennial women are the highest consumers of cosmetics.
- ❖ Online sales will account for about one half of all cosmetics sales by 2023.
- ❖ Marketing strategies for cosmetics should be data-driven and should reflect customer preferences.
- ❖ Applicable marketing mix variables must be aligned with an accurate knowledge of the position of each cosmetics item on the product life cycle.
- ❖ Return on Investments (ROI) of marketing assets in cosmetics business depends on market growth rate and market share.

- Finally, both the digital and sharing economies present important opportunities for the cosmetics market.
- Africa is a largely under-exploited market for the cosmetics industry and represents the "next frontier".

References

1. Fortune Business Insights. Cosmetics market size, share, and covid-19 impact analysis. [Cited 2021 Dec 10]; Available from: https://www.fortunebusinessinsights.com/cosmetics-market-102614
2. Fortune Business Insights. Cosmetics and personal care products direct selling market size, share and global trend by type and geography forecast till 2021-2028. [Cited 2021 Dec 14]; Available from: https://www.fortunebusinessinsights.com/industry-reports/cosmetics-personal-care-products-direct-selling-market-100183
3. TABS Industry Report. TABS Analytics Second Annual U.S. Cosmetics Study. [Cited 2021 Dec 12]; Availablefrom:https://cdn2.hubspot.net/hubfs/544043/2015_Cosmetics_Campaign/2015_Cosmetics_Study/study/TABS_Analytics_Second__Annual_U.S._Cosmetics_Study.pdf?t=1516735850975
4. Palmitier RW, Crecelius, A.T. The "first principles" of marketing strategy. AMS Rev. 2019; 9:5–26.
5. Kotler P, Keller K. Marketing Management. 15th Edition. Saddle River: Prentice Hall; 2018. 117–139.
6. Holdford D. Marketing for Pharmacists: Providing and Promoting Pharmacy Services. 3rd Ed. Washington DC: American Pharmacists Association; 2015. 169–193.
7. Das S, Hassan H. Impact of sustainable supply chain management and customer relationship management on organizational performance. Int J Product Perform Manag. 2021; In Print.
8. Aghazadeh H. Strategic marketing management: achieving superior business performance through intelligent marketing strategy. Procedia Soc. Behav. Sci. 2015; 207(2015):125–34.
9. Gomez A, Loar R, Kramer A. The impact of market segmentation and social marketing on uptake of preventive programmes: the example of voluntary medical male circumcision. A literature review. Gates Open Res. 2018;2(68). 121-137
10. Anekwe R, Onudugu V, Ndubuisi O, Akaegbobi G. Differentiation Strategy and Organizational Growth of Manufacturing Firm in Ebonyi State, Nigeria. Eur J Soc Sci. 2021; 61(3):175–181
11. Kotler P, Kartajaya H, Setiawan I. Marketing: From Products to Customers to Human Spirit. John Wiley & Sons Inc; 2010. 129-145
12. Moorman C, van Heerde H, Moreau C, Palmatier R. Challenging the boundaries of marketing. J Mark. 83(5):1–4.
13. Harvard Business Essentials. Marketer's Toolkit: The 10 strategies you need to succeed. Harvard Business School Publishing Corporation; 2006. 9–19.
14. Chapman B, Sisodia R. Everybody matters: Extraordinary power of caring for your people like family. Portfolio; 2015. 112-126

15. Brown L, Brown C. The customer culture imperative. A leader's guide to driving superior performance. McGraw-Hill; 2013. 112–146.
16. McAleamey A, Sieck C, Hefner JL AA Walker DM, Rizer, MK, Moffatt-Bruce, SD, Huerta, DR. High Touch and High Tech (HT2) Proposal: Transforming Patient Engagement Throughout the Continuum of Care by Engaging Patients with Portal Technology at the Bedside. JMIR Res Protoc. 2016 Dec;5(4): e221.
17. Ihekoronye R, Osemene K, Erhun W. Relationship marketing practices in community pharmacies in Nigeria. Malays J Pharm Sci. 2020;18(2):33–45.
18. Storbacka K, Moser T. The changing role of marketing: transformed propositions, processes and partnerships. AMS Rev. 2020; 10:299–310.
19. Kotler P, Armstrong G, Harris L, Piercy N. Principles of Marketing. 7th European Edition. Essex: Pearson Education Limited; 2017. 121–139.
20. Dye R, Sibony O, Truong V. Flaws in strategic decision making: McKinsey Global Survey results. McKinsey [Internet]. 2009 [cited 2021 Dec 10]; Available from: http://www.mckinsey.com/insights/strategy
21. Mohapatra S. IT and porter's competitive forces model and strategies. In: Information Systems Theory. New York: Springer; 2012. 265–281.
22. Islami X, Mustafa N, Topuzovska L. Linking Porter's generic strategies to firm performance. Futur Bus J. 2020;6(3). 47-61
23. Dini I, Laneri S. The New Challenge of Green Cosmetics: Natural Food Ingredients for Cosmetic Formulations. Molecules. 2021 Jul;26(13):3921.
24. Larry M, Shamir L, Johnson F. The 5 competitive forces framework in a technology mediated environment. Do these forces still hold in the industry of the 21st century? [Internet]. 2014. Available from: http://essay.utwente.nl/66196/1/Johnson_BA_MB.pdf
25. Sisodia R, Wolfe D, Sheth J. Firms of endearment: How world-class companies profit from passion and purpose. 2nd ed. Wharton School Publishing; 2007. 77- 93
26. Londhe B. Marketing mix for next generation marketing. Procedia Econ Finance. 2014;11(2014):335–340.
27. Al Badi K. The Impact of Marketing Mix on the Competitive Advantage of the SME Sector in the Al Buraimi Governorate in Oman. Bus Manag. 2018;8(3):19–41.
28. Foss N, Saebi T. Fifteen years of research on business model innovation: How far have we come, and where should we go? J Manag. 2017;43(1):200–227.
29. Antalo C, Priem R. Value creation through stakeholder synergy. Strateg Manag J. 2016;37(2):314–329.
30. Grewal D, Hulland J, Kopalle P, Karahanna E. The future of technology and marketing: A multidisciplinary perspective. J Acad Mark Sci. 2020;48(1):1–8.
31. Levitt T. EXPLOIT the Product Life Cycle. Harv Bus Rev. 1965;43(6):81–94.
32. L'Oreal Paris. Shop L'Oreal Paris bestsellers. [cited 2021 Dec 18]; Available from: https://www.caretobeauty.com/ng/loreal-paris/
33. Mohajan H. An analysis on BCG growth sharing matrix. Nobel Int J Bus Manag Res. 2018;2(1):1–6.
34. Bhayani S, Vachhani N. Internet Marketing Vs Traditional Marketing: A Comparative Analysis. FIIB Bus Rev. 2018;3(3):53–63.

35. Yasmin A, Tasneem S, Fatema K. Effectiveness of Digital Marketing in the Challenging Age: An Empirical Study. Int J Manag Sci Bus Adm. 2015;1(5):69–50.
36. Išorait M, Miniotienė N. Electronic Commerce: Theory and Practice. Integr J Bus Econ [Internet]. 2018;2(2). Available from: http://ojs.ijbe-research.com/index.php/IJBE/article/view/78
37. Grabner-Kräuter S. Consumer goods. In: The SAGE Encyclopaedia of Business Ethics and Society [Internet]. Thousand Oaks: SAGE Publications; 2018. 641–642. Available from: 10.4135/9781483381503.n236
38. Ledford J. SEO: Search Engine Optimization Bible. New Jersey: Wiley; 2008. 127–152.
39. Bala M, Verma D. A Critical Review of Digital Marketing. Int J Manag IT Eng. 2018;8(10):321–339.
40. Akram W, Kumar R. A Study on Positive and Negative Effects of Social Media on Society. Int J Comput Sci Eng. 2018; 5(10):347–360.
41. Hudak M, Kianickova E, Madlenak R. The Importance of E-mail Marketing in E-commerce. Procedia Eng. 2017; 192(2017):342–347.
42. Swieczak W. Content marketing as an important element of marketing strategy of scientific institutions. Trans Inst Aviat. 2012; 226(2012):133–150.
43. Mobile Marketing Association. The Brand Safety and Suitability Strategy Guide [Internet]. Mobile Marketing Association; 2019 [cited 2021 Dec 15]. Available from: https://www.mmaglobal.com/learning-library
44. Amirkhanpour M, Vrontis D, Thrassou A. Mobile marketing: a contemporary strategic perspective. Int J Technol Mark. 2014; 9(3):253–257.
45. Saima, Khan M. Effect of Social Media Influencer Marketing on Consumers' Purchase Intention and the Mediating Role of Credibility. J Promot Manag. 2021; 27(4):503–523.
46. Patrick Z, Hee O. Factors Influencing the Intention to Use Affiliate Marketing: A Conceptual Analysis. Int J Acad Res Bus Soc Sci. 2019; 9(2):701–710.
47. Keen P, Williams R. Value architectures for digital business: Beyond the business model. MIS Quaterly. 2013 Jun; 37(2):643–648.
48. Whitehouse L. Beauty and the sharing economy: what's the future? [Cited 2021 Dec. 28]. Available from: https://www.cosmeticsdesign-europe.com/Article/2016/10 /13/Beauty-and-the-sharing-economy-what-s-t he-future
49. Young R. How to Crack Nigeria's $1.2 Billion Beauty Market [Cited 2021 Dec 27]. Available from: https://www.businessoffashion.com/briefings/global-markets/ how-to-crack-nigerias-12-billion-beauty-market/
50. Daxue Consulting. Sharing economy meets digital innovation in China's beauty industry. [Cited 2021 Dec. 29]. Available from: https://daxueconsulting.com /beauty-booth-in-china-17beauty/.
51. Technavio Research Reports. Beauty and Personal Care Market in Africa to Grow by USD 1.26 bn | 17,000+.[Cited 2022 Mar 12]. Available from: https://www.prnewswire.com/news-releases/beauty-and-personal-care-market-in-africa-to-grow-by-usd-1-26-bn--17-000-technavio-research-reports-301405106.html

52. Africa Business Pages. The African beauty industry: Cosmetics in big demand in the African market [Cited 2022 Mar 12]. Available from: https://news.africa-business.com/post/the-african-beauty-market
53. UNIDO West African Competitiveness Program [Cited 2022 Mar 12]. Available from: https://wacompghana.org/publications/technical/#flipbook-df_324/11/1
54. Mordor Intelligence. Africa Cosmeceutical Market | 2022 - 27 | Industry Share, Size, Growth. [Cited 2022 Mar 12]. Available from: https://www.mordorintelligence.com/industry-reports/africa-cosmeceutical-market
55. The Guardian. Investing in Africa: Why beauty companies are swarming in | The Guardian Nigeria News - Nigeria and World News — Features — The Guardian Nigeria News – Nigeria and World News. [Cited 2022 Mar 12]. Available from: https://guardian.ng/features/investing-in-africa-why-beauty-companies-are-swarming-in/

List of abbreviations

Figures	
3D	3-dimentional
4-MBC	4-methyl-benzlidene Camphor
18-MEA	18-methyleicosanoic Acid
A	
AAPH	2,2-azobis-(2-amidino-propane) dihydrochloride
ABTS	2,2′-azino-bis(3-ethylbenzothiazoline-6-sulfonic acid)
ACD	Allergic Contact Dermatitis
AHAs	α-hydroxy Acids/alpha hydroxyl acids
AHTN	7-acetyl-1,1,3,4,4,6-hexamethyltetrahydronaphthalene
AKT	Serine/threonine Protein Kinase
AMPs	Antimicrobial Peptides
AON	Active Oxygen Number
APCON	Advertising Practitioners Council of Nigeria
API	Active Pharmaceutical Ingredient
ASEAN	Association of Southeast Asian Nations
ATD	Amino-Terminal Domain
ATM	Ataxia-Telangiectasia Mutated
ATP	Adenosine Triphosphate
AUC	Area Under the Curve
AUCI	Area Under the Curve Index
AVO	Avobenzone (Butyl methoxydibenzoylmethane)
Aw	Water Activity
B	
B-PE	b-phycoerythrin
BB	'Best before' date
BC	Breast Cancer
BCC	Basal Cell Carcinoma
BCG	Boston Consulting Group
BHA	Butylated hydroxyl anisole
BHAs	β-hydroxy acids/beta-hydroxy acids
BHT	Butylated hydroxytoluene

BMI	Body Mass Index
BNVISA	Brazilian National Health Surveillance Agency
BoNTs	Botulinum Neurotoxins
BPA	Bisphenol-A
BRCA1	Breast Cancer gene1
BRCA2	Breast Cancer gene2
BSTI	Baumann Skin Type Index
C	
C-S lyases	Chondroitin Sulphate Lyases
C-T Lyases	Cysteine-Thiol Lyases
CAGR	Composite Annual Growth Rate
CAS	Chemical Abstracts Services
CDK	Cyclin Dependent Kinases
CDSN	Corneodesmosin
CEO	Chief Executive Officer
CFCs	Chlorofluorocarbons
CFSAN	The Center for Food Safety and Applied Nutrition
CFU	Colony-forming Unit
cGMP	current Good Manufacturing practice
CGS	Centimetre-Gram-Second
CH8-LHA	C8-lipohydroxy acid
CIR	Cosmetic Ingredient Review
CL	Chemiluminescence
CLDN1	Claudin
CMC	Critical Micelle Concentration
CMR	Carcinogenic, Mutagenic or toxic to Reproduction
Co Q10	Coenzyme Q10
COX-2	Cyclooxygenase 2
cP	Centipoise
CPC	California Perfume Company
CPG	Consumer Packaged Goods
CSA	Chemical Safety Assessment
CTL	Cytotoxic T- Lymphocytes
Cu/Zn-SOD	Copper-Zinc Superoxide Dismutase

CYP 450	Cytochrome P450 Enzyme Systems
D	
D&C	Drug & Cosmetic certified colour additives
DBD	DNA-binding Domain
DCF	Dichlorofluorescein
DCM	Dicaprylyl Maleate
DDT	Dichlorodiphenyltrichloroethane
DEA	Diethanolamine
DEFI	Device for Exclusive Formula Integrity
DES	Diethylstilbesterol
DHI	Dihydroxyindole
DHICA	Dihydroxyindole-2-carboxylic acid
DLA	Dalton's Lymphoma Ascites
DMBA	7,12-dimethylbenz[a]anthracene
DMDM	Dimethylol-dimethyl
DNA	Deoxyribonucleic acid
DPPH	2,2′-diphenyl-1,1′-picrylhydrazyl
DQ	Dopaquinone
DSG1	Desmoglein 1
E	
E2	Oestradiol
EC	European Commission
ECHA	European Chemicals Agency
ECM	Extracellular Matrix
EDC	Endocrine Disrupting Chemicals
EDTA	Ethylenediamine tetraacetic Acid
EFAs	Essential Fatty Acids
EGFR	Epidermal Growth Factor Receptor
EMS	Electromagnetic spectrum
EMT	Epithelial-Mesenchymal Transition
EO	Exogenous Ochronosis
EO	Essential oils
EP	European Pharmacopoeia
EPR	Electron Spin Resonance

EPRI	Spectroscopy and Imaging
ET	Electron Transfer
EU	European Union
F	
FD&C	Food, Drug, and Cosmetic certified colour additives
FD&C Act /FD&CA	Food, Drug, and Cosmetic Act
FDA	Food and Drug Administration (United States of America)
FIFO	First in, first out
FMI	Fragrance Mix I
FO	Fragrance oils
FRP	Formaldehyde-Releasing Preservatives
G	
GAGs	Glycosaminoglycans
GHK	Glycyl-L-histidyl-L-lysine
GMOs	Genetically Modified Organisms
GMP	Good Manufacturing Practice
GP	Gland Poor
GPx1-8	Glutathione Peroxidases
GRAS	Generally Recognised As Safe
GSH	Glutathione
GSSG	Oxidized form of Gluthathione
H	
H2DCF-dA	2′, 7′-dichlorodihydrofluorescein Diacetate
HAT	Hydrogen Atom Transfer
HBD-3	Human β-defensin 3
HCFCs	Hydrochlorofluorocarbons
HD	High Definition
HDPE	High Density Polyethylene
HER2	Human Epidermal Growth Factor 2
HFCs	Hydrofluorocarbons
HHCB	1,3,4,6,7,8-hexahydro-4,6,6,7,8,8-hexamethylcyclopenta[g]-2-benzopyran
HIV	Human Immunodeficiency Virus

HLB	Hydrophile-Lipophile Balance
HPMC	Hydroxypropyl methylcellulose
HPTLC	High-Performance Thin Layer Chromatography
HPV	Human Papillomavirus
HQ	Hydroquinone
I	
IARC	International Agency for Research on Cancer
ICCR	International Cooperation on Cosmetics Regulation
ICD	Irritant Contact Dermatitis
IFNγ	Interferon Gamma
IGF	Insulin-like Growth Factor
IL	Interleukin
INCI	International Nomenclature for Cosmetic Ingredients
IPD	Immediate Pigment Darkening
IPF	Immune Protection Factor
IPQC	In-process Quality Control
ISO	International Organisation for Standardisation
IV	Intravenous
J	
JP	Japanese Pharmacopoeia
K	
KLKs	Kallikrein proteases
KRAS	Kristen Rat Sarcoma Viral Proto-oncogene
L	
LBD	Ligand-Binding Domain
LDPE	Low Density Polyethylene
LED	Light Emitting Diode
LFN	Laws of the Federal Republic of Nigeria
M	
MAAs	Mycosporine-like Amino Acids
MBEH	Monobenzyl Ether of Hydroquinone
MBV	Market-Based View
MCI	Methylchloroisothiazolinone
MEA	Middle East and Africa

MED	Minimal Erythemal Dose
MHLW	Ministry of Health, Labour and Welfare
MI	Methylisothiazolinone
MMS	Multimedia Messaging Service
mRNA	Messenger Ribonucleic Acid
MRSA	Methicillin-resistant *Staphylococcus Aureus*
N	
NaCMC	Sodium carboxymethylcellulose
NADP	Nicotinamide Adenine Dinucleotide Phosphate
NAFDAC	National Agency for Food and Drug Administration and Control
NF-κ	Nuclear Factor Kappa
NFκB	Nuclear Factor Kappa B
Nfd	Not Found
NFO	Natural Fragrance Oils
NK	Natural Killer
NLC	Nanostructured Lipid Carriers
O	
o/w	Oil-in-water
OCLN	Occludin
ORAC	Oxygen Radical Absorbance Capacity
OSA	Orthosilicic Acid
OTC	Over-the-counter
P	
Pa.s	Pascal.sec
PABA	Para-aminobenzoic Acid
PAH	Polyaromatic Hydrocarbons
Pal-KTTKS	Palmitoyl Pentapeptide-4
PAO	Period After Opening
PC	Prostate Cancer
PC	Polycarbonate
PCN	Pharmacy Council of Nigeria
PCPs	Personal Care Products
PCPC	Personal Care Products Council
PCR	Post-Consumer Recycled

PCx	The Pharmaceutical Codex
PDL1	Programmed Death Ligand 1
PEG	Polyethylene Glycol
PEGs	Polyethylene Glycols
PEST	Political, Economic, Social and Technology
PESTEL	Political, Economic, Social, Technological, Environmental, and Legal
PET or PETE	Polyethylene Terephthalate
PFAS	Per-and polyfluoroalkyl substances
PFOA	Perfluorooctanoic acid
PG	Propyl Gallate
PG	Propylene Glycol
PHAs	Polyhydroxy Acids
PIF	Product Information File
PLA	Poly (lactic acid)
PLGA	Poly-lactic-co-glycolic Acid
PMD Act	Pharmaceutical and Medical Devises Act
PMMA	Poly (methyl methacrylate)
PMS	Post-marketing Surveillance
PP	Polypropylene
PPD	Persistent Pigment Darkening
PPF	Phototoxic Protection Factor
PRC	People's Republic of China
PTEN	Phosphatase and Tensin Homolog
PUFAs	Polyunsaturated Fatty Acids
PVC	Polyvinyl Chloride
Q	
QA	Quality Assurance
QC	Quality Control
R	
R&D	Research and Development
RCT	Randomised Controlled Clinical Trials
RHE	Reconstructed Human Epidermis
RNase 7	Ribonuclease 7
RNS	Reactive Nitrogen Species

ROS	Reactive Oxygen Species
RPF	Radical Protection Factor
RSF	Radical Skin/status Factor
S	
SA	Scarring Alopecia
SA	Salicylic Acid
SACTFA	South African Cosmetics, Toiletry, and Fragrance Association
SC	Stratum Corneum
SCC	Squamous Cell Carcinoma
SCCNFP	Scientific Committee on Cosmetic Products and Non-Food Products
SCCS	Scientific Committee on Consumer Safety
SEER	Surveillance, Epidemiology, And End Results Programme
SEM	Search Engine Marketing
SEO	Search Engine Optimisation
SERP	Search Engine Results Page
SFO	Synthetic Fragrance Oils
SGR	Sebaceous Gland-rich
SI	System of Units
SLN	Solid Lipid Nanoparticles
SLS	Sodium Lauryl Sulphate
SMM	Social Media Marketing
SMS	Short Message Service
SOD	Superoxide Dismutase
SON	Standards Organisation of Nigeria
SOP	Standard Operating Procedure
SPF	Sun Protection Factor
Spp.	Species
SRI	Stanford Research Institute
STAT3	Signal Transducer and Activator of Transcription 3
SUEs	Serious and Undesirable Effects
SWOT	Strengths, Weaknesses, Opportunities and Threats
T	
T	Testosterone
TA	Traction Alopecia

TBHQ	Tertiary butylhydroquinone
TCA	Trichloro Acetic Acid
TEAC	Trolox Equivalent Antioxidant Capacity
TEWL	Trans-epidermal Water Loss
TGF β-1	Transforming Growth Factor beta-1
Th1	CD4 T Helper Type 1
TJs	Tight Junctions
TLR	Toll-like receptor
TN	Trichorrhexis nodosa
TNF-α	Tumour Necrosis Factor Alpha
TOC	Total Organic Carbon
TP53	Tumour Protein 53
TPA	12-O-tetradecanoylphorbol-13-acetate
TRAP	Total Radical-Trapping Antioxidant Parameter
TRP-1	Tyrosinase related Protein- 1
TRP-2	Tyrosinase related Protein-2
TRPM8	Transient Receptor Potential Melastatin 8
TXA2	Thromboxane
TYR	Tyrosinase
U	
UK	United Kingdom
US/ USA	United States of America
US-FDA	United States Food and Drug Administration
US-NNI	United States National Nanotechnology Initiative
USP	United States Pharmacopeia
UV	Ultraviolet
UVA	Ultraviolet A
UVB	Ultraviolet B
UVC	Ultraviolet C
UVR	Ultraviolet Radiation
V	
VEGF	Vascular Endothelial Growth Factor
VEGF-A	Vascular Endothelial Growth Factor-A
VOC	Volatile Organic Compounds

W

w/o	Water-in-oil
WHO	World Health Organisation
WMA	World Medical Association

INDEX

Made in the USA
Monee, IL
08 May 2026

49766021R00450